STREET [obscured]S
South Hampshire

Contents

III **Key to map symbols**

IV **Key to map pages**

VI **Route planning**

VIII **Administrative and Postcode boundaries**

1 **Street maps** at 3½ inches to 1 mile

215 **Street map of Portsmouth city centre** at 7 inches to 1 mile

216 **Town maps** of Winchester, Andover, Basingstoke, Farnborough and Newbury

219 **Index** of towns and villages

220 **Index** of streets, hospitals, industrial estates, railway stations, schools, shopping centres, universities and places of interest

First published in 1991 by

Philip's, a division of
Octopus Publishing Group Ltd
2–4 Heron Quays, London E14 4JP

Second colour edition 2002
First impression 2002

ISBN 0-540-08105-1 (hardback)
ISBN 0-540-08106-X (spiral)

Printed and bound in Spain
by Cayfosa-Quebecor

Digital Data

The exceptionally high-quality mapping found in this atlas is available as digital data in TIFF format, which is easily convertible to other bit mapped (raster) image formats.

The index is also available in digital form as a standard database table. It contains all the details found in the printed index together with the National Grid reference for the map square in which each entry is named.

For further information and to discuss your requirements, please contact Philip's on
020 7531 8439 or george.philip@philips-maps.co.uk

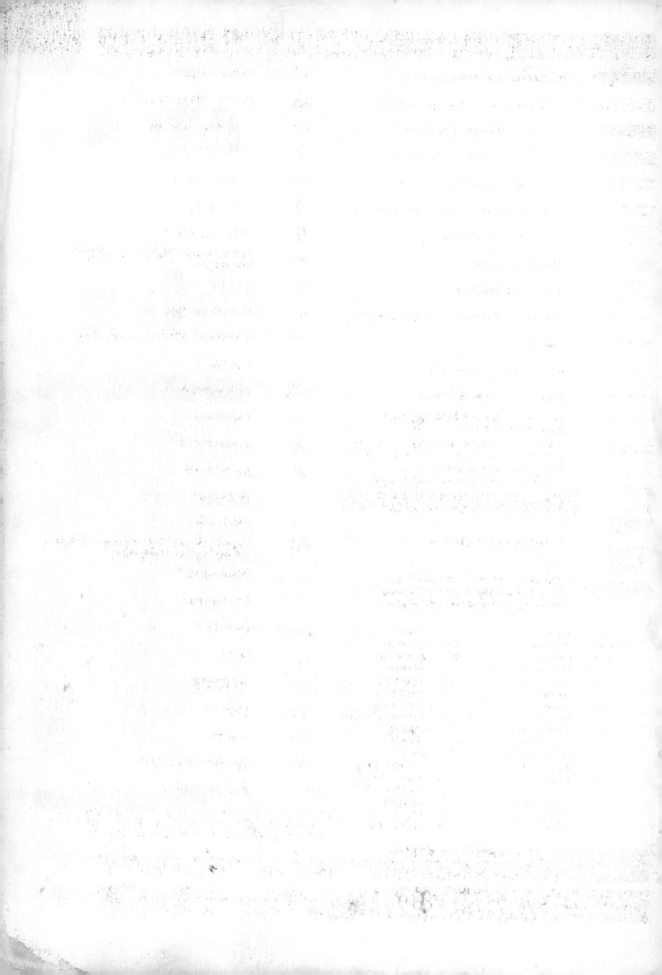

Key to map symbols

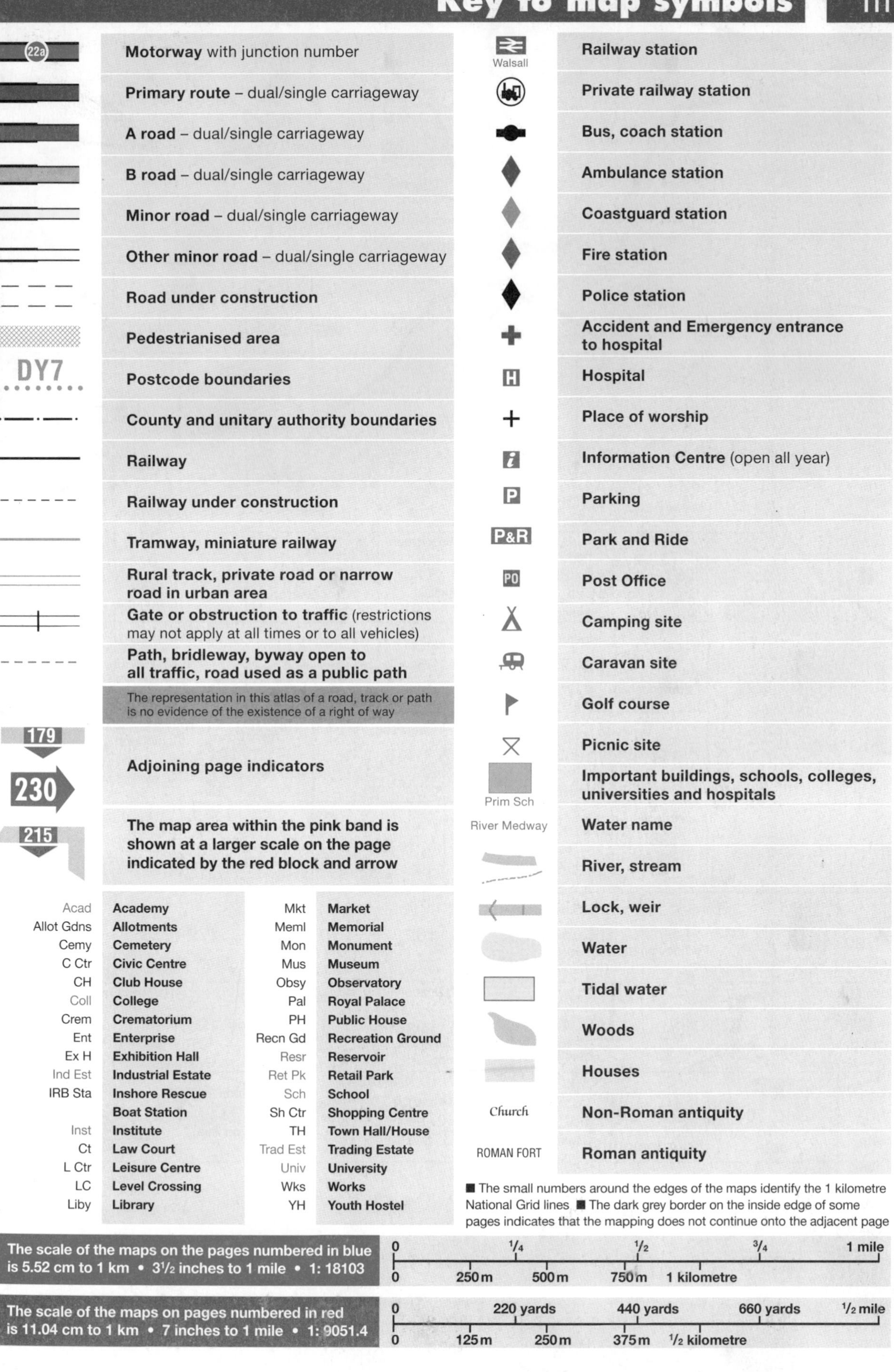

Acad	Academy	Mkt	Market
Allot Gdns	Allotments	Meml	Memorial
Cemy	Cemetery	Mon	Monument
C Ctr	Civic Centre	Mus	Museum
CH	Club House	Obsy	Observatory
Coll	College	Pal	Royal Palace
Crem	Crematorium	PH	Public House
Ent	Enterprise	Recn Gd	Recreation Ground
Ex H	Exhibition Hall	Resr	Reservoir
Ind Est	Industrial Estate	Ret Pk	Retail Park
IRB Sta	Inshore Rescue Boat Station	Sch	School
		Sh Ctr	Shopping Centre
Inst	Institute	TH	Town Hall/House
Ct	Law Court	Trad Est	Trading Estate
L Ctr	Leisure Centre	Univ	University
LC	Level Crossing	Wks	Works
Liby	Library	YH	Youth Hostel

■ The small numbers around the edges of the maps identify the 1 kilometre National Grid lines ■ The dark grey border on the inside edge of some pages indicates that the mapping does not continue onto the adjacent page

The scale of the maps on the pages numbered in blue is 5.52 cm to 1 km • 3½ inches to 1 mile • 1: 18103

0 – ¼ – ½ – ¾ – 1 mile
0 – 250 m – 500 m – 750 m – 1 kilometre

The scale of the maps on pages numbered in red is 11.04 cm to 1 km • 7 inches to 1 mile • 1: 9051.4

0 – 220 yards – 440 yards – 660 yards – ½ mile
0 – 125 m – 250 m – 375 m – ½ kilometre

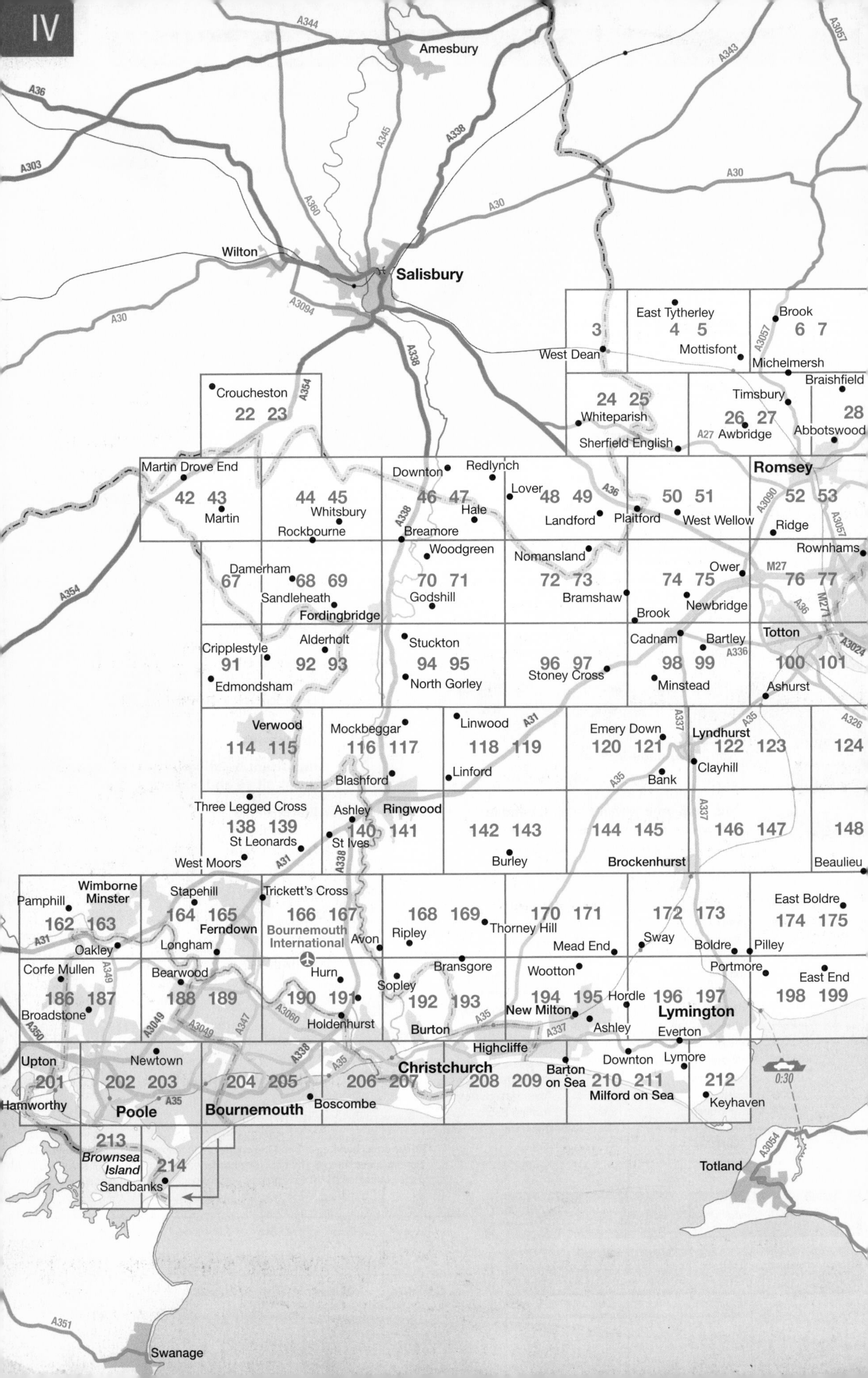
Amesbury
Salisbury
Wilton
A344
A36
A303
A345
A338
A360
A30
A3094
A343
A3057
A354
A27
A3090
A36
M27
M271
A3024
A336
A337
A31
A35
A326
A349
A350
A3049
A347
A3060
A351
A3054
West Dean
East Tytherley
Mottisfont
Brook
Michelmersh
Braishfield
Timsbury
Abbotswood
Whiteparish
Sherfield English
Awbridge
Romsey
Croucheston
Martin Drove End
Martin
Whitsbury
Rockbourne
Downton
Redlynch
Hale
Breamore
Lover
Landford
Plaitford
West Wellow
Ridge
Rownhams
Woodgreen
Nomansland
Ower
Damerham
Sandleheath
Fordingbridge
Godshill
Bramshaw
Brook
Newbridge
Totton
Cadnam
Bartley
Cripplestyle
Alderholt
Stuckton
Edmondsham
North Gorley
Stoney Cross
Minstead
Ashurst
Verwood
Mockbeggar
Linwood
Emery Down
Lyndhurst
Clayhill
Bank
Blashford
Linford
Three Legged Cross
Ashley
Ringwood
St Leonards
St Ives
West Moors
Burley
Brockenhurst
Beaulieu
Pamphill
Wimborne Minster
Stapehill
Trickett's Cross
Ferndown
Bournemouth International
Thorney Hill
East Boldre
Oakley
Longham
Avon
Ripley
Mead End
Sway
Boldre
Pilley
Corfe Mullen
Bearwood
Hurn
Bransgore
Sopley
Wootton
Portmore
East End
Broadstone
Holdenhurst
Burton
New Milton
Hordle
Ashley
Lymington
Everton
Highcliffe
Downton
Lymore
Upton
Newtown
Christchurch
Barton on Sea
Hamworthy
Poole
Bournemouth
Boscombe
Milford on Sea
Keyhaven
0:30
Brownsea Island
Sandbanks
Totland
Swanage
3
4 5
6 7
24 25
26 27
28
22 23
42 43
44 45
46 47
48 49
50 51
52 53
67
68 69
70 71
72 73
74 75
76 77
91
92 93
94 95
96 97
98 99
100 101
114 115
116 117
118 119
120 121
122 123
124
138 139
140
141
142 143
144 145
146 147
148
162 163
164 165
166 167
168 169
170 171
172 173
174 175
186 187
188 189
190 191
192 193
194 195
196 197
198 199
201
202 203
204 205
206 207
208 209
210 211
212
213
214

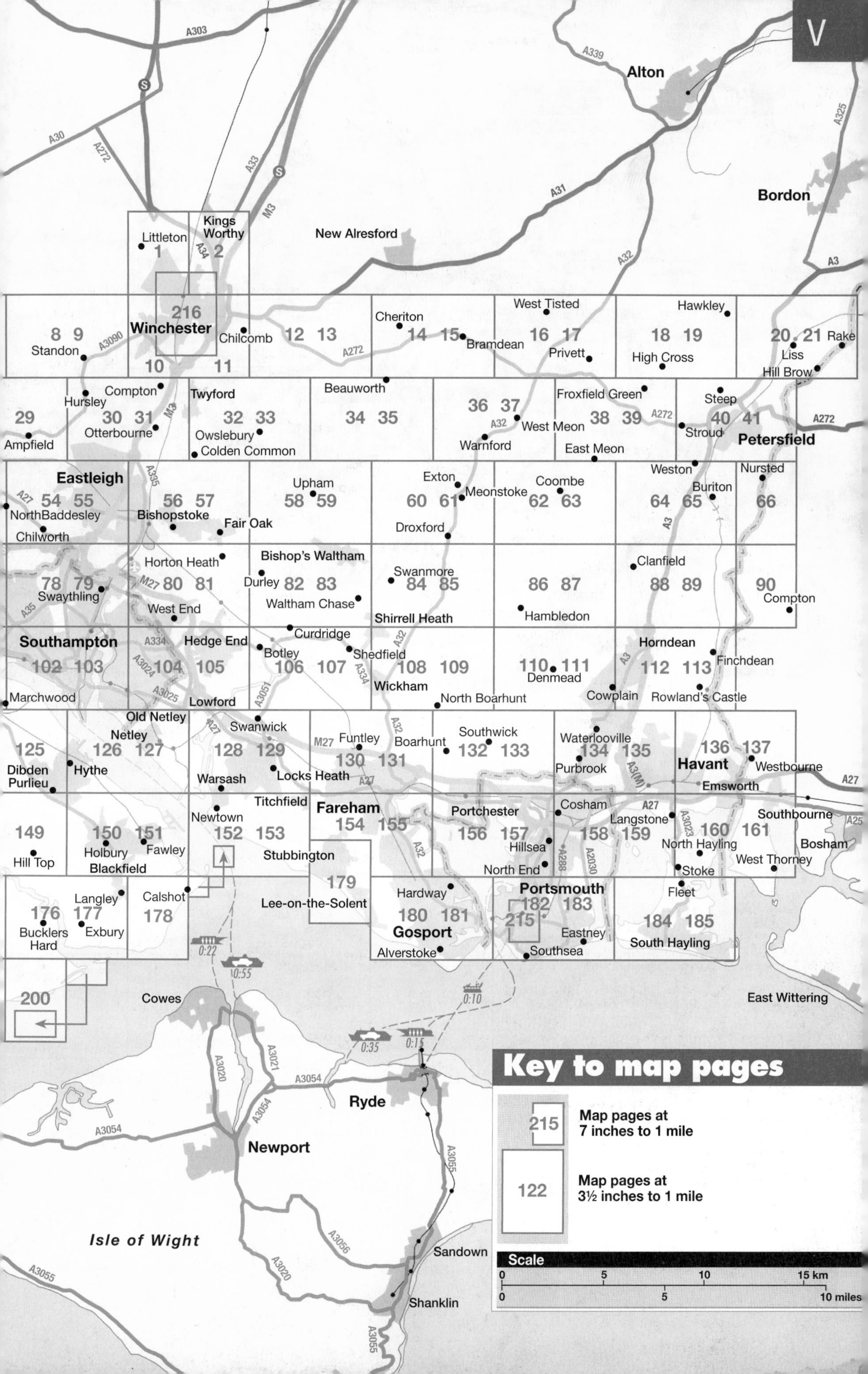

Key to map pages
215
Map pages at 7 inches to 1 mile
122
Map pages at 3½ inches to 1 mile
Scale
0
5
10
15 km
0
5
10 miles
Alton
Bordon
New Alresford
Littleton
1
Kings Worthy
2
216
Winchester
Chilcomb
10
11
8
9
Standon
12
13
Cheriton
14
15
Bramdean
West Tisted
16
17
Privett
Hawkley
18
19
High Cross
20
21
Rake
Liss
Hill Brow
Compton
Hursley
29
Ampfield
30
31
Otterbourne
Twyford
32
33
Owslebury
Colden Common
Beauworth
34
35
36
37
West Meon
Warnford
Froxfield Green
38
39
East Meon
Steep
40
41
Stroud
Petersfield
Eastleigh
54
55
NorthBaddesley
Chilworth
56
57
Bishopstoke
Fair Oak
Upham
58
59
Exton
60
61
Meonstoke
Droxford
Coombe
62
63
Weston
64
65
Buriton
Nursted
66
Horton Heath
78
79
Swaythling
80
81
West End
Bishop's Waltham
Durley
82
83
Waltham Chase
Swanmore
84
85
Shirrell Heath
86
87
Hambledon
Clanfield
88
89
90
Compton
Southampton
102
103
Marchwood
Hedge End
104
105
Curdridge
Botley
106
107
Shedfield
108
109
Wickham
110
111
Denmead
North Boarhunt
Horndean
112
113
Finchdean
Cowplain
Rowland's Castle
Lowford
Old Netley
Netley
125
126
127
Dibden Purlieu
Hythe
Swanwick
128
129
Warsash
Locks Heath
Funtley
130
131
Boarhunt
Southwick
132
133
Waterlooville
134
135
Purbrook
136
137
Havant
Westbourne
Emsworth
Titchfield
Newtown
149
Hill Top
150
151
Holbury
Fawley
Blackfield
152
153
Stubbington
Fareham
154
155
Portchester
156
157
Hillsea
North End
Cosham
Langstone
158
159
160
161
North Hayling
Southbourne
Bosham
West Thorney
Stoke
179
Lee-on-the-Solent
Hardway
180
181
Gosport
Alverstoke
Portsmouth
182
183
215
Eastney
Southsea
Fleet
184
185
South Hayling
176
177
Langley
Bucklers Hard
Exbury
Calshot
178
200
Cowes
East Wittering
Ryde
Newport
Isle of Wight
Sandown
Shanklin
0:22
0:55
0:10
0:35
0:15
A303
A339
A325
A30
A272
A33
M3
A31
A34
A32
A3
A3090
A27
A335
M27
A35
A334
A3024
A3025
A3051
A288
A2030
A3(M)
A3023
A25
A3054
A3020
A3021
A3055
A3056

Route planning
Scale
0 1 2 3 4 5 6 7 8 km
0 1 2 3 4 5 miles
Stonehenge
Codford St Mary
Yarnbury Castle
A303
Winterbourne Stoke
Berwick St James
Wilsford
Lake
Amesbury
Cholderton
Grateley
Newton Tony
Palestine
Goodworth Clatford
Allington
Boscombe
River Bourne
Over Wallop
Kentsboro
Fullerton
Great Durnford
Airfield
Danebury
Middle Wallop
Nether Wallop
Longstock
Leckford
Porton
Idmiston
Middle Woodford
A345
Winterbourne Dauntsey
Gomeldon
Winterbourne Gunner
Lopcombe Corner
A30
Stockbridge
A338
Figsbury Ring
Fonthill Bishop
Magna
Winterbourne Earls
Middle Winterslow
The Common
Whiteshoot Hill
Broughton
Chilmark
A36
Ford
Old Sarum
A30
West Winterslow
Houghton
Dinton
Baverstock
WILTON
Pitton
Ridge
Teffont Evias
Barford St Martin
Wilton Ho
Quidhampton
Laverstock
West Tytherley
Horsebridge
King's Somborne
Chicksgrove
Fovant
Compton Chamberlayne
Burcombe
Netherhampton
SALISBURY
Farley
East Tytherley
Lockerley Hall
Brook
Sutton Mandeville
Regimental Badges
Chiselbury
A3094
Harnham
Swallowcliffe
A30
East Grimstead
West Dean
Lockerley
Mottisfont Abbey
Michelmersh
Ansty
Stratford Tony
Coombe Bissett
Britford
Alderbury
Broad Chalke
River Ebble
Odstock
Bodenham
West Grimstead
Dean Hill
East Dean
Carter's Clay
Braishfield
Homington
Nunton
Whaddon
A36
White Sheet Hill
Bishopstone
Odstock Down
Timsbury
Ebbesbourne Wake
Clearbury Ring
Charlton-All-Saints
Whiteparish
Newtown
Kent's Oak
A27
Berwick St John
Alvediston
A338
Abbotswood
Bowerchalke
Wick Down
Downton
Newton
Morgan's Vale
Sherfield English
Awbridge
ROMSEY
Rockbourne Down
Woodminton
Winkelbury
Wick
Martin Drove End
Redlynch
Landford Manor
East Wellow
Woodfalls
Castle Ditches
North Charford
Lover
Woodyates
Martin
Tidpit
Whitsbury
Breamore House
Plaitford
West Wellow
Tollard Royal
Upper Street
Hale
Landford
Canada
Toothill
Deanland
Pentridge
Rockbourne
Breamore
B3080
A354
B3081
Nomansland
Lee
Sixpenny Handley
Pentridge Hill
Damerham
Woodgreen
B3078
Bramshaw
Ower
Newbridge
Copythorne
Testwood
Farnham
Sandleheath
Godshill
Fritham
Cadnam
M27
Calmore
M271
Monkton Up Wimborne
FORDINGBRIDGE
Stuckton
Blissford
Brook
TOTTON
Chettle
Cashmoor
Cranborne
B3078
Rufus Stone
Bartley
Gussage St Michael
Gussage All Saints
Wimborne St Giles
Edmondsham
Bickton
Alderholt
Hyde
Stoney Cross
Netley Marsh
Eling
Earthworks
North Gorley
Minstead
Woodlands
Long Crichel
South Gorley
Newtown
Ashurst
Pooksgreen
More Crichel
Verwood
Ringwood Forest
Ibsley
NEW FOREST
Tarrant Monkton
Linwood
Emery Down
Lyndhurst
Manswood
Woodlands
Moyles Court
A31
Horton
Linford
B3056
Beaulieu Road Station
Witchampton
Three Legged Cross
Blashford
Picket Post
Bank
Hinton Martell
Chalbury Common
Tarrant Rushton
Mannington
Ashley Heath
RINGWOOD
Gaunt's Common
Burley Street
New Park
Balmerlawn
Stanbridge
Holt
West Moors
St Ives
Burley
Bisterne Close
Badbury Rings
Broom Hill
B3055
Shapwick
Clapgate
St Leonards
Kingston
Brockenhurst
Kingston Lacy
Tadden
Colehill
Trickett's Cross
Setley
Pamphill
A31
Ferndown
Moors R.
Lymington R.
WIMBORNE MINSTER
Stapehill
Parley Common
Beaulieu Heath
East Boldre
Sturminster Marshall
Hampreston
A348
West Parley
Parley Cross
Bournemouth International Airport
Avon
Ripley
Thorney Hill
Sway
Battramsley
East End
Longham
Merley
Hurn
Sopley
Bransgore
Wootton
Bashley
Boldre
Norleywood
Corfe Mullen
Bearwood
Ensbury
River Stour
Neacroft
Portmore
East End
Lychett Matravers
Broadstone
Canford Heath
Kinson
Throop
River Avon
New Milton
Hordle
LYMINGTON
Beacon Hill
Waterloo
Moordown
Burton
Hinton
Everton
Lytchett Minster
A3049
Newtown
Winton
Highcliffe
Barton on Sea
A337
Lower Pennington
A35
Upton
Branksome
A338
Pokesdown
CHRISTCHURCH
Downton
Lymore
Keyhaven
Holton Heath
Hamworthy
A35
Parkstone
Boscombe
Wick
Priory
Southbourne
Mudeford
Christchurch Bay
Milford on Sea
Sconce Point
Yarmouth Castle
Branksome Park
Westbourne
BOURNEMOUTH
HENGISTBURY HEAD
B3058
POOLE
Poole Harbour
Brownsea Island
Canford Cliffs
POOLE BAY
Hurst Castle
Norton
Ningwood
Arne
Colwell Bay
Norton Green
Ridge
Totland
Totland Bay
Freshwater
Sandbanks
Toll
Alum Bay
A3055
Wytch Heath
THE NEEDLES
Tennyson's Monument
Freshwater Bay
Compton Bay
Norden
Newton Heath
Studland Bay
The Undercliff
Studland
ISLE OF PURBECK
The Foreland or Handfast Point
Church Knowle
Corfe Castle
Nine Barrow Down
B3351
Ballard Point
Swanage Bay
Kingston
Harman's Cross
SWANAGE
B3069
Peveril Point
Durlston Bay
Worth Matravers
Langton Matravers
DURLSTON HEAD
Seacombe Cliff
Tilly Whim Caves
ST ALDHELM'S OR ST ALBAN'S HEAD

Wherwell
Newton Stacey
Barton Stacey
Sutton Scotney Services
Wonston
Micheldever
East Stratton
Preston Candover
Bradley
Lower Wield
Bentworth
Holybourne
Binsted
Wheatley
Chilbolton
Sutton Scotney
Stoke Charity
Micheldever Wood
Brown Candover
Upper Wield
Thedden Grange
ALTON
Wyck
East Worldham
Kingsley
Beech
Medstead
Northington
The Grange
Winchester Services
Hattingley
South Town
Chawton
West Worldham
Sleaford
Lindford
Bordon Camp
South Wonston
Crawley
Worthy Down
Kings Worthy
Itchen Abbas
Old Alresford
Bighton
Soldridge
Lower Farringdon
Upper Farringdon
Oakhanger
Whitehill
Four Marks
Selborne
Littleton
Headbourne Worthy
Itchen Stoke
New Alresford
Gundleton
North Street
Kitwood
Newton Valence
Blackmoor
BORDON
Up Somborne
Ashley
Sparsholt
Easton
Ovington
Bishop's Sutton
Ropley
Ropley Dean
Monkwood
East Tisted
Longmoor Camp
WINCHESTER
Empshott
Hawkley
Greatham
Liss Forest
Langley
Farley Mount
Monument
Pitt Down
Chilcomb
Tichborne
Cheriton
New Cheriton
Bramdean
West Tisted
Liss
East Liss
Rake
Standon
Oliver's Battery
Longwood Warren
Beauworth
Hinton Ampner
Brockwood Park
Privett
High Cross
Steep
Froxfield Green
Sheet
Hill Brow
Hursley
Compton
Morestead
Kilmeston
West Meon
Langrish
Stroud
Ampfield
Twyford
Shawford
Otterbourne
Colden Common
Owslebury
Warnford
East Meon
Ramsdean
Weston
PETERSFIELD
Rogate
Chandler's Ford
North Baddesley
Exton
Corhampton
Old Winchester Hill
Butser Hill
Nursted
East Harting
Nyewood
Elsted
Fisher's Pond
Bishopstoke
Upham
Lower Upham
Dean
Meonstoke
Brockbridge
War Down
Buriton
South Harting
Treyford
Chilworth
EASTLEIGH
Fair Oak
Wintershill
Horton Heath
Bishop's Waltham
Palace
Droxford
Chidden
Uppark
Southampton International Airport
Durley
Swanmore
Soberton
Clanfield
Chalton
North Marden
Rownhams
Nursling
Bassett
Swaythling
West End
Long Common
Waltham Chase
Hambledon
Compton
Portswood
Curdridge
Shirrell Heath
Soberton Heath
Hoe Gate
Catherington
Blendworth
East Marden
West Marden
Shirley
Bitterne
Anthill Common
HORNDEAN
Finchdean
Millbrook
Northam
Thornhill
Hedge End
Botley
Shedfield
Newtown
Denmead
Cowplain
Rowlands Castle
Forestside
Stoughton
Sholing
Wickham
Curbridge
Hundred Acres
FOREST OF BERE
Marchwood
Woolston
Burridge
North Boarhunt
Walderton
SOUTHAMPTON
Bursledon
Swanwick
Waterlooville
Dibden
Netley
Lower Swanwick
Purbrook
HAVANT
Funtington
Westbourne
Woodmancote
Hythe
Sarisbury
Park Gate
Boarhunt
Southwick
Hamble-le-Rice
Locks Heath
Portsdown
Bedhampton
Dibden Purlieu
Wymering
Drayton
Cosham
Langstone
EMSWORTH
Hermitage
Hambrook
Southbourne
Beaulieu Heath
Hardley
Oil Refinery
Warsash
Titchfield
FAREHAM
Wallington
Portchester
Castle
Horsea Island
Hilsea
North Hayling
Thorney Island
Chidham
Hill Top
Fawley
Power Station
Calshot Castle
Stubbington
Bridgemary
Portsmouth Harbour
North End
Langstone Harbour
Stoke
West Thorney
Beaulieu
Holbury
Blackfield
Hardway
Whale Island
Portsea
Langley
Exbury
Calshot
Hill Head
Lee-on-the-Solent
GOSPORT
PORTSEA ISLAND
Fratton
HAYLING ISLAND
West Itchenor
Chichester Harbour
Bucklers Hard
South Hayling
Shipton Green
Stansore Point
Alverstoke
Eastney
Lepe
THE SOLENT
Stokes Bay
Southsea
PORTSMOUTH
Hayling Bay
West Wittering
Needs Ore Point
COWES
Cowes Roads
Gilkicker Point
Spitbank Fort
East Wittering
Gurnard Bay
Gurnard
East Cowes
Osborne Bay
SPITHEAD
Horse Sand Fort
Bracklesham Bay
Thorness Bay
Whippingham
No Man's land Fort
Ryde Roads
Fishbourne
RYDE
Northwood
Abbey
Puckpool Point
Parkhurst
Parkhurst Forest
Nettlestone Point
Hamstead
Newtown
Porchfield
Wootton Common
Wootton Bridge
Binstead
Seaview
Nettlestone
Cranmore
The Priory
Shalfleet
Havenstreet
St Helen's Fort
Bembridge Point
Carisbrooke
Staplers
NEWPORT
Newbridge
Downend
Nunwell House
St Helens
Brading
Bembridge
Wellow
Castle
FORELAND
ISLE OF WIGHT
Haseley Manor
River Yar
Alverstone
Whitecliff Bay
Calbourne
Bowcombe
Blackwater
Shalcombe
Brighstone Forest
Gatcombe
Merstone
Arreton
Newchurch
Yaverland
Culver Cliff
Brook
Chillerton
Rookley
Winford
SANDOWN
Moortown
Mottistone
Brighstone
Shorwell
Branstone
Apse Heath
Sandown Bay
Godshill
Chilton Chine
Yafford
Kingston
SHANKLIN
Little Atherfield
Roud
Appuldurcombe House
Shanklin Chine
Brighstone Bay
Wroxall
Luccombe Village
Pyle
Chale Green
Luccombe Chine
Atherfield Point
Whale Chine
Bierley
Chale
Stenbury Down
Whitwell
DUNNOSE
VENTNOR
Chale Bay
Blackgang Chine
Blackgang
Niton
St Lawrence
The Undercliff
Rocken End
ST CATHERINE'S POINT

Major administrative and Postcode boundaries

County and unitary authority boundaries
District boundaries
Postcode boundaries
Area covered by this atlas

Scale

0 5 10 15 km
0 5 10 miles

ST SU
SY SZ
Wiltshire
Dorset
West Berkshire
Wokingham
Bracknell Forest
Surrey
Rushmoor
Hart
Basingstoke and Deane
Test Valley
Hampshire
Winchester
East Hampshire
West Sussex
Eastleigh
New Forest
City of Southampton
Fareham
Gosport
Havant
City of Portsmouth
Bournemouth
Poole
Isle of Wight

Newbury
Mortimer
Wokingham
Camberley
Frimley
Farnborough
Aldershot
Farnham
Yateley
Tadley
Bramley
Burghclere
Kingsclere
Chineham
Hook
Fleet
Odiham
Basingstoke
Oakley
Vernham Green
Tangley
St Mary Bourne
Whitchurch
North Waltham
Ellisfield
Bentley
Thruxton
Andover
Wherwell
Micheldever
Bentworth
Alton
Medstead
Bordon
Grayshott
Haslemere
Liphook
East Tisted
Over Wallop
South Wonston
Itchen Abbas
New Alresford
Broughton
Winchester
Liss
West Dean
Mottisfont
Twyford
West Meon
Petersfield
Croucheston
Romsey
West Wellow
Meonstoke
Wick
Martin
Eastleigh
Bishop's Waltham
Fordingbridge
West End
Hambledon
Totton
Cadnam
Horndean
Southampton
Wickham
Lyndhurst
Ibsley
Verwood
Hythe
Netley
Fareham
Havant
Ringwood
Burley
Brockenhurst
Beaulieu
Fawley
Gosport
Thorney Island
Wimborne Minster
Ferndown
Portsmouth
Hayling Island
Sway
Lymington
Barton on Sea
Christchurch
Bournemouth
Poole

RG14
RG19
RG20
RG7
RG40
GU46
RG17
SN8
RG26
RG27
GU15
GU17
GU16
GU14
GU51
GU12
GU11
GU52
GU9
RG24
RG23
RG28
RG22
RG21
RG29
RG25
SP9
SP11
SP10
SP4
GU10
GU35
GU34
GU26
GU30
GU27
SO21
SO20
SO23
SO24
SP5
SO22
GU33
SO51
GU32
GU31
SO53
SO50
SO52
SO32
SP6
SO16
SO17
SO18
SO30
PO8
PO18
SO40
SO15
SO19
SO43
SO14
SO31
PO7
PO17
PO9
BH31
PO15
BH24
PO10
BH21
PO16
PO6
PO14
BH22
SO42
SO45
PO13
PO2
PO3
PO11
PO1
PO12
PO4
PO5
BH18
BH10
BH3
BH9
BH23
BH25
SO41
BH11
BH8
BH17
BH12
BH7
BH16
BH15
BH14
BH13
BH6
BH5
BH1
BH2

A272 Stockbridge (A30)
A34 Newbury
North Hampshire STREET ATLAS

A B C

4
33
3
32
2
31
1
30

Lower Farm Cottages
Down Farm
SO21
A272
A34
B3420
Littleton Stud
DOWN FARM LA
A34
Littleton Manor
CHURCH LA
The Running Horse (PH)
SO23
NEW RD
Littleton
1 WESTFIELD RD
2 UPHILL RD
3 HILL TOP
4 LAWN RD
5 HILLSIDE
Barracks
Sewage Works
ROZELLE CL
HOLM OAK CL
MAIN RD
HOLLANDS CL
THE HALLWAY
PITTER CL
FAIRCLOSE DR
HILDEN WAY
FYFIELD WAY
FLOWERDOWN CVN PK
LITTLETON LA
DALE CL
VALLEY RD
NORTH DR
BERCOTE CL
SO22
WELL HOUSE LA
SO21
SOUTH DR
CHESTNUT AVE
HARESTOCK CL
Well House Farm
PO
Flowerdown Barrows
FLOWERDOWN HO
CHAWTON CL
GRAYSHOTT CL
B3049
KENNEL LA
HICKORY DR
MINSTEAD CL
BEAULIEU CL
BURITON RD
ANDOVER RD N
DEANE DOWN DRO
ROCKBOURNE RD
HARESTOCK RD
LARG DR
BURLEY RD
PRIORS DEAN RD
SOUTHWICK CL
APPLESHAW CL
Harestock
HAMBLEDON CL
FROXFIELD CL
Henry Beaufort Sec Sch
LITTLETON RD
WINSLADE RD
BRADLEY RD
LITCHFIELD RD
WOODGREEN RD
REWLANDS DR
LYNDHURST CL
EAST WOODHAY RD
AMPORT CL
SWANMORE CL
ABBOTTS ANN RD
ASHURST CL
BRAMSHAW CL
UPTON GREY CL
LOVETT WLK
ASHLEY CL
Harestock Prim Sch
ELING CL
HALLS FARM CL
ORIENT DR
ROWLINGS RD
TAPLINGS CL
MOUNTBATTEN CT
HARESTOCK CNR
FLEMING RD
TAPLINGS RD
MOUNT CL
Barton Farm
SO23
SALTERS ACRES
GODWIN CL
FROMOND RD
TRUSSELL CL
GREAT FIELD
PEMERTON RD
DEVENISH RD
BEREWEEKE AVE
UPLANDS RD
WINCHESTER
STOCKBRIDGE RD
TRUSSELL CRES
WESTMAN RD
OLD GARDENS
SALTERS LA
RUFFIELD CL
Weeke Prim Sch
STONEY LA
PO
WOODLEA CL
PARK RD
WOODPECKERS DR
BURNETT CL
LYNFORD AVE
ABBOTTS CT
ORCHARD WLK
VERNHAM RD
Greenacres Specl Sch
ABBEY HILL CL
DEN HAM CL
WESTVIEW RD
DEAN LA
DEAN CL
ST MATTHEWS RD
WESSEX DR
WINTON CL
LAINSTON CL
ACORN CL
ST STEPHEN'S RD
LYNFORD WAY
MORNINGTON DR
PARKSIDE GDNS
WEEKE MANOR CL
KYNEGILS RD
BEREWEEKE AVE
LYNWOOD CT
DOWNSIDE RD
OLD HILLSIDE RD
LYNCH CL
HIGH TREES DR
NORTH HILL CL
BERE CL
Weeke
BEREWEEKE WAY
LANKHILLS RD
Lanham Down
MALMESBURY GDNS
HILLSIDE CL
TRAVELLER'S END
B3041
NORTH HILL CT
CROUCHER'S CROFT
BRADLEY PEAK
Mus
BUTTS CL
BEREWEEKE CL
EASTACRE
Lankhills Sch
SAWYER CL
GROVELANDS RD
SERMON RD
WESTLEY CL
BEREWEEKE RD
BOSCOBEL RD
BRASSEY RD
HYDE LODGE
LANHAM LA
BEECH COPSE
WEBSTER RD
HILLSIDE RD
GORING FIELD
HAMPTON LA
STOCKERS AVE
SILWOOD CL
CHANTRY MEAD
OWEN'S RD
P
Fulflood
B3041
CHILBOLTON AVE
Peter Symonds' Coll
ASHMORE RD
CHERITON CL
LANGTON CL
Nethercliffe Sch
Andover Road Ret Pk
B3045
TEG DOWN MEADS
WALNUT GR
LINKS RD
HATHERLEY RD
CRANWORTH RD
B3420
WORTHY LA
COPPICE CL
B3041
CHERITON RD
PILGRIMS GATE
FAIRFIELD RD
CONIFER CL
HYDE CL
Westgate Sec Sch
FORDINGTON RD
B3049
B3044
P P
VICTORIA RD

45 A 46 B 47 C

10
2

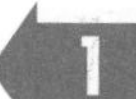

1

A
B
C
North Hampshire STREET ATLAS
A33 Basingstoke (A30)
M3 Basingstoke
M3
A33
A34
B3047
B3044
Springvale
Meadow Farm
Cemy
Woodhams Farm
Recn Gd
Kings Worthy Prim Sch
Kings Worthy
Prince's Mead Sch
Worthy Park
Abbots Worthy
Worthy Park Home Farm
Headbourne Worthy
Headbourne Worthy Ho
Upper Farm
Taylors Cnr
Lower Farm
Foresters Pk
Pudding House Farm
Easton Down
SO21
SO23
SO22
Three Castles Path
Itchen Way
Dairy Farm
Lone Barn
Winchester By Pass
River Itchen
Kings Way
Nuns Wlk
Abbots Barton House
Abbotts Barton
Winnall Cottage Farm
Shoulder of Mutton Farm
Abbots Barton Farm House
The Wykeham Ind Est
WINCHESTER
North Walls Recn Gd
Hyde
River Park L Ctr
Dykes Farm
Chaucer Ind Est
Erasmus Pk
Superstore
Winnall Trad Est
Dennet Ho
Spitfire Link
Winnall Down Copse
Basingstoke Rd
London Rd
Worthy Rd
Hyde St
Easton La
Long Wlk
Church La
Malthouse Cl
Springvale Rd
Springvale Ave
Bentley Cl
Down Farm La
Well House La
Green Cl
School La
Bedfield La
Bedfield Ho
Pudding La
Loveden La
Loader Cl
Holdaway Cl
Old Rectory Gdns
Park La
Mill La
St Mary's Cl
Court Rd
The Paddock
The Wood Lands
Willis Waye
Church La
Mount Pleasant
Mortimer Cl
Hinton Fields
St Nicholas Rise
Nations Hill
Lynn Way
Felmer Dr
Campion Way
Field End
Boyne Mead Rd
Meadowland
Legion La
Rampton Way
Wesley Rd
Haydn Cl
Tudor Way
Boyne Rise
Harwood Pl
Pound Rd
Sherbrook Cl
Ramsay Rd
Tovey Pl
Vian Pl
Mountbatten Pl
Fraser Rd
Forbes Rd
Brooke Cl
North
Somerville Rd
Fryers Cl
Larch Cl
Cedar Cl
Cundell Way
Maple Dr
Hookpit Farm La
Sycamore Dr
Lex Cl
Firs Cres
Laburnham Dr
1 Gillingham Cl
2 Cedarwood
Colley Cl
Stoke Rd
Mannington Cl
Wymmingford
Courtenay Rd
Cavendish Gr
Francis Gdns
Abbotts Rd
Abbotts Cl
Dyson Dr
Grosvenor Dr
Green Park Cl
Charles Cl
Chaundler Rd
Austen Cl
Park Rd
Park Cl
Denham Ct
Salcot Rd
Abbey Hill
Abbey Hill Cl
Northlands Dr
Russell Rd
Knight Rd
Oglander Rd
Hillier Way
Lankhills Rd
Edington Rd
Arthur Rd
Egbert Rd
Nuns Rd
Saxon Rd
Monks Rd
Birinus Rd
Worthy La
Hyde Church La
Hyde Cl
Hyde Gate
King Alfred Pl
Moorside Rd
Leicester Way
Winnall Cl
Winnall Manor Rd
PO
PH
P
9
48
49
50

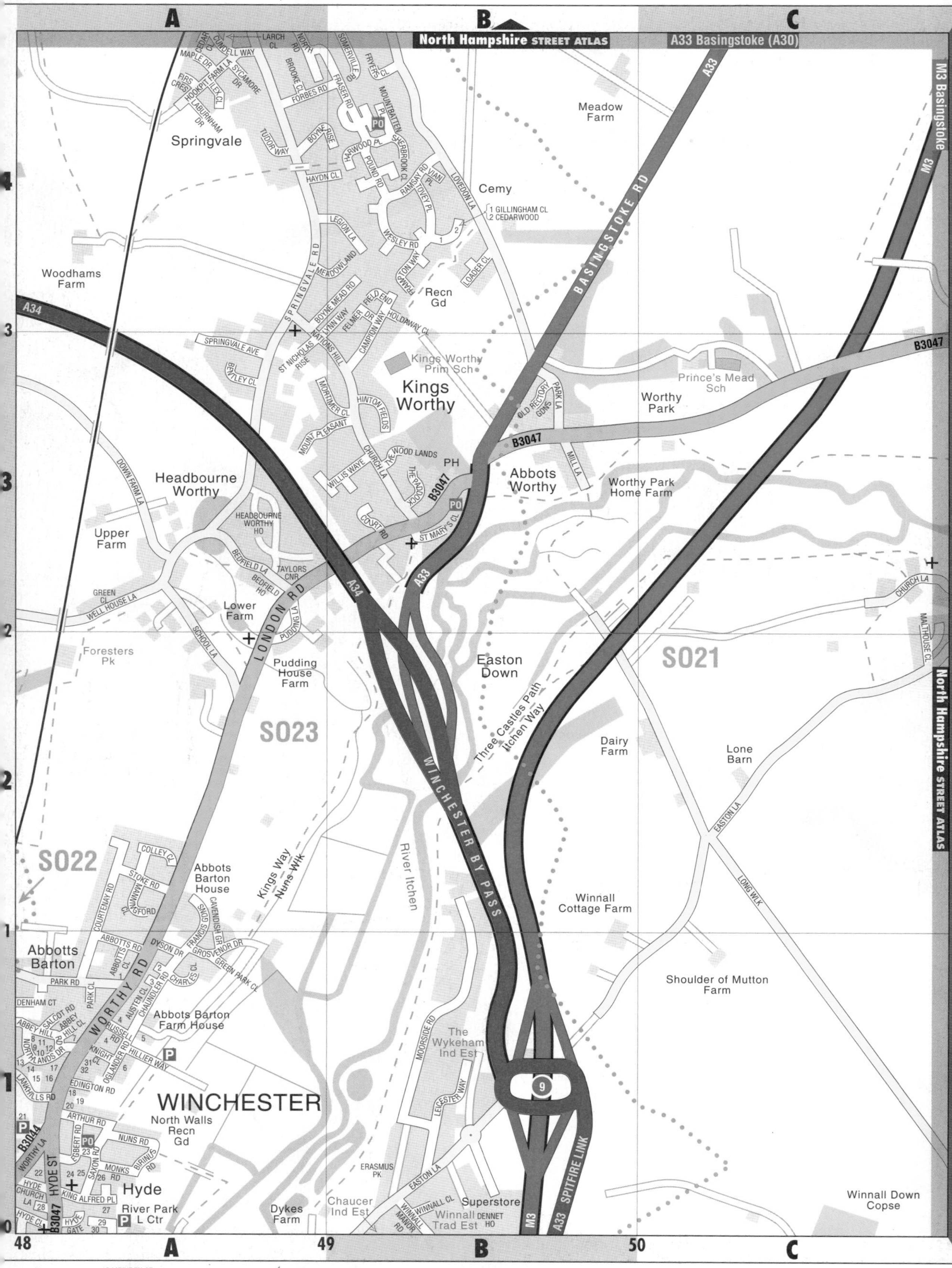

A1
1 PARK CT
2 HUSSEY CL
3 CORAM CL
4 CONEY GN
5 SIMONDS CT
6 COLBOURNE CT
7 COVENTRY CT
8 KENILWORTH CT
9 STRATFORD CT
10 MERIDEN CT
11 WARNER CT
12 ALTON CT
13 WARWICK CL
14 WARWICK CT
15 TWYFORD CT
16 FARINGDON CT
17 REGENT CT
18 WOODLANDS CT
19 DONNINGTON CT
20 THE TOLLGATE
21 HYDE LODGE
22 HYDE HOUSE GDNS
23 DANES RD
24 HYDE CHURCH PATH
25 BARTHOLOMEW CL
26 ST BEDE'S CT
27 ALSWITHA TERR
28 ROSEWARNE CT
29 KING ALFRED TERR

1

A1
30 ARLINGTON PL
31 DALZELL
32 YORK HO

11

4

A
B
C
North Hampshire STREET ATLAS
Wiltshire STREET ATLAS
Coalpits Copse
Park Lane
Park Copse
Redridge Copse
Bentley Wood
Beechwood Copse
Barnridge Copse
Elm's Copse
Howe Cottage
Howe Copse East
Hatchers Farm
Howe Farm
Heath Copse
Howe Copse West
Dean Copse
SP5
Hawks Grove
Fine Wood
STANDING HILL
Home Farm
Duck Ponds
Cole's Pond Farm
RED LA
Tytherley Common
South Lodge
DEAN RD
Drove Farm
Frenchmoor Farm
Rosewood Farm
FRENCHMOOR LA
Glebe Farm
ROOKERY COTTS
Church Farm
PO
RECTORY HILL
West Dean
Dean
Park Farm
LC
MOODY'S HILL
Green Acre
Windrush
DEAN RD
MOODY'S HILL
The Red Lion (PH)
Sawmills
HILLSIDE CL
FRENCHMOOR LA
Old Brewers (PH)
ASHMORE LA
4
3
29
28
2
1
24
25
26

24
4

3

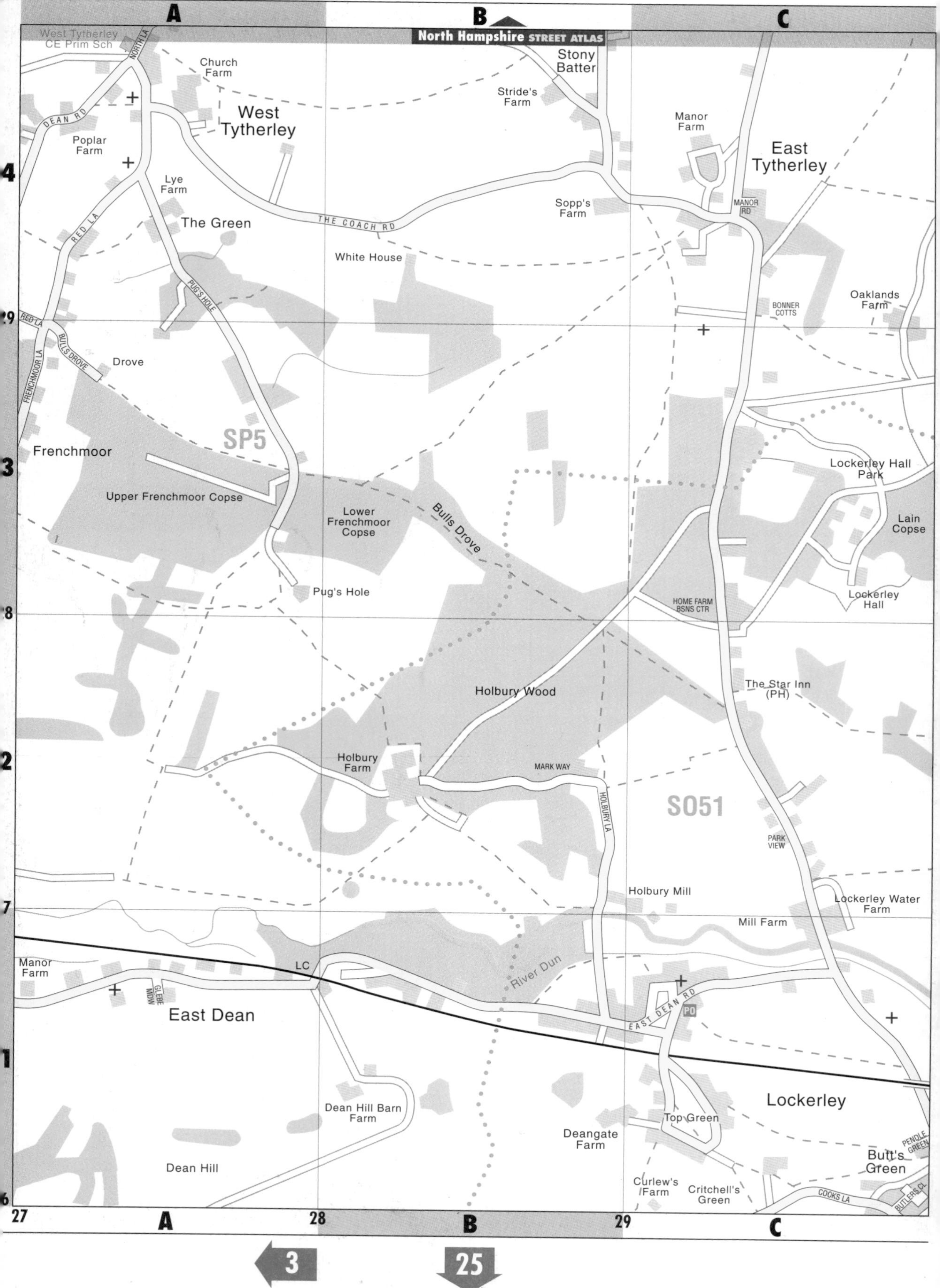
A
B
C
North Hampshire STREET ATLAS
West Tytherley CE Prim Sch
NORTH LA
Church Farm
West Tytherley
DEAN RD
Poplar Farm
Lye Farm
The Green
RED LA
Stony Batter
Stride's Farm
Manor Farm
East Tytherley
Sopp's Farm
MANOR RD
THE COACH RD
White House
PUG'S HOLE
BONNER COTTS
Oaklands Farm
RED LA
BULLS DROVE
FRENCHMOOR LA
Drove
SP5
Frenchmoor
Upper Frenchmoor Copse
Lower Frenchmoor Copse
Bulls Drove
Lockerley Hall Park
Lain Copse
Lockerley Hall
HOME FARM BSNS CTR
Pug's Hole
The Star Inn (PH)
Holbury Wood
Holbury Farm
MARK WAY
HOLBURY LA
SO51
PARK VIEW
Holbury Mill
Lockerley Water Farm
Mill Farm
Manor Farm
LC
River Dun
GLEBE MDW
East Dean
EAST DEAN RD
PO
Lockerley
Dean Hill Barn Farm
Top Green
Deangate Farm
PENDLE GREEN
Butt's Green
Dean Hill
Curlew's Farm
Critchell's Green
COOKS LA
BUTLERS CL
27
28
29
4
29
3
8
2
7
1
6

3

25

6

North Hampshire STREET ATLAS
A
B
C
Hackpits Copse
B3084
Deborah Copse
Redhills Copse
Pittleworth Manor
Pittleworth Farm
4
Little Bentley Farm
Great Bentley Farm
Holm Moor Copse
SP5
SO20
Bentley Firs
29
Blackpits Wood
The Bungalow
3
Great Copse
Lain Copse
Clapgate Copse
Newlyns Farm
BACK LA
Spearywell Wood
SO51
Snook's Copse
28
Bushy Copse
Blackmoor Firs
Culver Leaze
Woodland Walk
Cadbury Farm
2
Spearywell
Dummer Copse
Test Way
Mottisfont Abbey (National Trust)
Gardens
Priory
OAKLEY RD
BENGER'S LA
KEEPERS LA
Abbey Farm
Mottisfont
PO
HATT LA
Glebe Farm
River Dun
Drove Copse
Hatt Farm
Hatt Hill
Monarch's Way
CHURCH LA
1
River Test
Lockerley Endowed CE Prim Sch
Dunbridge
LOCKERLEY RD
The School Farm
LC
LC
Butt's Green
Dunbridge
Test Way
River Dun
OVAL RD
CLEM'S WAY
RUSSELL DR 1
MILL RISE 2
LOCKERLEY RD
PH
DUNBRIDGE LA
B3084
30
31
32

26
6

5
A
B
C
North Hampshire STREET ATLAS
A3057 Stockbridge
A3057
Lodge
Drovelands
ROMSEY RD
Compton Park
Humbers Wood
Test Way
Compton
Compton Manor
Compton Home Farm
Brook Dairy Farm
Horse Lynch
BROOK COTTS
Monarch's Way
Brook
River Test
SO20
News Wood
Oakley Copse
Eldon Firs
Lower Brook
Strouds Wood
Oakley Farm
Lower Eldon Farm
Michelmersh Wood
Park Farm Bungalow
SO51
Parnell Lane
Michelmersh Court
MESH RD
CHURCH RD
Stonymarsh Cottage
The Monarch's Way
Manor Farm
Oak Tree Farm
SCHOOL LA
Michelmersh
Stonymarsh
STAFF RD
HACKUPPS LA
MANOR FARM LA
Linhay Meads Dairy
A3057
4
29
3
8
2
7
1
6
33
34
35
27

A
B
C
North Hampshire STREET ATLAS
King's Somborne
Hoplands
Charlwood Copse
Clarendon Way
Bourne Farm
Hoplands Cottages
FURZEDOWN RD
FURZEDOWN COTTS
Furzedown Farm
FURZEDOWN HO
Humbers Wood
Combe Bottom
Luke Copse
Dirty Mount
Parnholt Wood
SO20
News Wood
ELDON RD
The Bungalow
Eldon House
Bailey's Down
Taunton Vale
Fishponds Farm
Bailey's Down Farm
PARNHOLT RD
Stubb's Copse
SO51
Farley House
Blue Haze Farm
Bull Grove Copse
Parnell La
Monarch's Way
Windmill Cottages
KINGS SOMBORNE RD
FARLEY LA
Hall Place
Pitt Farm
Braishfield Manor
Fern Hill La
Fernhill Farm
PAYNES HAY RD
BRAISHFIELD RD
4
29
3
28
2
27
1
26
36
37
38

7

A B C

4
9
3
8
2
7
1
6

39 A 40 B 41 C

7
29

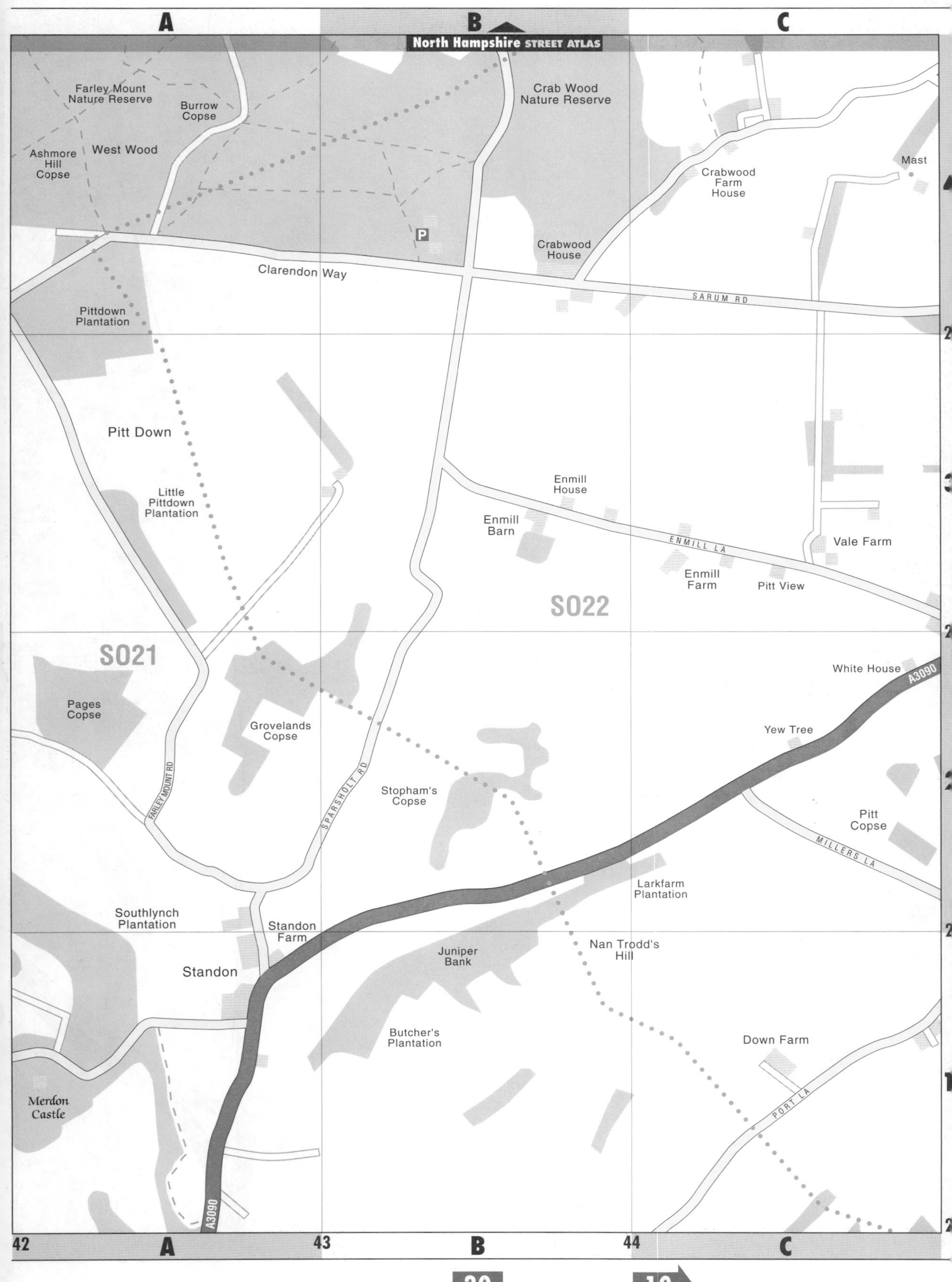
A
B
C
North Hampshire STREET ATLAS
Farley Mount Nature Reserve
Burrow Copse
Crab Wood Nature Reserve
Ashmore Hill Copse
West Wood
Crabwood Farm House
Mast
Crabwood House
Clarendon Way
SARUM RD
Pittdown Plantation
Pitt Down
Little Pittdown Plantation
Enmill House
Enmill Barn
ENMILL LA
Vale Farm
Enmill Farm
Pitt View
SO22
SO21
White House
A3090
Pages Copse
Grovelands Copse
Yew Tree
FARLEY MOUNT RD
SPARSHOLT RD
Stopham's Copse
Pitt Copse
MILLERS LA
Larkfarm Plantation
Southlynch Plantation
Standon Farm
Nan Trodd's Hill
Juniper Bank
Standon
Butcher's Plantation
Down Farm
Merdon Castle
PORT LA
A3090
42
A
43
B
44
C

C4
1 RONALD BOWKER CT
2 FULFLOOD CT
3 FORDINGTON RD
4 BANKSIDE HO
5 SPICERS CT
6 ABBOTS ROW
9
C4
7 KINGS ROW
8 EDINBURGH HO
9 RICHMOND HO
10 ALISON WAY
11 CAPITAL HO
12 EAGLE CT
1
C4
13 KINGSDALE CT
14 TOWER CT
15 BILBERRY CT
16 FABERS YD
17 PRINTERS ROW
18 CHARLECOTE MEWS
19 ST PAULS PL
20 BLACK SWAN BLDGS
21 ST CLEMENT ST
22 ST THOMAS MEWS
23 LIONS HALL
24 DUMMER MEWS
25 CULVERWELL GDNS
26 ST MICHAEL'S GDNS
27 FAIRLAWN HO
28 CONSTABLES GATE
29 BEAUMOND GN
30 QUEENS CT
31 THE MONS
32 CLIFTON LODGE NO 1
33 CLIFTON LODGE NO 2
34 ARBOUR CT
35 MACKLIN HO
36 HIGHFIELD TERR
37 CEDAR WLK
A
B
C
Teg Down
Mast
Royal Winchester
Sarum Farm
CH
Teg Down Farm
Sarum Road
Westgate Sec Sch
Western CE Prim Sch
CHILBOLTON AVE
B3041
Student Village
HM Prison
Cty Pol HQ
Winchester
Royal Hampshire County
King Alfred's Coll
Cemy
West Hill
Kings' Sch
SARUM RD
B3
1 WOOLFORD CL
2 WILBERFORCE CL
3 BIRCH CT
4 THE VALLEY CT
5 LENT HILL CT
6 GENERAL JOHNSON CT
Sleepers' Hill
WINCHESTER
VENTA BELGARVM
ROMSEY RD
Pitt Manor
St Peter's RC Prim Sch
Garage
B3040
Pitt
PITT RDBT
A3090
Manor Farm
South Winchester
Oliver Cromwell's Battery
Stanmore
SO22
Recn Gd
Stanmore Prim Sch
Badger Farm
Superstore
Whiteshute Lane
Clarendon Way
Oliver's Battery
Oliver's Battery Prim Sch
Maybush
The Old Kennels
BADGER FARM RD
Bushfield Camp
Bushfield Farm
Texas
Compton Down
Yew Hill
Silkstead Lane
Attwoods Drove Farm
Yew Tree Farm
SO21
St Cross
ST CROSS RD
B3335
St Cross Hospital
SO23
St Cross Farm
St Cross Mill
St Cross Bridge
River Itchen
HOCKLEY LINK
M3
The Itchen Navigation
Tumbling Bay
Ridding Meads
St Faith's CE Prim Sch
Winchester Coll
C3
1 CHRISTCHURCH GDNS
2 PALMERSTON CT
3 LANSDOWNE CT
4 ST CROSS CT
45
46
47
9
31

A4
1 HOMERISE HO
2 ARLINGTON PL
3 MATILDA PL
4 DANEMARK CT
5 MARSTON GATE
6 ROPEWALK HO
7 DE LUNN BLDGS
8 RICHARD MOSS HO
9 NORTHGATE CHAMBERS
10 PRINCESS CT
11 MILMAN CT
12 PRIORY GDNS
13 WESLEY HO
14 ST GEORGES' HO
15 SAXON CT
16 TROWBRIDGE CT
17 MERCHANTS PL
18 PRINCE'S BLDGS
19 HANDY VILLAS
20 COSSACK LA
21 LAWN HO
22 GARDEN LA
23 COSSACK LANE HO
24 GODSON HO
25 WINDSOR HO
26 GREYFRIARS
27 ST JOHN'S HOSPITAL (N)
28 TANNER ST
29 CROSS KEYS PAS
30 ST THOMAS ST
31 ST CLEMENT ST
32 KINGS HEAD YD
33 MINSTER LA
34 GREAT MINSTER ST

2

A4
35 CULVER RD
36 PATORNOSTER ROW
37 PATORNOSTER HO
38 ST JOHN'S HOSPITAL (S)
39 MILDWAY CT
40 ITCHEN CT

12

A4
41 DURGATE TERR
42 PARMITER HO
43 MANOR CL
44 RIVERSIDE HO
45 MAGDALEN MEWS
46 BRIDGE ST
47 EARLSDOWN
48 THE CONSERVATORY
49 WATERSMEET
50 ST MARY MAGDALEN ALMSHOUSES

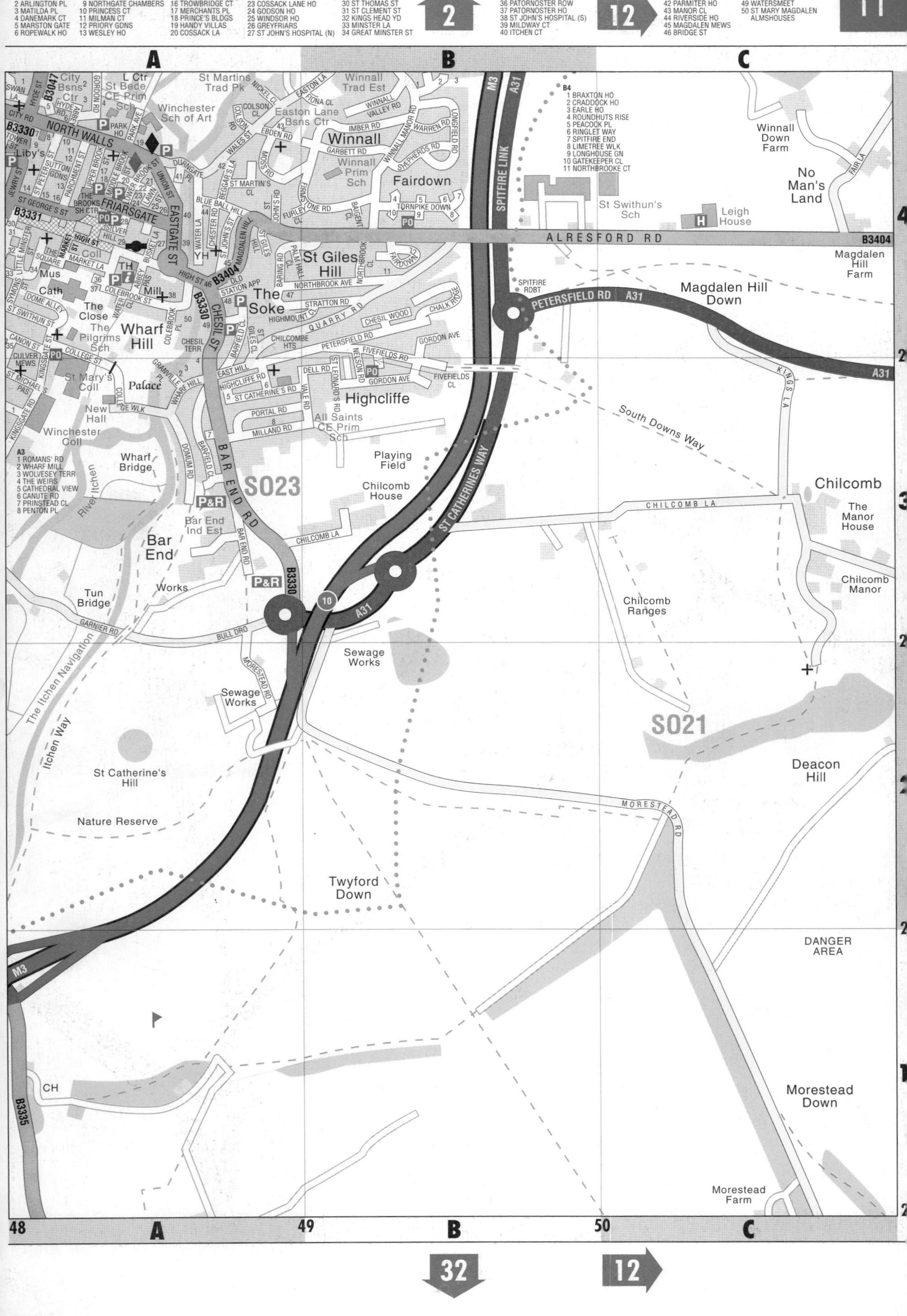

32
12

11

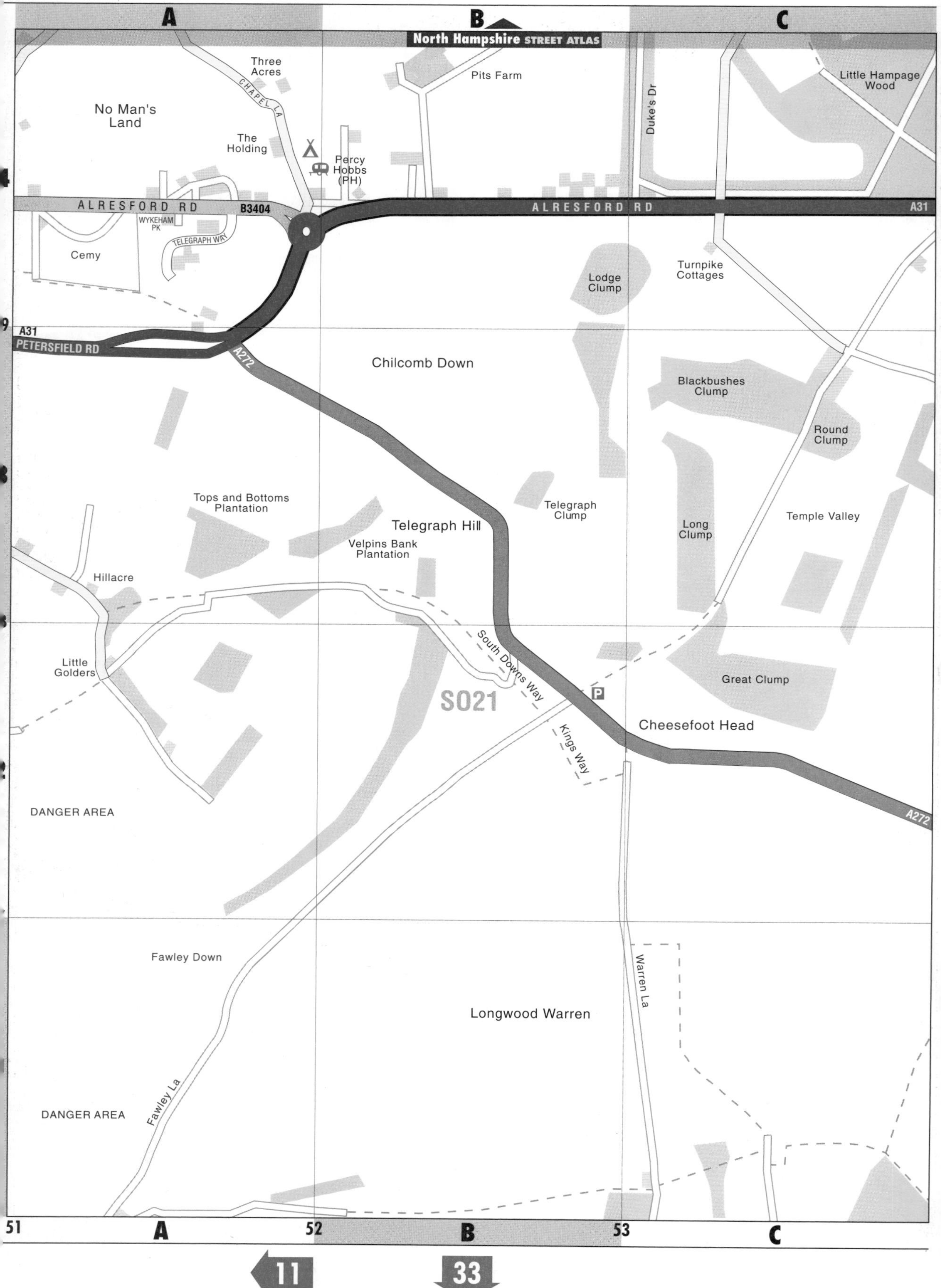
A
B
C
North Hampshire STREET ATLAS
Three Acres
Pits Farm
Little Hampage Wood
No Man's Land
CHAPEL LA
Duke's Dr
The Holding
Percy Hobbs (PH)
ALRESFORD RD
B3404
ALRESFORD RD
A31
WYKEHAM PK
TELEGRAPH WAY
Cemy
Lodge Clump
Turnpike Cottages
A31
PETERSFIELD RD
A272
Chilcomb Down
Blackbushes Clump
Round Clump
Tops and Bottoms Plantation
Telegraph Hill
Telegraph Clump
Long Clump
Temple Valley
Velpins Bank Plantation
Hillacre
South Downs Way
Little Golders
SO21
P
Great Clump
Cheesefoot Head
Kings Way
A272
DANGER AREA
Fawley Down
Warren La
Longwood Warren
Fawley La
DANGER AREA
51
A
52
B
53
C

11
33

14

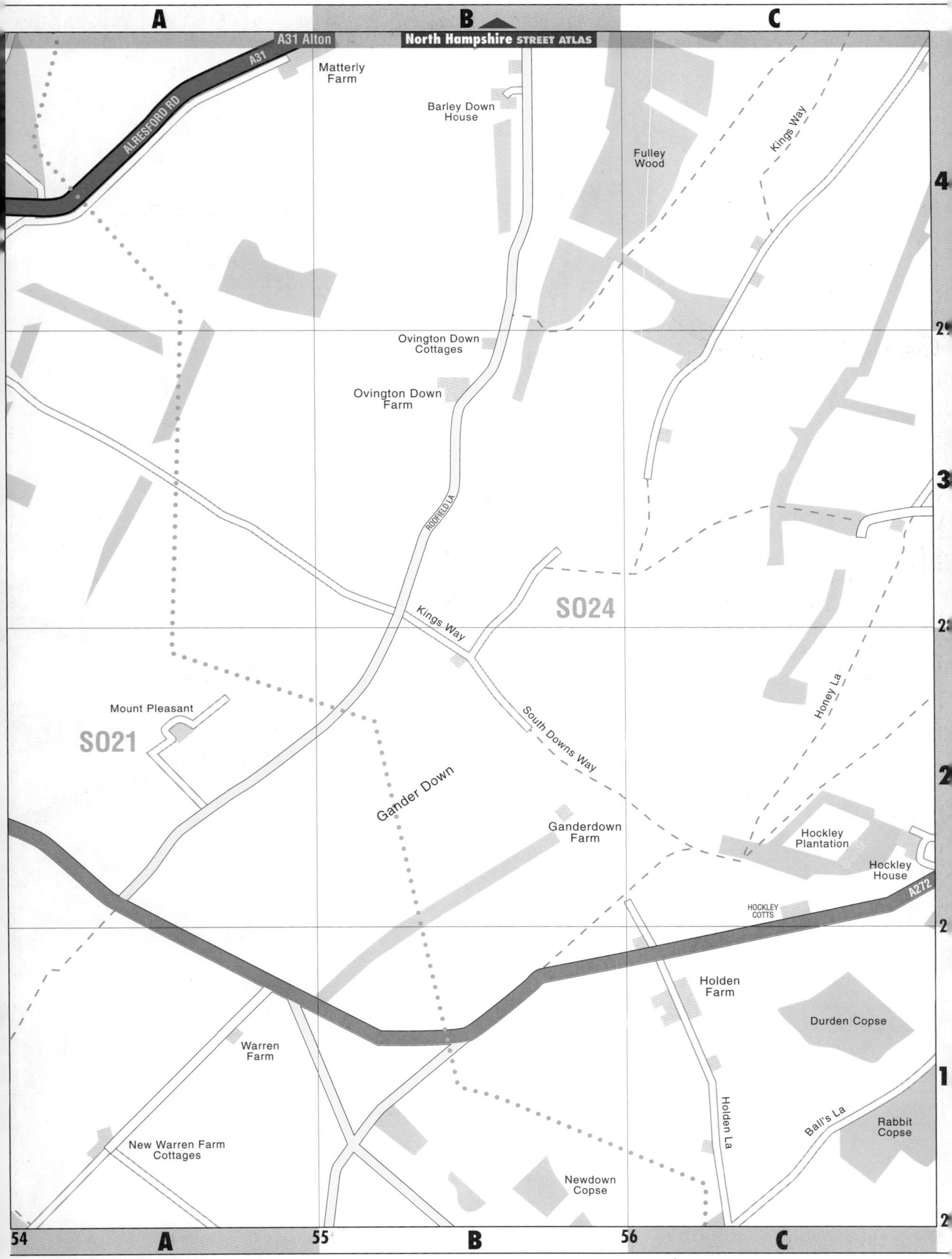

North Hampshire STREET ATLAS

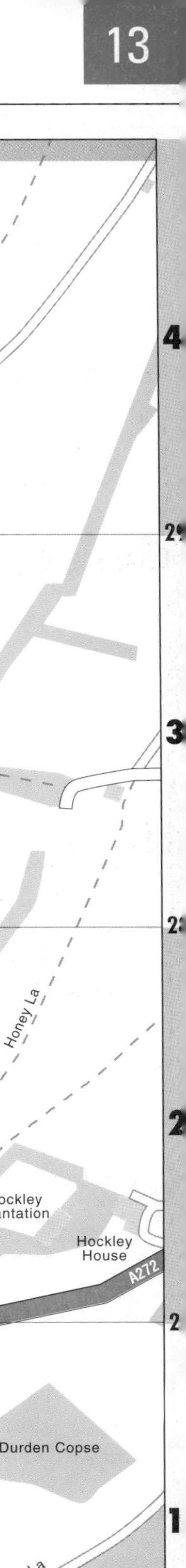

A B C

A31 Alton
A31
ALRESFORD RD
Matterly Farm
Barley Down House
Fulley Wood
Kings Way
Ovington Down Cottages
Ovington Down Farm
RODFIELD LA
Kings Way
SO24
South Downs Way
Honey La
Mount Pleasant
SO21
Gander Down
Ganderdown Farm
Hockley Plantation
Hockley House
A272
HOCKLEY COTTS
Holden Farm
Durden Copse
Warren Farm
Holden La
Ball's La
Rabbit Copse
New Warren Farm Cottages
Newdown Copse

54 A 55 B 56 C

34
14

13

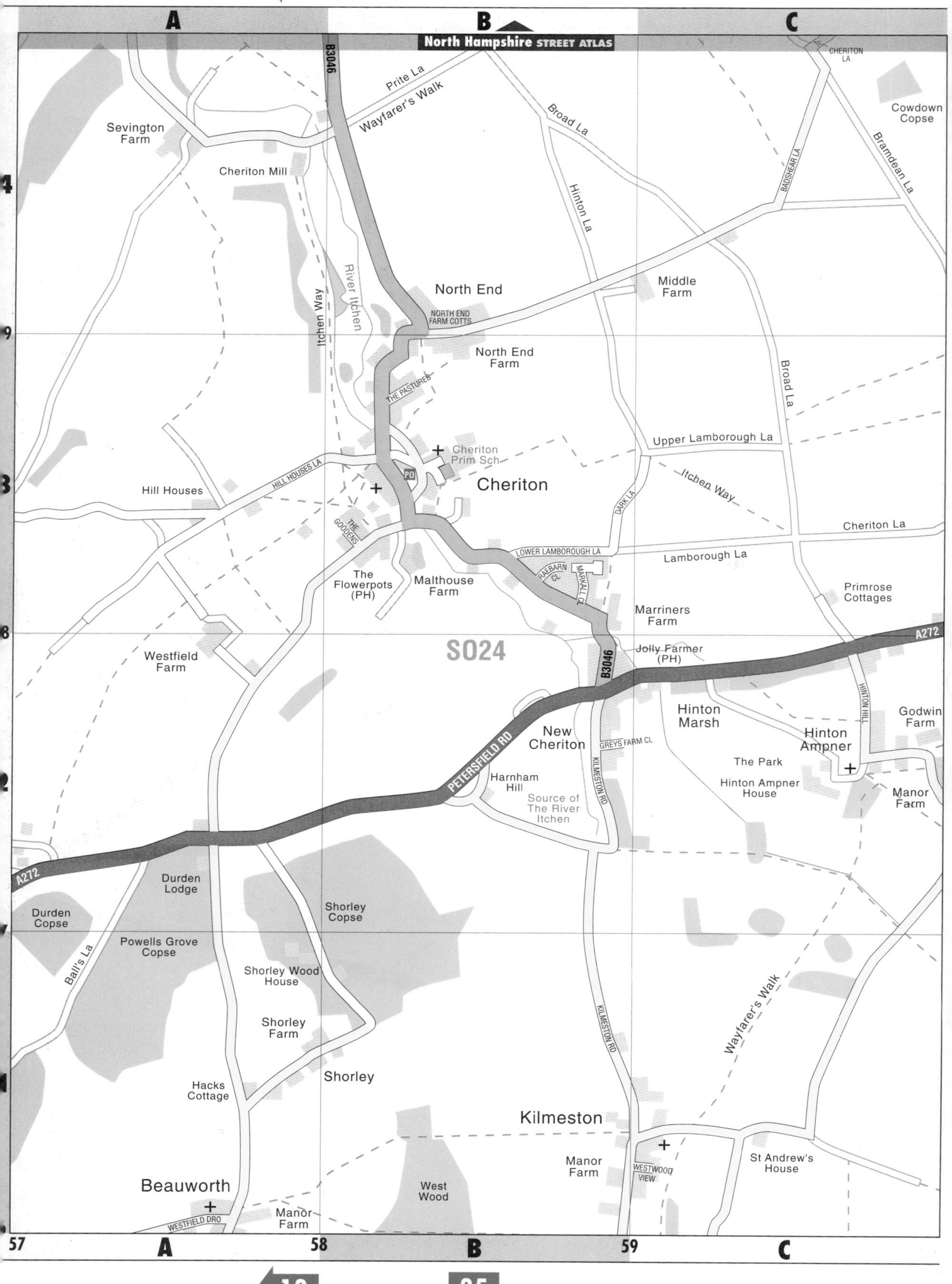
A
B
C
North Hampshire STREET ATLAS
B3046
Prite La
Wayfarer's Walk
Broad La
CHERITON LA
Cowdown Copse
Bramdean La
Sevington Farm
Cheriton Mill
Hinton La
BADSHEAR LA
Middle Farm
North End
NORTH END FARM COTTS
River Itchen
Itchen Way
North End Farm
THE PASTURES
Broad La
Upper Lamborough La
Cheriton Prim Sch
Cheriton
PO
Itchen Way
HILL HOUSES LA
Hill Houses
DARK LA
THE GOODENS
Cheriton La
LOWER LAMBOROUGH LA
Lamborough La
RAEBARN CL
MARKALL CL
The Flowerpots (PH)
Malthouse Farm
Primrose Cottages
Marriners Farm
A272
Jolly Farmer (PH)
SO24
Westfield Farm
B3046
HINTON HILL
Hinton Marsh
Godwin Farm
New Cheriton
Hinton Ampner
GREYS FARM CL
PETERSFIELD RD
KILMESTON RD
The Park
Harnham Hill
Hinton Ampner House
Manor Farm
Source of The River Itchen
A272
Durden Lodge
Durden Copse
Shorley Copse
Powells Grove Copse
Ball's La
Shorley Wood House
Wayfarer's Walk
KILMESTON RD
Shorley Farm
Shorley
Hacks Cottage
Kilmeston
Manor Farm
WESTWOOD VIEW
St Andrew's House
West Wood
Beauworth
WESTFIELD DRO
Manor Farm
57
A
58
B
59
C

13
35

A B C

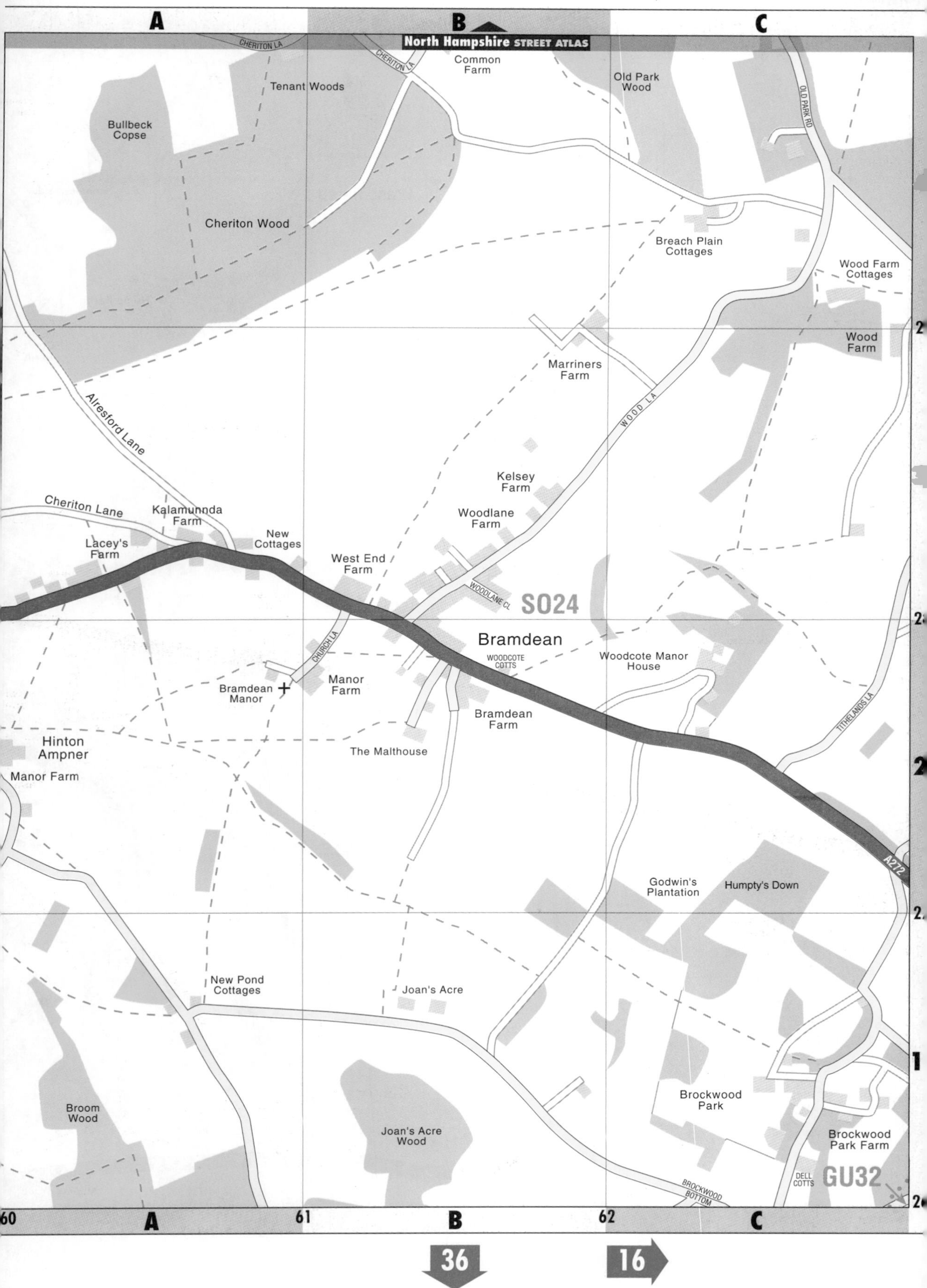
North Hampshire STREET ATLAS
CHERITON LA
Common Farm
Old Park Wood
OLD PARK RD
Tenant Woods
Bullbeck Copse
Cheriton Wood
Breach Plain Cottages
Wood Farm Cottages
Wood Farm
Marriners Farm
WOOD LA
Alresford Lane
Kelsey Farm
Woodlane Farm
Cheriton Lane
Kalamunnda Farm
New Cottages
Lacey's Farm
West End Farm
WOODLANE CL
SO24
Bramdean
CHURCH LA
WOODCOTE COTTS
Woodcote Manor House
Bramdean Manor
Manor Farm
Bramdean Farm
TITHELANDS LA
Hinton Ampner
Manor Farm
The Malthouse
A272
Godwin's Plantation
Humpty's Down
New Pond Cottages
Joan's Acre
Brockwood Park
Broom Wood
Joan's Acre Wood
Brockwood Park Farm
DELL COTTS
GU32
BROCKWOOD BOTTOM
60
61
62

A B C

15

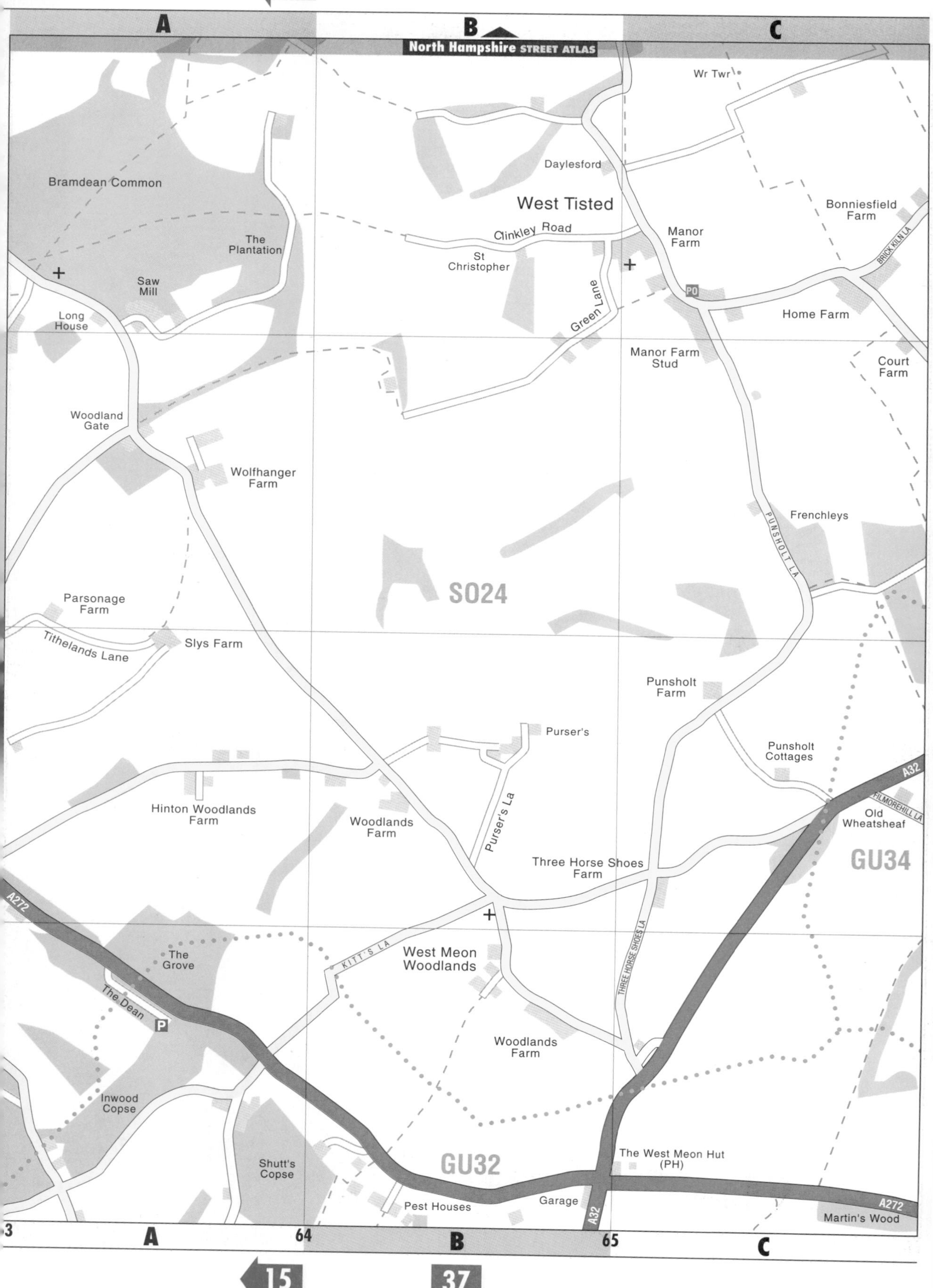
A
B
C
North Hampshire STREET ATLAS
Wr Twr
Bramdean Common
Daylesford
West Tisted
Bonniesfield Farm
Clinkley Road
Manor Farm
The Plantation
St Christopher
BRICK KILN LA
Saw Mill
Green Lane
PO
Home Farm
Long House
Manor Farm Stud
Court Farm
Woodland Gate
Wolfhanger Farm
Frenchleys
PUNSHOLT LA
Parsonage Farm
SO24
Tithelands Lane
Slys Farm
Punsholt Farm
Purser's
Punsholt Cottages
A32
FILMOREHILL LA
Old Wheatsheaf
Hinton Woodlands Farm
Woodlands Farm
Purser's La
GU34
Three Horse Shoes Farm
A272
KITT'S LA
West Meon Woodlands
The Grove
THREE HORSE SHOES LA
The Dean
P
Woodlands Farm
Inwood Copse
Shutt's Copse
GU32
The West Meon Hut (PH)
Pest Houses
Garage
A272
A32
Martin's Wood
3
A
64
B
65
C

15
37

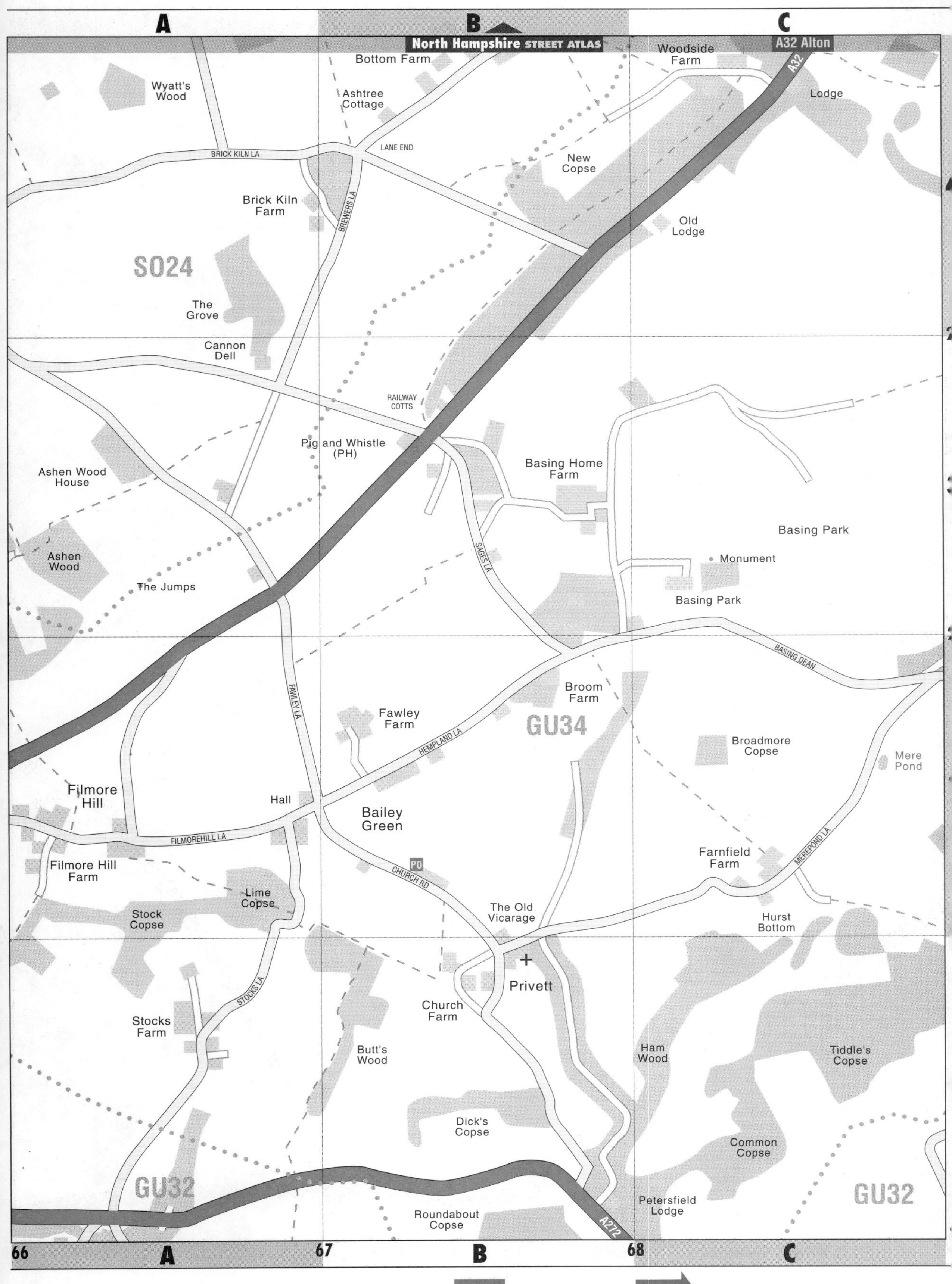
A
B
C
North Hampshire STREET ATLAS
A32 Alton
Bottom Farm
Woodside Farm
Wyatt's Wood
Ashtree Cottage
A32
Lodge
LANE END
BRICK KILN LA
New Copse
Brick Kiln Farm
BREWERS LA
Old Lodge
SO24
The Grove
Cannon Dell
RAILWAY COTTS
Pig and Whistle (PH)
Basing Home Farm
Ashen Wood House
Basing Park
Ashen Wood
SAGES LA
Monument
The Jumps
Basing Park
BASING DEAN
Broom Farm
FAWLEY LA
Fawley Farm
GU34
Broadmore Copse
HEMPLAND LA
Mere Pond
Filmore Hill
Hall
Bailey Green
FILMOREHILL LA
MEREPOND LA
Farnfield Farm
Filmore Hill Farm
PO
CHURCH RD
Lime Copse
Stock Copse
The Old Vicarage
Hurst Bottom
Privett
STOCKS LA
Church Farm
Stocks Farm
Butt's Wood
Ham Wood
Tiddle's Copse
Dick's Copse
Common Copse
GU32
Petersfield Lodge
GU32
Roundabout Copse
A272
66
A
67
B
68
C

17

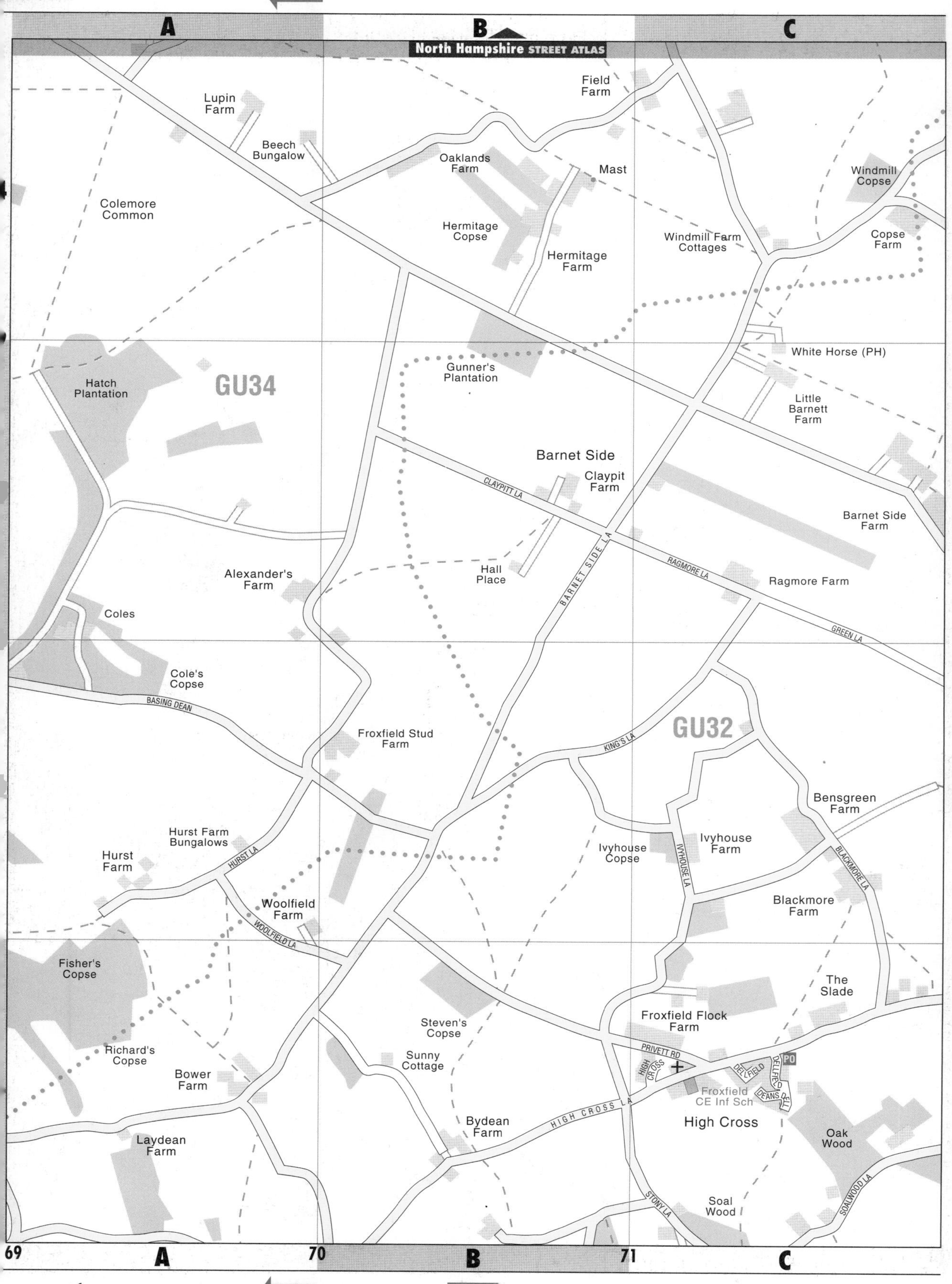
A
B
C
North Hampshire STREET ATLAS
Lupin Farm
Beech Bungalow
Field Farm
Oaklands Farm
Mast
Windmill Copse
Colemore Common
Hermitage Copse
Windmill Farm Cottages
Copse Farm
Hermitage Farm
White Horse (PH)
Gunner's Plantation
Hatch Plantation
GU34
Little Barnett Farm
Barnet Side
Claypit Farm
CLAYPITT LA
Barnet Side Farm
BARNET SIDE LA
RAGMORE LA
Alexander's Farm
Hall Place
Ragmore Farm
Coles
GREEN LA
Cole's Copse
BASING DEAN
GU32
Froxfield Stud Farm
KING'S LA
Bensgreen Farm
Hurst Farm Bungalows
Ivyhouse Copse
Ivyhouse Farm
Hurst Farm
HURST LA
IVYHOUSE LA
BLACKMORE LA
Woolfield Farm
Blackmore Farm
WOOLFIELD LA
Fisher's Copse
The Slade
Froxfield Flock Farm
Steven's Copse
Richard's Copse
PRIVETT RD
Sunny Cottage
HIGH CROSS
DELFIELD
DEANS DELL
PO
Bower Farm
Froxfield CE Inf Sch
HIGH CROSS LA
Bydean Farm
High Cross
Laydean Farm
Oak Wood
STONY LA
Soal Wood
SOALWOOD LA
69
70
71

17
39

20

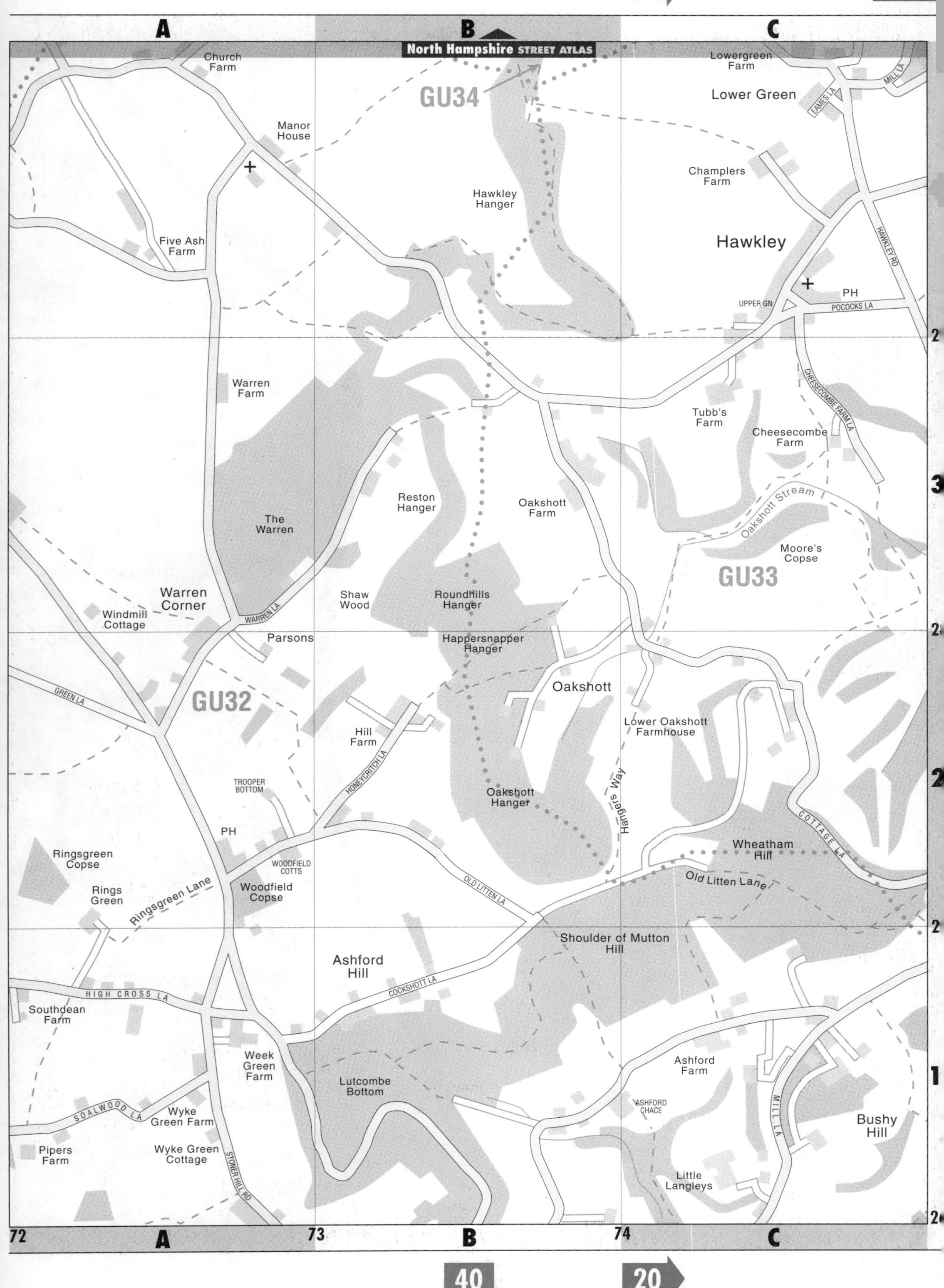
North Hampshire STREET ATLAS
A
B
C
Church Farm
Manor House
GU34
Hawkley Hanger
Lowergreen Farm
Lower Green
EAMES LA
MILL LA
Champlers Farm
Hawkley
HAWKLEY RD
PH
UPPER GN
POCOCKS LA
Five Ash Farm
Warren Farm
Tubb's Farm
CHEESECOMBE FARM LA
Cheesecombe Farm
Oakshott Stream
Reston Hanger
Oakshott Farm
The Warren
Moore's Copse
GU33
Warren Corner
Windmill Cottage
WARREN LA
Shaw Wood
Roundhills Hanger
Parsons
Happersnapper Hanger
Oakshott
GREEN LA
GU32
Hill Farm
Lower Oakshott Farmhouse
HONEYCRITCH LA
TROOPER BOTTOM
Oakshott Hanger
Hangers Way
COTTAGE LA
PH
Ringsgreen Copse
WOODFIELD COTTS
Wheatham Hill
Old Litten Lane
Rings Green
Ringsgreen Lane
Woodfield Copse
OLD LITTEN LA
Shoulder of Mutton Hill
Ashford Hill
HIGH CROSS LA
COCKSHOTT LA
Southdean Farm
Week Green Farm
Lutcombe Bottom
Ashford Farm
ASHFORD CHACE
MILL LA
Bushy Hill
SOALWOOD LA
Wyke Green Farm
Pipers Farm
Wyke Green Cottage
STONER HILL RD
Little Langleys
72
73
74
A
B
C

19

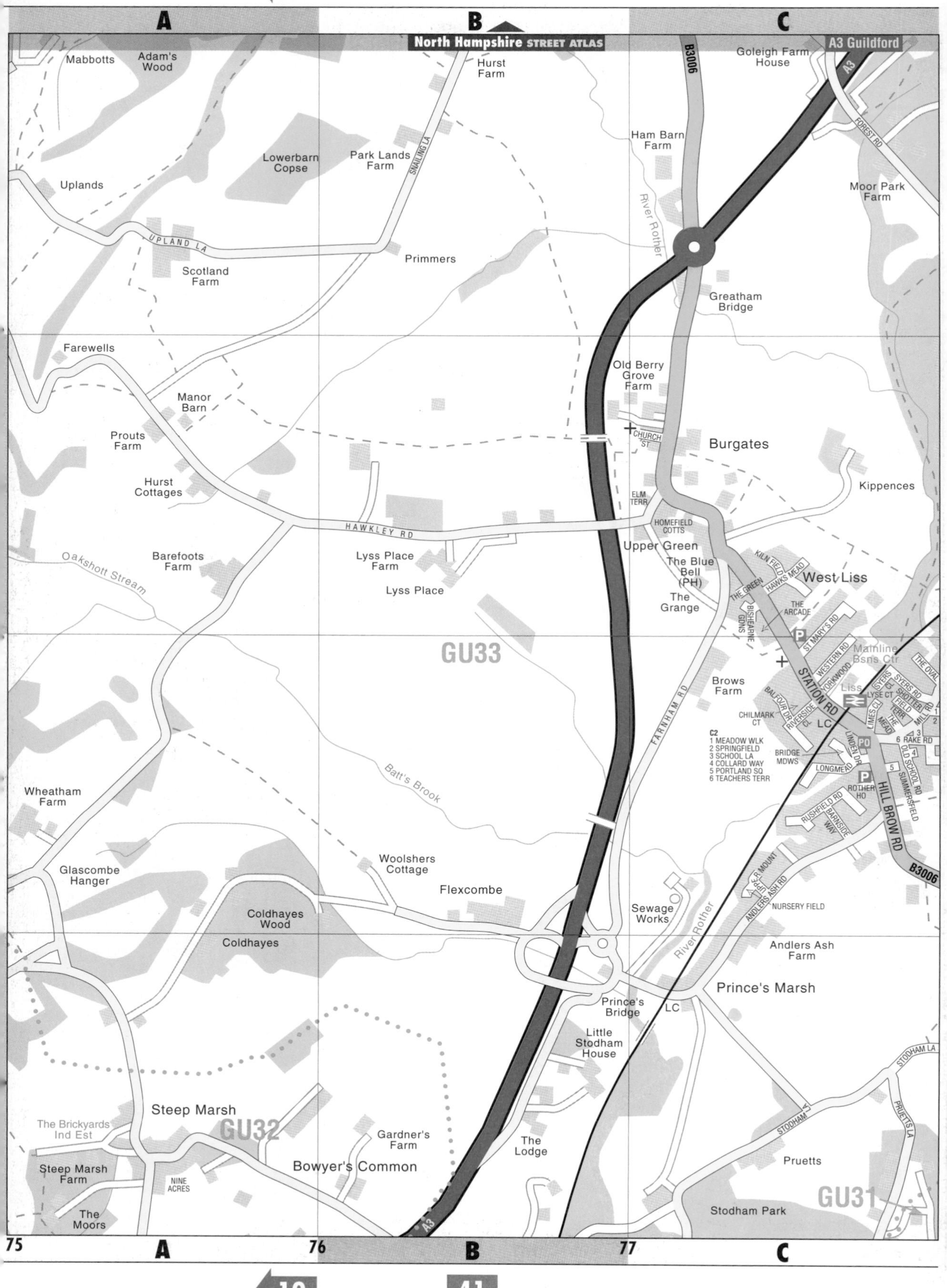
A
B
C
North Hampshire STREET ATLAS
A3 Guildford
Mabbotts
Adam's Wood
Hurst Farm
Goleigh Farm House
Ham Barn Farm
Lowerbarn Copse
Park Lands Farm
Uplands
Moor Park Farm
UPLAND LA
Scotland Farm
Primmers
Greatham Bridge
Farewells
Old Berry Grove Farm
Manor Barn
Prouts Farm
Burgates
Kippences
Hurst Cottages
HAWKLEY RD
Upper Green
Barefoots Farm
Lyss Place Farm
The Blue Bell (PH)
West Liss
Oakshott Stream
Lyss Place
The Grange
GU33
Brows Farm
Mainline Bsns Ctr
Liss
STATION RD
FARNHAM RD
C2
1 MEADOW WLK
2 SPRINGFIELD
3 SCHOOL LA
4 COLLARD WAY
5 PORTLAND SQ
6 TEACHERS TERR
Batt's Brook
Wheatham Farm
HILL BROW RD
B3006
Glascombe Hanger
Woolshers Cottage
Flexcombe
Sewage Works
Coldhayes Wood
Coldhayes
Andlers Ash Farm
Prince's Marsh
Prince's Bridge
Little Stodham House
Steep Marsh
The Brickyards Ind Est
GU32
Gardner's Farm
The Lodge
Steep Marsh Farm
Bowyer's Common
Pruetts
GU31
Stodham Park
The Moors
75
76
77

19
41

A
B
C
North Hampshire STREET ATLAS
Longmoor Inclosure
GU30
Little Dean Bottom
The Wylds
Warren Hill
The Lake
Wylds Farm
Langley
WARREN RD
Langley Bridge Farm
The Temple Inn (PH)
Liss Forest
The Mint
Mangers
Brewells Farm
Little Langley Farm
REEDS LA
Reeds
MINT RD
Home Farm
Whangerei Nursery Palmers Farm
Palmers
Newlands
LC
Wyld Green Farm
Ciddy Hall
ST PATRICK'S LA
Rake CE Prim Sch
East Liss
Liss
GU33
St Patrick's Copse
Rake Bsns Pk
The Flying Bull (PH)
B2070
High Firs House
Coldharbour Park Farm
Rake
HATCH LA
Highfield Farm
Highfield Wood
Sussex Border Path
East Hill
Liss Inf & Jun Schs
CANHOUSE LA
Pot Well
Hill Side
Black Pond
HILL BROW RD
Rake Common
Rake Hanger
Hill Brow
B3006
GU31
Hambledon Piece
Farther Commons
PH
Combe Hill
Clayton Court
Harting Combe
West Sussex STREET ATLAS
LONDON RD
B2070
79
80
78
West Sussex STREET ATLAS

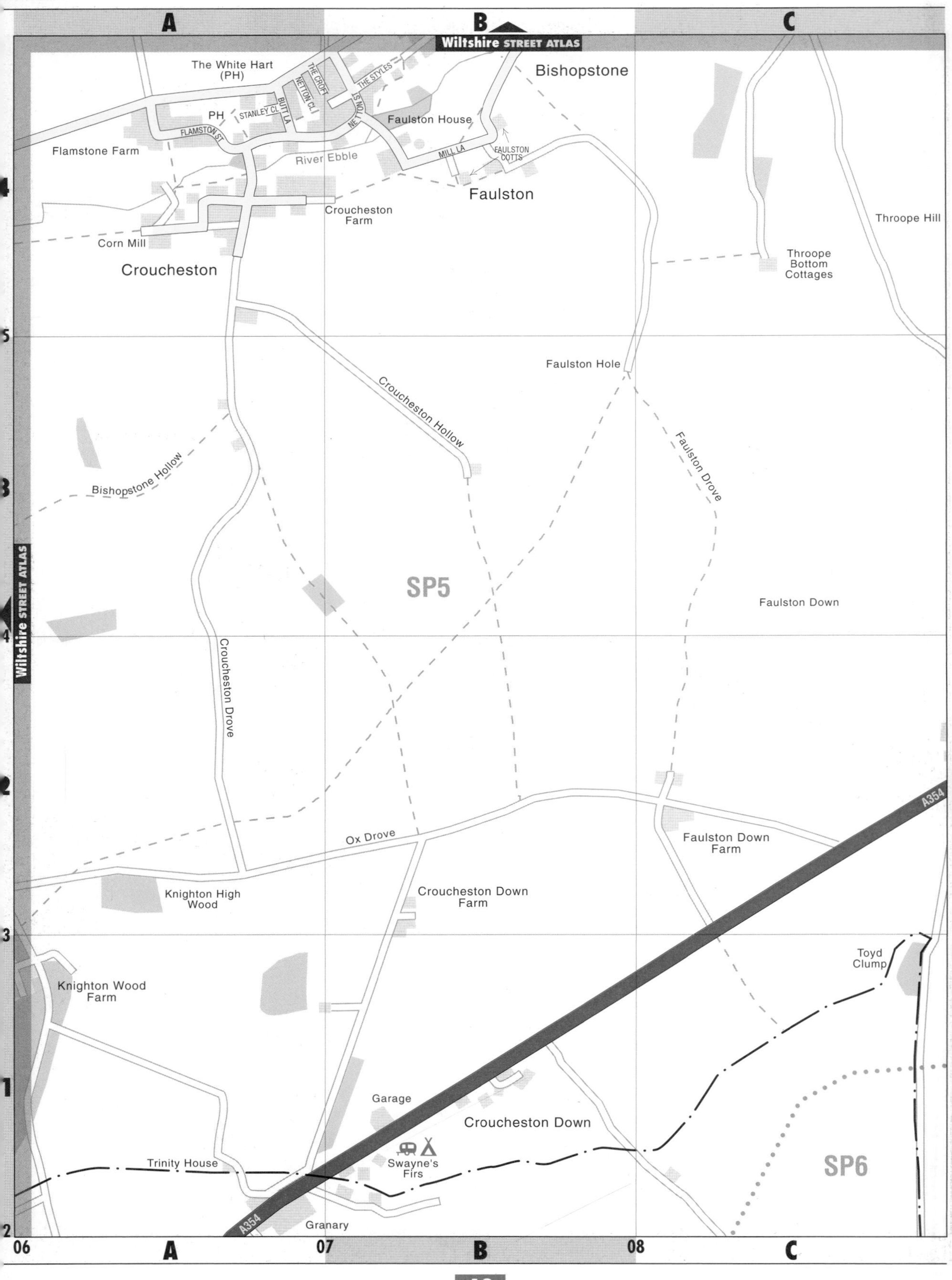
A
B
C
Wiltshire STREET ATLAS
The White Hart (PH)
Bishopstone
PH
STANLEY CL
BUTT LA
NETTON CL
THE CROFT
THE STYLES
NETTON ST
FLAMSTON ST
Faulston House
Flamstone Farm
River Ebble
MILL LA
FAULSTON COTTS
Faulston
Croucheston Farm
Corn Mill
Croucheston
Throope Hill
Throope Bottom Cottages
Faulston Hole
Croucheston Hollow
Faulston Drove
Bishopstone Hollow
SP5
Faulston Down
Croucheston Drove
Ox Drove
Faulston Down Farm
A354
Knighton High Wood
Croucheston Down Farm
Knighton Wood Farm
Toyd Clump
Garage
Croucheston Down
Trinity House
Swayne's Firs
SP6
Granary
06
07
08

43

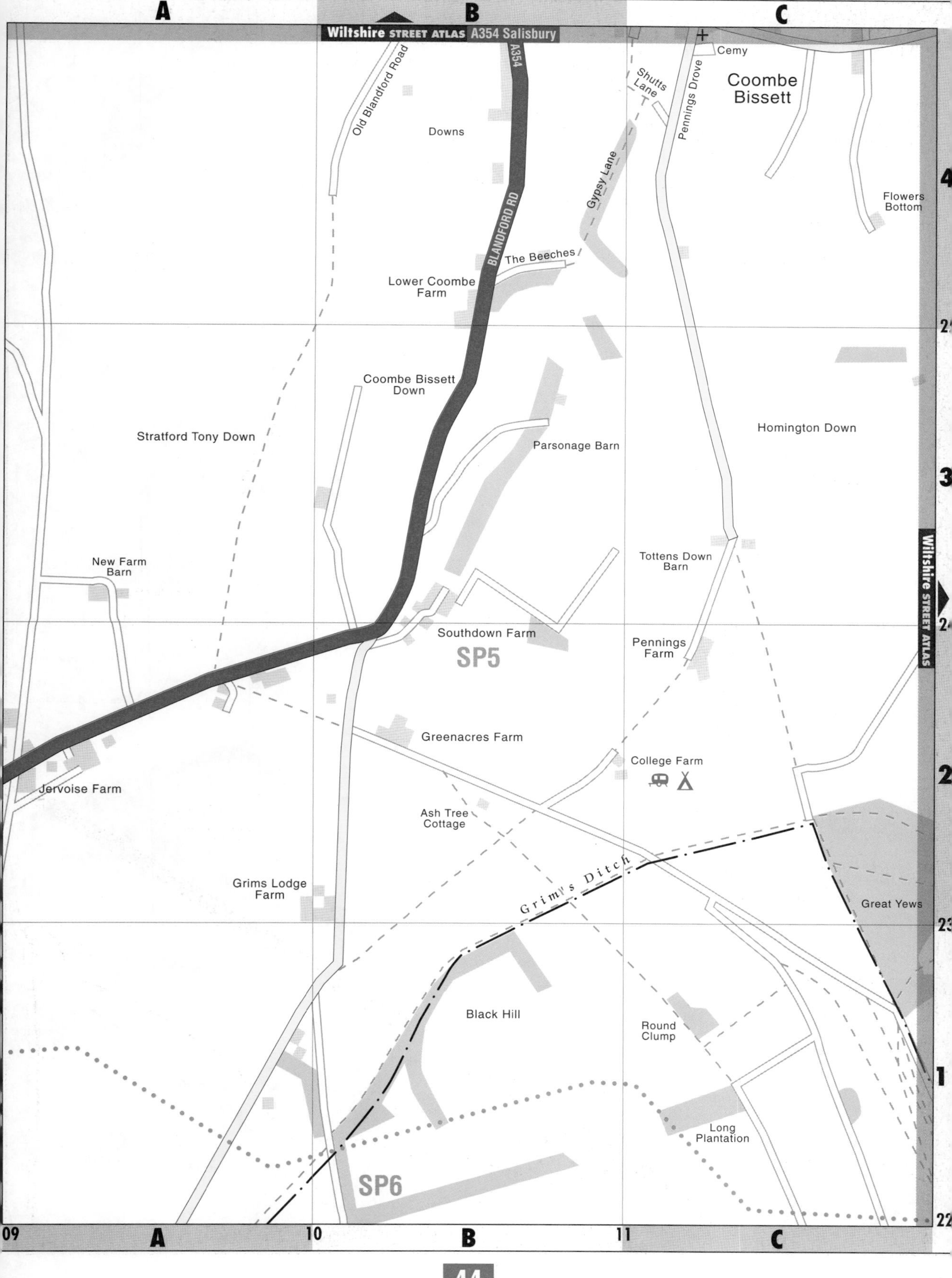
A
B
C
Wiltshire STREET ATLAS
A354 Salisbury
A354
Old Blandford Road
Shutts Lane
Pennings Drove
Cemy
Coombe Bissett
Downs
Gypsy Lane
Flowers Bottom
BLANDFORD RD
The Beeches
Lower Coombe Farm
Coombe Bissett Down
Homington Down
Stratford Tony Down
Parsonage Barn
New Farm Barn
Tottens Down Barn
Southdown Farm
SP5
Pennings Farm
Greenacres Farm
College Farm
Jervoise Farm
Ash Tree Cottage
Grims Lodge Farm
Grim's Ditch
Great Yews
Black Hill
Round Clump
Long Plantation
SP6
09
10
11
22
23
24
1
2
3
4
Wiltshire STREET ATLAS

44

3

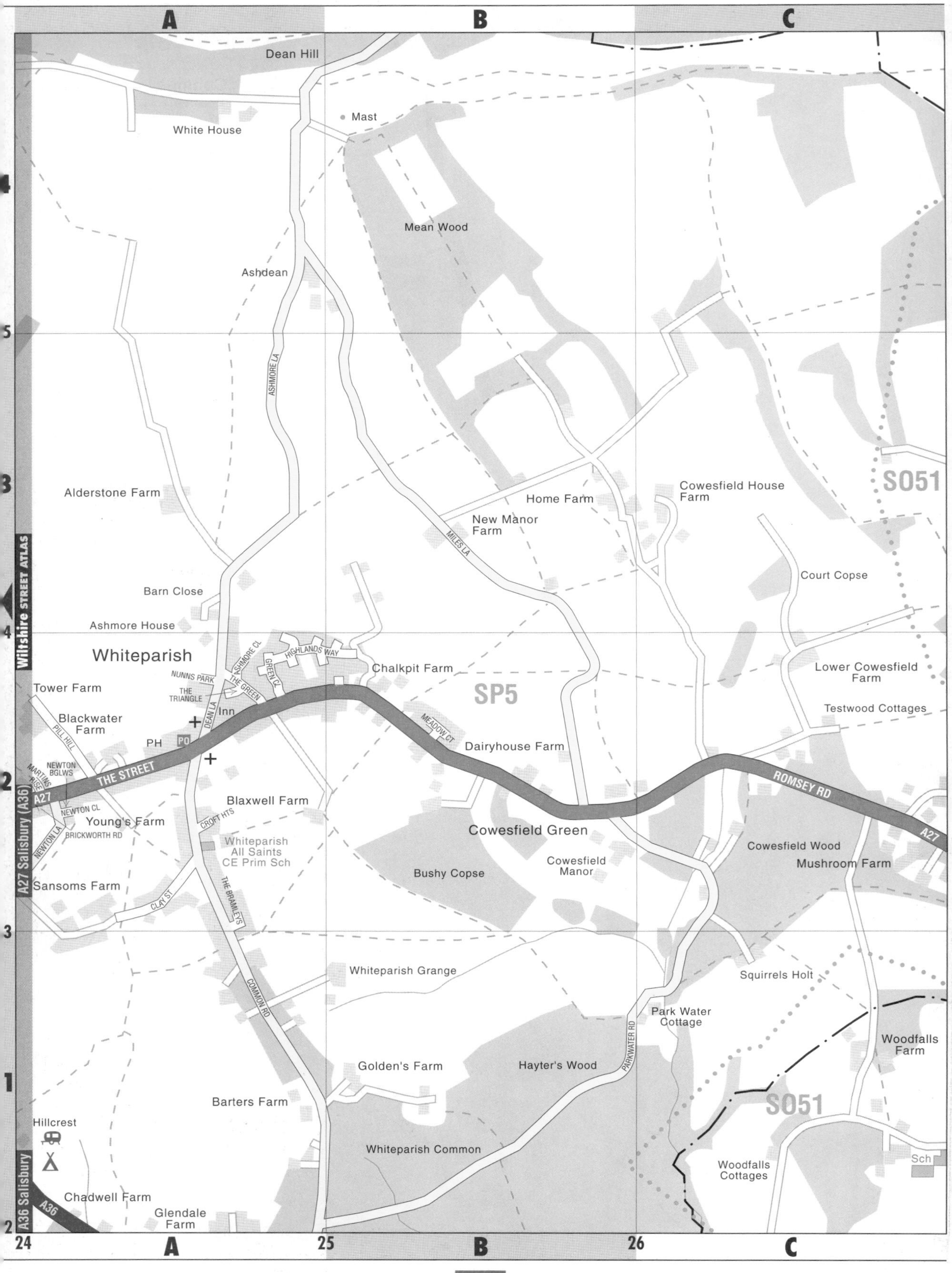
A
B
C
Dean Hill
White House
Mast
Mean Wood
Ashdean
ASHMORE LA
Alderstone Farm
Home Farm
Cowesfield House
Farm
New Manor
Farm
MILES LA
S051
Court Copse
Barn Close
Ashmore House
Whiteparish
HIGHLANDS WAY
ASHMORE CL
GREEN CL
NUNNS PARK
THE GREEN
THE TRIANGLE
Chalkpit Farm
SP5
Lower Cowesfield
Farm
Tower Farm
Inn
DEAN LA
Testwood Cottages
Blackwater
Farm
PILL HILL
MEADOW CT
PH
PO
Dairyhouse Farm
NEWTON BGLWS
MARTINS RISE
THE STREET
A27
ROMSEY RD
NEWTON CL
NEWTON LA
BRICKWORTH RD
Blaxwell Farm
Young's Farm
CROFT HTS
Cowesfield Green
Whiteparish
All Saints
CE Prim Sch
Cowesfield Wood
Mushroom Farm
Bushy Copse
Cowesfield
Manor
Sansoms Farm
CLAY ST
THE BRAMLEYS
Whiteparish Grange
Squirrels Holt
COMMON RD
Park Water
Cottage
PARKWATER RD
Woodfalls
Farm
Golden's Farm
Hayter's Wood
Barters Farm
S051
Hillcrest
Whiteparish Common
Sch
Woodfalls
Cottages
Chadwell Farm
Glendale
Farm
A36
A36 Salisbury
A27 Salisbury (A36)
Wiltshire STREET ATLAS
24
25
26
5
4
3
2
1

49

4
26

A
B
C
SP5
Deanhill Barn
Curlew's Farm
COOKS LA
New Barn
COOKS LA 1
OVAL RD 2
Lockerley Manor
Critchell's Green
Pits (disused)
Butler's Barn
4
Gatmore Copse
Painshill Farm
MOUNT LA
Gatmore Cottage
25
Mount Pleasant Farm
Chapel Farm
Brokes Copse
3
Owls Lodge
Little Fosters
Gambledown Farm
Rowden's Farm
Badgers
24
SO51
Broxmore Park
DOCTOR'S HILL
Bryce's Farm
Morrisholt Farm
2
BUNNY LA
SP5
Ash Hill House
Cowesfield Gate
Berryfield Copse
Deer Park Close
Watson's Farm
Sandy Close Farm
Manor Farm
Pound Farm
CHURCH LA
23
Warren Farm
Pound Hill
GRAEMAR LA
Sole Hill Farm
BRANCHES LA
Broxmore Farm
POUND LA
PO
Pinewood Farm
Glebe Farm
A27
1
Temple Park
Melchet Pond
Greenvale Farm
EASTWOOD
Rectory
St Edward's Sch
THE DRIVE
Sherfield English
Hatchet Inn (PH)
MELCHET CL
Blackwater Farm
STEPLAKE LA
Sack Hill Farm
Fouracres
MILL LA
Midfield Farm
DANDY'S FORD LA
22
27
28
29

25
5

A
B
C
River Dun
PH
COOKS LA
MOUNT LA
LOCKERLEY RD
Canefield
School Farm
Dunbridge Hill
B3084
Dunbridge Copse
Barley Hill Wood
Kimbridge Farm
Monarch's Way
LC
KIMBRIDGE LA
Kimbridge
Canefield Copse
Mount Copse
Mount Farm
DUNBRIDGE LA
Kents Oak Farm
Hatchers Farm
Carter's Clay
John's Hill Copse
Hyde Farm
SAUNDERS LA
New Farm
THE BANKS
CHAPEL LA
THE BEECHES
Awbridge Farm
COWLEAS CL
COUNCIL HOS
CARTER'S CLAY RD
Butler's Wood Farm
COWLEAS COTTS
Tote Hill
SO51
Kent's Oak
Awbridge Prim Sch
Yew Tree Farm
DOCTOR'S HILL
Hazelwood Farm
Wood Farm
B3084
Hansard Poultry Farm
THE SQUARE
PH
Awbridge
Horseshoe Farm
Doctor's Hill
Newtown
Upper Ratley
CHURCH LA
NEWTOWN RD
DOCTOR'S HILL
DANES RD
Doctor's Hill Farm
Lower Ratley
Awbridge Danes Lake
COOMBE LA
Danes Farm
Awbridge Danes
CH
Test Way
Dunwood Manor
Dunwood Fruit Farm
Baldwin's Copse
A27
Croylands
Dellens Farm
Birchwood House Farm
The Frenches
OLD SALISBURY LA
Frenchwood Farm
Dunwood Hill
FRENCHES LA
The Frenches Farm
Stanbridge-Ranvilles Farm
Lower Frenchwood Farm
Lower Shootash Farm
Shootash
Winacres Farm
TANNERS LA
A27
4
25
3
24
2
23
1
22
30
31
32
A
B
C

25
51

6
28

A
B
C
A3057
KIMBRIDGE CNR
STAFF RD
Meadow Farm
Monarch's Way
KIMBRIDGE LA
Bear & Ragged Staff (PH)
Works
HILL VIEW RD
Glenville
Meadow Cottages
CHAPEL LA
NEW RD
Hunt's Farm
RUDD LANE
THE MILBURNS
MANNYNGHAM WAY
The Malthouse Inn
Linhay Meads
Refuse Tip
Cranford Farm
Casbrook Common
Timsbury
Herons Mead
HERON LA
ST ANDREWS CL
Awbridge House
BUNNY LA
Timsbury Manor
LC
River Test
Brook Farm
JINNY LA
Timsbury Lake
Yokesford Hill Est
YOKESFORD HILL
SO51
Test Way
Lodge Farm
The White House
Wynford Ind Pk
BELBINS
COOKS LA
Parsonage Farm
Rookwood Copse
COOMBE LA
Coombe Farm
STANBRIDGE LA
Ashley Meadows
Belbins House
Tollgate Ests
Hilberry Farm
Rookwood Cottages
B3084
Duke's Head (PH)
Stanbridge Earls
Stanbridge Earls Sch
SOUTH DR
Lone Barn Farm
South Lodge Farm
Greatbridge House
Great Bridge
OLD SALISBURY LA
Greatbridge Mill
Roke Manor Farm
Fishlake Cottage
Fishlake Meadows
Test Way
GREATBRIDGE RD
Palmer's Copse
Fish Lake
ROBERT WHITWORTH DR 1
ROWSE CL 2
NEVILLE DR 3
WESTBROOKE GDNS 4
THE MEADOW 5
HORSECROFT 6
TITHE MEAD 7
Roke Manor
Budds Lane Trad Est
BUDDS LA
Frobisher Ind Cntr
A3057
Romsey Ind Est
FISHLAKE MEADOWS
GRAYLING MEAD
4
25
3
24
2
23
1
22
33
34
35

52
28

27
7
A
B
C
Malthouse Farm
Paynes Hay Farm
PAYNES HAY RD
Monarch's Way
Merrie Meade Farm
Fern Hill Lane
ELDON RD
WHITE LADIES
Sharpes Farm
Braishfield
CHURCH LA
Hawkes Farm
Churchers Barn
LOWER ST
DUMMER RD
Monarch's Way
BUNNY LA
NEWPORT LA
DORES LA
Pucknall
Pucknall Farm
The Newport Inn (PH)
CHAPEL CL
HILL VIEW RD
PO
P
COMMON HILL RD
Braishfield Prim Sch
Fairbourne Lake
KILN LA
The Wheatsheaf Inn (PH)
The Homestead
Round Copse
Fairbournes Farm
SO51
MEGANA WAY
Dog & Crook (PH)
Abbotswood Farm
Crookhill Farm
Sir Harold Hillier Gardens & Arboretum
BRAISHFIELD RD
The Bog
Jermyns House
JERMYNS LA
Outwood Lodge
BELBINS
SANDY LA
Bracken Wood
A3090
Belbins Bsns Pk
P
Cemy
Abbotswood
Nursery
Abbotswood House
South Holmes Copse
WOODLEY CLOSE FLATS
WOODLEY CL
THE STRAIGHT MILE
CUPERNHAM LA
Ganger Farm
GANGER FARM LA
ROMSEY
Oxlease
Cupernham
WOODLEY WAY
GANGER RD
FOOTNER CL
ANDERSON CL
Woodley
Woodlands
WOODLEY LA
CAVENDISH CL
HORSESHOE DR
NORRIS CL
BROOK WAY
STAPLEFORD CL
ABBOTS WOOD CL
HUNTERS CRES
DIBBEN WLK
SHORT HILL
KINVER CL
WARREN GDNS
ANSTEY RD
OAKWOOD CL
THE GREEN
NORTH CL
SOUTH CL
Ganger Wood
Crampmoor Farm
THE MEADOW
RICHMOND LA
BRANSLEY CL
SCHOOL RD
PINEWOOD CL
THE COPSE
PEEL CL
1 GRANGE MEWS
2 COWSLIP WAY
3 HALTERWORTH LA
4 ST SWITHUN'S CL
GROVELY WAY
FISHLAKE MDWS
OXLEASE CL
CARISBROOKE CT
Cupernham Schs
LINCOLN CL
WAVERLEY CL
WINTERBOURNE RD
ADDISON CL
BEVERLEY GDNS
CEDAR LAWN
A3090 WINCHESTER RD
CRAMPMOOR LA
Crampmoor
WESTERING
RALPH LA
CANAL CL
SMITH'S FIELD
DURBAN CL
FAIRVIEW DR
WINCHESTER HILL
BRIAR WAY
SORREL CL
COMFREY CL
COLTSFOOT WLK
CAMPION DR
BRAMBLE DR
FAIR FIELD
CUPERNHAM CL
FAIRVIEW CL
PRIMROSE WAY
CLOVER WAY
GREEN LA
36
37
38
A
B
C
A1
1 RIMINGTON GDNS
2 HALDEN CL
3 SELBORNE CT
4 TAVISTOCK CL
5 WINCHESTER CT
6 SUTHERLAND CL
7 HOGARTH CL
8 WOODLANDS GDNS
9 SAVERNAKE CL
10 CLARENDON CL
27
53

8
30
A
B
C
Upper Slackstead
Dores Copse
Sunlight Cottages
Waterloo Plantation
Slackstead Manor
Lower Slackstead
DORES LA
DOVE LA
Home Farm
Dell Copse
Home Farm Row
Woolley Green Farm
Hodge Copse
Clay Pit Road
Little Fir Hill
Keeper's Lodge
SO21
Red Gate
Ampfield Wood
Claypit Hill
Ampfield Copse
Portland Copse
Petty Priest Copse
Monarch's Way
SO51
Knapp
KNAPP LA
A3090
Great Close
Ampfield CE Prim Sch
MORLEYS LA
Ampfield Plantation
Nevil's Copse
Ratlake
Ampfield House
GREEN POND LA
Upper Ratlake Farmhouse
Lower Farm
LOWER FARM LA
CH
Ampfield
POTTERS HERON LA
POTTERS HERON CL
Potter's Heron Hotel
White Horse (PH)
Gosport Farm
Broadgate
HOOK RD
HOOKWOOD LA
WOODLEA WAY
Gosport
POUND LA
Purser's Great Copse
Bluebell Copse
GREEN LA
Green Lane Farm
SO53
Trodds Copse
SO52
Churchers Common Plantation
4
25
3
24
2
23
1
22
39
40
41
54
30

29
9

A
B
C
4
25
3
24
2
23
1
22
42
43
44
A3090
B3043
SO22
SO21
SO53
SO51
SO52
Hursley Park
Hursley
HURSLEY PARK RD
King's Head Inn
KEBLE CL
CATWAYS
HEATHCOTE PL
PORT LA
COLLINS' LA
Cemy
PO
MEREDUN CL
PELICAN CT
SOUTH END CL
Parsonage Farm
BUNSTEAD LA
Monarch's Way
Shawlands Farm
SILKSTEAD LA
Keble Meml CE Prim Sch
Bunstead
POLES LA
Shepherds Lane
Upper Silkstead Farm
Silkstead
Brooks Copse
Weedacre Copse
Hursley Forest
Lower Silkstead Farmhouse
Windmill Copse
Ladwell
Red House
Strowdens Copse
Freemantles Copse
Kent's Copse
Wells Row
Field House
Cranbury Park
Hawstead Farm
Cranbury House
Home Farm
Great Pond
Hocombe Plantation
Hocombe
Hocombe Bridge
Hocombe Upper Plantation
ROTHVILLE PL
HOOK RD
HOCOMBE PARK CL
ASHDOWN DR
HOCOMBE RD
Castle Copse
Upper Pond
HOOK WATER CL
HOOK WATER RD
HURSLEY RD
HOCOMBE DR
CHARNWOOD GDNS
ASHDOWN CL
HEATHFIELD CL
MAYTREE RD
RANDALL RD
Lower Pond
The Castle
HOOK CL
HOOK CRES
HOCOMBE WOOD RD
TITHEWOOD CL
CHARNWOOD CL
CHARNWOOD CRES
ASHDOWN RD
WALNUT CL
HEATHFIELD RD
NICHOL RD
WOODLANDS CL
COULTAS RD
BEECHWOOD CL
BEECHWOOD CRES
HURSLEY CT 1
ASHTON PL 2
HILTINGBURY CT 3
VANBURGH WAY 4
CLEVELANDS CL
RICHMOND CL
ELM CT
HAZEL CL
SYCAMORE AVE
PO STEWART HO
QUEEN'S RD
LAKEWOOD RD
MALCOLM RD
SHERWOOD RD
MARLBOROUGH RD
KINGSWAY
THE GLADE
THORNBURY WOOD
FLEXFORD CL
BADDESLEY RD
AVEBURY GDNS
ASHBRIDGE RISE
ROSEMOOR GR
5 CHILLINGTON GDNS
6 CRANBORNE GDNS
7 LAURISTON DR
8 ORMESBY DR
9 STRATFIELD DR
10 ALBURY PL
11 APSLEY PL
12 OAKLANDS
Hiltingbury
GORDON RD
HILTINGBURY RD
WESTERN RD
HILTINGBURY CL
HEATHERDENE RD
THOROLD RD
GROSVENOR RD
ST MARKS CL
THORNBURY HTS
WINCHESTER RD
N MILLERS DALE
KELMSCOTT GDNS
THE WOODLANDS
THE TANYARDS
Recn Gd
Cemy
Cuckoo Bushes
PINE RD
Hiltingbury Inf Sch
Hiltingbury Jun Sch
PINE CRES
OAKWOOD CT
BEECH CL
OAKWOOD CL
OAKWOOD RD
MALCOLM CL
FRESHWATER CT
BROXBURN CL
MALIBRES RD

29
55

10
32

A
B
C
Silkstead La
SO22
Compton End
Godwins Field
Martins Fields
Atwoods Dro
PO
Welshers La
Compton St
Compton
Compton All Saints CE Prim Sch
Carmans La
Otterbourne Rd
Place La
Appleshaw House
M3
The Itchen Navigation
River Itchen
Compton Lock
Shawford
Hurdle Way
Compton Down
Clease Way
Combe Down
Red La
Bridge La
Shepherds La
The Spinney
Field Wk
Cliff Way
Field Cl
Playing Field
PH
Shawford Rd
Meml
Shawford
Station Terr
Park View
Bridge Terr
Shawford Down
Shawford House
Norris's Bridge
Churchfields Rd
Shepherds La
Monarch's Way
P
Shepherds Down Specl Sch
Otterbourne Rd
Tilden Rd
South Down
The Itchen Navigation
Itchen Way
Riverside Cotts
Twyford St Mary CE Prim Sch
Finch's La
School Rd
Queen St
Segars La
Segars Farm
The Drove
Brewers La
Drove Cl
Manor Rd
Manor Flats
Manor Farm Gn
Four Dell Farm
Highways Rd
Fairfield Rd
Cross Way
Southdown Rd
Dean Copse
Captain Barnard (PH)
Grove Rd
Poles La
SO21
Itchen Way
Sparrowgrove
Richmond Pk
Norlands Dr
Copse Cl
Main Rd
Waterworks Rd
Regent Cl
Wks
Bourne Cl
1 Oakwood Lodge
2 Oakwood Ho
Oakwood Cl
Oakwood Ave
B3335
Matthew's Copse
Water Works
Weir
Twyford Moors
B3354
Old Parsonage Ct
Otterbourne Hill
Meadow Croft Cl
Brooklyn Cl
Greenacres Dr
Coles Mede
Otterbourne
Mews Ct 1
Cranbury Cl 2
Cranbourne Dr
Main Rd
Great Moorlands Copse
PH
Otterbourne CE Prim Sch
1 Otterbourne Ho
2 Otterbourne House Gdns
Main Rd B3354
Old House At Home (PH)
Otterbourne Farm
Kiln La
Cemy
Rosemary Leet
SO50
Highbridge Rd
Recn Gd
Manor House
Kingfisher Stream
Woodend Copse
Winchester Rd
Chapel La
3 Ivy Cotts
4 Stone Terr
5 Park View
6 Fleet Terr
The Close
F1
1 Frampton Cl
2 Chestnut Ave
3 Springfields Cl
4 Fountain Ct
Fleming Pl
Lower Moors Rd
Orchard Cl
New Rd
Colvedene Cl
Moors Cl
SO53
Hocombe Rd
Otterbourne Hill
Boyatt La
Park La
Brambridge Ho
Brambridge Park
Sunningdale Cvn Pk
Spring La
Winchester Rd
H
Wessex Nuffield
Otterbourne Park Wood
Miniature Rly
Sch
Hill La
SO50
Lincolns Rise
B3335
Upper Moors Rd
St Vigor Way
Birch Cl
4
3
2
1
25
24
23
22
45
46
47

56
32

31
11

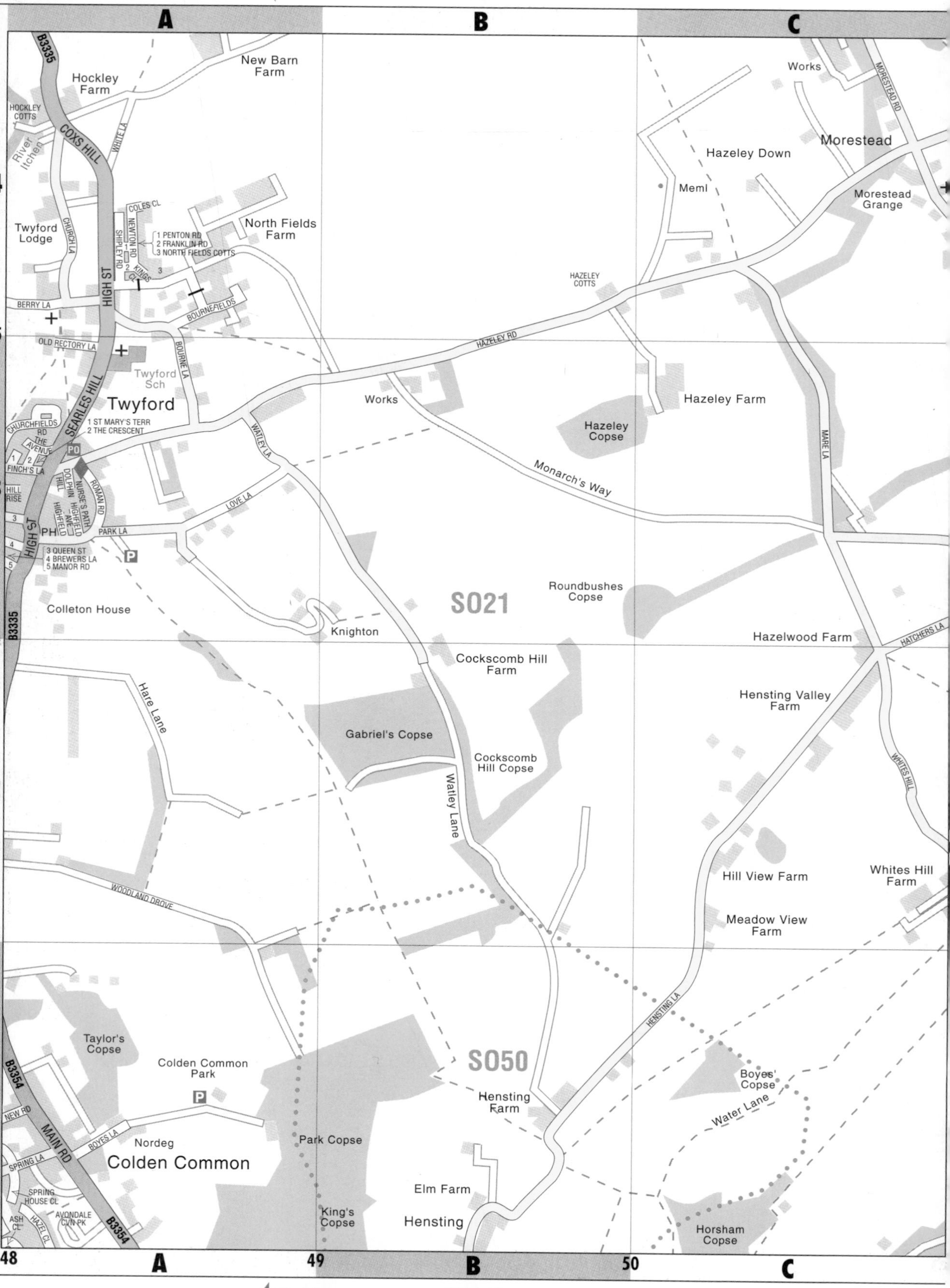

A
B
C
4
3
25
24
2
23
1
22
48
49
50
B3335
Hockley Farm
New Barn Farm
HOCKLEY COTTS
River Itchen
COXS HILL
WHITE LA
Twyford Lodge
CHURCH LA
COLES CL
NEWTON RD
SHIPLEY RD
1 PENTON RD
2 FRANKLIN RD
3 NORTH FIELDS COTTS
KINGS CL
North Fields Farm
BERRY LA
BOURNEFIELDS
OLD RECTORY LA
BOURNE LA
Twyford Sch
Twyford
SEARLES HILL
CHURCHFIELDS RD
THE AVENUE
1 ST MARY'S TERR
2 THE CRESCENT
PO
FINCH'S LA
HILL RISE
DOLPHIN HILL
NURSE'S PATH
HIGHFIELD AVE
HIGHFIELD
ROMAN RD
HIGH ST
PH
PARK LA
LOVE LA
WATLEY LA
3 QUEEN ST
4 BREWERS LA
5 MANOR RD
P
Colleton House
Knighton
Works
Hazeley Down
Morestead
MORESTEAD RD
Meml
Morestead Grange
HAZELEY COTTS
HAZELEY RD
Hazeley Farm
Hazeley Copse
Monarch's Way
MARE LA
Roundbushes Copse
SO21
Hazelwood Farm
HATCHERS LA
Cockscomb Hill Farm
Hensting Valley Farm
Hare Lane
Gabriel's Copse
Cockscomb Hill Copse
Watley Lane
WHITES HILL
Hill View Farm
Whites Hill Farm
Meadow View Farm
WOODLAND DROVE
HENSTING LA
Taylor's Copse
Colden Common Park
SO50
Boyes' Copse
B3354
NEW RD
MAIN RD
BOYES LA
Nordeg
Colden Common
Hensting Farm
Water Lane
Park Copse
SPRING LA
SPRING HOUSE CL
Elm Farm
AVONDALE CVN PK
King's Copse
Hensting
ASH CL
HAZEL CL
Horsham Copse

31
57

12
34

A
B
C
Ox Drove
Hydes Cottages
FAWLEY LA
Morestead Warren Farm
Grove Copse
WARREN LA
Old Down Plantation
4
The Manor House
Old Down Lane
Bushy Copse
Old Down Copse
Honeyman Lane
Warren Lane
25
Hill Farm
Hill Barn Copse
JACKMAN'S HILL
Bottom Pond Farm
Shortlands Copse
Morestead House
3
STAGS LA
SO21
Kings Way
Shearers Arms (PH)
OWSLEBURY BOTTOM
Pilgrims Ash
Bottom Farm
HATCHERS LA
LONGWOOD RD
24
Park Plantation
BELMORE LA
The Grove
Baybridge House
Whiteflood Farmhouse
BEECH GR
HILLY CL
GORSE DOWN
Owslebury Prim Sch
PO
Owslebury
BAYBRIDGE LA
2
MAIN RD
Boyes' Farm
PH
Lower Whiteflood Farm
WHITES HILL
PITCOT LANE
Monarch's Way
Baybridge
Upper Baybridge Farm
WHADDON LA
Lower Baybridge House
23
Blackdown Farm
Lower Farm
Sweetbriar Farm
Greenhill Farm
Blackdown House
LOWER BAYBRIDGE LA
Whaddon Farm
SO32
1
Greenhill
Phillips Farm
Greenhill Lane
Austin's Copse
Red Lane
22
51
52
53

58
34

33
13

A
B
C
Lane End Copse
Lane End Down
Hamilton Farm Cottages
Hamilton Farm
WESTFIELD DRO
Piddles Plantation
Ganderdown wood
Honeyman Farm
Lane End
4
Lane End Farm
South Downs Way
HOLDEN LA
Stonywalls Plantation
Stubb La
High Stoke
25
SO24
Windmill Farm
Greendowns
SO21
Loverdene
Lancen Cottages
The Milbury's (Inn)
3
Forest Copse
Millbarrow Plantation
Glasspools Farm House
Douglas Cottage
LONGWOOD DEAN LA
May Cottages
24
Longwood Dean Farm
Rookery
Long Wood
2
Dur Wood
Saltlane Plantation
West Lodge
Valley Walk
BELMORE LA
Durwood Cottages
SALT LA
The Holt
23
Lime Wood
High Wood
SO32
Monarch's Way
Stony Hard Farm
The Holt Lodge
Middle Preshaw
Hazards Copse
1
Well Copse
Priest Wood
Lower Preshaw Lane
Linches Rows
STAKE'S LA
Lower Preshaw Farm
22
54
55
56

33
59

14
36

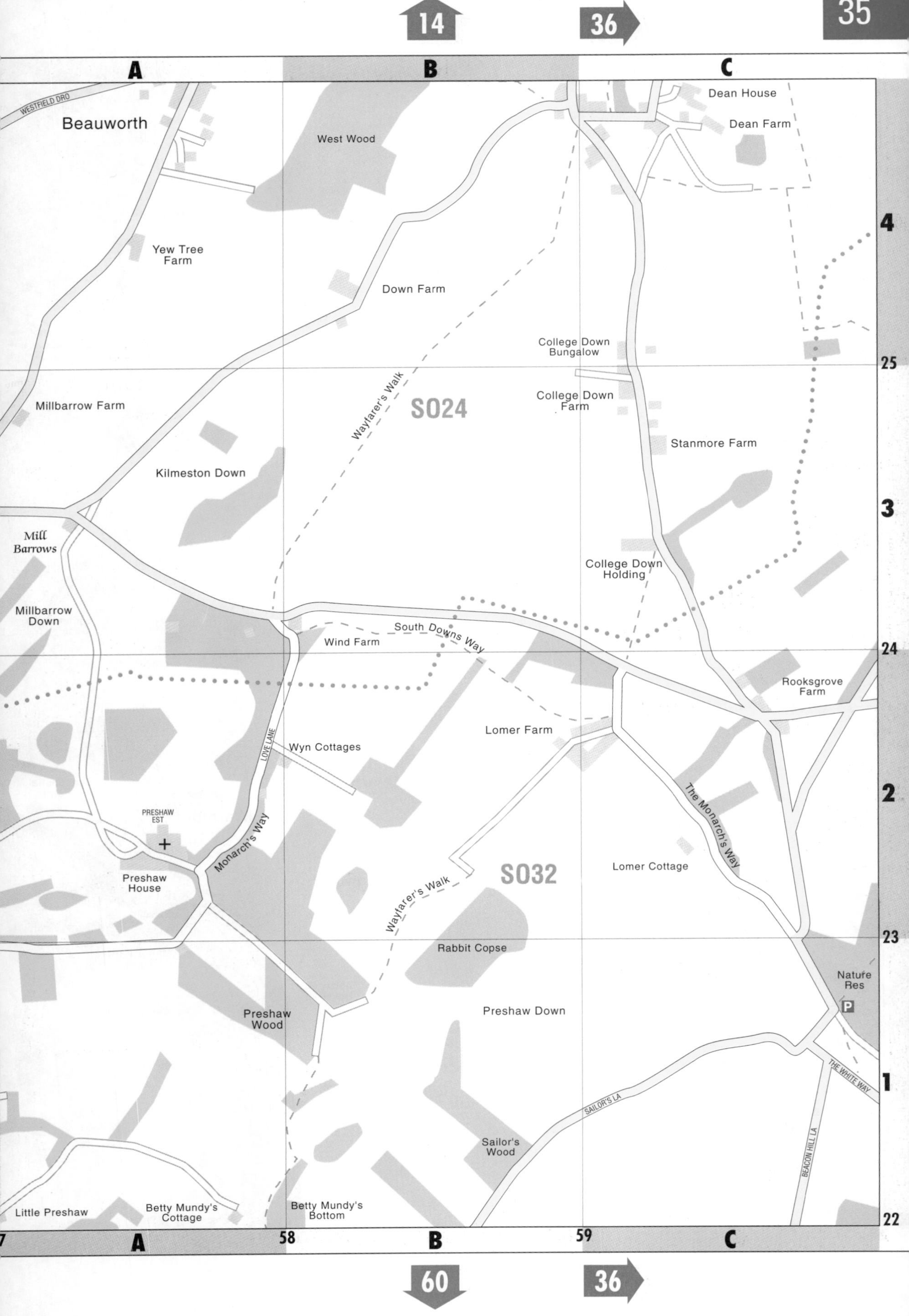
A
B
C
WESTFIELD DRO
Beauworth
West Wood
Dean House
Dean Farm
4
Yew Tree
Farm
Down Farm
College Down
Bungalow
25
Millbarrow Farm
SO24
College Down
Farm
Wayfarer's Walk
Stanmore Farm
Kilmeston Down
3
Mill
Barrows
College Down
Holding
Millbarrow
Down
South Downs Way
Wind Farm
24
Rooksgrove
Farm
Lomer Farm
LOVE LANE
Wyn Cottages
2
The Monarch's Way
PRESHAW
EST
Monarch's Way
Preshaw
House
SO32
Lomer Cottage
Wayfarer's Walk
23
Rabbit Copse
Nature
Res
P
Preshaw
Wood
Preshaw Down
THE WHITE WAY
1
SAILOR'S LA
Sailor's
Wood
BEACON HILL LA
Little Preshaw
Betty Mundy's
Cottage
Betty Mundy's
Bottom
22
A
58
B
59
C

60
36

35
15

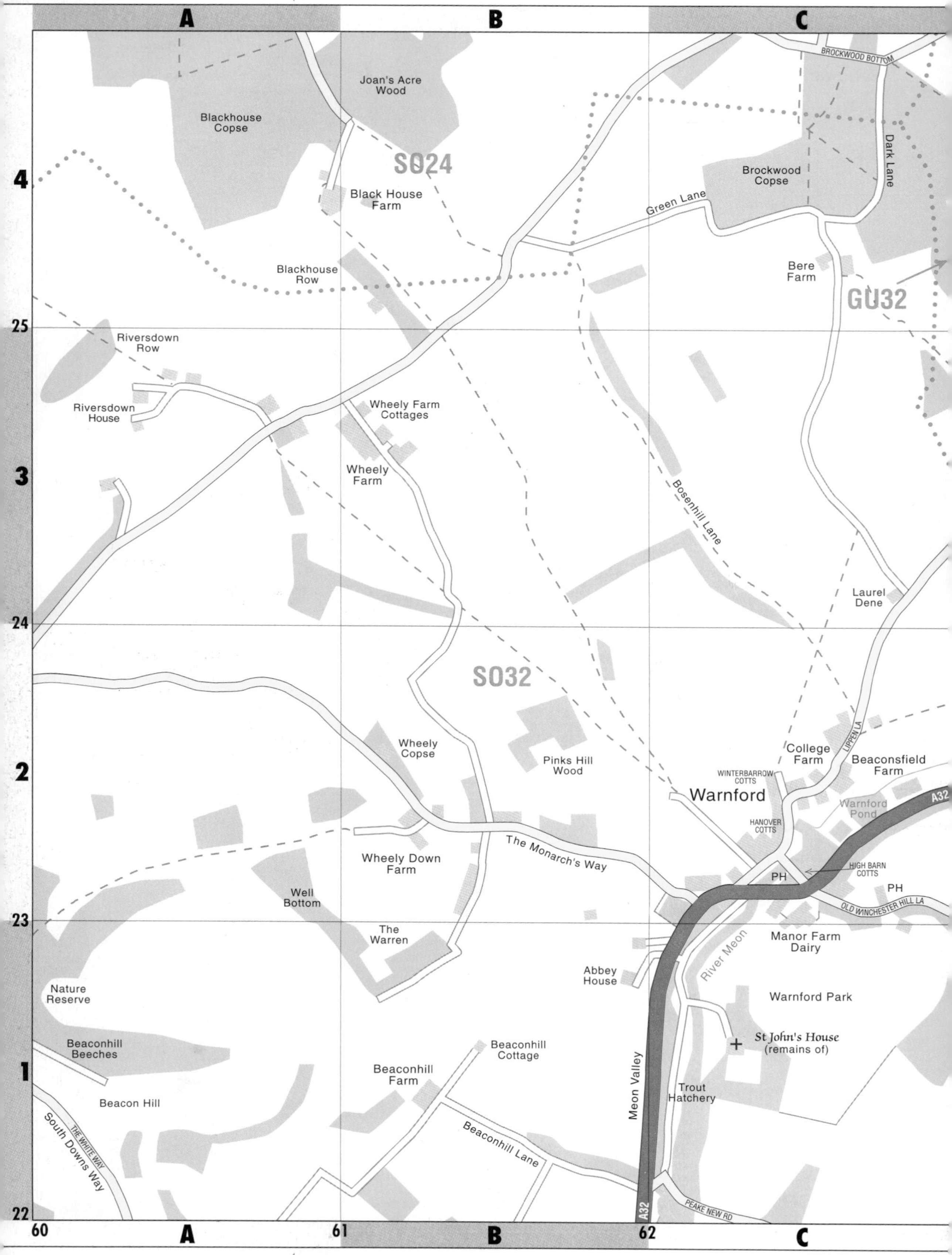

A B C

Joan's Acre Wood
Blackhouse Copse
SO24
Black House Farm
Blackhouse Row
BROCKWOOD BOTTOM
Dark Lane
Brockwood Copse
Green Lane
Bere Farm
GU32
Riversdown Row
Riversdown House
Wheely Farm Cottages
Wheely Farm
Bosenhill Lane
Laurel Dene
SO32
Wheely Copse
Pinks Hill Wood
College Farm
LIPPEN LA
Beaconsfield Farm
WINTERBARROW COTTS
Warnford
Warnford Pond
A32
HANOVER COTTS
Wheely Down Farm
The Monarch's Way
PH
HIGH BARN COTTS
PH
OLD WINCHESTER HILL LA
Well Bottom
The Warren
Manor Farm Dairy
River Meon
Abbey House
Nature Reserve
Warnford Park
Beaconhill Beeches
Beaconhill Cottage
St John's House (remains of)
Beaconhill Farm
Beacon Hill
Meon Valley
Trout Hatchery
THE WHITE WAY
South Downs Way
Beaconhill Lane
A32
PEAKE NEW RD

4 25 3 24 2 23 1 22

60 A 61 B 62 C

35
61

16
38

A
B
C
A32
Brick Kiln Farm
Great Headdon Copse
Westwood
Highfield
Headdon Farm
Sutton Park
Marlands
Hayling Wood
Marldell Farm
GU32
Court Farm
Lippen Wood
Lippen Cottages
Garretts Farm
VINNELLS LA
LONG PRIORS
KNAPPS HARD
Hall
Westbury Cottage
Floud Cottages
HEADON VIEW
CHURCH LA
DOCTORS LA
East End
Westbury Manor Farm
West Meon CE Prim Sch
PH
PO
HIGH ST
MEONWARA CRES
West Meon
Hall Place
St Nicholas's Chapel (rems of)
River Meon
Hall Farm
Westbury House
STATION RD
LYNCH LA
P
RAILWAY COTTS
Chappetts Farm
Westbury Park
Brocklands Farm
Sheepbridge Copse
Hayden Barn
SO32
OLD WINCHESTER HILL LA
The Monarch's Way
Hen Wood
Whitewool Hanger
Peake Farm
4
25
3
24
2
23
1
22
63
64
65

62
38

A B C

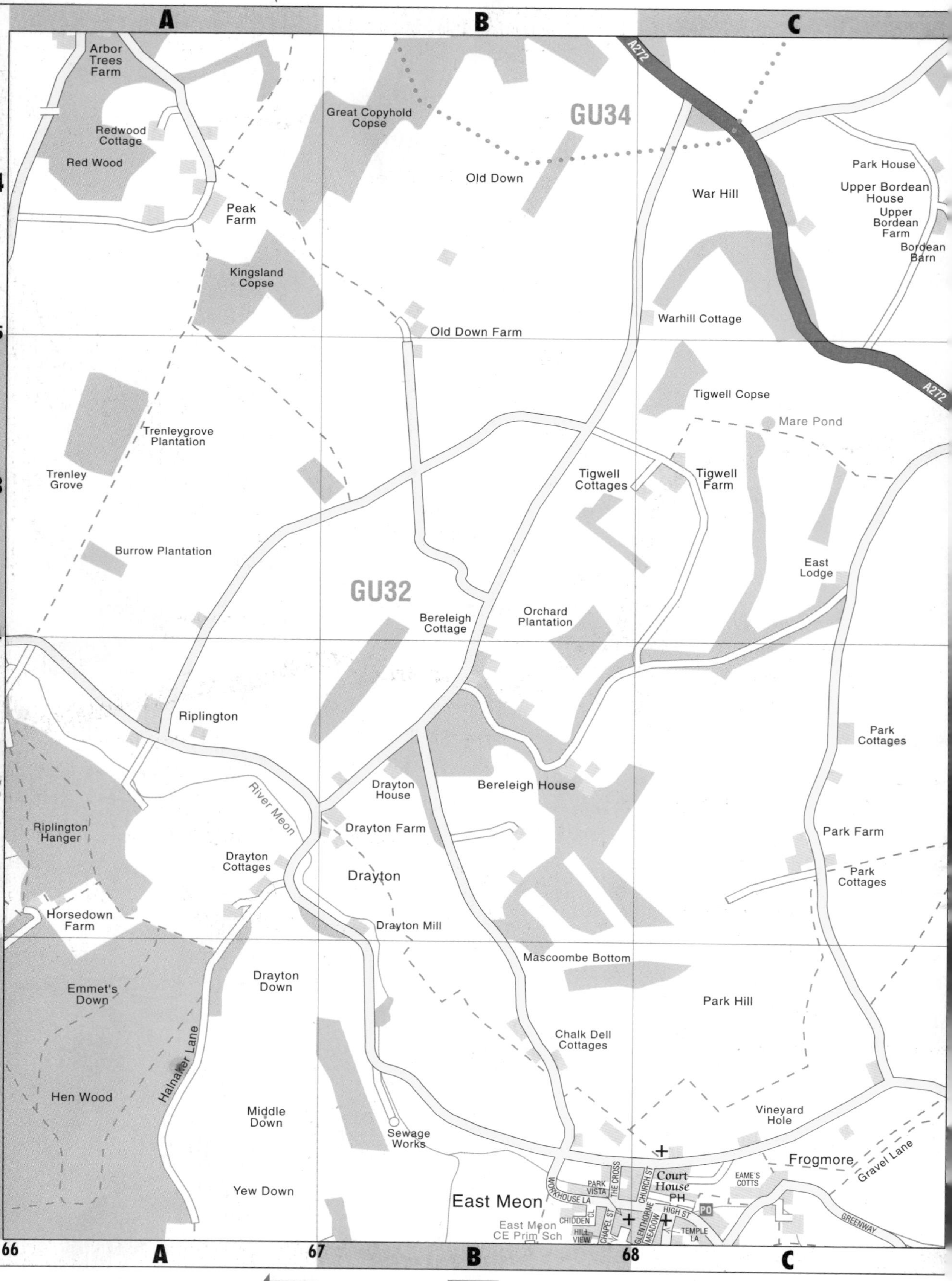

4
25
3
24
2
23
1
22

66 A 67 B 68 C

18
40

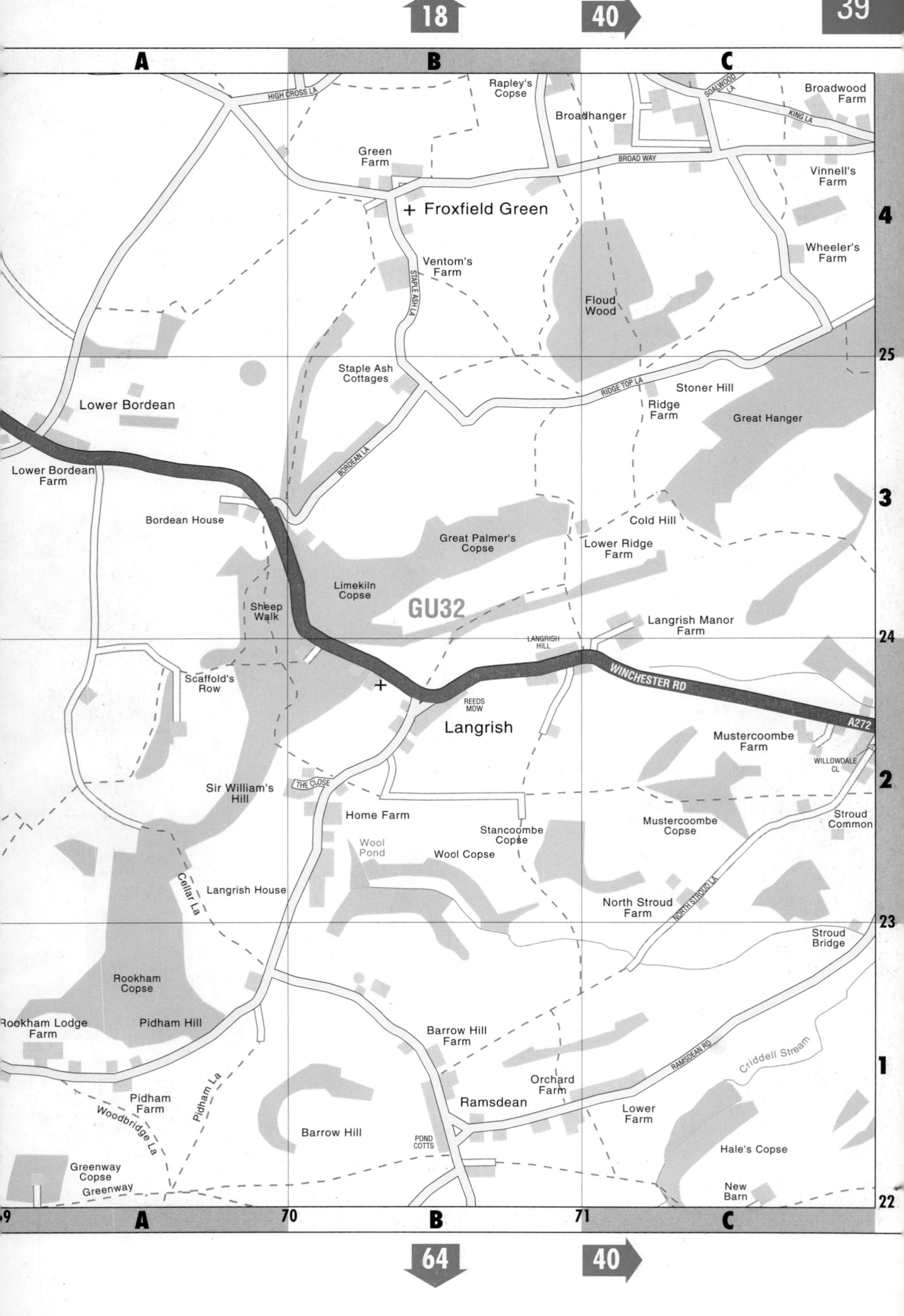
A
B
C
HIGH CROSS LA
Rapley's Copse
Broadhanger
SOALWOOD LA
KING LA
Broadwood Farm
Green Farm
BROAD WAY
Vinnell's Farm
Froxfield Green
4
Ventom's Farm
STAPLE ASH LA
Wheeler's Farm
Floud Wood
25
Staple Ash Cottages
RIDGE TOP LA
Stoner Hill
Lower Bordean
Ridge Farm
Great Hanger
BORDEAN LA
Lower Bordean Farm
3
Bordean House
Cold Hill
Great Palmer's Copse
Lower Ridge Farm
Limekiln Copse
Sheep Walk
GU32
Langrish Manor Farm
LANGRISH HILL
24
WINCHESTER RD
Scaffold's Row
REEDS MDW
Langrish
A272
Mustercoombe Farm
WILLOWDALE CL
THE CLOSE
Sir William's Hill
2
Home Farm
Stroud Common
Stancoombe Copse
Mustercoombe Copse
Wool Pond
Wool Copse
Cellar La
Langrish House
North Stroud Farm
NORTH STROUD LA
23
Stroud Bridge
Rookham Copse
Rookham Lodge Farm
Pidham Hill
Barrow Hill Farm
RAMSDEAN RD
Criddell Stream
1
Orchard Farm
Pidham Farm
Ramsdean
Lower Farm
Woodbridge La
Pidham La
Barrow Hill
POND COTTS
Hale's Copse
Greenway Copse
Greenway
New Barn
22
70
71

64
40

39
19

A B C

4 3 2 1 25 24 23 22

Stoner Hill
Island Farm
Island
Oakhurst Farm
MILL LA
KING LA
BROAD WAY
Vinnells Farm
Broadway Copse
Ridge Farm
Northfield Wood
Church Common
Steep Farm
Ridge Hanger
HAYS COTTS
Steep CE Prim Sch
Ridge Top Lane
CHURCH RD
The Cricketers Inn (PH)
Stonerwood Park
Lythe Hanger
Steep
Bedales Sch
Round Copse
Ridge Common
RIDGE COMMON LA
Lythe Farm
Dunhill Farm
Dunhurst (Bedales Jun Sch)
A3
HARROW LA
Collyers
Tilmore Brook
Tilmore Farm
Mellstock Farm
Soal Farm
SANDSBURY LA
Steep House
RESERVOIR LA
WHITE HOUSE GDNS
COXES MDW
BELL HILL RIDGE
Bell Hill
Hangers Way
TILMORE RD
THE PURROCKS
MONKS ORCH
MONKS WOOD
Tilmore Gardens
TILMORE GDNS
SELBOURNE CL
STAFFORD RD
LYTHE LA
BELL HILL
WOODBURY AVE
Aldersnapp Farm
GU32
Rothercombe Farm
BUCKMORE AVE
Buckmore Farm
STANTON RD
LYNTON RD
OAKLANDS RD
KIMBERS
HIGHFIELD RD
Cemy
ROTHERCOMBE LA
Stroud
STROUD END
Stroud Farm
BECKHAM LA
STONEHAM CL
STONEHAM PK
RUSHES FARM
BELVEDERE CL
MADELINE RD
NORTH STROUD LA
A272
WINCHESTER RD
A272
Petersfield
PENNS RD
BALMORAL WAY
BANNERMAN RD
WOOLNER AVE
NORTH RD
B2070
FINCHMEAD LA
DUKES CL
KINGS RD
PRINCES RD
QUEENS RD
MEON CL
FRENCHMANS RD
STATION RD
OSBORNE RD
SANDRINGHAM RD
WILLOWDALE CL
Seven Stars (PH)
REGENT MEWS
NOREVIL RD
RUSHES RD
DRUM LA
WINDSOR RD
WINTON RD
LYNDUM CL
KING GEORGE AVE
GRENEHURST WAY
COLLEGE ST
Langrish Prim Sch
New Buildings Farm
GLOUCESTER CL
VAUXHALL WAY
DRUM MEAD
CHARLES ST
LAVANT ST
CHAPEL ST
BARHAM RD
RAMSDEAN RD
YORK CL
BUCKINGHAM RD
BOROUGH HILL
SWAN ST
THE SQUARE
RAMS WALK
FOLLY LA
B2070
TOR WAY
Stroud Common
Amey Ind Est
Petersfield
CASTLE GDNS
Liby
HIGH ST
HEATH RD
THE SPAIN
SHEEP ST
ST PETER'S RD
Petersfield Bsns Pk
BOROUGH RD
HYLTON RD
DRAGON ST
THE AVENUE
Borough Hill
Churchers Coll Jun Sch
THE MALTINGS
BEDFORD RD
ALDERFIELD
Petersfield Cty Inf Sch
THE MINT
SUSSEX GDNS
SUSSEX RD
B2146
Stroudbridge Farm
Furzefield Copse
PETERSFIELD
THE MEAD
CRANFORD RD
GRANGE RD
The Petersfield Sch
OSIER RD
BOROUGH GR
HEATH CT
HEATH LODGE
BOROUGH RD
PADDOCK WAY
LARCOMBE RD
ITCHEN CL
STOUR CL
ORWELL RD
KENNET RD
ARUN CL
GU31
TEST CL
AVON CL
NIGHTINGALE RD
THE CAUSEWAY
Causeway
Widow Knight's Copse
Fairfield Farm
Landpits
A3
B2070
Dean's Farm

C2
1 ROTHERLEY
2 GARAGE COTTS
3 LAVANT CT
4 SPINNINGFIELD HO
5 WOODS HO
6 BRITNELL HO
7 KING GEORGE MEWS
8 GLOUCESTER CT
9 ASHCROFT CT
10 CREMORNE PL
11 WINTON CT
12 PARK CT
13 BURGESMEDE HO
14 THE COURTYARD
15 CHARTERGROVE HO
16 JOLLIFFE CT
17 ST PETER'S CT
18 SPAIN BLDGS
19 WESTON HO
20 SIWARD HO
21 PARK RD
22 BROWNFIELD HO
23 STABLE LA
24 CRAWTERS LA

72 A 73 B 74 C

39
65

A B C

Downgate Farm
Elmwood House
Tankerdale Farm
TANKERDALE LA
CH
GU33
Stodham Copse
Stodham Brows
STODHAM LA
PRUETTS LA
B2070
Budd's Copse
Ashford Stream
A3
Adhurst Wood
Upper Adhurst Farm
Durford Court
Burntash Farm
The Harrow Inn (PH)
HARROW LA
FARNHAM RD
GU32
Adhurst St Mary
LONDON RD
Birchwood
Lord's Farm
WATERWORKS RD
A272
LC
Sheet Prim Sch
THE VALE
MILL LA
SCHOOL LA
B2070
Plain
Sheet
BROADLAND COTTS
VILLAGE ST
RESERVOIR LA
LONG RD
LOCKYER CT
PORTLAND'S CL
PH
TOWN LA
INMANS LA
LONDON RD
KINGSFERNSDEN LA
PARSONAGE CL
Westmark Farm
B2199
Sheet Mill
1 ELMDALE
2 THE MEWS
3 ROOKES MEWS
B2070
SHEAR HILL
OLD MILL LA
HOGGARTH CL
RAMSHILL
Churcher's Coll
MERRYFIELD RD
CHURCHFIELD RD
HAZELBANK CL
PULENS LA
GU31
River Rother
Birch Copse
READON HO
READON CL
LOVE LA
ROTHER CL
COPSE CL
GEDDES WAY
PULENS CRES
TEG DOWN
UPPER WARDOWN
LONG DOWN
Tilmore Brook
Alder Copse
A272
Herne Jun Sch
HARTING DOWN
P
HOADLANDS
L Ctr
Penns Place (Office)
UPPER HEYSHOTT
LOWER HEYSHOTT
MOGGS MEAD
RIVERSIDE WLK
HANGER WAY
BUTSER WLK
BARNFIELD RD
HEATHFIELD RD
Durford Abbey Farm
BEPTON DOWN
HENWOOD DOWN
MARDEN WAY
WETHERDOWN
GRUNDLES
HOLT DOWN
HEAD DOWN
GREAT HANGER
B2
1 HAWTHORN CT
2 BRAMBLE CT
MONTAGUE GDNS
EASTLAKE CL
CLARE GDNS
HERNE RD
HEATH RD
HOME WAY
PO
DURFORD RD
Durford Mill
BRAMBLE RD
FERN CL
SANDY CL
RIVAL MOOR RD
RYEFIELD CL
WOOD LARK GDNS
The Old House
TORBERRY DR
GORSE RD
HEATHER RD
BROOM RD
THORN CL
TEAZLE CL
BRACKEN RD
WHEATEAR DR
LINNET CL
HARRIER WAY
RIVAL MOOR RD
STONECHAT CL
Sewage Works
Heath Pond
Heath Common
HEATH RD E
Ryefield
P
RUSSELL WAY
SUSSEX RD
B2199
Heath Farm
RYEFIELD COTTS
B2146
West Sussex STREET ATLAS
A272 Midhurst
76
77
3
2
1
22
23

A 76 B 77 C

A
B
C
Chicken Grove
Chickengrove Bottom
Verndritch Lodge
Verndritch Chase
A354
Sundown Farm
Haskells Farm
Martin Drove End
The Coote Arms (PH)
Bokerley Junction
SP6
Middle Lane
Dorset STREET ATLAS
SP5
A354
A354 Blandford Forum
TOWNSEND LA
Martin Down
National Nature Reserve
Bokerley Farm
SILLEN LA
Bowling Green Lane
Earthpits Lane
Jubilee Trail
Bokerley Down
Blagdon Plantation
Peaked Post
BH21
MORGAN'S LA
Pentridge
Whitey Top
4
21
3
20
2
19
1
18
03
04
05

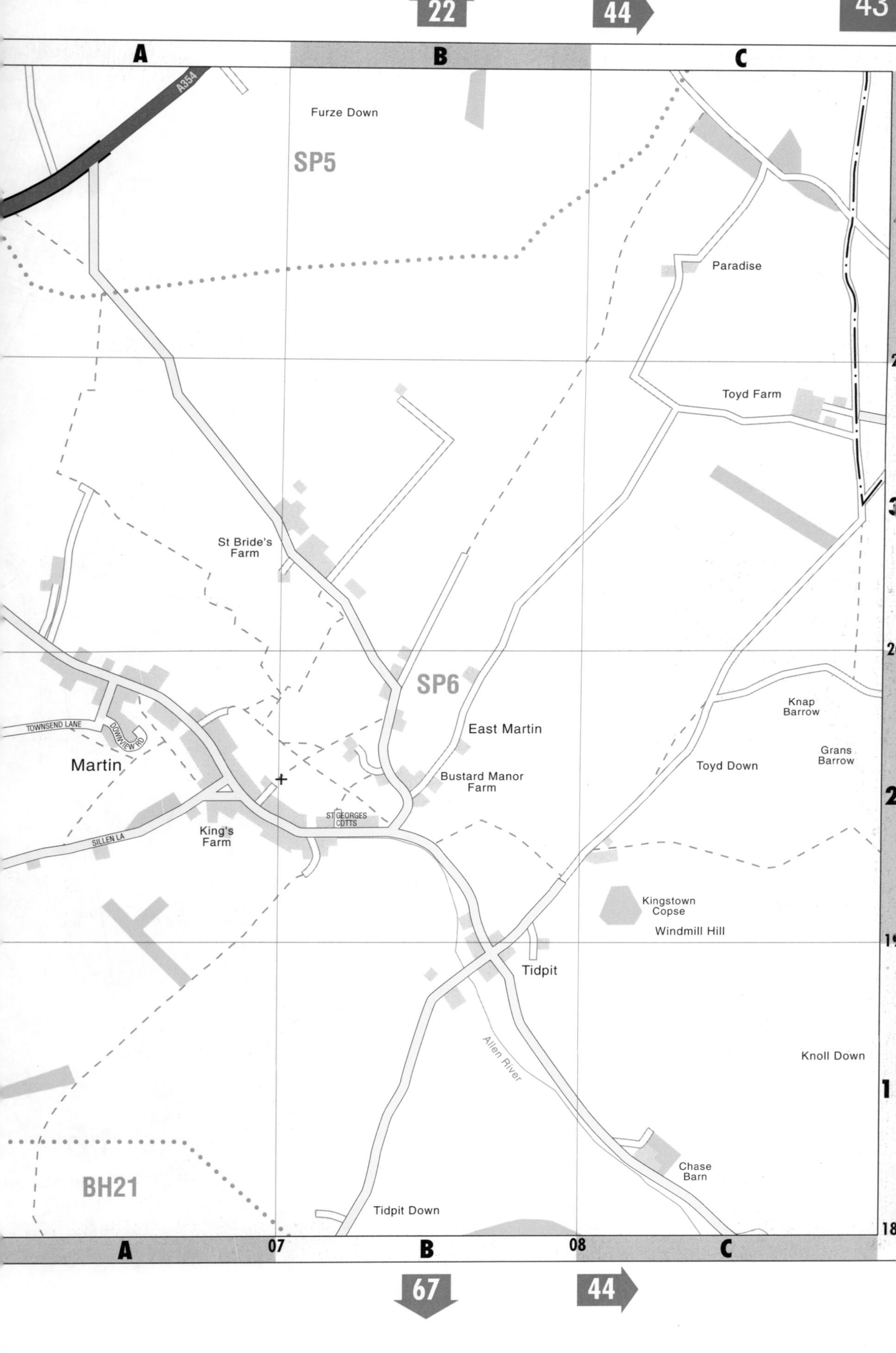
22
44
A
B
C
A354
Furze Down
SP5
Paradise
Toyd Farm
St Bride's Farm
SP6
East Martin
Bustard Manor Farm
Knap Barrow
Grans Barrow
Toyd Down
TOWNSEND LANE
DOWNVIEW RD
Martin
King's Farm
SILLEN LA
ST GEORGES COTTS
Kingstown Copse
Windmill Hill
Tidpit
Allen River
Knoll Down
1
Chase Barn
BH21
Tidpit Down
18
A
07
B
08
C
67
44

43
23

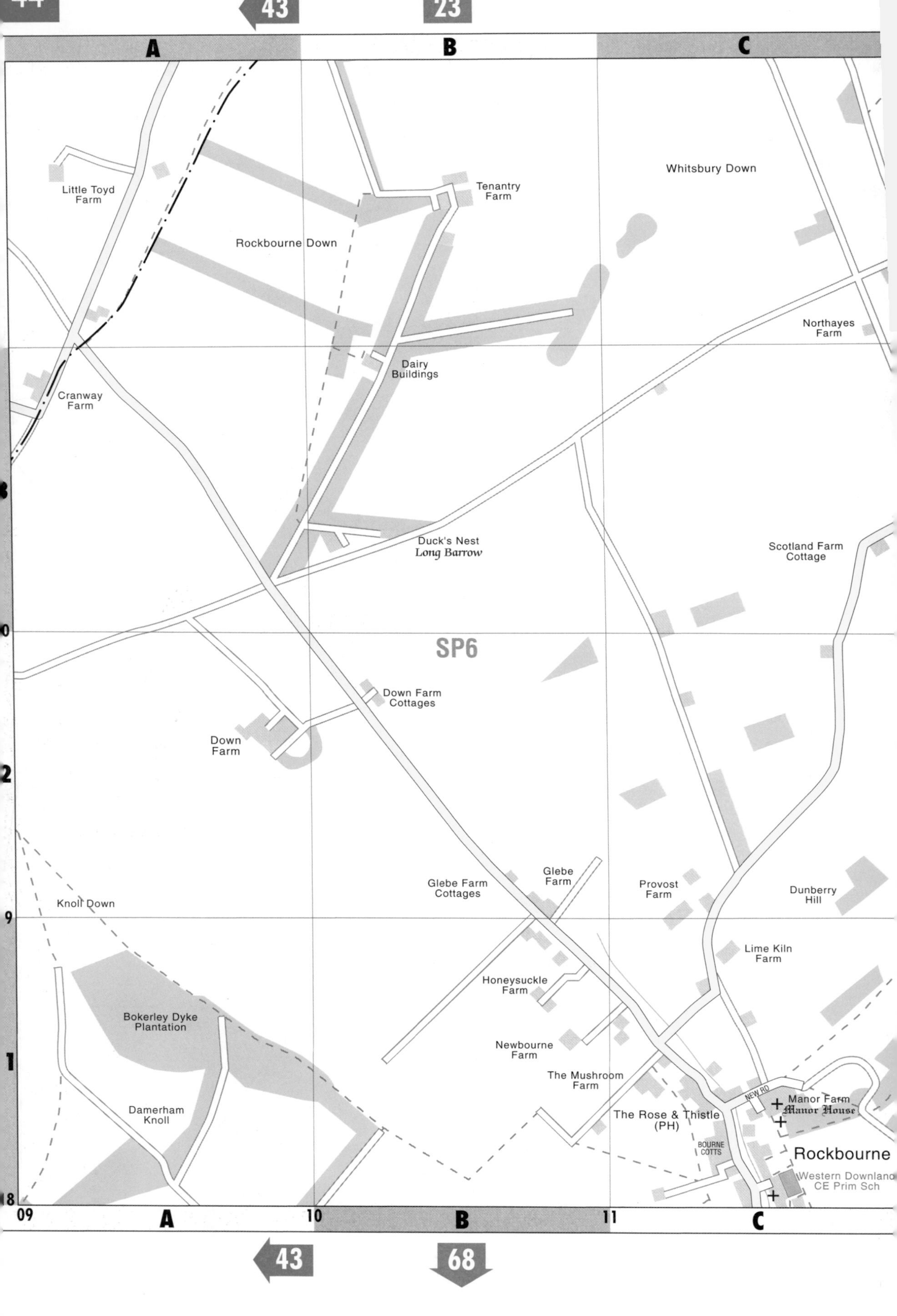
A
B
C
Little Toyd Farm
Rockbourne Down
Tenantry Farm
Whitsbury Down
Northayes Farm
Dairy Buildings
Cranway Farm
Duck's Nest
Long Barrow
Scotland Farm Cottage
SP6
Down Farm Cottages
Down Farm
Glebe Farm
Glebe Farm Cottages
Provost Farm
Dunberry Hill
Knoll Down
Lime Kiln Farm
Honeysuckle Farm
Bokerley Dyke Plantation
Newbourne Farm
The Mushroom Farm
Damerham Knoll
NEW RD
Manor Farm
Manor House
The Rose & Thistle (PH)
BOURNE COTTS
Rockbourne
Western Downland CE Prim Sch
09
10
11
A
B
C

43
68

46

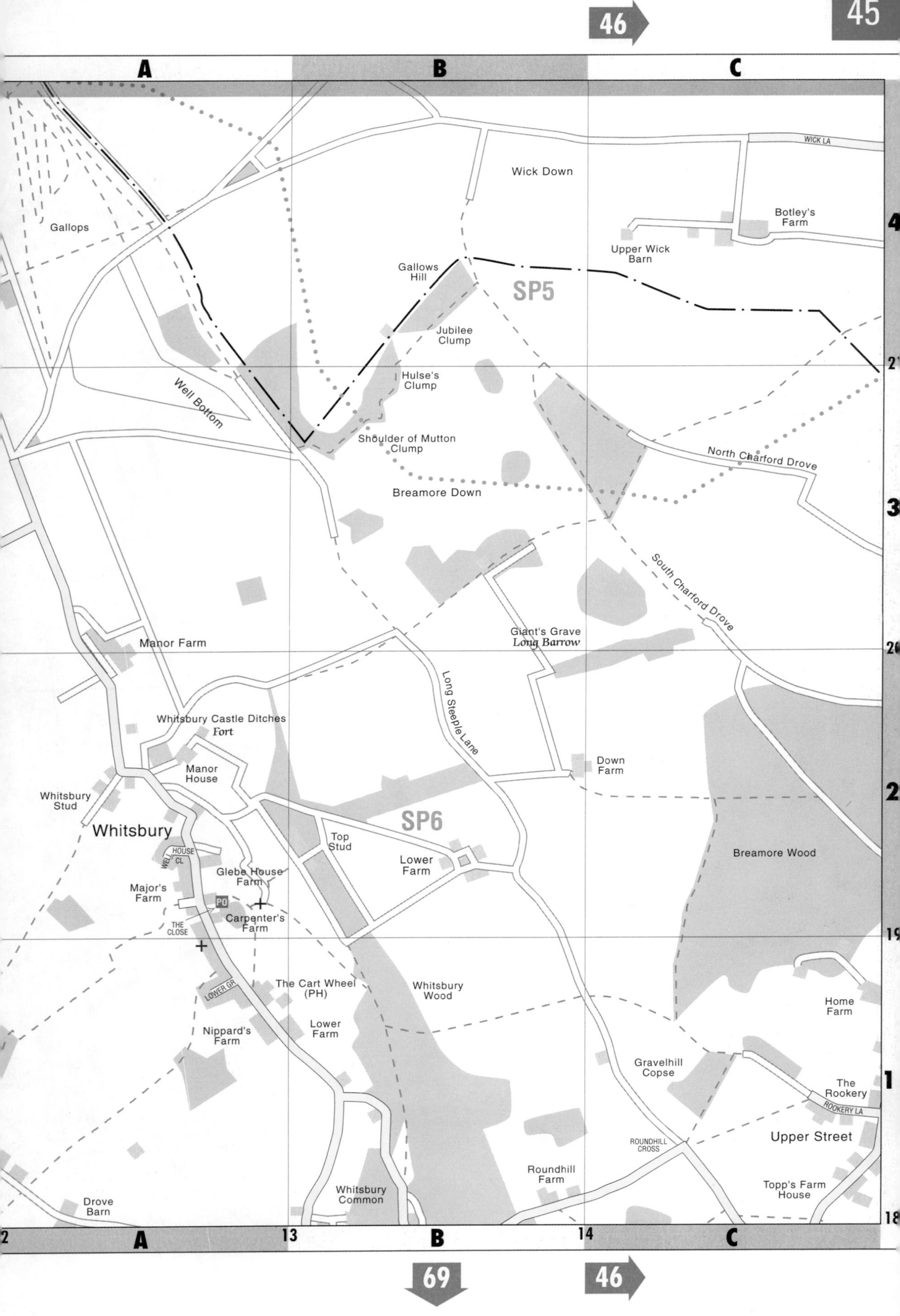
A
B
C
Wick Down
WICK LA
Gallops
Botley's Farm
Upper Wick Barn
Gallows Hill
SP5
Jubilee Clump
Hulse's Clump
Well Bottom
Shoulder of Mutton Clump
North Charford Drove
Breamore Down
South Charford Drove
Giant's Grave
Long Barrow
Manor Farm
Long Steeple Lane
Whitsbury Castle Ditches
Fort
Down Farm
Manor House
Whitsbury Stud
SP6
Whitsbury
Top Stud
Lower Farm
Breamore Wood
WELL HOUSE CL
Glebe House Farm
Major's Farm
PO
Carpenter's Farm
THE CLOSE
The Cart Wheel (PH)
Whitsbury Wood
LOWER GR
Home Farm
Nippard's Farm
Lower Farm
Gravelhill Copse
The Rookery
ROOKERY LA
Upper Street
ROUNDHILL CROSS
Roundhill Farm
Topp's Farm House
Whitsbury Common
Drove Barn
4
3
2
1
13
14

69
46

45

A338 Salisbury
Wick
Wick Farm
WICK LA
David Hart Bsns Ctr
Downton CE Prim Sch
Avon Valley Path
THE BOROUGH
B3080
THE HEADLANDS
Sports Ctr
The Bull Hotel
The Three Horse Shoes (PH)
Middle Wick Farm
Wick House
SP5
Downton Sec Sch
Sluices
Weir
Weirs
Sewage Works
North Charford Down Farm
South Charford Down Buildings
North Charford Drove
South Charford Drove
Lions Lodge
North Charford Manor House
River Avon
Searchfield Farm
Ford
Works
Breamore Wood
Yarnfield Pit
SP6
Breamore House
South Charford Farm
Breamore Park
North Street
Breamore Countryside Mus
SALISBURY RD
Breamore
Hulse Hall
Hale House
A338
15
16
17
A
B
C

45
70

A
B
C
Wiltshire STREET ATLAS
Cemy
Parsonage Farm
BARFORD LA
HAMILTON PK
CHURCH HATCH
Liby
THE SIDINGS
HIGH ST
B3080
PO
LODE HILL
Downton
Gdn
MOOT LA
SAXONHURST
CASTLE MDW
Moot Farm
SAXON MDW
MOOT CL
EASTMAN CL
TWYNHAM CL
Down House
MUDDYFORD RD
Templeman's Old Farmhouse
LANG FORD LA
Templeman Farm
Grove Copse
Paccombe Farm
THE ROW
SANDY LA
PH
PETTICOAT LA
GROVE LA
Cemy
BOWERS HILL
KILN LA
PRINCES CL
PRINCES HILL
CHALK CL
APPLETREE RD
MORGANS RISE RD
FOUNDARY RD
THE CLOSE
DOWNTON HILL
APPLE TREE CL
ORCHARD RD
Morgan's Vale & Woodfall's Prim Sch
MORGANS VALE RD
VICARAGE PK
Morgan's Vale
Redlynch
QUAVEY RD
GOGGS LA
Pensworth Farm
SLAB LA
PRIMROSE LA
THE RIDGE
HILBERT RD
ST BIRINUS RD
MITCHELLS CL
CASTLE WOODS
HILLCROFT
VALE RD
VALLEY CL
GREENS MEADE
CHAPEL LA
HARTHILL DRO
SP5
ELMFIELD CL
Church Close Copse
Woodfalls Farm
KINGSFORD CL
Inn
The Drove
CHURCH HILL
Lock's Farm
Lover
PO
Woodfalls
HIGHFIELD LA
Lodge Farm House
Ridge Farm
SPRINGFIELD CRES
Little Woodfalls Farmhouse
LITTLE WOODFALLS DR
PINE VIEW CL
TINNEYS CL
Tinney's Firs
BESOMER DRO
ST MARYS CL
SCHOOL RD
Rye Hill Copse
Lodge Copse
LODGE DRO
WHITESHOOT
WHITESHOOT HILL
Bohemia
Avon Valley Path
Whiteshoot Farm
North Charford
Hookers Copse
Hatchet Green
HATCHET CL
CARTER'S CL
BOHEMIA LA
LOOSEHANGER
TETHERING DRO
ST GEORGE'S COTTS
HALE LA
Cemy
Hale Prim Sch
FOREST RD
Home Farm
Hale
SP6
Hale Farm
QUEEN ST
MAYS FIRS
Hale Park
Hale
Folly Drove
B3080
Maydene
Hale Purlieu
8
19
20

47

A
B
C
Wiltshire STREET ATLAS
Titchborne Farm
MOOR LA
Mollcroft Copse
Gill's Hole
Great Sherwood Copse
Horse Pond Copse
Lower Pensworth Farm
4
Wall Copse
East Copse
Thorn's Copse
Newhouse
GROVE LA
Bagfield Copse
GOGG'S LA
1
Out Wood
River Blackwater
TIMBERLEY LA
Appsy Copse
Timbury Farm House
Homan's Copse
Shearwood Copse
Langley Wood
Round Copse
3
Badger's Copse
Brickkiln Cottage
Witterns Hill Farm
COLE'S LA
VICARAGE RD
Langley Wood
Lover
CHURCH WLK
Cole's Copse
Bishops Wood
CHURCH HILL
The Mount
SCHOOL RD
Redlynch CE Prim Sch
SP5
Ford
Moor Copse
Hamptworth Farm
BLACK LA
HAMPTWORTH RD
Loosehanger Farm
2
Hamptworth Lodge
Loosehanger Copse
Home Farm
Pimlico Firs
The Bog
SP6
Loosehanger Common
Pimlico Bottom
Radnor Firs
LYBURN RD
Lyburn Farm
Horse Common
Quar Hill Plantation
B3080
Windyeats Farm
Cloven Hill Plantation
21
A
22
B
23
C

47

72

A
B
C
A36
COMMON RD
Barnsell Copse
Broadlands Copse
Melchet Park
Earldoms Lodge
Glazier's Copse
Scotland La
The Earldoms
Bush Farm
Landford Wood
Landsbrook Farm
SO51
4
Whitehouse Farm
Furze Copse
The Beeches
21
Stocklane Farm
Nursery Farm
COMPTON'S DR
North Common
NORTH COMMON LA
Wicketsgreen Farm
STOCK LA
North Common Farm
The Four Winds
Sandown Farm
BARROWS LA
3
Furzy Close
Broom Park
Manor Farm
B3079
Landford Lodge
White House Farm
Landford Manor
SP5
20
CH
Elmtree Farmhouse
Highfield Farm
Glebe Farm
Newell's Park
River Blackwater
GLEBE LA
Bridge Farm
Brooklands
Elm Farm
The Cuckob Inn (PH)
Cuckoo Farm
BROOKSIDE
HAMPTWORTH RD
Smallbrook Farm
Landford CE Prim Sch
Park Farm
Cherry Tree Farm
A36
2
Hamptworth
Manor Farm
Landford
Captain's Copse
Latchmoor Dro
LYNDHURST RD
Mayfield
LYBURN RD
Lane End Farm
LANE END COTTS
19
BEECH GRANGE
PINE CL
PO
Lyburn Birches
Landford Larches
Landford Common Farm
BROOMHILL
NEW RD
Landford Common
1
Newlands Farm
Greenhill Farm
SCHOOL RD
Hamptworth Common
OAKLEIGH DR
B3079
24
A
25
B
26
C

49
25

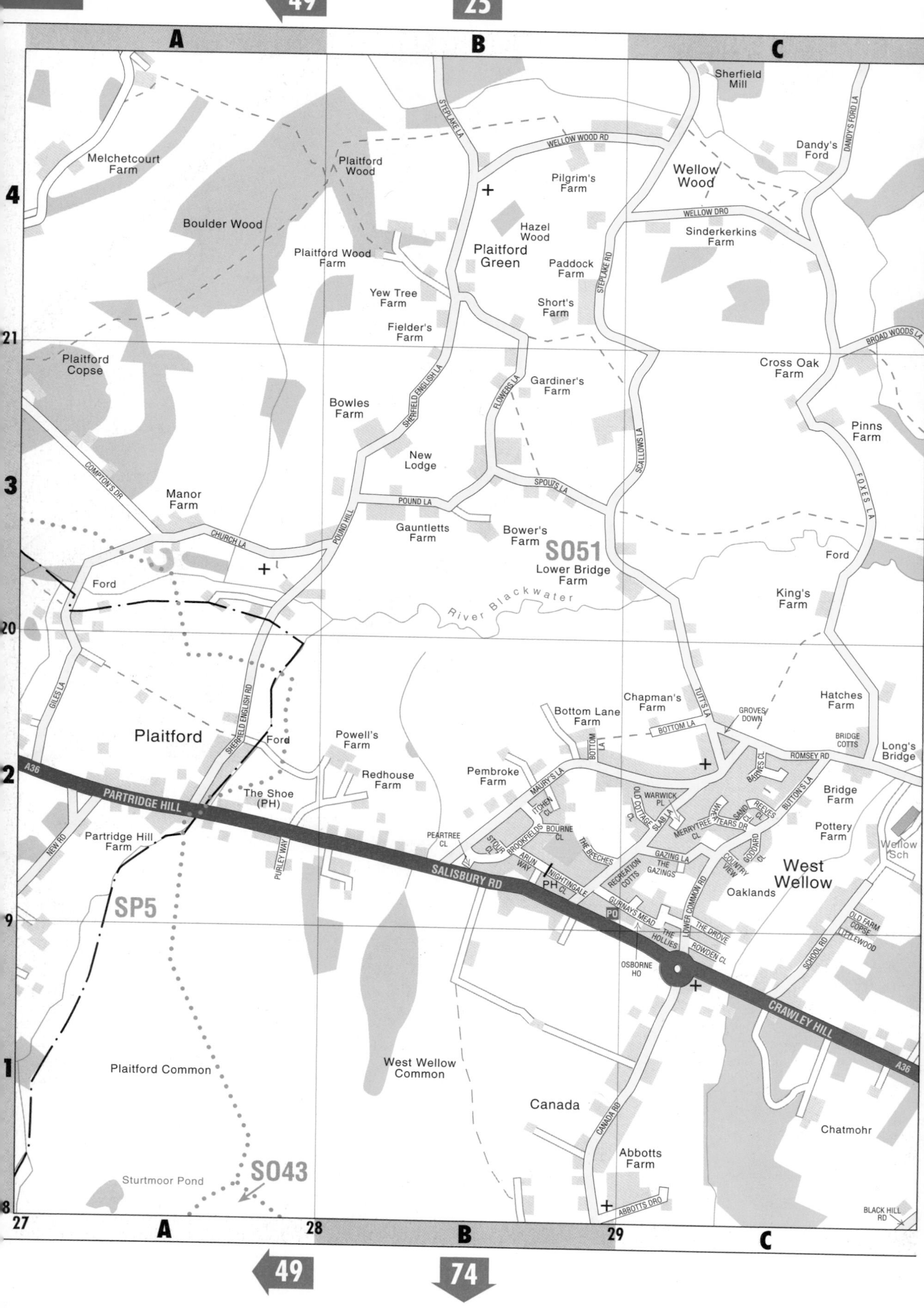
A
B
C
4
3
2
1
21
20
9
8
27
28
29
Sherfield Mill
Dandy's Ford
DANDY'S FORD LA
Melchetcourt Farm
Plaitford Wood
STEPLAKE LA
WELLOW WOOD RD
Pilgrim's Farm
Wellow Wood
WELLOW DRO
Sinderkerkins Farm
Boulder Wood
Hazel Wood
Plaitford Wood Farm
Plaitford Green
Paddock Farm
STEPLAKE RD
Yew Tree Farm
Short's Farm
Fielder's Farm
BROAD WOODS LA
Plaitford Copse
Cross Oak Farm
Gardiner's Farm
Bowles Farm
SHERFIELD ENGLISH LA
FLOWERS LA
Pinns Farm
SCALLOWS LA
New Lodge
COMPTON'S DR
FOXES LA
SPOUTS LA
Manor Farm
POUND LA
POUND HILL
Gauntletts Farm
Bower's Farm
CHURCH LA
SO51
Ford
Lower Bridge Farm
Ford
King's Farm
River Blackwater
Hatches Farm
Chapman's Farm
Bottom Lane Farm
TUTTS LA
GROVES DOWN
GILES LA
SHERFIELD ENGLISH RD
BOTTOM LA
Plaitford
Ford
Powell's Farm
BRIDGE COTTS
Long's Bridge
ROMSEY RD
A36
Pembroke Farm
Redhouse Farm
MAURY'S LA
BARNES CL
The Shoe (PH)
PARTRIDGE HILL
ITCHEN CL
WARWICK PL
OLD COTTAGE CL
SLAB LA
WHITEARS DR
SAND CL
REEVES CL
BUTTON'S LA
Bridge Farm
MERRYTREE CL
BOURNE CL
Partridge Hill Farm
PEARTREE CL
STOUR CL
BROOKFIELDS
Pottery Farm
NEW RD
PURLEY WAY
THE BEECHES
GAZING LA
THE GAZINGS
GODDARD CL
Wellow Sch
ARUN WAY
RECREATION COTTS
COUNTRY VIEW
West Wellow
SALISBURY RD
PH
NIGHTINGALE CL
Oaklands
SP5
PO
GURNAYS MEAD
LOWER COMMON RD
THE DROVE
OLD FARM COPSE
THE HOLLIES
LITTLEWOOD
ROWDEN CL
SCHOOL RD
OSBORNE HO
CRAWLEY HILL
A36
Plaitford Common
West Wellow Common
Canada
CANADA RD
Chatmohr
Abbotts Farm
SO43
Sturtmoor Pond
ABBOTTS DRO
BLACK HILL RD

49
74

A
B
C
Aldermoor Copse
FRENCHES LA
Merryhill Farm
Allen's Copse
A27
Kitts Merries Farm
SALISBURY RD
4
Smidmore Copse
Wellow Vineyard
Embley Poultry Farm
TANNERS LA
EMBLEY LA
Embley Manor
Embley Park Ind Est
Woodington Farm
A27
21
Embley Park
GARDENERS LA
Woodington
Withybed Farm
Embley Park Sch
BROAD WOODS LA
Withybed Copse
WOODINGTON RD
3
Hall Copse
Homefield
East Wellow
Mill Farm
Mill
HACKLEYS LA
Wellow Manor
20
SO51
CH
Chestnut Cottages
RYEDOWN LA
Nature Reserve
2
Warners Farm
ROMSEY RD
Wellow Mill
Kentford House
Kentford Lake
Kentford House Farm
River Blackwater
Hamdown Farm
Sewage Works
19
Cooper's Clump
Embley Wood
WOODLAND CL
HAMDOWN CRES
KOOYONG CL
WHINWHISTLE RD
FLORENCE CL
Ham Lake
Long Clump
FIELDERS WAY
Oakdene Farm
CROSFIELD CL
CHICHESTER CL
Hammond's Farm
COOPER'S CL
THE DRIVE
Great Pond
LODGE VALE
1
ASHTON CROSS
Lark Farm
CRAWLEY HILL
ELMDALE GR
PLANTS CL
SHELLEY LA
Blackhill
Blackhill Farm
BLACKHILL RD
SALISBURY RD
Fighting Cocks Farm
Shelley Bungalow
Romsey Common Farm
Shelley Common
A36
18
30
A
31
B
32
C

51
27

A
B
C
Squabb Wood
Monk's Cottages
Budds Lane Trad Est
Frobisher Ind Ctr
LANSDOWNE CT
A3057
GREATBRIDGE RD
THE CLOISTERS
LAURENCE MEWS
Romsey Ind Est
KINGFISHER WAY
OATLANDS
NEW RD
MERCER WAY
C4
1 ROBERT WHITWORTH DR
2 HORSECROFT
3 LANSDOWNE CL
4 FLEMING PL
5 SPRING PL
6 HOLBROOK PL
7 THE COURTYARD
8 LORTEMORE PL
9 ABBEY WATER
10 NARROW LA
11 DUKES MILL CTR
12 LINDEN CT
13 BARLING MEWS
14 BADEN POWELL WAY
15 PLAZA MEWS
16 ENGLISH CT
17 WAKEFORD CT
18 SOUTH FRONT
Mead Mill Farm
PRIESTLANDS
LANSDOWNE GDNS
B3398
CHERVILLE ST
ST CLEMENTS CL
DUTTON'S RD
MALMESBURY RD
CANAL WLK
Romsey
NELSON CT
LATHAM CT
MALLARD CL
4
The Romsey Sch
CHERVILLE MEWS
MALTHOUSE CL
PRINCE'S RD
JUBILEE RD
HOLLMAN DR
TEST MILLS
TEST HO
CHERVILLE CT
THE HORSEFAIR
HORSEFAIR MEWS
Liby
HORSEFAIR CT
STATION RD
ALBANY RD
ALMA RD
MITCHELLS CL
MOUNTBATTEN AVE
Romsey Inf Sch
Test Way
MILL LA
CHURCH LA
CHURCH RD
CHURCH ST
PORTERS
BRIDGE ST
ORCHARD LA
VICTORIA PL
Romsey Abbey CE Prim Sch
MILLSTREAM RISE
PO
P
Mus
LATIMER ST
PEMBROKE CL
LOVE LA
LINDEN RD
A3057
WINCHESTER RD
A3090
CHURCH PL
Abbey
LITTLEMEADS
RIVERMEAD CL
THE ABBEY
MKT PL
CORN MKT
STIRLING WALK
THE HUNDRED
KNATCHBULL CL
Spursholt Farm
Spursholt House
Sewage Works
THE MEADS
Embley Park Jun Sch
TH
NEWTON LA
BELL ST
BROADWATER RD
PALMERSTON ST
CRESSEY RD
THE HARRAGE
A27
21
A27
Saddler's Mill
Cvt
BRIDGE CT
BANNING ST
BURMA RD
The Rapids
Burnt Grove Cotts
SALISBURY RD
Saddler's Mill Farm
RIVERSIDE GDNS
MIDDLEBRIDGE ST
BY PASS RD
ROMSEY
1 ASHLEY HO
2 PAIMPOL PL
3 MOUNT PLEASANT
4 ST MARY'S
5 BERTHON HO
6 TADBURN GN
7 ST ANNES HO
8 BROOK CT
9 HOMEMEAD HO
10 STEPHENS CT
11 BARK HILL MEWS
Sports Ctr
Mast
CAUSEWAY
PH
MAINSTONE
3
River Test
A3090
Broadlands
Mainstone Farm
Burnt Grove
PAUNCEFOOT HILL
Broadlands Park
Pauncefoot House
20
SO51
GARDENERS LA
2
Cutters Barn
Broadlands Farm
Turlington
Town Copse
Test Way
Lee House
SPANIARD'S LA
Embley Ridge
Yewtree Cottage
9
Ranvilles Farm
Yewtree Copse
Semple House
1
Jack O' Lantern
RIDGE LA
Ridge Copse
Ridge Farm
Ridge
A3090
Lee Park Farm
Skidmore
8
33
A
34
B
35
C

51
76

A
B
C

OLD RD
NEW RD
MERCER WAY
LATHAM RD
Romsey Jun Sch
GREAT WELL DR
GREENWOOD
HAYTER GDNS
NIGHTINGALE HO
WOODLEY LA
CUPERNHAM LA
ASHLEY MDWS
Harefield
BARTON CL
WINDFIELD DR
HAREFIELD CT
A3090
WINCHESTER HILL
Romsey
H
DEANSFIELD
SELSDON AVE
NEROQUIS CL
THE CRESCENT
VINEY RD
VINEY AVE
ST BLAIZE RD
WESTERING
CLOVER WAY
LC
HESTIA CL
JENNER FELTHAM CL
JENNER WAY
SEWARD RISE
1 FABER MEWS
2 BRICKWOODS CL
3 STRONGS CL
HALTERWORTH CL
HIGH FIRS GDNS
HIGH FIRS RD
KENNET RD
KENNET CL
HALTERWORTH LA
MEON CL
MEON RD
Halterworth
SAXON WAY
ANTON CL
AVON CRES
HOLYBORNE RD
MEAD CL
EIGHT ACRES
ASHDOWN WAY
HEREWARD CL
WESSEX GDNS
SENLAC RD
BENEDICT CL
MONTFORT HTS
MONTFORT CL
THE VIKINGS
Halterworth Com Prim Sch
1 GROSVENOR CT
2 MONTFORT COLLEGE
HIGHWOOD LA
Stroud Sch
GREEN LA
Willow Farm
Warren Farm
FIELD CL
TADFIELD RD
TADFIELD CRES
QUEEN'S CL
ROSEDALE AVE
HILLSIDE AVE
SYMES RD
ALLAN GR
CHAMBERS AVE
OAKLEIGH GDNS
NIGHTINGALE CL
4 MINDEN HO
5 BLENHEIM HO
6 NORMANDY HO
7 SALERNO HO
Cemy
JACOBS CL
NURSERY GDNS
MOUNT TEMPLE
GRAYS CL
TADBURN CL
PETTY CL
KNIGHT CL
WILLS WAY
SYDMANTON CL
TADBURN RD
REYNOLDS CT
JAMES CT
ST BARBE CL
THE TYLESHADES
DAVID CT
BRIDGE RD
Whitenap Farm
WHITENAP CL
MAPLE CL
SYCAMORE CL
ASH CL
NORTHLANDS RD
WHITENAP LA
ELMTREE GDNS
ALDER CL
ROWAN CL
PINE RD
BOTLEY RD
CHESTNUT CL
MONTFORT CL
BEECH CL
BIRCH CL
PH
FIVE ELMS DR
THE COVERT
THE THICKET
The Mountbatten Sch
Whitenap
LUZBOROUGH LA
The Quadrangle
PARK CT
PREMIER WAY
The Premier Ctr
The Triton Ctr
Abbey Ent Ctr
Brooklyn
North Baddesley
HEATHERVIEW CL 1
LINDEN WLK 2
BADDESLEY CL
A27
SOUTHAMPTON RD
SO51
Beggars Wood
STRAGWYNE CL
WEST LA
BROAD LA
ORCHARD CL
WILLOW GDNS
HIGHLANDS CL
ST ANDREWS CL
POPLAR WAY
CEDAR CRES
JUNIPER CL
SYCAMORE CL
ASH CL
CEDAR CRES
Scrag Hill
DUNNINGS LA
OVERBROOK WAY
HILLCREST CL
THE BIRCHES CL
AMBERLEY CL
RINGWOOD DR
ROWNHAMS LA
CRESCENT RD
UPPER CRESCENT RD
PINE CL
FOREST CL
NORTHER WOOD CL
WYNYARDS GAP
FIRGROVE RD
FIRGROVE CL
WOODLANDS WAY
CERNE CL
HOLLYWOOD CL
COPSE CL
TUTLAND RD
SEYMOUR LA
Luzborough Plantation
Parker's Moor
SO52
QUEENS RIDE
FIELDEN CL
WOODSIDE RD
TORNAY GR
HEATHERBRAE GDNS
HULLES WAY
LANGHAM CL
TOTTEHALE CL
SYLVAN DR
PROCTOR DR
DIBBLE DR
MORTIMER WAY
LAUNCELYN CL
LAVINGTON GDNS
Hoe Farm
A3057
Lower Ashfield Farm
Ashfield
HOE LA
SPANIARD'S LA
Upper Ashfield Farm
LEE LA
Telegraph Wood
Lower Toothill
Toot Hill
Packridge Farm
Upper Toothill
TOOTHILL RD
PACKRIDGE LA
LEE DRO
Middle Farm
UPPER TOOTHILL RD
ROWNHAMS LA
Mast
SO16
Lee Manor Farm Cottage
Nightingale Wood
A3057

4
21
3
20
2
19
1
18

6
A
37
B
38
C

77
54

53
29

A
B
C
Broadgate Plantation
Woodend Copse
Thorn Hill
Tadburn Lake
Green Acres
Emer Bog
SO51
Newlands Copse
POUND LA
Bucket Corner
Knightwood Prim Sch
Castle Hill
Baddesley Common
FLEXFORD RD
Sky's Wood
Lights Copse
Manor Farm
Manor House
SO52
Test Valley Bsns Pk
BADDESLEY CL
A27
Dirty Drive
Zion Hill Farm
Zionshill Copse
SO53
WILD ARUM WAY
Nutburn
NUTBURN RD
SANDY LA
Great Covert
Ind Pk
Liby
BOTLEY RD
Works
Wrens Farm
Hogtrough Wood
CASTLE LA
North Baddesley Jun & Inf Schs
Misslebrooks Copse
Castle Lane Farm
CH
MISSLEBROOK LA
Austins Copse
SO16
HOE LA
RONNHAMS LA
Manor Farm
Calveslease Copse
Tanner's Brook
PACKRIDGE LA
Chilworth
Chilworth Old Village
The Clump
Hut Wood
CHILWORTH RD
Chilworth Manor Hotel & Con Ctr
The Clump Inn
Home Copse
Rownhams Plantation
Science and Research Centre
Kennels Farm
SO16
UNIVERSITY PARKWAY
MANOR RD
ROMAN RD
GREEN LA
M27
4
21
3
20
2
19
1
18
39
40
41

53
78

A B C

SO52
Flexford Nature Reserve
Ramalley Bridge
Cemy
Knight Wood
Badger's Copse
Monk's Brook
Leigh House
Chandler's Ford
Sherborne House Sch
The Lakes
Thornden Sch
Pitmore Sch
Woodhill Sch
Merdon Jun Sch
Scantabout Prim Sch
Chandler's Ford Inf Sch
Liby
Fryern Schs
Fryern Hill
Ind Est
The Central Precinct
Rex Est
Monks Brook Ind Pk
Chandler's Ford Ind Est
Brickfield Trad Est
SO53
Sports Ctr
St Francis CE Prim Sch
PH
Small Profits
Valley Park
Warrior Pk
The Toynbee Sch
Crestwood Com Sch
Ind Est
Superstores
Hampshire Fire Brigade HQ
SO50
Cemy
Hotel
TH
Sports Centre
EASTLEIGH
Works
Fleming Park
CH
Monks Brook
Velmore Farm
Hampshire Corporate Pk
Superstores
East Links
West Links
Works
Hut Wood
Hicknor Hill
SO16
Art Gal
Barton Peveril Coll
Alderman Quilley Sch
Nightingale Prim Sch
The Golf Academy
SO53

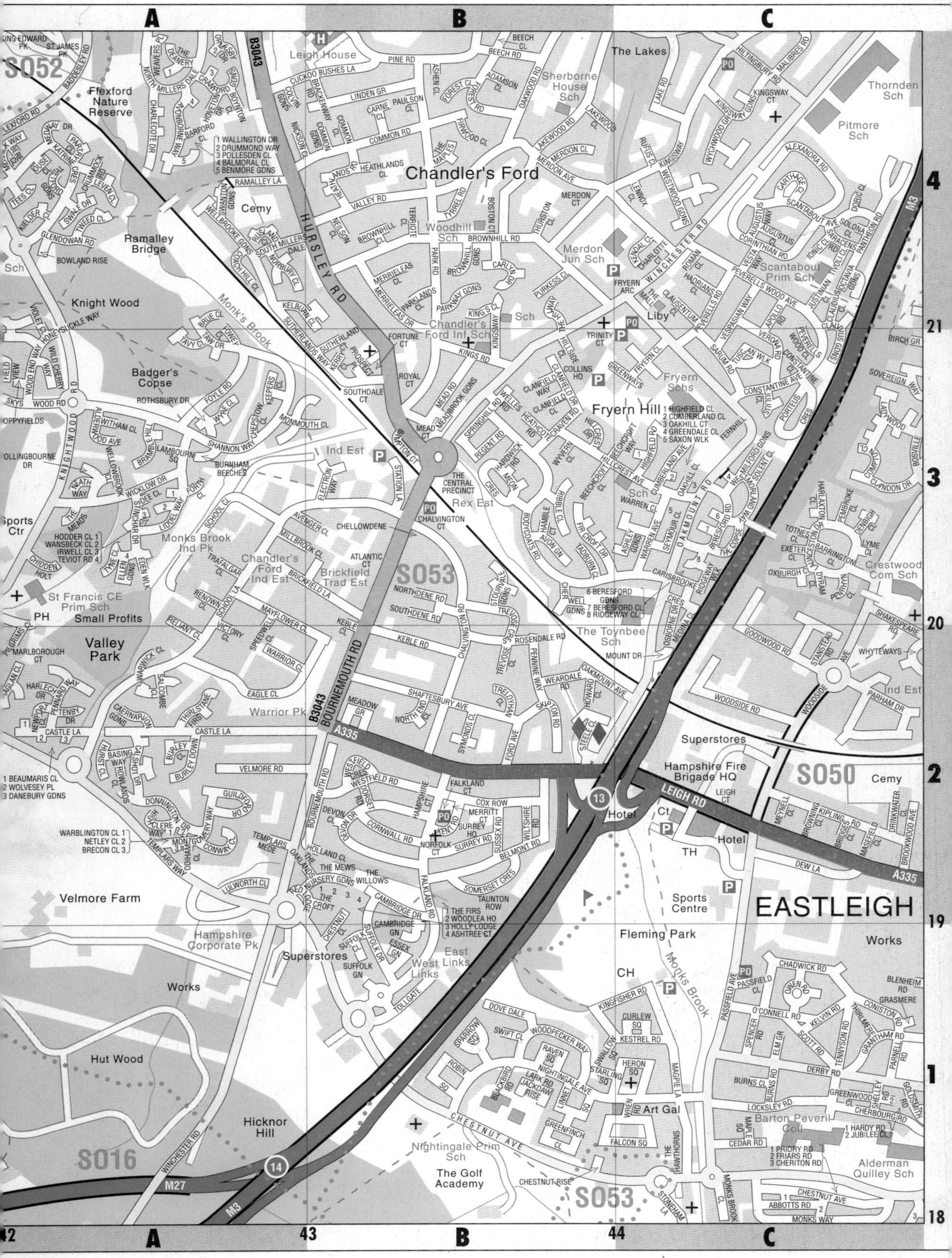

B3043 HURSLEY RD
B3043 BOURNEMOUTH RD
A335
LEIGH RD
M3
M27
13
14

1 WALLINGTON DR
2 DRUMMOND WAY
3 POLLESDEN CL
4 BALMORAL CL
5 BENMORE GDNS

1 HIGHFIELD CL
2 CUMBERLAND CL
3 OAKHILL CT
4 GREENDALE CL
5 SAXON WLK

HODDER CL 1
WANSBECK CL 2
IRWELL CL 3
TEVIOT RD 4

6 BERESFORD GDNS
7 BERESFORD CL
8 RIDGEWAY CL

1 BEAUMARIS CL
2 WOLVESEY PL
3 DANEBURY GDNS

WARBLINGTON CL 1
NETLEY CL 2
BRECON CL 3

1 THE FIRS
2 WOODLEA HO
3 HOLLY LODGE
4 ASHTREE CT

1 PRIORY RD
2 FRIARS RD
3 CHERITON RD

1 HARDY RD
2 JUBILEE CL

4 3 2 1
21 20 19 18

A 43 B 44 C

55
31

A
B
C
4
21
3
20
2
19
1
18
45
46
47
SO21
SO53
SO50
SO21
Otterbourne Grange
Broom Hill
Allbrook
Boyatt Wood
Shakespeare Schs
Newtown
Brookwood Ind Est
Crescent Prim Sch
Norwood Prim Sch
Eastleigh Coll of F Ed
The Park
Mus
The Swan Ctr
Liby
Eastleigh
Tankerville Specl Sch
Barton Park Ind Est
Phoenix Pk
Deacon Trad Est
The Tower Ind Est
Works
Locomotive Works
EASTLEIGH
Sewage Works
Recreation Ground
Barton River
The Itchen Way
The Itchen Navigation
River Itchen
Ham Farm (PH)
Highbridge
High Bridge
Highbridge Farm
Bugle Farm
Brambridge
Dog & Crook (PH)
Colden Common Prim Sch
Lord's Wood
Hill's Farm House
Breach Sling Copse
Breach Farm
Training Centre
Burrow Hill
The Mount
Stoke Common
Brick Kiln Copse
Stoke Park Farm
IDEAL PARK HOMES
Cemy
Stoke Park Wood
Bishopstoke
Stoke Park Inf Sch
Stoke Park Jun Sch
The River Inn
West Horton Farm
Shakespeare Bsns Ctr
ALLBROOK WAY
ALLBROOK HILL
TWYFORD RD
SOUTHAMPTON RD
ROMSEY RD
LEIGH RD
BISHOPSTOKE RD
FAIROAK RD
ALAN DRAYTON WAY
HIGHBRIDGE RD
BRAMBRIDGE RD
BISHOPSTOKE LA
CHURCH RD
A335
B3335
B3037
M3
A1
1 MAPLELEAF GDNS
2 ELMTREE GDNS
3 GRANTHAM CT
4 DERBY HO
5 MISSENDEN PL
6 BLENHEIM HO
7 ERRINGTON HO
A2
1 SALISBURY CT
2 CRESCENT HO
3 GODFREY OLSON HO
4 JOHN DARLING MALL
A3
1 CLAREMONT CL
2 BROWSHOLME CL
3 RAGLAN CT
4 DRUMMOND CT
5 BRAMBLE CL
6 ALBERT RD
7 BOYATT WOOD SHOPPING CTR
C1
1 LOFTING CL
2 GRIFFEN CL
3 MANOR FARM GR
4 MANOR FARM CL
5 DEVINE GDNS
6 SUNNINGDALE CL
7 SQUIRREL CL
8 PRINCE WILLIAM CT
9 HOLT VIEW
10 BADGER CT
11 DOLPHIN CL
12 AUDLEY PL
C4
1 CROWDERS GN
2 TEES GN
3 THACKING GN
4 CLAMP GN
5 SKINTLE GN
6 PIPING GN

55
80

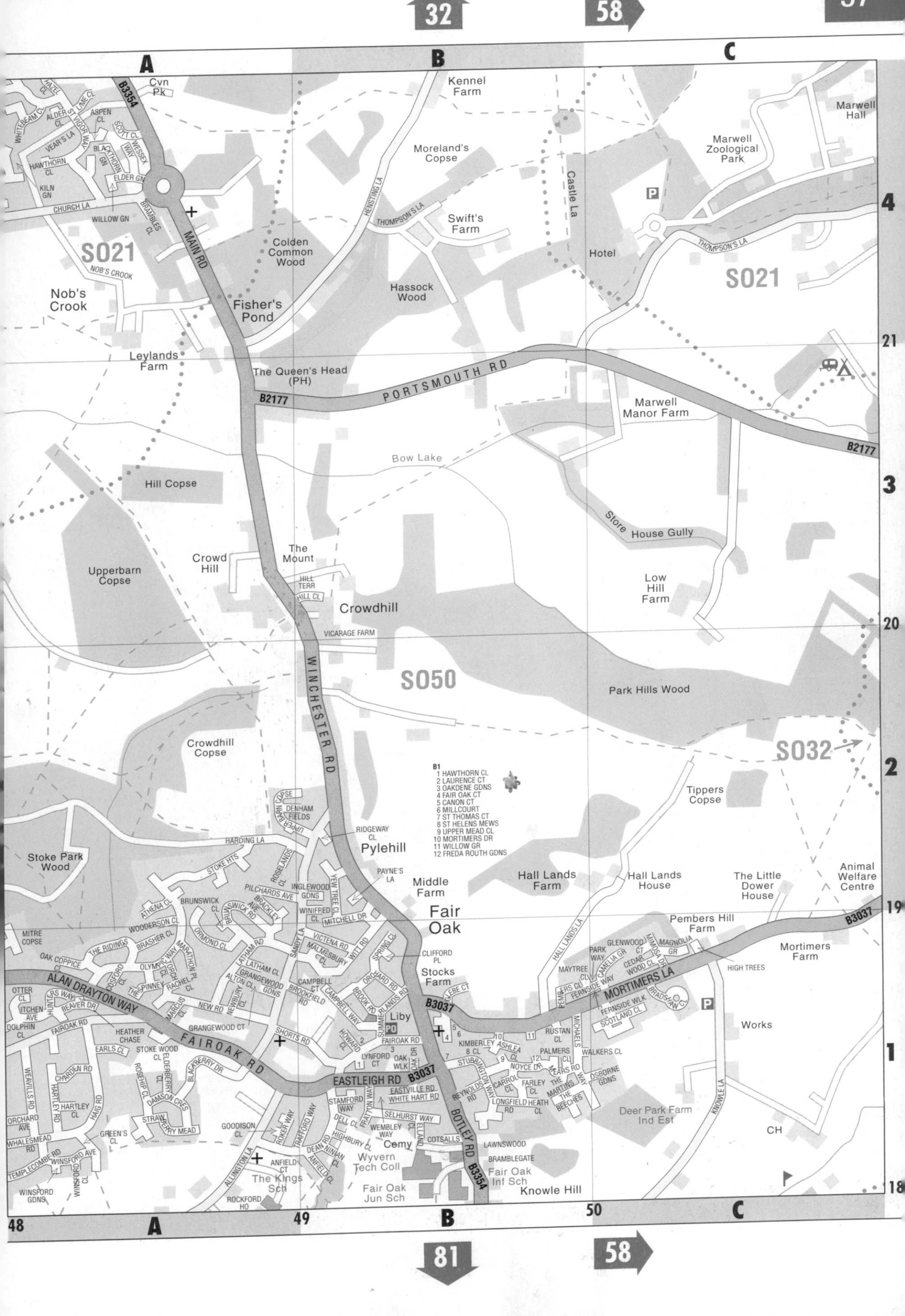
32
58
A
B
C
Kennel Farm
Marwell Hall
Moreland's Copse
Marwell Zoological Park
Castle La
Swift's Farm
Colden Common Wood
Hotel
SO21
Nob's Crook
Fisher's Pond
Hassock Wood
Leylands Farm
The Queen's Head (PH)
PORTSMOUTH RD
B2177
Marwell Manor Farm
Bow Lake
Hill Copse
Store House Gully
Crowd Hill
The Mount
Upperbarn Copse
Low Hill Farm
Crowdhill
VICARAGE FARM
SO50
Park Hills Wood
WINCHESTER RD
Crowdhill Copse
SO32
B1
1 HAWTHORN CL
2 LAURENCE CT
3 OAKDENE GDNS
4 FAIR OAK CT
5 CANON CT
6 MILLCOURT
7 ST THOMAS CT
8 ST HELENS MEWS
9 UPPER MEAD CL
10 MORTIMERS DR
11 WILLOW GR
12 FREDA ROUTH GDNS
Tippers Copse
Stoke Park Wood
Pylehill
Middle Farm
Hall Lands Farm
Hall Lands House
The Little Dower House
Animal Welfare Centre
Fair Oak
Pembers Hill Farm
Mortimers Farm
Stocks Farm
MORTIMERS LA
ALAN DRAYTON WAY
FAIROAK RD
EASTLEIGH RD
B3037
BOTLEY RD
B3354
MAIN RD
Works
Deer Park Farm Ind Est
CH
Cemy
Wyvern Tech Coll
The Kings Sch
Fair Oak Jun Sch
Fair Oak Inf Sch
Knowle Hill
21
20
19
18
4
3
2
1
48
49
50
81
58

57
33

A
B
C
Rowhay Wood
Woodlock's Down Farm
Leybushes Copse
Greenhill Lane
Lower Baybridge La
Whaddon La
Thompson's La
Marwell House
SO21
Hurst Farm
Red Lane
King's Way
Summerlands
Sladford's Copse
Monarch's Way
Roughay Farm
The Rookery
Hurst La
White Hill
Woodcote Lane
Rowhay Lane
Widlers Lane
SO50
Red La
Sweet Briar Cottage
Shoe La
B2177
Deeps Bushes Copse
Church St
PH
Thistle Ridge Farm
Deeps Copse
Cawtes Copse
Widlers La
West Hall
Elm Cres
Oak Cl
Upham
Hatchley La
Rowhay La
Upham Copse
Upham CE Prim Sch
Hatchley Lane
Bushy Copse
Pondside
Deeps Farm
Popes Farm
Upham St
Popes La
Upham Farm
Stroudwood Farm
SO32
Stroudwood Rd
New Farm
Ashbourne Stables
Winchester Rd
PO
Lower Upham
B3037
Stroudwood
Hoyle Cl
Alma Inn (PH)
Merry Orchard Farm
Woodman Inn (PH)
Redlands Copse
Stakes La
Stroudwood Dairy Farm
Mortimers La
King's Way
Cross La
Stakes Farm
Pond Farm
Torbay Farm
Oaklands Farm
Woolstreet Farm
Down Farm
Woodward Farm
Alma La
SO50
Woodley Farm
Meadowview
Coombs Farm
Scivier's La
The Crescent
Moplands Copse
Wintershill Hall
Kimbers Copse
Oakdale Farm
Woodlands
Greenwood La
Giles Farm
Winters Hill
Wintershill Farm
Durley Hall Rd
B2177
Job's Corner
Nursery
Winters Hill
Durley Hall Farm
Wintershill
4
21
3
20
2
19
1
18
51
52
53

57
82

34
60

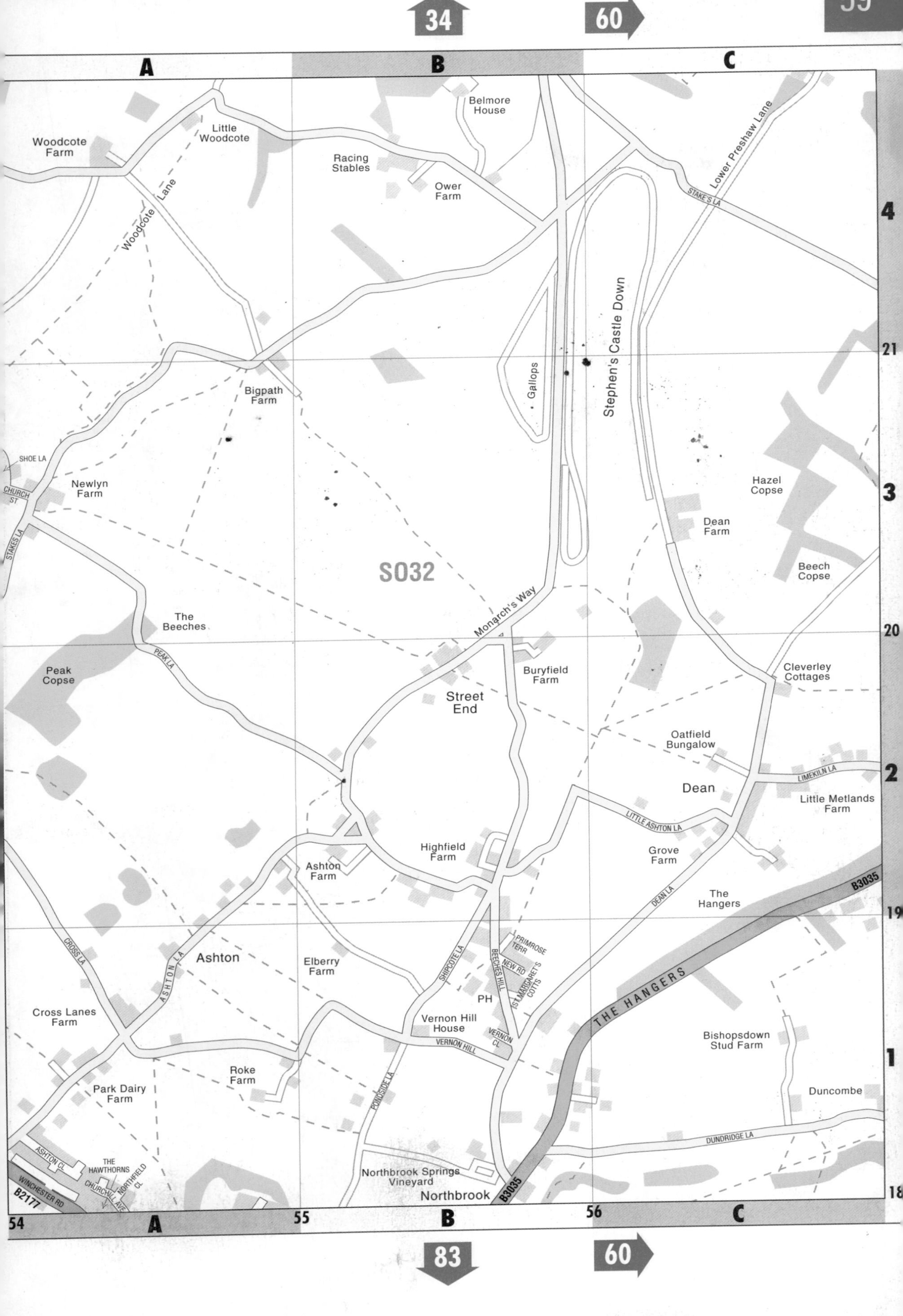
A
B
C
Belmore House
Little Woodcote
Woodcote Farm
Racing Stables
Ower Farm
Lower Preshaw Lane
STAKE'S LA
Woodcote Lane
4
Stephen's Castle Down
Gallops
21
Bigpath Farm
SHOE LA
CHURCH ST
Newlyn Farm
Hazel Copse
3
Dean Farm
STAKES LA
SO32
Beech Copse
Monarch's Way
The Beeches
20
PEAK LA
Peak Copse
Buryfield Farm
Cleverley Cottages
Street End
Oatfield Bungalow
LIMEKILN LA
2
Dean
Little Metlands Farm
LITTLE ASHTON LA
Highfield Farm
Ashton Farm
Grove Farm
B3035
DEAN LA
The Hangers
19
CROSS LA
PRIMROSE TERR
NEW RD
ASHTON LA
Ashton
Elberry Farm
SHIPCOTE LA
BEECHES HILL
ST MARGARET'S COTTS
THE HANGERS
PH
Cross Lanes Farm
Vernon Hill House
VERNON CL
Bishopsdown Stud Farm
VERNON HILL
1
Roke Farm
Park Dairy Farm
PONDSIDE LA
Duncombe
DUNDRIDGE LA
ASHTON CL
THE HAWTHORNS
NORTHFIELD CL
Northbrook Springs Vineyard
WINCHESTER RD
CHURCHILL AVE
B3035
B2177
Northbrook
18
54
A
55
B
56
C

83
60

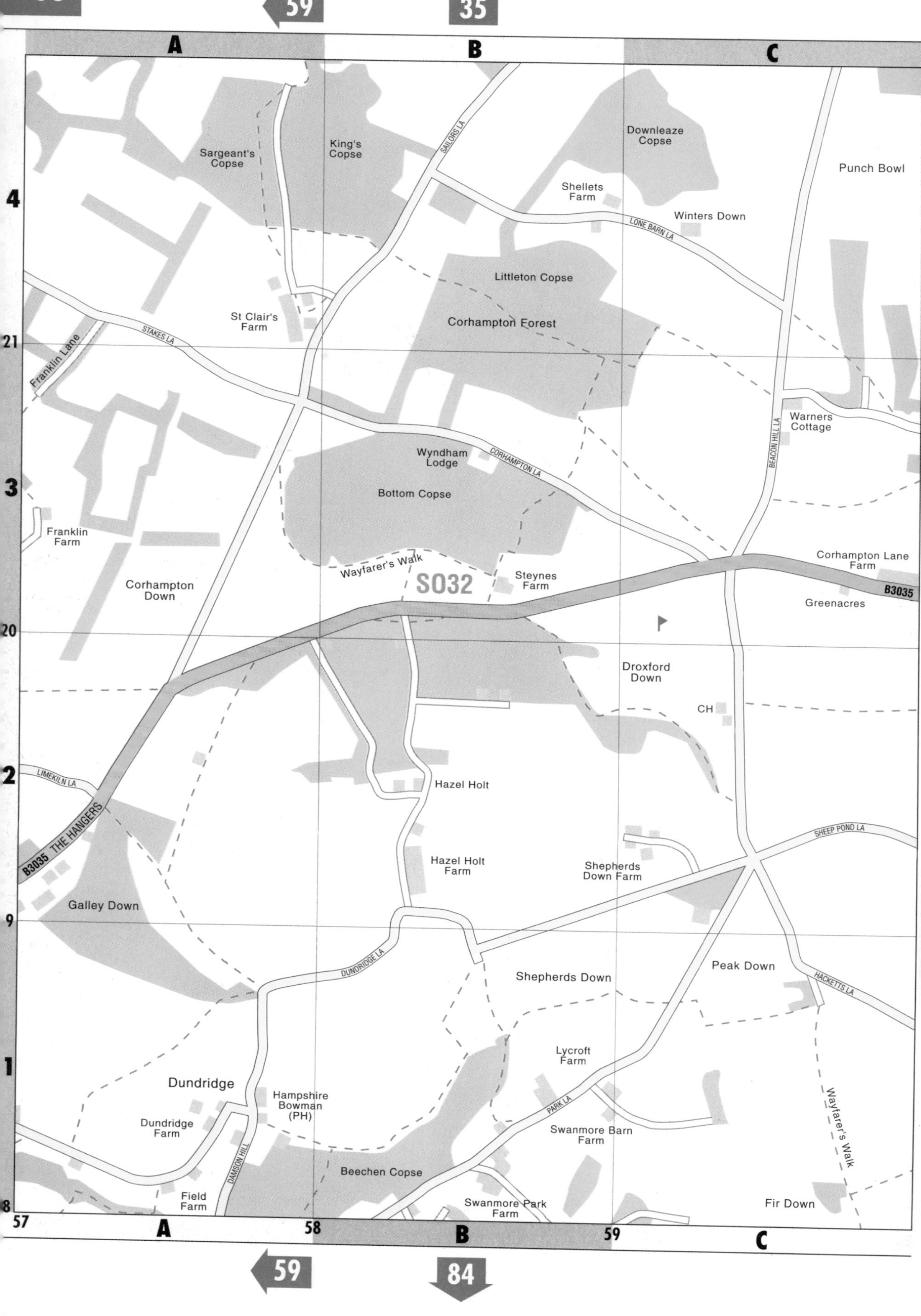
59
35
A
B
C
Sargeant's Copse
King's Copse
SAILORS LA
Downleaze Copse
Punch Bowl
Shellets Farm
Winters Down
LONE BARN LA
Littleton Copse
St Clair's Farm
Corhampton Forest
STAKES LA
Franklin Lane
Warners Cottage
BEACON HILL LA
Wyndham Lodge
CORHAMPTON LA
Bottom Copse
Franklin Farm
Corhampton Lane Farm
Wayfarer's Walk
SO32
Steynes Farm
B3035
Corhampton Down
Greenacres
Droxford Down
CH
LIMEKILN LA
Hazel Holt
B3035 THE HANGERS
SHEEP POND LA
Hazel Holt Farm
Shepherds Down Farm
Galley Down
DUNDRIDGE LA
Peak Down
Shepherds Down
HACKETTS LA
Lycroft Farm
Dundridge
Hampshire Bowman (PH)
PARK LA
Dundridge Farm
Swanmore Barn Farm
Wayfarer's Walk
DAMSON HILL
Beechen Copse
Field Farm
Swanmore Park Farm
Fir Down
4
21
3
20
2
9
1
8
57
58
59
59
84

36
62

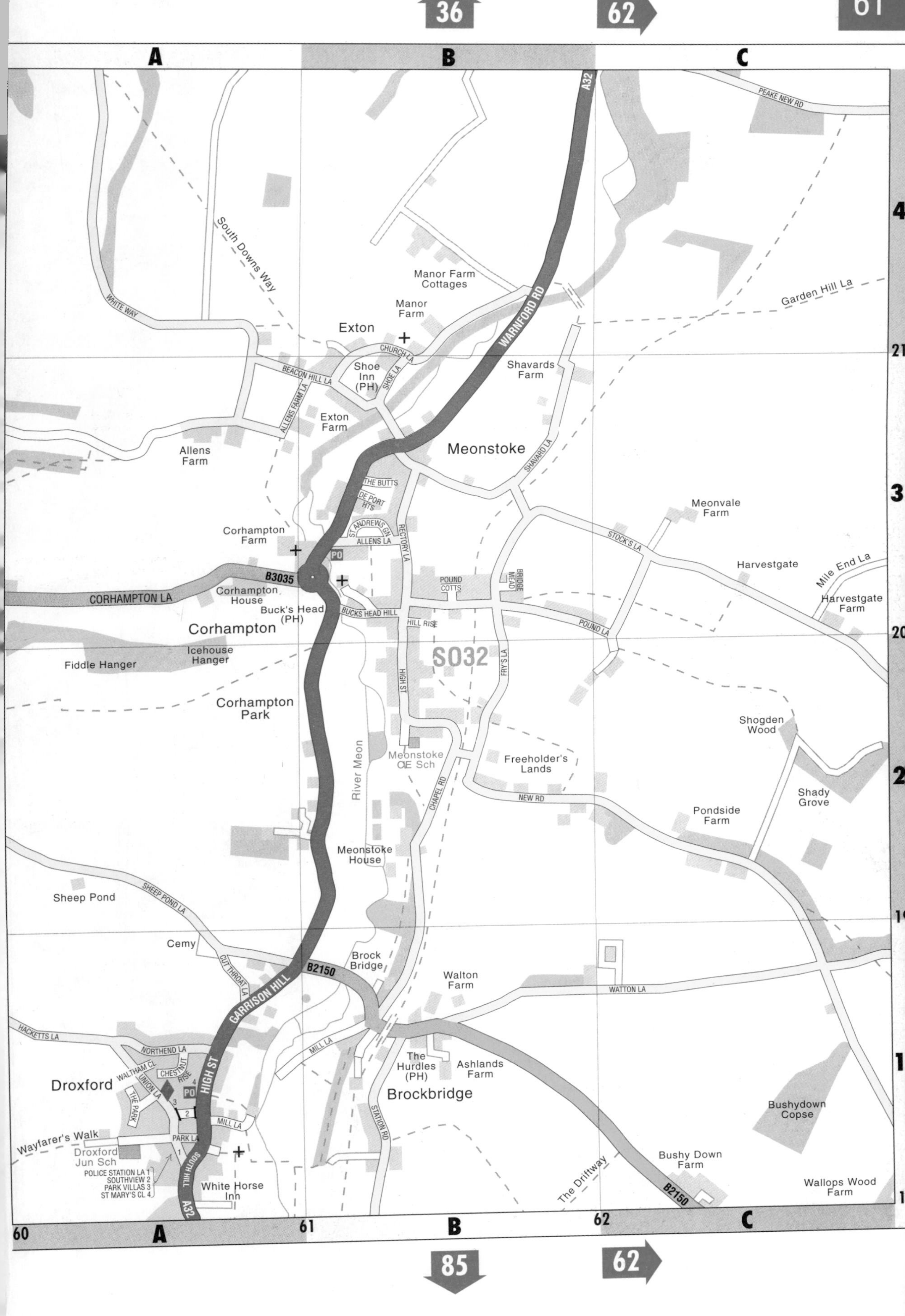
A
B
C
Exton
Manor Farm Cottages
Manor Farm
Shoe Inn (PH)
Exton Farm
Allens Farm
Shavards Farm
Meonstoke
Corhampton Farm
Corhampton House
Buck's Head (PH)
Corhampton
Fiddle Hanger
Icehouse Hanger
Corhampton Park
Meonvale Farm
Harvestgate
Harvestgate Farm
SO32
Shogden Wood
Freeholder's Lands
Meonstoke CE Sch
River Meon
Meonstoke House
Pondside Farm
Shady Grove
Sheep Pond
Cemy
Brock Bridge
Walton Farm
Droxford
The Hurdles (PH)
Ashlands Farm
Brockbridge
Droxford Jun Sch
White Horse Inn
Bushydown Copse
Bushy Down Farm
Wallops Wood Farm
South Downs Way
WHITE WAY
BEACON HILL LA
ALLENS FARM LA
CHURCH LA
SHOE LA
WARNFORD RD
A32
PEAKE NEW RD
Garden Hill La
SHAVARD LA
THE BUTTS
DE PORT HTS
ST ANDREWS GN
ALLENS LA
RECTORY LA
PO
B3035
CORHAMPTON LA
POUND COTTS
BRIDGE MEAD
STOCK'S LA
Mile End La
BUCKS HEAD HILL
HILL RISE
POUND LA
HIGH ST
FRY'S LA
CHAPEL RD
NEW RD
SHEEP POND LA
CUT THROAT LA
GARRISON HILL
B2150
WATTON LA
HACKETTS LA
NORTHEND LA
WALTHAM CL
CHESTNUT RISE
UNION LA
THE PARK
MILL LA
PARK LA
Wayfarer's Walk
SOUTH HILL
STATION RD
The Driftway
POLICE STATION LA 1
SOUTHVIEW 2
PARK VILLAS 3
ST MARY'S CL 4
4
21
3
20
2
1
60
61
62

85
62

61
37

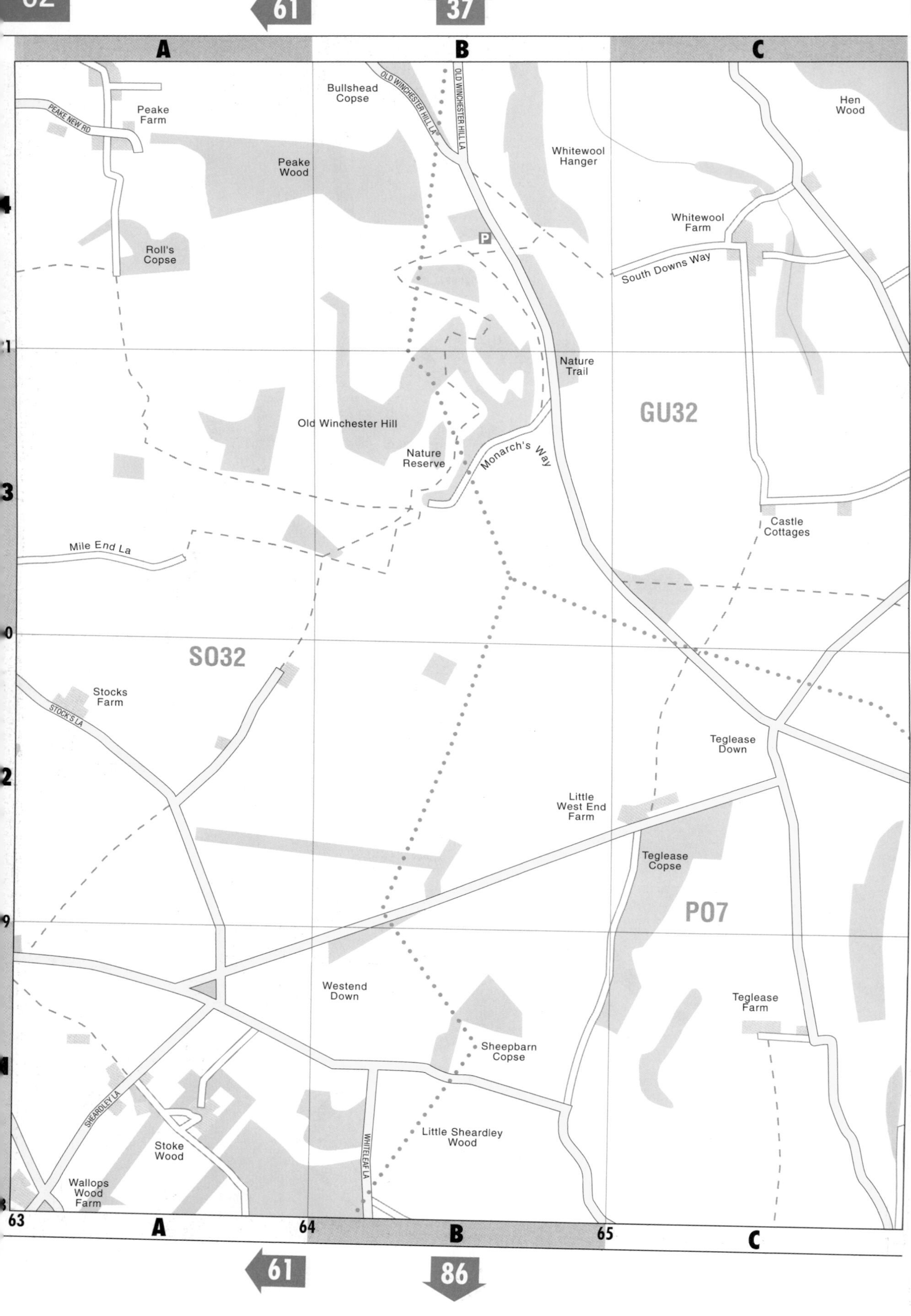
A
B
C
Peake Farm
PEAKE NEW RD
Bullshead Copse
OLD WINCHESTER HILL LA
OLD WINCHESTER HILL LA
Hen Wood
Whitewool Hanger
Peake Wood
Whitewool Farm
Roll's Copse
South Downs Way
Nature Trail
GU32
Old Winchester Hill
Nature Reserve
Monarch's Way
Castle Cottages
Mile End La
SO32
Stocks Farm
STOCK'S LA
Teglease Down
Little West End Farm
Teglease Copse
PO7
Westend Down
Teglease Farm
Sheepbarn Copse
SHEARDLEY LA
WHITELEAF LA
Little Sheardley Wood
Stoke Wood
Wallops Wood Farm
63
64
65
A
B
C

61
86

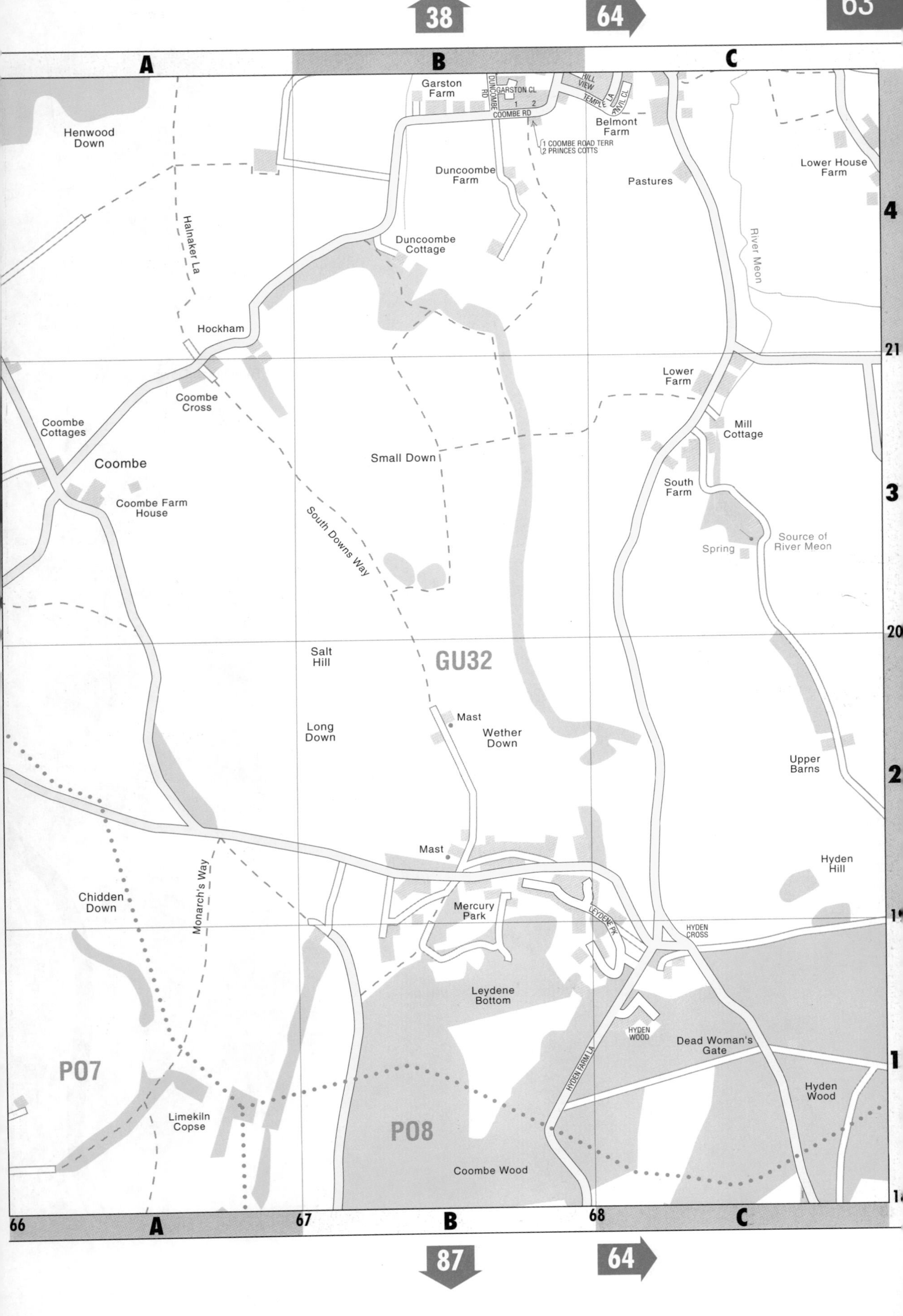
38
64
A
B
C
Garston Farm
GARSTON CL
DUNCOMBE RD
COOMBE RD
HILL VIEW
TEMPLE LA
ANVIL CL
Belmont Farm
1 COOMBE ROAD TERR
2 PRINCES COTTS
Henwood Down
Duncoombe Farm
Pastures
Lower House Farm
Halnaker La
Duncoombe Cottage
River Meon
4
Hockham
21
Coombe Cross
Lower Farm
Coombe Cottages
Mill Cottage
Small Down
Coombe
South Farm
3
Coombe Farm House
South Downs Way
Source of River Meon
Spring
20
Salt Hill
GU32
Mast
Long Down
Wether Down
Upper Barns
2
Mast
Hyden Hill
Chidden Down
Monarch's Way
Mercury Park
LEYDENE PK
HYDEN CROSS
Leydene Bottom
HYDEN WOOD
Dead Woman's Gate
HYDEN FARM LA
1
PO7
Hyden Wood
Limekiln Copse
PO8
Coombe Wood
66
A
67
B
68
C
87
64

63
39

A
B
C
Hill Hampton Farm
Twentyways Farm
Nutcombe Copse
Cumber's La
Hilhampton Copse
Oxenbourne Farm
Leythe House Farm
Nutcoombe Tower
Harroway Farm
Browning's Hill
Fishpond Cottages
The Nore
Rakefield Hanger
Parsonage Barn
Oxenbourne Leythe
Ramsdean Down
GU32
Lower Oxenbourne Farm
LIMEKILN LA
Rake Bottom
Preston Farm
Butser Hill
GU31
Stonylands Farm
HARVESTING LA
Radio Station Mast
P
South Downs Way
Queen Elizabeth Country Park
Hilhampton Down
Tegdown Bottom
A3
PO8
Hilhampton Bottom
Tegdown Hill
NORTH LA
Oxenbourne Down
Nine Corner Hanger
Blagdon Farm
Visitor Ctr
Newmans Farm
Wascoombe Bottom
Blagden Copse
Byden Copse
Hyden Wood
Ditch Acre Copse
Gravel Hill
4
21
3
20
2
9
1
8
69
70
71

63
88

40
66

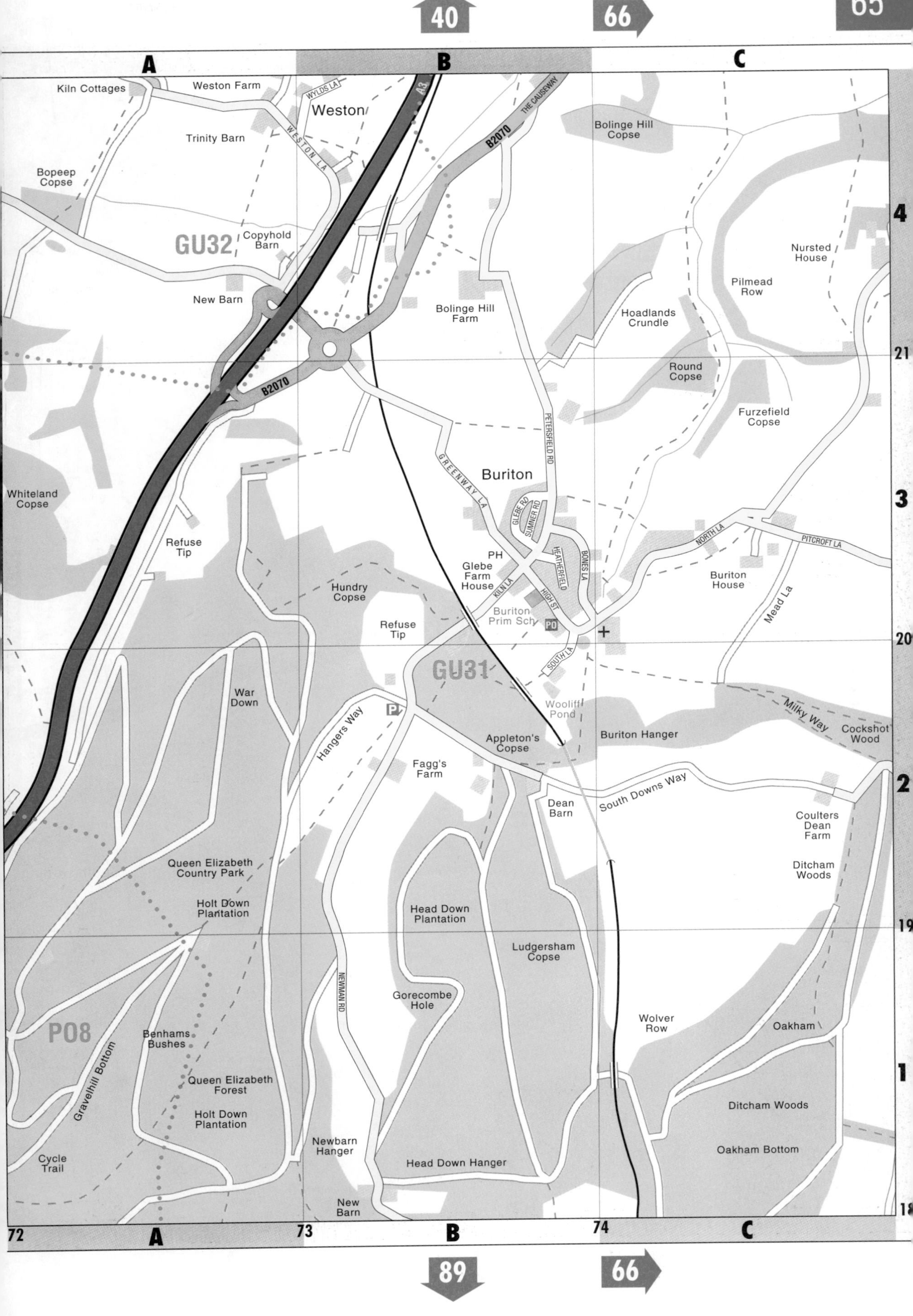
A
B
C
Kiln Cottages
Weston Farm
WYLDS LA
Weston
A3
THE CAUSEWAY
B2070
Bolinge Hill Copse
Trinity Barn
WESTON LA
Bopeep Copse
GU32
Copyhold Barn
Nursted House
Pilmead Row
New Barn
Bolinge Hill Farm
Hoadlands Crundle
Round Copse
B2070
Furzefield Copse
PETERSFIELD RD
GREENWAY LA
Buriton
Whiteland Copse
GLEBE RD
SUMNER RD
Refuse Tip
NORTH LA
PITCROFT LA
PH
HEATHERFIELD
BONES LA
Glebe Farm House
Buriton House
Hundry Copse
KILN LA
HIGH ST
Mead La
Buriton Prim Sch
PO
Refuse Tip
SOUTH LA
GU31
War Down
Wooliff Pond
Milky Way
Hangers Way
P
Buriton Hanger
Cockshot Wood
Appleton's Copse
Fagg's Farm
South Downs Way
Dean Barn
Coulters Dean Farm
Queen Elizabeth Country Park
Ditcham Woods
Holt Down Plantation
Head Down Plantation
Ludgersham Copse
NEWMAN RD
Gorecombe Hole
Wolver Row
Oakham
PO8
Benhams Bushes
Gravelhill Bottom
Queen Elizabeth Forest
Ditcham Woods
Holt Down Plantation
Oakham Bottom
Newbarn Hanger
Cycle Trail
Head Down Hanger
New Barn
4
21
3
20
2
19
1
18
72
73
74
A
B
C

89
66

65
41

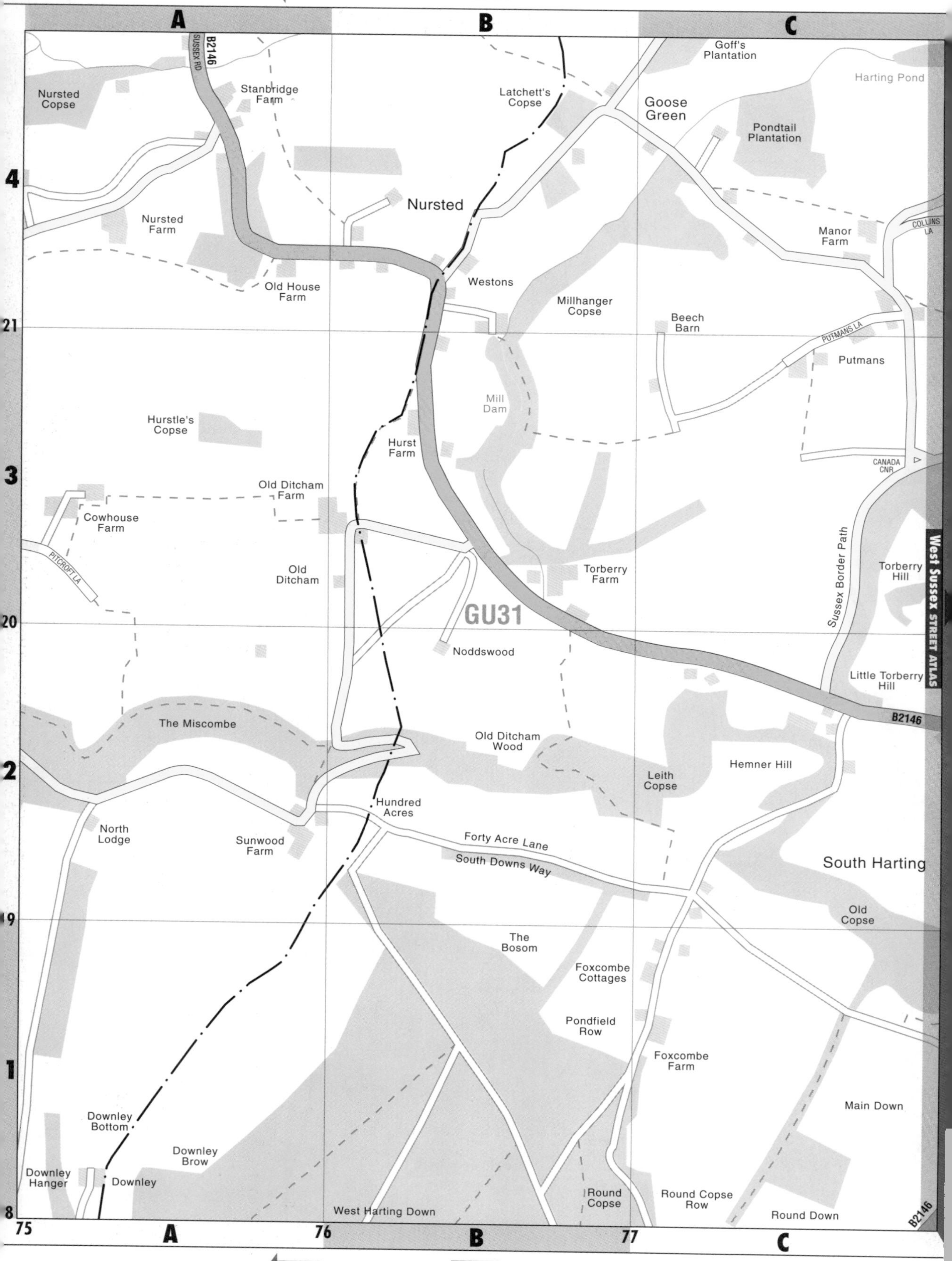

A
B
C
B2146
SUSSEX RD
Nursted Copse
Stanbridge Farm
Latchett's Copse
Goff's Plantation
Harting Pond
Goose Green
Pondtail Plantation
Nursted
Nursted Farm
Manor Farm
COLLINS LA
Old House Farm
Westons
Millhanger Copse
Beech Barn
PUTMANS LA
Putmans
Mill Dam
Hurstle's Copse
Hurst Farm
CANADA CNR
Old Ditcham Farm
Cowhouse Farm
PITCROFT LA
Old Ditcham
Torberry Farm
Sussex Border Path
Torberry Hill
GU31
Noddswood
Little Torberry Hill
The Miscombe
Old Ditcham Wood
B2146
Hemner Hill
Leith Copse
Hundred Acres
North Lodge
Sunwood Farm
Forty Acre Lane
South Downs Way
South Harting
Old Copse
The Bosom
Foxcombe Cottages
Pondfield Row
Foxcombe Farm
Main Down
Downley Bottom
Downley Brow
Downley Hanger
Downley
Round Copse
Round Copse Row
West Harting Down
Round Down
B2146
4
21
3
20
2
19
1
18
75
76
77
West Sussex STREET ATLAS

65
90

43
68
A
B
C
Tidpit Common Down
Allen River
Knight's Copse
Soldier's Ring
South Allenford Farm
Blackheath Down
Kites Nest Farm
New Road Plantation
Boulsbury Down
4
17
Blagdon Hill Wood
High Boulsbury Wood
Martin Wood
3
Boulsbury Cottages
Boulsbury Farm
SP6
Holm Hill Copse
Dorset STREET ATLAS
16
Stone Hill Wood
Kingland Copse
Peaked Plantation
Highwood Copse
Ball Hill Copse
BH21
Bottom Copse
2
Stapleton Farm
Buttons Copse
High Wood
Boulsbury Wood
Boveridge Farm
15
Boveridge House
Biddlesgate Copse
Noddle Hill
Boveridge
Bovis Row
Park Row
Hyde Cross
1
Hyde Farm
Perry Copse
Burwood
Biddlesgate Farm
Wadleys Dro
Pinetree Farm
Bratch Copse
14
06
07
08
91
68

67 44

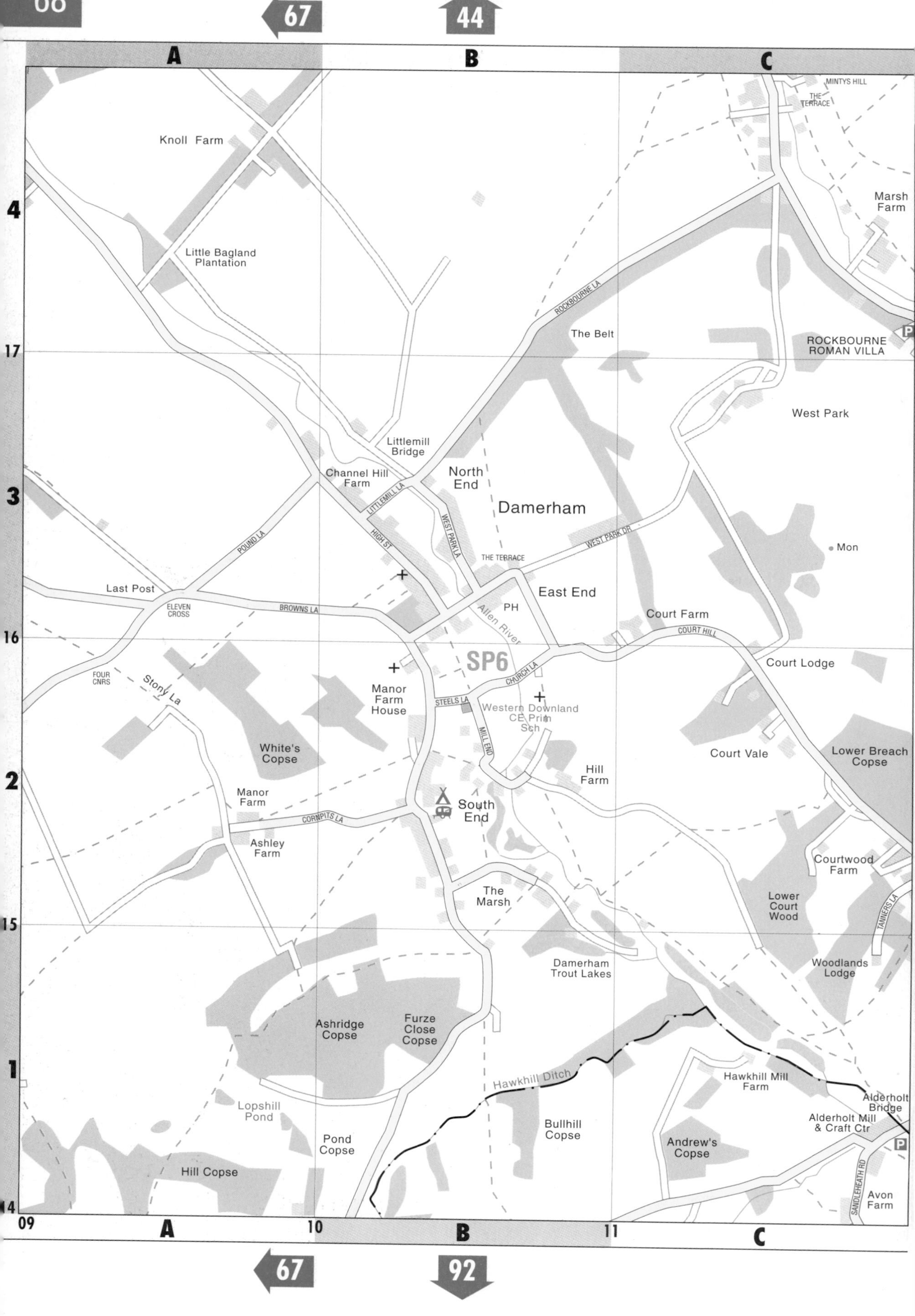
A
B
C
4
17
3
16
2
15
1
14
09
10
11
Knoll Farm
Little Bagland Plantation
MINTYS HILL
THE TERRACE
Marsh Farm
ROCKBOURNE LA
The Belt
ROCKBOURNE ROMAN VILLA
West Park
Littlemill Bridge
Channel Hill Farm
North End
Damerham
LITTLEMILL LA
WEST PARK LA
HIGH ST
POUND LA
THE TERRACE
WEST PARK DR
Mon
Last Post
ELEVEN CROSS
BROWNS LA
East End
PH
Allen River
Court Farm
COURT HILL
SP6
Court Lodge
FOUR CNRS
Stony La
Manor Farm House
CHURCH LA
STEELS LA
Western Downland CE Prim Sch
MILL END
White's Copse
Court Vale
Lower Breach Copse
Hill Farm
Manor Farm
South End
CORNPITS LA
Ashley Farm
Courtwood Farm
The Marsh
Lower Court Wood
TANNERS LA
Woodlands Lodge
Damerham Trout Lakes
Ashridge Copse
Furze Close Copse
Hawkhill Ditch
Hawkhill Mill Farm
Alderholt Bridge
Alderholt Mill & Craft Ctr
Lopshill Pond
Bullhill Copse
Pond Copse
Andrew's Copse
Hill Copse
SANDLEHEATH RD
Avon Farm

67 92

45
70

Whitsbury Common
Rockstead Copse
Whitsbury House
WHITSBURY CROSS
OUTWICK CROSS
Outwick
Kiln Wood
Rockstead Farm
Radnall Wood
Flood Street
Whip's Hill Copse
Brookheath
Clack La
Sagles Spring
Fryern Court Wood
Peasash Farm
Clack Barn
Sweatfords Water
Palmer's Copse
Mist Farm
Fryern Court Farm
Fryern Court
Allen's Farm
West Park Farm
SP6
Avon Vale Nurseries
Avon Valley Path
Brickhill
Wilkins's Coomb
Sandle Dairy Farm
TINKERS CROSS
Puddleslosh La
Arch Farm Ind Est
Fordingbridge Jun & Inf Schs
Hurley Farm
Sandle Manor
Sandleheath
Marl La
Sandleheath Ind Est
Forres Sandle Manor
Thorps Farm
Reeve's Copse
Ashford
Fordingbridge Bsns Pk
Ashford Water
Ashford Works Ind Est
Hotel
FORDINGBRIDGE
Fordingbridge
Mus
Liby
TH
B3078
River Avon
GARENDON CT 1
MEADOW CL 2
OAKLANDS CL 3
WILSON CT 4
AVON CT 5
HOMEBRIDGE HO 6
THE HUNDRED 7
SYCAMORE CT 8
A
B
C
4
3
2
1
17
16
15
14
12
13
14

93
70

69
46
A
B
C
Breamore Marsh
Breamore CE Prim Sch
PO
A338
PH
Breamore
Marsh Farm
Weir
Norton's Hole
Woodgreen
Barn's Farm
Dodgson Cl
Hale Rd
Lower Densome Wood
Hill Close Est
St Georges Cotts
Higher End Farm
PH
The Alley
Grace La
Love La
Trimm's Dro
Steels Dro
Brook La
Little Dro
High St
Woodgreen Common
Marsh La
Green's Farm
Mill
Arch Farm
The Shallows
The Shallows
Flood Street Farm
Cemy
Godshill Inclosure
Upper Burgate
Fryern Court Rd
Burgate Cross
Castle Hill
Avon Valley Path
River Avon
Godshill Wood
Castle Hill
Burgate Cross Farm
Salisbury Rd
Weir
SP6
Armsley
The Fairgate Ctr
Burgate Farm
Folds Farm
Godshill Wood Farm
Tudor Rose Inn (PH)
Burgate Court
Ford
The Burgate Sch
Millers Ford Farm
Burgate Manor Farm
Burgate Fields
Waverley Rd
Lower Burgate
Frankenbury
Furze Close Copse
Salisbury Rd
Langley Gdn
Pembridge Rd
Woodfern
Hall
PH
Roger Penny Way
B3078
Godshill Green
Lyster Rd
River Rd
Field Way
Rookham Bottom
Sandy Balls
Holiday Centre
Larch Row
The Pines
Godshill Farm
Bruyn Rd
Bruyn Ct
Ling Cres
Hart Hill
Well La
Salisbury Rd
East Mills
Godshill
Newgrounds
Weir
Avon View
Arniss Farm
Horseport
Southampton Rd
B3078
East Mill Farm
Criddlestyle
Strawberry Farm
Ditchend Brook
1 Bridge St
2 Ringwood Rd
Stuckton Rd
St Johns Farm
Blissford Rd
A338
4
17
3
16
2
15
1
14
15
16
17
69
94

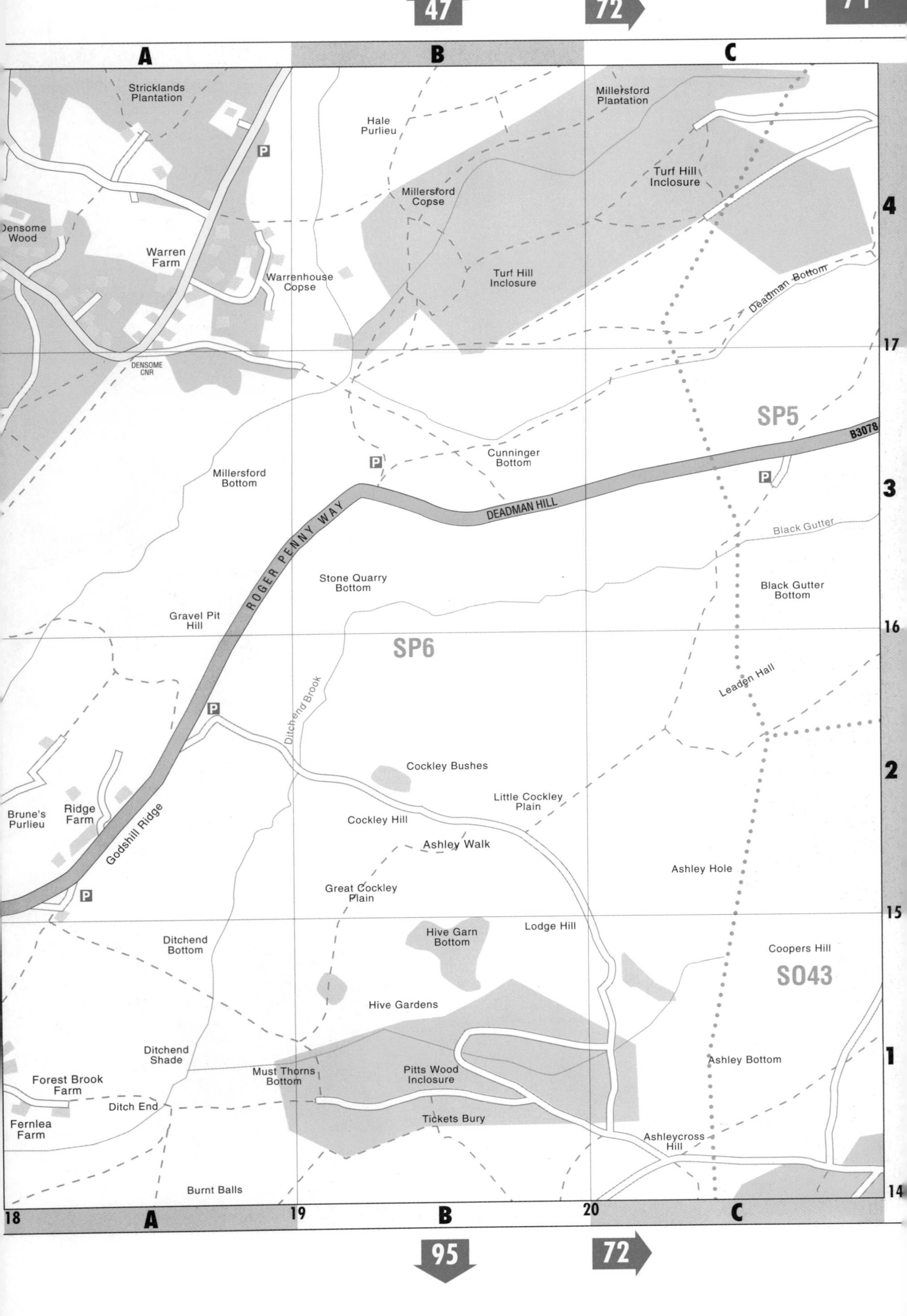
A
B
C
Stricklands Plantation
Hale Purlieu
Millersford Plantation
Turf Hill Inclosure
Millersford Copse
Densome Wood
Warren Farm
Warrenhouse Copse
Turf Hill Inclosure
Deadman Bottom
DENSOME CNR
SP5
B3078
Cunninger Bottom
Millersford Bottom
DEADMAN HILL
ROGER PENNY WAY
Black Gutter
Stone Quarry Bottom
Black Gutter Bottom
Gravel Pit Hill
SP6
Leaden Hall
Ditchend Brook
Cockley Bushes
Little Cockley Plain
Brune's Purlieu
Ridge Farm
Cockley Hill
Godshill Ridge
Ashley Walk
Ashley Hole
Great Cockley Plain
Hive Garn Bottom
Lodge Hill
Ditchend Bottom
Coopers Hill
SO43
Hive Gardens
Ditchend Shade
Ashley Bottom
Must Thorns Bottom
Pitts Wood Inclosure
Forest Brook Farm
Ditch End
Tickets Bury
Fernlea Farm
Ashleycross Hill
Burnt Balls
4
17
3
16
2
15
1
14
18
19
20
A
B
C

71
48

A
B
C
Golden Cross
Jacob's Barrow
B3080
Pound Bottom
Cloven Hill Plantation
Franchises Common
Tinney's Plantation
LYBURN RD
4
Rushy Flat
FOREST RD
Burnt Ground Wood
Franchises Lodge
Franchises Wood
17
B3078
B3080
ROGER PENNY WAY
Hope Cottage
Firs Hill Copse
SP5
Bramshaw Telegraph
Tucker's Hat
Picket Corner
Studley Head
3
Black Gutter
Claypits Bottom
Bur Bushes
Studley Wood
Studley Castle
16
Homy Ridge
B3078
The Butts
2
Howen Bottom
Eyeworth Wood
Islands Thorns Inclosure
15
SO43
Crock Hill
Eyeworth Pond
Latchmore Brook
Eyeworth Lodge
1
Howen Bushes
Fritham Bridge
Fritham Farm
The Royal Oak (PH)
Fritham
Gorley Bushes
4
21
A
22
B
23
C

71
96

49
74

A
B
C
Lyburn Rd
Short Hill
Lyburn Rd
School Rd
Nomansland & Hamptworth CE Sch
York Dro
Whitehorn Dr
Pear Tree Dr
Oakleigh Dr
New Rd
B3079
Woodside Bottom
Nomansland
North La
Forest Rd
South La
Lyburn Ho
PH
Chapel La
Lyburn Park
Deazle Wood
Barford Farms
Bramshaw Inclosure
SP5
Judd's Hill
Two Beeches Bottom
Bramshaw Wood
Parsonage Farm
Piper's Wait
Rushy Slab
Crow's Nest Bottom
Vice La
Bramble Hill Hotel
Black Bush
Bramshaw
Butcher's Cnr
Stock's Cross
Black Bush Plain
Great Wood
Longcross Pond
Shepherds Gutter
SO43
Longcross Plain
Long Cross
Court Farm
Aerial
Ravens Nest Inclosure
Roger Penny Way
Bramshaw Hill
Fountain Court
Broom Hill
Brook Wood
Salisbury Trench
Coppice of Linwood
Fritham House
Gibbet Wood
Round Hill
B3078
4
17
3
16
2
15
1
14
25
26

97
74

73
50

A B C

SP5
Rockingham Arms (PH)
CANADA RD
PLANTATION RD
Black Hill
Canada Common
Pitts Farm
Swallow Fields
SO51
BLACKHILL RD
Wicksmoor Farmhouse
Penn Common
Hungerford Farm
Cooper's Lane
Furzley
Penn Farm
Furzley Farm
FURZLEY LA
Half Moon Common
SO43
Mark's Farm
Furzley Common
Penn Copse
Duck Hill
Stagbury Hill
VICE LA
Porters Farm
Crock Hill
FURZLEY RD
Blenmans Farm
Newbridge
NEWBRIDGE RD
Cadnam Common
B3079
Warren's House
Warren's Park
Storm's Farm
Cadnam River
SO40
PO
Brook Hill
BROOK CNR
Warren's Farm
CADNAM LA
Cadnam Green
Withers Farm
KEWLAKE LA
B3079
CH
The Bell Inn Hotel
Brook
Manor Farm
Springer's Farm
Dairyhouse Farm
Manor Farm
B3078
B3079
Ford
WITTENSFORD LA
M27
OLD LYNDHURST RD

4 17 3 16 2 15 1 14

27 A 28 B 29 C

73
98

A B C

Tilhill
Foxbury Plantation
A36
SALISBURY RD
Pearce's Copse
Bricky Lake La
Allmoor Copse
Cooper's La
Home Farm
CH
SHELLEY LA
Shelley Farm
Shelley Nursery
River Blackwater
A3090
OLD SALISBURY RD
Hotel
Wigley
CHENEY'S FARM
Ower Bridge
Ower
SO43
Robins Copse
Cadnam River
Paultons Park
SO51
LAKESIDE
Mortimer's Ind Units
Wade Park Farm
M27
ROMSEY RD
Court Copse
Middle Copse
High Wood Copse
A31
Fuzzies Copse
Green Pastures Farm
Stonyford
Stonyford
Newbridge Inclosure
Copythorne Common
SO40
WHITEMOOR LA
BARROW HILL RD
COPYTHORNE CRES
Barrow Hills
Bunker's Hill
Whitemoor Pond
LOPERWOOD
NEWBRIDGE RD
Copythorne CE Inf Sch
Tatchbury
Tatchbury Mount
POUND LA
WINSOR RD
VICARAGE LA
Copythorne
James's Farm
TATCHBURY LA
POLLARDS MOOR RD
Dell Farm
Compass Inn (PH)
Tatchbury Manor
Pollards Moor
Kent's Farm
Winsor
WINSOR LA
Copied Hall Farm

4 17 3 16 2 15 1 14

0 A 31 B 32 C

75
52

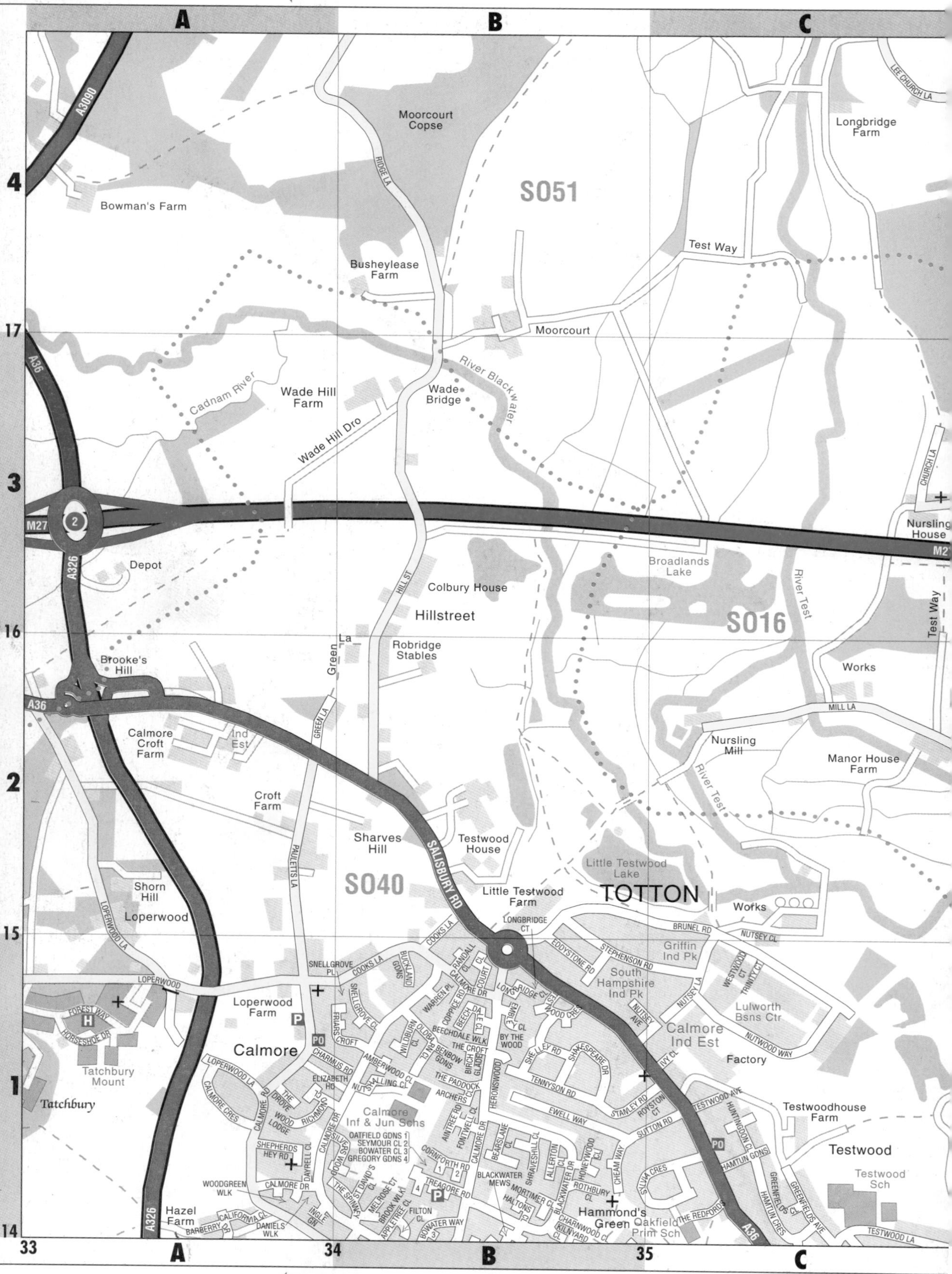
A
B
C
4
3
2
1
17
16
15
14
33
34
35
A3090
Moorcourt
Copse
SO51
Longbridge
Farm
LEE CHURCH LA
Bowman's Farm
RIDGE LA
Busheylease
Farm
Test Way
Moorcourt
A36
Cadnam River
Wade Hill
Farm
Wade
Bridge
River Blackwater
Wade Hill Dro
M27
2
CHURCH LA
Nursling
House
M27
A326
Depot
Broadlands
Lake
River Test
Colbury House
HILL ST
Hillstreet
SO16
Test Way
Green
La
Robridge
Stables
Brooke's
Hill
Works
A36
GREEN LA
MILL LA
Calmore
Croft
Farm
Ind
Est
Nursling
Mill
Manor House
Farm
River Test
Croft
Farm
Sharves
Hill
SALISBURY RD
Testwood
House
Little Testwood
Lake
PAULETTS LA
Shorn
Hill
SO40
Little Testwood
Farm
TOTTON
Works
LOPERWOOD LA
Loperwood
LONGBRIDGE
CT
BRUNEL RD
NUTSEY CL
COOKS LA
Griffin
Ind Pk
SNELLGROVE
PL
COOKS LA
BUCKLAND
GDNS
RANDALL
CL
COURT
CL
EDDYSTONE RD
STEPHENSON RD
WESTWOOD
CT
TRINITY CT
South
Hampshire
Ind Pk
LOPERWOOD
Loperwood
Farm
SNELLGROVE CL
WARREN PL
CALMORE DR
LONG
RIDGE CL
WOOD CRES
NUTSEY
AVE
NUTSEY LA
Lulworth
Bsns Ctr
FOREST WAY
H
HORSESHOE DR
P
PO
FRIARS CROFT
COPPICE RD
BEECH DA
LEE CL
EMBLEY CL
BY THE
WOOD
Calmore
Ind Est
NUTWOOD WAY
Calmore
WILDBURN
OLDBURN CL
BEECHDALE WLK
THE CROFT
Tatchbury
Mount
LOPERWOOD LA
CHARMUS RD
AMBERWOOD CL
BENBOW
GDNS
BIRCH
GLADE
SHELLEY RD
SHAKESPEARE DR
IVY CL
Factory
Tatchbury
CALMORE CRES
CALMORE RD
THE
DROVE
ELIZABETH
HO
NUTSHALLING CL
THE PADDOCK
ARCHERS
HERONSWOOD
TENNYSON RD
RICHMOND
WOOD
LODGE
Calmore
Inf & Jun Schs
AINTREE RD
FONTWELL CL
CALMORE DR
EWELL WAY
STANLEY RD
ROYSTON
CT
TESTWOOD AVE
HUNTINGDON CL
Testwoodhouse
Farm
OATFIELD GDNS 1
SEYMOUR CL 2
BOWATER CL 3
GREGORY GDNS 4
SUTTON RD
SHEPHERDS
HEY RD
DAYRELL CL
CALMORE DR
SILVER
CORNFORTH RD
BEARSLANE
SHRAVESHILL CL
ALLERTON
HONEYWOOD
CHEAM WAY
SYLVIA CRES
PO
HAMTUN GDNS
Testwood
WOODGREEN
WLK
CALMORE DR
THE SPINNEY
ST DAVID'S
MELROSE CT
BROOK WLK
TREAGORE RD
P
BLACKWATER
MEWS
MORTIMER CL
BLACKWATER DR
ROTHBURY
CL
GREENFIELDS CL
HAMTUN CRES
GREENFIELDS AVE
Testwood
Sch
A326
Hazel
Farm
CALIFORNIA CL
BARBERRY DR
DANIELS
WLK
INGLE
GN
APPLETREE CL
FILTON
CL
BOWATER WAY
HALTONS
CHARNWOOD CL
KILNYARD CL
Hammond's
Green
Oakfield
Prim Sch
THE REDFORDS
A36
TESTWOOD LA

75
100

A B C

Nightingale Wood
Old Canal
Lee Manor Farm
Lee
Malthouse Cotts
Coldharbour La
Lee La
Grove Farm
SO51
A3057
M271
CH
Fir Copse
Upton Cres
Upper Toothill Rd
Greenhill La
Rownhams Pk
Service Area
M27
Service Area
Parker's Farm
Rownhams
Rownhams La
Routs Way
Acorn Dr
Adcock Ct
Victory Way 1
Loreille Gdns 2
St Johns Cl 3
Armada Cl
Colts Rd
Hedgerow Cl
Prince Rd
Hann Rd
Balmoral Way
Hurricane Dr
Normandy Cl
St Johns Glebe
The Mews
1 Lucas Cl
2 Logan Cl
3 Blackbushe Cl
Upton
Upton La
Lymer La
Lymer Villas
Casa Aquila Farm
Atherley Sch
Horns Hill
Nutfield Rd
Beacon Cl
Barker Mill Cl
Rownhams House
Horns Dro
Rownhams Way
Rownhams Cl
Greenwood Ave
Paulet Lacave Ave
Horns Hill Cl
Betteridge Dr
Broadbent Cl
Phillips Cl
Rufus Cl
Laverstoke Cl
Rownhams CE Prim Sch
Michelmersh Cl
Westways Cl
Church Farm
Church La
Standen Rd
Lukin Dr
Testlands Ave
Blake Cl
Crawford Cl
Broadmead Rd
Winfrith Way
Home Field Dr
Mill Cl
Shepherds Way
Winstanley Rd
Nursling St
Broadmead Flats
Joe Bigwood Cl
Knowles Cl
Toogoods Way
Jeffries Cl
Horsebridge Way
Nutshalling Ave
Bossington Cl
Hazeldown Rd
Trowbridge Cl
Bakers Dro
Bridgers Cl
Lakeside Ave
Rosebank Cl
Fernyhurst Ave
Fyeford Cl
Bedwell Cl
Fairlawn Cl
Mosseleigh Ave
Evox Cl
Colt Cl
Welch Way
Redward Rd
Emmett Rd
Rownhams Rd N
Lennox Cl
Forbes Cl
Fraser Cl
Matheson Rd
Buchanan Rd
Chisholm Cl
Armstrong Ct
Sutherland Rd
Erskine Ct
Cameron Ct
Dunbar Cl
Menzies Ct
Lord's Hill Way
Cranwell Ct
Hornchurch Rd
Fairway Gdns
Rosebank Lodge
st Way
Four Horseshoes (PH)
Nursling CE Prim Sch
Recn Gd
Wilks Cl
Blann Cl
Tuffin Cl
Crammer Dr
Nursling
Watley Cl
Chambers Cl
SO16
Station Rd
Dairy La
Home Covert
Cromarty Rd
Fastnet Cl
Rockall Cl
Lundy Cl
Orkney Cl
Viking Cl
Malin Cl
Fairisle Rd
Oaklands Com Sch
Lord's Hill
Cardington Ct
Schs
Liby
Lord's Hill Centre W
Lord's Hill Centre E
Odiham Cl
The Cedar Specl Sch
Romsey Rd
Canberra Rd
Nursling Ind Est
Mauretania Rd
Majestic Rd
Oriana Way
Adanac Farm
Redbridge La
SOUTHAMPTON
Lordshill Rdbt
Lord's Hill Way
Andromeda Rd
Pegasus Cl
Saturn Cl
Neptune Ct
Manston Ct
Eastchurch Cl
Gemini Cl
Mercury Cl
Orion Cl
Jupiter Cl
Upper Brownhill Rd
Mill La
Weston La
Yewtree Farm
Hillyfields
Yewtree La
Danebury Way
Jerrett's La
Triangle Gdns
Tennis Ctr
Frogmore La
Portelet Ho
Boniface Cres
Sarnia Ct
Alderney Cl
Guernsey Cl
St Martin's Cl
Rozel Ct
Jersey Cl
St Brelade Pl
St Helier Pl
Brownhill Ct
Corbiere Cl
Nutfield Ct
Barons Mead
Kennedy Rd
Dolton Rd
Rosewall Rd
Lancaster Rd
Link Rd
Ashmead Rd
Rylandes Ct
Brightside Rd
Test Way
Andes Rd
Franconia Dr
River Test
Hotel
Bargain Farm
Brownhill Way
Lower Brownhill Rd
Holkham Cl
Millbrook Com Sch
LC
Flamborough Cl
Seafield Rd
Atherfield Rd
Tetney Cl
Selsey Cl
Green La
Watts Cl
Kern Cl
Rownhams Ct
Kingston Ct
Rownhams Rd
Maybush
Ordnance Survey Office
Coxford Rd
Thorndike Rd
New Cotts
Colburn Cl
Hayburn Rd
Blakeney Rd
Oldbury Ct
Colne Ave
Anderby Rd
Brean Cl
Windbury Rd
Colne Ct
Lulworth Gn
Lulworth Cl
Cowley Cl
Test Valley Bsns Ctr
Ruddy Mead
Holy Family RC Prim Sch
Mansel Rd W
Maplin Rd
Blyth Cl
Goodwin Cl
Canvey Ct
Buttermere Cl
Thirlmere Rd
Mansel Inf & Jun Schs
Maybush Rd
Grasmere Ct
Ennerdale Rd
Tindale Rd
Crabwood Ct
Glencoyne Gdns
Winston Cl
Hardwicke Cl
A3057
River Test
Redbridge La
Porlock Rd
Canford Cl
Culver Cl
Windermere Ave
Mansel Ct
Crabwood Rd
Timsbury Dr
Lockerley Cres
Braishfield Cl
Test La
Yeoman Pk
SO40
Thorness Cl
Seacombe Gn
Vellan Ct
Durlston Rd
Cromer Rd
Recn Gd
Ullswater Rd
Crabtree
Wimpson Gdns
Irving Rd
Hawswater Cl
Lower Test Nature Reserve
Playing Field
Kendal Ave
Sedberg Ho
Pevensey Cl
Bideford Cl
Evenlode Rd
Derwent Rd
Orwell Cl
Mansel Rd E
Newlands Inf & Jun Schs
Borrowdale Rd
Wimpson La
Redbridge Hill
Walnut Cl
Plaitford Wlk 1
Wimborne Ho 2
Blandford Ho 3
Barters Cl
Walnut Gr
Paignton Rd
Harlyn Rd
Western Com
Perran Rd
Ingleton Rd
Sedbergh Rd
Copeland Rd
Windrush Rd
Teme Cres
Ribble Ct
Oakley Rd
Ballard Cl
Studland Rd
Kendal Ct
Studland Cl
Waveney Gn
Gover Rd
Stirling Cl
M271

A 37 B 38 C

4 17 3 16 2 15 1 14

77
54

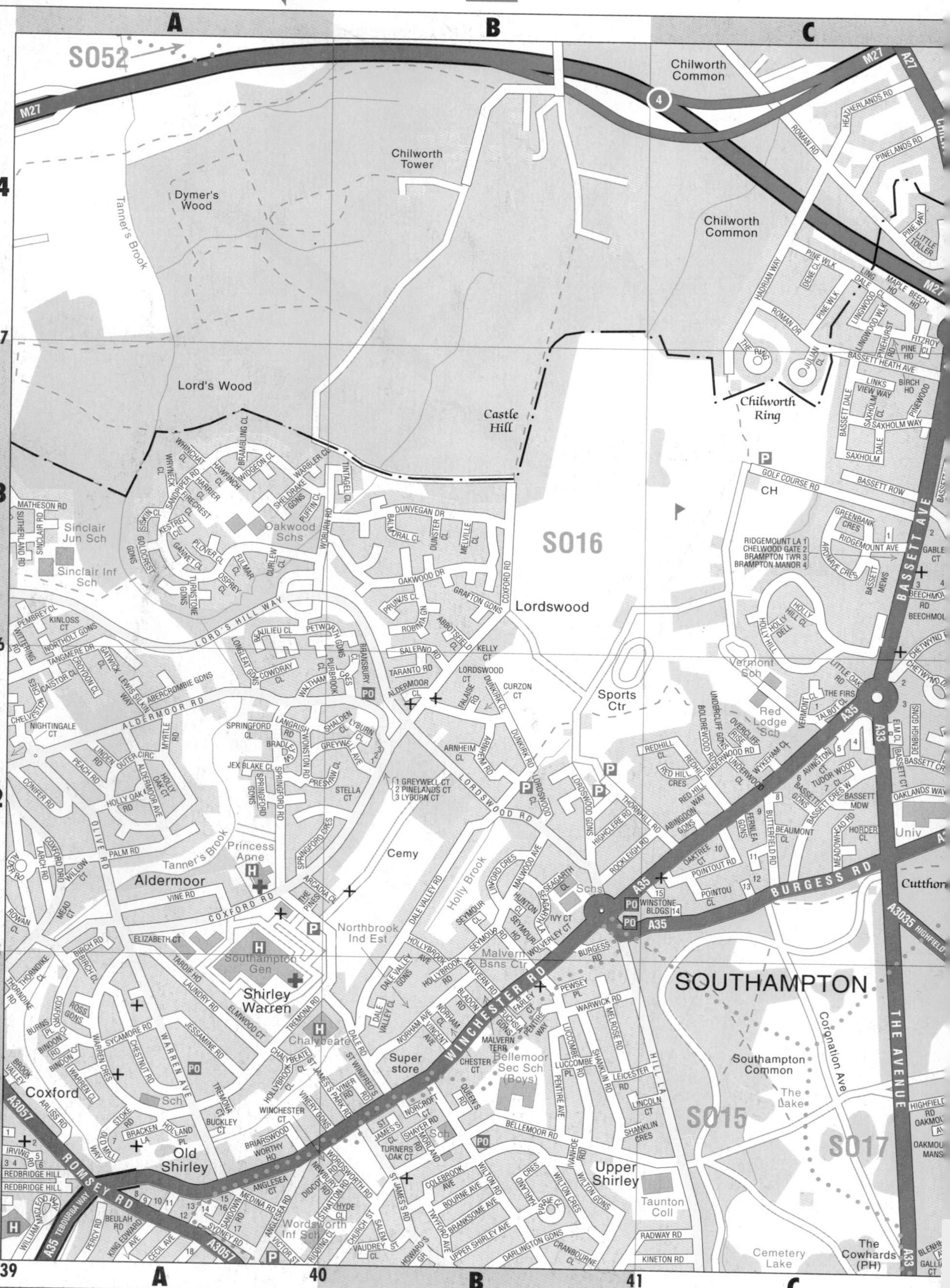

A B C

SO52
M27
Chilworth Common
Chilworth Tower
Dymer's Wood
Tanner's Brook
Chilworth Common
Lord's Wood
Castle Hill
Chilworth Ring
Sinclair Jun Sch
Sinclair Inf Sch
Oakwood Schs
SO16
Lordswood
Sports Ctr
Vermont Sch
Red Lodge Sch
Princess Anne
Aldermoor
Cemy
Northbrook Ind Est
Southampton Gen
Shirley Warren
Chalybeate
Malvern Bsns Ctr
SOUTHAMPTON
Southampton Common
Super store
Bellemoor Sec Sch (Boys)
Coxford
Old Shirley
Upper Shirley
Taunton Coll
SO15
SO17
The Lake
Cemetery Lake
The Cowhards (PH)
Wordsworth Inf Sch
WINCHESTER RD
ROMSEY RD
BURGESS RD
BASSETT AVE
THE AVENUE
LORD'S HILL WAY
ALDERMOOR RD
COXFORD RD
LORDSWOOD RD

39 A 40 B 41 C

A1
1 BRAISHFIELD CL
2 MAYBUSH CT
3 UPTON HO
4 STURMINSTER HO
5 BROUGHTON CL
6 CHARMOUTH TERR
7 CHALFONT CT
8 ROMSEY LODGE
9 THE MOUNT
10 THE GRANGE
11 GRANGE RD
12 LAWSON CT
13 HUNTER CT
14 YARMOUTH GDNS
15 RICHARDS CT
16 KINGSMEAD CT
17 SHINWELL CT
18 CLARENDON RD

77
102

C2
1 VECTIS CT
2 REDCOURT
3 FAIRLEA GRANGE
4 TOWER GDNS
5 THE MOUNT
6 CANADA PL
7 BASSETT WOOD MEWS
8 SHAWFORD CL
9 MARSHALL PL
10 WELLMAN CT
11 GLENCARROW WAY
12 CHESTNUT LODGE
13 SHERWOOD CL
14 BURGESS GDNS
15 ASHWOOD GDNS

55
80

A1
1 KINGFISHER CT
2 OMDURMAN CT
3 HIGHFIELD LODGE
4 BURLEY CT
5 CRANFORD HO
6 OAKDENE
7 ST ANNS CT
8 CHESTNUT CT
9 WESTBOURNE MANS
10 LEIGH MANS
11 LATIMER CT
12 COTSWOLD CT
13 PINEHURST
14 BROOKVALE CT
15 ABBOTTS CT
16 BENTLEY CT
17 WICKHAM HO
18 AUTUMN PL
19 MELBURY CT
20 SOVEREIGN CT
21 SANDRINGHAM CT
22 BERMUDA CT
23 HAMILTON CT
24 REGENT CT
25 WINN MANS
26 CHELTENHAM CT
27 TENNYSON CT
28 WESTWOOD MANS
29 ELM CT
30 GUARDIAN CT
31 BARRINGTON CT
32 SOMBORNE CT
33 CARRINGTON HO
34 SOBERTON HO
35 ADDIS SQ
36 PORTSWOOD CTR
37 TENNYSON CT
38 WICKHAM HO
39 WESTRIDGE CT

103

B1
1 WESTMARCH CT
2 THE NEWLANDS
3 KENSINGTON CT
4 MILL CT
5 GROSVENOR LODGE
6 RICHMOND HALL
7 GROSVENOR CT
8 GROSVENOR MEWS
9 SHAMROCK VILLAS

80

C1
1 JULIAN CT
2 CAMELLIA CT
3 CASTLE HTS
4 CASTLE CT
5 THE BROADWAY
6 PARKLANDS

79
56

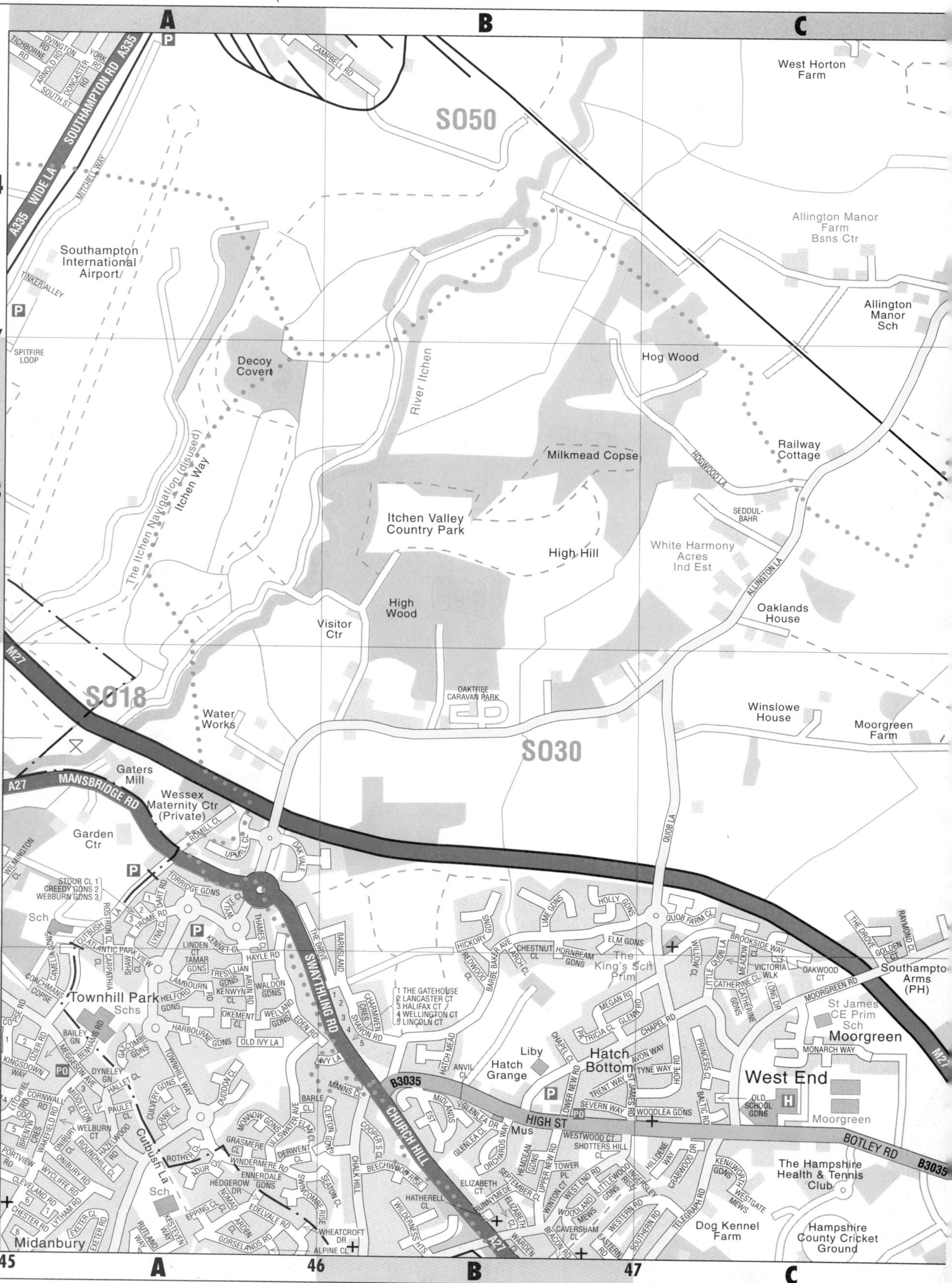
A
B
C
SO50
SO18
SO30
West Horton Farm
Allington Manor Farm Bsns Ctr
Allington Manor Sch
Southampton International Airport
SOUTHAMPTON RD
A335
WIDE LA
MITCHELL WAY
TINKER ALLEY
SPITFIRE LOOP
OVINGTON RD
TICHBORNE RD
ARNOLD RD
DONCASTER RD
YORK RD
SOUTH ST
CAMPBELL RD
Decoy Covert
River Itchen
Hog Wood
Railway Cottage
Milkmead Copse
HOGWOOD LA
SEDDUL-BAHR
The Itchen Navigation (disused)
Itchen Way
Itchen Valley Country Park
High Hill
White Harmony Acres Ind Est
ALLINGTON LA
Oaklands House
High Wood
Visitor Ctr
OAKTREE CARAVAN PARK
Water Works
Winslowe House
Moorgreen Farm
M27
A27
MANSBRIDGE RD
Gaters Mill
Wessex Maternity Ctr (Private)
Garden Ctr
QUOB LA
ROMILL CL
UPMILL CL
OAK VALE
WILMINGTON CL
STOUR CL 1
CREEDY GDNS 2
WEBBURN GDNS 3
TORRIDGE GDNS
Sch
Townhill Park
Schs
SWAYTHLING RD
THE DRIVE
BARNSLAND
HICKORY GDNS
REDWOOD CL
BARBE BAKER AVE
LARCH CL
CHESTNUT CL
HORNBEAM GDNS
LIME GDNS
HOLLY GDNS
ELM GDNS
QUOB FARM CL
The King's Sch Prim
WILLOW CL
LITTLE QUOB LA
MEADOW CL
BROOKSIDE WAY
VICTORIA WLK
CATHERINE CL
CATHERINE GDNS
LONG DR
OAKWOOD CT
THE DROVE
GOLDEN CT
RAYMOND CL
Southampton Arms (PH)
MOORGREEN RD
St James CE Prim Sch
Moorgreen
MONARCH WAY
1 THE GATEHOUSE
2 LANCASTER CT
3 HALIFAX CT
4 WELLINGTON CT
5 LINCOLN CT
SHARON RD
CHARMWEN CRES
EDEN RD
HATCH MEAD
Liby
Hatch Grange
Hatch Bottom
MEGAN RD
PATRICIA CL
GLENN RD
CHAPEL RD
AVON WAY
TYNE WAY
TRENT WAY
SEVERN WAY
HOPE RD
PRINCESS CL
BALTIC RD
West End
OLD SCHOOL GDNS
B3035
CHURCH HILL
HIGH ST
BOTLEY RD
Mus
WOODLEA GDNS
WESTWOOD CT
SHOTTERS HILL CL
HILLDENE WAY
CRABWOOD DR
KENILWORTH GDNS
WESTGATE MEWS
The Hampshire Health & Tennis Club
Hampshire County Cricket Ground
Dog Kennel Farm
TELEGRAPH RD
SOUTHERN RD
WESTERN RD
EASTERN RD
CAVERSHAM CL
BEACON RD
WARDEN CL
RUNNYMEDE
ELIZABETH CT
ELIZABETH CL
SEPTEMBER CL
HEMDEAN GDNS
UPPER NEW RD
TOWER PL
WINTON CT
WEST END RD
WOODLAND MEWS
LITTLEWOOD GDNS
INGERSLEY RISE
ORCHARDS WAY
GLENLEA DR
GLENLEA CL
MIDLANDS EST
ANVIL CL
LOWER NEW RD
ST JAMES RD
CHAPEL CL
HATHERELL CL
WILDERNESS HTS
BEECHWOOD RISE
COOPER'S CL
CHALK HILL
CLIFTON GDNS
SEATON CL
SWINCOMBE RISE
WHEATCROFT DR
ALPINE CL
BARLE CL
MANNS CL
IVY LA
OLD IVY LA
DERWENT CL
ULLSWATER AVE
ELAN CL
MONMOW GDNS
GRASMERE CL
WINDERMERE RD
ENNERDALE GDNS
HEDGEROW DR
EDELVALE RD
GORSELANDS RD
ARDEN CL
EPPING CL
NOMAD CL
ROTHER CL
ADUR CL
KESTEVEN WAY
RUTLAND WAY
Cutbush La
Midanbury
EXETER CL
EXETER RD
CHESTER RD
LYTHAM RD
CLEVELAND RD
PORTVIEW RD
WYCLIFFE RD
ONIBURY RD
ONIBURY CL
ROUNDHILL CL
HAZELWOOD RD
WELBURN CT
PAULET CL
HALLET CL
DYNELEY GN
MIDDLETON CL
MEGGESON AVE
BAILEY GN
BENHAMS RD
OZIER RD
KINGSDOWN WAY
WAKEFIELD RD
BRENTWOOD CRES
LITCHFIELD RD
CORNWALL RD
GALCOMBE GDNS
TOWNHILL WAY
CULVERY GDNS
CONE CL
DUDDON CL
HARBOURNE GDNS
OKEMENT CL
WELLAND GDNS
WALDON GDNS
ARUN RD
KENWYN CL
TRESILLIAN GDNS
LAMBOURN RD
HELFORD GDNS
HAYLE RD
TAMAR GDNS
LINDEN CT
KENNET CL
THAMES CL
WYLYE CL
FROME RD
LYNN CL
DART RD
ROSTRON CL
CUTBUSH LA
ATLANTIC PARK VIEW
CARPATHIA CL
SHAW CL
CAMELIA GDNS
COACHMANS COPSE
45
46
47
4
17
3
16
2
15
1
14

79
104

A1
1 LONGMEAD RD
2 ROWLANDS WLK
3 DEWSBURY CT
4 CORNWALL CL
5 GRASDEAN CL
6 WAKEFIELD CT
7 CLEVELAND CT
8 BENHAMS FARM CL

57
82

A
B
C
Quobleigh Pond
Lake Farm
ALLINGTON LA
Firtree Farm
Allington Manor Farm
FIRTREE LA
Foxholes Farm
Hearts Copse
Chalcroft Farm
Distribution Park
Little Moorgreen Farm
SO30
SO50
SO32
Berrywood Farm
Berrywood Bsns Village
MOORGREEN RD
Moorlands Farm
Dowd's Farm
TOLLBAR WAY
WELLINGTON PK
Nelson Ind Pk
Solent Ind Est
Herald Ind. Est
Hedge End Bsns Ctr
Waterloo Ind Est
BOTLEY RD
B3035
B3342
M27
B3354
BOTLEY RD
PAVILION CL
Whitetree Farm
Lapstone Farm
The Lapstone (PH)
KNOWLE LA
The Cockpit Farm
Horton Heath
Durley Copse
Greenwood Farm
Greenwood Farm
Copperbeach Farm
GREENWOOD LA
DURLEY RD
The Old Rectory
Church Croft Farm
CHURCH LA
DURLEY BROOK ROAD
BEECH CNR
Little Snakemoor Farm
STAPLEFORD LA
SNAKEMOOR LA
Snakemoor Farm
Brigadier Gerard (PH)
BURNETTS LA
BLIND LA
DENHAM'S CNR
B3342
BUBB LA
Jacksons Farm
Croft House
The Firs
SHAMBLEHURST LA N
WINCHESTER RD
CHANCELLORS LA
Park Farm
Braxells Farm
Hotel
Long Common
Pear Tree (PH)
Boorley Green
Hedge End
REGENT HO
CRANLEIGH HO
ANSON RD
EXMOUTH GDNS
CHAPEL DRO
FIR-TREE CL
THE LILIES
WILSON CT
YORK CL
FONTWELL GDNS
EPSOM CL
ASCOT RD
NEWMARKET CL
RIPON CT
HUNTINGDON GDNS
AINTREE CL
PO
BURNETTS FIELDS
BURNETTS GDNS
ANGELICA GDNS
CENTAURY GDNS
WESTFIELD CL
DUMPERS DRO
ROSEBAY CL
VALERIAN CL
BRAMLEY GDNS
AVENS CL
EYEBRIGHT CL
CRISPIN CL
BRYONY GDNS
MEADOWSWEET WAY
CAMPION CL
THE DROVE
ST ANDREWS PK
CHERRY DRO
ARTHURS GDNS
ADAMS CL
TERRIER CL
PEPPERCORN WAY
NELSONS GDNS
WAINWRIGHT GDNS
MARLBOROUGH GDNS
FAIRLIE CL
CHELTENHAM GDNS
BRITANNIA GDNS
GREYHOUND CL
STEPHENSON WAY
HACKWORTH GDNS
COLLETT CL
HEDLEY GDNS
MARSH GDNS
BLUESTAR GDNS
GRESLEY GDNS
STANIER WAY
CHURCHWARD GDNS
MARTLEY GDNS
MAUNSELL WAY
STROUDLEY WAY
GARRATT CL
MALLARD GDNS
OLD SHAMBLEHURST LA
ST LAWRENCE CL
MALVERN GDNS
ARDINGLY CRES
FELFORD GDNS
MALLET CL
REPTON GDNS
WATKIN RD
REPTON GDNS
LEATHERHEAD GDNS
BEATTIE RISE
ELLIOT RISE
STOWE CL
BILLINGTON GDNS
BRUNEL CL
STIRLING CRES
GILES CL
CHARTERHOUSE WAY
RADLEY CL
LOMAX CL
DRUMMOND RD
HAILEYBURY GDNS
ST LUKES CL
SHAMBLEHURST LA S
GRANGE PARK MOBILE HOMES
CUDWORTH MEAD
Berrywood Prim Sch
WALKER GDNS
CHICHESTER CL
LOCKE RD
NAVIGATORS WAY
HERALD RD
MANATON WAY
FLANDERS RD
PEAR TREE CL
MADDOXFORD LA
MADDOXFORD WAY
OATLANDS CL
OATLANDS RD
RAVENS WAY
FALCON WAY
KESTREL CL
CROFT
CROWS NEST LA
WINCHESTER ST
WOODHOUSE LA
4
17
3
16
2
15
1
14
49
50
105
82

81
58

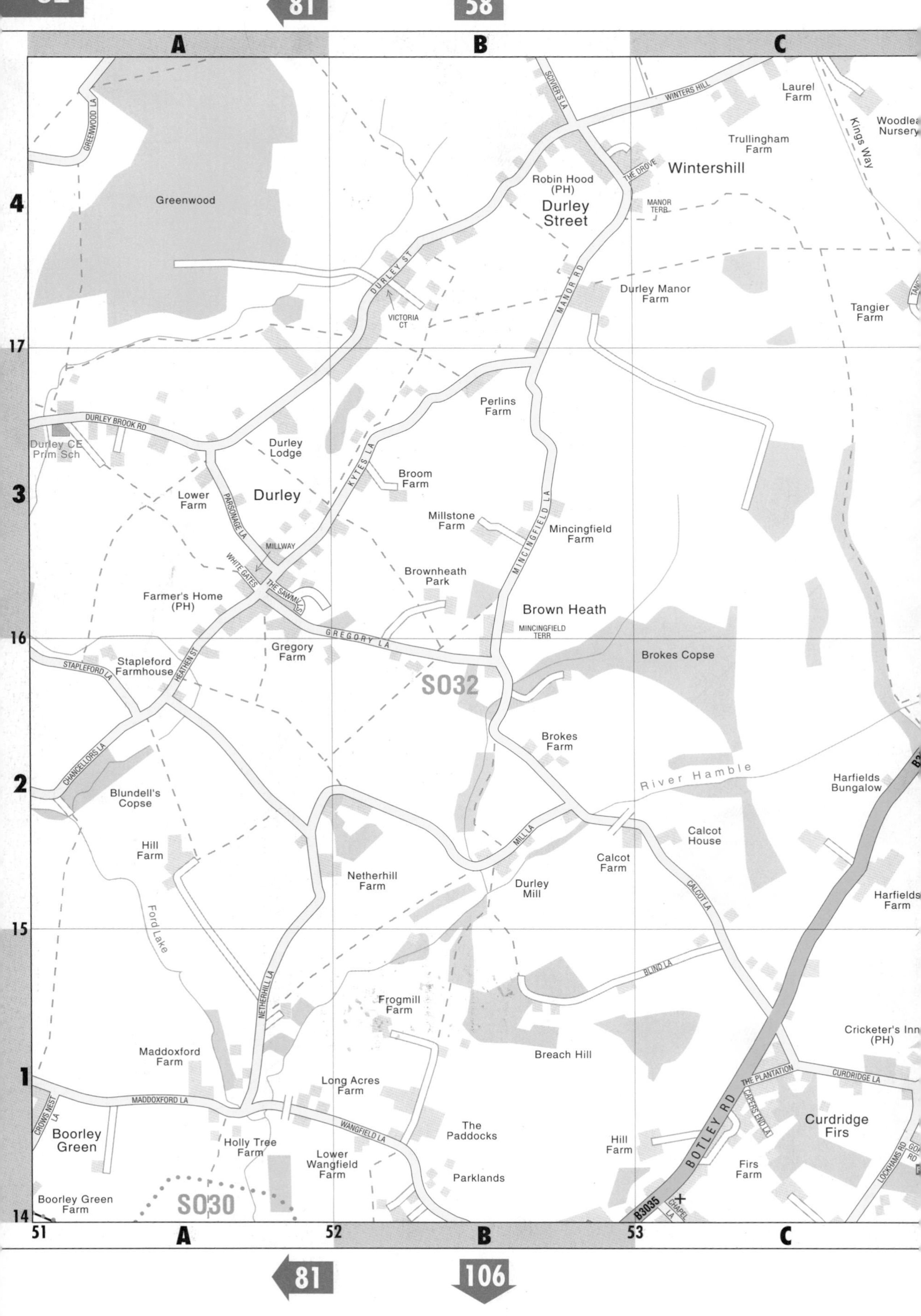
A
B
C
4
3
2
1
17
16
15
14
51
52
53
Greenwood
GREENWOOD LA
SCIVIER'S LA
WINTERS HILL
Laurel Farm
Woodlea Nursery
Kings Way
Trullingham Farm
Wintershill
THE DROVE
Robin Hood (PH)
Durley Street
MANOR TERR
DURLEY ST
VICTORIA CT
MANOR RD
Durley Manor Farm
Tangier Farm
DURLEY BROOK RD
Durley CE Prim Sch
Perlins Farm
Durley Lodge
Broom Farm
KYTES LA
Lower Farm
Durley
PARSONAGE LA
Millstone Farm
Mincingfield Farm
MINCINGFIELD LA
MILLWAY
WHITE GATES
THE SAWMILLS
Brownheath Park
Farmer's Home (PH)
Brown Heath
MINCINGFIELD TERR
GREGORY LA
Gregory Farm
Stapleford Farmhouse
STAPLEFORD LA
HEATHEN ST
Brokes Copse
SO32
Brokes Farm
CHANCELLORS LA
River Hamble
Harfields Bungalow
Blundell's Copse
Hill Farm
MILL LA
Calcot House
Calcot Farm
Netherhill Farm
Durley Mill
CALCOT LA
Harfields Farm
Ford Lake
BLIND LA
NETHERHILL LA
Frogmill Farm
Cricketer's Inn (PH)
Maddoxford Farm
Breach Hill
THE PLANTATION
CURDRIDGE LA
Long Acres Farm
MADDOXFORD LA
CROWS NEST LA
CAPERS END LA
Curdridge Firs
Boorley Green
Holly Tree Farm
WANGFIELD LA
The Paddocks
Hill Farm
BOTLEY RD
Lower Wangfield Farm
Firs Farm
LOCKHAMS RD
Parklands
Boorley Green Farm
SO30
B3035
CHAPEL LA

81
106

59
84

A
B
C
Claylands Road Ind Est
Works
Newtown
PRIORY SCHOOL 1
PRIORY CL 2
ST SWITHUN CL 3
CUNNINGHAMS HO 4
CLAYLANDS CT 5
VICTORIA BLDGS 6
CHURCHILL AVE 7
THE HAWTHORNS 8
Abbey Mill Bsns Site
Bishop's Waltham Palace
(remains of)
Bishop's Waltham
B4
1 WAYNFLETE CL
2 DENEWULF CL
3 MIDDLEBROOK
4 DUKES CT
5 SOUTHBROOK MEWS
6 CROSS ST
7 ST GEORGE'S SQ
8 BASING MEWS
9 PENFORDS PADDOCK
WINCHESTER RD
B2177
B3035
LOWER LA
COPPICE HILL
BOTLEY RD
PALACE MEWS
LADYSMITH TERR
Liby
Ridgemede Jun Sch
Sch
Cemy
Hoe
HOE RD
SWANMORE RD
JERVIS COURT LA
Little Hoe Farm
SUETTS LA
The Moors
Kings Way
Thickets House
Chase Moor Farm
PARADISE LA
Freehills Farm
Brooklands Farm
River Hamble
Locks Farm
Ford
Forest Farm
Fountain Inn (PH)
Swanmore Bsns Pk
Lower Chase Farm
Sewage Works
SO32
Ludwells Farm
Swanmore Sec Sch
Church House Farm
LOWER CHASE RD
LUDWELL'S LA
Clewers Hill
CLEWERS HILL
CLEWERS LA
Pine Lodge
Treefield Farm
Clay Hill Farm
Glebe
Glebe Farm
NEW RD
BRICKYARD RD
FOREST RD
Fillditch Farm
Woodmans Farm
CURDRIDGE LA
Waltham Chase
BULL LA
Nation's Farm
Oak Avenue
Poplars Farm House
Spencer Place
SANDY LA
LITTLE BULL LA
St John The Baptist CE Prim Sch
Gamblins Farm
SOLOMONS LA
Curdridge Grange
Stares Farm
The Vintage Inn (PH)
BLACKHORSE LA
Lyons Copse
4
3
2
1
17
16
15
14
55
56

107
84

83
60

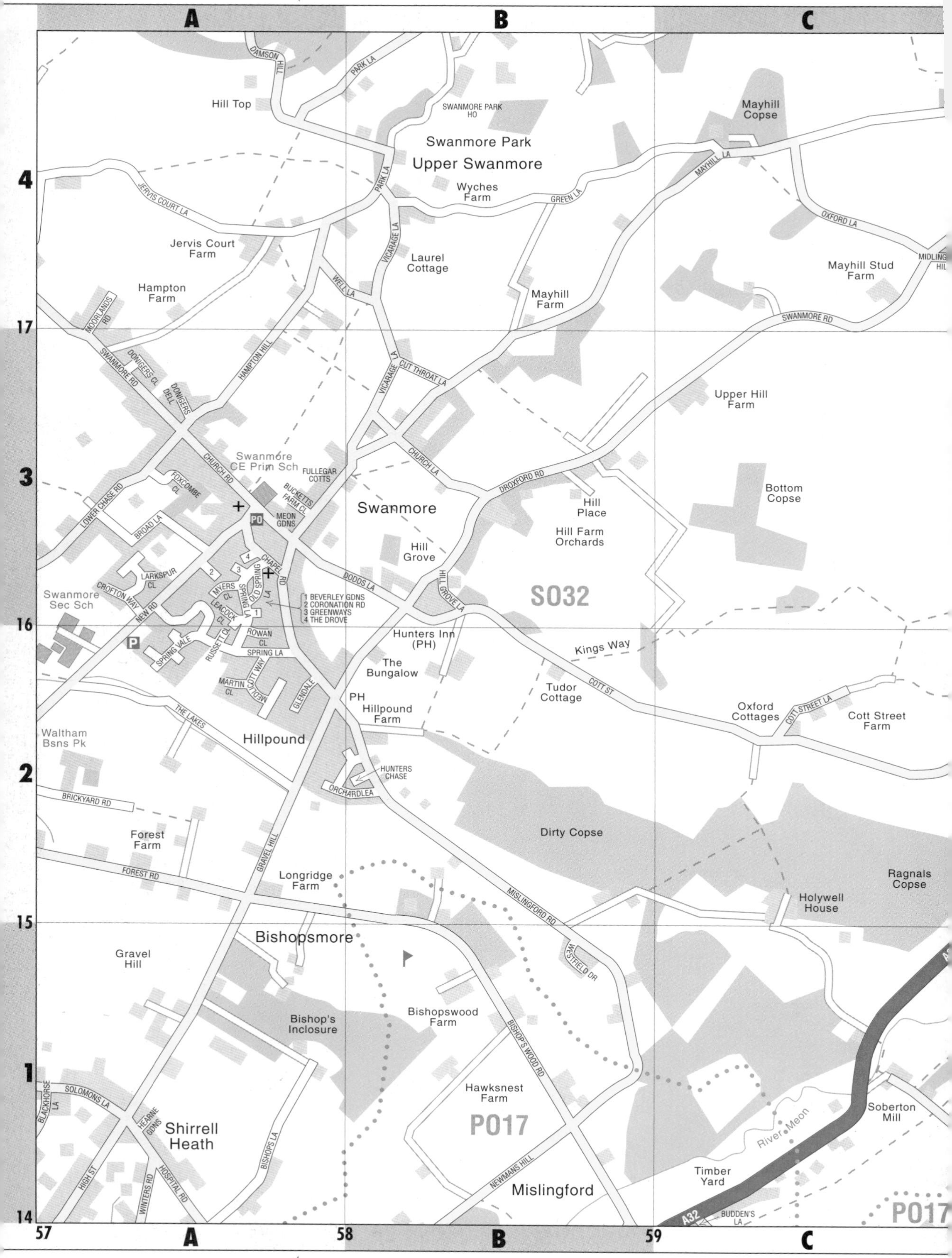

A B C

4
17
3
16
2
15
1
14

57 58 59

A B C

83
108

61
86

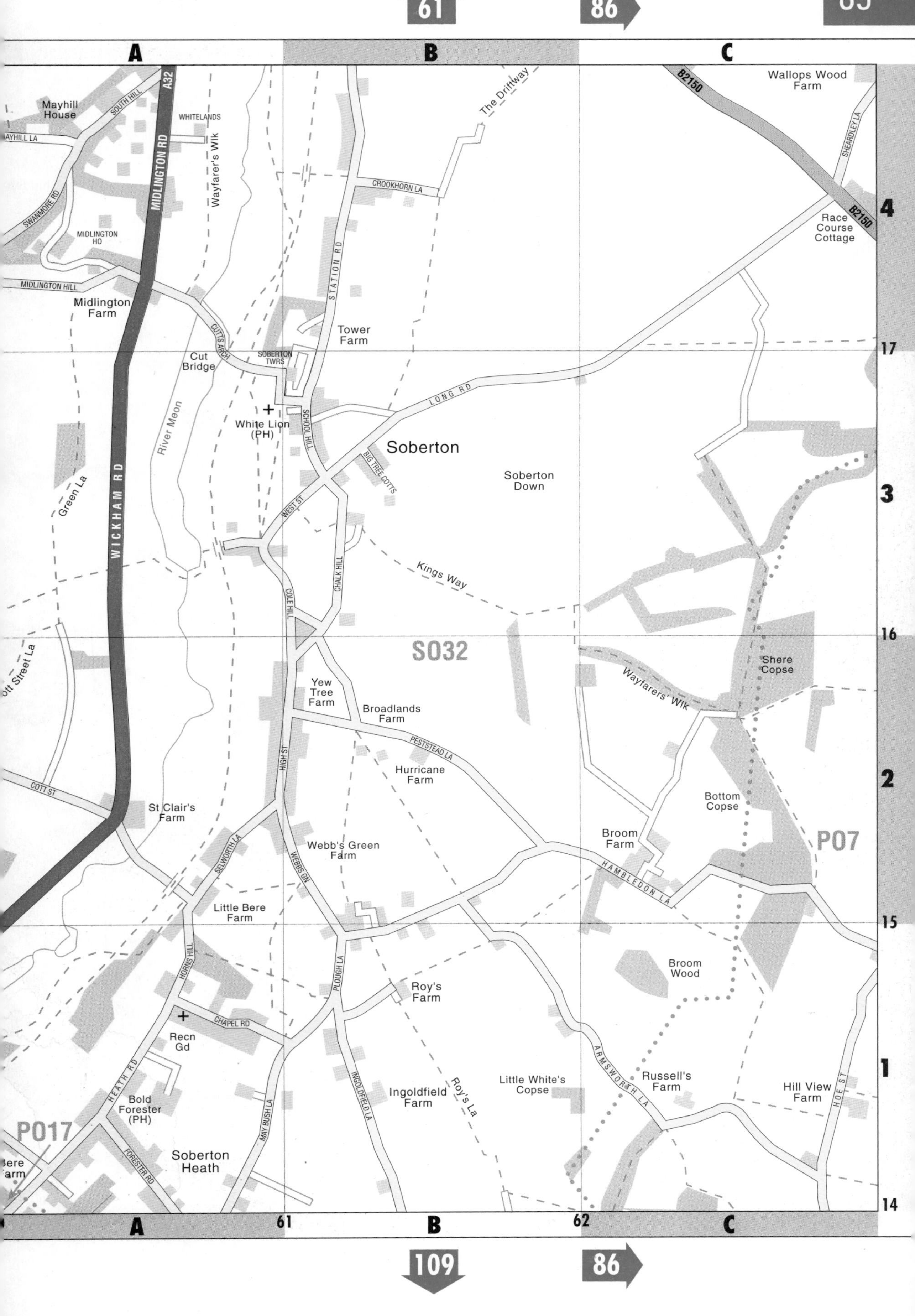
A
B
C
Mayhill House
SOUTH HILL
MAYHILL LA
A32
WHITELANDS
MIDLINGTON RD
Wayfarer's Wlk
SWANMORE RD
MIDLINGTON HO
MIDLINGTON HILL
Midlington Farm
The Driftway
CROOKHORN LA
STATION RD
Tower Farm
CUTTS ARCH
SOBERTON TWRS
Cut Bridge
White Lion (PH)
SCHOOL HILL
LONG RD
Soberton
BIG TREE COTTS
Soberton Down
River Meon
WICKHAM RD
Green La
WEST ST
Kings Way
CHALK HILL
COLE HILL
SO32
Yew Tree Farm
Broadlands Farm
PESTSTEAD LA
Hurricane Farm
HIGH ST
Cott Street La
COTT ST
St Clair's Farm
SELWORTH LA
Webb's Green Farm
WEBBS GN
Little Bere Farm
HORNS HILL
PLOUGH LA
Roy's Farm
CHAPEL RD
Recn Gd
HEATH RD
Bold Forester (PH)
P017
Bere Farm
FORESTER RD
Soberton Heath
MAY BUSH LA
INGOLDFIELD LA
Ingoldfield Farm
Roy's La
Little White's Copse
ARMSWORTH LA
Russell's Farm
Hill View Farm
HOE ST
Broom Wood
Broom Farm
HAMBLEDON LA
Bottom Copse
P07
Shere Copse
Wayfarers' Wlk
Wallops Wood Farm
B2150
SHEARDLEY LA
Race Course Cottage
4
17
3
16
2
15
1
14
61
62

109
86

85
62

A
B
C
4
3
2
1
17
16
15
14
63
64
65
SHEARDLEY LA
Wallops Wood Parlour
Stoke Wood
Stockram Copse
Big West End Farm
Chidden Farm
Chidden
WHITELEAF LA
SO32
B2150
Grenville Hall
Upper Grenville Copse
GREEN LA
Hook Cottage
Beckless Plantation
Lower Grenville Copse
Beckless Farm
Chidden Holt Farm
Brooks Copse
Chidden Holt
Park Wood
Three Corners
Home Down
BROOK LA
Windmill Down
Park Farm
PO7
EAST HOE RD
East Hoe Manor
Whitedale Farm
DOGKENNEL LA
Litheys Hanger
Whitedale House
Wayfarer's Walk
The Hangers
Hambledon Inf Sch
CHURCH LA
Fairfield House
GLIDDEN LA
LASHLEY MDW
STEWARTS GN
HIGH ST
EAST ST
VICARAGE LA
THE GARDENS
The Monarch's Way
Hoe Cross Farm
PH
PO
Hambledon House
HAMBLEDON LA
RUSHMERE GATE
WEST ST
COACHMANS HALT
SPELTHAM HILL
Little Hanger
HOE ST
Boarhuts Copse
Hambledon
Rushmere Stud Farm
OLD BARN CRES
Cams
Kings Way
CAMS HILL
Veniss Copse
Goldsmith's Plantation
Rushmere
MENSLANDS LA
Wayfarer's Walk
RUSHMERE LA
Rushmere Farm
PIT HILL LA
Bury Lodge
Glebeland Farm
Hole Farm
HOLE LA
HAMBLEDON RD

85
110

63
88

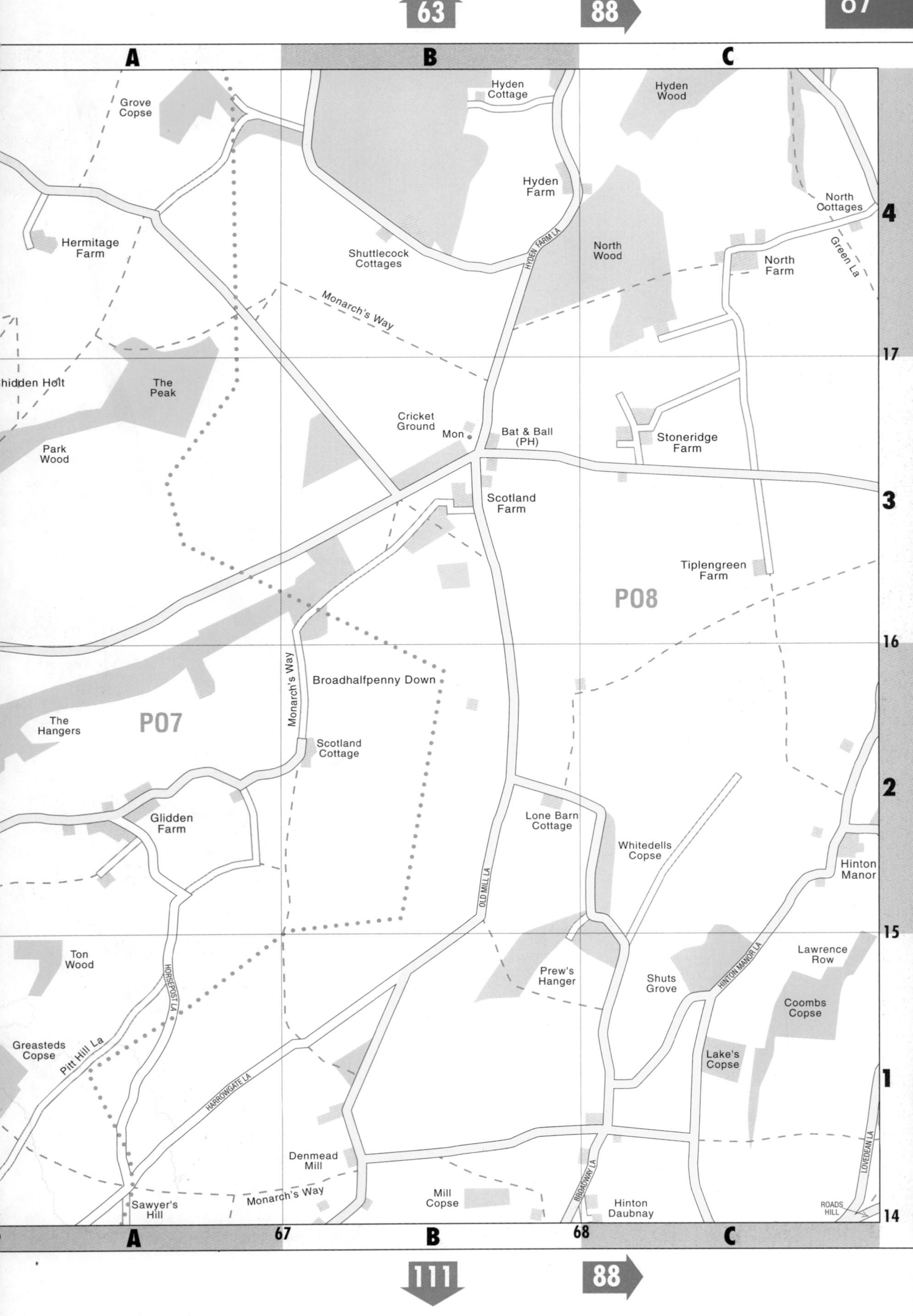
A
B
C
Grove Copse
Hyden Cottage
Hyden Wood
Hyden Farm
North Cottages
Hermitage Farm
Shuttlecock Cottages
North Wood
North Farm
Green La
HYDEN FARM LA
Monarch's Way
Shidden Holt
The Peak
Cricket Ground
Mon
Bat & Ball (PH)
Stoneridge Farm
Park Wood
Scotland Farm
Tiplengreen Farm
PO8
Monarch's Way
Broadhalfpenny Down
The Hangers
PO7
Scotland Cottage
Glidden Farm
Lone Barn Cottage
Whitedells Copse
Hinton Manor
OLD MILL LA
Ton Wood
Prew's Hanger
Shuts Grove
HINTON MANOR LA
Lawrence Row
Coombs Copse
HORSEPOST LA
Greasteds Copse
Pitt Hill La
Lake's Copse
HARROWGATE LA
Denmead Mill
Mill Copse
Monarch's Way
BROADWAY LA
Sawyer's Hill
Hinton Daubnay
LOVEDEAN LA
ROADS HILL
4
17
3
16
2
15
1
14
67
68

111
88

87
64

A
B
C
Lowton's Copse
Ditch Acre Copse
Smith's Copse
Chapel Farm
Thieves' Lane
Hog's Lodge Inn (PH)
New Buildings
PETERSFIELD RD
Clanfield Jun Sch
Manor Farm
Green La
Green Lane
PO8
CHALTON LA
Clanfield
Down Farm
Meadow Croft Farm
1 SLINDON CL
2 AMBERLEY RD
3 MIDDLETON RISE
4 HEYSHOTT GDNS
Clanfield Down
Butser Ancient Far
Chalton Windmill
Windmill Hill
Windmill Hill Farm
Windmill Down
LONDON RD
Charity Farm
Petersgate Inf Sch
Kennels
Snell's Corner
Horndean Down
Blendworth Down
White Dirt Farm
Munday's Row
New Barn Farm
Old Lane
Catherington Down
Nature Reserve
Catherington CE Inf Sch
St Catherines
Stubbins Down
Catherington
Kings Court Sch
Blendworth Lith
Crabden Row
A3
A3(M)
4
3
2
1
17
16
15
14
69
70
71

87
112

65
90

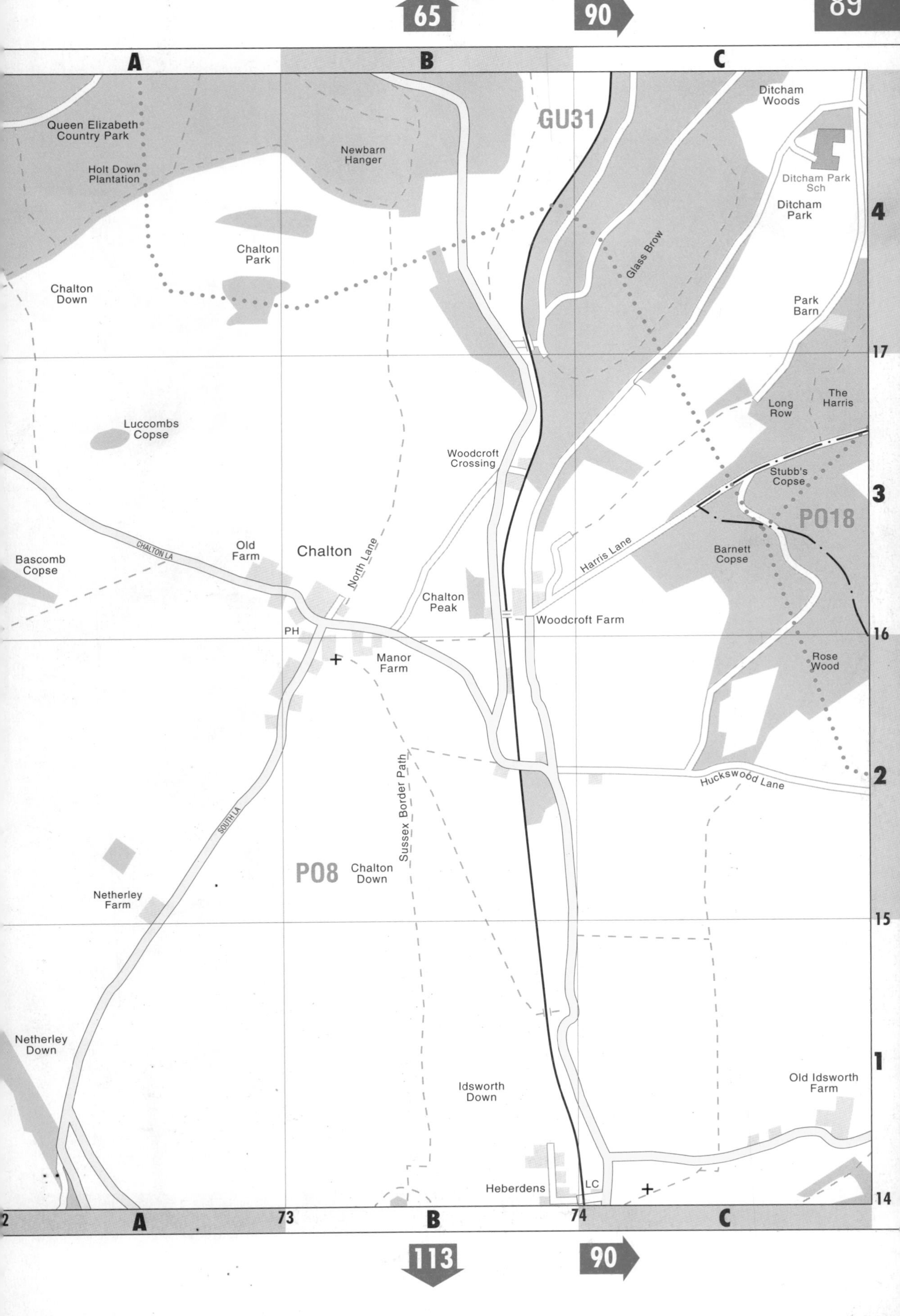
A
B
C
Queen Elizabeth Country Park
Holt Down Plantation
Newbarn Hanger
GU31
Ditcham Woods
Ditcham Park Sch
Ditcham Park
Chalton Park
Chalton Down
Glass Brow
Park Barn
Long Row
The Harris
Luccombs Copse
Woodcroft Crossing
Stubb's Copse
PO18
Bascomb Copse
CHALTON LA
Old Farm
Chalton
North Lane
Chalton Peak
Harris Lane
Barnett Copse
Woodcroft Farm
PH
Manor Farm
Rose Wood
Huckswood Lane
Sussex Border Path
SOUTH LA
PO8
Chalton Down
Netherley Farm
Netherley Down
Idsworth Down
Old Idsworth Farm
Heberdens
LC
4
17
3
16
2
15
1
14
2
73
74

113
90

89
66

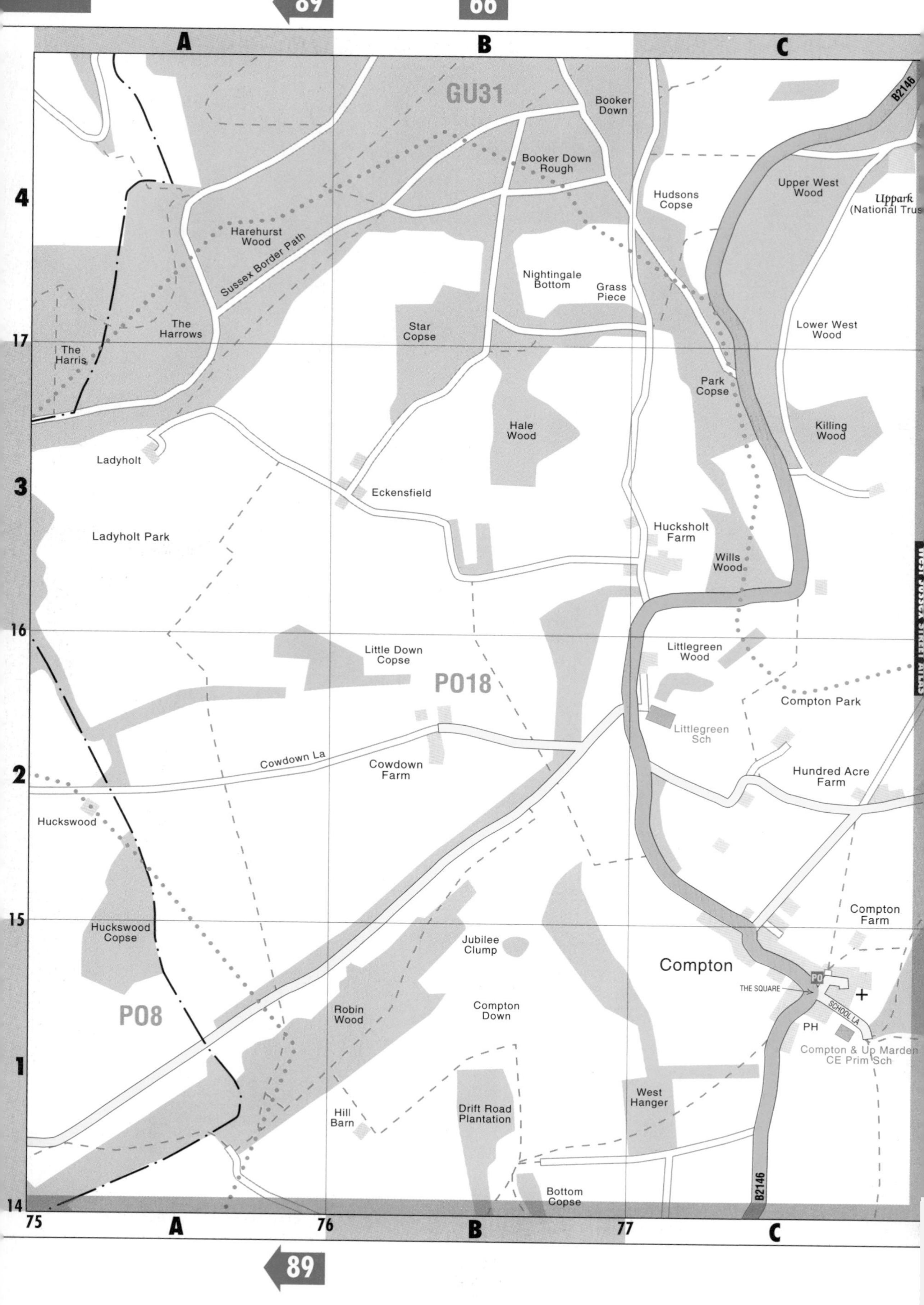
A
B
C
GU31
Booker Down
Booker Down Rough
B2146
Upper West Wood
Uppark (National Trus
Hudsons Copse
Harehurst Wood
Sussex Border Path
Nightingale Bottom
Grass Piece
The Harrows
The Harris
Star Copse
Lower West Wood
Park Copse
Hale Wood
Killing Wood
Ladyholt
Eckensfield
Ladyholt Park
Hucksholt Farm
Wills Wood
Little Down Copse
PO18
Littlegreen Wood
Compton Park
Littlegreen Sch
Cowdown La
Cowdown Farm
Hundred Acre Farm
Huckswood
Huckswood Copse
Compton Farm
Jubilee Clump
Compton
THE SQUARE
PO
SCHOOL LA
PH
PO8
Robin Wood
Compton Down
Compton & Up Marden CE Prim Sch
West Hanger
Hill Barn
Drift Road Plantation
Bottom Copse
B2146
4
17
3
16
2
15
1
14
75
76
77

89

67
92

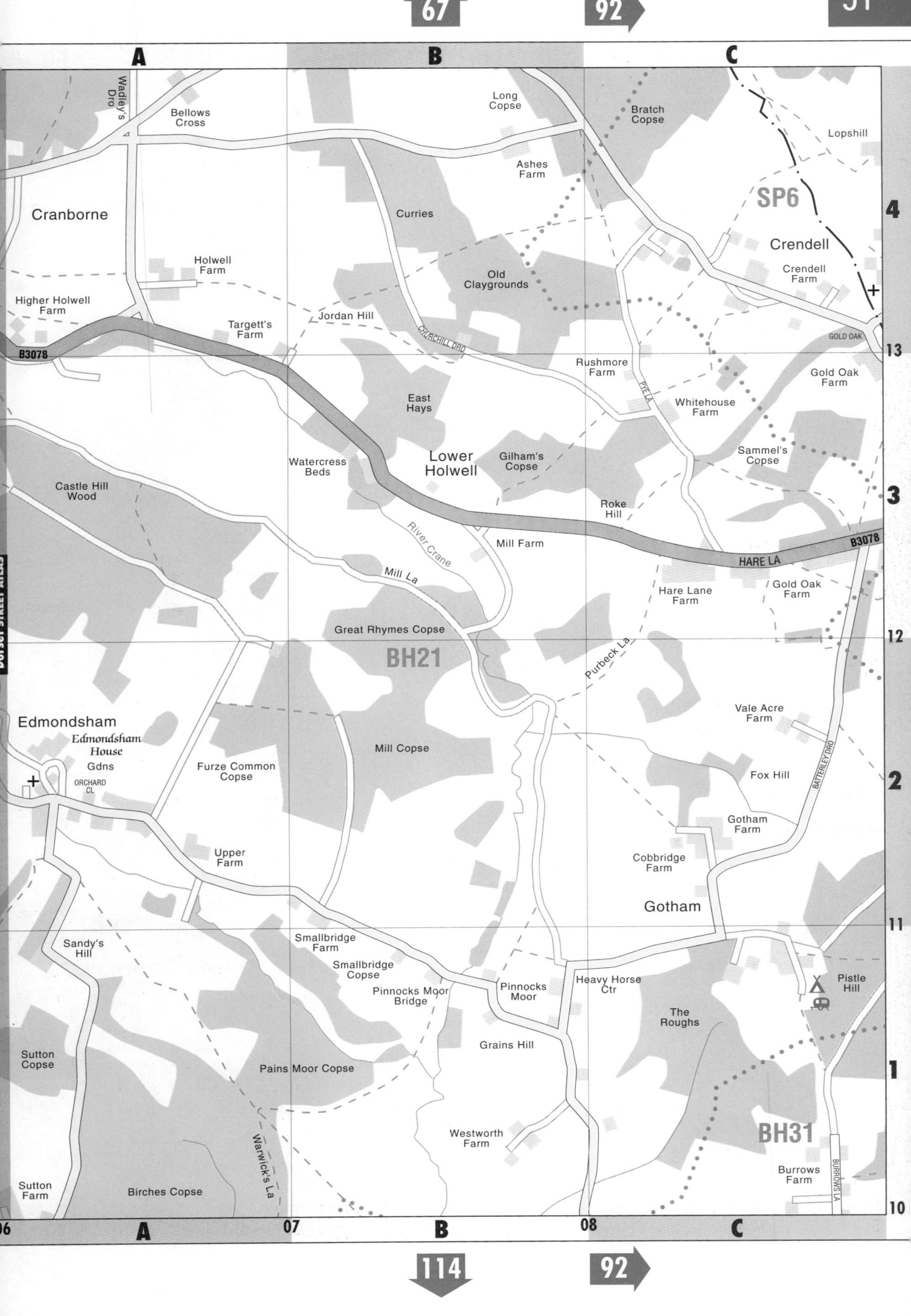
A
B
C
Wadley's Dro
Bellows Cross
Long Copse
Bratch Copse
Lopshill
Ashes Farm
SP6
Cranborne
Curries
4
Crendell
Holwell Farm
Old Claygrounds
Crendell Farm
Higher Holwell Farm
Jordan Hill
Targett's Farm
CHURCHILL DRO
GOLD OAK
B3078
Rushmore Farm
13
Gold Oak Farm
PYE LA
East Hays
Whitehouse Farm
Sammel's Copse
Watercress Beds
Lower Holwell
Gilham's Copse
Castle Hill Wood
Roke Hill
3
River Crane
Mill Farm
B3078
HARE LA
Mill La
Hare Lane Farm
Gold Oak Farm
Great Rhymes Copse
12
BH21
Purbeck La
Vale Acre Farm
Edmondsham
Edmondsham House
Gdns
Mill Copse
Furze Common Copse
Fox Hill
2
ORCHARD CL
BATTERLEY DRO
Gotham Farm
Upper Farm
Cobbridge Farm
Gotham
11
Smallbridge Farm
Sandy's Hill
Smallbridge Copse
Pistle Hill
Heavy Horse Ctr
Pinnocks Moor Bridge
Pinnocks Moor
The Roughs
Grains Hill
Sutton Copse
1
Pains Moor Copse
BH31
Westworth Farm
Warwick's La
Burrows Farm
BURROWS LA
Sutton Farm
Birches Copse
10
06
A
07
B
08
C

114
92

91
68

A
B
C
Higher Bullhill Farm
Pond Close
SANDLEHEATH RD
Cutts Copse
Lopshill Farm
CHEATER'S LA
Cheater's Gate
Lopshill Common
4
Lower Daggons
Alderholt Park
Hart's Farm
High Wood
Park Farm
Hill Cottage Farm
13
Hither Daggons Wood
Further Daggons Wood
Vicarage Farm
HIGHWOOD CL
Churchill Arms (PH)
APPLE TREE RD
B3078
PARK LA
STATION RD
STATION VD
OLD FORGE CL
DAGGONS RD
LIME TREE CL
PEAR TREE CL
Bittersweet Farm
STATION RD
PO
ALDER DR
3
Daggons
SP6
CHURCHILL CL
EARLSWOOD DR
B3078
CRANBORNE RD
BLACKWATER GR
ATTWOOD CL
PINE RD
OAK RD
Cripplestyle
RINGWOOD RD
King Barrow
Charing Cross
Alderholt
12
Sleepbrook Farm
Cross Roads Plantation
Ringwood Forest
2
Stanford Point
Alderholt Common
BH21
Telegraph Plantation
Cranborne Common
11
Sleep Brook
Decoy Pond
Sleep Bottom
Mast
BH31
1
Plumley Wood
BH24
Mount Ararat
10
09
A
10
B
11
C

91
115

69
94
A
B
C
4
13
3
12
2
11
1
10
12
13
14
116
94
Hill Farm
Home Farm
Salisbury Arms Farm
Cross Farm
Camel Green
St James CE Fst Sch
Bonfire Hill
Hillbury Farm
Oak Tree Farm
Sleepbrook Farm
Alderholt Common
Warren Park Farm
Plumley Wood
Whitefield Bottom
North Plumley Farmhouse
Hamer Copse
Hamer
Bowerwood House
BOWERWOOD COTTS
New Farm
Highfield Farm
Wolvercrate Copse
Hilbury Copse
Drove End Farm
Bleakhill Farm
Bleak Hill
Midgham Wood
SP6
Midgham Farm
Midgham Long Copse
BH24
Cobley Wood Farm
Cobley Hill
Kent Hill
Kent
Harbridge
Harbridge Green
Harbridge House
North End Farm
East Moor Copse
Avon Valley Path
River Avon
Bickton
Bickton Farm
Weir
Sewage Works
Padstow Farm
FORDINGBRIDGE RD
BOWERWOOD RD
STATION RD
RINGWOOD RD
HILLBURY RD
ASHFORD RD
LOMER LA
HARBRIDGE DRO
NORTH END LA
KENT LA
CHURCHFIELD LA
FROG LA
PADSTOW PL
CHURCH ST
B3078
BUSHELLS FARM
CHURCH FARM
MULBERRY GDNS
SANDLEHEATH RD
ANDLEHEATH RD
PRESSEYS CNR
DOWN LODGE CL
WINDSOR WAY
HAYTERS WAY
COPPERS CL
CAMEL GREEN RD
FIR TREE HILL
SOUTH HILL
ANTELL'S WAY
ASH CL
BRAMBLE CL
BEECH CL
TUDOR CL
SILVERDALE CRES
GREEN DR
GILBERT CL
WREN GDNS
BIRCHWOOD DR
HILLBURY PK
KESTREL WAY
SAXON WAY
HAZEL CL
FERN CL
BROOMFIELD DR
ARLSWOOD DR
1 YEW TREE CT
2 MULBERRY MEWS
3 DIAMOND CL
4 DIAMOND CT
5 QUADRANT
6 WEST ST
7 BROOK TERR
8 TIMBERMILL CT

93
70

A
B
C
4
13
3
12
2
11
1
10
15
16
17
Cemy
A338
Winnall's
Wood
BROADHILL
LA
BLISSFORD RD
Blissford Hill
STUCKTON RD
Rose
Farm
The
Merrie Thought
Newfoundland
Blissford
BLISSFORD
CROSS
Redbrook
The Three Lions
(PH)
Redbrook
Farm
REDBROOK
COTTS
Stuckton
Ditchend Brook
CHILLY
HILL
Frogham
BARTLETTS
COMM
BLISSFORD HILL
THE
CLOSE
ABBOTS WELL RD
Flaxfield
Farm
The Foresters Arms
(PH)
FROGHAM HILL
PENTONS HILL
THE
PADDOCK
HYDE LA
Abbots
Well
Ogdens
Farm
HERN LA
Hyde
Hyde Common
Hyde
CE Prim
Sch
SP6
HUNGERFORD HILL
Hungerford
Ogdens
Hern Gate
Farm
Dairy
Farm
GORLEY LYNCH
RINGWOOD RD
The Royal Oak
(PH)
Gunville
Holland
Bottom
RINGWOOD RD
GORLEY
CROSS
BUDDLE HILL
Buddle
Gorley Common
LAWRENCE LA
North
Gorley
THE
COTTAGES
Dorridge Hill
Gorley Hill
Huckles Brook
Furze Hill
Knutley
Copse
Brogenslade Bottom
King's
Copse
Ford
South
Gorley
BROOKSIDE
Hucklesbrook
Farm
Cuckoo Hill
Huckles
Bridge
Cuckoo
Hill
Railway
BLIND LA
BH24
Newtown
Farm
IBSLEY DRO
NEWTOWN LA
Ibsley Common
Little Chibden
Bottom
SALISBURY RD A338
Merrilea
Farm

93
117

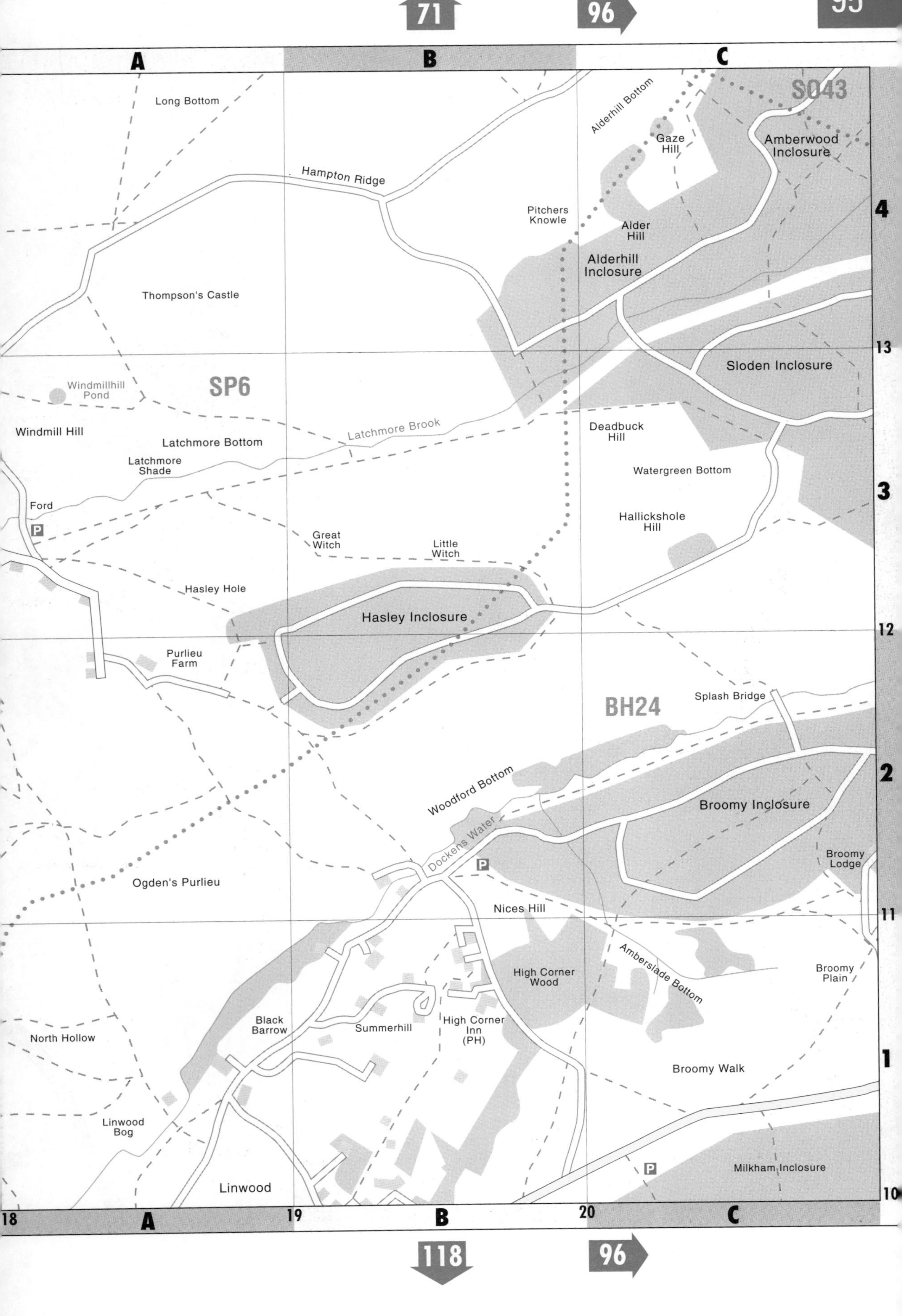
71
96
A
B
C
Long Bottom
Alderhill Bottom
Gaze Hill
SO43
Amberwood Inclosure
Hampton Ridge
Pitchers Knowle
Alder Hill
4
Alderhill Inclosure
Thompson's Castle
13
Sloden Inclosure
Windmillhill Pond
SP6
Windmill Hill
Latchmore Brook
Deadbuck Hill
Latchmore Bottom
Latchmore Shade
Watergreen Bottom
3
Ford
Hallickshole Hill
Great Witch
Little Witch
Hasley Hole
Hasley Inclosure
12
Purlieu Farm
Splash Bridge
BH24
2
Woodford Bottom
Broomy Inclosure
Dockens Water
Broomy Lodge
Ogden's Purlieu
Nices Hill
11
Ambersiade Bottom
High Corner Wood
Broomy Plain
Black Barrow
Summerhill
High Corner Inn (PH)
North Hollow
1
Broomy Walk
Linwood Bog
Milkham Inclosure
Linwood
10
18
19
20
118
96

95
72
A
B
C
Latchmore Brook
Whiteshoot Bottom
Hiscocks Hill
Amberwood Inclosure
Fritham Grange
Green Pond
Fritham Plain
Queen North Wood
North Bentley Inclosure
Sloden Inclosure
Freeworms Hill
South Bentley Inclosure
Rakes Brakes Bottom
Dockens Water
SO43
Anses Wood
Ragged Boys Hill
Cadmans Pool
Holly Hatch Cottage
Holly Hatch Inclosure
Ocknell Pond
BH24
Broomy Lodge
Ocknell Plain
Broomy Bottom
Winding Stonard
Bratley Water
Spreading Oak
Broomy Plain
A31
Slufters Inclosure
Slufters Bottom
Fritham Cross
4
13
3
12
2
11
1
0
21
22
23
119

73
98

A
B
C
Coppice of Linwood
The Butt
Brook Common
Lush's
King's Garn Gutter
Skers Farm
King's Garn Gutter Inclosure
Janesmoor Pond
Janesmoor Plain
Ford
Blackthorne's
Ford
Blackthorn Copse
13
Water Tower
Upper Canterton
Long Beech Hill
Long Beech Inclosure
Tom Pook's Hill
Sir Walter Tyrrell (PH)
Blackwool
Coalmeer Gutter
Stricknage Wood
3
SO43
12
A31
Hotel
Stoney Cross
Ocknell Inclosure
Bolderwood Walk
Highland Water
Stoney Cross Plain
The Grove
Asher's Bottom
Fox Hill
11
Ocknell Arch
King's Garn
Mill Stream
Long Brook
Withybed Bottom
1
Lucas Castle
Stonard Wood
Ringwood Ford Bottom
Ringwood Ford
Hart Hill
10
24
25
26
A
B
C

120
98

A
B
C
Wittensford
Cadnam River
Birchenwood Farm
Canterton Manor
Lower Canterton
Pipers Copse
Greys Farm
Bignell Wood
Cadnam
Rockram Wood
Works
Bartley Lodge Hotel
Shave Hat
SO40
Rufus Stone
Malwood Farm
Shave Green Inclosure
Shave Wood
Beechwood House
French's Bushes
Yolsham Hill
Malwood Castle
Mast
Malwood
Clay Hill
SO43
Seaman's Corner
Minstead Hall
Furzey Gdns
London Minstead
Hazel Hill
Brockis Hill
Home Farm
Minstead Lodge
Dogben Gutter
Minstead
Field House
The Old Rectory
Minstead Rural Studies Ctr
Ford
Newtown
Duell's Farm
Fleetwater Stud
Park Farm House
Manor Park
William's Hill
Fleet Water
Woodside
Manor Wood
The Kennels
Harcourt Wood
B3079
M27
A31
A336
A337
ROMSEY RD
LYNDHURST RD
OLD ROMSEY RD
SOUTHAMPTON RD
WHITE HART LA
THE PARADE
WELLINGTON PL
BARLEYCORN WLK
OLD LYNDHURST RD
LYNDHURST HILL
ORCHARD CT
KEWLAKE LA
CADNAM LA
WITTENSFORD LA
CANTERTON LA
BEECHWOOD RD
BROCKISHILL RD
SEAMANS LA
BULL LA
CONGLETON CL
CHURCH CL
FOOTBALL GN
MILL LA
PH
PO
P
4
13
3
12
2
11
1
10
27
28
29

A
B
C
Homestead
Oakhill
POLLARDS MOOR RD
Budds Farm
St Helen's Farm
Manor Farm
Stamford Hill Farm
THE BRICKYARD
WINSOR RD
Burnards Copse
Judds Farm
TATCHBURY LA
WINSOR LA
4
BARNEY HAYES LA
KENNINGTON LA
Bartley CE Jun Sch
PH
SOUTHAMPTON RD
ROCKRAM CL
Garden Centre
PH
EADENS LA
Bartley Grange
Saw Mill
NEW INN RD
OAKFIELD RD
NEW INN LA
ABBOTSFORD
RINGWOOD RD
Carlton House
A336
13
PO
CHINHAM RD
Forest House
BEECHWOOD RD
Bartley
PUNDLE GREEN EST
SHEPHERDS CL
RIVERSIDE CL
SHEPHERDS RD
BOURNE RD
PARADISE LA
Bourne Farm
Ford
BOURNE LA
Beechwood Park
3
The Copse Caravan Park
Ridge Farm
BROCKISHILL RD
Bartley Manor
The Orchard Caravan Park
ROSSITERS LA
WOODLANDS RD
Rossiters La
Rossiters Copse
PURKISS CL
LANESBRIDGE CL
12
GREEN CL
PH
Moorlands Farm
MILLVINA CL
Nicholas Corner
BARTLEY RD
Goldenhayes
SO40
Woodlands
Eaves Hill
Goldenhayes Park
2
Brockishill Inclosure
Foyers
Hotel
The Woodlands Lodge Hotel
WOODLANDS RD
THE CRESCENT
WOODLANDS DRO
P
ALPINE RD
HAZEL GR
Busketts Wood
11
FLETCHWOOD LA
Busketts Lawn Inclosure
Ford
Costicles Inclosure
Ford
SO43
Bartley Water
1
Furzy Lawn Inclosure
Gutter Heath
Ironshill Lodge
A35
10
0
A
31
B
32
C

99
76

A
B
C
4
3
2
1
13
12
11
10
33
34
35
TOTTON
Netley Marsh
Rushington
Brokenford
Hounsdown
Foxhills
Fletchwood
Ashurst
Colbury
Ashurst Bridge
S040
Vane's Copse
Hanger Farm
Meadow Farm
Netley Marsh CE Inf Sch
The White Horse (PH)
Thornlands Farm
Willswood Farm
Little Fletchwood Farm
Great Fletchwood Farm
Bartley Water
Two Oaks
Five Oaks
Martins Croft Farm
Nature Reserve
Fletchwood Copse
Busketts Inclosure
The New Forest Hotel (PH)
Ashurst (Geriatric)
Ashurst (New Forest)
Ashurst Farm
Prior's Bushes
Biddlecombe Farm
The Forest Inn (PH)
Longdown Dairy Farm
Deerleap Farm
Hunters Inn Hill
Foxhills Jun Sch
Foxhills Inf Sch
Colbury Farm
Pritchel's Copse
Durley Farm
Muttonsnow Farm
Blind Copse
Hounsdown Sec Sch
New Forest Ent Ctr
Rushington Bsns Pk
Recn Gnd
Totton Coll
Recn Ctr
Springdale Ct Ind Est
Bsn Ctr
A326
A336
A36
A35
B3076
RINGWOOD RD
TOTTON WESTERN BY-PASS
LYNDHURST RD
HUNTERS HILL
MAIN RD
SPICER'S HILL
SALISBURY RD
WATER LA
CALMORE RD
FLETCHWOOD LA
FLETCHWOOD RD
WOODLANDS RD
ASHURST BRIDGE RD
POUND LA
DEERLEAP LA
KNELLERS LA
FOXHILLS
WHARTONS LA
MARCHWOOD BY-PASS
TOTTON BY PASS
PERRYWOOD GDNS 1
FIELDFARE CT 2
HOLMSLEY CT 3
REDWING GDNS 4
LAPWING DR 5
THE LINNETS 6
CLYDESDALE WAY 7
SHIRES WLK 8
EXMOOR CL 9
BULLFINCH CL 10
THE BRAMBLINGS 11
GOLDCREST LA 12
THE DORRITS 1
COPPERFIELDS 2
NICKLEBY GDNS 3
1 HOLLAND RD
2 ASHWOOD GDNS
3 TIMSON CL
4 PEREGRINE CL
1 GOLDSMITH CL
2 LYDGATE
3 AUSTEN CL
4 THOMAS CL
5 HUDSON CT
6 KAYLEIGH CL

99
123

A
B
C
SOUTHAMPTON
Redbridge
Wimpson
Millbrook
Eling
Marchwood
Trotts
Pooksgreen
SO15
SO16
SO40
River Test
Southampton Docks
Prince Charles Container Port
REDBRIDGE CAUSEWAY
REDBRIDGE FLYOVER
REDBRIDGE RD
COMMERCIAL RD
TOTTON BY PASS
TEBOURBA WAY
MILLBROOK RD W
MILLBROOK FLYOVER
MARCHWOOD BY PASS
MARCHWOOD RD
BURY RD
JACOB'S GUTTER LA
TROTTS LA
TAVELL'S LA
The Furlongs
Red Bridge
Salterns Special Sch
Redbridge Vehicle Depot
Millbrook Trad Est
Trinity Ind Est
Eling Wharf
The Anchor Inn (PH)
Ealing Tide Mill
Cemy
Village Bells (PH)
The King Rufus (PH)
Colbury Manor
Bury Brickfield Park Caravan Site
Bury Brickfield Cottages
Jacob's Farm
Bury Farm
Trotts Farm
Bull's Copse
Golt's Copse
Great Cole Copse
Coffin's Farm
Langley Lodge
Heron's Hill
Dumper's Farm
Park's Farm
Tavell's Farm
Cork's Farm
Recycling Centre
Works
Marchwood Jun Sch
Luggy Creek
Tanner's Creek
36
37
38
10
11
12
13
4
3
2
1

102
A4
1 REGENT'S GR
2 CARLISLE CT
3 LASHAM HO
4 COMPTON HO
5 BURLEY HO
6 REGENTS CT
7 LEIGHTON AVE
8 DENNISON CT
9 NORTH CT
10 CENTRE CT
11 SOUTH CT
12 WEST CT
13 OAKLEY HO
14 CLIFTON GDNS
15 CLIFTON CT
16 ASHDENE
17 ENDEAVOUR CL
18 MEDLEY PL
19 KELSTON CL
20 STANTON BLDGS
101
B4
1 BURLINGTON MANS
2 WITHEWOOD MANS
3 LUMSDEN MANS
4 HATHERLEY MANS
78
B3
1 MINSTER CT
2 TRINITY CT
3 PARK CT FLATS
4 SOMERSET CT
5 RICHMOND HO
6 CROSSLEY CT
7 CHERITON CT
8 HESKETH HO
9 NIGHTINGDALE CT
10 ROMSEY CT
11 ALMOND CT
12 FREEMANTLE BSNS CTR
13 BROOK CT
C4
1 AVENUE CT
2 CAVENDISH MWS
3 MAYCROFT CT
4 HULSE LODGE
5 CARLTON CT
6 ST MARGARETS HO
7 BARKSHIRE CT
8 HILDA CT
9 ROXAN CT
10 GWEN-RHIAN CT
11 OAKLEY HO
12 BEAULIEU HO
13 BANISTER CT
14 MAYFLOWER CT
15 ABBEY CT
16 BANISTER GRANGE
17 DORRICK CT
18 WOODLAND PL
19 FOXLEA
20 PAVILION CT
21 DURBAN CT
22 SILVERDALE CT
23 DORVAL HO
24 DORVAL MANOR
25 OVERDELL CT
26 SHERFIELD HO
A
B
C
SO16
SO17
SO15
SO14
SO40
Shirley
Southampton Common
The Hawthorns Urban Wildlife Ctr
King Edward VI Sch
Cemy
Banister's Park
Gipsy Grove
St Mark's CE Jun Sch
Fitzhugh
Bedford Place
Freemantle
Solent Ind Ctr
Solent Bsns Ctr
Stanton Rd Ind Est
TA Ctr
Liners Ind Est
Hill
Springhill RC Prim Sch
The Polygon Sch
Polygon
Art Gall & Liby
Civic Ctr
Millbrook
King George V Graving Dock
Prince Charles Container Port
Mountbatten Bsns Ctr
Southampton Central
Hotels
City Ind Pk
Leisure World
Lansdowne Hill
The Quays
Hotel
Mus
Mayflower Park
Maritime Mus
IOW Ferry Terminal
Royal Pier
Town Quay
Docks
SOUTHAMPTON
River Test
Jetty
Marchwood Yacht Club
Marchwood Ind Pk
Southampton Institute of H Ed Marine Operations Ctr
Pier
Cracknore Hard
Works
Byams House
McMullen Barracks
Marchwood Military Port
Piers
MILLBROOK RD W
MOUNTBATTEN WAY
WESTERN ESPL
WEST QUAY RD
SHIRLEY HIGH ST
SHIRLEY RD
HERBERT WALKER AVE
A33
A35
A3057
A3024
4
13
3
12
2
11
1
10
39
40
41
C2
1 SCULLARDS LA
2 WEST BARGATE
3 ALBION PL
4 FOREST VIEW
5 MADDISON ST
6 CASTLE LA
7 CEMENT TERR
8 CASTLE SQ
9 LANSDOWNE HILL
10 BIDDLESGATE CT
11 HAMTUN ST
12 IRONSIDE CT
13 SIMNEL ST
14 POSTERN CT
15 BLUE ANCHOR LA
16 ST MICHAEL'S SQ
17 CHURCH LA
18 ST MICHAEL'S ST
19 WESTGATE ST
20 VYSE LA
21 MERCHANTS WLK
22 CUCKOO LA
C3
1 UPPER BANISTER ST
2 HANDFORD PL
3 SOUTHAMPTON ST
4 WINCHESTER ST
5 VERNON WLK
6 SALISBURY ST
7 LOWER BANISTER ST
8 THORNERS CT
9 HENSTEAD CT
10 DEVONSHIRE MANS
11 OAKVILLE MANS
12 EMILY DAVIS HALLS OF RESIDENCE
13 FITZHUGH ST
14 WYNDHAM PL
15 SOUTHBROOK RD
16 FOURPOSTS HILL
17 SPRING CT
18 TINTERN GR
101
125

103
A4
1 CLIFFORD DIBBEN MEWS
2 BUCKINGHAM CT
3 LINGDALE PL
4 MINSTEAD CT
5 HARTLEY CT
6 WINDSOR CT
7 BALMORAL CT
8 WESSEX CT
9 RANELAGH CT
10 KINTERBURY CT
11 ELFIN CT
12 WESTWOOD CT
13 CANDLEMAS PL
14 WINDSOR CT
15 PARKLAND PL
16 CHERRY CT
17 CAMBRIDGE CT
18 ST ANNES MEWS
19 HYNES CT
20 BARTLETT HO
21 ST ANDREWS HO
22 ST GEORGES HO
23 WOODSIDE CT
24 ASCUPART HO
25 BEVOIS MANS
26 BEVOIS MEWS
27 DARNAN HO
28 CHARLES WYATT HO
29 TEMPLAR CT
30 LAMWARD MANS
C4
1 MIDANBURY WLK
2 KELLY CT
3 FLORENCE CT
79
C4
4 DEAN CT
5 BINDON CT
6 CAUSEWAY CT
7 ABBEYFIELD HO
8 BIRCHWOOD CT
9 CHRISTINE CT
104
C4
10 MIDANBURY CT
11 WELLOW CT
12 THE GATEHOUSE
13 WINDSOR CT
14 MANOR PARK HO
15 COBBETT CT
16 ROSEBROOK CT
17 JUNIPER CT
A2
1 ALBION TWRS
2 JOHNSON ST
3 KINGSLAND SQ
4 KINGSLAND CT
A
B
C
4
13
3
12
2
11
1
10
SO17
SO18
SO15
SO14
SO19
Bevois Mount
Portswood Park
Bevois Town
St Denys'
Bevois Valley
Bitterne Manor
Bitterne
St Mary's Coll
Northam Bridge
Northam
Newtown
Bellevue
Queensland
Millbank
Belvidere
Kingsland Place
St Mary's Stadium
Chapel
Sussex Place
Crosshouse
The Itchen Bridge (Toll)
Ocean Village
Marina
Southampton Oceanography Ctr
Empress Dock
Weston Point
Jetty
Jurd's Lake
Peartree Green
Itchen
Woolston
Mayfield Park
Weston
Merry Oak
Recreation Ground
River Itchen
River Test
THOMAS LEWIS WAY
BEVOIS VALLEY RD
BITTERNE RD W
NORTHAM RD
PORTSMOUTH RD
CENTRAL BRIDGE
KINGSWAY
BRITANNIA RD
MARINE PAR
Itchen Way
RIVER VIEW HO 1
WHARNCLIFFE HO 2
HIGHLANDS HO 3
SHAMROCK RD 4
TANKERVILLE RD 5
DEFENDER WLK 6
LABURNUM CT 7
ROBERE HO 8
WESTCLIFF MEWS 9
COOPER'S LA 10
THE CLIFF 11
JACKMANS CL 12
MERLIN LODGE 13
SOMMERS CT 14
1 LONGBRIDGE IND PK
2 ASTURIAS WAY
3 CADLAND CT
4 MOORHEAD CT
5 CALSHOT CT
1 THE GREENWICH
2 THE ALBANY
3 ST JULIEN'S ALMHOUSES
4 BACK OF THE WALLS
5 MONUMENT CT
COBDEN MARINE CT 1
BELLAMY CT 2
RIVERSIDE CT 3
RIVERBOURNE CT 4
HOLLINGBOURNE CL 5
WHITWORTH CT 6
VESPASIAN CT 7
1 SCHOOL PL
2 PEARTREE CT
3 SEAWARD GDNS
4 THE HAVEN
BAGSHOT MEWS 5
WHITCHURCH CT 6
CRANBURY CT 7
ROWAN CT 8
BEECH CT 9
ELM CT 10
1 CHARLOTTE CT
2 SPRINGFIELD CT
5 SOMBORNE HO
6 KINGSCLERE CL
7 WEST CT
8 BARNFIELD FLATS
DUNCAN CL 3
NEW CLIFF HO 4
43
44
A2
5 BROAD GN
6 COSSACK GN
7 EAST BARGATE
8 BARGATE CTR
9 HIGH ST
10 MARKET PL
11 TALBOT CT
12 HOLYROOD HO
13 ORCHARD HO
14 CHANDOS HO
15 QUEENS HO
16 EAST STREET CTR
17 KING'S HO
18 CHALLIS CT
19 ALL SAINTS HO
20 MARSH HO
21 RUSSELL ST
22 ELDON HO
23 ST JAMES HO
24 ST BERNARD HO
25 CANUTE HO
26 CHANDOS ST
27 LATIMER GATE
28 JESSIE TERR
29 CITY COMMERCE CTR
30 COMMODORE CT
31 ST LAWRENCE RD
32 CONSULATE HO
33 BRIDGE TERR
A3
1 SOUTHCLIFFE HO
2 ROCKSTONE CT
3 THE CRANBURY
4 CRANBURY TERR
5 EMMADALE CT
6 CRANBURY TWRS
7 ST SWITHUNS CT
8 COLLEGE PL
9 BELLEVUE TERR
10 LOWER ALFRED ST
11 RADCLIFFE CT
12 JOSIAN WLK
13 CLIFFORD ST
14 WINTON ST
15 CRAVEN ST
16 NORTH FRONT
17 WOOLLEY HO
18 PRIORY HO
19 LEWIS HO
126
A3
20 KINGSLAND HO
21 THE CARRONADES
22 ST MATTHEWS CL
23 COMPTON WLK
B3
1 NORTHAM BSNS CTR
2 PRINCES CT
3 PRINCES HO
4 GRAHAM HO
104
B3
5 CLARENCE HO
6 COBURG HO
7 YORK HO
8 AVON HO
9 TEVIOT HO
10 SOLWAY HO
11 FORTH HO
12 BELVIDERE HO
13 MAURETANIA HO
14 MILLBANK HO
15 KENILWORTH HO
16 NORMAN HO
17 SAXON HO
18 CHARLIEJOY GDNS
19 ARUNDEL HO
20 ARMADALE HO
21 WARWICK HO
22 BRITANNIC HO
23 AQUITANIA HO
24 CLYDE HO
25 TRENT HO
26 SHANNON HO
27 KENT HO
28 HILDA PL
29 CABLE ST
30 GUILDFORD ST

A4
1 BRAMBLE MEWS
2 DEAN CT
3 MILLVERTON CT
4 JUSTINE CT
5 HONEYSUCKLE CT

103
80

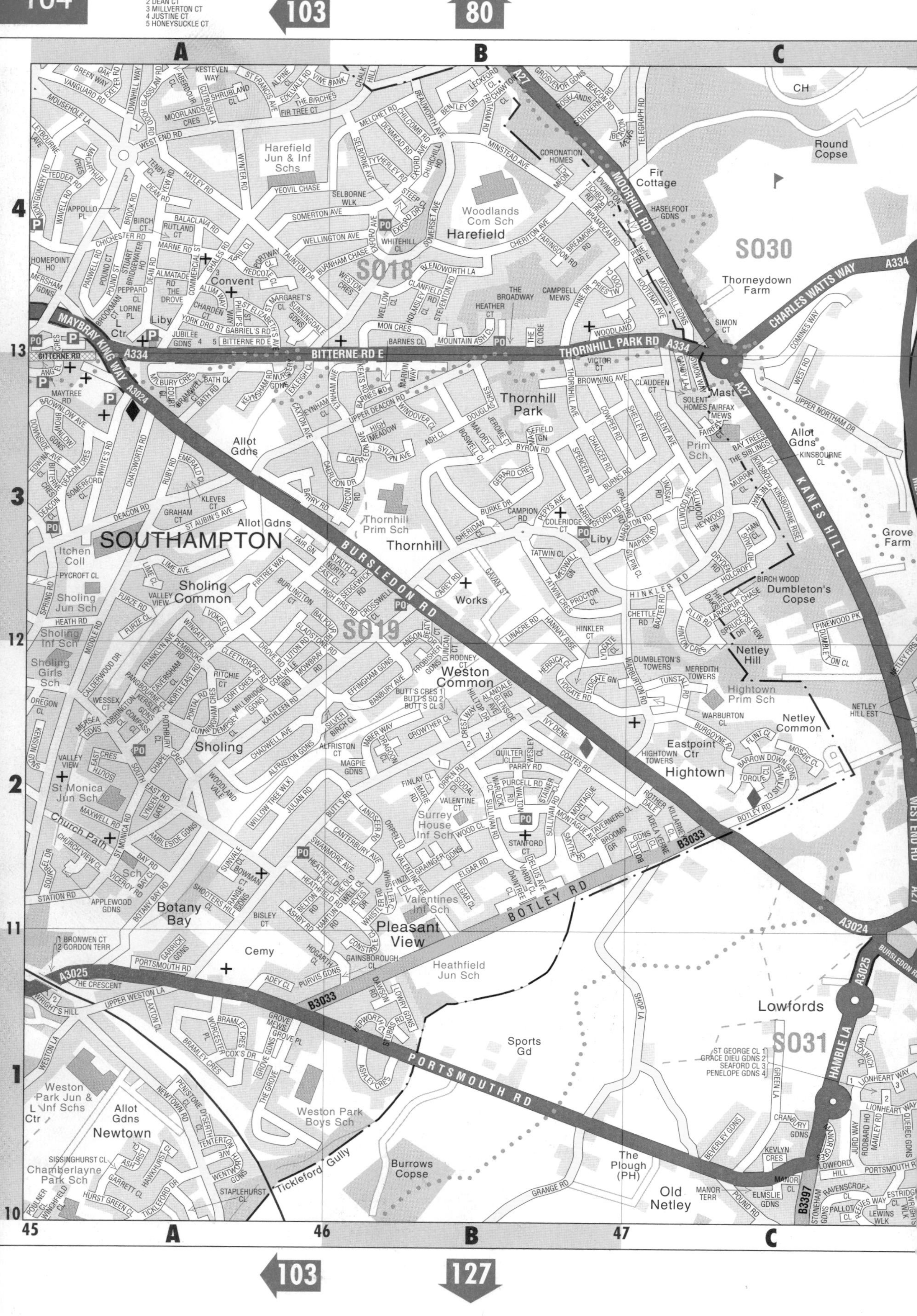

103
127

81
106

128
106

105
82

105
129

Row Ash
Rowash Farm House
Wickham Vineyard
Raglington Farm
Ferny Copse
HALL CT
Shedfield Grange
SANDY LA
Country Club
Shedfield House
Shedfield Lodge
Sandy Hills House
B2177
SMITHS LA
GAMBLINS LA
HIGH ST
NIGHTINGALE CRES
ST ANNES LA
ST JOHNS LA
UPPER CHURCH RD
Turkey Island
CHURCH VIEW
THE OLD FORGE
MURRAY COTTS
CHURCH RD
CANFORD CL
SLOANE PARK
Shedfield
Fairlands Montessori Sch
Shedfield Common
CULVERLANDS CL
PRICKETT HILL
WINCHESTER RD
SO32
Hallcourt Wood
Brook Wood
Redhill Copse
Biddenfield
BLIND LA
Biddenfield High Wood
Blacklands Copse
Tankerhill Copse
BIDDENFIELD LA
Mansfield Lane
Cold Harbour Farm
LITTLE PARK MANSIONS
Meon Park
Mansfield Barn
Hangman's Copse
Park Place Farm
SO30
Alder Moor
Marvane Cottage Farm
CH
A334
COLD HARBOUR CL
HOLT CL
ELIZABETH CL
TANFIELD PARK
Park Place Pastoral Centre
PO17
TITCHFIELD LA
Webb's Land Farm
TANFIELD LA
Quob Farm
Dimmock's Moor
Works
Mayles
Little Tapnage Farm
Sager's Down
Ridge Copse
River Meon
MAYLES LA
Tapnage
PO15
Botley Wood
The Lodge
Fiddlers Green
A
B
C
4
13
3
12
2
11
1
10
54
55
56

107
84

107
131

A B C

Forester Rd
May Bush La
Kiln Hill
Liberty Rd
Dradfield Copse
Adam's Farm
Southend La
Southend Farm
Roy's La
Southend
SO32
Square Copse
Clays Copse
East Croft Copse
Menslands La
Hole La
Haraldslea Farm
Forest Lodge Farm
Dradfield La
Kings Way
West Walk
PO
Southend Plain
Ingoldfield La
Huntbourne Farm
Hoe Manor Farm
Hoegate Farm
Hoe St
Hoe Gate
Kiln Copse
Fodderhouse Copse
Grove Copse
Huntbourn Corner
Hoegate Common
Clamp Farm
Church Rd
Newtown
Newtown Soberton Inf Sch
Rail Croft
Huntbourn Wood
The Purlieus
Rudley Mill
Hall's Copse
Lodge Hill
Hundred Acres Rd
Lodge Hill
Oak Tree Farm
Mill Copse
Clamp Kiln Farm
Martin's Corner
St Martin's Corner Farm
PO7
P
Retreat Farm
Traveller's Rest (PH)
Charles Wood
Hoe Moor Farm
Kings Way
Charleswood Farm
Forest Farm
PO17
Bunns La
Meadows Farm
Goathouse La
Kiln Farm
Hipley
Bunns Lane Farm
Apless La
Goathouse Farm
Hoemoor Farm
Chairmakers' Arms (PH)
Sand Pit
Trampers La
Ivy Cottage
Kiln La
Shoot Hill
Hipley Farm
Birch Hill
Little Forest
Horse & Jockey (PH)
Kings Way
Shoothill Lodge
Goathouse Copse
Kiln Wood
Russell's Copse
Hale Row
Hipley Copse
Pounds Farm
Houndels Row
Beckford Bridge
Winecross
Gravelpit Row
Orchard Bglws
North Boarhunt
Quagg Farm
Beckford La
Goldsmith's Copse
Ashlands
Mitchelland Copse
Kings Way
Wine Cross
PO
Dirty Ground Copse
Furzy Ground
Bonham Row
P
Blackhouse La
B2177
Walton Heath Plantation
Tylers Copse
Ashlands Plantation
Hipley Barn Farm

4
13
3
12
2
11
1
10

0 A 61 B 62 C

132
110

109 86

A B C

4
13
3
12
2
11
1
10

63 A 64 B 65 C

109 133

87
112

134
112

C2
1 THAMES CT
2 AVON CT
3 HAMBLE CT
4 ITCHEN CT
5 BEAULIEU CT
6 PATRICK HOWARD -DOBSON CT

111
88

111
135

A1
1 DORCAS CL
2 LYSANDER WAY
3 OLIVIA CL
4 JESSICA CL
5 OCTAVIUS CT
6 KEMPTON PK
7 PLUMPTON GR
8 HAYDOCK MEWS
9 CHEPSTOW CT
10 FONTWELL MEWS
11 RIPON GDNS
12 THE WESTBROOK CTR
13 BRACKEN HEATH
14 HITHERWOOD CL

89

A
B
C
Wick Farm
Oxleys Copse
Old Idsworth Garden
Wick Hanger
Murrants Copse
Sussex Border Path
South Holt Farm
Idsworth House
Idsworth Park
Finchdean
ASHCROFT LA
WOODHOUSE LA
Treadwheel Farm
The George (PH)
PO8
Finchdean Farm
Adam's Copse
TREADWHEEL RD
Woodhouse
Woods Copse
Forestside
DEAN LA
MAGPIE RD
Old Idworth School
Deanlane End
Motleys Copse
Calf Dell
MAGPIE COTTS
WOODHOUSE LA
Wellsworth Lane
Drews Farm
Sussex Border Path
Cherry Row
Broad Walk
Monarch's Way
Woodhouse Ashes Farm
Great Wellsworth
PO9
Stein Wood
FINCHDEAN RD
WELLSWORTH LA
HOLT GDNS
WELLSWOOD GDNS
MEADOWLANDS
Stansted Forest
GREATFIELD WAY
BOWES HILL
BROAD CROFT
UPLANDS RD
LINKS LA
THE PEAK
Rowlands Castle
STANSTED CT
Recn Gnd
Rowland's Castle
THE FAIRWAY
PO
THE GREEN
The Sling
CH
Monarch's Way
Sussex Border Path
The Forest
Red Hill
The Avenue
MANOR LODGE RD
KINGS CL
STANSTED CL
GLEN DALE
Staunton Country Park
ROYAL GDNS
KINGS WAY
NIGHTINGALE CL
CASTLE RD
LINKS CL
REDHILL RD
Horsepasture Farm
KINGFISHER CL
DUNNOCK CL
YARDLEA CL
COLLEGE CL
Furzy Plain
BLACKCAP CL
BRAMBLING RD
Lyels Wood
WOODBERRY LA
THE DRIFT
MALLARD RD
NUTHATCH CL
HILLBROW CL
HAZELDEAN CT
B2149
HAZELDEAN DR
Red Hill Farm
Nightingale Bottom
73
74
A
B
C
4
13
3
12
2
11
1
10
West Sussex STREET ATLAS

136

91

A
B
C
Sutton Holms
Birches Copse
B3081
Sutton Hill Farm
Warwick's Lane
The Inclosure
Ironmongers Copse
Chy
Eastworth Farm
Romford East Farm
Mill
The Albion Inn (PH)
West Farm
Romford Bridge
Romford
STATION RD
Dewlands Wood
CH
Burgess Farm Cottage
Woodlands Common
Ninney-cox Wood
Martin's Farm
Doe's Lane
Mount Pleasant Farm
Dewlands Common
Woodlands
Wedge Hill
River Crane
Verwood CE First Sch
Emmanuel CE Mid Sch
Bridge Farm
BH31
Verwood
Wedge Hill Farm
Heathy How
Homer's Wood
Manor Farm
David's Cross
Redman's Hill
Monmouth's Ash Farm
Horton Farm
Bog Farm
Horton Common
Horton Heath Farm
Crab Orchard Farm
Crab Orchard
BH21
Grixey Farm
Harkwood Farm
Horton Heath
Hope Lodge Farm
Bramble Farm
Silverwood
High Moon
Three Legged Cross First Sch
Chapel Farm
MANOR RD
B3072
VERWOOD RD
Bugden's Copse
L Ctr
Liby
Dorset STREET ATLAS
06
07
08
09
1
2
3
4

138

92
116

139
116

115
93

115
140

94
118
A
B
C
A338
SALISBURY RD
Ibsley Manor Farm
Cottage Plantation
Great Bottom
Summerlug Hill
PO
NEW RD
CUFFNELLS CL
Whitefield Plantation
Linwood Bog
Ibsley
Hearns Plantation
Cross Lanes Farm
Mockbeggar Farm
4
Digden Bottom
MOCKBEGGAR LA
Mockbeggar
CROSS LANES
Ibsley House
09
Avon Valley Path
Newlands Plantation
Dockens Water
Rodens Bottom
Fir Walk
Gravel Pit
Moyles Court Sch
Ford
Big Whitemoor Bottom
3
Works
Rockford Common
ELLINGHAM DRO
Wood Sorrel
Little Whitemoor Bottom
Alice Lisle Inn (PH)
Rockford
08
Rockford Green
BH24
Blashford Lakes Study Ctr
Gravel Pit
Waterslade Farm
Ivy Lake
Bigsburn Hill
Water Slade Bottom
P
IVY LA
Rockford Farm
2
Highwood
Highwood Copse
Bracken Hill
Forest Edge Farm
SNAILS LA
HIGHWOOD LA
LINFORD HO
Blashford
Linbrook Almshouses
07
Highwood Farm
Linbrook View
Linford
Lin Brook
SYCAMORE CT 1
OLD FARM CL 2
WOOLMER LA
Northfield Lake
LIN BROOK DR
COWPITTS LA
Linbank Farm
Headlands Bsns Pk
POULNER MOBILE HOME PK
North Poulner
Hangersley
1
NORTH POULNER RD
SHAW RD
LAWRENCE RD
Poulner Inf & Jun Schs
ROSS RD
WATERSIDE CL
KINGFISHER WAY
MORANT RD
CROFT RD
DENE CL
DENHOLM CL
PADGET RD
ST AUBYNS LA
Burcomb
FORESTSIDE GDNS
Headlands Adventure Ctr
Kingfisher Lake
Hangersley Hill
HOLM CL
A338
PO
LINFORD RD
BURCOMBE LA
HURST RD
NORTHFIELD RD
BUTLERS LA
EDWINA CL
LINBROOK CT
SEYMOUR RD
FAIRLIE
1 GRENVILLE CL
2 DRAKE CL
3 FROBISHER CL
4 CHICHESTER RD
5 POULNER PK
Forest Corner Farm
BROADSHARD LA
MEADOW CL
WANSTEAD CL
FAIRLIE PK
PARKERS CL
GORLEY RD
NARROW LA
SALISBURY RD
HIGHFIELD DR
HAMPTON DR
HAWKINS CL
06
16
17
141
118

117
95

A
B
C
Amie's Wood
Milkham Inclosure
Linwood
Webb's Copse
TOMS LA
Toms Farm
4
Appleslade Farm
The Red Shoot Inn (PH)
Linwood Farm
Amie's Corner
Appleslade Bottom
Lin Wood
King's Garden
Mount Hill
09
Castle Piece
Roe Inclosure
Appleslade Inclosure
Linford Brook
3
Red Shoot Plain
Red Shoot Wood
Green Ford
Buckherd Bottom
Greenford Bottom
08
Great Linford Inclosure
White Hill
BH24
Pinnick Wood
Collier's Thorns
A31
2
Handy Cross
Akercombe Bottom
Linford Bottom
Little Linford Inclosure
Handy Cross Plain
Marrowbones Hill
07
Linford
Picket Bottom
Ridley Plain
1
Old Gate
Brook Farm
Little Wood
Harvest Slade
Picket Hill
Shobley
Ridley Bottom
Ridley Wood
Shobley Bottom
Picket Post
A31
06
18
19
20

117
142

96
120
A
B
C
Linford Brook
A31
Slufters Inclosure
Milkham Bottom
Bratley Arch
Mogshade Hill
Bratley Inclosure
Bratley Plain
Bushy Bratley
SO43
Bolderwood Farm
Deer Sanctuary
Sandy Ridge
Bratley Wood
Upper Lazy Bushes
Bushy Bradley
Lazy Bushes
Backley Bottom
Smoky Hole
Backley Holmes
North Oakley Inclosure
Bratley Water
Backley Inclosure
BH24
Stinking Edge Wood
Blackensford Bottom
Blackensford Hill
Blackensford Lawn
Blackensford Brook
Backley Plain
Soarley Beeches
Beech Bed Inclosure
Harvest Slade Bottom
Soarley Bottom
Woolfield Hill
Dogwood Bottom
Old House
Mouse's Cupboard
South Oakley Inclosure
Woolfield Cottage
Burley Outer Rails Inclosure
Berry Beeches
4
09
3
08
2
07
1
06
22
23
143
120

119
97

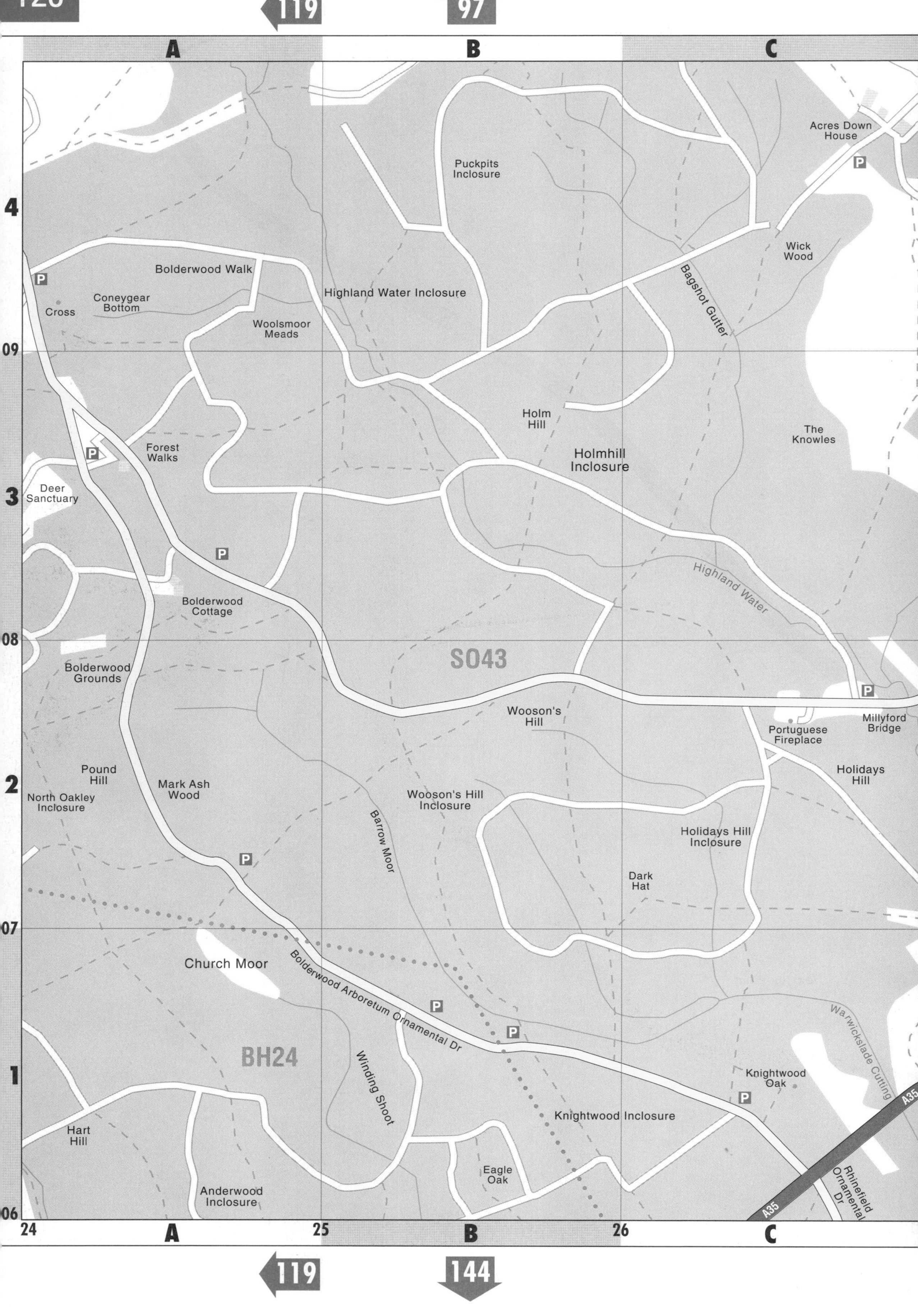
A
B
C
4
3
2
1
09
08
07
06
24
25
26
Acres Down House
P
Puckpits Inclosure
Wick Wood
Bolderwood Walk
Coneygear Bottom
Cross
Highland Water Inclosure
Woolsmoor Meads
Bagshot Gutter
Holm Hill
Holmhill Inclosure
The Knowles
Forest Walks
Deer Sanctuary
Bolderwood Cottage
Highland Water
SO43
Bolderwood Grounds
Wooson's Hill
Portuguese Fireplace
Millyford Bridge
Pound Hill
North Oakley Inclosure
Mark Ash Wood
Wooson's Hill Inclosure
Barrow Moor
Holidays Hill
Holidays Hill Inclosure
Dark Hat
Church Moor
Bolderwood Arboretum Ornamental Dr
Warwickslade Cutting
BH24
Winding Shoot
Knightwood Oak
A35
Hart Hill
Knightwood Inclosure
Eagle Oak
Anderwood Inclosure
Rhinefield Ornamental Dr

119
144

A
B
C
Fleet Water
Manor Park
Mill Stream
Acres Down Inclosure
Sinefield
Fish Pond Piece
Firry Piece Farm
Foldsgate Inclosure
Bunker's Hill
Pikes Hill
Beaulieu River
Pilmore Gate Heath
Acres Down
Fenwick
Pol HQ
Emery Down
Broom Hill
James Hill
Northerwood Park
Lyndhurst CE Inf Sch
Wood Crates
New Forest Inn (PH)
Lyndhurst Hill
Swan Green
Lyndhurst
PH
Liby
White Moor
Buckhill Hole
SO43
Cut Walk
White Shoot
Cuffnell's Farm
Foxlease Park
Foxlease House
New Forest Reptiliary
Allum Green
PH
Bank
Pinkney Farm
Warwick Slade
New Forest Gate House
Sewage Works
High Coxlease
Gritnam
Highland Water
Brick Kiln Inclosure
Gritnam Wood
A337
A35
ROMSEY RD
HIGH ST
BOURNEMOUTH RD
CHAPEL LA
SHRUBBS HILL RD
PINKNEY LA
SILVER ST
BOULTBEE COTTS
NORTHERWOOD HO
NORTHERWOOD AVE
GARDEN CL
WOODHAY
ROBERTSHAW HO
WESTWOOD RD
BROUGHTON RD
FOLDSGATE CL
PIKES HILL
PIKES HILL AVE
CALPE AVE
CUSTARDS RD
RACECOURSE VIEW
CLARENCE RD
CRANLEIGH PADDOCK
FOREST GDNS
QUEEN'S PAR
EMPRESS RD
KINGS CL
WELLANDS RD
KNIGHTWOOD CL
KNIGHTWOOD AVE
ELCOMBES CL
CHURCH LA
SHAGGS MDW
SHRUBBS HILL GDNS
HASKELLS CL
DEARING CL
SANDY LA
GREAT MEAD
THE MEADOWS
OAK CL
CEDARMOUNT
FIR CL
FOXLEASE TERR
4
09
3
08
2
07
1
06
27
28
29

121
99

121
146

A
B
C
Churchplace Inclosure
Church Place
Ashurst Wood
Deerleap Inclosure
Langley Cottage
New Forest Otter, Owl & Wildlife Pk
Langley Wood
DEERLEAP LA
The Homestead
NEW COTTS
Home Farm
Ashurst Lodge
Longdown Inclosure
Ashurst Walk
Fulliford Bog
SO40
Beaulieu River
Peel Hill
Matley Heath
Matley Wood
Matley Holms
Fulliford Passage
King's Passage
Withycombe Shade
Decoy Pond Farm
Matley Bog
Matley Passage
SO42
Church Place
SO43
Black Down
Hotel
STATION COTTS
Beaulieu Road
Stag Park
Shatterford Bottom
Denny Wood
B3056
4
09
3
08
2
07
1
06
33
34
35

123 101

123 148

125
102
126
A
B
C
SO14
SO40
SO45
SO42
River Test
Oaklands
LC
HYTHE RD
VEAL'S LA
Veal's Farm
Marchwood Priory
MARCHWOOD BY PASS
MAIN RD
CHURCH FARM CL
Church Farm
GARDEN CITY
Lock's Farm
Dibden
Dibden Manor Hotel
The Old Manor
LOCK'S COTTS
Talbot Farm
CH
West Cliff Hall
WATERSIDE SQ 1
JESSOP WLK 2
WESTCLIFFE WLK 3
PERCY CL 4
JESSOP CL
WEST ST
WEST HILL DR
DIBDEN LODGE CL
BEAUMARIS GDNS
SOUTHAMPTON RD
JONES LA
MANOR RD
Applemore Hill
Applemore
Roys Copse
ROOKSBRIDGE 1
RIDGEWOOD CL 2
ROCKRAM GDNS 3
RANMORE CT 4
ROUNDCOPSE 5
OCKNELL GR 6
EVEWORTH WLK 7
MAGNOLIA CL 8
ROCKERY CL
CLAYPITS LA
DRAPERS COPSE CVN SITE
Clayfields Sports Ctr
Draper's Copse
Home Farm
Depedene
MOUNTFIELD
LOWER MULLIN'S LA
DOUGLAS WAY
MICHAEL'S WAY
MALWOOD RD W
ROBERTS RD
MALWOOD RD
HOLLYBANK RD
HOLLYBANK CRES
SOLENT DR
FAIRWAY RD
FAIRFIELD CL
FERRY RD
DALE RD
WIDECOMBE DR
TAMAR GR
MERRIVALE CL
Fern Row
LAUREL CL
SYCAMORE RD
LANEHAYS RD
COPSEWOOD RD
HILLVIEW RD
CONIFER CL
FERN RD
HAWTHORN RD 1
BOUNDSTONE 2
UPPER MULLINS LA
THE MEAD
TORMEAD
MIDWAY
GLENSIDE
THE VALE
SUNNINGDALE
OVERBROOK
WHITTINGHAM CL
FAIRVIEW DR
Marchwood Inclosure
Sleepy Hollow
VAUGHAN RD
LATCHMORE DR
BROOMY CL
HAWKHILL
ROWHILL DR
RUSHPOLE CT
SIZER WAY
Superstore
CABOT DR
CYGNUS GDNS
COURTIER CL
CATHAY GDNS
CAVALIER CL
CHEVIOT DR
MORRIS CL
FLETCHER CL
ASHBURTON CL
CORSAIR DR
CAPELLA GDNS
CUMBERLAND WAY
CALEDONIA DR
CANTERBURY DR
CAMBRIA DR
COSWORTH DR
CORDELIA CL
CORINNA GDNS
Applemore Recn Ctr
Oak Lodge Specl Sch
Applemore Coll
REDWOOD CL
ALDER CL
FERNLEA WAY
THE SYLVANS
MOORLAND CL
THE BRACKENS
COTSWOLD CL
MALVERN DR
BRECON CL
Orchard Jun Sch
KILN CL
MARLBOROUGH CT
Orchard Inf Sch
OAKENBROW
PENNINE GDNS
KENSINGTON FIELDS
Noadswood Sec Sch
CHALLENGER WAY
BRENDON CL
MENDIP GDNS
MILNE CL
LEWIS CL
BUCHAN CT
HUXLEY CT
CROMALT CL
BRIARSWOOD RISE
OAKLANDS WAY
PENTLAND CL
CLEVELAND DR
BLACKDOWN CL
NORTH RD
WATER LA
LIME WLK
LIME CL
PEARTREE RD
ORCHARD WAY
BRAEHEAD
FOREST HILL WAY
PINE CL
THE WICKET
BYEWAYS
HEATH FIELD
GOLDEN HIND PK
DRAKES CL
HIGHLANDS WAY
VALLEYDENE
MILLERS WAY
SQUIRRELS WLK
BADGERS WLK
WHITEWATER RISE
DUKES WOOD DR
NOADS CL
NOADS WAY
Dibden Bottom
Dibden Inclosure
Horestone Hill
HYTHE BY PASS
ROMAN RD
BLENHEIM GDNS
NASH RD
NASH CL
DOWNWOOD CL 1
BROCKS CL 2
THE QUANTOCKS 3
ROMAN WAY
ROMAN GDNS
WELLINGTON CL
WEST RD
NORTH RD
BANFURLY GDNS
BEAULIEU RD
Dibden Purlieu
LAMBOURNE CL
WINDMILL COPSE
AMBERSLADE WLK
FOXTAIL DR
BULLRUSH CL
PARTRIDGE RD
LODGE DR
RATCLIFFE RD
Wildground Inf & Jun Schs
HAYNES WAY
MUIR HO
WOODLANDS CL
OAK CL
TALBOT RD
OAK RD
MANSELL CL
WHINFIELD RD
WATERMANS LA
CRETE COTTS
CRETE LA
CRETE RD
ARMITAGE AVE
HEATHERSTONE AVE
A326
P
PO
09
08
07
06
40
41
9
1
2
3
4
149
126
C1
1 MERRIEMEADE PAR
2 MERRIEMEADE CL
3 LONGWORTHY
4 THORNWORTHY
5 WOODLANDS CT
6 CHAVENEY CL

125
103
A
B
C
SO14
TEST RD
Docks
Mast
Ferry
Weston Shelf
Weston Hard
ROTHSCHILD CL
WESTON LA
HOLT CT
RIVERSDALE CL
INTERNATIONAL WAY
HAWKLEY GN
BURGHCLERE RD
SPARSHOLT RD
BRAMSHOTT RD
CROOKHAM RD
SO19
KINGSCLERE AVE
FOXCOTT CL
FULLERTON CL
HURSTBOURNE PL
CANBERRA TWRS
Weston Shore Inf Sch
Weston Park
WESTON PAR
Solent Way
C4
1 SQUIRES WLK
2 HAMPTON TWRS
3 HAVRE TWRS
4 OSLO TWRS
5 COPENHAGEN TWRS
6 ROTTERDAM TWRS
7 WESTON HOMES
8 GRATELEY CL
9 DRAYTON CL
SO31
MARINA VIEW
ABBEY HILL
4
09
Hythe Marina
Southampton Water
ENDEAVOUR WAY
SHAMROCK WAY
3
Hythe Pier Rly
Hythe Pier
Hythe Hard
Hythe
WEST ST
A3
1 WHITE HEATHER CT
2 VELSHEDA CT
3 ASTRA CT
4 WATERSIDE
5 MOUNT HOUSE CL
6 HAZELDALE VILLAS
7 HOMEBOROUGH HO
8 DRUMMOND CT
9 ADMIRALS WAY
DIBDEN LODGE CL
JONES LA
BRINTON LA
STEWART CL
PROSPECT PL
HIGH ST
THE PROMENADE
08
Hythe Prim Sch
PYLEWELL RD
THE MARSH
ST JOHN'S ST
SIR CHRISTOPHER CL
EMERALD CRES
SCOTT-PAINE DR
WADMORE CL
Liby
LC
SCHOOL RD
EDWARD RD
ALEXANDRA RD
ALEXANDRA CL
HOLLYDENE
LONGMEADOW GDNS
NEW RD
DOMINY CL
Pier
A2
1 MARSH PAR
2 NEW MARSH HO
3 DRUMMOND RD
4 COURT HOUSE CL
5 SIR CHRISTOPHER CT
6 LAWRENCE HO
7 MARINERS MEWS
8 HANOVER CT
9 THE SYCAMORES
10 FAIRFIELD CL
11 GREEN CL
12 HOLLYBANK CL
SOUTHAMPTON RD
ATHELING RD
CARPENTER CL
SOUTH ST
SPRING RD
PARK CL
SHORE RD
2
MALWOOD RD
FREEDOM CT
MOUSEHOLE LA
SO45
HOBART DR
GRAYS AVE
SEAWARD RD
HOLLYBANK CRES
KELVIN CL
COAT GDNS
LANGDOWN RD
HOWARD OLIVER HO
Langdown Jun Sch
ASHFORD CRES
ABBEY CL
HARVEY GDNS
FAIRVIEW DR
FAIRVIEW CL
LANGDOWN FIRS
LANGDOWN LAWN
WINDRUSH WAY
ELGIN CL
QUEENS CL
KNIGHTWOOD RD
HOME FARM CL
TATES RD
DEERLEAP CL
DEERLEAP WAY
07
LANGDOWN LAWN CL
WHITECROFT
ADAMS RD
BURNETT CL
TATES RD
GUILLEMOT CL
GANNET CL
CORMORANT DR
FULMAR DR
LC
Langdown
IPLEY WAY
LADYCROSS RD
LYTTON RD
CURLEW WLK
CURLEW DR
TERN CL
FAWLEY RD
BEAULIEU RD
GREATWOOD CL
FURZEY AVE
Langdown Inf Sch
Hythe
ROSE CL
FOXBURY CL
Furzey Piece
PINEWOOD CRES
BIRCH DALE PK
SPINNEY DALE
HIGHLANDS CL
BELVEDERE RD
MONT CL
BUTTS BRIDGE HILL
SUMMIT CL
ROSEBERY AVE
LAMMAS RD
PINEWOOD DR
FURZEDALE PK
SPINNEY GDNS
HARDY DR
HART HILL
1
DUKES RD
WINGLE DR
SADLERS LA
FROG HALL
LODGE DR
HARTLEY CL
ELIZABETH GDNS
GLEN
BUTTSBRIDGE RD
FERNHILLS RD
FURZEDALE GDNS
FROST LA
Furzedown Farm
Hotel
Frostlane
BUTTERCUP CL
ROSEBERY AVE
HEATHERSTONE AVE
CHALONER CRES
GRENVILLE GDNS
FAWLEY RD
Kitcher's Copse
Crampool Copse
BUTTS ASH GDNS
BUTTS ASH LA
FLEURET CL
Forest Lodge
Works
06
42
43
44
A
B
C
A1
1 FAIRVIEW PAR
2 KNIGHTSTONE GRANGE
3 HIGHLANDS WAY
4 FRAYSLEA
5 HARTLEY WLK
6 SILVERS END
7 ANDREW CL
8 WILDGROUND LA
9 NORTHBOURNE CL
10 SHOBLANDS WAY
11 SANDILANDS WAY
12 NELSON CT
13 FURZEDOWN MEWS
14 TRAFALGAR WAY
15 HAMILTON MEWS
16 CURLEW CL
125
150

104
128
A
B
C
Netley
Butlocks Heath
Hound
S019
S031
Chamberlayne Park Sch
West Wood
Abbey Fruit Farm
Ridge Farm
The Roll Call (PH)
Kestrel Farm
The Grange (PH)
Schs
Priors Heath Copse
Netley Abbey
Netley Castle (Conv Home)
Hound Farm
Hound Corner Fruit Farm
Abbey Hall
Hound Corner Ecology Park
Hamble Sec Sch
Netley Court Sch
Liby
Police Training Ctr
Hamble
Min Rly
Royal Victoria Country Park
Heritage Centre
Cemy
Airfield (disused)
West Wood
Hamble Prim Sch
LC
Recn Gd
Hamble Court Bsns Pk
Southampton Water
Works
Hamble Cliff
Solent Way
Depot
Works
Hamble Common
HAMBLE LA
B3397
1 DRAYTON CL
2 LONGSTOCK CL
3 LAMBERHURST CL
CHAMBERLAYNE RD 1
ASH CL 2
MAPLE CL 3
NIGHTINGALE CL 4
BATCHELOR GN 5
WOODLAND VIEW 6
THE OAKS 7
FOUNDRY CRES 8
SHOREWELL 1
NETTLESTONE 2
A3
1 MANCHESTER RD
2 ROSS MEWS
3 VICTORIA CT
4 ENGLEFIELD CT
5 GARFIELD RD
6 WYKEHAM CL
7 WINCHESTER CL
8 HOLMES CL
9 MORTIMER CL
10 CHAMBERLAYNE HO
11 CRICHTON HO
12 ASHBURTON HO
4
09
3
08
2
07
1
06
45
46
47
151
128

127
105

A
B
C
4
09
3
08
2
07
1
06
48
49
50
Bursledon
Bursledon Jun & Inf Schs
Cemy
Fox & Hounds (PH)
The Jolly Sailor (PH)
Yacht Marina
Lower Swanwick
Swanwick Bsns Ctr
Air Traffic Control Ctr
Works
Swanwick Nature Reserve
Swanwick Lodge
Hackett's Marsh
Jetty
Brooklands
Brooklands Farm
Lincegrove Marsh
Badnam Copse
UNIVERSAL MARINA
SO31
Sarisbury
Sarisbury CE Jun Sch
Coldeast
Lord Wilson Sch
Sarisbury Inf Sch
Brookfield Com Sch
Holly Hill Mansions
Wendleholme Nature Reserve
Holly Hill Woodland Park
Winnard's Copse
Cawte's Copse
River Hamble
Satchell Marsh
Hamble-le-Rice
IRB Sta
Solent Way
Ferry P
The Rising Sun (PH)
Hamble Common
Warsash
Fleetend
BRIDGE RD
A27
M27
B3397
1 YACHTSMAN CL
2 SWAN CT
1 LUKES CL
2 MARINA DR
1 ADMIRALS CT
2 HAMBLE MANOR
3 SOLENT MDWS
MALLOW CL 1
WOODBIND WLK 2
BURGUNDY CL 3
THE FAIRWAY 4
STONE CROP CL 5
SNAPDRAGON CL 6
LARKSPUR CL 7
SILVERWEED CT 8
WILLOW HERB CL 9
1 NORMANDY CT
2 TOWER CT
3 NEWTOWN CT
4 HAVELOCK CT
5 WARSASH CT
WEYBRIDGE CL 1
EDENBRIDGE WAY 2
UXBRIDGE CL 3

127
152

106
130

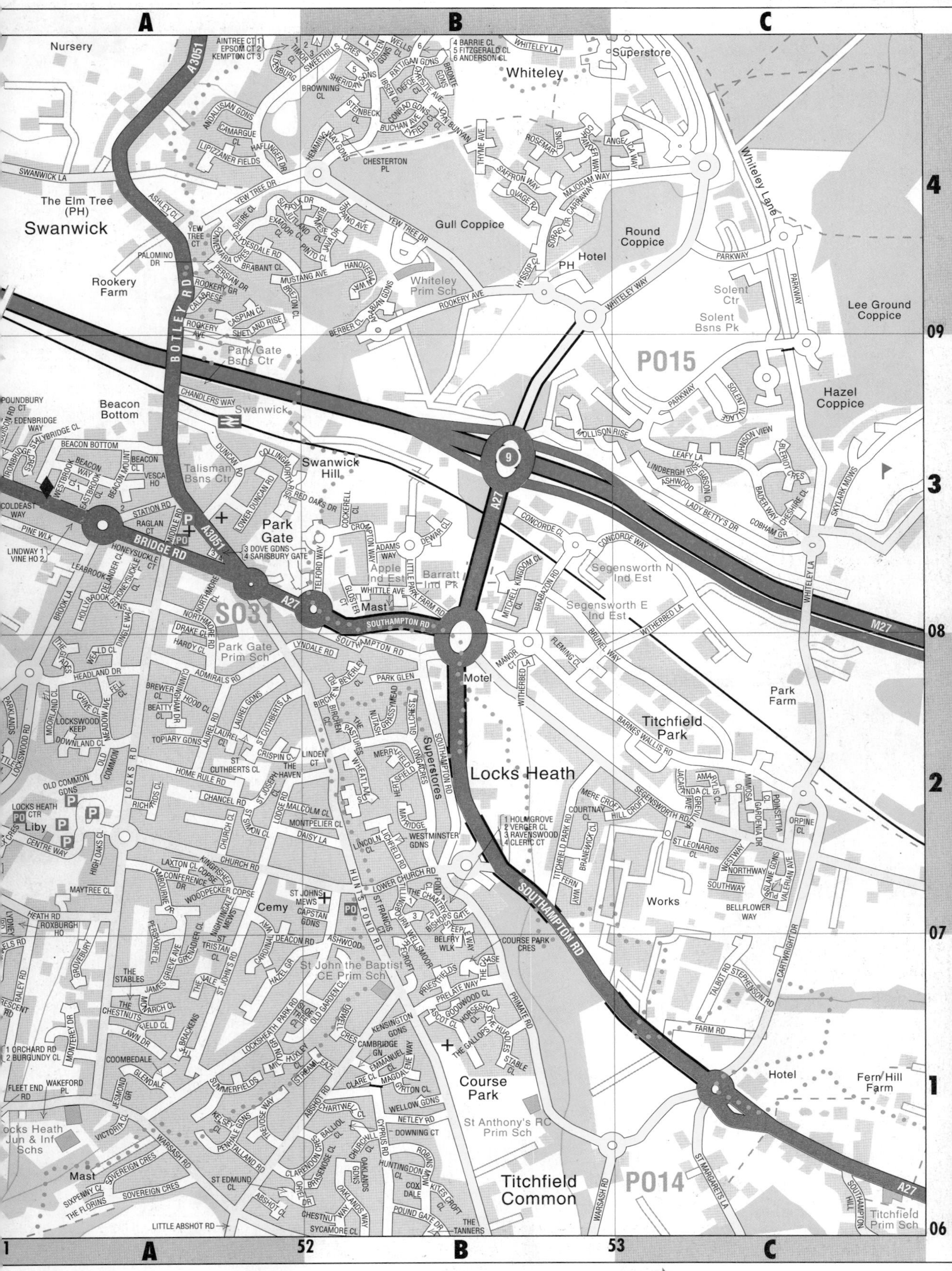

153
130

129
107

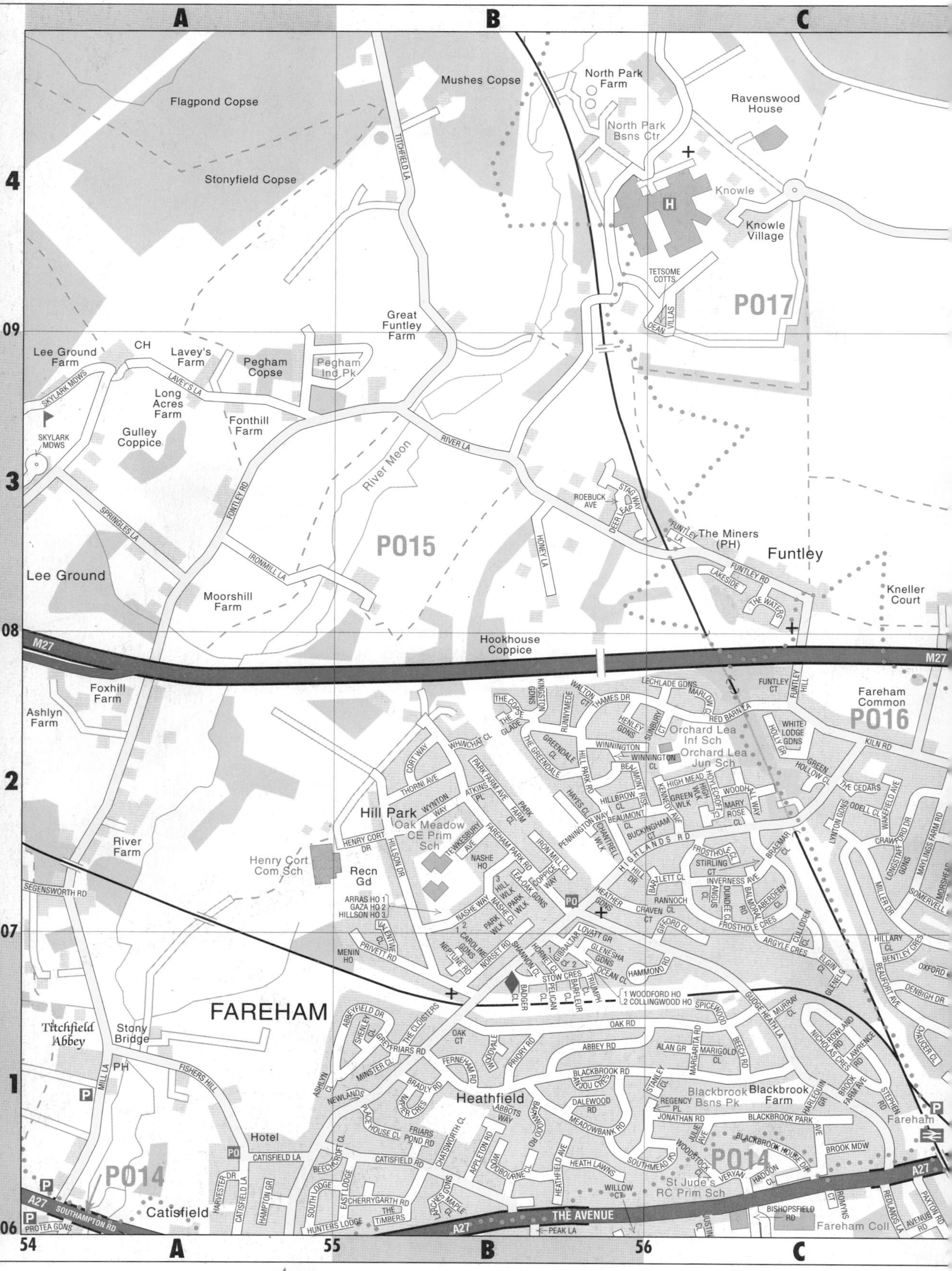

129
154

A1
1 ASHWOOD LODGE
2 ELMWOOD LODGE
3 BEECHWOOD LODGE
4 REDWOOD LODGE
5 PINEWOOD LODGE
6 CEDARWOOD LODGE
7 BIRCHWOOD LODGE
8 NORTHWOOD SQ
9 DARREN CT
10 KELLY CT
11 VICTORIA HO
12 MEADOW TERR
13 WEST END COTTS
14 WESTERN CT
15 DELME CT
16 MAYTREE RD
17 THE GILLIES
18 BURY HO
19 HOMEFAYRE HO
20 CHEQHERS HO
21 MORESBY CT
22 SAVOY BLDGS
23 DELME SQ
24 WESTBURY MALL
25 WESTBURY SQ
26 THACKERAY MALL

B1
1 TIVERTON CT
2 FERN COTTS
3 WALLINGTON HILL
4 THACKERAY SQ
5 OSBORN SQ
6 OSBORN MALL
7 CROOD CT
8 WESTQUAY HO
9 ADELAIDE PL

B1
10 MADISON CT
11 BATH LA
12 CEDAR CT
13 BATH LA (LOWER)
14 WALLINGTON SHORE RD
15 CHARLEMONT DR

131
109

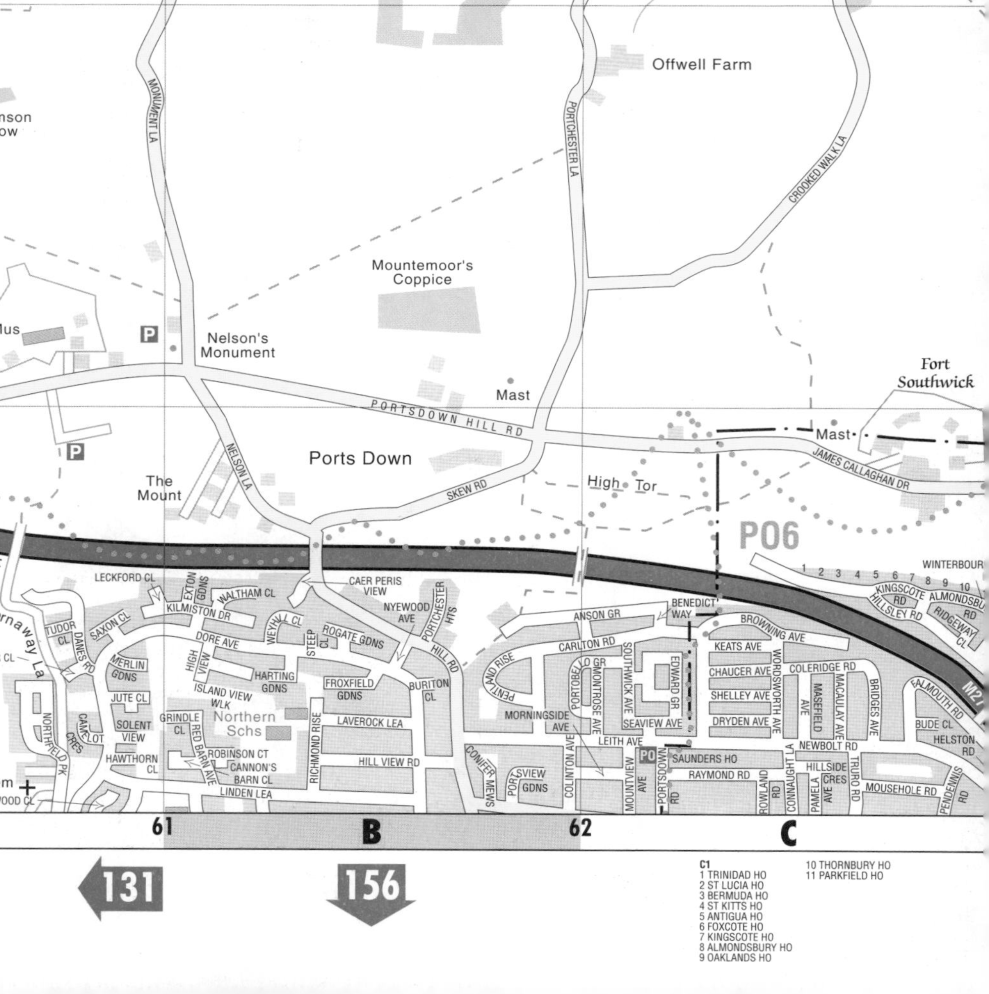

131
156

C1
1 TRINIDAD HO
2 ST LUCIA HO
3 BERMUDA HO
4 ST KITTS HO
5 ANTIGUA HO
6 FOXCOTE HO
7 KINGSCOTE HO
8 ALMONDSBURY HO
9 OAKLANDS HO
10 THORNBURY HO
11 PARKFIELD HO

133
110
134
A
B
C
Wynn's Copse
Jays Copse
Little Belney Copse
Belney Farm
Great Belney Copse
Place Wood
Assells Coppice
ssells Row
Hazelhook Coppice
Wanstead Farm
Sheepwash Farm
SHEEPWASH LA
Graysland Hummock
Short's Coppice
Ward's Coppice
Dunsland Coppice
Hobern Coppice
Lyeheath Farm
BOULTER LA
NORTH RD W
WOOD LA
NORTH RD E
WEST RD
MAIN DR
SOUTH RD
PRIORY RD
EAST RD
HMS Dryad
Southwick House
CH
Southwick Park Naval Recreation Centre
PO17
Lye Heath
Littlehunts Coppice
Wayfarer's Walk
Newlandsmoor Coppice
Comphouse Moor Coppice
Portland Coppice
Cooper Hill
Comphouse Farm
Sawyer's Wood
PINSLEY DR
Greathunts Coppice
Southwick Park Lake
PURBROOK HEATH RD
Broomground Coppice
Potwell Coppice
Hookheath Farm
Broomfield House
PIGEON HOUSE LA
Potwell Farm
DROVE RD
PITYMOOR LA
Pitymoor Coppice
Pinsley Coppice
Miller's Coppice
Pinsley Plantation
Potwell House
Ford
New Barns
Bushy Coppice
PO7
MILL LA
Mill Farm
Pigeon House Farm
WIDLEY WLK
SOUTHWICK RD
JAMES CALLAGHAN DR
Paulsgrove Chalk Pit
PO6
Ports Down
Fort Widley
Mast
Mus
PORTSDOWN HILL RD
B2177
SOUTHWICK HILL RD
ROCKROSE WAY
BUTTERFLY DR
CHALKPIT RD
LIME GR
LEOMINSTER HO
Paulsgrove
LEOMINSTER RD
DORSTONE RD
BLAKEMERE CRES
MEADOWSWEET WAY
HOLBEACH CL
DERSINGHAM CL
HARLESTON RD
SHERINGHAM RD
MABLETHORPE RD
FORT WIDLEY MARRIED QUARTERS
DORMINGTON RD
BREDENBURY CRES
LOWESTOFT RD
Wymering
LEDBURY RD
WILLERSLEY CL
WALSINGHAM CL
BOSTON RD
ARRAN CL
KINTYRE RD
SHETLAND CL
Queen Alexandra
CHEDWORTH CRES
HATHERLEY RD
WOOFFERTON RD
BRESLER HO
ELKSTONE RD
WINCHCOMBE RD
SEVERN CL
TARLETON RD
CLEEVE
MORTIMER RD
LUDLOW RD
COLLINGTON CRES
NORWICH RD
CROMER RD
PETERBOROUGH RD
HARWICH RD
COLCHESTER RD
ASHFORD CL
CAVELL DR
ORKNEY RD
COLESBOURNE RD
KINGSLAND CL
CREDENHILL RD
RAPSON CL
MAIDSTONE CRES
SEVENOAKS RD
ISLAY GDNS
BIRDLIP RD
NAILSWORTH RD
HEMPSTED RD
ARTILLERY CL
WALFORD RD
ABBEYDORE RD
BROMYARD CRES
FITZPATRICK CT
WASHBROOK RD
TUNSTALL RD
WYMERING LA
BRAINTREE RD
HYTHE RD
DEAL RD
H
A3
M27
ALMOUTH RD
BEVERSTON RD
DEERHURST CRES
MONDSBURY RD
INTERN
ILLSLEY RD
ILBURY HO
09
08
07
06
4
3
2
1
64
65
157
134
A1
1 LONGDEAN CL
2 WATERSHED CT
3 DEERHURST HO
4 BEVERSTON HO
5 NASEBY CL
6 AUSTIN CT
7 CAMCROSS CL
8 WITHINGTON CL
9 DESBOROUGH CL
10 BRAUNSTON CL
11 BRIXWORTH CL
12 ROTHWELL CL
13 NEWBOLT RD
14 DELLFIELD CL
15 ULLSWATER HO
16 ESKDALE HO
17 POTTERDALE HO
18 GRASMERE HO
19 CONISTON HO
20 RYDAL CL
21 LOWESWATER HO
22 RYDAL HO
23 THIRLMERE HO
24 BUTTERMERE HO
25 WASTWATER HO
26 SEATHWAITE HO
27 LUDLOW RD
28 ST MICHAEL'S CT
29 EDWARD'S CL
30 HUNTLEY CL
31 WESTBURY CL
32 CINDERFORD CL

133
111

C3
1 MILLENNIUM CT
2 DOGWOOD DELL
3 ROSEBAY CT
4 COLTSFOOT DR

C4
1 HINTON HO
2 DILLINGTON HO
3 REDWOOD CT
4 THE BEECHES
5 MARIE CT
6 JADE CT
7 HOMEWATER HO
8 QUEEN'S PAR
9 WELLINGTON WAY
10 ST GEORGES WLK
11 CLOCK HO
12 CHAPEL LA
13 DUKES WLK SERVICE RD
14 DUKES WLK

A
B
C
66
67
68

C1
1 BROOKFIELD CL
2 CHIDHAM WLK
3 WHYKE CT
4 COMPTON CT
5 WESTBOURNE CT
6 THE FORUM
7 RIVERSDALE GDNS
8 WELLINGTON CT
9 EAST VIEW TERR
10 MANOR CL
11 NORTH STREET ARC
12 MERIDIAN CTR
13 EMPIRE CT
14 GROVE CT
15 SLINDON GDNS
16 CLARENDON RD

135
113

A3
1 HOUGHTON CL
2 SYDMONTON CT
3 FOUR MARKS GN
4 WYEFORD CL
5 SOLDRIDGE CL
6 WARNBOROUGH CT
7 HEDGE END WLK
8 SHALDON RD
9 KIMPTON CT
10 BRADLEY CT
11 FREEFOLK GN
12 BLACKMOOR WLK
13 WARBROOK CT
14 CHILBOLTON CT
15 HURN CT
16 MONXTON GN
17 BURLEY CL
18 IFORD CT
19 SOPLEY CT
20 TIPTOE GN
21 SCOTNEY CT
22 WOODHAY WLK
23 YALDHURST CT
24 TYTHERLEY GN
25 HOLBURY CT
26 FULLERTON CL
27 MUSCLIFFE CT
28 TISTED CT
29 HECKFIELD CL

135

A3
30 WOOLMER CT
31 WHITE OAK WLK
32 OAKFIELD CT
33 WHERWELL CT
34 PENWOOD GN
35 MINLEY CT
36 SUMMERLANDS WLK
37 BRAMSHAW CT
38 FROYLE CT

160

A3
39 SWAY CT
40 PASSFIELD WLK
41 DEANE CT
42 STANFORD CT
43 FAWLEY CT
44 ROPLEY RD
45 KITWOOD GN
46 WORTHY CT
47 LASHAM GN
48 GOSPORT HO
49 LIPHOOK HO
50 ALDERSHOT HO
51 EILEEN BEARD HO
52 CURDRIDGE CL
53 HILTINGBURY RD
54 FURZEDOWN CRES
55 WOODINGTON CL
56 BROXHEAD RD
57 BROADMERE AVE
58 SOUTHAMPTON HO
59 BOURNEMOUTH HO
60 WINCHESTER HO

West Sussex STREET ATLAS
Holme Farm
Sussex Border Path
PO9
The Groves
Stubbermere
Racton Common
Pond Cottage
Pond Copse
Brickkiln Ponds
EMSWORTH COMMON RD
PARK LA
Sindle's Farm
New Barn Cottage
NEWBARN LA
Walderton
PO18
MONUMENT LA
Racton Mon
B2147
Aldsworth
Ell Bridge
Ellbridge Buildings
Ractonpark Wood
Aldsworth Manor
Aldsworth Common
Didmans Copse
COMMON RD
Westbourne Common
Valley Farm
Cricket Gd
Monk's Farm
MONK'S HILL
1 SILVERLOCK PL
2 LANSDOWN TERR
COMMONSIDE
Commonside
Hollybank Farm
LONG COPSE LA
Westbourne Cty Prim Sch
River Ems
FOXBURY LA
Woodmancote
PO10
Deepsprings
BECKENHAM TERR
MALLARD WAY
Westbourne
Woodmancote Farm
Bishop Barn Farm
Manor House
WOODMANCOTE LA
The Woodmancote Arms (PH)
EAST ST
Cemy
Chantry Farm
CEMETERY LA
South Lane Farm
WALNUT TREE DR
DUFFIELD LA
Hampshire Farm
The Wren Ctr
WESTBOURNE RD
RIVERMEAD CT
CHURCH VIEW 1
VICTORIA TERR 2
JUBILEE TERR 3
Lumley Farm
New Brighton
SOUTH LA
A27
A27 Chichester
OLD FARM LA
BROOK COTTS
WEST VIEW COTTS
HITHER GN
FRASER GDNS
BREACH AVE
PO18
MILL LA
Lumley Croft
Lumley Mill Farm
Works
Bourne Com Coll
Breach
Loveders Farm
Lumley
1 VICTORIA TERR
2 RAGLAN TERR
3 LUMLEY TERR
PRIORS LEAZE LA
Inlands Farm
Inlands
COOKS LA
HURSTWOOD AVE
GUILDFORD CL
MANOR WAY
MANOR RD
A
B
C
4
09
3
08
2
07
1
06
76
77

161

A B C

4
05
3
04
2
03
1
02

06 07 08

Clump Hill Farm
Skies Farm
Upper Mannington Farm
Mannington
BURT'S LA
Jubilee Farm
Lower Mannington
Mannington Copse
Mannington Farm
Cross Keys (PH)
Summerlug Hill
Holt Heath
Holt Heath
Ferndown Forest
Clayford Farm
Hamwoods Copse
Dolman's Crossing
Uddens Plantation
FOREST LINKS RD
AMEYSFORD RD
Ameysford
Uddens Water
A31
A31
Dolman's Farm
Broadmoor Coppice
Pennington's Copse
HORTON RD
HOLT RD
BH21
Barewood Copse
Haddons Farm
HADDONS DR
Newman's Farm
NEWMAN'S LA
Newman's Farm South
BH22
Gullivers Farm
Sturt's Farm
WEST MOORS RD
WEST MOORS RD
THREE CROSS RD
NEWMANS CL
PAYNE CL
ALBANY DR
WEST AVE
FRYER
RD
CHURCH RD
BAY CL
EVERGREEN CL
JOYS RD
JUNIPER CL
PO
B3072
VERWOOD RD
FURZELANDS RD
Earles Rd
Three Legged Cross
Homestead Farm
PH
1 BRACKENDALE CT
2 GREYCOT CL
3 HERMITAGE CL
4 SAINTS CL
RINGWOOD RD
DYMEWOOD RD
Gundry's Farm
Nursery
Kingfisher Pk
COLLINGWOOD RD
Minster Pk
Depot
JIMMY BROWN AVE
SARUM AVE
SARUM AVE
WOODSIDE RD
HIGHFIELD RD
DENEWOOD RD
BOND AVE
RITCHIE PL
DENEWOOD COPSE
PINE WLK
West Moors
THE AVENUE
BLACKFIELD LA
FIR CL
HARRISON WAY
West Moors St Mary's CE Fst Sch
HESTON WAY
ASHURST RD
ARNOLD CL
ARNOLD RD
BRIDGES CL
MOORLANDS RISE
BRAESIDE RD
FOREST RD
West Moor Plantation
GARDEN COURT COTTS
CASTLEMAN CT
PO
NEWCOMBE RD
CHARNWOOD CL
MOORLANDS RD
SUMMERCROFT WAY
MARY LA
RIVERSIDE RD
PULLMAN CT
Liby
GLENWOOD WAY
KNIGHTSTONE GR
STATION RD
GLENWOOD CL
GLENWOOD RD
BELLE VUE GR
KINGFISHER CL
OAKHURST CL
OAKHURST LA
GLENWOOD LA
FIRS GLEN RD
SHIRLEY CL
OAKHURST RD
UPLANDS RD
MANNINGTON WAY
FARM RD
BIRCH GR
PENN CT
PARK WAY
PENNINGTON RD
PENNINGTON CRES
PENNINGTON CL
QUEENS CL
KINGS CL
MOORSIDE RD
AVON RD
FERNSIDE RD
Sch
SHAFTESBURY CL
SHAFTESBURY RD
HARDY CL
HARDY RD
ELMHURST RD
ELMHURST WAY
HEATHFIELD WAY
SPINNERS CL
WEAVERS CL
TEASEL WAY
PINEHURST RD
WOOLSLOPE GDNS
SOUTHDOWN WAY
WOOLSLOPE RD
WOOLSLOPE CL
CANTERBURY CL
MERINO WAY
BEECHWOOD RD
West Moors Mid Sch
B3072

115
140
Lower Common
Visitor Centre
Moors Valley Country Park
BH21
Ashley Heath
Homeland Farm
Ashley Heath Ind Est
RINGWOOD RD
PH
Woolsbridge Manor Farm
CRANE WAY
VICTORY CL
THORNE WAY
Woolsbridge
Depot
Woolsbridge Ind Est
LIBERTY CL
Wools Bridge
Ashley Heath Caravan Park
Ashley Heath
HORTON RD
Woolsbridge Farm
AZURA CL
CONDOR CL
Egypt
Little Lions Farm
Castleman Trailway
Lions Hill
Lions Hill Farm
Lions Hill Way
Moors River
BH24
St Leonards
Racehorse Heath
Hotel
West Moors Plantation
BH22
Oakhill Farm
Hill Farm
Shamba
East Moors Farm
RINGWOOD RD
Barnsfield Wood
Mast
BOUNDARY LA
St Leonards
Grange Estate
A31
166
140

139
116

A B C

4
05
3
04
2
03
1
02

LINDEN GDNS 1
MANOR GDNS 2
LINDEN CT 3
THE SWEEP 4
FURLONG MEWS 5
ELMSDOWN CT 6
MONMOUTH CT 7
NORTHUMBERLAND CT 8
PEDLARS WLK 9
MANSFIELD RD 10
STEPHENS WLK 11
MARY MITCHELL CL 12
KING'S ARMS ROW 13
FRIDAY'S CT 14
THE GRANARY 15
GRANARY MEWS 16

QUAKER CT 1
ANDROSE GDNS 2

1 GREENWOOD WAY
2 GREENWOOD COPSE

Baker's Hanging
Ashley Heath
Watchmoor Wood
Ashley Trailway
Castleman Trailway
Holly Grove Farm
Ringwood Waldorf Sch
The Sheiling Sch
Ashley
St Ives House
St Ives Fst Sch
St Ives
BH24
David's Hill
Whitehouse Wood
The Rowans
The Warren
Avon Heath Country Park (North Park)
The Chalet
Barnsfield Wood
Visitor Ctr
Nature Reserve
Avon Heath Country Park (South Park)
Caravan & Camping Site
Leybrook Common
Avon Heath Country Park (South Park)
Kitten's Farm
Oakford Coppice
Avon Castle
Westover Farm
King Stream
Weir
PH
River Avon
Bickerley Mill Stream
Avon Valley Path
Black Firs
Kingston North Common
Haskell's Pond
Moorhouse Farm
Kingston Farm
Lib

B3081
VERWOOD RD
RINGWOOD RD
A31
A338
SALISBURY RD
B3347
HORTON RD
HURN RD
HURN LA
AVON PARK
HURN CL
WESTOVER LA
WARREN DR
WARREN CL
WARREN LA
GREEN ACRES CL
CASTLE MEWS
CASTLEWOOD
DAVID'S LA
THE CHASE
THE CLOSE
WINDMILL LA
WINDMILL CL
AVON CASTLE DR
AVON AVE
AVON CASTLE
EGMONT DR
EGMONT CL
EGMONT GDNS
CHAPEL RISE
FOLLY FARM LA
STRUAN GDNS
ASHLEY PARK
STRUAN DR
STRUAN CT
WHITFIELD PARK
ST IVES WOOD
ST IVES PARK
STRODE GDNS
RUSSELL GDNS
HESKETH CL
SANDY LA
PINEHOLT CL
FRINWOOD CL
LANGLEY CHASE
COMPTON BEECHES
LARCH CL
AZALEA CL
POST OFFICE LA
SCHOOL LA
THE CLOSE
ST IVES END LA
GLENIVES CL
BIRCH RD
PLANT PARK RD
ALPINE RD
EUCALYPTUS AVE
BARNSFIELD RD
BOUNDARY LA
MERTON GR
GRAVEL LA
SOUTHAMPTON RD
STALLARDS LA
THE FURLONG
CENTRE PL
HOUSE LA
MEETING HOUSE LA
STAR LA
MARKET PL
WEST ST
HIGH ST
THE CLOSE
NEW CT
STRIDES LA
HANDLEY CT
THE BRIDGES
WHITE LION CTYD
DEWEYS LA
LYNE'S LA
KING'S ARMS LA
KINGSBURY'S LA
GOOSEBERRY LA
EBENEZER LA
CHRISTCHURCH RD
BICKERLEY TERR
BICKERLEY RD
BICKERLEY GDNS
EYNON MEWS
RIVERSIDE
OLD MILL HO

12 13 14
A B C

139
167

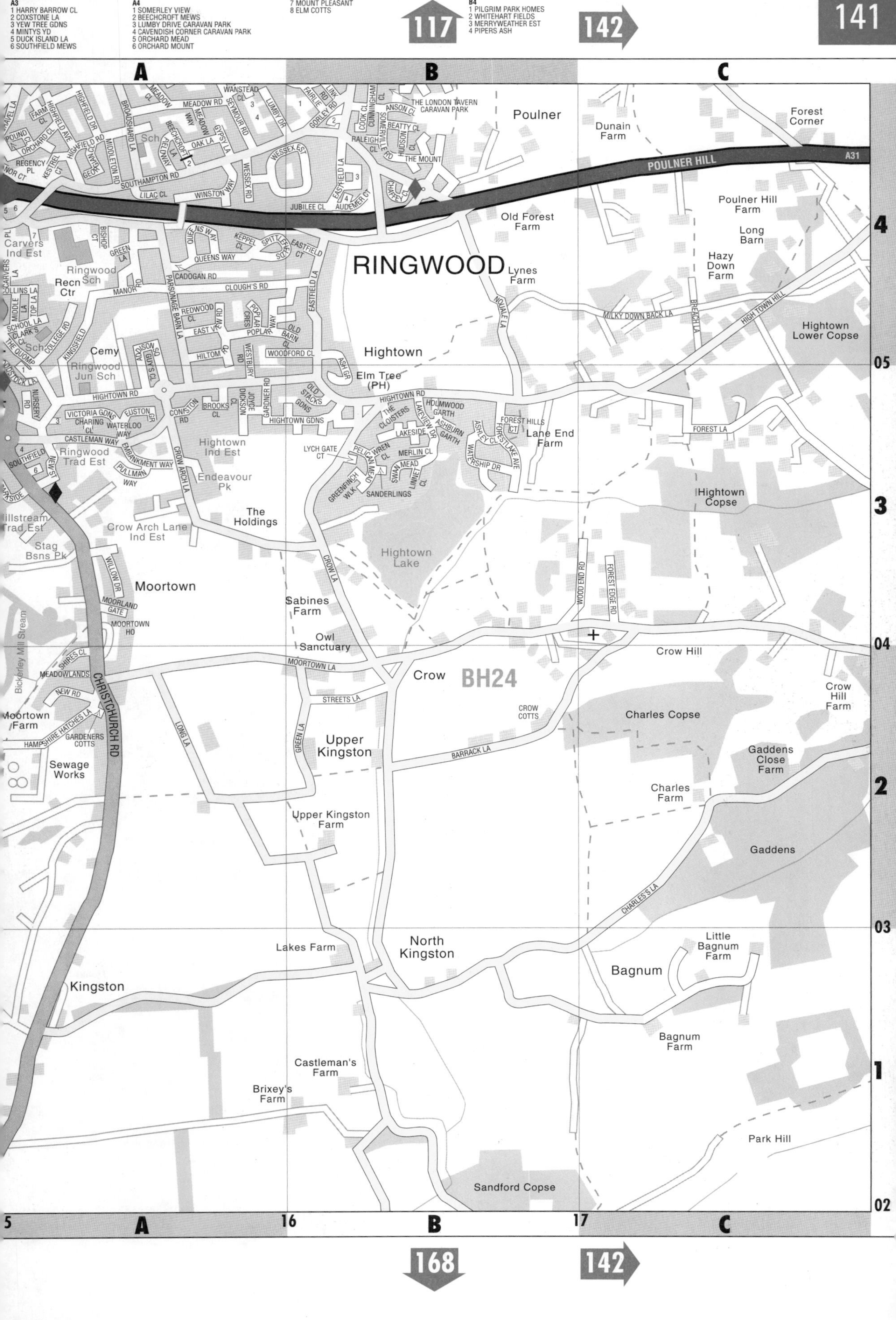

141
117
142
168
A3
1 HARRY BARROW CL
2 COXSTONE LA
3 YEW TREE GDNS
4 MINTYS YD
5 DUCK ISLAND LA
6 SOUTHFIELD MEWS
A4
1 SOMERLEY VIEW
2 BEECHCROFT MEWS
3 LUMBY DRIVE CARAVAN PARK
4 CAVENDISH CORNER CARAVAN PARK
5 ORCHARD MEAD
6 ORCHARD MOUNT
7 MOUNT PLEASANT
8 ELM COTTS
B4
1 PILGRIM PARK HOMES
2 WHITEHART FIELDS
3 MERRYWEATHER EST
4 PIPERS ASH
A
B
C
RINGWOOD
Poulner
Dunain Farm
Forest Corner
POULNER HILL
A31
Poulner Hill Farm
Old Forest Farm
Long Barn
Hazy Down Farm
Lynes Farm
Hightown Lower Copse
Hightown
Elm Tree (PH)
Lane End Farm
Hightown Copse
Hightown Lake
Hightown Ind Est
Endeavour Pk
The Holdings
Ringwood Trad Est
Crow Arch Lane Ind Est
Stag Bsns Pk
Carvers Ind Est
Ringwood Sch
Recn Ctr
Cemy
Ringwood Jun Sch
Moortown
Sabines Farm
Owl Sanctuary
Crow
BH24
Crow Hill
Crow Hill Farm
Charles Copse
Gaddens Close Farm
Charles Farm
Gaddens
Upper Kingston
Upper Kingston Farm
Moortown Farm
Sewage Works
CHRISTCHURCH RD
Lakes Farm
North Kingston
Kingston
Bagnum
Little Bagnum Farm
Bagnum Farm
Castleman's Farm
Brixey's Farm
Park Hill
Sandford Copse
MILKY DOWN BACK LA
HIGH TOWN HILL
BREACH LA
FOREST LA
HIGHTOWN RD
CROW LA
MOORTOWN LA
STREETS LA
GREEN LA
LONG LA
BARRACK LA
CHARLES'S LA
WOOD END RD
FOREST EDGE RD
NOVALE LA
CROW ARCH LA
CROW COTTS
05
04
03
02
4
3
2
1
5
16
17

141
118

A
B
C
A31
Picket Plain
Ridley Wood
Ridley Green
Picket Hill
Foulford
Foulford Bottom
Mill Lawn Brook
Vereley Wood
Vereley Farm
Turf Croft Farm
Foulford Farm
Mast
Vereley
Box Berry Hill
Vereley Hill
Smugglers Road
Burley Croft
Whitemoor
COACH HILL LA
Hurn Farm
FOREST LA
Common Moor
Broad Bottom
FOREST RD
RINGWOOD RD
Forest Farm
Vales Moor
RANDALL'S LA
PO
Little Castle Common
Knaves Ash
Burley Street
Stocks Farm
TYRELLS LA
CROW HILL TOP
Castle Hill
CHARLES'S LA
BH24
Sandys
LONGMEAD RD
Gritenbury Farm
Strodgemoor Bottom
Black Bush
Sandy Shoot
Burley Hill House
Coffins Holms
CASTLE HILL LA
CLOUGH LA
ESDAILE LA
GARDEN RD
HONEY LA
Church Moor
Campden House
Bagnum Rough
Cranes Moor
COPSE RD
Burley Beacon
WARNES LA
POUND LA
Kingston Great Common
Burnt Axon
MEADOW CL
Shappen
Pound Farm
SHAPPEN HILL LA
Bagnum Bog
Muddy Lane
Brown Loaf
Chubb's Farm
Slap
4
05
3
04
2
03
1
02
18
19
20

141
169

119
144
A
B
C
Sir Dudley's Ride
Berry Wood
Burley Outer Rails Inclosure
Burley Lodge
Springwood Cottages
South Oakley Inclosure
Southmead Cottage
Turf Croft
Burley Walk
White Moor Bottom
Great Early
Depot
Black Hill
Burley New Inclosure
LYNDHURST RD
Lucy Hill
Burley Moor
WOOD'S CNR
Brookside Farm
FOREST RD
North Farm
Little Early
Cockroad Hill
Burley Grange
Mill Lawn House
Redrise Hill
MILL LA
Mill Lawn
BURLEY LAWN
Mill Lawn Brook
Burley Manor Hotel
Fords
Burley Lawn
CHAPEL LA
Burley
Burley Rocks
The Queens Head Hotel
BEECHWOOD LA
LESTER SQ
DOVEYS CL
THE MALL
RINGWOOD RD
Shoot Wood
HOWARD CL
THE CROSS
CHURCH LA
Burley Prim Sch
POUND LA
PO
CH
Creek Bottom
Bisterne Close
The White Buck Inn
SOUTHFIELD LA
COTT LA
YH
BENNETTS LA
BISTERNE CL
Rock Hills
MOORHILL RD
Shappen Farm
The Burrows
Hotel
Pigsty Hill
Turf Hill
Clay Hill
Cot Bottom
STATION RD
Shappen Hill
Broadoak Bottom
Shappen Bottom
Holman's Bottom
21
22
23
170
144

143
120

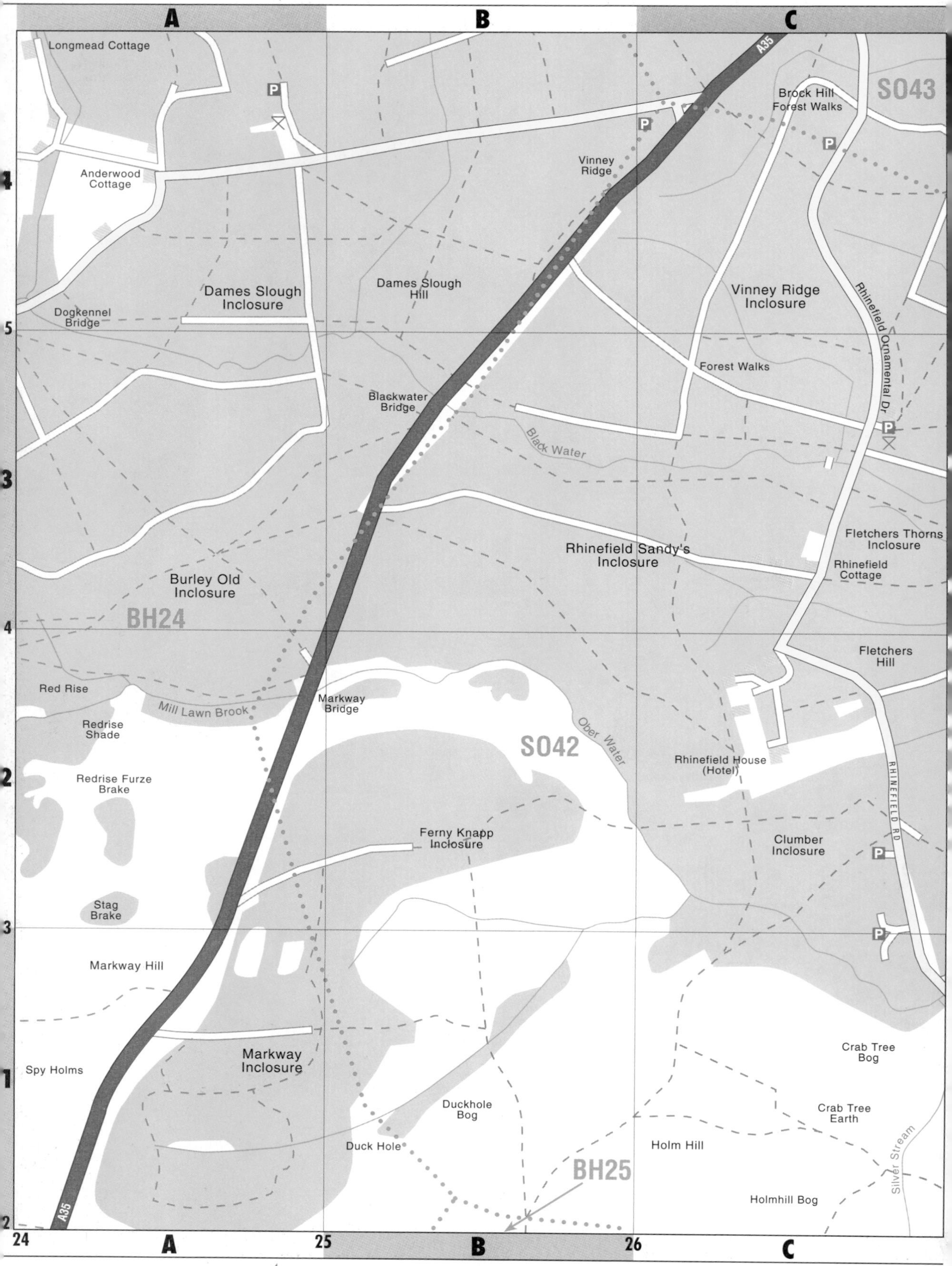

143
171

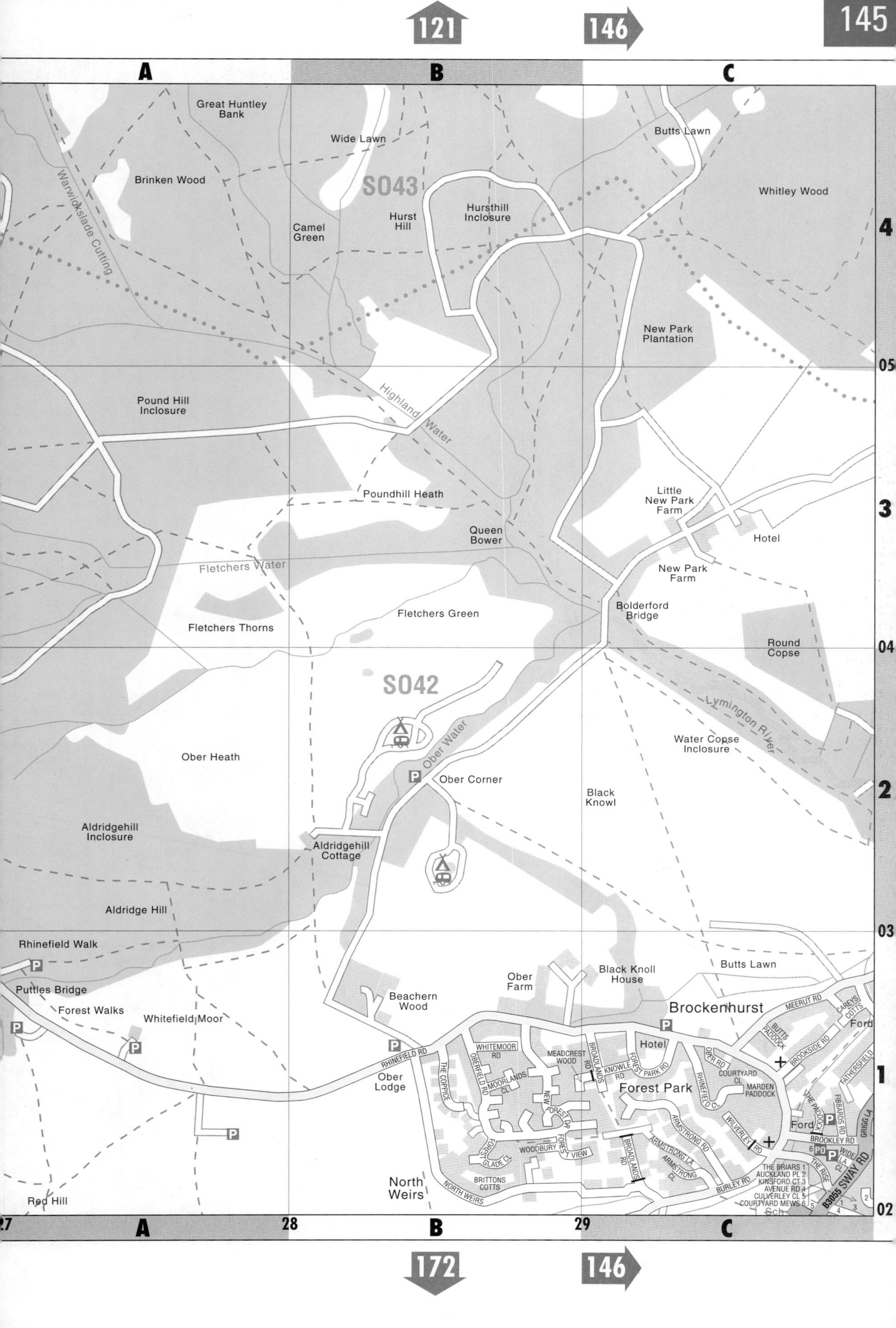
145
121
146
A
B
C
Great Huntley Bank
Wide Lawn
Butts Lawn
Brinken Wood
Warwickslade Cutting
SO43
Hurst Hill
Hursthill Inclosure
Camel Green
Whitley Wood
4
New Park Plantation
05
Pound Hill Inclosure
Highland Water
Poundhill Heath
Little New Park Farm
Hotel
3
Queen Bower
Fletchers Water
New Park Farm
Bolderford Bridge
Fletchers Thorns
Fletchers Green
Round Copse
04
SO42
Lymington River
Water Copse Inclosure
Ober Water
Ober Heath
Ober Corner
Black Knowl
2
Aldridgehill Inclosure
Aldridgehill Cottage
Aldridge Hill
03
Rhinefield Walk
Butts Lawn
Black Knoll House
Ober Farm
Puttles Bridge
Beachern Wood
Brockenhurst
Forest Walks
Whitefield Moor
MEERUT RD
CAREYS COTTS
BUTTS PADDOCK
Ford
Hotel
WHITEMOOR RD
RHINEFIELD RD
MEADCREST WOOD
BROADLANDS RD
KNOWLE RD
FOREST PARK RD
OBER RD
BROOKSIDE RD
COURTYARD CL
MARDEN PADDOCK
1
Ober Lodge
THE COPPICE
OBERFIELD RD
MOORLANDS CL
Forest Park
RHINEFIELD CL
FATHERSFIELD
NEW FOREST DR
THE PADDOCK
FIBBARDS RD
GRIGG LA
Ford
ARMSTRONG RD
WILVERLEY RD
BROOKLEY RD
FOREST GLADE CL
WOODBURY CL
FOREST VIEW
ARMSTRONG LA
BROADLANDS RD
PO
WIDE LA CL
THE RISE
B3055 SWAY RD
ARMSTRONG CL
THE BRIARS 1
AUCKLAND PL 2
KINSFORD CT 3
AVENUE RD 4
CULVERLEY CL 5
COURTYARD MEWS 6
BRITTONS COTTS
BURLEY RD
North Weirs
NORTH WEIRS
Red Hill
Sch
02
27
28
29
172
146

145
122

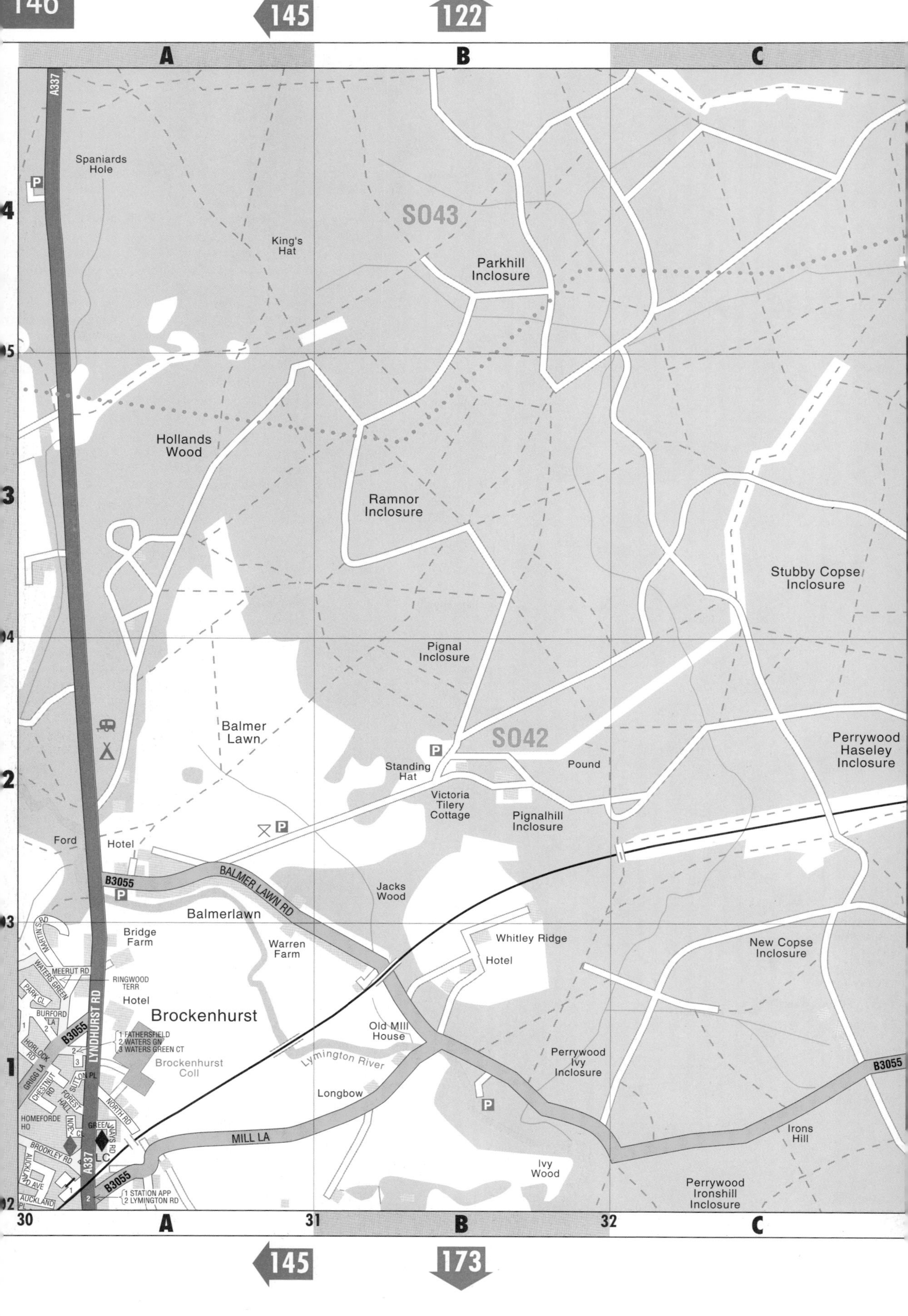

145
173

123
148

A
B
C
Denny Wood
Denny Lodge
B3056
Stephill Bottom
4
Woodfidley Passage
Furzy Brow
05
Bishop of Winchester's Purlieu
Denny Lodge Inclosure
Penny Moor
3
Woodfidley
Rowbarrow
SO42
04
LC
Frame Heath Inclosure
2
Frame Wood
03
Ladycross Inclosure
Moon Hill
Ladycross Lodge
1
Worts Gutter
Hawkhill Inclosure
Lodge Heath
Stockley Inclosure
Little Wood
B3055
02
33
34
35

174
148

147
124

A
B
C
SO40
Buck Hill
King's Hat Cottage
King's Hat Inclosure
Ferny Crofts (Scout Ctr)
B3056
Gurnetfields Furzebrake
Ford
Starpole Pond
Culverley Old Farm
Pig Bush
Culverley Farm
Foxhunting Inclosure
NORTH LA
Honey Hill
Halfpenny Green
Shepton Bridge
Gurnet Fields
North Gate
Shepton Water
The House in the Wood
Penerley Water
Penerley Wood
SO42
Beaulieu River
Little Goswell Copse
Little Honeyhill Wood
Penerley Gate
Penerley Farm
Hides Hill La
Tantany Wood
Hartford Bridge
Penerley Lodge
Leygreen Farm
Hides Close
Stubbs Wood
Black Bridge
Hartford Copse
Abbotstanding Wood
Wood La
The National Motor Mus
Beaulieu Abbey (remains of)
Works Gutter
Palace House
PALACE LA
B3054
Furzey Lodge
FURZEY LA
Pit Copse
Hotel
Mill
PONDSIDE FLATS 1
DITTON COTTS 2
CLITHEROE COTTS 3
HIGH ST
PO
Beaulieu
B3056
B3054
Beaulieu Village Prim Sch
4
05
3
04
2
03
1
02
36
37
38

147
175

A
B
C
Dibden Inclosure
The Noads
Crabhat Inclosure
A326
B3054
HYTHE BY PASS
Solent Way
Fawley Inclosure
Flash Pond
Nature Reserve
BEAULIEU RD
Harford House
Hartford Heath
Beaulieu Heath
SO45
SO42
Stonyford Pond
Holbury Purlieu
Great Goswell Copse
Hilltop Farm
Hill Top
Hilltop Wood
Hilltop House
Royal Oak (PH)
Boarman Pond
Moonhills Gate
Moonhills Copse
MOONHILLS LA
PALACE LA
Home Farm
Carpenters Cottage
DOCK LA
Otterwood
Otterwood Gate
Otterwood Farm House
SUMMER LA
Stock Water
Cowleys La
Cowleys Copse
4
05
3
04
2
03
1
02
40
41

149
126
A
B
C
Forest Lodge Farm
Gringo's Copse
Buttsash
Works
Factory
Lammas Wood
Reservoir
Hardley Lane
Solent Way
HYTHE BY PASS
A326
Mast
Hardley Ind Est
Hardley Bridge (ford)
Hardley
Chevron Bsns Pk
Flare
Little Holbury Farmhouse
The Old Mill (PH)
Hardley Sch & Sixth Form
Little Holbury
SO45
LONG LA
Oil Refinery
Holbury Purlieu
Manor Inf Sch
Dark Water
Holbury
Holbury Manor
Holbury Schs
Flares
Stonyford Hill
Kennels Row
B3053
FAWLEY RD
Ipers Bridge Farm
Bridge Tavern (PH)
ROLLESTONE RD
Rollestone Farm
Gang Warily Recn Ctr
Beaulieu Heath
Green Lane
Green Rollestone Copse
Roughdown
Blackfield Jun Sch
Blackfield Inf Sch
Blackfield
King's Copse Inclosure
Row Down
Cutler's Copse
Liby
Bsns Ctr
42
43
44
149
177

127
152
A
B
C
Jetty
Southampton Water
Cadland Creek
4
05
Pier
Marine Terminal
Pier
Pier
3
FORESHORE N
FORESHORE S
NORTH TRESTLE RD
PLPH RD
BURMAH RD N
BURMAH RD S
JETTY RD
SOUTH TRESTLE RD
E AVE
J AVE
CADLAND RD
OLD AGWI RD
AGITATOR RD
SEPS 4 RD
BITUMEN RD
FLUME RD
D AVE
C AVE
2ND ST
1ST ST
B AVE
A AVE
04
SO45
2
Fawley
MARSH LA
RYE PADDOCK LA
CHURCHFIELDS
COPTHORNE COTTS
COPTHORNE LA
GRAHAM
SHERRIN CL
CHURCH LA
ADMIRALS CL
ASHLETT CL
ASHLETT RD
STONEHILLS
Liby
PO
Fawley Inf Sch
Fawley Bsns Ctr
SOUTH AVE
ORCHARD CL
WOODVILLE RD
COLEVILLE AVE
LINDA RD
FOREST EDGE
SCHOOL RD
DENNY CL
FIELDS
FALCON
THE LANE
CALSHOT RD
FAWLEY RD
FAWLEY BY PASS
THE PENTAGON
CHAPEL LA
P
Ashlett Creek
The Jolly Sailor (PH)
Ashlett
03
HAMLET CT 1
MEADOW WAY 2
THE PADDOCKS 3
CHARLES LEY CT 4
WHITES LA 5
FORGE LA 6
ASHLETT MEWS 7
RHYME HALL MEWS 8
Stone Hill Farm
Stonehills
NORTHERN ACCESS RD
NORTHERN RD
SWITCH HOUSE RD
EASTERN RD
CENTRAL WAY N
HALFWAY RD
WRIGHT WAY
BOILER RD
WESTERN RD
CHANNEL MOUTH RD
Fawley Power Station
1
Fields Farm
Badminston Farm
Fields Heath
BADMINSTON LA
Swing Bridge
Chy
Tom's Down
Badminston Common
BADMINSTON DRO
B3053
LOWER LA
SOUTHERN RD
QUAYSIDE RD
02
45
A
46
B
47
C
178
152

151
128

A
B
C
S031
Hamble Point Marina
River Hamble
Newtown
Sch
Hook Lake
Warsash Maritime Ctr (Southampton Inst)
Nature Reserve
Hamble Spit
Hook Park
Solent Way
Workman's Lane
S031
Solent Court Farm
Solent Court
Solent Breezes Cvn Site
Southampton Water
NEWTOWN RD
QUEEN'S RD
BEVIS CL
SHELLCROFT
MEADCROFT CL
OSBORNE RD
HEWETTS RISE
PITCHPONDS RD
UPPER SPINNEY
LOWER SPINNEY
GLENDA CL
ROMFORD RD
ROSSAN AVE
JUMAR CL
HOWERTS CL
HORNBY CL
SPENSER CL
CHEVIOT GN
CHURCH RD
ASPEN AVE
ELMDALE CL
SPRUCE CL
OAKWOOD CL
NEW RD
DIBLES RD
FLEET END BOTTOM
FLEET END RD
HOOK COTTS
1 BEECHWOOD CL
2 LARCHDALE CL
3 BIRCHDALE CL
4 SANDYCROFT
GILCHRIST GDNS
HOOK PARK RD
SOLENT DR
COWES LA
CHILLING LA
S045
Nature Reserve
Lifeboat Sta
Pier
Calshot Castle
S045
Calshot Activities Ctr
S045
Calshot
Hillhead
B3053
Stanswood Bay
02
01
48
49
4
05
3
04
2
03
1
02
48
A
49
B
50
C

151

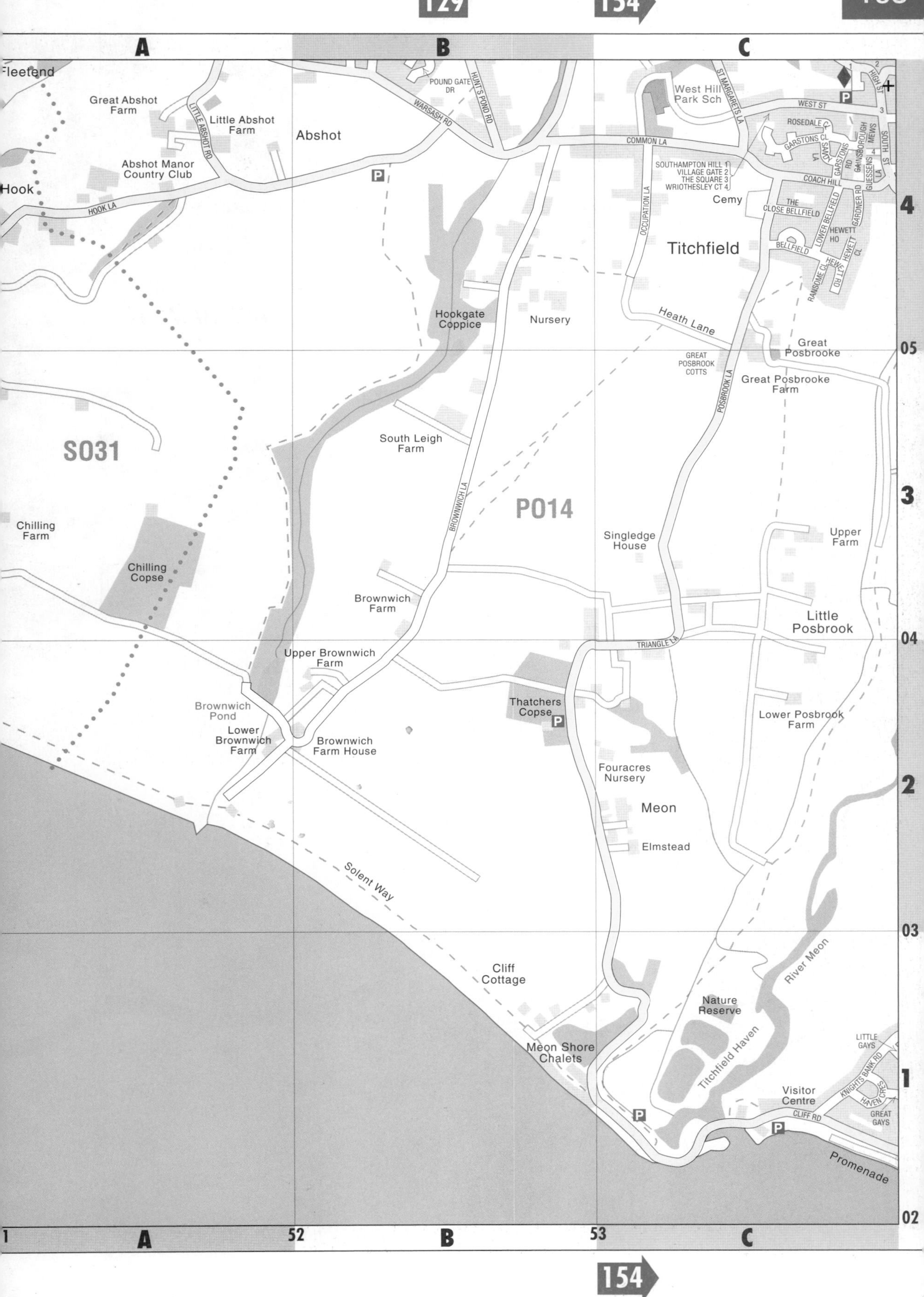
A
B
C
Fleetend
Great Abshot Farm
Little Abshot Farm
LITTLE ABSHOT RD
Abshot
POUND GATE DR
HUNT'S POND RD
WARSASH RD
West Hill Park Sch
ST MARGARETS LA
WEST ST
HIGH ST
ROSEDALE CL
GARSTONS CL
COMMON LA
Abshot Manor Country Club
Hook
HOOK LA
SOUTHAMPTON HILL 1
VILLAGE GATE 2
THE SQUARE 3
WRIOTHESLEY CT 4
COACH HILL
Cemy
OCCUPATION LA
THE CLOSE BELLFIELD
Titchfield
BELLFIELD
LOWER BELLFIELD
GARDNER RD
HEWETT HO
HEWETT CL
RANSOME CL
4
Hookgate Coppice
Nursery
Heath Lane
GREAT POSBROOK COTTS
Great Posbrooke
Great Posbrooke Farm
POSBROOK LA
05
SO31
South Leigh Farm
PO14
BROWNWICH LA
3
Chilling Farm
Chilling Copse
Singledge House
Upper Farm
Brownwich Farm
Little Posbrook
04
TRIANGLE LA
Upper Brownwich Farm
Thatchers Copse
Brownwich Pond
Lower Brownwich Farm
Brownwich Farm House
Lower Posbrook Farm
Fouracres Nursery
2
Meon
Elmstead
Solent Way
03
River Meon
Cliff Cottage
Nature Reserve
Titchfield Haven
LITTLE GAYS
KNIGHTS BANK RD
HAVEN CRES
Meon Shore Chalets
1
Visitor Centre
CLIFF RD
GREAT GAYS
Promenade
02
52
53

153
130
C4
1 FLANDERS HO
2 WHITEBEAM CL
3 VIMY HO
4 BLAVEN WLK
5 JASMINE WLK
6 TEBOURBA HO
7 CAEN HO
8 ST MICHAEL'S HO
9 MARNE HO
10 MIDDLETON WLK
11 RAMILLIES HO
12 ST QUENTIN HO
13 MITRE CT
14 BROADLAW WALK PREC
15 SICILY HO
16 CANNOCK WLK
17 COTSWOLD WLK
18 TUDOR CT
A
B
C
A27
SOUTHAMPTON RD
THE AVENUE
B3334
Titchfield Industries
Mast
St Francis Sch
Heathfield Sch
Schs
Fareham Coll
Wallisdean Jun & Inf Schs
Neville Lovett Com Sch
PO15
Hollam Farm
BRIDGE ST
ROWAN WAY
Oxleys Coppice
TAMMYS TURN 1
GAYLYN WAY 2
FAIRACRE WLK 3
RANVILLES LA
PEAK LA
1 PURBECK WLK
2 LASHAM WLK
3 DUNSTABLE WLK
LONGFIELD AVE
West End
FAREHAM
Hollam Hill Farm
WALLINGTON CT 1
WIDLEY CT 2
REDOUBT CT 3
PO14
TITCHFIELD RD
Crofton Manor Farm
River Meon
OAKCROFT LA
Newlands Farm
STROUD GREEN LA
HMS Collingwood
TANNERS LA
Cemy
Meoncross Sch
Stubbington
Sewage Works
Meon View Farm
Liby
Park La
Crofton Sch
Peel Common
B3385
Crofton Anne Dale Jun & Inf Schs
179
Baycroft Sch
GOSPORT RD
Hill Head
Crofton Hammond Jun & Inf Schs
Daedalus Airfield
Seafield Park
Hammond Ind Pk
PO13
B3334
HILL HEAD RD
SEAFIELD PARK RD
MONKS WAY
4
05
3
04
2
03
1
02
54
55
56
153
179

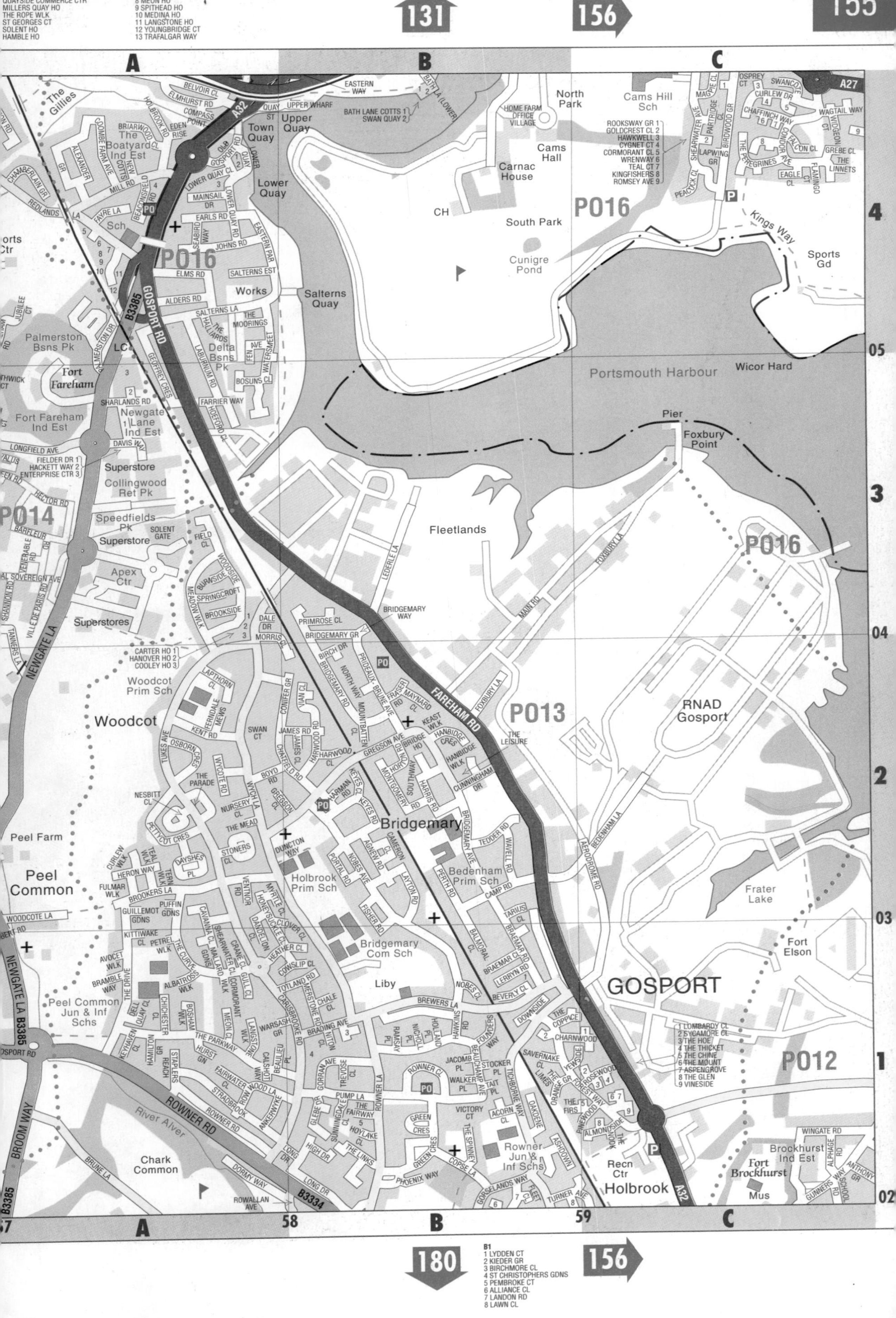

A
B
C
Town Quay
Upper Quay
Lower Quay
Salterns Quay
North Park
Cams Hill Sch
Cams Hall
Carnac House
South Park
Cunigre Pond
PO16
Portsmouth Harbour
Wicor Hard
Pier
Foxbury Point
Fleetlands
RNAD Gosport
PO13
PO14
PO12
Bridgemary
Bedenham Prim Sch
Bridgemary Com Sch
Holbrook Prim Sch
Woodcot
Woodcot Prim Sch
Peel Farm
Peel Common
Peel Common Jun & Inf Schs
Chark Common
River Alver
GOSPORT
Holbrook
Recn Ctr
Rowner Jun & Inf Schs
Frater Lake
Fort Elson
Fort Brockhurst
Brockhurst Ind Est
Fort Fareham
Fort Fareham Ind Est
Newgate Lane Ind Est
Palmerston Bsns Pk
Delta Bsns Pk
Collingwood Ret Pk
Speedfields Pk
Apex Ctr
Superstore
Superstores
Sports Gd
Kings Way
FAREHAM RD
GOSPORT RD
ROWNER RD
NEWGATE LA
BROOM WAY
A32
A27
B3385
B3334
ROOKSWAY GR 1
GOLDCREST CL 2
HAWKWELL 3
CYGNET CT 4
CORMORANT CL 5
WRENWAY 6
TEAL CT 7
KINGFISHERS 8
ROMSEY AVE 9
FIELDER DR 1
HACKETT WAY 2
ENTERPRISE CTR 3
CARTER HO 1
HANOVER HO 2
COOLEY HO 3
BATH LANE COTTS 1
SWAN QUAY 2
1 LOMBARDY CL
2 SYCAMORE CL
3 THE HOE
4 THE THICKET
5 THE CHINE
6 THE MOUNT
7 ASPENGROVE
8 THE GLEN
9 VINESIDE
4
05
3
04
2
03
1
02
57
58
59

155
132
A
B
C
A27
PORTCHESTER RD
WINNHAM DR
SEVERN CL
Crem
DORE AVE
BOXWOOD CL
SIMPSON CL
Red Barn
Com Prim Sch
THE HILLWAY
Portchester
HILL RD
KELVIN GR
PORTSVIEW AVE
PORTSDOWN RD
JUBILEE AVE
Westfield
Jun Sch
CONNAUGHT LA
ALLAWAY AVE
King Richard
Sch
PO6
Saxon Shore
Inf Sch
ROCKINGHAM WAY
Cornaway Bridge
BEAULIEU AVE
ROMSEY AVE
ASHTEAD CL
HATHERLEY CRES
QUINTRELL AVE
THE QUEENSWAY
THE CLOSE
THE KINGSWAY
THE FAIRWAY
THE CROSSWAY
THE DOWNSWAY
RUSSELL BLDGS 1
NEW PAR 2
RUSHIN HO 3
THE LEAWAY
ST HELENA WAY
STATION RD
NEW TOWN
GARDEN CT
Murrills
Est
NEELANDS GR
SEDGEFIELD CL
COLTSMEAD
SHOREHAVEN
BEECH DR
FARMLE RD
EAST ST
SOUTHAMPTON RD
A27
THE THICKET 1
WINNHAM DR 2
TRENT WLK 3
AVON WLK 4
MERROW CL 5
RUDGEWICK CL 6
STONELEIGH CL 7
Wicor Prim
Sch
HATHERLEY DR
CORNAWAY LA
NELSON AVE
WEST ST
ST JAMES WAY
Liby
WEST ST
POSTERN CL
THE KEEP
Castle
Trad Est
HAMILTON RD
1 PRIORY CT
2 PARRY CL
3 HOPKINS CL
4 ELGAR CL
5 SULLIVAN CL
4
Portchester
PRIORY GDNS
KING GEORGE RD
JUBILEE RD
ASSHETON CT
BRENCHLEY CL
CENTRAL RD
WESSEX GDNS
WHITEHAVEN
WESTLANDS GR
ALLENBY GR
QUEEN MARY RD
VINCENT GR
WELLINGTON GR
PO16
Portchester
Com Sch
SUNNINGDALE RD
KENYA RD
KING JOHN AVE
CLIVE GR
FROBISHER GR
SHRUBBERY CL
CRANLEIGH RD
ORCHARD GR
SANDPORT GR
SISSINGHURST RD
TATTERSHALL CRES
GATE HOUSE RD
HERITAGE GDNS
SEAFIELD RD
FOXBURY GR
NORGETT WAY
CARBERRY DR
MARLBOROUGH GR
GLADSTONE GDNS
CASTLE GR
MYRTLE AVE
Castle
Prim Sch
COW LA
CASTLE ST
05
WHITE HART LA
Wicor Path
MORAUNT DR
WICOR MILL LA
CORAL CL
SEAWAY GR
MARINA GR
COPPINS GR
KENT GR
GROVE AVE
MERTON AVE
OLIVE CRES
NEVILLE AVE
EDGAR CRES
WINDSOR CT
YORK GDNS
BAYLY AVE
Jetty
ALBION CL
CADOR DR
AUDRET CL
Works
KILWICH WAY
WINDMILL GR
HARBOUR VIEW
WESTBROOK RD
COOPER GR
BENHAM GR
MERTON CRES
DENVILLE AVE
NORMAN CL
CASTLEVIEW RD
PH
Wicor Path
ROMAN GR
Kings Way
ALTON GR
LANSDOWNE AVE
LONSDALE AVE
WICOR PATH
WEBB RD
KENWOOD RD
BEACHWAY
Cemy
HOSPITAL LA
WATERSIDE LA
CHURCH RD
Portchester Castle
and remains of
ROMAN FORT
3
04
Pewit
Island
2
Portsmouth Harbour
03
RNAD
Gosport
1
PO12
GUNNERS WAY
BLACKTHORN DR
HAMLET WAY
FRATER LA
WANDESFORD PL
RICHARD GR
CEDAR CL
PARKER CL
ANTHONY GR
ORCHARD CL
STANLEY CL
HAM LA
NASH DR
CHESTNUT WLK
QUAY LA
02
60
A
61
B
62
C
155
181

B4
1 ARTILLERY CL
2 DOWNTON HO
3 COTSWOLD HO
4 MELLOR CL
5 MALDON RD
6 HADLEIGH RD
7 HOCKLEY CL
8 PEBMARSH RD
9 WYMERING MANOR CL
10 BLACKWATER CL
C4
1 GLEBEFIELD GDNS
2 TANKERTON CL
133
C4
3 DYMCHURCH HO
4 NEPTUNE HO
5 MALLOW CL
6 ELIZABETH CT
7 STUART CT
8 TUDOR CT
158
C4
9 WINDSOR CT
10 ODEON BLDGS
11 CHIPSTEAD RD
12 CHIPSTEAD HO
13 NORTHERN BLDGS
14 ALDROKE ST
15 BEATRICE MEWS
16 VICTORIA TERR
17 ORFORD CT
18 GLENLEIGH CT
19 GLENLEIGH AVE
20 MEGAN CT
21 SELWYN CT
22 VINE CT
A
B
C
Queen Alexandra
Portsdown Prim Sch
St Pauls RC Prim Sch
Paulsgrove Prim Sch
Paulsgrove Ent Ctr
Paulsgrove Ind Ctr
A3 SOUTHAMPTON RD
Hotel
Superstore
Oak Park Ind Est
Acorn Bsns Ctr
Medina Prim Sch
P06
Works
WESTERN RD
NORTHERN RD
Cosham
Port Solent
Horsea Island
HMS Excellent (Horsea Island)
M27
A27
A3
A397
M275
Lido
P03
TA Ctr
Allot Gdns
Hilsea
City of Portsmouth Boys Sch
P02
PORTSMOUTH
Northern Parade Inf & Jun Schs
Sports Gd
Tipner Point
Waterside Sch
Pier
Tipner
Quay
Mountbatten Ctr
Portsea Island
DANGER AREA
Range
Stamshaw Jun Sch
Cliffdale Prim Sch
Mayfield Sch
North End
Corpus Christi Sch
College Park Inf Sch
Lyndhurst Jun Sch
Stamshaw
HMS Excellent (Whale Island)
Hard
LONDON RD
NORTHERN PAR
COPNOR RD
TWYFORD AVE
STAMSHAW RD
WHALE ISLAND WAY
A2047
A288
05
04
03
02
4
3
2
1
63
64
65
B1
1 SOMERVILLE PL
2 SCOTT HO
3 HASTINGS HO
4 OAK LODGE
5 STAMPSEY CT
6 BILL STILLWELL CT
7 SMEATON ST
8 NEWCOMEN CT
9 SHADWELL CT
10 EDEN TERR
11 PENROSE CL
12 HARRISON HO
13 WEYMOUTH RD
14 STAMSHAW CT
15 MEYRICK HO
16 ST JOHN'S CT
17 RUDMORE CT
18 ST NICHOLAS FLATS
19 WHITES CT
20 THE PROMENADE
182
158
C1
1 BURGUNDY TERR
2 SHACKLETON HO
3 VERNON CT
4 KIRBY CT
C2
1 FALKLANDS RD
2 ST FRANCIS CT
3 DAME ELIZABETH KELLY CT
4 CORONATION EVENTIDE HOMES
5 EASTWOOD RD
6 GERARD HO
7 LORING HO
8 OLDGATE GDNS
9 WALBERANT BLDGS
10 KNIGHTSTONE CT
11 GARRICK HO
12 BREECH CL
13 BENHAM DR
14 WHITECROSS GDNS
15 BALDERTON CL
16 DOYLE CT
17 PARK ROYAL
18 KIPLING BLDGS
19 MAGDALEN CT
20 BRIGHAM CL
21 HAIG CT
22 WOODFIELD HO

A4
1 WALBERTON CT
2 DORNEY CT
3 PARK MANS
4 WIDLEY CT

157
134

157
183

135
160

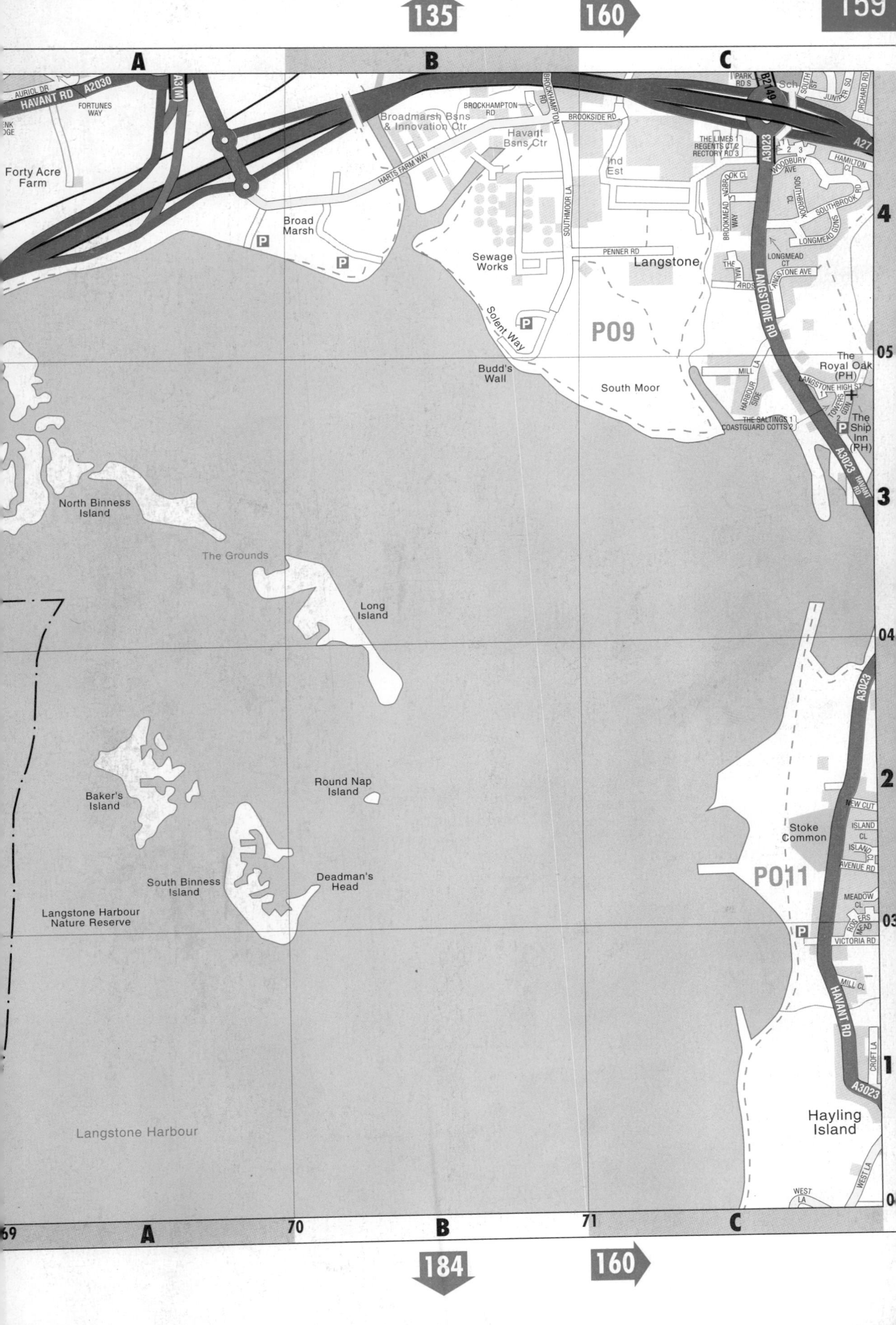

184
160

159
136

159
185

A
B
C
Hermitage
Caravan Park
Gosden Green
Southbourne
Southbourne Jun & Inf Schs
MAIN RD
Prinsted
New Farm
Marina
Thornham Farm
Nutbourne
PO18
A259 Chichester
Marsh Farm
Wks
Slipper Hovel
Thornham Grange
Boat Yard
Little Deep
Eames Farm
Sussex Border Path
Thornham Point
Prinsted Point
Chidham Point
Great Deep
PO10
Wickor Barn
Sports Ground
Thorney Island
Thorney Island Com Prim Sch
Stanbury Point
Baker Barracks
Airfield (disused)
Thorney Channel
West Thorney
CHURCH RD
A4
1 SPRING GDNS
2 PELHAM TERR
3 FRANKLAND TERR
4 ST PETERS CT
5 CHEQUERS QUAY
6 RIVERSIDE TERR
West Sussex STREET ATLAS
4
05
3
04
2
03
1
02
76
77

A
B
C
Dorset STREET ATLAS
B3082
BLANDFORD RD
River Allen
Pound Farm
Hound Hill
Chilbridge
TADDEN COTTS
Kingston Lacy Park
Lodge
Pound Farm
Coneygar Copse
Kingston Lacy Ho
(National Trust)
Obelisks
PO
Hillbutts
Pamphill Farm
Queen Elizabeth's Sch
ABBOTT ST
Kingston Lacy Home Farm
Kingston Lacy Gardens
Pamphill
L Ctr
SANDY LA
Pamphill CE Fst Sch
Stour Valley Wlk
All Fools Lane
Wynne Copse
Vine Inn (PH)
Little Pamphill
Manor House
Holly Lane
VINE HILL
COWGROVE RD
Poplar Farm
Firs Farm
Walnut Farm
Star Cottage Gdn
ROMAN WAY
Weir
Cowgrove
Cowgrove Common
Cowgrove Farm
BH21
Netherwood Mead
Chaw Meadow
Eye Mead
River Stour
B3078
A31
WILLETT RD
Sewage Works
Candys Farm
CANDYS LA
Lambs' Green
LAMBSGREEN LA
Weir
Coventry Arms (PH)
Court House
Court Farm
CANDYS CL
CORFE HALT CL
A31 MILL ST
A31 Bere Regis
WIMBORNE RD
WAYGROUND RD
STOUR VIEW GDNS
PINE RD
B3074
Mill Farm
BROG ST
BLANDFORD RD
East End
BRICKYARD LA
KNOLL LA
Water Works
RECTORY AVE
SLEIGHT LA
Sleight
Happy Bottom
4
01
3
00
2
99
1
98
97
98
99

186

A3
1 FARMERS WLK
2 COWDRYS FIELD
3 KNOBCROOK RD
4 SHEPPARDS FIELD
5 HAMILTON CT
6 BARTLEY CT
7 PRIORS WLK
8 CROWN CT
9 KINGSMEAD CT
10 CHURCH ST
11 WEST STREET CT
12 THREE LIONS CL
13 WESTFIELD
14 MORAY CT
B3
1 GULLIVER CT
2 HELIC HO
3 MARLBOROUGH CT
4 QUEENSMEAD
5 MILLBANK HO
6 JESSOPP HO
164
Dorset STREET ATLAS
A
B
C
Wilksworth Farm
Catley Copse
Sunday's Barn
CRANBORNE RD
B3078
FURZEHILL
DOGDEAN
Dogdean Farm
Long Lane Farm
LONG LA
Dumpton Sch
Deans Grove
Deans Grove Farm
DEANS GR
Merry Field Hill
MERRIFIELD
NEW MERRIFIELD
MARSHFIELD
SMUGGLERS LA
Colehill
Colehill Farm
COLEHILL LA
LITTLE LONNEN
LONNEN RD
ROTARY CL
WESTON RD
HOWELL HO
MIDDLEHILL RD
River Allen
The Row
Horns Inn (PH)
St Michael's CE Mid Sch
BURTS HILL
GREENHILL RD
GREENHILL CL
COBB'S RD
Beaucroft Sch
WIMBORNE RD
KYRCHIL LA
KYRCHIL WAY
PARK HOMER RD
PARK HOMER DR
WIMBORNE MINSTER
Stone
Long Close Farm
Stone Farmhouse
Stone Lane Ind Est
Craft Ctr
STONE LA
WALFORD GDNS
WALFORD CL
MILTON RD
SHAKESPEARE RD
TENNYSON RD
CHAUCER
RIVER CL
BYRON RD
VENATOR PL
CHERITON WAY
LACY CL
LACY DR
GIDDY LAKE
BELLS HO
ONSLOW HO
ONSLOW GDNS
BOUNDARY DR
GREENHILL LA
TOWER LA
BEAUCROFT RD
WHITEWAYS
NORTHLEIGH LA
VINERIES CL
THE VINERIES
COLBORNE AVE
ST MARGARETS HILL
CULVERHAYES PL
CULVERHAYES RD
Cemy
ST MARGARETS CL
ST MARGARET'S ALMSHOUSES
CEMETERY RD
BLIND LA
CHAPEL LA
EAST BOROUGH
WIMBORNE RD
Allenbourn Mid Sch
ELIZABETH RD
ALLENVIEW RD
COURTENAY DR
GLENDALE CL
BADBURY VIEW
BEAUFORT DR
MINSTER VIEW
Rowlands
MARLBOROUGH PL
ROWLANDS HILL
HIGHLAND RD
HIGHLAND VIEW CL
QUINCE LA
WESLEY RD
MELVERLEY GDNS
ROYSTON DR
Wimborne Fst Sch
REDCOTTS RD
SCHOOL LA
NETHERWOOD PL
COWGROVE RD
Victoria
WEST BOROUGH
B3073
ALLEN CT
GREENHAYS RISE
Ct
GRANGEWOOD HALL
POPLAR CL
ASHDENE CL
PINE TREE CL
HORNBEAM WAY
BEAUCROFT LA
FAIRFIELD CL
LEIGH LA
Leigh Common
CUTHBURY GDNS
VICTORIA RD
VICTORIA PL
WESTFIELD CL
REDCOTTS LA
Allotment Gdns
B3082
HANHAM RD
EAST BOROUGH
THE SQUARE
MILL LA
East Brook
BOURNE CT
RYDAL MEWS
CRANFIELD AVE
OAKDENE CL
BIRCHDALE RD
GREENCLOSE LA
OLD MANOR CL
BH21
LEIGH COMM
WEST ST
OLD RD
CUTHBURY CL
HIGH ST
Mus
CROWN MEAD
EASTBROOK ROW
LEVENS CL
LEVENS LA
YEW TREE CL
CUTHBURGA RD
ST JOHN'S HILL
RETREAT RD
FAIRFIELD RD
OLD HIGHWAY MEWS
B3078
PYE CNR
Minst
KING ST
Liby
EAST ST
PARK LA
PARKWOOD RD
LEGG LA
Sch
WELLAND RD
CHENE RD
LEIGH RD
B3073
PARMITER RD
PARMITER DR
PARMITER WAY
BROOKSIDE RD
Leigh
Julian's Bridge
JULIAN'S RD
Model Town & Gdns
DEANS COURT LA
MILLSTREAM CL
RODWAY
CRESCENT RD
ST CATHERINES
GROVE RD
ASHMORE AVE
ST JOHN'S CL
AVENUE RD
GRENVILLE RD
RICHMOND RD
BEECH CT
LIVINGSTONE RD
GORDON RD
DAY'S CT
LEIGH GDNS
WEST ROW MEWS 1
PYE LA 2
WEST ROW 3
COOK ROW 4
BEAUFORT MEWS 5
GRAMMAR SCHOOL LA 6
QUEEN ELIZABETH CT 7
The Leaze
St Johns
POOLE RD
ALLEN RD
OSBORNE RD
ETHELBERT RD
MARKET WAY
STATION TERR
NEW BOROUGH RD
EDEN GR
STATION RD
CHARLES KEIGHTLEY CT
HARDY CRES
TAPPER CT
Leigh Park
BARNES CRES
BROOK RD
Brook Road Depot
Trinity Ind Est
Sewage Works
CHURCHILL RD
Stour Valley Wlk
Riverside Pk Ind Est
A31
River Stour
Merley Hall Farm
Castleman Trailway
WILLETT RD
ULLSWATER RD
DERWENTWATER RD
MERLEY WAYS
WHITEHOUSE RD
OAKLEY RD
Willett Rd
OAKLEY HILL
Boat Houses
Oakley
Merley Pond
Dirty Lane Coppice
SILVERWOOD CL
CRUXTON FARM CTYD
OAKLEY LA
FLORAL FARM
MOUNTJOY CL
DE HAVILAND CL
SOPWITH CRES
ASHINGTON LA
Merley Park
MERLEY HOUSE LA
HARRIER DR
COBHAM WAY
The Willett Arms (PH)
Merley Fst Sch
OAKLEY STRAIGHT
CHICHESTER WLK
Sports Gd
Ashington
MERLEY HO
Merley House (Mus)
Merley
COCKERELL CL
BRABAZON RD
HAWKER CL
MERLEY LA
SEDKIRK CL
Harvey Rd
LYNWOOD DR
MERLEY PARK RD
GRAVEL HILL
A349
CHRISTOPHERS
REMPSTONE RD
DE MONTFORT RD
MERLEY GDNS
LAYARD DR
ROSAMUND AVE
HUNTINGDON DR
A341
4
01
3
00
2
99
1
98
0
01
02
B2
1 QUARTERJACK MEWS
2 SHAMROCK CT
3 STEVENSONS CL
4 BROADWAY PK
5 COPPERCOURT LEAZE
6 BROADWAY GDNS
7 ROBINS CT
8 RIVERSDALE
9 SAVILLE CT
187
B2
10 FLOWER CT
11 STOUR WLK
12 GRIFFIN CT
13 INGRAM WLK
14 MOORHILLS
15 MEADOW CT
16 CROMWELL RD
17 HARLESTON VILLAS
164

163

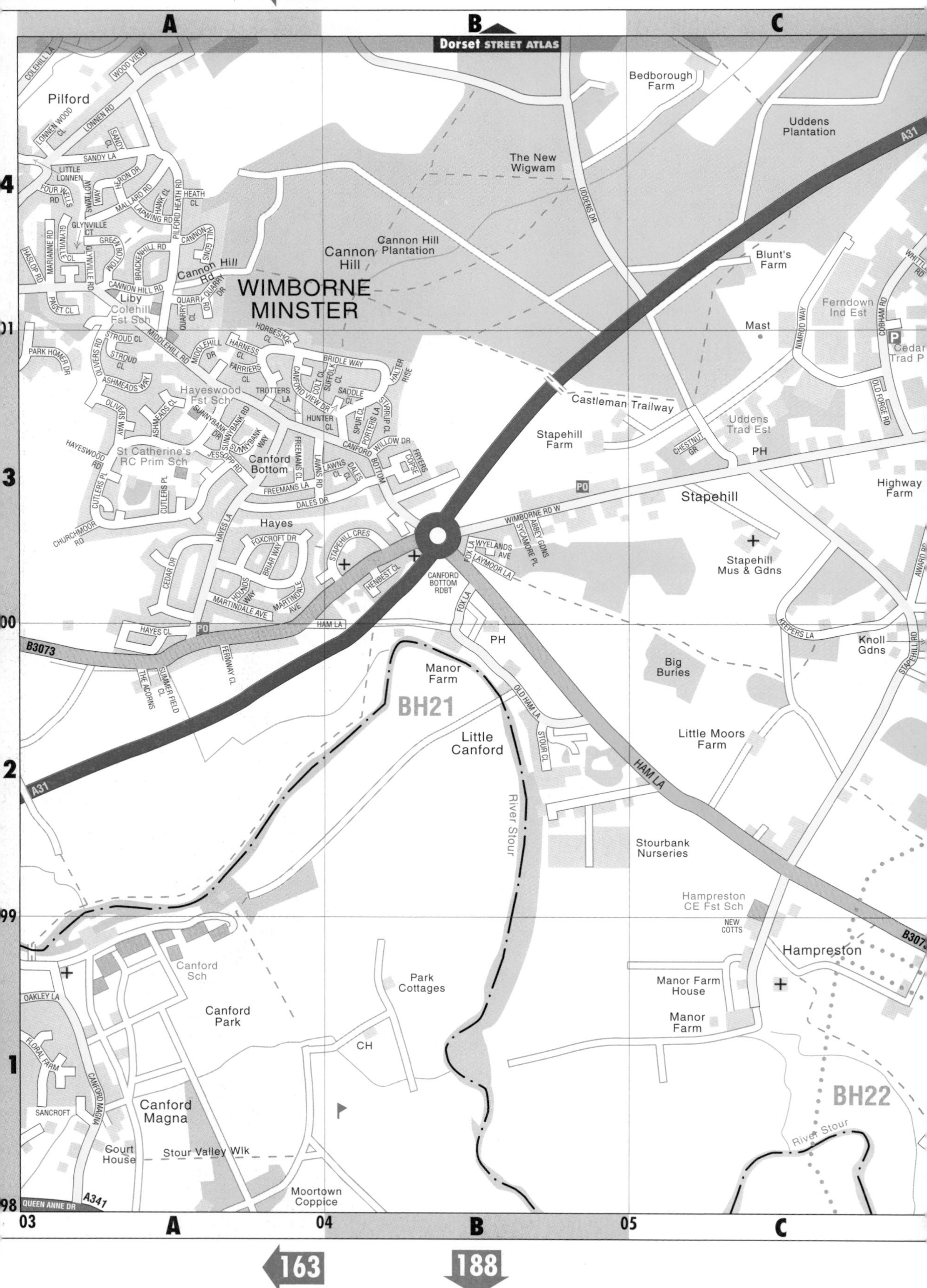
Dorset STREET ATLAS
A
B
C
Pilford
Bedborough Farm
Uddens Plantation
The New Wigwam
Cannon Hill
Cannon Hill Plantation
WIMBORNE MINSTER
Blunt's Farm
Ferndown Ind Est
Mast
Liby
Colehill Fst Sch
Hayeswood Fst Sch
St Catherine's RC Prim Sch
Canford Bottom
Castleman Trailway
Stapehill Farm
Uddens Trad Est
PH
Stapehill
Highway Farm
Hayes
Stapehill Mus & Gdns
CANFORD BOTTOM RDBT
Manor Farm
BH21
Little Canford
River Stour
Big Buries
Knoll Gdns
Little Moors Farm
Stourbank Nurseries
Hampreston CE Fst Sch
Hampreston
Manor Farm House
Manor Farm
Canford Sch
Canford Park
Park Cottages
CH
Canford Magna
Court House
Stour Valley Wlk
Moortown Coppice
BH22
A31
B3073
A341
HAM LA
WIMBORNE RD W
03
04
05
98
99
1
2
3
4
00
01

163

188

138
166

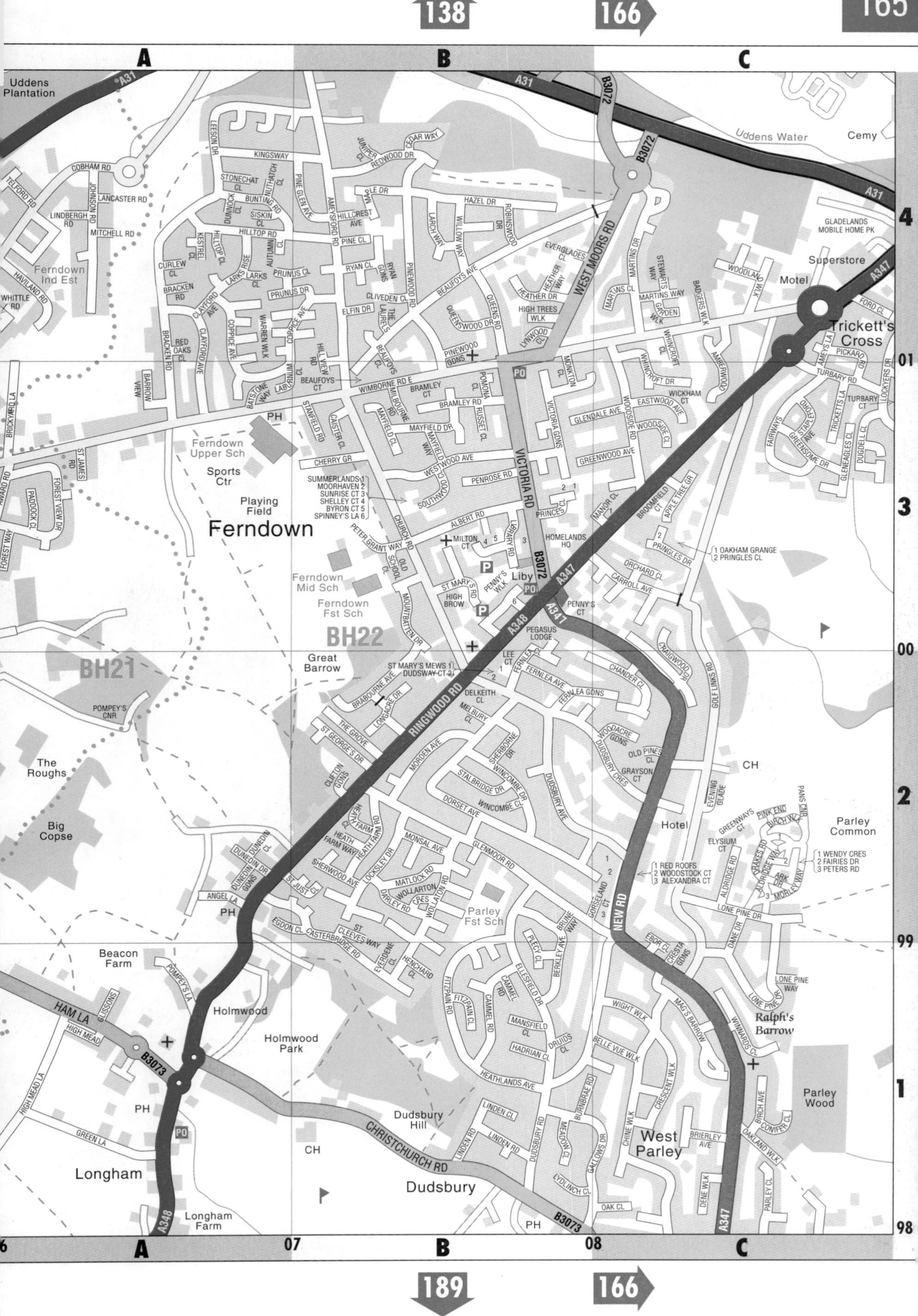

189
166

165
139

165
190

140 168

191 168

167
141
A
B
C
Wilkin's Farm
Sandford
DRAGON LA
4
Upper Bisterne Farm
BH24
Keepers Copse
Selfsown Firs
Three Corner Copse
01
Bisterne Manor
Hain Hill
Broad Heath
Gardens Cottage
3
Ripley Wood
Ringwood Lodge
Lower Bisterne Farm
B3347
Summergates
Ripley
00
Bunnybrook
North Ripley Farm
Blackberry Farm
Whistlers Copse
Ball's Copse
Ford
ANNA LA
North Ripley
2
BH23
Tinker's Copse
Ripley Plantations
Tinkers Farm
Martin's Copse
THATCHERS LA
99
Coules Farm
Salway's Plantation
Avon Valley Path
Ripley
Legg's Row
South Ripley Farm
Middle Ripley Farm
1
Hackthorn Plantation
Sopley Prim Sch
Long Acre Plantation
Parsonage Farm
Twobridges Plantation
98
DERRIT LA
15
16
17
167
192

142
170
A
B
C
BH24
Slap Bottom
Burbush Hill
Dur Hill Inclosure
Dur Hill Down
POUND LA
Whitten Pond
Bisterne Common
Lugden Bottom
Whitten Bottom
Avon Clump
Whitefield Hill
Avon Tyrell
Hillside Farm
Thorney Hill Holms
White Lodge
Home Farm
CROSS WAYS
Magpie Green
Black Firs
BH23
SCHOOL LA
BRUSHERS
SCHOOL RD
Devils Den
Shirley Common
BRICK LA
VALLEY LA
FOREST RD
Pigsty Hill
Thorneywood Farm
WHITELANDS
Thorney Hill
Lane End Farm
Thorneywood
North Braggers
WILLOW LA
King Braggers
Purlieu
BURLEY RD
Hill Farm
Shirley House
BLACK LA
HATCHERS LA
Shirley Farm
Nature Reserve
Prink's Wood
Howen Copse
DIAL CL
Hill Farm
Shirley
Stibb's Copse
Tothill
Jopps Plantation
Burnt House Farm
Poors Common
BURNT HOUSE LA
STIBBS WAY
MT PLEASANT DR
WEDGWOOD GDNS
CEDAR PL
ELMERS WAY
BRAMBLE WAY
AVON GDNS
TYRRELLS CT
BRANSGORE GDNS
Poors Copse
Heathfield Farm
New Merryfield Farm
SHIRLEY CL
ROSEHILL DR
BETSY CL
BETSY LA
SHACKLETON SQ
ROSEHILL CL
SHEARS BROOK CL
STOUTS LA
CANUTE DR
FURZY WHISTLERS
DERRITT LA
WEST RD
BROOKSIDE RD
HUNGERFORD CL
RINGWOOD RD
OAKTREE PAR
CRANWELL CL
BENSON CL
POPLAR CL
CUCKOO HILL WAY
HEATHFIELD HO
LYNDHURST RD
01
00
99
98
19
20
4
3
2
1
193
170

169
143
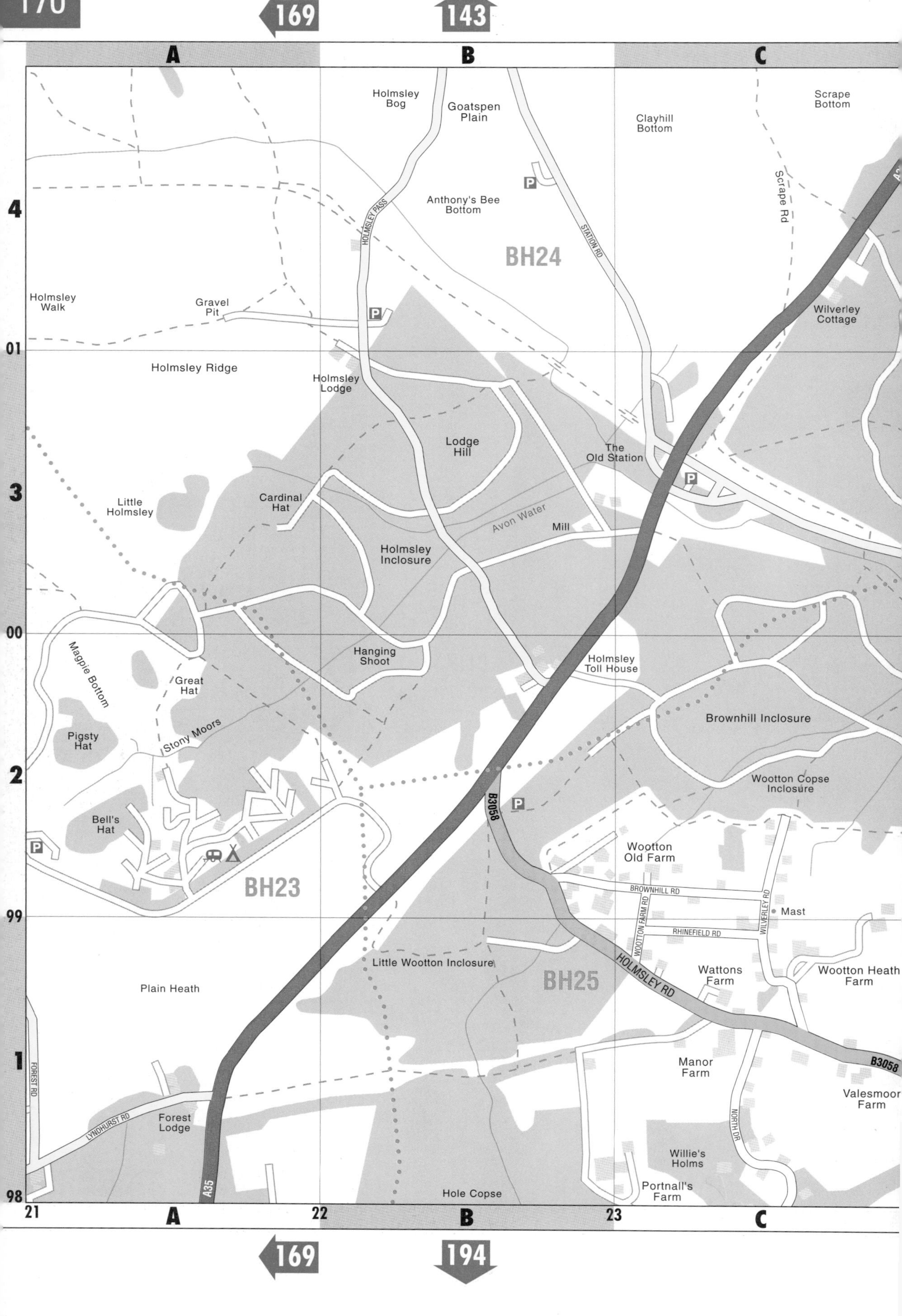

169
194

144
172

195
172

171
145

A B C

White Moor
Five Thorns Hill
Furzey Cottage
Pound Farm
Brockenhurst CE Prim Sch
Brookley Farm
B3055
PARTRIDGE RD
RAILWAY TERR 1
AVENUE RD 2
HIGHWOOD RD
Highwood PRU
TATTENHAM RD
THE LAURELS
ADDISON RD
COLLYERS RD
WOODLANDS RD
BURLEY RD
Furzy Hill
South Weirs
SOUTH WEIRS
Worthys Farmhouse
SWAY RD
Westbeams Stables
Trenley Lawn
Farm Cottage
Brokenhurst Copse
SO42
Blackhamsley House
CH
Brokenhurst Manor Golf Club
Hinchesla Wood
Lymington Junction
TILEBARN LA
Hinchesla Bog
BH25
Cater's Cottage
Latchmoor House
Blackhamsley Hill
Setley Plain
Three Beech Bottom
Cemy
QUARR HO
Milking Pound Bottom
Widden Bottom
BULDOWNE WLK
FOREST EDGE CL
ISLAND VIEW
BOND CL
MANCHESTER RD
OXFORD TERR
JORDANS LA
BRIGHTON RD
RHINERS CL
KITCHERS CL
DURRANT WAY
OAKENBROW
GILPIN HILL
HIGHFIELD CL
LITTLE BURN
SO41
ADLAMS LA
THE CLOSE
HAWTHORN DR
HIGHFIELD GDNS
NORMANDY CL
STANFORD RISE
MIDDLE RD
WIDDEN CL
ST JAMES RD
BADGERS CL
MEAD END RD
ANDERWOOD DR
DURNSTOWN
PH
CRUSE CL
SET THORNS RD
HYDE CL
CENTENARY CL
Durns Town
St Luke's CE Prim Sch
CRITTALL CL
BACK LA
HERON CL
PITMORE LA
SHIRLEY HOLMS
Sway
WESTBEAMS RD
CHURCH LA
PO
Hotel
CHAPEL LA
Rushcroft Farm
ROWAN CL
STATION RD
Little Purley Farm
Sway Park Ind Est
Hilltop
BIRCHY HILL
COOMBE LA
HOLLIES CL
Sway
JUBILEE CT
TEBOURBA COTTS
B3055
OLD VICARAGE LA
Manor Farm
Eastwoods

4
01
3
00
2
99
1
98

27 A 28 B 29 C

171
196

146
174

197
174

173
147

173
198

A
B
C
B3054
B3055
Hatchet Gate
Hazelcopse Farm
HATCHET LA
The Lodge
FURZEY LA
Hatchet Pond
Bunkers Hill
Jarvis's Copse
Hatchet Mill
MASSEYS LA
Swinesleys Farm
Beufre Farm
HEATH LA
WITHERS LA
PAGES LA
GAZA AVE
MATTHEWS LA
SWEYNS LEASE
EAST BOLDRE RD
CHAPEL LA
PO
WARTON CL
WALLACE LA
Grindingstone Cottages
Cemy
Sewage Works
Knights Copse
STRAWBERRY FIELDS
Bagshot Moor
NEW INN LA
NEW INN COTTS
The Turfcutters Arms (PH)
CRIPPLE GATE LA
CHURCH LA
Newhouse Farm
High Wood
East Boldre
SO42
Peaked Bottom
Peaked Hill
Gravelly Copse
Lodge Farm
Newhouse Copse
Newlands Cottage
Harepath
Wormstall Hill
Newlands Plantation
Longmead Copse
Newlands
Horsebush Bottom
Ford
Broom Hill
Broomhill Farm
Bergerie Rough
Horsemoor Copse
Upper Beckheath Plantation
SO41
4
01
3
00
2
99
1
98
36
37
38

175
149

175
200

Row Down
KING'S COPSE RD
East Stock Copse
SO42
Kings Copse Inclosure
Meadow Close Copse
Cemy
Ford
Blackwell Common
Gatewood Bridge
Gatewood Farm House
Gatewood Hill
Blackfield
Recn Gd
Langley
1 ST FRANCIS CL
2 THE MEWS
3 FOXY PADDOCK
4 FOXLANDS
5 FOX'S WLK
6 FOXGLADE
PH
West Common
Whitefield Farm
Dark Water
Nursery
Yard Wood
Main Drive
SUMMER LA
Exbury Bridge
Exbury Gardens
Witchers Copse
Exbury House
THE CRESCENT
CRESCENT COTTS
NEW COTTS
Chale Wood
East Wood
Whitefield Rough
SO45
Recn Gd
Exbury
Upper Exbury
St Mary's Spring
East Hill Farm
The Green
Salterns Copse
Haxland Pits
Lepe Farm
Grassy Copse
Pophams Wood
Aldermoor
The Moor
Lower Exbury House
Three Stones
Little Haxland Copse
Inchmery House
Lower Exbury
Lepe House
Quay
Groynes
A
B
C
4
01
3
00
2
99
1
98
43
44

177
151

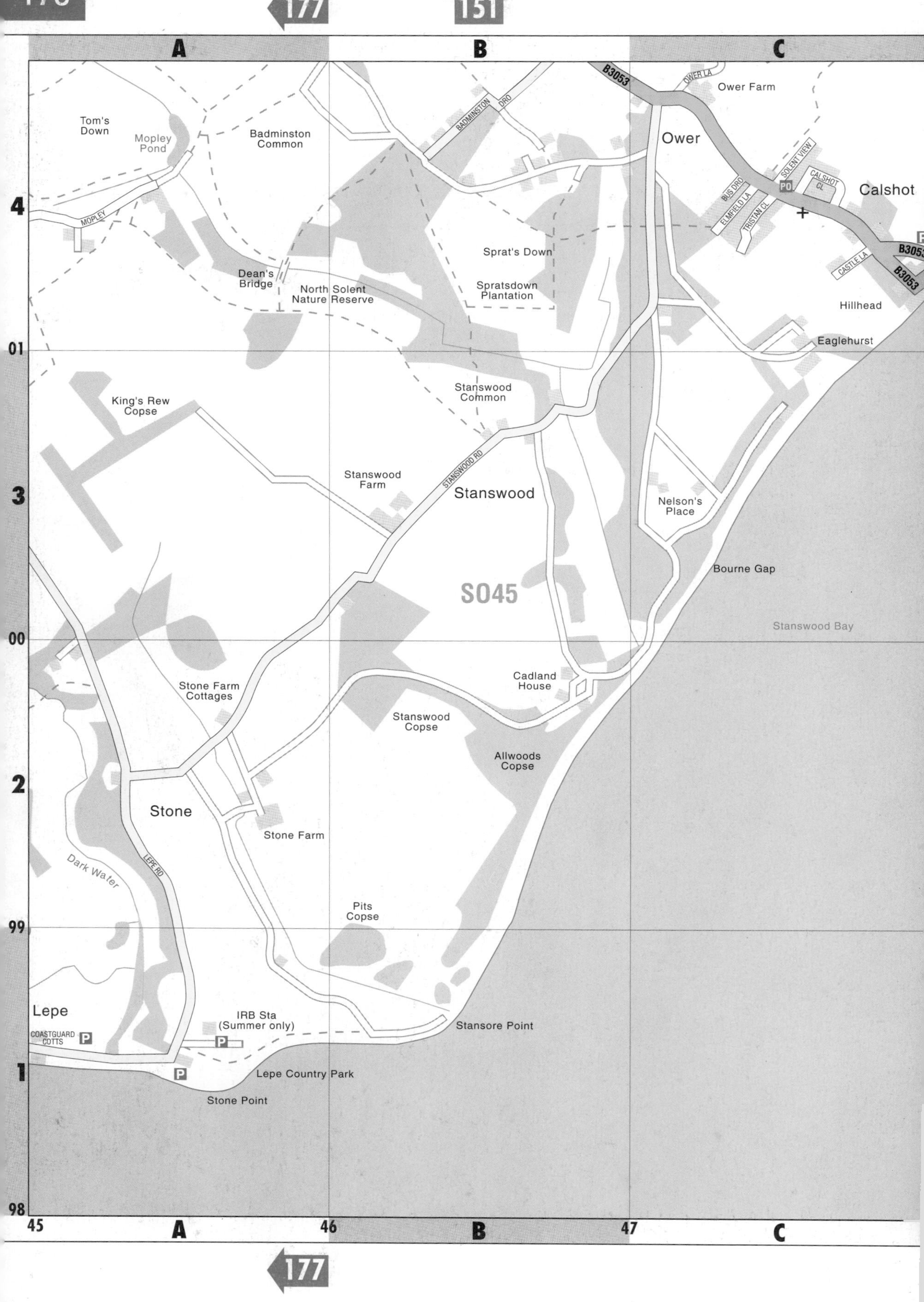
A
B
C
Tom's Down
Mopley Pond
Badminston Common
BADMINSTON DRO
B3053
OWER LA
Ower Farm
Ower
SOLENT VIEW
CALSHOT CL
PO
Calshot
BUS DRO
ELMFIELD LA
TRISTAN CL
MOPLEY
4
Sprat's Down
B3053
CASTLE LA
Dean's Bridge
North Solent Nature Reserve
Spratsdown Plantation
Hillhead
Eaglehurst
01
King's Rew Copse
Stanswood Common
STANSWOOD RD
Stanswood Farm
Stanswood
3
Nelson's Place
Bourne Gap
SO45
Stanswood Bay
00
Cadland House
Stone Farm Cottages
Stanswood Copse
Allwoods Copse
2
Stone
Stone Farm
Dark Water
LEPE RD
Pits Copse
99
Lepe
IRB Sta (Summer only)
Stansore Point
COASTGUARD COTTS
P
1
Lepe Country Park
Stone Point
98
45
46
47

177

154
180

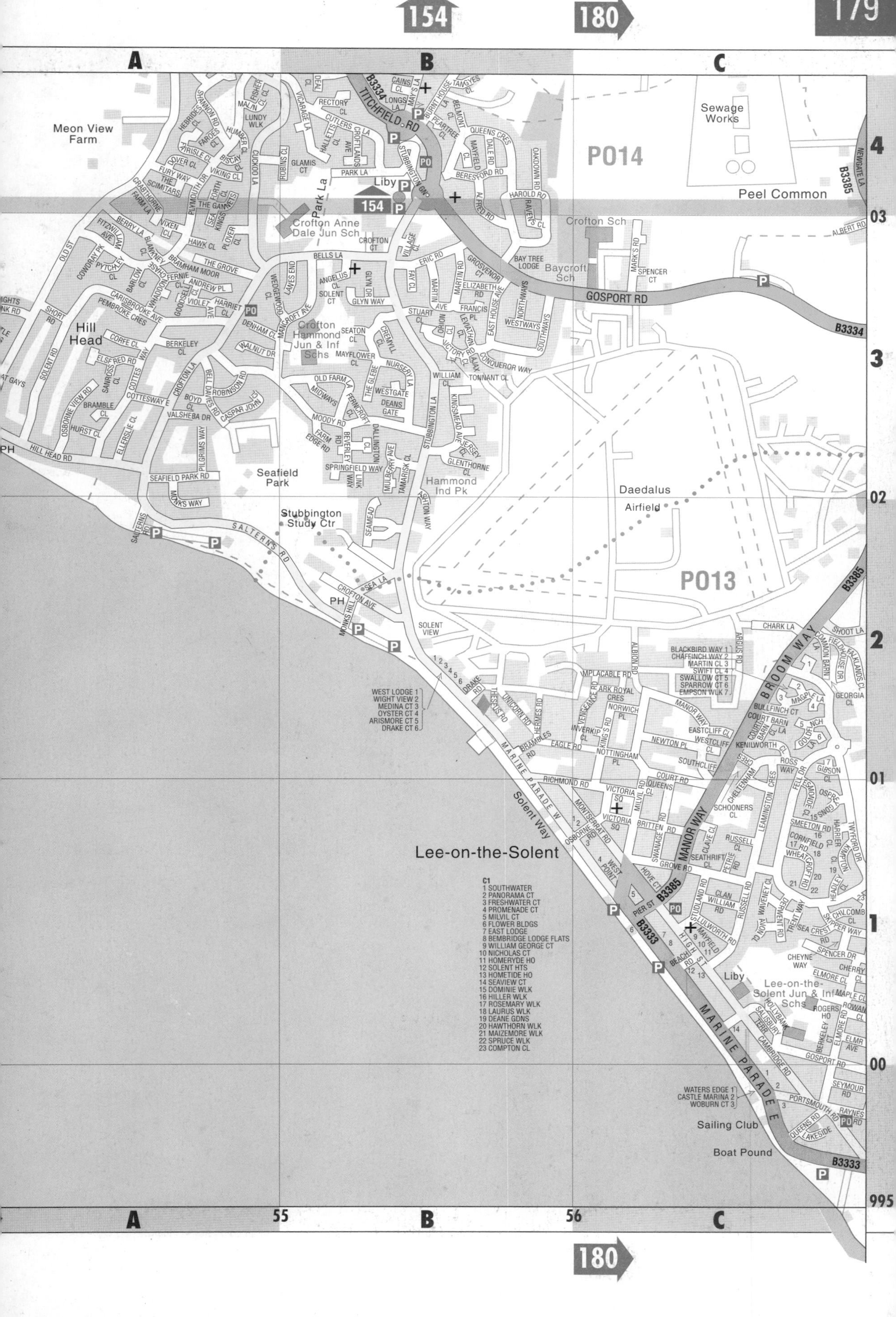
A
B
C
4
3
2
1
03
02
01
00
995
55
56
Meon View Farm
Hill Head
Seafield Park
Stubbington Study Ctr
Crofton Anne Dale Jun Sch
Crofton Hammond Jun & Inf Schs
Hammond Ind Pk
Crofton Sch
Baycroft Sch
Sewage Works
Peel Common
PO14
PO13
Daedalus Airfield
Lee-on-the-Solent
Lee-on-the-Solent Jun & Inf Schs
Sailing Club
Boat Pound
Liby
PH
TITCHFIELD RD
GOSPORT RD
STUBBINGTON LA
STUBBINGTON GN
SALTERNS RD
HILL HEAD RD
CROFTON AVE
MARINE PARADE W
MARINE PARADE E
Solent Way
BROOM WAY
MANOR WAY
HIGH ST
PIER ST
B3334
B3385
B3333
Park La
WEST LODGE 1
WIGHT VIEW 2
MEDINA CT 3
OYSTER CT 4
ARISMORE CT 5
DRAKE CT 6
BLACKBIRD WAY 1
CHAFFINCH WAY 2
MARTIN CL 3
SWIFT CL 4
SWALLOW CT 5
SPARROW CT 6
EMPSON WLK 7
C1
1 SOUTHWATER
2 PANORAMA CT
3 FRESHWATER CT
4 PROMENADE CT
5 MILVIL CT
6 FLOWER BLDGS
7 EAST LODGE
8 BEMBRIDGE LODGE FLATS
9 WILLIAM GEORGE CT
10 NICHOLAS CT
11 HOMERYDE HO
12 SOLENT HTS
13 HOMETIDE HO
14 SEAVIEW CT
15 DOMINIE WLK
16 HILLER WLK
17 ROSEMARY WLK
18 LAURUS WLK
19 DEANE GDNS
20 HAWTHORN WLK
21 MAIZEMORE WLK
22 SPRUCE WLK
23 COMPTON CL
WATERS EDGE 1
CASTLE MARINA 2
WOBURN CT 3

179
155

A B C

Rowner
Grange Inf & Jun Schs
Brune Park Com Sch
Brockhurst
Fort Rowner
HMS Sultan
Shoot Farm
Wild Grounds Nature Reserve
Grange Farm
Works
River Alver
PO13
PO12
Fort Grange
Siskin Inf & Jun Schs
Nature Trail
Mus
Cemy
Ann's Hill
Westfield Ind Est
Privett
Schs
Browndown
Browndown Training Camp
Browndown Point
Solent Way
Browndown Battery
Bay House Sec Sch
Stokes Bay
The Pebble Beach (PH)
Sailing Club
Promenade

ROWNER RD
PORTSMOUTH RD
PRIVETT RD
BROCKHURST RD
FAREHAM RD
MILITARY RD
GRANGE RD
GOMER LA
STOKES BAY RD
WESTERN WAY
ST NICHOLAS AVE
BROWNDOWN RD
SANDHILL LA
BRUNE LA
SHOOT LA

CHAPEL SQ 1
THAMESMEAD CL 2
CLARE HO 3
RUSSELL CHURCHER CT 4
GAYOA HO 5
BAGOT HO 6

JADE CT 1
JASMINE CT 2
COBALT CT 3
MAGENTA CT 4
CARMINE CT 5
CORAL CT 6

1 TWYFORD DR
2 COMPTON CL

1 CHERRY CL
2 MAPLE CL

BATH AND WELLS CT 1
BRADFORD CT 2
WORCESTER CT 3
HEREFORD CT 4
SHEFFIELD CT 5

ROCHESTER CT 1
LIVERPOOL CT 2
LICHFIELD CT 3
BLACKBURN CT 4
ST EDMONDSBURY CT 5
BIRMINGHAM CT 6
ELY CT 7
LINCOLN CT 8
MANCHESTER CT 9
LEICESTER CT 10
PETERBOROUGH CT 11
WINCHESTER CT 12
ST ALBANS CT 13
GUILDFORD CT 14

NASMITH CL 1
MILFORD CT 2
WHITECLIFFE CT 3
MOAT CT 4

CHURCHER WLK 5
WICKHAM CT 6
WOOLSTON CT 7
FAIR OAK CT 8
CADNAM CT 9
SHIRREL CT 10
MARCHWOOD CT 11
SEAVIEW CT 12
ASHURST CT 13

BURNETT RD 1
CLIFTON ST 2
CLAUDIA CT 3

NORMANDY GDNS 1
DROXFORD CL 2
SELBOURNE GDNS 3
WARNFORD CL 4
WILTON CL 5
ARDEN CL 6
CANBERRA CT 7
PILBROW CT 8

1 WAVERLEY PATH
2 GOMER CT

4
01
3
00
2
99
1
98

57 A 58 B 59 C

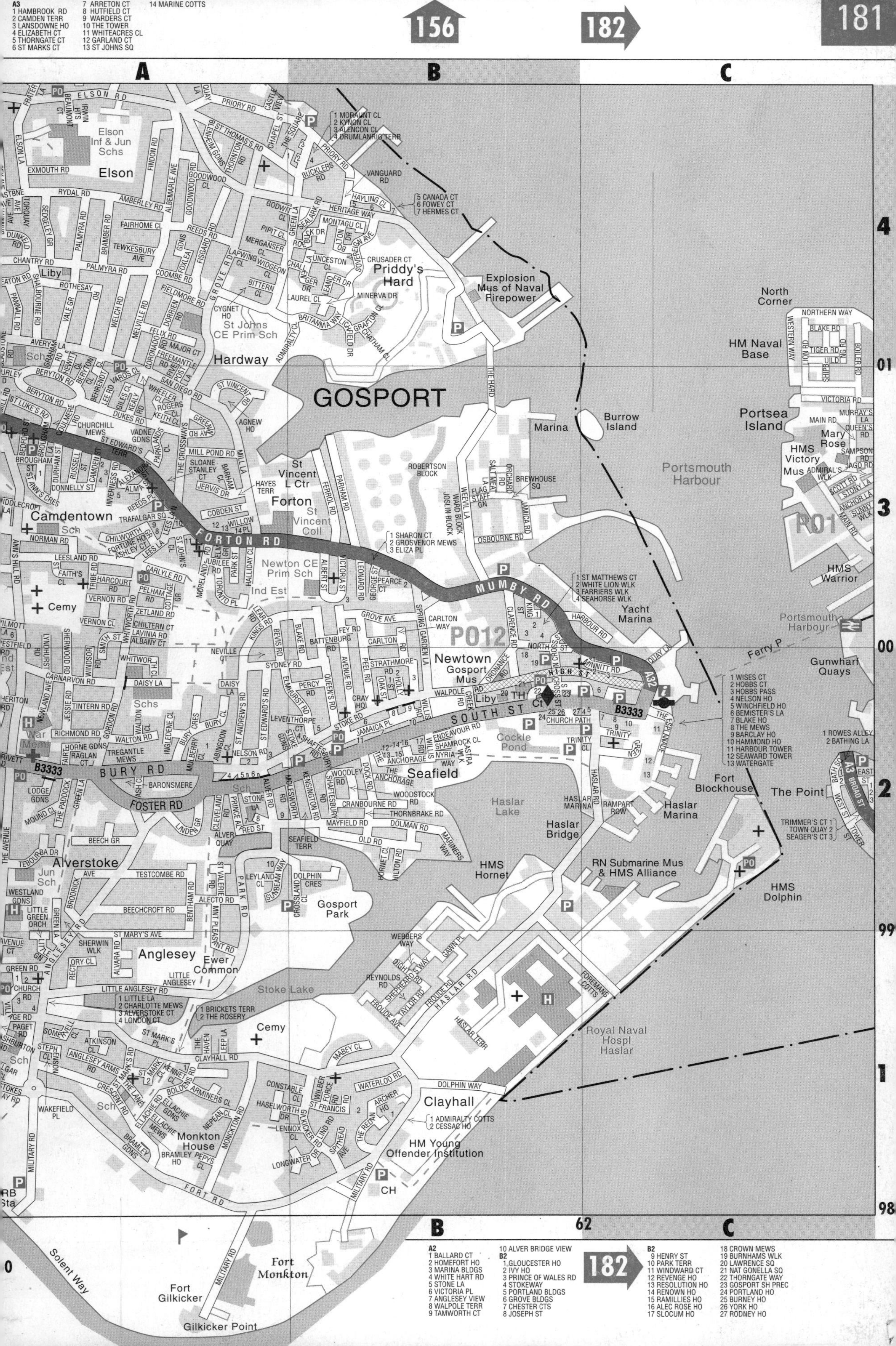

181
156
182
A3
1 HAMBROOK RD
2 CAMDEN TERR
3 LANSDOWNE HO
4 ELIZABETH CT
5 THORNGATE CT
6 ST MARKS CT
7 ARRETON CT
8 HUTFIELD CT
9 WARDERS CT
10 THE TOWER
11 WHITEACRES CL
12 GARLAND CT
13 ST JOHNS SQ
14 MARINE COTTS
A
B
C
4
01
3
00
2
99
1
98
62
GOSPORT
Elson
Hardway
Priddy's Hard
Explosion Mus of Naval Firepower
Burrow Island
Portsmouth Harbour
HM Naval Base
North Corner
Portsea Island
HMS Victory
Mary Rose
HMS Warrior
PO1
PO12
Forton
Camdentown
Newtown
Gosport Mus
Seafield
Haslar Lake
Haslar Marina
Haslar Bridge
Fort Blockhouse
The Point
Gunwharf Quays
Yacht Marina
HMS Hornet
RN Submarine Mus & HMS Alliance
HMS Dolphin
Gosport Park
Stoke Lake
Alverstoke
Anglesey
Ewer Common
Royal Naval Hospl Haslar
Clayhall
HM Young Offender Institution
Monkton House
Fort Monkton
Fort Gilkicker
Gilkicker Point
Solent Way
FORTON RD
MUMBY RD
SOUTH ST
BURY RD
FOSTER RD
HIGH ST
B3333
A32
A3
B
62
C
A2
1 BALLARD CT
2 HOMEFORT HO
3 MARINA BLDGS
4 WHITE HART RD
5 STONE LA
6 VICTORIA PL
7 ANGLESEY VIEW
8 WALPOLE TERR
9 TAMWORTH CT
10 ALVER BRIDGE VIEW
B2
1 GLOUCESTER HO
2 IVY HO
3 PRINCE OF WALES RD
4 STOKEWAY
5 PORTLAND BLDGS
6 GROVE BLDGS
7 CHESTER CTS
8 JOSEPH ST
182
B2
9 HENRY ST
10 PARK TERR
11 WINDWARD CT
12 REVENGE HO
13 RESOLUTION HO
14 RENOWN HO
15 RAMILLIES HO
16 ALEC ROSE HO
17 SLOCUM HO
18 CROWN MEWS
19 BURNHAMS WLK
20 LAWRENCE SQ
21 NAT GONELLA SQ
22 THORNGATE WAY
23 GOSPORT SH PREC
24 PORTLAND HO
25 BURNEY HO
26 YORK HO
27 RODNEY HO

A3
1 STATION APP
2 HALF MOON ST
3 OLD STAR PL
4 DRAKE HO
5 BENBOW PL
6 BENBOW HO
7 CARTER HO
8 UNION ST
9 FROBISHER HO
10 CLOCK ST
11 POWELL SQ
12 SHIP LEOPARD ST
13 CRADDOCK HO
14 BENEFICIAL ST
15 COCHRANE HO
16 COLLEGE LA
17 VICTORY RD
18 ROSEMARY LA
19 MILL GATE HO
20 MARGERY'S CT
21 THREE TUN CL
22 GRENVILLE HO
23 DUCKWORTH HO
24 SEA MILL GDNS
25 RALEIGH HO
26 EVA ALLAWAY CT
27 DAVIDSON CT
28 ST GEO BSNS CTR
29 TED KELLY CT
30 JOSEPH NYE CT
31 ROBERT MACK CT
32 MONTAGUE WALLIS CT
33 FRANK JUDD CT
34 RICHMOND HO

157

35 DELAVAL HO
36 FOUNDRY CT
37 WILLIAM BOOTH HO
38 WARD HO
39 SARAH ROBINSON HO

B4
1 SILVERLOCK CL
2 HASLEGRAVE HO
3 FLYING BULL CL
4 GLADSTONE PL
5 KILBRIDE PATH
6 KILPATRICK CL
7 CHAPEL CT
8 PROVIDENCE CT
9 CONSORT HO
10 NICKLEBY HO
11 BARKIS HO
12 MICAWBER HO
13 PICKWICK HO
14 MAITLAND ST
15 BLACKWOOD HO
16 WELLER HO
17 PEGGOTTY HO
18 TUPMAN HO
19 CHEERYBLE HO
20 BRISBANE HO
21 COPPERFIELD HO
22 CHERRY BLOSSOM CT
23 BARRINGTON HO
24 THE LION BREWERY

A2
1 MARTELLS CT
2 WARBLINGTON CT
3 A'BECKETT CT
4 SOUTH NORMANDY
5 ST THOMAS'S CT
6 HIGHBURY ST
7 HANOVER CT
8 LOMBARD CT
9 KING CHARLES ST
10 WALTON CT
11 HAYWARDS CT
12 REGENCY CT
13 OYSTER MEWS
14 FRENCH ST
15 CAPTAINS ROW
16 SPICE QUAY
17 CAMBER PL
18 THE RELDAS
19 THE GEORGE CT
20 LINGFIELD CT

B1
1 CUNNINGHAM CT
2 THEATRE MEWS
3 DOCK MILL COTTS
4 ADMIRAL'S CNR
5 GARDEN TERR
6 RAVENSWOOD GDNS
7 CHILTERN CT
8 TUDOR CT

181

B1
9 CLARENDON CT
10 BEAUFORT RD
11 FURNESS RD
12 JAMES BUTCHER CT
13 FASTNET HO
14 JACK COCKERILL WAY
15 ST MARTIN'S HO
16 PALM CT
17 QUEENS KEEP
18 HAMILTON CT
19 ADMIRALS CT
20 NETLEY TERR
21 NETLEY RD
22 PARK HO
23 HOMEHEIGHTS
24 CLIFTON TERR
25 CLIFTON RD
26 SERPENTINE RD
27 PORTLAND TERR
28 PALMERSTON MANS
29 PALMERSTON RD PREC
30 THE FRIARY
31 FRIARY CL
32 FONTWELL RD
33 TRAFALGAR CT
34 CHESTER PL
35 LINDSAY HO
36 FREESTONE RD

C1
1 KING COTE VILLAS
2 MANSION CT
3 ROSTREVOR LA
4 CRANESWATER GATE
5 CRANESWATER MEWS
6 NORMAN CT
7 DOLPHIN CT
8 CHARMINSTER
9 SOLENT GATE
10 CRESTA CT

For full street detail of the highlighted area see page 215.

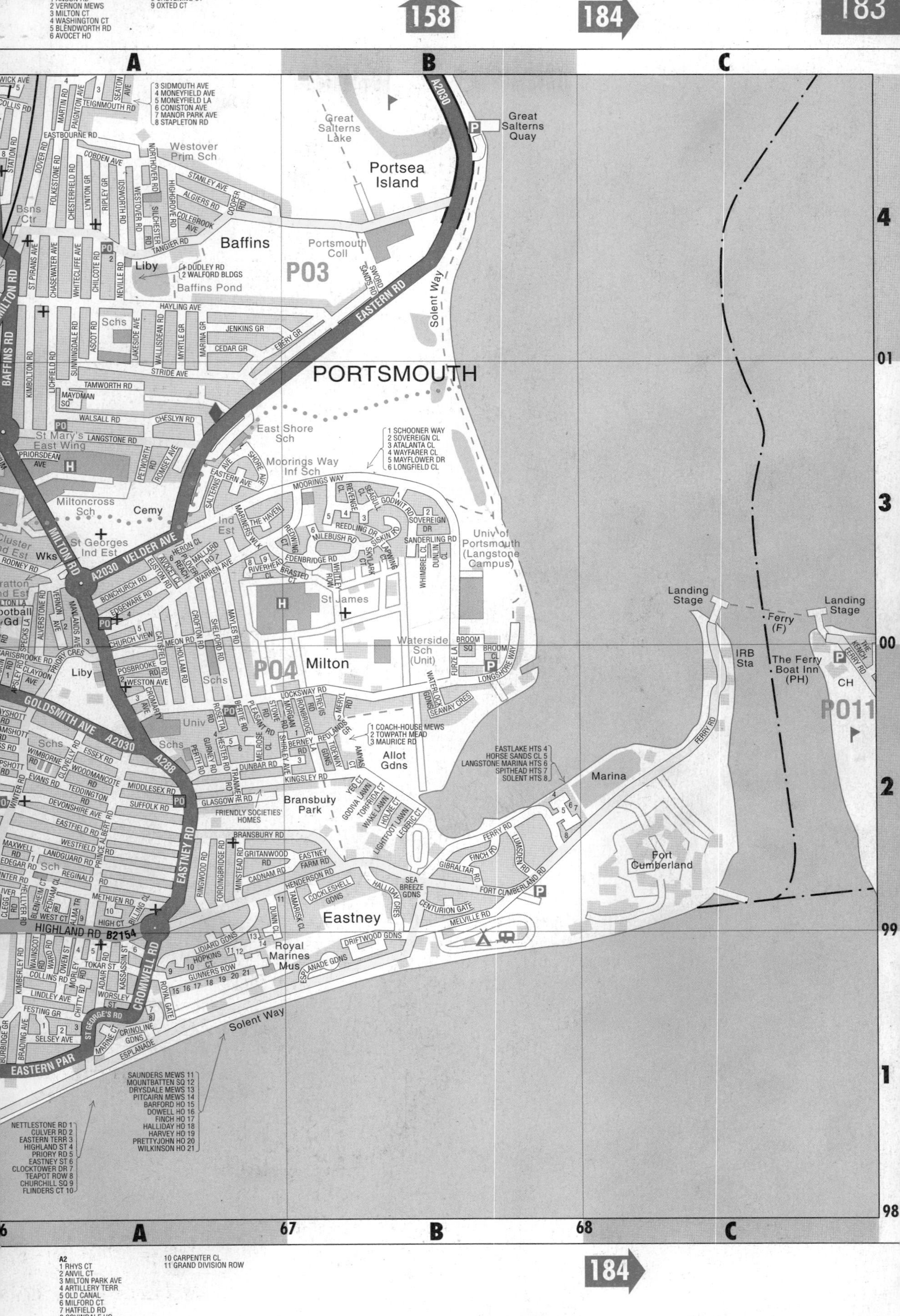
A3
1 ANSON RD
2 VERNON MEWS
3 MILTON CT
4 WASHINGTON CT
5 BLENDWORTH RD
6 AVOCET HO
7 CURLEW PATH
8 CHEVENING CT
9 OXTED CT
158
184
A
B
C
3 SIDMOUTH AVE
4 MONEYFIELD AVE
5 MONEYFIELD LA
6 CONISTON AVE
7 MANOR PARK AVE
8 STAPLETON RD
Great Salterns Lake
Great Salterns Quay
Westover Prim Sch
Portsea Island
A2030
Baffins
Portsmouth Coll
PO3
Liby
1 DUDLEY RD
2 WALFORD BLDGS
Baffins Pond
EASTERN RD
Solent Way
Schs
PORTSMOUTH
01
4
East Shore Sch
1 SCHOONER WAY
2 SOVEREIGN CL
3 ATALANTA CL
4 WAYFARER CL
5 MAYFLOWER DR
6 LONGFIELD CL
Moorings Way Inf Sch
St Mary's East Wing
Miltoncross Sch
Cemy
3
St Georges Ind Est
VELDER AVE
MILTON RD
Univ of Portsmouth (Langstone Campus)
St James
Landing Stage
Ferry (F)
00
Waterside Sch (Unit)
PO4
Milton
IRB Sta
The Ferry Boat Inn (PH)
CH
PO11
1 COACH-HOUSE MEWS
2 TOWPATH MEAD
3 MAURICE RD
Allot Gdns
GOLDSMITH AVE
EASTLAKE HTS 4
HORSE SANDS CL 5
LANGSTONE MARINA HTS 6
SPITHEAD HTS 7
SOLENT HTS 8
Marina
2
Bransbury Park
FRIENDLY SOCIETIES' HOMES
Fort Cumberland
EASTNEY RD
Eastney
HIGHLAND RD B2154
CROMWELL RD
Royal Marines Mus
99
Solent Way
EASTERN PAR
SAUNDERS MEWS 11
MOUNTBATTEN SQ 12
DRYSDALE MEWS 13
PITCAIRN MEWS 14
BARFORD HO 15
DOWELL HO 16
FINCH HO 17
HALLIDAY HO 18
HARVEY HO 19
PRETTYJOHN HO 20
WILKINSON HO 21
1
NETTLESTONE RD 1
CULVER RD 2
EASTERN TERR 3
HIGHLAND ST 4
PRIORY RD 5
EASTNEY ST 6
CLOCKTOWER DR 7
TEAPOT ROW 8
CHURCHILL SQ 9
FLINDERS CT 10
98
A
67
B
68
C
184
A2
1 RHYS CT
2 ANVIL CT
3 MILTON PARK AVE
4 ARTILLERY TERR
5 OLD CANAL
6 MILFORD CT
7 HATFIELD RD
8 COVINDALE HO
9 WYN SUTCLIFFE CT
10 CARPENTER CL
11 GRAND DIVISION ROW

183
159

A
B
C
4
01
3
00
2
99
1
98
69
70
71
DAW LA
WEST LA
A3023
MANOR RD
WOODLANDS LA
BRIGHTS LA
HIGWORTH LA
Higworth Cvn Site
DENHILL CL
SALTMARSH LA
WARDENS CL
DOVER CT
GLEBE CL
ATHERLEY RD
Newtown
CHARLESTON CL
GILBERT MEAD
SYCAMORE DR
NORTH SHORE RD
PO11
FURNISS WAY
DANCES WAY
NEWTOWN LA
HAMFIELD DR
AUBREY CL
SPINNAKER CL
FATHOMS REACH
Rook Farm
THE KENCH
The Kench
Pier
Sinah Farm
Holiday Village
WARREN CL
SINAH LA
PARK RD
STATION RD
PO
HARBOUR RD
FERRY RD
RICHMOND DR
RICHMOND CL
JAMES CL
GRAYLAND CL
LEXDEN GDNS
SOUTHLEIGH GR
ST MARY'S RD
LIME GR
ST CATHERINE'S RD
ST AUBIN'S PK
ST THOMAS AVE
STAUNTON AVE
West Town
BENWELL CT
HILDEN CT
ELWELL GN
BRIARWOOD GDNS
OAKWOOD R
Sinah Common
ST CATHERINES CT
ST HELEN'S RD
THE GORSEWAY
FERNHURST CL
BEACH RD
GARDEN CL
SOUTH RD
ELM CLOSE EST
LINKS LA
ST GEORGE'S RD
GORSEWAY
BATHURST CL
BACON LA
STAMFORD AVE
WINSTON CL
MAGDALA RD
GREEN LA
OLD TIMBERS
HOLLOW LA
CH
WEST MEAD CL
WESTFIELD AVE
VICTORIA AVE
ALEXANDRA AVE
BAY VIEW CT
SEA FRONT
NORFOLK CRES
SOLENT DR
ORCHARD CL
TUDOR CL
Gunner Point
Hotel
PH
Westfield
The Beach
CHICHESTER AVE
South Hayling
Hayling Bay
BAY VIEW MEWS 1
WARD CT 2
NORFOLK MEWS 3
THE ROYAL 4
LAUREN MEWS 5
ANNES CT 6
STAMFORD LODGE 7
ROPLEY CT 8
FAIRMEAD CT 9
OCEAN CT 10
NICHOLAS CL 11
PADWICK CT 12
VICTORIA CT 13
MARK ANTHONY CT 14
WESTFIELD OAKS 15
ST JOHNS CL 16
HOLM CT 17

183

A
B
C
HAYLING ISLAND
Verner Common
Fleet
HAVANT RD
A3023
Emsworth Channel
Mill Rythe Jun & Inf Sch
Pound Marsh
Mill Rythe Holiday Village
Middle Marsh
Manor Farm
Manor House
P011
The Hayling Sch
Tourner Bury Marsh
Tournerbury Farm
Tourner Bury
Tourner Bury Wood
Tourner Bury Plantations
Gable Head
Mengham Jun Sch
Meringham Salterns
My Lord's Pond
Mengham House
Mengham
Selsmore
Yacht Harbour
Black Point
Holiday Village
Boating Lake
Eastoke
Caravan Park
Sea View
Prom
IRB Sta
West Sussex STREET ATLAS
4
3
2
1
01
00
73
74

162

Corfe Mullen
Newtown
Mount Pleasant
Barrow Hill
Ashington
Corfe Hills
Hill View
Naked Cross
Beacon Hill Clay Pits
Upton Heath
Beacon Hill
Beacon Heath
Poor Common
Allen Hill
Mountain Clump
BH16
BH21
BH18
BH17
BLANDFORD RD
HIGHER BLANDFORD RD
WAREHAM RD
SPRINGDALE RD
Castleman Trailway
A350 Blandford Forum
Dorset STREET ATLAS

201

163
188

202
188

187 164

187 203

C1
1 EVELYN MEWS
2 ST JOHN'S GDNS
3 NORWAY CL

C2
1 REDHILL PARK HOMES
2 WHEATPLOT PARK HOMES
3 KINGFISHER PARK HOMES
4 RIVERSIDE
5 WIMBORNE RD
6 MAGNOLIA HO
7 WISTERIA HO
8 LABURNUM HO

189
166
A
B
C
B3073 CHRISTCHURCH RD
BARRACK RD
East Parley
Bournemouth Sports Club
CHAPEL LA
ENTERPRISE WAY
CHAPEL GATE
Bournemouth International Airport
BH22
PARLEY LA
New Cottages
BH23
College of Air Traffic Control
MERRITOWN LA
Alice in Wonderland Family Park
Merritown
B3073
Parley Court
Parley Green
DALES LA
River Stour
West Hurn
HURN COURT LA
Hurn Court Farm
Works
BH10
A2
1 REDHILL CT
2 PORTSWOOD DR
3 THE CIRCLE
4 THE AVENUE
5 COMBER RD
6 MEADOW CT
7 PRIORY VIEW PL
8 CHARNWOOD AVE
9 WARMWELL CL
10 STURMINSTER RD
11 SIDNEY GDNS
BH9
Berry Hill
Muccleshell Farm
PIG SHOOT LA
West Lodge
THE FRANK WAREHAM COTTAGE HOMES
MUSCLIFFE LA
Hicks Farm
WOOD ROW
Leaden Stour
Weir
Throop Mill
Nursery
BOURNEMOUTH
Muscliffe
Muscliff Prim Sch
Cemy
River Farm
Throop
THROOP RD
BH8
1 DOWNTON CL
2 CALMORE CL
3 FRITHAM GDNS
4 BRAMSHAW GDNS
A3060
Blue Roof Farm
VICARAGE COTTS
HOLDENHURST RD
Nurseries
MOUNTBATTEN GDNS 1
IBBERTSON CL 2
BOURNEMOUTH MEMORIAL HOMES 3
LUCKHAM GDNS
B3063
CASTLE LA W
The Hampshire Ctr
Yeomans Ind Pk
SHAWFORD GDNS 1
MICHELMARSH GN 2
SHERFIELD CL 3
WHITSBURY CL 4
Bournemouth Gram Sch (Girls)
Charminster
Moordown
EVENTIDE HOMES
Strouden
Bournemouth Gram Sch (Boys)
Sports Ctr
EAST WAY
Summerbee Comp Sch
Summerbee First & Jun Schs
Liby
Haddon Hill
Cemy
CHARMINSTER RD
09
10
11
A1
1 ROSEBUD AVE
2 MC WILLIAM RD
3 MINTERNE RD
4 MALVERN CT
5 CHARMINSTER CL
189
205

A
B
C
Bournemouth Aviation Mus
THEOBOLD RD
A338
B3347
Avon Causeway (Bridge)
Dayman's Wood
Sopley Common
PH
MATCHAMS LA
MOORS CL
AVON CSWY
PUSSEX LA
Watermeadows
Hurn
Hurnbridge Farm
Hurn Bridge
PO
PARLEY LA
P
97
Mill Copse
MILL LA
Ramsdown Plantation
Mast
Home Farm
CHRISTCHURCH RD
Ford
Moors River
HURN COURT LA
BH23
North Lodge
Quomp Copse
Blackwater Hill
Town Common
Blackwater
96
HURN CT
Leaden Stour
Weir
ORFORD CL
HESTAN CL
FORELAND CL
BLYTH CL
WHITBY CL
DRESWICK CL
WT Sta
Mast
VALENCIA CL
Reservoirs
New Bridge
HURN RD
ASTON MEAD
RYDAL CL
HILLSIDE DR
LYNTON CRES
1 CHALFONT AVE
2 GRASMERE CL
3 HIGHVIEW CL
4 AMBLESIDE
5 MARLOW DR
St Catherine's Hill
DUDMOOR LA
DUDMOOR FARM RD
Wood Farm
HOLDENHURST RD
River Stour
CONIFER CL
ST CATHERINE'S WAY
WOODBURY CL
VALLEY CL
CATHERINE WHEEL GDNS
BH8
Holdenhurst
MANOR FARMYARD
Sewage Works
Weir
GLENDALE CT
GLENDALE CL
OLD BARN CL
OLD BARN RD
95
SANDY LA
HUNTINGDON GDNS
TYRRELL GDNS
HOPKINS CL
Townsend
BIRCH DR
SWANS
Manor House
PO
Com Ctr
Townsend Prim & Com Sch
IBBERTSON CL
NOYCE GDNS
VICKERS CL
WILKINSON DR
JEWELL RD
THROOP RD
THROOP CL
CHESHIRE
DUKESFIELD
SQUIRREL'S CL
RIVER WAY
SPRINGFIELD AVE
KATTERNS CL
RIVERMEAD GDNS
BOSLEY CL
BOSLEY WAY
PIPPIN CL
APPLE GR
ST CATHERINE'S PAR
LINCOLN AVE
MARSH LA
HAMPSHIRE CL
SURREY CL
NORFOLK AVE
SUFFOLK AVE
CAMBRIDGE GDNS
BH7
Elderly Nurses National Home
HURN WAY
STOUR WAY
STOURCROFT DR
THE GROVE
Jumpers Common
PO
ESSEX AVE
Fairmile
LYNDON CT
ASHWELL CT
LANGHAM CT
WALCOTT AVE
1
Recn Gd
The Royal Bournemouth General
RIVERSIDE AVE
Bournemouth Crown & Cty Cts
THE ROSE GDN
CROSS WAY
DARWIN AVE
NORMANTON CL
MELBOURNE RD
FAIRMILE RD
FAIRMILE PAR
CASTLE LA W
A338
WESSEX WAY
CASTLE LA E A3060
H
LINKS DR
ELM AVE
CANBERRA RD
ENDFIELD RD
ALBION RD
KINGSWAY
RAMBARD AVE
EMILY CL
COOPER DEAN RDBT
LONGBARROW CL 1
COOPER DEAN DR 2
DEANSLEIGH RD
Superstore
BURFORD CL
WILTON CL
PERTH CL
BRISBANE RD
CROFTON CL
ARCADIA RD
ENDFIELD RD
Christchurch
B3073
H
94
12
13
14

191
168

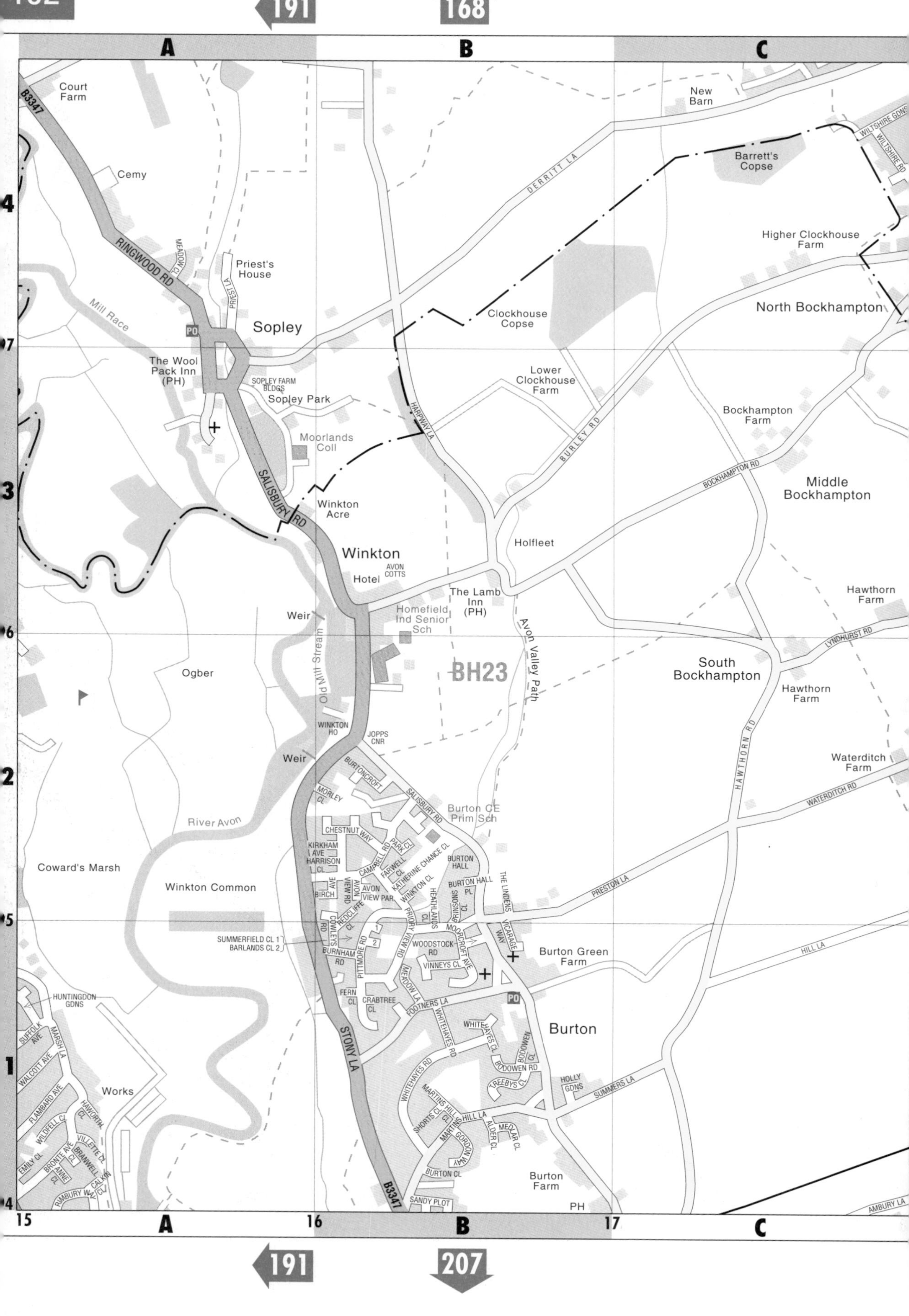

191
207

169
194
A
B
C
Bransgore
The Three Tuns (PH)
Bransgore CE Prim Sch
River Mude
PH
Harrow Wood
Harrow Farm
Beech House
Home Close
Bockhampton Corner
Waterhouse Farm
Harrow Lodge Hotel
Colbornes Wood
HARROW RD
Neacroft
Little Harrow
LYNDHURST RD
Shears Wood
Keeper's Lodge
CROFT RD
CHISELS LA
BROOK LA
HARROW CL
Godwinscroft
New Close Farm
RINGWOOD RD
Waterditch
BH23
Hinton Park
WATERDITCH RD
Allensworth Wood
Hinton Admiral
Waterditch Farm
Dark Firs
Tilley's Plantation
A35
Donkey Bottom
Burton Common
Burton Rough
The Cat & Fiddle (PH)
RINGWOOD RD
STATION RD
HINTONWOOD LA
Hinton Admiral
STATION RD
LYNDHURST RD
CHRISTCHURCH
ROESHOT HILL
Highcliffe
1 COLOMBINE CL
2 BURDOCK CL
3 SUNDEW CL
4 MONKSHOOD CL
5 SNOWDROP GDNS
Highcliffe Sch
Highcliffe Jun Sch
HAVELOCK WAY
THE MEADWAY
CLIVE RD
HINTON ADMIRAL MEWS
ROSSLEY CL
MILVERTON CL
WOODHAYES AVE
BROOKSIDE WAY
CRANEMOOR AVE
CRANEMOOR GDNS
AMBERWOOD DR
TALBOT DR
DUNBAR CRES
CHANTRY CL
LATIMERS CL
PINEWOOD RD
HOLMHURST AVE
SHEPHERD CL
BRAEMAR DR
DENHAM DR
GREENWAYS
THURSBY RD
LAKEWOOD RD
THORNFIELD DR
HINTON WOOD AVE
CARISBROOKE WAY
MOONRAKERS WAY
MARSTON GR
HURSTBOURNE AVE
TERRINGTON AVE
ASHMORE GR
LANGLEY RD
SMUGGLERS LA N
ROESHOT CRES
RIDGEFIELD GDNS
FOREST WAY
PARKSIDE
WOODFIELD GDNS
BAY TREE WAY
WINGFIELD AVE
FOREST RISE
WINSFORD CL
WESTBURY CL
TREESIDE
HAZEL CL
NADA RD
SMUGGLERS WOOD RD
LAUREL CL
HOBURNE CT
HOBURNE GDNS
HOBURNE LA
MANNING AVE
VERNO LA
BUTTERCUP DR
SAFFRON DR
CORNFLOWER DR
WESTFIELD GDNS
TUCKS CL
PEACE CL
PEAR TREE CL
BETSY LA
HALTON CL
ST GEORGES CL
BLACKBIRD WAY
POPLAR LA
ST MARYS CL
THE ORCHARD
POPLAR CL
CLARE LODGE CL
COLBOURNE CL
WOODLANDS RD
BROOKSIDE RD
CHAPEL LA
WESTLANDS CT
WILTSHIRE GDNS
MERRYFIELD CL
WEST RD
HILL LA
HILL CL
MEADOW CL
MEYRICK CL
WESTBURY CL
BURLEY RD
BOCKHAMPTON RD
HILL LA
4
97
3
96
2
95
1
94
8
19
20
208
194

193
170

193
209

196

A B C

4
3
2
1

97
96
95
94

Bashley
Marlpit Farm
Wootton
Danelea
Tiptoe Prim Sch
Tiptoe
Broadley House
Arnewood Common
Crabbswood Farm
Deemster Farm
Bashley Park
Brockhills Farm
Oak Farm
The Plough (PH)
Meadow Farm
Danestream Farm
ARNEWOOD BRIDGE RD
SWAY RD
Stanleys Park (Caravan & Chalet Site)
Danebury Farm
Stanley's Copse
Tiptoe Farm
Hordle Grange
BH25
Vaggs Farm
SO41
Ballard Coll
Golden Hill Farm
Three Bells (PH)
Ashley Inf Sch
Lavender Farm
New Milton
Golden Hill
Hordle
Ashley Jun Sch
Ashley
Noah's Ark Farm
Cemy
Peter's Farm
White Croft
Superstore
Sand and Gravel Pit
Breakhill Copse
LYMINGTON RD
Ashley Manor Farm

1 SUMMERTREES CT
2 DINHAM CT
3 BLACKTHORN WAY
4 COPPICE CL

A 25 B 26 C

A1
1 VINCENT RD
2 VINCENT CL
3 CHARLOTTE CL
4 ELM CT
5 SPENCER CT
6 ORCHARD LEIGH
7 CORNERWAYS CT
8 JACMAR CT
9 ASHLEY ARNEWOOD CT
10 WESTCROFT PAR
11 ELIZABETH CT
12 WAVERLEY HO
13 HOMEFIELD HO
14 ELIOT HO
15 SHELLEY HO
16 BYRON HO
17 KEATS HO
18 SHENSTONE CT
19 CLIFTON CT
20 WINSTON CT
21 SOLENT LO
22 WINSTON PAR
23 BOUVERIE CL
24 EDMUNDS CL
25 BARTON COURT AVE
26 SPINDLEWOOD CL
27 HAZEL CT
28 ST DENYS
29 DUDLEY PL
30 YEW TREE CT
31 CHERRY TREE CT
32 GREENWOODS
33 CASSELLES CT

A2
1 WHITEFIELD LO
2 HEATHER LO
3 RUSSELL CT
4 OSBOURNE HO
5 HOMEMILL HO

210

A2
6 MALLARD BLDGS
7 RICHMOND CT
8 PEGASUS CT
9 BEAU CT
10 ORCHARD CT
11 TANGLEWOOD CT
12 ALVANDI GDNS
13 ASHTON CT
14 MORANT CT

196

A2
15 TREVONE
16 FREMINGTON CT
17 YORK PL
18 FAIRCOURT
19 MERLEWOOD CT
20 CONWAY CT
21 STIRLING CT

195
172

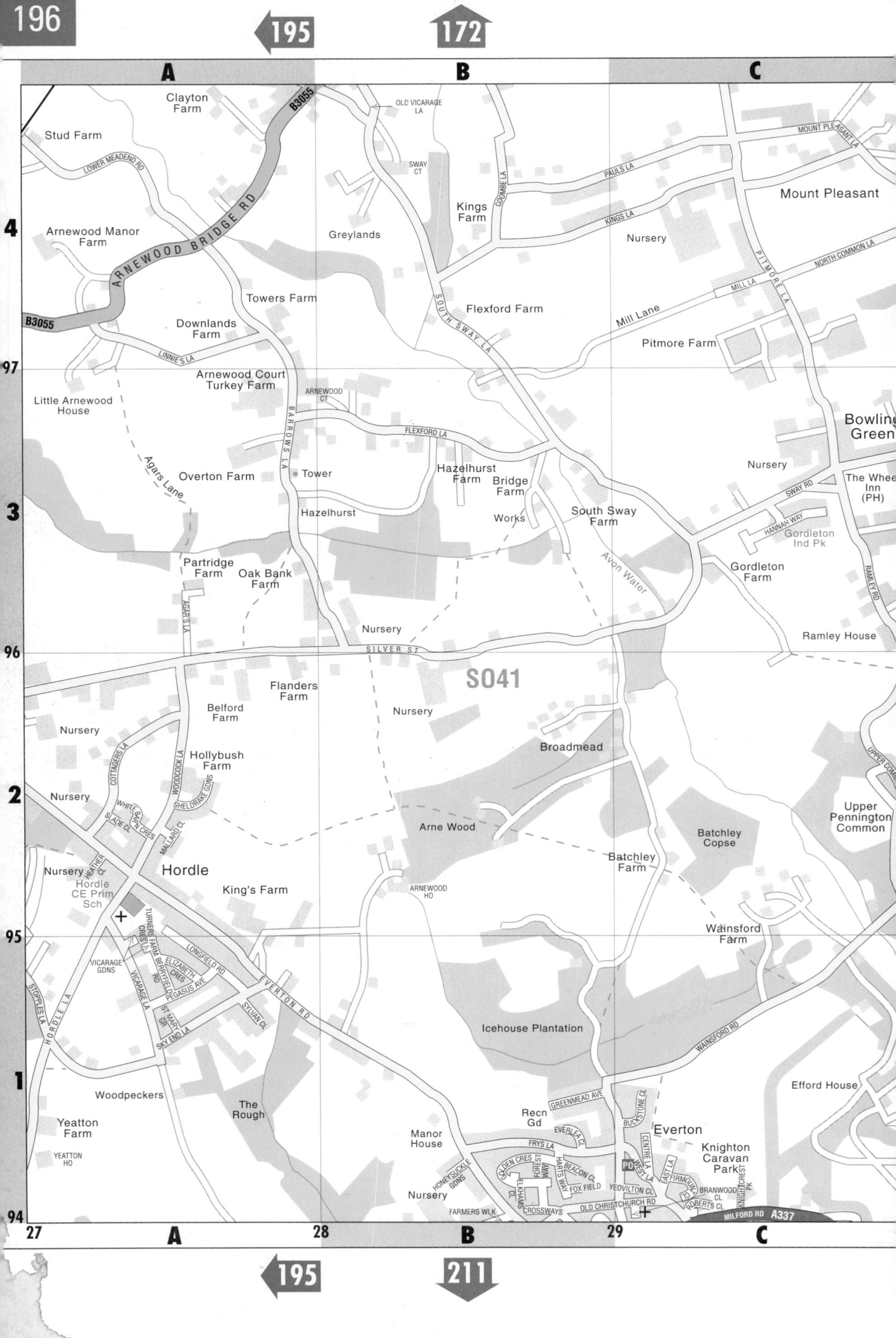

195
211

197
173
198
212
198
A
B
C
4
3
2
1
97
96
95
94
31
32
Passford House Hotel
Mount Pleasant
Springhill
St Austins
Starve Croft Bottom
Galley Hill
Tuckermill Copse
Passford Hill
Passford Water
Nursery
Great Fry's Hill Copse
Vicars Hill Farm
Warborne
Southlands Sch
Vicars Hill
Works
St Rose
SWAY RD
Wr Twr
Buckland Rings
Buckland Manor Farm
Buckland
S041
LYMINGTON
Yaldhurst Copse
Lower Buckland
Lymington River
Cowley Farm
Yaldhurst
Recn Gd
Cemy
Upper Pennington
War Meml
Liby
Lymington Jun & Inf Schs
Infmy & Day
Lymington Town
Pennington Inf Sch
Pennington CE Jun Sch
Priestlands Sch
Upper Rough
Newlease Copse
Vineyard
Avon Water
Pennington
Efford Farm House
Works
Efford Bridge
Nursery
Manor Farm House
Woodside Gdns
Woodside
De La Warr House
SOUTHAMPTON RD
AVENUE RD
EAST HILL
BRIDGE RD
MARSH LA
MILFORD RD
A337
B3054
1 RIVER CT
2 RIVERSIDE BSNS PK
3 ADELAIDE CT
4 BRITANNIA PL
5 HAMILTON MEWS
6 TRAFALGAR PL
1 OAK CT
2 WILLOW TREE HO
3 BILLINGTON PL
4 KINGSTON PK
5 GAINSBOROUGH CT
C1
1 PYRFORD GDNS
2 VICTORIA PL
3 GOLD MEAD CL
4 PEARMAIN DR
5 PEARTREE CT
6 PIPPIN CL
7 WORCESTER PL
8 BROADMEAD CL
9 RUSSET CL
10 MONKS CT
11 CONFERENCE PL
12 CHURCH MEAD
13 WOODSIDE CL

197
174

A
B
C
Norley Inclosure
NORLEYWOOD RD
Norleywood
SWEDISH HOS
JOYS LA
THATCHERS LA
B3054
Bull Hill Farm
WARBORNE LA
JORDANS LA
MAIN RD
Brick Kiln Clump
Portmore
HUNDRED LA
Newtown Park Farm
Ford
Carters Farm
Pleasure Copse
BROOK HILL
B3054 WALHAMPTON HILL
Portmore Pond
Newtown Park
Winter's Wood
Plummers Water
Hordle Walhampton Sch
South Baddesley
B3054
MAIN RD
WALHAMPTON HILL
South Baddesley CE Prim Sch
Pike Lake
SNOOKS LA
SO41
Solent Way
Dod's Pond
MONUMENT LA
Snooks Farm
Shotts Copse
Pylewell Park
Pylewell Home Farm
MILL LA
Mon
Walhampton
UNDERSHORE RD
FERRYPOINT
SOUTH BADDESLEY RD
SHOTTS LA
Pylewell House
Bampton's Farm
Marina
Lymington Pier
Country Club
Lisle Court Farm
LISLE COURT RD
Ferry Terminal
1 SOLENT VIEW
2 HOLBEIN LODGE
Lisle Court
SOLENT AVE
BATH RD
SPRINGFIELD CL
SPRING RD
MAYFLOWER CL
IRB Sta
STANLEY RD
KING'S SALTERN RD
WESTFIELD RD
KINGSFIELD
Yacht Haven
Lymington River
COASTGUARD COTTS
NORMANDY LA
Waterford
Normandy Farm
Solent Way
A
34
B
35
C
33
1
2
3
4
94
95
96
97

197

175
200
A
B
C
SO42
Upper Beckheath Plantation
Beck Farm House
Thorns Corner Cottages
Beck Farm
Norley Copse
MAIN RD
SO42
NORLEYWOOD RD
ST LEONARDS RD
4
Coombes Gate Farm Kennels
Hardings Wood
Forestside Farm
LYMINGTON RD
BROOM HILL
ROWES LA
East End
Thorns Cottages
East End Bridge
Thorns Farm
Bridge Farm
Ravensbeck Farm
Solent Way
97
East End Arms (PH)
THORNS LA
Sowley Pond
3
Sowley Brooms
SO41
Whitehouse Copse
SOWLEY LA
Sowley House
SO42
Solent Way
SANDPIT LA
Sowley Farm
MILL LA
BROWNS LA
96
PITTS DEEP LA
Colgrims
Otters Hill Copse
Boscoppa
Pitts Deep
TANNERS LA
Quay
2
95
1
94
A
37
B
38
C
200

199
176

A
B
C
Bergerie Farm
Solent Way
The Log House
Gins House
Black Water
Rye Errish
Park
PARK LA
Black Water House
WARREN LA
Thorns Copse
Rye Errish Copse
Warren Farm
SO41
SO42
Park Farm
Gravelly Marsh
Great Marsh
Thorns Marsh
Thorns Beach
Warren House
Park Shore
THORNS LA
Little Marsh
Beaulieu River
Gull Island
Bird Sanctuary
Needs Ore Cottages
Needs Ore Point
WARREN LA
Bird Sanctuary
97
42
43
4
97
3
96
2
95
1
94
39
40
41

199

A
B
C
1 DOUGLAS MEWS
2 LLEWELLIN CT
3 SHIRLEY RD
4 UPTON PARK MOBILE HOME PK
5 ELIZABETH RD
6 CHRIS CRES
7 MAPLE LO
Cemy
A350
A35
B3068
B3067
BLANDFORD RD N
DORCHESTER RD
The Marsh
Upton
Liby
PO
Yarrells Sch
Upton Inf & Jun Schs
Castleman Trailway
Creekmoor
BH17
UPTON RD
Upton House
Upton Park Farm
Upton Country Park
Boat House
Pergins Island
POOLE
Holes Bay
BH16
Ind Est
Lytchett Bay
Turlin Moor
Turlin Moor Fst & Mid Schs
RICE GDNS 1
RICE TERR 2
Hamworthy
BLANDFORD RD
Dawkins Bsns Ctr
Holton Point
Rockley Viaduct
Ham Hill
Rockley Sands
Rockley Point
Ham Common
BH15
Marina
Cobb Quay
Carter Com Sch
Sch
Pier
Lake
MORICONIUM QUAY
Wareham Channel
Hamworthy Mid Sch
Promenade
LC
98
99

A1
1 WEST BUTTS ST
2 MARSTON RD
3 ST AUBYNS CT
4 GUILDHALL CT
5 LEVET'S LA
6 POPLAR CL
7 ST JAMES CL
8 BARBERS PILES
9 NEW ST
10 CINNAMON LA
11 ST GEORGE'S ALMSHOS
12 THAMES MEWS
13 THAMES ALLEY
14 SARUM ST
15 BARBERS GATE
16 BARBERS WHARF
17 PARADISE ST
18 BELL LA
19 DENNETTS LA
20 GRAND PAR
21 KEY LA
22 BENNETT'S ALLEY
23 HOSIER'S LA

B1
1 TOWNGATE SH CTR
2 FALKLAND SQ
3 WINCHESTER PL
4 NIGHTINGALE LA
5 OLD TOWN MEWS
6 POST OFFICE LA
7 THE BROMBYS
8 WESTONS LA
9 CARTER'S LA
10 NELSON CT
11 GRENVILLE CT
12 LAGLAND CT
13 DANIEL GDNS
14 PROSPEROUS ST
15 THE SEED WAREHOUSE
16 BULL LA
17 BALL LA
18 BUTTON'S LA
19 QUAY POINT
20 THE KIOSKS
21 TAYLOR'S BLDGS
22 DRAKE CT
23 GRAY'S YD

C2
1 BANOCROFT CT
2 CROWE HILL CT
3 MERTON CT
4 THOROGOOD CT
5 BIRDS HILL GDNS
6 LANSDELL CT
7 GARDENS CT
8 SUNNINGDALE
9 PARK VIEW

203
188
204
A
B
C
BH17
BH15
BH12
BH14
BH13
Acorn Bsns Pk
Works
Trad Est
Wessex Trad Ctr
Newtown
Chalwyn Ind Est
Newtown Bsns Ctr
Foxholes
Kinson Pottery Ind Est
The Martin Kemp-Welch Sch
Trinidad Fst Sch
Recn Gd
L Ctr
Rossmore
St Joseph's RC Comb Sch
Liby
Cemy
Branksome Heath Mid Sch
Sylvan Fst Sch
Heatherlands Fst Sch
Upper Parkstone
Mast
Branksome
Poole Commerce Ctr
Courthill Fst Sch
Parkstone
Baden Powell & St Peter's Mid Sch
Lower Parkstone
Uplands Sch
Parkstone Bay
Blue Lagoon
Luscombe Valley
CH
Branksome Park
ASHLEY RD
CASTLE HILL
BOURNEMOUTH RD
COMMERCIAL RD
POOLE RD
RINGWOOD RD
SEA VIEW RD
ALDER RD
SANDBANKS RD
DORSET WAY
B3068
B3061
B3369
A3049
A3040
A35
04
05
90
91
1
2
3
214
204
10 WESTBURY CT
11 CHALBURY CT
12 HIGHFIELD HO
13 FAR ENDS

203
189

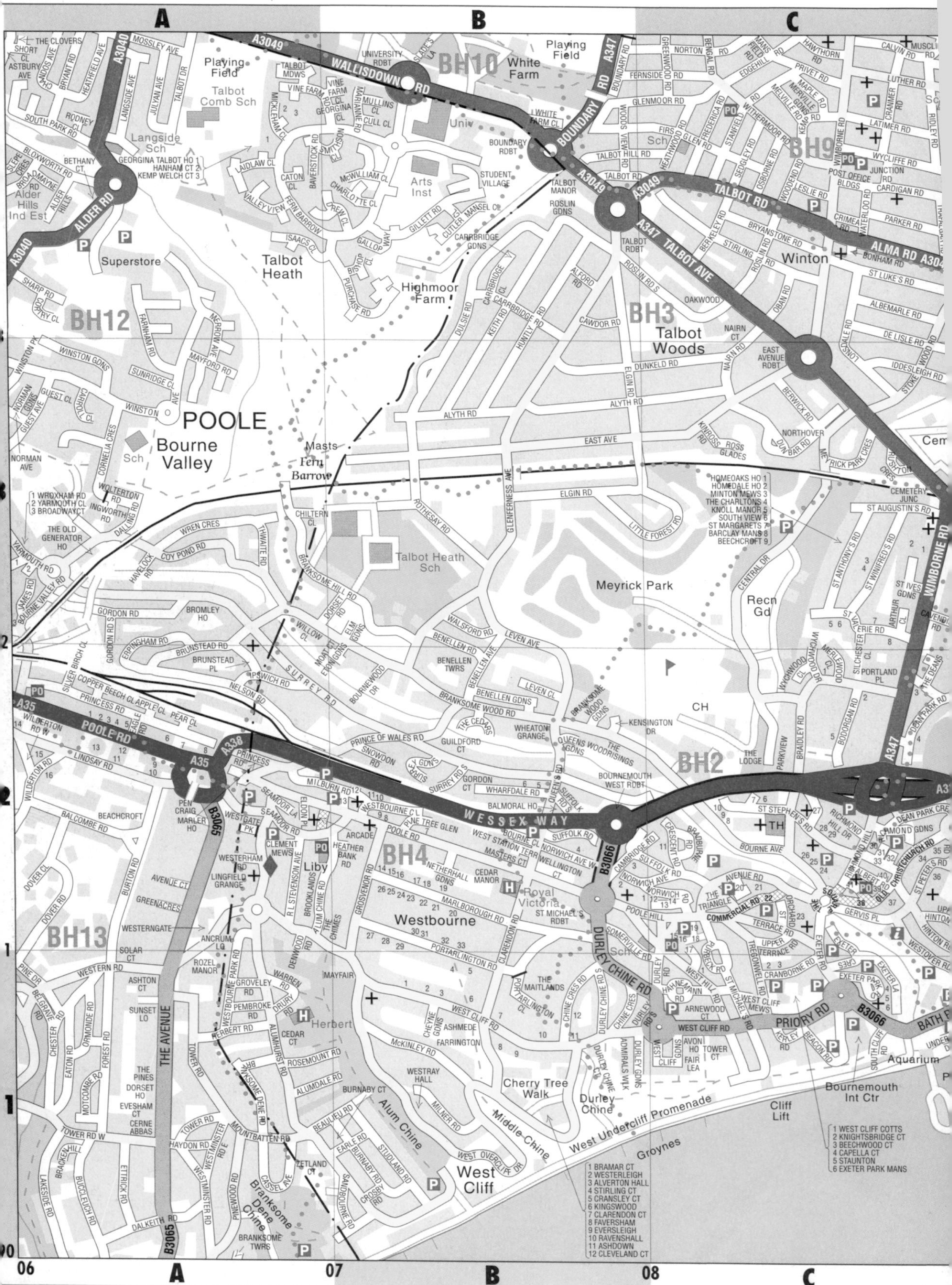
A
B
C
06
07
08
POOLE
Bourne Valley
Talbot Heath
Talbot Woods
Highmoor Farm
White Farm
Winton
Westbourne
Meyrick Park
Alder Hills Ind Est
Superstore
Talbot Comb Sch
Talbot Heath Sch
Langside Sch
Arts Inst
Univ
Masts
Fern Barrow
Playing Field
Recn Gd
Royal Victoria
Herbert
Alum Chine
Middle Chine
Durley Chine
Branksome Dene Chine
Cherry Tree Walk
West Cliff
Cliff Lift
Groynes
Aquarium
Bournemouth Int Ctr
West Undercliff Promenade
BH2
BH3
BH4
BH9
BH10
BH12
BH13
A3049
A3040
A347
A35
A338
B3065
B3066
WALLISDOWN RD
TALBOT RD
TALBOT AVE
ALMA RD
WIMBORNE RD
BOUNDARY RD
ALDER RD
POOLE RD
WESSEX WAY
DURLEY CHINE RD
PRIORY RD
BATH RD
THE AVENUE
WEST CLIFF RD
ELGIN RD
EAST AVE
ALYTH RD
DUNKELD RD
HOMEOAKS HO 1
HOMEDALE HO 2
MINTON MEWS 3
THE CHARLTONS 4
KNOLL MANOR 5
SOUTH VIEW 6
ST MARGARETS 7
BARCLAY MANS 8
BEECHCROFT 9
1 WROXHAM RD
2 YARMOUTH CL
3 BROADWAY CT
1 GEORGINA TALBOT HO
2 HANHAM CT
3 KEMP WELCH CT
1 BRAMAR CT
2 WESTERLEIGH
3 ALVERTON HALL
4 STIRLING CT
5 CRANSLEY CT
6 KINGSWOOD
7 CLARENDON CT
8 FAVERSHAM
9 EVERSLEIGH
10 RAVENSHALL
11 ASHDOWN
12 CLEVELAND CT
1 WEST CLIFF COTTS
2 KNIGHTSBRIDGE CT
3 BEECHWOOD CT
4 CAPELLA CT
5 STAUNTON
6 EXETER PARK MANS

A2
1 BURLING TERR
2 CORAL CT
3 LINDUM CT
4 DARWIN CT
5 EAGLHURST
6 PRINCES CT
7 MARLBOROUGH CT
8 BARONS CT
9 RUTLAND MANOR
10 LINDSAY MANOR
11 KILBRIDE
12 THE OASIS
13 HOLLY LO
14 MELTON CT
15 LINDSAY PK
16 PINE PARK MANS

B2
1 THE MEWS
2 ST MICHAEL'S
3 RIVIERA CT
4 NORWICH MANS
5 QUEENS CT
6 GRENVILLE CT
7 QUARRY CHASE
8 WEST MANS
9 ANGLEWOOD MANS
10 BICKNELL CT
11 BENNETT HO
12 MILBURN CL

B2
13 LANDSEER RD
14 CRANBORNE CT
15 THORNBURY
16 WOLVERLEY CT
17 STOURTON CT
18 ALINGTON
19 CLIVE CT
20 KENT HO
21 MARLBOROUGH CT
22 BOSTON LO
23 BROWNLOW CT
24 TIVERTON CT
25 BLENHEIM CT
26 BELMOUR LO
27 LANGTON DENE
28 BRIARFIELD
29 BEVERLEY GRANGE
30 BEECHFIELD
31 BEAU CT
32 CURZON CT
33 WESLEY GRANGE

C2
1 WYCHWOOD GRANGE
2 FAIRTHORN CT
3 BOURNE PINES
4 HORSESHOE CT
5 MEYRICK PARK MANS
6 ST STEPHEN'S CT
7 DURRANT RD
8 SUNBURY CT
9 AMIRA CT
10 TRYSTWORTHY
11 MAJORCA MANS
12 NORWICH CT
13 UPPER NORWICH RD
14 PARK GATE MEWS
15 WEST HILL PL
16 ST MICHAEL'S MEWS
17 SOUTH VIEW PL
18 ST MICHAEL'S PL
19 MANNINGTON PL
20 AVENUE LA
21 THE AVENUE SH CTR
22 ORCHARD WLK
23 EDMONSHAM HO
24 BOURNE CT
25 HAMPSHIRE HO
26 HAMPSHIRE CT
27 ST STEPHEN'S WAY
28 FERN BANK
29 FERNHILL FLATS
30 MOUNT HEATHERBANK
31 VERULAM PL
32 GRANVILLE PL
33 YELVERTON RD
34 BURLINGTON ARC
35 OLD CHRISTCHURCH LA
36 ST PETER'S CRES
37 THE ARCADE
38 ST PETER'S WLK
39 CRITERION ARC
40 ADELAIDE LA
41 POST OFFICE RD

214

A3
1 CULFORD CT
2 APSLEY CT
3 TRELOEN CT
4 RAVANA CT
5 HOMELEIGH HO
6 BEECHY CT
7 WELLINGTON CT
8 MORINGTON CT
9 PARSONAGE CT
10 HAMILTON CT
11 MOORLEA
12 PORCHESTER CT
B3
1 OPHIR GDNS
2 METHUEN CL
3 LOWTHER GDNS
4 THE LANE
5 STEWART CL
6 HENVILLE RD
7 MALMESBURY PARK PL
8 WESLEY CL
190
206
A
B
C
BH9
BH8
BH7
BH1
BH5
Cemy
Queen's Park
Recn Gd
Linwood Mixed Sch
CH
1 SHELBOURNE CL
2 CAPSTONE PL
3 AVON CL
4 RICHMOND PARK CL
5 EGERTON GDNS
6 ST LEDGER'S PL
King's Park
Dean Court (Bournemouth FC)
Athletic Ctr
Kings Park Comm
King's Park Sch
Malmesbury Park Prim Sch
Springbourne
Bournemouth
Bournemouth Central Bsns Pk
Schs
Mus
Liby
Cricket Ground
Dean Park
Sports Ctr
Boscombe
Nuffield
Cts Coll
Coll
Promenade
Pier
Russell -Cotes Art Gall & Mus
Cliff Lift
1 WOODBURY
2 HINTON WOOD
BOURNEMOUTH
RICHMOND PARK ROAD
WESSEX WAY
CHRISTCHURCH RD
CHARMINSTER RD
LANSDOWNE RD
ASHLEY RD A3049
ALMA RD
ST PAUL'S RD
BATH RD
CENTENARY WAY
QUEEN'S PARK AVE
A338
A35
A3049
B3063
B3064
B3066
10
11
90
SHBOURNE CT
RINITY
T PETERS CT
NE GRANGE
JCKINGHAM MANS
EXANDRA LO
JEENSBURY MANS
MBERLEY CT
TH HILL CT
10 LITTLE FOREST MANS
11 BERNE CT
12 ELIZABETH CT
13 LANSDOWNE HO
14 CODOGAN CT
15 BURFORD CT
16 GRANGE CT
17 GARDEN HO
18 ATHELNEY CT
19 GROSVENER CT
20 EDEN CT
21 GROVE MANS
22 RIVIREA
B2
1 WILLOW LO
2 GROSVENOR CT
3 PINE MANS
4 VALE MONS
5 KNOLE CT
6 COURTLEIGH MANOR
7 GORSECLIFF CT
C2
1 DONOUGHMORE RD
2 RANDOLPH RD
3 THE CRESCENT
4 CARNARVON RD
5 ROYAL ARC
6 PENNY LA
7 FLORIN MALL
8 SOVEREIGN SQ
9 CROWN WLK
10 HORACE RD
11 ARGYLL MANS
12 FAIRHAVON CT
13 CLIFTON CT
14 WARWICK CT
15 RICHMOND CT
16 GRANTLEY RD
17 THESSALY CT
18 ST GEORGES MANS
206
C2
19 WATKIN RD
20 ST JAMES'S
21 MARINA CT
22 MERMAID CT
23 SAN REMO TWRS
24 MARINA TWRS
25 WOLLSTONECRAFT RD
26 CLEASBY GRANGE
27 LAVERSTOCK
28 OCEAN HTS
29 CARLINFORD
C3
1 ST ANN'S CT
2 ST GEORGE'S CT
3 ST DAVID'S CT
4 ST JOHN'S CT
5 HAVILAND RD W

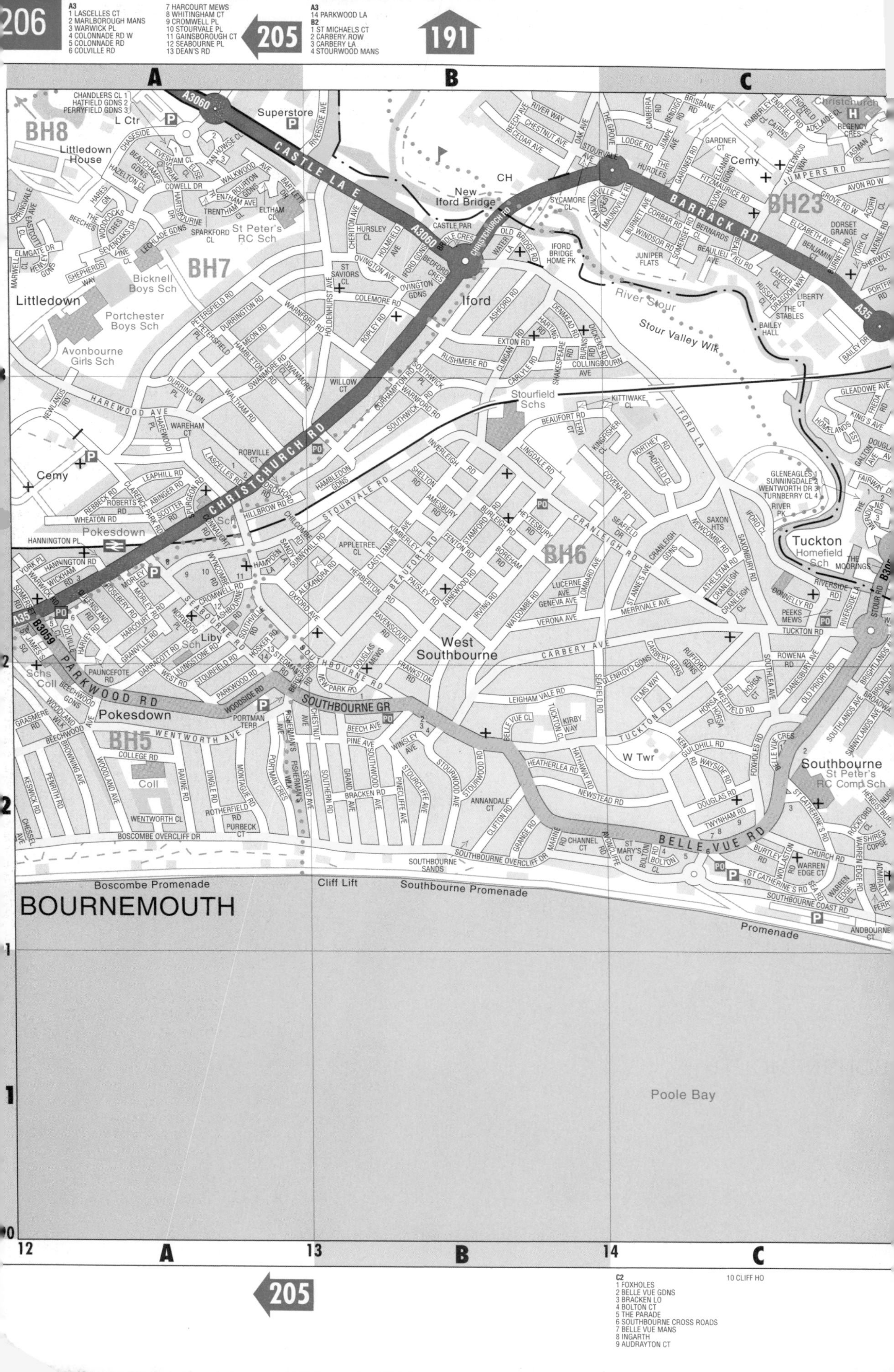
206
A3
1 LASCELLES CT
2 MARLBOROUGH MANS
3 WARWICK PL
4 COLONNADE RD W
5 COLONNADE RD
6 COLVILLE RD
7 HARCOURT MEWS
8 WHITINGHAM CT
9 CROMWELL PL
10 STOURVALE PL
11 GAINSBOROUGH CT
12 SEABOURNE PL
13 DEAN'S RD
205
A3
14 PARKWOOD LA
B2
1 ST MICHAELS CT
2 CARBERY ROW
3 CARBERY LA
4 STOURWOOD MANS
191
A
B
C
BH8
BH7
BH6
BH5
BH23
Littledown House
Littledown
L Ctr
Superstore
CASTLE LA E
A3060
New Iford Bridge
CH
Christchurch
Cemy
BARRACK RD
A35
Iford
River Stour
Stour Valley Wlk
Bicknell Boys Sch
Portchester Boys Sch
Avonbourne Girls Sch
St Peter's RC Sch
Stourfield Schs
CHRISTCHURCH RD
Pokesdown
Tuckton
Homefield Sch
West Southbourne
SOUTHBOURNE GR
PARKWOOD RD
B3059
Southbourne
St Peter's RC Comp Sch
BELLE VUE RD
W Twr
Coll
Liby
Schs Coll
Boscombe Promenade
Cliff Lift
Southbourne Promenade
Promenade
BOURNEMOUTH
Poole Bay
12
13
14
A
B
C
205
C2
1 FOXHOLES
2 BELLE VUE GDNS
3 BRACKEN LO
4 BOLTON CT
5 THE PARADE
6 SOUTHBOURNE CROSS ROADS
7 BELLE VUE MANS
8 INGARTH
9 AUDRAYTON CT
10 CLIFF HO

A
B
C
Latch Farm
Avon Valley Path
River Avon
Christchurch
Mus
Sch
Recn Gd
Liby
Castle
Priory
Mus
Twynham Sch
Quomps
Ferry (F)
River Stour
Recn Gd
Liby
Wick
Caravan Park
St Katharine's CE Prim Sch
CH
Stour Valley Wlk
BH6
BH23
Works
The Manor Arms (PH)
CHRISTCHURCH BY-PASS
A35
B3059
B3347
B3073
FAIRMILE RD
BARRACK RD
STOUR RD
BARGATES
FOUNTAIN WAY
STONY LA
PUREWELL CROSS RD
SOMERFORD RD
MUDEFORD LA
MUDEFORD
Purewell
Somerford
The Grange Comp Sch
Schs
Silver Bsns Pk
Airfield Ind Est
C Ctr
L Ctr
Marsh Lane
Ship in Distress (PH)
Bsns Ctr
Sch
Mudeford Jun Sch
CHRISTCHURCH
Stanpit
Fisherman's Bank
Stanpit Marsh Nature Reserve
Crouch Hill
Grimbury Marsh
Ferry (F)
Christchurch Harbour
Wick Hams
Nature Trail
Promenade
SOUTHBOURNE COAST RD
BROADWAY
Coastguard Lookout Sta
Nature Reserve
Warren Hill
Hengistbury Head
16
17
A
B
C

207
193

A
B
C
A35
CHRISTCHURCH BY-PASS
Superstore
Prim Sch
Rec Gd
PH
EDWARD RD
AMEYTHST RD
B3059 SOMERFORD RD
A337
SPEEDWELL DR 1
OK MOBILE HOME PK 2
Sea Vixen Ind Est
Ind Est
Grange Road Bsns Ctr
Somerford
Somerford Bsns Pk
Hughes Bsns Ctr
Ind Est
Beaver Ind Est
River Mude
Ambassador Ind Est
1 MARINERS CT
2 RODNEY CT
REDLANDS
DAKOTA CL 1
VULCAN WAY 2
BRITANNIA WAY 3
Priory Ind Pk
HALIFAX WAY
HIGHCLIFFE RD
BH23
Bure Brook
SHELLEY HILL
LYMINGTON RD
Highcliffe
NEA RD
SMUGGLERS LA N
SMUGGLERS LA S
ROWAN DR
WOODLAND WAY
SOMERFORD CT
CH
HIGH PINES
SHELLEY HAMLETS
ELIZABETH GDNS
Friars Cliff
FRESHWATER RD
PENNY WAY
Highcliffe Castle
ROTHESAY DR
RANELAGH CT 1
BEACON CT 2
HARRINGTON CT 3
WHARNCLIFFE CT 4
Groynes
BURE HOMAGE LA
BURE LA
SOUTHCLIFFE RD
FRIARS GATE
CLIFF DR
ISLAND VIEW AVE
PROMENADE
CHRISTCHURCH
Groynes
RICARDO CRES
BURE HAVEN DR
SHELDRAKE RD
MUDEFORD
Mudeford
ORESTES GATE
Hotel
SMUGGLERS REACH
MOUNT PLEASANT
CHICHESTER WAY
VIKING WAY
Sandhills
IRB Sta
Little Haven
Haven House Inn (PH)
Ferry (F)
BH6
Groynes
Stour Valley Wlk
Hengistbury Head
4
3
2
1
0
18
19
20

194
210

A
B
C
BH23
BH25
LYMINGTON RD
CHRISTCHURCH RD
A337
Chewton Bunny
Naish Holiday Village
High Cliff
Barton Cliff
Barton on Sea
Groynes
Groynes
A4
1 LAVENDER VILLAS
2 BUCKINGHAM CT
3 CASTLE CT
4 CARISBROOKE CT
5 WINDSOR CT
6 HURST CT
7 BALMORAL CT
8 MERTON CT
9 BERMUDA CT
10 EXETER CT
11 PEMBROKE CT
12 HERTFORD CT
13 FRANCES CT
14 ROSEMARY CT
15 KENNETH CT
16 ALAN CT
17 WILLIAM CT
18 PENELOPE CT
19 STELLA CT
1 TRACEY CT
2 DIANA CT
3 CLAIRE CT
WESTMINSTER CT 1
CRESCENT CT 2
CLIFF TERR 3
4
3
2
1
93
92
91
90
22
23

210

209
195

A
B
C
Barton on Sea
Barton Cliff
Barton Common
Durlston Court Sch
BH25
CH
Becton Bunny
Angel Cottage
Home Farm
Ashley Bridge
Ashley Clinton House
Downton
S041
Dane Stream
Taddiford Farm
Hordle Bridge
Hordle Manor Farm
PH
B3058
MILFORD RD
A337 LYMINGTON RD
CHRISTCHURCH RD
CLIFF RD
ANGEL LA
BARTON COMMON RD
BARTON COMMON LA
HIGHLANDS RD
CHESTNUT AVE
SOLENT DR
GROVE RD
MARINE DR E
WILLOW WLK
1 ALDBURY CT
2 DOLPHIN PL
3 HIGH MARRYATS
4 LYNRIC CL
5 WHITE KNIGHTS
Christchurch Bay
4
93
3
92
2
91
1
90
24
25
26

209

A
B
C
Leagreen
Leagreen Farm
Downton Manor Farm
CHRISTCHURCH RD
MILFORD RD A337
Everton Grange
RODBOURNE CL 1
ASH GR 2
OAK GDNS 3
CHERRY TREE CL 4
CYPRESS GR 5
LABURNUM DR 6
MULBERRY GR 7
PLANTATION 8
Newlands Manor
Buona Vista Farm
BRAXTON CTYD
NEWLANDS MANOR
Cox's Bridge
Lymore
Barnes Farm
Blackbush Copse
SO41
Nursery
Hotel
LYMINGTON RD
Milford on Sea Prim Sch
Lymore Farm
Knold
B3
1 ADDINGTON CT
2 BLANDFORD CT
3 DACRES WLK
4 DRYDEN PL
5 WINDMILL CL
6 GLEBEFIELDS
Danes Stream
AMBERWOOD
Recn Gd
The Vicarage
Studland Common
1 THE LYDGATE
2 SEAWINDS
1 MOLEFIELDS
2 MILFORD HO
Hordle Cliff
CLIFF RD
HIGH ST
MILFORD CRES
PARK LA
Rook Cliff
A2
1 CAMDEN HURST
2 SOLENT PINES
3 MARYLAND CT
4 WHITBY CT
5 BEATRICE CT
6 ALLISON CT
E2
1 KIVERNELL PL
2 HOLLY GDNS
3 ROOKWOOD
4 HAVEN CT
5 HURST CT
6 SOLENT CT
7 OSBORNE CT
8 TOTLAND CT
9 SEA PINES
10 PINEHURST
11 NEEDLES CT
12 RICHMOND CT
13 ROOKCLIFF
14 PARK CT
15 HOMEGRANGE HO
16 THE BOLTONS
17 HURDLES MEAD
War Meml
Milford Trad Est
Milford on Sea
Sturt Pond
Solent Way
4
93
3
92
2
91
1
90
28
29

211
197

A
B
C
MILFORD RD
A337
Efford Experimental
Horticulture Station
Great Newbridge
Copse
Sadlers Farm
Lower Pennington
Lower Farm
Pennington
House
LOWER PENNINGTON LA
Iley La
RIDGEWAY LA
PLATOFF RD
The
Chequers Inn
(PH)
LOWER WOODSIDE
The
Salterns
Oxey Marsh
AGARTON LA
Avon Water
SO41
Saltworks
Nature
Reserve
Pennington
Marshes
Jetty
Solent Way
Vidle Van
Farm
LYMORE LA
Saltworks
Keyhaven Marshes
Keyhaven
AUBREY FARM
COTTS
KEYHAVEN RD
HAREWOOD GN
NEW RD
Aubrey
House
SHIPWRIGHTS
WLK
PH
Jetty
Lyndon
Keyhaven
House
Salt
Grass
SALTGRASS LA
Ferry (F)
(Summer Only)
The Mount
Solent Way
Hurst Beach
Hurst
Castle
4
93
3
92
2
91
1
90
30
31
32
A
B
C

211

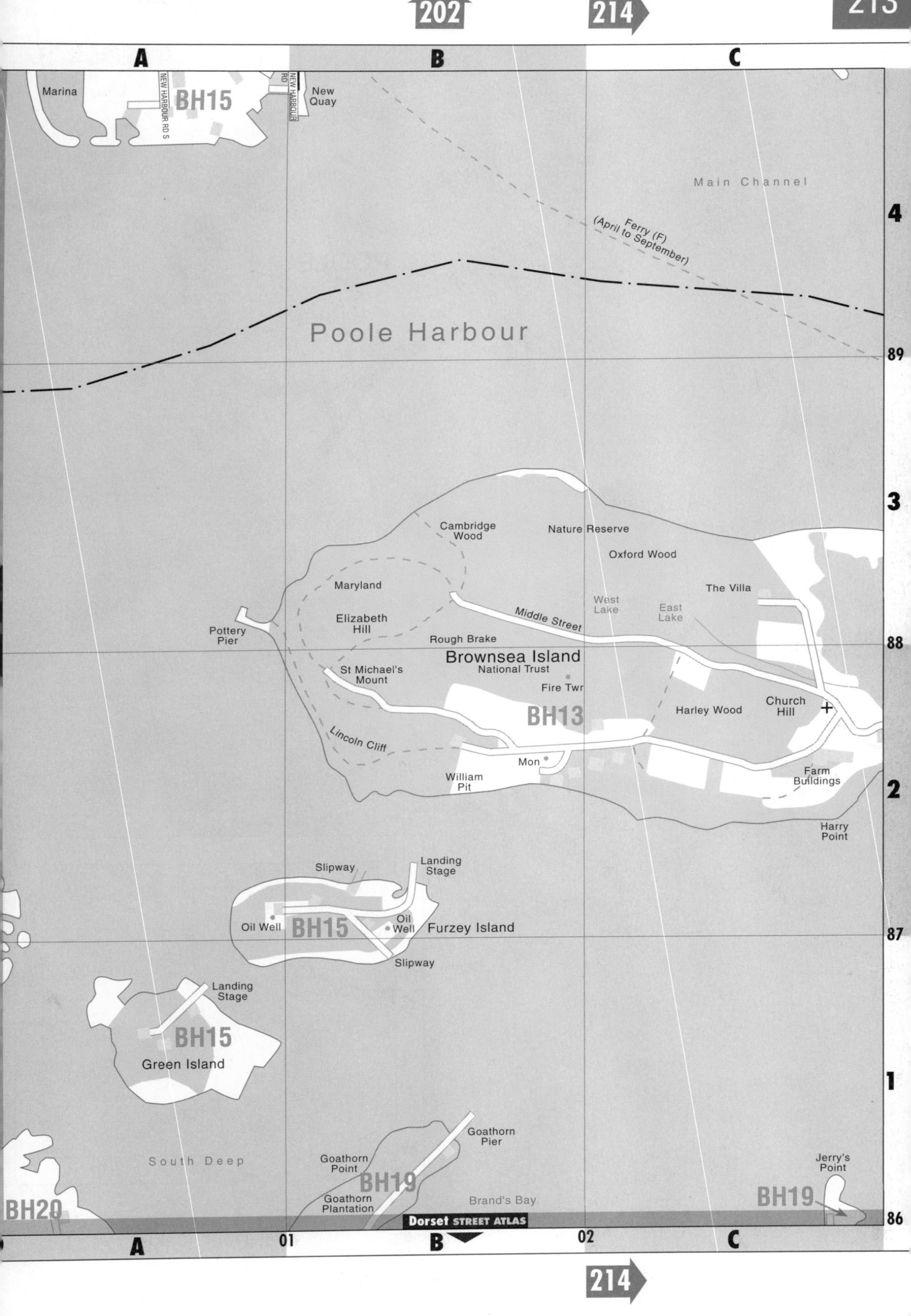
A
B
C
Marina
BH15
NEW HARBOUR RD S
NEW HARBOUR RD
New Quay
Main Channel
Ferry (F) (April to September)
Poole Harbour
4
89
3
Cambridge Wood
Nature Reserve
Oxford Wood
Maryland
The Villa
West Lake
East Lake
Elizabeth Hill
Middle Street
Pottery Pier
Rough Brake
88
Brownsea Island
National Trust
St Michael's Mount
Fire Twr
BH13
Harley Wood
Church Hill
Lincoln Cliff
Mon
Farm Buildings
William Pit
2
Harry Point
Slipway
Landing Stage
Oil Well
BH15
Oil Well
Furzey Island
87
Slipway
Landing Stage
BH15
Green Island
1
Goathorn Pier
South Deep
Goathorn Point
BH19
Jerry's Point
BH20
Goathorn Plantation
Brand's Bay
BH19
86
01
02
A
B
C

213
203

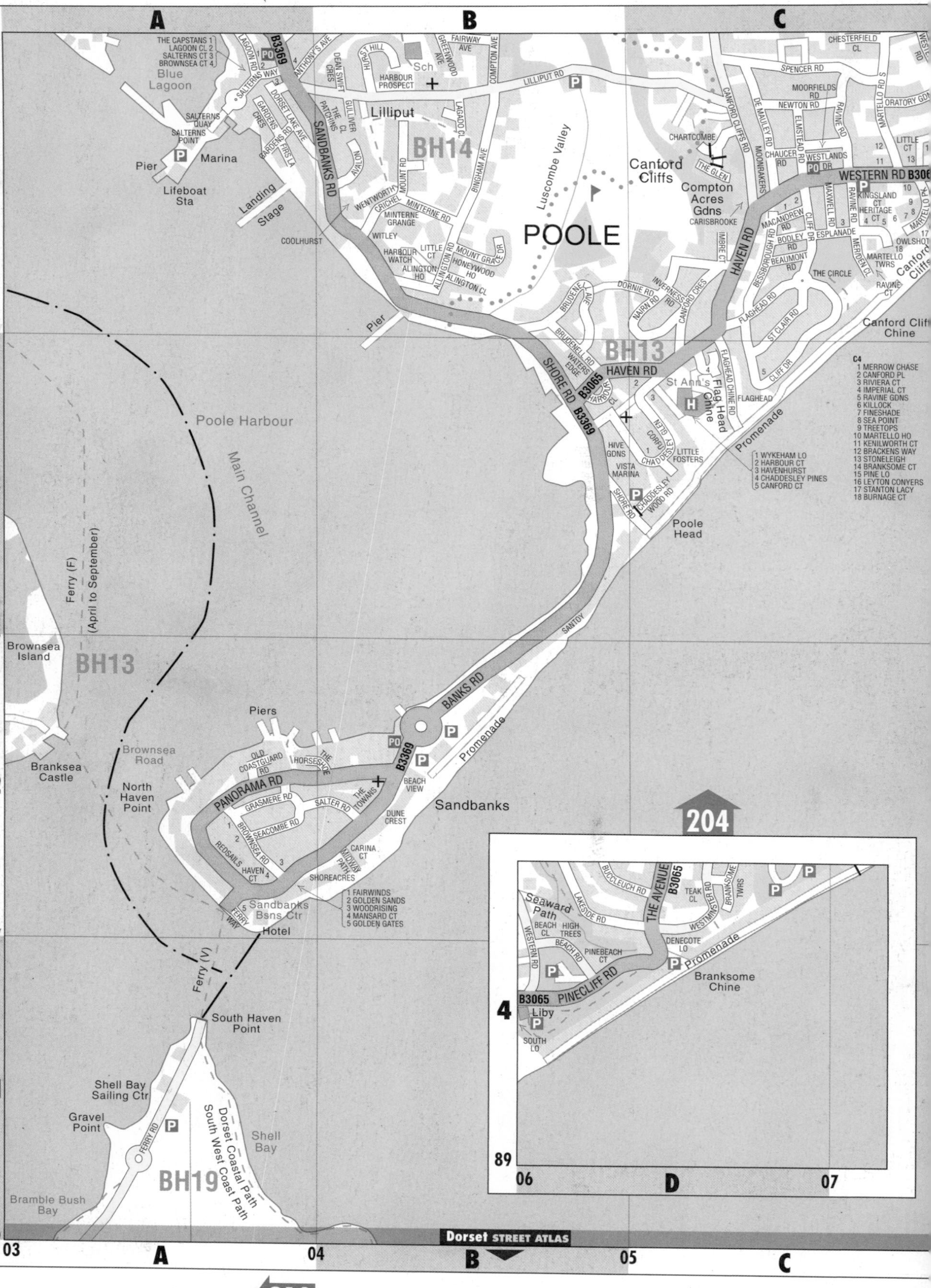

A B C

THE CAPSTANS 1
LAGOON CL 2
SALTERNS CT 3
BROWNSEA CT 4

Blue Lagoon
SALTERNS WAY
SALTERNS QUAY
SALTERNS POINT
Pier
Marina
Lifeboat Sta
Landing Stage
LAGOON RD
DORSET LAKE AVE
GARDENS CRES
GARDENS RD
FIRS LA
B3369
SANDBANKS RD
ANTHONY'S AVE
DEAN SWIFT CRES
THE PATCHINS
GULLIVER CL
HURST HILL
HARBOUR PROSPECT
Sch
FAIRWAY AVE
GREENWOOD AVE
COMPTON AVE
LILLIPUT RD
Lilliput
LAGADO CL
AVALON
MOUNT RD
BH14
BINGHAM AVE
WENTWORTH
CRICHEL
MINTERNE RD
MINTERNE GRANGE
WITLEY
COOLHURST
HARBOUR WATCH
LITTLE CT
ALINGTON HO
ALINGTON RD
ALINGTON CL
MOUNT GRACE DR
HONEYWOOD HO
Luscombe Valley
POOLE
Canford Cliffs
Compton Acres Gdns
CARISBROOKE
CHARTCOMBE
THE GLEN
CANFORD CLIFFS RD
DE MAULEY RD
MOONRAKERS
CHESTERFIELD CL
SPENCER RD
MOORFIELDS RD
NEWTON RD
ELMSTEAD RD
RAVINE RD
MARTELLO RD S
ORATORY GDNS
CHAUCER RD
WESTLANDS DR
LITTLE CT
WESTERN RD B3065
KINGSLAND CT
HERITAGE CT
MACANDREW RD
CLIFF DR
MAXWELL RD
ESPLANADE
BODLEY RD
BEAUMONT RD
BESSBOROUGH RD
MERIDEN CL
OWLSHOTT
MARTELLO TWRS
THE CIRCLE
RAVINE CT
Canford Cliffs
IMBRE CT
HAVEN RD
DORNIE RD
INVERNESS RD
NAIRN RD
CANFORD CRES
BRUDENELL AVE
BRUDENELL RD
WATERS EDGE
FLAGHEAD RD
ST CLAIR RD
Canford Cliffs Chine
Pier
BH13
SHORE RD
B3065
HAVEN RD
HARBOUR CL
St Ann's
H
Flag Head Chine
FLAGHEAD CHINE RD
FLAGHEAD
CLIFF DR
B3369
CORFU
GLEN
CHADDESLEY GLEN
HIVE GDNS
LITTLE FOSTERS
VISTA MARINA
CHADDESLEY WOOD RD
SHORE RD
Promenade
Poole Head

1 WYKEHAM LO
2 HARBOUR CT
3 HAVENHURST
4 CHADDESLEY PINES
5 CANFORD CT

C4
1 MERROW CHASE
2 CANFORD PL
3 RIVIERA CT
4 IMPERIAL CT
5 RAVINE GDNS
6 KILLOCK
7 FINESHADE
8 SEA POINT
9 TREETOPS
10 MARTELLO HO
11 KENILWORTH CT
12 BRACKENS WAY
13 STONELEIGH
14 BRANKSOME CT
15 PINE LO
16 LEYTON CONYERS
17 STANTON LACY
18 BURNAGE CT

Poole Harbour
Main Channel
Ferry (F) (April to September)
Brownsea Island
BH13
SANTOY
BANKS RD
Piers
Brownsea Road
Branksea Castle
North Haven Point
OLD COASTGUARD RD
HORSESHOE
THE
B3369
PANORAMA RD
GRASMERE RD
SALTER RD
THE TOWANS
BEACH VIEW
Promenade
Sandbanks
DUNE CREST
SEACOMBE RD
BROWNSEA RD
REDSAILS
HAVEN CT
CARINA CT
MIDWAY PATH
SHOREACRES
Sandbanks Bsns Ctr
FERRY WAY
Hotel

1 FAIRWINDS
2 GOLDEN SANDS
3 WOODRISING
4 MANSARD CT
5 GOLDEN GATES

Ferry (V)
South Haven Point
Shell Bay Sailing Ctr
Gravel Point
FERRY RD
Dorset Coastal Path
South West Coast Path
Shell Bay
BH19
Bramble Bush Bay

204

BUCCLEUCH RD
THE AVENUE B3065
TEAK CL
WESTMINSTER RD
BRANKSOME TWRS
Seaward Path
LAKESIDE RD
BEACH CL
HIGH TREES
WESTERN RD
BEACH RD
PINEBEACH CT
DENECOTE LO
Promenade
Branksome Chine
B3065 PINECLIFF RD
Liby
SOUTH LO
4
89
06 D 07

89 88 87 86
4 3 2 1
03 04 05
A B C

213

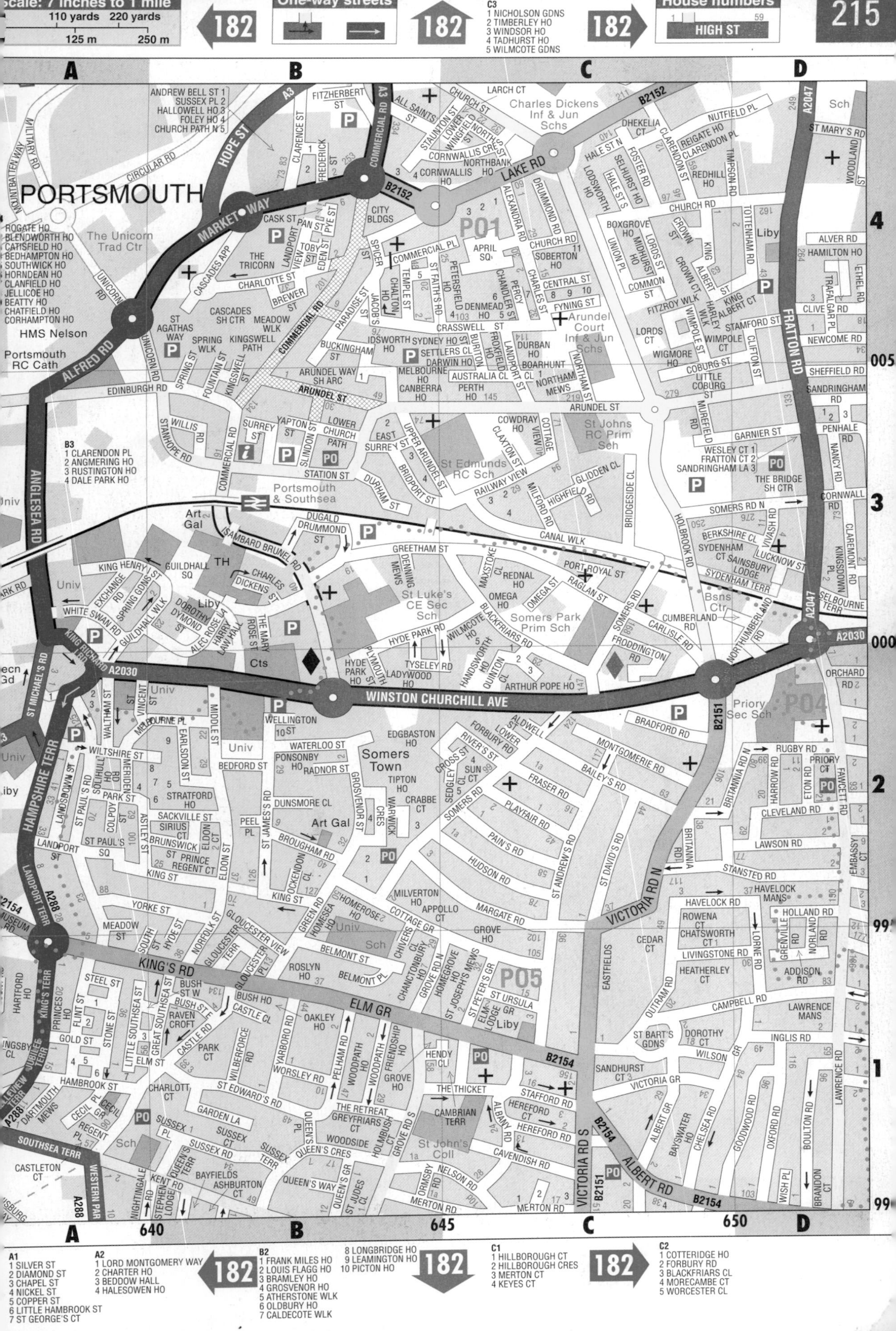

Scale: 7 inches to 1 mile
110 yards
220 yards
125 m
250 m
182
One-way streets
182
C3
1 NICHOLSON GDNS
2 TIMBERLEY HO
3 WINDSOR HO
4 TADHURST HO
5 WILMCOTE GDNS
182
House numbers
1
59
HIGH ST
215
A
B
C
D
PORTSMOUTH
The Unicorn Trad Ctr
HMS Nelson
Portsmouth RC Cath
ANDREW BELL ST 1
SUSSEX PL 2
HALLOWELL HO 3
FOLEY HO 4
CHURCH PATH N 5
ROGATE HO
BLENDWORTH HO
CATISFIELD HO
BEDHAMPTON HO
SOUTHWICK HO
HORNDEAN HO
CLANFIELD HO
JELLICOE HO
BEATTY HO
CHATFIELD HO
CORHAMPTON HO
Charles Dickens Inf & Jun Schs
Arundel Court Inf & Jun Schs
St Johns RC Prim Sch
St Edmunds RC Sch
Portsmouth & Southsea
Art Gal
GUILDHALL SQ
TH
Liby
Univ
St Luke's CE Sec Sch
Somers Park Prim Sch
Bsns Ctr
Priory Sec Sch
Somers Town
Art Gal
St John's Coll
B3
1 CLARENDON PL
2 ANGMERING HO
3 RUSTINGTON HO
4 DALE PARK HO
WESLEY CT 1
FRATTON CT 2
SANDRINGHAM LA 3
THE BRIDGE SH CTR
CASCADES SH CTR
THE TRICORN
CITY BLDGS
LAKE RD
MARKET WAY
HOPE ST
ALFRED RD
ANGLESEA RD
COMMERCIAL RD
ARUNDEL ST
FRATTON RD
WINSTON CHURCHILL AVE
KING'S RD
ELM GR
VICTORIA RD N
VICTORIA RD S
ALBERT RD
HAMPSHIRE TERR
LANDPORT TERR
SOUTHSEA TERR
CANAL WLK
A3
A2047
A2030
A288
B2152
B2151
B2154
P01
P04
P05
005
000
99
4
3
2
1
640
645
650
A1
1 SILVER ST
2 DIAMOND ST
3 CHAPEL ST
4 NICKEL ST
5 COPPER ST
6 LITTLE HAMBROOK ST
7 ST GEORGE'S CT
A2
1 LORD MONTGOMERY WAY
2 CHARTER HO
3 BEDDOW HALL
4 HALESOWEN HO
182
B2
1 FRANK MILES HO
2 LOUIS FLAGG HO
3 BRAMLEY HO
4 GROSVENOR HO
5 ATHERSTONE WLK
6 OLDBURY HO
7 CALDECOTE WLK
8 LONGBRIDGE HO
9 LEAMINGTON HO
10 PICTON HO
182
C1
1 HILLBOROUGH CT
2 HILLBOROUGH CRES
3 MERTON CT
4 KEYES CT
182
C2
1 COTTERIDGE HO
2 FORBURY RD
3 BLACKFRIARS CL
4 MORECAMBE CT
5 WORCESTER CL

Abbotts Barton
Abbots Barton Farm House
Weeke
Weeke Prim Sch
Greenacres Specl Sch
Lankhills Sch
North Walls Recn Gd
Kings Way
Hyde
River Park L Ctr
Dykes Farm
St Martins Trad Pk
Winchester Sch of Art
St Bede CE Prim Sch
City Bsns Ctr
Fulflood
Peter Symonds' Coll
Nethercliffe Sch
Andover Road Ret Pk
Teg Down
Westgate Sec Sch
Western CE Prim Sch
Winchester
HM Prison
Cty Pol HQ
Mus
Liby's
Student Village
Sarum Road
Royal Hampshire County
Cemy
West Hill
Mus's
Mus
Cath
The Close
The Pilgrims Sch
Wharf Hill
The Soke
King Alfred's Coll
Sleepers' Hill
St Mary's Coll
Palace
New Hall
Winchester Coll
Wharf Bridge
All Saints CE Prim Sch
Recn Gd
Ridding Meads
Bar End
Bar End Ind Est
Works
Stanmore
SO22
Stanmore Prim Sch
St Faith's CE Prim Sch
Tun Bridge
St Cross
Badger Farm
Whiteshute Lane
Clarendon Way
Superstore
St Cross Hospital
SO23
Sewage Works
The Itchen Navigation
Itchen Way
River Itchen
St Catherine's Hill
Nature Reserve
Oliver's Battery Prim Sch
Maybush
South View Park Homes
Bushfield Camp
St Cross Farm
St Cross Mill
St Cross Bridge
SO21
Stockbridge Rd
Bereweeke Rd
Andover Rd
Worthy Rd
Worthy La
Hyde St
North Walls
City Rd
High St
Friarsgate
Eastgate St
Chesil St
Romsey Rd
Chilbolton Ave
Sussex St
Southgate St
Bar End Rd
St Cross Rd
Stanmore La
Badger Farm Rd
Christchurch Rd
Kingsgate St
B3049
B3041
B3420
B3044
B3045
B3047
B3330
B3040
B3331
B3335
B3404
A3090
M3

Winchester

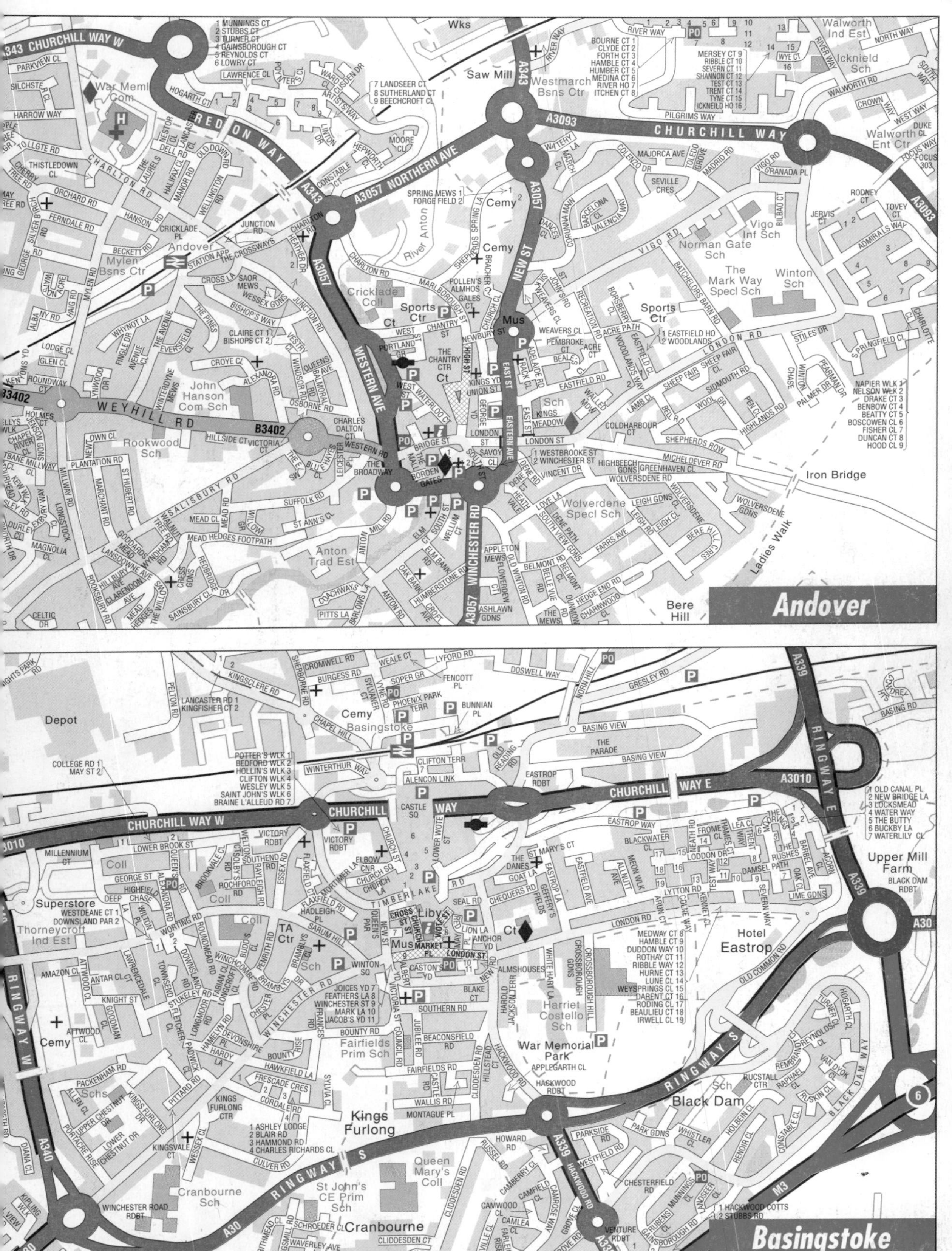
Andover
A343 CHURCHILL WAY W
Wks
Saw Mill
Westmarch Bsns Ctr
A3093
CHURCHILL WAY
Walworth Ind Est
Icknield Sch
Walworth Ent Ctr
War Meml Com
REDON WAY
A3057 NORTHERN AVE
Cemy
River Anton
Andover
Mylen Bsns Ctr
Cricklade Coll
Sports Ctr
Ct
Mus
NEW ST
WESTERN AVE
Vigo Inf Sch
Norman Gate Sch
The Mark Way Specl Sch
Winton Sch
Sports Ctr
LONDON RD
John Hanson Com Sch
WEYHILL RD
B3402
Rookwood Sch
Sch
Iron Bridge
Wolverdene Specl Sch
Ladies Walk
Anton Trad Est
WINCHESTER RD
A3057
Bere Hill
SALISBURY RD
Basingstoke
Depot
Cemy
Basingstoke
THE PARADE
BASING VIEW
CHURCHILL WAY E
A3010
CHURCHILL WAY W
CHURCHILL WAY
RINGWAY E
A339
Upper Mill Farm
BLACK DAM RDBT
A30
Coll
Superstore
Thorneycroft Ind Est
Coll
TA Ctr
Sch
Liby
Mus
Ct
Hotel Eastrop
RINGWAY W
Cemy
Harriet Costello Sch
War Memorial Park
Fairfields Prim Sch
RINGWAY S
Black Dam
Sch
Kings Furlong
Queen Mary's Coll
Cranbourne Sch
St John's CE Prim Sch
Cranbourne
A340
A30
M3
6

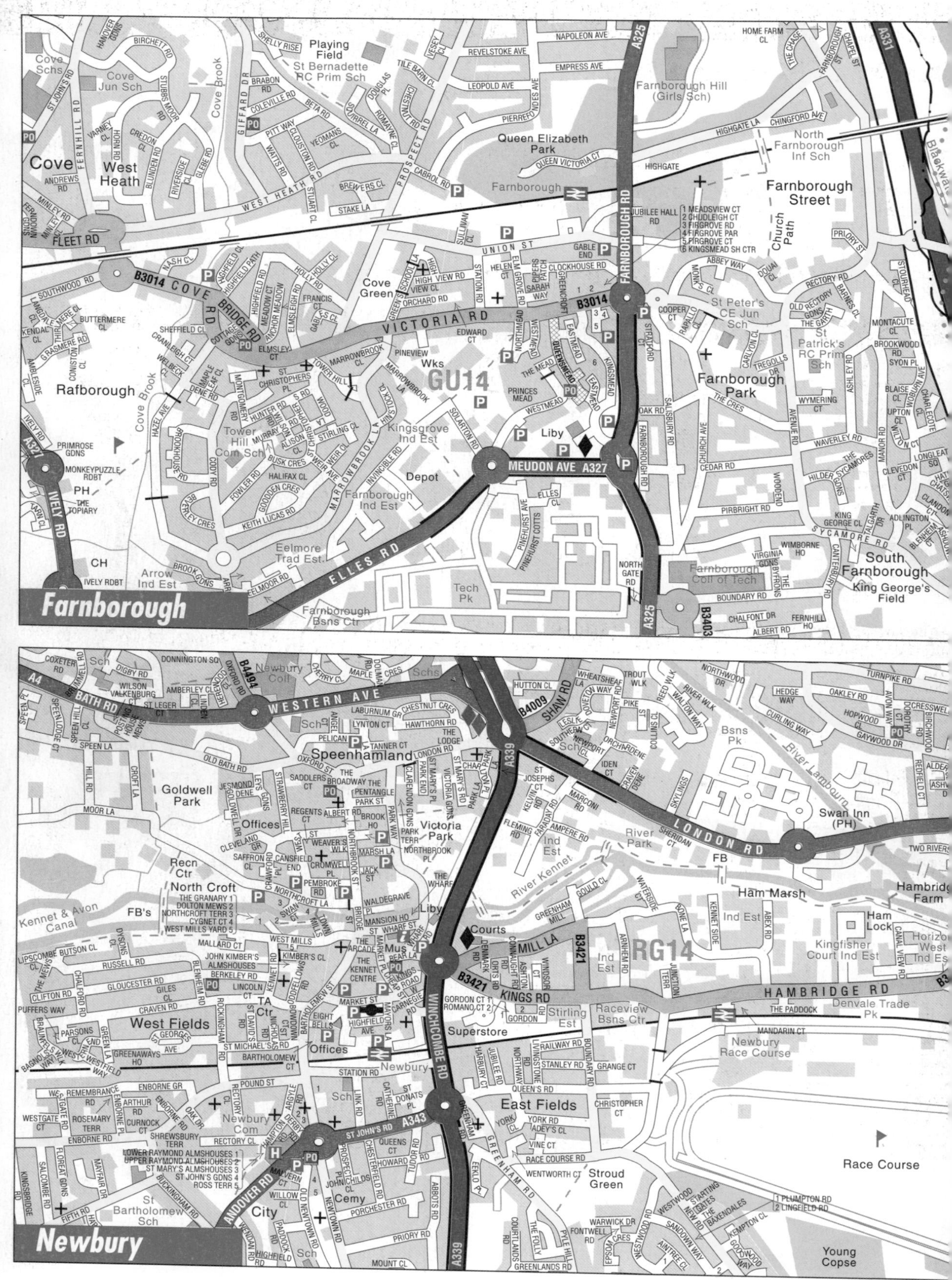
Farnborough
Cove
West Heath
Rafborough
Cove Green
Farnborough Park
Farnborough Street
South Farnborough
Queen Elizabeth Park
Farnborough Hill (Girls Sch)
North Farnborough Inf Sch
St Peter's CE Jun Sch
St Patrick's RC Prim Sch
Kingsgrove Ind Est
Farnborough Ind Est
Eelmore Trad Est.
Arrow Ind Est
Farnborough Bsns Ctr
Tech Pk
Farnborough Coll of Tech
King George's Field
Tower Hill Com Sch
Playing Field
St Bernadette RC Prim Sch
Cove Jun Sch
Cove Schs
GU14
VICTORIA RD
FARNBOROUGH RD
MEUDON AVE A327
ELLES RD
B3014 COVE RD
FLEET RD
WEST HEATH RD
IVELY RD
A325
A331
B3403
1 MEADSVIEW CT
2 CHUDLEIGH CT
3 FIRGROVE RD
4 FIRGROVE PAR
5 FIRGROVE CT
6 KINGSMEAD SH CTR
Newbury
Speenhamland
Goldwell Park
Victoria Park
North Croft
West Fields
East Fields
Stroud Green
City
Newbury Com
St Bartholomew Sch
Ham Marsh
Hambridge Farm
Ham Lock
Kingfisher Court Ind Est
Denvale Trade Pk
Raceview Bsns Ctr
Stirling Est
Newbury Race Course
Race Course
Young Copse
Swan Inn (PH)
River Park
River Kennet
River Lambourn
Kennet & Avon Canal
Newbury Coll
Bsns Pk
Superstore
Cemy
RG14
WESTERN AVE
LONDON RD
HAMBRIDGE RD
KINGS RD
WINCHCOMBE RD
ANDOVER RD
BATH RD
A4
A339
A343
B4494
B4009
B3421
THE GRANARY 1
DOLTON MEWS 2
NORTHCROFT TERR 3
CYGNET CT 4
WEST MILLS YARD 5
LOWER RAYMOND ALMSHOUSES 1
UPPER RAYMOND ALMSHOUSES 2
ST MARY'S ALMSHOUSES 3
ST JOHN'S GDNS 4
ROSS TERR 5
1 PLUMPTON RD
2 LINGFIELD RD

Index

Church Rd **6** Beckenham BR2.........**53** C6

Place name	Location number	Locality, town or village	Postcode district	Page and grid square
May be abbreviated on the map	Present when a number indicates the place's position in a crowded area of mapping	Shown when more than one place has the same name	District for the indexed place	Page number and grid reference for the standard mapping

Public and commercial buildings are highlighted in magenta **Places of interest** are highlighted in blue with a star★

Abbreviations used in the index

Acad	Academy	Comm	Common	Gd	Ground	L	Leisure	Prom	Prom
App	Approach	Cott	Cottage	Gdn	Garden	La	Lane	Rd	Road
Arc	Arcade	Cres	Crescent	Gn	Green	Liby	Library	Recn	Recreation
Ave	Avenue	Cswy	Causeway	Gr	Grove	Mdw	Meadow	Ret	Retail
Bglw	Bungalow	Ct	Court	H	Hall	Meml	Memorial	Sh	Shopping
Bldg	Building	Ctr	Centre	Ho	House	Mkt	Market	Sq	Square
Bsns, Bus	Business	Ctry	Country	Hospl	Hospital	Mus	Museum	St	Street
Bvd	Boulevard	Cty	County	HQ	Headquarters	Orch	Orchard	Sta	Station
Cath	Cathedral	Dr	Drive	Hts	Heights	Pal	Palace	Terr	Terrace
Cir	Circus	Dro	Drove	Ind	Industrial	Par	Parade	TH	Town Hall
Cl	Close	Ed	Education	Inst	Institute	Pas	Passage	Univ	University
Cnr	Corner	Emb	Embankment	Int	International	Pk	Park	Wk, Wlk	Walk
Coll	College	Est	Estate	Intc	Interchange	Pl	Place	Wr	Water
Com	Community	Ex	Exhibition	Junc	Junction	Prec	Precinct	Yd	Yard

Index of localities, towns and villages

Abbotswood 28 A2
Alderholt 92 A3
Ampfield 29 A1
Ashington 163 A1
Ashurst 100 A1
Awbridge 26 B2
Barton on Sea 209 A4
Beaulieu 148 A4
Beauworth 35 C4
Bishop's Waltham 83 A4
Bishopstoke 56 B2
Blackfield 177 B4
Blashford 117 A2
Boldre 173 A1
Botley 106 A3
Bournemouth 206 A2
Braishfield 28 A4
Bramdean 15 B2
Bramshaw 73 C2
Bransgore 193 A2
Breamore 70 A3
Broadstone 187 A1
Brockbridge 61 B1
Brockenhurst 145 A1
Brook 74 A1
Bucklers Hard 176 B3
Buriton 65 B2
Burley 143 A1
Bursledon 128 A4
Burton 192 B1
Cadnam 98 B4
Calshot 178 C4
Chalton 89 B3
Chandler's Ford 55 A2
Cheriton 14 A3
Chilcomb 11 B4
Chilworth 54 B1
Christchurch 207 A3
Clanfield 88 A3
Colden Common 32 A1
Compton (Hants) 31 B2
Compton (Sussex) 90 C1
Coombe Bissett 23 B4
Corfe Mullen 186 A1
Cosham 158 A4
Cowplain 111 C2
Cranborne 91 B4
Croucheston 22 A4
Curdridge 106 B4
Damerham 68 A2
Dean 59 C2
Denmead 111 A1
Dibden Purlieu 125 C1
Downton 47 A3
Droxford 61 A1
Durley 82 A1
East Boldre 175 B3
East Dean 4 A1
East End 199 A4
East Meon 38 B1
East Tytherley 4 B2
East Wellow 51 A3
Eastleigh 55 A2
Edmondsham 91 A2
Emery Down 121 B3
Emsworth 136 A1
Exbury 177 A3
Fair Oak 57 A1
Fareham 131 A1
Fawley 151 A1
Ferndown 165 B3
Finchdean 113 B3
Fordingbridge 69 A1
Fratton 182 C2
Fritham 72 C1
Froxfield Green 39 B3
Godshill 70 C1
Gosport 181 A1
Hamble-le-Rice 128 A1
Hambledon 86 A1
Hamworthy 201 A2
Havant 135 A1
Hawkley 19 C2
Hayling Island 185 A4
Hedge End 105 A2
Hermitage 161 A3
High Cross 18 C1
Highcliffe 208 C4
Hill Brow 21 A1
Holbury 150 A2
Holt Heath 138 A4
Hordle 195 C2
Horndean 112 A3
Horton Heath 81 B4
Hurn 191 A3
Hursley 30 A3
Hythe 126 A1
Ibsley 117 A4
Keyhaven 212 A2
Kilmeston 14 B1
Kings Worthy 2 A2
Kingston 167 C4
Landford 49 A3
Langrish 39 B1
Langstone 159 C4
Lee-on-the-Solent 179 B1
Lepe 178 A1
Linwood 118 A4
Liss 21 A2
Littleton 1 A2
Lockerley 4 B2
Locks Heath 129 A1
Lover 48 A3
Lymington 197 A1
Lyndhurst 121 A2
Marchwood 101 B1
Martin 43 A2
Meonstoke 61 A3
Michelmersh 6 A1
Milford on Sea 211 A2
Minstead 98 A1
Mottisfont 5 B1
Netley 127 A3
Netley Marsh 100 A3
New Milton 194 C1
Newbridge 74 C2
Nomansland 73 A4
North Baddesley 53 A3
North Boarhunt 109 A1
North Hayling 160 A1
Nursling 77 A2
Oakley 163 C1
Otterbourne 31 A1
Ower 75 B2
Owslebury 33 A2
Pamphill 162 A3
Pentridge 42 A1
Petersfield 40 C2
Plaitford 50 A2
Poole 202 A1
Portchester 156 A3
Portmore 198 A4
Portsea Island 182 B3
Portsmouth 157 A1
Privet 17 B1
Purbrook 134 C2
Rake 21 B2
Ramsdean 39 B1
Redlynch 47 B2
Ringwood 141 A2
Ripley 168 B1
Rockbourne 44 C1
Romsey 52 A2
Rowland's Castle 113 A1
Rownhams 77 B3
St Leonards 139 B1
Sandleheath 69 C1
Shedfield 107 A4
Sherfield English 25 A1
Soberton 85 A1
Sopley 192 A3
South Harting 66 C3
South Hayling 184 A2
Southampton 102 A3
Southbourne 161 A4
Southsea 182 B1
Southwick 132 A2
Standon 9 A1
Steep 40 C4
Steep Marsh 20 A1
Stubbington 154 A2
Swanmore 84 A2
Swanwick 129 A4
Sway 172 A1
Thorney Island 161 A1
Three Legged Cross 138 C4
Timsbury 27 B3
Titchfield 153 C3
Totton 100 A2
Twyford 32 A3
Upham 58 A1
Upton 201 A3
Verwood 114 A1
Walderton 137 C4
Waltham Chase 83 B1
Warnford 36 C2
Warsash 128 B1
Waterlooville 134 A1
West Dean 3 A1
West End 80 A1
West Meon 37 A3
West Moors 138 A1
West Parley 189 C4
West Tisted 16 B1
West Tytherley 4 A3
West Wellow 50 B1
Westbourne 137 A1
Whiteparish 24 A1
Whitsbury 45 A1
Wick 46 C4
Wickham 108 A1
Wimborne Minster 163 A1
Winchester 10 A1
Woodgreen 70 C4
Woodlands 114 A3
Wootton 171 A1

1
1st St SO45 .....151 A2

2
2nd St SO45 .....151 A2

3
3rd St SO45 .....150 C2

4
4th St SO45 .....150 C2

5
5th St SO45 .....150 C2

6
6th St Fawley SO45 .....150 C2
Fawley SO45 .....150 C3

7
7th St SO45 .....150 C2

8
8th St SO45 .....150 C2

9
9th St SO45 .....150 B2

1
10th St SO45 .....150 B3
11th St SO45 .....150 B3
12th St SO45 .....150 B3
13th St SO45 .....150 B3
14th St SO45 .....150 B3
17th Centure Experience Mus★ PO13 .....180 B3

A
A Ave SO45 .....150 B2
A'beckett Ct 3 PO1 .....182 A2
Aaron Cl BH17 .....202 C4
Aaron Ct SO40 .....101 C1
Abbas Gr PO9 .....135 B4
Abbey Cl SO45 .....126 A2
Abbey Ct 15 SO15 .....102 C4
Abbey Ent Ctr SO51 .....53 B3
Abbey Gdns BH21 .....164 B3
Abbey Hill SO31 .....127 A4
Abbey Hill Cl SO23 .....2 A1
Abbey Hill Rd SO23 .....1 C1
Abbey Mill Bsns Site SO32 .....83 A4
Abbey Pas SO23 .....11 A4
Abbey Rd Fareham PO15 .130 B1
West Moors BH22 .....166 A4
Abbey The SO51 .....52 C4
Abbey Water 9 SO51 .....52 C4
Abbeyfield Dr PO15 .....130 B1
Abbeyfield Ho 7 SO18 .103 C4
Abbeyfields Cl SO31 .....127 B3
Abbots Cl
Christchurch BH23 .....208 C4
Waterlooville PO7 .....134 B2
Abbots Row 6 SO22 .....10 C4
Abbots Way
Fareham PO15 .....130 B1
Netley SO31 .....127 B3
Abbots Well Rd SP6 .....94 C4
Abbotsbury Rd
Bishopstoke SO50 .....56 C1
Broadstone BH18 .....186 C3
Abbotsfield SO40 .....100 C4
Abbotsfield Cl SO16 .....78 B3
Abbotsford SO40 .....99 A3
Abbotstone Ave PO9 .....136 A2
Abbotswood Cl SO51 .....28 B1
Abbotswood Jun Sch SO40 .....100 C4
Abbott Cl BH9 .....205 A4
Abbott Rd BH9 .....205 A4
Abbott St BH21 .....162 B3
Abbotts Ann Rd SO22 .....1 B2
Abbotts Cl SO23 .....2 A1
Abbotts Ct
15 Southampton SO17 .....79 A1
Winchester SO22 .....1 C1
Abbotts Dro SO51 .....50 C1
Abbotts Rd Eastleigh SO50 55 C1
Winchester SO23 .....2 A1
Abbotts Way
Southampton SO17 .....79 A1
West Moors BH22 .....166 A4
Abercrombie Gdns SO16 .78 A2
Aberdare Ave PO6 .....158 A4
Aberdare Rd BH10 .....189 C2
Aberdeen Cl PO15 .....130 C2
Aberdeen Rd SO17 .....79 B1
Aberdour Cl SO18 .....104 A4
Abingdon Cl PO12 .....181 A2
Abingdon Dr BH23 .....209 B4
Abingdon Gdns SO16 .....78 C2
Abingdon Rd BH17 .....202 B4
Abinger Rd BH7 .....206 A3
Abney Rd BH10 .....189 B2
Above Bar St SO14 .....102 C3
Abraham Cl SO30 .....105 B3
Abshot Cl PO14 .....129 A1
Abshot Rd PO14 .....129 B1
Acacia Ave BH31 .....115 B2
Acacia Gdns PO8 .....112 A3
Acacia Rd Hordle SO41 .195 C2
Southampton SO19 .....103 C3
Acer Way PO9 .....136 A2
Ackworth Rd PO3 .....158 A3
Acland Rd BH9 .....205 A4
Acorn Bsns Ctr PO6 .....157 B4
Acorn Bsns Pk BH12 .....203 A4
Acorn Cl
Christchurch BH23 .....206 C4
Cosham PO6 .....158 C4
Gosport PO13 .....155 B1
Marchwood SO40 .....102 A1
New Milton BH25 .....195 B2
St Leonards BH24 .....139 C2
Acorn Cotts BH31 .....114 C4
Acorn Ct SO31 .....127 C2
Acorn Dr SO16 .....77 C4
Acorn Gdns PO8 .....112 A3
Acorn Gr SO53 .....54 C2
Acorn Way BH31 .....115 A3
Acorn Workshops SO14 103 A4
Acorns The
Bursledon SO31 .....127 C4
Wimborne Minst BH21 .....164 A2
Acre La PO7 .....112 B1
Acres Rd BH11 .....189 A1
Acton Rd BH10 .....189 A1
Ad Astro Fst Sch BH17 .187 C1
Adair Rd PO4 .....183 A1
Adames Rd PO1 .....182 C3
Adams Cl SO30 .....81 A2
Adams Rd SO45 .....126 A1
Adams Terr PO6 .....158 B3
Adams Way PO15 .....129 B3
Adams Wood Dr SO40 .....101 C1
Adamsfield Gdns BH10 .189 B1
Adamson Cl SO53 .....55 B4
Adastral Rd BH17 .....202 C4
Adastral Sq BH17 .....202 C4
Adcock Ct SO16 .....77 C4
Adderbury Ave PO10 .....136 C2
Addington Ct 1 SO41 .....211 B3
Addington Pl BH23 .....207 B3
Addis Sq 35 SO17 .....79 A1
Addiscombe Rd BH23 .....207 A4
Addison Cl Romsey SO51 .28 A1
Winchester SO22 .....10 B3
Addison Rd
Brockenhurst SO42 .....172 C4
Eastleigh SO50 .....56 A3
Locks Heath SO31 .....128 C3
Portsmouth PO5 .....215 D1
Addison Sq BH24 .....141 A4
Adelaide Cl BH23 .....206 C4
Adelaide Ct SO41 .....197 C2
Adelaide La 40 BH1 .....204 C2
Adelaide Pl 9 PO16 .....131 B1
Adelaide Rd SO17 .....103 B4
Adeline Rd BH5 .....205 C2
Adey Cl SO19 .....104 A1
Adhurst Rd PO9 .....136 A2
Adlam's La SO41 .....172 A1
Admiral Lord Nelson Sch PO3 .....158 A1
Admiral Park The PO3 .158 A2
Admiral's Cnr 4 PO5 .....182 B1
Admiral's Wlk PO1 .....181 C3
Admirals Cl SO45 .....151 A2
Admirals Ct
Hamble-le-Rice SO31 .....128 A1
Lymington SO41 .....197 C2
19 Portsmouth PO5 .....182 B1
Admirals Rd SO31 .....129 A2
Admirals Way 9 SO45 .....126 A3
Admirals Wlk
Bournemouth BH2 .....204 B1
Gosport PO12 .....180 C2
Admiralty Cl PO12 .....181 B4
Admiralty Cotts PO12 .....181 B1
Admiralty Ho SO14 .....103 A1
Admiralty Rd
Bournemouth BH6 .....206 C2
Portsmouth PO1 .....182 A3
Admiralty Way SO40 .....101 C2
Adsdean Cl PO9 .....135 C2
Adstone La PO3 .....158 B2
Adur Cl Gosport PO12 .....180 C4
West End SO18 .....80 A1
Aerodrome Rd PO13 .....155 C2
Africa Dr SO40 .....124 C4
Agar's La SO41 .....196 A3
Agarton La SO41 .....211 C3
Aggis Farm BH31 .....114 C3
Agincourt Rd PO2 .....182 B4
Agitator Rd SO45 .....151 B2
Agnew Ho PO12 .....181 A3
Agnew Rd PO13 .....155 B2
Aikman La SO40 .....100 A4
Ailsa La SO19 .....103 B2
Ainsdale Rd PO6 .....134 B1
Ainsley Gdns SO50 .....56 A3
Aintree Cl SO50 .....81 B4
Aintree Ct SO31 .....129 A4
Aintree Dr PO7 .....112 A1
Aintree Rd SO40 .....76 B1
Airetons Cl BH18 .....187 B2
Airfield Ind Est BH23 .....207 C3
Airfield Rd BH23 .....207 C3
Airfield Way BH23 .....207 C4
Airlie Cnr SO22 .....10 C3
Airlie Rd SO22 .....10 C3
Airport Service Rd PO3 158 A2
Airspeed Rd
Christchurch BH23 .....208 A4
Portsmouth PO3 .....158 B1
Ajax Cl PO14 .....179 B3
Akeshill Cl BH25 .....195 A3
Alameda Rd PO7 .....134 B2
Alameda Way PO7 .....134 B2
Alan Chun Ho SO31 .....127 B4
Alan Ct 16 BH23 .....209 A4
Alan Drayton Way SO50 .56 C1
Alan Gr PO15 .....130 C1
Alandale Rd SO19 .....104 B2
Albacore Ave SO31 .....128 C1
Albany BH1 .....205 B2
Albany Cl BH25 .....194 C1
Albany Ct
Bishop's Waltham SO32 .....83 A4
Gosport PO12 .....181 A3
Albany Dr
Bishop's Waltham SO32 .....83 A4
Three Legged Cross BH21 114 C1
Albany Gdns BH15 .....201 C1
Albany Park Ct SO17 .....102 C4
Albany Pk BH17 .....202 A4
Albany Rd
Bishop's Waltham SO32 .....83 A4
Holbury SO45 .....150 B2
Portsmouth PO5 .....215 C1
Romsey SO51 .....52 C4
Southampton SO15 .....102 B3
Albany The SO14 .....103 A2
Albatross Wlk PO13 .....155 A1
Albemarle Ave PO12 .....181 A4
Albemarle Rd BH3 .....204 C4
Albermarle Ct SO17 .....79 B2
Albert Cl SO31 .....127 B3
Albert Ct SO17 .....79 B1
Albert Gr PO5 .....215 C1
Albert Rd
Bishop's Waltham SO32 .....83 A4
Bournemouth BH1 .....204 C2
Corfe Mullen BH21 .....186 B3
Cosham PO6 .....157 C4
6 Eastleigh SO50 .....56 A3
Ferndown BH22 .....165 B3
Hedge End SO30 .....105 A3
New Milton BH25 .....194 C1
Poole BH12 .....203 B3
Portsmouth PO4, PO5 .....182 C1
Stubbington PO14 .....179 C3
Albert Rd N SO14 .....103 A2
Albert Rd S SO14 .....103 A2
Albert St PO12 .....181 B3
Albion Cl Poole BH12 .....203 A4
Portchester PO16 .....156 A3
Albion Pl 3 SO14 .....102 C2
Albion Rd
Christchurch BH23 .....191 C1
Fordingbridge SP6 .....69 C1
Lee-on-the-Solent PO13 .....179 C2
Albion Twrs 1 SO14 .....103 A2
Albion Way BH31 .....114 B4
Albretia Ave PO8 .....111 C2
Albury Pl SO53 .....30 A1
Alby Rd BH12 .....203 C3
Alcantara Cres SO14 .....103 A2
Alcester Rd BH12 .....203 B3
Alchorne Pl PO3 .....158 A2
Aldbury Ct BH25 .....210 A4
Alder Cl Burton BH23 .....192 B1
Colden Common SO21 .....57 A4
Hythe SO45 .....125 B2
Marchwood SO40 .....101 C1
Romsey SO51 .....53 B3
Alder Cres BH12 .....203 C4
Alder Dr SP6 .....92 C3
Alder Hill Dr SO40 .....100 A4
Alder Hills BH12 .....204 A4
Alder Hills Ind Est BH12 204 A4
Alder La PO12,PO13 .....180 B3
Alder Rd Poole BH12 .....203 C3
Southampton SO16 .....78 A2
Alderbury Ct 5 BH23 .....207 C3
Alderfield GU32 .....40 C2
Alderholt Mill & Craft Ctr★ SP6 .....68 C1
Alderholt Rd SP6 .....69 A1
Alderley Rd BH10 .....189 C2
Alderman Quilley Sch SO50 .....55 C1
Alderman Quilley Sch The SO50 .....56 A1
Aldermoor Ave SO16 .....78 A2
Aldermoor Cl SO16 .....78 B2
Aldermoor Rd
Gosport PO13 .....180 B4
Southampton SO16 .....78 A2
Waterlooville PO7 .....134 B2
Aldermoor Rd E PO7 .....134 B3
Alderney Ave BH12 .....188 B1
Alderney Cl SO16 .....77 C2
Alderney Hospl BH12 .....188 B1
Alderney Mid Sch BH12 188 B1
Alderney Rdbt BH12 .....188 B1
Alders Rd PO16 .....155 A4
Aldershot Ho 50 PO9 .....136 A3
Alderwood Ave SO53 .....55 A3
Alderwood Cl PO9 .....135 A2
Aldis Gdns BH15 .....201 C1
Aldrich Rd PO1 .....182 A3
Aldridge Cl PO8 .....88 B3
Aldridge Rd
Bournemouth BH10 .....189 B3
Ferndown BH22 .....165 C2
Aldridge Way BH22 .....165 C2
Aldroke St 14 PO6 .....157 C4
Aldsworth Cl PO6 .....158 B4
Aldsworth Gdns PO6 .....158 B4
Aldwell St PO5 .....215 C2
Alec Rose Ho 16 PO12 .....181 B2
Alec Rose La PO1 .....215 B3
Alec Wintle Ho PO2 .....182 B4
Alecto Rd PO12 .....181 A2
Alencon Cl PO12 .....181 B4
Alexander Cl
Christchurch BH23 .....207 C3
Totton SO40 .....100 B4
Waterlooville PO7 .....134 B3
Alexander Ct
Southampton SO15 .....102 B3
Southampton, Woolston SO19 .....103 C1
Alexander Gr PO16 .....155 A4
Alexander Ho PO11 .....185 C1
Alexandra Ave PO11 .....184 C1
Alexandra Cl SO45 .....126 A2
Alexandra Lo 6 BH1 .....205 A2
Alexandra Rd
Bournemouth BH6 .....206 B3
Chandler's Ford SO53 .....55 C4
Fordingbridge SP6 .....69 C1
Hedge End SO30 .....105 A3
Hythe SO45 .....126 A2
Lymington SO41 .....197 B3
Poole BH14 .....203 C2
Portsmouth PO1 .....215 C4
Southampton SO15 .....102 C3
Alexandra St PO12 .....181 A3
Alexandra Terr SO23 .....10 C4
Alexandra Way SO30 .....106 A4
Alexandria Ct BH22 .....165 C2
Alford Rd BH3 .....204 B4
Alfred Cl SO40 .....100 B4
Alfred Rd
Portsmouth PO1 .....215 A4
Stubbington PO14 .....154 B2
Alfred Rose Ct SO18 .....79 C2
Alfred St SO14 .....103 A3
Alfrey Cl PO10 .....161 B4
Alfriston Ct SO19 .....104 B2
Alfriston Gdns SO19 .....104 A2
Algiers Rd PO3 .....183 A4
Alhambra Rd PO4 .....182 C1
Alice in Wonderland Family Pk★ BH23 .....190 C4
Alington 18 BH4 .....204 B2
Alington Cl BH14 .....214 B4
Alington Ho BH14 .....214 B4
Alington Rd BH3 .....205 A3
Alipore Cl BH14 .....203 B2
Alipore Hts BH14 .....203 B2
Alison Way 10 SO22 .....10 C4
All Saints CE Prim Sch SO23 .....11 A3
All Saints Ho 19 SO14 .....103 A2
All Saints Rd SO41 .....197 C1
All Saints' Rd PO1 .....182 B4
All Saints' St PO1 .....215 B4
Allan Gr SO51 .....53 A4
Allaway Ave PO6 .....157 A4
Allbrook Ct 12 PO9 .....135 B3
Allbrook Hill SO50 .....56 A4
Allbrook Knoll SO50 .....56 A4
Allbrook Way SO50 .....56 A4
Allcot Rd PO3 .....158 A1
Allen Ct BH21 .....163 B3
Allen Rd Hedge End SO30 105 B4
Wimborne Minst BH21 .....163 B2
Allen Water Dr SP6 .....69 C1
Allen's Rd PO4 .....182 C1
Allenbourn Mid Sch BH21 .....163 B3
Allenby Cl BH17 .....187 A1
Allenby Gr PO16 .....156 B4
Allenby Rd Gosport PO12 180 C3
Poole BH17 .....187 A1
Allendale Ave PO10 .....136 C2
Allens Farm La SO32 .....61 A3
Allens La Meonstoke SO32 .61 B3
Upton BH16 .....201 B3
Allens Rd BH16 .....201 B3
Allenview Rd BH21 .....163 B3
Allerton Cl SO40 .....76 B1
Alley The SP6 .....70 C4
Alliance Cl PO13 .....180 B4
Allington La SO30 .....80 C3
Allington Manor Farm Bsns Ctr SO50 .....80 C4
Allington Rd Poole BH14 214 B4
Southampton SO15 .....101 B4
Allison Ct 6 SO41 .....211 A2
Allison Ho SO30 .....105 B4
Allmara Dr PO7 .....134 C2
Allotment Rd
Hedge End SO30 .....105 A3
Locks Heath SO31 .....128 C3
Alma Ho SO14 .....103 A4
Alma La SO32 .....58 A1
Alma Rd
Bournemouth BH9 .....205 A4
Romsey SO51 .....52 C4
Southampton SO14 .....103 A4
Alma St PO12 .....181 A3
Alma Terr PO4 .....183 A2
Almatade Rd SO18 .....104 A4
Almer Rd BH15 .....201 C2
Almond Cl Cosham PO9 .158 C4
Waterlooville PO8 .....112 B2
Almond Ct 11 SO15 .....102 B3
Almond Gr BH12 .....203 B4
Almond Rd SO15 .....102 B3
Almondsbury Ho 8 PO6 .....132 C1
Almondsbury Rd PO6 .....132 C1
Almondside PO13 .....155 C1
Almshouses BH10 .....189 B1
Alpha Ctr The BH17 .....202 A4
Alphage Rd PO12 .....155 C1
Alpine Cl SO18 .....104 A4
Alpine Rd Ashurst SO40 .....99 C2
St Leonards BH24 .....140 B1
Alresford Rd
Chilcomb SO21, SO23 .....12 B4
Havant PO9 .....135 C2
Winchester SO21, SO23 .....11 B4
Alsford Rd PO7 .....134 B3
Alswitha Terr 27 SO23 .....2 A1
Alten Rd PO7 .....111 B1
Althorpe Dr PO3 .....158 B2
Alton Cl SO50 .....57 A1
Alton Ct 12 SO23 .....2 A1
Alton Gr PO16 .....156 B3
Alton Ho SO18 .....103 C4
Alton Rd
Bournemouth BH10 .....189 A1
Poole BH14 .....203 B2
Alton Rd E BH14 .....203 B1
Alum Chine Rd BH4 .....204 A2
Alum Cl SO45 .....150 B2
Alum Way
Portchester PO16 .....131 C1
Southampton SO18 .....104 A4
Alumdale Rd BH4 .....204 A1
Alumhurst Rd BH4 .....204 A1
Alvandi Gdns 12 BH25 .....195 A2
Alvara Rd PO12 .....181 A1
Alver Bridge View 10 PO12 .....181 A2
Alver Quay PO12 .....181 A2
Alver Rd Gosport PO12 .181 A2
Portsmouth PO1 .....182 C3
Alvercliffe Dr PO12 .....180 C1
Alverstoke CE Jun Sch PO12 .....181 A2
Alverstoke Ct PO12 .....181 A1
Alverstoke Inf Sch PO12 .....181 A1
Alverstone Rd PO4 .....183 A3
Alverton Ave BH15 .....202 C2
Alverton Hall BH4 .....204 B1
Alveston Ave PO14 .....154 B4
Alyne Ho SO15 .....102 C4
Alyth Rd BH3 .....204 B3
Amarylis Cl PO15 .....129 C2
Ambassador Cl BH23 .....208 A3
Ambassador Ind Est BH23 .....208 A3
Amber Rd BH21 .....186 B2
Amberley Cl Botley SO30 106 A4
Christchurch BH23 .....208 C4
North Baddesley SO52 .....53 C3
Amberley Ct
8 Bournemouth BH1 .....205 A2
Totton SO40 .....100 C3
Amberley Rd Clanfield PO8 88 B3
Gosport PO12 .....181 A4
Portsmouth PO2 .....157 C2
Amberslade Wlk SO45 .....125 C1
Amberwood
Ferndown BH22 .....165 C3
Milford on Sea SO41 .....211 A3
Amberwood Cl SO40 .....76 B1
Amberwood Dr BH23 .....193 C1
Amberwood Gdns BH23 194 A1
Amberwood Ho BH23 .....194 A1
Ambledale SO31 .....128 C2
Ambleside
Bishop's Waltham SO32 .....83 A4
Christchurch BH23 .....191 C2
Hedge End SO30 .....105 B3
Ambleside Gdns SO19 .....104 A2
Ambleside Rd SO41 .....197 C2
Ambury La BH23 .....207 C4
Amersham Cl PO12 .....180 C2
Amesbury Rd BH6 .....206 B3
Amethyst Gr PO7 .....135 A4
Amethyst Rd BH23 .....207 C4
Amey Ind Est GU32 .....40 C2
Ameys La BH22 .....165 C4
Ameysford Rd BH22 .....165 B4
Amira Ct 9 BH2 .....204 C2
Amoy St SO15 .....102 C3
Ampfield CE Prim Sch SO51 .....29 B2
Ampfield Cl PO9 .....135 A2
Ampfield Rd BH8 .....190 B2
Amport Cl SO22 .....1 B2
Amport Ct PO9 .....135 B3
Ampress La SO41 .....197 B3
Ampthill Rd SO15 .....102 A4
Amsterdam Sq BH23 .....207 B3
Amyas Ct PO4 .....183 B2
Ancasta Rd SO14 .....103 A4
Anchor Cl
Bournemouth BH11 .....188 C3
Christchurch BH23 .....208 A3
Anchor La PO1 .....182 A3
Anchor Mews SO41 .....197 C2
Anchor Rd BH11 .....188 C3
Anchorage Rd PO3 .....158 A2
Anchorage The PO12 .....181 B2
Anchorage Way SO41 .....197 B2

Ancrum Lo BH4 .204 A2
Andalusian Gdns SO31 .129 A4
Andbourne Ct BH6 .206 C2
Anderby Rd SO16 .77 B1
Anderson Cl Havant PO9 136 A2
Romsey SO51 .28 B1
Swanwick PO15 .129 B4
Anderson's Rd SO14 .103 A2
Anderwood Dr SO41 .172 A1
Andes Cl SO14 .103 B2
Andes Rd SO16 .77 A2
Andlers Ash Rd GU33 .20 C2
Andover Cl BH23 .208 A4
Andover Ho PO9 .136 A3
Andover Rd
Portsmouth PO4 .182 C1
Southampton SO15 .102 B3
Winchester SO21, SO22, SO23 .1 C1
Andover Rd N SO22 .1 C2
Andover Road Ret Pk SO23 .1 C1
Andree Ct BH23 .209 A4
Andrew Bell St PO1 .215 B4
Andrew Cl
[7] Hythe SO45 .126 A1
Portsmouth PO1 .182 C3
Totton SO40 .100 B4
Andrew Cres PO7 .111 B1
Andrew La BH25 .195 B1
Andrew Pl PO14 .179 A3
Andrewes Cl SO32 .83 B4
Andrews Cl BH11 .189 A2
Andromeda Rd SO16 .77 C2
Androse Gdns BH24 .140 C3
Anfield Cl SO50 .57 B1
Anfield Ct SO50 .57 A1
Angel Cres SO18,SO19 .104 A3
Angel Ct SO41 .197 C2
Angel La
Barton on Sea BH25 .210 B4
Ferndown BH22 .165 A2
Angelica Ct PO7 .135 A3
Angelica Gdns SO50 .81 B4
Angelica Way PO15 .129 C4
Angeline Cl BH23 .208 C4
Angelo Cl PO7 .135 A4
Angelus Cl PO14 .179 B3
Angerstein Rd PO2 .157 B1
Anglers Way SO31 .128 B4
Anglesea Ct SO15 .78 A1
Anglesea Rd
Lee-on-the-Solent PO13 .180 A2
Portsmouth PO1 .215 A3
Southampton SO15 .78 A1
Anglesea Terr SO14 .103 A2
Anglesey Arms Rd PO12 .181 A1
Anglesey Rd PO12 .181 A1
Anglesey View [7] PO12 .181 A2
Anglewood Mans [9] BH4 .204 B2
Anglo-European Coll of Chiropractic BH5 .206 A2
Angmering Ho [2] PO1 .215 B3
Angus Cl PO15 .130 C2
Anjou Cl BH11 .188 B3
Anjou Cres PO15 .130 B1
Anker La PO14 .154 B2
Ankerwyke PO13 .155 A1
Anmore Cl PO9 .135 B2
Anmore Cnr PO7 .111 A2
Anmore Dr PO7 .111 B1
Anmore La PO7,PO8 .111 B3
Anmore Rd PO7 .111 A2
Ann's Hill Rd PO12 .181 A3
Anna La BH23 .168 A2
Annandale Ct BH6 .206 B2
Anne Cl BH23 .192 A1
Anne Cres PO7 .134 C3
Annerley Rd BH1 .205 B2
Annes Ct PO11 .184 C1
Annet Cl BH15 .201 C1
Anson Cl
Christchurch BH23 .207 C3
Gosport PO13 .180 B3
Ringwood BH24 .141 B4
Anson Dr SO19 .104 B3
Anson Gr PO16 .132 C1
Anson Ho SO14 .103 A2
Anson Rd
Horton Heath SO50 .81 B4
[1] Portsmouth PO4 .183 A3
Anstey Cl BH11 .189 A3
Anstey Rd
Bournemouth BH11 .189 A3
Romsey SO51 .28 A1
Antell's Way SP6 .93 A3
Anthill Cl PO7 .110 B3
Anthony Gr PO12 .156 A1
Anthony Way PO10 .136 C2
Anthony's Ave BH14 .203 B1
Antigua Ho [5] PO6 .132 C1
Antler Dr BH25 .194 C2
Anton Cl SO51 .53 B4
Anvil Cl East Meon GU32 .63 C4
Waterlooville PO7 .112 B1
West End SO30 .80 B1
Anvil Cres BH18 .186 C3
Anvil Ct [2] PO4 .183 A2
Anzac Cl PO14 .154 B2
Apex Ctr PO14 .155 A3
Apless La PO7 .110 A2
Apollo Cl BH12 .203 B4
Apollo Dr PO7 .134 C2
Apollo Rd SO53 .55 C4
Apple Cl BH12 .204 A2
Apple Gr
Christchurch BH23 .191 C1
Emsworth PO10 .161 A4
Apple Ind Est PO15 .129 B3
Apple Tree Cl SP5 .47 B4
Apple Tree Gr BH22 .165 C3
Apple Tree Rd SP6 .92 C3
Applegate Pl PO8 .112 A3
Applemore Coll SO45 .125 B2
Applemore Recn Ctr SO45 .125 B2
Appleshaw Cl SO22 .1 B2
Appleshaw Gn PO9 .135 B2
Appleslade Way BH25 .195 A3
Appleton Rd
Fareham PO15 .130 B1
Southampton SO18 .79 C1
Appletree Cl
Bournemouth BH6 .206 B3
New Milton BH25 .195 A1
Totton SO40 .76 B1
Appletree Ct SO30 .106 A4
Appletree Rd SP5 .47 B4
Applewood Gdns SO19 .104 A2
Applewood Gr PO7 .134 B2
Applewood Pl SO40 .100 B3
Applewood Rd PO9 .135 B2
Appollo Ct PO5 .215 B2
Appollo Pl SO18 .104 A4
Approach Rd BH14 .203 A2
Approach The PO3 .158 A1
April Cl
Bournemouth BH11 .189 A2
Southampton SO18 .104 A4
April Gr SO31 .128 C2
April Sq PO1 .215 C4
Apsley Cres BH17 .187 B1
Apsley Ct [2] BH8 .205 A3
Apsley Pl SO53 .30 A1
Apsley Rd PO4 .183 A2
Aquila Way SO31 .127 C1
Aquitania Ho [23] SO14 .103 B3
Arabian Gdns PO15 .129 B4
Aragon Way BH9 .190 A2
Arbour Ct [34] SO22 .10 C4
Arcade BH4 .204 A2
Arcade The
[37] Bournemouth BH1 .204 C2
Liss GU33 .20 C3
Arcadia Ave BH8 .205 A4
Arcadia Cl SO16 .78 B2
Arcadia Rd BH23 .191 C1
Arch Farm Ind Est SP6 .69 C2
Archdale Cl BH10 .189 B1
Archer Ho PO12 .181 B1
Archers SO15 .102 C3
Archers Cl SO40 .76 B1
Archers Rd Eastleigh SO50 56 A2
Southampton SO15 .102 C4
Archery Gdns SO19 .103 C1
Archery Gr SO19 .103 C1
Archery La
Fareham PO16 .131 B1
Winchester SO22 .10 C4
Archery Rd SO19 .103 C1
Archgate SO41 .197 C2
Archway Rd BH14 .203 C2
Arden Cl Gosport PO12 .180 C2
Southampton SO18 .80 A1
Arden Rd BH9 .189 C2
Arden Wlk BH25 .195 A1
Ardingly Cres SO30 .81 B1
Ardington Rise PO7 .134 C2
Ardmore Rd BH14 .203 A2
Ardnave Cres SO16 .78 C3
Argosy Cl SO31 .128 C1
Argus Rd PO13 .179 C2
Argyle Cres PO15 .130 C1
Argyle Rd
Christchurch BH23 .207 C3
Southampton SO14 .103 A3
Argyll Mans [11] BH5 .205 C2
Argyll Rd
Bournemouth BH5 .205 C2
Poole BH12 .203 B3
Ariel Cl BH6 .207 A2
Ariel Dr BH6 .207 A2
Ariel Rd PO1 .182 C3
Arismore Ct PO13 .179 B2
Ark Dr BH22 .165 C2
Ark Royal Cres PO13 .179 C2
Arle Cl PO8 .88 B2
Arley Rd BH14 .203 A1
Arlington Ct BH25 .210 A4
Arlington Pl [2] SO23 .11 A4
Arliss Rd SO16 .78 A1
Arlott Ct SO15 .102 C4
Armada Cl SO16 .77 C4
Armada Dr SO45 .125 C1
Armadale Ho [20] SO14 .103 B3
Arminers Cl PO12 .181 A1
Armitage Ave SO45 .125 C1
Armory La PO1 .182 A2
Armoury The SO40 .102 A2
Armstrong Cl
Brockenhurst SO42 .145 C1
Waterlooville PO7 .111 B1
Armstrong Ct SO16 .77 C3
Armstrong La SO42 .145 C1
Armstrong Rd SO42 .145 C1
Armsworth La PO7,SO32 .85 C1
Arnaud Cl PO2 .182 B4
Arne Ave BH12 .203 C4
Arne Cres BH12 .203 C4
Arnewood Bridge Rd SO41 .196 A4
Arnewood Ct
Bournemouth BH2 .204 C1
Arnewood Ct *continued*
Sway SO41 .196 B3
Arnewood Ho SO41 .196 B2
Arnewood Rd BH6 .206 B3
Arnewood Sch The BH25 .194 C1
Arnheim Cl SO16 .78 B2
Arnheim Rd SO16 .78 B2
Arnold Cl BH22 .138 C2
Arnold Rd Eastleigh SO50 .80 A4
Southampton SO17 .79 B1
West Moors BH22 .138 C2
Arnolds Cl BH25 .209 C4
Arnside Rd PO7 .134 C4
Arnwood Ave SO45 .149 C4
Arragon Ct PO7 .135 A4
Arran Cl PO6 .133 C1
Arran Way BH23 .194 A1
Arras Ho PO15 .130 B2
Arreton SO31 .127 B3
Arreton Ct [7] PO12 .181 A3
Arrow Cl Eastleigh SO50 .56 A2
Southampton SO19 .103 B1
Arrowsmith Ct BH18 .187 A2
Arrowsmith La BH21 .187 C4
Arrowsmith Rd BH21 .187 C4
Arters Lawn SO40 .124 B3
Arthur Cl BH2 .204 C3
Arthur Kille Ho PO7 .134 B3
Arthur La [3] BH23 .207 A4
Arthur Pope Ho PO5 .215 C2
Arthur Rd
Christchurch BH23 .207 A4
Eastleigh SO50 .56 A2
Southampton SO15 .102 B3
Winchester SO23 .2 A1
Arthur St PO2 .182 C4
Arthurs Gdns SO30 .81 A2
Artillery Cl [1] PO6 .157 B4
Artillery Terr [4] PO4 .183 A2
Arts Inst of Bournemouth The BH12 .204 B4
Arun Cl GU31 .40 C1
Arun Rd SO18 .80 A1
Arun Way SO51 .50 B2
Arundel Cl BH25 .194 C2
Arundel Ct Inf Sch PO1 215 C4
Arundel Ct Jun Sch PO1 .215 C4
Arundel Dr PO16 .131 A1
Arundel Ho
Southampton, Banister's Pk SO15 .102 C4
[19] Southampton, Northam SO14 .103 B3
Arundel Rd Eastleigh SO50 56 A3
Gosport PO12 .180 C3
Totton SO40 .101 A4
Arundel St PO1 .215 C3
Arundel Way BH23 .208 C4
Arundel Way Sh Arc PO1 .215 B3
Ascham Rd BH8 .205 A3
Ascot Cl PO14 .129 B1
Ascot Rd
Broadstone BH18 .187 A2
Fair Oak SO50 .81 B4
Portsmouth PO3 .183 A4
Ascupart Ho [24] SO17 .103 A4
Ascupart St SO14 .103 A2
Asford Gr SO50 .56 B2
Ash Cl Alderholt SP6 .93 A3
Bursledon SO31 .127 C4
Colden Common SO21 .32 A1
Fareham PO14 .154 C4
Gosport PO12 .181 A2
Hythe SO45 .150 A4
North Baddesley SO52 .53 C3
Romsey SO51 .53 B3
Southampton SO19 .104 B3
Upton BH16 .201 A4
Waterlooville PO8 .111 C1
Ash Gr Ashurst SO40 .100 B2
Hordle SO41 .211 B4
Ringwood BH24 .141 B4
Ash Rd SO40 .100 A1
Ash Tree Rd SO18 .79 C1
Ashbarn Cres SO22 .10 C3
Ashbourne Ct [1] BH1 .205 A2
Ashbourne Rd BH5 .206 A3
Ashbridge Rise SO53 .30 A1
Ashburn Garth BH24 .141 B3
Ashburnham Cl SO19 .103 B3
Ashburton Cl SO45 .125 B2
Ashburton Ct PO5 .215 B1
Ashburton Gdns BH10 .189 B1
Ashburton Ho [12] SO31 .127 A3
Ashburton Rd
Gosport PO12 .180 C1
Portsmouth PO5 .182 B1
Ashby Cres SO40 .100 B4
Ashby Pl PO5 .182 B1
Ashby Rd
Southampton SO19 .104 A2
Totton SO40 .100 B4
Ashcroft Ct [9] GU32 .40 C2
Ashcroft La PO8 .113 B3
Ashdene [16] SO15 .102 A4
Ashdene Cl BH21 .163 B3
Ashdene Rd SO40 .100 B2
Ashdown
Bournemouth BH2 .204 B1
Fawley SO45 .150 C2
Gosport PO13 .155 B1
Ashdown Cl
Chandler's Ford SO53 .30 B1
Poole BH17 .187 C1
Ashdown Dr SO53 .30 B1
Ashdown Rd
Blackfield SO45 .150 C1
Chandler's Ford SO53 .30 B1
Ashdown Sch BH17 .187 C1
Ashdown Way SO51 .53 A4
Ashdown Wlk BH25 .195 B1
Ashe Rd PO9 .136 A3
Ashen Cl SO53 .55 B4
Ashford Chace GU32 .19 C1
Ashford Cl Cosham PO6 .133 C1
Fordingbridge SP6 .69 B1
Ashford Cres SO45 .126 A2
Ashford Rd
Bournemouth BH6 .206 B4
Fordingbridge SP6 .93 B4
Ashford Works Ind Est SP6 .69 B1
Ashington Cl PO8 .112 A2
Ashington Gdns BH21 .186 C4
Ashington La BH21 .163 A1
Ashington Pk BH25 .195 A1
Ashlea Cl SO50 .57 B1
Ashleigh Cl SO45 .150 A4
Ashleigh Rise BH10 .189 B1
Ashlett Cl SO45 .151 B2
Ashlett Gdns BH25 .195 B2
Ashlett Lawn [4] PO9 .135 B3
Ashlett Mews SO45 .151 A2
Ashlett Rd SO45 .151 B2
Ashley Arnewood Ct [9] BH25 .195 A1
Ashley Cl
Bournemouth BH1 .205 C3
Havant PO9 .135 B2
Horndean PO8 .111 C3
Ringwood BH24 .141 B3
Swanwick SO31 .129 A4
Winchester SO22 .1 B2
Ashley Common Rd BH25 .195 B2
Ashley Cres SO19 .104 B1
Ashley Ct
Bursledon SO31 .105 A1
Gosport PO12 .181 A3
West Moors BH22 .166 A4
Ashley Dr BH24 .116 B2
Ashley Drive N BH24 .139 C3
Ashley Drive S BH24 .139 C3
Ashley Drive W BH24 .139 C3
Ashley Gdns
Chandler's Ford SO53 .55 C3
Waltham Chase SO32 .83 C2
Ashley Heath Ind Est BH21 .139 A4
Ashley Ho SO51 .52 C3
Ashley Inf Sch BH25 .195 B2
Ashley Jun Sch BH25 .195 B2
Ashley La Hordle SO41 .195 C2
Lymington SO41 .197 C2
New Milton BH25 .195 C2
Ashley Mdws SO51 .53 A4
Ashley Meads BH25 .195 B2
Ashley Park BH24 .140 A3
Ashley Rd
Bournemouth BH1, BH7 .205 C3
New Milton BH25 .195 B2
Poole BH14 .203 B3
Ashleycross Cl SO45 .150 B2
Ashling Cl
Bournemouth BH8 .205 B4
Denmead PO7 .110 C2
Ashling Cres BH8 .205 A4
Ashling Gdns PO7 .110 C2
Ashling La PO2 .157 B1
Ashling Park Rd PO7 .110 C2
Ashlyn Cl PO15 .130 B1
Ashmead Rd SO16 .77 C2
Ashmeads Cl BH21 .164 A3
Ashmeads Way BH21 .164 A3
Ashmede BH4 .204 B1
Ashmore BH21 .163 B2
Ashmore Ave
Barton on Sea BH25 .210 A4
Hamworthy BH15 .201 C1
Ashmore Cl SP5 .24 A2
Ashmore Cres BH15 .201 C1
Ashmore Gr BH23 .193 C1
Ashmore La
West Dean SP5 .24 A3
Whiteparish SP5 .24 A3
Ashmore Rd SO22 .1 B1
Ashridge Ave [1] BH10 .189 B3
Ashridge Cl SO15 .102 C4
Ashridge Gdns BH10 .189 B3
Ashridge Par [2] BH10 .189 B3
Ashtead Cl PO16 .156 A4
Ashton Cl SO32 .59 A1
Ashton Cross SO51 .51 A1
Ashton Ct
[13] New Milton BH25 .195 A2
Poole BH13 .204 A1
Ashton Ho SO19 .103 C1
Ashton La SO32 .59 A1
Ashton Pl SO53 .30 A1
Ashton Rd BH9 .189 C1
Ashton Way PO14 .179 B2
Ashtree Cl BH25 .195 B1
Ashtree Ct SO53 .55 B2
Ashurst (New Forest) Sta SO40 .100 A1
Ashurst Bridge Rd SO40 .100 B3
Ashurst Cl Ashurst SO40 .100 A1
Southampton SO19 .104 A1
Winchester SO22 .1 B2
Ashurst Ct PO12 .180 B2
Ashurst Hospl (Geriatric) SO40 .100 A1
Ashurst Rd
Bournemouth BH8 .190 B2
Cosham PO6 .157 C4
West Moors BH22 .138 C2
Ashwell Ct BH23 .191 C1
Ashwood
Swanwick, Whiteley PO15 .129 C3
Titchfield SO31 .129 B1
Ashwood Cl Havant PO9 .135 A2
South Hayling PO11 .185 A2
Ashwood Dr BH18 .187 B2
Ashwood Gdns
[15] Southampton SO16 .78 C2
Totton SO40 .100 B4
Ashwood Lodge [1] PO16 .131 A1
Aspen Ave SO31 .152 B4
Aspen Cl
Colden Common SO21 .57 A4
Hedge End SO30 .105 B4
Aspen Dr BH31 .115 A3
Aspen Gdns BH12 .203 C4
Aspen Holt SO16 .79 A3
Aspen Pl BH25 .195 A1
Aspen Rd BH12 .203 C4
Aspen Way Poole BH12 .203 C4
Waterlooville PO8 .112 A3
Aspen Wlk SO40 .100 A4
Aspengrove PO13 .155 C1
Asquith Cl BH23 .207 B3
Assheton Ct PO16 .156 B4
Astbury Ave BH12 .189 A1
Aster Rd SO16 .79 B2
Astley St PO5 .215 A2
Aston Mead BH23 .191 C2
Aston Rd
Portsmouth PO4 .182 C2
Waterlooville PO7 .134 B4
Astra Ct [3] SO45 .126 A3
Astra Wlk PO12 .181 B2
Astral Gdns SO31 .127 C2
Astrid Cl PO11 .185 B2
Asturias Way SO14 .103 B2
Asylum Rd SO15 .103 A3
Atalanta Cl PO4 .183 B3
Atheling Rd SO45 .126 A2
Athelney Ct [18] BH1 .205 A2
Athelstan Rd
Bournemouth BH6 .206 C3
Southampton SO19 .103 C3
Athelston Ct SO41 .197 B2
Athena Ave PO7 .134 C2
Athena Cl SO50 .57 A2
Atherfield Rd SO16 .77 C2
Atherley Ct SO15 .102 C4
Atherley Rd
South Hayling PO11 .184 C3
Southampton SO15 .102 B3
Atherley Sch SO16 .77 A3
Atherstone Wlk [5] PO5 .215 B2
Atkins Pl PO15 .130 B2
Atkinson Cl PO12 .181 A1
Atlantic Cl SO14 .103 A1
Atlantic Ct SO53 .55 B3
Atlantic Park View SO18 .80 A1
Atlantis Ave PO7 .134 C1
Attwood Cl SP6 .92 C3
Attwoods Dro SO21 .10 B1
Aubrey Cl
Milford on Sea SO41 .211 C2
South Hayling PO11 .184 C2
Aubrey Farm Cotts SO41 .212 A2
Auckland Ave SO42 .146 A1
Auckland Pl SO42 .146 A1
Auckland Rd
Christchurch BH23 .208 B4
Southampton SO15 .101 C4
Auckland Rd E PO5 .182 B1
Auckland Rd W PO5 .182 B1
Audemer Ct BH24 .141 B4
Audley Pl [12] SO50 .56 C1
Audrayton Ct [9] BH6 .206 C2
Audret Cl PO16 .156 A3
Augustine Rd
Cosham PO6 .158 B4
Southampton SO14 .103 A3
Augustus Cl SO53 .55 C4
Augustus Way SO53 .55 C4
Auriol Dr PO9 .159 A4
Aust Rd PO14 .154 B4
Austen Ave
Bournemouth BH10 .189 C3
Winchester SO22 .10 B2
Austen Cl Totton SO40 .100 B3
Winchester SO23 .2 A1
Austen Gdns PO15 .129 B4
Auster Cl BH23 .208 A4
Austerberry Way PO13 .180 C4
Austin Ave BH14 .203 A1
Austin Cl BH1 .205 B3
Austin Ct [6] PO6 .133 A1
Australia Cl PO1 .215 C3
Autumn Cl BH22 .165 A4
Autumn Copse BH25 .195 B1
Autumn Pl [18] SO17 .79 A1
Autumn Rd
Bournemouth BH11 .188 B2
Marchwood SO40 .102 A1
Avalan Ct SO23 .10 C3
Avalon BH14 .214 B4
Avalon Ct PO10 .136 C1
Avebury Ave BH10 .189 C3
Avebury Gdns SO53 .30 A1
Avenger Cl SO53 .55 A3

Avens Cl SO50 ... 81 B3
Avenue C SO45 ... 150 C4
Avenue Campus (Univ of Southampton) SO17 ... 79 A1
Avenue Ct Gosport PO12 ... 181 A1
Poole BH13 ... 204 A2
1 Southampton SO17 ... 102 C4
Avenue D SO45 ... 150 C4
Avenue De Caen PO5 ... 182 B1
Avenue E SO45 ... 150 C4
Avenue La 20 BH2 ... 204 C2
Avenue Rd
Bournemouth BH2 ... 204 C2
Brockenhurst SO42 ... 172 C4
Christchurch BH23 ... 206 C4
Christchurch, Walkford BH23 ... 194 B1
Fareham PO14 ... 130 C1
Gosport PO12 ... 181 B2
Lymington SO41 ... 197 C2
New Milton BH25 ... 195 A2
North Hayling PO11 ... 160 A2
Southampton SO14 ... 103 A4
Wimborne Minst BH21 ... 163 B2
Winchester SO22 ... 10 C4
Avenue Sh Ctr The 21 BH2 ... 204 C2
Avenue The
Bishop's Waltham SO32 ... 83 A4
Bournemouth BH9 ... 189 C2
Fareham PO14 ... 130 B1
Gosport PO12 ... 181 A2
Petersfield GU31 ... 40 C2
Poole BH13 ... 204 A1
Southampton SO17 ... 102 C4
Twyford SO21 ... 32 A3
West Moors BH22 ... 138 C2
Avery La PO12 ... 181 A4
Avington Cl SO50 ... 56 B3
Avington Ct SO16 ... 78 C2
Avington Gn PO9 ... 136 A3
Avocet Cl PO4 ... 183 A3
Avocet Ho 6 PO4 ... 183 A3
Avocet Quay PO10 ... 161 A4
Avocet Way PO8 ... 112 A4
Avocet Wlk PO13 ... 155 A1
Avon Ave BH24 ... 140 B2
Avon Bldgs BH23 ... 207 A4
Avon Castle BH24 ... 140 B2
Avon Castle Dr BH24 ... 140 B2
Avon Cl
Bournemouth BH8 ... 205 B3
Lee-on-the-Solent PO13 ... 179 C1
Lymington SO41 ... 197 B2
Petersfield GU31 ... 40 C1
Avon Cotts BH23 ... 192 B3
Avon Cres SO51 ... 53 B4
Avon Cswy BH23 ... 191 B4
Avon Ct
Christchurch BH23 ... 207 B3
Fordingbridge SP6 ... 69 C1
Netley SO31 ... 127 B3
2 Waterlooville PO8 ... 111 C2
Avon Dyke SP5 ... 46 C3
Avon Farm Cotts BH23 ... 167 C2
Avon Gdns BH23 ... 169 A1
Avon Gn SO53 ... 55 B3
Avon Heath Ctry Park Visitor Ctr* BH24 ... 140 A1
Avon Heath Ctry Pk (North Pk) BH24 ... 140 A2
Avon Heath Ctry Pk (South Pk) BH24 ... 167 A4
Avon Ho
Bournemouth BH2 ... 204 C1
8 Southampton SO14 ... 103 B3
Avon Mdw SP5 ... 46 C4
Avon Meade SP6 ... 69 C1
Avon Mews BH8 ... 205 B3
Avon Park BH24 ... 140 B3
Avon Rd
Bournemouth BH8 ... 205 B3
Southampton SO18 ... 79 C1
West Moors BH22 ... 138 C1
Avon Rd E BH23 ... 207 A4
Avon Rd W BH23 ... 206 C4
Avon Run Cl BH23 ... 208 A3
Avon Run Rd BH23 ... 208 A3
Avon View SP6 ... 70 B1
Avon View Par BH23 ... 192 B2
Avon View Rd BH23 ... 192 B2
Avon Way SO30 ... 80 C1
Avon Wharf BH23 ... 207 B3
Avon Wlk PO16 ... 156 A4
Avonborne Way SO53 ... 55 A4
Avonbourne Girls Sch BH7 ... 206 A4
Avoncliffe Rd BH6 ... 206 C2
Avondale Ct SO17 ... 79 A1
Avondale Cvn Pk SO21 ... 32 A1
Avondale Rd
Portsmouth PO1 ... 182 C4
Waterlooville PO7 ... 134 C4
Avonlea Sch BH24 ... 141 A4
Award Rd BH21 ... 164 C3
Awbridge Prim Sch SO51 ... 26 B3
Awbridge Rd PO9 ... 135 B2
Axford Cl BH8 ... 190 B2
Aylen Rd PO3 ... 158 A1
Aylesbury Rd
Bournemouth BH1 ... 205 C2
Portsmouth PO2 ... 182 C4
Ayling Cl PO13 ... 180 B4
Aylward St PO1 ... 182 A3
Aynsley Ct SO15 ... 102 B4
Aysgarth Rd PO7 ... 134 C4
Aysha Cl BH25 ... 195 A1
Azalea Cl Havant PO9 ... 136 B2
St Leonards BH24 ... 140 A3
Azura Cl BH21 ... 139 A3

B

B Ave Fawley SO45 ... 150 B3
Fawley SO45 ... 150 C2
Back La Mottisfont SO51 ... 5 C3
Southwick PO17 ... 132 C3
Sway SO41 ... 172 B1
Back of the Walls
Southampton SO14 ... 103 A1
Southampton SO14 ... 103 A2
Back St SO23 ... 10 C2
Bacon Cl SO19 ... 103 C1
Bacon La PO11 ... 184 C2
Badbury Cl BH18 ... 187 B2
Badbury Ct 7 BH23 ... 207 C3
Badbury View BH21 ... 163 B3
Badbury View Rd BH21 ... 186 B4
Baddesley Cl SO52 ... 53 C3
Baddesley Gdns PO9 ... 135 B3
Baddesley Rd SO53 ... 30 A1
Baden Cl BH25 ... 195 A1
Baden Powell & St Peter's Mid Sch BH14 ... 203 A2
Baden Powell Way 14 SO51 ... 52 C4
Bader Cl SO30 ... 105 B4
Bader Rd BH17 ... 202 C4
Bader Way PO15 ... 129 C3
Badger Brow PO7 ... 135 A3
Badger Cl
Bishopstoke SO50 ... 56 C1
Fareham PO15 ... 130 B1
Badger Ct 10 SO50 ... 56 C1
Badger Farm Rd SO22, SO23 ... 10 B2
Badger Rd PO14 ... 154 C3
Badger Way BH31 ... 114 C3
Badger Wood Pl SO18 ... 79 C1
Badgers Cl
St Leonards BH24 ... 139 C3
Sway SO41 ... 172 B1
Badgers Copse BH25 ... 195 B3
Badgers Run SO31 ... 128 C3
Badgers The SO31 ... 127 B3
Badgers Wlk
Ferndown BH22 ... 165 C4
Hythe SO45 ... 125 C1
Badminston Dro SO45 ... 178 B4
Badminston La SO45 ... 151 B1
Badshear La SO24 ... 14 C4
Baffins Rd PO3 ... 183 A4
Bagber Rd SO40 ... 100 C4
Bagot Ho PO12 ... 180 C3
Bagshot Mews SO19 ... 103 C2
Baigent Cl SO23 ... 11 B4
Bailey Cl Botley SO30 ... 106 A3
New Milton BH25 ... 195 B2
Winchester SO22 ... 10 B3
Bailey Cres BH15 ... 202 B4
Bailey Dr BH23 ... 206 C4
Bailey Gn SO18 ... 80 A1
Bailey Hall BH23 ... 206 C4
Bailey's Rd PO5 ... 215 C2
Baiter Gdns BH15 ... 202 B1
Baker Rd BH11 ... 189 A3
Baker St PO1 ... 182 B4
Bakers Dro SO16 ... 77 C3
Bakers Farm Rd BH31 ... 114 C4
Balaclava Rd SO18 ... 104 A4
Balcombe Rd BH13 ... 204 A2
Balderton Cl 15 PO2 ... 157 C2
Baldwin Cl BH23 ... 207 B3
Balena Cl BH17 ... 202 A4
Balfour Cl
Christchurch BH23 ... 208 B4
Gosport PO13 ... 180 B3
Balfour Dr GU33 ... 20 C2
Balfour Rd
Bournemouth BH9 ... 189 C1
Portsmouth PO2 ... 157 C1
Southampton SO19 ... 104 B2
Balfour Red Cross Mus* SO22 ... 1 B1
Ball La 17 BH15 ... 202 B1
Ballam Cl BH16 ... 201 B4
Ballard Cl
New Milton BH25 ... 195 A2
Poole BH15 ... 202 B1
Southampton SO16 ... 77 B1
Ballard Coll BH25 ... 195 A2
Ballard Ct 1 PO12 ... 181 A2
Ballard Rd BH15 ... 202 B1
Ballard Sch BH25 ... 195 A2
Balliol Cl PO14 ... 129 B1
Balliol Rd PO2 ... 182 C4
Balmer Lawn Rd SO42 ... 146 A2
Balmoral Ave BH8 ... 190 C1
Balmoral Cl
Chandler's Ford SO53 ... 55 A4
Gosport PO13 ... 155 B1
Southampton SO16 ... 78 B3
Balmoral Ct
7 Christchurch BH23 ... 209 A4
7 Southampton SO17 ... 103 A4
Southampton, Millbrook SO15 ... 102 A3
Balmoral Dr PO7 ... 134 B2
Balmoral Ho BH2 ... 204 B2
Balmoral Rd
Fareham PO15 ... 130 C2
Poole BH14 ... 203 B2
Balmoral Way
Petersfield GU32 ... 40 C2
Rownhams SO16 ... 77 C3
Balmoral Wlk BH25 ... 194 C2
Balston Rd BH14 ... 203 A3
Balston Terr BH15 ... 202 A1
Baltic Rd SO30 ... 80 C1
Bambridge Pk Gdn Ctr Miniature Rly* SO50 ... 31 C1
Bamford Ho PO4 ... 183 A1
Bampton Cl SO16 ... 101 C4
Bampton Ct SO53 ... 55 B3
Banbury Ave SO19 ... 104 B2
Banbury Rd BH17 ... 202 B4
Banfurly Gdns SO45 ... 125 C1
Bangor Rd SO15 ... 102 A3
Banister Ct 13 SO15 ... 102 C4
Banister Gdns SO15 ... 102 C4
Banister Grange 16 SO15 ... 102 C4
Banister Inf Sch SO15 ... 102 C4
Banister Mews SO15 ... 102 C4
Banister Rd SO15 ... 102 C4
Bank Chambers BH14 ... 203 C2
Bank Cl BH23 ... 207 A3
Bank Side SO18 ... 79 B2
Bank St SO32 ... 83 B4
Bankhill Dr SO41 ... 197 B3
Banks Rd BH13 ... 214 B2
Banks The SO51 ... 26 A3
Bankside SO41 ... 197 B3
Bankside Ho 4 SO22 ... 10 C4
Bankside Rd BH9 ... 190 A2
Bankview SO41 ... 197 B3
Bannerman Rd GU32 ... 40 C2
Banning St SO51 ... 52 C3
Bannister Ct SO40 ... 101 A4
Banocroft Ct 1 BH15 ... 202 C2
Banstead Rd BH18 ... 187 A3
Bapaume Rd PO3 ... 157 C3
Bar End Ind Est SO23 ... 11 A3
Bar End Rd SO23 ... 11 A3
Bar Gate & Guildhall (Mus)* SO14 ... 102 C2
Barbe Baker Ave SO30 ... 80 B1
Barberry Dr SO40 ... 76 A1
Barberry Way BH31 ... 115 B3
Barbers Gate 15 BH15 ... 202 A1
Barbers Piles 8 BH15 ... 202 A1
Barbers Wharf 16 BH15 ... 202 A1
Barclay Ho PO12 ... 181 C2
Barclay Mans BH2 ... 204 C3
Barclay Mews
Hythe SO45 ... 149 C4
Hythe SO45 ... 150 A4
Bardon Way PO14 ... 154 B4
Barfield Cl SO23 ... 11 A3
Barfields SO41 ... 197 C2
Barfields Ct SO41 ... 197 C2
Barfleur Cl PO15 ... 130 B1
Barfleur Rd PO14 ... 155 A3
Barford Cl SO53 ... 55 A4
Barford La SP5 ... 47 A4
Bargate Ctr 8 SO14 ... 103 A2
Bargate St SO14 ... 102 C2
Bargates BH23 ... 207 A4
Barham Cl PO12 ... 181 A3
Barham Rd GU32 ... 40 C2
Barham Way PO2 ... 157 B2
Baring Rd
Bournemouth BH6 ... 207 A2
Winchester SO23 ... 11 A4
Bark Hill Mews SO51 ... 52 C3
Barker Mill Cl SO16 ... 77 C3
Barkis Ho 11 PO1 ... 182 B4
Barkshire Ct 7 SO15 ... 102 C4
Barlands Cl BH23 ... 192 B1
Barle Cl SO18 ... 80 A1
Barley Down Dr SO22 ... 10 B2
Barleycorn Wlk SO40 ... 98 C4
Barling Mews 13 SO51 ... 52 C4
Barlow Cl PO14 ... 179 A3
Barn Cl Emsworth PO10 ... 160 B4
Upton BH16 ... 201 A4
Barn Fold PO7 ... 112 B1
Barn Piece SO53 ... 54 C3
Barn Rd BH18 ... 187 A2
Barnaby Cl SP5 ... 46 B4
Barnbrook Rd SO31 ... 128 C2
Barncroft Inf Sch PO9 ... 135 B2
Barncroft Jun Sch PO9 ... 135 B2
Barncroft Way PO9 ... 135 B2
Barnes Cl
Bournemouth BH10 ... 189 B2
Locks Heath SO31 ... 128 B2
Southampton SO18 ... 104 B3
West Wellow SO51 ... 50 C2
Winchester SO23 ... 10 C3
Barnes Cres
Bournemouth BH10 ... 189 B2
Wimborne Minst BH21 ... 163 C2
Barnes La
Locks Heath SO31 ... 128 C2
Milford on Sea SO41 ... 211 B3
Barnes Rd
Bournemouth BH10 ... 189 B2
Portsmouth PO1 ... 182 C3
Southampton SO19 ... 104 B3
Barnes Wallis Rd PO15 ... 129 C2
Barnes Way PO9 ... 135 B2
Barnet Side La GU32 ... 18 B3
Barney Evans Cres PO8 ... 111 B2
Barney Hayes La SO40 ... 99 A4
Barnfield BH23 ... 208 B4
Barnfield Cl
Southampton SO19 ... 103 C1
Southbourne PO10 ... 137 C1
Barnfield Ct
Fareham PO14 ... 154 C4
Southampton SO19 ... 103 C1
Barnfield Flats SO19 ... 103 C1
Barnfield Rd
Petersfield GU31 ... 41 B2
Southampton SO19 ... 103 C1
Barnfield Way SO19 ... 103 C1
Barnfields Flats SO19 ... 103 C1
Barns Rd BH22 ... 166 A3
Barnsfield Cres SO40 ... 100 B4
Barnsfield Rd BH24 ... 140 A2
Barnside Way GU33 ... 20 C2
Barnsland SO30 ... 80 B2
Barnwood Rd PO15 ... 130 B1
Baron Rd SO31 ... 127 C2
Barons Ct 8 BH12 ... 204 A2
Barons Mead SO16 ... 77 C2
Barons Rd BH11 ... 188 B3
Baronsmere PO12 ... 181 A2
Barrack La BH24 ... 141 B2
Barrack Rd
Christchurch BH23 ... 206 C4
Ferndown BH22 ... 166 A1
Barratt Ind Pk PO15 ... 129 B3
Barrie Cl PO15 ... 129 B4
Barrie Rd BH9 ... 189 C2
Barrington Cl SO50 ... 55 C3
Barrington Ct 31 SO17 ... 79 A1
Barrington Ho 23 PO1 ... 182 B4
Barrow Down Gdns SO19 ... 104 C2
Barrow Dr BH8 ... 190 C1
Barrow Hill Rd SO40 ... 75 B2
Barrow Rd BH8 ... 190 C1
Barrow View BH22 ... 165 A3
Barrow Way BH8 ... 190 C1
Barrowgate Rd BH8 ... 190 B2
Barrowgate Way BH8 ... 190 B2
Barrows La Landford SP5 ... 49 B3
Sway SO41 ... 196 A3
Barrs Ave BH25 ... 195 A2
Barrs Wood Dr BH25 ... 195 A2
Barrs Wood Rd BH25 ... 195 A2
Barry Gdns BH18 ... 186 C3
Barry Rd SO19 ... 104 A3
Barters Cl SO16 ... 77 C1
Barters La BH18 ... 186 C2
Bartholomew Cl 25 SO23 ... 2 A1
Bartlett Cl PO15 ... 130 C2
Bartlett Dr BH7 ... 206 A4
Bartlett Ho 20 SO17 ... 103 A4
Bartletts Comm SP6 ... 94 C4
Bartletts The SO31 ... 128 A1
Bartley Ave SO40 ... 100 C3
Bartley CE Jun Sch SO40 ... 99 A4
Bartley Ct 6 BH21 ... 163 A3
Bartley Rd SO40 ... 99 B2
Barton Cl SO51 ... 53 A4
Barton Common La BH25 ... 210 A4
Barton Common Rd BH25 ... 210 A4
Barton Court Ave BH25 ... 210 A4
Barton Court Rd BH25 ... 195 A1
Barton Cres SO18 ... 79 C1
Barton Croft BH25 ... 210 A4
Barton Cross PO8 ... 112 A4
Barton Ct BH25 ... 210 A3
Barton Dr
Barton on Sea BH25 ... 209 C4
Hamble-le-Rice SO31 ... 127 C2
Hedge End SO30 ... 105 B4
Barton Gn BH25 ... 210 A3
Barton Gr PO3 ... 158 A2
Barton Ho BH25 ... 209 C4
Barton La BH25 ... 209 C4
Barton Lo BH12 ... 203 A3
Barton Park Ind Est SO50 ... 56 B1
Barton Peveril Coll SO50 ... 55 C1
Barton Rd SO50 ... 56 B2
Barton Way BH25 ... 209 C4
Barton Wood Rd BH25 ... 209 C4
Bartons Rd
Fordingbridge SP6 ... 69 C1
Havant PO9 ... 136 A2
Bartons The
Fordingbridge SP6 ... 69 C1
Hedge End SO30 ... 105 A3
Bartonside Rd BH25 ... 209 B4
Bartram Rd SO40 ... 101 A3
Barwell Gr PO10 ... 136 C2
Barwell Terr 10 SO30 ... 105 B3
Bascott Cl BH11 ... 189 A1
Bascott Rd BH11 ... 189 A1
Bashley Common Rd BH25 ... 195 A4
Bashley Cross Rd BH25 ... 194 C3
Bashley Dr BH25 ... 195 A3
Bashley Rd BH25 ... 195 A3
Basin St PO2 ... 182 B4
Basing Dean GU34 ... 17 C2
Basing Ho SO15 ... 102 B4
Basing Mews 8 SO32 ... 83 B4
Basing Rd PO9 ... 135 C2
Basing Way SO53 ... 55 A2
Basingstoke Rd SO23 ... 2 B4
Basingwell St SO32 ... 83 B4
Bassett Ave SO16 ... 78 C3
Bassett Cl SO16 ... 78 C2
Bassett Cres E SO16 ... 78 C2
Bassett Cres W SO16 ... 78 C2
Bassett Ct SO16 ... 78 C2
Bassett Dale SO16 ... 78 C3
Bassett Gdns SO16 ... 78 C2
Bassett Gn SO16 ... 79 A3
Bassett Green Cl SO16 ... 79 A3
Bassett Green Ct SO16 ... 79 A3
Bassett Green Dr SO16 ... 79 A3
Bassett Green Prim Sch SO16 ... 79 A2
Bassett Green Rd SO16 ... 79 A3
Bassett Heath Ave SO16 ... 78 C3
Bassett Mdw SO16 ... 78 C2
Bassett Mews SO16 ... 78 C3
Bassett Rd BH12 ... 203 A3
Bassett Row SO16 ... 78 C3
Bassett Wlk 8 PO9 ... 135 B3
Bassett Wood Dr SO16 ... 79 A3
Bassett Wood Mews 7 SO16 ... 78 C2
Bassett Wood N SO16 ... 79 A3
Bassett Wood Rd SO16 ... 79 A3
Bastone Way BH22 ... 165 A3
Batchelor Cres BH11 ... 188 C2
Batchelor Gn SO31 ... 127 C4
Batchelor Rd BH11 ... 188 C2
Batcombe Cl BH11 ... 188 C2
Bath & Wells Ct PO13 ... 180 B3
Bath Cl SO19 ... 104 A3
Bath Hill Ct 9 BH1 ... 205 A2
Bath Hill Rdbt BH1 ... 205 A1
Bath La 11 PO16 ... 131 B1
Bath La (lower) 13 PO16 ... 131 B1
Bath Lane Cotts PO16 ... 155 B4
Bath Rd
Bournemouth BH1 ... 205 A2
Emsworth PO10 ... 160 C4
Lymington SO41 ... 197 C2
Portsmouth PO4 ... 182 C2
Southampton SO19 ... 104 A3
Bath Sq PO1 ... 181 C2
Bath St SO14 ... 103 A4
Bathing La PO1 ... 181 C2
Bathurst Cl PO11 ... 184 C2
Bathurst Way PO2 ... 157 A1
Batten Cl BH23 ... 207 B4
Batten Rd SP5 ... 46 C4
Battenburg Ave PO2 ... 157 C1
Battenburg Rd PO12 ... 181 B3
Battens Way PO9 ... 135 C2
Batterley Dro BH21 ... 91 C2
Battery Cl PO12 ... 180 C4
Battery Hill
Bishop's Waltham SO32 ... 83 A4
Winchester SO22 ... 10 B3
Battery Row PO1 ... 182 A2
Battle Cl SO31 ... 129 A2
Battramsley Cross SO41 ... 173 B1
Baverstock Rd BH12 ... 204 A4
Baxter Rd SO19 ... 104 C3
Bay Cl Southampton SO19 ... 104 A2
Three Legged Cross BH21 ... 138 C4
Upton BH16 ... 201 A3
Bay Hog La BH15 ... 202 A1
Bay House Sec Sch PO12 ... 180 C2
Bay Rd Gosport PO12 ... 180 C2
Southampton SO19 ... 104 A2
Bay Tree Lodge PO14 ... 179 B3
Bay Tree Way BH23 ... 193 B1
Bay Trees SO19 ... 104 C3
Bay View Ct PO11 ... 184 B1
Bay View Mews PO11 ... 184 B1
Baybridge La SO21 ... 33 B2
Baybridge Rd PO9 ... 136 A3
Baycroft Sch PO14 ... 179 C3
Bayfields PO5 ... 215 B1
Bayly Ave PO16 ... 156 B3
Bays Ct SO41 ... 197 B2
Bays Rd SO41 ... 197 B2
Bayswater Ho PO5 ... 215 C1
Baythorn Cl PO2 ... 182 B4
Beach Ave BH25 ... 209 C4
Beach Cl BH13 ... 214 D4
Beach La SO31 ... 127 A3
Beach Rd
Emsworth PO10 ... 160 C4
Lee-on-the-Solent PO13 ... 179 C1
Poole BH13 ... 214 D4
Portsmouth PO5 ... 182 B1
South Hayling PO11 ... 184 C2
Upton BH16 ... 201 A3
Beach View BH13 ... 214 B2
Beachcroft BH13 ... 204 A2
Beachway PO16 ... 156 B3
Beacon Bottom SO31 ... 129 A3
Beacon Cl Hordle SO41 ... 196 B1
Locks Heath SO31 ... 129 A3
Rownhams SO16 ... 77 B3
Beacon Ct
Christchurch BH23 ... 208 C4
Fordingbridge SP6 ... 69 C2
Beacon Dr BH23 ... 208 C4
Beacon Gdns BH18 ... 186 C2
Beacon Hill La
Corfe Mullen BH21 ... 186 A2
Droxford SO32 ... 60 C3
Meonstoke SO32 ... 61 B3
Beacon Mews SO30 ... 104 B4
Beacon Mount SO31 ... 129 A3
Beacon Park Cres BH16 ... 201 A4
Beacon Park Rd BH16 ... 201 A4
Beacon Rd
Bournemouth BH2 ... 204 C1
Broadstone BH18 ... 186 C2
Upton BH16 ... 201 A4
West End SO30 ... 104 B4
Beacon Sq PO10 ... 160 C4
Beacon Way
Broadstone BH18 ... 186 C2
Locks Heath SO31 ... 129 A3
Beaconsfield Ave PO6 ... 158 A4
Beaconsfield Rd
Christchurch BH23 ... 207 A4

Beaconsfield Rd *continued*
Fareham PO16 .....155 A4
Poole BH12 .....203 B3
Waterlooville PO7 .....134 C4
Bealing Cl SO16 .....79 A2
Beamish Rd BH17 .....202 C4
Bear Cross Ave BH11 .....188 C3
Bear Cross Rdbt BH11 .....188 C3
Bearslane Cl SO40 .....76 B1
Bearwood Prim Sch
BH11 .....188 B3
Beatrice Ct 5 SO41 .....211 A2
Beatrice Mews 15 PO6 .....157 C4
Beatrice Rd
Portsmouth PO4 .....182 C1
Southampton SO15 .....102 B4
Beatrice Royal Art Gal★
SO50 .....55 C1
Beattie Rise SO30 .....81 B1
Beatty Cl
Locks Heath SO31 .....129 A2
Ringwood BH24 .....141 B4
Beatty Dr PO12 .....180 C2
Beatty Ho 9 PO1 .....215 C4
Beatty Rd BH9 .....190 A1
Beaty Ct SO19 .....104 B3
Beau Ct
31 Bournemouth BH4 .....204 B2
9 New Milton BH25 .....195 A2
Beauchamp Ave PO13 .....155 B1
Beauchamps Gdns BH7 .....206 A4
Beaucroft La BH21 .....163 C3
Beaucroft Rd
Waltham Chase SO32 .....83 C2
Wimborne Minst BH21 .....163 C3
Beaucroft Sch BH21 .....163 C3
Beaufort Ave PO16 .....130 C1
Beaufort Cl BH23 .....208 A4
Beaufort Dr
Bishop's Waltham SO32 .....83 B4
Wimborne Minst BH21 .....163 B3
Beaufort Mews BH21 .....163 A2
Beaufort Rd
Bournemouth BH6 .....206 B3
Havant PO9 .....135 B1
10 Portsmouth PO5 .....182 B1
Winchester SO23 .....10 C3
Beaufoys Ave BH22 .....165 B4
Beaufoys Cl BH22 .....165 B4
Beaufoys Ct BH22 .....165 B3
Beaulieu Abbey★ SO42 .....148 C1
Beaulieu Ave
Christchurch BH23 .....206 C4
Havant PO9 .....135 B3
Portchester PO16 .....156 A4
Beaulieu Cl
New Milton BH25 .....194 C2
Southampton SO16 .....78 A3
Winchester SO22 .....1 B2
Beaulieu Ct 5 PO8 .....111 C2
Beaulieu Ho 12 SO15 .....102 C4
Beaulieu Pl PO13 .....155 A1
Beaulieu Rd
Beaulieu SO42,SO45 .....149 B3
Bournemouth BH4 .....204 A1
Christchurch BH23 .....206 C4
Eastleigh SO50 .....56 A2
Hamble-le-Rice SO31 .....127 C2
Hythe SO45 .....125 C1
Lyndhurst SO42 .....122 B2
Marchwood SO40 .....124 C3
Portsmouth PO2 .....157 C1
Beaulieu Road Sta
SO42 .....123 B1
Beaulieu Village Prim Sch
SO42 .....148 C1
Beaumaris Cl SO53 .....55 A2
Beaumaris Gdns SO40 .....125 C3
Beaumond Gn 29 SO22 .....10 C4
Beaumont Cl
Fareham PO15 .....130 B2
Southampton SO16 .....78 C2
Beaumont Ct PO12 .....181 A4
Beaumont Pl SO40 .....101 A4
Beaumont Rd
Poole BH13 .....214 C4
Totton SO40 .....101 A4
Beaumont Rise PO15 .....130 B2
Beauworth Ave SO18 .....104 B4
Beaver Dr SO50 .....57 A1
Beaver Ind Est BH23 .....208 A3
Beccles Cl BH15 .....201 C1
Becher Rd BH14 .....203 C2
Beck Cl SO31 .....128 C2
Beck St PO1 .....182 A3
Beckenham Terr PO10 .....137 A2
Beckford La PO17 .....109 C1
Beckham La GU32 .....40 B2
Beckhampton Rd BH15 .....201 C2
Beckley Copse BH23 .....194 A1
Becton La BH25 .....210 A4
Becton Mead BH25 .....195 A1
Bedale Way BH15 .....202 C3
Bedales Sch GU32 .....40 C4
Beddow Hall 3 PO5 .....215 A2
Bedenham La PO13 .....155 C2
Bedenham Prim Sch
PO13 .....155 B2
Bedfield Ho SO23 .....2 A3
Bedfield La SO23 .....2 A3
Bedford Ave SO19 .....103 C1
Bedford Cl
Fordingbridge SP6 .....69 C2
Havant PO9 .....160 A4
Hedge End SO30 .....105 B3
Bedford Cres BH7 .....206 B4
Bedford Pl SO15 .....102 C3
Bedford Rd GU32 .....40 B2
Bedford Rd N BH12 .....188 B1
Bedford Rd S BH12 .....188 B1
Bedford St Gosport PO12 .....181 A3
Portsmouth PO5 .....215 B2
Bedhampton Hill PO9 .....135 A1
Bedhampton Hill Rd
PO9 .....135 A1
Bedhampton Ho 4 PO1 .....215 C4
Bedhampton Rd
Havant PO9 .....135 B1
Portsmouth PO2 .....182 C4
Bedhampton Sta PO9 .....135 B1
Bedhampton Way PO9 .....135 C2
Bedwell Cl SO16 .....77 C3
Beech Ave
Bournemouth BH6 .....206 B2
Christchurch BH23 .....206 B4
Southampton SO18 .....103 C4
Beech Cl Alderholt SP6 .....93 A3
Broadstone BH18 .....186 C2
Chandler's Ford SO53 .....30 B1
Hamble-le-Rice SO31 .....127 C1
Hordle SO41 .....211 B4
Romsey SO51 .....53 B3
Verwood BH31 .....114 C3
Waterlooville PO8 .....111 C1
Winchester SO22 .....10 A2
Beech Cnr SO32 .....81 C3
Beech Copse SO22 .....1 A1
Beech Cres SO45 .....150 A4
Beech Ct
Southampton SO19 .....103 C2
Wimborne Minst BH21 .....163 C2
Beech Dr PO6 .....156 C4
Beech Gdns SO31 .....127 C1
Beech Gr Gosport PO12 .....181 A2
Owslebury SO21 .....33 A2
South Hayling PO11 .....185 A2
Beech Grange SP5 .....49 B1
Beech Ho SO16 .....78 C4
Beech La BH24 .....139 C1
Beech Rd Ashurst SO40 .....100 A1
Chandler's Ford SO53 .....55 B4
Clanfield PO8 .....88 B3
Fareham PO15 .....130 C1
Hedge End SO30 .....105 B4
Southampton SO15 .....102 A3
Beech Way PO8 .....112 A3
Beech Wood Cl BH18 .....187 A2
Beecham Rd PO1 .....182 C4
Beechbank Ave BH17 .....186 C1
Beechcroft BH1 .....205 A3
Beechcroft Cl
Chandler's Ford SO53 .....55 B3
Fareham PO15 .....130 B1
Beechcroft La BH24 .....141 A4
Beechcroft Mews 2
BH24 .....141 A4
Beechcroft Rd PO12 .....181 A2
Beechcroft Way SO53 .....55 B4
Beechdale Cl SO40 .....76 B1
Beechdale Wlk SO40 .....76 B1
Beechen La SO43 .....122 A2
Beeches Hill SO32 .....59 B1
Beeches The
Awbridge SO51 .....26 C3
Bournemouth BH7 .....206 A4
Fair Oak SO50 .....57 B1
4 Waterlooville PO7 .....134 C4
West Wellow SO51 .....50 B2
Beechey Ct 6 BH8 .....205 A3
Beechey Rd BH8 .....205 A3
Beechfield 30 BH4 .....204 B2
Beechfield Ct SO15 .....102 A4
Beechmount SO16 .....78 C3
Beechmount Rd SO16 .....78 C3
Beechwood SP6 .....69 B1
Beechwood Ave
Bournemouth BH5 .....205 C2
New Milton BH25 .....194 C2
Waterlooville PO7 .....134 C3
Beechwood Cl
Chandler's Ford SO53 .....30 A1
Locks Heath SO31 .....152 B4
Beechwood Cres SO53 .....30 A1
Beechwood Ct
Bournemouth BH2 .....204 C1
Liss GU33 .....21 A3
Beechwood Gdns
Bournemouth BH5 .....206 A2
Southampton SO18 .....103 C4
Beechwood Ho SO17 .....103 B4
Beechwood Jun Sch
SO18 .....103 C4
Beechwood La BH24 .....143 A2
Beechwood Lodge 3
PO16 .....131 A1
Beechwood Rd
Cadnam SO40 .....99 A3
Holbury SO45 .....150 B2
Portsmouth PO2 .....157 C2
West Moors BH22 .....138 C1
Beechwood Rise SO18 .....80 B1
Beechwood Way SO45 .....125 B1
Beechworth Rd 3 PO9 .....136 A1
Beehive Cotts PO16 .....131 A2
Beehive Wlk PO1 .....182 A2
Beeston Ct PO1 .....182 C4
Beggar's La SO23 .....11 A4
Begonia Rd SO16 .....79 A2
Behrendt Cl PO12 .....181 A3
Belben Cl BH12 .....188 B1
Belben Rd BH12 .....188 B1
Belbins SO51 .....27 C2
Belbins Bsns Pk SO51 .....28 A2
Belfield Rd BH6 .....207 A2
Belfry Wlk PO14 .....129 B1
Belgrave Ct BH1 .....205 B2
Belgrave Ind Est SO17 .....79 B1
Belgrave Rd Poole BH13 .....204 A1
Southampton SO17 .....79 B1
Belgravia Rd PO2 .....157 C1
Bell Cl SO45 .....150 C1
Bell Cres PO7 .....134 C3
Bell Davies Rd PO14 .....179 A3
Bell Heather Cl BH16 .....201 A4
Bell Hill GU32 .....40 C3
Bell Hill Ridge GU32 .....40 C3
Bell Ho PO18 .....161 C4
Bell La 18 BH15 .....202 A1
Bell Rd PO6 .....157 B4
Bell St Romsey SO51 .....52 C4
Southampton SO14 .....103 A2
Bellair Ho PO9 .....136 A1
Bellair Rd PO9 .....136 A1
Bellamy Ct SO17 .....103 B4
Belle Vue Cl BH6 .....206 B2
Belle Vue Cres BH6 .....206 C2
Belle Vue Gdns 2 BH6 .....206 C2
Belle Vue Gr BH22 .....138 C1
Belle Vue Mans 7 BH6 .....206 C2
Belle Vue Rd
Bournemouth BH6 .....206 C2
Poole BH14 .....203 B2
Belle Vue Wlk BH22 .....165 C1
Bellemoor Rd SO15 .....78 B1
Bellemoor Sec Sch (Boys)
SO15 .....78 B1
Belleview Terr PO5 .....215 A1
Bellevue La PO10 .....136 C1
Bellevue Rd
Eastleigh SO50 .....56 A2
Southampton SO15 .....103 A3
Bellevue Terr 9 SO14 .....103 A3
Bellfield PO14 .....153 C4
Bellflower Cl BH23 .....208 A4
Bellflower Way SO53 .....54 C4
Bells Ho BH21 .....163 B3
Bells La PO14 .....179 B3
Belmont Ave BH8 .....190 B1
Belmont Cl Horndean PO8 .....88 B2
Hythe SO45 .....126 A1
Stubbington PO14 .....154 B2
Verwood BH31 .....115 A3
Belmont Gr PO9 .....135 B1
Belmont Pl PO5 .....215 B1
Belmont Rd
Chandler's Ford SO53 .....55 B2
New Milton BH25 .....195 B2
Poole BH14 .....203 B3
Southampton SO17 .....103 A4
Belmont St PO5 .....215 B1
Belmore Cl PO1 .....182 C4
Belmore La
Lymington SO41 .....197 C2
Owslebury SO21 .....33 C2
Upham SO32 .....34 A2
Belmore Rd SO41 .....197 B2
Belmour Lo 26 BH4 .....204 B2
Belney Ho PO6 .....157 A4
Belstone Rd SO40 .....100 C4
Belton Rd SO19 .....104 A2
Belvedere Cl GU32 .....40 C2
Belvedere Rd
Bournemouth BH3 .....205 A3
Christchurch BH23 .....207 A4
Hythe SO45 .....126 A1
Belvidere Ho 12 SO14 .....103 B3
Belvidere Rd SO14 .....103 B3
Belvidere Terr SO14 .....103 B3
Belvoir Cl PO16 .....155 A4
Bembridge SO31 .....127 B3
Bembridge Cl SO16 .....79 B3
Bembridge Cres PO4 .....182 C1
Bembridge Ct PO11 .....185 B1
Bembridge Dr PO11 .....185 B1
Bembridge Ho PO11 .....185 B1
Bembridge Lodge Flats 8
PO13 .....179 C1
Bemister Rd BH9 .....205 A4
Bemister's La PO12 .....181 C2
Benbow Cl PO8 .....112 B4
Benbow Cres BH12 .....188 C1
Benbow Gdns SO40 .....76 B1
Benbow Ho 6 PO1 .....182 A3
Benbow Pl 5 PO1 .....182 A3
Benbridge Ave BH11 .....188 C3
Bencraft Ct SO16 .....79 A3
Bendigo Rd BH23 .....206 C4
Benedict Cl SO51 .....53 B4
Benedict Way PO16 .....132 C1
Beneficial St 14 PO1 .....182 A3
Benellen Ave BH4 .....204 B2
Benellen Gdns BH4 .....204 B2
Benellen Rd BH4 .....204 B3
Benellen Twrs BH4 .....204 B2
Bengal Rd BH9 .....204 C4
Benger's La SO51 .....5 B1
Benham Dr 13 PO3 .....157 C2
Benham Gr PO16 .....156 B3
Benhams Farm Cl 8
SO18 .....80 A1
Benhams Rd SO18 .....80 A1
Benjamin Ct BH23 .....206 C4
Benjamin Rd BH15 .....201 C1
Benmoor Rd BH17 .....202 A4
Benmore Cl BH25 .....195 B1
Benmore Gdns SO53 .....55 A4
Benmore Rd BH9 .....190 A1
Bennett Ho 11 BH4 .....204 B2
Bennett Rd BH8 .....205 B3
Bennett's Alley 22 BH15 .....202 A1
Bennetts La BH24 .....143 B1
Bennion Rd BH10 .....189 B2
Benridge Cl BH18 .....187 A2
Benson Cl BH23 .....169 A1
Benson Rd Poole BH17 .....202 B4
Southampton SO15 .....102 A4
Bent La PO7 .....110 A4
Bentham Rd PO12 .....181 A2
Bentham Way SO31 .....128 B4
Benthem Ct SO16 .....79 A2
Bentley Cl Horndean PO8 .....112 B4
Kings Worthy SO23 .....2 A3
Bentley Cres PO16 .....130 C1
Bentley Ct Havant PO9 .....136 A3
16 Southampton SO17 .....79 A1
Bentley Gr SO18 .....104 B4
Bentley Rd BH9 .....189 C2
Bentworth Cl PO9 .....135 B2
Benwell Ct PO11 .....184 C2
Bepton Down GU31 .....41 A2
Berber Cl PO15 .....129 B4
Bercote Cl SO22 .....1 A3
Bere Cl
North Baddesley SO53 .....55 A4
Poole BH17 .....187 B1
Winchester SO22 .....1 B1
Bere Farm La PO17 .....131 C4
Bere Rd PO7 .....110 C2
Beresford Cl
Chandler's Ford SO53 .....55 C3
Poole BH12 .....203 B3
Waterlooville PO7 .....134 C3
Beresford Gdns
Chandler's Ford SO53 .....55 C3
Christchurch BH23 .....207 C3
Beresford Rd
Bournemouth BH6 .....206 A2
Chandler's Ford SO53 .....55 C3
Lymington SO41 .....197 B2
Poole BH12 .....203 B3
Portsmouth PO2 .....157 C1
Stubbington PO14 .....154 B2
Bereweeke Ave SO22 .....1 C1
Bereweeke Cl SO22 .....1 C1
Bereweeke Rd SO22 .....1 C1
Bereweeke Way SO22 .....1 C1
Bergen Cres SO30 .....105 B3
Berkeley Ave BH12 .....203 B4
Berkeley Cl
Southampton SO15 .....102 C4
Stubbington PO14 .....179 A3
Verwood BH31 .....114 C4
Berkeley Ct PO13 .....179 C1
Berkeley Gdns SO30 .....105 B3
Berkeley Rd
Bournemouth BH3 .....204 C4
Southampton SO15 .....102 C3
Berkeley Sq PO9 .....136 A1
Berkeley The PO5 .....182 C1
Berkley Ave BH22 .....165 B1
Berkshire Cl PO1 .....215 D3
Bermuda Ct
9 Christchurch BH23 .....209 A4
22 Southampton SO17 .....79 A1
Bermuda Ho 3 PO6 .....132 C1
Bernard Ave PO6 .....158 A4
Bernard Powell Ho PO9 .....136 A1
Bernard St SO14 .....103 A2
Bernards Cl BH23 .....206 C4
Berne Ct 11 BH1 .....205 A2
Berney Rd PO4 .....183 B2
Bernina Ave PO7 .....111 B1
Bernina Cl PO7 .....111 B1
Bernwood Gr SO45 .....177 C4
Beron Ct BH15 .....202 C2
Berrans Ave BH11 .....189 A3
Berrans Ct BH11 .....189 A3
Berry Cl SO30 .....105 B3
Berry La
Stubbington PO14 .....179 A3
Twyford SO21 .....32 A4
Berrydown Rd PO9 .....135 B4
Berryfield Rd SO41 .....196 A1
Berrylands GU33 .....21 A4
Berrywood Bsns Village
SO30 .....81 A2
Berrywood Gdns SO30 .....105 A4
Berrywood Prim Sch
SO30 .....81 B1
Berthon Ho SO51 .....52 C3
Bertie Rd PO4 .....183 A2
Bertram Rd BH25 .....195 B2
Berwick Rd BH3 .....204 C3
Berwyn Ct BH18 .....187 A2
Berwyn Wlk PO14 .....154 C4
Beryl Ave PO12 .....180 C4
Beryton Cl PO12 .....181 A3
Beryton Rd PO12 .....181 A3
Besomer Dro SP5 .....47 C3
Bessborough Rd BH13 .....214 C4
Bessemer Cl BH31 .....115 B2
Beswick Ave BH10 .....189 B1
Bethany Ct BH12 .....204 A4
Bethany Ho BH1 .....205 B3
Bethany Jun CE Sch
BH1 .....205 B3
Bethia Cl BH8 .....205 B3
Bethia Rd BH8 .....205 B3
Betsy Cl BH23 .....169 A1
Betsy La BH23 .....169 A1
Betteridge Dr SO16 .....77 B3
Bettesworth Rd PO1 .....182 C4
Bettiscombe Cl BH17 .....187 C1
Betula Cl PO7 .....135 A3
Beulah Rd SO16 .....78 A1
Bevan Cl SO19 .....103 C1
Bevan Rd PO8 .....112 A3
Beverley Cl PO14 .....129 B2
Beverley Gdns
Bournemouth BH10 .....189 B2
Bursledon SO31 .....104 C1
Romsey SO51 .....28 B1
Beverley Gdns *continued*
Swanmore SO32 .....84 A3
Beverley Gr PO6 .....134 C1
Beverley Grange 29
BH4 .....204 B2
Beverley Hts SO18 .....79 C2
Beverley Rd Hythe SO45 .....149 C4
Stubbington PO14 .....179 B3
Beverly Cl PO13 .....155 B1
Beverston Ho 4 PO6 .....133 A1
Beverston Rd PO6 .....133 A1
Bevis Cl Blackfield SO45 .....150 C1
Locks Heath SO31 .....152 B4
Bevis Rd Gosport PO12 .....181 A3
Portsmouth PO2 .....157 B1
Bevis Rd N PO2 .....157 B1
Bevois Gdns SO14 .....103 A4
Bevois Hill SO14 .....103 A4
Bevois Mans 25 SO14 .....103 A4
Bevois Mews 26 SO14 .....103 A4
Bevois Town Prim Sch
SO14 .....103 A4
Bevois Valley Rd SO14 .....103 A4
Bexington Cl BH11 .....188 C2
Beyne Rd SO22 .....10 A2
Bickerley Gdns BH24 .....140 C3
Bickerley Rd BH24 .....140 C3
Bickerley Terr BH24 .....140 C4
Bicknell Boys Sch BH7 .....206 A4
Bicknell Ct 10 BH4 .....204 B2
Bickton Wlk 9 PO9 .....135 B3
Bicton Rd BH10 .....189 A2
Bidbury Inf Sch PO9 .....135 B1
Bidbury Jun Sch PO9 .....135 B1
Bidbury La PO9 .....135 B1
Biddenfield La SO32,
PO17 .....107 B3
Biddlecombe Cl PO13 .....180 B4
Biddlesgate Ct 10 SO14 .....102 C2
Bideford Cl SO16 .....77 C1
Big Tree Cotts SO32 .....85 B3
Biggin Wlk PO14 .....154 C4
Bilberry Cl SO31 .....128 C1
Bilberry Ct 15 SO22 .....10 C4
Bilberry Dr SO40 .....101 C1
Bill Stillwell Ct 6 PO2 .....157 B1
Billett Ave PO7 .....134 C4
Billing Cl PO4 .....183 A2
Billington Gdns SO30 .....81 B1
Billington Pl SO41 .....197 B1
Billy Lawn Ave PO9 .....135 C3
Bilton Bsns Pk PO3 .....158 B1
Bilton Way PO3 .....158 B1
Bindon Cl Poole BH12 .....203 C4
Southampton SO16 .....78 A1
Bindon Ct 5 SO18 .....103 C4
Bindon Rd SO16 .....78 A1
Bingham Ave BH14 .....214 B4
Bingham Cl
Christchurch BH23 .....207 C4
Verwood BH31 .....115 A2
Bingham Dr
Lymington SO41 .....197 C2
Verwood BH31 .....115 A2
Bingham Rd
Bournemouth BH9 .....205 A4
Christchurch BH23 .....207 C4
Verwood BH31 .....115 A2
Binnacle Way PO6 .....157 A4
Binness Way PO6 .....158 C4
Binnie Rd BH12 .....203 C3
Binstead Cl SO16 .....79 B3
Binsteed Rd PO2 .....182 C4
Birch Ave Burton BH23 .....192 B2
Ferndown BH22 .....165 C1
New Milton BH25 .....194 B3
Birch Cl
Colden Common SO21 .....56 C4
Corfe Mullen BH21 .....186 B3
Liss GU33 .....21 A2
Poole BH14 .....203 C2
Romsey SO51 .....53 B3
Southampton SO16 .....78 A1
St Leonards BH24 .....139 B2
Waterlooville PO8 .....111 C2
Birch Ct
Southampton SO18 .....104 A4
3 Winchester SO22 .....10 B3
Birch Dale SO45 .....126 A1
Birch Dr
Bournemouth BH8 .....191 A1
Gosport PO13 .....155 B2
Birch Gr Eastleigh SO50 .....56 A3
New Milton BH25 .....195 A1
West Moors BH22 .....138 B1
Birch Hill PO17 .....109 A2
Birch Ho SO16 .....78 C4
Birch Rd Chilworth SO16 .....79 A4
Hedge End SO30 .....105 B4
Southampton SO16 .....78 A2
St Leonards BH24 .....140 A2
Birch Tree Cl PO10 .....136 C2
Birch Tree Dr PO10 .....136 C2
Birch Wlk BH22 .....165 C2
Birch Wood SO19 .....104 C3
Birchdale Cl SO31 .....152 B4
Birchdale Rd BH21 .....163 B3
Birchen Cl SO31 .....129 B2
Birchen Rd SO31 .....129 B2
Birches Cl The SO52 .....53 C3
Birches The SO18 .....104 A4
Birchglade SO40 .....76 B1
Birchlands SO40 .....100 B3
Birchmore Cl 3 PO13 .....155 B1
Birchwood Cl BH23 .....208 C4

Birchwood Ct 8 SO18 ..103 C4
Birchwood Dr SP6 ......93 A3
Birchwood Gdns SO30 ..105 B4
Birchwood Lodge 7
PO16 ....131 A1
Birchwood Mews BH14 .203 B2
Birchwood Rd
Poole BH14 ....203 B2
Upton BH16 ....201 A3
Birchy Hill SO41 ......172 B1
Bird Field SO53 ....54 C4
Bird's Hill Rd BH15 ....202 C2
Birdham Rd PO11 ......185 C1
Birdlip Cl PO8 ....112 A3
Birdlip Rd PO6 ....133 A1
Birds Hill Gdns 5 BH15 202 C2
Birdwood Gr PO16 .....155 C4
Birinus Rd SO23 ....2 A1
Birkdale Ave PO6 ......134 B1
Birkdale Ct BH18 ......187 A3
Birkdale Rd BH18 ......187 A3
Birmingham Ct PO13 ...180 B3
Biscay Cl PO14 ....154 A2
Bishearne Gdns GU33 ...20 C3
Bishop Cl BH12 ....204 B4
Bishop Ct BH24 ....141 A4
Bishop Rd BH9 ....205 A4
Bishop St PO1 ....182 A3
Bishop's La SO32 ....83 B4
Bishop's Waltham Inf Sch
SO32 ....83 B4
Bishop's Waltham Pal★
SO32 ....83 B4
Bishop's Wood Rd PO17 .84 B1
Bishops Cl
Bournemouth BH7 ......205 C4
Totton SO40 ....100 C4
Bishops Cres SO19 .....103 C2
Bishops Ct SO50 ....56 B3
Bishops Gate PO14 .....129 B2
Bishops La SO32 ....84 A1
Bishops Rd SO19 ....103 C2
Bishopsfield Rd PO14 ..154 C4
Bishopstoke La SO50 ....56 C4
Bishopstoke Manor SO50 56 B2
Bishopstoke Rd
Eastleigh SO50 ....56 B2
Havant PO9 ....135 C3
Bisley Ct SO19 ....104 A2
Bisterne Cl BH24 ......143 C1
Bittern Cl PO12 ....181 A4
Bitterne CE Inf & Jun Sch
SO19 ....103 C3
Bitterne Cl PO9 ....135 C3
Bitterne Cres SO19 ....104 A3
Bitterne Manor Ho
SO18 ....103 B4
Bitterne Manor Prim Sch
SO18 ....103 B4
Bitterne Park Inf Sch
SO17 ....79 B1
Bitterne Park Jun Sch
SO17 ....79 B1
Bitterne Park Sec Sch
SO18 ....79 C1
Bitterne Park Triangle
SO18 ....79 B1
Bitterne Rd SO18 ......104 A3
Bitterne Rd E SO18 ....104 B4
Bitterne Rd W SO18 ...103 C4
Bitterne Sta SO18 .....103 B4
Bitterne Way
Lymington SO41 ....197 B1
Southampton SO19 .....103 C3
Verwood BH31 ....115 A3
Bitumen Rd SO45 ......151 A2
Black Hill BH31 ....115 A3
Black La Bransgore BH23 169 C2
Redlynch SP5 ....48 A2
Black Moor Rd BH31 ...115 B2
Black Swan Bldgs 20
SO22 ....10 C4
Blackberry Cl PO8 ......88 B2
Blackberry Dr SO50 .....57 A1
Blackberry La BH23 ....207 C3
Blackberry Terr SO14 ..103 A4
Blackbird Cl
Broadstone BH17 ......201 C4
Waterlooville PO8 .....111 C2
Blackbird Rd SO50 ......55 B1
Blackbird Way
Bransgore BH23 ....193 B4
Lee-on-the-Solent PO13 ..179 C2
Blackbrook Bsns Pk
PO15 ....130 C1
Blackbrook House Dr
PO14,PO15 ....130 C1
Blackbrook Park Ave
PO15 ....130 C1
Blackbrook Rd PO15 ...130 B1
Blackburn Ct PO13 ....180 B3
Blackburn Rd BH12 ....203 A3
Blackbush Rd SO41 ....211 A3
Blackbushe Cl SO16 ....77 C3
Blackcap Cl PO9 ......113 A1
Blackdown Cl SO45 ....125 B1
Blackdown Cres PO9 ...135 C2
Blackfield Inf Sch SO45 150 C1
Blackfield Jun Sch
SO45 ....150 B1
Blackfield La BH22 ....138 C2
Blackfield Rd
Blackfield SO45 ....150 C1
Bournemouth BH8 ......190 B2
Blackfriars Cl 3 PO1 ..215 C2
Blackfriars Rd PO1 ....215 C3
Blackhill Rd SO51 ......74 C4
Blackhorse La SO32 .....83 C1
Blackhouse La PO17 ...109 A1
Blackmoor Wlk 12 PO9 .136 A3
Blackmore La GU32 .....18 C2
Blacksmith Cl BH21 ...186 B3
Blackthorn Cl
Lymington SO41 ....197 A1
Southampton SO19 .....103 C3
Blackthorn Dr
Gosport PO12 ....156 A1
South Hayling PO11 ....185 B2
Blackthorn Gn SO21 ....57 A4
Blackthorn Rd
South Hayling PO11 ....185 B1
Southampton SO19 .....103 C3
Blackthorn Terr PO1 ..182 A3
Blackthorn Way
New Milton BH25 ......195 B2
Verwood BH31 ....115 A3
Blackthorn Wlk PO7 ...112 B1
Blackwater Cl 10 PO6 ..157 B4
Blackwater Dr
Oakley BH21 ....187 B4
Totton SO40 ....76 B1
Blackwater Gr SP6 ......92 C3
Blackwater Mews SO40 ..76 B1
Blackwood Ho 15 PO1 ..182 B4
Bladon Cl PO9 ....136 B2
Bladon Rd SO16 ....78 B1
Blair Ave BH14 ....203 B2
Blair Cl BH25 ....194 C2
Blake Cl SO16 ....77 B3
Blake Dene Rd BH14 ...203 A1
Blake Hill Ave BH14 ...203 B1
Blake Hill Cres BH14 ..203 B1
Blake Ho PO12 ....181 C2
Blake Rd Cosham PO6 ..134 B1
Gosport PO12 ....181 B3
Portsmouth PO1 ....181 C4
Blakemere Cres PO6 ...133 B1
Blakeney Rd SO16 ......77 B1
Blakesley La PO3 .....158 B2
Blanchard Rd SO32 .....83 A4
Blandford Cl BH15 ....201 C1
Blandford Ct 2 SO41 ..211 B3
Blandford Ho SO16 .....77 C1
Blandford Rd
Coombe Bissett SP5 .....23 B4
Corfe Mullen BH21 ....186 B4
Hamworthy BH15,BH16 ..201 B2
Pamphill BH21 ....162 B4
Blandford Rd N BH16 ..201 A4
Blaney Way BH21 ......186 B3
Blankney Cl PO14 .....179 A3
Blann Cl SO16 ....77 B3
Blashford Lakes Study Ctr
BH24 ....117 A2
Blaven Wlk 4 PO14 ...154 C4
Bleaklow Cl SO16 .....101 C4
Blechynden Terr SO15 ..102 C3
Blencowe Dr SO53 ......54 C3
Blendworth Cres PO9 ..135 C2
Blendworth Ho 2 PO1 .215 C4
Blendworth La
Horndean PO8 ....112 C4
Southampton SO18 ....104 B4
Blendworth Rd 5 PO4 ..183 A3
Blenheim Ave SO17 .....79 A1
Blenheim Cl
Chandler's Ford SO53 ...54 C2
Totton SO40 ....100 C3
Blenheim Cres SO41 ...195 C2
Blenheim Ct
25 Bournemouth BH4 ...204 B2
Christchurch BH23 ....207 A4
Portsmouth PO4 ......183 A2
Southampton SO17 .....79 A1
Blenheim Dr BH23 .....208 A3
Blenheim Gdns
Gosport PO12 ....181 A4
Havant PO9 ....136 B1
Hythe SO45 ....125 B1
Southampton SO17 .....79 A1
Blenheim Ho
6 Eastleigh SO50 ....56 A1
Romsey SO51 ....53 A4
Blenheim Rd
Eastleigh SO50 ....56 A1
Waterlooville PO8 .....112 A3
Blenhem Barn PO7 ....110 C1
Bleriot Cres PO15 .....129 C3
Blighmont Ave SO15 ...102 A3
Blighmont Cres SO15 ..102 A3
Blind La Curdridge SO32 ..82 C1
Fair Oak SO30 ....81 B3
Ibsley SP6 ....94 B1
Wickham PO17 ....107 C3
Wimborne Minst BH21 ..163 A3
Bliss Cl PO7 ....134 C3
Blissford Cl PO9 ......136 A3
Blissford Cross SP6 ....94 C4
Blissford Hill SP6 ......94 C4
Blissford Rd SP6 ....94 C4
Bloomfield Ave BH9 ...189 C1
Bloomfield Pl BH9 ....189 C1
Bloomsbury Wlk SO19 .103 C1
Blossom Cl SO30 ......105 C3
Blount Rd PO1 ....182 A2
Bloxworth Rd BH12 ...203 C4
Blue Anchor La 15
SO14 ....102 C2
Blue Ball Hill SO23 .....11 A4
Bluebell Cl
Christchurch BH23 ....208 A4
Waterlooville PO7 .....135 A3
Bluebell Copse SO31 ..128 C1
Bluebell La BH17 ......186 C1
Bluebell Rd SO16 ....79 B2
Blueprint Portfield Rd
PO3 ....158 A1
Bluestar Gdns SO30 ....81 B1
Blundell La SO31 .....105 B1
Blyth Cl
Christchurch BH23 ....191 B2
Southampton SO16 .....77 B1
Blythe Rd BH21 ....186 B3
Blythswood Ct BH25 ..209 C4
Boakes Pl SO40 ....100 B1
Boardwalk The PO6 ...157 A4
Boardwalk Way SO40 ..102 A2
Boarhunt Cl PO1 .....215 C3
Boarhunt Rd PO17 ....131 C2
Boatyard Ind Est The
PO16 ....155 A4
Bob Hann Cl BH12 ....203 B3
Bockhampton Rd BH23 .192 C3
Bodley Rd BH13 ......214 C4
Bodmin Rd
Bishopstoke SO50 ......56 C1
Portchester PO6 ......157 A4
Bodorgan Rd BH2 .....204 C2
Bodowen Cl BH23 .....192 B1
Bodowen Rd BH23 ....192 B1
Bodycoats Rd SO53 ....55 B3
Bognor Rd BH18 ......186 C2
Bohemia La SP5 ....47 C2
Boiler Rd Fawley SO45 .151 C1
Portsmouth PO1 ......181 C4
Bolde Cl PO3 ....158 A2
Boldens Rd PO12 .....181 A1
Bolderwood Arboretum
Ornamental Dr★ SO43 120 B1
Bolderwood Cl SO50 ...56 C1
Boldre Cl
Barton on Sea BH25 ...209 B4
Havant PO9 ....135 B2
Poole BH12 ....203 B4
Boldre La SO41 ....197 B4
Boldrewood Rd SO16 ...78 C2
Boleyn CL BH9 ....190 A2
Bolhinton Ave SO40 ..101 B1
Bolton Cl BH6 ....206 C2
Bolton Cres BH22 ....166 A3
Bolton Ct 4 BH6 .....206 C2
Bolton Dr PO12 ......181 B4
Bolton Rd BH6 ....206 C2
Boltons The
16 Milford on Sea SO41 .211 B2
Waterlooville PO7 ....134 C2
Bonchurch Cl SO16 ....79 B3
Bonchurch Rd PO4 ....183 A3
Bond Ave BH22 ......138 B2
Bond Cl SO41 ....172 A2
Bond Rd Poole BH15 ..202 C3
Southampton SO18 .....79 C1
Bond St SO14 ....103 B3
Bondfields Cres PO9 ..135 C3
Bones La GU31 ....65 B3
Bonfire Cnr PO1 .....182 A3
Bonham Rd BH3 ......204 C4
Boniface Cl SO40 ....100 B4
Boniface Cres SO16 ...77 C2
Bonington Cl BH23 ..207 C4
Bonner Cotts SP5 ......4 C4
Boothby Cl SO40 .....101 A3
Border Dr BH16 ......201 B3
Border Lo BH23 ......194 B1
Border Rd BH16 ......201 B3
Bordon Rd PO9 ....135 C3
Boredean La
Froxfield Green GU32 ...39 B3
Langrish GU32 ....39 B3
Boreham Rd BH6 .....206 B3
Borley Rd BH17 ......202 A4
Borough Gr GU32 ......40 C1
Borough Hill GU32 .....40 C2
Borough Rd
Petersfield GU32 ....40 B1
Petersfield GU32 ....40 C2
Borough The SP5 ......46 C4
Borrowdale Rd SO16 ...77 C1
Borthwick Rd BH1 ....205 C3
Boscobel Rd SO22 ......1 C1
Boscombe Cliff Rd BH5 205 C2
Boscombe Gr Rd BH1 .205 B3
Boscombe Overcliff Dr
BH5 ....206 A2
Boscombe Spa Rd BH5 .205 B2
Bosham Rd PO2 ......182 C4
Bosham Wlk PO13 ....155 A1
Bosley Cl BH23 ......191 C1
Bosley Way BH23 ....191 C1
Bosmere Gdns PO10 ..136 C1
Bosmere Jun Sch PO9 .159 C4
Bosmere Rd PO11 ....185 C1
Bossington Cl SO16 ...77 C3
Boston Ct SO53 ....55 B4
Boston Lo 22 BH4 ....204 B2
Boston Rd PO6 ....133 C1
Bosuns Cl PO16 ......155 A3
Bosville SO50 ....56 A3
Boswell Cl Botley SO30 .106 A3
Southampton SO19 ....104 B3
Bosworth Mews BH9 ..190 A2
Botany Bay Rd SO19 ..104 A2
Botley CE Prim Sch
SO30 ....106 A4
Botley Dr PO9 ....135 B3
Botley Gdns SO19 ....104 C2
Botley Hill SO30 .....106 A3
Botley Rd Curdridge SO32 .82 C1
Fair Oak SO50 ....57 B1
Fair Oak, Wildern SO50 ..81 B4
North Baddesley SO52 ...53 B3
Botley Rd *continued*
Romsey SO51 ....53 B3
Southampton SO19 ....104 B2
Swanwick SO31 ....129 A4
West End SO30 ....81 A1
Botley Sta SO30 ......106 B4
Bottings Est SO30 ....106 A4
Bottom La SO51 ....50 C2
Boulnois Ave BH14 ...203 C2
Boultbee Cotts SO43 ..121 B3
Boulter La PO17 ......133 A4
Boulton Rd PO5 ......215 D1
Bound La PO11 ....185 A1
Boundary Acre SO31 ..105 A2
Boundary Cl SO15 ....101 C4
Boundary Dr BH21 ....163 B3
Boundary La BH24 ....139 C1
Boundary Oak Prep Sch
PO17 ....131 B3
Boundary Rd
Bournemouth BH10,BH9 .189 C1
Bursledon SO31 ......127 C4
Boundary Rdbt BH3,
BH10 ....204 B4
Boundary Way
Havant PO9 ....135 C1
Waterlooville PO6 ....134 A1
Boundstone SO45 .....125 C2
Boundway SO41 ......171 C1
Bountys La BH12 .....203 C3
Bourne Ave
Bournemouth BH2 .....204 C2
Southampton SO15 .....78 B1
Bourne Cl
Bournemouth BH4 .....204 B2
Otterbourne SO21 ......31 A2
Waterlooville PO8 ....112 A3
West Wellow SO51 .....50 B2
Bourne Com Coll PO10 .137 B1
Bourne Cotts SP6 ......44 C1
Bourne Ct
24 Bournemouth BH2 ..204 C2
Wimborne Minst BH21 .163 B3
Bourne La
Netley Marsh SO40 .....99 B3
Twyford SO21 ....32 A3
Bourne Pines 8 BH1 ..204 C2
Bourne Rd Cosham PO6 .157 A4
Netley Marsh SO40 .....99 B3
Southampton SO15 ....102 B3
Bourne Valley Rd BH12 .204 A3
Bourne View PO10 ....137 B1
Bournefields SO21 .....32 A4
Bournemouth & Poole Coll
Annexe The BH1 .....205 A2
Bournemouth & Poole Coll of
F Ed BH14 ....202 C2
Bournemouth & Poole Coll of
F Ed (Annex) BH14 ..202 C3
Bournemouth & Poole Coll
The BH1 ....205 A2
Bournemouth Aquarium★
BH2 ....204 C1
Bournemouth Ave PO12 181 A4
Bournemouth Aviation Mus★
BH23 ....191 A4
Bournemouth Central Bsns
Pk BH1 ....205 B3
Bournemouth Crown & Cty
Cts BH7 ....191 B1
Bournemouth Gram Sch
(Boys) BH8 ....190 B1
Bournemouth Gram Sch
(Girls) BH8 ....190 B1
Bournemouth Ho 59
PO9 ....136 A3
Bournemouth Int Airport
BH23 ....190 C4
Bournemouth Int Ctr★
BH2 ....204 C1
Bournemouth Meml Homes
BH8 ....190 C1
Bournemouth Nuffield Hospl
BH8 ....205 A3
Bournemouth Rd
Chandler's Ford SO53 ...55 B2
Lyndhurst SO43 ....121 C3
Poole BH14 ....203 B2
Bournemouth Sta BH1 .205 A2
Bournemouth Univ
BH12 ....204 B4
Bournemouth West Rdbt
BH2 ....204 B2
Bournewood Dr BH4 ..204 B2
Bourton Gdns BH7 ....206 A4
Bouverie Cl 23 BH25 ..195 A1
Boveridge Gdns BH9 ..190 A2
Bovington Cl BH17 ...187 C1
Bowater Cl SO40 ......76 B1
Bowater Way SO40 .....76 B1
Bowcombe SO31 ......127 B4
Bowden La SO17 ....79 B1
Bowden Rd BH12 .....188 B1
Bower Cl Holbury SO45 .150 B2
Southampton SO19 ....103 C1
Bower Rd BH8 ....205 B4
Bowers Cl PO8 ....112 A2
Bowers Hill SP5 ....47 C4
Bowerwood Cotts SP6 ...93 B4
Bowerwood Rd SP6 .....93 B4
Bowes Hill PO9 ......113 B2
Bowes-Lyon Ct PO8 ..112 A4
Bowland Rise
New Milton BH25 .....195 B1
North Baddesley SO53 ..55 A4
Bowland Way SO45 ...177 C4
Bowler Ave PO1 .....182 C3
Bowler Ct PO1 ....182 C3
Bowman Ct SO19 .....104 A2
Box Cl BH17 ....202 A4
Boxgrove Ho PO1 ....215 C4
Boxwood Cl
Portchester PO16 .....132 A1
Waterlooville PO7 ....134 C3
Boyatt Cres SO50 ......56 A4
Boyatt La Eastleigh SO50 .56 A4
Otterbourne SO21,SO50 ..31 A1
Boyatt Wood Sh Ctr 7
SO50 ....56 A3
Boyd Cl PO14 ....179 A3
Boyd Rd Gosport PO13 .155 A2
Poole BH12 ....203 C3
Boyes La SO21 ....32 A1
Boyle Cres PO7 ......134 B3
Boyne Mead Rd SO23 ....2 B4
Boyne Rise SO23 ....2 A4
Boynton Cl SO53 ......55 A4
Brabant Cl PO15 .....129 A4
Brabazon Dr BH23 ....208 A4
Brabazon Rd
Locks Heath PO15 ....129 B3
Oakley BH21 ....163 C1
Brabourne Ave BH22 ..165 B2
Bracken Cl
North Baddesley SO52 ..54 A2
St Leonards BH24 ....139 B2
Bracken Cres SO50 ....56 C1
Bracken Glen BH15 ...202 C3
Bracken Hall SO16 .....79 A4
Bracken Heath 13 PO7 .112 A1
Bracken La SO16 ......78 A1
Bracken Lodge 3 BH6 .206 C2
Bracken Pl SO16 ......79 A4
Bracken Rd
Bournemouth BH6 ....206 B2
Ferndown BH22 ......165 A4
North Baddesley SO52 ..54 A2
Petersfield GU31 ......41 B1
Bracken Way BH23 ...194 A1
Brackendale Ct BH21 .138 C4
Brackendale Rd BH8 ..205 B4
Brackenhill BH13 ....204 A1
Brackenhill Rd BH21 .164 A4
Brackens The
Hythe SO45 ....125 B2
Locks Heath SO31 ....129 A1
Brackens Way
Lymington SO41 ......197 C1
12 Poole BH13 ....214 C4
Brackenway Rd SO53 ...55 B4
Bracklesham Cl SO19 .103 C2
Bracklesham Rd
Gosport PO13 ....180 B4
South Hayling PO11 ...185 C1
Brackley Ave SO50 ....57 A2
Brackley Cl BH23 ....191 A4
Brackley Way SO40 ...100 B4
Bradbourne Rd BH2 ..204 C2
Bradford Ct PO13 ....180 B3
Bradford Rd
Bournemouth BH9 ....190 B2
Portsmouth PO5 ......215 C2
Brading Ave
Gosport PO13 ....155 B1
Portsmouth PO4 ......183 A1
Brading Cl SO16 ....79 B3
Bradley Ct 10 PO9 ...136 A3
Bradley Gn SO16 ......78 A2
Bradley Peak SO22 .....1 B1
Bradley Rd SO22 ....1 B2
Bradly Rd PO15 ......130 B1
Bradpole Rd BH8 .....190 C1
Bradshaw Cl SO50 .....57 C1
Bradstock Cl BH12 ...203 C4
Braehead SO45 ....125 C1
Braemar Ave
Bournemouth BH6 ....207 A2
Cosham PO6 ....158 A4
Braemar Cl
Bournemouth BH6 ....207 A2
Fareham PO15 ....130 C2
Gosport PO13 ....155 B1
Braemar Dr BH23 ....193 C1
Braemar Rd PO13 ....155 B1
Braeside Cl
Southampton SO19 ....103 C3
Winchester SO22 ....10 A2
Braeside Cres SO19 ..103 C3
Braeside Rd
Southampton SO19 ....103 C3
St Leonards BH24 ....139 C2
West Moors BH22 .....138 C2
Braidley Rd BH2 .....204 C2
Brailswood Rd BH15 ..202 C2
Braintree Rd PO6 ....133 B1
Braishfield Cl SO16 ...77 C1
Braishfield Gdns BH8 .190 B1
Braishfield Prim Sch
SO51 ....28 B3
Braishfield Rd
Havant PO9 ....136 A2
Romsey SO51 ....28 B2
Brake Ho PO9 ....135 B1
Bramar Ct BH4 ....204 B1
Bramber Rd PO12 ....181 A4
Bramble Cl Alderholt SP6 .93 A3
5 Eastleigh SO50 ......56 A3
Havant PO9 ....136 B2
Holbury SO45 ....150 B2
Stubbington PO14 ....179 A3
Bramble Ct
2 Petersfield GU31 ....41 B2
West Moors BH22 .....138 B1
Bramble Dr SO51 ......28 B1
Bramble Hill SO53 .....55 A3

Bramble La
Christchurch BH23 194 A1
Clanfield PO8 88 A4
Locks Heath SO31 128 C3
Bramble Mews 1 SO18 104 A4
Bramble Rd
Petersfield GU31 41 B2
Portsmouth PO4 182 C2
Bramble Way
Bransgore BH23 169 A1
Gosport PO13 155 A1
Bramble Wlk SO41 197 B3
Bramblegate SO50 57 B1
Brambles Bsns Ctr The PO7 111 B1
Brambles Cl SO21 57 A4
Brambles Ent Ctr The PO7 111 B1
Brambles Farm Ind Est PO7 134 B4
Brambles Rd PO13 179 B2
Brambling Cl SO16 78 A3
Brambling Rd PO9 113 A1
Bramblings The SO40 100 B4
Brambridge SO50 56 C4
Brambridge Ho SO21 31 B1
Brambridge Rd SO21, SO50 56 C4
Bramdean Dr PO9 135 B3
Bramdean Mews SO19 103 C3
Bramdean Rd SO18 104 B4
Bramham Moor PO14 179 A3
Bramley Cl
Lymington SO41 197 C1
Waterlooville PO7 134 C4
Bramley Cres SO19 104 A1
Bramley Ct BH22 165 B3
Bramley Gdns
Fair Oak SO50 81 B3
Gosport PO12 181 A1
Hermitage PO10 161 A4
Bramley Ho
Gosport PO12 181 A1
Hedge End SO30 105 A3
3 Portsmouth PO5 215 B2
Bramley Rd
Bournemouth BH10 189 B3
Ferndown BH22 165 B3
Bramleys The SP5 24 A2
Brampton La PO3 158 B2
Brampton Manor SO16 78 C3
Brampton Rd BH15 202 B3
Brampton Twr SO16 78 C3
Bramshaw Cl SO22 1 B2
Bramshaw Ct 37 PO9 136 A3
Bramshaw Gdns BH8 190 B2
Bramshaw Way BH25 209 B4
Bramshott Rd
Portsmouth PO4 182 C2
Southampton SO19 126 C4
Bramston Rd SO15 102 B4
Bramwell Ct SO18 104 A3
Branches La SO51 25 C2
Branders Cl BH6 207 A2
Branders La BH6 207 A3
Brandon Ct PO5 215 D1
Brandon Rd PO5 182 B1
Brandwood Ct 4 BH14 203 A2
Branewick Cl PO15 129 B2
Branksea Ave BH15 201 C1
Branksea Cl BH15 201 C1
Branksome Ave SO15 78 B1
Branksome Cl
New Milton BH25 195 A1
Winchester SO22 10 A3
Branksome Ct 14 BH13 214 C4
Branksome Dene Rd BH4 204 A1
Branksome Heath Mid Sch BH12 203 B3
Branksome Hill Rd
Bournemouth BH4 204 A3
Poole BH12 204 A3
Branksome Sta BH12 203 C2
Branksome Twrs BH13 214 D4
Branksome Wood Gdns BH2 204 B2
Branksome Wood Rd
Bournemouth BH2,BH4 204 B2
Poole BH12 204 B2
Bransbury Cl SO16 78 B2
Bransbury Rd PO4 183 A2
Bransgore Ave PO9 135 B2
Bransgore CE Prim Sch BH23 193 B4
Bransgore Gdns BH23 169 B1
Bransley Cl SO51 28 A1
Branwell Cl BH23 192 A1
Branwood Cl SO41 196 C1
Brasenose Cl PO14 129 B1
Brasher Cl SO50 57 A1
Brassey Cl BH9 190 A1
Brassey Rd
Bournemouth BH9 190 A1
Winchester SO22 1 C1
Brassey Terr BH9 189 C1
Brasted Ct PO4 183 B3
Braunston Cl 10 PO6 133 A1
Braxall Lawn PO9 135 B3
Braxton Ctyd SO41 211 C4
Braxton Ho 1 SO23 11 B4
Breach Ave PO10 137 C1
Breach La BH24 141 C4
Breamore CE Prim Sch SP6 70 A4
Breamore Cl
Eastleigh SO50 56 A3
New Milton BH25 194 C2
Breamore Countryside Mus* SP6 46 A1
Breamore Ho* SP6 46 A2
Breamore Rd SO18 104 B4
Brean Cl SO16 77 C1
Brearley Ct BH23 209 A4
Brecon Ave PO6 158 A4
Brecon Cl
Bournemouth BH10 189 C3
Chandler's Ford SO53 55 A2
Fareham PO14 154 C4
Hythe SO45 125 C2
New Milton BH25 195 B1
Brecon Rd SO19 104 B3
Bredenbury Cres PO6 133 B1
Bredon Wlk PO14 154 C4
Bredy Cl BH17 187 B1
Breech Cl 12 PO3 157 C2
Bremble Cl BH12 188 B1
Brenchley Cl PO16 156 A4
Brendon Cl
Bournemouth BH8 190 C1
Hythe SO45 125 B1
Brendon Gr SO16 101 C4
Brendon Rd PO14 154 B4
Brent Ct PO10 160 C4
Brentwood Cres SO18 80 A1
Breton Cl PO15 129 A4
Brewells La GU33 21 C2
Brewer Cl SO31 129 A2
Brewer St PO1 215 B4
Brewers La
Gosport PO13 155 B1
Twyford SO21 31 C3
West Tisted SO24 17 B4
Brewhouse Sq PO12 181 B3
Brewster Cl PO8 112 A2
Briar Cl
Christchurch BH23 207 C3
Gosport PO12 180 C2
Poole BH15 202 C3
Waterlooville PO8 112 A3
Briar Way Romsey SO51 28 B1
Wimborne Minst BH21 164 A3
Briar Wood GU33 21 A4
Briar's The PO7 111 B1
Briardene Ct SO40 100 C4
Briarfield 28 BH4 204 B2
Briarfield Gdns PO8 112 A3
Briars The SO42 145 C1
Briarswood SO16 78 A1
Briarswood Rd BH16 201 B4
Briarswood Rise SO45 125 B1
Briarwood Cl PO16 155 A4
Briarwood Gdns PO11 184 C2
Briarwood Rd SO40 100 B3
Brick Kiln La SO24 17 A4
Brick La BH23 169 C2
Brickets Terr PO12 181 A1
Brickfield La
Chandler's Ford SO53 55 B3
Lymington SO41 197 C3
Brickfield Rd SO17 79 B1
Brickfield Trad Est SO53 55 B3
Brickmakers Rd SO21 56 C4
Brickwoods Cl SO51 53 A4
Brickworth Rd SP5 24 A2
Brickyard La
Broadstone BH21 162 A1
Ferndown BH21 165 A3
Brickyard Rd SO32 84 A2
Brickyard The SO40 99 A4
Brickyards Ind Est The GU32 20 A1
Bridefield Cl PO8 111 B2
Bridefield Cres PO8 111 B2
Bridge App BH15 202 A1
Bridge Cl SO31 105 A1
Bridge Cotts SO51 50 C2
Bridge Ct SO51 52 C3
Bridge Ho Gosport PO13 155 B2
Southampton SO15 102 B3
Bridge Industries PO16 131 B2
Bridge La SO21 31 C4
Bridge Mdws GU33 20 C2
Bridge Mead SO32 61 B3
Bridge Pl BH10 189 B4
Bridge Rd
Emsworth PO10 136 C1
Locks Heath SO31 128 B3
Lymington SO41 197 C3
Romsey SO51 53 A4
Southampton SO19 103 B2
Bridge Sh Ctr The PO1 215 D3
Bridge St
Christchurch BH23 207 B3
Fordingbridge SP6 69 C1
Southwick PO17 132 C3
Titchfield PO14 154 A4
Wickham PO17 108 A2
46 Winchester SO23 11 A4
Bridge Terr
Compton (Hants) SO21 31 C3
33 Southampton SO14 103 A2
Bridgefoot Dr PO16 131 B1
Bridgefoot Path PO10 160 C4
Bridgemary Ave PO13 155 B2
Bridgemary Com Sch PO13 155 B1
Bridgemary Gr PO13 155 B3
Bridgemary Rd PO13 155 B2
Bridgemary Way PO13 155 B3
Bridgers Cl SO16 77 C3
Bridges Ave PO6 132 C1
Bridges Cl Eastleigh SO50 55 C2
West Moors BH22 138 C2
Bridges The BH24 140 C4
Bridgeside Cl PO1 215 C3
Bridget Cl PO8 112 B4
Bridgewater Rd BH12 203 B3
Bridgeway Ct SO40 101 A4
Bridgwater Ct SO15 102 B3
Bridle Cl BH16 201 B4
Bridle Cres BH7 206 B4
Bridle Way BH21 164 B3
Bridleways BH31 114 C3
Bridlington Ave SO15 102 B4
Bridport Ct SO15 102 B3
Bridport Rd Poole BH12 203 C4
Verwood BH31 114 C3
Bridport St PO1 215 B3
Brierley Ave BH22 165 C1
Brierley Cl BH10 189 C3
Brierley Rd BH10 189 C2
Brigantine Rd SO31 128 C1
Brigham Cl 20 PO2 157 C2
Brighstone Cl SO16 79 B3
Bright Rd BH15 202 B3
Brightlands Ave BH6 206 C3
Brighton Ave PO12 180 C4
Brighton Rd
Southampton SO15 102 C4
Sway SO41 172 A2
Brights La PO11 184 C3
Brightside PO7 134 B3
Brightside Rd SO16 77 C1
Brightstone Rd PO6 157 C4
Brindle Cl SO16 79 A3
Brinsons Cl BH23 192 B2
Brinton La SO45 126 A3
Brinton's Rd SO14 103 A3
Brinton's Terr SO14 103 A3
Brisbane Ho 20 PO1 182 B4
Brisbane Rd BH23 191 C1
Bristol Ct PO13 180 B3
Bristol Rd PO4 182 C1
Britain St PO1 182 A3
Britannia Ct BH12 203 A4
Britannia Gdns SO30 81 A2
Britannia Pl SO41 197 C2
Britannia Rd Poole BH14 203 A2
Portsmouth PO5 215 C2
Southampton SO14 103 A3
Britannia Rd N PO5 215 C2
Britannia Way
Christchurch BH23 208 A4
Gosport PO12 181 B4
Britannic Ho 22 SO14 103 B3
Britnell Ho 6 GU31 40 C2
Briton St SO14 103 A2
Britten Rd PO13 179 C1
Britten Way PO7 134 C2
Brittons Cotts SO42 145 B1
Brixey Cl BH12 203 B4
Brixey Rd BH12 203 B4
Brixworth Cl 11 PO6 133 A1
Broad Ave BH8 205 B4
Broad Chalke Down SO22 10 B2
Broad Croft PO9 113 B2
Broad Gdns PO6 158 C4
Broad Gn 5 SO14 103 A2
Broad La Denmead PO7 110 A3
Lymington SO41 197 C1
North Baddesley SO52 53 C3
Southampton SO14 102 C2
Swanmore SO32 84 A3
Broad Mead Rd GU23 114 C1
Broad Oak SO30 105 C4
Broad St PO1 181 C2
Broad View La SO22 10 A2
Broad Way
Froxfield Green GU32 39 C4
Hamble-le-Rice SO31 127 C3
Broad Woods La SO51 51 A3
Broadbent Cl SO16 77 C3
Broadcut PO16 131 B1
Broadfields Cl SO41 211 B3
Broadhill La SP6 94 B4
Broadhurst Ave BH10 189 C2
Broadland Cotts GU32 41 A3
Broadlands* SO51 52 C3
Broadlands Ave
Bournemouth BH6 206 C2
Eastleigh SO50 56 A3
Waterlooville PO7 134 C4
Broadlands Cl
Bournemouth BH8 190 B2
Christchurch BH23 194 A1
Broadlands Rd
Brockenhurst SO42 145 C1
Southampton SO17 79 A2
Broadlaw Walk Prec 14 PO14 154 C4
Broadley Cl SO45 150 B2
Broadly Cl SO41 197 A1
Broadmarsh Bsns & Innovation Ctr PO9 159 B4
Broadmayne Rd BH12 204 A4
Broadmead Cl 8 SO41 197 C1
Broadmead Flats SO16 77 B3
Broadmead Rd SO16 77 B3
Broadmeadow Cl SO40 100 C4
Broadmeadows La 8 PO7 135 A4
Broadmere Ave PO9 135 C3
Broadmoor Rd BH21 186 B4
Broadoak Cl SO45 150 B2
Broads The BH21 162 C3
Broadsands Dr PO12 180 B2
Broadsands Wlk PO12 180 C2
Broadshard La BH24 141 A4
Broadstone Fst Sch BH18 187 A2
Broadstone Mid Sch BH18 187 B3
Broadstone Way
Broadstone BH18,NH17 186 C1
Broadstone, Fleet's Cnr BH15,BH17 202 A4
Broadwater Ave BH14 203 B1
Broadwater Rd
Romsey SO51 52 C3
Southampton SO18 79 C2
Broadway BH6 207 A2
Broadway Ct BH12 204 A3
Broadway Gables BH14 203 C2
Broadway Gdns 6 BH21 163 B2
Broadway La
Bournemouth BH8 190 B2
Horndean PO8 111 B4
Broadway Mews BH14 202 C2
Broadway Pk 4 BH21 163 B2
Broadway The
Bournemouth BH10 189 B3
5 Southampton, Bitterne Pk SO18 79 C1
Southampton, Portswood SO17 79 A1
Southampton, Thornhill Pk SO18 104 B4
Winchester SO23 11 A4
Brock Hill Forest Wlks* SO43 144 C4
Brockenhurst Ave PO9 135 B3
Brockenhurst CE Prim Sch SO42 172 C4
Brockenhurst Coll SO42 146 A1
Brockenhurst Rd BH9 190 A1
Brockenhurst Sta SO42 173 A4
Brockhampton La PO9 135 C1
Brockhampton Rd PO9 135 B1
Brockhills La BH25 195 B3
Brockhurst Ind Est PO12 155 C1
Brockhurst Inf Sch PO12 180 C4
Brockhurst Jun Sch PO12 181 A4
Brockhurst Rd PO12 180 C4
Brockishill Rd SO40 99 A3
Brocklands PO9 135 B1
Brockley Rd BH10 189 C2
Brocks Cl SO45 125 B1
Brocks Pine BH24 139 C2
Brockwood Bottom SO32 36 C4
Brodrick Ave PO12 181 A2
Brog St BH21 162 B1
Brokenford Ave SO40 101 A4
Brokenford Bsns Ctr SO40 100 C4
Brokenford La SO40 100 C4
Brombys The 7 BH15 202 B1
Bromley Ho BH12 204 A3
Bromley Rd SO18 79 C1
Brompton Rd PO4 182 C2
Bromyard Cres PO6 133 B1
Bronte Ave BH23 192 A1
Bronte Cl SO40 100 B3
Bronte Gdns PO15 129 B4
Bronte Way SO19 103 C3
Bronwen Ct SO19 104 A1
Brook Ave
Locks Heath SO31 128 B2
New Milton BH25 195 A2
Brook Ave N BH25 195 A2
Brook Cl
Bournemouth BH10 189 B2
Locks Heath SO31 128 C2
North Baddesley SO52 54 A2
Brook Cnr SO43 74 A1
Brook Cotts
King's Somborne SO51 6 B3
Westbourne PO10 137 A2
Brook Ct Romsey SO51 52 C3
13 Southampton SO15 102 B3
Brook Dr BH31 115 A2
Brook Farm Ave PO15 130 C1
Brook Gdns PO10 160 B4
Brook Hill SO41 198 C4
Brook La Botley SO30 105 C3
Bransgore BH23 193 A4
Corfe Mullen BH21 186 B3
Hambledon PO7 86 B3
Locks Heath SO31 128 C2
Woodgreen SP6 70 C4
Brook Mdw PO15 130 C1
Brook Rd
Bournemouth BH10 189 B2
Fair Oak SO50 57 B1
Lymington SO41 197 C1
Poole BH12 203 B3
Southampton SO18 104 A4
Wimborne Minst BH21 163 C2
Brook Road Depot BH21 163 C2
Brook St SO32 83 B4
Brook Terr SP6 93 C4
Brook Valley SO16 78 A1
Brook Way
Christchurch BH23 208 B4
Romsey SO51 28 A1
Brook Wlk SO40 76 B1
Brookdale Cl
Broadstone BH18 187 A2
Waterlooville PO7 134 C4
Brookdale Farm BH18 187 A2
Brooke Cl SO23 2 A4
Brookers La PO13 155 A2
Brookfield Cl 1 PO9 135 C1
Brookfield Com Sch SO31 128 C2
Brookfield Gdns SO31 128 C2
Brookfield Pl SO17 79 A1
Brookfield Rd
Fair Oak SO50 57 B1
Portsmouth PO1 182 C3
Brookfields SO51 50 B2
Brookland Cl SO41 197 B2
Brooklands
Bournemouth BH4 204 A2
Lyndhurst SO43 122 A2
Brooklands Rd
Bishop's Waltham SO32 83 B4
Havant PO9 135 A1
Brookley Rd SO42 146 A1
Brooklyn Cl SO21 31 B2
Brooklyn Ct BH25 194 C2
Brooklyn Dr PO7 134 C4
Brooklynn Cl SO32 83 C1
Brookman Ct SO18 104 A4
Brookmead Way PO9 159 C4
Brooks Cl BH24 141 A3
Brooks Sh Ctr The SO23 11 A4
Brookside
Fordingbridge SP6 69 A1
Gosport PO13 155 A3
Ibsley SP6 94 B1
Landford SP5 49 B2
Totton SO40 100 C3
Brookside Ave SO15 101 C4
Brookside Cl
Bransgore BH23 169 A1
Denmead PO7 110 C2
Brookside Ho SO18 79 C2
Brookside Park Homes BH21 186 A2
Brookside Rd
Bransgore BH23 193 A4
Brockenhurst SO42 145 C1
Havant, Bedhampton PO9 135 B1
Havant, Langstone PO9 159 C4
Wimborne Minst BH21 163 C2
Brookside Way
Christchurch BH23 193 C1
Southampton SO18 79 C2
West End SO30 80 C2
Brookvale Ct 14 SO17 79 A1
Brookvale Rd SO17 79 A1
Brookwood Ave SO50 55 C2
Brookwood Ind Est SO50 56 A2
Brookwood Rd SO16 101 B4
Broom Cl
Portsmouth PO4 183 B2
Waterlooville PO7 135 A3
Broom Hill SO41 199 A4
Broom Hill Way SO50 56 A4
Broom Rd
Petersfield GU31 41 B1
Poole BH12 188 B1
Broom Sq PO4 183 B3
Broom Way PO13 179 C2
Broomfield Cres PO13 180 A4
Broomfield Ct BH22 165 C3
Broomfield Dr SP6 93 A3
Broomfield La SO41 197 C2
Broomhill SP5 49 B1
Broomhill Cl SO41 197 A1
Brooms Gr SO19 104 B2
Broomy Cl SO45 125 B2
Brougham La PO12 181 A3
Brougham Rd PO5 215 B2
Brougham St PO12 181 A3
Broughton Ave BH10 189 C2
Broughton Cl
Bournemouth BH10 189 C2
5 Southampton SO16 78 A1
Broughton Ct PO3 158 B2
Broughton Rd SO43 121 C3
Brow The PO7 134 B1
Browndown Rd PO13 180 B2
Brownen Rd BH9 205 A4
Brownfield Ho 22 GU31 40 C2
Brownhill Cl SO53 55 B4
Brownhill Ct SO16 77 C2
Brownhill Gdns SO53 55 B4
Brownhill Rd
Brockenhurst BH25 170 C2
Chandler's Ford SO53 55 B4
North Baddesley SO52 54 A2
Brownhill Way SO16 77 B2
Browning Ave
Bournemouth BH5 206 A2
Portchester PO6 132 C1
Southampton SO19 104 B3
Browning Cl
Eastleigh SO50 55 C2
Swanwick PO15 129 B4
Totton SO40 100 B4
Browning Dr SO22 10 B4
Browning Rd BH12 203 B3
Brownings Cl SO41 197 A2
Brownlow Ave SO19 104 A3
Brownlow Cl PO1 182 B4
Brownlow Ct 23 BH4 204 B2
Brownlow Gdns SO19 104 A3
Browns La Beaulieu SO41 199 B3
Damerham SP6 68 A3
Brownsea Ave BH21 186 B3
Brownsea Cl BH25 194 C2
Brownsea Ct BH14 214 A4
Brownsea Island (NT)* BH15 213 B2
Brownsea Rd BH13 214 A2
Brownsea View Ave BH14 203 B1
Brownsea View Cl BH14 203 B1
Brownwich La PO14 153 B3

Browsholme Cl 2 SO50 56 A3
Broxburn Cl SO53 30 C1
Broxhead Rd 56 PO9 136 A3
Bruce Cl PO16 131 A2
Bruce Rd PO4 182 C1
Brudenell Ave BH13 214 B4
Brudenell Rd BH13 214 B3
Brue Cl SO53 55 A4
Brune La Gosport PO13 180 A4
Stubbington PO13 155 A1
Brune Park Com Sch PO12 180 C4
Brune Way BH22 165 B2
Brunei Ho SO16 79 A3
Brunel Cl Hedge End SO30 81 C1
Verwood BH31 115 B2
Brunel Rd
Portsmouth PO2 157 C2
Southampton SO15 101 B4
Totton SO40 76 C2
Brunel Way PO15 129 B2
Brunstead Pl BH12 204 A2
Brunstead Rd BH12 204 A2
Brunswick Cl SO50 57 A2
Brunswick Gdns PO9 135 B1
Brunswick Pl
Lymington SO41 197 C2
Southampton SO15 103 A3
Brunswick Rd SO50 57 A2
Brunswick Sq SO14 103 A2
Brunswick St PO5 215 B2
Brushers BH23 169 C2
Bruyn Ct SP6 70 A1
Bruyn Rd SP6 70 A1
Bryanston Rd SO19 103 C3
Bryanstone Rd BH3 204 C4
Bryant Rd BH12 204 A4
Bryher Br PO6 157 A4
Bryher Island PO6 157 A4
Brympton Cl SP6 69 B1
Bryony Cl
Broadstone BH18 186 C2
Locks Heath SO31 128 C1
Bryony Gdns SO50 81 B3
Bryony Way PO7 135 A4
Bryson Rd PO6 157 B4
Bub La BH23 207 C3
Bubb La SO32 81 B2
Buccaneers Cl BH23 207 C3
Buccleuch Rd BH13 204 A1
Bucehayes Cl BH23 209 A4
Buchan Ave PO15 129 B4
Buchan Ct SO45 125 B1
Buchanan Ave BH7 205 C3
Buchanan Rd SO16 77 C3
Buckby La PO3 158 B2
Bucketts Farm Cl SO32 84 A3
Buckingham Ct
2 Christchurch BH23 209 A4
Fareham PO15 130 C2
Poole BH15 202 B2
2 Southampton SO17 103 A4
Buckingham Gr PO1 182 B4
Buckingham Mans 5 BH1 205 A2
Buckingham Rd
Petersfield GU32 40 B2
Poole BH12 203 B4
Buckingham St PO1 215 B4
Buckingham Wlk BH25 194 C2
Buckland Cl
Eastleigh SO50 56 A3
Waterlooville PO7 111 B1
Buckland Ct SO41 197 C3
Buckland Dene SO41 197 B3
Buckland Gdns SO40 76 B1
Buckland Gr BH23 193 C1
Buckland Path PO2 182 B4
Buckland Rd BH12 203 B3
Buckland St PO2 182 C4
Buckland Terr BH12 203 B3
Buckland View SO41 197 C3
Bucklers Ct Havant PO9 135 B4
Lymington SO41 197 B2
Portsmouth PO2 157 B1
Bucklers Hard Maritime Mus★ SO42 176 B3
Bucklers Mews SO41 197 B2
Bucklers Rd PO12 181 B4
Bucklers The SO41 211 A3
Bucklers Way BH8 190 B2
Buckley Ct SO16 78 A1
Buckmore Ave GU32 40 B2
Bucks Head Hill SO32 61 B3
Bucksey Rd PO13 180 B4
Buckstone Cl SO41 196 C1
Buckthorn Cl
Broadstone BH17 186 C1
Totton SO40 100 A4
Budden's La PO17 108 C4
Buddens Rd PO17 108 A2
Buddle Hill SP6 94 B2
Budds La SO51 27 C1
Budds Lane Trad Est SO51 27 C1
Bude Cl PO6 132 C1
Buffalo Mews BH15 202 A1
Bugdens La BH31 115 A3
Bugle St SO14 102 C2
Bulbarrow Wlk PO14 154 C4
Bulbeck Rd PO9 135 C1
Buldowne Wlk SO41 172 A2
Bull Dro SO23 11 A3
Bull Hill Boldre SO41 174 A1
Rake GU33 21 C2
Bull La Minstead SO43 98 B2
16 Poole BH15 202 B1
Waltham Chase SO32 83 B2
Bullar Rd SO18 103 C4
Bullar St SO14 103 A3
Bullfinch Cl
Broadstone BH17 186 C1
Totton SO40 100 B4
Bullfinch Ct PO13 179 C2
Bullrush Cl SO45 125 C1
Bulls Copse La PO8 112 A3
Bulls Dro SP5 4 A3
Bunkers Hill PO7 110 B2
Bunns La PO7 109 C3
Bunny La
Michelmersh SO51 27 C3
Sherfield English SO51 25 A2
Bunstead La SO21 30 B4
Bunting Gdns PO8 111 C2
Bunting Rd BH22 165 A4
Bupa Hospl PO9 136 B3
Burbidge Gr PO4 183 A1
Burbridge Cl BH17 202 C4
Burbush Cl SO45 150 B2
Burcombe La BH24 117 C1
Burcombe Rd BH10 189 B3
Burcote Dr PO3 158 A2
Burdale Dr PO11 185 B2
Burdock Cl BH23 193 A1
Bure Cl BH23 208 A3
Bure Haven Dr BH23 208 A3
Bure Homage Gdns BH23 208 A3
Bure Homage La BH23 208 A3
Bure La BH23 208 A3
Bure Pk BH23 208 A3
Bure Rd BH23 208 A3
Burford Cl BH23 191 B1
Burford Ct 15 BH1 205 A2
Burford La SO42 146 A1
Burgate Cl PO9 135 B2
Burgate Cross SP6 70 A3
Burgate Fields SP6 70 A3
Burgate Sch The SP6 70 A2
Burgesmede Ho 13 GU32 40 C2
Burgess Cl
Bournemouth BH11 188 C2
South Hayling PO11 185 B1
Burgess Ct SO16 79 A2
Burgess Fld BH21 114 A3
Burgess Gdns 14 SO16 78 C2
Burgess Rd SO16,SO17 79 A2
Burghclere Rd
Havant PO9 136 A3
Southampton SO19 126 C4
Burgoyne Rd
Portsmouth PO5 182 B1
Southampton SO19 104 C2
Burgundy Cl SO31 128 C1
Burgundy Terr 1 PO2 157 C1
Buriton Cl PO16 132 B1
Buriton Ct SO19 103 C2
Buriton Prim Sch GU31 65 B3
Buriton Rd SO22 1 B2
Buriton St PO1 215 C4
Burke Dr SO19 104 B3
Burleigh Rd
Bournemouth BH6 206 B3
Portsmouth PO1 182 C4
Burley Cl Ashurst SO40 100 A4
Barton on Sea BH25 209 B4
Chandler's Ford SO53 55 A2
17 Havant PO9 136 A3
Verwood BH31 114 C3
Burley Ct 4 SO17 79 A1
Burley Down SO53 55 A2
Burley Ho 5 SO16 102 A4
Burley Lawn BH24 143 A2
Burley Prim Sch BH24 143 A2
Burley Rd
Bransgore BH23 193 A4
Brockenhurst SO42 172 B4
Burton BH23 192 B3
Poole BH12 203 B3
Winchester SO22 1 B2
Burley YH★ BH24 143 B1
Burling Terr 1 BH12 204 A2
Burlington Arc 34 BH1 204 C2
Burlington Ct SO19 104 A3
Burlington Mans 1 SO15 102 B4
Burlington Rd
Portsmouth PO2 157 C1
Southampton SO15 102 C3
Burma Ho SO18 79 C2
Burma Rd SO51 52 C3
Burmah Rd N SO45 151 B3
Burmah Rd S SO45 151 A3
Burmese Cl PO15 129 B4
Burn Cl BH31 115 A2
Burnaby Ct BH4 204 B1
Burnaby Rd
Bournemouth BH4 204 B1
Portsmouth PO1 182 A2
Burnage Ct 18 BH13 214 C4
Burnbake Rd BH31 115 A3
Burnbank Gdns SO40 100 C4
Burnbrae Rd BH22 165 B1
Burnett Ave BH23 206 C4
Burnett Cl Hythe SO45 126 A1
Southampton SO18 79 C1
Winchester SO22 1 B1
Burnett Rd
Christchurch BH23 206 C4
Gosport PO12 180 C3
Burnetts Fields SO50 81 B4
Burnetts Gdns SO50 81 B4
Burnetts La SO50,SO30 81 B3
Burney Ho 25 PO12 181 B2
Burney Rd PO12 180 C2
Burngate Rd BH15 201 C1
Burnham Beeches SO53 55 A3
Burnham Chase SO18 104 B4
Burnham Dr BH8 205 B4
Burnham Rd
Burton BH23 192 B1
Cosham PO6 134 B1
Fordingbridge SP6 69 C2
Burnham Wood PO16 131 A2
Burnhams Wlk 19 PO12 181 B2
Burnleigh Gdns BH25 195 B2
Burns Cl SO50 55 C1
Burns Pl SO16 78 A1
Burns Rd
Bournemouth BH6 206 B4
Eastleigh SO50 55 C1
Southampton SO19 104 B3
Burnside
Christchurch BH23 208 B4
Gosport PO13 155 A3
Waterlooville PO7 112 A1
Burnt House La
Boldre SO41 174 A1
Bransgore BH23 169 A1
Stubbington PO14 154 B2
Burr Cl SO21 56 C4
Burrard Gr SO41 197 C1
Burrfields Rd PO3 158 A1
Burridge Rd SO31 106 A1
Burrill Ave PO6 158 A4
Burrows Cl PO9 136 A2
Burrows La BH31 114 C4
Bursledon Hts SO31 105 A1
Bursledon Jun & Inf Sch SO31 128 A4
Bursledon Pl PO7 134 B3
Bursledon Rd
Hedge End SO30 105 A3
Southampton SO19,SO31 104 B3
Waterlooville PO7 134 B3
Bursledon Sta SO31 128 A4
Bursledon Windmill★ SO31 105 A1
Burt's La Holt Heath BH21 138 A4
Verwood BH21 138 A4
Burtley Rd BH6 206 C2
Burton CE Prim Sch BH23 192 B2
Burton Cl Burton BH23 192 B1
St Leonards BH24 139 C3
Burton Hall BH23 192 B2
Burton Hall Pl BH23 192 B2
Burton Rd
Christchurch BH23 207 C4
Poole BH13 204 A2
Southampton SO15 102 C3
Burtoncroft BH23 192 B2
Burts Hill BH21 163 B3
Burwood Gr PO11 185 A2
Bury Cl PO12 181 A2
Bury Cres PO12 181 A2
Bury Farm SO30 106 B2
Bury Hall La PO12 180 C2
Bury Ho 18 PO16 131 A1
Bury La SO40 101 A3
Bury Rd Gosport PO12 181 A2
Marchwood SO40 101 C2
Poole BH13 203 C1
Bus Dro SO45 178 C4
Bush Ho PO5 215 B1
Bush St E PO5 215 B1
Bush St W PO5 215 B1
Bushell Rd BH15 202 B4
Bushells Farm SP6 93 C4
Bushey Rd BH8 190 B1
Bushmead Dr BH24 139 C3
Bushy Mead PO7 134 B2
Busket La SO23 11 A4
Busketts Way SO40 100 A1
Butcher St PO1 182 A3
Butcher's Cnr SO43 73 C2
Bute Dr BH23 209 A4
Butlers Cl SO51 4 C1
Butlers La BH24 117 B1
Butser Ancient Farm★ PO8 88 C3
Butser Ct PO8 88 B2
Butser Wlk
Fareham PO14 154 C4
Petersfield GU31 41 A2
Butt La SP5 22 A4
Butt's Cl SO19 104 B2
Butt's Cres SO19 104 B2
Butt's Rd SO19 104 B2
Butt's Sq SO19 104 B2
Buttercup Cl
Hedge End SO30 105 A3
Hythe SO45 126 A1
Buttercup Dr BH23 193 A1
Buttercup Way SO31 128 C2
Butterfield Rd SO16 78 C2
Butterfly Dr PO6 133 A1
Buttermere Cl SO16 77 C1
Buttermere Ho 24 PO6 133 A1
Buttery The BH23 207 B4
Button's La
18 Poole BH15 202 B1
West Wellow SO51 50 C2
Butts Ash Gdns SO45 126 A1
Butts Ash La SO45 149 C4
Butts Bridge Hill SO45 126 A1
Butts Farm La SO32 83 B4
Butts Paddock SO42 145 C1
Butts Rd SO22 1 B1
Butts The SO32 61 B3
Buttsash Ave SO45 150 A4
Buttsbridge Rd SO45 126 A1
By Pass Rd SO51 52 C3
By The Wood SO40 76 B1
Byams La SO40 102 A1
Bye Rd SO31 128 B4
Byerley Cl PO10 137 A3
Byerley Rd PO1 182 C3
Byeways SO45 125 C1
Byrd Cl PO7 134 C3
Byres The PO14 154 B2
Byron Ave SO22 10 B4
Byron Cl
Bishop's Waltham SO32 83 C4
Fareham PO16 131 A1
Byron Ct Ferndown BH22 165 B3
Southampton SO15 102 C3
Byron Ho 16 BH25 195 A1
Byron Rd
Barton on Sea BH25 209 C4
Bournemouth BH5 205 C2
Eastleigh SO50 56 A2
Portsmouth PO2 182 C4
Southampton SO19 104 B3
Wimborne Minst BH21 163 B3

C

C Ave SO45 150 C2
Cable St 29 SO14 103 B3
Cabot Bsns Village BH17 202 A4
Cabot Dr SO45 125 B2
Cabot La BH17 202 A4
Cabot Way BH25 194 C2
Cadgwith Pl PO6 157 A4
Cadhay Cl BH25 194 C2
Cadland Ct SO14 103 B1
Cadland Rd Fawley SO45 151 A3
Holbury SO45 150 B4
Cadlands Park Est SO45 150 B3
Cadnam Ct PO12 180 B2
Cadnam La SO40 74 C1
Cadnam Lawn PO9 135 B3
Cadnam Rd PO4 183 A2
Cadnam Way BH8 190 B2
Cadogan Rd BH24 141 A4
Cador Dr PO16 156 A3
Caen Ho 7 PO14 154 C4
Caer Peris View PO16 132 B1
Caerleon Ave SO19 104 B3
Caerleon Dr SO19 104 B3
Caernarvon Gdns SO53 55 A2
Caesar's Way BH18 186 C2
Cains Cl PO14 154 B2
Caird Ave BH25 195 B1
Cairns Cl BH23 206 C4
Cairo Terr PO2 182 B4
Caister Cl BH22 165 B3
Caistor Cl SO16 78 A2
Calabrese SO31 129 A4
Calbourne SO31 127 B4
Calcot La SO32 82 C2
Caldecote Wlk 7 PO5 215 B2
Calder Cl SO16 101 C4
Calder Rd BH17 202 C4
Calderwood Dr SO19 104 A2
Caledon Rd BH14 203 C2
Caledonia Dr SO45 125 B2
Caledonian Cl BH23 208 A4
California Cl SO40 76 A1
Calkin Cl BH23 192 A1
Calluna Rd BH12 203 A4
Calmore Cl BH8 190 B2
Calmore Cres SO40 76 A1
Calmore Dr SO40 76 A1
Calmore Gdns SO40 100 B4
Calmore Ind Est SO40 76 C1
Calmore Inf Sch SO40 76 B1
Calmore Jun Sch SO40 76 B1
Calmore Rd SO40 100 B4
Calpe Ave SO43 121 C3
Calshot Activities Ctr SO45 152 A1
Calshot Castle★ SO45 152 A1
Calshot Cl SO45 178 C4
Calshot Ct SO14 103 B1
Calshot Dr SO53 55 A2
Calshot Rd Fawley SO45 151 A2
Havant PO9 135 B4
Calshot Way PO13 155 A1
Calvin Rd BH9 204 C4
Camargue Cl SO31 129 A4
Camber Pl 17 PO1 182 A2
Cambria Dr SO45 125 B2
Cambrian Cl SO31 105 A1
Cambrian Terr PO5 215 C1
Cambrian Wlk PO14 154 C4
Cambridge Ct 17 SO14 103 A4
Cambridge Dr SO53 55 B2
Cambridge Gdns BH23 191 C1
Cambridge Gn
Chandler's Ford SO53 55 B1
Titchfield PO14 129 B1
Cambridge Junc PO1 182 A2
Cambridge Rd
Bournemouth BH2 204 B2
Gosport PO12 180 C3
Lee-on-the-Solent PO13 179 C1
Portsmouth PO1 182 A2
Southampton SO14 103 A4
Camcross Cl 7 PO6 133 A1
Camden Cl BH9 190 A1
Camden Hurst 1 SO41 211 A2
Camden St PO12 181 A3
Camden Terr 2 PO12 181 A3
Camel Green Rd SP6 93 A3
Camelia Cl Havant PO9 136 A2
Camelia Cl *continued*
North Baddesley SO52 54 A3
Camelia Gdns SO18 80 A1
Camelia Gr SO50 57 C1
Camellia Cl BH21 114 C1
Camellia Ct 2 SO18 79 C1
Camellia Gdns BH25 195 A1
Camelot Cres PO16 132 A1
Cameron Cl PO13 155 B2
Cameron Ct SO16 77 C3
Cameron Rd BH23 207 B4
Camley Cl SO19 103 C1
Cammel Rd BH22 165 B1
Camp Rd PO13 155 B2
Campbell Cres PO7 134 B3
Campbell Ct SO50 57 B1
Campbell Mews SO18 104 B4
Campbell Rd
Bournemouth BH1 205 C3
Burton BH23 192 B2
Eastleigh SO50 56 A1
Portsmouth PO5 215 D1
Campbell St SO14 103 B3
Campbell Way SO50 57 B1
Campion Cl Fair Oak SO50 81 B3
Locks Heath SO31 128 C1
Waterlooville PO7 135 A3
Campion Dr SO51 28 B1
Campion Gr BH23 207 C3
Campion Rd SO19 104 B3
Campion Way
Kings Worthy SO23 2 B4
Lymington SO41 197 C3
Cams Bay Cl PO16 131 C1
Cams Hill Hambledon PO7 86 A1
Portchester PO16 131 C1
Cams Hill Sch PO16 155 C4
Canada Cnr GU31 66 C3
Canada Ct PO12 181 B4
Canada Pl 6 SO16 78 C2
Canada Rd
Southampton SO19 103 C1
West Wellow SO51 50 B1
Canal Cl SO51 28 A1
Canal Wlk
Portsmouth PO1 215 C3
Romsey SO51 52 C4
Southampton SO14 103 A2
Canberra Cl PO12 180 C2
Canberra Ct PO12 180 C2
Canberra Ho PO1 215 B3
Canberra Rd
Christchurch BH23 191 C1
Nursling SO16 77 A2
Thorney Island PO10 161 A2
Canberra Twrs SO19 126 C4
Candlemas Pl 13 SO17 103 A4
Candover Ct SO19 127 A4
Candy La SO19 104 C3
Candys Cl BH21 162 C1
Candys La BH21 162 C1
Canford Ave BH11 189 A1
Canford Bottom BH21 164 B3
Canford Bottom Rdbt BH21 164 B3
Canford Cl
Shedfield SO32 107 C4
Southampton SO16 77 B1
Canford Cliffs Ave BH14 203 C1
Canford Cliffs Rd BH13 203 C1
Canford Cres BH13 214 C4
Canford Ct BH13 214 C3
Canford Gdns BH11 189 A1
Canford Heath Fst & Mid Schs BH17 202 B4
Canford Heath Nature Reserve★ BH11 188 A2
Canford Heath Rd BH17 187 C1
Canford Magna BH21 164 A1
Canford Pl 2 BH13 214 C4
Canford Rd
Bournemouth BH11 189 A1
Poole BH15 202 B2
Canford Sch BH21 164 A1
Canford View Dr BH21 164 A3
Canford Way BH12 188 B1
Canhouse La GU33 21 C2
Cannock Wlk 16 PO14 154 C4
Cannon Cl BH18 187 A1
Cannon Hill Gdns BH21 164 A4
Cannon Hill Rd BH21 164 A4
Cannon Ho SO41 197 C2
Cannon St
Lymington SO41 197 C2
Southampton SO15 102 B4
Cannon's Barn Cl PO16 132 B1
Canoe Cl SO31 128 C1
Canon Ct 5 SO50 57 B1
Canon St SO23 10 C4
Canons Wlk SO41 211 B3
Cantell Sec Sch SO16 79 A2
Canterbury Ave SO19 104 B2
Canterbury Cl
Lee-on-the-Solent PO13 180 A2
West Moors BH22 138 C1
Canterbury Dr SO45 125 B2
Canterbury Rd
Portsmouth PO4 182 C2
Stubbington PO14 154 B2
Canterton La SO43 98 A4
Canton St SO15 102 C3
Canute Dr BH23 169 A1
Canute Ho 25 SO14 103 A2
Canute Rd
Southampton SO14 103 A2
6 *Winchester* SO23 11 A[illegible]
Canvey Ct SO16 77 [illegible]

Capel Ley PO7 134 C2
Capella Ct BH2 204 C1
Capella Gdns SO45 125 B2
Capers End La SO32 82 C1
Capesthorne BH23 208 A3
Capital Ho [11] SO22 10 C4
Capon Cl SO18 79 C2
Capstan Gdns SO31 129 B2
Capstans The BH14 214 A4
Capstone Pl BH8 205 B3
Capstone Rd BH8 205 A3
Captain's Pl SO14 103 A2
Captain's Row SO41 197 C2
Captains Cl PO12 180 C4
Captains Row [15] PO1 182 A2
Caradon Pl BH31 114 B4
Carberry Dr PO16 156 B4
Carbery Ave BH6 206 B3
Carbery Ct PO9 135 B4
Carbery Gdns BH6 206 C3
Carbery La [3] BH6 206 B2
Carbery Row [2] BH6 206 B2
Carbis Cl PO6 157 A4
Cardew Rd GU33 21 A2
Cardiff Rd PO2 157 B1
Cardigan Rd
Bournemouth BH9 204 C4
Poole BH12 203 C2
Cardinal Dr PO7 112 A1
Cardinal Way SO31 129 A1
Cardington Ct SO16 77 C2
Carey Rd
Bournemouth BH9 189 C2
Southampton SO19 104 B3
Careys Cotts SO42 145 C1
Careys Rd BH8 190 B2
Carina Ct BH13 214 B2
Carisbrook Cres BH15 201 B2
Carisbrooke Netley SO31 127 B4
Poole BH13 214 C4
Carisbrooke Ave PO14 179 A3
Carisbrooke Cl [2] PO9 136 A1
Carisbrooke Cres SO53 55 C3
Carisbrooke Ct
[4] Christchurch BH23 209 A4
New Milton BH25 194 C2
Romsey SO51 28 A1
Carisbrooke Dr SO19 103 C3
Carisbrooke Rd
Gosport PO13 155 B1
Portsmouth PO4 183 A2
Carisbrooke Way BH23 193 C1
Carless Cl PO13 180 B4
Carlinford [29] BH5 205 C2
Carlisle Ct [2] SO16 102 A4
Carlisle Rd
Portsmouth PO1 215 C3
Southampton SO16 102 A4
Carlton Ave BH25 209 C4
Carlton Commerce Ctr The
SO14 103 A4
Carlton Cres SO15 102 C3
Carlton Ct [5] SO15 102 C4
Carlton Gr BH12 203 B3
Carlton Ho SO41 197 C2
Carlton Pl SO15 102 C3
Carlton Rd
Bournemouth BH1 205 B2
Gosport PO12 181 B3
Portchester PO16 132 C1
Southampton SO15 102 C4
Carlton Way PO12 181 B3
Carlyle Rd
Bournemouth BH6 206 B3
Gosport PO12 181 A3
Carlyn Dr SO53 55 B4
Carmans La SO21 31 B4
Carmarthen Ave PO6 158 A4
Carmel Cl BH15 201 B1
Carmine Ct PO13 180 B3
Carnarvon Rd
[4] Bournemouth BH1 205 C2
Gosport PO12 181 A2
Portsmouth PO2 182 C4
Carnation Rd SO16 79 B2
Carne Cl SO53 55 B4
Carne Pl PO6 157 A4
Carnegie Cl BH14 203 B3
Caroline Ave BH23 207 C3
Caroline Gdns PO15 130 B1
Caroline Rd BH11 189 A2
Carolyn Cl SO19 103 C1
Carpathia Cl SO18 80 A1
Carpenter Cl Hythe SO45 126 A2
Lymington SO41 197 B3
[10] Portsmouth PO4 183 A2
Carradale BH23 208 A4
Carran Wlk PO14 154 C4
Carraway PO15 129 B4
Carrbridge Cl BH3 204 B4
Carrbridge Gdns BH3 204 B4
Carrbridge Rd BH3 204 B4
Carrick Way BH25 195 B1
Carrington Cl SO41 211 C3
Carrington Ho [33] SO17 79 A1
Carrington La SO41 211 C2
Carrol Cl SO50 57 B1
Carroll Ave BH22 165 C3
Carroll Cl BH12 204 A3
Carronade Wlk PO3 157 C3
Carronades The [21]
SO14 103 A3
Carshalton Ave PO6 158 A4
Carsworth Way BH17 188 A1
Carter Com Sch BH15 201 C1
Carter Ho Gosport PO13 155 A3
[7] Portsmouth PO1 182 A3
Carter's Cl SP6 47 B2
Carter's Clay Rd SO51 26 A3
Carter's Copse Nature Trail*
PO13 180 B3
Carter's La [9] BH15 202 B1
Carters Ave BH15 201 B2
Carthage Cl SO53 55 C4
Cartref Cl BH31 114 C3
Cartwright Cl BH10 189 B2
Cartwright Dr PO14,
PO15 129 C1
Carvers Ind Est BH24 141 A4
Carvers La BH24 141 A4
Carysfort Rd BH1 205 B2
Cascades App PO1 215 B4
Cascades Sh Ctr PO1 215 B4
Cases Bakery Cl PO17 108 A2
Cashmoor Cl BH12 203 C4
Cask St PO1 215 B4
Caslake Cl BH25 194 C1
Caspar John Cl PO14 179 A3
Caspian Cl SO31 129 A4
Cassel Ave BH13 204 A1
Casselles Ct [33] BH25 195 A1
Casterbridge Rd BH22 165 B2
Castle Ave
Christchurch BH23 208 C4
Havant PO9 136 A1
Winchester SO23 10 C4
Castle Cl
Milford on Sea SO41 211 C2
Portsmouth PO5 215 B1
Castle Court Sch BH21 186 A4
Castle Ct
[3] Christchurch BH23 209 A4
[4] Southampton, Bitterne Pk
SO18 79 C1
Southampton, Millbrook
SO15 102 A3
Castle Farm La PO17 108 A1
Castle Gate Cl BH8 190 B1
Castle Gdns GU32 40 C2
Castle Gr PO16 156 B4
Castle Hill Poole BH14 203 A2
Winchester SO22 10 C4
Castle Hill La BH24 142 C2
Castle Hts [3] SO18 79 C1
Castle La
Chandler's Ford SO53 55 A2
Fawley SO45 178 C4
North Baddesley SO53,SO52 54 B2
[6] Southampton SO14 102 C2
Castle La E BH7 206 B4
Castle La W BH8, BH9 190 B1
Castle Marina PO13 179 C1
Castle Mdw SP5 46 C4
Castle Mews
Southampton SO14 102 C2
St Leonards BH24 140 B3
Castle Par BH7 206 B4
Castle Prim Sch PO16 156 B4
Castle Rd
Bournemouth BH9 190 A1
Netley SO31 127 A3
Portsmouth PO5 215 B1
Rowland's Castle PO9 113 A1
Southampton SO18 79 C1
Southwick PO17 132 C3
Castle Sq [8] SO14 102 C2
Castle St
Christchurch BH23 207 B3
Poole BH15 202 B1
Portchester PO16 156 B4
Southampton SO14 103 A4
Titchfield PO14 154 A4
Castle Trad Est PO16 156 C4
Castle View PO12 181 A4
Castle View Rd PO16 156 C3
Castle Way SO14 102 C2
Castle Woods SP5 47 B3
Castledene Cres BH14 203 A1
Castlemain Ave BH6 206 B3
Castleman Ct BH22 138 B2
Castleman Way BH24 141 A3
Castlemans La PO11 160 A1
Castleshaw Cl SO16 101 C4
Castleton Ave BH10 189 B3
Castleton Ct PO5 215 A1
Castleway PO9 136 A1
Castlewood BH24 140 B3
Catalina Cl BH23 208 A3
Catalina Dr BH15 202 C1
Catamaran Cl SO31 128 C1
Cateran Cl SO16 101 C4
Cathay Gdns SO45 125 B2
Cathedral View [5] SO23 11 A3
Catherine Cl SO30 80 C1
Catherine Cres SP5 46 B4
Catherine Gdns SO30 80 C1
Catherine Wheel Gdns
BH23 191 C2
Catherington CE Inf Sch
PO8 88 A1
Catherington Hill PO8 88 A2
Catherington La
Horndean PO8 112 A4
Waterlooville PO8 112 A4
Catherington Way PO9 135 C2
Catisfield Ho [3] PO1 215 C4
Catisfield La PO15 130 A1
Catisfield Rd
Fareham PO15 130 B1
Portsmouth PO4 183 A2
Catmint Cl SO53 54 C4
Caton Cl BH12 204 A4
Cattistock Rd BH8 190 C1
Catways SO21 30 A4
Causeway SO51 52 B3
Causeway Cres SO40 101 A4
Causeway Ct [6] SO18 103 C4
Causeway Farm PO8 112 A3
Causeway The
Petersfield GU31 40 C1
Portchester PO16 131 C1
Cavalier Cl SO45 125 B2
Cavalier Ct PO6 158 B4
Cavan Cres BH17 187 A1
Cavanna Cl PO13 155 A2
Cavell Dr PO6 133 C1
Cavendish Cl
Romsey SO51 28 A1
Waterlooville PO7 134 C4
Cavendish Corner Cvn Pk [4]
BH24 141 A4
Cavendish Dr PO7 134 C4
Cavendish Gr
Southampton SO17 102 C4
Winchester SO23 2 A2
Cavendish Hall BH1 205 A3
Cavendish Mews [2]
SO15 102 C4
Cavendish Pl BH1 205 A3
Cavendish Rd
Bournemouth BH1 205 A3
Portsmouth PO5 215 C1
Caversham Cl
Hamworthy BH15 201 C2
Southampton SO19 104 A2
West End SO30 80 B1
Cawdor Rd BH3 204 B4
Cawte Rd SO15 102 B3
Cawte's Pl PO16 131 B1
Caxton Ave SO19 104 A3
Caxton Cl BH23 208 A4
Cecil Ave Ashurst SO40 100 B1
Bournemouth BH8 205 B4
Southampton SO16 78 A1
Cecil Cl BH21 186 C3
Cecil Ct BH8 205 A4
Cecil Gr PO5 215 A1
Cecil Hill BH8 205 A4
Cecil Pl PO5 215 A1
Cecil Rd
Bournemouth BH5 205 C2
Poole BH12 203 B3
Southampton SO19 103 C2
Cecil Villas SO17 79 B1
Cedar Ave
Bournemouth BH10 189 B3
Christchurch BH23 206 B4
Southampton SO15 102 B4
St Leonards BH24 139 C2
Cedar Cl Bursledon SO31 127 C4
Gosport PO12 156 A1
Hedge End SO30 105 B4
Kings Worthy SO23 2 A4
Upton BH16 201 A4
Waterlooville PO7 134 C3
Cedar Cres
North Baddesley SO52 53 C3
Waterlooville PO8 112 B3
Cedar Ct
Bournemouth BH4 204 A1
[12] Fareham PO16 131 B1
Portsmouth PO5 215 C1
Cedar Dr Hordle SO41 211 B4
Wimborne Minst BH21 164 A3
Cedar Gdns
Barton on Sea BH25 194 C1
Havant PO9 136 A1
Southampton SO14 103 A4
Cedar Gr PO3 183 A4
Cedar Lawn SO51 28 B1
Cedar Manor BH4 204 B2
Cedar Pl BH23 169 A1
Cedar Rd Eastleigh SO50 55 C1
Hythe SO45 150 A4
Southampton SO14 103 A4
Cedar Specl Sch The
SO16 77 C2
Cedar St SO32 83 B4
Cedar Trad Pk BH21 164 C3
Cedar Way
Fareham PO14 154 C4
Ferndown BH22 165 B4
Cedar Wlk [37] SO22 10 C4
Cedar Wood Cl
Fair Oak SO50 57 C1
Totton SO40 100 B4
Cedarmount SO43 121 C2
Cedars The
Bournemouth BH4 204 B2
Fareham PO16 130 C2
Cedarwood SO23 2 B4
Cedarwood Lodge [6]
PO16 131 A1
Ceder Ho SO14 103 A2
Cedric Cl SO45 177 C4
Celandine Ave
Locks Heath SO31 128 C1
Waterlooville PO8 112 A2
Celandine Cl
Chandler's Ford SO53 54 C3
Christchurch BH23 208 A4
Celia Cl PO7 135 A4
Cellars Farm Rd BH6 207 A2
Cement Terr [7] SO14 102 C2
Cemetery Ave BH15 202 C3
Cemetery Junc BH2 204 C3
Cemetery La
Denmead PO7 110 C3
Westbourne PO10 137 B2
Cemetery Rd
Southampton SO15 102 C4
Wimborne Minst BH21 163 A3
Centaur St PO2 182 B3
Centaury Gdns SO50 81 B4
Centenary Cl SO41 172 B1
Centenary Ho [6] BH23 207 A4
Centenary Way BH1, 205 C3
Central Ave
Corfe Mullen BH21 186 B4
Poole BH12 203 C3
Central Bridge SO14 103 A2
Central Dr BH2 204 C3
Central Prec The SO53 55 B3
Central Rd Cosham PO6 158 B4
Portchester PO16 156 A4
Southampton SO14 103 A1
Central St PO1 215 C4
Central Station Bridge
SO15 102 C3
Central Way N SO45 151 C1
Centre La SO41 196 C1
Centre Pl BH24 140 C4
Centre Way SO31 129 A2
Centurian Ind Pk SO18 103 B4
Centurion Gate PO4 183 B2
Cerdic Mews SO31 128 A2
Cerne Abbas BH13 204 A1
Cerne Cl
Bournemouth BH9 190 A2
North Baddesley SO52 53 C2
West End SO18 80 A1
Cessac Ho PO12 181 B1
CH La SO32 83 C2
Chadderton Gdns PO1 182 A2
Chaddesley Glen BH13 214 C3
Chaddesley Pines BH13 214 C3
Chaddesley Wood Rd
BH13 214 C3
Chadswell Mdw PO9 135 B1
Chadwell Ave SO19 104 A2
Chadwick Rd SO50 55 C1
Chafen Rd SO18 103 B4
Chaffey Cl BH24 141 B4
Chaffinch Cl
Broadstone BH17 186 C1
New Milton BH25 194 C1
Totton SO40 100 B4
Chaffinch Gn PO8 111 C2
Chaffinch Way
Lee-on-the-Solent PO13 179 C2
Portchester PO16 155 C4
Chalbury Cl BH17 188 A1
Chalbury Ct
[6] Christchurch BH23 207 C3
[11] Poole BH14 203 A2
Chaldecott Gdns BH10 189 B2
Chaldon Rd BH17 187 C1
Chale Cl PO13 155 B1
Chalewood Rd SO45 177 C4
Chalfont Ave BH23 191 B2
Chalfont Ct [7] SO16 78 A1
Chalice Cl BH14 203 A2
Chalice Ct SO30 105 A3
Chalk Cl SP5 47 B4
Chalk Hill Soberton SO32 85 B3
West End SO18 80 B1
Chalk Hill Rd PO8 112 B4
Chalk La PO17 131 A4
Chalk Pit Cotts PO17 131 A4
Chalk Ridge Horndean PO8 88 B2
Winchester SO23 11 B4
Chalkpit Rd PO6 133 A1
Chalkridge Rd PO6 134 A1
Challenge Ent Ctr The
PO3 158 A2
Challenger Dr PO12 181 B4
Challenger Way SO45 125 B1
Challis Ct [18] SO14 103 A2
Chalmers Way SO31 127 C2
Chaloner Cres SO45 126 A1
Chalton Cres PO9 135 B2
Chalton Ho PO1 215 B4
Chalton La PO8 88 B3
Chalvington Ct SO53 55 B3
Chalvington Rd SO53 55 B2
Chalwyn Ind Est BH12 203 A4
Chalybeate Cl SO16 78 A1
Chalybeate Hospl SO16 78 A1
Chamberlain Gr PO14 155 A4
Chamberlain Hall SO16 79 A2
Chamberlain Rd SO17 79 A2
Chamberlayne Ct SO52 54 A2
Chamberlayne Ho [10]
SO31 127 A3
Chamberlayne Park Sch
Southampton SO19 104 A1
Southampton SO19 127 A4
Chamberlayne Rd
Bursledon SO31 127 C4
Eastleigh SO50 56 A1
Netley SO31 127 A3
Chambers Ave SO51 53 A4
Chambers Cl SO16 77 B3
Champion Cl SO41 211 C2
Chancel Rd SO31 129 A2
Chancellors La SO32 81 C2
Chanctonbury Ho PO5 215 B1
Chander Cl BH22 165 C2
Chandler's Ford Ind Est
SO53 55 A3
Chandler's Ford Inf Sch
SO53 55 B3
Chandler's Ford Inf Sch
(Annexe) SO53 55 B4
Chandlers Cl
Bournemouth BH7 206 A4
South Hayling PO11 185 B1
Chandlers Way SO31 129 A3
Chandos Ave BH12 204 A4
Chandos Ho [14] SO14 103 A2
Chandos St [26] SO14 103 A2
Channel Ct
Barton on Sea BH25 209 C4
Bournemouth BH6 206 B2
Channel Mouth Rd
SO45 151 C1
Channel Way SO14 103 B2
Channels Farm Rd SO16 79 B3
Chant Cl BH23 207 B4
Chantrell Wlk PO15 130 B2
Chantry Cl BH23 193 C1
Chantry Mead SO22 1 C1
Chantry Rd
Gosport PO12 181 A4
Horndean PO8 112 A4
Southampton SO14 103 A2
Chantry The
Bournemouth BH1 205 A2
Locks Heath PO14 129 B2
Chapel Cl Braishfield SO51 28 B3
Corfe Mullen BH21 186 B3
West End SO30 80 B1
Chapel Cres SO19 104 A2
Chapel Ct [7] PO1 182 B4
Chapel Dro Fair Oak SO50 81 B4
Hedge End SO30 105 A3
Chapel Gate BH23 190 B4
Chapel La
Blackfield SO45 177 C4
Bransgore BH23 193 A4
Burley BH24 143 A2
Chilcomb SO21, SO23 12 A4
Corfe Mullen BH21 186 B3
Curdridge SO32 106 C4
East Boldre SO42 175 B3
Fawley SO45 151 A1
Hurn BH23 190 B4
Lockerley SO51 26 A3
Lyndhurst SO43 121 C2
Michelmersh SO51 27 B4
Nomansland SP5 73 B4
Otterbourne SO21 31 A1
Poole BH15 202 B1
Redlynch SP5 47 C3
Sway SO41 172 B1
Totton SO40 100 C3
[13] Waterlooville PO7 134 C4
Wimborne Minst BH21 163 A3
Chapel Rd Droxford SO32 61 B2
Locks Heath SO31 128 C3
Poole BH14 203 A2
Soberton SO32 85 A1
Southampton SO14 103 A2
Swanmore SO32 84 A3
West End SO30 80 C1
Chapel Rise BH24 140 B1
Chapel Sq PO12 180 C4
Chapel St East Meon GU32 38 B1
Gosport PO12 181 A4
Petersfield GU32 40 C2
[3] Portsmouth PO2 215 A1
Southampton SO14 103 A2
Chapelside PO14 154 A4
Chaplains Ave PO8 111 B2
Chaplains Cl PO8 111 B2
Charborough Rd BH18 187 A2
Charden Ct SO18 104 A4
Charden Rd
Bishopstoke SO50 57 A1
Gosport PO13 180 B4
Charfield Cl
Fareham PO14 154 B4
Winchester SO22 10 C3
Charielote Ho SO15 102 B3
Charing Cl BH24 141 A3
Chark La PO13 179 C2
Charlcot Lawn PO9 135 B3
Charlecote Dr SO53 55 A4
Charlecote Mews [18]
SO22 10 C4
Charlemont Dr [15] PO16 131 B1
Charles Cl
Waterlooville PO7 134 B3
Winchester SO23 2 A1
Charles Cres BH25 195 A3
Charles Dickens Birthplace
Mus* PO1 182 B4
Charles Dickens Inf Sch
PO1 182 B4
Charles Dickens Jun Sch
PO1 182 B4
Charles Dickens St PO1 215 B3
Charles Gdns BH10 189 B1
Charles Keightley Ct
BH21 163 B2
Charles Knott Gdns
SO15 102 C4
Charles Ley Ct SO45 151 A2
Charles Rd
Christchurch BH23 207 C4
Poole BH15 202 B2
Charles St
Petersfield GU32 40 C2
Portsmouth PO1 215 C4
Southampton SO14 103 A2
Charles Watts Way
SO30 105 A4
Charles Wyatt Ho [28]
SO14 103 A4
Charles's La BH24 141 C2
Charlesbury Ave PO12 180 C2
Charleston Cl PO11 184 C2
Charleston Rd SO45 150 B4
Charlesworth Dr PO7 111 B1
Charlesworth Gdns PO7 111 B1

Charliejoy Gdns 18 SO14 ... 103 B3
Charlott Ct PO5 ... 215 B1
Charlotte Cl
 Christchurch BH23 ... 208 A3
 3 New Milton BH25 ... 195 A1
 Poole BH12 ... 204 B4
Charlotte Ct
 Chandler's Ford SO53 ... 55 C4
 Southampton SO19 ... 103 C1
Charlotte Mews PO12 ... 181 A1
Charlotte Pl SO14 ... 103 A3
Charlotte St PO1 ... 215 B4
Charlton Cl
 Bournemouth BH9 ... 190 B2
 Hordle SO41 ... 195 C2
Charlton Rd SO15 ... 102 B4
Charltons The BH2 ... 204 C3
Charminster 8 PO5 ... 182 B1
Charminster Ave BH9 ... 190 A1
Charminster Cl
 5 Bournemouth BH8 ... 190 A1
 Waterlooville PO7 ... 134 C4
Charminster Pl BH8 ... 190 B1
Charminster Rd BH8 ... 205 A4
Charmouth Gr BH14 ... 203 A2
Charmouth Terr 6 SO16 ... 78 A1
Charmus Rd SO40 ... 76 A1
Charnwen Cres SO30 ... 80 B1
Charnock Cl SO41 ... 195 C2
Charnwood PO13 ... 155 B1
Charnwood Ave 8 BH9 ... 190 A2
Charnwood Cl
 Chandler's Ford SO53 ... 30 B1
 Totton SO40 ... 76 B1
 West Moors BH22 ... 138 C1
Charnwood Cres SO53 ... 30 B1
Charnwood Dr SP6 ... 69 C2
Charnwood Gdns SO53 ... 30 B1
Charnwood Way SO45 ... 177 C4
Chartcombe BH13 ... 214 C4
Charter Ho 2 PO5 ... 215 A2
Charter Rd BH11 ... 188 B3
Chartergrove Ho 15 GU31 ... 40 C2
Charterhouse Way SO30 ... 81 B1
Chartwell Cl
 Eastleigh SO50 ... 56 A3
 Titchfield PO14 ... 129 B1
Chartwell Dr PO9 ... 136 B2
Chase Cl GU33 ... 21 A2
Chase Farm Cl SO32 ... 83 C2
Chase Gr SO32 ... 83 C2
Chase Rd GU33 ... 21 A2
Chase The Gosport PO12 ... 180 C2
 Locks Heath PO14 ... 129 B1
 St Leonards BH24 ... 140 B3
 Verwood BH31 ... 115 B3
Chaseside BH7 ... 206 A4
Chasewater Ave PO3 ... 183 A4
Chatburn Ave PO8 ... 111 C2
Chatfield Ho 10 PO1 ... 215 C4
Chatfield Rd PO13 ... 155 B2
Chatham Cl PO12 ... 181 B4
Chatham Dr PO1 ... 182 A2
Chatham Rd SO22 ... 10 B3
Chatsworth Ave PO6 ... 158 A3
Chatsworth Cl PO15 ... 130 B1
Chatsworth Ct PO5 ... 215 C1
Chatsworth Rd
 Bournemouth BH8 ... 205 B3
 Eastleigh SO50 ... 56 A3
 Poole BH14 ... 203 A3
 Southampton SO19 ... 104 A3
Chatsworth Way BH25 ... 194 C2
Chaucer Ave PO6 ... 132 C1
Chaucer Cl
 Fareham PO16 ... 130 C1
 Waterlooville PO7 ... 111 C1
 Wimborne Minst BH21 ... 163 B3
Chaucer Dr SO41 ... 211 B3
Chaucer Ind Est SO23 ... 2 B1
Chaucer Rd Poole BH13 ... 214 C4
 Southampton SO19 ... 104 B3
Chaucombe Pl BH25 ... 194 C1
Chaundler Rd SO23 ... 2 A1
Chaveney Cl 6 SO45 ... 125 C1
Chawton Cl
 Southampton SO18 ... 104 B4
 Winchester SO22 ... 1 B2
Cheam Rd BH18 ... 186 C2
Cheam Way SO40 ... 76 B1
Cheater's La SP6 ... 92 B4
Cheddar Cl SO19 ... 103 C2
Cheddington Rd BH9 ... 190 A2
Chedington Cl BH17 ... 187 C1
Chedworth Cres PO6 ... 133 A1
Cheeryble Ho 19 PO1 ... 182 B4
Cheesecombe Farm La GU33 ... 19 C3
Chellowdene SO53 ... 55 B3
Chelmsford Rd
 Portsmouth PO2 ... 157 C1
 Upton BH16 ... 201 A4
Chelsea Rd PO5 ... 215 C1
Cheltenham Cres PO13 ... 179 C2
Cheltenham Ct 26 SO17 ... 79 A1
Cheltenham Gdns SO30 ... 81 B2
Cheltenham Rd
 Cosham PO6 ... 157 B4
 Poole BH12 ... 203 B3
Chelveston Cres SO16 ... 78 A2
Chelwood Gate SO16 ... 78 C3
Chene Rd BH21 ... 163 B2
Cheney's Farm SO51 ... 75 C3
Cheping Gdns SO30 ... 106 A3
Chepstow Cl
 North Baddesley SO53 ... 55 A3
 Totton SO40 ... 100 B4
Chepstow Ct 9 PO7 ... 112 A1
Chequers Cl SO41 ... 197 B2
Chequers Ho 20 PO16 ... 131 A1
Chequers Quay 5 PO10 ... 161 A4
Cherbourg Prim Sch SO50 ... 56 A1
Cherbourg Rd SO50 ... 56 A1
Cherford Rd BH11 ... 189 A1
Cherita Ct BH15 ... 202 C3
Cheriton Ave
 Bournemouth BH7 ... 206 B4
 Southampton SO18 ... 104 B4
Cheriton Cl Havant PO9 ... 135 B2
 Horndean PO8 ... 112 A4
 Winchester SO22 ... 1 B1
Cheriton Ct 7 SO15 ... 102 B3
Cheriton La SO24 ... 15 A4
Cheriton Prim Sch SO24 ... 14 B3
Cheriton Rd
 Eastleigh SO50 ... 55 C1
 Gosport PO12 ... 180 C2
 Winchester SO22 ... 10 C4
Cheriton Way BH21 ... 163 B3
Cherque La PO13 ... 180 A4
Cherrett Ct BH11 ... 188 C2
Cherries Dr BH9 ... 189 C1
Cherry Blossom Ct 22 PO1 ... 182 B4
Cherry Cl
 Lee-on-the-Solent PO13 ... 180 A3
 Poole BH14 ... 203 A2
Cherry Ct Poole BH14 ... 203 A3
 16 Southampton SO17 ... 103 A4
Cherry Dro SO50 ... 81 B3
Cherry Gdns SO32 ... 83 B4
Cherry Gr BH22 ... 165 B3
Cherry Hill Gdns BH16 ... 201 A3
Cherry Hill Gr BH16 ... 201 A3
Cherry Tree Ave
 Fareham PO14 ... 154 B4
 Waterlooville PO8 ... 112 A1
Cherry Tree Cl
 Hordle SO41 ... 211 B4
 St Leonards BH24 ... 139 B2
Cherry Tree Ct 31 BH25 ... 195 A1
Cherry Tree Dr BH25 ... 194 C3
Cherry Wlk SO15 ... 102 B4
Cherrygarth Rd PO15 ... 130 B1
Cherryton Gdns SO45 ... 150 A2
Cherrywood SO30 ... 105 A3
Cherrywood Gdns
 South Hayling PO11 ... 185 A2
 Totton SO40 ... 100 B4
Chervil Cl
 Chandler's Ford SO53 ... 54 C3
 Horndean PO8 ... 88 B1
Cherville Ct SO51 ... 52 C4
Cherville Mews SO51 ... 52 C4
Cherville St SO51 ... 52 C4
Cherwell Cres SO16 ... 101 C4
Cherwell Gdns SO53 ... 55 B3
Cherwell Ho SO16 ... 101 C4
Cheshire Cl PO15 ... 129 C3
Cheshire Dr BH8 ... 191 A1
Cheshire Way PO10 ... 137 B1
Chesil St SO23 ... 11 A4
Chesil Terr SO23 ... 11 A4
Chesil Wood SO23 ... 11 B4
Chesildene Ave BH8 ... 190 B2
Chesildene Dr BH8 ... 190 B2
Cheslyn Rd PO3 ... 183 A3
Chessel Ave
 Bournemouth BH5 ... 205 C2
 Southampton SO19 ... 103 C3
Chessel Cres SO19 ... 103 C4
Chester Cres PO13 ... 180 A2
Chester Ct SO16 ... 78 B1
Chester Cts 7 PO12 ... 181 B2
Chester Pl 34 PO5 ... 182 B1
Chester Rd Poole BH13 ... 204 A1
 Southampton SO18 ... 80 A1
 Winchester SO23 ... 11 A4
Chesterfield Cl BH13 ... 214 C4
Chesterfield Ct BH1 ... 205 B2
Chesterfield Rd PO3 ... 183 A4
Chesterton Gdns PO8 ... 111 C2
Chesterton Pl SO31 ... 129 B4
Chestnut Ave
 Ashurst SO40 ... 100 B2
 Barton on Sea BH25 ... 210 A4
 Bournemouth BH6 ... 206 B2
 Christchurch BH23 ... 206 B4
 2 Colden Common SO21 ... 31 C1
 Eastleigh SO50,SO53 ... 55 B1
 Havant PO9 ... 135 A2
 Ibsley BH24 ... 116 A3
 Littleton SO22 ... 1 A2
 Portsmouth PO4 ... 182 C2
 Waterlooville PO8 ... 112 B3
Chestnut Cl
 Chandler's Ford SO53 ... 55 B2
 Denmead PO7 ... 110 C2
 Romsey SO51 ... 53 B3
 West End SO30 ... 80 B2
Chestnut Ct
 Rowland's Castle PO9 ... 136 A4
 8 Southampton SO17 ... 79 A1
Chestnut Gr BH21 ... 164 C3
Chestnut Lodge 12 SO16 ... 78 C2
Chestnut Rd
 Brockenhurst SO42 ... 146 A1
 Southampton SO16 ... 78 A1
Chestnut Rise
 Droxford SO32 ... 61 A1
Chestnut Rise *continued*
 Eastleigh SO53 ... 55 B1
Chestnut Way
 Burton BH23 ... 192 B2
 Titchfield PO14 ... 129 B1
Chestnut Wlk
 Botley SO30 ... 105 C4
 Gosport PO12 ... 156 A1
Chestnuts The SO31 ... 129 A1
Chetnole Cl BH17 ... 188 A1
Chettle Rd SO19 ... 104 C3
Chetwode Way BH17 ... 187 A1
Chetwynd Dr SO16 ... 78 C2
Chetwynd Rd
 Portsmouth PO4 ... 182 C2
 Southampton SO16 ... 78 C3
Chevening Ct 8 PO4 ... 183 A3
Cheviot Court Flats BH23 ... 207 C4
Cheviot Cres SO16 ... 101 C4
Cheviot Dr SO45 ... 125 B2
Cheviot Gn SO31 ... 152 B4
Cheviot Rd SO16 ... 101 C4
Cheviot Way BH31 ... 114 C3
Cheviot Wlk PO14 ... 154 C4
Cheviots The BH14 ... 203 B2
Chevron Bsns Pk SO45 ... 150 A3
Chewter Cl PO4 ... 182 C1
Chewton Common Rd BH23 ... 209 A4
Chewton Farm Rd BH23 ... 194 B1
Chewton Lodge BH23 ... 209 A4
Chewton Way BH23 ... 194 A1
Cheyne Gdns BH4 ... 204 B1
Cheyne Way PO13 ... 179 C1
Chichester Ave PO11 ... 185 A2
Chichester Cl
 Gosport PO13 ... 155 A1
 Hedge End SO30 ... 81 B1
 Locks Heath SO31 ... 128 C2
 West Wellow SO51 ... 51 A1
Chichester Ho PO9 ... 136 A2
Chichester Rd
 North Hayling PO11 ... 160 B1
 Portsmouth PO2 ... 182 C4
 Ringwood BH24 ... 117 B1
 Southampton SO18 ... 104 A4
Chichester Way BH23 ... 208 A3
Chichester Wlk BH21 ... 163 C1
Chickenhall La SO50 ... 56 B1
Chickerell Cl BH9 ... 190 A2
Chidden Cl GU32 ... 38 B1
Chidden Holt SO53 ... 55 A3
Chideock Cl BH12 ... 203 C3
Chideock Ct BH12 ... 203 C3
Chidham Cl PO9 ... 135 C1
Chidham Dr PO9 ... 135 C1
Chidham Rd PO6 ... 134 A1
Chidham Sq PO9 ... 135 C1
Chidham Wlk 2 PO9 ... 135 C1
Chigwell Rd BH8 ... 190 A1
Chilbolton Ave SO22 ... 10 B4
Chilbolton Ct
 14 Havant PO9 ... 136 A3
 Winchester SO22 ... 10 B4
Chilcomb Cl PO13 ... 179 C1
Chilcomb La
 Chilcomb SO21 ... 11 C3
 Winchester SO23 ... 11 B3
Chilcomb Rd SO18 ... 104 B4
Chilcombe Cl PO9 ... 135 C2
Chilcombe Hts SO23 ... 11 A4
Chilcombe Rd BH6 ... 206 A3
Chilcote Rd PO3 ... 183 A4
Childe Sq PO2 ... 157 B1
Chilfrome Cl BH17 ... 187 B1
Chilgrove Rd PO6 ... 158 B4
Chilham Cl SO50 ... 56 A4
Chillenden Ct SO40 ... 100 B3
Chillerton SO31 ... 127 B4
Chilling La SO31 ... 152 C3
Chillington Gdns SO53 ... 30 A1
Chilly Hill SP6 ... 94 C4
Chilmark Ct GU33 ... 20 C2
Chilsdown Way PO7 ... 134 C2
Chiltern Cl
 Barton on Sea BH25 ... 194 C1
 Poole BH12 ... 204 A3
 Totton SO40 ... 100 B3
Chiltern Ct
 5 Christchurch BH23 ... 207 C4
 Gosport PO12 ... 181 A3
 7 Portsmouth PO5 ... 182 B1
Chiltern Dr
 Barton on Sea BH25 ... 209 C4
 Verwood BH31 ... 114 C3
Chiltern Gr SO16 ... 101 C4
Chiltern Wlk PO14 ... 154 C4
Chilworth Cl SO16 ... 54 B1
Chilworth Gdns PO8 ... 88 B2
Chilworth Gr PO12 ... 181 A3
Chilworth Rd SO16 ... 54 C1
Chimes The BH4 ... 204 A2
Chine Ave SO19 ... 103 C3
Chine Cl SO31 ... 129 A2
Chine Cres BH2 ... 204 B1
Chine Cres Rd BH2 ... 204 B1
Chine The PO13 ... 155 C1
Chine Wlk BH22 ... 165 C1
Chinham Rd SO40 ... 99 B3
Chipstead Ho 12 PO6 ... 157 C4
Chipstead Rd 11 PO6 ... 157 C4
Chisels La BH23 ... 193 A3
Chisholm Cl SO16 ... 77 C3
Chiswell Rd BH17 ... 187 B1
Chitty Rd PO4 ... 183 A1
Chivers Cl PO5 ... 215 B1
Chorley Cl BH15 ... 202 B3
Chris Cres BH16 ... 201 B4
Christ the King RC Prim Sch BH11 ... 189 A3
Christchurch Bay Rd BH25 ... 209 C4
Christchurch By-Pass BH23 ... 207 B4
Christchurch Castle* BH23 ... 207 B3
Christchurch Cty Jun Sch BH23 ... 207 A4
Christchurch Cty Prim Sch BH23 ... 207 A4
Christchurch Gdns
 Waterlooville PO7 ... 134 A1
 1 Winchester SO23 ... 10 C3
Christchurch Hospl BH23 ... 206 C4
Christchurch Priory* BH23 ... 207 B3
Christchurch Rd
 Barton on Sea BH25 ... 209 B4
 Bournemouth BH1, BH7 ... 205 B2
 Ferndown BH22 ... 165 B1
 Hordle SO41 ... 211 B4
 Hurn BH23 ... 191 B3
 Ringwood BH24 ... 141 A2
 Winchester SO23 ... 10 C3
Christchurch Ski Ctr BH23 ... 167 A2
Christchurch Sta BH23 ... 207 A4
Christie Ave PO15 ... 129 B4
Christine Ct 9 SO18 ... 103 C4
Christopher Cres BH15 ... 202 B3
Christopher Way PO10 ... 136 C1
Christophers BH21 ... 163 B1
Christyne Ct PO7 ... 134 B2
Church Cl
 Bishopstoke SO50 ... 56 B2
 Clanfield PO8 ... 88 A3
 Locks Heath SO31 ... 129 A2
 Minstead SO43 ... 98 B1
 North Baddesley SO52 ... 54 A2
Church End SO15 ... 102 B4
Church Farm SP6 ... 93 C4
Church Farm Cl SO45 ... 125 A3
Church Hatch SP5 ... 47 A4
Church Hill
 Milford on Sea SO41 ... 211 C2
 Redlynch SP5 ... 47 C3
 Verwood BH31 ... 114 C3
 West End SO18,SO30 ... 80 B1
Church La Awbridge SO51 ... 26 C2
 Boldre SO41 ... 173 C1
 Botley SO30 ... 106 A3
 Braishfield SO51 ... 28 B4
 Bramdean SO24 ... 15 B2
 Brockenhurst SO42 ... 173 A4
 Burley BH24 ... 143 A2
 Bursledon SO31 ... 128 A4
 Christchurch BH23 ... 207 A3
 Colden Common SO21 ... 56 C4
 Curdridge SO32 ... 106 B4
 Damerham SP6 ... 68 B2
 Durley SO32 ... 81 C3
 East Boldre SO42 ... 175 B3
 Fawley SO45 ... 151 A2
 Ferndown BH22 ... 189 C4
 Hambledon PO7 ... 86 B2
 Havant PO9 ... 160 A4
 Hedge End SO30 ... 105 A3
 Kings Worthy SO23 ... 2 B3
 Littleton SO22 ... 1 A3
 Lymington SO41 ... 197 C2
 Lyndhurst SO43 ... 121 C3
 Meonstoke SO32 ... 61 B4
 Mottisfont SO51 ... 5 C1
 New Milton BH25 ... 194 C1
 North Hayling PO11 ... 160 B2
 Nursling SO16 ... 76 C3
 Plaitford SO51 ... 50 A3
 Romsey SO51 ... 52 C4
 Sherfield English SO51 ... 25 B2
 17 Southampton SO14 ... 102 C2
 Southampton, Highfield SO17 ... 79 A1
 Swanmore SO32 ... 84 B3
 Sway SO41 ... 172 A1
 Twyford SO21 ... 32 A4
 West Meon GU32 ... 37 B3
 Winchester SO21 ... 2 C3
Church Mead 12 SO41 ... 197 C1
Church Path
 3 Emsworth PO10 ... 160 C4
 Fareham PO16 ... 131 B1
 Gosport PO12 ... 181 B2
 Horndean PO8 ... 112 B3
 Titchfield PO14 ... 154 A4
Church Path N PO1 ... 215 C4
Church Pl SO51 ... 52 C4
Church Rd
 Bishopstoke SO50 ... 56 B3
 Bournemouth BH6 ... 206 C2
 Ferndown BH22 ... 165 B3
 Froxfield GU34 ... 17 B2
 Gosport PO12 ... 181 A1
 Locks Heath SO31 ... 129 A2
 Locks Heath, Newtown SO31 ... 152 B4
 Michelmersh SO51 ... 6 B1
 Poole BH14 ... 203 A2
 Portchester PO16 ... 156 C3
 Portsmouth PO1 ... 215 C4
 Romsey SO51 ... 52 C4
 Shedfield SO32 ... 107 C4
 Soberton PO17 ... 109 B3
 South Hayling PO11 ... 185 A3
 Southampton SO19 ... 103 B1
Church Rd *continued*
 Southbourne PO10 ... 161 C4
 Steep GU32 ... 40 C4
 Swanmore SO32 ... 84 A3
 Thorney Island PO10 ... 161 B1
 Three Legged Cross BH21 ... 114 C1
 Westbourne PO10 ... 137 A2
Church St
 Christchurch BH23 ... 207 A3
 East Meon GU32 ... 38 C1
 Fordingbridge SP6 ... 93 C4
 Liss GU33 ... 20 C3
 Poole BH15 ... 202 A1
 Portsmouth PO1 ... 215 C4
 Romsey SO51 ... 52 C4
 Southampton SO15 ... 78 B1
 Titchfield PO14 ... 154 A4
 Upham SO32 ... 58 C3
 10 Wimborne Minst BH21 ... 163 A3
Church View
 Portsmouth PO4 ... 183 A3
 Shedfield SO32 ... 107 C4
 Westbourne PO10 ... 137 A2
Church View Cl SO19 ... 104 A2
Church Wlk SP5 ... 48 A3
Churcher Cl PO12 ... 180 B2
Churcher Rd PO10 ... 137 A2
Churcher Wlk PO12 ... 180 B2
Churcher's Coll GU31 ... 41 A2
Churchers Coll Jun Sch GU32 ... 40 C2
Churchfield BH31 ... 114 C3
Churchfield Cres BH15 ... 202 C2
Churchfield Ct BH15 ... 202 C2
Churchfield La BH24 ... 93 C1
Churchfield Rd
 Petersfield GU31 ... 41 A2
 Poole BH15 ... 202 C2
Churchfields SO45 ... 151 A2
Churchfields Rd SO21 ... 32 A3
Churchill Ave SO32 ... 59 A1
Churchill Cl Alderholt SP6 ... 92 C3
 Titchfield PO14 ... 129 B1
Churchill Cres BH12 ... 203 B3
Churchill Ct Cosham PO6 ... 158 C4
 New Milton BH25 ... 194 C1
 Waterlooville PO8 ... 112 A3
Churchill Dr PO10 ... 136 C2
Churchill Dro BH21 ... 91 B4
Churchill Gdns BH12 ... 203 B3
Churchill Ho SO18 ... 104 B4
Churchill Mews PO12 ... 181 A3
Churchill Rd
 Bournemouth BH1 ... 205 B3
 Poole BH12 ... 203 B3
 Wimborne Minst BH21 ... 163 C2
Churchill Sq PO4 ... 183 A1
Churchill Yard Ind Est PO7 ... 111 C1
Churchmoor Rd BH21 ... 164 A3
Churchward Gdns SO30 ... 81 B1
Cinderford Cl 32 PO6 ... 133 A1
Cinnamon Ct SO15 ... 102 C3
Cinnamon La 10 BH15 ... 202 A1
Circle The
 3 Bournemouth BH9 ... 190 A2
 Poole BH13 ... 214 C4
 Portsmouth PO5 ... 182 B1
 Wickham PO17 ... 108 A2
Circular Rd PO1 ... 182 B4
Cirrus Gdns SO31 ... 127 C1
City Bldgs PO1 ... 215 B4
City Bsns Ctr SO23 ... 11 A4
City Commerce Ctr 29 SO14 ... 103 A2
City Ind Pk SO15 ... 102 C2
City of Portsmouth Boys Sch PO2 ... 157 C2
City of Portsmouth Girls' Sch PO1 ... 182 C3
City of Toronto Homes SO16 ... 101 C4
City Rd SO23 ... 10 C4
Civic Centre Rd
 Havant PO9 ... 135 C1
 Southampton SO14 ... 102 C3
Civic Way PO16 ... 131 B1
Clacton Rd PO6 ... 157 B4
Claire Ct BH23 ... 209 A4
Claire Gdns PO8 ... 88 B1
Clamp Gn 4 SO21 ... 56 C4
Clandon Dr SO50 ... 55 C3
Clanfield Cl SO53 ... 55 B3
Clanfield Dr SO53 ... 55 B3
Clanfield Ho 7 PO1 ... 215 C4
Clanfield Jun Sch PO8 ... 88 A4
Clanfield Rd SO18 ... 104 B4
Clanfield Way SO53 ... 55 B3
Clanwilliam Rd PO13 ... 179 C1
Clare Cl PO14 ... 129 B1
Clare Gdns
 Blackfield SO45 ... 177 C4
 Petersfield GU31 ... 41 B2
Clare Ho PO12 ... 180 C4
Clare Lodge Cl BH23 ... 169 A1
Claremont Ave BH9 ... 190 A1
Claremont Cl 1 SO50 ... 56 A3
Claremont Cres SO15 ... 102 A4
Claremont Gdns PO7 ... 134 C2
Claremont Rd
 Bournemouth BH9 ... 190 A1
 Portsmouth PO1 ... 215 D3
 Southampton SO15 ... 102 A4
Clarence Espl PO5 ... 182 B1
Clarence Ho 5 SO14 ... 103 B3
Clarence Par PO5 ... 182 B1
Clarence Park Rd BH7 ... 206 A3

larence Rd
iosport PO12 181 B3
yndhurst SO43 121 C3
3 Poole BH14 203 A2
Portsmouth PO5 182 B1
larence St PO1 215 B4
larendon Cl
Broadstone BH18 187 A2
10 Romsey SO51 28 A1
larendon Cres PO14 129 B1
larendon Ct
Bournemouth BH2 204 B1
9 Portsmouth PO5 182 B1
arendon Pk SO41 197 B1
arendon Pl PO1 215 C4
arendon Rd
Bournemouth BH4 204 B2
Broadstone BH18 186 C2
Christchurch BH23 207 A4
6 Havant PO9 135 C1
Portsmouth PO5 182 B1
outhampton SO16 102 A4
arendon St PO1 215 C4
ark's Cl BH24 141 A4
arke's Rd PO1 182 C3
aude Ashby Cl SO18 79 C2
audeen Cl SO18 79 C3
audeen Ct SO19 104 C3
audia Ct PO12 180 C3
audius Cl SO53 55 C4
audius Gdns SO53 55 C4
ausen Way SO41 197 B1
ausentum Cl SO53 55 C4
ausentum Rd
outhampton SO14 103 A4
Vinchester SO23 10 C3
ave Cl PO13 179 C1
axton St PO1 215 C3
ay Hill SO43 122 A2
ay St SP5 24 A2
aybank Rd PO3 158 A1
aybank Spur PO3 158 A1
aydon Ave PO4 183 A2
ayfields Sports Ctr
O45 125 B2
ayford Ave BH22 165 A4
ayford Cl BH17 187 B1
ayhall Rd PO12 181 A1
ayhill Cl SO32 83 B2
aylake Dr BH31 115 A3
aylands Ct SO32 83 A4
aylands Rd SO32 83 A4
aylands Road Ind Est
O32 83 A4
aypit La GU32 18 B3
aypits La SO45 125 B2
easby Cl SO16 101 C4
easby Grange 26 BH5 205 C2
ease Way SO21 31 B4
ee Ave PO14 154 B4
eethorpes Rd SO19 104 A2
eeve Cl PO6 133 A1
eeves Cl BH12 188 B1
eeves The SO40 100 B3
egg Rd PO4 183 A2
em's Way SO51 5 A1
ematis Cl BH23 208 B4
ement Atlee Way PO6 157 A4
ement Mews BH4 204 A2
eric Ct PO14 129 B2
eveland Cl BH25 209 B4
eveland Ct
ournemouth BH2 204 B1
7 Southampton SO18 80 A1
eveland Dr
areham PO14 154 B4
ythe SO45 125 B1
eveland Gdns BH1 205 B3
eveland Rd
ournemouth BH1 205 B3
osport PO12 181 A2
ortsmouth PO5 215 D2
outhampton SO18 79 C1
evelands Cl SO53 30 A1
ewers Hill SO32 83 B2
ewers La SO32 83 C2
iff Cres BH25 209 C4
iff Dr
Christchurch BH23 208 B3
Poole BH13 214 C3
iff Ho 10 BH6 206 C2
iff Rd
Milford on Sea SO41 211 A2
Southampton SO15 102 B3
Stubbington PO14 153 C1
liff Terr BH25 209 C3
liff The SO19 103 B2
liff Way SO21 31 B4
liffdale Prim Sch PO2 157 C1
liffe Ave SO31 127 C2
liffe Rd BH25 209 C4
lifford Dibben Mews 1
SO14 103 A4
lifford Pl SO50 57 B1
lifford Rd BH9 190 A1
lifford St 13 SO14 103 A3
lifton Cres PO7 111 A2
lifton Ct
18 Bournemouth BH5 205 C2
19 New Milton BH25 195 A1
15 Southampton SO15 102 A4
Clifton Gdns
Ferndown BH22 165 B2
14 Southampton SO15 102 A4
West End SO18 80 B1
Clifton Hill SO22 10 C4
Clifton Lodge SO15 102 A4
Clifton Lodge No 1 32
SO22 10 C4
Clifton Lodge No 2 33
SO22 10 C4
Clifton Rd
Bournemouth BH6 206 B2
Lee-on-the-Solent PO13 180 A2
Poole BH14 203 C1
25 Portsmouth PO5 182 B1
Southampton SO15 102 A4
Winchester SO22 10 C4
Clifton St Gosport PO12 180 C3
Portsmouth PO1 215 D4
Clifton Terr
24 Portsmouth PO5 182 B1
Winchester SO23 10 C4
Clingan Rd BH6 206 B4
Clinton Cl BH23 194 A1
Clinton Rd
Lymington SO41 197 C3
Waterlooville PO7 111 B1
Clipper Cl SO31 128 C1
Clitheroe Cotts SO42 148 C1
Clive Ct 19 BH4 204 B2
Clive Gr PO16 156 B4
Clive Rd
Bournemouth BH9 189 C1
Christchurch BH23 193 C1
Portsmouth PO1 182 C3
Cliveden Cl BH22 165 B4
Clock Ho 12 PO7 134 C4
Clock St 10 PO1 182 A3
Clocktower Dr PO4 183 A1
Cloisters The
Christchurch BH23 207 A3
Fareham PO15 130 B1
Lymington SO41 197 C2
Ringwood BH24 141 B3
Romsey SO51 52 C4
Southampton SO16 79 A2
Close Bellfield The
PO14 153 C4
Close The
Barton on Sea BH25 210 A4
Broadstone BH18 186 C2
Colden Common SO21 31 B1
Cosham PO6 158 A4
Fordingbridge SP6 94 B4
Hamble-le-Rice SO31 128 A2
Hedge End SO30 105 A3
Holbury SO45 150 B2
Langrish GU32 39 B2
Portchester PO16 156 B4
Redlynch SP5 47 B4
Ringwood BH24 140 C4
Southampton SO18 104 B4
St Leonards, Avon Castle
BH24 140 B2
St Leonards, St Ives BH24 140 A2
Sway SO41 172 A1
Whitsbury SP6 45 A2
Closewood Rd PO7 111 A1
Clough La BH24 142 C2
Clough's Rd BH24 141 A4
Clovelly Rd
Emsworth PO10 160 C4
North Hayling PO11 160 B2
Portsmouth PO4 183 A2
Southampton SO14 103 A3
Southbourne PO10 137 B1
Clover Cl
Christchurch BH23 208 A4
Gosport PO13 155 A2
Locks Heath SO31 128 C1
Clover Ct
New Milton BH25 195 B2
Waterlooville PO7 135 A3
Clover Dr BH17 186 C1
Clover Nooke SO15 101 B4
Clover Way
Hedge End SO30 105 A3
Romsey SO51 53 B4
Clovers The BH12 204 A4
Clowes Ave BH6 207 A2
Clump Hill BH21 114 A1
Cluster Ind Est PO4 183 A3
Clyde Ct PO12 180 C3
Clyde Ho 24 SO14 103 B3
Clyde Rd Gosport PO12 180 C3
Poole BH17 187 A1
Clydebank Rd PO2 182 B4
Clydesdale Rd PO15 129 A4
Clydesdale Way SO40 100 A4
Coach Hill PO14 153 C4
Coach Hill Cl SO53 55 A4
Coach Hill La BH24 142 C3
Coach House Pl BH1 205 A3
Coach Rd SO31 127 C2
Coach Rd The
East Tytherley SP5 4 B4
West Tytherley SP5 4 B4
Coach-House Mews
PO4 183 B2
Coachmans Copse SO18 80 A1
Coachmans Halt PO7 86 B1
Coal Park La SO31 128 B4
Coalville Rd SO19 104 A2
Coastguard Cl PO12 180 C1
Coastguard Cotts
Exbury SO45 178 A1
Havant PO9 159 C3
Lymington SO41 198 A1
Coastguard Way BH23 207 C3
Coat Gdns SO45 126 A2
Coates Rd SO19 104 B2
Coates Way PO7 134 C3
Cobalt Ct PO13 180 B3
Cobb's Rd BH21 163 C3
Cobbett Cl SO22 10 B3
Cobbett Ct 15 SO18 103 C4
Cobbett Rd SO18 103 C4
Cobbett Way SO30 105 C4
Cobblers Cnr SO41 173 A2
Cobblewood PO10 136 C2
Cobbs La BH15 202 C3
Cobden Ave
Portsmouth PO3 183 A4
Southampton SO18 103 C4
Cobden Cres SO18 103 C4
Cobden Ct SO18 103 C4
Cobden Gdns SO18 79 C1
Cobden Hts SO18 79 C1
Cobden Marine Ct SO17 103 B4
Cobden Rise SO18 79 C1
Cobden St PO12 181 A3
Cobham Gr PO15 129 C3
Cobham Rd
Bournemouth BH9 190 A2
Ferndown BH21 165 A4
Cobham Way BH21 163 C1
Coblands Ave SO40 100 B4
Coburg Ho 6 SO14 103 B3
Coburg St
Portsmouth PO1 215 C4
Southampton SO14 103 B3
Cochrane Cl PO13 180 B3
Cochrane Ho 15 PO1 182 A3
Cockerell Cl
Locks Heath PO15 129 B3
Oakley BH21 163 C1
Cockleshell Cl SO31 128 C1
Cockleshell Gdns PO4 183 B2
Cocklydown La SO40 100 B3
Cockshott La GU32 19 B1
Codogan Ct 14 BH1 205 A2
Cogdean Cl BH21 186 C4
Cogdean Way BH21 186 C4
Cogdean Wlk BH21 186 C4
Cogdeane Rd BH17 187 B1
Coghlan Cl PO16 131 A1
Coker Cl SO22 10 C4
Colborne Ave BH21 163 C3
Colborne Cl SO41 197 C3
Colbourne Cl
Bransgore BH23 193 A4
Poole BH15 202 B1
Colbourne Ct 6 SO23 2 A1
Colburn Cl SO16 77 B1
Colbury Gr PO9 135 B2
Colchester Ave SO50 56 C2
Colchester Rd PO6 133 C1
Cold East Cl SO31 128 C3
Cold Harbour Cl PO17 107 C2
Coldeast Hospl SO31 128 C3
Coldeast Way SO31 128 C3
Colden Common Prim Sch
SO21 56 C4
Coldharbour Farm Rd
PO10 136 C1
Coldharbour La SO16,
SO51 77 A4
Coldhill La PO8 111 C4
Cole Hill SO32 85 B3
Cole's La SP5 48 C3
Colebrook Ave
Portsmouth PO3 183 A4
Southampton SO15 78 B1
Colebrook Pl SO23 11 A4
Colebrook St SO23 11 A4
Colehill Cres BH9 190 A2
Colehill Fst Sch BH21 164 A4
Colehill La BH21 163 C4
Coleman Rd BH11 189 A2
Coleman St SO14 103 A2
Colemore Rd BH7 206 B4
Colemore Sq PO9 135 C2
Colenso Rd PO16 131 A1
Coleridge Cl SO31 128 B1
Coleridge Ct SO19 104 B3
Coleridge Gdns PO8 111 C2
Coleridge Gn BH23 207 C4
Coleridge Rd PO6 132 C1
Coles Ave BH15 201 C1
Coles Cl SO21 32 A4
Coles Gdns BH15 201 C1
Coles Mede SO21 31 A2
Colesbourne Rd PO6 133 A1
Coleson Rd SO18 103 C4
Coleville Ave SO45 151 A2
Colin Cl BH21 186 B3
Colinton Ave PO16 132 B1
Coll of Air Traffic Control
BH23 190 C4
Collard Way 4 GU33 20 C2
College Cl
Hamble-le-Rice SO31 127 C1
Rowland's Castle PO9 113 B1
College Keep SO14 103 A2
College La 16 PO1 182 A3
College Park Inf Sch
PO2 157 C1
College Pl 8 SO15 103 A3
College Rd
Bournemouth BH5 206 A2
Portsmouth PO1 182 A3
Ringwood BH24 141 A4
Southampton SO19 103 C1
Waterlooville PO7 134 C2
College St
Petersfield GU31, GU32 40 C2
Portsmouth PO1 182 A3
Southampton SO14 103 A2
Winchester SO23 11 A4
College Wlk SO23 11 A3
Collett Cl SO30 81 A1
Colley Cl SO23 2 A2
Collier Cl SO17 103 B4
Collingbourne Ave BH6 206 A4
Collingbourne Dr SO53 55 A3
Collington Cres PO6 133 A1
Collingwood Ho PO15 130 B1
Collingwood Rd
Portsmouth PO5 182 B1
West Moors BH21 138 C3
Collingwood Ret Pk
PO14 155 A3
Collingworth Rise SO31 129 A3
Collins Cl SO53 54 C3
Collins Ho SO53 55 B3
Collins La
Ringwood BH24 141 A4
South Harting GU31 66 C4
Collins Rd PO4 183 A1
Collins' La SO21 30 B4
Collis Rd PO3 183 A4
Collwood Cl BH15 202 B4
Collyers Rd SO42 172 C4
Colman Ct BH1 205 B2
Colne Ave SO16 77 B1
Colne Ct SO16 77 C1
Colombine Cl BH23 193 A1
Colonnade Rd 5 BH5 206 A3
Colonnade Rd W 4
BH5 206 A3
Colonnade The SO19 103 B2
Colpoy St PO5 215 A2
Colson Cl SO23 11 A4
Colson Rd SO23 11 A4
Colt Cl Rownhams SO16 77 C3
Wimborne Minst BH21 164 A3
Colton Copse SO53 54 C3
Colts Rd SO16 77 C4
Coltsfoot Cl SO30 105 A4
Coltsfoot Dr
Locks Heath SO31 128 C1
4 Waterlooville PO7 134 C3
Coltsfoot Wlk SO51 28 B1
Coltsmead PO6 156 C4
Columbia Rd BH10 189 B1
Columbia Trees La
BH10 189 B1
Columbian Way BH10 189 B1
Colvedene Cl SO21 31 C1
Colville Cl BH5 206 A3
Colville Dr SO32 83 B4
Colville Rd
6 Bournemouth BH5 206 A3
Cosham PO6 158 A4
Colvin Gdns SO53 55 A4
Colwell Cl SO16 101 B4
Colwell Rd PO6 157 C4
Combe Down SO21 31 C4
Combe Rd GU33 21 A1
Comber Rd 5 BH9 190 A2
Comet Way BH23 208 A3
Comfrey Cl Horndean PO8 88 B1
Romsey SO51 28 B1
Comines Way SO30 104 C4
Comley Hill PO9 136 B3
Comley Rd BH9 189 C1
Commercial Pl PO1 215 B4
Commercial Rd
Bournemouth BH2 204 C2
Poole BH14 203 A2
Portsmouth PO1 215 B4
Southampton SO15 102 C3
Totton SO40 101 A4
Commercial St SO18 104 A4
Commodore Ct 30 SO14 103 A2
Common Barn La PO13 179 C2
Common Cl SO53 55 B4
Common Gdns SO53 55 B4
Common Hill Rd SO51 28 B3
Common La
Southwick PO17 132 C4
Titchfield PO14 153 C4
Common Rd
Chandler's Ford SO53 55 B4
Westbourne PO10 137 C3
Whiteparish SP5 24 A1
Common St PO1 215 C4
Commonside PO10 137 A3
Compass Cl
Gosport PO13 180 B3
Southampton SO19 104 A2
Compass Point
Fareham PO16 155 A4
Hamble-le-Rice SO31 127 C1
Compass Rd PO6 157 A4
Compton & Up Marden CE
Prim Sch PO18 90 C1
Compton Acres Gdns*
BH13 214 C4
Compton All Saints CE Prim
Sch SO21 31 B4
Compton Ave BH14 203 B1
Compton Beeches
BH24 140 A3
Compton Cl
Eastleigh SO50 55 C3
Havant PO9 135 C2
23 Lee-on-the-Solent
PO13 179 C1
Verwood BH31 114 C3
Winchester SO22 10 A2
Compton Cres BH22 139 A1
Compton Ct
4 Havant PO9 135 C1
Poole BH14 203 B2
Compton Dr BH14 203 B1
Compton Gdns BH14 203 B1
Compton Ho 4 SO16 102 A4
Compton Rd
New Milton BH25 195 A1
Compton Rd *continued*
Portsmouth PO2 157 C2
Totton SO40 101 A4
Winchester SO23 10 C4
Compton St SO21 31 B4
Compton Way SO22 10 A2
Compton Wlk 23 SO14 103 A3
Compton's Dr SO51 50 A3
Conan Rd PO2 157 C2
Concorde Cl PO15 129 B3
Concorde Way PO15 129 B3
Condor Ave PO16 155 C4
Condor Cl
Southampton SO19 103 B2
Three Legged Cross BH21 139 A3
Coney Gn 4 SO23 2 A1
Conference Dr SO31 129 A2
Conference Pl 11 SO41 197 C1
Conford Ct PO9 135 B3
Congleton Cl SO43 98 B2
Conifer Ave BH14 203 A1
Conifer Cl
Christchurch BH23 191 B2
Ferndown BH22 165 C1
Hythe SO45 125 C2
St Leonards BH24 139 B2
Waterlooville PO8 112 A1
Winchester SO22 1 C1
Conifer Cres SO41 197 A2
Conifer Gr PO13 155 B2
Conifer Mews PO16 132 B1
Conifer Rd SO16 78 A2
Conigar Rd PO10 136 C2
Coniston Ave
Bournemouth BH11 188 C3
Portsmouth PO3 183 A4
Coniston Cl BH31 114 C3
Coniston Gdns SO30 105 A3
Coniston Ho 19 PO6 133 A1
Coniston Rd
Eastleigh SO50 55 C1
Ringwood BH24 141 A3
Southampton SO16 101 B4
Coniston Wlk PO14 154 C4
Connaught Cl BH25 194 C1
Connaught Cres BH12 203 C3
Connaught Hall SO18 79 B2
Connaught La PO6 156 C4
Connaught Pl 5 PO9 136 A1
Connaught Rd
Bournemouth BH5 206 A3
Havant PO9 136 A1
Portsmouth PO2 157 B1
Connell Rd BH15 202 B3
Connemara Cres PO15 129 A4
Connigar Cl PO13 180 B4
Conqueror Way PO14 179 B3
Conrad Gdns PO15 129 B4
Conservatory The 48
SO23 11 A4
Consort Cl Eastleigh SO50 56 A3
Poole BH12 203 B3
Consort Ho 9 PO1 182 B4
Consort Rd SO50 56 A3
Constable Cl
Gosport PO12 181 B1
Southampton SO19 104 B1
Constables Gate 28 SO22 10 C4
Constantine Ave SO53 55 C3
Constantine Cl SO53 55 C3
Constitution Hill Gdns
BH14 203 A3
Constitution Hill Rd
BH14 203 A3
Consulate Ho 32 SO14 103 A2
Convent Ct PO10 160 C4
Convent La PO10 160 C4
Conway Cl
Chandler's Ford SO53 55 A2
New Milton BH25 195 A2
Conway Ct 20 BH25 195 A2
Conways Dr BH14 203 A2
Cook Cl BH24 141 B4
Cook Row BH21 163 A2
Cook St SO14 103 A2
Cooke Gdns BH12 203 C3
Cooke Rd BH12 203 C3
Cooks La Awbridge SO51 27 A2
Lockerley SO51 25 C4
Southbourne PO10 137 B1
Totton SO40 76 B1
Cooley Ho PO13 155 A3
Coolhurst BH14 214 B4
Coombe Ave BH10 189 C2
Coombe Farm Ave
PO16 155 A4
Coombe Gdns BH10 189 C1
Coombe La SO41 196 B4
Coombe Rd
East Meon GU32 63 B4
Gosport PO12 181 A4
Coombe Road Terr GU32 63 B4
Coombedale SO31 129 A1
Coombs Cl PO8 88 B1
Cooper Dean Dr BH8 190 C1
Cooper Dean Rdbt BH7,
BH8 191 A1
Cooper Gr PO16 156 B3
Cooper Rd Ashurst SO40 100 B2
Portsmouth PO3 183 A4
Cooper's Cl
West End SO18 80 B1
West Wellow SO51 51 A1
Cooper's La SO19 103 B2
Coopers Ct SO14 103 A2

Coopers La BH31 ....114 C4
Copeland Dr BH14 ....203 A1
Copeland Rd SO16 ....77 B1
Copenhagen Twrs 5 SO19 ....126 C4
Copinger Cl SO40 ....100 B3
Copnor Bridge Bsns Ctr PO3 ....183 A4
Copnor Inf & Jun Sch PO3 ....158 A1
Copnor Rd PO3 ....157 C2
Copper Beech Cl BH12 .204 A2
Copper Beech Dr PO6 ..158 C4
Copper Beech Gdns BH10 ....189 B1
Copper Beeches SO45 ..150 C1
Copper St 5 PO5 ....215 A1
Coppercourt Leaze 5 BH21 ....163 B2
Copperfield Ho 21 PO1 .182 B4
Copperfield Rd SO16 ....79 A3
Copperfields SO40 ....100 A4
Coppers Cl SP6 ....93 A3
Coppice Ave BH22 ....165 A4
Coppice Cl
New Milton BH25 ....195 B2
St Leonards BH24 ....139 C2
Winchester SO22 ....1 B1
Coppice Hill SO32 ....83 B4
Coppice Rd SO40 ....76 B1
Coppice The
Brockenhurst SO42 ....145 B1
Christchurch BH23 ....208 A3
Gosport PO13 ....155 B1
Waterlooville PO8 ....112 A3
Coppice View BH10 ....189 C2
Coppice Way PO15 ....130 B2
Coppins Gr PO16 ....156 B3
Copse Ave BH25 ....195 A1
Copse Cl Liss GU33 ....21 A2
North Baddesley SO52 ....53 C2
Otterbourne SO21 ....31 B2
Petersfield GU31 ....41 B2
Poole BH14 ....202 C2
Totton SO40 ....100 C3
Waterlooville PO7 ....134 B1
Copse Cvn Pk The SO40 .99 B3
Copse La Chilworth SO16 ..54 C1
Gosport PO13 ....155 B1
Hamble-le-Rice SO31 ....127 C1
North Hayling PO11 ....160 A1
Copse Rd Burley BH24 ..142 C1
New Milton BH25 ....195 A1
Southampton SO18 ....80 A1
Verwood BH31 ....114 C3
Copse The
Chandler's Ford SO53 ....55 C3
Fareham PO15 ....130 B2
Romsey SO51 ....28 B1
Copse View SO19 ....104 C3
Copse Way BH23 ....208 C4
Copsewood Ave BH8 ..190 C1
Copsewood Rd
Ashurst SO40 ....100 B2
Hythe SO45 ....125 C2
Southampton SO18 ....79 C1
Copsey Cl PO6 ....158 B4
Copsey Gr PO6 ....158 B4
Copthorne Cotts SO45 ..151 B2
Copthorne La SO45 ....151 A2
Copythorn Rd PO2 ....157 C1
Copythorne CE Inf Sch SO40 ....75 A1
Copythorne Cl BH8 ....190 B1
Copythorne Cres SO40 ..75 B2
Coracle Cl SO31 ....128 C1
Coral Cl PO16 ....156 B3
Coral Ct Gosport PO13 ..180 B3
2 Poole BH12 ....204 A2
Coralin Gr PO7 ....112 A1
Coram Cl 3 SO23 ....2 A1
Corbar Rd BH23 ....206 C4
Corbett Rd PO7 ....134 B3
Corbiere Ave BH12 ....188 B1
Corbiere Cl SO16 ....77 C2
Corbin Ave BH22 ....166 A3
Corbin Ct SO41 ....197 A1
Corbin Rd SO41 ....197 A1
Corbould Rd SO45 ....149 C4
Corby Cres PO3 ....158 A2
Cordelia Cl SO45 ....125 B2
Corfe Cl PO14 ....179 A3
Corfe Halt Cl BH21 ....162 C1
Corfe Hills Sch BH18 ....186 C3
Corfe Lodge Rd BH18, BH21 ....186 B2
Corfe Mews BH15 ....202 B2
Corfe View Rd
Corfe Mullen BH21 ....186 B3
Poole BH14 ....203 B2
Corfe Way BH18 ....186 C2
Corfu BH13 ....214 C3
Corhampton Cres PO9 .135 B2
Corhampton Ho 11 PO1 215 C4
Corhampton La
Droxford SO32 ....60 B3
Meonstoke SO32 ....61 A3
Corhampton Rd BH6 ..206 B3
Coriander Dr SO40 ....100 B4
Coriander Way PO15 ....129 B4
Corinna Gdns SO45 ....125 B2
Corinthian Rd SO53 ....55 C4
Cork La SO40 ....101 C1
Cormorant Cl PO16 ....155 C4
Cormorant Dr SO45 ....126 B1
Cormorant Wlk PO13 ...155 A1
Corn Mkt SO51 ....52 C4
Cornaway La PO16 ....156 A4
Cornbrook Gr PO7 ....112 B1
Cornel Rd SO19 ....103 C3
Cornelia Cres BH12 ....204 A3
Cornelius Dr PO7 ....112 A1
Corner Mead PO7 ....110 C2
Cornerways Ct 7 BH25 .195 A1
Cornes Cl SO22 ....10 B4
Cornfield PO16 ....131 A2
Cornfield Cl SO53 ....54 C3
Cornfield Rd PO13 ....179 C1
Cornflower Cl SO31 ....128 C2
Cornflower Dr BH23 ....208 B4
Cornford Way BH23 ....208 B4
Cornforth Rd SO40 ....76 B1
Cornish Gdns BH10 ....189 B1
Cornpits La SP6 ....68 B2
Cornwall Cl 4 SO18 ....80 A1
Cornwall Cres SO18 ....79 C1
Cornwall Rd
Chandler's Ford SO53 ....55 B2
Portsmouth PO1 ....182 C3
Southampton SO18 ....79 C1
Cornwallis Cres PO1 ...215 C4
Cornwallis Ho PO1 ....215 B4
Cornwallis Rd SO41 ....211 A2
Cornwell Cl
Gosport PO13 ....180 B4
Portsmouth PO2 ....157 A1
Coronado Rd PO12 ....181 A4
Coronation Ave
Bournemouth BH9 ....189 C1
Upton BH16 ....201 A4
Coronation Cl BH31 ....114 C4
Coronation Eventide Homes 4 PO2 ....157 C2
Coronation Homes SO18 ....104 B4
Coronation Par SO31 ...127 C2
Coronation Rd
South Hayling PO11 ....185 C1
Swanmore SO32 ....84 A3
Verwood BH31 ....114 C4
Waterlooville PO7 ....134 C4
Coronation Terr SP6 ....69 A1
Corporation Rd BH1 ...205 B3
Corpus Christi RC Prim Sch
Bournemouth BH5 ....206 A3
Portsmouth PO2 ....157 B1
Corsair Dr SO45 ....125 B2
Corscombe Cl BH17 ....187 C1
Cort Way PO15 ....130 B2
Cortina Way SO30 ....105 B3
Cortry Cl BH12 ....204 A4
Corvette Ave SO31 ....128 C1
Cosford Cl SO50 ....57 A1
Cosham Park Ave PO6 .157 C4
Cosham Sta PO6 ....157 C4
Cossack Gn 6 SO14 ....103 A2
Cossack La 20 SO23 ....11 A4
Cossack Lane Ho 23 SO23 ....11 A4
Cosworth Dr SO45 ....125 B2
Cotes Ave BH14 ....203 A3
Cotes Ct BH14 ....203 A3
Cotlands Rd BH1 ....205 A2
Cotsalls SO50 ....57 B1
Cotswold Cl Havant PO9 .135 C3
Hythe SO45 ....125 B2
Verwood BH31 ....114 C3
Cotswold Ct
6 Christchurch BH23 ....207 C4
12 Southampton SO17 ....79 A1
Cotswold Ho 3 PO6 ....157 B4
Cotswold Rd SO16 ....101 C4
Cotswold Wlk 17 PO14 ..154 C4
Cott La BH24 ....143 A1
Cott St SO32 ....84 B2
Cott Street La SO32 ....84 C2
Cottage Cl PO7 ....110 C2
Cottage Gdns BH12 ....203 B3
Cottage Gr Gosport PO12 181 A3
Portsmouth PO5 ....215 B2
Cottage Grove Prim Sch PO5 ....215 B1
Cottage La GU32 ....19 C2
Cottage Mews SP6 ....69 C1
Cottage View PO1 ....215 C3
Cottagers La SO41 ....196 A2
Cottagers The SP6 ....94 A2
Cotteridge Ho 1 PO1 ..215 C2
Cottes Way PO14 ....179 A3
Cottesway E PO14 ....179 A3
Cotton Cl
Bishopstoke SO50 ....56 C2
Corfe Mullen BH18 ....186 C3
Cotton Dr PO10 ....136 C2
Cotwell Ave PO8 ....112 A2
Coulmere Rd PO12 ....181 A3
Coulsdon Rd SO30 ....105 B3
Coultas Rd SO53 ....30 C1
Council Hos
Lockerley SO51 ....26 A3
Sopley BH23 ....167 C1
Countess Cl BH21 ....187 C4
Countess Gdns BH7 ....205 C4
Country View
Stubbington PO14 ....154 A2
West Wellow SO51 ....50 C2
County Gdns PO14 ....154 B4
Course Park Cres PO14 .129 B1
Court Barn Cl PO13 ....179 C2
Court Barn La PO13 ....179 C2
Court Cl
12 Christchurch BH23 ....207 C4
Cosham PO6 ....158 A4
Court Cl *continued*
Lymington SO41 ....197 B1
Southampton SO18 ....104 A3
Totton SO40 ....76 B1
Court Cotts SO41 ....197 B1
Court Hill SP6 ....68 C3
Court House Cl 4 SO45 126 A2
Court La PO6 ....158 A4
Court Lane Inf Sch PO6 158 A4
Court Lane Jun Sch PO6 ....158 A4
Court Mead PO6 ....158 A4
Court Rd
Bournemouth BH9 ....190 A1
Kings Worthy SO23 ....2 B3
Lee-on-the-Solent PO13 ..179 C2
Southampton SO15 ....102 C4
Court Royal Mews SO15 102 C4
Courtenay Dr BH21 ....163 B3
Courtenay Pl SO41 ....197 C2
Courtenay Rd
Poole BH14 ....203 A2
Winchester SO23 ....2 A2
Courthill Fst Sch BH14 .203 B2
Courthill Rd BH14 ....203 B2
Courtier Cl SO45 ....125 B2
Courtland Gdns SO16 ....79 A3
Courtlands SO41 ....197 C2
Courtlands Terr PO8 ...112 A2
Courtleigh Manor 6 BH5 ....205 B2
Courtmount Gr PO6 ....158 A4
Courtnay Cl PO15 ....129 B2
Courtney Pl BH21 ....186 B3
Courtyard Cl SO42 ....145 C1
Courtyard Mews SO42 ..145 C1
Courtyard The
Christchurch BH23 ....207 B3
14 Petersfield GU31 ....40 C2
Poole BH12 ....188 B1
7 Romsey SO51 ....52 C4
Cousins Gr PO4 ....182 C1
Cove Rd BH10 ....189 B1
Covena Rd BH6 ....206 C3
Coventry Cl BH21 ....186 B2
Coventry Cres BH17 ....187 A1
Coventry Ct
Gosport PO13 ....180 B3
7 Winchester SO23 ....2 A1
Coventry Rd SO15 ....102 C3
Coverack Way PO6 ....157 A4
Covert Gr PO7 ....135 A3
Covert The SO51 ....53 A3
Covindale Ho 8 PO4 ....183 A2
Covington Rd PO10 ....137 A3
Cow La Cosham PO6 ....157 B4
Portchester PO16 ....156 B4
Cowan Rd PO7 ....134 B3
Coward Rd PO12 ....180 C1
Cowdray Cl
Bishopstoke SO50 ....56 C1
Southampton SO16 ....78 A2
Cowdray Ho PO1 ....215 C3
Cowdray Pk PO14 ....179 A3
Cowdrey Gdns BH8 ....190 C1
Cowdrys Field 2 BH21 .163 A3
Cowell Dr BH7 ....206 A4
Cowes La SO31 ....152 B3
Cowgrove Rd BH21 ....162 C3
Cowleas Cl SO51 ....26 C3
Cowleas Cotts SO51 ....26 C3
Cowley Cl SO16 ....77 C1
Cowley Rd
Lymington SO41 ....197 B2
Poole BH17 ....202 B4
Cowleys Rd BH23 ....192 B1
Cowper Ave BH25 ....195 A1
Cowper Rd
Bournemouth BH9 ....189 C1
Portsmouth PO1 ....182 C4
Southampton SO19 ....104 B3
Cowpitts La BH24 ....117 B1
Cowplain Sch PO8 ....111 C1
Cowslip Cl Gosport PO13 155 B1
Locks Heath SO31 ....128 C1
Cowslip Rd BH18 ....186 C1
Cowslip Way SO51 ....28 B1
Cox Ave BH9 ....190 A2
Cox Cl BH9 ....190 A2
Cox Dale PO14 ....129 B1
Cox Row SO53 ....55 B2
Cox's Dr SO19 ....104 A1
Cox's La SO19 ....103 B2
Coxes Mdw GU32 ....40 C3
Coxford Cl SO16 ....78 A1
Coxford Dro SO16 ....78 A2
Coxford Rd SO16 ....78 A2
Coxs Hill SO21 ....32 A4
Coxstone La 2 BH24 ...141 A3
Coy Pond Rd BH12 ....204 A3
Cozens Cl SO19 ....103 C1
Crab Orchard Way BH21 ....114 C1
Crabapple Cl SO40 ....100 B4
Crabbe Ct PO5 ....215 B2
Crabbs Way SO40 ....100 A4
Crabbswood La SO41 ..195 C4
Crabden La PO8 ....88 C1
Crableck La SO31 ....128 B3
Crabthorne Farm La PO14 ....154 A2
Crabton Close Rd BH5 .205 C2
Crabtree SO16 ....77 C1
Crabtree Cl BH23 ....192 B1
Crabwood Cl SO16 ....77 C1
Crabwood Ct PO9 ....135 B4
Crabwood Dr SO30 ....80 C1
Crabwood Rd SO16 ....77 C1
Cracknore Hard SO40 ..102 A1
Cracknore Hard La SO40 ....102 A1
Cracknore Rd SO15 ....102 B3
Craddock Ho
13 Portsmouth PO1 ....182 A3
2 Winchester SO23 ....11 B4
Craigmoor Ave BH8 ....190 C1
Craigmoor Cl BH8 ....190 C1
Craigmoor Way BH8 ....190 C1
Craigside Rd BH24 ....139 B2
Craigwell Rd PO7 ....134 B2
Craigwood Dr BH22 ....165 C2
Crampmoor La SO51 ....28 C1
Cranberry Cl SO40 ....101 C1
Cranborne Cres BH12 ..203 C4
Cranborne Ct
Bournemouth BH9 ....205 A4
14 Bournemouth, Westbourne BH4 ....204 B2
Cranborne Gdns SO53 ...30 A1
Cranborne Pl BH25 ....194 C2
Cranborne Rd
Alderholt SP6, BH21 ....92 A3
Bournemouth BH2 ....204 C1
Cosham PO6 ....134 A1
Wimborne Minst BH21 ....163 B4
Cranborne Wlk PO14 ...154 C4
Cranbourne Cl SO15 ....78 B1
Cranbourne Ct BH17 ....188 A1
Cranbourne Dr SO21 ....31 A2
Cranbourne Pk SO30 ....105 B2
Cranbourne Rd PO12 ....181 B2
Cranbrook Mews BH12 .203 A3
Cranbrook Rd BH12 ....203 A3
Cranbury Ave SO14 ....103 A3
Cranbury Cl Downton SP5 .46 C3
Otterbourne SO21 ....31 A2
Cranbury Ct SO19 ....103 C2
Cranbury Gdns SO31 ....104 C1
Cranbury Pl SO14 ....103 A3
Cranbury Rd
Eastleigh SO50 ....56 A1
Southampton SO19 ....103 C2
Cranbury Terr 4 SO14 ..103 A3
Cranbury The 3 SO14 ..103 A3
Cranbury Twrs 6 SO14 .103 A3
Crane Cl Gosport PO13 ....155 A1
Verwood BH31 ....114 C3
Crane Dr BH31 ....114 C4
Crane Way BH21 ....139 A3
Cranemoor Ave BH23 ....193 C1
Cranemoor Cl BH23 ....193 C1
Cranemoor Gdns BH23 .193 C1
Cranes Mews BH15 ....202 B2
Craneswater Ave PO4 ..182 C1
Craneswater Gate 4 PO4 ....182 C1
Craneswater Jun Sch PO4 ....182 C1
Craneswater Mews 5 PO4 ....182 C1
Craneswater Pk PO4 ..182 C1
Cranfield Ave BH21 ....163 B3
Cranford Gdns SO53 ....55 A4
Cranford Ho 5 SO17 ....79 A1
Cranford Rd GU32 ....40 B1
Cranford Way SO17 ....79 A1
Cranleigh Ave PO1 ....182 C3
Cranleigh Cl BH6 ....206 C3
Cranleigh Ct BH6 ....206 C3
Cranleigh Gdns BH6 ...206 C3
Cranleigh Ho
Hedge End SO30 ....81 B2
Southampton SO17 ....103 A4
Cranleigh Paddock SO43 ....121 C3
Cranleigh Rd
Bournemouth BH6 ....206 C3
Hedge End SO30 ....105 B3
Portchester PO16 ....156 A4
Portsmouth PO1 ....182 C3
Cranmer Dr SO16 ....77 B3
Cranmer Rd BH9 ....204 C4
Cranmore SO31 ....127 B4
Cransley Ct BH4 ....204 B1
Crantock Gr BH8 ....190 C1
Cranwell Cl
Bournemouth BH11 ....188 C2
Bransgore BH23 ....169 A1
Cranwell Ct SO16 ....77 C3
Cranworth Rd SO22 ....1 C1
Crasswell St PO1 ....215 C4
Craven Ct PO15 ....130 C2
Craven Rd SO53 ....55 B3
Craven St 15 SO14 ....103 A3
Crawford Cl SO16 ....77 B3
Crawford Dr PO16 ....130 C2
Crawley Ave PO9 ....136 A3
Crawley Hill SO51 ....50 C1
Crawshaw Rd BH14 ....203 A1
Crawte Ave SO45 ....150 B1
Crawters La 24 GU31 ....40 C2
Cray Ho PO12 ....181 B2
Creasey Rd BH11 ....189 A3
Credenhill Rd PO6 ....133 B1
Creech Rd BH12 ....203 B3
Creech View PO7 ....110 C2
Creech Wood Forest Wlk★ PO7 ....110 B2
Creedy Gdns SO18 ....80 A2
Creek End PO10 ....160 C4
Creek Rd Gosport PO12 ..181 B2
South Hayling PO11 ....185 B1
Creekmoor La BH17 ....202 A4
Creighton Rd SO15 ....101 C3
Cremorne Pl 10 GU32 ...40 C2
Cremyll Cl PO14 ....179 B3
Crescent Cl SO22 ....10 A2
Crescent Cotts SO45 ...177 A3
Crescent Ct BH25 ....209 C4
Crescent Dr BH25 ....209 C4
Crescent Ho 2 SO50 ....56 A2
Crescent Prim Sch SO50 .56 A2
Crescent Rd
Bournemouth BH2 ....204 C2
Fareham PO16 ....131 A1
Gosport PO12 ....181 A1
Locks Heath SO31 ....128 C1
North Baddesley SO52 ....53 C3
Poole BH14 ....203 C2
Verwood BH31 ....115 A3
Wimborne Minst BH21 ...163 B2
Crescent The
Barton on Sea BH25 ....209 B4
3 Bournemouth BH7 ....205 C2
Eastleigh SO50 ....56 A2
Exbury SO45 ....177 A3
Marchwood SO40 ....101 C1
Netley SO31 ....127 B3
Netley Marsh SO40 ....99 C2
Romsey SO51 ....53 A4
Southampton SO19 ....104 A1
Southbourne PO10 ....161 B4
Twyford SO21 ....32 A3
Upham SO32 ....58 B1
Waterlooville PO7 ....134 B2
Crescent Wlk BH22 ....165 C1
Cressey Rd SO51 ....52 C4
Cressy Rd PO2 ....182 B4
Crest Cl PO16 ....131 B1
Crest Rd BH12 ....203 B3
Crest The PO7 ....134 B1
Crest Way SO19 ....104 B2
Cresta Ct 8 PO4 ....182 C1
Cresta Gdns BH22 ....165 C1
Crestland Cl PO8 ....112 A2
Crestwood Com Sch SO50 ....55 C3
Crete Cotts SO45 ....125 C1
Crete La SO45 ....125 C1
Crete Rd SO45 ....125 C1
Cribb Cl BH17 ....202 C4
Crichel Mount Rd BH14 214 B4
Crichel Rd BH9 ....205 A4
Crichton Ho 11 SO31 ....127 A3
Cricket Cl BH23 ....207 C3
Cricket Dr PO8 ....112 A3
Cricklemede SO32 ....83 B4
Cricklewood Cl SO32 ...83 B4
Crigdon Cl SO16 ....101 C4
Crimea Rd BH9 ....204 C4
Cringle Ave BH6 ....207 A2
Crinoline Gdns PO4 ....183 A1
Cripple Gate La
Beaulieu SO42 ....175 B3
East Boldre SO42 ....175 B3
Cripstead La SO23 ....10 C3
Crispen Cl BH23 ....208 C4
Crispin Cl Fair Oak SO50 ..81 B3
Locks Heath SO31 ....129 A2
Crisspyn Cl PO8 ....112 A3
Criterion Arc 39 BH1 ..204 C2
Crittall Cl SO41 ....172 B1
Crockford Cl BH25 ....195 A3
Crockford Rd PO10 ....137 A2
Croft Cl BH21 ....186 B4
Croft Hts SP5 ....24 A2
Croft La PO11 ....159 C1
Croft Rd
Bournemouth BH9 ....189 C1
Bransgore BH23 ....193 A3
Christchurch BH23 ....207 C4
Poole BH12 ....203 A3
Portsmouth PO2 ....157 B1
Ringwood BH24 ....117 B1
Croft The
Chandler's Ford SO53 ....55 B2
Croucheston SP5 ....22 A4
Stubbington PO14 ....154 B2
Totton SO40 ....76 B1
Croftlands Ave PO14 ...154 B2
Crofton Anne Dale Jun Sch PO14 ....179 B3
Crofton Ave PO13 ....179 B2
Crofton Cl
Christchurch BH23 ....191 C1
Southampton SO17 ....79 A1
Waterlooville PO7 ....134 B3
Crofton Ct PO14 ....179 B3
Crofton Hammond Jun & Inf Schs PO14 ....179 B3
Crofton La PO14 ....179 A3
Crofton Rd
Portsmouth, Milton PO4 ..183 A3
Portsmouth, North End PO2 ....157 C1
Crofton Sch PO14 ....179 C3
Crofton Way
Locks Heath SO31 ....128 B1
Swanmore SO32 ....84 A3
Cromalt Cl SO45 ....125 B1
Cromarty Ave PO4 ....183 A2
Cromarty Cl PO14 ....154 A2
Cromarty Rd SO16 ....77 C3
Crombie Cl PO8 ....111 C2
Cromer Gdns BH12 ....203 C3
Cromer Rd
Bournemouth BH8 ....205 B4
Cosham PO6 ....133 C1
Poole BH12 ....203 C3
Southampton SO16 ....77 B1
Cromhall Cl PO14 ....154 B4
Crompton Way PO15 ....129 B3
Cromwell Pl 9 BH5 ....206 A3

omwell Rd
ournemouth BH5 206 A3
oole BH12 203 B3
ortsmouth PO4 183 A1
outhampton SO15 102 C4
6 Wimborne Minst BH21 163 B2
Vinchester SO22 10 C3
ondall Ave PO9 135 C3
ood Ct 7 PO16 131 B1
ooked Hays Cl SO40 101 C1
ooked Walk La PO17 132 C2
ookham Cl PO9 135 B2
ookham Rd SO19 126 C4
ookhorn Com Sch The PO7 134 C2
ookhorn La
oberton SO32 85 B4
Vaterlooville PO7 134 C2
osby Rd BH4 204 B1
osfield Cl SO51 51 A1
oss House Ctr SO14 103 B2
oss Keys Pas 29 SO23 11 A4
oss La
Bishop's Waltham SO32 59 A1
Vaterlooville PO8 112 A3
oss Lanes BH24 117 B4
oss Rd
ee-on-the-Solent PO13 180 A2
Southampton SO19 103 C4
oss St
3 Bishop's Waltham SO32 83 B4
Portsmouth PO5 215 C2
Portsmouth, Portsea PO1 182 A3
Winchester SO23 10 C4
oss The Burley BH24 143 A2
East Meon GU32 38 B1
oss Trees SP6 46 A1
oss Way
Christchurch BH23 191 B1
Compton(Hants) SO21 31 B3
Havant PO9 135 C1
oss Ways BH23 169 B3
ossbill Cl PO8 112 A4
ossfell Wlk PO14 154 C4
osshouse Rd SO14 103 B2
rossland Cl PO12 181 B2
rossland Dr PO9 136 A2
rossley Ct 6 SO15 102 B3
rossmead Ave BH25 195 A1
rossway The PO16 156 B4
rossways SO41 196 B1
rossways Cl SP5 46 C4
rossways The
Denmead PO7 111 A4
Gosport PO12 181 A3
Upton BH16 201 B4
rosswell Cl SO19 104 B3
rouch La PO8 112 A4
roucher's Croft SO22 1 B1
row Arch La BH24 141 A3
row Arch Lane Ind Est BH24 141 A3
row Cotts BH24 141 B2
row Hill Top BH24 142 A2
row La BH24 141 B3
rowder Terr SO22 10 C4
rowders Gn 1 SO21 56 C4
rowe Hill Ct 2 BH15 202 C2
rown Cl Poole BH12 203 B3
Waterlooville PO7 134 C2
rown Ct
Portsmouth PO1 215 C4
8 Wimborne Minst BH21 163 A3
rown Mead BH21 163 B2
rown Mews 18 PO12 181 B2
rown St
Portsmouth PO1 215 C4
Southampton SO15 102 A4
rown Wlk 9 BH7 205 C2
rows Nest La SO32 81 C1
rowsbury Cl PO10 136 C2
rowsport SO31 128 A2
rowther Cl SO19 104 B2
roydon Cl SO16 78 A2
rummock Rd SO53 55 A4
rusader Ct PO12 181 B4
rusader Rd
Bournemouth BH11 188 B2
Hedge End SO30 105 B3
rusader Way SO53 54 C3
ruse Cl SO41 172 A1
ruxton Farm Ctyd BH21 163 B1
Crystal Way PO7 135 A4
Cucklington Gdns BH9 190 A2
Cuckmere La SO16 101 B4
Cuckoo Bushes La SO53 55 B4
Cuckoo Hill Rly★ SP6 94 B1
Cuckoo Hill Way BH23 169 B1
Cuckoo La
22 Southampton SO14 102 C2
Stubbington PO14 154 A2
Cuckoo Rd BH12 203 A4
Cudnell Ave BH11 189 A3
Cudworth Mead SO30 81 B1
Cuffnells Cl BH24 117 A4
Cul-de-sac BH25 209 B4
Culford Ave SO40 100 C3
Culford Cl BH8 190 C1
Culford Ct 1 BH8 205 A3
Culford Way SO40 100 C3
Cull Cl BH12 204 B4
Cull La BH25 195 A3
Culliford Cres BH17 187 C1
Culloden Cl PO15 130 C1
Culloden Rd PO14 154 C3
Cullwood La BH25 195 B3
Culver SO31 127 B4
Culver Cl SO16 77 B1
Culver Dr PO11 185 B1
Culver Mews SO23 11 A4
Culver Rd
New Milton BH25 194 C1
Portsmouth PO4 183 A1
35 Winchester SO23 11 A4
Culverhayes Pl BH21 163 A3
Culverhayes Rd BH21 163 A3
Culverin Sq PO3 158 A2
Culverlands Cl SO32 107 C4
Culverley Cl SO42 145 C1
Culverwell Gdns 25 SO23 10 C4
Culvery Gdns SO18 80 A1
Cumber Rd SO31 128 C2
Cumberland Ave
Chandler's Ford SO53 55 C3
Emsworth PO10 136 C2
Cumberland Bsns Ctr PO1 215 C3
Cumberland Cl SO53 55 C3
Cumberland Ho PO1 182 A4
Cumberland House Natural History Mus★ PO5 182 C1
Cumberland Inf Sch PO4 183 A2
Cumberland Pl SO15 102 C3
Cumberland Rd PO1 215 D3
Cumberland St
Portsmouth PO1 182 A3
Southampton SO14 103 A2
Cumberland Way SO45 125 B2
Cumbrian Way SO16 101 C4
Cummins Gn SO31 105 A1
Cumnor Rd BH1 205 A2
Cunard Ave SO15 102 B4
Cunard Rd SO14 103 A1
Cundell Way SO23 2 A4
Cunningham Ave SO32 83 A4
Cunningham Cl
Bournemouth BH11 189 A2
Christchurch BH23 208 A3
Portsmouth PO2 157 B2
Ringwood BH24 141 B4
Cunningham Cres
Bournemouth BH11 189 A2
Southampton SO19 104 A2
Cunningham Ct
New Milton BH25 194 C2
1 Portsmouth PO5 182 B1
Cunningham Dr
Gosport PO13 155 B2
Locks Heath SO31 129 A2
Cunningham Gdns SO31 127 C4
Cunningham Ho SO32 83 A4
Cunningham Pl BH11 189 A2
Cunningham Rd
Horndean PO8 112 B4
Waterlooville PO7 134 B3
Cupernham Cl SO51 28 A1
Cupernham Inf Sch SO51 28 A1
Cupernham Jun Sch SO51 28 A1
Cupernham La SO51 28 A1
Curdridge Cl 52 PO9 136 A3
Curdridge La SO32 83 B2
Curdridge Prim Sch SO32 106 B4
Curlew Cl
Emsworth PO10 160 C4
Ferndown BH22 165 A4
16 Hythe SO45 126 A1
Southampton SO16 78 A3
Curlew Dr Hythe SO45 126 A1
Portchester PO16 155 C4
Curlew Gdns PO8 111 C2
Curlew Path 7 PO4 183 A3
Curlew Rd
Bournemouth BH8 190 B1
Christchurch BH23 208 A3
Curlew Sq SO50 55 C1
Curlew Wlk
Gosport PO13 155 A2
Hythe SO45 126 A1
Curlews The BH31 115 A3
Curlieu Rd BH15 202 B3
Curtis Mead PO2 157 C2
Curtis Rd BH12 203 B3
Curtiss Gdns PO12 180 C2
Curve The Gosport PO13 155 A1
Horndean PO8 111 C3
Curzon Ct
32 Bournemouth BH4 204 B2
Southampton SO16 78 B2
Curzon Howe Rd PO1 182 A3
Curzon Pl SO41 197 B1
Curzon Rd
Bournemouth BH1 205 B3
Poole BH14 203 A2
Waterlooville PO7 134 C4
Curzon Way BH23 208 B4
Custards Rd SO43 121 C3
Custards The SO43 122 A3
Cut Throat La
Droxford SO32 61 A1
Swanmore SO32 84 B3
Cutbush La
Southampton SO18 104 A4
West End SO18 80 A2
Cuthbert Rd PO1 182 C3
Cuthburga Rd BH21 163 B2
Cuthbury Cl BH21 163 A2
Cuthbury Gdns BH21 163 A3
Cutler Cl
New Milton BH25 195 B2
Poole BH12 204 B4
Cutlers La PO14 154 B2
Cutlers Pl BH21 164 A3
Cutter Ave SO31 128 C1
Cutts Arch Droxford SO32 85 A3
Soberton SO32 85 A3
Cygnet Ct PO16 155 C4
Cygnet Ho PO12 181 A4
Cygnet Rd PO6 158 C4
Cygnus Gdns SO45 125 B2
Cynthia Cl BH12 203 A4
Cynthia Ho BH12 203 A4
Cynthia Rd BH12 203 A4
Cypress Ave SO19 103 C3
Cypress Cres PO8 112 A3
Cypress Gdns
Botley SO30 106 A4
Totton SO40 100 B4
Cypress Gr SO41 211 B4
Cyprus Rd
Portsmouth PO2 182 C4
Titchfield PO14 129 B1
Cyril Rd BH8 205 B3

D

D Ave SO45 150 C3
D-Day Mus★ PO5 182 B1
Dacombe Cl BH16 201 B4
Dacombe Dr BH16 201 B4
Dacres Wlk 3 SO41 211 B3
Daffodil Rd SO16 79 B2
Daggons Rd SP6 92 B3
Dahlia Rd SO17 79 A2
Daintree Cl SO19 104 B2
Dairy Cl
Christchurch BH23 207 B4
Corfe Mullen BH21 186 A2
Dairy La SO16 77 A3
Dairymoor PO17 108 A2
Daisy La Gosport PO12 181 A2
Locks Heath SO31 129 B2
Daisy Mead PO7 135 A4
Daisy Rd SO16 79 A2
Dakota Cl BH23 208 A4
Dale Cl Littleton SO22 1 A3
Poole BH15 202 C3
Dale Dr PO13 155 A3
Dale Park Ho 4 PO1 215 B3
Dale Rd Hythe SO45 125 C2
Poole BH15 202 C3
Southampton SO16 78 B1
Stubbington PO14 154 B2
Dale The PO7 134 B1
Dale Valley Cl SO16 78 B1
Dale Valley Gdns SO16 78 B1
Dale Valley Rd
Poole BH15 202 C4
Southampton SO16 78 B2
Dales Cl BH21 164 B3
Dales Dr BH21 164 A3
Dales La BH23 190 C4
Dales Way SO40 100 A4
Dalewood Ave BH11 188 C3
Dalewood Rd PO15 130 B1
Dalkeith Rd
Corfe Mullen BH21 186 B2
Poole BH13 204 A1
Dalling Rd BH12 204 A3
Dallington Cl PO14 179 B3
Dalmally Gdns SO18 103 C4
Dalmeny Rd BH6 207 A2
Dalzell 31 SO23 2 A1
Damask Gdns PO7 112 A1
Dame Elizabeth Kelly Ct 3 PO2 157 C2
Damen Cl SO30 105 A3
Damerham Rd BH8 190 B2
Damerham Trout Lakes★ SP6 68 B1
Dampier Cl PO13 180 B4
Damson Cres SO50 57 A1
Damson Hill SO32 60 A1
Danbury Ct PO10 137 A1
Dances Way PO11 184 C2
Dandelion Cl PO13 155 A1
Dando Rd PO7 111 A2
Dandy's Ford La SO51 25 C1
Dane Cl SO45 150 C1
Dane Ct BH14 203 A2
Dane Dr BH22 165 C2
Dane Rd SO41 211 A3
Danebury Cl PO9 135 C3
Danebury Gdns SO53 55 A2
Danebury Way SO16 77 B2
Danecourt Cl BH14 202 C2
Danecourt Rd BH14 202 C2
Danecrest Rd SO41 195 C2
Danehurst SO41 211 A3
Danehurst New Rd SO41 195 B4
Danemark Ct 4 SO23 11 A4
Danes Cl BH25 210 A4
Danes Rd Awbridge SO51 26 B2
Portchester PO16 132 A1
23 Winchester SO23 2 A1
Danesbrook La PO7 135 A4
Danesbury Ave BH6 206 C2
Danesbury Mdws BH25 195 B3
Danestream Cl SO41 211 B2
Danestream Ct SO41 211 C2
Daneswood Rd BH25 195 B2
Daniel Gdns 13 BH15 202 B1
Daniell's Cl SO41 197 C2
Daniell's Wlk SO41 197 C2
Daniels Wlk SO40 76 A1
Dansie Cl BH14 203 A2
Dapple Pl SO40 102 A1
Darby's Cl BH15 202 B3
Darby's Cnr BH17 187 B1
Darby's La BH15 202 B3
Darby's La N BH17 202 B4
Dark La Blackfield SO45 150 C1
Bransgore BH23 194 A2
Cheriton SO24 14 B3
Darley Rd BH22 165 B2
Darlington Gdns SO15 78 B1
Darlington Rd PO4 182 C2
Darnan Ho 27 SO14 103 A4
Darracott Rd BH5 206 A3
Darren Cl PO14 154 B2
Darren Ct 9 PO16 131 A1
Darrian Ct BH16 201 A4
Dart Ho SO18 103 C4
Dart Rd SO18 80 A2
Dartington Rd SO50 56 B3
Dartmouth Mews PO5 215 A1
Dartmouth Rd PO3 158 A1
Darwin Ave BH23 191 C1
Darwin Ct 4 BH12 204 A2
Darwin Ho PO1 215 C4
Darwin Rd Eastleigh SO50 56 A2
Southampton SO15 102 C4
Darwin Way PO13 180 B3
Daubney Gdns 3 PO9 135 B3
Daulston Rd PO1 182 C4
Davenport Cl
Gosport PO13 180 B3
Upton BH16 201 B4
Daventry La PO3 158 B2
David Ct SO51 53 A3
David Hart Bsns Ctr SP5 46 C4
David Way BH15 201 C1
David's La BH24 140 B3
Davidia Ct PO7 135 A3
Davidson Ct 27 PO1 182 A3
Davis Cl PO13 180 B4
Davis Ct BH12 203 C3
Davis Field BH25 194 C1
Davis Rd BH12 203 C3
Davis Way PO14 155 A3
Daw La PO11 184 C4
Dawkins Bsns Ctr BH15 201 B2
Dawkins Rd BH15 201 B2
Dawkins Way BH25 195 A1
Dawlish Ave SO15 102 B4
Dawn Chorus BH14 203 A2
Dawn Cl BH10 189 B1
Dawn Gdns SO22 10 B3
Dawnay Cl SO16 79 B3
Daws Ave BH11 189 A1
Dawson Rd SO19 104 B1
Day La PO8 111 C4
Day's Ct BH21 163 B2
Daylesford Cl BH14 203 A1
Dayrell Cl SO40 76 A1
Dayshes Cl PO13 155 A2
Dayslondon Rd PO7 134 B3
De Courtenai Cl BH11 188 C3
De Grouchy La SO17 79 A1
De Haviland Cl BH21 163 C1
De Havilland Ho BH23 208 A3
De Havilland Way BH23 208 A3
De La Warr Rd SO41 211 B2
De Lisle Cl PO2 157 C2
De Lisle Rd BH3 204 C4
De Lunn Bldgs 7 SO23 11 A4
De Mauley Rd BH13 214 C4
De Montfort Rd BH21 163 B1
De Mowbray Way SO41 197 B1
De Port Hts SO32 61 B3
De Redvers Rd BH14 203 B1
Deacon Cl SO19 104 A3
Deacon Cres SO19 104 A3
Deacon Gdns BH11 189 A3
Deacon Rd
Bournemouth BH11 189 A3
Locks Heath SO31 129 A1
Southampton SO19 104 A3
Deacon Trad Est SO50 56 B1
Deadman Hill SP6 71 B3
Deal Cl PO14 154 B2
Deal Rd PO6 133 C1
Dean Cl Hamworthy BH15 201 C2
Winchester SO22 1 B1
Dean Court (Bournemouth FC) BH7 205 C3
Dean Ct Hedge End SO30 105 B4
2 Southampton SO18 104 A4
4 Southampton, Bitterne Manor SO18 103 C4
Dean La
Bishop's Waltham SO32 59 C2
Rowland's Castle PO8 113 B3
Whiteparish SP5 24 A2
Winchester SO22 1 A1
Dean Park Cres BH1 204 C2
Dean Park Rd BH1 204 C2
Dean Rd Cosham PO6 157 C4
Fair Oak SO50 57 B1
Southampton SO18 104 A4
West Dean SP5 3 A1
West Tytherley SP5 3 C3
Dean St PO1 182 A3
Dean Sta SP5 3 B2
Dean Swift Cres BH14 214 B4
Dean Villas PO17 130 C4
Dean's Rd 13 BH5 206 A3
Deane Ct 41 PO9 136 A3
Deane Down Dro SO22 1 A2
Deane Gdns 19 PO13 179 C1
Deane's Park Rd PO16 131 B1
Deanery The SO53 55 A4
Deanfield Cl SO31 127 C2
Deans Court La BH21 163 B2
Deans Ct SO41 211 B3
Deans Dell GU32 18 C1
Deans Gate PO14 179 B3
Deans Gr BH21 163 B4
Deans The BH1 204 C2
Deanscroft Rd BH10 189 C2
Deansfield Cl SO51 53 A4
Deansleigh Rd BH7 191 A1
Deanswood Dr PO7 111 C1
Dear Hay La BH15 202 B1
Dearing Cl SO43 121 C2
Debney Lodge PO7 134 C4
Decies Rd BH14 203 A3
Dee Cl SO53 55 A3
Dee Way BH15 202 A1
Deep Dell PO8 112 A3
Deepdene SO18 103 C4
Deepdene La BH11 188 C3
Deeping Cl SO19 103 C1
Deeping Gate PO7 135 A4
Deer Leap PO15 130 B3
Deer Park Cl BH25 194 C2
Deer Park Farm Ind Est SO50 57 C1
Deer Sanctuary★ BH24 119 C3
Deerhurst Cl SO40 100 B3
Deerhurst Ho 3 PO6 133 A1
Deerleap Cl SO45 126 A2
Deerleap La SO40 100 B1
Deerleap Way
Hythe SO45 126 A2
New Milton BH25 195 A3
Defender Rd SO19 103 B2
Defender Wlk SO19 103 B2
Defoe Cl PO15 129 B4
Delamere Gdns BH10 189 C2
Delamere Rd PO4 182 C2
Delaval Ho 35 PO1 182 A3
Delft Cl SO31 128 C2
Delft Gdns PO8 111 B1
Delft Mews BH23 207 B3
Delhi Cl BH14 203 B2
Delhi Rd BH9 189 C1
Delilah Rd BH15 201 B1
Delius Ave SO19 104 B2
Delius Wlk PO7 134 C3
Delkeith Ct BH22 165 B2
Dell Cl Broadstone BH18 186 C2
Fair Oak SO50 57 B1
Waterlooville PO7 134 A1
Dell Cotts SO24 15 C1
Dell Piece E PO8 112 B3
Dell Piece W PO8 112 B3
Dell Quay Cl PO13 155 A1
Dell Rd Southampton SO18 79 C1
Winchester SO23 11 B3
Dell The
Barton on Sea BH25 209 B4
Havant PO9 135 A1
Portchester PO16 131 B1
Dellcrest Path PO6 134 A1
Dellfield Cl 14 PO6 133 A1
Delme Ct 15 PO16 131 A1
Delme Dr PO16 131 B1
Delme Sq 28 PO16 131 A1
Delph Rd BH21 187 B4
Delph Woods Woodland Trail★ BH21 187 B4
Delphi Way PO7 134 C1
Delta Bsns Pk PO16 155 A4
Delta Cl BH23 208 A4
Dempsey Cl SO19 104 A2
Denbigh Cl Eastleigh SO50 55 C3
Totton SO40 100 B3
Denbigh Dr PO16 130 C1
Denbigh Gdns SO16 78 C2
Denby Rd BH15 202 C2
Dene Cl Chilworth SO16 78 C4
Locks Heath SO31 128 C2
Ringwood BH24 117 B1
Dene Hollow PO6 158 B4
Dene Rd SO40 100 B1
Dene Way SO40 100 B2
Dene Wlk BH22 165 C1
Denecote Lo BH13 214 D4
Deneside Copse SO41 197 A1
Deneve Ave BH17 187 B1
Denewood Copse BH22 138 B2
Denewood Rd BH22 138 B2
Denewulf Cl 2 SO32 83 B4
Denham Cl Poole BH17 187 C2
Stubbington PO14 179 A3
Winchester SO23 1 C1
Denham Ct SO23 2 A1
Denham Dr BH23 193 C1
Denham Fields SO50 57 A2
Denham Gdns SO31 127 A3
Denham's Cnr SO32 81 B3
Denhill Cl PO11 184 C3
Denholm Cl BH24 117 B1
Denison Rd BH17 187 B1
Denmark La BH15 202 B2
Denmark Rd
Bournemouth BH9 189 C1
Poole BH15 202 B2
Denmark Terr BH1 205 C3
Denmead BH25 195 B2
Denmead Cvn Pk PO7 111 A2
Denmead Ho PO1 215 C4
Denmead Inf Sch PO7 111 A2
Denmead Jun Sch PO7 111 A2
Denmead Rd
Bournemouth BH6 206 B4
Southampton SO18 104 B4
Dennet Ho SO23 2 B1
Dennetts La 19 BH15 202 A1
Denning Mews PO1 215 B3

Dennis Rd BH21 ....186 B3
Dennis Way GU33 ....21 A2
Dennison Ct 8 SO15 .....102 A4
Dennistoun Ave BH23 ...207 C4
Denny Cl SO45 ....151 A2
Densome Cnr SP6 ....71 A3
Denville Ave PO16 .....156 B3
Denville Cl PO6 ....158 C4
Denvilles Cl PO9 ....136 A1
Denwood Rd BH4 ......204 A2
Denzil Ave Netley SO31 ..127 B3
Southampton SO14 ....103 A3
Depedene Cl SO45 ......150 B2
Derby Ct PO13 ....180 B3
Derby Ho 4 SO50 ....56 A1
Derby Rd
Bournemouth BH1 ....205 B2
Eastleigh SO50 ....55 C1
Portsmouth PO2 ....157 B1
Southampton SO14 ......103 A3
Dereham Way BH12 ....203 C3
Deridene Ct SO40 ....100 B3
Derlyn Rd PO16 ....131 A1
Derritt La BH23 ....192 B4
Derrybrian Gdns BH25 .195 A1
Dersingham Cl PO6 ....133 C1
Derwent Cl
Bournemouth BH9 ......190 A1
Ferndown BH22 ....166 A3
Horndean PO8 ....88 B1
Stubbington PO14 ......154 B2
West End SO18 ....80 A1
Derwent Dr SO40 ......100 A4
Derwent Rd
Lee-on-the-Solent PO13 ..179 C1
New Milton BH25 ......195 A3
Southampton SO16 ....77 C1
Derwentwater Rd BH21 .163 B1
Desborough Cl 9 PO6 ..133 A1
Desborough Rd SO50 ....56 A1
Devenish Rd SO22 ....1 B2
Deverel Cl BH23 ....207 A4
Deverell Pl PO7 ....134 B2
Devine Gdns 5 SO50 ....56 C1
Devon Cl SO53 ....55 B2
Devon Dr SO53 ....55 B2
Devon Rd
Christchurch BH23 ......206 C4
Poole BH15 ....202 C3
Portsmouth PO3 ....158 A2
Devonshire Ave PO4 ...183 A2
Devonshire Gdns
Bursledon SO31 ....105 A1
Hythe SO45 ....150 A4
Devonshire Inf Sch PO4 182 C2
Devonshire Mans 10
SO15 ....102 C3
Devonshire Rd SO15 ...102 C3
Devonshire Sq PO4 ....182 C2
Devonshire Way PO14 ..154 B4
Dew La SO50 ....55 C2
Dewar Cl PO15 ....129 B3
Deweys La BH24 ....140 C4
Dewlands Pk BH31 .....114 B3
Dewlands Rd BH31 .....114 B3
Dewlands Way BH31 ...114 C3
Dewlish Cl BH17 ....188 A1
Dewsbury Ct 3 SO18 ....80 A1
Dhekelia Ct PO1 ....215 C4
Dial Cl BH23 ....169 B1
Diamond Cl SP6 ....93 C4
Diamond Ct
Fordingbridge SP6 ....93 C4
Waterlooville PO7 ......134 C4
Diamond St 2 PO5 ....215 A1
Diana Cl Gosport PO12 ..180 C2
Havant PO10 ....136 C2
Diana Ct BH23 ....209 A4
Diana Way BH21 ....186 C4
Dibben Wlk SO51 ....28 B1
Dibble Dr SO52 ....53 C2
Dibden Cl
Bournemouth BH8 ......190 B2
Havant PO9 ....135 B2
Dibden Lodge Cl SO45 .125 C3
Dibles Rd SO31 ....128 C1
Dickens Cl PO2 ....182 B4
Dickens Dell SO40 .....100 A4
Dickens Dr PO15 ....106 B1
Dickens Rd BH6 ....206 B4
Dickson Pk PO17 ....108 A2
Didcot Rd Poole BH17 ..202 B4
Southampton SO15 ....78 B1
Dieppe Cres PO2 ....157 C2
Dieppe Gdns PO12 .....180 C2
Dight Rd PO12 ....181 B1
Diligence Cl SO31 .....105 A1
Dillington Ho 2 PO7 ...134 C4
Dilly La BH25 ....210 A4
Dimond Cl SO18 ....79 C1
Dimond Hill SO18 ....79 C1
Dimond Rd SO18 ....79 C1
Dingle Rd BH5 ....206 A2
Dingle Way SO31 ....129 A3
Dingley Rd BH15 ....202 B3
Dinham Ct BH25 ....195 B2
Dinham Rd BH25 ....195 B2
Dinsey Cl SO16 ....101 C4
Diprose Rd BH21 ....186 C4
Disa Ho SO15 ....102 C3
Discovery Cl PO14 .....154 B3
Disraeli Rd BH23 ....207 B3
Ditcham Cres PO9 .....135 C2
Ditcham Park Sch GU31 .89 C4
Ditchbury SO41 ....197 B3
Ditton Cl PO14 ....154 B2
Ditton Cotts SO42 ......148 C1
Dock La SO42 ....149 A1
Dock Mill Cotts 3 PO5 .182 B1
Dock Rd PO12 ....181 B2
Dockenfield Cl PO9 ....135 B2
Doctor's Hill SO51 ......26 A2
Doctors La GU32 ....37 B3
Dodds La SO32 ....84 B3
Dodgson Cl SP6 ....70 C4
Dodwell La SO31 ....105 A2
Doe Copse Way BH25 ..194 C2
Dogdean BH21 ....163 B4
Dogkennel La PO7 ....86 C2
Dogwood Dell 2 PO7 ..134 C3
Dogwood Rd BH18 .....186 C1
Dolbery Rd N BH12 ....188 B1
Dolbery Rd S BH12 ....188 B1
Dolman Rd PO12 ....181 B2
Dolphin Ave BH10 .....189 C3
Dolphin Cl 11 SO50 .....56 C1
Dolphin Cres PO12 .....181 B2
Dolphin Ct
7 Portsmouth PO5 .....182 C1
Stubbington PO14 ......154 A2
Dolphin Ctr BH15 ......202 B1
Dolphin Hill SO21 ....32 A3
Dolphin Pl BH25 ....210 A4
Dolphin Way PO12 .....181 B1
Dolton Rd SO16 ....77 C2
Dome Alley SO23 ....11 A4
Dominie Wlk 15 PO13 ..179 C1
Dominion Ctr BH11 ....188 C2
Dominion Rd BH11 .....188 C2
Dominy Cl SO45 ....126 A2
Domum Rd
Portsmouth PO2 ....157 C1
Winchester SO23 ....11 A3
Domvilles App PO2 ....157 A1
Donaldson Rd PO6 .....157 C3
Doncaster Rd SO50 ......80 A4
Donigers Cl SO32 ....84 A3
Donigers Dell SO32 ......84 A3
Donkey La SO30 ....106 A4
Donnelly Rd BH6 ....206 C3
Donnelly St PO12 ......181 A3
Donnington Ct 19 SO23 ...2 A1
Donnington Dr
Chandler's Ford SO53 ....55 A2
Christchurch BH23 ......208 A4
Donnington Gr SO17 ....79 B1
Donoughmore Rd 1
BH1 ....205 C2
Dorcas Cl 1 PO7 ....112 A1
Dorchester Ct SO15 ...102 C4
Dorchester Gdns BH15 .202 C3
Dorchester Mans BH1 ..205 B2
Dorchester Rd
Poole BH15 ....202 C3
Upton BH16 ....201 A4
Dore Ave PO16 ....132 B1
Dores La Braishfield SO51 .29 A4
Hursley SO51 ....29 A4
Doric Cl SO53 ....55 C4
Dorking Cres PO6 ......157 C4
Dorland Gdns SO40 ....100 B3
Dorlands Rd PO8 ......112 B4
Dormers The BH25 .....194 C1
Dormington Rd PO6 ...133 B1
Dormy Cl SO31 ....128 B2
Dormy Way PO13 ....155 A1
Dorney Ct 2 PO6 ......158 A4
Dornie Rd BH13 ....214 C4
Dornmere La PO7 ......135 A4
Dorothy Ct PO5 ....215 C1
Dorothy Dymond St
PO1 ....215 B3
Dorrick Ct 17 SO15 ....102 C4
Dorrien Rd PO12 ....181 A4
Dorrita Ave PO8 ....112 A2
Dorrita Cl PO4 ....182 C1
Dorrits The SO40 ......100 A4
Dorset Ave BH22 ....165 B2
Dorset Cl PO8 ....112 A3
Dorset Grange BH23 ...206 C4
Dorset Heavy Horse & Animal
Ctr★ BH21 ....91 B1
Dorset Ho BH13 ....204 A1
Dorset Lake Ave BH14 .214 A4
Dorset Lake Manor
BH14 ....203 A1
Dorset Rd
Bournemouth BH4 ......204 B3
Chandler's Ford SO53 ....55 B2
Christchurch BH23 .....207 C4
Dorset St SO14 ....103 A3
Dorstone Rd PO6 ......133 B1
Dorval Ho 23 SO15 ....102 C4
Dorval Manor 24 SO15 ..102 C4
Douglas Ave BH23 .....207 A3
Douglas Cl BH16 ....201 B4
Douglas Cres SO19 ....104 B3
Douglas Gdns
Havant PO9 ....136 A2
Poole BH12 ....203 C3
Douglas Mews
Bournemouth BH6 ......206 B3
Upton BH16 ....201 B4
Douglas Rd
Bournemouth BH6 ......206 C2
Poole BH12 ....203 C3
Douglas Way SO45 ....125 C2
Doulton Gdns BH14 ...203 A1
Doussie Cl BH16 ....201 A4
Dove Cl PO8 ....111 C2
Dove Dale SO50 ....55 B1
Dove Gdns SO31 ....129 A3
Dove La SO51 ....29 A4
Dover Cl Poole BH13 ...204 A2
Stubbington PO14 ......154 A2
Dover Ct PO11 ....184 C3
Dover Rd Poole BH13 ...204 A2
Portsmouth PO3 ....183 A4
Dover St SO14 ....103 A4
Dovercourt Rd PO6 ....158 A3
Doveshill Cres BH10 ...189 B2
Doveshill Gdns BH10 ..189 B2
Doveshill Mobile Home Pk
BH10 ....189 B2
Doveys Cl BH24 ....143 A2
Dowds Cl SO30 ....105 A4
Dowell Ho PO4 ....183 A1
Dowlands Cl BH10 .....189 B2
Dowlands Rd BH10 ....189 B2
Down End PO6 ....134 B1
Down End Rd PO6 .....134 B1
Down Farm La SO22,SO23 .1 C4
Down Farm Pl PO8 ......88 B1
Down Lodge Cl SP6 .....93 A3
Down Rd Horndean PO8 ...88 A1
Horndean PO8 ....112 B4
Down's Park Ave SO40 .101 A3
Down's Park Cres SO40 101 A3
Down's Park Rd SO40 ..101 A3
Downend Rd PO16 .....131 C1
Downey Cl BH11 ....188 C1
Downham Cl PO8 ......111 C2
Downhouse Rd PO8 .....88 A2
Downing Ct PO14 ......129 B1
Downland Cl
Botley SO30 ....105 C4
Locks Heath SO31 ......129 A2
Downland Pl SO30 .....105 A3
Downlands Cl SP5 ....46 C3
Downlands Pl BH17 ....202 C4
Downlands Rd SO22 .....10 A2
Downley Point PO9 ....136 A2
Downley Rd PO9 ....136 A2
Downs Cl PO7 ....134 C2
Downscroft Gdns SO30 .105 A4
Downside PO13 ....155 B1
Downside Ave SO19 ...104 A3
Downside Rd
Waterlooville PO7 ......134 B2
Winchester SO22 ....1 A1
Downsway The PO16 ...156 B4
Downton CE Prim Sch
SP5 ....46 C4
Downton Cl BH8 ....190 B2
Downton Hill SP5 ....47 B4
Downton Ho 2 PO6 ....157 B4
Downton La SO41 .....210 C4
Downton Rd SO18 ....79 C1
Downton Sec Sch SP5 ...46 C4
Downview Rd SP6 ....43 A2
Downwood Cl
Fordingbridge SP6 ....69 B1
Hythe SO45 ....125 B1
Downwood Way PO8 ....88 B1
Doyle Ave PO2 ....157 C2
Doyle Cl PO2 ....157 C2
Doyle Ct
16 Portsmouth PO2 .....157 C2
Southampton SO19 .....103 C1
Doyle Ho PO9 ....135 A2
Doyne Rd BH14 ....203 C2
Dradfield La SO32 .....109 B4
Draffatts Ho SO15 .....102 B4
Dragon Est PO6 ....158 C4
Dragon La BH23 ....168 A4
Dragon St GU31,GU32 ...40 C2
Dragoon Cl SO19 ......104 B2
Dragoon Way BH23 ...206 C4
Drake Cl
Christchurch BH23 .....207 C3
Locks Heath SO31 ......129 A3
Marchwood SO40 ......102 A1
New Milton BH25 ......194 C2
Ringwood BH24 ....117 B1
Drake Ct
Lee-on-the-Solent PO13 ..179 B2
22 Poole BH15 ....202 B1
Drake Ho 4 PO1 ....182 A3
Drake Rd
Bishopstoke SO50 ....56 C2
Lee-on-the-Solent PO13 ..179 B2
Poole BH15 ....202 B1
Drakes Cl SO45 ....125 C1
Drakes Ct SO40 ....102 A2
Drakes Rd BH22 ....165 C2
Draper Rd
Bournemouth BH11 .....189 A2
Christchurch BH23 .....207 C4
Drapers Copse Cvn Site
SO45 ....125 B2
Draycote Rd PO8 ....88 B2
Draycott Rd BH10 .....189 B1
Drayton Cl 9 SO19 ....126 C4
Drayton La PO6 ....134 A1
Drayton Pl SO40 ....100 B4
Drayton Rd PO2 ....157 C1
Drayton St SO22 ....10 B3
Dreadnought Rd PO14 .154 C3
Dresden Dr PO8 ....111 C2
Dreswick Cl BH23 .....191 B2
Drew Cl BH12 ....204 B4
Drewitt Ind Est BH11 ..188 C2
Drift Rd Clanfield PO8 ....88 B2
Fareham PO16 ....131 B1
Drift The PO9 ....113 A1
Driftwood Gdns
Portsmouth PO4 ....183 B1
Totton SO40 ....100 B3
Drill Shed Rd PO2 .....157 A1
Drinkwater Cl SO50 .....55 C2
Drive The Fareham PO16 .131 A1
Drive The continued
Gosport PO13 ....155 A1
Havant PO9 ....135 C2
Poole BH12 ....203 B3
Sherfield English SO51 ...25 A1
Southbourne PO10 .....161 B4
Totton SO40 ....100 C3
West End SO30 ....80 A2
West Wellow SO51 ....51 A1
Drove Cl SO21 ....31 C3
Drove Rd
Southampton SO19 .....104 A2
Southwick PO17 ....133 A2
Drove The
Blackfield SO45 ....150 C1
Durley SO32 ....82 B4
Fair Oak SO50 ....81 B3
Southampton SO18 .....104 A4
Swanmore SO32 ....84 A3
Totton SO40 ....76 A1
Twyford SO21 ....31 C3
West End SO30 ....80 C2
West Wellow SO51 ....50 C2
Droxford Cl PO12 ......180 C2
Droxford Jun Sch SO32 ...61 A1
Droxford Rd
Bournemouth BH6 ......206 A3
Swanmore SO32 ....84 B3
Druids Cl BH22 ....165 B1
Druitt Rd BH23 ....207 C4
Drum La GU32 ....40 C2
Drum Mead GU32 ....40 C2
Drumlanrig Terr PO12 ..181 B4
Drummond Cl SO22 .....10 C3
Drummond Ct
4 Eastleigh SO50 ....56 A3
8 Hythe SO45 ....126 A3
Southampton SO19 .....103 C2
Drummond Dr SO14 ....103 B4
Drummond Rd
Bournemouth BH1 ....205 B2
Hedge End SO30 ....81 B1
3 Hythe SO45 ....126 A2
Portsmouth PO1 ....215 C4
Drummond Way SO53 ...55 A4
Drury Rd BH4 ....204 A1
Dryden Ave PO6 ....132 C1
Dryden Cl Fareham PO16 131 A1
St Leonards BH24 ....139 C3
Waterlooville PO7 ....111 C1
Dryden Pl 4 SO41 ......211 B3
Dryden Rd SO19 ....104 C3
Drysdale Mews PO4 ....183 A1
Duart Ct BH25 ....195 B2
Duck Island La 5 BH24 141 A3
Duck La BH11 ....188 C2
Ducking Stool La BH23 .207 A3
Duckmead La GU33 ......21 A3
Duckworth Ho 23 PO1 ..182 A3
Duddon Cl SO18 ....80 A1
Dudleston Heath Dr
PO8 ....112 A1
Dudley Ave
Fordingbridge SP6 ....69 C2
Hordle SO41 ....195 C2
Dudley Gdns BH10 .....189 B3
Dudley Pl 29 BH25 .....195 A1
Dudley Rd
Bournemouth BH10 .....189 B3
Portsmouth PO3 ....183 A4
Dudley Terr GU33 ....21 A3
Dudmoor Farm Rd
BH23 ....191 C2
Dudmoor La BH23 .....191 C2
Dudsbury Ave BH22 ....165 B2
Dudsbury Cres BH22 ...165 C2
Dudsbury Ct 8 BH23 ..207 C3
Dudsbury Gdns BH22 ..189 C4
Dudsbury Rd BH22 .....165 B1
Dudsway Ct BH22 ......165 B2
Duffield La PO10 ....137 C2
Dugald Drummond St
PO1 ....215 B3
Dugdell Cl BH22 ....165 C3
Duisburg Way PO5 .....182 A1
Duke Cres PO1 ....182 B4
Duke of Edinburgh Ho
PO1 ....182 A3
Duke Rd SO30 ....105 B3
Duke St SO14 ....103 A2
Duke Terr PO9 ....135 B2
Dukes Cl GU32 ....40 B2
Dukes Ct 4 SO32 ....83 B4
Dukes Dr BH11 ....188 C3
Dukes Mill Ctr 11 SO51 ..52 C4
Dukes Rd Gosport PO12 .181 A3
Southampton SO14 ......103 A4
Dukes Wlk 14 PO7 .....134 C4
Dukes Wlk Service Rd 13
PO7 ....134 C4
Dukes Wood Dr SO45 ..126 A1
Dukesfield BH23 ....191 B1
Dulsie Rd BH3 ....204 B4
Dumbarton Cl PO2 .....182 B4
Dumbleton Cl SO19 ....104 C2
Dumbleton's Twrs SO19 104 C2
Dummer Ct PO9 ....135 B3
Dummer Mews 24 SO23 ..10 C4
Dummer Rd SO51 ....28 B4
Dumpers Dro SO50 ......81 B3
Dumpton Sch BH21 ....163 B4
Dunbar Cl SO16 ....77 C3
Dunbar Cres BH23 .....193 C1
Dunbar Rd
Bournemouth BH3 ......204 C3
Portsmouth PO4 ....183 A2
Dunbridge La SO51 .....26 C4
Dunbridge Sta SO51 ......5 B1
Duncan Cl SO19 103
Duncan Cooper Ho PO7 134
Duncan Ct SO19 104
Duncan Rd
Locks Heath SO31 129
New Milton BH25 195
Portsmouth PO5 182
Duncans Dr PO14 154
Duncliff Rd BH6 207
Duncombe Dr BH24 116
Duncombe Rd GU32 63
Duncton Rd PO8 88
Duncton Way PO13 155
Dundas Cl PO3 158
Dundas La PO3 158
Dundas Rd BH17 202
Dundas Spur PO3 158
Dundee Cl PO15 130
Dundee Rd SO17 79
Dundonald Cl
South Hayling PO11 185
Southampton SO19 103
Dundridge La SO32 60
Dundry Way SO30 105
Dune Crest BH13 214
Dunedin Cl BH22 165
Dunedin Dr BH22 165
Dunedin Gdns BH22 ...165
Dunedin Gr BH23 208
Dunfield Way SO45 150
Dunford Cl
Barton on Sea BH25 209
New Milton BH25 194
Dunford Rd BH12 203
Dunhurst (Bedales Jun Sch)
GU32 40
Dunhurst Cl PO9 136
Dunkeld Rd
Bournemouth BH3 204
Gosport PO12 181
Dunkirk Cl SO16 78
Dunkirk Rd SO16 78
Dunlin Cl
Christchurch BH23 208
Portsmouth PO4 183
Dunn Cl PO4 183
Dunnings La SO52 53
Dunnock Cl
Ferndown BH22 165
Rowland's Castle PO9 ...113
Dunsbury Way PO9 135
Dunsmore Cl PO5 215
Dunstable Wlk PO14 ...154
Dunstans La BH15 203
Dunster Cl SO16 78
Dunvegan Dr SO16 78
Dunvegan Rd SO16 78
Dunvegan Way SO16 78
Dunyeats Rd BH18 187
Dunyeats Rdbt BH18 ...187
Durban Cl SO51 28
Durban Ct 21 SO15 102
Durban Ho PO1 215
Durban Rd PO1 182
Durdells Ave BH11 189
Durdells Gdns BH11 ...189
Durford Ct PO9 135
Durford Rd GU31 41
Durham Gdns PO7 134
Durham St Gosport PO12 181
Portsmouth PO1 215
Durland Cl BH25 195
Durley Ave PO8 111
Durley Brook Rd
Durley SO32 81
Durley SO32 82
Durley CE Prim Sch
SO32 82
Durley Chine Ct BH2 ...204
Durley Chine Rd BH2 ..204
Durley Chine Rd S BH2 .204
Durley Cres SO40 100
Durley Gdns BH2 204
Durley Hall Rd SO32 58
Durley Rd
Bournemouth BH2 204
Durley SO32,SO50 81
Gosport PO12 181
Durley Rd S BH2 204
Durley St SO32 82
Durlston Court Sch
BH25 210
Durlston Cres BH23 ...191
Durlston Rd Poole BH14 .203
Southampton SO16 77
Durnford Rd SO14 103
Durngate Pl SO23 11
Durngate Terr 41 SO23 ...11
Durnstown SO41 172
Durrant PRU PO9 136
Durrant Rd
7 Bournemouth BH2 204
Poole BH14 203
Durrant Way SO41 172
Durrants Gdns PO9 136
Durrants Rd PO9 136
Durrington Pl BH7 206
Durrington Rd BH7 206
Dursley Cres PO6 157
Durweston Cl BH9 190
Dutton La SO50 56
Dutton's Rd SO51 52
Dyer Rd SO15 102
Dymchurch Ho 3 PO6 ..157
Dymewood Rd BH21 ...138
Dymoke St PO10 136
Dymott Cl SO15 102
Dyneley Gn SO18 ....80 A1

n Cl SO50 55 C3
rt Ave PO6 158 A4
rth Cl SO19 104 A1
n Dr SO23 2 A1

e SO45 150 C3
ns La SO40 99 B4
e Ave PO8 111 C2
e Cl
ndler's Ford SO53 55 A2
chester PO16 155 C4
e Ct 12 SO23 10 C4
e House Sch BH14 203 A2
e Rd
on-the-Solent PO13 179 B2
e BH12 204 A2
hurst 5 BH12 204 A2
e's Cotts GU32 38 C1
es La GU33 19 C4
e Ho 3 SO23 11 B4
e Rd BH4 204 B1
ey Ct SO41 197 C2
nam Dr BH14 203 B2
s Cl SO50 57 A1
s Rd Fareham PO16 155 A4
thampton SO14 103 A4
sdon St PO5 215 B2
sdon Way BH23 208 C4
sdown 47 SO23 11 A4
swood Dr SP6 92 C3
swood Pk BH25 195 B2
ley Rd PO11 185 C1
Ave
ton on Sea BH25 209 B4
rnemouth BH3 204 B3
Avenue Rdbt BH3 204 C3
Bank Rd SO42 173 A4
Bargate 7 SO14 103 A2
Boldre Rd SO42 175 B3
Borough BH21 163 A3
Cams Cl PO16 131 C1
Cl BH25 209 B4
Cliff Way BH23 208 B4
Cosham Rd PO6 158 A4
Ct Cosham PO6 158 A4
tsmouth PO1 182 C4
Dean Rd SO51 4 C1
Dr SO50 56 C2
Field Cl PO10 137 C1
Hill Lymington SO41 197 C2
nchester SO23 11 A3
Hill Cl PO16 131 B1
Hill Dr GU33 21 A2
Hoe Rd PO7 86 A2
House Ave PO14 179 B3
Howe La BH10 189 B2
La SO41 196 C1
Links SO53 55 B1
Lodge
eham PO15 130 B1
Lee-on-the-Solent
013 179 C1
Lodge Pk PO6 158 C4
t Meon CE Prim Sch
32 38 B1
Meon Rd PO8 88 A3
Overcliff Dr BH1 205 B2
Park Terr SO14 103 A3
st Quay BH15 202 B1
st Quay Rd BH15 202 B1
st Rd Fawley SO45 150 B4
uthwick PO17 133 A3
st Shore Sch PO4 183 A3
st St Fareham PO16 131 B1
mbledon PO7 86 B2
avant PO9 135 C1
ole BH15 202 B1
rtchester PO16 156 C4
rtsmouth PO1 182 A2
uthampton SO14 103 A2
tchfield PO14 154 A4
estbourne PO10 137 A2
imborne Minst BH21 163 B2
st Street Ctr 16 SO14 103 A2
st Surrey St PO1 215 B3
st View Rd BH24 141 A4
st View Terr 9 PO9 135 C1
st Way
ournemouth BH8 190 B1
orfe Mullen BH21 186 B3
st Woodhay Rd SO22 1 B2
stacre SO22 1 C1
stbourne Ave
osport PO12 180 C4
outhampton SO15 102 B4
stbourne Rd PO3 183 A4
stbrook Cl
osport PO12 180 C4
ocks Heath SO31 129 A3
stbrook Row BH21 163 B2
stbury Ct BH23 207 C2
stchurch Cl SO16 77 C2
stcliff Cl PO13 179 C2
stcot Cl SO45 150 B2
stcott Cl BH7 206 A4
stcroft Rd PO12 180 C3
aster Rd BH9 190 A1
astern Ave PO4 183 A3
astern Ind Ctr PO6 158 B3
astern Par
areham PO16 155 A4
ortsmouth PO4 182 C1
astern Rd Fawley SO45 151 C1
avant PO9 136 A1
ymington SO41 197 B2

Eastern Rd *continued*
Portsmouth PO3, PO6 158 B2
Portsmouth, Whale Is PO2 157 A1
West End SO30 80 B1
Eastern Terr PO4 183 A1
Eastern Villas Rd PO4 182 B1
Eastern Way
Fareham PO16 131 B1
Milford on Sea SO41 211 C2
Eastfield Ave PO14 154 C4
Eastfield Ct BH24 141 B4
Eastfield La BH24 141 B4
Eastfield Rd
Portsmouth PO4 183 A2
Southampton SO17 103 B4
Eastfields PO5 215 C1
Eastgate St
Southampton SO14 103 A2
Winchester SO23 11 A4
Eastlake Ave BH12 203 B3
Eastlake Cl GU31 41 B2
Eastlake Hts PO4 183 B2
Eastlands BH25 195 A1
Eastleigh Coll SO50 56 A1
Eastleigh Coll of F Ed
SO50 56 A1
Eastleigh Lakeside Rly★
SO50 79 C4
Eastleigh Rd
Fair Oak SO50 57 B1
Havant PO9 136 B2
Eastleigh Sta SO50 56 A2
Eastleigh Town Mus★
SO50 56 A1
Eastman Cl SP5 47 A3
Eastmeare Ct SO40 100 B3
Eastney Farm Rd PO4 183 B2
Eastney Rd PO4 183 A2
Eastney St PO4 183 A1
Eastoke Ave PO11 185 B1
Easton La SO21 2 C2
Easton Lane Bsns Ctr
SO23 11 A4
Eastover Ct 10 PO9 135 B3
Eastville Rd SO50 57 B1
Eastways SO32 83 B4
Eastwood SO51 25 B1
Eastwood Ave BH22 165 C3
Eastwood Cl PO11 185 A3
Eastwood Rd 5 PO2 157 C2
Eastworth Rd BH31 114 C4
Eaton Rd BH13 204 A1
Ebblake Ent Pk BH31 115 B3
Ebblake Ind Est BH31 115 B2
Ebden Rd SO23 11 A4
Ebenezer La BH24 140 C4
Ebery Gr PO3 183 B4
Ebor Cl BH22 165 C1
Ebor Rd BH12 203 B3
Eccles Rd BH15 202 A1
Ecton La PO3 158 B2
Eddystone Rd SO40 76 B1
Edelvale Rd SO18 80 A1
Eden Ct 20 BH1 205 A2
Eden Gr BH21 163 B2
Eden Rd SO18 80 A1
Eden Rise PO16 155 A4
Eden St PO1 215 B4
Eden Terr 10 PO2 157 B1
Eden Wlk SO53 55 A3
Edenbridge Rd PO4 183 B3
Edenbridge Way SO31 128 C3
Edgar Cres PO16 156 B3
Edgar Rd SO23 10 C3
Edgar Villas SO23 10 C3
Edgarton Rd BH17 187 B2
Edgbaston Ho PO5 215 B2
Edgecombe Cres PO13 180 B4
Edgefield Gr PO7 112 B1
Edgehill Rd
Bournemouth BH9 189 C1
Southampton SO18 79 C1
Edgell Rd PO10 137 A2
Edgemoor Rd BH22 139 A1
Edgerly Gdns PO6 157 C3
Edgeware Rd PO4 183 A3
Edgewood Ct GU33 21 A1
Edifred Rd BH9 190 A2
Edinburgh Ct SO15 102 A3
Edinburgh Ho 8 SO22 10 C4
Edinburgh Rd PO1 215 A3
Edington Cl SO32 83 A4
Edington Rd SO23 2 A1
Edith Haisman Cl SO15 102 B3
Edmondsham Ho Gdns★
BH21 91 A2
Edmondsham Rd BH31 114 C4
Edmonsham Ho 23 BH2 204 C2
Edmund Rd PO4 182 C2
Edmunds Cl
Barton on Sea BH25 195 A1
Hedge End SO30 105 B3
Edneys La PO7 111 A3
Edward Ave SO50 56 B2
Edward Cl SO45 150 C1
Edward Gdns PO9 135 B1
Edward Gr PO16 132 C1
Edward Rd
Bournemouth BH11 189 A2
Christchurch BH23 207 C4
Hythe SO45 126 A2
Poole BH14 203 B3
Southampton SO15 102 B4
Winchester SO23 10 C3
Edward Way Ct BH11 189 A2
Edward's Cl 29 PO6 133 A1
Edwards Cl SO41 197 A2
Edwin Jones Gn SO15 102 C4

Edwina Cl
North Baddesley SO52 54 A2
Ringwood BH24 117 B1
Southampton SO19 104 A3
Edwina Dr BH17 187 A1
Edwina Ho SO18 79 C2
Effingham Gdns SO19 104 B2
Efford Ct SO41 197 A1
Efford Farm Cotts SO41 197 A1
Efford Way SO41 197 A1
Egan Cl PO2 157 C2
Egbert Rd SO23 2 A1
Egdon Cl BH22 165 A2
Egdon Ct BH16 201 A4
Egdon Dr BH21 187 C4
Egerton Gdns BH8 205 B3
Egerton Rd BH8 205 B3
Eglantine Cl PO8 112 A2
Eglantine Wlk PO8 112 B2
Egmont Cl BH24 140 B1
Egmont Dr BH24 140 B1
Egmont Gdns BH24 140 B1
Egmont Rd BH16 201 A2
Eight Acres SO51 53 A4
Eileen Beard Ho 51 PO9 136 A3
Elaine Gdns PO8 112 A3
Elan Cl SO18 80 A1
Elcombes Cl SO43 121 C3
Elder Cl
Locks Heath SO31 128 C1
Marchwood SO40 102 A1
Winchester SO22 10 B2
Elder Gn SO21 57 A4
Elder Rd PO9 136 A2
Elderberry Cl
Clanfield PO8 88 B2
Fair Oak SO50 57 A1
Elderberry La BH23 207 C3
Elderberry Way PO8 112 B2
Elderfield Cl PO10 137 A2
Elderfield Rd PO9 135 B4
Eldon Ave BH25 209 C4
Eldon Cl BH25 209 C4
Eldon Ct 9 Poole BH14 203 A2
Portsmouth PO5 215 B2
Eldon Ho 22 SO14 103 A2
Eldon Pl BH4 204 A2
Eldon Rd
Bournemouth BH9 189 C1
Braishfield SO20, SO51 7 A3
King's Somborne SO20 7 A3
Eldon St PO5 215 B2
Eldridge Gdns SO51 52 C4
Eleanor Dr BH11 188 B3
Eleanor Gdns BH23 206 C4
Electron Way SO53 55 B3
Elettra Ave PO7 134 B4
Eleven Cross SP6 68 A3
Elfin Ct 11 SO17 103 A4
Elfin Dr BH22 165 B4
Elgar Cl Gosport PO12 181 A1
Portchester PO6 156 C4
Southampton SO19 104 B2
Elgar Ct SO41 197 C2
Elgar Rd
Bournemouth BH10 189 B2
Southampton SO19 104 B2
Elgar Wlk PO7 134 C3
Elgin Cl Fareham PO15 130 C1
Hythe SO45 126 A2
Elgin Rd
Bournemouth BH3,BH4 204 B3
Cosham PO6 157 C3
Poole BH14 203 B1
Southampton SO15 102 B3
Elijah Cl BH15 201 C1
Eling Cl SO22 1 B2
Eling Ct PO9 135 B3
Eling Hill SO40 101 A3
Eling Inf Sch SO40 101 A3
Eling La SO40 101 A3
Eling Tide Mill★ SO40 101 A3
Eling View SO15 101 B4
Elingfield Ct SO40 101 A4
Eliot Ho
14 New Milton BH25 195 A1
Southampton SO17 79 B1
Elise Cl BH7 206 A4
Eliza Pl PO12 181 B3
Elizabeth Ave BH23 206 C4
Elizabeth Cl Downton SP5 46 B4
West End SO30 80 B1
Wickham PO17 107 C2
Elizabeth Cres SO41 196 A1
Elizabeth Ct
12 Bournemouth BH1 205 A2
6 Cosham PO6 157 C4
Eastleigh SO50 56 A2
Fareham PO14 154 C4
4 Gosport PO12 181 A3
11 New Milton BH25 195 A1
Southampton, Aldermoor
SO16 78 A2
Southampton, Portswood
SO17 79 B1
West End SO30 80 B1
Elizabeth Gdns
Christchurch BH23 208 B4
Hythe SO45 126 A1
Portsmouth PO4 182 C1
Elizabeth Ho SO40 76 B1
Elizabeth Rd Poole BH15 202 B2
Stubbington PO14 179 B3
Upton BH16 201 B4
Waterlooville PO7 134 C3
Wickham PO17 108 A2
Wimborne Minst BH21 163 B3

Elizabeth Way
Bishop's Waltham SO32 83 A4
Eastleigh SO50 56 A3
Elkhams Cl SO41 196 B1
Elkstone Rd PO6 133 A1
Ellachie Gdns PO12 181 A1
Ellachie Mews PO12 181 A1
Ellachie Rd PO12 181 A1
Elland Cl SO50 57 B1
Elldene Ct SO40 100 C3
Ellen Gdns SO53 55 A3
Ellen Wren Ho SO18 79 C2
Ellerslie Cl PO14 179 A3
Ellery Gr SO41 197 C3
Ellesfield Dr BH22 165 B1
Ellesmere Orch PO10 137 A3
Ellingham Cross BH24 116 C3
Ellingham Dr BH24 116 B3
Ellingham Dro BH24 117 A3
Ellingham Rd BH25 209 B4
Elliot Cl SO40 100 B4
Elliot Rd BH11 188 C2
Elliot Rise SO30 81 B1
Ellis Rd SO19 104 C3
Ellisfield Rd PO9 135 C2
Ellwood Ave SO19 104 C3
Ellwood Cl SO19 104 C3
Elm Ave
Christchurch BH23 191 C1
Lymington SO41 197 B1
New Milton BH25 195 A1
Elm Cl
South Hayling PO11 185 A2
Southampton SO16 78 C2
Elm Close Est PO11 184 C2
Elm Cotts 8 BH24 141 A4
Elm Cres Hythe SO45 150 A4
Upham SO32 58 C3
Elm Ct
Chandler's Ford SO53 30 B1
4 New Milton BH25 195 A1
Southampton, Sholing
SO19 103 C2
29 Southampton, Westwood Pk
SO17 79 A1
Winchester SO22 10 C4
Elm Gdns
Bournemouth BH4 204 B3
West End SO30 80 B2
Elm Gr Eastleigh SO50 55 C1
Gosport PO12 181 A3
Portsmouth PO5 215 B1
South Hayling PO11 185 A2
Elm La PO9 135 C1
Elm Lodge PO5 215 C1
Elm Park Rd PO9 135 C1
Elm Rd
Bishop's Waltham SO32 83 C4
Havant PO9 160 A4
Winchester SO22 10 C4
Elm St Portsmouth PO1 215 A1
Southampton SO14 103 A2
Elm Terr Liss GU33 20 C3
Southampton SO14 103 A2
Elm Tree Wlk BH22 189 C4
Elmdale GU31 41 A2
Elmdale Cl SO31 152 B4
Elmdale Gr SO51 51 A1
Elmers Way BH23 169 A1
Elmes Dr SO15 101 C4
Elmes Rd BH9 189 C1
Elmeswelle Rd PO8 112 A3
Elmfield Cl SP5 47 B3
Elmfield La SO45 178 C4
Elmgate Dr BH7 206 A4
Elmhurst Rd
Bournemouth BH11 189 A3
Fareham PO16 155 A4
Gosport PO12 181 B2
West Moors BH22 138 C1
Elmhurst Way BH22 138 C1
Elmleigh Rd PO9 135 C1
Elmore Ave PO13 180 A3
Elmore Cl PO13 179 C1
Elmore Dr BH24 139 C3
Elmore Rd PO13 179 C1
Elmrise Prim Sch BH11 189 A2
Elms Ave BH14 203 A1
Elms Cl Fordingbridge SP6 69 A1
Poole BH14 203 A1
Elms Rd PO16 155 A4
Elms Way BH6 206 C2
Elmsdown Ct BH24 140 C4
Elmsleigh Ct SO17 79 A2
Elmsleigh Gdns SO16 79 A2
Elmslie Gdns SO31 104 C1
Elmstead Rd BH13 214 C4
Elmtree Cl SO40 100 A1
Elmtree Gdns
2 Eastleigh SO50 56 A1
Romsey SO51 53 B3
Elmtree Rd PO6 158 C4
Elmwood Ave
Fordingbridge SP6 69 B1
Waterlooville PO7 134 C3
Elmwood Ct SO16 78 A1
Elmwood Lodge 2
PO16 131 A1
Elmwood Rd PO2 157 C2
Elmwood Way BH23 209 A4
Elphinstone Rd
Christchurch BH23 194 A1
Portsmouth PO5 182 B1
Elsfred Rd PO14 179 A3
Elson Inf Sch PO12 181 A4
Elson Jun Sch PO12 181 A4
Elson La PO12 181 A4
Elson Rd PO12 181 A4

Elstead Gdns PO7 134 B2
Elstree Rd SO19 103 C3
Eltham Cl BH7 206 A4
Elvin Cl SO41 195 C2
Elwell Gn PO11 184 C2
Elwyn Rd BH1 205 B3
Ely Ct PO13 180 B3
Elysium Ct BH22 165 C2
Emanuel St PO2 182 B4
Embankment Way BH24 141 A3
Embassy Ct PO4 215 D2
Emberley Cl BH22 166 A3
Embley Cl SO40 76 B1
Embley La SO51 51 C4
Embley Park Ind Est
SO51 51 C4
Embley Park Jun Sch
SO51 52 C4
Embley Park Sch SO51 51 C3
Embsay Rd SO31 128 B4
Emer Cl SO52 54 A3
Emerald Cl
Southampton SO19 104 A3
St Leonards BH24 139 C3
Waterlooville PO7 135 A4
Emerald Cres SO45 126 A2
Emerson Cl BH15 202 B1
Emerson Rd BH15 202 B1
Emily Cl BH23 192 A1
Emily Ct BH14 203 C3
Emily Davis Halls Of
Residence 12 SO14 102 C3
Emmadale Ct 5 SO14 103 A3
Emmanuel CE Mid Sch
BH31 114 C3
Emmanuel Cl PO14 129 B1
Emmett Rd SO16 77 C3
Emmons Cl SO31 128 A1
Empire Ct 13 PO9 135 C1
Empress Pk SO14 103 A4
Empress Rd
Lyndhurst SO43 121 C3
Southampton, Bevois Valley
SO14 103 A4
Empshott Rd PO4 182 C2
Empson Wlk PO13 179 C2
Emsbrook Dr PO10 136 C1
Emsworth Common Rd
PO9,PO10 136 C3
Emsworth House Cl
PO10 136 C1
Emsworth Mus★ PO10 160 C4
Emsworth Prim Sch
PO10 136 C1
Emsworth Rd
Havant PO9 136 A1
Lymington SO41 197 C2
Portsmouth PO2 157 C1
Southampton SO15 102 A4
Thorney Island PO10 161 A1
Emsworth Sta PO10 136 C1
Encombe Cl BH12 203 C4
Endeavour Cl 17 SO15 102 A4
Endeavour Pk BH24 141 A3
Endeavour Rd PO12 181 B2
Endeavour Way SO45 126 A3
Enderleigh Ho PO9 135 C1
Enderwood Cl SO40 100 A4
Endfield Cl BH23 191 C1
Endfield Rd
Bournemouth BH9 190 A1
Christchurch BH23 191 C1
Endle St SO14 103 A2
Endofield Cl PO14 154 C3
Enfield Cres BH15 202 C3
Enfield Gr SO19 103 C2
Enfield Rd BH15 202 C3
Englands Way BH11 188 B2
Englefield Ct 4 SO31 127 A3
Englefield Rd SO18 103 B4
English Ct 16 SO51 52 C4
English Rd SO15 102 A4
Enmill La SO22 9 C3
Ennel Copse SO52 54 A2
Ennerdale Cl PO8 88 B1
Ennerdale Gdns SO18 80 A1
Ennerdale Rd
Southampton SO16 77 C1
Stubbington PO14 154 B2
Ensbury Ave BH10 189 B1
Ensbury Cl BH10 189 B1
Ensbury Ct BH10 189 C1
Ensbury Park Rd BH9 189 C1
Ensign Dr PO13 180 B3
Ensign Pk SO31 127 C1
Ensign Way SO31 127 C1
Enterprise Cl SO31 128 C1
Enterprise Ctr
Fareham PO14 155 A3
Portsmouth PO3 158 A2
Enterprise Ind Est PO8 112 B4
Enterprise Rd
Chilworth SO16 54 B1
Horndean PO8 112 B4
Enterprise Way
Hurn BH23 190 B4
Southampton SO14 103 A1
Eperston Rd PO8 112 A3
Epiphany CE Prim Sch
BH9 190 A2
Epping Cl SO18 80 A1
Epsom Cl SO50 81 B4
Epsom Ct PO15 129 B4
Epworth Rd PO2 157 C1
Erasmus Pk SO23 2 B1

Eric Rd PO14 179 B3
Erica Cl
Locks Heath SO31 128 C2
Waterlooville PO8 112 A2
Erica Dr BH21 186 B3
Erica Way PO8 112 A2
Ericksen Rd BH11 189 B2
Erinbank Mans BH1 205 B2
Ernest Cl PO10 136 C1
Ernest Rd Havant PO9 135 B2
Portsmouth PO1 182 C4
Erpingham Rd BH12 204 A3
Errington Ho 7 SO50 56 A1
Erskine Ct SO16 77 C3
Erskine Rd SO22 10 C4
Escombe Rd SO50 56 B2
Escur Cl PO2 157 C2
Esdaile La BH24 142 C2
Esher Gr PO7 111 B1
Eskdale Cl PO8 88 B1
Eskdale Ho 16 PO6 133 A1
Esmond Cl PO10 160 C4
Esmonde Cl PO13 179 C1
Esmonde Way BH17 202 C4
Esplanade Poole BH13 214 C4
Portsmouth PO4 183 A1
Esplanade Gdns PO4 183 B1
Esplanade The PO12 181 C2
Essex Ave BH23 191 C1
Essex Gn SO53 55 B1
Essex Rd PO4 183 A2
Esslemont Rd PO4 182 C2
Estella Rd PO2 182 B4
Estridge Cl SO31 105 A1
Ethel Rd PO1 215 D4
Ethelbert Rd BH21 163 B2
Ethelburt Ave SO16 79 B3
Ethelred Gdns SO40 100 B3
Eton Gdns BH4 204 B2
Eton Rd PO5 215 D2
Ettrick Rd BH13 204 A1
Eucalyptus Ave BH24 140 A1
European Way SO14 103 A1
Euryalus Rd PO14 155 A3
Euston Gr BH24 141 A3
Euston Rd PO4 183 A3
Eva Allaway Ct 26 PO1 182 A3
Evans Cl
Bournemouth BH11 188 C1
Portsmouth PO2 157 A1
St Leonards BH24 139 C3
Evans Rd PO4 183 A2
Evans St SO14 103 A2
Evelegh Rd PO6 158 B4
Evelyn Cl SO32 83 C2
Evelyn Cres SO15 102 B4
Evelyn Mews 1 BH9 189 C1
Evelyn Rd BH9 190 A1
Evening Glade BH22 165 C2
Evenlode Rd SO16 77 C1
Eventide Homes BH8 190 C1
Everdene Cl BH22 165 B1
Everdon La PO3 158 B2
Everest Rd BH23 207 C4
Everglades Ave PO8 111 C2
Everglades Cl BH22 165 B4
Evergreen Cl
Marchwood SO40 101 C1
Three Legged Cross BH21 138 C4
Waterlooville PO7 134 B4
Evergreens
St Leonards BH24 139 C3
Totton SO40 101 A3
Evering Ave BH12 188 B1
Evering Gdns BH12 188 B1
Everlea Cl SO41 196 B1
Everon Gdns BH25 195 A1
Evershot Rd BH8 190 C1
Eversleigh BH2 204 B1
Eversley Cres PO9 135 C2
Eversley Pl SO22 10 B3
Everton Rd SO41 196 A1
Evesham Cl
Bournemouth BH7 206 A4
Southampton SO16 79 A3
Evesham Ct BH13 204 A1
Ewart Ct SO45 126 A3
Ewart Rd PO1 182 C4
Ewell Way SO40 76 B1
Ewhurst Cl PO9 135 B2
Exbourne Manor BH1 205 B2
Exbury Cl SO50 56 C1
Exbury Dr BH11 188 C3
Exbury Gdns* SO45 177 A3
Exbury Rd
Blackfield SO45 150 C1
Havant PO9 136 A3
Excellent Rd PO14 154 C3
Excelsior Rd BH14 203 B2
Exchange Rd PO1 215 A3
Exeter Cl Eastleigh SO50 55 C3
Emsworth PO10 136 C1
Locks Heath SO31 128 C2
Southampton SO18 80 A1
Exeter Cres BH2 204 C2
Exeter Ct
10 Christchurch BH23 209 A4
Gosport PO13 180 B3
Exeter La BH2 204 C1
Exeter Park Mans BH2 204 C1
Exeter Park Rd BH2 204 C1
Exeter Rd
Bournemouth BH2 204 C2
Portsmouth PO4 182 C1
Southampton SO18 104 A4
Exford Ave SO18 104 B4
Exford Dr SO18 104 B4
Exleigh Cl SO18 104 A3
Exmoor Cl
Swanwick PO15 129 A4
Totton SO40 100 A4
Exmoor Rd SO14 103 A3
Exmouth Gdns SO50 81 B4
Exmouth Rd
Gosport PO12 181 A4
Portsmouth PO5 182 B1
Exmouth St SO14 103 A3
Explosion Mus of Naval Firepower* PO12 181 B4
Exton Gdns PO16 132 B1
Exton Rd
Bournemouth BH6 206 B4
Havant PO9 136 A3
Eyebright Cl SO50 81 B3
Eyeworth Wlk SO45 125 B2
Eynham Ave SO19 104 B3
Eynham Cl SO19 104 B3
Eynon Mews BH24 140 C3
Eyre Cl SO40 100 B3

F

F Ave SO45 150 C3
Faber Cl PO9 136 A2
Faber Mews SO51 53 A4
Fabers Yd 16 SO22 10 C4
Fabian Cl PO7 135 A4
Factory Rd Eastleigh SO50 56 A1
Upton BH16 201 B3
Fair Field SO51 28 A1
Fair Gn SO19 104 A3
Fair Isle Cl PO14 154 A2
Fair La SO21 11 C4
Fair Lea BH2 204 C1
Fair Oak Ct
4 Fair Oak SO50 57 B1
Gosport PO12 180 B2
Fair Oak Dr PO9 135 C2
Fair Oak Inf Sch SO50 57 B1
Fair Oak Jun Sch SO50 57 B1
Fairacre Rise PO14 154 A4
Fairacre Wlk PO14 154 A4
Fairbairn Wlk SO53 54 C3
Fairbourne Cl PO8 111 C1
Fairclose Dr SO22 1 A3
Faircourt 18 BH25 195 A2
Faircross Cl SO45 150 B2
Fairdown Cl SO23 11 B4
Fairfax Cl SO22 10 A3
Fairfax Ct SO19 104 C3
Fairfax Mews SO19 104 C3
Fairfield
Christchurch BH23 207 A4
Denmead PO7 110 C3
Fairfield Ave PO14 154 C4
Fairfield Cl
Christchurch BH23 207 A4
Emsworth PO10 136 C1
Hythe SO45 125 C2
Lymington SO41 197 C2
Wimborne Minst BH21 163 C3
Fairfield Inf Sch PO9 136 A1
Fairfield Rd
Barton on Sea BH25 209 C4
Compton(Hants) SO21 31 B3
Havant PO9 135 C1
Wimborne Minst BH21 163 B2
Winchester SO21 1 C1
Fairfield Sq PO6 157 C4
Fairgate Ctr The SP6 70 A2
Fairhaven Ct 12 BH5 205 C2
Fairhome Cl PO12 181 A4
Fairies Dr BH22 165 C2
Fairisle Inf Sch SO16 77 C2
Fairisle Jun Sch SO16 77 C2
Fairisle Rd SO16 77 C2
Fairlands Montessori Sch SO32 107 C4
Fairlawn Cl SO16 77 C3
Fairlawn Ho 27 SO22 10 C4
Fairlea Grange 3 SO16 78 C2
Fairlea Rd
Emsworth PO10 136 C2
Lymington SO41 197 C3
Fairlead Dr PO13 180 B3
Fairlie BH24 117 B1
Fairlie Cl SO30 81 B2
Fairlie Pk BH24 117 A1
Fairlight La SO41 195 B4
Fairmead Ct PO11 184 C2
Fairmead Way SO40 100 C3
Fairmead Wlk PO8 112 A2
Fairmile Par BH23 191 C1
Fairmile Rd BH23 191 C1
Fairoak Rd
Bishopstoke SO50 57 A1
Fair Oak SO50 57 A1
Fairthorn Ct 2 BH2 204 C2
Fairthorne Gdns PO12 181 A2
Fairview Cl Hythe SO45 126 A2
Romsey SO51 28 A1
Fairview Cres BH18 187 A3
Fairview Ct PO12 180 C2
Fairview Dr
Broadstone BH18 187 A3
Hythe SO45 126 A2
Romsey SO51 28 A1
Fairview Par 1 SO45 126 A1
Fairview Pk BH14 203 B2
Fairview Rd BH18 187 A3
Fairwater Cl PO13 155 A1
Fairway Ave BH14 214 B4
Fairway Bsns Ctr PO3 158 B1
Fairway Dr BH23 206 C3
Fairway Gdns SO16 77 C3
Fairway Rd SO45 125 C2
Fairway The
Barton on Sea BH25 210 A4
Gosport PO13 155 B1
Locks Heath SO31 128 C1
Portchester PO16 156 B4
Rowland's Castle PO9 113 B1
Fairways BH22 165 C3
Fairwinds BH13 214 A2
Fairwood Rd BH31 115 B3
Fairy Cross Way PO8 112 A1
Falaise Rd SO16 78 B2
Falcon Cl PO16 155 C4
Falcon Dr BH23 208 A3
Falcon Fields SO45 151 A2
Falcon Gn PO6 158 C4
Falcon Rd PO8 112 A4
Falcon Sq SO50 55 C1
Falcon View SO22 10 B2
Falcon Way SO32 81 C1
Falconer Ct SO45 150 B3
Falconer Dr BH15 201 C2
Falconwood Cl SP6 69 B1
Falkland Ct SO53 55 B2
Falkland Rd
Chandler's Ford SO53 55 B2
Southampton SO15 102 A4
Falkland Sq 2 BH15 202 B1
Falklands Cl PO13 179 C2
Falklands Rd 1 PO2 157 C2
Fallow Field SO22 10 B2
Fallows The BH25 195 A3
Falstaff Way SO40 100 C3
Fancy Rd BH12 203 A4
Fanshawe St SO14 103 A3
Far Ends 13 BH14 203 A2
Far Meadow Way PO10 160 B4
Farcroft Rd BH12 203 A3
Fareham Coll PO14 130 C1
Fareham Hts PO16 131 B2
Fareham Ind Pk PO16 131 B2
Fareham Park Rd PO15 130 B2
Fareham Rd
Gosport PO13 155 B2
Southwick PO17 132 C3
Wickham PO17 108 A2
Fareham Sta PO15 130 C1
Faringdon Ct 16 SO23 2 A1
Faringdon Rd SO18 104 B4
Farleigh Cl PO9 135 B3
Farley Cl Fair Oak SO50 57 B1
Winchester SO22 10 A2
Farley Ct SO15 78 B1
Farley La SO51 7 C1
Farley Mount Nature Reserve* SO21 9 A4
Farley Mount Rd SO21 9 A2
Farlington Ave PO6 134 B1
Farlington Marshes (Nature Reserve)* PO6 158 C3
Farlington Rd PO2 157 C1
Farm Cl
Hamble-le-Rice SO31 128 A1
Ringwood BH24 141 A4
Farm Edge Rd PO14 179 B3
Farm House Cl PO14 154 B3
Farm La
Christchurch BH23 208 A3
Southbourne PO18 161 C4
Farm La (N) BH25 210 A4
Farm La S BH25 210 A4
Farm Lane Cl PO7 134 B3
Farm Rd
Titchfield PO14,PO15 129 C1
West Moors BH22 138 B1
Farm View PO10 136 C2
Farm View Ave PO8 88 A3
Farmdene Cl BH23 208 B4
Farmers Wlk
Hordle SO41 211 B4
1 Wimborne Minst BH21 163 A3
Farmery Cl SO18 79 B2
Farmhouse Way PO8 112 A3
Farmlea Rd PO6 157 A4
Farmside Gdns PO3 157 C2
Farnham Rd Liss GU33 20 C2
Poole BH12 204 A4
Steep GU32 41 A4
Farnleys Mead SO41 197 C1
Faroes Cl PO14 154 A2
Farrier Way PO16 155 A3
Farriers Cl BH21 164 A3
Farriers Way PO7 112 B1
Farriers Wlk PO12 181 B3
Farringdon Rd PO9 136 A2
Farringford Rd SO19 104 B3
Farrington BH4 204 B1
Farthing La PO1 182 A2
Farthings Gate PO7 134 C2
Farwell Cl BH23 192 B2
Farwell Rd BH12 188 B1
Fastnet Cl SO16 77 C3
Fastnet Ho 13 PO5 182 B1
Fastnet Way PO14 154 A2
Fathersfield SO42 145 C1
Fathoms Reach PO11 184 C2
Faulston Cotts SP5 22 B4
Faversham BH2 204 B1
Fawcett Rd
Barton on Sea BH25 194 C1
Portsmouth PO4 215 D2
Fawley Bsns Ctr SO45 151 A2
Fawley By Pass SO45 151 A2
Fawley Ct 43 PO9 136 A3
Fawley Gn BH8 190 B2
Fawley Inf Sch SO45 151 A2
Fawley La Froxfield GU34 17 A2
Owslebury SO21 33 A4
Fawley Rd Fawley SO45 150 C2
Hythe SO45 150 A4
Portsmouth PO2 157 C3
Southampton SO15 102 A3
Fawn Gdns BH25 194 C2
Fay Cl PO14 179 B3
Fayre La PO16 155 A4
Fayrewood Ct BH31 114 C4
Fearon Rd PO2 157 C1
Felix Rd PO12 181 A4
Fell Cl SO31 129 A2
Fell Dr PO13 179 C2
Felmer Dr SO23 2 B4
Feltham Cl SO51 53 B4
Felton Cres BH23 208 C4
Felton Ct BH14 202 C3
Felton Rd BH14 202 C3
Feltons Pl PO3 157 C3
Fen Ave PO16 155 A4
Fenleigh Cl BH25 195 A1
Fennel Gdns SO41 197 C3
Fennell Cl PO7 111 B1
Fenton Rd BH6 206 B3
Fenwick Ct BH8 205 A3
Fenwick Hospl SO43 121 C3
Fern Bank 28 BH2 204 C2
Fern Barrow BH12 204 A4
Fern Cl Alderholt SP6 93 A3
Burton BH23 192 B1
Petersfield GU31 41 B2
Fern Cotts 2 PO16 131 B1
Fern Ct SO18 103 C4
Fern Dr PO9 136 A1
Fern Rd Hythe SO45 125 C2
Southampton SO19 103 C1
Fern Way PO15 129 B2
Ferncroft Cl PO14 179 B3
Ferncroft Gdns BH10 189 B3
Ferncroft Rd BH10 189 B3
Ferndale Hedge End SO30 105 B3
Waterlooville PO7 135 A4
Ferndale Mews PO13 155 A2
Ferndale Rd
Marchwood SO40 101 C1
New Milton BH25 195 A3
Ferndene Way SO18 103 C4
Ferndown Ct SP6 69 B1
Ferndown Fst Sch BH22 165 B3
Ferndown Ind Est BH21 164 C4
Ferndown Mid Sch BH22 165 B3
Ferndown Upper Sch BH22 165 A3
Ferneham Rd PO15 130 B1
Fernglade BH25 195 A2
Fernheath Cl BH11 189 A2
Fernheath Rd BH11 189 A2
Fernhill SO53 55 C3
Fernhill Cl BH17 188 A1
Fernhill Flats 29 BH2 204 C2
Fernhill Gate BH25 195 A3
Fernhill La BH25 195 A2
Fernhill Rd BH25 195 A2
Fernhills Rd SO45 126 A1
Fernhurst Cl PO11 184 B2
Fernhurst Jun Sch PO4 182 C2
Fernhurst Rd PO4 182 C2
Fernie Cl PO14 179 A3
Fernlea Ave BH22 165 B2
Fernlea Cl
Ferndown BH22 165 B2
St Leonards BH24 139 C2
Fernlea Gdns
Ferndown BH22 165 B2
Southampton SO16 78 C2
Fernlea Way SO45 125 B2
Fernside Ave BH14 202 C2
Fernside Cl
Holbury SO45 150 B2
Southampton SO16 101 C4
Fernside Ct BH15 202 C2
Fernside Rd
Bournemouth BH9 204 C4
Poole BH15 202 C2
West Moors BH22 138 C1
Fernside Way SO50 57 C1
Fernside Wlk SO50 57 C1
Fernway Cl BH21 164 A2
Fernwood Cl BH24 140 A3
Fernwood Cres SO18 103 C4
Fernwood Ho PO8 112 A1
Ferny Crofts (Scout Ctr) SO42 148 A4
Fernyhurst Ave SO16 77 C3
Ferris Ave BH8 190 B1
Ferris Cl BH8 190 B1
Ferris Pl BH8 190 B1
Ferrol Rd PO12 181 B3
Ferry Rd
Bournemouth BH6 206 C2
Hamworthy BH15 202 A1
Hythe SO45 125 C2
Poole BH19 214 A1
Portsmouth PO4 183 B2
Portsmouth PO4 183 C2
South Hayling PO11 184 A2
Ferry Way BH13 214 A2
Ferrybridge Gn 4 SO30 105 B3
Ferrymans Quay SO31 127 A3
Ferrypoint SO41 198 A2
Festing Gr PO4 183 A1
Festing Rd PO4 182 C1
Feversham Ave BH8 190 C1
Fey Rd PO12 181 B3
Fibbards Rd SO42 145 C1
Field Cl
Compton (Hants) SO21 3
Gosport PO13 15
Locks Heath SO31 12
Romsey SO51 5
Southampton SO16 7
Field End SO23
Field Pl
Barton on Sea BH25 20
Verwood BH31 11
Field View SO53 5
Field Way
Christchurch BH23 19
Compton (Hants) SO21 3
Corfe Mullen BH21 18
Denmead PO7 11
Fordingbridge SP6 7
Field Wlk SO41 19
Fielden Cl SO52 5
Fielder Dr PO14 15
Fielders Ct PO7 13
Fielders' Way SO51 5
Fieldfare Cl PO8 8
Fieldfare Ct SO40 10
Fieldhouse Dr PO13 17
Fieldmore Rd PO12 18
Fields Cl SO45 15
Fields The BH31 11
Fieldway BH24 14
Fifth Ave Cosham PO6 15
Havant PO9 13
Fifth St PO1 18
Filmer Cl PO13 18
Filmorehill La GU34 1
Filton Cl SO40 7
Filton Rd SO41 19
Finch Ho PO4 18
Finch Rd PO4 18
Finch's La SO21 3
Finchdean Rd
Havant PO9 13
Rowland's Castle PO9 11
Finches The SO17 7
Finchfield Ave BH11 18
Finchmead La GU32 4
Finchwood Farm Ind Units PO11 16
Findon Rd PO12 18
Fineshade 7 BH13 21
Finisterre Cl PO14 15
Finlay Cl SO19 10
Fiona Cl SO23 1
Fir Ave BH25 195
Fir Cl Lyndhurst SO43 121
West Moors BH22 138
Fir Copse Rd PO7 134
Fir Croft Dr SO53 55
Fir Rd SO40 100
Fir Tree Cl Fair Oak SO50 81
St Leonards BH24 139
Fir Tree Cotts GU33 21
Fir Tree Ct SO18 104
Fir Tree Gdns PO8 112
Fir Tree Gr SO45 150
Fir Tree Hill SP6 93
Fir Tree La BH23 193
Fir Tree Rd Cadnam SO40 99
South Hayling PO11 185
Fir Vale Rd BH1 204
Firbank Rd BH9 205
Firecrest Cl SO16 78
Firgrove Cl SO52 53
Firgrove Cres PO3 157
Firgrove Ct SO15 102
Firgrove La PO17 108
Firgrove Rd
North Baddesley SO52 54
Southampton SO15 102
Firlands Rise PO9 135
Firmain Rd BH12 188
Firmount Cl SO41 196
Firs Ave PO8 111
Firs Cres SO23 2
Firs Dr SO30 105
Firs Glen Rd
Bournemouth BH9 204
Verwood BH31 115
West Moors BH22 138
Firs La BH14 214
Firs The
Bournemouth BH1, 205
Chandler's Ford SO53 55
Gosport PO13 155
Southampton SO16 78
Firshill BH23 208
Firside Rd BH21 186
First Ave Cosham PO6 157
Cosham, Farlington PO6 158
Havant PO9 136
Horndean PO8 88
Southampton SO15 101
Southbourne PO10 161
First Marine Ave BH25 209
First St SO45 150
Firsway BH16 201
Firtree Cres SO41 195
Firtree La SO50 81
Firtree Way SO19 104
Firwood Cl SO53 55
Fisgard Rd PO12 181
Fisher Cl PO14 154
Fisher Rd PO13 155
Fisher's Rd SO40 101
Fisherman's Ave BH5, BH6 206
Fisherman's Wlk BH5 206
Fishermans Rd BH15 202
Fishermans The PO10 161

ermans Wlk PO11 . .185 C1
ers Gr PO6 . . . . . . .158 C4
ers Hill PO15 . . . . .130 A1
ery La PO11 . . . . . .185 B1
lake Mdws SO51 . . . .28 A1
gerald Cl PO15 . . . .129 B4
harris Ave BH9 . . . .205 A4
herbert Rd PO6 . . . .158 B4
herbert Spur PO6 . .158 C4
herbert St PO1 . . . .215 B4
hugh Ho SO15 . . . . .102 C3
hugh Pl SO15 . . . . .102 C4
hugh St 13 SO15 . . . .102 C3
maurice Rd BH23 . . .206 C4
pain Cl BH22 . . . . . .165 B1
pain Rd BH22 . . . . . .165 B1
patrick Ct PO6 . . . . .133 B1
roy Cl SO16 . . . . . . .78 C4
roy Wlk PO1 . . . . . .215 C4
william Ave PO14 . . .179 A3
william Cl BH11 . . . .188 C3
worth Ave BH16 . . . .201 B2
wygram Cres PO9 . .135 C2
e Bridges Rd SO23 . . .10 C2
e Elms Dr SO51 . . . . .53 B3
e Heads Rd PO8 . . . .112 B4
e Post La PO12 . . . .181 A3
efields Cl SO23 . . . . .11 B3
efields Rd SO23 . . . . .11 B4
g Staff Gn PO12 . . . .181 B3
g Wlk PO8 . . . . .111 C3
ghead BH13 . . . . . . .214 C3
ghead Chine Rd
13 . . . . .214 C3
ghead Rd BH13 . . . .214 C4
mbard Ave BH23 . . .192 A1
mbard Rd BH14 . . . .203 B2
mborough Cl SO16 . . .77 B2
mingo Ct PO16 . . . .155 C4
mston St SP5 . . . . . .22 A4
nders Ho 1 PO14 . . .154 C4
nders Ind Pk SO30 . .105 A4
nders Rd SO30 . . . . .105 A4
thouse Rd PO1 . . . . .182 B4
xfields End SP6 . . . . .69 C1
zen Cl BH11 . . . . . . .188 B2
et Cl PO13 . . . . .155 B1
et End Bottom SO31 152 C4
et End Rd SO31 . . . .152 C4
et Terr SO21 . . . . . . .31 A1
et's Cnr BH17 . . . . .202 A4
etend Cl PO9 . . . . . .135 C3
etpoint Bsns Ctr
H15 . . . . .202 A3
ets Est BH15 . . . . . .202 A3
ets La BH15 . . . . . . .202 B3
eetsbridge Bsns Ctr
H17 . . . . .202 A4
etwood Ct BH15 . . . .202 B4
ming Ave SO52 . . . . . .54 A2
ming Cl PO15 . . . . . .129 B2
ming Ct
orth Baddesley SO52 . . . .54 A2
outhampton SO19 . . . . .103 B1
eming Pl
olden Common SO21 . . . . .31 C1
Romsey SO51 . . . . .52 C4
eming Rd SO17 . . . . . .79 B2
etcher Cl
ournemouth BH10 . . . . .189 B2
ythe SO45 . . . . .125 B2
etcher Rd BH10 . . . . .189 B2
etchwood La SO40 . . .100 A2
etchwood Rd SO40 . . .100 A3
euret Cl SO45 . . . . . .126 A1
exford Cl SO53 . . . . . .30 A1
exford Gdns PO9 . . . .136 A2
exford La SO41 . . . . .196 B3
exford Rd SO52,SO53 . . .54 C4
inders Ct PO4 . . . . . .183 A1
int Cl SO19 . . . . . . .104 C2
int St PO5 . . . . .215 A1
oating Bridge Rd
O14 . . . . .103 B2
oral Farm BH21 . . . . .164 A1
orence Cl SO51 . . . . . .51 A1
orence Ct 3 SO18 . . . .103 C4
orence Rd
Bournemouth BH5 . . . . .205 C2
Poole BH14 . . . . .203 B2
Portsmouth PO5 . . . . . .182 B1
Southampton SO19 . . . . .103 B1
orentine Way PO7 . . . .135 A4
orin Mall 7 BH7 . . . . .205 C2
lorins The
Locks Heath PO14 . . . . . .129 A1
Waterlooville PO7 . . . . . .134 C2
loriston Gdns BH25 . . . .195 B2
lower Bldgs 6 PO13 . . .179 C1
lower Ct 10 BH21 . . . . .163 B2
lowerdown Cl SO40 . . .100 B4
lowerdown Cvn Pk SO22 .1 B3
lowerdown Ho SO22 . . . . .1 B2
lowers Cl SO31 . . . . . .127 C2
lowers La SO51 . . . . . . .50 B3
lum' E Rd SO45 . . . . . .151 B2
lushards SO41 . . . . . . .197 C2
lying Bull Cl 3 PO2 . . .182 B4
lying Bull Inf Sch PO2 .182 B4
lying Bull Jun Sch
PO2 . . . . .182 B4
lying Bull La PO2 . . . .182 B4
oldsgate Cl SO43 . . . . .121 C3
oley Ho PO1 . . . . .215 B4
olkestone Rd PO3 . . . .183 A4
olly Farm La BH24 . . . .140 B3
olly Field SO32 . . . . . . .83 B4
olly La GU32 . . . . .40 C2

Font Cl PO14 . . . . .129 B2
Fontley Rd PO15 . . . . . .130 A3
Fontmell Rd BH18 . . . . .187 B2
Fontwell Cl SO40 . . . . . . .76 B1
Fontwell Gdns SO50 . . . .81 B4
Fontwell Mews 10 PO7 . .112 A1
Fontwell Rd 32 PO5 . . . .182 B1
Foord Rd SO30 . . . . . . .105 A3
Football Gn SO43 . . . . . .98 B2
Footner Cl SO51 . . . . . . .28 B1
Footners La BH23 . . . . .192 B1
Forbes Cl SO16 . . . . .77 C3
Forbes Rd SO23 . . . . .2 A4
Forbury Rd 2 PO1 . . . . .215 C2
Ford Ave SO53 . . . . .55 B2
Ford Cl BH22 . . . . .165 C4
Ford La BH22 . . . . .166 A4
Ford Rd PO12 . . . . .180 C3
Fordingbridge Bsns Pk
SP6 . . . . .69 B1
Fordingbridge Hospl
SP6 . . . . .69 C1
Fordingbridge Inf Sch
SP6 . . . . .69 C2
Fordingbridge Jun Sch
SP6 . . . . .69 C2
Fordingbridge Rd
Alderholt SP6 . . . . .93 A4
Portsmouth PO4 . . . . . . .183 A2
Fordington Ave SO22 . . . .10 C4
Fordington Rd 3 SO22 . . .10 C4
Foreland Cl BH23 . . . . . .191 B2
Foreland Ct PO11 . . . . . .185 B1
Foreland Rd BH16 . . . . . .201 B2
Forelle Ctr The BH31 . . .115 B2
Foremans Cotts PO12 . . .181 C1
Foreshore N SO45 . . . . .151 A3
Foreshore S SO45 . . . . .151 A3
Forest Ave PO8 . . . . . . .112 A2
Forest Cl
Chandler's Ford SO53 . . . . .55 B4
Christchurch BH23 . . . . . .193 B1
North Baddesley SO52 . . . . .53 C3
Verwood BH31 . . . . .115 B2
Waltham Chase SO32 . . . . .83 C2
Waterlooville PO8 . . . . . .111 C2
Forest Cnr GU33 . . . . .21 A4
Forest Ct
Fordingbridge SP6 . . . . . . .69 C1
New Milton BH25 . . . . . . .195 A1
Forest Edge SO45 . . . . . .151 A2
Forest Edge Cl
St Leonards BH24 . . . . . .139 B3
Sway SO41 . . . . .172 A2
Forest Edge Dr BH24 . . .139 B3
Forest Edge Rd BH24 . . .141 C3
Forest Edge Sch SO40 . .100 C4
Forest End PO7 . . . . . . .134 B4
Forest Front SO45 . . . . .150 A4
Forest Gate SO45 . . . . . .177 C4
Forest Gate Gdns SO41 . .197 B1
Forest Gdns
Lyndhurst SO43 . . . . .121 C3
Waltham Chase SO32 . . . . .83 C2
Forest Glade Cl SO42 . . .145 B1
Forest Hall SO42 . . . . . .146 A1
Forest Hill Way SO45 . . .125 C1
Forest Hills Ct BH24 . . .141 B3
Forest Hills Dr SO18 . . . .79 C2
Forest La Fareham PO17 . .131 A4
Holbury SO45 . . . . .150 A3
Ringwood BH24 . . . . .141 C3
Verwood BH31 . . . . .114 C4
Forest Links Rd BH22 . . .138 A1
Forest Mdw SO45 . . . . . .150 A4
Forest Mead PO7 . . . . . .110 C2
Forest Oak Dr BH25 . . . .195 A3
Forest Park Rd SO42 . . . .145 C1
Forest Pines BH25 . . . . .195 A2
Forest Rd
Bransgore BH23 . . . . .169 C2
Burley BH24 . . . . .142 C3
Chandler's Ford SO53 . . . . .55 B4
Denmead PO7 . . . . .110 B2
Liss GU33 . . . . .21 A3
Nomansland SP5 . . . . .73 B4
Poole BH13 . . . . .204 A1
Waltham Chase SO32 . . . . .83 C2
Waterlooville PO7 . . . . . .134 B4
West Moors BH22 . . . . . .138 C2
Woodgreen SP6 . . . . .47 C2
Forest Rise
Christchurch BH23 . . . . . .193 B1
Liss GU33 . . . . .21 A3
Forest View
Brockenhurst SO42 . . . . . .145 B1
New Milton BH25 . . . . . . .194 B3
4 Southampton SO14 . . . . .102 C2
Forest View Cl BH9 . . . .190 A1
Forest View Dr BH21 . . .165 A3
Forest View Rd BH9 . . . .190 A1
Forest Walks (Rhinefield)★
SO42 . . . . .145 A1
Forest Way
Christchurch BH23 . . . . . .193 B1
Ferndown BH21 . . . . .165 A3
Gosport PO13 . . . . .155 C1
Hordle SO41 . . . . .196 B1
Totton SO40 . . . . .76 A1
Forest Wlks (Blackwater)★
SO42 . . . . .144 C3
Forester Rd SO32 . . . . . . .85 A1
Foresters Gate SO45 . . .177 B4
Foresters Pk SO23 . . . . . . .2 A2
Foresters Rd SO45 . . . . .150 C1
Forestlake Ave BH24 . . .141 B3
Forestside Ave PO9 . . . .136 A3
Forestside Gdns BH24 . . .117 B1

Forestside The BH31 . . .115 B3
Forge Cl SO31 . . . . .105 A1
Forge La SO45 . . . . .151 A2
Forge Rd SO45 . . . . .177 C4
Forneth Gdns PO15 . . . .154 A4
Forres Sandle Manor
SP6 . . . . .69 B1
Forster Rd SO14 . . . . . .103 A4
Forsyth Gdns BH10 . . . .189 B1
Forsythia Cl Havant PO9 .136 A2
Hedge End SO30 . . . . . . .105 A4
Hythe SO45 . . . . .150 A4
Forsythia Pl SO19 . . . . .103 C3
Fort Brockhurst★ PO12 155 C1
Fort Cumberland Pl
BH15 . . . . .201 B1
Fort Cumberland Rd
PO4 . . . . .183 B2
Fort Fareham Ind Est
PO14 . . . . .155 A3
Fort Fareham Rd PO14 . .154 C3
Fort Nelson★ PO16 . . . .132 A2
Fort Nelson Mus★
PO17 . . . . .132 A2
Fort Rd Gosport PO12 . . .181 A1
Southampton SO19 . . . . . .103 C2
Fort Wallington Ind Est
PO16 . . . . .131 B1
Fort Widley Married Quarters
PO6 . . . . .133 C1
Fortescue Rd
Bournemouth BH3 . . . . . .205 A3
Poole BH12 . . . . .203 B3
Forth Cl
North Baddesley SO53 . . . .55 A3
Stubbington PO14 . . . . . .154 A2
Forth Ho 11 SO14 . . . . .103 B3
Forties Cl PO14 . . . . . .154 A2
Forton Rd Gosport PO12 .181 A3
Portsmouth PO1 . . . . . . .182 C3
Fortune Ct SO53 . . . . . . .55 B3
Fortune Ho PO12 . . . . . .181 A3
Fortunes Way PO9 . . . . .134 C1
Forum The 6 PO9 . . . . . .135 C1
Forward Dr SO41 . . . . . .197 B1
Foster Cl PO14 . . . . . . .154 B2
Foster Rd Gosport PO12 . .181 A2
Portsmouth PO1 . . . . . . .215 C4
Founders Way PO13 . . . .155 B1
Foundry Cres SO31 . . . .127 C4
Foundry Ct 36 PO1 . . . . .182 A3
Foundry La SO15 . . . . . .102 A4
Foundry Lane Prim Sch
SO15 . . . . .102 A4
Foundry Rd SP5 . . . . . . .47 B4
Fountain Ct
4 Colden Common SO21 . . .31 C1
Hedge End SO30 . . . . . . .105 A3
Fountain St PO1 . . . . . .215 B3
Fountain Way BH23 . . . .207 A3
Fountains Pk SO31 . . . . .127 A4
Four Acre SO30 . . . . . . .106 A3
Four Cnrs SP6 . . . . .68 A2
Four Marks Gn 3 PO9 . . .136 A3
Four Wells Rd BH21 . . . .164 A4
Fourposts Hill 16 SO15 . .102 C3
Fourshells Cl SO45 . . . .150 C1
Fourth Ave Cosham PO6 . .157 C4
Havant PO9 . . . . .136 A1
Fourth St PO1 . . . . .182 C3
Fowey Cl SO53 . . . . .55 A3
Fowey Ct PO12 . . . . . . .181 B4
Fowey The SO45 . . . . . .150 C1
Fowlers Rd SO30 . . . . . .105 A4
Fowlers Wlk SO16 . . . . . .54 B1
Fox Cl SO50 . . . . .56 C1
Fox Field SO41 . . . . . . .196 B1
Fox La Ferndown BH21 . . .164 B3
Winchester SO22 . . . . .10 B3
Fox Pond La SO41 . . . . .197 B1
Fox's Wlk SO45 . . . . . . .177 C4
Foxbury Cl SO45 . . . . . .126 A1
Foxbury Gr PO16 . . . . . .156 A4
Foxbury La Gosport PO13 155 B2
Gosport PO13 . . . . .155 C3
Westbourne PO10 . . . . . .137 B2
Foxbury Rd BH24 . . . . . .166 C4
Foxcombe Cl SO32 . . . . . .84 A3
Foxcote Gdns BH25 . . . .194 C2
Foxcote Ho 6 PO6 . . . . .132 C1
Foxcott Cl SO19 . . . . . .126 C4
Foxcott Gr PO9 . . . . . . .135 C3
Foxcroft Dr
Holbury SO45 . . . . .150 A2
Wimborne Minst BH21 . . . .164 A3
Foxes Cl Verwood BH31 . .114 C3
Waterlooville PO7 . . . . . .134 C3
Foxes La SO51 . . . . .50 C3
Foxglade SO45 . . . . . . .177 C4
Foxglove Cl BH23 . . . . .208 B4
Foxglove Pl BH25 . . . . .195 B2
Foxgloves Fareham PO16 131 B2
Upton BH16 . . . . .201 A4
Foxgloves The SO30 . . . .105 B3
Foxhayes La SO45 . . . . .177 C4
Foxhills Ashurst SO40 . . .100 B2
Verwood BH31 . . . . .115 A3
Foxhills Cl SO40 . . . . . .100 B2
Foxhills Inf Sch SO40 . . .100 B2
Foxhills Jun Sch SO40 . .100 B2
Foxholes 1 BH6 . . . . . . .206 C2
Foxholes Rd
Bournemouth BH6 . . . . . .206 C2
Poole BH15 . . . . .202 C3
Foxlands SO45 . . . . .177 C4
Foxlea 19 SO15 . . . . . . .102 C4
Foxlea Gdns PO12 . . . . .181 A4
Foxlease Terr SO43 . . . . .121 C2

Foxley Dr PO3 . . . . .158 A2
Foxtail Dr SO45 . . . . . . .125 C1
Foxwood Ave BH23 . . . . .207 C3
Foxy Paddock SO45 . . . . .177 C4
Foy Gdns SO31 . . . . .128 B1
Foyes Ct SO15 . . . . .102 B3
Foyle Rd SO53 . . . . .55 A3
Frampton Cl
1 Colden Common SO21 . . .31 C1
New Milton BH25 . . . . . . .195 B3
Frampton Pl BH24 . . . . .141 A4
Frampton Rd BH9 . . . . . .205 A4
Frampton Way
Kings Worthy SO23 . . . . . . .2 B4
Totton SO40 . . . . .100 C3
Frances Ct 13 BH23 . . . .209 A4
Frances Rd
Bournemouth BH1 . . . . . .205 B2
Waterlooville PO7 . . . . . .134 B2
Francesca Ct 14 BH23 . . .207 C4
Francesca Grange 13
BH23 . . . . .207 C4
Francesca Lo 1 BH23 . . .207 C3
Francis Ave
Bournemouth BH11 . . . . . .188 B2
Portsmouth PO4 . . . . . . .182 C2
Francis Avenue Ind Est
BH11 . . . . .188 B2
Francis Cl PO13 . . . . . . .180 A3
Francis Gdns SO23 . . . . . . .2 A2
Francis Pl PO14 . . . . . . .179 B3
Francis Rd Horndean PO8 . .88 B2
Poole BH12 . . . . .203 C3
Franconia Dr SO16 . . . . . .77 A2
Frank Judd Ct 33 PO1 . . .182 A3
Frank Miles Ho 1 PO5 . .215 B2
Frank Wareham Cottage
Homes The BH9 . . . . . .190 A2
Frankland Cres BH14 . . .203 C2
Frankland Terr 3 PO10 . .161 A4
Franklin Rd
Bournemouth BH9 . . . . . .190 A2
Gosport PO13 . . . . .180 B4
New Milton BH25 . . . . . . .195 B2
Twyford SO21 . . . . .32 A4
Franklyn Ave SO19 . . . . .104 A2
Franklyn Cl BH16 . . . . . .201 A4
Franks Way BH12 . . . . . .203 A4
Frankston Rd BH6 . . . . . .206 B2
Frarydene PO10 . . . . . . .161 B4
Fraser Cl SO16 . . . . .77 C3
Fraser Ct BH25 . . . . . . .194 C2
Fraser Gdns PO10 . . . . .137 C1
Fraser Rd Gosport PO13 . .155 B2
Havant PO9 . . . . .135 B1
Kings Worthy SO23 . . . . . . .2 B4
Poole BH12 . . . . .203 C4
Portsmouth PO5 . . . . . . .215 C2
Portsmouth,Whale Is PO2 . .157 A1
Frater La PO12 . . . . . . .156 A1
Fratton Ct PO1 . . . . . . .215 D3
Fratton Park (Portsmouth
FC) PO4 . . . . .183 A3
Fratton Rd PO1 . . . . . . .215 D4
Fratton Sta PO1 . . . . . .182 C3
Fratton Way SO50 . . . . . .57 B1
Frattton Ind Est PO4 . . .183 A3
Frayslea 4 SO45 . . . . . .126 A1
Freda Rd BH23 . . . . . . .206 C3
Freda Routh Gdns 12
SO50 . . . . .57 B1
Frederica Rd BH9 . . . . .204 C4
Frederick St
Portsmouth PO1 . . . . . . .215 B4
Southampton SO14 . . . . . .103 A3
Free St SO32 . . . . .83 B4
Freedom Ct SO45 . . . . . .126 A2
Freefolk Gn 11 PO9 . . . .136 A3
Freegrounds Ave SO30 . . .105 B3
Freegrounds Cl 1 SO30 105 B3
Freegrounds Inf Sch
SO30 . . . . .105 B3
Freegrounds Jun Sch
SO30 . . . . .105 B3
Freegrounds Rd SO30 . . .105 B3
Freemans Cl BH21 . . . . .164 A3
Freemans La BH21 . . . . .164 A3
Freemantle Bsns Ctr 12
SO15 . . . . .102 B3
Freemantle CE Inf Sch
SO15 . . . . .102 B3
Freemantle Cl SO19 . . . .103 C3
Freemantle Common Rd
SO19 . . . . .103 C3
Freemantle Rd PO12 . . . .181 A4
Freestone Rd 36 PO5 . . .182 B1
Fremington Ct 16 BH25 . .195 A2
French Rd BH17 . . . . . . .187 A1
French St
14 Portsmouth PO1 . . . . .182 A2
Southampton SO14 . . . . . .102 C2
French's Farm Rd BH16 201 A4
Frenches La SO51 . . . . . . .51 B4
Frenchmans Rd GU32 . . . .40 C2
Frenchmoor La
East Dean SP5 . . . . .3 C1
West Tytherley SP5 . . . . . . .3 C2
Frendstaple Rd PO7 . . . .135 A3
Frensham Cl
Bournemouth BH10 . . . . . .189 C2
Hedge End SO30 . . . . . . .105 B3
Frensham Ct
Hedge End SO30 . . . . . . .105 B3
Portsmouth PO4 . . . . . . .182 C2
Frensham Rd PO4 . . . . . .182 C2
Freshfield Gdns PO7 . . . .134 C4
Freshfield Rd SO15 . . . . .102 A4
Freshfield Sq SO15 . . . . .102 A4

Freshwater Ct
Chandler's Ford SO53 . . . . .30 C1
3 Lee-on-the-Solent
PO13 . . . . .179 C1
Freshwater Dr BH15 . . . .201 B2
Freshwater Rd
Christchurch BH23 . . . . . .208 B3
Cosham PO6 . . . . .157 C4
Frewen Liby PO1 . . . . . .182 A2
Friars Croft SO40 . . . . . . .76 B1
Friars Gate BH23 . . . . . .208 B3
Friars Pond Rd PO15 . . . .130 B1
Friars Rd
Christchurch BH23 . . . . . .208 A3
Eastleigh SO50 . . . . .55 C1
Friars Way SO18 . . . . . . .79 B2
Friars Wlk BH25 . . . . . . .210 A4
Friarscroft SO31 . . . . . .127 A4
Friarsgate SO23 . . . . .11 A4
Friary Cl 31 PO5 . . . . . .182 B1
Friary The 30 PO5 . . . . .182 B1
Friday's Ct BH24 . . . . . .140 C4
Friendly Societies' Homes
PO4 . . . . .183 A2
Friendship Ho PO5 . . . . .215 B1
Frimstone Rd SO23 . . . . . .11 B4
Frinton Ct 6 BH14 . . . . .203 A2
Frith La PO17 . . . . .108 A4
Frith Lane End PO17 . . . .108 A4
Fritham Cl SO40 . . . . . .100 B4
Fritham Gdns BH8 . . . . .190 B2
Fritham Rd SO18 . . . . . .104 B4
Frobisher Ave BH12 . . . .188 C1
Frobisher Cl
Christchurch BH23 . . . . . .207 C3
Gosport PO13 . . . . .180 B3
Ringwood BH24 . . . . .117 B1
Frobisher Ct SO40 . . . . .102 A2
Frobisher Gdns
7 Emsworth PO10 . . . . . .160 C4
Southampton SO19 . . . . . .104 B2
Frobisher Gr PO16 . . . . .156 B4
Frobisher Ho 9 PO1 . . . .182 A3
Frobisher Ind Cntr SO51 . .27 C1
Froddington Rd PO1 . . . .215 C2
Frog La SP6 . . . . .93 C4
Froghall SO45 . . . . .126 A1
Frogham Gn PO9 . . . . . .135 B3
Frogham Hill SP6 . . . . . . .94 B3
Frogmore PO14 . . . . . . .154 B4
Frogmore La
Nursling SO16 . . . . .77 B2
Waterlooville PO8 . . . . . .112 A3
Frogmore Rd PO4 . . . . . .183 A3
Frome Cl SO40 . . . . .102 A1
Fromond Cl SO41 . . . . . .197 C3
Fromond Rd SO22 . . . . .1 B2
Front Lawn Inf Sch PO9 135 C3
Front Lawn Jun Sch
PO9 . . . . .135 C3
Frost La SO45 . . . . .126 A1
Frost Rd BH11 . . . . .188 C2
Frosthole Cl PO15 . . . . .130 C2
Frosthole Cres PO15 . . . .130 C2
Froud Way BH21 . . . . . . .186 B2
Froude Ave PO12 . . . . . .181 B1
Froude Rd PO12 . . . . . . .181 B1
Froxfield CE Inf Sch
GU32 . . . . .18 C1
Froxfield Cl SO22 . . . . . . .1 B2
Froxfield Gdns PO16 . . . .132 B1
Froxfield Ho PO1 . . . . . .215 C4
Froxfield Rd PO9 . . . . . .136 A3
Froyle Ct 38 PO9 . . . . . .136 A3
Fry Cl Blackfield SO45 . . .150 C1
Hamble-le-Rice SO31 . . . .128 A2
Fry's La SO32 . . . . .61 B2
Fryer Cl BH11 . . . . .189 A3
Fryern Arc SO53 . . . . . . .55 C4
Fryern Cl SO53 . . . . .55 C3
Fryern Court Rd SP6 . . . .69 C3
Fryern Inf Sch SO53 . . . . .55 C3
Fryern Jun Sch SO53 . . . .55 C3
Fryers Cl SO23 . . . . .2 B4
Fryers Copse BH21 . . . . .164 B3
Fryers Rd BH21 . . . . . . .138 B4
Frys La SO41 . . . . .196 B1
Fuchsia Gdns SO16 . . . . . .78 B1
Fulflood Ct 2 SO22 . . . . . .10 C4
Fulflood Rd PO9 . . . . . . .135 C3
Fullegar Cotts SO32 . . . . .84 A3
Fullerton Cl
26 Havant PO9 . . . . .136 A3
Southampton SO19 . . . . . .126 C4
Fullerton Rd SO41 . . . . .197 B2
Fulmar Cl SO16 . . . . .78 A3
Fulmar Dr SO45 . . . . . . .126 A1
Fulmar Rd BH23 . . . . . . .208 A3
Fulmar Wlk PO13 . . . . . .155 A2
Fulmer Wlk PO8 . . . . . . .111 C2
Fulwood Ave BH11 . . . . .188 C3
Funtington Rd PO2 . . . . .182 C4
Funtley Ct PO16 . . . . . . .130 C2
Funtley Hill PO16 . . . . . .130 C2
Funtley La PO17 . . . . . . .130 C3
Funtley Rd PO15,PO17 . . .130 C3
Furdies PO7 . . . . .110 C2
Furley Cl SO23 . . . . .11 A4
Furlong Mews BH24 . . . .140 C4
Furlong The BH24 . . . . .140 C4
Furlonge Ho PO10 . . . . .136 C1
Furneaux Gdns PO16 . . . .131 A2
Furnell Rd BH15 . . . . . . .202 B1
Furness Rd 11 PO5 . . . . .182 B1
Furniss Way PO11 . . . . . .184 B2

Furnston Gr PO10 137 C1
Fury Way PO14 154 A2
Furze Cl SO19 104 A3
Furze Croft BH25 195 A1
Furze Hall PO16 131 A2
Furze Hill Dr BH14 203 B1
Furze La PO4 183 B2
Furze Rd SO19 104 A3
Furze Way PO8 112 A2
Furzebrook Cl BH17 187 C2
Furzedale Gdns SO45 126 A1
Furzedale Pk SO45 126 A1
Furzedown Cotts SO20 7 A4
Furzedown Cres 54 PO9 136 A3
Furzedown Ho SO20 7 A3
Furzedown Mews 13 SO45 126 A1
Furzedown Rd
King's Somborne SO20 7 A4
Southampton SO17 79 A1
Furzehall Ave PO16 131 A2
Furzehill BH21 163 B4
Furzelands Rd BH21 138 C4
Furzeley Rd PO7 110 C1
Furzey Ave SO45 126 A1
Furzey Cl SO45 150 C1
Furzey Gdns★ SO43 98 A2
Furzey La SO42 148 A1
Furzey Rd BH16 201 A3
Furzley Ct PO9 135 B3
Furzley La SO43 74 B3
Furzley Rd SO40, SO43 74 C2
Furzy Whistlers Cl BH23 169 A1
Fushia Cl PO9 136 B2
Futcher Sch PO6 158 B4
Fyeford Cl SO16 77 C3
Fyfield Cl PO15 129 B4
Fyning St PO1 215 C4

G

G Ave SO45 150 C3
Gable Mews PO11 185 A2
Gables Ct SO16 78 C3
Gage Cl SO40 102 A1
Gain's Rd PO4 182 C1
Gainsborough Ave BH25 195 A3
Gainsborough Cl SO19 104 B1
Gainsborough Ct
11 Bournemouth BH5 206 A3
Lymington SO41 197 B1
North Baddesley SO52 54 A2
Gainsborough Mews PO14 153 C4
Gainsborough Rd
Bournemouth BH7 205 C4
St Leonards BH24 139 C3
Gainsford Rd SO19 103 C3
Galaxie Rd PO8 112 A2
Gale Moor Ave PO12 180 B2
Galleon Cl SO31 128 C1
Gallia Ct SO17 78 C1
Gallop Way BH12 204 B4
Gallops The PO14 129 B1
Galloway Rd BH15 201 B2
Gallows Dr BH22 165 C1
Galsworthy Rd SO40 100 B4
Galt Rd PO6 158 B4
Galton Ave BH23 206 C3
Gamble Cl SO19 103 C2
Gamble Rd PO2 182 B4
Gamblins La SO32 107 C4
Gang Warily Recn Ctr SO45 150 C2
Ganger Farm La SO51 28 B1
Ganger Rd SO51 28 B1
Gannet Cl Hythe SO45 126 A1
Southampton SO16 78 A3
Gannets The PO14 154 A2
Gar St SO22 10 C4
Garage Cotts 2 GU32 40 C2
Garbett Rd SO23 11 B4
Garden City SO45 125 A3
Garden Cl
Lyndhurst SO43 121 C3
New Milton BH25 195 A1
South Hayling PO11 184 C2
Garden Court Cotts BH22 138 B2
Garden Ct
Bournemouth BH1 205 B3
Portchester PO16 156 B4
Garden Downton Moot★ SP5 47 A4
Garden Ho 17 BH1 205 A2
Garden La
Portsmouth PO5 215 B1
St Leonards BH24 139 C2
22 Winchester SO23 11 A4
Garden Mews SO31 128 B1
Garden Rd BH24 142 C2
Garden Terr 5 PO5 182 B1
Garden Wlk BH22 165 C4
Gardeners Cotts BH24 141 A2
Gardeners La
Awbridge SO51 52 A2
Romsey SO51 52 A2
Gardenia Dr PO15 129 C2
Gardens Cres BH14 214 A4
Gardens Ct 7 BH15 202 C2
Gardens Rd BH14 214 A4
Gardens The
Hambledon PO7 86 B2
Havant PO9 136 A1
Gardiner Cl SO40 102 A1
Gardner Ct BH23 206 C4
Gardner Rd
Christchurch BH23 206 C4
Ringwood BH24 141 A3
Titchfield PO14 153 C4
Garendon Ct SP6 69 C1
Garfield Ave BH1 205 B3
Garfield Cl SO32 83 B4
Garfield Rd
Bishop's Waltham SO32 83 B4
5 Netley SO31 127 A3
Portsmouth PO2 182 B4
Southampton SO19 103 C4
Garland Ave PO10 136 C2
Garland Ct 12 PO12 181 A3
Garland Rd BH15 202 B2
Garland Way SO40 100 A4
Garnett Cl PO14 154 B2
Garnier Pk PO17 108 A2
Garnier Rd SO23 11 A3
Garnier St PO1 215 D3
Garnock Rd SO19 103 B1
Garratt Cl SO30 81 B1
Garrett Cl SO19 104 A1
Garrick Gdns SO19 104 A1
Garrick Ho 11 PO2 157 C2
Garrison Hill SO32 61 A1
Garrow Dr SO41 197 C3
Garsdale Cl BH11 189 A3
Garsons Rd PO10 161 B4
Garston Cl GU32 63 B4
Garstons Cl PO14 153 C4
Garstons Rd PO14 153 C4
Garth Cl BH24 139 B2
Garth Rd BH9 190 A1
Garton Rd SO19 103 B2
Gashouse Hill SO31 127 B3
Gaston Gdns SO51 52 C4
Gatcombe SO31 127 B4
Gatcombe Ave PO3 158 A1
Gatcombe Dr PO2 157 C2
Gatcombe Gdns
Fareham PO14 154 A4
West End SO18 80 A1
Gatcombe Park Inf Sch PO2 157 C2
Gate House Rd PO16 156 A4
Gatehouse The
12 Southampton SO18 103 C4
West End SO30 80 B1
Gatekeeper Cl 10 SO23 11 B4
Gateway The BH13 203 C2
Gatwick Cl SO16 78 A2
Gaulter Cl PO9 136 A2
Gavan St SO19 104 B3
Gawn Pl PO12 181 B1
Gayda Ho PO12 180 C3
Gaydon Rise BH11 188 C2
Gaylyn Way PO14 154 A4
Gaza Ave SO42 175 B3
Gaza Ho PO15 130 B2
Gazelle Cl PO13 180 B3
Gazing La SO51 50 C2
Gazings The SO51 50 C2
Geddes Way GU31 41 B2
Gemini Cl SO16 77 C2
General Johnson Ct 6 SO22 10 B3
Geneva Ave BH6 206 B3
Genoa Cl SO41 197 B1
Genoa Ho PO6 157 A4
Gento Cl SO30 105 C3
Geoffrey Ave PO7 134 A1
Geoffrey Cres PO16 155 A3
George Byng Way PO2 182 B4
George Ct The 19 PO1 182 A2
George Curl Way SO18 79 C3
George Eyston Dr SO22 10 B3
George Rd SO41 211 B3
George Rdbt The BH15 202 B2
George St Eastleigh SO50 56 A2
Gosport PO12 181 B3
Portsmouth PO1, PO2 182 C4
Georges Mews BH21 186 B4
Georgia Cl PO13 179 C2
Georgian Cl BH24 141 A4
Georgian Way BH10 189 C2
Georgina Cl BH12 204 B4
Georgina Talbot Ho BH12 204 A4
Gerald Rd BH3 205 A3
Gerard Cres SO19 104 B3
Gerard Ho 6 PO2 157 C2
Germaine Cl BH23 208 C4
Gervis Cres BH14 203 A2
Gervis Pl BH2 204 C2
Gervis Rd BH1 205 A2
Gibbs Rd SO14 102 C3
Gibraltar Cl PO15 130 B1
Gibraltar Rd
Gosport PO14 154 C3
Portsmouth PO4 183 B2
Gibson Cl
Lee-on-the-Solent PO13 179 C2
Swanwick PO15 129 C3
Gibson Rd BH17 202 C4
Giddylake BH21 163 B3
Gifford Cl PO15 130 C2
Gilbert Cl Alderholt SP6 93 A3
Gosport PO13 180 B4
Lymington SO41 197 B1
Gilbert Ct 5 BH23 207 A4
Gilbert Mead PO11 184 C2
Gilbert Rd BH1 205 B3
Gilbert Way PO7 134 C3
Gilbury Cl SO18 79 C2
Gilchrist Gdns SO31 152 B4
Giles Cl Fareham PO16 131 A2
Gosport PO12 181 A3
Hedge End SO30 81 B1
Giles La SP5 50 A2
Gilkicker Rd PO12 181 B1
Gillam Rd BH10 189 B3
Gillcrest PO14 129 B2
Gillett Rd BH12 204 B4
Gillies The 17 PO16 131 A1
Gillingham Cl
Bournemouth BH9 190 B2
Kings Worthy SO23 2 B4
Gillingham Rd SO41 211 B2
Gillion Ct 2 BH23 207 C3
Gillman Rd PO6 134 C1
Gilpin Cl Boldre SO41 173 C1
Southampton SO19 104 C3
Gilpin Hill SO41 172 A1
Gins La SO42 176 C1
Girton Cl PO14 129 B1
Gitsham Gdns PO7 134 B2
Gladdis Rd BH11 188 C2
Glade The
Blackfield SO45 177 C4
Chandler's Ford SO53 30 C1
Fareham PO15 130 B2
South Hayling PO11 185 B1
St Leonards BH24 139 C3
Waterlooville PO7 135 A4
Gladelands Cl BH18 186 C2
Gladelands Mobile Home Pk BH22 165 C4
Gladelands Way BH18 186 C2
Glades The SO31 129 A2
Gladstone Cl BH23 207 B3
Gladstone Gdns PO16 156 B4
Gladstone Pl 4 PO2 182 B4
Gladstone Rd
Bournemouth BH7 205 C3
Gosport PO12 181 A4
Poole BH12 203 B3
Southampton SO19 104 A3
Gladstone Rd E BH7 205 C3
Gladstone Rd W BH1 205 C3
Gladstone St SO23 10 C4
Gladys Ave
Portsmouth PO2 157 B1
Waterlooville PO8 112 A2
Glamis Ave BH10 189 C3
Glamis Cl PO7 135 A4
Glamis Ct PO14 154 B2
Glamorgan Rd PO8 88 A2
Glasgow Rd PO4 183 A2
Glasslaw Rd SO18 104 A4
Glasspool PO7 110 C3
Gleadowe Ave BH23 206 C3
Glebe Cl PO11 184 C3
Glebe Cnr PO17 108 A2
Glebe Ct Botley SO30 106 A4
Fair Oak SO50 57 B1
Southampton SO17 79 A1
Glebe Dr PO13 155 B1
Glebe La SP5 49 B2
Glebe Mdw SP5 4 A1
Glebe Park Ave PO9 135 A1
Glebe Rd GU31 65 B3
Glebe The PO14 179 B3
Glebefield Gdns 1 PO6 157 C4
Glebefields 6 SO41 211 B3
Glen Cl BH25 209 B4
Glen Dale PO9 113 B1
Glen Eyre Cl SO16 79 A2
Glen Eyre Dr SO16 79 A3
Glen Eyre Hall SO16 79 A3
Glen Eyre Rd SO16 78 C3
Glen Eyre Way SO16 79 A2
Glen Fern Rd BH1 205 A2
Glen Ho PO12 180 C2
Glen Rd
Bournemouth BH5 205 C2
Locks Heath SO31 128 C3
Poole BH14 203 A2
Southampton SO19 103 B1
Swanwick SO31 128 C4
Glen Spey BH25 195 B1
Glen The Gosport PO13 155 C1
Poole BH12 203 B3
Poole, Canford Cliffs BH13 214 C4
Glenair Ave BH14 203 A2
Glenair Cres BH14 203 A2
Glenair Rd BH14 203 A2
Glenavon BH25 195 B1
Glenavon Rd BH23 193 C1
Glenbrook Wlk PO14 154 B4
Glencarron Way 11 SO16 78 C2
Glencoe Rd
Bournemouth BH7 205 C4
Poole BH12 203 B3
Portsmouth PO1 182 C4
Glencoyne Gdns SO16 77 C1
Glenda Cl SO31 152 B4
Glendale
Locks Heath SO31 129 A1
Swanmore SO32 84 A2
Glendale Ave BH22 165 C3
Glendale Cl
Christchurch BH23 191 B2
Wimborne Minst BH21 163 B3
Glendale Ct BH23 191 B2
Glendale Rd BH6 207 A2
Glendon Ave BH10 189 B3
Glendowan Rd SO53 55 A4
Glendrive BH25 209 B4
Gleneagles BH23 206 C3
Gleneagles Ave BH14 203 B1
Gleneagles Cl BH22 165 C3
Gleneagles Dr PO7 112 A1
Glenelg PO15 130 C1
Glenesha Gdns PO15 130 B1
Glenferness Ave BH3, BH4 204 B3
Glenfield Ave SO18 103 C4
Glenfield Cres SO18 103 C4
Glenfield Inf Sch SO18 103 C4
Glenfield Way SO18 103 C4
Glengariff Rd BH14 203 B2
Glengarry BH25 195 B1
Glengarry Way BH23 208 B3
Glenhurst Sch PO9 136 A1
Glenives Cl BH24 140 A2
Glenlea Cl SO30 80 B1
Glenlea Dr SO30 80 B1
Glenleigh Ave 19 PO6 157 C4
Glenleigh Ct 18 PO6 157 C4
Glenleigh Pk PO9 136 A1
Glenmeadows Dr BH10 189 A3
Glenmoor (Girls) Sch BH10 189 B1
Glenmoor Cl BH10 189 B1
Glenmoor Rd
Bournemouth BH9 204 C4
Ferndown BH22 165 B2
Glenmore Ct SO17 103 A4
Glenmount Dr BH14 203 A2
Glenn Rd SO30 80 B1
Glenroyd Gdns BH6 206 C2
Glenside
Barton on Sea BH25 209 A4
Hythe SO45 125 C2
Glenside Ave SO19 104 B2
Glenthorne Cl PO14 179 B3
Glenthorne Mdw GU32 38 C1
Glenthorne Rd PO3 158 A1
Glenville Cl BH23 194 A1
Glenville Gdns BH10 189 B1
Glenville Rd
Bournemouth BH10 189 B1
Christchurch BH23 194 A1
Glenwood Ave SO16 79 A3
Glenwood Cl BH22 138 C1
Glenwood Ct SO50 57 C1
Glenwood Gdns PO8 111 C2
Glenwood La BH22 138 C1
Glenwood Rd
Southbourne PO10 137 C1
Verwood BH31 114 C3
West Moors BH22 138 C1
Glenwood Sch PO10 136 C1
Glenwood Way BH22 138 C1
Glidden Cl PO1 215 C3
Glidden La PO7 86 C2
Glissons BH22 165 A1
Globe La BH15 202 B1
Gloster Ct PO14 129 B3
Gloucester Cl GU32 40 B2
Gloucester Ct 8 GU32 40 C2
Gloucester Ho 1 PO12 181 B2
Gloucester Pl PO5 215 B1
Gloucester Rd
Bournemouth BH7 205 C3
Poole BH12 203 C3
Portsmouth PO1 182 A3
Waterlooville PO7 134 C3
Gloucester Terr PO5 215 B1
Gloucester View PO5 215 B2
Glyn Dr PO14 179 B3
Glyn Jones Cl SO45 150 C1
Glyn Way PO14 179 B3
Glynville Cl BH21 164 A4
Glynville Ct BH21 164 A4
Glynville Rd BH21 164 A4
Goathorn Cl BH16 201 B2
Goathouse La PO17 109 A2
Goddard Cl SO51 50 C2
Godfrey Olson Ho 3 SO50 56 A2
Godfrey Pink Way SO32 83 B4
Godiva Lawn PO4 183 B2
Godmanston Cl BH17 188 A1
Godshill Cl BH8 190 B2
Godson Ho 24 SO23 11 A4
Godwin Cl
Emsworth PO10 136 C2
Winchester SO22 1 B1
Godwin Cres PO8 88 B2
Godwins Field SO21 31 B4
Godwit Cl PO12 181 A4
Godwit Rd PO4 183 B3
Gofton Ave PO6 158 A4
Goggs La SP5 47 C3
Gold Mead Cl 3 SO41 197 C1
Gold Oak SP6 91 C4
Gold St PO5 215 A1
Goldcrest Cl
Horndean PO8 112 A4
Portchester PO16 155 C4
Goldcrest Gdns SO16 78 A3
Goldcrest La SO40 100 B4
Golden Cres SO41 196 B1
Golden Ct SO30 80 C2
Golden Gates BH13 214 A2
Golden Gr SO14 103 A3
Golden Hind Pk SO45 125 C1
Golden Sands BH13 214 A2
Goldenleas Ct BH11 188 B2
Goldenleas Dr BH11 188 B2
Goldfinch Cl BH25 194 C1
Goldfinch La PO13 179 C2
Goldfinch Rd BH17 201 C4
Goldring Cl PO11 185 A2
Goldsmith Ave PO4 182 C2
Goldsmith Cl SO40 100 B4
Goldsmith Inf Sch PO4 182 C2
Goldsmith Rd SO50 5
Goldsmiths Ct SO14 10
Goldwire Dr SO53 5
Golf Course Rd SO16 7
Golf Links Rd
Broadstone BH18 18
Ferndown BH22 16
Goliath Rd BH15 20
Gomer Ct PO12 18
Gomer Inf Sch PO12 18
Gomer Jun Sch PO12 18
Gomer La PO12 18
Good Acre Dr SO53 5
Good Rd BH12 20
Goodens The SO24 1
Goodison Cl SO50 5
Goodlands Vale SO30 10
Goodsell Cl PO14 17
Goodwin Cl SO16 7
Goodwood Cl
Gosport PO12 18
Titchfield PO14 12
Waterlooville PO8 11
Goodwood Ct PO10 16
Goodwood Gdns SO40 10
Goodwood Rd
Eastleigh SO50 5
Gosport PO12 18
Portsmouth PO5 21
Gooseberry La BH24 14
Gordleton Ind Pk SO41 19
Gordon Ave
Southampton SO14 10
Winchester SO23 1
Gordon Bldgs SO15 10
Gordon Ct BH4 20
Gordon Mount BH23 20
Gordon Rd
Bournemouth BH1 20
Chandler's Ford SO53 3
Christchurch BH23 20
Curdridge SO32 8
Fareham PO16 13
Gosport PO12 18
Hermitage PO10 16
Lymington SO41 19
Poole BH12 204
Portsmouth PO1 182
Waterlooville PO7 134
Wimborne Minst BH21 163
Winchester SO23 11
Gordon Rd S BH12 204
Gordon Terr SO19 104
Gordon Way BH23 192
Gore Grange BH25 194
Gore Rd BH25 194
Gore Rd Ind Est BH25 194
Gorey Ave BH12 188
Goring Ave PO8 88
Goring Field SO22 1
Gorleston Rd BH12 203
Gorley Cross SP6 94
Gorley Ct PO9 135
Gorley Lynch SP6 94
Gorley Rd BH24 117
Gorran Ave PO13 155
Gorse Cl
Locks Heath SO31 128
New Milton BH25 195
St Leonards BH24 139
Gorse Down SO21 33
Gorse Hill Cl BH15 202
Gorse Hill Cres BH15 202
Gorse Hill Rd BH15 202
Gorse Knoll Dr BH31 114
Gorse La BH16 201
Gorse Rd
Corfe Mullen BH21 186
Petersfield GU31 41
Gorsecliff Ct 7 BH5 205
Gorsecliff Rd BH10 189
Gorsefield Rd BH25 195
Gorseland Ct BH22 165
Gorselands Rd SO18 80
Gorselands Way PO13 180
Gorseway PO11 184
Gorseway The PO11 184
Gort Cres SO19 104
Gort Rd
Bournemouth BH11 189
Poole BH17 187
Gosling Cl BH17 202
Gosport Ho 48 PO9 136
Gosport La SO43 122
Gosport Mus★ PO12 181
Gosport Rd
Fareham PO16 155
Lee-on-the-Solent PO13 179
Stubbington PO14 179
Gosport Sh Prec 23 PO12 181 B
Gosport St SO41 197 C
Gough Cres BH17 187 A
Gover Rd SO16 101 B
Grace Dieu Gdns SO31 104 C
Grace La SP6 70 C
Gracefields PO15 154 A
Graddidge Way SO40 100 B
Graemar La SO51 25 B
Grafton Cl
Bournemouth BH3 205 A
Christchurch BH23 207 B
Gosport PO12 181 B
Grafton Gdns
Lymington SO41 197 B
Southampton SO16 78 B
Grafton Rd
Bournemouth BH3 205 A

ton Rd *continued*
:hester SO23 10 C3
ton St PO2 182 B4
am Ct SO19 104 A3
am Ho 4 SO14 103 B3
am Norris Bsns Ctr The
5 150 C1
am Rd
port PO12 181 A4
smouth PO4 182 C2
thampton SO14 103 A3
am St SO14 103 B3
nger Gdns SO19 104 B2
nmar School La
1 163 A2
ada Cl PO8 112 A2
ada Rd
ge End SO30 105 A3
smouth PO4 182 C1
ary Mews BH24 140 C4
ary The BH24 140 C4
by Gr SO17 79 A2
by Rd BH9 190 A2
d Ave BH6 206 B2
d Division Row 11
183 A2
d Par
Poole BH15 202 A1
tsmouth PO1 182 A2
th Hayling PO11 185 A1
nge Cl Gosport PO12 180 C3
ant PO9 136 A1
dle SO41 211 C4
thampton SO18 79 C2
chester SO23 10 C2
nge Cotts SO30 105 C4
nge Cres PO12 180 C3
nge Ct
Bournemouth BH1 205 A2
ley SO31 127 A4
nge Dr SO30 105 B4
nge Gdns BH12 203 C4
nge Inf Sch PO13 180 B4
nge Jun Sch PO13 180 B4
nge La PO13 180 B4
nge Mews SO51 28 B1
nge Park Mobile Homes
30 81 B1
nge Rd
urnemouth BH6 206 B2
oadstone BH18 187 A2
ristchurch BH23 208 A4
sport PO13 180 B3
dge End SO30 105 B4
tley SO31 127 B4
tersfield GU32 40 C1
rtsmouth PO2 157 B1
Southampton SO16 78 A1
Leonards BH24 139 C1
nchester SO23 10 C2
nge Road Bsns Ctr
23 208 A4
nge Sch The BH23 207 C4
nge The Hordle SO41 211 C4
Southampton SO16 78 A1
angewood Ct SO50 57 A1
angewood Gdns SO50 57 A1
angewood Hall BH21 163 B3
ant Rd PO6 158 B4
ant's Ave BH1 205 B3
antham Ave SO31 127 C2
antham Ct 3 SO50 56 A1
antham Rd
ournemouth BH1 205 C3
astleigh SO50 56 A1
outhampton SO19 103 C3
antley Rd 16 BH5 205 C2
ants Cl BH1 205 C3
anville Cl PO9 136 A1
anville Pl
2 Bournemouth BH1 204 C2
Vinchester SO23 11 A3
anville Rd
ournemouth BH5 206 A3
oole BH12 203 A3
anville St SO14 103 A2
asdean Cl 5 SO18 80 A1
asmere SO50 55 C1
asmere Cl
hristchurch BH23 191 B2
West End SO18 80 A1
asmere Ct SO16 77 C1
asmere Gdns BH25 195 A3
asmere Ho 18 PO6 133 A1
asmere Rd
ournemouth BH5 206 A2
oole BH13 214 A2
asmere Way PO14 154 B2
assmere Way PO7 112 B1
assymead PO14 129 B2
ateley Cl 8 SO19 126 C4
ateley Cres PO9 135 B2
avel Cl SP5 46 C4
avel Hill
Broadstone BH18 187 B3
Swanmore SO32 84 A2
avel La BH24 140 C4
ray Cl Locks Heath SO31 128 C1
Poole BH17 202 C4
ray's Yd 23 BH15 202 B1
raycot Cl BH10 189 B3
rayland Cl PO11 184 C2
rays Ave SO45 126 A2
rays Cl
Colden Common SO21 56 C4
Gosport PO12 180 C2
Romsey SO51 53 A4
rays Ct PO1 182 A2

Grayshott Cl SO22 1 B2
Grayshott Rd
Gosport PO12 180 C2
Portsmouth PO4 182 C2
Grayson Ct BH22 165 C2
Great Copse Dr PO9 135 C3
Great Elms Cl SO45 150 A2
Great Field Rd SO22 1 B2
Great Gays PO14 179 A3
Great Hanger GU31 41 A2
Great Mead
Denmead PO7 111 A2
Lyndhurst SO43 121 C2
Great Minster St 34 SO23 11 A4
Great Posbrook Cotts
PO14 153 C3
Great Southsea St PO5 215 B1
Great Well Dr SO51 53 A4
Greatbridge Rd SO51 27 C1
Greatfield Way PO9 113 A2
Greatwood Cl SO45 126 A1
Greaves Cl BH10 189 B2
Grebe Cl
Broadstone BH17 201 C4
Christchurch BH23 208 A3
Milford on Sea SO41 211 C2
Portchester PO16 155 C4
Waterlooville PO8 111 C2
Westbourne PO10 137 A2
Green Acres BH23 207 C4
Green Acres Cl BH24 140 B3
Green Bottom BH21 164 A4
Green Cl 11 Hythe SO45 126 A2
Kings Worthy SO23 2 A3
Netley Marsh SO40 99 C2
Poole BH15 202 B1
Whiteparish SP5 24 A2
Green Cres PO13 155 B1
Green Dr SP6 93 A3
Green Farm Gdns PO3 157 C2
Green Gdns BH15 202 B1
Green Hollow Cl PO16 130 C2
Green Jacket Cl SO22 10 C3
Green La Ampfield SO51 29 A1
Barton on Sea BH25 210 A4
Bishop's Waltham SO32 83 B4
Blackfield SO45 177 C4
Bournemouth BH10 189 B2
Bursledon SO31 104 C1
Chilworth SO16 54 C1
Clanfield PO8 88 B3
Denmead PO7 110 C2
Downton SP5 46 C4
Ferndown BH22 165 A1
Fordingbridge SP6 69 C1
Froxfield Green GU32 18 C3
Gosport PO12 181 B4
Gosport, Alverstoke PO12 181 A2
Hamble-le-Rice SO31 128 A1
Hambledon PO7 86 A2
Locks Heath SO31 128 C1
New Milton BH25 194 C4
Ower SO40 76 A2
Portsmouth PO3 158 A2
Ringwood BH24 141 A4
Ringwood, Upper Kingston
BH24 141 B2
Soberton PO7 86 B4
South Hayling PO11 184 C2
Southampton SO16 77 C1
Swanmore SO32 84 B4
Swanwick SO31 106 A1
Swanwick, Lwr Swanwick
SO31 128 B4
Whitsbury SP6 69 B4
Green Loaning 4 BH23 207 C3
Green Park Cl SO23 2 A1
Green Park Rd SO16 101 C4
Green Pk BH1 205 B2
Green Pond Cnr 9 PO9 136 A1
Green Pond La SO51 29 B2
Green Rd
Bournemouth BH9 205 A4
Gosport PO12 181 A1
Poole BH15 202 B1
Portsmouth PO5 215 B2
Stubbington PO14 154 B2
Green The Liss GU33 20 C3
Locks Heath SO31 128 C3
Romsey SO51 28 B1
Rowland's Castle PO9 113 B1
Whiteparish SP5 24 A2
Green Wlk PO15 130 C2
Green's Cl SO50 57 A1
Greenacre BH25 210 A4
Greenacre Cl BH16 201 B3
Greenacre Gdns PO7 134 B2
Greenacres Downton SP5 46 B4
Poole BH13 204 A2
Greenacres Cl BH10 189 C3
Greenacres Dr SO21 31 B2
Greenacres Specl Sch
SO22 1 C1
Greenaway La
Locks Heath SO31 128 B1
Locks Heath SO31 128 C1
Greenbank Cres SO16 78 C3
Greenbanks Cl SO41 211 B2
Greenbanks Gdns PO16 131 B1
Greenclose La BH21 163 B2
Greendale Cl
Chandler's Ford SO53 55 C3
Fareham PO15 130 B2
Greendale The PO15 130 B2
Greenfield Cres PO8 112 B2
Greenfield Gdns BH25 210 A4
Greenfield Rd BH15 202 C4
Greenfield Rise PO8 112 A2

Greenfields Liss GU33 21 A2
Poole BH12 203 C4
Greenfields Ave SO40 76 C1
Greenfields Cl SO40 76 C1
Greenfinch Cl
Broadstone BH17 186 C1
Eastleigh SO50 55 B1
Greenfinch Wlk BH24 141 B3
Greenhayes BH18 187 B1
Greenhays Rise BH21 163 B3
Greenhill Ave SO22 10 C4
Greenhill Cl
Wimborne Minst BH21 163 B3
Winchester SO22 10 C4
Greenhill La
Rownhams SO16 77 C4
Wimborne Minst BH21 163 B3
Greenhill Rd
Wimborne Minst BH21 163 B3
Winchester SO22 10 B4
Greenhill Terr SO22 10 C4
Greenlea Cl PO7 134 A1
Greenlea Cres SO16 79 B3
Greenlea Rd PO12 180 C4
Greenmead Ave SO41 196 B1
Greens Cl SO32 83 A4
Greens Meade SP5 47 B3
Greenside Ct BH25 210 A3
Greensleeves Ave BH18 187 A3
Greensome Dr BH22 165 C3
Greenway GU32 38 C1
Greenway Cl SO41 197 B2
Greenway Cres BH16 201 A4
Greenway La GU31 65 B3
Greenway Rd PO12 181 A3
Greenway The PO10 136 C2
Greenways
Chandler's Ford SO53 55 C3
Christchurch BH23 208 C4
Milford on Sea SO41 211 B3
Southampton SO16 79 B3
Swanmore SO32 84 A3
Greenways Ave BH8 190 B2
Greenways Ct BH22 165 C2
Greenways Rd SO42 146 A1
Greenwich The
Blackfield SO45 150 C1
Southampton SO14 103 A2
Greenwood Ave
Cosham PO6 157 B4
Ferndown BH22 165 C3
Poole BH14 214 B4
Rownhams SO16 77 B3
Greenwood Cl
Eastleigh SO50 55 C1
Fareham PO16 131 A2
Romsey SO51 53 A4
Greenwood Copse
BH24 140 A2
Greenwood La SO32 82 A4
Greenwood Rd BH9 204 C4
Greenwood Way BH24 140 A2
Greenwoods 32 BH25 195 A1
Greetham St PO1 215 B3
Gregory Gdns SO40 76 B1
Gregory La SO32 82 B3
Gregson Ave PO13 155 B2
Gregson Cl PO13 155 B2
Grenadier Cl SO31 129 A1
Grendon Cl SO16 79 A3
Grenehurst Way GU31 40 C2
Grenfell Rd BH9 189 C2
Grenfield Ct PO10 136 C2
Grenville Cl BH24 117 B1
Grenville Ct
6 Bournemouth BH4 204 B2
11 Poole BH15 202 B1
Southampton, SO15 102 C4
Southampton, Bitterne Pk
SO18 79 C2
Grenville Gdns SO45 126 A1
Grenville Ho 22 PO1 182 A3
Grenville Rd
Portsmouth PO5 215 D1
Wimborne Minst BH21 163 B2
Gresham Rd BH9 190 A1
Gresley Gdns SO30 81 B1
Greville Gn PO10 136 C2
Greville Rd SO15 102 B4
Grevillea Ave PO15 129 C2
Greycot Cl BH21 138 C4
Greyfriars 26 SO23 11 A4
Greyfriars Ct PO5 215 B1
Greyfriars Rd PO15 130 B1
Greyhound Cl SO30 81 A2
Greyladyes SO31 128 A4
Greys Farm Cl SO24 14 B2
Greyshott Ave PO14 154 B4
Greystoke Ave BH11 188 C3
Greywell Ave SO16 78 B2
Greywell Ct SO16 78 B2
Greywell Sq PO9 135 C3
Griffen Cl 2 SO50 56 C1
Griffin Ct
Southampton SO17 103 B4
12 Wimborne Minst BH21 163 B2
Griffin Ind Pk SO40 76 C1
Griffin Wlk PO13 180 B3
Griffiths Gdns BH10 189 A3
Griffon Cl SO31 105 A1
Grigg La SO42 146 A1
Grindle Cl PO16 132 B1
Gritanwood Rd PO4 183 A2
Grosvener Ct 19 BH1 205 A2
Grosvenor Cl
Southampton SO17 79 B1
St Leonards BH24 139 B3

Grosvenor Ct
2 Bournemouth BH1 205 B2
Christchurch BH23 209 A4
Cosham PO6 158 C4
Romsey SO51 53 B4
7 Southampton SO17 79 B1
Stubbington PO14 179 B3
Grosvenor Dr SO23 2 A1
Grosvenor Gdns
Bournemouth BH1 205 C2
Southampton SO17 79 B1
West End SO30 104 B4
Grosvenor Ho 4 PO5 215 B2
Grosvenor Lodge 5
SO17 79 B1
Grosvenor Mews
Gosport PO12 181 B3
Lymington SO41 197 B3
8 Southampton SO17 79 B1
Grosvenor Rd
Bournemouth BH4 204 B2
Chandler's Ford SO53 30 C1
Southampton SO17 79 B1
Grosvenor Sq SO15 102 C3
Grosvenor St PO5 215 B2
Grove Ave Gosport PO12 181 B3
Portchester PO16 156 B3
Grove Bldgs 6 PO12 181 B2
Grove Ct 14 PO9 135 C1
Grove Gdns SO19 104 A1
Grove Ho
Portsmouth PO5 215 B1
Portsmouth PO5 215 C1
Grove La SP5 47 C4
Grove Mans 21 BH1 205 A2
Grove Mews SO19 104 A1
Grove Pastures SO41 197 C2
Grove Pl Lymington SO41 197 C2
Southampton SO19 104 A1
Grove Rd
Barton on Sea BH25 210 A4
Bournemouth BH1 205 A2
Compton (Hants) SO21 31 B3
Cosham PO6 158 B4
Fareham PO16 131 A1
Gosport PO12 181 A4
Havant PO9 135 C1
Lee-on-the-Solent PO13 179 C1
Lymington SO41 197 C2
Poole BH12 203 A3
Southampton SO15 102 B4
Wimborne Minst BH21 163 B2
Grove Rd E BH23 207 A4
Grove Rd N PO5 215 B1
Grove Rd S PO5 215 B1
Grove Rd W BH23 206 C4
Grove St SO14 103 A2
Grove The
Bournemouth BH9 189 C2
Bursledon SO31 105 A1
Christchurch BH23 191 C1
Ferndown BH22 165 B2
Netley SO31 127 B4
Southampton SO19 104 A1
Stubbington PO14 179 A3
Verwood BH31 115 A3
Westbourne PO10 137 A2
Grovebury SO31 129 A1
Grovelands Rd SO22 1 A1
Groveley Bsns Ctr BH23 207 C3
Groveley Rd
Bournemouth BH4 204 A1
Christchurch BH23 207 C3
Groveley Way SO51 28 C1
Grovely Ave BH5 205 C2
Groves Down SO51 50 C2
Grower Gdns BH11 189 A2
Grundles GU31 41 A2
Gruneisen Rd PO2 157 B1
Guardhouse Rd PO1 182 A4
Guardian Ct 30 SO17 79 A1
Guardroom Rd PO2 157 A1
Gudge Heath La
PO15 130 C1
Guelders The PO7 134 C2
Guernsey Cl SO16 77 C2
Guernsey Rd BH12 188 B1
Guessens La PO14 153 C4
Guest Ave BH12 204 A3
Guest Cl BH12 204 A3
Guest Rd
Bishopstoke SO50 56 B2
Upton BH16 201 A4
Guildford Cl PO10 137 C1
Guildford Ct
Bournemouth BH4 204 B2
Gosport PO13 180 B3
Guildford Dr SO53 55 A2
Guildford Rd PO1 182 C3
Guildford St 30 SO14 103 B3
Guildhall Ct 4 BH15 202 A1
Guildhall Sq PO1 215 B3
Guildhall Wlk PO1 215 B3
Guildhill Rd BH6 206 C2
Guillemot Cl SO45 126 A1
Guillemot Gdns PO13 155 A2
Gull Cl PO13 155 A1
Gulliver Cl BH14 214 B4
Gulliver Ct 1 BH21 163 B3
Gulls The SO40 101 C1
Gullycroft Mead SO30 105 A4
Gunners Bldgs PO3 157 C2
Gunners Pk SO32 83 C4
Gunners Row PO4 183 A1
Gunners Way PO12 155 C1
Gunstore Rd PO3 158 A2
Gunville Cres BH9 190 A2
Gunwharf Rd PO1 182 A2

Gurjun Cl BH16 201 A4
Gurkha Mus The★ SO23 10 C4
Gurnard Rd PO6 157 C4
Gurnays Mead SO51 50 C2
Gurney Rd
Corfe Mullen BH21 186 C3
Portsmouth PO4 183 A2
Southampton SO15 102 B4
Gussage Rd BH12 203 C4
Gutner La PO11 160 B1
Guy's Cl BH24 141 A3
Gwatkin Cl PO9 135 B2
Gwen-Rhian Ct 10 SO15 102 C4
Gwenlyn Rd BH16 201 B3
Gwynne Rd BH12 203 C3
Gypsy La BH24 141 A4

H

H Ave SO45 150 C3
Ha'penny Dell PO7 134 C2
Haarlem Mews BH23 207 B4
Hack Dr SO21 56 C4
Hackett Way PO14 155 A3
Hacketts La SO32 60 C1
Hackleys La SO51 51 A3
Hackupps La SO51 6 B1
Hackworth Gdns SO30 81 B2
Hadden Rd BH8 205 B4
Haddon Cl PO15 130 C1
Haddon Dr SO50 56 A3
Haddons Dr BH21 138 B4
Hadleigh Gdns SO50 56 A3
Hadleigh Rd 6 PO6 157 B4
Hadley Field SO45 150 A3
Hadley Way BH18 186 C2
Hadow Rd BH10 189 B2
Hadrian Cl BH22 165 B1
Hadrian Way
Chilworth SO16 78 C4
Corfe Mullen BH21 186 C4
Hadrians Cl SO53 55 C4
Haflinger Dr PO15 129 A4
Haglane Copse SO41 197 B1
Hahnemann Rd BH2 204 C1
Haig Ave BH13 203 C1
Haig Ct 21 PO2 157 C2
Haig Rd SO50 57 A1
Haileybury Gdns SO30 81 B1
Hainault Dr BH31 115 A3
Haking Rd BH23 207 B4
Halcyon Ct BH15 202 B3
Halden Cl 2 SO51 28 A1
Hale Ave BH25 195 A1
Hale Ct PO1 182 C4
Hale Gdns BH25 195 A1
Hale La SP6 47 A2
Hale Prim Sch SP6 47 B2
Hale St N PO1 215 C4
Hale St S PO1 215 C4
Hales Dr SO30 105 A3
Halesowen Ho 4 PO5 215 A2
Halewood Way BH23 206 C4
Half Moon St 2 PO1 182 A3
Halfpenny La PO1 182 A2
Halfway Rd SO45 151 C1
Halifax Ct SO30 80 B1
Halifax Rise PO7 134 C4
Halifax Way BH23 208 A4
Hall Cl SO32 83 B4
Hall Ct SO32 107 A4
Hall Lands La SO50 57 B1
Hall of Aviation (Mus)★
SO14 103 A2
Hall Rd BH11 188 C2
Hall Way The SO22 1 A3
Hallet Cl SO18 80 A1
Hallett Rd PO9 136 A1
Halletts Cl PO14 154 B2
Halliards The PO16 155 A4
Halliday Cl PO12 181 A3
Halliday Cres PO4 183 B2
Halliday Ho PO4 183 A1
Hallowell Ho PO1 215 B4
Halsey Cl PO12 180 C2
Halstead Rd Cosham PO6 157 B4
Southampton SO18 79 C1
Halstock Cres BH17 187 B1
Halter Path BH15 201 C2
Halter Rise BH21 164 B3
Halterworth Cl SO51 53 A4
Halterworth Com Prim Sch
SO51 53 B4
Halterworth La SO51 53 B4
Halton Cl BH23 193 A4
Haltons Cl SO40 76 B1
Halyard Cl PO13 180 B4
Halyards SO31 128 A2
Ham La Ferndown BH21 164 C2
Gosport PO12 156 A1
Horndean PO8 112 A4
Southbourne PO10 161 B4
Hambert Way SO40 100 C3
Hamble Cl SO31 128 B1
Hamble Court Bsns Pk
SO31 127 C2
Hamble Ct
Chandler's Ford SO53 55 B3
Stubbington PO14 154 A2
3 Waterlooville PO8 111 C2
Hamble Ho 6 PO16 155 A4
Hamble House Gdns
SO31 128 A1

Hamble La
Bursledon SO31 .127 C4
Hamble-le-Rice SO31 .127 C1
Southampton SO31 .104 C1
Waterlooville PO7 .134 C3
Hamble Manor SO31 .128 A1
Hamble Prim Sch SO31 .127 C2
Hamble Rd Gosport PO12 180 C2
Poole BH15 .203 A3
Hamble Sec Sch SO31 .127 C3
Hamble Springs SO32 .83 B4
Hamble Sta SO31 .127 C3
Hamblecliff Ho SO31 .127 B2
Hambledon Cl SO22 .1 B2
Hambledon Gdns BH6 .206 B3
Hambledon Inf Sch PO7 .86 B2
Hambledon La PO7,SO32 .85 C2
Hambledon Par PO7 .111 B1
Hambledon Rd
Clanfield PO8 .88 A3
Denmead PO7 .111 A2
Hambledon PO7 .110 B4
Waterlooville PO7 .111 A2
Hambleside Ct SO31 .127 C1
Hambleton Rd BH7 .206 A4
Hamblewood SO30 .106 A3
Hamblewood Ct SO30 .106 A3
Hambrook Rd 1 PO12 .181 A3
Hambrook St PO5 .215 A1
Hamdown Cres SO51 .51 A1
Hameldon Cl SO16 .101 C4
Hamfield Dr PO11 .184 C2
Hamilton Cl
Bournemouth BH1 .205 B3
Christchurch BH23 .207 C2
Hamworthy BH15 .201 C1
Havant PO9 .159 C4
Hamilton Cres BH15 .201 C1
Hamilton Ct
10 Bournemouth BH8 .205 A3
Milford on Sea SO41 .211 B2
18 Portsmouth PO5 .182 B1
23 Southampton SO17 .79 A1
5 Wimborne Minst BH21 .163 A3
Hamilton Gr PO13 .155 A1
Hamilton Ho PO1 .215 D4
Hamilton Mews
15 Hythe SO45 .126 A1
Lymington SO41 .197 C2
Hamilton Pk SP5 .47 A4
Hamilton Rd
Bishopstoke SO50 .56 B2
Bournemouth BH1 .205 B2
Corfe Mullen BH21 .186 C3
Hamworthy BH15 .201 C1
Hythe SO45 .150 A4
Portchester PO6 .156 C4
Portsmouth PO5 .182 B1
Hamilton Way BH25 .194 C1
Hamlet Ct SO45 .151 A2
Hamlet Way PO12 .156 A1
Hamlon Cl BH11 .189 A2
Hammond Ho PO12 .181 C2
Hammond Ind Pk PO14 .179 B3
Hammond Rd PO15 .130 C1
Hammond's Gr SO40 .100 B4
Hammonds Cl SO40 .100 C4
Hammonds La SO40 .100 C4
Hammonds Way SO40 .100 C4
Hampage Gn PO9 .135 B4
Hampden La BH6 .206 A3
Hampreston CE Fst Sch BH21 .164 C2
Hampshire Cl BH23 .191 C1
Hampshire Corporate Pk SO53 .55 A1
Hampshire County Cricket Ground★ SO30 .80 C1
Hampshire Ct
26 Bournemouth BH2 .204 C2
Chandler's Ford SO53 .55 B2
Hampshire Ctr The BH8 190 C1
Hampshire Hatches La BH24 .141 A2
Hampshire Ho 25 BH2 .204 C2
Hampshire St PO1 .182 C4
Hampshire Terr PO1 .215 A2
Hampton Cl
Blackfield SO45 .177 C4
Waterlooville PO7 .135 A4
Hampton Dr BH24 .117 A1
Hampton Gdns SO45 .177 C4
Hampton Gr PO15 .130 A1
Hampton Hill SO32 .84 A3
Hampton La
Blackfield SO45 .150 C1
Winchester SO22 .1 B1
Hampton Twrs 2 SO19 .126 C4
Hamptworth Rd SP5 .48 B2
Hamtun Cres SO40 .76 C1
Hamtun Gdns SO40 .76 C1
Hamtun Rd SO19 .104 B2
Hamtun St 11 SO14 .102 C2
Hamworthy Fst Sch BH15 .201 C1
Hamworthy Mid Sch BH15 .201 C1
Hamworthy Sta BH16 .201 B2
Hanbidge Cres PO13 .155 B2
Hanbidge Wlk PO13 .155 B2
Handel Rd SO15 .102 C3
Handel Terr SO15 .102 C3
Handford Pl 2 SO15 .102 C3
Handley Ct BH24 .140 C4
Handley Lodge BH12 .203 C4
Handley Rd PO12 .180 C3
Handsworth Ho PO5 .215 C2
Handy Villas 19 SO23 .11 A4
Hanger Way GU31 .41 A2
Hangers The SO32 .59 C1
Hanham Ct BH12 .204 A4
Hanham Rd
Corfe Mullen BH21 .186 B3
Wimborne Minst BH21 .163 B3
Hankinson Rd BH9 .205 A4
Hanley Rd SO15 .102 B4
Hann Rd SO16 .77 C3
Hannah Gdns PO7 .134 C4
Hannah Way SO41 .196 C3
Hannay Rise SO19 .104 B3
Hannington Pl BH7 .206 A3
Hannington Rd
Bournemouth BH7 .206 A3
Havant PO9 .135 B4
Hanns Way SO50 .56 A1
Hanover Bldgs SO14 .103 A2
Hanover Cotts SO32 .36 C2
Hanover Ct
8 Hythe SO45 .126 A2
7 Portsmouth PO1 .182 A2
Hanover Gdns PO16 .131 A2
Hanover Gn BH17 .202 C4
Hanover Ho
Gosport PO13 .155 A3
Poole BH15 .202 B2
Totton SO40 .101 A4
Hanover Lodge SO23 .10 C3
Hanover St PO1 .182 A3
Hanoverian Way PO15 .129 B4
Hanway Rd PO1, PO2 .182 C4
Harbeck Rd BH8 .190 B2
Harborough Rd SO15 .102 C3
Harbour Cl BH13 .214 B3
Harbour Cres BH23 .207 C3
Harbour Ct
Barton on Sea BH25 .209 C4
Christchurch BH23 .207 C3
Poole BH13 .214 C3
Harbour Hill Cres BH15 202 C3
Harbour Hill Rd BH15 .202 C3
Harbour Hospl The BH15 .202 B2
Harbour Lights BH15 .202 C2
Harbour Par SO15 .102 C2
Harbour Prospect BH14 214 B4
Harbour Rd
Bournemouth BH6 .207 A2
Gosport PO1 .181 C3
South Hayling PO11 .184 B2
Harbour Twr PO12 .181 C2
Harbour View PO16 .156 B3
Harbour View Cl BH14 .203 A3
Harbour View Ct BH23 .207 A3
Harbour View Rd BH14 .203 A2
Harbour Watch BH14 .214 B4
Harbour Way
Emsworth PO10 .161 A4
Portsmouth PO2 .157 B1
Harbour Wlk PO1 .182 A2
Harbourne Gdns SO18 .80 A1
Harbourside PO9 .159 C3
Harbridge Ct PO9 .135 B4
Harbridge Dro BH24 .93 B2
Harcombe Cl BH17 .187 C2
Harcourt Cl PO8 .112 A2
Harcourt Mews 7 BH5 .206 A3
Harcourt Rd
Bournemouth BH5 .206 A3
Fareham PO14 .154 A4
Gosport PO12 .181 A3
Portsmouth PO1 .182 C4
Southampton SO18 .103 C4
Hard The Gosport PO12 .181 B3
Portsmouth PO1 .182 A3
Harding La SO50 .57 A2
Harding Rd PO12 .180 C3
Hardley Ind Est SO45 .150 A3
Hardley La SO45 .150 A4
Hardley Rdbt SO45 .150 A3
Hardley Sch & Sixth Form SO45 .150 B3
Hardman Ct PO3 .158 A2
Hardwick Rd SO53 .55 B3
Hardwicke Cl SO16 .77 C1
Hardwicke Way SO31 .127 C2
Hardy Cl
Locks Heath SO31 .129 A2
New Milton BH25 .194 C2
Southampton SO15 .102 A3
West Moors BH22 .138 C1
Hardy Cres BH21 .163 B2
Hardy Dr SO45 .126 A1
Hardy Rd Cosham PO6 .158 C4
Eastleigh SO50 .56 A1
Poole BH14 .203 B2
West Moors BH22 .138 C1
Hare La Alderholt BH21 .91 C3
Hordle SO41 .195 C2
New Milton BH25 .195 C2
Harebell Cl PO16 .131 B2
Harefield Ct SO51 .53 A4
Harefield Inf Sch SO18 .104 A4
Harefield Jun Sch SO18 104 A4
Harefield Rd SO17 .79 B2
Hares Gn BH7 .206 A4
Harestock Cl SO22 .1 B3
Harestock Cnr SO22 .1 B2
Harestock Prim Sch SO22 .1 B2
Harestock Rd
Havant PO9 .135 B2
Winchester SO22 .1 B2
Harewood Ave BH7 .206 A3
Harewood Cl SO50 .56 A3
Harewood Cres BH7 .205 C4
Harewood Gdns BH7 .205 C4
Harewood Gn SO41 .212 A2
Harewood Pl BH7 .206 A3
Harford Cl SO41 .197 B1
Harford Rd BH12 .203 B4
Harkness Dr PO7 .135 A4
Harkwood Dr BH15 .201 C2
Harland Cres SO15 .78 B1
Harland Rd BH6 .207 A2
Harlaxton Cl SO50 .55 C3
Harlech Dr SO53 .55 A2
Harlequin Gr PO15 .130 C1
Harleston Rd PO6 .133 B1
Harleston Villas 17 BH21 .163 B2
Harley Ct SO31 .128 B1
Harley Wlk PO1 .215 C4
Harlyn Rd SO16 .77 C1
Harman Rd PO13 .155 B2
Harness Cl BH21 .164 A3
Harold Cl SO40 .100 B3
Harold Rd
Portsmouth PO4 .182 C2
South Hayling PO11 .185 A1
Southampton SO15 .102 B4
Stubbington PO14 .154 B2
Westbourne PO10 .137 A2
Harold Terr PO10 .136 C1
Harpway La BH23 .192 B3
Harrage The SO51 .52 C4
Harrier Cl Horndean PO8 112 A4
Lee-on-the-Solent PO13 .179 C1
Southampton SO16 .78 A3
Harrier Dr BH21 .163 B1
Harrier Gn SO45 .150 A3
Harrier Way
Holbury SO45 .150 A3
Petersfield GU31 .41 B1
Harriers Cl BH23 .208 B4
Harriet Cl PO14 .179 A3
Harrington Ct BH23 .208 C4
Harris Ave SO30 .105 B4
Harris Rd PO13 .155 B2
Harris Way BH25 .195 A3
Harrison Ave BH1 .205 B3
Harrison Cl BH23 .192 B2
Harrison Ho 12 PO2 .157 B1
Harrison Prim Sch PO16 .131 A1
Harrison Rd
Fareham PO16 .131 A1
Southampton SO17 .79 B2
Harrison Way BH22 .138 C2
Harrison's Cut SO14 .103 A2
Harrow Cl BH23 .193 A4
Harrow Down SO22 .10 B2
Harrow La GU32 .40 C3
Harrow Rd
Bransgore BH23 .193 A3
Portsmouth PO5 .215 D2
Harrowgate La PO7,PO8 .87 A1
Harry Barrow Cl 1 BH24 .141 A3
Harry Law Hall PO1 .215 B3
Hart Cl BH25 .194 C2
Hart Ct SO19 .103 C2
Hart Hill SO45 .126 B1
Hart Plain Ave PO8 .111 C1
Hart Plain Jun & Inf Schs PO7,PO8 .111 C1
Hartford Ho PO1 .215 A1
Harthill Dro SP5 .47 C3
Harting Cl PO8 .88 B2
Harting Down GU31 .41 A2
Harting Gdns PO16 .132 B1
Harting Rd BH6 .206 B4
Hartington Rd
Gosport PO12 .180 C3
Southampton SO14 .103 A3
Hartland Ct PO10 .137 B1
Hartland's Rd PO16 .131 A1
Hartley Ave SO17 .79 A2
Hartley Cl
Bishopstoke SO50 .57 A1
Hythe SO45 .126 A1
Hartley Ct 5 SO17 .103 A4
Hartley Grange SO16 .79 A2
Hartley Rd
Bishopstoke SO50 .57 A1
Portsmouth PO2 .157 C2
Hartley Wlk 5 SO45 .126 A1
Hartnell Ct BH21 .186 B3
Harts Farm Way PO9 .159 B4
Harts Way SO41 .196 B1
Hartsbourne Dr BH7 .206 A4
Hartsgrove Ave SO45 .150 C1
Hartsgrove Cl SO45 .150 C1
Hartwell Rd PO3 .158 A2
Hartwood Gdns PO8 .111 C1
Harvest Cl SO22 .10 B2
Harvest Rd
Chandler's Ford SO53 .54 C3
Denmead PO7 .110 C2
Harvester Dr PO15 .130 A1
Harvester Way SO41 .197 B3
Harvestgate Wlk 5 PO9 .135 B3
Harvesting La GU32,PO8 .64 B3
Harvey Brown Ho PO11 .185 A3
Harvey Cres SO31 .128 C1
Harvey Ct SO45 .150 C1
Harvey Gdns SO45 .126 A2
Harvey Ho PO4 .183 A1
Harvey Rd
Bishopstoke SO50 .56 C1
Bournemouth BH5 .206 A3
Oakley BH21 .187 C4
Harwell Rd BH17 .202 B4
Harwich Rd PO6 .133 B1
Harwood Cl
Gosport PO13 .155 B2
Totton SO40 .100 B4
Harwood Ct BH25 .194 C2
Harwood Pl SO23 .2 B4
Harwood Rd PO13 .155 B2
Haselbury Rd SO40 .100 C4
Haselfoot Gdns SO30 .104 C4
Haselworth Dr PO12 .181 A1
Haselworth Prim Sch PO12 .181 A2
Haskells Cl SO43 .121 C2
Haskells Rd BH12 .203 A4
Haslar Cres PO7 .111 B1
Haslar Marina PO12 .181 C2
Haslar Rd PO12 .181 B1
Haslar Terr PO12 .181 B1
Haslegrave Ho 2 PO2 .182 B4
Haslemere Ave BH23 .209 A4
Haslemere Gdns PO11 .185 C1
Haslemere Pl BH23 .209 A4
Haslemere Rd
Portsmouth PO4 .182 C2
Southbourne PO10 .137 B1
Hasler Rd BH17 .187 B1
Haslop Rd BH21 .164 A4
Hassocks The 9 PO7 .135 A4
Hastings Ave PO12 .180 C4
Hastings Ho 3 PO2 .157 B1
Hastings Rd
Bournemouth BH8 .190 C1
Poole BH17 .187 A1
Hatch Ct PO9 .135 B4
Hatch La GU33 .21 B2
Hatch Mead SO30 .80 B1
Hatch Pond Rd BH17 .202 B4
Hatchers La SO21 .33 A3
Hatchet Cl SP6 .47 B2
Hatchet La
Beaulieu SO42 .175 B4
East Boldre SO42 .175 B4
Hatchley La SO21 .58 A3
Hatfield Ct BH25 .194 C2
Hatfield Gdns BH7 .206 A4
Hatfield Rd 7 PO4 .183 A2
Hathaway Cl SO50 .56 A2
Hathaway Gdns PO7 .112 A1
Hathaway Rd BH6 .206 B2
Hatherden Ave BH14 .202 C3
Hatherell Cl SO30 .80 B1
Hatherley Cres PO16 .156 A4
Hatherley Dr PO16 .156 A4
Hatherley Mans 4 SO15 .102 B4
Hatherley Rd
Cosham PO6 .133 A1
Winchester SO22 .1 C1
Hatley Rd SO18 .104 A4
Hatt La SO51 .5 C1
Havant Bsns Ctr PO9 .159 B4
Havant Coll PO9 .135 C1
Havant Education PRU PO8 .111 C1
Havant Farm Cl PO9 .135 C2
Havant Mus & Arts Ctr★ PO9 .136 A1
Havant Rd Cosham PO6 .158 B4
Emsworth PO10 .160 C4
Horndean PO8 .112 B3
North Hayling PO11 .159 C1
Portsmouth PO2 .182 C4
Havant St PO1 .182 A3
Havant Sta PO9 .135 C1
Havant War Meml Hospl PO9 .135 C1
Havant-by-pass PO9 .160 A4
Havelock Ct SO31 .128 B1
Havelock Mans PO5 .215 D2
Havelock Rd
Locks Heath SO31 .128 B1
Poole BH12 .204 A3
Portsmouth PO5 .215 C2
Southampton SO14 .102 C3
Havelock Way BH23 .193 B1
Haven Cres PO14 .153 C1
Haven Ct
4 Milford on Sea SO41 .211 B2
Poole BH13 .214 A2
Haven Gdns BH25 .195 A1
Haven Rd
Corfe Mullen BH21 .186 B3
Poole BH13 .214 C4
South Hayling PO11 .185 C1
Haven The Eastleigh SO50 .56 A3
Gosport PO12 .181 A1
Locks Heath SO31 .129 A2
Portsmouth PO4 .183 A3
Southampton SO19 .103 C2
Havendale SO30 .105 B3
Havenhurst BH13 .214 C3
Havenstone Way SO18 .79 B2
Haverstock Rd BH9 .190 A2
Haviland Mews BH7 .205 C3
Haviland Rd
Bournemouth BH1, BH7 .205 C3
Ferndown BH21 .165 A4
Haviland Rd E BH7 .205 C3
Haviland Rd W 5 BH7 .205 C3
Havisham Rd PO2 .182 B4
Havre Twrs 3 SO19 .126 C4
Hawden Rd BH11 .189 A1
Hawfinch Cl SO16 .78 A3
Hawk Cl
Stubbington PO14 .179 A3
Wimborne Minst BH21 .164 A4
Hawkchurch Gdns BH17 .18
Hawke St PO1 .18
Hawker Cl BH21 .16
Hawkeswood Rd SO18 .10
Hawkewood Ave PO7 .11
Hawkhill SO45 .12
Hawkhurst Cl SO19 .10
Hawkins Cl BH24 .11
Hawkins Ct SO40 .10
Hawkins Rd
Gosport PO13 .15
Poole BH12 .18
Hawkley Gn SO19 .12
Hawkley Rd Hawkley GU33 2
Liss GU33 .2
Hawks Mead GU33 .2
Hawkwell PO16 .15
Hawkwood Rd BH5 .20
Hawley Cl PO9 .13
Haworth Cl BH23 .19
Hawstead Gn 14 PO9 .13
Hawswater Cl SO16 .7
Hawthorn Cl
Colden Common SO21 .5
1 Fair Oak SO50 .5
Hedge End SO30 .10
New Milton BH25 .19
Hawthorn Cres PO6 .15
Hawthorn Ct 1 GU31 .4
Hawthorn Dr
Broadstone BH17 .18
Sway SO41 .17
Hawthorn La SO31 .12
Hawthorn Rd
Bournemouth BH9 .204
Burton BH23 .192
Denmead PO7 .110
Horndean PO8 .88
Hythe SO45 .125
Southampton SO17 .79
Hawthorn Wlk 20 PO13 .179
Hawthorne Gr PO11 .185
Hawthorne Rd SO40 .100
Hawthorns The
Bishop's Waltham SO32 .83
Christchurch BH23 .207
Eastleigh SO50 .55
Marchwood SO40 .102
Hawthorns The Urban Wildlife Ctr★ SO15 .102
Hayburn Rd SO16 .77
Haydens Ct SO41 .197
Haydn Cl SO23 .2
Haydock Cl SO40 .100
Haydock Mews 8 PO7 .112
Haydon Rd BH13 .204
Hayes Ave BH7 .205
Hayes Cl Fareham PO15 .130
Wimborne Minst BH21 .164
Hayes La BH21 .164
Hayes Mead SO45 .150
Hayes Terr PO12 .181
Hayeswood Fst Sch BH21 .164
Hayeswood Rd BH21 .164
Hayle Rd SO18 .80
Hayley Cl SO45 .149
Hayling Ave PO3 .183
Hayling Cl Fareham PO14 154
Gosport PO12 .181
Hayling Sch The PO11 .185
Haymoor Mid Sch BH17 187
Haymoor Rd BH15 .203
Haynes Ave BH15 .202
Haynes Way SO45 .125
Hays Cotts GU32 .40
Haysoms Cl BH25 .195
Hayter Gdns SO51 .53
Hayters Way SP6 .93
Hayton Ct SO40 .100
Hayward Bsns Ctr PO9 .136
Hayward Cl SO40 .100
Hayward Cres BH31 .114
Hayward Ct SO45 .150
Hayward Way BH31 .114
Haywards Ct 11 PO1 .182
Haywards Farm Cl BH31 .114
Haywards La BH21 .186
Hazel Cl Alderholt SP6 .93
Chandler's Ford SO53 .30
Christchurch BH23 .193
Colden Common SO21 .32 A
Hazel Ct
Bournemouth BH9 .190 B
27 New Milton BH25 .195 A
Portsmouth PO4 .182 C
Hazel Dr BH22 .165 B
Hazel Farm Rd SO40 .100 B
Hazel Gr Ashurst SO40 .99 C
Clanfield PO8 .88 B
Locks Heath SO31 .129 A
Winchester SO22 .10 B
Hazel Rd Clanfield PO8 .88 B
Lymington SO41 .197 A
Southampton SO19 .103 B
Hazel Wood Inf Sch SO40 .100 B
Hazelbank Cl GU31 .41 A
Hazeldale Villas 6 SO45 .126 A
Hazeldean Ct PO9 .113 A
Hazeldean Dr PO9 .113 A
Hazeldene BH18 .187 A
Hazeldown Rd SO16 .77 C
Hazeleigh Ave SO19 .103 C
Hazeley Cotts SO21 .32 B

Hazeley Gn PO9 136 A3
Hazeley Rd SO21 32 B3
Hazelholt Dr PO9 135 B2
Hazell Ave BH10 189 A1
Hazelton Cl BH7 206 A4
Hazelwood PO14 154 A3
Hazelwood Ave
Havant PO9 135 A2
New Milton BH25 194 C2
Hazelwood Dr BH31 115 A2
Hazelwood Rd SO18 80 A1
Hazlebury Rd BH17 202 A4
Hazlemere Dr BH24 139 C2
Hazleton Way PO8 112 A2
Head Down GU31 41 A2
Head's La BH10 189 C3
Headbourne Worthy Ho SO23 2 A3
Headland Dr SO31 129 A2
Headlands Bsns Pk BH24 117 A1
Headlands The SP5 46 C4
Headless Cross BH10 189 B3
Headley Cl PO13 179 C1
Headon View GU32 37 B3
Heads Farm Cl BH10 189 C3
Headswell Ave BH10 189 C2
Headswell Cres BH10 189 C2
Headswell Gdns BH10 189 C2
Heanor Cl BH10 189 B1
Hearne Gdns SO32 84 A1
Hearts of Oak Mews SO41 197 B2
Heath Ave BH15 202 B3
Heath Cl Fair Oak SO50 57 B1
Horndean PO8 112 A4
Wimborne Minst BH21 164 A4
Heath Ct GU31 40 C1
Heath Farm Cl BH22 165 B2
Heath Farm Rd BH22 165 B2
Heath Farm Way BH22 165 B2
Heath Gdns SO31 127 B4
Heath House Cl SO30 105 A2
Heath House Gdns SO30 105 A2
Heath House La SO30 105 B2
Heath La SO42 175 B4
Heath Lawns PO15 130 B1
Heath Lodge GU31 40 C1
Heath Rd
Christchurch BH23 194 A1
Hordle SO41 195 C2
Locks Heath SO31 129 A2
North Baddesley SO52 54 A2
Petersfield GU31 41 A2
Soberton SO32 85 A1
Southampton SO19 104 A3
St Leonards BH24 139 B2
Heath Rd E GU31 41 A1
Heath Rd N SO31 128 C2
Heath Rd S SO31 128 C2
Heath Rd W GU31 41 A1
Heath The PO7 111 A2
Heathcote Pl SO21 30 A4
Heathcote Rd
Bournemouth BH5 205 C2
Chandler's Ford SO53 55 B3
Portsmouth PO2 157 C1
Heathen St SO32 82 A2
Heather Chase SO50 57 A1
Heather Cl
Bournemouth BH8 190 B2
Christchurch BH23 194 A1
Corfe Mullen BH21 186 C3
Gosport PO13 155 A1
Hordle SO41 196 A2
St Leonards BH24 139 C2
Totton SO40 100 C4
Waterlooville PO7 134 C3
Heather Ct SO18 104 B4
Heather Dell BH16 201 A3
Heather Dr BH22 165 B4
Heather Gdns PO15 130 B2
Heather Lo 2 BH25 195 A2
Heather Rd
Blackfield SO45 150 C1
Bournemouth BH10 189 B2
Petersfield GU31 41 B2
Heather View Rd BH12 203 C4
Heather Way BH22 165 B4
Heatherbank Rd BH4 204 B2
Heatherbrae Gdns SO52 53 C2
Heatherbrae La BH16 201 A3
Heatherdeane Rd SO17 79 A1
Heatherdene Rd SO53 30 C1
Heatherdown Rd BH22 139 A1
Heatherdown Way BH22 139 A1
Heatherfield GU31 65 B3
Heatherlands Fst Sch BH12 203 C3
Heatherlands Rd SO16 78 C4
Heatherlands Rise BH12 203 B3
Heatherlea Rd BH6 206 B2
Heatherley Ct PO5 215 C1
Heatherstone Ave SO45 125 C1
Heatherton Mews PO10 136 C1
Heatherview Cl SO52 53 C3
Heathfield SO45 125 C1
Heathfield Ave
Fareham PO15 130 B1
Poole BH12 204 A4
Heathfield Cl
Chandler's Ford SO53 30 B1
Southampton SO19 104 A2
Heathfield Ho BH23 169 C1
Heathfield Jun Sch SO19 104 B1
Heathfield Rd
Chandler's Ford SO53 30 B1
Petersfield GU31 41 B2
Portsmouth PO2 157 B1
Southampton SO19 104 B2
West Moors BH22 139 A1
Heathfield Specl Sch PO14 154 B4
Heathfield Way BH22 138 C1
Heathlands Ave BH22 165 B1
Heathlands Cl
Burton BH23 192 B2
Chandler's Ford SO53 55 B4
Verwood BH31 115 A3
Heathlands Prim Sch BH11 189 A2
Heathlands Rd SO53 55 B4
Heathwood Ave BH25 209 C4
Heathwood Rd BH9 204 C4
Heathy Cl BH25 209 C4
Heaton Rd
Bournemouth BH10 189 A1
Gosport PO12 181 A4
Heavytree Rd BH14 203 A2
Hebrides Cl PO14 154 A2
Heckfield Cl 29 PO9 136 A3
Heckford La BH15 202 B2
Heckford Rd
Corfe Mullen BH21 186 B3
Poole BH15 202 B2
Hector Cl PO7 134 C1
Hector Rd PO14 155 A3
Hedera Rd SO31 128 C2
Hedge End Bsns Ctr SO30 81 A1
Hedge End Sta SO30 81 B2
Hedge End Wlk 7 PO9 136 A3
Hedgerley BH25 210 A4
Hedgerow Cl SO16 77 C4
Hedgerow Dr SO18 80 A1
Hedgerow Gdns PO10 136 C2
Hedley Cl SO45 150 C1
Hedley Gdns SO30 81 A2
Heidelberg Rd PO4 182 C2
Heights App BH16 201 B4
Heights Rd BH16 201 B4
Heights The
Fareham PO16 131 B1
Hedge End SO30 105 A3
Helena Rd PO4 182 C1
Helford Gdns SO18 80 A1
Helic Ho 2 BH21 163 B3
Hellyer Rd PO4 183 A2
Helm Cl PO13 180 B3
Helsby Cl PO14 154 C4
Helsted Cl PO12 180 C2
Helston Dr PO10 136 C2
Helston Rd PO6 132 C1
Helvellyn Rd SO16 101 C4
Helyar Rd BH8 190 C1
Hemdean Gdns SO30 80 B1
Hemlock Rd PO8 111 C2
Hemlock Way SO53 54 C3
Hemming Cl SO40 100 C3
Hemmingway Gdns PO15 129 B4
Hempland La GU34 17 B2
Hempsted Rd PO6 133 A1
Hemsley Wlk PO8 112 A2
Henbest Cl BH21 164 B3
Henbury Cl
Corfe Mullen BH21 186 B3
Poole BH17 188 A1
Henbury Rise BH21 186 B3
Henbury View Fst Sch BH21 186 B3
Henbury View Rd BH21 186 B3
Henchard Cl BH22 165 B1
Henderson Rd PO4 183 B2
Hendford Gdns BH10 189 B1
Hendford Rd BH10 189 B1
Hendy Cl PO5 215 B1
Hengist Rd BH1 205 B2
Hengistbury Head Nature Reserve* BH6 207 C1
Hengistbury Head Nature Trail* BH6 207 B2
Hengistbury Rd
Barton on Sea BH25 209 C4
Bournemouth BH6 207 A2
Henley Ct SO41 211 C2
Henley Gdns
Bournemouth BH7 206 A4
Fareham PO15 130 B2
Henley Rd PO4 182 C2
Henning's Park Rd BH15 202 C3
Henry Beaufort Sec Sch SO22 1 C2
Henry Cl SO45 150 A3
Henry Cort Com Sch PO15 130 A2
Henry Cort Dr PO15 130 B2
Henry Rd
Bishopstoke SO50 56 B2
Southampton SO15 102 B4
Henry St
9 Gosport PO12 181 B2
Southampton SO15 102 C3
Henstead Ct 9 SO15 102 C3
Henstead Rd SO15 102 C3
Hensting La
Colden Common SO21,SO50 32 C1
Owslebury SO21 58 C1
Henty Rd SO16 102 A4
Henville Cl PO13 180 B4
Henville Rd 6 BH8 205 B3
Henwood Down GU31 41 A2
Hepworth Cl SO19 104 B1
Herald Ind Est SO30 81 A1
Herald Rd SO30 81 A1
Herbert Ave BH12 203 B4
Herbert Ct BH12 203 B4
Herbert Hospl BH4 204 A1
Herbert Rd
Bournemouth BH4 204 A1
Gosport PO12 180 C3
New Milton BH25 195 A2
Poole BH13 204 A1
Portsmouth PO4 182 C1
Redlynch SP5 47 B3
Herbert St PO1 182 B4
Herbert Walker Ave SO15 102 B2
Herberton Rd BH6 206 B3
Hercules Rd BH15 201 B2
Hercules St PO2 182 B4
Hereford Ct
Gosport PO13 180 B3
Portsmouth PO5 215 C1
Hereford Rd PO5 215 C1
Hereward Cl SO51 53 A4
Heritage Ct BH13 214 C4
Heritage Ctr* SO31 127 B2
Heritage Gdns PO16 156 A4
Heritage Way PO12 181 B4
Herm Rd BH12 188 B1
Hermes Ct PO12 181 B4
Hermes Rd PO13 179 B2
Hermitage Cl
Bishop's Waltham SO32 83 A4
Havant PO9 135 C2
Three Legged Cross BH21 138 C4
Hermitage Gdns PO7 134 C4
Hermitage Rd BH14 203 A3
Hermitage The BH14 203 A3
Hern La SP6 94 A3
Herne Jun Sch GU31 41 A2
Herne Rd Cosham PO6 157 C4
Petersfield GU31 41 A2
Heron Cl Portsmouth PO4 183 A3
Sway SO41 172 A1
Heron Court Rd BH3, BH9 205 A4
Heron Dr BH21 164 A4
Heron La SO51 27 B3
Heron Quay PO10 161 A4
Heron Sq SO50 55 C1
Heron Way PO13 155 A2
Herons Cl PO14 154 B2
Herons Ct PO11 185 A3
Heronswood SO40 76 B1
Herrick Cl SO19 104 B2
Herriot Cl PO8 112 A3
Herriot Ho PO8 112 A1
Herstone Cl BH17 187 C1
Hertford Cl SP6 69 C2
Hertford Ct 12 BH23 209 A4
Hertford Pl PO1 182 B4
Hertsfield PO14 129 B2
Hesketh Cl BH24 140 A3
Hesketh Ho 8 SO15 102 B3
Hestan Cl BH23 191 B2
Hester Rd PO4 183 A2
Hestia Cl SO51 53 B4
Heston Way BH22 138 B2
Heston Wlk PO12 180 C2
Hewett Cl PO14 153 C4
Hewett Ho PO14 153 C4
Hewett Rd
Portsmouth PO2 157 C1
Titchfield PO14 153 C4
Hewetts Rise SO31 152 B4
Hewitt Cl PO12 181 A4
Hewitt Rd BH15 201 C2
Hewitt's Rd SO15 102 B3
Heyes Dr SO19 104 B2
Heysham Rd
Broadstone BH18 187 A2
Southampton SO15 102 A4
Heyshott Gdns PO8 88 B2
Heyshott Rd PO4 182 C2
Heytesbury Rd BH6 206 B3
Heyward Rd PO4 182 C2
Heywood Gdns PO9 135 B3
Heywood Gr SO19 104 C3
Hibberd Way BH10 189 B1
Hibbs Cl BH16 201 B4
Hickes Cl BH11 188 C2
Hickory Cl BH16 201 A4
Hickory Dr SO22 1 B2
Hickory Gdns SO30 80 B2
High Barn Cotts SO32 36 C2
High Brow BH22 165 B3
High Cross GU32 18 C1
High Cross La GU32 18 B1
High Ct PO4 183 A2
High Dr PO13 155 B1
High Firs Gdns SO51 53 B4
High Firs Rd Romsey SO51 53 B4
Southampton SO19 104 B3
High Howe Cl BH11 188 C2
High Howe Gdns BH11 188 C2
High Howe La BH11 188 C2
High Lawn Way PO9 135 C3
High Marryats BH25 210 A4
High Mdw SO19 104 B3
High Mead
Fareham PO15 130 C2
Ferndown BH22 165 A1
High Mead La BH22 165 A1
High Oaks Cl SO31 129 A2
High Oaks Gdns BH11 188 C2
High Park Rd BH18 186 C2
High Pines BH23 208 B4
High Point SO18 103 C4
High Rd SO16 79 B2
High Ridge Cres BH25 195 B1
High St Beaulieu SO42 148 C1
Bishop's Waltham SO32 83 B4
Botley SO30 106 A4
Buriton GU31 65 B3
Bursledon SO31 128 A4
Christchurch BH23 207 A3
Cosham PO6 157 C4
Damerham SP6 68 B3
Downton SP5 47 A4
Droxford SO32 61 A1
East Meon GU32 38 C1
Eastleigh SO50 56 A1
Emsworth PO10 160 C4
Fareham PO16 131 B1
Fordingbridge SP6 69 C1
Gosport PO12 181 B2
Hamble-le-Rice SO31 128 A1
Hambledon PO7 86 B2
Hythe SO45 126 A3
Lee-on-the-Solent PO13 179 C1
Lymington SO41 197 C2
Lyndhurst SO43 121 C3
Meonstoke SO32 61 B2
Milford on Sea SO41 211 B2
Petersfield GU32 40 C2
Poole BH15 202 B1
Portsmouth PO1 182 A2
Ringwood BH24 140 C4
Shedfield SO32 107 C4
Soberton SO32 85 A2
9 Southampton SO14 103 A2
Southwick PO17 132 C3
St Leonards BH24 139 C3
Titchfield PO14 153 C4
Totton SO40 101 A4
Twyford SO21 32 A3
Twyford SO21 32 A4
West End SO30 80 B1
West Meon GU32 37 B3
Wimborne Minst BH21 163 A2
Winchester SO23 11 A4
Woodgreen SP6 70 C4
High St N BH15 202 B2
High Town Hill BH24 141 C4
High Trees Fair Oak SO50 57 C1
Poole BH13 214 D4
Waterlooville PO7 134 C4
High Trees Dr SO22 1 C1
High Trees Wlk BH22 165 B4
High View PO16 132 B1
High View Way SO18 103 C4
High Walls PO16 131 B1
High Way BH18 186 C2
High Wlk PO15 130 C2
Highbank Ave PO7 134 B2
Highbank Gdns SP6 69 C1
Highbridge Rd
Colden Common, Highbridge SO50, SO21 56 B4
Colden Common, Twyford Moors SO21 31 C1
Poole BH14 203 B2
Highbury Bldgs PO6 157 C3
Highbury Cl Fair Oak SO50 57 B1
New Milton BH25 195 A1
Highbury Coll PO6 158 A3
Highbury Gr PO6 158 A3
Highbury Prim Sch PO6 158 A3
Highbury St 6 PO1 182 A2
Highbury Way PO6 157 C3
Highclere Ave PO9 135 C2
Highclere Rd SO16 78 B2
Highclere Way SO53 55 A2
Highcliff Ave SO14 103 A4
Highcliffe Castle* BH23 208 C4
Highcliffe Cnr BH23 209 A4
Highcliffe Dr SO50 56 A4
Highcliffe Jun Sch BH23 193 C1
Highcliffe Rd
Christchurch BH23 208 B4
Gosport PO12 180 C2
Winchester SO23 11 A3
Highcliffe Sch BH23 193 B1
Highcroft Ind Est PO8 112 B4
Highcroft La PO8 112 B4
Highcrown Mews SO17 79 A1
Highcrown St SO17 79 A1
Higher Blandford Rd BH18,BH21 186 C3
Higher Merley La BH21 186 C4
Highfield Lymington SO41 197 B2
Twyford SO21 32 A3
Highfield Ave
Fareham PO14 154 C4
Lymington SO41 197 B2
Ringwood BH24 141 A4
Southampton SO16,SO17 78 C2
Twyford SO21 32 A3
Waterlooville PO7 111 C1
Highfield Campus (Univ of Southampton) SO17 79 A2
Highfield CE Inf Sch SO17 79 A1
Highfield CE Prim Sch SO17 79 A1
Highfield Cl
Chandler's Ford SO53 55 C3
Corfe Mullen BH21 186 C3
Southampton SO17 79 A1
Sway SO41 172 A1
Waterlooville PO7 111 C1
Highfield Cres SO17 79 A1
Highfield Ct SO32 83 A4
Highfield Dr BH24 141 A4
Highfield Gdns Liss GU33 21 A2
Sway SO41 172 A1
Highfield Hall SO17 79 A1
Highfield Ho 12 BH14 203 A2
Highfield La Redlynch SP5 47 B3
Southampton SO17 79 A1
Highfield Lodge 3 SO17 79 A1
Highfield Par PO7 112 A1
Highfield Rd
Bournemouth BH9 189 C1
Chandler's Ford SO53 55 C3
Corfe Mullen BH21 186 C3
Gosport PO12 180 C3
Lymington SO41 197 B2
Petersfield GU32 40 C2
Portsmouth PO1 215 C3
Ringwood BH24 141 A4
Southampton SO17 79 A1
West Moors BH22 138 C2
Highfield Terr 36 SO22 10 C4
Highfields SO31 128 C1
Highgate Rd PO3 158 A1
Highgrove Cl SO40 100 B3
Highgrove Ind Pk PO3 158 A2
Highgrove Rd PO3 183 A4
Highland Ave BH23 194 A1
Highland Cl PO10 160 C4
Highland Rd
Emsworth PO10 136 C1
Poole BH14 203 A3
Portsmouth PO4 183 A2
Wimborne Minst BH21 163 B3
Highland St PO4 183 A1
Highland Terr PO4 182 C2
Highland View Cl BH21 163 B3
Highlands Cl Hythe SO45 126 A1
North Baddesley SO52 53 C3
Highlands Cres BH10 189 B2
Highlands Ho SO19 103 B2
Highlands Rd
Barton on Sea BH25 210 A4
Cosham PO6 158 B4
Fareham PO15,PO16 130 B2
Highlands Way
Hythe SO45 125 C1
Whiteparish SP5 24 A2
Highmoor Cl
Corfe Mullen BH21 186 B3
Poole BH14 203 A2
Highmoor Rd
Bournemouth BH11 189 A1
Corfe Mullen BH21 186 B3
Poole BH14 203 B2
Highmount Cl SO23 11 B4
Highnam Gdns SO31 128 C2
Hightown Gdns BH24 141 B3
Hightown Ind Est BH24 141 A3
Hightown Prim Sch SO19 104 C2
Hightown Rd BH24 141 A3
Hightown Twrs SO19 104 C2
Hightrees Ave BH8 190 C1
Highview Cl BH23 191 C2
Highview Gdns BH12 203 B4
Highways Rd SO21 31 B3
Highwood Cl SP6 92 B3
Highwood La
North Baddesley SO51 53 B4
Ringwood BH24 117 C2
Highwood Lawn PO9 135 B4
Highwood PRU SO42 172 C4
Highwood Rd
Brockenhurst SO42 172 C4
Gosport PO13 180 B4
Poole BH14 203 C2
Higworth La PO11 184 C3
Hilary Ave PO6 158 A4
Hilary Cl SO43 122 A2
Hilary Ct PO13 180 B3
Hilary Rd BH17 187 B1
Hilda Ct 8 SO15 102 C4
Hilda Gdns PO7 111 A2
Hilda Pl 28 SO14 103 B3
Hilda Rd BH12 203 C4
Hilden Ct PO11 184 C2
Hilden Way SO22 1 A3
Hiley Rd BH15 202 B3
Hill Brow Rd GU33 21 A1
Hill Cl Bransgore BH23 193 A4
Fair Oak SO50 57 B3
Hill Close Est SP6 70 C4
Hill Croft PO15 129 C2
Hill Dr PO15 130 B2
Hill Farm Rd SO15 102 C3
Hill Grove La SO32 84 B3
Hill Head Rd PO14 179 A3
Hill House Sch SO41 173 B1
Hill Houses La SO24 14 A3
Hill La Bransgore BH23 193 A4
Burton BH23 192 C1
Colden Common SO21 31 C1
Southampton SO15 78 C1
Hill Park Rd
Fareham PO15 130 B2
Gosport PO12 180 C3
Hill Pl SO31 128 A4
Hill Rd PO16 132 B1
Hill Rise Meonstoke SO32 61 B3
Twyford SO21 32 A3
Hill St Ower SO40 76 B3
Poole BH15 202 B1
Hill Terr SO50 57 B3
Hill Top SO22 1 B3

Hill View GU32 .38 B1
Hill View Prim Sch BH10 .189 C2
Hill View Rd
Braishfield SO51 .28 B3
Ferndown BH22 .165 B4
Michelmersh SO51 .27 B4
Portchester PO16 .132 B1
Hill Way BH24 .139 C3
Hill Wlk PO15 .130 B2
Hillary Cl PO16 .130 C1
Hillary Rd BH23 .207 C4
Hillborough Cres 2 PO5 .215 C1
Hillborough Ct 1 PO5 .215 C1
Hillbourne Fst & Mid Schs BH17 .187 A1
Hillbourne Rd BH17 .187 A1
Hillbrow Cl
Fareham PO15 .130 B2
Rowland's Castle PO9 .113 A1
Hillbrow Rd BH6 .206 A3
Hillbury Pk SP6 .93 A3
Hillbury Rd SP6 .93 A3
Hillcrest Ave
Chandler's Ford SO53 .55 C3
Ferndown BH22 .165 B4
Hillcrest Cl
Bournemouth BH9 .190 A2
North Baddesley SO52 .53 C3
Hillcrest Dr SO53 .55 B3
Hillcrest Gdns SO32 .83 B2
Hillcrest Hospl BH10 .189 B1
Hillcrest Rd
Bournemouth BH9 .190 A2
Corfe Mullen BH21 .186 B3
Hillcroft SP5 .47 B3
Hilldene Way SO30 .80 C1
Hillditch SO41 .197 B3
Hilldown Rd SO17 .79 A1
Hilldowns Ave PO2 .157 B1
Hiller Wlk 16 PO13 .179 C1
Hillgrove Rd SO18 .79 C2
Hillier Way SO23 .2 A1
Hillman Rd BH14 .203 B3
Hillmead Gdns PO9 .135 A1
Hillmeadow BH31 .115 A2
Hillside Curdridge SO32 .106 C4
Littleton SO22 .1 B3
Hillside Ave Romsey SO51 53 A4
Southampton SO18 .79 C1
Waterlooville PO7 .134 A1
Hillside Cl
Chandler's Ford SO53 .55 B3
Horndean PO8 .88 B2
West Dean SP5 .3 B1
Winchester SO22 .1 B1
Hillside Cres PO6 .132 C1
Hillside Dr BH23 .191 B2
Hillside First Sch BH31 .114 C4
Hillside Gdns BH21 .186 B2
Hillside Ind Est PO8 .112 B4
Hillside Mews BH21 .186 B2
Hillside Rd
Corfe Mullen BH21 .186 B3
Lymington SO41 .197 B2
Poole BH12 .188 C1
Verwood BH31 .114 C4
Winchester SO22 .1 B1
Woodlands BH21 .114 A3
Hillside Wlk BH21 .114 A3
Hillsley Rd PO6 .132 C1
Hillson Dr PO15 .130 B2
Hillson Ho PO15 .130 B2
Hillsons Rd SO30 .106 A4
Hilltop Cl BH22 .165 A4
Hilltop Cres PO6 .134 B1
Hilltop Dr SO19 .104 B2
Hilltop Gdns PO8 .88 B2
Hilltop Rd
Corfe Mullen BH21 .186 C3
Ferndown BH22 .165 A4
Hillview PO8 .112 B3
Hillview Rd
Bournemouth BH10 .189 B2
Hythe SO45 .125 C2
Hillway The
Chandler's Ford SO53 .55 B4
Portchester PO16 .156 B4
Hilly Cl SO21 .33 A2
Hillyfields SO16 .77 B2
Hilsea Cres PO2 .157 C3
Hilsea Mkt PO2 .157 C3
Hilsea Sta PO3 .158 A2
Hiltingbury Cl SO53 .30 B1
Hiltingbury Ct SO53 .30 A1
Hiltingbury Inf Sch SO53 30 B1
Hiltingbury Jun Sch SO53 .30 B1
Hiltingbury Rd
Chandler's Ford SO53 .30 B1
53 Havant PO9 .136 A3
Hiltom Rd BH24 .141 A4
Hilton Cl BH15 .203 A3
Hilton Rd Gosport PO12 .181 B2
Hedge End SO30 .105 B4
New Milton BH25 .195 A2
Hinchcliffe Cl BH15 .201 C1
Hinchcliffe Rd BH15 .201 C1
Hinkler Ct SO19 .104 B2
Hinkler Rd SO19 .104 C3
Hinton Admiral Mews BH23 .193 C1
Hinton Admiral Sta BH23 .193 C1
Hinton Ampner Ho★ SO24 .14 C2
Hinton Cl PO9 .135 B2
Hinton Cres SO19 .104 C2
Hinton Hill SO24 .14 C2
Hinton Ho 1 PO7 .134 C4
Hinton Manor La PO8 .87 C1
Hinton Rd BH1 .204 C2
Hinton Wood BH1 .205 A1
Hinton Wood Ave BH23 .193 C1
Hintonwood La BH23 .193 C1
Hipley Rd PO9 .136 A2
Hirst Rd SO45 .126 A2
Hispano Ave PO15 .129 B4
Hither Gn PO10 .137 C1
Hitherwood Cl 14 PO7 .112 A1
Hive Gdns BH13 .214 B3
Hives Way SO41 .197 B3
HMS Victory★ PO1 .181 C3
HMS Warrior★ PO1 .181 C3
Hoad's Hill PO17 .108 A1
Hoadlands GU31 .41 A2
Hobart Dr SO45 .126 A2
Hobart Rd BH25 .194 C1
Hobb La SO30 .105 B3
Hobbs Ct PO12 .181 C2
Hobbs Pass PO12 .181 C2
Hobbs Pk BH24 .139 C2
Hobbs Rd BH12 .203 B4
Hobby Cl PO3 .158 A2
Hobson Way SO45 .150 B2
Hoburne Ct BH23 .193 B1
Hoburne Gdns BH23 .193 B1
Hoburne La BH23 .208 B4
Hockham Ct PO9 .135 B4
Hockley Cl 7 PO6 .157 B4
Hockley Cotts
Cheriton SO24 .13 C2
Twyford SO21 .32 A4
Hockley Link SO21 .10 C1
Hocombe Dr SO53 .30 A1
Hocombe Park Cl SO53 .30 A1
Hocombe Rd SO53 .30 B1
Hocombe Wood Rd SO53 30 A1
Hodder Cl SO53 .55 A3
Hodges Cl Havant PO9 .136 A2
Poole BH17 .202 C4
Hoe La SO52 .53 B2
Hoe Rd SO32 .83 C4
Hoe St PO7 .109 C4
Hoe The PO13 .155 C1
Hoeford Cl PO16 .155 A3
Hogarth Cl
7 Romsey SO51 .28 A1
Southampton SO19 .104 B1
Hogarth Way BH8 .191 A1
Hoggarth Cl GU32 .41 A2
Hogs Lodge La PO8 .88 C4
Hogue Ave BH10 .189 B3
Hogwood La SO30 .80 C3
Holbeach Cl PO6 .133 C1
Holbein Lodge SO41 .198 A2
Holbrook Pl 6 SO51 .52 C4
Holbrook Prim Sch PO13 .155 B2
Holbrook Rd
Fareham PO16 .155 A4
Portsmouth PO1 .215 C3
Holbury Cl BH8 .190 C2
Holbury Ct 25 PO9 .136 A3
Holbury Dro SO45 .150 B2
Holbury Inf Sch SO45 .150 B2
Holbury Jun Sch SO45 .150 B2
Holbury La
East Tytherley SO51 .4 B2
Lockerley SO51 .4 B2
Holcombe Rd BH16 .201 A3
Holcot La PO3 .158 B2
Holcroft Rd SO19 .104 C3
Holdaway Cl SO23 .2 B4
Holden La SO24 .34 C4
Holdenbury Ct PO3 .158 B2
Holdenhurst Ave BH7 .206 B4
Holdenhurst Cl PO8 .88 B1
Holdenhurst Rd
Bournemouth BH8 .205 B3
Bournemouth, Holdenhurst BH8 .191 A2
Hole La Curdridge SO32 .83 A1
Soberton PO7 .110 A4
Holes Bay North Rdbt BH17 .202 A3
Holes Bay Rd BH15 .202 A2
Holes Bay Rdbt BH15 .202 A3
Holes Cl SO41 .195 C2
Holkham Cl SO16 .77 C2
Hollam Cl PO14 .154 A4
Hollam Cres PO14 .154 A4
Hollam Dr PO14 .154 A4
Hollam Rd PO4 .183 A2
Holland Cl SO53 .55 A2
Holland Pk SO31 .128 C2
Holland Pl Gosport PO13 155 B1
Southampton SO16 .78 A1
Holland Rd
Portsmouth PO5 .215 D2
Southampton SO19 .103 B1
Totton SO40 .100 B4
Holland Way BH18 .186 C3
Hollands Cl SO22 .1 A3
Hollands Wood Dr BH25 .195 A3
Hollies Cl SO41 .172 A1
Hollies The SO51 .50 C2
Hollingbourne Cl SO18 .103 B4
Hollman Dr SO51 .52 B4
Hollow La PO11 .184 C2
Holloway Ave BH11 .188 C3
Holly Cl Hythe SO45 .150 A4
Locks Heath SO31 .128 C2
St Leonards BH24 .139 B2
Upton BH16 .201 A4
Holly Ct BH15 .202 B2
Holly Dell SO16 .78 C3
Holly Dr PO7 .135 A3
Holly Gdns Burton BH23 .192 B1
Milford on Sea SO41 .211 B3
West End SO30 .80 B2
Holly Gr Fareham PO16 .130 C2
Verwood BH31 .114 C3
Holly Green Rise BH11 .188 C2
Holly Hatch Rd SO40 .100 C3
Holly Hedge La BH17 .202 B4
Holly Hill SO16 .78 C3
Holly Hill Cl SO16 .78 C3
Holly Hill La SO31 .128 B3
Holly Hill Mans SO31 .128 C2
Holly Hill Woodland Pk★ SO31 .128 B2
Holly Ho SO19 .103 C1
Holly La Boldre SO41 .174 A1
Christchurch BH23 .194 B1
New Milton BH25 .195 B2
Holly Lo 13 BH12 .204 A2
Holly Lodge
Chandler's Ford SO53 .55 B2
Southampton SO17 .79 A1
Holly Oak Ct SO16 .78 A2
Holly Oak Rd SO16 .78 A2
Holly Rd Ashurst SO40 .100 A1
Blackfield SO45 .177 C4
Holly St PO12 .181 B2
Hollybank PO13 .179 C1
Hollybank Cl
12 Hythe SO45 .126 A2
Waterlooville PO8 .112 B3
Hollybank Cres SO45 .125 C2
Hollybank La PO10 .136 C2
Hollybank Rd SO45 .125 C2
Hollybrook Ave SO16 .78 B2
Hollybrook Cl SO16 .78 A1
Hollybrook Gdns SO31 .129 A3
Hollybrook Inf Sch SO16 .78 B2
Hollybrook Jun Sch SO16 .78 B2
Hollybrook Rd SO16 .78 B1
Hollydene SO45 .126 A2
Hollywell Dr PO6 .157 A4
Hollywood Cl SO52 .53 C2
Hollywood Ct SO41 .197 B3
Hollywood La SO41 .197 B3
Holm Cl BH24 .117 B1
Holm Ct PO11 .184 C1
Holm Hill La BH23 .194 A4
Holm Oak Cl Littleton SO22 .1 A3
Verwood BH31 .114 C4
Holman Cl PO8 .112 A1
Holmbush Ct PO5 .215 B1
Holmdale Rd PO12 .180 C4
Holme Cl SO41 .197 B1
Holme Rd BH23 .209 A4
Holmes Cl 8 SO31 .127 A3
Holmesland Dr SO30 .105 C4
Holmesland La SO30 .105 C4
Holmesland Wlk SO30 .105 C4
Holmfield SO43 .122 A3
Holmfield Ave
Bournemouth BH7 .206 B4
Fareham PO14 .154 C4
Holmgrove PO14 .129 B2
Holmhurst Ave BH23 .193 C1
Holmsley Cl
Lymington SO41 .197 A1
Southampton SO18 .104 B4
Holmsley Ct SO40 .100 A4
Holmsley Pass BH24 .170 B4
Holmsley Rd BH25 .170 C1
Holmwood Garth BH24 .141 B3
Holne Ct PO4 .183 B2
Holnest Rd BH17 .187 B1
Holst Way PO7 .134 C3
Holt Cl PO17 .107 C2
Holt Ct SO19 .126 C4
Holt Down GU31 .41 A2
Holt Gdns PO9 .113 A2
Holt Rd Poole BH12 .203 C3
Southampton SO15 .102 C3
Verwood BH21 .138 B4
Holt View 9 SO50 .56 C1
Holworth Cl BH11 .188 C2
Holy Family RC Prim Sch SO16 .77 B1
Holy Rood Est SO14 .103 A2
Holyborne Rd SO51 .53 A4
Holybourne Rd PO9 .135 C2
Holyrood Ave SO17 .79 A1
Holyrood Cl
Broadstone BH17 .202 A4
4 Waterlooville PO7 .135 A4
Holyrood Ho 12 SO14 .103 A2
Holywell Cl BH17 .187 B2
Home Farm Bsns Ctr SP5 .4 C3
Home Farm Cl SO45 .126 A2
Home Farm La SO45 .177 C3
Home Farm Office Village PO16 .155 B4
Home Farm Rd BH31 .114 C3
Home Farm Way BH31 .114 C3
Home Field Dr SO16 .77 B3
Home Mead PO7 .110 C2
Home Rd BH11 .189 A3
Home Rule Rd SO31 .129 A2
Home Way GU31 .41 B2
Homeborough Ho 7 SO45 .126 A3
Homebridge Ho SP6 .69 C1
Homedale Ho BH2 .204 C3
Homedene Ho BH15 .202 B2
Homefayre Ho 19 PO16 .131 A1
Homefield SO51 .28 A1
Homefield Cotts GU33 .20 C3
Homefield Ho 18 BH25 .195 A1
Homefield Ind Prep Sch BH6 .206 C3
Homefield Ind Senior Sch BH23 .192 B3
Homefield Rd
Cosham PO6 .158 B4
Westbourne PO10 .137 A2
Homefield Way PO8 .88 A3
Homeforde Ho SO42 .146 A1
Homefort Ho 2 PO12 .181 A2
Homegrange Ho 15 SO41 .211 B2
Homegrove Ho PO5 .215 C1
Homeheights 23 PO5 .182 B1
Homelake Ho BH14 .203 A2
Homelands Est BH23 .206 C3
Homelands Ho BH22 .165 B3
Homeleigh Ho 5 BH8 .205 A3
Homemead Ho SO51 .52 C3
Homemill Ho 5 BH25 .195 A2
Homeoaks Ho BH2 .204 C3
Homepoint Ho SO18 .104 A4
Homer Cl Gosport PO13 .180 A4
Waterlooville PO8 .111 C1
Homer Mobile Home Pk SO45 .177 C3
Homerise Ho 1 SO23 .11 A4
Homerose Ho PO5 .215 B2
Homeryde Ho 11 PO13 .179 C1
Homesea Ho PO5 .215 B2
Homeside Rd BH9 .190 A1
Homespinney Ho SO18 .79 B1
Homestour Ho 1 BH23 .207 A3
Hometide Ho 13 PO13 .179 C1
Homeview Ho BH15 .202 B2
Homewater Ho 7 PO7 .134 C4
Homeway Cotts SO40 .101 A3
Homewell PO9 .135 C1
Homewood Cl BH25 .195 B2
Homewood Ho SO41 .197 B1
Honey La Burley BH24 .142 C1
Fareham PO15 .130 B3
Honeybourne Cres BH6 207 A2
Honeycritch La GU32 .19 B2
Honeysuckle Cl
Gosport PO13 .155 A2
Locks Heath SO31 .129 A3
Winchester SO22 .10 C2
Honeysuckle Ct
Locks Heath SO31 .129 A3
5 Southampton SO18 .104 A4
Waterlooville PO7 .135 A3
Honeysuckle Gdns SO41 .196 B1
Honeysuckle La BH17 .186 C1
Honeysuckle Rd SO16 .79 A2
Honeysuckle Way
Christchurch BH23 .208 A4
North Baddesley SO53 .55 A3
Honeywood Cl
Portsmouth PO3 .157 C2
Totton SO40 .76 B1
Honeywood Ho BH14 .214 B4
Honister Cl SO16 .101 C4
Hood Cl
Bournemouth BH10 .189 A1
Locks Heath SO31 .129 A2
Hood Cres BH10 .189 A1
Hood Rd SO18 .104 A4
Hook Cl SO51 .30 A1
Hook Cotts SO31 .152 C4
Hook Cres SO51 .30 A1
Hook La PO14,SO31 .153 A4
Hook Park Rd SO31 .152 C3
Hook Rd Ampfield SO51 .29 C1
Chandler's Ford SO51 .29 C1
Hook Water Cl SO53 .30 A1
Hook Water Rd SO53 .30 A1
Hook with Warsash CE Prim Sch SO31 .152 B4
Hook's Farm Way PO9 .135 B2
Hook's La PO9 .135 B2
Hooke Cl BH17 .188 A1
Hookpit Farm La SO23 .2 A4
Hookwood La SO51 .29 C1
Hop Cl BH16 .201 A4
Hope Lodge Sch SO18 .103 C4
Hope Rd SO30 .80 C1
Hope St PO1 .215 B4
Hopfield Cl PO7 .134 C4
Hopfield Ho PO7 .134 C3
Hopfield Mews PO7 .134 C3
Hopkins Cl
Bournemouth BH8 .191 A1
Portchester PO6 .156 C4
Hopkins Ct PO4 .183 A1
Horace Rd 10 BH5 .205 C2
Horder Cl SO16 .78 C2
Hordle CE Prim Sch SO41 .196 A2
Hordle Ho Sch SO41 .210 C3
Hordle La SO41 .196 A1
Hordle Rd PO9 .135 B2
Hordle Walhampton Sch SO41 .198 A3
Horlock Rd SO42 .146 A1
Hornbeam Cl 9 SO30 .105 B3
Hornbeam Gdns SO30 .80 B2
Hornbeam Rd
Chandler's Ford SO53 .54 C3
Havant PO9 .136 A2
Hornbeam Way BH21 .163 C3
Hornby Cl SO31 .152
Hornchurch Rd SO16 .77
Horndean CE Jun Sch PO8 .112
Horndean Com Sch PO8 .112
Horndean Ho 6 PO1 .215
Horndean Inf Sch PO8 .112
Horndean Prec PO8 .112
Horndean Rd
Emsworth PO10 .136
Horndean PO8 .112
Hornet Cl Fareham PO15 .130
Gosport PO12 .181
Hornet Rd Gosport PO14 .154
Thorney Island PO10 .161
Horning Rd BH12 .203
Horns Dro SO16 .77
Horns Hill Nursling SO16 .77
Soberton SO32 .85
Horns Hill Cl SO16 .77
Horsa Cl BH6 .206
Horsa Ct BH6 .206
Horsa Rd BH6 .206
Horse Sands Cl PO4 .183
Horsea La PO2 .157
Horsea Rd PO2 .157
Horsebridge Rd PO9 .136
Horsebridge Way SO16 .77
Horsecroft 2 SO51 .52
Horsefair Ct SO51 .52
Horsefair Mews SO51 .52
Horsefair The SO51 .52
Horsehoe Bridge SO14 .103
Horsepost La PO7,PO8 .87
Horseshoe Cl
Titchfield PO14 .129
Wimborne Minst BH21 .164
Horseshoe Ct
4 Bournemouth BH1 .204
Downton SP5 .46
Horseshoe Dr
Romsey SO51 .28
Totton SO40 .76
Horseshoe Lodge SO31 .128
Horseshoe The BH13 .214
Horsham Ave BH10 .189
Horton Cl BH9 .190
Horton Rd Gosport PO13 .155
St Leonards BH24 .139
Verwood BH21 .114
Horton Way
Bishopstoke SO50 .56
Verwood BH31 .114
Hosier's La 23 BH15 .202 A
Hosker Rd BH5 .206 A
Hospital La PO16 .156 C
Hospital Rd SO32,PO17 .108 A
Hotspur Cl SO45 .125 C
Houchin St SO32 .83 B
Houghton Cl 1 PO9 .136 A
Houlton Rd BH15 .202 C
Hound Cl SO31 .127 B
Hound Manor SO31 .127 C
Hound Rd SO31 .127 B
Hound Road Gdns SO31 127 B
Hound Way SO31 .127 B
Hounds Way BH21 .164 A
Houndwell Pl SO14 .103 A
Hounsdown Ave SO40 .100 C
Hounsdown Cl SO40 .100 C
Hounsdown Sec Sch SO40 .100 C
Hounslow Cl BH15 .201 C
House Farm Rd PO12 .180 C
Hove Ct PO13 .179 C
Hoveton Gr SO53 .55 A
Howard Cl Burley BH24 .143 A
Chandler's Ford SO53 .55 B
Christchurch BH23 .207 C
Fair Oak SO50 .57 B
Southampton SO18 .79 C
Howard Oliver Ho SO45 126 A
Howard Rd
Bournemouth BH8 .205 B4
Portsmouth PO2 .157 C2
Southampton SO15 .102 B3
Verwood BH31 .114 C3
Howard's Gr SO15 .102 B4
Howards Mead SO41 .197 A1
Howe Cl
Christchurch BH23 .207 C3
New Milton BH25 .194 C2
Howe La BH31 .114 C3
Howe Rd PO13 .180 B3
Howell Ho BH21 .163 C4
Howerts Cl SO31 .152 B4
Howeth Cl BH10 .189 B2
Howeth Rd BH10 .189 B2
Howlett Cl SO41 .197 B2
Howton Cl BH10 .189 B3
Howton Rd BH10 .189 B3
Hoxley Rd BH10 .189 B2
Hoyal Rd BH15 .201 B2
Hoylake Cl PO13 .155 B1
Hoylake Rd PO6 .134 B1
Hoyle Cl SO32 .58 B2
Hoylecroft Cl PO15 .130 C2
Hubert Rd SO23 .10 C2
Hudson Cl Gosport PO13 .180 B3
Poole BH12 .188 B1
Ringwood BH24 .141 B4
Hudson Ct SO40 .100 B3
Hudson Davies Cl SO41 173 C1
Hudson Rd PO5 .215 C2
Hughes Bsns Ctr BH23 .208 A4
Hughes Cl SO45 .150 C1
Hulbert Jun Sch PO7 .134 C3

Hulbert Rd Havant PO9 135 A2
Waterlooville PO7 134 C4
Hull Cres BH11 188 C2
Hull Rd BH11 188 C2
Hull Way BH11 188 C2
Hulles Way SO52 53 C2
Hulse Lodge 4 SO15 102 C4
Hulse Rd SO15 102 C4
Hulton Cl SO19 103 B1
Humber Cl PO14 154 A2
Humber Gdns SO31 105 A1
Humber Rd BH22 166 A3
Hummicks The SO42 176 B4
Hundred Acres PO17 108 C2
Hundred Acres Rd
PO17 108 C2
Hundred La SO41 198 A4
Hundred The
Fordingbridge SP6 69 C1
Romsey SO51 52 C4
Waterlooville PO7 111 B1
Hunger Hill BH15 202 B1
Hungerfield Cl BH23 169 A1
Hungerford SO31 128 A4
Hungerford Hill SP6 94 B3
Hungerford Rd BH8 190 B2
Hunt Ave SO31 127 B3
Hunt Rd
Christchurch BH23 207 C4
Poole BH15 202 C2
Hunter Cl
Christchurch BH23 208 A4
Gosport PO13 180 B4
Holbury SO45 150 A3
Wimborne Minst BH21 164 B3
Hunter Ct 13 SO16 78 A1
Hunter Rd
Portsmouth PO4 183 A2
Thorney Island PO10 161 A2
Hunters Chase SO32 84 B2
Hunters Cl BH31 115 B3
Hunters Cres SO51 28 B1
Hunters Ct SO31 105 A2
Hunters Hill SO40 100 B2
Hunters Lodge PO15 130 B1
Hunters Ride PO7 134 C3
Hunters Way SO50 57 A1
Huntfield Rd BH9 190 A1
Huntingdon Cl
Titchfield PO14 129 B1
Totton SO40 76 C1
Huntingdon Dr BH21 163 C1
Huntingdon Gdns
Christchurch BH23 192 A1
Horton Heath SO50 81 B4
Huntley Cl 30 PO6 133 A1
Huntly Rd BH3 204 B4
Huntly Way SO18 103 C4
Hunton Cl SO16 78 B2
Hunts Pond Rd SO31,
PO14 129 B2
Huntsbottom La GU33 21 A2
Huntsman Cl PO8 111 C3
Huntvale Rd BH9 190 A2
Hurdle Way SO21 31 B4
Hurdles Mead 17 SO41 211 B2
Hurdles The
Christchurch BH23 206 C4
Titchfield PO14 129 B1
Hurlingham Gdns SO16 79 A3
Hurn Cl BH24 140 B3
Hurn Court La BH23 190 C3
Hurn Ct
Bournemouth BH8 191 A2
15 Havant PO9 136 A3
Hurn La BH24 140 B3
Hurn Rd
Christchurch BH23 191 B2
St Leonards BH24 140 B2
Hurn Way BH23 191 B1
Hurricane Dr SO16 77 C3
Hursley Cl BH7 206 B4
Hursley Ct SO53 30 A1
Hursley Dr SO45 177 C4
Hursley Park Rd
Hursley SO21 30 A3
Hursley SO21 30 A4
Hursley Rd
Chandler's Ford SO53 55 B4
Havant PO9 135 B3
Hurst Castle★ SO41 212 B1
Hurst Cl
Barton on Sea BH25 209 B4
Chandler's Ford SO53 55 A2
Christchurch BH23 194 B1
Stubbington PO14 179 A3
Totton SO40 100 C4
Hurst Ct
6 Christchurch BH23 209 A4
5 Milford on Sea SO41 211 B2
Hurst Gn PO13 155 A1
Hurst Green Cl
Southampton SO19 104 A1
Waterlooville PO8 112 A1
Hurst Hill BH14 214 B4
Hurst La
Colden Common SO21 58 A4
Froxfield GU34 18 A2
Hurst Rd
Milford on Sea SO41 211 C2
Ringwood BH24 117 A1
Hurstbourne Ave BH23 193 C1
Hurstbourne Cl PO9 135 B3
Hurstbourne Pl SO19 126 C4
Hurstdene Rd BH8 190 B1
Hurstly La SO41 173 A2
Hurstville Dr PO7 134 C4
Hurstwood Ave PO10 137 C1
Hussar Cl BH23 206 C4
Hussar Ct PO7 111 B1
Hussey Cl 2 SO23 2 A1
Hutfield Ct 8 PO12 181 A3
Hutwood Rd SO16 79 A4
Huxley Cl SO31 129 A1
Huxley Ct SO45 125 B1
Hyacinth Cl BH17 186 C1
Hyde Abbey Rd SO23 11 A4
Hyde CE Prim Sch SP6 94 B3
Hyde Church La SO23 2 A1
Hyde Church Path 24
SO23 2 A1
Hyde Cl Southampton SO15 78 B1
Sway SO41 172 A1
Totton SO40 100 A4
Winchester SO23 1 C1
Hyde Gate SO23 2 A1
Hyde House Gdns 22 SO23 2 A1
Hyde La Downton SP5 46 B4
Fordingbridge SP6 94 B3
Hyde Lodge SO22 1 C1
Hyde Park Ho PO1 215 B2
Hyde Park Rd PO1 215 B3
Hyde Rd BH10 189 B3
Hyde St Portsmouth PO5 215 B2
Winchester SO23 2 A1
Hyde The BH25 194 C2
Hyden Cross GU32 63 C1
Hyden Farm La PO8 87 B4
Hyden Wood GU32 63 C1
Hylton Rd GU32 40 C2
Hyman Way SO40 100 C4
Hynes Ct 19 SO17 103 A4
Hynesbury Rd BH23 208 B4
Hyssop Cl PO15 129 B4
Hythe By Pass SO45 149 C4
Hythe Bypass SO45 150 A4
Hythe Hospl SO45 126 A1
Hythe Prim Sch SO45 126 A2
Hythe Rd Cosham PO6 157 C4
Marchwood SO40 124 C4
Poole BH15 203 A4

I

Ibbertson Cl BH8 190 C1
Ibbertson Rd BH8 190 C1
Ibbertson Way BH8 190 C1
Ibbett Rd BH10 189 B2
Ibbotson Way SO40 100 B3
Ibsen Cl PO15 129 B4
Ibsley Cl BH8 205 B3
Ibsley Dro BH24 94 A1
Ibsley Gr PO9 135 B2
Icarus Pl PO7 134 C1
Iddesleigh Rd BH3 205 A3
Ideal Park Homes SO50 56 C3
Idsworth Cl PO8 112 C3
Idsworth Ho PO1 215 B4
Idsworth Rd
Portsmouth PO3 183 A4
Waterlooville PO8 112 A1
Iford Bridge Home Pk
BH6 206 B4
Iford Cl BH6 206 C3
Iford Ct 18 PO9 136 A3
Iford Gdns BH7 206 B4
Iford La BH6 206 C3
Ilex Cres SO31 128 C2
Ilex Wlk PO11 185 B1
Imber Dr BH23 208 C4
Imber Rd SO23 11 B4
Imber Way SO19 104 B2
Imbre Ct BH13 214 C4
Imperial Ave SO15 102 A4
Imperial Ct 4 BH13 214 C4
Imperial Pk SO14 103 A4
Imperial Rd SO14 103 A4
Imperial Way SO15 102 B3
Implacable Rd PO13 179 C2
Ingarth 8 BH6 206 C2
Ingle Glen SO45 126 A1
Ingle Gn SO40 76 A1
Ingledene Cl
Gosport PO12 181 A2
Havant PO9 135 B1
Inglegreen Cl BH25 194 C1
Inglesham Way BH15 201 C2
Ingleside SO31 127 B4
Ingleside Cl PO14 154 A4
Ingleton Rd SO16 77 B1
Inglewood Ave BH8 190 C1
Inglewood Dr BH25 195 A1
Inglewood Gdns SO50 57 B2
Inglis Rd PO5 215 D1
Ingoldfield La
PO17&SO32 109 B4
Ingram Ct SO17 103 B4
Ingram Wlk 18 BH21 163 B2
Ingworth Rd BH12 204 A3
Inhams La PO7 110 B3
Inhurst Ave PO7 135 A4
Inhurst Rd PO2 157 C1
Inkerman Rd SO19 103 B2
Inkpen Wlk PO9 135 B4
Inlands Rd PO18 161 C4
Inmans La GU32 41 A3
Insley Cres BH18 186 C3
International Pk SO18 79 C3
International Way SO19 126 C4
Inveravon BH23 207 C2
Inverclyde Ho BH14 203 A2
Inverclyde Rd BH14 203 B2
Invergordon Ave PO6 158 A4
Inverkip Cl PO13 179 C2
Inverleigh Rd BH6 206 B3
Inverness Ave PO15 130 C2
Inverness Rd
Gosport PO12 181 A3
Poole BH13 214 C4
Portsmouth PO1 182 C4
Inwood Rd GU33 21 A2
Ionic Cl SO53 55 C4
IOW Ferry Terminal
SO14 102 C1
Iping Ave PO9 135 C2
Ipley Way SO45 126 A1
Ipswich Rd BH4 204 A2
Ireland Way PO7 134 C3
Iris Rd Bournemouth BH9 189 C1
Southampton SO16 79 A2
Iron Mill Cl PO15 130 B2
Ironbridge Cres SO31 129 A3
Ironbridge La PO4 183 B2
Ironmill La PO15 130 A3
Ironside Ct 12 SO14 102 C2
Irvine Cl PO16 131 A2
Irvine Way BH23 207 C4
Irving Rd
Bournemouth BH6 206 B3
Southampton SO16 77 C1
Irwell Cl SO53 55 A3
Irwin Hts PO12 181 A4
Isaacs Cl BH12 204 A4
Isambard Brunel Jun Sch
PO2 182 C4
Isambard Brunel Rd
PO1 215 B3
Isis Cl SO16 101 C4
Island Cl PO11 160 A2
Island Point SO41 197 C2
Island View SO41 172 A2
Island View Ave BH23 208 A3
Island View Cl SO41 211 C2
Island View Rd BH25 209 A4
Island View Terr PO2 157 B1
Island View Wlk PO16 132 B1
Islay Gdns PO6 133 C1
Itchen Ave SO50 56 C1
Itchen Cl Petersfield GU31 40 C1
West Wellow SO51 50 B2
Itchen Coll SO19 104 A3
Itchen Ct
4 Waterlooville PO8 111 C2
40 Winchester SO23 11 A4
Itchen Rd PO9 136 A3
Itchen Valley Ctry Pk
SO30 80 B3
Itchen View SO18 79 C2
Itchenor Rd PO11 185 C1
Itchenside Cl SO18 79 C2
Itchin Cl SO40 100 B3
Ithica Cl PO11 185 A2
Ivamy Pl BH11 188 C1
Ivanhoe Rd SO15 78 B1
Ivor Cl SO45 150 B2
Ivor Rd
Corfe Mullen BH21 186 B2
Poole BH15 202 A1
Ivy Cl St Leonards BH24 139 B2
Totton SO40 76 C1
Winchester SO22 10 C3
Ivy Cotts SO21 31 A1
Ivy Ct Southampton SO16 78 B2
Waterlooville PO7 134 B2
Ivy Dene SO19 104 B2
Ivy Ho 2 PO12 181 B2
Ivy La Portsmouth PO1 182 A3
Ringwood BH24 117 A2
West End SO18 80 B1
Ivy Orch PO8 88 A3
Ivy Rd Oakley BH21 187 B4
Southampton SO17 103 B4
Ivydene Gdns PO8 112 A2
Ivyhouse La GU32 18 C2
Iwerne Cl BH9 190 A2

J

J Ave SO45 151 A3
Jacaranda Cl PO15 129 C2
Jack Cl SO53 54 C3
Jack Cockerill Way 14
PO5 182 B1
Jackdaw Cl PO8 111 C2
Jackdaw Rise SO50 55 B1
Jackie Wigg Gdns SO40 101 A4
Jacklin Ct BH18 187 A3
Jackman's Hill SO21 33 A3
Jackmans Cl SO19 103 B2
Jackson Cl PO6 158 B3
Jackson Gdns BH12 203 B3
Jackson Rd BH12 203 B3
Jacmar Ct 8 BH25 195 A1
Jacob's Gutter La SO40 101 A2
Jacob's St PO1 215 B4
Jacobean Cl BH23 194 A1
Jacobs Cl Clanfield PO8 88 B3
Romsey SO51 53 A4
Jacobs Rd BH15 201 C1
Jacobs Wlk SO40 100 C3
Jacomb Pl PO13 155 B1
Jacqueline Ave PO7 134 B2
Jacqueline Rd BH12 203 B4
Jade Ct Gosport PO13 180 B3
6 Waterlooville PO7 134 C4
Jago Rd PO1 181 C3
Jamaica Pl PO12 181 B2
James Butcher Ct 12
PO5 182 B1
James Callaghan Dr
Cosham PO6 133 A1
Portchester PO17 132 C1
James Cl Gosport PO13 155 B2
South Hayling PO11 184 C2
James Copse Rd PO8 111 C3
James Ct SO51 53 A3
James Grieve Ave SO31 129 A1
James Howell Ct PO7 110 C2
James Rd Gosport PO13 155 B2
Havant PO9 135 C1
Poole BH12 204 A3
James St SO14 103 A2
Jameson Rd
Bournemouth BH9 189 C1
Southampton SO19 103 C2
Jamica Rd PO12 181 B3
Janaway Gdns SO17 103 B4
Janes Cl SO45 177 C4
Janred Ct BH25 209 C4
Janson Rd SO15 102 B4
Japonica Way PO9 136 B2
Jarndyce Wlk PO2 182 B4
Jarvis Fields SO31 128 A4
Jasmine Ct
Gosport PO13 180 B3
Lymington SO41 197 C2
Jasmine Gr PO7 135 A3
Jasmine Rd SO30 105 A4
Jasmine Way PO8 88 B3
Jasmine Wlk 5 PO14 154 C4
Jasmond Rd PO6 157 C3
Jason Pl PO7 134 C1
Jason Way PO12 180 C4
Jaundrells Cl BH25 195 B2
Java Dr PO15 129 B4
Javelin Rd PO10 161 A2
Jay Cl Horndean PO8 112 A4
Stubbington PO14 154 A3
Jay's Ct BH23 209 A4
Jealous La SO41 173 A1
Jefferson Ave BH1 205 B3
Jeffries Cl SO16 77 C3
Jellicoe Ave PO12 180 C2
Jellicoe Cl BH14 202 C3
Jellicoe Dr BH23 207 C3
Jellicoe Ho 8 PO1 215 C4
Jenkins Cl SO30 106 A4
Jenkins Gr PO3 183 A4
Jenner Way SO51 53 B4
Jennings Rd Poole BH14 203 B1
Totton SO40 101 A4
Jensen Ct SO15 102 C4
Jephcote Rd BH11 188 C2
Jermyns La SO51 28 C2
Jerome Ct SO19 104 B3
Jerram Cl PO12 180 C2
Jerrett's La SO16 77 B2
Jersey Cl Poole BH12 188 B1
Southampton SO16 77 C2
Stubbington PO14 179 B3
Jersey Rd Poole BH12 188 B1
Portsmouth PO2 182 C4
Jervis Court La SO32 84 A4
Jervis Dr PO12 181 A3
Jervis Rd PO2 157 B1
Jesmond Ave BH23 208 C4
Jesmond Gr SO31 129 A1
Jessamine Rd SO16 78 A1
Jessica Ave BH31 114 B4
Jessica Cl 4 PO7 112 A1
Jessie Rd Gosport PO12 181 A2
Havant PO9 135 B2
Portsmouth PO4 182 C2
Jessie Terr 28 SO14 103 A2
Jessop Cl
Bournemouth BH10 189 C2
Hythe SO45 125 C3
Jessop Rd BH21 164 A3
Jessop Wlk SO45 125 C3
Jessopp Ho 6 BH21 163 B3
Jetty Rd SO45 151 A3
Jewell Rd BH8 191 A1
Jewry St SO23 11 A4
Jex Blake Cl SO16 78 A4
Jimmy Brown Ave BH22 138 C3
Jinny La SO51 27 C3
Joanna Cl SP5 46 B4
Jockey La SO50 56 C3
Jodrell Cl PO8 112 B4
Joe Bigwood Cl SO16 77 B3
John Bunyan Cl PO15 129 B4
John Darling Mall 4
SO50 56 A2
John King Shipyard
PO10 161 A4
John St SO14 103 A2
John's Rd SO19 103 B2
Johns Rd PO16 155 A4
Johnson Rd BH21 165 A4
Johnson St 2 SO14 103 A2
Johnson View PO15 129 C3
Johnston Rd BH15 202 B4
Johnstone Rd BH23 207 C3
Jolliffe Ave BH15 202 B2
Jolliffe Ct 16 GU32 40 C2
Jolliffe Rd BH15 202 B2
Jonas Nichols Sq SO14 103 A2
Jonathan Cl SO41 197 C3
Jonathan Rd PO15 130 C1
Jones La SO45 126 A3
Jopps Cnr BH23 192 B2
Jordan Ho SO15 102 B3
Jordans La Boldre SO41 198 A4
Sway SO41 172 B1
Joseph Nye Ct 30 PO1 182 A3
Joseph St 8 PO12 181 B2
Joshua Cl BH15 201 C1
Josian Wlk 12 SO14 103 A3
Joslin Block PO12 181 B3
Jowitt Dr BH25 194 C1
Joyce Dickson Cl BH24 141 A3
Joys La SO41 198 C4
Joys Rd BH21 138 C4
Jubilee Ave PO6 156 C4
Jubilee Bsns Ctr PO7 134 C4
Jubilee Cl
Corfe Mullen BH21 186 C4
Eastleigh SO50 55 C1
Fordingbridge SP6 69 B1
Ringwood BH24 141 B4
Jubilee Cres BH12 203 B3
Jubilee Ct Fareham PO14 155 A4
Sway SO41 172 A1
Jubilee Gdns
Bournemouth BH10 189 B1
Southampton SO18 104 A4
Jubilee Ho PO10 136 C1
Jubilee Rd
Corfe Mullen BH21 186 C4
Fordingbridge SP6 69 B1
Gosport PO12 181 A3
Poole BH12 203 B3
Portchester PO16 156 B4
Portsmouth PO4 182 C2
Romsey SO51 52 C4
Waterlooville PO7 111 C1
Jubilee Terr
Portsmouth PO5 215 A1
Westbourne PO10 137 A2
Julia Cl BH23 208 C4
Julian Cl SO16 78 C3
Julian Ct 1 SO18 79 C1
Julian Rd SO19 104 A2
Julian's Rd BH21 163 A2
Julie Ave PO15 130 C1
Juliet Ct PO7 135 A4
Julius Cl SO53 55 C3
Julyan Ave BH12 204 A4
Jumar Cl SO31 152 B4
Jumpers Ave BH23 206 C4
Jumpers Rd BH23 206 C4
Junction Rd
Bournemouth BH9 204 C4
Hamworthy BH16 201 B2
Totton SO40 101 A4
Juniper Cl
Ferndown BH22 165 B4
Lymington SO41 197 A1
North Baddesley SO52 53 C3
Three Legged Cross BH21 138 C4
Winchester SO22 10 B3
Juniper Ct 17 SO18 103 C4
Juniper Flats BH23 206 C4
Juniper Rd Horndean PO8 88 B1
Southampton SO18 103 C4
Juniper Sq PO9 159 C4
Jupiter Cl SO16 77 C2
Jupiter Ct PO1 182 A2
Jupiter Way BH21 186 C4
Jura Cl PO6 133 C1
Jurd Way SO31 104 C1
Jurds Lake Way SO19 103 C1
Justin Cl PO14 154 C4
Justin Gdns BH10 189 C2
Justine Ct 4 SO18 104 A4
Justinian Cl SO53 55 C4
Jute Cl PO16 132 A1
Jutland Cl PO15 129 A4
Juventu Cl PO9 136 A2

K

Kamptee Copse BH25 195 A3
Kanes Hill SO19 104 C3
Kanes Hill Prim Sch
SO19 104 C3
Kangaw Pl BH15 201 B1
Karen Ave PO6 158 B3
Kassassin St PO4 183 A1
Kassel Cl PO7 135 A4
Katherine Chance Cl
BH23 192 B2
Kathleen Rd SO19 104 A2
Katrina Gdns PO11 185 A3
Katrine Cres SO53 55 A4
Katterns Cl BH23 191 C1
Kay Cl BH23 207 C3
Kayak Cl SO31 128 C1
Kayleigh Cl SO40 100 B3
Kealy Rd PO12 181 A3
Kearsney Ave PO2 157 C2
Keast Wlk PO13 155 B2
Keats Ave
Milford on Sea SO41 211 B3
Portchester PO6 132 C1
Keats Cl Swanwick PO15 106 A1
Waterlooville PO8 111 C2
Winchester SO22 10 B2
Keats Ho Havant PO9 135 C2
17 New Milton BH25 195 A1
Keats Rd SO19 104 B3
Keble Cl
Chandler's Ford SO53 55 B2
Hursley SO21 30 A4
Keble Meml CE Prim Sch
SO21 30 A3
Keble Rd SO53 55 B2
Keble St SO22 10 B3
Keeble Cl BH10 189 B3
Keeble Cres BH10 189 B3
Keeble Rd BH10 189 B3
Keel Cl Gosport PO13 180 B3
Portsmouth PO3 158 B2
Keelan Ct PO5 182 B1

Keep The PO16 ....156 C4
Keepers Cl SO53 ....55 A3
Keepers La
Ferndown BH21 ....164 C2
Mottisfont SO51 ....5 B1
Kefford Cl PO8 ....112 A3
Keighley Ave BH18 ....186 C1
Keith Cl PO12 ....181 A3
Keith Rd BH3 ....204 B4
Kelburn Cl SO53 ....55 A4
Kellaway Rd BH17 ....202 C4
Kellett Rd SO15 ....102 C4
Kelly Cl BH17 ....202 C4
Kelly Ct
10 Fareham PO16 ....131 A1
Southampton SO16 ....78 B3
2 Southampton, Bitterne SO18 ....103 C4
Kelly Ho SO18 ....79 C2
Kelly Rd PO7 ....134 C3
Kelmscott Gdns SO53 ....30 A1
Kelsall Gdns BH25 ....195 A2
Kelsey Ave PO10 ....137 C1
Kelsey Cl Liss GU33 ....21 A3
Locks Heath PO14 ....129 A1
Kelsey Head PO6 ....157 A4
Kelston Cl
19 Southampton SO15 ....102 A4
Southampton SO15 ....102 A4
Kelvin Cl SO45 ....126 A2
Kelvin Gr Netley SO31 ....127 B3
Portchester PO16 ....156 B4
Kelvin Rd SO50 ....55 C1
Kemp Rd BH9 ....204 C4
Kemp Welch Ct BH12 ....204 A4
Kemps Quay Ind Pk SO18 ....103 B4
Kempton Ct PO15 ....129 B4
Kempton Pk 6 PO7 ....112 A1
Kemshott Ct PO9 ....135 B3
Ken Berry Ct PO9 ....136 A3
Ken Rd BH6 ....206 C2
Kench The PO11 ....183 C2
Kendal Ave
Portsmouth PO3 ....158 A1
Southampton SO16 ....101 B4
Kendal Cl
Chandler's Ford SO53 ....55 C4
Waterlooville PO8 ....112 A2
Kendal Ct SO16 ....77 B1
Kenilworth Cl
Lee-on-the-Solent PO13 ....179 C2
New Milton BH25 ....195 A2
Kenilworth Ct
2 Christchurch BH23 ....207 A4
11 Poole BH13 ....214 C4
8 Winchester SO23 ....2 A1
Kenilworth Dr SO50 ....56 A3
Kenilworth Gdns SO30 ....80 C1
Kenilworth Ho 15 SO14 ....103 B3
Kenilworth Rd
Portsmouth PO5 ....182 B1
Southampton SO15 ....102 C3
Kenmore Cl SO40 ....100 C3
Kennard Ct BH25 ....194 C2
Kennard Rd BH25 ....194 C2
Kennart Rd BH17 ....202 A4
Kennedy Ave PO15 ....130 C2
Kennedy Cl PO7 ....134 C2
Kennedy Cres PO12 ....180 C1
Kennedy Rd SO16 ....77 C2
Kennel La SO22 ....1 B2
Kennet Cl Gosport PO12 ....181 A1
Romsey SO51 ....53 B4
West End SO18 ....80 A2
Kennet Rd
Petersfield GU31 ....40 C1
Romsey SO51 ....53 B4
Kenneth Ct 15 BH23 ....209 A4
Kennington La SO40 ....99 A4
Kennington Rd BH17 ....202 B4
Kensington Cl SO50 ....56 B3
Kensington Ct 3 SO17 ....79 B1
Kensington Dr BH2 ....204 B2
Kensington Fields SO45 ....125 B1
Kensington Gdns PO14 ....129 B1
Kensington Pk SO41 ....211 B2
Kensington Rd
Gosport PO12 ....181 B2
Portsmouth PO2 ....157 C1
Kenson Gdns SO19 ....104 A2
Kent Gdns SO40 ....100 B3
Kent Gr PO16 ....156 B3
Kent Ho
20 Bournemouth BH4 ....204 B2
27 Southampton SO14 ....103 B3
Kent La BH24 ....93 B1
Kent Rd
Chandler's Ford SO53 ....55 B2
Gosport PO13 ....155 A2
Poole BH12 ....203 C3
Portsmouth PO5 ....215 B1
Southampton SO17 ....79 B1
Kent St Portsmouth PO1 ....182 A3
Southampton SO14 ....103 B3
Kentidge Rd PO7 ....134 B3
Kentish Rd SO15 ....102 B4
Kenwood Rd PO16 ....156 B3
Kenwyn Cl SO18 ....80 A1
Kenya Rd PO16 ....156 A4
Kenyon Cl BH15 ....202 C4
Kenyon Rd Poole BH15 ....202 C4
Portsmouth PO2 ....157 C1
Keppel Cl BH24 ....141 A4
Kerley Rd BH2 ....204 C1
Kern Cl SO16 ....77 C2
Kerrfield SO22 ....10 B4
Kerrfield Mews SO22 ....10 B4
Kerrigan Ct SO17 ....103 A4
Kerry Cl
Chandler's Ford SO53 ....55 B3
Lymington SO41 ....197 B2
Kerry Gdns SP6 ....69 A1
Kersley Gdns SO19 ....104 A2
Kesteven Way SO18 ....104 A4
Kestrel Cl
Bishop's Waltham SO32 ....83 A4
Botley SO32 ....81 C1
Clanfield PO8 ....88 B2
Ferndown BH22 ....165 A4
Marchwood SO40 ....101 C1
Southampton SO16 ....78 A3
Stubbington PO14 ....154 A2
Upton BH16 ....201 A4
Winchester SO22 ....10 B2
Kestrel Ct BH24 ....141 A4
Kestrel Dr BH23 ....208 A3
Kestrel Pl PO6 ....158 C4
Kestrel Rd Eastleigh SO50 ....55 C1
Portsmouth PO3 ....158 A2
Kestrel Way SP6 ....93 A3
Keswick Ave PO3 ....183 A4
Keswick Ct BH25 ....195 A3
Keswick Rd
Bournemouth BH5 ....206 A2
New Milton BH25 ....195 A3
Southampton SO19 ....103 B1
Keswick Way BH31 ....114 C3
Kettering Terr PO2 ....182 B4
Keverstone Ct BH1 ....205 B2
Kevlyn Cres SO31 ....104 C1
Kew La SO31 ....128 A4
Kewlake La SO40 ....74 B1
Key La 21 BH15 ....202 A1
Keydell Ave PO8 ....112 A3
Keydell Cl PO8 ....112 A3
Keyes Cl
Christchurch BH23 ....207 C3
Gosport PO13 ....155 B2
Poole BH12 ....188 C1
Keyes Ct 4 PO5 ....215 C1
Keyes Rd PO13 ....155 B2
Keyhaven Cl PO13 ....155 A1
Keyhaven Dr PO9 ....135 B3
Keyhaven Rd SO41 ....211 C2
Keynsham Rd SO19 ....104 A3
Keysworth Ave BH25 ....209 C4
Keysworth Rd BH16 ....201 B2
Khandala Gdns PO7 ....134 C2
Khartoum Rd SO17 ....79 A1
Khyber Rd BH12 ....203 B3
Kidmore La PO7 ....110 C3
Kielder Cl SO53 ....55 A4
Kielder Gr 2 PO13 ....155 B1
Kilbride 11 BH12 ....204 A2
Kilbride Path 5 PO2 ....182 B4
Kilford Ct SO30 ....106 A3
Kilham La SO22 ....10 A3
Killarney Cl SO19 ....104 C2
Killock 6 BH13 ....214 C4
Kilmarnock Rd BH9 ....189 C1
Kilmeston Cl PO9 ....135 C3
Kilmeston Rd
Cheriton SO24 ....14 B2
Kilmeston SO24 ....14 B1
Kilmington Way BH23 ....208 C4
Kilmiston Dr PO16 ....132 B1
Kilmiston Rd PO1 ....182 C4
Kiln Acre PO16 ....131 A2
Kiln Cl Corfe Mullen BH21 ....186 B2
Hythe SO45 ....125 C2
Kiln Field GU33 ....20 C3
Kiln Gn SO21 ....57 A4
Kiln Hill SO32 ....109 A4
Kiln La Braishfield SO51 ....28 B3
Buriton GU31 ....65 B3
Otterbourne SO21 ....31 B1
Redlynch SP5 ....47 C4
Southwick PO7 ....109 B2
Kiln Rd Fareham PO16 ....131 A2
Portsmouth PO3 ....158 A1
Kiln Way BH31 ....115 B2
Kilnside PO7 ....110 C2
Kilnyard Cl SO40 ....76 B1
Kilpatrick Cl 6 PO2 ....182 B4
Kilwich Way PO16 ....156 A3
Kimber Rd BH11 ....188 C2
Kimberley Cl
Christchurch BH23 ....206 C4
Fair Oak SO50 ....57 B1
Kimberley Ct SO19 ....103 C1
Kimberley Rd
Bournemouth BH6 ....206 B3
Poole BH14 ....203 A2
Portsmouth PO4 ....183 A1
Kimbers GU32 ....40 C2
Kimbolton Rd PO3 ....183 A3
Kimbridge Cnr SO51 ....27 A4
Kimbridge Cres PO9 ....136 A3
Kimbridge La SO51 ....27 A4
Kimmeridge Ave BH12 ....203 B4
Kimpton Cl PO13 ....179 C1
Kimpton Ct 9 PO9 ....136 A3
Kineton Rd SO15 ....78 C1
King Albert Ct PO1 ....215 C4
King Albert St PO1 ....215 C4
King Alfred Pl SO23 ....2 A1
King Alfred Terr 29 SO23 ....2 A1
King Alfred's Coll SO22 ....10 C4
King Arthur's Ct PO6 ....158 B4
King Charles St 9 PO1 ....182 A2
King Cl BH24 ....139 C2
King Cote Villas 1 PO5 ....182 C1
King Cup Ave SO31 ....128 C2
King Edward Ave
Bournemouth BH9 ....190 A1
Southampton SO16 ....102 A4
King Edward Ct BH9 ....189 C1
King Edward Pk (Cvn Pk) SO53 ....55 A4
King Edward VI Sch SO15 ....102 C4
King Edward's Cres PO2 ....157 B1
King Fisher Way BH23 ....208 A3
King George Ave
Bournemouth BH9 ....189 C1
Petersfield GU32 ....40 C2
King George Mews 7 GU32 ....40 C2
King George Mobile Home Pk BH25 ....194 C1
King George Rd PO16 ....156 B4
King George's Ave SO15 ....101 C4
King Harold Ct SO23 ....10 C3
King Henry I St PO1 ....215 A3
King John Ave
Bournemouth BH11 ....188 B3
Portchester PO16 ....156 A4
King John Cl BH11 ....188 B3
King La GU32 ....39 C4
King Richard 1 Rd PO1 ....182 A2
King Richard Cl PO6 ....157 B4
King Richard Dr BH11 ....188 B3
King Richard I Rd PO1 ....215 A3
King Richard Sch PO6 ....156 C4
King St Emsworth PO10 ....161 A4
Gosport PO12 ....181 B3
Portsmouth PO5 ....215 B2
Southampton SO14 ....103 A2
Westbourne PO10 ....137 A2
Wimborne Minst BH21 ....163 A2
King William St PO1 ....182 A3
King's Arms La BH24 ....140 C4
King's Arms Row BH24 ....140 C4
King's Ave BH23 ....206 C3
King's Cl SO53 ....55 B4
King's Copse Rd SO45 ....177 B4
King's Cres BH14 ....203 C1
King's Croft La PO9 ....135 B1
King's Ho 17 SO14 ....103 A2
King's La GU32 ....18 B2
King's Park Athletic Ctr* BH7 ....205 C3
King's Park Dr BH7 ....205 C3
King's Park Rd
Bournemouth BH7 ....205 C3
Southampton SO15 ....103 A3
King's Park Sch BH1 ....205 C3
King's Rd
Bournemouth BH3 ....205 A4
Emsworth PO10 ....160 C4
Fareham PO16 ....131 A1
Lee-on-the-Solent PO13 ....179 C2
Portsmouth PO5 ....215 B1
Winchester SO22 ....10 B3
King's Saltern Rd SO41 ....198 A1
King's Sch Prim The SO30 ....80 C2
King's Terr
1 Emsworth PO10 ....160 C4
Portsmouth PO1 ....215 A1
Kingcup Cl BH18 ....186 C1
Kingdom Cl PO15 ....129 B3
Kingfisher Cl
Bournemouth BH6 ....206 C3
Hamble-le-Rice SO31 ....128 A2
Rowland's Castle PO9 ....113 A1
South Hayling PO11 ....185 B1
Waterlooville PO8 ....111 C2
West Moors BH22 ....138 C1
Kingfisher Copse SO31 ....129 A2
Kingfisher Ct
1 Havant PO9 ....136 A1
Portsmouth PO3 ....158 A2
1 Southampton SO17 ....79 A1
Kingfisher Dr PO10 ....137 A2
Kingfisher Park Homes 3 BH10 ....189 C2
Kingfisher Pk BH21 ....138 C3
Kingfisher Rd SO50 ....55 C1
Kingfisher Way
Marchwood SO40 ....101 C1
Ringwood BH24 ....117 A1
Romsey SO51 ....52 C4
Kingfishers
9 Christchurch BH23 ....207 A3
Portchester PO16 ....155 C4
Kingfishers The BH31 ....115 A3
Kinghton Heath Ind Est BH11 ....188 C2
Kingland Cres BH15 ....202 B1
Kingland Rd BH15 ....202 B1
Kings Ave
Hamble-le-Rice SO31 ....127 C2
Poole BH14 ....203 B1
Winchester SO22 ....10 C3
Kings Bench Alley PO1 ....182 A3
Kings Cl Lymington SO41 ....197 B2
Lyndhurst SO43 ....121 C3
Rowland's Castle PO9 ....113 A1
Twyford SO21 ....32 A4
West Moors BH22 ....138 C1
Kings Copse Ave SO30 ....105 B3
Kings Copse Prim Sch SO30 ....105 B3
Kings Copse Rd SO30 ....105 B3
Kings Court Sch PO8 ....88 A1
Kings Cres SO41 ....197 B2
Kings Ct SP6 ....69 C1
Kings Field SO31 ....105 A1
Kings Field Gdns SO31 ....105 A1
Kings Head Yd 32 SO23 ....11 A4
Kings Huts SO41 ....197 A2
Kings La Chilcomb SO21 ....11 C3
Sway SO41 ....196 C4
Kings Mede PO8 ....112 A3
Kings Mews PO5 ....182 B1
Kings Park Com Hospl BH7 ....205 C3
Kings Rd
Chandler's Ford SO53 ....55 B3
Gosport PO12 ....181 A3
Lymington SO41 ....197 B2
New Milton BH25 ....195 B2
Petersfield GU32 ....40 B2
South Hayling PO11 ....185 A3
Kings Ride SO45 ....177 C4
Kings Row 7 SO22 ....10 C4
Kings Royal Hussars Mus The* SO23 ....10 C4
Kings Sch The SO50 ....57 A1
Kings Somborne Rd SO51 ....7 B1
Kings Way PO9 ....113 A1
Kings Worthy Prim Sch SO23 ....2 B3
Kings' Sch SO22 ....10 A4
Kingsbere Ave BH10 ....189 A1
Kingsbere Gdns BH23 ....209 A4
Kingsbere Rd BH15 ....202 C3
Kingsbridge Rd BH14 ....203 B2
Kingsbury Ct PO8 ....88 A3
Kingsbury Rd SO14 ....103 A4
Kingsbury's La BH24 ....140 C4
Kingsclere Ave
Havant PO9 ....135 B3
Southampton SO19 ....126 C4
Kingsclere Cl SO19 ....103 C1
Kingscote Ho 7 PO6 ....132 C1
Kingscote Rd
Cosham PO6 ....132 C1
Waterlooville PO8 ....111 B2
Kingscroft Ct PO9 ....135 B1
Kingsdale Ct 13 SO22 ....10 C4
Kingsdown Pl PO1 ....215 D3
Kingsdown Rd PO7 ....111 B1
Kingsdown Way SO18 ....80 A1
Kingsey Ave PO10 ....160 C4
Kingsfernsden La GU32 ....41 A3
Kingsfield
Lymington SO41 ....198 A1
Ringwood BH24 ....141 A4
Kingsfold Ave SO18 ....79 C2
Kingsford Cl SP5 ....47 B3
Kingsgate Rd SO23 ....10 C3
Kingsgate St SO23 ....11 A3
Kingsland Cl PO6 ....133 B1
Kingsland Ct Poole BH13 ....214 C4
4 Southampton SO14 ....103 A2
Kingsland Ho 20 SO14 ....103 A3
Kingsland Mkt SO14 ....103 A2
Kingsland Sq 3 SO14 ....103 A2
Kingsleigh Fst Sch BH10 ....189 B2
Kingsleigh Jun Sch BH10 ....189 B2
Kingsleigh Sec Sch BH10 ....189 B2
Kingsley Ave BH6 ....207 A2
Kingsley Cl BH6 ....207 A2
Kingsley Gdns SO40 ....100 A4
Kingsley Gn PO9 ....135 C3
Kingsley Pl SO22 ....10 C3
Kingsley Rd
Gosport PO12 ....180 C4
Portsmouth PO4 ....183 B2
Southampton SO15 ....102 A4
Kingsmead PO17 ....108 B4
Kingsmead Ave PO14 ....179 B3
Kingsmead Ct
16 Southampton SO15 ....78 A1
9 Wimborne Minst BH21 ....163 A3
Kingsmill Cl PO12 ....180 C2
Kingsmill Rd BH17 ....202 C4
Kingston SO31 ....127 B4
Kingston Cres PO2 ....182 B4
Kingston Cross PO2 ....182 B4
Kingston Ct SO16 ....77 C1
Kingston Gdns PO15 ....130 B2
Kingston Lacy Ho (NT)* BH21 ....162 A4
Kingston Pk SO41 ....197 B1
Kingston Rd
Gosport PO12 ....180 C3
Poole BH15 ....202 B2
Portsmouth PO1, PO2 ....182 C4
Southampton SO15 ....102 B3
Kingsway
Chandler's Ford SO53 ....55 C4
Ferndown BH22 ....165 A4
North Hayling PO11 ....160 A2
Southampton SO14 ....103 A3
Kingsway Cl BH23 ....191 C1
Kingsway Ct SO53 ....55 C4
Kingsway Gdns SO53 ....55 C4
Kingsway The PO16 ....156 B4
Kingswell Cl BH10 ....189 B1
Kingswell Gdns BH10 ....189 A1
Kingswell Gr BH10 ....189 A1
Kingswell Path PO1 ....215 B4
Kingswell Rd BH10 ....189 B1
Kingswell St PO1 ....215 B4
Kingswood
Bournemouth BH4 ....204 B1
Marchwood SO40 ....102 A1
Kingsworthy Rd PO9 ....135 C2
Kinloss Ct SO16 ....78 A3
Kinnell Cl PO10 ....160 C4
Kinross Cres PO6 158
Kinross Rd
Bournemouth BH3 204
Totton SO40 100
Kinsbourne Ave BH10 189
Kinsbourne Cl SO19 104
Kinsbourne Rise SO19 104
Kinsbourne Way SO19 104
Kinsford Ct SO42 145
Kinson Ave BH15 203
Kinson Gr BH10 189
Kinson Park Rd BH10 189
Kinson Pottery Ind Est BH14 203
Kinson Prim Sch BH11 189
Kinson Rd BH10 189
Kinterbury Ct 10 SO17 103
Kintyre Rd PO6 133
Kinver Cl SO51 28
Kiosks The 20 BH15 202
Kipling Bldgs 18 PO2 157
Kipling Cl PO15 106
Kipling Ct SO19 103
Kipling Rd Eastleigh SO50 55
Poole BH14 203
Portsmouth PO2 157
Kirby Cl BH15 202
Kirby Ct 4 PO2 157
Kirby Rd PO2 157
Kirby Way BH6 206
Kirk Gdns SO40 100
Kirkham Ave BH23 192
Kirkstall Rd PO4 182
Kirkway BH18 187
Kirtley Cl PO6 158
Kirton Rd PO6 158
Kitchener Cres BH17 187
Kitchener Rd SO17 79
Kitchers Cl SO41 ....172 A
Kite Cl PO8 111
Kites Croft Cl PO14 ....129 B
Kitnocks Hill SO32 106
Kitscroft Rd BH10 ....189 B
Kitt's La SO24 ....16 B
Kittiwake Cl
Bournemouth BH6 ....206 C
Gosport PO13 ....155 A
Kitwalls La SO41 ....211 B
Kitwood Gn 45 PO9 ....136 A
Kivernell Pl 1 SO41 ....211 B
Kivernell Rd SO41 ....211 B
Kiwi Cl BH15 ....202 C
Kleves Ct SO19 ....104 A
Knapp Cl BH23 ....207 A
Knapp La SO51 ....29 B
Knapp Mill Ave BH23 ....207 A
Knapps Hard GU32 ....37 A
Knatchbull Cl SO51 ....52 C
Knellers La SO40 ....100 B
Knight Cl SO23 ....2 A
Knightcrest Pk SO41 ....196 C
Knighton Cnr PO8 ....112 B
Knighton Heath Cl BH11 ....188 C
Knighton Heath Rd BH11 ....188 C
Knighton La BH21 ....188 B
Knighton Pk BH25 ....209 C
Knighton Rd SO19 ....103 C
Knights Bank Rd PO14 ....153 C
Knights Cl SO31 ....128 C
Knights Rd BH11 ....188 B
Knightsbridge Ct BH2 ....204 C
Knightstone Ct 10 PO2 ....157 C
Knightstone Gr BH22 ....138 B
Knightstone Grange 2 SO45 ....126 A
Knightwood Ave
Havant PO9 ....136 A
Lyndhurst SO43 ....121 C
Knightwood Cl
Ashurst SO40 ....100 A
Christchurch BH23 ....208 B
Lyndhurst SO43 ....121 C
Knightwood Oak* SO43 ....120 C
Knightwood Prim Sch SO53 ....54 C
Knightwood Rd
Chandler's Ford SO52 ....55 A
Hythe SO45 ....126 A
North Baddesley SO52 ....55 A
Knobcrook Rd 3 BH21 ....163 A
Knole Ct 5 BH1 ....205 B
Knole Gdns BH1 ....205 B
Knole Rd BH1 ....205 B
Knoll Gdns*
Ferndown BH21 ....164 C
St Leonards BH24 ....139 C
Knoll La BH21 ....186 A
Knoll Manor BH2 ....204 C
Knotgrass Rd SO31 ....128 C
Knowland Dr SO41 ....211 B
Knowle Hill SO50 ....56 A
Knowle Hospl PO17 ....130 C
Knowle La SO50 ....57 C
Knowle Rd SO42 ....145 C
Knowles Cl
Christchurch BH23 ....207 C
Southampton SO16 ....77 B
Knowles Mdw GU33 ....21 A
Knowlton Gdns BH9 ....190 A
Knowlton Rd BH17 ....187 C
Knowsley Cres PO6 ....158 A
Knowsley Rd PO6 ....157 C
Knox Rd Havant PO9 ....135 B
Portsmouth PO2 ....157 B
Knyght Cl SO51 ....53 A

veton Ho BH1 .205 A2
veton Rd BH1 .205 B2
tenay Ave SO18 .104 C4
yong Cl SO51 .51 A1
egils Rd SO22 .1 C1
on Cl PO12 .181 B4
chil La BH21 .163 C3
chil Way BH21 .163 C4
es La SO32 .82 B3

rador Dr BH15 .202 B1
urnham Dr SO23 .2 A4
urnum Ave PO6 .158 B4
urnum Cl
rndown BH22 .165 A3
rth Baddesley SO52 .54 A3
rwood BH31 .115 B3
urnum Cres SO45 .150 A4
urnum Ct SO19 .103 B2
urnum Dr SO41 .211 C4
urnum Gr
stleigh SO50 .56 A2
rtsmouth PO2 .157 C1
uth Hayling PO11 .185 A2
urnum Ho
Bournemouth BH10 .189 C2
dge End SO30 .105 B3
urnum Rd
reham PO16 .155 A3
dge End SO30 .105 B3
uthampton SO16 .79 B2
aterlooville PO7 .134 B3
cey Cres BH15 .203 A3
ckford Ave SO40 .100 C3
con Cl SO18 .103 C4
cy Cl BH21 .163 B3
cy Dr BH21 .163 B3
dram Rd PO12 .180 C2
dy Betty's Dr PO15 .129 C3
dybridge Rd PO7 .134 B2
dycross Rd SO45 .126 A1
dysmith Rd BH23 .207 C4
dysmith Terr SO32 .83 B4
dywood SO50 .55 C3
dywood Ho PO1 .215 B2
gado Cl BH14 .214 B4
gland Ct 12 BH15 .202 B1
gland St BH15 .202 B1
goon Cl BH14 .214 A4
goon Rd BH14 .214 A4
idlaw Cl BH12 .204 A4
ke Ave BH15 .201 B1
ke Cres BH15 .201 C2
ke Dr BH15 .201 B1
ke Farm Cl SO30 .105 B4
ke Grove Rd BH25 .195 A2
ke Ho SO15 .102 B3
ke Rd
ournemouth BH11 .189 A3
handler's Ford SO53 .55 C4
urdridge SO32 .106 C4
amworthy BH15 .201 C1
ortsmouth PO1 .215 C4
outhampton SO19 .103 B1
erwood BH31 .115 A3
ke View Manor BH25 .195 A2
keland Gdns SO40 .101 C1
kelands Dr SO15 .102 B3
kes The SO32 .84 A2
keside Fareham PO17 .130 C3
ee-on-the-Solent PO13 .179 C1
wer SO51 .75 B3
ingwood BH24 .141 B3
keside Ave
ortsmouth PO3 .183 A4
ownhams SO16 .77 C3
keside Ctry Pk★ SO50 .79 C4
keside Gdns PO9 .136 A1
keside Pines BH25 .195 A2
keside Rd BH13 .204 A1
kesmere Rd PO8 .112 B3
keview Dr BH24 .141 B3
kewood Cl SO53 .55 B4
kewood Rd
shurst SO40 .100 B2
handler's Ford SO53 .30 C1
hristchurch BH23 .193 C1
amberhurst Cl SO19 .127 A4
ambert Cl PO7 .134 C3
ambourn Cl PO14 .154 B4
ambourn Sq SO53 .55 A3
ambourne Cl SO45 .125 C1
ambourne Dr SO31 .129 A2
ambourne Ho SO30 .105 A3
ambourne Rd SO18 .80 A1
ambs Cl BH17 .187 B1
ambs Lease GU33 .21 A2
ambsgreen La BH21 .162 C1
ammas Rd SO45 .126 A1
ampeter Ave PO6 .158 A4
ampton Gdns BH9 .189 C1
amward Mans 30 SO14 103 A4
ancaster Cl
Bursledon SO31 .105 A1
Christchurch BH23 .208 B4
Corfe Mullen BH18 .186 C3
Lee-on-the-Solent PO13 .180 A2
Portchester PO16 .132 A1
ancaster Ct SO30 .80 B1
ancaster Dr
Corfe Mullen BH18 .186 C3
Verwood BH31 .114 C3
ancaster Rd
Ferndown BH21 .165 A4
Southampton SO16 .77 C2

Lancaster Way PO7 .134 C3
Lance's Hill SO18 .103 C4
Lancer Cl BH23 .206 C4
Lander Cl BH15 .202 B1
Landford CE Prim Sch
SP5 .49 B2
Landford Common Farm
SP5 .49 C1
Landford Gdns BH8 .190 B1
Landford Way BH8 .190 B1
Landguard Rd
Portsmouth PO4 .183 A2
Southampton SO15 .102 B3
Landon Rd PO13 .180 B4
Landport St
Portsmouth PO1 .215 C4
Portsmouth, Southsea
PO5 .215 A2
Landport Terr PO1 .215 A2
Landport View PO1 .215 B4
Lands End Rd SO31 .128 B4
Landsdowne St PO5 .215 A2
Landseer Rd
13 Bournemouth BH4 .204 B2
Southampton SO19 .104 B2
Lane End SO24 .17 B4
Lane End Cotts SP5 .49 B2
Lane End Dr PO10 .160 C4
Lane The
4 Bournemouth BH8 .205 B3
Fawley SO45 .151 A2
Gosport PO12 .181 A1
Portsmouth PO4 .182 C1
Lanehays Rd SO45 .125 C2
Lanes End PO14 .179 B3
Lanes The BH25 .195 A3
Lanesbridge Cl SO40 .99 C3
Langbar Cl SO19 .103 C3
Langbrook Cl PO9 .159 C4
Langdale Ave PO6 .158 A4
Langdale Cl SO16 .101 C4
Langdon Ct BH14 .203 B2
Langdon Rd BH14 .203 B2
Langdown Firs SO45 .126 A2
Langdown Inf Sch SO45 126 A1
Langdown Jun Sch
SO45 .126 A2
Langdown Lawn SO45 .126 A2
Langdown Lawn Cl
SO45 .126 A1
Langdown Rd SO45 .126 A2
Langford La SP5 .47 C4
Langford Rd PO1 .182 C4
Langham Cl SO52 .53 C2
Langham Ct BH23 .191 C1
Langhorn Rd SO16 .79 B2
Langley Chase BH24 .140 A3
Langley Gdn SP6 .70 A2
Langley Lodge Gdns
SO45 .177 C4
Langley Rd
Christchurch BH23 .193 C1
Poole BH14 .203 C2
Portsmouth PO2 .182 C4
Southampton SO15 .102 A3
Langrish Cl PO9 .136 A3
Langrish Hill GU32 .39 B2
Langrish Prim Sch GU32 .40 A2
Langrish Rd SO16 .78 A2
Langside Ave BH12 .204 A4
Langside Sch BH12 .204 A4
Langstone Ave PO9 .159 C4
Langstone High St PO9 159 C3
Langstone Ho
11 Fareham PO16 .155 A4
Havant PO9 .136 A2
Langstone Inf Sch PO3 .183 A4
Langstone Jun Sch PO3 183 A4
Langstone Marina Hts
PO4 .183 B2
Langstone Rd
Havant PO9 .159 C4
Portsmouth PO3 .183 A3
Langstone Wlk
Fareham PO14 .154 B4
Gosport PO13 .155 A1
Langton Cl
Barton on Sea BH25 .210 A4
Winchester SO22 .1 C1
Langton Dene 27 BH4 .204 B2
Langton Farm Gdns
PO1 .182 C4
Langton Rd
Bishop's Waltham SO32 .83 B4
Bournemouth BH7 .205 C3
Lanham La SO22 .1 A1
Lankhills Rd SO23 .2 A1
Lankhills Sch SO22 .1 C1
Lansdell Ct 6 BH15 .202 C2
Lansdown Ave PO16 .156 B3
Lansdown Terr PO10 .137 A3
Lansdowne Ave
Waterlooville PO7 .134 A1
Winchester SO23 .10 C3
Lansdowne Cl 3 SO51 .52 C4
Lansdowne Cres BH1 .205 A2
Lansdowne Ct
Romsey SO51 .52 C4
3 Winchester SO23 .10 C3
Lansdowne Gdns
Bournemouth BH1 .205 A2
Romsey SO51 .52 C4
Lansdowne Hill 9
SO14 .102 C2
Lansdowne Ho
13 Bournemouth BH1 .205 A2
3 Gosport PO12 .181 A3

Lansdowne Rd
Bournemouth BH1 .205 A3
Southampton SO15 .102 A4
Lansdowne The BH1 .205 A2
Lantana Cl PO7 .134 C3
Lantern Ct SO23 .10 C3
Lanyard Dr PO13 .180 B3
Lapthorn Cl PO13 .155 A2
Lapwing Cl
Gosport PO12 .181 A4
Horndean PO8 .112 A4
Portsmouth PO4 .183 B3
Lapwing Dr SO40 .100 B4
Lapwing Gr PO16 .155 C4
Lapwing Rd BH21 .164 A4
Lara Cl BH8 .190 B2
Larch Ave SO45 .150 B3
Larch Cl
Broadstone BH17 .186 C1
Hordle SO41 .195 C2
Kings Worthy SO23 .2 A4
Lee-on-the-Solent PO13 .180 A3
St Leonards BH24 .140 A2
West End SO30 .80 B1
Larch Ct PO1 .215 C4
Larch Rd SO16 .78 A2
Larch Row SP6 .70 B1
Larch Way
Bursledon SO31 .127 C4
Ferndown BH22 .165 B4
Larchdale Cl SO31 .152 B4
Larches Gdns PO15 .130 B1
Larchfield Way PO8 .112 B3
Larchwood Ave PO9 .135 A2
Larchwood Rd SO40 .100 B3
Larcombe Rd GU32 .40 B1
Larg Dr SO22 .1 B2
Lark Hill Rise SO22 .10 B2
Lark Rd
Christchurch BH23 .208 A3
Eastleigh SO50 .55 B1
Lark Way PO10 .137 B2
Larkhill Rd PO3 .157 C2
Larks Cl BH22 .165 A4
Larks Rise BH22 .165 A4
Larksfield Ave BH9 .190 B2
Larkshill Cl BH25 .195 A2
Larkspur Chase SO19 .104 C3
Larkspur Cl
Locks Heath SO31 .128 C1
Swanmore SO32 .84 A3
Larkspur Dr
Chandler's Ford SO53 .54 C3
Marchwood SO40 .124 C4
Larkspur Gdns
7 Hedge End SO30 .105 B3
Holbury SO45 .150 A2
Larkwhistle Wlk PO9 .135 B4
Lascelles Ct 1 BH7 .206 A3
Lascelles Rd BH7 .206 A3
Laser Cl SO31 .128 C1
Lasham Gn 47 PO9 .136 A3
Lasham Ho 3 SO16 .102 A4
Lasham Wlk PO14 .154 B4
Lashley Mdw PO7 .86 B2
Latch Farm Ave BH23 .207 A4
Latchmore Dr SO45 .125 B2
Latchmore Forest Gr
PO8 .112 A2
Latchmore Gdns PO8 .111 C2
Latelie Cl SO31 .127 B3
Latham Cl SO50 .57 A1
Latham Ct SO15 .102 A4
Latham Rd Fair Oak SO50 .57 A1
Romsey SO51 .53 A4
Latimer Ct
Portsmouth PO3 .158 A2
11 Southampton SO17 .79 A1
Latimer Gate 27 SO14 .103 A2
Latimer Rd BH9 .204 C4
Latimer St Romsey SO51 .52 C4
Southampton SO14 .103 A2
Latimers Cl BH23 .193 C1
Lauder Cl PO10 .137 C1
Launcelyn Cl SO52 .53 C2
Launceston Cl PO12 .181 B4
Launceston Dr SO50 .55 C3
Laundry La SO41 .211 C2
Laundry Rd SO16 .78 A1
Laurel Cl
Christchurch BH23 .193 B1
Corfe Mullen BH21 .186 B3
Gosport PO12 .181 B4
Hordle SO41 .195 C2
Hythe SO45 .125 C2
Locks Heath SO31 .129 A2
Southampton SO19 .103 B2
St Leonards BH24 .139 C2
Laurel Dr BH18 .187 B2
Laurel Gdns
Broadstone BH18 .187 B2
Locks Heath SO31 .129 A2
Laurel La BH24 .139 C2
Laurel Rd
Locks Heath SO31 .129 A2
Waterlooville PO8 .112 B2
Laurels The
Brockenhurst SO42 .172 C4
Ferndown BH22 .165 B4
Lauren Mews PO11 .184 C1
Laurence Ct 2 SO50 .57 B1
Laurence Gn PO10 .136 C2
Laurence Mews SO51 .52 C4
Lauriston Dr SO53 .30 A1
Laurus Cl PO7 .135 A3
Laurus Wlk 18 PO13 .179 C1
Lavant Cl PO8 .112 A1
Lavant Ct 3 GU32 .40 C2

Lavant Dr PO9 .136 A2
Lavant St GU32 .40 C2
Lavender Cl
Southampton SO19 .103 C3
Verwood BH31 .115 B3
Lavender Rd
Bournemouth BH8 .190 B2
Hordle SO41 .195 C2
Waterlooville PO7 .135 A3
Lavender Villas 1
BH23 .209 A4
Lavender Way BH18 .186 B2
Laverock Lea PO16 .132 B1
Laverstock 27 BH5 .205 C2
Laverstoke Cl SO16 .77 C3
Lavey's La PO15 .130 A3
Lavington Gdns SO52 .53 C2
Lavinia Rd Gosport PO12 181 A3
Poole BH12 .203 B4
Lawford Rd BH9 .190 A2
Lawford Way SO40 .100 C4
Lawn Cl Gosport PO13 .180 B4
Milford on Sea SO41 .211 C2
Lawn Ct SO17 .103 A4
Lawn Dr SO31 .129 A1
Lawn Ho 21 SO23 .11 A4
Lawn Rd Eastleigh SO50 .56 A3
Littleton SO22 .1 B2
Lymington SO41 .197 A2
Milford on Sea SO41 .211 C2
Southampton SO17 .103 A4
Lawn St SO23 .11 A4
Lawn View BH25 .194 B3
Lawns Cl BH21 .164 B3
Lawns Rd BH21 .164 A3
Lawns The BH23 .209 A4
Lawnside Rd SO15 .102 A4
Lawnswood SO50 .57 B1
Lawnswood Cl PO8 .111 C1
Lawrence Ave PO8 .111 C1
Lawrence Ct
Bournemouth BH8 .205 B3
Southampton SO19 .103 C1
Lawrence Dr BH13 .203 C1
Lawrence Gr SO19 .103 C1
Lawrence Ho 6 SO45 .126 A2
Lawrence La SP6 .94 A2
Lawrence Mans PO5 .215 D1
Lawrence Rd
Fareham PO15 .130 C1
Portsmouth PO5 .215 D1
Ringwood BH24 .117 B1
Lawrence Sq 20 PO12 .181 B2
Lawrence Wlk PO13 .180 B3
Lawson Cl SO31 .128 B4
Lawson Ct 12 SO16 .78 A1
Lawson Rd Poole BH12 .203 A3
Portsmouth PO5 .215 D2
Laxton Cl
Locks Heath SO31 .129 A2
Southampton SO19 .104 A1
Layard Dr BH21 .163 B1
Laymoor La BH21 .164 B3
Layton Ct BH12 .203 B3
Layton Rd Gosport PO13 .155 B2
Poole BH12 .203 B3
Lazy Acre PO10 .161 B4
Le Patourel Cl BH23 .207 B4
Lea Rd SO45 .177 C4
Lea The BH31 .115 A3
Lea Way BH11 .188 C3
Lea-Oak Gdns PO15 .130 B2
Leabrook SO31 .129 A3
Leacock Cl SO32 .84 A3
Leafy La PO15 .129 C3
Lealand Gr PO6 .158 B4
Lealand Rd PO6 .158 B4
Leamington Cres PO13 .179 C1
Leamington Ho 9 PO5 .215 B2
Leamington Rd BH9 .205 A4
Leander Cl SO50 .56 A3
Leander Dr PO12 .181 B4
Leaphill Rd BH7 .206 A3
Lear Rd PO12 .181 A3
Learoyd Rd BH17 .202 C4
Leaside Way SO16 .79 B3
Leatherhead Gdns SO30 .81 B1
Leaway The PO16 .156 B4
Lebanon Rd SO15 .101 B4
Lechlade Gdns
Bournemouth BH7 .206 A4
Fareham PO15 .130 C2
Leckford Cl
Portchester PO16 .132 A1
Southampton SO18 .104 B4
Leckford Rd PO9 .136 A3
Ledbury Rd
Christchurch BH23 .207 C3
Cosham PO6 .133 B1
Lederle La PO13 .155 B3
Ledgard Cl BH14 .203 A2
Lee Church La SO51 .76 C4
Lee Ct BH22 .165 B2
Lee Dro SO51 .53 A1
Lee La SO51 .77 A4
Lee Rd PO12 .181 A3
Lee-on-the-Solent Inf Sch
PO13 .179 C1
Lee-on-the-Solent Jun Sch
PO13 .179 C1
Leedam Rd BH10 .189 B2
Leelands SO41 .197 B1
Leep La PO12 .181 A1
Lees Cl BH23 .191 B2
Lees La PO12 .181 A3
Lees La N PO12 .181 A3
Leesland CE Inf Sch
PO12 .181 A2

Leesland CE Jun Sch
PO12 .181 A2
Leesland Rd PO12 .181 A3
Leeson Dr BH22 .165 A4
Leeson Rd BH7 .205 C4
Legg La BH21 .163 B2
Legion Cl
Hamworthy BH15 .201 C1
Southampton SO16 .79 B2
Legion La SO23 .2 B4
Legion Rd
Hamworthy BH15 .201 C1
South Hayling PO11 .185 A2
Leicester Ct PO13 .180 B3
Leicester Rd Poole BH13 203 C2
Southampton SO15 .78 B1
Leicester Way SO23 .2 B1
Leigh Comm BH21 .163 C3
Leigh Ct SO50 .55 C2
Leigh Gdns BH21 .163 B2
Leigh House Hospl
Chandler's Ford SO53 .55 B4
Winchester SO21 .11 C4
Leigh La BH21 .163 C3
Leigh Mans 10 SO17 .79 A1
Leigh Pk SO41 .197 B2
Leigh Rd
Eastleigh SO50, SO53 .55 C2
Fareham PO16 .131 A1
Havant PO9 .135 C1
New Milton BH25 .195 A2
Southampton SO17 .79 A1
Wimborne Minst BH21 .163 C2
Leigham Vale Rd BH6 .206 B2
Leighton Ave 7 SO15 .102 A4
Leighton Rd SO19 .103 C2
Leisure The PO13 .155 B2
Leith Ave PO16 .132 C1
Lemon Rd SO15 .102 A4
Lendorber Ave PO6 .158 A4
Lennox Cl
Chandler's Ford SO53 .55 C4
Gosport PO12 .181 B1
Southampton SO16 .77 C3
Lennox Rd N PO5 .182 B1
Lennox Rd S PO5 .182 B1
Lensyd Gdns PO8 .111 C3
Lent Hill Ct 5 SO22 .10 B3
Lentham Cl BH17 .187 B1
Lentune Way SO41 .197 B1
Leofric Ct PO4 .183 B2
Leominster Rd PO6 .133 A1
Leonard Rd PO12 .181 B3
Leonards Ct SO16 .101 B4
Leopold Dr SO32 .83 A4
Leopold St PO4 .182 C1
Lepe Ctry Pk★ SO45 .178 A1
Lepe Rd SO45 .178 A2
Leroux Cl SO15 .102 C3
Lerryn Rd PO13 .155 B1
Leslie Loader Ct SO50 .56 A2
Leslie Loader Ho SO19 .103 C3
Leslie Rd
Bournemouth BH9 .204 C4
Poole BH14 .203 A2
Lester Ave PO9 .135 B1
Lester Rd PO12 .180 C3
Lester Sq BH24 .143 B2
Leven Ave BH4 .204 B3
Leven Cl
Bournemouth BH4 .204 B2
North Baddesley SO53 .55 A4
Leventhorpe Ct PO12 .181 B2
Leveson Cl PO12 .180 C2
Levet's La 5 BH15 .202 A1
Leviathan Cl PO14 .179 B3
Lewens Cl BH21 .163 B2
Lewens La BH21 .163 B2
Lewes Cl SO50 .56 A3
Lewesdon Dr BH18 .186 C2
Lewin Cl SO21 .56 C4
Lewins Wlk SO31 .104 C1
Lewis Cl SO45 .125 B1
Lewis Ho 19 SO14 .103 A3
Lewis Rd PO10 .137 A2
Lewis Silkin Way SO16 .78 A2
Lewry Cl SO30 .105 B4
Lexby Rd SO40 .101 A3
Lexden Gdns PO11 .184 C2
Leybourne Ave
Bournemouth BH10 .189 B2
Southampton SO18 .104 A4
Leybourne Cl BH10 .189 B3
Leydene Ave BH8 .190 C1
Leydene Cl BH8 .190 C1
Leydene Pk GU32 .63 C2
Leyland Cl PO12 .181 A2
Leyland Rd BH12 .188 C1
Leyside BH23 .207 C3
Leyton Conyers 16
BH13 .214 C4
Leyton Rd SO14 .103 B3
Liam Cl PO9 .136 A2
Liberty Cl BH21 .139 A3
Liberty Ct BH23 .206 C4
Liberty Rd PO17 .109 A4
Liberty Row SO31 .128 A1
Library Mews BH12 .203 B3
Library Rd
Bournemouth BH9 .189 C1
Ferndown BH22 .165 B3
Poole BH12 .203 C3
Totton SO40 .101 A4
Lichen Way SO40 .101 C1
Lichfield Ct PO13 .180 B3

Lichfield Dr PO12 ... 181 B4
Lichfield Rd
Locks Heath PO14 ... 129 B2
Portsmouth PO3 ... 183 A3
Liddel Way SO53 ... 55 A3
Liddiards Way PO7 ... 134 C2
Lidiard Gdns PO4 ... 183 A1
Liederbach Dr BH31 ... 115 B2
Lightfoot Lawn PO4 ... 183 B2
Lightning Cl SO45 ... 150 C1
Lilac Cl Havant PO9 ... 136 B2
Ringwood BH24 ... 141 A4
Lilac Rd SO16 ... 79 A2
Lilies The SO50 ... 81 B4
Lilley Cl SO40 ... 101 C1
Lilliput CE Fst Sch BH14 ... 214 B4
Lilliput Ct BH14 ... 203 A2
Lilliput Rd BH14 ... 214 B4
Lily Ave PO7 ... 134 A1
Limberline Rd PO3 ... 158 A2
Limberline Spur PO3 ... 158 A3
Lime Ave SO19 ... 104 A3
Lime Cl
Colden Common SO21 ... 57 A4
Hythe SO45 ... 125 C1
Poole BH15 ... 202 C3
Southampton SO19 ... 104 A3
Lime Gdns SO30 ... 80 B2
Lime Gr Cosham PO6 ... 133 A1
Hordle SO41 ... 211 B4
South Hayling PO11 ... 184 B2
Lime Kiln La SO45 ... 150 A3
Lime Kiln Lane Mobile Home Pk SO45 ... 150 A3
Lime St SO14 ... 103 A2
Lime Tree Cl SP6 ... 92 C3
Lime Tree Ho SO41 ... 197 C2
Lime Wlk Botley SO30 ... 105 C4
Hythe SO45 ... 125 C1
Limekiln La
Bishop's Waltham SO32 ... 59 C2
East Meon GU32 ... 64 B3
Limes Cl GU33 ... 20 C2
Limes The Gosport PO13 ... 155 B1
Havant PO9 ... 159 C4
Marchwood SO40 ... 102 A1
Waterlooville PO7 ... 134 B2
Limetree Wlk 8 SO23 ... 11 B4
Limited Rd BH9 ... 190 A1
Lin Brook Dr BH24 ... 117 B1
Linacre Rd SO19 ... 104 B3
Linbrook Ct BH24 ... 117 A1
Lincoln Ave
Bournemouth BH1 ... 205 B3
Christchurch BH23 ... 191 C1
Lincoln Cl
Locks Heath PO14 ... 129 B2
Romsey SO51 ... 28 A1
Lincoln Ct Gosport PO13 ... 180 B3
Southampton SO15 ... 78 C1
West End SO30 ... 80 B1
Lincoln Rd Poole BH12 ... 203 B4
Portsmouth PO1 ... 182 C3
Lincoln Rise PO8 ... 112 A2
Lincolns Rise SO50 ... 31 A1
Lind Cl PO7 ... 134 C2
Lind Rd PO12 ... 181 B1
Linda Gr PO8 ... 111 C2
Linda Rd SO45 ... 151 A2
Lindbergh Cl PO13 ... 180 B3
Lindbergh Rd BH21 ... 165 A4
Lindbergh Rise PO15 ... 129 C3
Linden Cl Ferndown BH22 ... 165 B1
Waltham Chase SO32 ... 83 C2
Linden Ct
Locks Heath SO31 ... 129 B2
Ringwood BH24 ... 140 C4
12 Romsey SO51 ... 52 C4
West End SO18 ... 80 A2
Linden Dr GU33 ... 20 C2
Linden Gdns
Hedge End SO30 ... 105 B3
Ringwood BH24 ... 140 C4
Linden Gr
Chandler's Ford SO53 ... 55 B4
Gosport PO12 ... 181 A2
South Hayling PO11 ... 185 A2
Linden Lea PO16 ... 132 B1
Linden Rd
Bournemouth BH9 ... 190 A2
Ferndown BH22 ... 165 B1
Poole BH12 ... 203 B3
Romsey SO51 ... 52 C4
Southampton SO16 ... 78 A2
Linden Way Havant PO9 ... 135 C2
Lymington SO41 ... 197 B2
Waterlooville PO8 ... 112 B3
Linden Wlk SO52 ... 53 C3
Lindens Cl PO10 ... 136 C1
Lindens The BH23 ... 192 B2
Lindisfarne Cl PO6 ... 158 A4
Lindley Ave PO4 ... 183 A1
Lindsay Ho 35 PO5 ... 182 B1
Lindsay Manor 10 BH12 ... 204 A2
Lindsay Pk 15 BH13 ... 204 A2
Lindsay Rd Poole BH13 ... 204 A2
Southampton SO19 ... 104 C3
Lindum Ct 3 BH12 ... 204 A2
Lindway SO31 ... 129 A3
Liners Ind Est SO15 ... 102 B3
Lineside BH23 ... 207 B4
Linford Cl BH25 ... 195 A2
Linford Cres SO16 ... 78 B2
Linford Ct Fair Oak SO50 ... 57 B1
Linford Ct *continued*
Havant PO9 ... 135 B4
Linford Ho BH24 ... 117 C2
Linford Rd BH24 ... 117 B1
Ling Dale SO16 ... 78 C4
Ling Rd BH12 ... 188 A1
Lingdale Pl 3 SO17 ... 103 A4
Lingdale Rd BH6 ... 206 B3
Lingfield Ct 20 PO1 ... 182 A2
Lingfield Gdns SO18 ... 79 C1
Lingfield Grange BH4 ... 204 A2
Lingwood Ave BH23 ... 207 C3
Lingwood Cl SO16 ... 78 C4
Lingwood Wlk SO16 ... 78 C4
Linhorns La BH25 ... 195 A3
Link Rd Ringwood BH24 ... 141 B4
Southampton SO16 ... 77 C2
Link Rise BH21 ... 186 C3
Link The PO7 ... 112 A1
Link Way PO14 ... 179 B3
Linkenholt Way PO9 ... 135 B2
Linklater Path PO1 ... 182 B4
Links Cl PO9 ... 113 A1
Links Dr BH23 ... 191 B1
Links La
Rowland's Castle PO9 ... 113 A1
South Hayling PO11 ... 184 B2
Links Rd Poole BH14 ... 203 B1
Winchester SO22 ... 1 B1
Links The PO13 ... 155 B1
Links View Ave BH14 ... 203 C1
Links View Way SO16 ... 78 C3
Linkside Ave BH8 ... 205 C4
Linmead Dr BH11 ... 189 A3
Linnet Cl Petersfield GU31 ... 41 B1
Ringwood BH24 ... 141 B3
Waterlooville PO8 ... 111 C2
Linnet Ct Gosport PO12 ... 180 C3
New Milton BH25 ... 194 C2
Linnet Rd BH17 ... 201 C4
Linnet Sq SO50 ... 55 B1
Linnets The
Portchester PO16 ... 155 C4
Totton SO40 ... 100 B4
Linnies La SO41 ... 196 A4
Linthorpe Rd BH15 ... 202 C2
Linwood Cl SO45 ... 126 A1
Linwood Mix Sch BH9 ... 205 A4
Linwood Rd BH9 ... 205 A4
Lion Brewery The 24 PO2 ... 182 B4
Lion Ho PO17 ... 108 A2
Lion Rd PO1 ... 181 C4
Lion St PO1 ... 182 A3
Lion Terr PO1 ... 182 A3
Lionheart Cl BH11 ... 188 B3
Lionheart Way SO31 ... 105 A1
Lions Hall 23 SO22 ... 10 C4
Lions La BH24 ... 139 B3
Lions Wood BH24 ... 139 C2
Liphook Ho 49 PO9 ... 136 A3
Lipizzaner Fields SO31 ... 129 A4
Lippen La SO32 ... 36 C2
Lisbon Rd SO15 ... 102 B3
Lisle Cl Lymington SO41 ... 197 B2
Winchester SO22 ... 10 A2
Lisle Court Rd SO41 ... 198 B2
Lisle Ct SO22 ... 10 C3
Lisle Way PO10 ... 136 C2
Liss Inf & Jun Schs GU33 ... 21 A2
Liss Rd PO4 ... 182 C2
Liss Sta GU33 ... 20 C2
Litchfield Cres SO18 ... 79 C1
Litchfield Rd
Southampton SO18 ... 79 C1
Winchester SO22 ... 1 B2
Litchford Rd BH25 ... 195 B2
Lith Ave PO8 ... 112 B4
Little Abshot Rd PO14 ... 153 A4
Little Anglesey PO12 ... 181 A1
Little Anglesey Rd PO12 ... 181 A1
Little Arthur St PO2 ... 182 C4
Little Ashton La SO32 ... 59 C2
Little Barn Pl GU33 ... 21 A2
Little Barrs Dr BH25 ... 195 A2
Little Bull La SO32 ... 83 B1
Little Burn SO41 ... 172 A1
Little Cnr PO7 ... 111 A2
Little Coburg St PO1 ... 215 C3
Little Croft Rd BH12 ... 203 A3
Little Ct Poole BH14 ... 214 B4
Poole, Canford Cliffs BH13 ... 214 C4
Little Dene Copse SO41 ... 197 A1
Little Dewlands BH31 ... 114 B3
Little Dro SP6 ... 70 C4
Little Forest Mans 10 BH1 ... 205 A2
Little Forest Rd BH4 ... 204 C3
Little Fosters BH13 ... 214 C3
Little Gays PO14 ... 179 A3
Little George St PO1 ... 182 C4
Little Gr PO12 ... 181 A1
Little Green Orch PO12 ... 181 A1
Little Hambrook St 6 PO5 ... 215 A1
Little Holbury Park Mobile Home Pk SO45 ... 150 A3
Little Hyden La PO8 ... 88 A4
Little Kimble Wlk 3 SO30 ... 105 B3
Little La PO12 ... 181 A1
Little Lance's Hill SO19 ... 103 C3
Little Lonnen BH21 ... 163 C4
Little Mead PO7 ... 111 A2
Little Minster St SO23 ... 11 A4
Little Oak Rd SO16 ... 78 C2
Little Park Cl SO30 ... 105 A3
Little Park Farm Rd PO15 ... 129 B3
Little Park Mans PO17 ... 107 C2
Little Quob La SO30 ... 80 C1
Little Reynolds SO40 ... 100 B3
Little Shore La SO32 ... 83 B4
Little Southsea St PO5 ... 215 A1
Little Toller SO16 ... 78 C4
Little Woodfalls Dr SP5 ... 47 B2
Little Woodham La PO13 ... 180 B3
Littlecroft Ave BH9 ... 190 A2
Littledown Ave BH7 ... 205 C4
Littledown Dr BH7 ... 205 C4
Littlefield Cres SO53 ... 54 C3
Littlegreen Ave PO9 ... 136 A2
Littlegreen Sch PO18 ... 90 C2
Littlemead Cl BH17 ... 202 A4
Littlemeads SO51 ... 52 B4
Littlemill La SP6 ... 68 B3
Littlemoor Ave BH11 ... 188 B2
Littlepark Ave PO9 ... 135 A2
Littleton Gr PO9 ... 135 C2
Littleton La SO21 ... 1 A3
Littleton Rd SO22 ... 1 A2
Littlewood SO51 ... 50 C2
Littlewood Gdns
Locks Heath SO31 ... 128 C2
West End SO30 ... 80 B1
Liverpool Ct PO13 ... 180 B3
Liverpool Rd
Gosport PO14 ... 154 C3
Portsmouth PO1 ... 182 C3
Liverpool St SO14 ... 103 A4
Livesay Gdns PO1 ... 182 C3
Livingston Rd BH12 ... 203 B3
Livingstone Ct PO13 ... 180 B3
Livingstone Rd
Bournemouth BH5 ... 206 A3
Christchurch BH23 ... 207 B4
Portsmouth PO5 ... 215 C1
Southampton SO14 ... 103 A4
Wimborne Minst BH21 ... 163 C2
Llewellin Cl BH16 ... 201 B4
Llewellin Ct BH16 ... 201 B4
Lloyd Ave SO40 ... 101 C1
Loaders Cl BH9 ... 205 A4
Loane Rd SO19 ... 103 C2
Lobelia Ct PO7 ... 135 A3
Lobelia Rd SO16 ... 79 B3
Locarno Rd PO3 ... 158 A1
Loch Rd BH14 ... 203 C3
Lock App PO6 ... 157 A4
Lock View PO6 ... 157 A4
Lock's Cotts SO45 ... 125 B3
Locke Rd SO30 ... 105 B4
Lockerley Cl SO41 ... 197 C1
Lockerley Cres SO16 ... 77 C1
Lockerley Endowed CE Prim Sch SO51 ... 5 A1
Lockerley Rd PO9 ... 136 A2
Lockerly Ct SO15 ... 102 C4
Lockhams Rd SO32 ... 106 C4
Locks Heath Ctr SO31 ... 129 A2
Locks Heath Jun & Inf Schs SO31 ... 129 A1
Locks Rd SO31 ... 129 A2
Locksheath Cl 6 PO9 ... 135 B3
Locksheath Park Rd SO31 ... 129 A1
Locksley Dr BH22 ... 165 B2
Locksley Rd SO50 ... 55 C1
Locksway Rd PO4 ... 183 B2
Lockswood Keep SO31 ... 129 A2
Lockswood Rd SO31 ... 128 C2
Lockyer Ct GU32 ... 41 A3
Lockyer's Mid Sch BH21 ... 186 B4
Lockyer's Rd BH21 ... 186 C4
Lockyers Dr BH22 ... 165 C3
Lode Hill SP5 ... 47 A4
Loders Cl BH17 ... 187 B2
Lodge Ave PO6 ... 158 A4
Lodge Cl BH14 ... 203 C2
Lodge Ct BH14 ... 203 C2
Lodge Dr SO45 ... 126 A1
Lodge Dro SP5 ... 47 B2
Lodge Gdns PO12 ... 181 A2
Lodge Hill PO17 ... 109 A3
Lodge Rd
Christchurch BH23 ... 206 C4
Havant PO9 ... 135 A1
Locks Heath SO31 ... 129 A2
Lymington SO41 ... 197 A2
Southampton SO14 ... 103 A4
Lodge The
Bournemouth BH2 ... 204 C2
Southampton SO15 ... 102 C4
Waterlooville PO7 ... 135 A3
Lodge Vale SO51 ... 51 A1
Lodgebury Cl PO10 ... 161 C4
Lodsworth Cl PO8 ... 88 B2
Lodsworth Ho PO1 ... 215 C4
Loewy Cres BH12 ... 188 B1
Lofting Cl 1 SO50 ... 56 C1
Logan Cl SO16 ... 77 C3
Lomax Cl SO30 ... 81 B1
Lombard Ave BH6 ... 206 B3
Lombard Ct 8 PO1 ... 182 A2
Lombard St PO1 ... 182 A2
Lombardy Cl
Gosport PO13 ... 155 C1
Verwood BH31 ... 115 A3
Lombardy Rise PO7 ... 134 C3
Lomer La BH24 ... 93 B2
Lomond Cl PO2 ... 182 B4
Londesborough Rd PO4 ... 182 C2
London Ave PO2 ... 157 B1
London Ct PO12 ... 181 A1
London La BH23 ... 167 C1
London Rd Clanfield PO8 ... 88 B2
Cosham PO7 ... 134 B2
Hill Brow GU33 ... 21 A1
Horndean PO8 ... 88 B2
Kings Worthy SO23 ... 2 A3
Petersfield GU31 ... 41 A3
Portsmouth PO2 ... 157 C2
Southampton SO15 ... 103 A3
Steep GU31 ... 41 B3
Waterlooville PO7, PO6 ... 134 B2
London Tavern Cvn Pk The BH24 ... 141 B4
Lone Barn La SO32 ... 60 C4
Lone Pine Dr BH22 ... 165 C2
Lone Pine Way BH22 ... 165 C1
Lone Valley PO7 ... 134 B2
Long Acre Ct PO1 ... 182 C4
Long Beech Dr SO40 ... 100 B3
Long Cl Downton SP5 ... 46 C4
Winchester SO23 ... 10 C3
Long Copse SO45 ... 150 C2
Long Copse Ct PO10 ... 136 C2
Long Copse La PO10 ... 137 A2
Long Curtain Rd PO5 ... 182 A1
Long Down GU31 ... 41 A2
Long Dr Gosport PO13 ... 155 B1
West End SO30 ... 80 C1
Long La Bursledon SO31 ... 105 A1
Holbury SO45 ... 150 B3
Marchwood SO40 ... 101 B1
Ringwood BH24 ... 141 A2
Wimborne Minst BH21 ... 163 C4
Long Lane Cl SO45 ... 150 B2
Long Priors GU32 ... 37 A3
Long Rd
Bournemouth BH10 ... 189 B3
Petersfield GU32 ... 41 A3
Soberton SO32 ... 85 B3
Long Water Dr PO12 ... 181 B1
Long Wlk
Portsmouth PO1 ... 182 B4
Winchester SO21 ... 2 C2
Longacre Cl GU33 ... 21 A2
Longacre Dr BH22 ... 165 B2
Longacres PO14 ... 129 B2
Longbarrow Cl BH8 ... 191 A1
Longbridge Cl SO40 ... 76 B1
Longbridge Ct SO40 ... 76 B1
Longbridge Ho 8 PO5 ... 215 B2
Longbridge Ind Pk SO14 ... 103 B2
Longclose Rd SO30 ... 105 B4
Longcroft PO9 ... 135 C1
Longdean Cl 1 PO6 ... 133 A1
Longdown Dairy Farm* SO40 ... 100 B1
Longespee Rd BH21 ... 187 C4
Longfield Ave PO14 ... 154 C4
Longfield Cl PO4 ... 183 B3
Longfield Dr
Bournemouth BH11 ... 189 A3
Ferndown BH22 ... 189 C4
Longfield Rd
Emsworth PO10 ... 136 C2
Fair Oak SO50 ... 57 B1
Hordle SO41 ... 196 A1
Winchester SO23 ... 11 B4
Longfleet CE Comb Sch BH15 ... 202 B2
Longfleet Rd BH15 ... 202 C2
Longford Pl SO41 ... 197 B1
Longhouse Gn 9 SO23 ... 11 B4
Longlands Rd PO10 ... 161 B4
Longleat Gdns
New Milton BH25 ... 194 C2
Southampton SO16 ... 78 A2
Longmead GU33 ... 20 C2
Longmead Ave SO50 ... 56 B2
Longmead Ct PO9 ... 159 C4
Longmead Gdns PO9 ... 159 C4
Longmead Rd
Burley BH24 ... 142 C2
1 Southampton SO18 ... 80 A1
Longmeadow Gdns SO45 ... 126 A2
Longmeadow La BH17 ... 201 C4
Longmore Ave SO19 ... 103 B1
Longmore Cres SO19 ... 103 B1
Longmynd Dr PO14 ... 154 B4
Longridge Rd SO30 ... 105 B3
Longs La PO14 ... 154 B2
Longshore Way PO4 ... 183 B2
Longspee Sch BH17 ... 202 B4
Longstaff Gdns PO16 ... 130 C2
Longstock Cl SO19 ... 127 A4
Longstock Cres SO40 ... 100 C4
Longstock Rd PO9 ... 136 A3
Longwood Ave PO8 ... 112 A2
Longwood Dean La SO32, SO23 ... 34 A3
Longwood Rd SO21 ... 33 B3
Longworthy 3 SO45 ... 125 C1
Lonnen Rd BH21 ... 164 A4
Lonnen Wood Cl BH21 ... 164 A4
Lonsdale Ave
Cosham PO6 ... 158 A4
Portchester PO16 ... 156 B3
Lonsdale Rd BH3 ... 204 C3
Loosehanger SP5 ... 47 C2
Loperwood SO40 ... 76 A1
Loperwood La Ower SO40 ... 76 A2
Totton SO40 ... 76 A1
Loraine Ave BH23 ... 209 B4
Lord Cl BH17 ... 202 C4
Lord Montgomery Way 1 PO1 ... 215 A2
Lord Mountbatten Cl SO18 ... 79
Lord Wilson Sch SO31 ... 128
Lord's Hill Ctr E SO16 ... 77
Lord's Hill Ctr W SO16 ... 77
Lord's Hill Way SO16 ... 78
Lordington Cl PO6 ... 158
Lords Ct PO1 ... 215
Lords St PO1 ... 215
Lordswood SO50 ... 56
Lordswood Cl SO16 ... 78
Lordswood Ct SO16 ... 78
Lordswood Gdns SO16 ... 78
Lordswood Rd SO16 ... 78
Loreille Gdns SO16 ... 77
Loring Ho 7 PO2 ... 157
Lorne Park Rd BH1 ... 205
Lorne Pl SO18 ... 104
Lorne Rd PO5 ... 215
Lortemore Pl 8 SO51 ... 52
Loughwood Cl SO50 ... 56
Louis Flagg Ho 2 PO5 ... 215
Lovage Gdns SO40 ... 100
Lovage Way PO8 ... 88
Lovatt Gr PO15 ... 130
Love La
Milford on Sea SO41 ... 211
Petersfield GU31 ... 41
Romsey SO51 ... 52
Twyford SO21 ... 32
Upham SO24,SO32 ... 35
Woodgreen SP6 ... 70
Lovedean La
Horndean PO8 ... 111
Waterlooville PO8 ... 111
Lovedon La SO23 ... 2
Lovett Rd PO3 ... 158
Lovett Wlk SO22 ... 1
Lowcay Rd PO5 ... 182
Lowden Cl SO22 ... 10
Lower Alfred St 10 SO14 ... 103
Lower Ashley Rd BH25 ... 195
Lower Banister St 7 SO15 ... 102
Lower Bartons SP6 ... 69
Lower Baybridge La SO21 ... 33
Lower Bellfield PO14 ... 153
Lower Bere Wood PO7 ... 134
Lower Blandford Rd BH18 ... 187
Lower Brook St SO23 ... 11
Lower Brookfield Rd PO1 ... 182
Lower Brownhill Rd SO16 ... 77
Lower Buckland Rd SO41 ... 197
Lower Canal Wlk SO14 ... 103
Lower Chase Rd SO32 ... 83
Lower Church Path PO1 ... 215
Lower Church Rd PO14 ... 129
Lower Common La BH21 ... 139
Lower Common Rd SO51 ... 50
Lower Crabbick La PO7 ... 110
Lower Densome Wood SP6 ... 70
Lower Derby Rd PO2 ... 157
Lower Drayton La PO6 ... 158
Lower Duncan Rd SO31 ... 129
Lower Farlington Rd PO6 ... 158
Lower Farm La SO51 ... 29
Lower Forbury Rd PO5 ... 215
Lower Golf Links Rd BH18 ... 187
Lower Gr SP6 ... 45
Lower Grove Rd PO9 ... 160
Lower Heyshott GU31 ... 41
Lower La SO32 ... 83
Lower Lamborough La SO24 ... 14
Lower Mead GU31 ... 41
Lower Mead End Rd SO41 ... 171
Lower Moors Rd SO21 ... 31
Lower Mortimer Rd SO19 ... 103
Lower Mullin's La SO45 ... 125
Lower New Rd SO30 ... 80
Lower Northam Rd SO30 ... 105
Lower Pennington La SO41 ... 212
Lower Quay PO16 ... 155
Lower Quay Cl PO16 ... 155
Lower Quay Rd PO16 ... 155
Lower Rd PO9 ... 135
Lower Sandy Down La SO41 ... 173
Lower Spinney SO31 ... 152
Lower St SO51 ... 28
Lower St Helens Rd SO30 ... 105
Lower Stanmore La SO23 ... 10
Lower Swanwick Rd SO31 ... 128
Lower Vicarage Rd SO19 ... 103
Lower Wardown GU31 ... 41
Lower William St SO14 ... 103
Lower William St Ind Est SO14 ... 103

wer Wingfield St
01 215 C4
wer Woodside SO41 212 C4
wer York St SO14 103 B3
wesmore Ct BH14 203 B2
westoft Rd PO6 133 B1
weswater Ho 21 PO6 133 A1
wford Hill SO31 104 C1
wland Rd PO7 110 C2
wry Gdns SO19 104 B1
wther Gdns 3 BH8 205 B3
wther Rd BH8 205 A3
xwood Rd PO8 111 C3
ard Ct 11 PO9 136 A1
cas Cl SO16 77 C3
cas Rd Poole BH15 202 A1
oole, Upper Parkstone
BH12 203 B3
ccombe Pl SO15 78 B1
ccombe Rd SO15 78 B1
cerne Ave
ournemouth BH6 206 B3
Vaterlooville PO7 111 B1
cerne Gdns SO30 105 A4
cerne Rd SO41 211 B2
ckham Cl BH9 190 A1
ckham Gdns BH9 190 B1
ckham Pl BH9 190 A1
ckham Rd BH9 190 A1
ckham Rd E BH9 190 A1
cknow St PO1 215 D3
cky La SO41 174 A1
dcombe PO7 110 C3
dlow Inf Sch SO19 103 C2
dlow Jun Sch SO19 103 C2
dlow Rd Cosham PO6 133 B1
outhampton SO19 103 C2
dwell's La SO32 83 C2
gano Cl PO7 111 B1
kes Cl SO31 128 A1
kin Dr SO16 77 B3
lworth Ave BH15 201 C1
lworth Bsns Ctr SO40 76 C1
lworth Cl
handler's Ford SO53 55 A2
amworthy BH15 201 C1
outh Hayling PO11 185 A3
outhampton SO16 77 C1
lworth Cres BH15 201 C1
lworth Gn SO16 77 C1
lworth Rd PO13 179 C1
mby Dr BH24 141 A4
mby Drive Cvn Pk 3
H24 141 A4
mley Gdns PO10 161 A4
mley Rd PO10 137 A1
mley Terr PO10 137 A1
msden Ave SO15 102 B4
msden Mans 3 SO15 102 B4
msden Rd PO4 183 B2
ndy Cl SO16 77 C3
ndy Wlk PO14 154 A2
nedale Rd SO45 149 C4
pin Rd SO16 79 B3
scombe Rd BH14 203 B1
ther Rd BH9 204 C4
tman St PO10 136 C2
ton Rd SO19 104 A2
xton Cl SO30 105 C4
zborough La SO51 53 B3
yburn Cl SO16 78 B2
yburn Ct SO16 78 B2
yburn Ho SP5 73 A4
yburn Rd SP5 48 C1
ych Gate Ct BH24 141 B3
ychgate Dr PO8 112 A4
ychgate Gn PO14 154 B3
ydden Ct 1 PO13 155 B1
ydford Gdns BH11 189 A1
ydford Rd BH11 189 A1
ydgate SO40 100 B4
ydgate Cl SO19 104 B2
ydgate Gn SO19 104 B2
ydgate Rd SO19 104 B2
ydgate The SO41 211 A3
ydiard Cl SO50 56 A3
ydlinch Cl BH22 165 B1
ydlynch Inf Sch SO40 100 C4
ydlynch Rd SO40 100 C4
ydney Cl PO6 157 B4
ydney Rd SO31 128 C2
ydwell Cl BH11 188 C3
yell Rd BH12 203 B3
ymbourn Rd PO9 136 A1
yme Cl SO50 55 C3
yme Cres BH23 208 C4
ymefields SO41 211 C3
ymer La SO16 77 B3
ymer Villas SO16 77 B3
ymington Cath Sch
SO41 197 C2
ymington CE Inf Sch
SO41 197 B2
ymington Hospl SO41 197 B2
ymington Infmy & Day Hospl
SO41 197 C2
ymington Jun Sch
SO41 197 B2
ymington Pier Sta
SO41 198 A2
ymington Rd
Barton on Sea BH25 195 B1
Brockenhurst SO42 146 A1
Christchurch BH23 208 C4
East Boldre SO41 199 A4
Milford on Sea SO41 211 C3
ymington Town Sta
SO41 197 C2

Lymington Vineyard★
SO41 197 A1
Lymore La SO41 211 C3
Lymore Valley SO41 211 C3
Lynch Cl SO22 1 C1
Lynch La GU32 37 B2
Lyndale Cl SO41 211 C3
Lyndale Rd SO31 129 B2
Lynden Cl PO14 154 A4
Lynden Gate SO19 104 A2
Lyndhurst CE Inf Sch
SO43 121 C3
Lyndhurst Cl
South Hayling PO11 185 A2
Winchester SO22 1 B2
Lyndhurst Hill SO40 98 C4
Lyndhurst Ho PO9 135 C3
Lyndhurst Jun Sch PO2 157 C1
Lyndhurst Rd
Ashurst SO40 100 A1
Bransgore BH23 193 B3
Brockenhurst SO42 146 A1
Burley BH24 143 B3
Burton BH23 193 B3
Cadnam SO40 98 C4
Christchurch BH23 193 B1
Gosport PO12 181 A2
Landford SP5 49 B2
Portsmouth PO2 157 C1
Lyndock Cl SO19 103 C1
Lyndock Pl SO19 103 C1
Lyndon Ct BH23 191 C1
Lyndum Cl GU32 40 C2
Lyne Pl PO8 112 A3
Lyne's La BH24 140 C4
Lynford Ave SO22 1 C1
Lynford Way SO22 1 C1
Lynn Cl SO18 80 A2
Lynn Rd Poole BH17 187 C1
Portsmouth PO2 182 C4
Lynric Cl BH25 210 A4
Lynton Cres BH23 191 B2
Lynton Ct SO40 100 C3
Lynton Gdns PO16 130 C2
Lynton Gr PO3 183 A4
Lynton Rd
Hedge End SO30 105 B4
Petersfield GU32 40 C2
Lynwood Ave PO8 111 B2
Lynwood Cl BH22 165 B4
Lynwood Ct
Lymington SO41 197 B2
Winchester SO22 1 C1
Lynwood Dr BH21 187 C4
Lynx Cl SO50 56 C1
Lyon Ave BH25 195 A2
Lyon Rd BH12 188 C1
Lyon St SO14 103 A3
Lysander Cl BH23 208 B4
Lysander Ct PO1 182 A2
Lysander Way PO7 135 A4
Lyse Ct GU33 20 C2
Lysses Ct PO16 131 B1
Lyster Rd SP6 70 A1
Lystra Rd BH9 190 A2
Lytchett Dr BH18 187 A2
Lytchett Way BH16 201 A3
Lyteltane Rd SO41 197 B1
Lytham Rd
Broadstone BH18 187 A2
Southampton SO18 80 A1
Lythe La GU32 40 A3
Lytton Rd
Bournemouth BH1 205 B3
Hythe SO45 126 A1

M

Mabey Ave BH10 189 B1
Mabey Cl PO12 181 B1
Mablethorpe Rd PO6 133 C1
Macandrew Rd BH13 214 C4
Macarthur Cres SO18 104 A4
Macaulay Ave PO6 132 C1
Macaulay Rd BH18 187 A2
Macklin Ho 35 SO22 10 C4
Maclaren Rd BH9 189 C2
Maclean Rd BH11 188 C2
Macnaghten Rd SO18 103 B4
Madden Cl PO12 180 C2
Maddison St 5 SO14 102 C2
Maddoxford La SO32 82 A1
Maddoxford Way SO32 81 C1
Madeira Rd
Bournemouth BH1 205 A2
Poole BH14 203 B3
Portsmouth PO2 157 C2
Madeline Cl BH12 203 A4
Madeline Cres BH12 203 A4
Madeline Rd GU31 40 C2
Madison Ave BH1 205 B3
Madison Cl PO13 180 C4
Madison Ct 10 PO16 131 B1
Madrisa Ct SO41 197 C2
Mafeking Rd PO4 182 C2
Maffey Ct SO30 106 A4
Mag's Barrow BH22 165 C1
Magazine La SO40 102 A2
Magdala Rd Cosham PO6 157 C4
South Hayling PO11 184 C2
Magdalen Ct 19 PO2 157 C2
Magdalen Hill SO23 11 A4
Magdalen La BH23 207 A3
Magdalen Mews 45 SO23 11 A4
Magdalen Rd PO2 157 C2
Magdalene Way PO14 129 B1
Magennis Cl PO13 180 B4

Magenta Ct PO13 180 B3
Magna Cl BH11 188 C3
Magna Gdns BH11 188 C3
Magna Rd BH11 188 B4
Magnolia Cl
Bournemouth BH6 207 A3
Fareham PO14 154 C4
Hythe SO45 125 B2
Verwood BH31 115 B2
Magnolia Gr SO50 57 C1
Magnolia Ho 6 BH10 189 C2
Magnolia Rd SO19 103 C3
Magnolia Terr PO7 134 C3
Magnolia Way PO8 112 B2
Magpie Cl
Bournemouth BH8 190 B2
Fareham PO16 131 C1
Magpie Cotts PO8 113 B2
Magpie Dr SO40 100 B4
Magpie Gdns SO19 104 B2
Magpie Gr BH25 194 C1
Magpie La Eastleigh SO50 55 C1
Lee-on-the-Solent PO13 179 C2
Magpie Rd PO8 113 B3
Magpie Wlk PO8 111 B2
Maiden La SO41 197 C1
Maidford Gr PO3 158 B2
Maidment Cl BH11 188 C2
Maidstone Cres PO6 133 C1
Main Dr PO17 133 A3
Main Rd
Colden Common SO21 32 A1
Compton(Hants) SO21 31 B2
East Boldre SO41,SO42 199 A4
Fawley SO45 150 B3
Gosport PO13 155 B3
Hermitage PO10,PO18 161 B4
Hythe SO45 125 B3
Littleton SO22 1 A3
Marchwood SO40 101 C1
Otterbourne SO21 31 A2
Owslebury SO21 33 A2
Portsmouth PO1 181 C3
Southbourne PO10,PO18 161 B4
Totton SO40 100 C2
Boldre SO41 198 A4
Mainline Bsns Ctr GU33 20 C2
Mainsail Dr PO16 155 A4
Mainstone SO51 52 B3
Mainstream Ct SO50 56 B2
Maisemore Gdns PO10 160 B4
Maitland Cres PO1 182 B4
Maitland Ct SO41 197 B2
Maitland St 14 PO1 182 B4
Maitlands The BH2 204 B1
Maizemore Wlk 21
PO13 179 C1
Majestic Rd SO16 77 A2
Major Ct PO12 181 A4
Majoram Way PO15 129 B4
Majorca Mans 11 BH2 204 C2
Malan Cl BH17 202 C4
Malcolm Cl
Chandler's Ford SO53 30 C1
Locks Heath SO31 129 A2
Malcolm Rd SO53 30 C1
Malcomb Cl BH6 207 A2
Malcroft Mews SO40 102 A1
Maldon Cl SO50 56 B2
Maldon Rd
5 Cosham PO6 157 B4
Southampton SO19 103 C2
Malibres Rd SO53 55 C4
Malin Cl
Southampton SO16 77 C2
Stubbington PO14 154 A2
Malins Rd PO2 182 B4
Mall The Burley BH24 143 A2
Chandler's Ford SO53 55 C4
Portsmouth PO2 157 B1
Mallard Bldgs 6 BH25 195 A2
Mallard Cl
Bishop's Waltham SO32 83 A4
Bournemouth BH8 190 B1
Christchurch BH23 208 A3
Hordle SO41 196 A2
Romsey SO51 52 C4
Mallard Gdns
Gosport PO13 155 A1
Hedge End SO30 81 B1
Mallard Rd
Bournemouth BH8 190 B1
Portsmouth PO4 183 A3
Rowland's Castle PO9 113 A1
Wimborne Minst BH21 164 A4
Mallard Way PO10 137 B2
Mallards Rd SO31 127 C4
Mallards The
Fareham PO16 131 A2
Havant PO9 159 C4
Mallet Cl SO30 81 C1
Mallory Cl BH23 207 C4
Mallory Cres PO16 131 A2
Mallow Cl
Broadstone BH18 186 C2
Christchurch BH23 208 B4
5 Cosham PO6 157 C4
Locks Heath SO31 128 C1
Waterlooville PO7 134 C3
Mallow Rd SO30 105 A3
Mallows The BH25 195 B2
Malmesbury Cl SO50 57 B1
Malmesbury Ct BH8 205 B3
Malmesbury Gdns SO22 1 B1
Malmesbury Park Pl 7
BH8 205 B3
Malmesbury Park Prim Sch
BH8 205 A3

Malmesbury Park Rd
BH8 205 A3
Malmesbury Pl SO15 102 B4
Malmesbury Rd
Romsey SO51 52 C4
Southampton SO15 102 B4
St Leonards BH24 139 C2
Maloney Mews PO11 185 C1
Maloren Way BH22 139 A1
Malory Cl SO19 104 B3
Malt La SO32 83 B4
Malta Rd PO2 182 C4
Malthouse BH15 202 B1
Malthouse Cl
Romsey SO51 52 C4
Winchester SO21 2 C2
Malthouse Cotts SO51 77 A4
Malthouse Gdns SO40 101 C1
Malthouse La PO16 131 A1
Malthouse Rd PO2 182 B4
Maltings The
Bournemouth BH11 188 C3
Fareham PO16 131 B1
Petersfield GU31 40 C2
Poole BH15 202 C2
Malus Cl PO14 154 C4
Malvern Ave PO14 154 C4
Malvern Bsns Ctr SO16 78 B1
Malvern Cl
Bishop's Waltham SO32 83 B4
Bournemouth BH9 190 A2
Malvern Ct
4 Bournemouth BH9 190 A1
2 Christchurch BH23 207 C4
Malvern Dr SO45 125 B2
Malvern Gdns SO30 81 B1
Malvern Mews PO10 136 C1
Malvern Rd
Bournemouth BH9 190 A1
Gosport PO12 180 C3
Hill Brow GU33 21 A1
Portsmouth PO5 182 B1
Southampton SO16 78 B1
Malvern Terr SO16 78 B1
Malwood Ave SO16 78 B2
Malwood Cl PO9 136 A3
Malwood Gdns SO40 100 B4
Malwood Rd SO45 126 A2
Malwood Rd W SO45 125 C2
Manaton Way SO30 81 A1
Manchester Ct PO13 180 B3
Manchester Rd
1 Netley SO31 127 A3
Portsmouth PO1 182 C3
Sway SO41 172 A2
Manchester Terr PO10 137 A2
Mancroft Ave PO14 179 B3
Mandalay Cl BH31 114 C3
Mandale Cl BH11 189 A2
Mandale Rd BH11 188 C2
Mandarin Way PO13 180 B3
Mandela Way SO15 102 C3
Manderley SO41 211 C2
Manley Rd SO31 104 C1
Manners La PO4 182 C2
Manners Rd PO4 182 C2
Manning Ave BH23 193 B1
Manning's Heath Rd
BH12 188 A1
Manningford Cl SO23 2 A2
Mannings Heath Rdbt
BH17 188 A1
Mannings Heath Works
BH12 188 A1
Mannington Pl 19 BH2 204 C2
Mannington Way BH22 138 B1
Manns Cl SO18 80 B1
Mannyngham Way SO51 27 B4
Manor Ave BH12 188 B1
Manor Cl Bursledon SO31 104 C1
Ferndown BH22 165 C3
Fordingbridge SP6 69 C1
10 Havant PO9 135 C1
Milford on Sea SO41 211 B3
Totton SO40 100 C3
Wickham PO17 108 A2
43 Winchester SO23 11 A4
Manor Cres
Bursledon SO31 104 C1
Cosham PO6 158 A4
Manor Ct Havant PO9 135 B1
Locks Heath PO15 129 B2
Ringwood BH24 140 C4
Verwood BH31 114 C3
Manor Farm Cl
4 Bishopstoke SO50 56 C1
New Milton BH25 194 C1
Manor Farm Ctry Pk★
SO31 105 B2
Manor Farm Gn SO21 31 C3
Manor Farm Gr 3 SO50 56 C1
Manor Farm La SO51 6 C1
Manor Farm Mus★
SO30 105 C2
Manor Farm Rd
Bournemouth BH10 189 B4
Fordingbridge SP6 69 B1
Southampton SO18 79 B1
Manor Farmyard BH8 191 A2
Manor Flats SO21 31 C3
Manor Gdns
Ringwood BH24 140 C4
Southbourne PO10 137 B1
1 Verwood BH31 114 C3
Manor House Ave SO15 101 C3
Manor Inf Sch
Holbury SO45 150 A2
Portsmouth PO1 182 C4

Manor La BH31 114 C3
Manor Lodge Rd PO9 113 A1
Manor Mews PO6 158 B4
Manor Park Ave PO3 183 A4
Manor Park Ho 14 SO18 103 C4
Manor Pk BH15 202 A3
Manor Rd
Bishopstoke SO50 56 C1
Bournemouth BH1 205 B2
Chilworth SO16 54 B1
Christchurch BH23 207 A3
Durley SO32 82 B4
East Tytherley SP5 4 C4
Holbury SO45 150 B2
Hythe SO45 125 A2
Milford on Sea SO41 211 B3
New Milton BH25 195 A2
North Hayling PO11 184 C3
Portsmouth PO1 182 C4
Ringwood BH24 141 A4
Southbourne PO10 137 B1
Twyford SO21 31 C3
Verwood BH31 114 C3
Manor Rd N SO19 103 C2
Manor Rd S SO19 103 C2
Manor Terr
Bursledon SO31 104 C1
Durley SO32 82 C4
Manor Villas PO17 108 A2
Manor Way
Lee-on-the-Solent PO13 179 C1
Lee-on-the-Solent PO13 179 C2
South Hayling PO11 185 A1
Southbourne PO10 137 B1
Verwood BH31 114 C4
Manor Wks SO40 101 A4
Mansard Ct BH13 214 A2
Mansbridge Prim Sch
SO18 79 C2
Mansbridge Rd
Eastleigh SO50 56 A1
Southampton SO18 79 C2
Mansel Cl BH12 204 B4
Mansel Ct SO16 77 C1
Mansel Inf Sch SO16 77 B1
Mansel Jun Sch SO16 77 B1
Mansel Rd E SO16 77 C1
Mansel Rd W SO16 77 B1
Mansell Cl SO45 125 C1
Mansergh Wlk SO40 100 A4
Mansfield Ave BH14 203 B2
Mansfield Cl
Ferndown BH22 165 B1
Poole BH14 203 B2
Mansfield Rd
Bournemouth BH9 189 C1
Gosport PO13 180 B4
Poole BH14 203 B2
Ringwood BH24 140 C4
Mansion Ct 2 PO4 182 C1
Mansion Rd
Portsmouth PO4 182 C1
Southampton SO15 102 B3
Manston Ct SO16 77 C2
Mansvid Ave PO6 158 A4
Mantle Cl PO13 180 B4
Mantle Sq PO2 157 A1
Manton Cl BH15 201 C2
Manton Rd BH15 201 C2
Maple Cl
Barton on Sea BH25 210 A4
Bursledon SO31 127 C4
Christchurch BH23 208 C4
Emsworth PO10 136 C1
Fareham PO15 130 B1
Lee-on-the-Solent PO13 179 C1
Romsey SO51 53 B3
Maple Cres PO8 88 B3
Maple Ct SO19 103 C1
Maple Dr Denmead PO7 111 A2
Ferndown BH22 165 B4
Kings Worthy SO23 2 A4
Maple Gdns SO40 100 B3
Maple Ho SO16 78 C4
Maple Lo BH16 201 B4
Maple Rd
Bournemouth BH9 204 C4
Hythe SO45 150 A4
Poole BH15 202 B2
Portsmouth PO5 182 B1
Southampton SO18 103 C4
Maple Sq SO50 55 C1
Maple Wood PO9 135 A1
Mapleleaf Gdns 1 SO50 56 A1
Maples The SO53 55 B4
Mapleton Rd SO30 105 B3
Mapletree Ave PO8 112 B2
Maplewood Cl SO40 100 B3
Maplin Rd SO16 77 B1
Mapperton Cl BH17 187 C1
Marabout Cl BH23 207 B4
Maralyn Ave PO7 134 C3
Marathon Pl SO50 57 A1
Marazan Rd PO3 158 A1
Marbream Cl SP6 69 B1
Marchesi Ct PO14 154 B2
Marchwood By Pass
Marchwood SO40 124 C4
Totton SO40 101 A2
Marchwood CE Inf Sch
SO40 124 C4
Marchwood Ct PO12 180 B2
Marchwood Ind Pk
SO40 102 A2

Marchwood Jun Sch
SO40 .101 C1
Marchwood Rd
Bournemouth BH10 .189 B2
Havant PO9 .135 C3
Southampton SO15 .102 A3
Totton SO40 .101 B2
Marchwood Terr SO40 .101 C1
Marcus Cl SO50 .57 A1
Mardale Rd SO16 .101 B4
Mardale Wlk SO16 .101 B4
Marden Paddock SO42 .145 C1
Marden Way GU31 .41 A2
Mardon Cl SO18 .79 C3
Mare La SO21 .32 C3
Margam Ave SO19 .103 C3
Margards La BH31 .114 C3
Margaret Cl PO7 .111 B1
Margarita Rd PO15 .130 C1
Margate Rd PO5 .215 C2
Margery's Ct 20 PO1 .182 A3
Marian Cl BH21 .186 B2
Marian Rd BH21 .186 B2
Marianne Cl SO15 .101 C3
Marianne Rd Poole BH12 204 B4
Wimborne Minst BH21 .164 A4
Marie Ave SP5 .46 B4
Marie Cl BH12 .203 B4
Marie Ct 5 PO7 .134 C4
Marie Rd SO19 .104 B2
Marigold Cl PO15 .130 C1
Marina Bldgs 3 PO12 .181 A2
Marina Cl PO10 .161 A4
Marina Ct
21 Bournemouth BH5 .205 C2
Christchurch BH23 .209 A4
Marina Dr
Hamble-le-Rice SO31 .128 A1
Poole BH14 .203 A1
Marina Gr
Portchester PO16 .156 B3
Portsmouth PO3 .183 A4
Marina Keep PO6 .157 A3
Marina The BH5 .205 C2
Marina Twrs 24 BH5 .205 C2
Marina View
6 Christchurch BH23 .207 A3
Netley SO31 .126 C4
Marine Cotts 14 PO12 .181 A3
Marine Ct
Barton on Sea BH25 .209 B4
Portsmouth PO4 .183 A1
Marine Dr BH25 .209 C4
Marine Dr E BH25 .210 A3
Marine Drive W BH25 .209 C4
Marine Par SO14 .103 A2
Marine Parade E PO13 .179 C1
Marine Parade W PO13 .179 B1
Marine Rd BH6 .206 B2
Marine Wlk PO11 .185 B2
Mariner's Cl SO31 .128 A2
Mariners Ct
Christchurch BH23 .208 A3
Lymington SO41 .197 C1
Mariners Mews 7
SO45 .126 A2
Mariners Way
Gosport PO12 .181 B2
Locks Heath SO31 .128 B1
Mariners Wlk PO4 .183 A3
Marion Ct BH23 .207 A4
Marion Rd PO4 .182 C1
Maritime Ave SO40 .102 A2
Maritime Mus★ SO14 .102 C2
Maritime Way SO14 .103 A1
Maritime Wlk SO14 .103 A1
Marjoram Cres PO8 .112 A2
Mark Anthony Ct PO11 .184 C2
Mark Cl Portsmouth PO3 .157 C2
Southampton SO15 .102 A4
Mark Ct PO7 .134 C4
Mark Way SO51 .4 B2
Mark's La BH25 .195 A3
Mark's Rd PO14 .179 C3
Markall Cl SO24 .14 B3
Marken Cl SO31 .128 C2
Market Bldgs SO16 .79 B2
Market Cl BH15 .202 B1
Market La SO23 .11 A4
Market Par PO9 .135 C1
Market Pl
Fordingbridge SP6 .69 C1
Ringwood BH24 .140 C4
Romsey SO51 .52 C4
10 Southampton SO14 .103 A2
Market St Eastleigh SO50 .56 A1
Poole BH15 .202 A1
Winchester SO23 .11 A4
Market Way BH21 .163 B2
Marketway PO1 .215 B4
Markham Ave BH10 .189 B4
Markham Cl BH10 .189 B3
Markham Rd BH9 .205 A4
Marks Rd BH9 .189 C2
Marks Terr SO32 .83 A4
Marks Tey Rd PO14 .154 B3
Markway Cl PO10 .136 B1
Marlands Lawn PO9 .135 B3
Marlands The (Sh Ctr)
SO14 .102 C2
Marlborough Cl PO7 .134 B3
Marlborough Ct
21 Bournemouth BH4 .204 B2
Chandler's Ford SO53 .55 A2
Hythe SO45 .125 C1
Marlborough Ct *continued*
7 Poole BH12 .204 A2
3 Wimborne Minst BH21 .163 B3
Marlborough Gdns SO30 .81 B2
Marlborough Gr PO16 .156 B4
Marlborough Ho SO15 .102 C4
Marlborough Mans 2
BH7 .206 A3
Marlborough Pk PO9 .136 B2
Marlborough Pl
Lymington SO41 .197 B3
Wimborne Minst BH21 .163 B3
Marlborough Rd
Bournemouth BH4 .204 B2
Chandler's Ford SO53 .30 C1
Gosport PO12 .180 C3
Poole BH14 .203 B2
Southampton SO15 .102 A4
Marlborough Row PO1 .182 A3
Marldell Cl PO9 .136 A3
Marler Ho BH4 .204 A2
Marles Cl PO13 .180 B4
Marley Ave BH25 .194 C2
Marley Cl BH25 .194 C2
Marley Mount SO41 .171 C1
Marlhill Cl SO18 .79 C1
Marlin Cl PO13 .180 B3
Marline Rd BH12 .203 B3
Marlott Rd BH15 .202 B3
Marlow Cl PO15 .130 C2
Marlow Dr BH23 .191 C2
Marlow Rd SO32 .83 A4
Marlowe Ct
Southampton SO19 .103 C1
Waterlooville PO7 .111 B1
Marlpit Dr BH23 .194 A1
Marlpit La BH25 .195 A4
Marls Rd SO30 .105 C3
Marmion Ave PO5 .182 B1
Marmion Gn BH23 .207 C4
Marmion Rd PO5 .182 B1
Marne Ho 9 PO14 .154 C4
Marne Rd SO18 .104 A4
Marnhull Rd BH15 .202 B2
Marpet Cl BH11 .188 C3
Marples Way PO9 .135 B1
Marquis Way BH11 .188 B3
Marram Cl SO41 .197 C3
Marrelswood Gdns PO7 134 B2
Marryat Ct
Christchurch BH23 .209 A4
New Milton BH25 .194 C2
Marryat Rd BH25 .194 C2
Marsden Rd PO6 .157 A4
Marsh Cl PO6 .158 B3
Marsh Gdns SO30 .81 B1
Marsh Ho 20 SO14 .103 A2
Marsh La Breamore SP6 .70 A4
Christchurch BH23 .191 C1
Fawley SO45 .151 A2
Lymington SO41 .197 C3
Southampton SO14 .103 A2
Upton BH16 .201 A4
Marsh Par 1 SO45 .126 A2
Marsh The SO45 .126 A2
Marshal Rd BH17 .187 A1
Marshall Pl 9 SO16 .78 C2
Marshall Rd PO11 .185 B1
Marshfield BH21 .163 C4
Marshfield Cl SO40 .101 B1
Marshfield Ho PO6 .158 B4
Marshlands Cl BH23 .207 B3
Marshlands Rd PO6 .158 B4
Marshlands Spur PO6 .158 C4
Marshwood Ave
Poole BH17 .187 C2
Waterlooville PO7 .135 A4
Marston Cl BH25 .195 A3
Marston Gate 5 SO23 .11 A4
Marston Gr BH23 .193 C1
Marston La PO3 .158 A2
Marston Rd
New Milton BH25 .195 A3
2 Poole BH15 .202 A1
Southampton SO19 .104 C3
Martello Cl PO12 .180 B2
Martello Ho 10 BH13 .214 C4
Martello Pk BH13 .214 C4
Martello Rd BH13 .203 C1
Martello Rd S BH13 .214 C4
Martello Twrs BH13 .214 C4
Martells Ct 1 PO1 .182 A2
Martells The BH25 .210 A4
Martin Ave
Denmead PO7 .111 A2
Stubbington PO14 .179 B3
Martin Cl
Broadstone BH17 .201 C4
Lee-on-the-Solent PO13 .179 C2
Swanmore SO32 .84 A2
Martin Down National Nature Reserve★ SP5,SP6 .42 B2
Martin Kemp-Welch Sch The
BH12 .203 B4
Martin Rd Havant PO9 .136 A2
Portsmouth PO3 .183 A4
Stubbington PO14 .179 B3
Martin St SO32 .83 A4
Martin's Rd SO42 .146 A1
Martindale Ave BH21 .164 A3
Martindale Terr SO16 .101 C4
Martingale Cl BH16 .201 B4
Martins Cl BH22 .165 C4
Martins Dr BH22 .165 C4
Martins Fields SO21 .10 B1
Martins Hill Cl BH23 .192 B1
Martins Hill La BH23 .192 B1
Martins Rise SP5 .24 A2
Martins The SO50 .57 B1
Martins Way BH22 .165 C4
Martley Gdns SO30 .81 B1
Marvic Ct PO9 .135 C3
Marvin Cl SO30 .105 C4
Marvin Way
Hedge End SO30 .105 B4
Southampton SO18 .104 B3
Marwell Cl BH7 .206 A4
Marwell Zoological Pk★
SO21 .57 C4
Mary La BH22 .138 B1
Mary Mitchell Cl BH24 .140 C4
Mary Rose★ PO1 .181 C3
Mary Rose Cl PO15 .130 C2
Mary Rose St The PO1 .215 B3
Marybridge Cl SO40 .100 C3
Marycourt Sch PO12 .181 A1
Maryfield SO14 .103 A2
Maryland Cl SO18 .79 C2
Maryland Ct 3 SO41 .211 A2
Maryland Gdns SO41 .211 A2
Maryland Rd BH16 .201 B2
Masefield Ave PO6 .132 C1
Masefield Cl SO50 .55 C2
Masefield Cres PO8 .111 C2
Masefield Gr SO19 .104 B3
Mason Moor Prim Sch
SO16 .101 C4
Masseys La SO42 .175 B4
Masten Cres PO13 .180 B4
Masters Ct BH4 .204 B2
Masterson Cl BH23 .207 B4
Matapan Rd PO2 .157 C2
Matchams Cl BH24 .167 A4
Matchams La BH23 .167 A2
Matheson Rd SO16 .78 A3
Matilda Pl 3 SO23 .11 A4
Matley Gdns SO40 .100 A4
Matlock Rd BH22 .165 B2
Matthews Cl PO9 .135 B2
Matthews La SO42 .175 B3
Maturin Cl SO41 .197 B2
Maundeville Cres BH23 .206 B4
Maundville Rd BH23 .206 C4
Maunsell Way SO30 .81 B1
Maureen Cl BH12 .203 A4
Maurepas Way PO7 .134 C4
Mauretania Ho 13 SO14 .103 B3
Mauretania Rd SO16 .77 A2
Maurice Rd
Bournemouth BH8 .205 B4
Portsmouth PO4 .183 B2
Maury's La SO51 .50 B2
Mavis Cres PO9 .135 C1
Mavis Rd BH9 .190 A1
Maxstoke Cl PO1 .215 C3
Maxwell Rd
Bournemouth BH9 .205 A4
Broadstone BH18 .186 C2
Poole BH13 .214 C4
Portsmouth PO4 .183 A2
Southampton SO19 .104 A2
May Ave SO41 .197 B3
May Bush La SO32 .85 A1
May Cl SO45 .150 B2
May Copse SO45 .150 B2
May Cres SO45 .150 B2
May Gdns
Bournemouth BH11 .188 C2
Christchurch BH23 .194 A1
May La SO41 .174 A1
May Rd SO15 .102 B4
May Tree Cl SO22 .10 B2
May's La PO14 .154 B2
Maybray King Way
SO18 .104 A4
Maybush Ct 2 SO16 .78 A1
Maybush Rd SO16 .77 C1
Maycroft Ct 3 SO15 .102 C4
Maydman Sq PO3 .183 A3
Mayfair BH4 .204 B1
Mayfair Ct SO30 .106 A4
Mayfair Gdns
Bournemouth BH11 .189 A2
Southampton SO15 .102 C4
Mayfield PO13 .179 C1
Mayfield Ave Poole BH14 203 C2
Totton SO40 .100 C4
Mayfield Cl
Ferndown BH22 .165 B3
Stubbington PO14 .154 B2
Mayfield Dr BH22 .165 B3
Mayfield Rd
Bournemouth BH9 .190 A1
Fordingbridge SP6 .69 B1
Gosport PO12 .181 B2
Portsmouth PO2 .157 C1
Southampton SO17 .79 B2
Mayfield Sch PO2 .157 C1
Mayfield Way BH22 .165 B3
Mayflower Cl
Chandler's Ford SO53 .55 A3
Lymington SO41 .198 A1
Stubbington PO14 .179 B3
Mayflower Ct 14 SO15 .102 C4
Mayflower Dr PO4 .183 B3
Mayflower Rd SO15 .102 A4
Mayflowers The SO17 .79 A2
Mayfly Cl SP6 .69 C1
Mayford Rd BH12 .204 A3
Mayhall Rd PO3 .158 A1
Mayhill La SO32 .84 C4
Maylands Ave PO4 .183 A3
Maylands Rd PO9 .135 A1
Mayles Cl PO17 .108 A2
Mayles La PO17 .107 C1
Mayles Rd PO4 .183 A3
Maylings Farm Rd PO16 130 C2
Maynard Cl PO13 .155 B2
Maynard Pl PO8 .112 A4
Maynard Rd SO40 .100 C4
Mayo Cl PO1 .182 B4
Maypole Villas SO50 .56 A4
Mayridge PO14 .129 B2
Mays Firs SP6 .47 C1
Maytree Cl Fair Oak SO50 .57 B1
Locks Heath SO31 .129 A2
Maytree Gdns PO8 .111 C2
Maytree Inf Sch SO14 .103 A3
Maytree Rd
Chandler's Ford SO53 .30 B1
16 Fareham PO16 .131 A1
Southampton SO19 .104 A3
Waterlooville PO8 .111 C2
Mayvale Cl SO40 .101 C1
Mayville High Sch PO5 .182 B1
Mc William Rd 2 BH9 .190 A1
McIntyre Rd BH23 .191 A4
McKinley Rd BH4 .204 B1
McWilliam Cl BH12 .204 B4
Meacher Cl SO40 .100 C4
Mead Cl
Broadstone BH18 .187 A1
Romsey SO51 .53 A4
Mead Cres SO18 .79 B2
Mead Ct
Chandler's Ford SO53 .55 B3
Southampton SO16 .78 A2
Mead End Rd
Denmead PO7 .111 A2
Sway SO41 .171 C1
Mead Rd
Chandler's Ford SO53 .55 B3
Lymington SO41 .197 A1
Winchester SO23 .10 C2
Mead The Gosport PO13 .155 A2
Hythe SO45 .125 C2
Liss GU33 .20 C2
Petersfield GU32 .40 B1
Mead Way PO16 .131 A2
Meadbrook Gdns SO53 .55 B3
Meadcrest Wood SO42 .145 B1
Meadcroft Cl SO31 .152 B4
Meadend Cl PO9 .136 A3
Meadow Ave
Fordingbridge SP6 .69 C1
Locks Heath SO31 .129 A2
Meadow Cl
Bransgore BH23 .193 A4
Burley BH24 .142 C1
Ferndown BH22 .165 B1
Fordingbridge SP6 .69 C1
North Baddesley SO52 .54 A2
North Hayling PO11 .159 C2
Ringwood BH24 .141 A4
Sopley BH23 .192 A4
Totton SO40 .100 C3
Waltham Chase SO32 .83 C2
West End SO30 .80 C1
Meadow Court Cl BH9 .190 A2
Meadow Croft Cl SO21 .31 B2
Meadow Ct
6 Bournemouth BH9 .190 A2
2 Emsworth PO10 .160 C4
Fordingbridge SP6 .69 C1
Whiteparish SP5 .24 B2
15 Wimborne Minst BH21 .163 B2
Meadow Edge PO7 .134 A1
Meadow Farm La BH21 .186 B4
Meadow Gdns SO32 .83 C2
Meadow Gr
Chandler's Ford SO53 .55 B2
Verwood BH31 .115 A3
Meadow La Burton BH23 192 B1
Hamble-le-Rice SO31 .128 A1
Meadow Rd
Lymington SO41 .197 B1
New Milton BH25 .195 A2
Ringwood BH24 .141 A4
Meadow Rise
Corfe Mullen BH18 .186 C3
Waterlooville PO8 .112 A2
Meadow St PO5 .215 A2
Meadow Terr 12 PO16 .131 A1
Meadow The
Denmead PO7 .110 C2
Romsey SO51 .28 A1
Meadow View Rd BH11 .188 C2
Meadow Way
Barton on Sea BH25 .210 A4
Fawley SO45 .151 A2
Ringwood BH24 .141 A4
Verwood BH31 .115 A3
Winchester SO22 .10 B3
Meadow Wlk
Gosport PO13 .155 A3
1 Liss GU33 .20 C2
Portsmouth PO1 .215 B4
Meadowbank BH16 .201 B4
Meadowbank Rd PO15 .130 B1
Meadowhead Rd SO16 .78 C2
Meadowland
Christchurch BH23 .207 C3
Kings Worthy SO23 .2 A4
Meadowlands
Havant PO9 .136 A1
Lymington SO41 .197 B2
Ringwood BH24 .141 A2
Rowland's Castle PO9 .113 B2
Meadowlands Jun & Inf Schs
PO8 .111 C3
Meadowmead Ave
SO15 .102 A4
Meadows Cl BH16 .201 B4
Meadows Dr BH16 .201 B4
Meadows The
Fareham PO16 .131
Lyndhurst SO43 .122
Waterlooville PO7 .134
Meadowside Cl SO18 .79
Meadowsweet PO7 .112
Meadowsweet Rd BH17 201
Meadowsweet Way
Cosham PO6 .133
Fair Oak SO50 .81
Meads The
North Baddesley SO53 .55
Romsey SO51 .52
Meadway The BH23 .193
Mears Rd SO50 .57
Meath Cl PO11 .185
Medina Cl SO53 .55
Medina Ct PO13 .179
Medina Ho 10 PO16 .155
Medina Prim Sch PO6 .157
Medina Rd Cosham PO6 .157
Southampton SO15 .78
Medina Way BH23 .208
Medlar Cl Burton BH23 .192
8 Hedge End SO30 .105
Medley Pl 18 SO15 .102
Medlicott Way SO32 .84
Medstead Rd PO9 .135
Medwall Gr SO19 .104
Medway Dr SO53 .55
Medway Rd BH22 .166
Meerut Rd SO42 .145
Meeting House La
BH24 .140
Megan Ct 20 PO6 .157
Megan Rd SO30 .80
Megana Way SO51 .28
Meggeson Ave SO18 .80
Melboure Rd BH23 .191
Melbourne Gdns 6
SO30 .105
Melbourne Ho PO1 .215
Melbourne Pl PO5 .215
Melbourne Rd
Bournemouth BH8 .205
5 Hedge End SO30 .105
Melbourne St SO14 .103
Melbury Ave BH12 .203
Melbury Cl
Ferndown BH22 .165
Lymington SO41 .197
Melbury Ct 19 SO17 .79
Melchet Cl SO51 .25
Melchet Rd SO18 .104
Melford Ct BH1 .205
Melick Cl SO40 .101
Mellor Cl 4 PO6 .157
Mellstock Rd BH15 .202
Melrose Cl PO4 .183
Melrose Ct
New Milton SO40 .195
Totton SO40 .76
Melrose Gdns PO12 .180
Melrose Rd SO15 .78
Melton Ct BH13 .203
Melverley Gdns BH21 .163
Melville Cl SO16 .78
Melville Rd
Bournemouth BH9 .204
Gosport PO12 .181
Portsmouth PO4 .183
Melvin Jones Ho PO14 .154
Mendip Cl
New Milton BH25 .195
Verwood BH31 .114
Mendip Ct 4 BH23 .207
Mendip Gdns SO45 .125
Mendip Rd
Southampton SO16 .101
Verwood BH31 .114
Mendips Rd PO14 .154
Mendips Wlk PO14 .154
Mengham Ave PO11 .185
Mengham Ct PO11 .185
Mengham Inf Sch PO11 185
Mengham Jun Sch
PO11 .185
Mengham La PO11 .185
Mengham Rd PO11 .185
Menin Ho PO15 .130
Menslands La
Hambledon PO7 .86
Soberton PO7 .109
Mentone Rd 2 BH14 .203
Menzies Cl SO16 .77
Meon Cl Clanfield PO8 .88
Gosport PO13 .155
Petersfield GU32 .40
Romsey SO51 .53
Meon Cres SO53 .55
Meon Ct SO18 .104
Meon Gdns SO32 .84
Meon Ho 8 PO16 .155
Meon Jun & Inf Schs
PO4 .183
Meon Rd
Bournemouth BH7 .206
Portsmouth PO4 .183
Romsey SO51 .53
Meoncross Sch PO14 .154
Meonstoke CE Sch SO32 .61
Meonwara Cres GU32 .37
Mercer Way SO51 .53
Merchants Pl 17 SO23 .11
Merchants Wlk 21 SO14 102
Merchistoun Rd PO7 .112
Mercury Cl SO16 .77
Mercury Gdns SO31 .128

ercury Pl PO7 134 C1
erdon Ave SO53 55 B4
erdon Cl SO53 55 B4
erdon Ct SO53 55 B4
erdon Jun Sch SO53 55 B4
ere Croft PO15 129 C2
eredith Cl BH23 207 B4
eredith Gdns SO40 100 B3
eredith Inf Sch PO2 182 C4
eredith Lodge 7 PO7 135 A4
eredith Rd PO2 157 C2
eredith Twrs SO19 104 C2
eredun Cl SO21 30 A4
erepond La GU34 17 C2
erganser Cl PO12 181 A4
eriden Cl BH13 214 C4
eriden Ct 10 SO23 2 A1
eriden Rd PO5 215 A2
eridian Ctr 12 PO9 135 C1
eridians The BH23 206 C3
erino Way BH22 138 C1
erlewood Cl BH2 204 C2
erlewood Ct 19 BH25 195 A2
erley Dr BH23 209 A4
erley Fst Sch BH21 163 B1
erley Gdns BH21 163 C1
erley Ho BH21 163 A1
erley House La BH21 163 B1
erley House Mus★
H21 163 A1
erley La BH21 163 C1
erley Park Rd
orfe Mullen BH21 186 C4
Vimborne Minst BH21 163 B1
erley Ways BH21 163 B1
erlin Cl
ishop's Waltham SO32 83 A4
ingwood BH24 141 B3
erlin Dr PO3 158 A2
erlin Gdns
edge End SO30 105 A4
ortchester PO16 132 A1
erlin Lodge SO19 103 B2
erlin Way
handler's Ford SO53 54 C4
hristchurch BH23 208 A3
ermaid Ct 22 BH5 205 C2
ermaid Rd PO14 154 C3
ermaid Way SO14 103 A1
errick Way SO53 55 A4
erridale Rd SO19 103 C3
erriefield Ave BH18 187 A3
erriefield Cl BH18 187 A3
erriefield Dr BH18 187 A3
errieleas Cl SO53 55 B4
errieleas Dr SO53 55 B4
erriemeade Cl 2
045 125 C1
erriemeade Par 1
045 125 C1
errifield BH21 163 C4
erritown La BH23 190 B4
erritt Ct SO53 55 B2
errivale Ave BH6 206 C3
errivale Cl SO45 125 C2
errivale Ct PO10 137 B1
errivale Rd PO2 157 C2
errow Ave BH12 204 A4
errow Chase 1 BH13 214 C4
errow Cl PO16 156 A4
erry Gdns SO52 54 A3
erryfield PO14 129 B2
erryfield Ave PO9 135 B3
erryfield Cl
ransgore BH23 193 A4
erwood BH31 114 C3
erryfield Ct BH10 189 B2
erryfield La BH10 189 B2
erryfield Rd GU31 41 A2
erryoak Gn SO19 103 C3
erryoak Rd SO19 103 C3
errytree Cl SO51 50 C2
erryweather Est 3
BH24 141 B4
ersea Gdns SO19 104 A2
ersham Gdns SO18 104 A4
erstone Rd PO13 155 B1
erthyr Ave PO6 158 A4
erton Ave PO16 156 B3
erton Cl SP6 69 C2
erton Cres PO16 156 B3
erton Ct
8 Christchurch BH23 209 A4
3 Poole BH15 202 C2
3 Portsmouth PO5 215 C1
erton Gr BH24 140 C4
erton Rd
Portsmouth PO5 215 C1
Southampton SO17 79 A2
erville Gdns BH9 204 C4
eryl Rd PO4 183 B2
esh Pond SP5 46 B4
esh Rd SO51 6 A1
etcalfe Ave PO14 154 B2
eteor Rd PO10 161 A2
ethuen Cl 2 BH8 205 B3
ethuen Rd
Bournemouth BH8 205 A3
Poole BH17 187 A1
Portsmouth PO4 183 A2
ethuen St SO14 103 A4
etuchen Way SO30 105 B2
ews Ct SO21 31 A2
ews La SO22 10 C4
ews The
Blackfield SO45 177 C4
1 Bournemouth BH2 204 B2
Chandler's Ford SO53 55 B2

Mews The *continued*
Gosport PO12 181 C2
Havant PO9 135 C2
Petersfield GU31 41 A2
Rownhams SO16 77 C3
Mewsey Ct PO9 135 B4
Mey Cl PO7 135 A4
Meynell Cl SO50 55 C2
Meyrick Cl BH23 193 A4
Meyrick Ho 15 PO2 157 B1
Meyrick Park Cres BH3 204 C3
Meyrick Park Mans 5
BH2 204 C2
Meyrick Rd
Bournemouth BH1 205 A2
Havant PO9 135 B1
Portsmouth PO2 157 B1
Micawber Ho 12 PO1 182 B4
Michael Crook Cl PO9 135 B2
Michael's Way SO45 125 C2
Michaels Way SO50 57 B1
Michelgrove Rd BH5 205 C2
Michelmersh Cl SO16 77 C3
Michelmersh Gn BH8 190 B1
Michigan Way SO40 100 A4
Mickleham Cl BH12 204 A4
Midanbury Cres SO18 79 C1
Midanbury Ct 10 SO18 103 C4
Midanbury La SO18 103 C4
Midanbury Wlk 1 SO18 103 C4
Midas Cl PO7 134 C2
Middle Brook BH11 189 A3
Middle Brook St SO23 11 A4
Middle Common Rd
SO41 197 A2
Middle Ct PO1 182 C4
Middle La BH24 141 A4
Middle Mdw GU33 21 A2
Middle Mead PO14 154 A4
Middle Park Way PO9 135 B3
Middle Rd
Bournemouth BH10 189 B3
Locks Heath SO31 129 A3
Lymington SO41 197 B2
New Milton SO41 195 C4
North Baddesley SO52 54 A2
Poole BH15 202 C3
Southampton SO19 104 A2
Sway SO41 172 A1
Sway, Tiptoe SO41 195 C4
Winchester SO22 10 C4
Middle St
Portsmouth PO5 215 B2
Southampton SO14 103 A4
Middlebere Cres BH16 201 B2
Middlebridge St SO51 52 C3
Middlebrook 3 SO32 83 B4
Middlecroft La PO12 180 C3
Middlehill Dr BH21 164 A3
Middlehill Rd BH21 164 A3
Middlesex Rd PO4 183 A2
Middleton Cl
Fareham PO14 154 C4
Southampton SO18 80 A1
Middleton Rd
Bournemouth BH9 189 C1
Ringwood BH24 141 A4
Middleton Rise PO8 88 B2
Middleton Wlk 10 PO14 154 C4
Midfield Cl PO14 154 C4
Midhurst Ho PO1 215 C4
Midland Rd BH9 189 C1
Midlands Est SO30 80 B1
Midlington Hill SO32 85 A4
Midlington Ho SO32 85 A4
Midlington Rd SO32 85 A4
Midway SO45 125 C2
Midway Path BH13 214 B2
Midway Rd PO2 157 C3
Midways PO14 179 B3
Midwood Ave BH8 190 C1
Milbeck Cl PO8 112 A2
Milborne Cres BH12 203 C4
Milbourne Rd BH22 165 B3
Milburn Cl 12 BH4 204 B2
Milburn Rd BH4 204 A2
Milburns The SO51 27 B4
Milbury Cres SO18 104 A3
Milbury Ho PO6 133 A1
Mildmay Ct 39 SO23 11 A4
Mildmay St SO22 10 B3
Mile End Rd PO2 182 B4
Milebush Rd PO4 183 B3
Miles Ct PO11 185 B1
Miles La SP5 24 B3
Milestone Rd BH15 202 B3
Milford Cl Havant PO9 135 B2
West Moors BH22 138 C1
Milford Cres SO41 211 C2
Milford Ct Gosport PO12 180 B2
Milford on Sea SO41 211 C2
6 Portsmouth PO4 183 A2
Milford Dr BH11 188 C3
Milford Gdns SO53 55 C3
Milford Ho SO41 211 C3
Milford on Sea Prim Sch
SO41 211 C3
Milford Rd
Barton on Sea BH25 210 A4
Lymington SO41 197 A1
Portsmouth PO1 215 C3
Milford Trad Est SO41 211 C2
Military Rd
Fareham PO16 131 B1
Gosport PO12 181 A1
Gosport, Brockhurst PO13 180 C3
Gosport, Clayhall PO12 181 B1
Portsmouth, Hilsea PO3 157 C3

Military Rd *continued*
Portsmouth, Landport PO1 182 A4
Milkwood Ct SO40 100 B4
Milky Down Back La
BH24 141 C4
Mill Cl Denmead PO7 111 A2
North Hayling PO11 159 C1
Nursling SO16 77 B3
Mill Ct Fordingbridge SP6 69 C1
4 Southampton SO17 79 B1
Mill End Damerham SP6 68 B2
Hermitage PO10 161 A4
Mill Gate Ho 19 PO1 182 A3
Mill Hill SO30 106 A3
Mill Hill Cl BH14 203 A2
Mill House Bsns Ctr
SO19 103 B2
Mill House Ctr SO40 101 A4
Mill House Lodge SO50 56 B2
Mill La Boldre SO41 198 C3
Brockbridge SO32 61 B1
Brockenhurst SO42 146 A1
Burley BH24 143 B2
Christchurch BH23 209 A4
Croucheston SP5 22 B4
Droxford SO32 61 A1
Durley SO32 82 B2
Gosport PO12 181 A3
Havant PO9 159 C3
Havant, Bedhampton PO9 135 B1
Hawkley GU33 19 C4
Hermitage PO10 137 A1
Hurn BH23 191 A3
Kings Worthy SO21 2 B3
Lymington SO41 197 C2
Minstead SO43 98 C1
Nursling SO16 76 C2
Petersfield GU32 41 A3
Poole BH14 203 A2
Portsmouth PO1 182 B4
Romsey SO51 52 B4
Sherfield English SO51 25 C1
Southwick PO7 133 C2
Steep GU32 40 C4
Steep Marsh GU32 19 C1
Sway SO41 196 C4
Titchfield PO15 130 A1
Westbourne PO10 137 A1
Wickham PO17 108 A3
Wimborne Minst BH21 163 A3
Mill Mdw SO41 211 B3
Mill Pond Rd PO12 181 A3
Mill Pond The SO45 150 A3
Mill Quay PO10 161 A4
Mill Race View SP5 46 C4
Mill Rd
Christchurch BH23 207 A4
Denmead PO7 111 A2
Fareham PO16 155 A4
Gosport PO12 181 A3
Liss GU33 21 A3
Southampton SO15 102 A4
Totton SO40 101 A4
Waterlooville PO7 134 C3
Westbourne PO10 137 A2
Mill Rd N BH8 190 B2
Mill Rd S BH8 190 B1
Mill Rise SO51 5 B1
Mill Rythe Inf Sch PO11 185 A3
Mill Rythe Jun Sch
PO11 185 A3
Mill Rythe La PO11 185 A4
Mill St Broadstone BH21 162 A1
Eastleigh SO50 56 A2
Titchfield PO14 154 A4
Mill Way SO40 100 C3
Millais Rd SO19 103 C2
Milland Rd SO23 11 A3
Millbank Ho
14 Southampton SO14 103 B3
5 Wimborne Minst BH21 163 B3
Millbank St SO14 103 B3
Millbridge Gdns SO19 104 A2
Millbrook Cl
Chandler's Ford SO53 55 A3
Liss GU33 21 A2
Millbrook Com Sch SO16 77 C2
Millbrook Dr PO9 136 A3
Millbrook Flyover SO15 101 C4
Millbrook Point Rd
SO15 102 A3
Millbrook Rd E SO15 102 B3
Millbrook Rd W SO15 102 A3
Millbrook Sta SO15 102 A3
Millbrook Trad Est
SO15 101 B4
Millcourt 6 SO50 57 B1
Millennium Ct 1 PO7 134 C3
Miller Cl BH25 195 B2
Miller Dr PO16 130 C1
Miller Rd BH23 207 B4
Miller's Pond Gdns
SO19 103 C2
Millers La SO22 9 C2
Millers Quay Ho 2
PO16 155 A4
Millers Way SO45 125 C1
Millfield
Broadstone BH17 202 A4
New Milton BH25 194 C2
Millhams Cl BH10 189 A3
Millhams Dr BH10 189 A3
Millhams Rd BH10 189 A3
Millhams St BH23 207 A3
Millhams St N BH23 207 A3
Milliken Cl SO45 150 C1
Mills Rd PO2 157 B1
Mills The BH12 203 C4

Millstream Cl
Broadstone BH17 202 A4
Wimborne Minst BH21 163 B2
Millstream Rise SO51 52 B4
Millstream Trad Est
BH24 141 A3
Millverton Ct 3 SO18 104 A4
Millvina Cl SO40 99 C2
Millway SO32 82 A3
Millyford Cl BH25 209 B4
Milman Ct 11 SO23 11 A4
Milne Cl SO45 125 B1
Milne Rd BH17 187 A1
Milner Ct SO15 102 B4
Milner Pl SO22 10 C3
Milner Rd BH4 204 B1
Milnthorpe La SO22 10 C4
Milton Cl BH14 203 B2
Milton Ct Ferndown BH22 165 B3
3 Portsmouth PO4 183 A3
Milton Gr
Locks Heath SO31 129 A1
New Milton BH25 195 A1
Milton Mead BH25 194 C1
Milton Par PO7 111 C1
Milton Park Ave 3 PO4 183 A2
Milton Park Jun & Inf Schs
PO4 183 A2
Milton Rd
Bournemouth BH8 205 A3
Eastleigh SO50 56 A3
Poole BH14 203 B2
Portsmouth PO3,PO4 183 A3
Southampton SO15 102 C3
Waterlooville PO7,PO8 111 C1
Wimborne Minst BH21 163 B3
Milton Villas BH8 205 A3
Miltoncross Sch PO3 183 A3
Milverton Cl
Christchurch BH23 193 C1
Totton SO40 101 A3
Milverton Ho PO5 215 B2
Milverton Rd
Totton SO40 101 A3
Winchester SO22 10 C4
Milvil Ct 5 PO13 179 C1
Milvil Rd PO13 179 C1
Mimosa Ave BH21 187 C4
Mimosa Ct PO15 129 C2
Mimosa Dr SO50 57 C1
Mincingfield La SO32 82 B3
Mincingfield Terr SO32 82 B3
Minden Ho
Fareham PO14 154 C4
Romsey SO51 53 A4
Minden Way SO22 10 B3
Minerva Cl PO7 134 C1
Minerva Cres PO1 182 A2
Minerva Dr PO12 181 B4
Minley Ct 35 PO9 136 A3
Minnitt Rd PO12 181 C2
Minstead Ave SO18 104 B4
Minstead Cl SO22 1 B2
Minstead Ct 4 SO17 103 A4
Minstead Rd
Bournemouth BH10 189 B2
Portsmouth PO4 183 A2
Minstead Rural Studies Ctr
SO43 98 A1
Minster Cl PO15 130 B1
Minster Ct 1 SO15 102 B3
Minster La 33 SO23 11 A4
Minster Pk BH21 138 C3
Minster The★ BH21 163 A2
Minster View BH21 163 B3
Minster Way BH16 201 A4
Mint Rd GU33 21 A3
Mint The GU31,GU32 40 C1
Minter's Lepe PO7 134 C2
Mintern Cl SO50 56 B3
Minterne Grange BH14 214 B4
Minterne Rd
3 Bournemouth BH9 190 A1
Christchurch BH23 207 C3
Poole BH14 214 B4
Minton Mews BH2 204 C3
Mintys Hill SP6 68 C4
Mintys Yd 4 BH24 141 A3
Mirror Cl SO31 128 C1
Mislingford Rd SO32 84 B2
Missenden Acres SO30 105 B4
Missenden Pl 5 SO50 56 A1
Mission La PO8 112 A2
Mission Rd BH18 187 A1
Misslebrook La SO52,
SO16 54 B2
Mistletoe Gdns SO31 128 C3
Mitchell Cl
Barton on Sea BH25 210 A4
Locks Heath PO15 129 B3
Mitchell Dr SO50 57 B2
Mitchell Point SO31 127 C1
Mitchell Rd
Eastleigh SO50 56 A1
Ferndown BH21 165 A4
Havant PO9 135 A2
Poole BH17 202 C4
Mitchell Way
Eastleigh SO18 79 C3
Portsmouth PO3 158 A2
Mitchells Cl Redlynch SP5 47 B3
Romsey SO51 52 C4
Mitre Copse SO50 56 C1
Mitre Ct 13 PO14 154 C4
Mizen Ho PO6 157 A4
Mizen Way PO13 180 B3
Mizoah Villas SO32 83 C2
Moat Cl SO45 150 A2

Moat Ct
Bournemouth BH4 204 B3
Gosport PO12 180 B2
Moat Dr PO12 180 B2
Moat Hill SO18 79 C2
Moat La BH25 209 C4
Moat Wlk PO12 180 B2
Mockbeggar La BH24 117 A4
Moffat Rd BH23 207 B4
Moggs Mead GU31 41 A2
Mole Hill PO7 134 C3
Molefields SO41 211 C3
Molesworth Rd PO12 181 B2
Mollison Rise PO15 129 B3
Molyneux Rd BH25 195 B2
Momford Rd SO22 10 A2
Mon Cres SO18 104 B4
Monaco Ct BH9 205 A4
Monarch Cl
Locks Heath SO31 129 A1
5 Waterlooville PO7 135 A4
Monarch Way
West End SO30 80 C1
Winchester SO22 10 B3
Monastery Rd SO18 103 C4
Monckton Rd
Gosport PO12 181 A1
Portsmouth PO3 158 A1
Moneyfield Ave PO3 158 A1
Moneyfield La PO3 183 A4
Moneyfly Rd BH31 115 A3
Monk's Hill PO10 137 A3
Monks Brook Cl SO50 55 C1
Monks Brook Ind Pk
SO53 55 A3
Monks Cl BH22 166 A4
Monks Ct 10 SO41 197 C1
Monks Hill PO13 179 B2
Monks Orch GU32 40 C3
Monks Pl SO40 100 B3
Monks Rd Netley SO31 127 A3
Winchester SO23 2 A1
Monks Way
Bournemouth BH11 188 B3
Eastleigh SO50 55 C1
Southampton SO18 79 C2
Stubbington PO14 179 A2
Monks Wlk SO45 149 C4
Monks Wood GU32 40 C3
Monks Wood Cl SO16 79 A3
Monkshood Cl BH23 193 A1
Monkswell Gn BH23 207 B3
Monkton Cl BH22 165 B3
Monkton Cres BH12 203 C4
Monkton Ho PO12 181 A1
Monkton La SO40 100 B3
Monkwood Cl PO9 135 B3
Monkworthy Dr BH24 139 C3
Monmouth Cl
North Baddesley SO53 55 A3
Verwood BH31 115 A2
Monmouth Ct
Lymington SO41 197 C2
Ringwood BH24 140 C4
Monmouth Dr BH31 115 A2
Monmouth Gdns SO40 100 B3
Monmouth Rd PO2 157 B1
Monmouth Sq SO22 10 A3
Monnow Gdns SO18 80 A1
Monroe Cl PO12 180 C2
Mons The 31 SO23 10 C4
Monsal Ave BH22 165 B2
Montacute Sch BH17 187 B1
Montacute Way BH21 187 C4
Montagu Cl PO12 181 B4
Montagu Pk BH23 209 A4
Montagu Rd BH23 209 A4
Montague Ave SO19 104 B2
Montague Cl SO19 104 B2
Montague Ct SO45 149 C4
Montague Gdns GU31 41 B2
Montague Rd
Bishopstoke SO50 56 B2
Bournemouth BH5 206 A2
Portsmouth PO2 157 C1
Montague Wallis Ct 31
PO1 182 A3
Montana Ct PO7 135 A3
Montefiore Ho SO18 79 B2
Monterey Dr Havant PO9 136 A2
Hordle SO41 195 C2
Locks Heath SO31 129 A1
Montfort Cl SO51 53 B4
Montfort Coll SO51 53 B4
Montfort Hts SO51 53 B4
Montfort Rd SO51 53 B3
Montgomerie Rd PO5 215 C2
Montgomery Ave
Bournemouth BH11 189 A2
Totton SO40 100 B4
Montgomery Cl SO22 10 B3
Montgomery Rd
Gosport PO13 155 B2
Havant PO9 136 A1
Southampton SO18 104 A4
Montgomery Way SO53 55 A2
Montgomery Wlk PO7 134 B3
Montpelier Cl SO31 129 B2
Montrose Ave PO16 132 C1
Montrose Cl
Hedge End SO30 105 C3
2 Verwood BH31 114 C3
Montrose Dr BH10 189 A1
Montserrat Rd PO13 179 C1
Monument Ct SO14 103 A1

Monument La
Boldre SO41 198 A3
Southwick PO17 132 B2
Walderton PO18 137 C4
Monxton Gn 16 PO9 136 A3
Moody Rd PO14 179 B3
Moody's Hill SP5 3 B1
Moon Cl SO40 101 C1
Moonhills La SO42 149 A1
Moonrakers BH13 214 C4
Moonrakers Way BH23 193 C1
Moonscross Ave SO40 100 C2
Moor La SP5 48 B4
Moor Pk PO7 112 A1
Moor Rd BH18 187 A3
Moor View Rd BH15 202 C4
Moorcroft Ave BH23 192 B1
Moordown Cl BH9 190 A2
Moordown St John's CE Prim Sch BH9 189 C1
Moore Ave BH11 189 A2
Moore Cl BH25 194 C1
Moore Cres SO31 127 B4
Moore Gdns PO12 180 C2
Moorfield Gr BH9 189 C1
Moorfields Rd BH13 214 C4
Moorgreen Hospl SO30 80 C1
Moorgreen Rd
Havant PO9 136 A3
West End SO30 80 C1
Moorhaven BH22 165 B3
Moorhead Ct SO14 103 B1
Moorhill Gdns SO18 104 C4
Moorhill Rd Burley BH24 143 A1
West End SO30 104 B4
Moorhills 14 BH21 163 B2
Moorings Cl BH15 201 C1
Moorings The
7 Christchurch BH23 207 A3
Fareham PO16 155 A4
Moorings Way PO4 183 B3
Moorings Way Inf Sch PO4 183 B3
Moorland Ave BH25 209 C4
Moorland Cl Hythe SO45 125 B2
Locks Heath SO31 129 A2
Moorland Cres BH16 201 A4
Moorland Gate BH24 141 A3
Moorland Par BH16 201 A4
Moorland Rd
Bournemouth BH1 205 B2
Portsmouth PO1 182 C3
Moorland Way BH16 201 A4
Moorlands Cl SO42 145 B1
Moorlands Coll BH23 192 A3
Moorlands Cres SO18 104 A4
Moorlands Inf Sch SO18 80 A1
Moorlands Rd
Swanmore SO32 84 A4
Verwood BH31 114 C4
West Moors BH22 138 C2
Moorlands Rise BH22 138 C2
Moorlea 11 BH8 205 A3
Moors Cl
Colden Common SO21 31 C1
Hurn BH23 191 A4
Moors Valley Ctry Park Visitor Ctr* BH24 139 B4
Moors Valley Ctry Pk*
St Leonards BH24 139 B4
Verwood BH24 115 C1
Moors Valley Rly* BH24 115 B1
Moorside Cl BH11 189 A2
Moorside Rd
Bournemouth BH11 189 A2
Corfe Mullen BH21 186 B3
West Moors BH22 138 C1
Winchester SO23 2 B1
Moortown Ave PO6 134 B1
Moortown Dr BH21 188 A4
Moortown Ho BH24 141 A3
Moortown La BH24 141 B2
Moorvale Rd BH9 190 A1
Moot Cl SP5 47 A4
Moot Gdns SP5 46 C3
Moot La SP5 46 C3
Mopley SO45 177 C4
Mopley Cl SO45 177 C4
Morant Ct 14 BH25 195 A2
Morant Rd BH24 117 A1
Moraunt Cl PO12 181 B4
Moraunt Dr PO16 156 A3
Moray Ct 14 BH21 163 A3
Mordaunt Rd SO14 103 A4
Morden Ave BH22 165 B2
Morden Rd BH9 189 C1
Morecombe Ct 4 PO5 215 C2
Moreland Rd PO12 181 A3
Morelands Ct PO7 134 C2
Morelands Prim Sch PO7 134 C1
Morelands Rd PO7 134 C2
Moresby Ct 21 PO16 131 A1
Morestead Rd
Winchester SO21 11 C2
Winchester SO23 11 A2
Moreton Rd BH9 190 A2
Morgan Le Fay Dr SO53 54 C4
Morgan Rd
Hedge End SO30 105 B3
Portsmouth PO4 183 B2
Morgan's La SP5 42 A1
Morgan's Vale & Woodfall's Prim Sch SP5 47 B4
Morgans Dr PO14 154 B3
Morgans Rise Rd SP5 47 B4
Morgans Vale Rd SP5 47 B3
Moriconium Quay BH15 201 B1
Morington Ct 8 BH8 205 A3
Morland Rd SO15 78 B1
Morley Cl
Bournemouth BH5 206 A3
Burton BH23 192 B2
Southampton SO19 103 C3
Morley Cres PO8 112 A2
Morley Dr SO32 83 B4
Morley Rd
Bournemouth BH5 206 A3
Portsmouth PO4 183 A1
Morley Way BH22 165 C2
Morleys La SO51 29 B2
Morningside Ave PO16 132 C1
Mornington Dr SO22 1 B1
Mornish Rd BH13 203 C1
Morpeth Ave SO40 100 C4
Morris Cl Gosport PO13 155 A3
Hythe SO45 125 B2
Morris Rd Poole BH17 202 B4
Southampton SO15 102 C3
Morrison Ave BH12 203 C3
Morse Ct SO31 127 A3
Morshead Cres PO16 130 C2
Mortimer Cl
Christchurch BH23 208 A3
Kings Worthy SO23 2 A3
9 Netley SO31 127 A3
Totton SO40 76 B1
Mortimer Lawn PO9 135 B4
Mortimer Rd
Botley SO30 106 A3
Bournemouth BH8 190 A1
Cosham PO6 133 B1
Southampton SO19 103 C2
Mortimer Way SO52 53 C2
Mortimer's Ind Units SO51 75 C3
Mortimers Dr 10 SO50 57 B1
Mortimers La SO32 58 A2
Mortimore Rd PO12 180 C3
Mosaic Cl SO19 104 C2
Mosdell Rd PO10 161 C4
Mosedale Wlk SO16 101 C4
Moselle Ct SO15 102 B3
Moss Cl GU33 21 A2
Moss Dr SO40 101 C1
Moss Rd SO23 11 A4
Mossleigh Ave SO16 77 C3
Mossley Ave BH12 189 A1
Motcombe Rd BH13 204 A1
Mottisfont Abbey (NT)* SO51 5 C1
Mottisfont Abbey Gdns* SO51 5 C2
Mottisfont Cl SO15 102 A3
Mottisfont Rd SO50 56 A2
Moulin Ave PO5 182 C1
Mound Cl PO12 181 A2
Mount Ave BH25 195 A1
Mount Cl
New Milton BH25 195 A1
Winchester SO22 1 C2
Mount Dr
Chandler's Ford SO53 55 C2
Fareham PO15 154 A4
Mount Grace Dr BH14 214 B4
Mount Heatherbank 30 BH1 204 C2
Mount Hospl The SO50 56 B3
Mount House Cl 5 SO45 126 A3
Mount La SO51 25 C4
Mount Pleasant
Christchurch BH23 208 A3
Denmead PO7 110 C1
Kings Worthy SO23 2 B3
7 Ringwood BH24 141 A4
Romsey SO51 52 C3
Mount Pleasant Dr BH8 190 C1
Mount Pleasant Ind Pk SO14 103 A4
Mount Pleasant Jun Sch SO14 103 A4
Mount Pleasant La
Lymington SO41 197 A4
Sway SO41 197 A4
Mount Pleasant Rd
Gosport PO12 181 A2
Southampton SO14 103 A3
Mount Rd
Bournemouth BH11 189 A2
Poole BH14 203 A3
Mount Temple SO51 53 A4
Mount The Gosport PO13 155 C1
Ringwood BH24 141 B4
5 Southampton, Bassett SO16 78 C2
9 Southampton, Shirley SO16 78 A1
Mount View SO50 56 A2
Mount View Rd SO22 10 A2
Mountain Ash Cl SO18 104 B4
Mountbatten Ave SO51 52 C4
Mountbatten Bsns Ctr SO15 102 B3
Mountbatten Bsns Pk PO6 158 B3
Mountbatten Cl
Christchurch BH23 208 A3
Gosport PO13 155 B2
Mountbatten Ct
New Milton BH25 194 C2
Winchester SO22 1 C2
Mountbatten Dr
Ferndown BH22 165 B3
Waterlooville PO7 134 B3
Mountbatten Gdns BH8 190 C1
Mountbatten Pl SO23 2 B4
Mountbatten Rd
Eastleigh SO50 56 A3
Poole BH13 204 A1
Totton SO40 100 B4
Mountbatten Sch The SO51 53 B3
Mountbatten Sq PO4 183 A1
Mountbatten Way
Portsmouth PO1 215 A4
Southampton SO15 102 B3
Mountfield SO45 125 C2
Mountjoy Cl BH21 163 C1
Mountview Ave PO16 132 C1
Mountwood Rd PO10 137 B1
Mousehole La
Hythe SO45 126 A2
Southampton SO18 103 C4
Mousehole Rd PO6 132 C1
Mowbray Rd SO19 104 A2
Moxhams SP6 69 C1
Moyles Court Sch BH24 117 B3
Mt Pleasant Dr BH23 169 B1
Mt Pleasant Rd BH15 202 B2
Muccleshell Cl PO9 136 A2
Muddyford Rd SP5 47 B4
Mude Gdns BH23 208 A3
Mudeford BH23 208 A3
Mudeford Cty Inf Sch BH23 207 C3
Mudeford Cty Jun Sch BH23 207 C3
Mudeford Green Cl BH23 207 C3
Mudeford La BH23 207 C3
Muir Ho SO45 125 C1
Muira Est SO14 103 B3
Mulberry Ave
Cosham PO6 158 A4
Stubbington PO14 179 B3
Mulberry Cl PO12 181 A2
Mulberry Ct 4 BH23 207 A4
Mulberry Gdns SP6 93 C4
Mulberry Gr SO41 211 B4
Mulberry La
Cosham PO6 158 A4
Locks Heath SO31 128 C3
Mulberry Mews SP6 93 C4
Mulberry Rd SO40 101 C1
Mulberry Wlk SO15 102 B4
Mullen Cl SO19 103 C2
Mullins Cl BH12 204 B4
Mullion Cl PO6 157 A4
Mumby Rd PO12 181 B3
Mundays Row PO8 88 B1
Munro Cres SO15 101 C4
Munster Rd Poole BH14 203 B2
Portsmouth PO2 157 B1
Murefield Rd PO1 215 C3
Muriel Rd PO7 134 C4
Murley Rd BH9 205 A4
Murray Cl Fareham PO15 130 C1
Southampton SO19 104 C3
Murray Cotts SO32 107 B4
Murray Rd PO8 112 A3
Murray's La PO1 181 C3
Murrills Est PO16 156 C4
Mus of Childhood* BH8 205 C3
Mus of Electricity* BH23 207 A4
Muscliff Prim Sch BH9 190 B2
Muscliffe Ct 27 PO9 136 A3
Muscliffe La BH9 190 A3
Muscliffe Rd BH9 189 C1
Museum of Archaeology* SO14 103 A1
Museum Rd PO1 182 A2
Mussett Cl SO40 100 C4
Mustang Ave PO15 129 B4
My Lords La PO11 185 A2
Myers Cl SO32 84 A3
Myrtle Ave
Portchester PO16 156 B4
Totton SO40 100 B3
Myrtle Cl Gosport PO13 155 A2
Hordle SO41 195 C2
Myrtle Gr PO3 183 A4
Myrtle Rd
Bournemouth BH8 205 B3
Southampton SO16 78 A2
Myvern Cl SO45 150 B2

N

Nada Rd BH23 193 B1
Nailsworth Rd PO6 133 A1
Nairn Ct BH3 204 C4
Nairn Rd
Bournemouth BH3 204 C3
Poole BH13 214 C4
Naish Ct PO9 135 B4
Naish Dr PO12 156 A1
Naish Holiday Village* BH25 209 B4
Naish Rd BH25 209 C4
Namu Rd BH9 189 C1
Nancy Rd PO1 215 D3
Nansen Ave BH15 202 B3
Napier Cl PO13 180 B3
Napier Cres PO15 130 B1
Napier Rd
Hamworthy BH15 201 B2
Napier Rd *continued*
Horndean PO8 112 B3
Portsmouth PO5 182 B1
Southampton SO19 104 C3
Narrow La
Ringwood BH24 117 B1
10 Romsey SO51 52 C4
Narvik Rd PO2 157 B2
Naseby Cl 5 PO6 133 A1
Naseby Rd BH9 190 A1
Nash Cl SO45 125 B1
Nash Rd SO45 125 B1
Nashe Cl PO15 130 B2
Nashe Ho PO15 130 B2
Nashe Way PO15 130 B2
Nasmith Cl PO12 180 B2
Nat Gonella Sq 21 PO12 181 B2
Nathen Gdns BH15 201 B2
National Motor Mus The* SO42 148 C1
Nations Hill SO23 2 B3
Navarac Ct BH14 203 B2
Navigator's Way SO30 105 B4
Navy Rd PO1 182 A3
Nea Cl BH23 208 B4
Nea Dr BH24 116 A3
Nea Rd BH23 208 C4
Neacroft Cl BH25 209 B4
Neath Way SO53 55 A3
Needles Ct 11 SO41 211 B2
Needles Ho 7 PO16 155 A4
Needles Point SO41 211 B2
Neelands Gr PO6 156 C4
Neighbourhood Ctr BH17 187 C1
Neilson Cl SO53 55 B4
Nelson Ave
Portchester PO16 156 A4
Portsmouth PO2 157 B1
Nelson Cl Holbury SO45 150 B2
New Milton BH25 194 C2
Romsey SO51 52 C4
Nelson Cres PO8 112 B4
Nelson Ct Fareham PO14 154 C3
12 Hythe SO45 126 A1
10 Poole BH15 202 B1
Nelson Ctr The PO3 158 A1
Nelson Dr BH23 207 C3
Nelson Ho PO12 181 B2
Nelson Ind Pk SO30 81 A1
Nelson La PO16 132 B1
Nelson Pl SO41 197 C2
Nelson Rd
Bishopstoke SO50 56 B2
Bournemouth BH4 204 A2
Gosport PO12 181 A2
Poole BH12 204 A2
Portsmouth PO5 215 C1
Southampton SO15 102 B3
Winchester SO23 11 B3
Nelson's Gdns SO30 81 B2
Nepean Cl PO12 181 A1
Neptune Ct
Portsmouth PO1 182 A2
Southampton SO16 77 C2
Neptune Ho 4 PO6 157 C4
Neptune Rd
Fareham PO15 130 B1
Gosport PO14 154 C3
Neptune Way SO14 103 A1
Nerissa Cl 2 PO7 135 A4
Nerquis Cl SO51 53 A4
Nesbitt Cl PO13 155 A2
Nessus St PO2 182 B4
Nest Bsns Pk PO9 136 A2
Nethercliffe Sch SO22 1 C1
Netherfield Cl PO9 136 A1
Netherhall Gdns BH4 204 B2
Netherhill La SO32 82 A1
Netherton Rd PO12 180 C4
Netherwood Pl BH21 163 A3
Netley Abbey Inf Sch SO31 127 A4
Netley Abbey Jun Sch SO31 127 A4
Netley Cl
Chandler's Ford SO53 55 A2
Poole BH15 203 A4
Netley Cliff SO31 127 A3
Netley Court Sch SO31 127 A3
Netley Firs Cl SO19 104 C2
Netley Firs Rd SO30 105 A3
Netley Hill Est SO19 104 C2
Netley Lodge Cl SO31 127 B3
Netley Marsh CE Inf Sch SO40 100 A4
Netley Rd
21 Portsmouth PO5 182 B1
Titchfield PO14 129 B1
Netley Sta SO31 127 B3
Netley Terr 20 PO5 182 B1
Nettlecombe Ave PO4 182 C1
Nettlestone SO31 127 B4
Nettlestone Rd PO4 183 A1
Nettleton Cl BH17 202 C4
Netton Cl SP5 22 A4
Netton St SP5 22 B4
Neva Rd SO18 103 C4
Neville Ave PO16 156 B3
Neville Ct PO12 181 A2
Neville Gdns PO10 136 C2
Neville Lovett Com Sch PO14 154 C4
Neville Rd PO3 183 A4
Neville Shute Rd PO3 158 A2
New Borough Rd BH21 163 B2
New Brighton Rd PO10 136 C1
New Cliff Ho SO19 103 C1
New Cliffe Gdns SO30 105
New Coll (Univ of Southampton) SO15 102
New Cotts Ashurst SO40 123
Boldre SO41 199
Exbury SO45 177
Fareham PO16 155
Ferndown BH21 164
Nursling SO16 77
New Ct BH24 140
New Cut PO11 159
New Down La PO6,PO7 134
New Fields Bsns Pk BH17 202
New Forest Dr SO42 145
New Forest Ent Ctr SO40 100
New Forest Mus & Visitor Ctr* SO43 122
New Forest Otter, Owl & Wildlife Pk* SO40 123
New Forest Owl Sanctuary* BH24 141
New Forest Reptiliary* SO43 121
New Hall SO23 11
New Harbour Rd BH15 202
New Harbour Rd S BH15 213
New Harbour Rd W BH15 202
New Inn Cotts SO42 175
New Inn La Cadnam SO40 99
East Boldre SO42 175
New Inn Rd SO40 99
New La Havant PO9 136
Milford on Sea SO41 211
New Milton BH25 194
New Marsh Ho 2 SO45 126
New Merrifield BH21 163
New Milton Inf Sch BH25 195
New Milton Jun Sch BH25 195
New Milton Sta BH25 195
New Orch BH15 202
New Par
Bournemouth BH10 189
Portchester PO16 156
New Park Rd BH6 206
New Quay Rd BH15 202
New Rd Ashurst SO40 100
Bishop's Waltham SO32 59
Blackfield SO45 150
Bournemouth BH10 189
Clanfield PO8 88
Colden Common SO21 31
Fair Oak SO50 57
Fareham PO16 131
Ferndown BH22 165
Havant PO9 135
Holbury SO45 150
Horndean PO8 111
Hythe SO45 126
Hythe, Hardley SO45 150
Ibsley BH24 117
Landford SP5 49
Littleton SO22 1
Locks Heath SO31 152
Meonstoke SO32 61
Michelmersh SO51 27
Milford on Sea SO41 212
Netley SO31 127
Poole BH12 203
Portsmouth PO2 182
Ringwood BH24 141
Rockbourne SP6 44
Romsey SO51 53
Southampton SO14 103
Southbourne PO10 161
Swanmore SO32 84
Swanwick SO31 128
Westbourne PO10 137
Woodlands BH21 114
New Rd E PO2 182
New St Lymington SO41 197
9 Poole BH15 202
Ringwood BH24 141
New Street Mews SO41 197
New Town PO16 156
New Valley Rd SO41 211
Newbarn La PO18 137
Newbarn Rd PO9 135
Newbolt Cl PO8 111
Newbolt Rd
13 Cosham PO6 133
Portchester PO6 132
Newbridge SO31 127
Newbridge Jun Sch PO1 182
Newbridge Rd SO40 75
Newbridge Way SO41 197
Newbroke Rd PO13 180
Newburgh St SO23 10
Newbury Cl SO50 57
Newbury Dr BH10 189
Newbury Pl SO31 128
Newbury Rd SO15 78
Newcombe Rd
Bournemouth BH6 206
Southampton SO15 102
West Moors BH22 138
Newcome Rd PO1 182
Newcomen Ct 8 PO2 157
Newcomen Rd PO2 157
Newcroft Gdns BH23 207
Newenham Rd SO41 197
Newfield Rd GU33 21

Newfoundland Dr BH15 .202 B1
Newfoundland Drive Rdbt
BH15 .202 B1
Newgate La PO14 .155 A2
Newgate Lane Ind Est
PO14 .155 A3
Newland Ave PO12 .181 A2
Newlands PO15 .130 B1
Newlands Ave SO15 .102 B4
Newlands Cl
Blackfield SO45 .150 C1
Chandler's Ford SO53 .54 C3
Newlands Copse SO45 .150 C1
Newlands Inf Sch SO16 .77 C1
Newlands Jun Sch SO16 .77 C1
Newlands La PO7 .134 A3
Newlands Manor SO41 .211 B4
Newlands Rd
Blackfield SO45 .150 C1
Bournemouth BH7 .206 A3
Christchurch BH23 .207 C4
New Milton BH25 .195 A1
Waterlooville PO7 .134 B3
Newlands The 2 SO17 .79 B1
Newlands Way BH18 .186 B2
Newlease Rd PO7 .134 C3
Newlyn Way Poole BH12 .203 C4
Portsmouth PO6 .157 A4
Newlyn Wlk SO51 .28 A1
Newman St SO16 .102 A4
Newman's La BH22 .138 B2
Newmans Cl BH22 .138 C3
Newmans Hill PO17 .84 B1
Newmarket Cl SO50 .81 B4
Newmer Ct 1 PO9 .135 B3
Newmorton Rd BH9 .190 A2
Newney Cl PO2 .157 C2
Newnham Ct PO9 .136 A3
Newport Cl SO53 .55 A2
Newport La SO51 .28 B3
Newport Rd PO12 .180 C3
Newstead Rd BH6 .206 B2
Newton Bglws SP5 .24 A2
Newton CE Prim Sch
PO12 .181 B3
Newton Cl
Stubbington PO14 .154 B2
Whiteparish SP5 .24 A2
Newton La Romsey SO51 .52 C3
Whiteparish SP5 .24 A2
Newton Morrell BH14 .203 B2
Newton Pl PO13 .179 C2
Newton Rd
Barton on Sea BH25 .210 A4
Poole BH13 .214 C4
Southampton SO18 .79 C1
Twyford SO21 .32 A4
Newtown Bsns Ctr
BH12 .203 A4
Newtown Ct SO31 .128 B1
Newtown La
Corfe Mullen BH21 .186 B4
Ibsley SP6,BH24 .94 B1
South Hayling PO11 .184 C2
Verwood BH31 .115 A3
Newtown Rd
Eastleigh SO50 .56 A2
Locks Heath SO31 .152 B4
Sherfield English SO51 .26 A2
Southampton SO19 .104 A1
Verwood BH31 .115 A3
Newtown Soberton Inf Sch
PO17 .109 B3
Nichol Rd SO53 .30 B1
Nicholas Cl BH23 .194 A1
Nicholas Cres PO15 .130 C1
Nicholas Ct
10 Lee-on-the-Solent
PO13 .179 C1
South Hayling PO11 .184 C2
Nicholas Gdns BH10 .189 B1
Nicholas Rd SO45 .177 C4
Nichole Ct BH12 .203 A4
Nicholl Pl PO13 .155 B1
Nichols Rd SO14 .103 A3
Nicholson Cl BH17 .202 C4
Nicholson Gdns 1 PO1 .215 C3
Nicholson Way PO9 .135 C2
Nicholson Wlk SO16 .77 B3
Nickel Cl SO23 .11 A4
Nickel St 4 PO5 .215 A1
Nickleby Gdns SO40 .100 A4
Nickleby Ho 10 PO1 .182 B4
Nickleby Rd PO8 .88 A3
Nickson Cl SO53 .55 A4
Nightingale Ave SO50 .55 B1
Nightingale Cl
Bursledon SO31 .127 C4
Gosport PO12 .180 C3
Romsey SO51 .53 A4
Rowland's Castle PO9 .113 A1
Verwood BH31 .115 A3
West Wellow SO51 .50 B2
Winchester SO22 .10 B3
Nightingale Cres SO32 .107 C4
Nightingale Ct SO16 .78 A2
Nightingale Dr SO40 .100 B4
Nightingale Gr SO15 .102 B4
Nightingale Ho SO51 .53 A4
Nightingale La 4 BH15 .202 B1
Nightingale Mews
Locks Heath SO31 .129 A2
Netley SO31 .127 B3
Nightingale Pk 8 PO9 .136 A1
Nightingale Prim Sch
SO50 .55 B1
Nightingale Rd
Petersfield GU32 .40 B1
Nightingale Rd *continued*
Portsmouth PO5 .182 A1
Southampton SO15 .102 B4
Nightingale Wlk SO31 .127 B2
Nightingdale Ct 9
SO15 .102 B3
Nightjar Cl
Broadstone BH17 .201 C4
Waterlooville PO8 .112 A3
Nile Rd SO17 .79 A1
Nile St PO10 .160 C4
Nimrod Dr PO13 .180 B3
Nimrod Way BH21 .164 C3
Nine Acres GU32 .20 A1
Nine Elms La PO17 .131 C2
Ninian Cl SO50 .57 B1
Ninian Park Rd PO3 .158 A1
Niton Cl PO13 .155 B1
Noads Cl SO45 .125 C1
Noads Way SO45 .125 C1
Noadswood Sec Sch
SO45 .125 C1
Nob's Crook SO21 .57 A4
Nobbs La PO1 .182 A2
Nobes Ave PO13 .155 B2
Nobes Cl PO13 .155 B1
Noble Cl BH11 .188 C1
Noble Rd SO30 .105 B3
Noel Cl SO42 .146 A1
Noel Rd BH10 .189 A1
Noel The BH25 .195 B2
Nomansland & Hamptworth
CE Sch SP5 .73 B4
Nook The Eastleigh SO50 .56 A3
Gosport PO13 .155 C1
Noon Gdns BH31 .115 A3
Noon Hill Dr BH31 .115 A3
Noon Hill Rd BH31 .115 A3
Norbury Cl SO53 .55 A4
Norbury Gdns SO31 .127 C1
Norcliffe Cl BH10 .189 A2
Norcliffe Rd SO17 .103 A4
Norcroft Ct SO15 .78 B1
Nordik Gdns SO30 .105 B3
Nore Cres PO10 .136 B1
Nore Farm Ave PO10 .136 B1
Norevil Rd GU32 .40 B2
Norfolk Ave BH23 .191 C1
Norfolk Cres PO11 .184 C1
Norfolk Ct SO53 .55 B2
Norfolk Ho 4 PO9 .136 A1
Norfolk Mews PO11 .184 C1
Norfolk Rd Gosport PO12 180 C4
Southampton SO15 .102 B4
Norfolk St PO5 .215 B2
Norgett Way PO16 .156 A4
Norham Ave SO16 .78 B1
Norham Cl SO16 .78 B1
Norland Rd PO4 .215 D1
Norlands Dr SO21 .31 B2
Norley Cl PO9 .135 C3
Norleywood BH23 .208 C4
Norleywood Rd SO41 .198 C4
Norman Ave BH12 .204 A3
Norman Cl PO16 .156 B3
Norman Ct 6 PO4 .182 C1
Norman Gdns
Hedge End SO30 .105 A3
Poole BH12 .204 A3
Norman Ho 16 SO14 .103 B3
Norman Rd
Blackfield SO45 .177 C4
Gosport PO12 .181 A3
Portsmouth PO4 .182 C2
South Hayling PO11 .185 A1
Southampton SO15 .102 B3
Winchester SO23 .10 C3
Norman Way PO9 .135 B1
Normandy Cl
Rownhams SO16 .77 C3
Sway SO41 .172 A1
Normandy Ct
Locks Heath SO31 .128 B1
Wickham PO17 .108 A2
Normandy Dr BH23 .207 B4
Normandy Gdns PO12 .180 C2
Normandy Ho SO51 .53 A4
Normandy La SO41 .197 C1
Normandy Rd PO2 .157 C2
Normandy Way
Fordingbridge SP6 .69 C1
Hamworthy BH15 .201 B1
Marchwood SO40 .102 A1
Normanhurst Ave BH8 .190 C1
Normans SO23 .10 C3
Normanton Cl BH23 .191 C1
Norris Cl Romsey SO51 .28 B1
St Leonards BH24 .139 C2
Norris Gdns Havant PO9 .160 A4
New Milton BH25 .195 A1
Norris Hill SO18 .79 C1
Norrish Ct PO2 .182 C4
Norrish Rd BH12 .203 B3
Norset Rd PO15 .130 B1
North Ave
Bournemouth BH10 .189 B3
Portsmouth PO2 .157 C3
North Baddesley Inf Sch
SO52 .54 A2
North Baddesley Jun Sch
SO52 .54 A2
North Battery Rd PO2 .157 A1
North Bay PO10 .161 A2
North Block SO15 .102 B3
North Cl Gosport PO12 .180 C2
Havant PO9 .160 A4
Lymington SO41 .197 C2
Romsey SO51 .28 B1
North Common La
Landford SP5 .49 A3
Sway SO41 .196 C4
North Cres PO11 .185 A2
North Cross St PO12 .181 B2
North Ct PO1 .182 C4
North Dr Littleton SO22 .1 A3
New Milton BH25 .170 C1
North East Cl SO19 .104 B3
North East Rd SO19 .104 A2
North End Ave PO2 .157 B1
North End Cl SO53 .55 B2
North End Farm Cotts
SO24 .14 B4
North End Gr PO2 .157 B1
North End La SP6,BH24 .93 B2
North Fields Cotts SO21 .32 A4
North Front 16 SO14 .103 A3
North Greenlands SO41 197 B1
North Head SO41 .211 A3
North Hill PO16 .131 A2
North Hill Cl SO22 .1 C1
North Hill Ct SO22 .1 C1
North La Beaulieu SO42 .148 C3
Buriton GU31 .65 C3
Clanfield PO8 .88 B4
East Meon PO8 .64 B1
Nomansland SP5 .73 B4
West Tytherley SP5 .4 A4
North Lodge Rd BH14 .203 C2
North Millers Dale SO53 .55 A4
North Park Bsns Ctr
PO17 .130 B4
North Poulner Rd BH24 117 A1
North Rd
Bournemouth BH7 .205 C3
Brockenhurst SO42 .146 A1
Horndean PO8 .88 B1
Hythe SO45 .125 C1
Kings Worthy SO23 .2 A4
Petersfield GU32 .40 C2
Poole BH14 .203 A2
Southampton SO17 .103 B4
North Rd E PO17 .133 A3
North Rd W PO17 .133 A3
North Shore Rd PO11 .184 B2
North St Emsworth PO10 .136 C1
Gosport PO12 .181 B2
Havant PO9 .135 C1
Havant, Bedhampton PO9 .135 B1
Lymington SO41 .197 B1
Poole BH15 .202 B1
Portsmouth PO1 .215 C4
Portsmouth, Portsea PO1 .182 A3
Westbourne PO10 .137 A2
North Street Arc 11
PO9 .135 C1
North Stroud La GU32 .39 C2
North Trestle Rd SO45 .151 B3
North View SO22 .10 C4
North Wallington PO16 .131 B1
North Walls SO23 .11 A4
North Way Gosport PO13 155 B2
Havant PO9 .135 C1
Locks Heath PO15 .129 C2
North Weirs SO42 .145 B1
Northam Bsns Ctr 1
SO14 .103 B3
Northam Mews PO1 .215 C3
Northam Prim Sch
SO14 .103 B3
Northam Rd SO14 .103 A3
Northam St PO1 .215 C3
Northampton La SO45 .177 C4
Northarbour Rd PO6 .157 B4
Northarbour Spur PO6 .157 B4
Northbank Ho PO1 .215 C4
Northbourne Ave BH10 .189 B3
Northbourne Cl 9
SO45 .126 A1
Northbourne Gdns
BH10 .189 C3
Northbourne Pl 3
BH10 .189 B3
Northbourne Rdbt
BH10 .189 C3
Northbrook Ave SO23 .11 B4
Northbrook Cl
Portsmouth PO1 .182 B4
Winchester SO23 .11 B4
Northbrook Ind Est SO16 78 B1
Northbrook Rd
Broadstone BH18 .187 A1
Southampton SO14 .103 A3
Northbrook Springs
Vineyard★ SO32 .59 A1
Northbrooke Ct 11 SO23 .11 B4
Northcote Rd
Bournemouth BH1 .205 A2
Portsmouth PO4 .182 C2
Southampton SO17 .79 B1
Northcott Cl PO12 .180 C2
Northcroft Rd PO12 .180 C3
Northdene Rd SO53 .55 B3
Northend La SO32 .61 A1
Northern Access Rd
SO45 .151 B1
Northern Anchorage
SO19 .103 B2
Northern Bldgs 18 PO6 .157 C4
Northern Inf Sch PO16 .132 B1
Northern Jun Sch PO16 132 B1
Northern Par PO2 .157 C2
Northern Parade Inf Sch
PO2 .157 C2
Northern Parade Jun Sch
PO2 .157 C2
Northern Rd
Cosham PO6 .157 C4
Fawley SO45 .151 C1
Northern Way PO1 .181 C4
Northerwood Ave SO43 .121 C3
Northerwood Cl SO52 .53 C2
Northerwood Ho SO43 .121 C3
Northey Rd BH6 .206 C3
Northfield Ave PO14 .154 C4
Northfield Cl
Bishop's Waltham SO32 .59 A1
Horndean PO8 .88 B1
Northfield Pk PO16 .132 A1
Northfield Rd
Milford on Sea SO41 .211 C2
Ringwood BH24 .117 A1
Southampton SO18 .79 C1
Northfields Farm La
PO17 .108 A3
Northgate Ave PO2 .182 C4
Northgate Chambers 9
SO23 .11 A4
Northlands Cl SO40 .100 B4
Northlands Dr SO23 .2 A1
Northlands Gdns SO15 .102 C4
Northlands Rd
Eastleigh SO50 .56 A2
Romsey SO51 .53 B3
Southampton SO15, SO40 .102 C4
Totton SO40 .100 C4
Northleigh Cnr SO18 .79 C3
Northleigh La BH21 .163 C3
Northmead Dr BH17 .201 C4
Northmere Dr BH12 .203 C4
Northmere Rd BH12 .203 C4
Northmore Cl SO31 .129 A3
Northmore Rd SO31 .129 A3
Northney La PO11 .160 B2
Northney Rd PO11 .160 A2
Northolt Gdns SO16 .78 A3
Northover BH3 .204 C3
Northover La SO41 .195 C4
Northover Rd
Lymington SO41 .197 A2
Portsmouth PO3 .183 A4
Northumberland Ct
BH24 .140 C4
Northumberland Rd
Portsmouth PO1 .215 D3
Southampton SO14 .103 A3
Northways PO14 .179 B3
Northwood Cl SO16 .79 A3
Northwood La PO11 .160 A1
Northwood Rd PO2 .157 C3
Northwood Sq 8 PO16 .131 A1
Nortoft Rd BH8 .205 A3
Norton Cl
Christchurch BH23 .207 B4
Southampton SO19 .103 C2
Southwick PO17 .132 C3
Waterlooville PO7 .134 B4
Norton Dr PO16 .131 A2
Norton Rd
Bournemouth BH9 .204 C4
Southwick PO17 .132 C3
Norton Welch Cl SO52 .54 A2
Norway Cl 3 BH9 .189 C1
Norway Rd PO3 .158 A2
Norwich Ave BH2 .204 B2
Norwich Ave W BH2 .204 B2
Norwich Cl SO31 .128 C2
Norwich Ct 12 BH2 .204 C2
Norwich Mans 4 BH2 .204 B2
Norwich Pl PO13 .179 C2
Norwich Rd
Bournemouth BH2 .204 C2
Cosham PO6 .133 B1
Southampton SO18 .79 C1
Norwood Pl BH5 .206 A3
Norwood Prim Sch SO50 56 A2
Nottingham Pl PO13 .179 C2
Nouale La BH24 .141 B4
Novello Gdns PO7 .134 C3
Noyce Dr SO50 .57 B1
Noyce Gdns BH8 .191 A1
Nuffield Hospl BH5 .205 C2
Nuffield Ind Est BH17 .202 B4
Nuffield Rd BH17 .202 B4
Nugent Rd BH6 .207 A2
Nunns Pk SP5 .24 A2
Nuns Rd SO23 .2 A1
Nurse's Path SO21 .32 A3
Nursery Cl
Emsworth PO10 .136 C2
Gosport PO13 .155 A2
Nursery Field GU33 .20 C2
Nursery Gdns
Chandler's Ford SO53 .55 B2
Romsey SO51 .53 A4
Southampton SO19 .104 A3
Waterlooville PO8 .112 A3
Winchester SO22 .10 B4
Nursery Gr SO30 .105 B3
Nursery La PO14 .179 B3
Nursery Rd
Bournemouth BH9 .190 A2
Havant PO9 .135 B1
Ringwood BH24 .141 A3
Southampton SO18 .79 B1
Nursling CE Prim Sch
SO16 .77 B3
Nursling Cres PO9 .136 A3
Nursling Gn BH8 .190 B1
Nursling Ind Est SO16 .77 A2
Nursling St SO16 .77 B3
Nutash PO14 .129 B2
Nutbeem Rd SO50 .56 A1
Nutbourne Ho PO6 .158 B4
Nutbourne Pk PO18 .161 C4
Nutbourne Rd
Cosham PO6 .158 B4
South Hayling PO11 .185 C1
Nutburn Rd SO52 .54 A3
Nutfield Ct SO16 .77 C2
Nutfield Pl PO1 .215 C4
Nutfield Rd SO16 .77 B3
Nuthatch Cl
Broadstone BH17 .201 C4
Ferndown BH22 .165 A4
Rowland's Castle PO9 .113 A1
Nutley Cl BH11 .188 C2
Nutley Rd PO9 .135 B3
Nutley Way BH11 .188 C2
Nutsey Ave SO40 .76 B1
Nutsey Cl SO40 .76 C2
Nutsey La SO40 .76 C1
Nutshalling Ave SO16 .77 C3
Nutshalling Cl SO40 .76 B1
Nutwick Rd PO9 .136 A2
Nutwood Way SO40 .76 C1
Nyewood Ave PO16 .132 B1
Nyria Way PO12 .181 B2

O

O' Jays Ind Pk PO3 .158 A1
O'connell Rd SO50 .55 C1
Oak Ave BH23 .206 B4
Oak Cl Corfe Mullen BH21 186 B3
Ferndown BH22 .165 C1
Hythe SO45 .125 C1
Lyndhurst SO43 .121 C2
Southampton SO15 .101 B4
Upham SO32 .58 C3
Waterlooville PO8 .111 C1
Oak Coppice Cl SO50 .57 A1
Oak Ct Fareham PO15 .130 B1
Lymington SO41 .197 B1
Oak Dr SO50 .57 B1
Oak Gdns SO41 .211 B4
Oak Green Way SO18 .104 A4
Oak La BH24 .141 A4
Oak Lodge 4 PO2 .157 B1
Oak Lodge Specl Sch
SO45 .125 B2
Oak Meadow CE Prim Sch
PO15 .130 B2
Oak Mews BH12 .203 B3
Oak Park Dr PO9 .136 A2
Oak Park Ind Est PO6 .157 B4
Oak Rd Alderholt SP6 .92 C3
Bishop's Waltham SO32 .83 C4
Bournemouth BH8 .205 B3
Bursledon SO31 .127 C4
Clanfield PO8 .88 B3
Fareham PO15 .130 B1
Hythe SO45 .125 C1
New Milton BH25 .195 B2
Southampton SO19 .103 C1
Upton BH16 .201 B3
Oak St PO12 .181 B2
Oak Tree Cl SO21 .56 C4
Oak Tree Dr
Emsworth PO10 .136 C2
Liss GU33 .21 A2
Oak Tree Gdns SO30 .105 A3
Oak Tree Rd SO18 .79 C1
Oak Tree Way SO50 .56 A3
Oak Vale SO30 .80 A2
Oak Wlk SO50 .57 B1
Oakapple Gdns PO6 .158 C4
Oakbank Rd
Bishopstoke SO50 .56 B2
Southampton SO19 .103 B2
Oakcroft La PO14 .154 B3
Oakdale Rd BH15 .202 C3
Oakdale South Road Mid Sch
BH15 .202 B3
Oakdene Gosport PO13 .155 B1
6 Southampton SO17 .79 A1
Totton SO40 .100 B4
Oakdene Cl BH21 .163 B3
Oakdene Gdns 3 SO50 .57 B1
Oakdown Rd PO14 .154 B2
Oakenbrow Hythe SO45 .125 B1
Sway SO41 .172 A1
Oakes The PO14 .154 A2
Oakfield Ct 32 PO9 .136 A3
Oakfield Prim Sch SO40 .76 C1
Oakfield Rd Cadnam SO40 .99 A4
Poole BH15 .202 B3
Totton SO40 .100 C4
Oakfields SO50 .56 A4
Oakford Ct BH8 .190 B2
Oakgrove Gdns SO50 .56 C1
Oakgrove Rd SO50 .56 C1
Oakham Grange BH22 .165 C3
Oakhill SO31 .105 A1
Oakhill Cl
Bursledon SO31 .105 A1
Chandler's Ford SO53 .55 C3
Oakhill Ct SO53 .55 C3
Oakhill Terr SO31 .105 A1
Oakhurst Cl Netley SO31 .127 B3
West Moors BH22 .138 C1
Oakhurst Dr PO7 .135 A4
Oakhurst Fst Sch BH22 .138 C1
Oakhurst Gdns PO7 .134 A1
Oakhurst La BH22 .138 C1
Oakhurst Rd
Southampton SO17 .79 A2
West Moors BH22 .138 C1

Oakhurst Way SO31 127 B3
Oakland Dr SO40 101 C1
Oakland Wlk BH22 165 C1
Oaklands
  Chandler's Ford SO53 30 A1
  Lymington SO41 197 C1
  Waterlooville PO7 135 A3
Oaklands Ave SO40 100 C4
Oaklands Cl
  Fordingbridge SP6 69 C1
  Verwood BH31 114 C3
  Winchester SO22 10 B3
Oaklands Com Sch SO16 77 C3
Oaklands Gdns PO14 129 B1
Oaklands Gr PO8 111 C2
Oaklands Ho 9 PO6 132 C1
Oaklands RC Comp Sch PO7 134 C3
Oaklands Rd Havant PO9 136 A1
  Petersfield GU32 40 C2
Oaklands The SO53 55 B2
Oaklands Way
  Hythe SO45 125 B1
  Southampton SO16 78 C2
  Titchfield PO14 129 B1
Oaklea Cl PO7 134 A1
Oakleaf Cl SO40 124 C4
Oakleigh Cres SO40 100 C3
Oakleigh Dr SP5 73 B4
Oakleigh Gdns SO51 53 A4
Oakleigh Way BH23 208 C4
Oakley Cl SO45 150 B2
Oakley Gdns BH16 201 A4
Oakley Hill BH21 163 B1
Oakley Ho
  Portsmouth PO5 215 B1
  11 Southampton, Banister's Pk SO15 102 C4
  13 Southampton, Shirley SO16 102 A4
Oakley La BH21 163 C1
Oakley Rd Havant PO9 135 B3
  Mottisfont SO51 5 C2
  Southampton SO16 102 A4
  Wimborne Minst BH21 163 B1
Oakley Straight BH21 163 C1
Oakmead Coll of Tech BH11 188 C2
Oakmead Gdns BH11 188 C2
Oakmead Rd BH17 201 C4
Oakmeadow Cl PO10 137 A2
Oakmount Ave
  Chandler's Ford SO53 55 B2
  Southampton SO17 79 A1
  Totton SO40 100 C4
Oakmount Dr PO8 111 C1
Oakmount Mans SO17 78 C1
Oakmount Rd SO53 55 C3
Oakridge Rd SO15 101 B4
Oaks Coppice PO8 112 A3
Oaks Dr BH24 139 B2
Oaks Mead BH31 115 A3
Oaks The Bursledon SO31 127 C4
  Southampton SO19 103 C3
  Verwood BH31 114 C4
  Waterlooville PO8 112 A1
Oakshott Dr PO9 136 A3
Oakthorn Cl PO13 180 B3
Oaktree Ct
  Milford on Sea SO41 211 B2
  Southampton SO16 78 C2
Oaktree Cvn Pk SO30 80 B2
Oaktree Par BH23 169 A1
Oakum Ho PO3 183 A3
Oakville Mans 11 SO15 102 C3
Oakwood BH3 204 C4
Oakwood Ave
  Havant PO9 135 A2
  New Milton BH25 195 B2
  Otterbourne SO21 31 B2
Oakwood Cl
  Bournemouth BH9 190 A1
  Chandler's Ford SO53 30 B1
  Locks Heath SO31 152 B4
  Otterbourne SO21 31 B2
  Romsey SO51 28 B1
Oakwood Ct
  Chandler's Ford SO53 30 B1
  New Milton BH25 195 B2
  West End SO30 80 C1
Oakwood Ctr The PO9 136 A2
Oakwood Dr SO16 78 B3
Oakwood Ho SO21 31 B2
Oakwood Inf Sch SO16 78 A3
Oakwood Jun Sch SO16 78 A3
Oakwood Lodge SO21 31 B2
Oakwood Rd
  Bournemouth BH9 190 A1
  Chandler's Ford SO53 55 B4
  Christchurch BH23 193 C1
  Portsmouth PO2 157 C2
  South Hayling PO11 184 C2
Oakwood Way SO31 128 A2
Oasis Mews BH16 201 A4
Oasis The 12 BH12 204 A2
Oates Rd BH9 189 C1
Oatfield Gdns SO40 76 B1
Oatlands SO51 52 C4
Oatlands Cl SO32 81 C1
Oatlands Rd SO32 81 C1
Oban Rd BH3 204 C4
Obelisk Ct SO19 103 B1
Obelisk Rd SO19 103 C1
Ober Rd SO42 145 C1
Oberfield Rd SO42 145 B1
Oberland Ct SO41 197 B2
Oberon Cl PO7 135 A4
Occupation La PO14 153 C4
Ocean Cl PO15 130 B1
Ocean Ct PO11 184 C2
Ocean Hts 28 BH5 205 C2
Ocean Pk PO3 158 A1
Ocean Rd Gosport PO14 154 C3
  Southampton SO14 103 A1
Ocean Way SO14 103 A1
Ockendon Cl PO5 215 B2
Ocknell Gr SO45 125 B2
Octavia Gdns SO53 55 C4
Octavia Hill SO22 10 B3
Octavia Rd SO18 79 C2
Octavius Ct 5 PO7 112 A1
Odell Cl PO16 130 C2
Odeon Bldgs 10 PO6 157 C4
Odiham Cl
  Chandler's Ford SO53 55 A2
  Southampton SO16 77 C2
Oelander Cl SO31 129 A3
Oglander Rd SO23 2 A1
Ogle Rd SO14 102 C2
OK Mobile Home Pk BH23 208 A4
Okeford Rd BH18 187 B2
Okement Cl SO18 80 A1
Old Agwi Rd SO45 151 B3
Old Barn Cl
  Christchurch BH23 191 B1
  Ringwood BH24 141 B4
Old Barn Cres PO7 86 B1
Old Barn Farm Rd BH21 139 A3
Old Barn Gdns PO8 111 C3
Old Barn Rd BH23 191 B1
Old Bound Rd BH16 201 B3
Old Brickyard Rd SP6 69 A1
Old Bridge Cl SO31 128 A4
Old Bridge House Rd SO31 128 A4
Old Bridge Rd
  Bournemouth BH6 206 B4
  Portsmouth PO4 182 C1
Old Canal 5 PO4 183 A2
Old Christchurch La 35 BH1 204 C2
Old Christchurch Rd
  Bournemouth BH1,BH2 204 C2
  Hordle SO41 196 B1
Old Coastguard Rd BH13 214 A2
Old Comm SO31 129 A2
Old Commercial Rd PO1 182 B4
Old Common Gdns SO31 129 A2
Old Copse Rd PO9 136 A2
Old Cottage Cl SO51 50 C2
Old Court Mews BH14 203 A2
Old Courts The SO16 79 A3
Old Cracknore Cl SO40 102 A1
Old Cricket Mews SO15 102 C4
Old Farm Cl BH24 117 B1
Old Farm Copse SO51 50 C2
Old Farm Dr SO18 79 C2
Old Farm La
  Stubbington PO14 179 B3
  Westbourne PO10 137 B2
Old Farm Rd BH15 202 C3
Old Farm Way PO6 158 C4
Old Farm Wlk SO41 197 B2
Old Farmhouse Mews SO41 197 C3
Old Forge Cl SP6 92 C3
Old Forge Ct SO41 197 B1
Old Forge Rd BH21 164 C3
Old Forge The SO32 107 B4
Old Garden Cl SO31 129 B1
Old Gdns SO22 1 C1
Old Generator Ho The BH12 204 A3
Old Gosport Rd PO16 155 A4
Old Granary The SP5 46 C4
Old Ham La BH21 164 B2
Old Highway Mews BH21 163 B2
Old Hillside Rd SO22 1 B1
Old Infirmary Ho PO1 182 A2
Old Ivy La SO18 80 A1
Old Kennels Cl SO22 10 A2
Old Kennels La SO22 10 A2
Old Kiln Rd BH16 201 B3
Old Lifeboat House (Mus)★ BH15 202 B1
Old Litten La GU32 19 B2
Old London Rd PO2 157 C2
Old Lyndhurst Rd SO40 98 C4
Old Magazine Cl SO40 101 C1
Old Maltings The SO41 197 B2
Old Manor Cl BH21 163 B2
Old Manor Farm PO9 135 A1
Old Manor Way PO6 158 A4
Old Market Rd BH21 186 A4
Old Mill Ho BH24 140 C3
Old Mill La
  Hambledon PO8 87 B2
  Petersfield GU31 41 A3
Old Mill Way SO16 78 A1
Old Milton Gn BH25 194 C1
Old Milton Rd BH25 195 A1
Old Mulberry Cl BH10 189 A1
Old Orch BH15 202 B1
Old Orchards SO41 197 C1
Old Parsonage Ct SO21 31 B2
Old Pines Cl BH22 165 C2
Old Priory Cl SO31 128 A1
Old Priory Rd BH6 206 C2
Old Rd Gosport PO12 181 B2
  Romsey SO51 53 A4
  Southampton SO14 103 A1
  Wimborne Minst BH21 163 A3
Old Rectory Cl
  Corfe Mullen BH21 186 B4
  Westbourne PO10 137 A2
Old Rectory Ct SO40 101 A3
Old Rectory Gdns SO21 2 B3
Old Rectory La SO21 32 A3
Old Rectory Rd PO6 158 C4
Old Redbridge Rd SO15 101 B4
Old Reservoir Rd PO6 158 B4
Old River PO7 110 C2
Old Road The PO6 157 C3
Old Romsey Rd SO40 98 C4
Old Rope Wlk The BH15 201 C1
Old Ropewalk BH15 202 A1
Old Salisbury La SO51 27 A1
Old Salisbury Rd SO51 75 C4
Old Sandpit La BH16 186 A1
Old Sawmill Cl BH31 114 B4
Old School Cl
  Ferndown BH22 165 B3
  Holbury SO45 150 A3
  Netley SO31 127 B4
  Poole BH14 203 A2
Old School Dr PO11 185 A1
Old School Gdns SO30 80 C1
Old School Rd GU33 20 C2
Old Shamblehurst La SO30 81 B1
Old Spring La SO32 84 A3
Old St PO14 154 A2
Old St John's Mews BH9 189 C2
Old Stacks Gdns BH24 141 B3
Old Star Pl 3 PO1 182 A3
Old Station App SO23 11 A4
Old Swanwick La SO31 128 B4
Old Timbers PO11 184 C2
Old Town Mews 5 BH15 202 B1
Old Turnpike PO16 131 A2
Old Turnpike Bsns Pk PO16 131 A1
Old Van Diemans Rd PO7 134 B3
Old Vicarage Cl BH10 189 C3
Old Vicarage La SO41 196 B4
Old Vineries The SP6 69 B1
Old Wareham Rd
  Corfe Mullen BH21 186 A2
  Poole BH12 203 A4
Old Well Cl The SO19 104 B2
Old Winchester Hill La
  Warnford SO32, GU32 37 A1
  West Meon GU32 37 B1
Old Winchester Hill Nature Reserve★ SO32 62 B3
Old Winchester Hill Nature Trail★ GU32 62 B3
Old Wymering La PO6 157 C4
Oldbarn Cl SO40 76 B1
Oldbury Ct SO16 77 B1
Oldbury Ho 6 PO5 215 B2
Oldbury Way PO14 154 B4
Oldenburg SO31 129 A4
Oldgate Gdns 8 PO2 157 C2
Oleander Dr SO40 100 A4
Olinda St PO1 182 C3
Olive Cres PO16 156 B3
Olive Ct PO2 182 C4
Olive Rd SO16 78 A2
Oliver Rd Lymington SO41 197 B2
  Portsmouth PO4 183 A2
  Southampton SO18 79 B2
Oliver's Battery Cres SO22 10 A2
Oliver's Battery Gdns SO22 10 A2
Oliver's Battery Prim Sch SO22 10 B2
Oliver's Battery Rd N SO22 10 A3
Oliver's Battery Rd S SO22 10 A2
Olivers Cl SO40 100 A4
Olivers Rd BH21 164 A3
Olivers Way BH21 164 A3
Olivia Cl 3 PO7 112 A1
Olympic Way SO50 57 A1
Omdurman Ct 2 SO17 79 A1
Omdurman Rd SO17 79 A1
Omega Ho PO1 215 C3
Omega St PO1 215 C3
Onibury Cl SO18 80 A1
Onibury Rd SO18 80 A1
Onslow Gdns BH21 163 B3
Onslow Ho BH21 163 B3
Onslow Rd
  Portsmouth PO5 182 B1
  Southampton SO14 103 A3
Ophir Gdns 1 BH8 205 B3
Ophir Rd
  Bournemouth BH8 205 A3
  Portsmouth PO2 157 C2
Oracle Dr PO7 134 C2
Orange Gr PO13 155 B1
Orange Row PO10 160 C4
Oratory Gdns BH13 214 C4
Orchard Ave
  Bishopstoke SO50 56 C1
  Poole BH14 202 C1
Orchard Bglws PO17 109 A1
Orchard Cl
  Christchurch BH23 207 A3
  Colden Common SO21 31 C1
Orchard Cl *continued*
  Corfe Mullen BH21 186 B4
  Edmondsham BH21 91 A2
  Fawley SO45 151 A2
  Ferndown BH22 165 C3
  Fordingbridge SP6 69 C1
  Gosport PO12 156 A1
  Horndean PO8 112 B3
  North Baddesley SO52 53 C3
  Ringwood BH24 141 A4
  South Hayling PO11 184 C1
  Totton SO40 100 C3
Orchard Ct Cadnam SO40 98 C4
  Hedge End SO30 105 C4
  10 New Milton BH25 195 A2
  Verwood BH31 115 A3
Orchard Cvn Pk The SO40 99 B3
Orchard Gdns SP6 69 C1
Orchard Gr
  New Milton BH25 195 A1
  Portchester PO16 156 A4
  Waterlooville PO8 111 C2
Orchard Ho 13 SO14 103 A2
Orchard Inf Sch SO45 125 C1
Orchard Jun Sch SO45 125 C2
Orchard La
  Corfe Mullen BH21 186 B4
  Hermitage PO10 161 A4
  Romsey SO51 52 C4
  Southampton SO14 103 A2
Orchard Lea Inf Sch PO15 130 C2
Orchard Lea Jun Sch PO15 130 C2
Orchard Leigh 6 BH25 195 A1
Orchard Mead 5 BH24 141 A4
Orchard Mews 2 BH23 207 A3
Orchard Mount 6 BH24 141 A4
Orchard Pl SO14 103 A2
Orchard Rd Fair Oak SO50 57 B1
  Gosport PO12 181 B3
  Havant PO9 159 C4
  Locks Heath SO31 128 C1
  Portsmouth PO4 182 C2
  Redlynch SP5 47 B3
  South Hayling PO11 185 A1
Orchard St BH2 204 C2
Orchard The
  Bournemouth BH11 188 B3
  Bransgore BH23 193 B4
  Chilworth SO16 54 C1
  Cosham PO6 157 C4
  Denmead PO7 110 C2
  Milford on Sea SO41 211 B2
  Southampton SO16 79 A3
Orchard Way SO45 125 C1
Orchard Wlk
  22 Bournemouth BH2 204 C2
  Winchester SO22 1 B1
Orchardlea SO32 84 B2
Orchards Way
  Southampton SO17 79 A1
  West End SO30 80 B1
Orcheston Rd BH8 205 B3
Orchid Way BH23 207 B4
Ordnance Ct PO3 158 A3
Ordnance Rd
  Gosport PO12 181 B2
  Southampton SO15 103 A3
Ordnance Row PO1 182 A3
Ordnance Way SO40 102 A2
Oregon Cl SO19 104 A2
Orestes Gate BH23 208 A3
Orford Cl BH23 191 B2
Orford Ct 17 PO6 157 C4
Oriana Way SO16 77 A2
Oriel Dr PO14 129 A1
Oriel Rd PO2 157 B1
Orient Dr SO22 1 B2
Orion Cl
  Southampton SO16 77 C2
  Stubbington PO14 179 B3
Orion Ind Ctr SO18 79 C3
Orkney Cl SO16 77 C2
Orkney Rd PO6 133 C1
Ormesby Dr SO53 30 A1
Ormond Cl SO50 57 A1
Ormonde Rd BH13 204 A1
Ormsby Rd PO5 215 B1
Orpen Rd SO19 104 B2
Orpine Cl PO15 129 C2
Orsmond Cl PO7 134 C3
Orwell Cl SO16 77 C1
Orwell Cres PO14 129 B1
Orwell Rd GU31 40 C1
Osborn Cres PO13 155 A2
Osborn Ct PO3 158 A2
Osborn Mall 6 PO16 131 B1
Osborn Rd PO16 131 A1
Osborn Sq 5 PO16 131 B1
Osborne Cl Netley SO31 127 B3
  3 Waterlooville PO7 135 A4
Osborne Ct
  7 Milford on Sea SO41 211 B2
  Southampton SO17 79 B1
Osborne Dr SO53 55 C3
Osborne Gdns
  Fair Oak SO50 57 C1
  Southampton SO17 79 B1
Osborne Ho
  Southampton SO14 103 A2
  West Wellow SO51 50 C2
Osborne Rd
  Bournemouth BH9 204 C4
  Lee-on-the-Solent PO13 179 C1
  Locks Heath SO31 152 B4
  New Milton BH25 195 A2
Osborne Rd *continued*
  Petersfield GU32 40 C2
  Poole BH14 203 A2
  Portsmouth PO5 182 B1
  Totton SO40 101 A4
  Wimborne Minst BH21 163 B2
Osborne Rd N SO17 79 B1
Osborne Rd S
  Fareham PO16 131 A1
  Southampton SO17 103 B4
Osborne View Rd PO14 179 A3
Osbourne Ho 4 BH25 195 A2
Osbourne Rd PO12 181 B3
Osier Cl PO2 157 B2
Osier Rd GU31 40 B1
Oslands La SO31 128 B4
Oslo Twrs 4 SO19 126 C4
Osprey Cl
  Christchurch BH23 208 A3
  Cosham PO6 158 C4
  Marchwood SO40 101 C1
  Southampton SO16 78 A3
Osprey Ct PO16 155 C4
Osprey Dr PO11 185 A2
Osprey Gdns PO13 179 C1
Osprey Quay PO10 161 A4
Ossemsley Manor Ho BH23 194 B3
Ossemsley South Dr BH25 194 C4
Osterley Cl SO30 105 C3
Osterly Rd SO19 103 C3
Oswald Cl BH9 189 C1
Oswald Rd BH9 189 C1
Othello Dr PO7 135 A4
Otter Cl Bishopstoke SO50 57 A1
  Gosport PO13 180 B3
  Upton BH16 201 A3
  Verwood BH31 115 A3
Otter Rd BH15 202 C3
Otterbourne CE Prim Sch SO21 31 A1
Otterbourne Cres PO9 135 B3
Otterbourne Hill SO21 31 B2
Otterbourne Ho SO21 31 A1
Otterbourne House Gdns SO21 31 A1
Otterbourne Rd SO21 31 B3
Otters Wlk BH25 195 B3
Ouse Cl SO53 55 A4
Outer Circ SO16 78 A2
Outlands La SO30 106 B4
Outram Rd PO5 215 C1
Outwick Cross SP6 69 C4
Oval Gdns PO12 180 C2
Oval Rd SO51 5 A1
Oval The GU33 20 C2
Over Links Dr BH14 203 B1
Overbrook SO45 125 C2
Overbrook Way SO52 53 C3
Overbury Rd BH14 203 B2
Overcliff Rise SO16 78 C2
Overcliffe Mans BH1 205 B2
Overcombe Cl BH17 187 C1
Overdell Ct 25 SO15 102 C4
Overstrand Cres SO41 211 B2
Overton Cres PO9 135 B3
Overton Rd PO10 137 C1
Oviat Cl SO40 100 A4
Ovington Ave BH7 206 B4
Ovington Ct SO18 104 B4
Ovington Gdns BH7 206 B4
Ovington Rd SO50 56 A1
Owen Cl PO13 180 B4
Owen Rd SO50 55 C1
Owen St PO4 183 A1
Owen's Rd SO22 1 C1
Ower La SO45 178 C4
Owls Rd
  Bournemouth BH5 205 C2
  Verwood BH31 115 A3
Owlshotts BH13 214 C4
Owslebury Bottom SO21 33 A3
Owslebury Gr PO9 135 C3
Owslebury Prim Sch SO21 33 A2
Oxburgh Cl SO50 55 C3
Oxenwood Gn 7 PO9 135 B3
Oxey Cl BH25 195 A1
Oxford Ave
  Bournemouth BH6 206 A3
  Southampton SO14 103 A3
Oxford Cl PO16 131 A1
Oxford La
  Bournemouth BH11 189 A3
  Swanmore SO32 84 C4
Oxford Rd
  Bournemouth BH1 205 A2
  Gosport PO12 180 C3
  Portsmouth PO5 215 D1
  Southampton SO14 103 A4
Oxford St SO14 103 A2
Oxford Terr SO41 172 A1
Oxlease Cl SO51 28 A1
Oxleys Cl PO14 154 A4
Oxted Ct 9 PO4 183 A3
Oyster Ct PO13 179 B2
Oyster Est The PO6 158 B3
Oyster Mews
  5 Emsworth PO10 160 C4
  13 Portsmouth PO1 182 A2
Oyster Quay PO6 157 A4
Oyster St PO1 182 A2
Ozier Rd SO18 80 A1

acific Cl SO14 103 B1
ackridge La SO51,SO52 53 C1
adbury Cl PO2 157 C2
addington Cl BH11 188 B2
addington Gr BH11 188 B2
addington Rd PO2 157 C1
addock Cl
erndown BH21 165 A3
t Leonards BH24 139 C2
addock End PO7 110 C2
addock Gdns SO41 197 B3
addock Gr BH31 115 A3
addock The
rockenhurst SO42 145 C1
astleigh SO50 56 A3
ordingbridge SP6 94 C3
osport PO12 181 A2
ings Worthy SO23 2 B3
tubbington PO14 154 B2
otton SO40 76 B1
addock Way GU32 40 B1
addock Wlk PO6 157 A4
addocks Cl BH12 203 A4
addocks The
ournemouth BH10 189 B2
awley SO45 151 A2
adfield Cl BH6 206 C3
adget Rd BH24 117 B1
adnell Ave PO8 112 A1
adnell Inf Sch PO8 112 A2
adnell Jun Sch PO8 112 A2
adnell Pl PO8 112 A1
adnell Rd PO8 112 A2
adstow Pl SP6 93 C4
adwell Rd SO14 103 A4
adwick Ave PO6 158 A4
adwick Ct PO11 184 C2
affard Cl PO13 180 B4
age Cl SO45 150 B1
ages La SO42 175 B3
aget Cl BH21 164 A4
aget Rd
ournemouth BH11 189 A2
osport PO12 181 A1
aget St SO14 103 A2
agham Cl PO10 161 A4
agham Gdns PO11 185 C1
aignton Ave PO3 183 A4
aignton Rd SO16 77 C1
aimpol Pl SO51 52 C3
ain's Rd PO5 215 C2
ainswick Cl
Cosham PO6 157 B4
ocks Heath SO31 128 C3
ainter Cl PO3 158 A2
ainters Field SO23 10 C2
aisley Rd BH6 206 B3
alace Ho★ SO42 148 C1
alace La SO42 148 C1
alace Mews SO32 83 B4
alfrey Rd BH10 189 B3
aling Bsns Pk SO30 105 A2
alk Rd PO9 135 B1
allant Gdns PO16 131 B1
allant The PO9 135 C1
allet Cl SO21 56 C4
allot Cl SO31 104 C1
alm Ct 16 PO5 182 B1
alm Hall Cl SO23 11 B4
alm Rd SO16 78 A2
alma Ct BH23 209 A4
almer Pl BH25 195 A2
almer Rd BH15 202 B3
almer's Rd PO10 136 C1
almers Cl SO50 57 B1
almerston Ave
Christchurch BH23 207 B3
Fareham PO16 131 A1
almerston Bsns Pk
PO14 155 A4
almerston Cl BH16 201 B4
almerston Ct 2 SO22,
SO23 10 C3
almerston Dr PO14 155 A4
almerston Mans 28
PO5 182 B1
almerston Rd
Bournemouth BH1 205 C3
Poole BH14 203 B2
Portsmouth PO5 182 B1
South Hayling PO11 185 A2
Southampton SO14 103 A2
Upton BH16 201 B4
almerston Road Prec 29
PO5 182 B1
almerston St SO51 52 C4
almerston Way PO12 180 C1
almyra Rd PO12 181 A4
alomino Dr PO15 129 A4
amphill CE Fst Sch
BH21 162 C3
amplyn Cl SO41 197 B2
an St PO1 215 B4
angbourne Ave PO6 158 A4
angbourne Cl SO19 104 A2
annall Rd PO12 181 A4
anorama Ct 2 PO13 179 C1
anorama Rd BH13 214 A2
ans Cnr BH22 165 C2
ansy Rd SO16 79 A2
antheon Rd SO53 55 C4
antiles The SP6 69 B1
anton Cl PO10 136 C2
anwell Rd SO18 104 A4
arade Ct PO2 157 C3

Parade The
Barton on Sea BH25 194 C1
5 Bournemouth BH6 206 C2
Cadnam SO40 98 C4
Gosport PO13 155 A2
New Milton BH25 195 B2
Poole BH17 187 A1
Portsmouth PO1 182 A3
Paradise La
Bishop's Waltham SO32 83 C3
Netley Marsh SO40 99 B3
Portchester PO16 131 C1
Westbourne PO10 137 A2
Paradise St
17 Poole BH15 202 A1
Portsmouth PO1 215 B4
Parchment St SO23 11 A4
Parchment The PO9 135 C1
Pardoe Cl SO30 105 B3
Pardys Hill BH21 186 B4
Parham Cl BH25 194 C2
Parham Dr SO50 55 C2
Parham Rd
Bournemouth BH10 189 B1
Gosport PO12 181 B3
Parish Ct SO41 197 C2
Parish Rd BH15 202 C2
Park Ave
Bournemouth BH10 189 B3
Lymington SO41 197 B2
Waterlooville PO7 134 B2
Winchester SO23 11 A4
Park Cl
Brockenhurst SO42 146 A1
Burton BH23 192 B2
Gosport PO12 180 C3
Hythe SO45 126 A2
Lyndhurst SO43 122 A2
Marchwood SO40 101 B1
Milford on Sea SO41 211 C2
New Milton BH25 195 B3
Winchester SO23 2 A1
Park Com Sch PO9 135 B3
Park Cotts PO17 108 A2
Park Court Flats 3
SO15 102 B3
Park Cres PO10 136 B1
Park Ct
14 Milford on Sea SO41 211 B2
North Baddesley SO51 53 B3
12 Petersfield GU32 40 C2
Portsmouth PO5 215 B1
1 Winchester SO23 2 A1
Park Dr BH31 114 C4
Park Farm Ave PO15 130 B2
Park Farm Cl PO15 130 B2
Park Farm Rd PO7 134 B2
Park Gate Bsns Ctr
SO31 129 A3
Park Gate Mews 14
BH2 204 C2
Park Gate Prim Sch
SO31 129 A2
Park Gdns BH23 207 C4
Park Glen SO31 129 B2
Park Gr PO6 157 C4
Park Hill Cl SO45 150 B2
Park Ho
22 Portsmouth PO5 182 B1
Winchester SO23 11 A4
Park Homer Dr BH21 164 A3
Park Homer Rd BH21 163 C3
Park House Farm Way
PO9 135 B3
Park House Prim Sch
PO9 135 B3
Park La Alderholt SP6 92 C3
Beaulieu SO41 200 A4
Bournemouth BH10 189 C2
Cosham PO6 158 A4
Droxford SO32 61 A1
Fareham PO16 131 A1
Havant PO7,PO9 135 B4
Havant PO9 135 B2
Holbury SO45 150 A2
Kings Worthy SO21 2 B3
Marchwood SO40 101 B1
Milford on Sea SO41 211 B2
Otterbourne SO21 31 A1
Rowland's Castle PO10 137 B4
Stubbington PO14 154 B2
Swanmore SO32 60 B1
Twyford SO21 32 A3
Waterlooville PO8 112 A1
Wimborne Minst BH21 163 B2
Park Lane Rd BH15 202 C1
Park Mans 3 PO6 158 A4
Park Par PO9 135 C2
Park Pl BH14 202 C2
Park Rd
Barton on Sea BH25 194 C1
Bishop's Waltham SO32 83 A4
Bournemouth BH8 205 A3
Chandler's Ford SO53 55 B4
Denmead PO7 110 C3
Fordingbridge SP6 69 C1
Gosport PO12 181 A2
Lymington SO41 197 B2
Milford on Sea SO41 211 C2
New Milton BH25 195 B3
21 Petersfield GU31 40 C2
Poole BH14 202 C2
Portsmouth PO1 182 A3
South Hayling PO11 184 B2
Southampton SO15 102 B3
Southbourne PO10 137 B1
Waterlooville PO7 134 B2
Winchester SO22,SO23 1 C1

Park Rd N PO9 135 C1
Park Rd S PO9 135 C1
Park Royal 17 PO2 157 C2
Park St Gosport PO12 181 A3
Portsmouth PO5 215 A2
Southampton SO15, SO16 102 A4
Park Terr 10 PO12 181 B2
Park The
Barton on Sea BH25 209 B4
Droxford SO32 61 A1
Park View Botley SO30 106 A4
Compton (Hants) SO21 31 C3
Hedge End SO30 105 A4
Lockerley SO21 4 C2
New Milton BH25 195 A1
Otterbourne SO21 31 A1
9 Poole BH15 202 C2
Portsmouth PO2 157 B2
Rowland's Castle PO9 136 A4
Park View Mews BH25 195 A1
Park Villas SO32 61 A1
Park Vista GU32 38 B1
Park Way Fair Oak SO50 57 C1
Havant PO9 135 C1
West Moors BH22 138 C1
Park Wlk Fareham PO15 130 B2
Southampton SO14 103 A3
Parker Cl PO12 156 A1
Parker Gdns PO7 134 B1
Parker Rd BH9 204 C4
Parkers Cl BH24 117 B1
Parkfield Ho 11 PO6 132 C1
Parkland Cl BH31 115 B2
Parkland Dr BH25 209 C4
Parkland Pl
New Milton BH25 195 A1
15 Southampton SO17 103 A4
Parklands
Locks Heath SO31 129 A2
6 Southampton SO18 79 C1
Totton SO40 101 A4
Parklands Ave PO8 112 A3
Parklands Bsns Pk PO7 110 C2
Parklands Cl
Chandler's Ford SO53 55 B4
Gosport PO12 181 A3
Parkside
Christchurch BH23 193 B1
Havant PO9 135 B1
Ringwood BH24 141 A3
Totton SO40 100 C3
Parkside Ave SO16 101 B4
Parkside Gdns
Bournemouth BH10 189 C1
Winchester SO22 1 B1
Parkside Rd BH14 203 B2
Parkside The SO15 102 A4
Parkstone Ave
Poole BH14 203 B2
Portsmouth PO4 182 C1
Parkstone Gram Sch
BH17 187 A1
Parkstone Hts
Poole BH14 202 C3
Poole BH14 203 A3
Parkstone Rd BH15 202 C2
Parkstone Sta BH14 203 A2
Parkview BH2 204 C2
Parkville Rd SO16 79 B2
Parkway PO15 129 C4
Parkway Dr BH8 205 C4
Parkway Gdns SO53 55 B4
Parkway The
Gosport PO13 155 A1
Southampton SO16 79 A3
Parkwood Cl SO30 105 B4
Parkwood Ctr PO7 134 C4
Parkwood La 14 BH5 206 A3
Parkwood Rd
Bournemouth BH5 206 A2
Wimborne Minst BH21 163 B2
Parley Cl BH22 165 C1
Parley Cross BH22 189 C4
Parley Fst Sch BH22 165 B2
Parley La BH23 190 B4
Parley Rd BH9 190 A1
Parliament Pl SO22 10 B2
Parmiter Dr BH21 163 C2
Parmiter Ho 42 SO23 11 A4
Parmiter Rd BH21 163 C2
Parmiter Way BH21 163 C2
Parnell Rd SO50 55 C1
Parnholt Rd SO51 7 C2
Parr Ho 5 BH14 203 A2
Parr Rd PO6 157 B4
Parr St BH14 203 A2
Parry Cl PO6 156 C4
Parry Rd SO19 104 B2
Parsonage Barn La
BH24 141 A4
Parsonage Cl
Fordingbridge SP6 69 C1
Petersfield GU32 41 A3
Parsonage Ct 9 BH8 205 A3
Parsonage La SO32 82 A3
Parsonage Park Dr SP6 69 C1
Parsonage Rd
Bournemouth BH1 205 A2
Southampton SO14 103 B3
Parsons Cl PO3 157 C2
Partridge Cl
Christchurch BH23 208 A3
Portchester PO16 155 C4
Partridge Down SO22 10 A2
Partridge Dr BH14 203 B1
Partridge Gdns PO8 111 B2
Partridge Gr BH25 195 A3
Partridge Hill SP5 50 A2

Partridge Rd
Brockenhurst SO42 172 C4
Hythe SO45 125 C1
Partridge Wlk BH14 203 A1
Partry Cl SO53 55 A4
Pascoe Cl BH14 203 A2
Passage La SO31 128 A1
Passfield Ave SO50 55 C1
Passfield Cl SO50 55 C1
Passfield Wlk 40 PO9 136 A3
Passingham Wlk PO8 112 A2
Pastures The
Cheriton SO24 14 B3
Denmead PO7 110 C2
Locks Heath PO14 129 B2
Pat Bear Cl SO15 101 B4
Patchins Rd BH16 201 A2
Patchins The BH14 214 B4
Patchway Dr PO14 154 B4
Paternoster Ho 37 SO23 11 A4
Paternoster Row 36
SO23 11 A4
Patricia Cl SO30 80 B1
Patricia Dr SO30 105 B4
Patrick Howard- Dobson Ct
6 PO8 111 C2
Patrick's Cl GU33 21 A2
Patrick's Copse Rd GU33 21 A2
Paulet Cl SO18 80 A1
Paulet Lecave Ave SO16 77 B3
Paulet Pl SO22 10 C3
Pauletts La SO40 76 A2
Pauls La SO41 196 C4
Paulsgrove Ent Ctr PO6 157 A4
Paulsgrove Ind Ctr PO6 157 A4
Paulsgrove Prim Sch
PO6 157 B4
Paulsgrove Rd PO2 182 C4
Paulson Cl SO53 55 B4
Paultons Pk★ SO51 75 B3
Pauncefoot Hill SO51 52 B3
Pauncefote Rd BH5 206 A3
Pauntley Rd BH23 207 C3
Pavan Gdns BH10 189 B1
Pavilion Cl SO50 81 B4
Pavilion Ct 20 SO15 102 C4
Pavilion Rd SO30 105 B4
Paxton Cl SO30 105 B3
Paxton Rd PO14 155 A4
Payne Cl BH22 138 C3
Payne's La SO50 57 B2
Payne's Rd SO15 102 B3
Paynes Hay Rd SO51 28 B4
Peace Cl BH23 193 A4
Peach Rd SO16 78 A2
Peacock Cl PO16 155 C4
Peacock La PO1 182 A2
Peacock Pl 5 SO23 11 B4
Peak Cl SO16 101 C4
Peak Dr PO14 154 B4
Peak La
Bishop's Waltham SO32 59 A2
Fareham PO14 154 B4
Peak Rd PO8 88 A3
Peak The PO9 113 B1
Peake New Rd SO32 61 C4
Peakfield PO7 110 C2
Pealsham Gdns SP6 69 C1
Pear Cl BH12 204 A2
Pear Tree Cl
Alderholt SP6 92 C3
Botley SO32 81 C1
Bransgore BH23 193 A4
Pear Tree Dr SP5 73 B4
Pearce Ave BH14 203 A1
Pearce Ct PO12 181 B3
Pearce Gdns BH14 203 A1
Pearce Rd BH16 201 A3
Pearce-Smith Ct BH25 209 C4
Pearl Gdns BH10 189 B2
Pearl Rd BH10 189 B2
Pearmain Dr 4 SO41 197 C1
Pearman Ct SO41 197 B1
Pearson Ave BH14 203 A3
Pearson Gdns BH10 189 B3
Peartree Ave SO19 103 C3
Peartree Cl
Southampton SO19 103 B2
Stubbington PO14 154 B2
West Wellow SO51 50 B2
Peartree Ct
5 Lymington SO41 197 C1
Southampton SO19 103 C2
Peartree Rd Hythe SO45 125 C1
Southampton SO19 103 B2
Pebble Cl PO11 185 A1
Pebble Ct
Marchwood SO40 101 C1
South Hayling PO11 185 B1
Pebmarsh Rd 8 PO6 157 B4
Peckham Ave BH25 195 A1
Pedham Cl PO4 183 A2
Pedlars Wlk BH24 140 C4
Pedula Way SO50 56 C3
Peeks Mews BH6 206 C3
Peel Cl Poole BH12 203 B3
Romsey SO51 28 B1
Peel Common Jun & Inf Schs
PO13 155 A1
Peel Pl PO5 215 B2
Peel Rd PO12 181 B2
Peel St SO14 103 B3
Peewit Hill SO31 105 A2
Peewit Hill Cl SO31 105 A2
Pegasus Ave SO41 196 A1
Pegasus Cl Gosport PO13 180 B3
Hamble-le-Rice SO31 127 C1
Southampton SO16 77 C2

Pegasus Ct
Bournemouth BH1 205 A3
8 New Milton BH25 195 A2
Pegasus Lodge BH22 165 B3
Peggotty Ho 17 PO1 182 B4
Pegham Ind Pk PO15 130 A3
Pelham Cl BH23 207 B3
Pelham Rd Gosport PO12 181 A3
Portsmouth PO5 215 B1
Pelham Terr 2 PO10 161 A4
Pelican Cl PO15 130 B1
Pelican Ct SO21 30 A4
Pelican Mead BH24 141 B3
Pelican Rd PO14 154 C3
Pembers Cl SO50 57 B1
Pemberton Rd SO43 122 A3
Pembrey Cl SO16 78 A3
Pembridge Rd SP6 70 A1
Pembroke Cl
Eastleigh SO50 55 C3
Portsmouth PO1 182 A2
Romsey SO51 52 C4
Totton SO40 101 A4
Pembroke Cres PO14 179 A3
Pembroke Ct
11 Christchurch BH23 209 A4
5 Gosport PO13 155 B1
Southampton SO17 79 A1
Pembroke Rd
Bournemouth BH4 204 A1
Poole BH12 203 B4
Portsmouth PO1 182 A2
Southampton SO19 104 A2
Pembury Rd Havant PO9 160 A4
Stubbington PO14 154 B2
Pemerton Rd SO22 1 B2
Penarth Ave PO6 158 A4
Pencraig BH13 204 A2
Pendennis Rd PO6 132 C1
Pendle Cl SO16 101 C4
Pendle Gn SO51 4 C1
Pendleton Gdns SO45 150 C1
Penelope Ct 18 BH23 209 A4
Penelope Gdns SO31 104 C1
Penfords Paddock 9
SO32 83 B4
Pengelly Ave BH10 189 C3
Penhale Gdns PO14 129 A1
Penhale Inf Sch PO1 182 C3
Penhale Rd PO1 182 C3
Penhale Way SO40 100 C3
Penhurst Rd PO9 135 A1
Peninsula Rd SO22 10 C4
Peninsula Sq SO23 10 C4
Penistone Cl SO19 104 A1
Penjar Ave PO7 134 B2
Penk Ridge PO9 158 C4
Penn Cl BH25 194 C1
Penn Ct BH22 138 B1
Penn Hill Ave BH14 203 B2
Penn Way PO12 180 C2
Pennant Hills PO9 135 A1
Pennant Pk PO16 131 B2
Pennant Way BH23 207 C4
Pennard Way SO53 55 A2
Penner Rd PO9 159 C4
Pennerley Ct PO9 135 B4
Pennine Ct 8 BH23 207 C4
Pennine Gdns SO45 125 B1
Pennine Ho SO16 101 C4
Pennine Rd SO16 101 C4
Pennine Way
Chandler's Ford SO53 55 B2
Lee-on-the-Solent PO13 180 A2
Verwood BH31 114 C3
Pennine Wlk PO14 154 C4
Pennington CE Jun Sch
SO41 197 B2
Pennington Cl
Colden Common SO21 56 C4
Lymington SO41 197 B1
West Moors BH22 138 B1
Pennington Cres BH22 138 B1
Pennington Cross SO41 197 B1
Pennington Inf Sch
SO41 197 B2
Pennington Oval SO41 197 A1
Pennington Rd BH22 138 B1
Pennington Way PO15 130 B2
Penns Rd GU32 40 C2
Penny Hedge BH25 210 A4
Penny La
6 Bournemouth BH7 205 C2
Hermitage PO10 161 A4
Penny Pl PO7 134 C2
Penny St PO1 182 A2
Penny Way BH23 208 B3
Penny's Cl SP6 69 C2
Penny's Cnr SO41 195 C2
Penny's Cres SP6 69 C2
Penny's Ct BH22 165 B3
Penny's Wlk BH22 165 B3
Pennycress SO31 128 C1
Pennys La SP6 69 C2
Pennywell Gdns BH25 195 B2
Penrhyn Ave PO6 158 A4
Penrhyn Cl SO50 55 C3
Penrith Cl BH31 114 C3
Penrith Ct SO16 101 C4
Penrith Rd BH5 206 A2
Penrose Cl 11 PO2 157 B1
Penrose Rd BH22 165 B3
Penshurst Way SO50 56 A3
Pentagon The SO45 151 A1
Pentere Rd PO8 112 A3

Pentire Ave SO15 78 B1
Pentire Way SO15 78 B1
Pentland Cl SO45 125 B1
Pentland Rise PO16 132 B1
Penton Ct PO9 136 A3
Penton Pl 8 SO23 11 A3
Penton Rd SO21 32 A4
Pentons Hill SP6 94 B3
Pentridge Way SO40 100 C3
Penwood Gn 34 PO9 136 A3
Peper Harow PO8 112 A3
Peppard Cl SO18 104 A4
Peppercorn Way SO30 81 B2
Pepys Ave SO19 104 B3
Pepys Cl Gosport PO12 181 A1
Portsmouth PO4 182 C2
Percival Rd PO2 182 C4
Percivale Rd SO53 54 C2
Percy Chandler St PO1 215 C4
Percy Cl SO45 125 C3
Percy Rd
Bournemouth BH5 205 C2
Gosport PO12 181 B2
Portsmouth PO4 182 C2
Southampton SO16 102 A4
Peregrine Cl SO40 100 B3
Peregrine Rd BH23 208 A3
Peregrines The PO16 155 C4
Pergin Cres BH17 202 A4
Pergin Way BH17 202 A4
Pern Dr SO30 106 A4
Peronne Cl PO3 157 C3
Peronne Rd PO3 157 C3
Perran Rd SO16 77 B1
Perry Gdns BH15 202 B1
Perry's Ct SO40 102 A1
Perryfield Gdns BH7 206 A4
Perrywood Cl SO45 150 B2
Perrywood Gdns SO40 100 A4
Perseus Pl PO7 134 C2
Perseus Terr PO1 182 A2
Pershore Cl SO31 129 A2
Persian Dr PO15 129 A4
Persley Rd BH10 189 C2
Perth Cl BH23 191 C1
Perth Ho PO1 215 C3
Perth Rd Gosport PO13 155 B2
Portsmouth PO4 183 A2
Pervin Rd PO6 157 C4
Peststead La SO32 85 B2
Peter Ashley Activity Ctr
PO6 134 B1
Peter Ashley Rd PO6 134 B1
Peter Grant Way BH22 165 B3
Peter Symonds' Coll SO22 1 C1
Peterborough Ct PO13 180 B3
Peterborough Rd
Cosham PO6 133 C1
Southampton SO14 103 A4
Peters Cl
Locks Heath SO31 128 C2
Upton BH16 201 B3
Peters Rd
Ferndown BH22 165 C2
Locks Heath SO31 128 C2
Peterscroft Ave SO40 100 A1
Petersfield Bsns Pk
GU32 40 B2
Petersfield Ho PO1 215 C4
Petersfield Hospl GU32 40 C2
Petersfield Inf Sch GU32 40 C2
Petersfield Pl BH7 206 A4
Petersfield Rd
Bournemouth BH7 206 A4
Buriton GU31 65 B3
Cheriton SO24 14 B2
Clanfield PO8 88 B4
Havant PO9 136 A3
Winchester SO21, SO23 11 B4
Petersfield Sch The
GU32 40 C1
Petersfield Sta GU32 40 C2
Petersgate Inf Sch PO8 88 B2
Petersham Rd BH17 202 A4
Petit Rd BH9 190 A2
Petrel Wlk PO13 155 A1
Petrie Rd PO13 179 C1
Petticoat La SP5 47 C4
Pettinger Gdns SO17 103 B4
Petty Cl SO51 53 A3
Pettycot Cres PO13 155 A2
Petworth Gdns
Eastleigh SO50 56 A3
Southampton SO16 78 B3
Petworth Rd PO3 183 A3
Petwyn Cl BH22 166 A3
Pevensey Cl SO16 77 B1
Peverell Rd BH16 201 A2
Peverells Rd SO53 55 C4
Peverells Wood Ave
SO53 55 C4
Peverells Wood Cl SO53 55 C3
Peveril Cl BH24 139 C3
Peveril Rd SO19 103 C2
Pewsey Pl SO15 78 B1
Phelipps Rd BH21 186 C3
Philip Rd PO7 134 C3
Phillimore Rd SO16 79 B2
Phillips Cl SO16 77 C3
Philpott Dr SO40 101 C1
Phoenix Bldgs PO3 158 A1
Phoenix Cl SO31 105 A1
Phoenix Pk SO50 56 B1
Phoenix Pupil Referral Unit
SO45 149 C4
Phoenix Sq PO2 157 C2
Phoenix Way PO13 155 B1
Phyldon Cl BH12 203 A3
Phyldon Rd BH12 203 A3
Pickard Rd BH22 165 C4
Pickering Cl BH18 187 A1
Picket Cl SP6 69 C1
Pickford Rd BH9 189 C1
Pickwick Cl SO40 100 A4
Pickwick Ho 13 PO1 182 B4
Picton Ho 10 PO5 215 B2
Pier Head Rd PO2 157 A1
Pier Rd PO1 182 A2
Pier St PO13 179 C1
Pig Shoot La BH23 190 C3
Pigeon House La PO7 133 B2
Pikes Hill SO43 121 C3
Pikes Hill Ave SO43 121 C3
Pilbrow Ct PO12 180 C2
Pilchards Ave SO50 57 A2
Pilford Heath Rd BH21 164 A4
Pilgrim Park Homes 1
BH24 141 B4
Pilgrim Pl SO18 79 C2
Pilgrim's Cl BH25 195 B2
Pilgrims Cl SO53 55 A3
Pilgrims Gate SO22 1 C1
Pilgrims Sch The SO23 11 A4
Pilgrims Way
Broadstone BH17 202 A4
Stubbington PO14 179 A3
Pill Hill SP5 24 A2
Pilley Bailey SO41 174 A1
Pilley Gn SO41 174 A1
Pilley Hill SO41 173 C1
Pilley St SO41 174 A1
Pilning Cl PO14 154 B4
Pilot Hight Rd BH11 189 A2
Pilsdon Dr BH17 187 C2
Pimpern Cl BH17 187 C1
Pimpernel Cl SO31 128 C1
Pine Ave
Bournemouth BH6 206 B2
Poole BH12 203 C3
Pine Cl Ashurst SO40 100 B2
Barton on Sea BH25 209 C4
Ferndown BH22 165 B4
Hythe SO45 125 C1
Landford SP5 49 B1
North Baddesley SO52 53 C3
Winchester SO22 10 A2
Pine Cotts GU33 21 A4
Pine Cres
Chandler's Ford SO53 30 B1
Christchurch BH23 208 C4
Pine Ct PO10 136 C2
Pine Dr Clanfield PO8 88 B3
Poole BH13 203 C2
Southampton SO18 104 B4
St Leonards BH24 139 C2
Pine Dr E SO18 104 C4
Pine Glen Ave BH22 165 B4
Pine Gr PO9 136 A1
Pine Grange 4 BH1 205 A2
Pine Ho New Milton BH25 195 A2
Southampton SO16 78 C4
Pine Lo 15 BH13 214 C4
Pine Manor Rd BH24 139 B3
Pine Mans 3 BH1 205 B2
Pine Park Mans 16
BH13 204 A2
Pine Rd Alderholt SP6 92 C3
Bishop's Waltham SO32 83 B4
Bournemouth BH9 205 A4
Broadstone BH21 162 C1
Chandler's Ford SO53 55 B4
Romsey SO51 53 B3
Pine Tree Cl BH21 163 B3
Pine Tree Gdns PO8 112 A1
Pine Tree Glen BH4 204 B2
Pine Trees Cl PO14 154 B4
Pine Vale Cres BH10 189 C2
Pine View Cl Redlynch SP5 47 B2
Upton BH16 201 B3
Verwood BH31 114 B4
Pine View Rd BH31 114 B4
Pine Way SO16 78 C4
Pine Wlk Chilworth SO16 78 C4
Liss GU33 21 A3
Locks Heath SO31 129 A3
Verwood BH31 115 A3
West Moors BH22 138 C2
Pinebeach Ct BH13 214 D4
Pinecliff Rd BH13 214 D4
Pinecliffe Ave BH6 206 B2
Pinecliffe Rd BH25 209 B4
Pinefield Rd SO18 79 C1
Pinegrove Rd SO19 103 C2
Pineholt Cl BH24 140 A3
Pinehurst
10 Milford on Sea SO41 211 B2
13 Southampton SO17 79 A1
Pinehurst Ave BH23 207 C3
Pinehurst Cl PO7 112 B1
Pinehurst Rd
Southampton SO16 78 C4
West Moors BH22 138 C1
Pinelands Ct SO16 78 B2
Pinelands Rd SO16 78 C4
Pines The
Fordingbridge SP6 70 B1
Poole BH13 204 A1
Portchester PO16 132 A1
Southampton SO16 78 A2
Pineside BH9 205 A4
Pinesprings Dr BH18 186 C1
Pinetops Cl SO41 197 A2
Pinetree Wlk BH17 201 C4
Pineview Cl SO31 105 A1
Pinewood Gosport PO13 155 C1
Southampton SO16 78 C3
Pinewood Ave
Bournemouth BH10 189 B3
Havant PO9 135 A2
Pinewood Cl
Bournemouth BH10 189 B3
Christchurch BH23 194 A1
Romsey SO51 28 B1
Stubbington PO14 154 B2
Upton BH16 201 A4
Pinewood Cres SO45 126 A1
Pinewood Dr SO45 126 A1
Pinewood Gdns BH22 165 B4
Pinewood Lodge 5
PO16 131 A1
Pinewood Pk SO19 104 C3
Pinewood Rd
Christchurch BH23 193 C1
Ferndown BH22 165 B4
Hordle SO41 195 C2
Poole BH13 204 A1
St Leonards BH24 139 C2
Upton BH16 201 A4
Pink End BH22 165 C2
Pink Rd PO2 182 C4
Pinkney La SO43 121 C2
Pinks Hill PO16 131 B1
Pinsley Dr PO17 133 A3
Pinto Cl PO15 129 B4
Pipers Ash 4 BH24 141 B4
Pipers Cl SO40 100 B3
Pipers Dr BH23 208 A4
Pipers Mead PO8 88 A3
Pipers Wood Ind Est
PO7 134 B4
Piping Cl SO21 56 C4
Piping Gn 6 SO21 56 C4
Piping Rd SO21 56 C4
Pipit Cl Gosport PO12 181 A4
Waterlooville PO8 112 A3
Pippin Cl
Christchurch BH23 191 C1
6 Lymington SO41 197 C1
Pirelli St SO15 102 C2
Pirrie Cl SO15 78 B1
Pit Hill La PO7 86 C1
Pitcairn Mews PO4 183 A1
Pitchponds Rd SO31 152 B4
Pitcot La SO21 33 A2
Pitcroft La GU31 65 C3
Pitcroft Rd PO2 157 B1
Pitmore Cl SO50 56 A4
Pitmore La SO41 172 B1
Pitmore Rd SO50 56 A4
Pitmore Sch SO53 55 C4
Pitreavie Rd PO6 157 C3
Pitt Rd SO15 102 B3
Pitt Rdbt SO22 10 A3
Pitter Cl SO22 1 A3
Pittmore Rd BH23 192 B1
Pitts Deep La SO41 199 B2
Pitts Pl BH25 195 B1
Pitwines Cl BH15 202 B1
Pitymoor La PO17 133 A2
Place Cres PO7 134 C3
Place House Cl PO15 130 B1
Place La SO21 31 C4
Plaitford Gr PO9 135 B3
Plaitford Wlk SO16 77 C1
Plant Park Rd BH24 140 B1
Plantaganet Cres BH11 188 B3
Plantation SO41 211 C4
Plantation Ct
Lymington SO41 197 B2
Poole BH17 187 B1
Plantation Dr
Christchurch BH23 194 A1
Marchwood SO40 101 C1
Plantation Rd
Hill Brow GU33 21 A1
Poole BH17 187 B1
West Wellow SO51 74 B4
Plantation The SO32 82 C1
Plants Cl SO51 51 A1
Plassey Cres BH10 189 B3
Platform Rd SO14 103 A1
Platoff Rd SO41 212 C4
Player Ct SP6 69 C2
Players Cres SO40 100 C3
Playfair Rd PO5 215 C2
Playfields Dr BH12 203 C3
Plaza Mews 15 SO51 52 C4
Pleasance Way BH25 194 C2
Pleasant La PO10 161 B1
Pleasant Rd PO4 183 A2
Plecy Cl BH22 165 B1
Plemont Cl BH12 188 C1
Pless Rd SO41 211 A3
Plough La SO32 85 B1
Plough Way SO22 10 B2
Plover Cl
Southampton SO16 78 A3
Stubbington PO14 179 A3
Plover Dr SO41 211 C2
Plover Rd SO40 100 B4
Plover Reach PO4 183 A3
Plovers Down SO22 10 A2
Plovers Rd PO8 112 A4
PLPH Rd SO45 151 A3
Plumer Rd BH17 187 A1
Plumley Wlk PO9 135 B4
Plumpton Gdns PO3 158 A2
Plumpton Gr 7 PO7 112 A1
Plymouth Dr PO14 154 A2
Plymouth St PO1 215 B2
Pococks La GU33 19 C4
Poets Way SO22 10 B4
Poinsettia Cl PO15 129 C2
Pointout Cl SO16 78 C2
Pointout Rd SO16 78 C2
Pokesdown Com Prim Sch
BH5 206 A3
Pokesdown Sta BH7 206 A3
Poles La Hursley SO21 30 B3
Lymington SO41 197 C1
Otterbourne SO21 31 A3
Police Station La SO32 61 A1
Police Training Ctr
SO31 127 B2
Pollards Moor Rd SO40 75 A1
Pollesden Cl SO53 55 A4
Polygon Ct SO15 102 C3
Polygon Special Sch The
SO15 102 C3
Polygon The SO15 102 C3
Pomona Cl BH22 165 B3
Pompey's Cnr BH21 165 A2
Pompey's La BH22 165 A1
Pond Cl Marchwood SO40 101 C1
New Milton BH25 195 A2
Pond Cotts GU32 39 B1
Pond La PO8 88 A3
Pond Piece PO7 110 C2
Pond Rd SO31 128 C3
Pondhead Cl SO45 150 B2
Pondside Flats SO42 148 C1
Pondside La SO32 83 B4
Ponsonby Ho PO5 215 B2
Ponsonby Rd BH14 203 B2
Pony Dr BH16 201 B4
Pook La Fareham PO17 131 B2
Havant PO9 160 A4
Pooksgreen SO40 101 B1
Pool La Rdbt BH11 188 C2
Poole Aquarium &
Serpentarium★ BH15 202 B1
Poole Commerce Ctr
BH12 203 C3
Poole Gram Sch BH17 187 B1
Poole High Sch BH15 202 B2
Poole Hill BH2 204 C2
Poole Hospl BH15 202 B2
Poole La BH11 189 A3
Poole Rd
Bournemouth BH2,BH4 204 B2
Poole BH12 204 A2
Southampton SO19 103 C2
Upton BH16, BH17 201 B4
Wimborne Minst BH21 163 B2
Poole Sta BH15 202 B2
Popes La Totton SO40 100 C4
Upham SO32 58 B2
Popes Rd BH15 202 B3
Popham Ct PO9 135 B3
Poplar Cl
Bransgore BH23 193 B4
Christchurch BH23 209 A4
6 Poole BH15 202 A1
Wimborne Minst BH21 163 B3
Poplar Cres BH24 141 A4
Poplar Dr Fareham PO14 154 C4
Marchwood SO40 101 B1
Poplar Gr PO11 185 A2
Poplar La BH23 193 B4
Poplar Rd
New Milton BH25 195 B2
Southampton SO19 103 C3
Poplar Way
Hedge End SO30 105 B3
North Baddesley SO52 53 C3
Ringwood BH24 141 A4
Poplars The SO32 83 C2
Poppy Cl
Christchurch BH23 208 B4
Locks Heath SO31 128 C1
Poppy Rd SO16 79 B3
Poppyfields SO53 55 A3
Porchester Ct 12 BH1 205 A3
Porchester Pl BH8 205 A3
Porchester Rd
Bournemouth BH8 205 A3
Southampton SO19 103 C2
Porlock Rd SO16 77 B1
Port La Hursley SO21 30 B4
Winchester SO22 10 A1
Port Royal St PO1 215 C3
Port Way PO6 157 A4
Portal Rd
Bishopstoke SO50 56 B2
Gosport PO13 155 B2
Southampton SO19 104 A2
Totton SO40 100 B4
Winchester SO23 11 A3
Portarlington Cl BH2 204 B1
Portarlington Rd BH4 204 B1
Portchester Boys Sch
BH7 206 A4
Portchester Castle★
PO16 156 C3
Portchester Com Sch
PO16 156 B4
Portchester Hts PO16 132 B1
Portchester La PO17 132 B2
Portchester Rd
Portchester PO16 156 A4
Portsmouth PO2 182 C4
Portchester Rise SO50 56 A4
Portchester Sta PO16 156 B4
Portcreek Cotts PO6 158 A3
Portelet Cl BH12 188 B1
Portelet Ho SO16 77 B2
Portelet Pl SO30 105 B3
Porter Rd BH17 202 A4
Porter's La SO14 102 C2
Porters La BH21 164
Portersbridge St SO51 52
Portesham Gdns BH9 190
Portesham Way BH17 187
Porteus Cres SO53 55
Portfield Cl BH23 207
Portfield Rd
Christchurch BH23 207
Portsmouth PO3 158
Portfield Sch
Christchurch BH23 207
Christchurch BH23 207
Portiere Ho BH11 189
Portland Bldgs 5 PO12 181
Portland Dr PO12 180
Portland Ho 24 PO12 181
Portland Pl BH2 204
Portland Rd
Bournemouth BH9 205
Portsmouth PO5 182
Waterlooville PO7 134
Portland Sq 5 GU33 20
Portland St
Fareham PO16 131
Portsmouth PO1 182
Southampton SO14 102
Portland Terr
27 Portsmouth PO5 182
Southampton SO14 102
Portland's Cl GU32 41
Portman Cres BH5 206
Portman Rd BH7 205
Portman Terr BH5 206
Portmore Cl BH18 187
Portobello Gr PO16 132
Portsdown Ave PO6 158
Portsdown Hill Rd
Havant PO9 135
Portchester PO17 132
Portsdown Prim Sch
PO6 157
Portsdown Rd PO16 156
Portside Cl SO40 102
Portsmouth & Southsea Sta
PO1 215
Portsmouth Cath (CE)
PO1 182
Portsmouth Cath(RC)
PO1 182
Portsmouth City Mus & Art
Gallery★ PO1 182
Portsmouth Coll PO3 183
Portsmouth Gram Sch
PO1 182
Portsmouth Harbour Sta
PO1 181
Portsmouth High Sch for
Girls PO5 215
Portsmouth High Sch for
Girls(Juns) PO5 182
Portsmouth Print Workshop
PO1 182
Portsmouth RC Cath★
PO1 215
Portsmouth Rd
Bursledon SO31 105
Colden Common SO50,
SO21 57
Horndean PO8 112
Lee-on-the-Solent PO13 180
Southampton SO19,SO31 104
Portsmouth Sea Life Ctr★
PO5 182
Portsview Ave PO16 156
Portsview Gdns PO16 132
Portswood Ave SO17 103
Portswood Ctr 36 SO17 79
Portswood Dr 2 BH9 190
Portswood Pk SO17 103
Portswood Prim Sch
SO17 79
Portswood Rd
Havant PO9 135
Portsmouth PO2 157
Southampton SO17 79
Portuguese Fireplace★
SO43 120
Portview Rd SO18 79
Portway Cl SO18 104
Posbrook La PO14 153
Posbrooke Rd PO4 183
Post Office Bldgs BH9 204
Post Office La
6 Poole BH15 202
St Leonards BH24 140
Post Office Rd
41 Bournemouth BH1 204
Waterlooville PO7 134
Postern Cl PO16 156
Postern Ct 14 SO14 102
Potash Terr PO9 135
Potterdale Ho 17 PO6 133
Potteries The PO16 131
Potterne Way BH21 115
Potterne Wood Cl BH31 115
Potters Ave PO16 131
Potters Field GU33 21
Potters Heron Cl SO51 29
Potters Heron La SO51 29
Potters Way BH14 203
Pottery Junc BH14 203
Pottery Rd BH14 203
Poulner Cl SO19 104
Poulner Ct PO9 135
Poulner Hill BH24 141
Poulner Inf & Jun Schs
BH24 117

Poulner Mobile Home Pk
BH24 .... 117 B1
Poulner Pk BH24 ....117 B1
Pound Cl Gosport PO13 ..180 B4
Poole BH15 ....202 C3
Ringwood BH24 ....141 A4
Pound Cotts SO32 ......61 B3
Pound Ct SO18 ....104 A4
Pound Gate Dr PO14 ...153 B4
Pound Hill SO51 ....50 B3
Pound La Ampfield SO51 ..29 A1
Ashurst SO40 ....100 C2
Burley BH24 ....142 C1
Cadnam SO40 ....75 B1
[3] Christchurch BH23 ....207 A3
Damerham SP6 ....68 A3
Meonstoke SO32 ....61 B3
Plaitford SO51 ....50 B3
Poole BH15 ....202 C3
Sherfield English SO51 ....25 C1
Pound Lea PO11 ....185 A3
Pound Rd
Bursledon SO31 ....104 C1
Kings Worthy SO23 ....2 B4
Lymington SO41 ....197 A1
Pound St SO18 ....104 A4
Pound Tree Rd SO14 ...103 A2
Poundbury Ct SO31 .....129 A3
Pounds Terr PO1 ....182 A3
Powell Cres SO40 ......100 C3
Powell Rd BH14 ....203 A2
Powell Sq [11] PO1 ......182 A3
Power Rd PO1 ....182 C3
Powerscourt Rd
Barton on Sea BH25 .....209 C4
Portsmouth PO2 ....182 C4
Powis Cl BH25 ....195 A2
Powlett Rd SO41 ....197 C2
Poyner Cl PO16 ....131 A1
Poynings Pl PO1 ....182 A2
Precinct The
Holbury SO45 ....150 B2
[10] Waterlooville PO7 ....134 C4
Precosa Rd SO30 ....105 C3
Prelate Way PO14 ......129 B1
Premier Ctr The SO51 ....53 B3
Premier Par SO18 ....79 C2
Premier Way SO51 ....53 B3
Preshaw Cl SO16 ....78 B2
Preshaw Est SO32 ....35 A2
Presseys Cnr SP6 ....93 A4
Preston Cl BH16 ....201 B4
Preston La BH23 ....192 B2
Preston Rd Poole BH15 ..202 B3
Portsmouth PO2 ....182 C4
Preston Way BH23 ......208 B4
Prestwood Cl BH25 .....194 C1
Prestwood Rd SO30 .....105 B3
Pretoria Rd
Hedge End SO30 ....105 A3
Portsmouth PO4 ....182 C2
Prettyjohn Ho PO4 .....183 A1
Pricketts Hill PO17 .....108 A3
Prideaux - Brune Ave
PO13 ....155 B2
Priest Croft SO45 ......150 C1
Priest Croft Dr SO45 ...150 C1
Priest La BH23 ....192 A4
Priest's House Mus & Gdns★
BH21 ....163 A2
Priestfields PO14 ....129 B1
Priestlands SO51 ....52 C4
Priestlands Cl SO40 .....100 A3
Priestlands La SO41 ....197 B2
Priestlands Pl SO41 ....197 B2
Priestlands Rd SO41 ....197 B2
Priestlands Sch SO41 ...197 B1
Priestley Cl SO40 ....100 B4
Priestley Rd BH10 ......189 A1
Priestwood Cl SO18 .....104 B4
Primate Rd PO14 ....129 B1
Primrose Cl
Chandler's Ford SO53 .....54 C2
Gosport PO13 ....155 B3
Hedge End SO30 ....105 B3
Primrose Ct PO7 ....135 A3
Primrose Gdns BH17 ....186 C1
Primrose La Rake GU33 ....21 B2
Redlynch SP5 ....47 B3
Primrose Rd SO16 ....79 A2
Primrose Terr SO32 ......59 B1
Primrose Way
Christchurch BH23 ......208 B4
Corfe Mullen BH21 ......186 C4
Locks Heath SO31 ....128 C1
Romsey SO51 ....28 B1
Prince Albert Rd PO4 ...183 A2
Prince Alfred St PO12 ..181 A2
Prince George St PO1 ..182 A3
Prince George's St PO9 135 C1
Prince of Wales Ave
SO15 ....102 A4
Prince of Wales Cl [6]
PO7 ....135 A4
Prince of Wales Rd
Bournemouth BH4 ....204 B2
[3] Gosport PO12 ....181 B2
Prince Rd Gosport PO14 .154 C3
Rownhams SO16 ....77 C3
Prince Regent Ct PO5 ..215 B2
Prince William Ct [8]
SO50 ....56 C1
Prince's Bldgs [18] SO23 ...11 A4
Prince's Mead Sch SO23 ..2 C3
Prince's Pl
New Milton BH25 ....195 B2
Portsmouth PO1 ....182 B4
Prince's Rd SO51 ....52 C4
Prince's St
Portsmouth PO1 ....182 B4
Southampton SO14 ......103 B3
Princes Cl
Bishop's Waltham SO32 ...83 A4
Ferndown BH22 ....165 B3
Redlynch SP5 ....47 C4
Princes Cotts GU32 ......63 B4
Princes Cres SO43 ......122 A3
Princes Ct
Lyndhurst SO43 ....122 A3
[6] Poole BH12 ....204 A2
[2] Southampton SO14 ...103 B3
Princes Dr PO7 ....112 A1
Princes Hill SP5 ....47 C4
Princes Ho
Portsmouth PO5 ....215 A1
[3] Southampton SO14 ...103 B3
Princes Pl SO22 ....10 C3
Princes Rd
Petersfield GU32 ....40 B2
Southampton SO15 ......102 B3
Princess Anne Hospl
SO16 ....78 A2
Princess Ave BH23 ......207 A3
Princess Cl SO30 ....80 C1
Princess Ct [10] SO23 .....11 A4
Princess Gdns PO8 .....112 B4
Princess Rd
Ashurst SO40 ....100 A1
Bournemouth BH4 ....204 A2
Poole BH12 ....204 A2
Pringles Cl BH22 ....165 C3
Pringles Dr BH22 ....165 C3
Prinstead Cl [7] SO23 .....11 A3
Prinsted Cres PO6 ......158 B4
Prinsted La PO10 ....161 B4
Prinsted Wlk PO14 ......154 B4
Printers Row [17] SO23 ....10 C4
Priors Barton SO23 ......10 C3
Priors Cl
Christchurch BH23 ......208 B4
Southbourne PO10 ......137 C1
Priors Dean Rd SO22 ......1 B2
Priors Hill La SO31 .....127 C4
Priors Leaze La PO18 ...137 C1
Priors Rd BH17 ....202 A4
Priors Way SO22 ....10 A2
Priors Wlk [7] BH21 .....163 A2
Priorsdean Ave PO3 .....183 A3
Priorsdean Cres PO9 ...135 B2
Priory Ave SO17 ....79 B1
Priory CE Prim Sch The
BH23 ....207 A3
Priory Cl
Bishop's Waltham SO32 ...83 A4
Southampton SO17 ....79 B1
Priory Cres PO4 ....183 A2
Priory Ct
Bishop's Waltham SO32 ...83 A4
Portchester PO6 ....156 C4
Portsmouth PO5 ....215 D2
Priory Gdns
Portchester PO16 ....156 B4
Waterlooville PO7 ....111 C1
West Moors BH22 ....166 A4
[12] Winchester SO23 .....11 A4
Priory Ho
Christchurch BH23 ......207 B3
[18] Southampton SO14 ...103 A3
Priory Ind Pk BH23 .....208 A4
Priory Quay BH23 ......207 B3
Priory Rd
Bournemouth BH2 ....204 C1
Eastleigh SO50 ....55 C1
Fareham PO15 ....130 B1
Gosport PO12 ....181 A4
Netley SO31 ....127 A3
Portsmouth PO4 ....183 A1
Southampton SO17 ......103 B4
West Moors BH22 ....166 A4
Priory Sch SO32 ....83 A4
Priory Sec Sch PO5 ....215 D2
Priory View Ct [5] BH23 .207 A3
Priory View Pl [7] BH9 ..190 A2
Priory View Rd
Bournemouth BH9 ....190 A2
Burton BH23 ....192 B1
Private Rd SO41 ....197 C3
Privet Rd BH9 ....204 C4
Privett Ho PO1 ....182 A3
Privett Pl PO12 ....180 C2
Privett Rd Fareham PO15 130 B1
Froxfield Green GU32 .....18 C1
Gosport PO12,PO13 .....180 C2
Waterlooville PO7 ....134 B2
Prochurch Rd PO8 ......112 A2
Proctor Cl SO19 ....104 B3
Proctor Dr SO52 ....53 C2
Proctor La PO1 ....182 C3
Promenade BH23 ....208 A3
Promenade Ct [4] PO13 .179 C1
Promenade The
Emsworth PO10 ....160 C4
Hythe SO45 ....126 A3
[20] Portsmouth PO2 ......157 B1
Prospect La PO9 ....136 A3
Prospect Pl
Chandler's Ford SO50 .....55 B3
Hythe SO45 ....126 A3
Prospect Rd PO1 ....182 B4
Prosperous St [14] BH15 .202 B1
Protea Gdns PO14 ....130 A1
Provene Cl SO32 ....83 C2
Provene Gdns SO32 ......83 C2
Providence Ct [8] PO1 ...182 B4
Providence Hill SO31 ...105 A1
Provost St SP6 ....69 C1
Pruetts La GU33 ....20 C1
Prunus Cl
Ferndown BH22 ....165 A4
Southampton SO16 ....78 B3
Prunus Dr BH22 ....165 A4
Pudbrook Ho SO30 ......106 A3
Pudbrooke Gdns SO30 ...105 A4
Pudding La SO23 ....2 A3
Puddletown Cres BH17 .187 C1
Puffin Cl SO16 ....78 A3
Puffin Cres PO14 ....154 A2
Puffin Gdns PO13 ....155 A2
Puffin Wlk PO8 ....111 B2
Pug's Hole SP5 ....4 A3
Pulens Cres GU31 ....41 B2
Pulens La GU31 ....41 A2
Pullman Ct BH22 ....138 B1
Pullman Way BH24 ......141 A3
Pump La Gosport PO13 ..155 B1
Waterlooville PO8 ....112 A3
Pundle Green Est SO40 ...99 A3
Punsholt La SO24 ....16 C3
Purbeck Ave BH15 ......201 C1
Purbeck Cl BH16 ....201 A4
Purbeck Ct
Bournemouth BH5 ....206 A2
[3] Christchurch BH23 ....207 C4
Purbeck Dr
Fareham PO14 ....154 B4
Verwood BH31 ....114 C3
Purbeck Gdns BH14 ....202 C3
Purbeck Hts BH14 ....203 A3
Purbeck Rd
Barton on Sea BH25 .....209 B4
Bournemouth BH2 ....204 C1
Purbeck St PO1 ....182 A3
Purbeck Wlk PO14 ......154 B4
Purbrook Chase Prec
PO7 ....134 C2
Purbrook Cl SO16 ....78 B2
Purbrook Gdns PO7 ....134 B3
Purbrook Heath Rd
PO7 ....134 A3
Purbrook Ho PO7 ....134 B3
Purbrook Inf Sch PO7 ...134 B3
Purbrook Jun Sch PO7 ..134 B3
Purbrook Park Sch PO7 134 B2
Purbrook Rd PO1 ....182 C3
Purbrook Way PO7,PO9 .135 B2
Purcell Cl PO7 ....134 C3
Purcell Rd SO19 ....104 B2
Purchase Rd BH12 ......204 B4
Purewell BH23 ....207 B3
Purewell Cl BH23 ....207 C3
Purewell Cross BH23 ....207 C3
Purewell Cross Rd
BH23 ....207 B4
Purewell Ct [11] BH23 ....207 C4
Purkess Cl SO53 ....55 B4
Purkiss Cl SO40 ....99 B3
Purley Way SO51 ....50 A2
Purrocks The GU32 ......40 C3
Purvis Gdns SO19 ......104 A1
Pussex La BH23 ....191 A4
Putmans La GU31 ....66 C4
Pycroft Cl
North Hayling PO11 .....160 B2
Southampton SO19 ......104 A3
Pye Cl BH21 ....186 C4
Pye Cnr BH21 ....163 A2
Pye La Alderholt BH21 ....91 C3
Wimborne Minst BH21 ...163 A2
Pye St PO1 ....215 B4
Pylands La SO31 ....105 A2
Pyle Cl PO8 ....112 A2
Pylewell Rd SO45 ....126 A2
Pyramid Ctr PO3 ......158 A2
Pyramids L Ctr The PO5 182 B1
Pyrford Cl Gosport PO12 .180 C2
Waterlooville PO7 ....111 C1
Pyrford Gdns [1] SO41 ...197 C1
Pyrford Mews SO41 .....197 C1
Pytchley Cl PO14 ....179 A3

Q

Quadra Point PO3 ......158 A2
Quadrangle The
Eastleigh SO50 ....56 A2
North Baddesley SO51 .....53 B3
Quadrant SP6 ....93 C4
Quail Way PO8 ....112 A3
Quaker Ct BH24 ....140 C3
Quantock Ct [7] BH23 ...207 C4
Quantock Rd SO16 ......101 C4
Quantocks The SO45 ....125 B1
Quarely Rd PO9 ....135 B3
Quarr Ho SO41 ....172 A2
Quarry Chase [7] BH4 ...204 B2
Quarry Cl BH21 ....164 A4
Quarry Dr BH21 ....164 A4
Quarry Rd
Wimborne Minst BH21 ...164 A4
Winchester SO23 ....11 B4
Quarterdeck Ave PO2 ..157 A1
Quarterjack Mews [1]
BH21 ....163 B2
Quartremaine Rd PO3 ..158 A2
Quavey Rd SP5 ....47 C3
Quay 2000 SO14 ....103 B4
Quay Haven SO31 ....128 B4
Quay Hill SO41 ....197 C2
Quay Ho SO31 ....128 A1
Quay La Gosport PO12 ...181 C2
Gosport, Elson PO12 .....156 A1
Quay Point
[19] Poole BH15 ....202 B1
Quay Point *continued*
Portsmouth PO6 ....157 B4
Quay Rd
Christchurch BH23 ......207 A3
Lymington SO41 ....197 C2
Quay St Fareham PO16 ..131 B1
Fareham PO16 ....155 B4
Lymington SO41 ....197 C2
Quay The
Hamble-le-Rice SO31 ....128 A1
Poole BH15 ....202 B1
Quayle Dr BH11 ....188 C3
Quayside SO30 ....106 A3
Quayside Commerce Ctr [1]
PO16 ....155 A4
Quayside Rd
Fawley SO45 ....151 C1
Southampton SO18 ......103 B4
Quayside Wlk SO40 .....101 C2
Quebec Gdns SO31 .....104 C1
Queen Alexandra Hospl
PO6 ....157 C4
Queen Anne Dr BH21 ...187 C4
Queen Anne's Dr PO9 ..135 B1
Queen Elizabeth Ave
SO41 ....197 B2
Queen Elizabeth Ct
Southampton SO17 ....79 B2
Wimborne Minst BH21 ...163 A2
Queen Elizabeth Ctry Pk★
PO8 ....64 C2
Queen Elizabeth's Sch
BH21 ....162 C3
Queen Katherine Rd
SO41 ....197 C2
Queen Mary Ave BH9 ..189 C1
Queen Mary Rd PO16 ..156 B4
Queen Rd PO14 ....154 C3
Queen St Emsworth PO10 161 A4
Lymington SO41 ....197 B2
Portsmouth PO1 ....182 A3
Twyford SO21 ....31 C3
Woodgreen SP6 ....47 A1
Queen's Ave BH23 ......207 A3
Queen's Cl SO51 ....53 A4
Queen's Cres PO5 ....215 B1
Queen's Ct SO15 ....102 C3
Queen's Gr PO5 ....215 B1
Queen's Inclosure Prim Sch
PO8 ....112 A1
Queen's Par
Lyndhurst SO43 ....121 C3
[8] Waterlooville PO7 ....134 C4
Queen's Park Ave BH8 205 B4
Queen's Park Gdns BH8 205 B4
Queen's Park Rd BH8 ..205 B4
Queen's Park South Dr
BH8 ....205 B4
Queen's Park West Dr
BH8 ....205 B4
Queen's Pl PO5 ....215 B1
Queen's Rd
Bournemouth BH4 ....204 B2
Chandler's Ford SO53 .....30 B1
Christchurch BH23 ......207 C3
Corfe Mullen BH21 ......186 B3
Fareham PO16 ....131 A1
Gosport PO12 ....181 B2
Locks Heath SO31 ....152 B4
Poole BH14 ....203 B2
Portsmouth PO1 ....181 C3
Portsmouth, Buckland PO2 182 C4
Southampton SO15 ....78 B1
Waterlooville PO7 ....111 C1
Winchester SO22 ....10 B4
Queen's Terr PO5 ......215 B1
Queen's Terr SO14 ......103 A2
Queen's Way PO5 ....215 B1
Queens Cl Hythe SO45 ...126 A2
Lee-on-the-Solent PO13 ..179 C1
West Moors BH22 ....138 B1
Queens Cres
Horndean PO8 ....112 B4
Stubbington PO14 ....154 B2
Queens Ct
[5] Bournemouth BH4 ....204 B2
Bournemouth, Charminster
BH9 ....205 A4
New Milton BH25 ....195 B2
[30] Winchester SO23 ......10 C4
Queens Gdns
Bournemouth BH2 ....204 B2
Fordingbridge SP6 ....69 C1
Queens Gr
New Milton BH25 ....195 B2
Waterlooville PO7 ....134 B3
Queens Ho [15] SO14 ....103 A2
Queens Keep [17] PO5 ...182 B1
Queens Mead SO22 ....10 B3
Queens Par PO12 ....180 C2
Queens Rd
Ferndown BH22 ....165 B4
Lee-on-the-Solent PO13 ..179 C1
Lyndhurst SO43 ....122 A3
Petersfield GU32 ....40 B2
Queens Ride SO52 ....53 C2
Queens View SO31 ......127 A3
Queens Way BH24 ......141 A4
Queensbury Mans [7]
BH1 ....205 A2
Queensland Rd BH5 ....206 A3
Queensmead [4] BH21 ....163 B3
Queenstown Rd SO15 ...102 B3
Queensway
New Milton BH25 ....194 C2
North Hayling PO11 .....160 A2
Southampton SO14 ......103 A2
Queensway The PO16 ..156 A4
Queenswood Ave BH8 ..190 C1
Queenswood Dr BH22 ..165 B4
Querida Cl SO31 ....128 B4
Quilter Cl SO19 ....104 B2
Quince La BH21 ....163 C3
Quinton Cl
Christchurch BH23 ......208 C4
Portsmouth PO1 ....215 C2
Quintrell Ave PO16 .....156 A4
Quob Farm Cl SO30 ......80 C2
Quob La SO30 ....80 C2
Quomp The BH24 ....141 A4

R

R L Stevenson Ave BH4 204 A2
Racecourse View SO43 .121 C3
Rachel Cl Fair Oak SO50 ..57 A1
Poole BH12 ....203 B4
Rachel Madocks Sch
PO8 ....111 B2
Racton Ave PO6 ....158 A4
Racton Rd PO10 ....136 C2
Radcliffe Ct [11] SO14 ...103 A3
Radcliffe Rd SO14 ......103 A3
Radclyffe Rd PO16 ......131 B1
Radipole Rd BH17 ......188 A1
Radleigh Gdns SO40 ....100 A4
Radley Cl SO30 ....81 B1
Radnor St PO5 ....215 B2
Radstock Rd SO19 ......103 C2
Radway Cres SO15 ......102 B4
Radway Rd SO15 ....78 C1
Raebarn Cl SO24 ....14 B3
Raeburn Dr SO30 ....105 B4
Raglan Cl SO53 ....55 A2
Raglan Ct
[3] Eastleigh SO50 ....56 A3
Gosport PO12 ....181 A2
Locks Heath SO31 ....129 A3
Raglan Gdns BH11 ......189 A1
Raglan St PO1 ....215 C3
Raglan Terr PO10 ....137 A1
Ragmore La GU32 ....18 C3
Rails La PO11 ....185 B1
Railway Cotts
Southampton SO15 ......101 B4
West Meon GU32 ....37 B2
West Tisted GU34 ....17 B3
Railway Flats PO1 ......182 C3
Railway Terr SO42 ......172 C4
Railway Triangle Ind Est
PO6 ....158 A3
Railway View PO1 ......215 C3
Railway View Rd SO17 ..103 B4
Rainbow Pl SO15 ....102 B3
Rake Bsns Pk GU33 ......21 C2
Rake CE Prim Sch GU33 .21 C3
Rake Rd GU33 ....21 A2
Raleigh Cl
Christchurch BH23 ......207 C3
New Milton BH25 ....194 C2
Ringwood BH24 ....141 B4
Raleigh Ho [25] PO1 .....182 A3
Raleigh Rd BH12 ....188 C1
Raleigh Wlk PO13 ......180 B3
Raley Rd SO31 ....129 A1
Ralph La SO51 ....28 A1
Ralph Rd BH21 ....186 C4
Ramalley La SO53 ....55 A4
Rambler Dr PO13 ....180 B3
Ramblers Way PO7 .....112 B1
Ramillies Ho
[11] Fareham PO14 ....154 C4
[15] Gosport PO12 ....181 B2
Ramley Rd SO41 ....197 A2
Rampart Gdns PO3 .....157 C3
Rampart Rd SO18 ......103 B4
Rampart Row PO12 .....181 C2
Rampart The SO41 .....197 B3
Rams Wlk GU32 ....40 C2
Ramsay Pl PO13 ....155 B1
Ramsay Rd SO23 ....2 B4
Ramsdale Ave PO9 .....135 B3
Ramsdean Rd GU32 ......39 C1
Ramsey Ct BH25 ....194 C2
Ramsey Rd PO11 ....185 A2
Ramshill GU31 ....41 A2
Rances Way SO22 ....10 C3
Randall Cl SO40 ....76 B1
Randall Rd SO53 ....30 B1
Randall's La BH24 ......142 C3
Randolph Rd
[2] Bournemouth BH1 ....205 C2
Poole BH14 ....203 B3
Portsmouth PO2 ....157 C1
Randolph St SO15 ......102 B4
Ranelagh Ct
Christchurch BH23 ......208 C4
[9] Southampton SO17 ...103 A4
Ranelagh Gdns SO15 ...102 C4
Ranelagh Rd
Christchurch BH23 ......208 C4
Havant PO9 ....135 B1
Portsmouth PO2 ....157 B1
Winchester SO23 ....10 C3
Range Gdns SO19 ......104 A2
Range Gn PO2 ....157 B2
Ranmore Ct SO45 ......125 B2
Rannoch Cl PO15 ....130 C2
Ransome Cl PO14 ....153 C4
Ranvilles Jun & Inf Schs
PO14 ....154 B4
Ranvilles La PO14 ......154 A4

Rapson Cl PO6 133 B1
Rareridge La SO32 83 C4
Ratcliffe Rd
Hedge End SO30 105 B4
Hythe SO45 125 C1
Rattigan Gdns PO15 129 B4
Ravana Ct 4 BH8 205 A3
Raven Cl PO13 180 B3
Raven Croft PO5 215 B1
Raven Rd SO14 103 A3
Raven Sq SO50 55 B1
Raven Way BH23 208 A3
Ravens Cl PO14 179 B3
Ravens Way SO41 211 B2
Ravenscourt Rd
Bournemouth BH6 206 B3
Lymington SO41 197 B1
Ravenscroft Cl SO31 104 C1
Ravenscroft Way SO32 81 C1
Ravensdale Cl BH12 203 B3
Ravenshall BH2 204 B1
Ravenswood PO14 129 B2
Ravenswood Gdns 6
PO5 182 B1
Ravine Ct BH13 214 C4
Ravine Gdns 5 BH13 214 C4
Ravine Rd
Bournemouth BH5 206 A2
Poole BH13 214 C4
Raymond Cl
Holbury SO45 150 B2
Verwood BH31 115 A3
West End SO30 80 C2
Raymond Rd
Portchester PO6 132 C1
Southampton SO15 102 B4
Rayners Dr BH12 203 B3
Rayners Gdns SO16 79 B2
Raynes Rd PO13 180 A2
Reading Room La SO32 106 B4
Readon Cl GU31 41 A2
Readon Ho GU31 41 A2
Rebbeck Rd BH7 206 A3
Recess The SO50 56 A3
Record Rd PO10 136 C1
Recreation Cotts SO51 50 C2
Recreation Rd BH12 203 C3
Rectory Ave BH21 162 B1
Rectory Cl Gosport PO12 181 A1
Stubbington PO14 154 B2
Rectory Ct SO30 105 C4
Rectory Hill SP5 3 B2
Rectory La Breamore SP6 46 A1
Meonstoke SO32 61 B3
Rectory Rd Havant PO9 159 C4
Poole BH15 202 B3
Red Barn Ave PO16 132 B1
Red Barn Com Prim Sch
PO16 156 B4
Red Barn La PO15,PO16 130 C2
Red Hill Cres SO16 78 C2
Red Hill Way SO16 78 C2
Red Horn Cl BH16 201 B2
Red House Mews SO41 197 C2
Red House Mus & Gdns★
BH23 207 A3
Red La
Compton (Hants) SO21 31 C4
Corfe Mullen BH21 186 A4
Owslebury SO21 58 A3
West Tytherley SP5 4 A4
Red Leaves SO32 83 C1
Red Lodge SO53 55 A2
Red Lodge Sch SO16 78 C2
Red Oaks Cl BH22 165 A4
Red Oaks Dr SO31 129 A3
Red Roofs BH22 165 C2
Redan Cl BH23 208 C4
Redan The PO12 181 B1
Redbreast Rd BH9 190 A2
Redbreast Rd N BH9 190 A2
Redbridge Causeway
SO15,SO40 101 A4
Redbridge Com Sch
SO16 101 B4
Redbridge Flyover
SO15 101 B4
Redbridge Gr PO9 135 B2
Redbridge Hill SO16 77 C1
Redbridge La SO16 77 B2
Redbridge Prim Sch
SO16 101 B4
Redbridge Rd SO15 101 B4
Redbridge Sta SO15 101 B4
Redbridge Twrs SO16 101 B4
Redbrook Cotts SP6 94 A4
Redcar Ave PO3 158 A1
Redcar St SO15 102 A4
Redcliffe Cl BH23 192 B2
Redcote Cl SO18 104 A4
Redcotts La BH21 163 A3
Redcotts Rd BH21 163 A3
Redcourt 2 SO16 78 C2
Redcroft La SO31 105 A1
Redfords The SO40 76 C1
Redhill SO16 78 C2
Redhill Ave BH9,BH10 189 C2
Redhill Cl
Bournemouth BH10 189 C2
Southampton SO16 78 C2
Redhill Cres BH9 189 C2
Redhill Ct BH10 189 C2
Redhill Dr BH10 189 C2
Redhill Ho PO1 215 C4
Redhill Park Homes 1
BH10 189 C2
Redhill Rd PO9 113 A1
Redhill Rdbt BH10 189 C2
Redhoave Rd BH17 187 C1
Redhouse Park Gdns
PO12 180 C4
Redlands
Christchurch BH23 208 A4
Poole BH12 203 C3
Redlands Dr SO19 103 C3
Redlands Gr PO4 183 B2
Redlands La
Emsworth PO10 136 C2
Fareham PO14,PO16 155 A4
Redlands Prim Sch
PO16 155 A4
Redlynch CE Prim Sch
SP5 48 A3
Redlynch Cl PO9 136 A2
Redmans View BH31 114 C3
Redmoor Cl SO19 103 C3
Rednal Ho PO1 215 C3
Redoubt Ct PO14 154 C3
Redrise Cl SO45 150 B2
Redsails BH13 214 A2
Redshank Cl BH17 186 C1
Redshank Rd PO8 112 A4
Redvers Cl SO41 197 B1
Redvers Rd BH23 207 C4
Redward Rd SO16 77 C3
Redwing Ct PO4 183 B3
Redwing Gdns SO40 100 B4
Redwing Rd PO8 88 B2
Redwood Cl Hythe SO45 125 B2
Lymington SO41 197 B3
Ringwood BH24 141 A4
West End SO30 80 B1
Redwood Ct 3 PO7 134 C4
Redwood Dr
Ferndown BH22 165 B4
Portchester PO16 156 A4
Redwood Gdns SO40 100 B4
Redwood Gr PO9 136 A2
Redwood Lodge 4
PO16 131 A1
Redwood Park Sch PO6 158 A3
Redwood Rd BH16 201 A4
Redwood Way SO16 79 A3
Reed Dr SO40 101 C1
Reeder Cl SP6 69 C1
Reedling Dr PO4 183 B3
Reedmace Cl PO7 135 A3
Reeds La GU33 21 B3
Reeds Mdw GU32 39 B2
Reeds Pl PO12 181 A3
Reeds Rd PO12 181 A4
Reeves Cl SO51 50 C2
Reeves Way SO31 104 C1
Regal Cl PO6 157 C4
Regency Cres BH23 206 C4
Regency Ct 12 PO1 182 A2
Regency Gdns PO7 134 B3
Regency Pl
Fareham PO15 130 C1
Ringwood BH24 141 A4
Regent Cl SO21 31 B2
Regent Ct
24 Southampton SO17 79 A1
17 Winchester SO23 2 A1
Regent Dr BH7 205 C4
Regent Ho SO30 81 B2
Regent Mews GU32 40 B2
Regent Pl PO5 215 A1
Regent Rd SO53 55 B3
Regent St
Portsmouth PO1 182 B4
Southampton SO14 102 C2
Regent Way BH23 207 A3
Regent's Gr 1 SO15 102 A4
Regent's Park Gdns
SO15 102 A4
Regent's Park Rd SO15 102 A4
Regents Ct Havant PO9 159 C4
6 Southampton SO16 102 A4
Regents Gate SO31 128 C3
Regents Park Girls Sch
SO16 102 A4
Reginald Rd PO4 183 A2
Reid St BH23 207 A4
Reigate Ho PO1 215 C4
Relay Rd PO7 134 B4
Reldas The 18 PO1 182 A2
Reliant Cl SO53 55 A3
Rempstone Rd BH21 187 B4
Renault Dr BH18 187 A1
Renda Rd SO45 150 B2
Renny Rd PO1 182 C3
Renouf Cl SO41 197 B2
Renown Cl SO53 55 A3
Renown Gdns PO8 111 C3
Renown Ho 14 PO12 181 B2
Repton Cl PO12 180 C2
Repton Gdns SO30 81 B1
Reservoir La
Hedge End SO30 105 A3
Petersfield GU32 40 C3
Resolution Ho 13 PO12 181 B2
Rest-a-wyle Ave PO11 185 A3
Restharrow BH1, 205 A2
Restynge Ho BH31 114 C4
Retreat Rd BH21 163 B2
Retreat The
Eastleigh SO50 56 A2
Portsmouth PO5 215 B1
Totton SO40 101 A3
Revenge Cl PO4 183 B3
Revenge Ho 12 PO12 181 B2
Rewlands Dr SO22 1 B2
Rex Est SO53 55 B3
Reynard Ct BH15 202 C2
Reynolds Ct SO51 53 A3
Reynolds Dale SO40 100 B3
Reynolds Rd
Fair Oak SO50 57 B1
Gosport PO12 181 B1
Southampton SO15 102 B4
Rhinefield Cl
Bishopstoke SO50 56 C1
Brockenhurst SO42 145 C1
Havant PO9 135 B2
Rhinefield Ornamental Dr★
SO42 144 C3
Rhinefield Rd
Brockenhurst SO42 145 B1
New Milton BH25 170 C1
Rhiners Cl SO41 172 A1
Rhyme Hall Mews SO45 151 A2
Rhys Ct 1 PO4 183 A2
Ribble Cl
Broadstone BH18 187 A1
Chandler's Ford SO53 55 B3
Ribble Ct SO16 77 C1
Ribbonwood Hts BH14 203 A2
Ricardo Cres BH23 208 A3
Rice Gdns BH16 201 B2
Rice Terr BH16 201 B2
Richard Cl BH16 201 A4
Richard Gr PO12 156 A1
Richard Moss Ho 8
SO23 11 A4
Richard Taunton Pl SO17 79 A1
Richards Cl
Blackfield SO45 150 C1
Locks Heath SO31 129 A2
Richards Ct 15 SO15 78 A1
Richlans Rd SO30 105 B3
Richmond Cl
Chandler's Ford SO53 30 B1
South Hayling PO11 184 C2
Totton SO40 76 A1
Richmond Ct
15 Bournemouth BH5 205 C2
12 Milford on Sea SO41 211 B2
7 New Milton BH25 195 A2
Richmond Dr PO11 184 C2
Richmond Gdns
Bournemouth BH1 204 C2
Southampton SO17 79 A1
Waterlooville PO7 134 B3
Richmond Hall 6 SO17 79 B1
Richmond Hill BH1,BH2 204 C2
Richmond Hill Dr BH2 204 C2
Richmond Ho
34 Portsmouth PO1 182 A3
5 Southampton SO15 102 B3
9 Winchester SO22 10 C4
Richmond La SO51 28 A1
Richmond Park Ave
BH8 205 B4
Richmond Park Cl BH8 205 B3
Richmond Park Cres
BH8 205 B4
Richmond Park Rd BH8 205 B4
Richmond Pk SO21 31 B2
Richmond Pl PO1 182 A3
Richmond Rd
Gosport PO12 181 A2
Lee-on-the-Solent PO13 179 C1
Poole BH14 203 B2
Portsmouth PO5 182 B1
Southampton SO15 102 B3
Wimborne Minst BH21 163 B2
Richmond Rise
Bournemouth BH8 205 B3
Portchester PO16 132 B1
Richmond St SO14 103 A2
Richmond Wood Rd
BH8 205 B4
Richville Rd SO16 102 A4
Ridding Cl SO15 78 B1
Riders Inf Sch PO9 135 C3
Riders Jun Sch PO9 135 C3
Riders La PO9 135 C2
Rideway PO9 135 B1
Ridge Cl PO8 88 B2
Ridge Common La GU32 40 B3
Ridge La Botley SO30 106 B2
Romsey SO51 76 B4
Ridge The SP5 47 B3
Ridge Top La GU32 39 C3
Ridgefield Gdns BH23 208 B4
Ridgemede Jun Sch
SO32 83 B4
Ridgemount Ave SO16 78 C3
Ridgemount Gdns BH15 201 C2
Ridgemount La SO16 78 C3
Ridgeway
Broadstone BH18 187 A2
Corfe Mullen BH21 186 B4
Ferndown BH22 189 C4
Winchester SO22 10 B3
Ridgeway Cl
Chandler's Ford SO53 55 C3
Cosham PO6 132 C1
Fair Oak SO50 57 B2
Ridgeway House Specl Sch
SO19 103 C3
Ridgeway La SO41 197 B1
Ridgeway The PO16 131 C1
Ridgeway Wlk SO53 55 C3
Ridgewood Cl SO45 125 B2
Ridings The Fair Oak SO50 57 A1
Liss GU33 21 A2
Portsmouth PO2 157 C2
Waltham Chase SO32 83 C2
Ridley Cl SO45 150 B2
Ridley Rd BH9 204 C4
Ridout Cl BH10 189 A1
Rigby Rd SO17 103 A4
Riggs Gdns BH11 188 C1
Rigler Rd BH15 202 A1
Rimbury Way BH23 207 A4
Rimington Gdns 1 SO51 28 A1
Rimington Rd PO8 111 C2
Ring The SO16 78 C4
Ringbury SO41 197 B3
Ringlet Way 6 SO23 11 B4
Ringwood CE Inf Sch
BH24 141 A4
Ringwood Dr SO52 53 C3
Ringwood Ho PO9 135 C3
Ringwood Jun Sch
BH24 141 A3
Ringwood Rd
Alderholt SP6 93 A2
Bournemouth BH11 188 C2
Bransgore BH23 193 B3
Burley BH24 142 C3
Christchurch BH23 194 A1
Ferndown BH22 165 B2
Fordingbridge SP6 94 A2
Fordingbridge SP6 94 B2
Poole BH12,BH14 203 A4
Portsmouth PO4 183 A2
Sopley BH23 192 A4
St Leonards BH24 139 B1
Three Legged Cross BH22 138 C4
Totton SO40 100 B4
Verwood BH31 115 A3
Ringwood Ret Pk BH11 188 C2
Ringwood Sch BH24 141 A4
Ringwood Terr SO42 146 A1
Ringwood Trad Est
BH24 141 A3
Ringwood Waldorf Sch
BH24 140 B3
Ripley Gr PO3 183 A4
Ripon Ct SO50 81 B4
Ripon Gdns 11 PO7 112 A1
Ripon Rd BH9 190 A1
Ripplewood SO40 102 A1
Ripstone Gdns SO17 79 A2
Rise The
Brockenhurst SO42 145 C1
Waterlooville PO7 134 B1
Ritchie Cl PO11 185 A2
Ritchie Ct SO19 104 A2
Ritchie Pl BH22 138 B2
Ritchie Rd BH11 189 A2
Rival Moor Rd GU31 41 B1
River Cl BH21 163 B3
River Ct SO41 197 C2
River Gdns SO41 211 C2
River Gn SO31 128 A1
River La PO15 130 B3
River Mews SO50 56 B2
River Park L Ctr SO23 2 A1
River Pk BH6 206 C3
River Rd SP6 70 B1
River St PO10 137 A2
River View Ho SO19 103 B2
River View Rd SO18 79 B1
River Way
Christchurch BH23 191 B1
Havant PO9 136 A2
River Wlk SO18 79 C2
River's St PO5 215 C2
Riverbourne Ct SO18 103 B4
Riverdale Ave PO7 135 A4
Riverdale Cl SP6 69 C1
Riverdale Cotts PO16 131 B2
Riverdale La BH23 207 A3
Riverdene Pl SO18 103 B4
Riverhead Cl PO4 183 A3
Riverlea Rd BH23 207 A3
Rivermead Cl SO51 52 B4
Rivermead Ct PO10 137 A2
Rivermead Gdns BH23 191 C1
Riverpark Ct SO18 79 B1
Rivers Reach SO41 197 C2
Riversdale 8 BH21 163 B2
Riversdale Cl SO19 126 C4
Riversdale Gdns 7 PO9 135 C1
Riversdale Rd BH6 207 A2
Riverside
Bishopstoke SO50 56 B2
4 Bournemouth BH10 189 C2
Ringwood BH24 140 C3
Riverside Ave
Bournemouth BH7 191 B1
Fareham PO16 131 B2
Riverside Bsns Pk SO41 197 C2
Riverside Cl Cadnam SO40 99 B3
Liss GU33 20 C2
Riverside Cotts SO21 31 C3
Riverside Ct SO18 103 B4
Riverside Gdns SO51 52 C3
Riverside Ho 44 SO23 11 A4
Riverside La BH6 206 C3
Riverside Mews PO17 108 A2
Riverside Pk BH23 207 A3
Riverside Pk Ind Est
BH21 163 B2
Riverside Pl SP6 69 C1
Riverside Rd
Bournemouth BH6 206 C3
West Moors BH22 138 B1
Riverside Sch PO7 134 C2
Riverside Terr 6 PO10 161 A4
Riverside Wlk GU31 41 A2
Riverslea Mews BH23 207 B3
Riversmeet Ct BH23 207 B3
Riverview SO40 100 C3
Riverview Terr SO31 128
Riviera Ct
3 Bournemouth BH2 204
3 Poole BH13 214
Rivirea 22 BH1 205
RN Submarine Mus & HMS
Alliance★ PO12 181
Road View PO2 182
Roads Hill PO8 88
Robere Ho SO19 103
Robert Cecil Ave SO18 79
Robert Mack Ct 32 PO1 182 A
Robert Whitworth Dr
SO51 27
Roberts Cl Hordle SO41 196
Wickham PO17 108 A
Roberts La BH17 202 A
Roberts Rd
Bournemouth BH7 206 A
Gosport PO12 180
Hythe SO45 125
Poole BH17 187 A
Southampton SO15 102
Totton SO40 100 C
Robertshaw Ho SO43 121 C
Robertson Block PO12 181 B
Robin Cres BH25 194 B
Robin Ct SO15 102 C
Robin Gdns Totton SO40 100 B
Waterlooville PO8 111 B
Robin Gr BH25 194 C
Robin Sq SO50 55 B
Robina Cl PO7 135 A
Robinia Gn SO16 78 B
Robins Cl PO14 154 B
Robins Ct 7 BH21 163 B
Robins Mdw PO14 129 B
Robins Way BH23 208 A
Robinson Ct PO16 132 B
Robinson Rd PO14 179 A
Robinson Way PO3 158 B
Robinswood Dr BH22 165 B
Robsall Cl BH12 203 C
Robville Ct BH6 206 A
Rochester Ct PO13 180 B
Rochester Rd
Bournemouth BH11 189 A
Portsmouth PO4 182 C
Rochester St SO14 103 B
Rochford Rd PO6 157 B
Rockall Cl SO16 77 C
Rockbourne Cl PO9 135 B
Rockbourne Gdns BH25 209 B
Rockbourne La
Damerham SP6 68 B
Rockbourne SP6 68 B
Rockbourne Rd SO22 1 B
Rockbourne Roman Villa★
SP6 68 C
Rockery Cl SO45 125 B
Rockford Cl BH6 206 C
Rockford Ho SO50 57 A
Rockingham Way PO16 156 A
Rockleigh Dr SO40 100 B
Rockleigh Rd SO16 78 B
Rockley Rd BH15 201 C
Rockpit Cotts GU33 21 A
Rockram Cl SO40 99 A
Rockram Gdns SO45 125 B
Rockrose Way PO6 133 A
Rockstone Ct 2 SO14 103 A
Rockstone La SO14 103 A
Rockstone Pl SO15 102 C
Rockville Dr PO7 134 C
Rodbard Ho SO31 104 C
Rodbourne Cl SO41 211 B
Rodfield La SO24 13 B
Rodlease La SO41 173 C
Rodney Cl Gosport PO13 180 B
Poole BH12 204 A
Rodney Ct
Christchurch BH23 208 A
Poole BH15 202 B
Southampton SO19 104 B
Rodney Dr BH23 207 C
Rodney Ho 27 PO12 181 B
Rodney Rd PO4 183 A
Rodney Way PO8 112 A
Rodway BH21 163 B
Rodwell Cl BH10 189 B
Roebuck Ave PO15 130 B
Roebuck Cl Cosham PO6 157 C4
New Milton BH25 195 A2
Roebuck Dr PO12 181 B4
Roeshot Cres BH23 193 C1
Roeshot Hill BH23 193 B1
Roewood Cl SO45 150 B2
Roewood Rd SO45 150 B2
Rogate Gdns PO16 132 B1
Rogate Ho 1 PO1 215 C4
Roger Penny Way
Brook SO43 73 B1
Fordingbridge, Bramshaw
SP6 72 B3
Fordingbridge, Godshill SP6 71 A3
Rogers Cl
Bishopstoke SO50 56 C2
Gosport PO12 181 A3
Rogers Ho PO13 179 C1
Rogers Rd SO50 56 C2
Roker Way SO50 57 A1
Roland Cl PO8 112 A3
Rollestone Rd SO45 150 B1
Rolls Dr BH6 207 A2
Roman Cl SO53 55 C4
Roman Ct PO10 137 B1
Roman Dr SO16 78 C4
Roman Gdns SO45 125 B1

oman Gn PO7 110 C2
oman Gr PO16 156 B3
oman Ho SO18 103 B4
oman Hts BH21 186 C4
oman Mdw SP5 46 C4
oman Quay SP6 69 C1
oman Rd Chilworth SO16 78 C4
Corfe Mullen BH18 186 C3
Havant PO10 136 B1
Holbury SO45 150 A3
Hythe SO45 125 B1
Twyford SO21 32 A3
oman Row SO32 83 B4
oman Way Havant PO9 135 B1
Hythe SO45 125 B1
Hamphill BH21 162 B3
omans' Rd 1 SO23 11 A3
omford Rd SO31 152 B4
omill Cl SO30 80 A2
omney Cl BH10 189 C2
omney Rd BH10 189 C2
omsey Abbey★ SO51 52 C4
omsey Abbey CE Prim Sch
SO51 52 C4
omsey Ave
Portchester PO16 156 A4
Portsmouth PO3 183 A3
omsey Cl SO50 56 A2
omsey Ct 10 SO15 102 B3
omsey Hospl SO51 53 A4
omsey Ind Est SO51 52 C4
omsey Inf Sch SO51 52 C4
omsey Jun Sch SO51 53 A4
omsey Lodge 8 SO16 78 A1
omsey Rd Cadnam SO51 75 C3
Eastleigh SO50 56 A2
Horndean PO8 88 B1
King's Somborne SO51 6 B4
Lyndhurst SO43 121 C3
Ower SO40,SO51 75 B2
Southampton SO16 77 C2
West Wellow SO51 51 A2
Whiteparish SP5 24 C2
Winchester SO22, SO23 10 B3
omsey Sch The SO51 52 C4
omsey Sta SO51 52 C4
omyns Ct PO14 130 C1
onald Bowker Ct 1
SO22 10 C4
onald Pugh Ct SO18 79 C2
ook Hill Rd BH23 208 B3
ookcliff 13 SO41 211 B2
ookcliff Way SO41 211 B2
ookery Ave
Swanwick PO15 129 B4
Swanwick PO15,SO31 129 A4
ookery Cotts SP5 3 B2
ookery Gr PO15 129 A4
ookery La SP6 45 C1
ookery The PO10 137 A1
ookes Cl PO8 112 A3
ookes La SO41 197 B1
ookes Mews GU31 41 A2
ookesbury Park Sch
PO17 108 B2
ookley SO31 127 B4
ooks Down Rd SO22 10 B3
ooksbridge SO45 125 B2
ooksbury Croft PO9 136 A3
ooksway Gr PO16 155 C4
ookwood 3 SO41 211 B2
ookwood Cl SO50 56 A3
ookwood Gdns SP6 69 B1
ookwood View PO7 110 C3
oosevelt Cres BH11 189 A3
ope Hill SO41 173 B1
ope Wlk SO31 128 A1
ope Wlk The 3 PO16 155 A4
opers La BH16 201 B4
opewalk Ho 6 SO23 11 A4
opley Cl SO19 127 A4
opley Ct PO11 184 C2
opley Rd
Bournemouth BH7 206 B4
44 Havant PO9 136 A3
osamund Ave BH21 163 C1
oscrea Cl BH6 207 A2
oscrea Dr BH6 207 A2
ose Cl Hedge End SO30 105 B4
Hythe SO45 126 A1
ose Cott PO8 112 B4
ose Cres BH15 202 C3
ose Ct BH15 202 C2
ose Gdn The BH23 191 B1
ose Gdns BH9 190 A2
ose Hill PO8 112 A3
ose Rd
Southampton SO14 103 A4
Totton SO40 101 A3
osebank Cl SO16 77 C3
osebank Lodge SO16 77 C3
osebay Cl SO50 81 B3
osebay Ct 3 PO7 134 C3
osebery Ave
Cosham PO6 158 A4
Hythe SO45 126 A1
osebery Cl BH31 115 B3
osebery Cres SO50 56 A3
osebery Rd BH5 206 A3
osebrook Ct 16 SO18 103 C4
osebud Ave 1 BH9 190 A1
osecrae Cl BH25 194 C2
osedale Ave SO51 53 A4
osedale Cl
3 Christchurch BH23 207 C3
Titchfield PO14 153 C4
osehill Cl BH23 169 A1
osehill Dr BH23 169 A1
Roseship Cl SO50 57 A1
Roselands
Waterlooville PO8 112 A3
West End SO30 104 B4
Roselands Cl SO50 57 A2
Roselands Gdns SO17 79 A1
Roseleigh Dr SO40 100 C3
Rosemary Ct 14 BH23 209 A4
Rosemary Gdns
Hedge End SO30 105 B3
Poole BH12 203 A4
Swanwick PO15 129 B4
Rosemary La 18 PO1 182 A3
Rosemary Rd BH12 203 B4
Rosemary Way PO8 112 A3
Rosemary Wlk 17 PO13 179 C1
Rosemoor Gr SO53 30 A1
Rosemount Rd BH4 204 A1
Rosendale Rd SO53 55 B2
Rosery The PO12 181 A1
Rosetta Rd PO4 183 A2
Rosewall Rd SO16 77 C2
Rosewarne Ct 28 SO23 2 A1
Rosewood PO13 155 C1
Rosewood Gdns
Clanfield PO8 88 B3
Marchwood SO40 102 A1
New Milton BH25 194 C2
Rosina Cl PO7 135 A4
Roslin Gdns BH3 204 B4
Roslin Rd BH3 204 C4
Roslin Rd S BH3 204 C4
Roslyn Ho PO5 215 B1
Rosoman Ct SO19 103 C2
Rosoman Rd SO19 103 C2
Ross Gdns
Bournemouth BH11 188 B3
Southampton SO16 78 A1
Ross Glades BH3 204 C3
Ross Mews 2 SO31 127 A3
Ross Rd BH24 117 B1
Ross Way PO13 179 C2
Rossan Ave SO31 152 B4
Rossington Ave SO18 103 C4
Rossington Way SO18 103 C4
Rossiters La SO40 99 C3
Rossiters Quay BH23 207 B3
Rossley Cl BH23 193 C1
Rosslyn Cl SO52 54 A2
Rossmore Par BH12 203 A4
Rossmore Rd BH12 203 B4
Rostrevor La 3 PO4 182 C1
Rostron Cl SO18 80 A1
Rosyth Rd SO18 103 C4
Rotary Cl BH21 163 C4
Rotary Ct SO31 127 A3
Rotary Ho SO15 102 B4
Rothbury Cl
Southampton SO19 104 A2
Totton SO40 76 B1
Rothbury Pk BH25 195 A1
Rother Cl Petersfield GU31 41 B2
West End SO18 80 A1
Rother Dale SO19 104 C2
Rother Ho GU33 20 C2
Rotherbank Farm La
GU33 21 A3
Rothercombe La GU32 40 A2
Rotherfield Rd
Bournemouth BH5 206 A2
Christchurch BH23 194 A1
Rotherley 1 GU32 40 C2
Rotherwick Cl PO9 136 A3
Rothesay Dr BH23 208 C4
Rothesay Rd
Bournemouth BH4 204 B3
Gosport PO12 181 A4
Rothsbury Dr SO53 55 A3
Rothschild Cl SO19 103 C1
Rothville Pl SO53 30 A1
Rothwell Cl 12 PO6 133 A1
Rotterdam Dr BH23 207 B4
Rotterdam Twrs 6
SO19 126 C4
Roughdown La SO45 150 B1
Roumelia La BH5 205 C2
Round Hill SP6 69 C1
Roundabouts The GU33 21 A3
Roundcopse SO45 125 B2
Roundhaye Rd BH11 188 C3
Roundhill Cl SO18 80 A1
Roundhill Cross SP6 45 C1
Roundhouse Ct PO11 185 A1
Roundhouse Dr SO40 100 A3
Roundhouse Mdw PO10 161 A4
Roundhuts Rise 4 SO23 11 B4
Roundway PO7 134 C4
Roundways BH11 188 C2
Routs Way SO16 77 C4
Row The SP5 47 B4
Row Wood La PO13 155 A1
Rowallan Ave PO13 180 B4
Rowan Ave PO8 112 A1
Rowan Cl
Bursledon SO31 127 C4
Christchurch BH23 208 B4
Lee-on-the-Solent PO13 179 C1
Romsey SO51 53 B3
Southampton SO16 78 A2
St Leonards BH24 139 B2
Swanmore SO32 84 A2
Sway SO41 172 A1
Totton SO40 100 B3
Rowan Ct
Portsmouth PO4 182 C2
Southampton SO19 103 C2
Rowan Dr
Broadstone BH17 186 C1
Rowan Dr *continued*
Christchurch BH23 208 B4
Verwood BH31 115 A2
Rowan Gdns SO30 105 B3
Rowan Tree Cl GU33 21 A2
Rowan Way
Fareham PO14 154 B4
Havant PO9 136 A2
Rowans Pk SO41 197 B2
Rowans The SO40 101 C1
Rowbarrow Cl BH17 187 C1
Rowborough Rd SO18 103 C4
Rowbury Rd PO9 135 B3
Rowden Cl SO51 50 C1
Rowe Asheway SO31 128 C2
Rowena Ct PO5 215 C2
Rowena Rd BH6 206 C3
Rowes Alley PO1 181 C2
Rowes La SO41 199 A4
Rowhay La SO32 58 B3
Rowhill Dr SO45 125 B2
Rowin Cl PO11 185 B1
Rowland Ave BH15 202 C3
Rowland Rd
Fareham PO15 130 C1
Portchester PO6 132 C1
Rowlands Ave PO7 111 C1
Rowlands Castle Rd
PO8 112 C3
Rowlands Castle St John's CE
Prim Sch PO9 136 A4
Rowlands Castle Sta
PO9 113 B1
Rowlands Cl SO53 55 A2
Rowlands Hill BH21 163 B3
Rowlands Wlk 2 SO18 80 A1
Rowley Cl SO30 105 C4
Rowley Ct SO30 105 C4
Rowley Dr SO30 105 C4
Rowlings Rd SO22 1 B2
Rowner Cl PO13 155 B1
Rowner Jun & Inf Schs
PO13 155 B1
Rowner La Gosport PO13 155 B1
Gosport, Rowner PO13 180 B4
Rowner Rd Gosport PO13 155 A1
Stubbington PO13 155 A1
Rownhams CE Prim Sch
SO16 77 C3
Rownhams Cl SO16 77 C3
Rownhams Ct SO16 77 C2
Rownhams La SO52,SO16 53 C1
Rownhams Pk SO16 77 C4
Rownhams Rd
Bournemouth BH8 190 B2
Havant PO9 135 B3
North Baddesley SO52 54 A2
Southampton SO16 77 C2
Rownhams Rd N SO16 77 C3
Rownhams Way SO16 77 C3
Roxan Ct 9 SO15 102 C4
Roxburgh Ho SO31 129 A2
Royal Arc 5 BH7 205 C2
Royal Bournemouth Gen
Hospl The BH7 191 A1
Royal Crescent Rd
SO14 103 A2
Royal Ct
Chandler's Ford SO53 55 B3
Southampton SO17 79 B1
Royal Gate PO4 183 A1
Royal Gdns PO9 113 A1
Royal Greenjackets Mus★
SO23 10 C4
Royal Hampshire Cty Hospl
SO22 10 C4
Royal Hampshire Regiment
Mus★ SO23 10 C4
Royal London Pk SO30 105 A4
Royal Marines Mus★
PO4 183 A1
Royal Naval Cotts PO17 132 C3
Royal Naval Hospl Haslar
PO12 181 B1
Royal Naval Mus★ PO1 181 C3
Royal Oak Rd BH10 189 B3
Royal South Hants Hospl
SO14 103 A3
Royal Sovereign Ave
PO14 155 A3
Royal The PO11 184 C1
Royal Victoria Ctry Pk★
SO31 127 B2
Royal Victoria Hospl
BH4 204 B2
Royal Way PO7 135 A4
Royden La SO41 173 B2
Roydon Cl SO22 10 C3
Royster Cl BH17 187 B1
Royston Ave SO50 56 A3
Royston Cl SO17 79 A1
Royston Ct SO40 76 C1
Royston Dr BH21 163 B3
Royston Pl BH25 210 A4
Rozel Ct SO16 77 C2
Rozel Manor BH13 204 A1
Rozelle Cl SO22 1 A3
Rozelle Rd BH14 203 B2
Ruben Dr BH15 201 B1
Rubens Cl BH25 195 A2
Ruby Ct PO7 134 C4
Ruby Rd SO19 104 A3
Rudd La SO51 27 C4
Rudgewick Cl PO16 156 A4
Rudmore Ct 17 PO2 157 B1
Rudmore Rd PO2 182 B4
Rudmore Sq PO2 182 B4
Ruffield Cl SO22 1 B1
Rufford Cl SO50 56 A3
Rufford Gdns BH6 206 C3
Rufus Cl
Chandler's Ford SO53 55 C4
Rownhams SO16 77 B3
Rufus Ct SO43 122 A3
Rufus Gdns SO40 100 B4
Rufus Stone★ SO43 98 A3
Rugby Rd Poole BH17 187 A1
Portsmouth PO5 215 D2
Rumbridge Gdns SO40 101 A4
Rumbridge St SO40 101 A3
Runnymede
Fareham PO15 130 B2
West End SO30 80 B1
Runnymede Ave BH11 188 C3
Runton Rd BH12 203 C3
Runway The BH23 208 A4
Rushall La BH21 186 A3
Rushcombe Fst Sch
BH21 186 B3
Rushcombe Way BH21 186 C3
Rushes Farm GU32 40 C2
Rushes Rd GU32 40 C2
Rushes The SO40 101 C1
Rushford Warren BH23 207 C2
Rushin Ho PO16 156 B4
Rushington Ave SO40 100 C3
Rushington Bsns Pk
SO40 100 C3
Rushington La SO40 100 C3
Rushmere Gate PO7 86 B1
Rushmere La PO7 110 C4
Rushmere Rd BH6 206 B4
Rushmere Wlk 11 PO9 135 B3
Rushpole Ct SO45 125 B2
Rushton Cres BH3 204 C3
Ruskin Ave BH9 190 A2
Ruskin Rd Eastleigh SO50 56 A3
Portsmouth PO4 183 A2
Ruskin Way PO8 111 C2
Rusland Cl SO53 55 A4
Russel Rd BH10 189 B3
Russell Bldgs PO16 156 B4
Russell Churcher Ct
PO12 180 C4
Russell Cl PO13 179 C1
Russell Cotes Art Gall &
Mus★ BH1 205 A1
Russell Cotes Rd BH1 205 A1
Russell Ct 3 BH25 195 A2
Russell Dr
Christchurch BH23 207 B3
Mottisfont SO51 5 B1
Russell Gdns
Hamworthy BH16 201 B2
St Leonards BH24 140 A3
Russell Pl Fareham PO16 131 A1
Southampton SO17 79 A1
Russell Rd Havant PO9 135 C1
Lee-on-the-Solent PO13 179 C1
Winchester SO23 2 A1
Russell St Gosport PO12 181 A3
21 Southampton SO14 103 A2
Russell Way GU31 41 A1
Russet Cl Ferndown BH22 165 B3
9 Lymington SO41 197 C1
Russet Gdns PO10 161 A4
Russet Ho SO30 105 A3
Russett Cl SO32 84 A2
Rustan Cl Fair Oak SO50 57 B1
Hedge End SO30 105 A3
Rustington Ho PO1 215 B3
Rutland Ct SO18 104 A4
Rutland Gdns SO31 105 A1
Rutland Manor 9 BH12 204 A2
Rutland Rd
Bournemouth BH9 205 A4
Christchurch BH23 191 C1
Rutland Way SO18 80 A1
Ruxley Cl SO45 150 B2
Ryall Rd BH17 187 B1
Ryan Cl BH22 165 B4
Ryan Gdns
Bournemouth BH11 189 A3
Ferndown BH22 165 B4
Rydal Cl
Christchurch BH23 191 B2
20 Cosham PO6 133 A1
Rydal Ho 22 PO6 133 A1
Rydal Mews BH21 163 B3
Rydal Rd PO12 181 A4
Ryde Pl PO13 180 A2
Ryde Terr SO14 103 A2
Rye Cl SO53 54 C3
Rye Dale SO40 100 B2
Rye Paddock La SO45 151 A2
Ryecroft Havant PO9 136 A1
Titchfield PO14 129 B1
Ryecroft Ave BH11 188 C3
Ryedown La SO51 51 C2
Ryefield Cl GU31 41 B2
Ryefield Cotts GU31 41 C1
Rylandes Ct SO16 77 C2

S

Sabre Rd PO10 161 A2
Sackville St PO5 215 B2
Saddle Cl BH21 164 B3
Saddlers Cl SO50 56 A3
Sadlers La SO45 126 A1
Sadlers Wlk PO10 161 A4
Saffron Ct
Bournemouth BH11 188 B2
Locks Heath SO31 128 C1
Saffron Dr BH23 208 A4
Saffron Way
Bournemouth BH11 188 B2
Swanwick PO15 129 B4
Sage Cl PO7 135 A3
Sages La GU34 17 B3
Sailors La SO32 60 B4
Sainsbury Lodge PO1 215 D3
Saints Cl BH21 138 C4
St Adlem's CE Comb Sch
BH12 204 A3
St Agatha's Rd SO31 128 A2
St Agathas Way PO1 215 B4
St Alban's Ave BH8 205 B4
St Alban's CE Prim Sch
PO9 136 A2
St Alban's Cres BH8 205 A4
St Alban's Rd
Bournemouth BH8 205 A4
Havant PO9 136 A2
Portsmouth PO4 182 C2
Southampton SO14 103 A3
St Albans Ct PO13 180 B3
St Aldhelm's BH14 203 C2
St Aldhelm's Cl BH13 203 C2
St Aldhelm's Rd BH13 203 C2
St Andrew Cl PO8 88 B1
St Andrew's Bldgs SO31 128 A1
St Andrew's Rd
Cosham PO6 158 C4
Gosport PO12 181 A2
Portsmouth PO5 215 C2
South Hayling PO11 185 A1
St Andrews BH23 207 A3
St Andrews Cl
Michelmersh SO51 27 B3
North Baddesley SO52 53 C3
St Andrews Gn SO32 61 B3
St Andrews Ho 21 SO17 103 A4
St Andrews Pk SO50 81 B3
St Andrews Rd
Broadstone BH18 187 A3
Southampton SO14 103 A3
St Ann's Cres PO12 181 A3
St Ann's Ct 1 BH1, 205 C3
St Ann's Hospl BH13 214 C3
St Ann's Rd PO8 112 B4
St Anne's Ave BH6 206 C3
St Anne's Convent RC Girls
Sch SO15 102 C3
St Anne's Gdns SO19 103 C1
St Anne's Gr PO14 154 C4
St Anne's Rd
Portsmouth PO4 182 C2
Southampton SO19 103 C1
Upton BH16 201 A4
St Annes Cl SO22 10 B2
St Annes Gdns SO41 197 B2
St Annes Ho SO51 52 C3
St Annes La SO32 107 C4
St Annes Mews 18 SO14 103 A4
St Anns Ct 7 SO17 79 A1
St Anthony's RC Prim Sch
PO14 129 B1
St Anthony's Rd BH2 204 C3
St Aubin's Ave SO19 104 A3
St Aubin's Pk PO11 184 B2
St Aubyns Ct 3 BH15 202 A1
St Aubyns La BH24 117 C1
St Augustin's Rd BH2 204 C3
St Augustine Gdns SO17 79 B1
St Augustine Rd PO4 182 C2
St Austell Cl SO50 56 C2
St Barbara Way PO2 157 C2
St Barbe Cl SO51 53 A3
St Barbe Mus★ SO41 197 C2
St Bartholomew's Gdns
PO5 215 C1
St Bede CE Prim Sch
SO23 11 A4
St Bede's Ct 26 SO23 2 A1
St Bernard Ho 24 SO14 103 A2
St Birinus Rd SP5 47 B3
St Blaize Rd SO51 53 B4
St Boniface Ct SO52 54 A2
St Bonnet Dr SO32 83 B4
St Brelade Pl SO16 77 B2
St Brelades BH14 203 B1
St Brelades Ave BH12 188 B1
St Catherine St PO5 182 B1
St Catherine's Par BH23 191 C1
St Catherine's RC Prim Sch
BH21 164 A3
St Catherine's Rd
Bournemouth BH6 206 C2
South Hayling PO11 184 B2
Southampton SO18 79 C1
Winchester SO23 11 A3
St Catherine's Way
BH23 191 B2
St Catherines BH21 163 B2
St Catherines Ct PO11 184 B2
St Catherines Rd SO50 56 A3
St Catherines View
SO30 105 A3
St Catherines Way
Portchester PO16 131 C1
Winchester SO23,SO21 11 B3
St Chads Ave PO2 157 C1
St Christopher Ave
PO16 131 B2
St Christopher's Rd
PO9 135 B2
St Christophers Cl SO52 54 A2
St Christophers Gdns 4
PO13 155 B1

St Christophers Hospl PO16 ... 131 A2
St Christophers Sch SO18 ... 103 C4
St Clair Rd BH13 ... 214 C4
St Clares Ave PO9 ... 135 B4
St Cleeves Way BH22 ... 165 B2
St Clement & St John CE Inf Sch BH8 ... 205 B3
St Clement St
21 Winchester SO22 ... 10 C4
31 Winchester SO23 ... 11 A4
St Clement's Gdns BH1 ... 205 B3
St Clement's Rd BH8 ... 205 B3
St Clements Cl SO51 ... 52 C4
St Clements La BH15 ... 202 A1
St Clements Rd BH15 ... 203 A4
St Colman's Ave PO6 ... 158 A4
St Cross Ct 4 SO23 ... 10 C3
St Cross Hospl★ SO23 ... 10 C2
St Cross Mede SO23 ... 10 C2
St Cross Rd SO22 ... 10 C3
St Cuthberts Cl SO31 ... 129 A2
St Cuthberts La SO31 ... 129 A2
St Cyres Meml Cotts SO41 ... 197 C3
St David's Cl SO40 ... 76 B1
St David's Ct
3 Bournemouth BH1, ... 205 C3
Gosport PO13 ... 180 B3
North Baddesley SO52 ... 54 A2
St David's Rd
Clanfield PO8 ... 88 B3
Portsmouth PO5 ... 215 C2
Upton BH16 ... 201 A4
St Davids Rd SO31 ... 128 C2
St Denys 28 BH25 ... 195 A1
St Denys Prim Sch SO17 ... 79 B1
St Denys Rd SO17,SO18 ... 79 B1
St Denys Wlk 18 PO9 ... 135 B3
St Denys' Sta SO17 ... 103 B4
St Edmondsbury Ct PO13 ... 180 B3
St Edmund Cl PO14 ... 129 A1
St Edmund's Rd SO16 ... 102 A4
St Edmunds RC Sch PO1 ... 215 C3
St Edward's RC/CE Sch BH15 ... 202 C4
St Edward's Rd
Gosport PO12 ... 181 A2
Portsmouth PO5 ... 215 B1
St Edward's Sch SO51 ... 25 A1
St Edward's Terr PO12 ... 181 A3
St Edwards Rd SO31 ... 127 A4
St Elizabeth's Ave SO18 ... 104 A4
St Evox Cl SO16 ... 77 C3
St Faith's CE Prim Sch SO22 ... 10 C3
St Faith's Cl PO12 ... 181 A3
St Faith's Rd
Portsmouth PO1 ... 215 B4
Winchester SO22 ... 10 C3
St Francis Ave SO18 ... 104 A4
St Francis CE Prim Sch SO53 ... 55 A3
St Francis Cl SO45 ... 177 C4
St Francis Ct
Locks Heath PO14 ... 129 B2
2 Portsmouth PO2 ... 157 C2
St Francis Pl PO9 ... 135 C2
St Francis Rd
Blackfield SO45 ... 177 C4
Gosport PO12 ... 181 B1
St Francis Specl Sch PO14 ... 154 B4
St Gabriel's Rd SO18 ... 104 A4
St George Cl SO31 ... 104 C1
St George RC Sch (Boys) SO17 ... 79 B3
St George's Almshos 11 BH15 ... 202 A1
St George's Ave
Bournemouth BH8 ... 205 B4
Havant PO9 ... 136 A1
Poole BH12 ... 203 A4
St George's Beneficial CE Prim Sch PO1 ... 182 A3
St George's Bsns Ctr 28 PO1 ... 182 A3
St George's Cl
Bournemouth BH8 ... 205 B4
Christchurch BH23 ... 208 B4
St George's Cotts SP6 ... 47 B2
St George's Cres SP6 ... 69 C1
St George's Ct
2 Bournemouth BH1, ... 205 C3
North Baddesley SO52 ... 54 A2
7 Portsmouth PO5 ... 215 A1
St George's Dr BH22 ... 165 B2
St George's Ho 14 SO23 ... 11 A4
St George's Rd
Cosham PO6 ... 157 C4
Portsmouth PO1 ... 182 A2
Portsmouth, Southsea PO4 ... 183 A1
South Hayling PO11 ... 184 B2
St George's Sq 7 SO32 ... 83 B4
St George's St
Southampton SO14 ... 103 A2
Winchester SO23 ... 11 A4
St George's Way PO1 ... 182 A3
St George's Wlk 11 PO7 ... 134 C4
St Georges Cl BH23 ... 193 A4
St Georges Cotts
Martin SP6 ... 43 B2
Woodgreen SP6 ... 70 C4
St Georges Ct 4 PO16 ... 155 A4
St Georges Ho 22 SO17 ... 103 A4
St Georges Ind Est PO4 ... 183 A3
St Georges Mans 18 BH5 ... 205 C2
St Georges Rd
Fordingbridge SP6 ... 69 C1
Locks Heath SO31 ... 128 C2
St Georges Sq PO1 ... 182 A3
St Giles Cl SO23 ... 11 A4
St Giles Hill SO23 ... 11 A4
St Giles Way PO8 ... 88 B1
St Helen's Cl PO4 ... 182 C1
St Helen's Par PO4 ... 182 C1
St Helen's Rd
Gosport PO12 ... 180 C2
South Hayling PO11 ... 184 B2
St Helena Gdns SO18 ... 79 C2
St Helena Way PO16 ... 156 B4
St Helens Mews 8 SO50 ... 57 B1
St Helier Pl SO16 ... 77 C2
St Helier Rd BH12 ... 188 B1
St Hellen's Rd PO6 ... 158 B4
St Hermans Mans PO11 ... 185 B1
St Hermans Rd PO11 ... 185 B1
St Hilda Ave PO8 ... 88 B1
St Hubert Rd PO8 ... 88 B1
St Ives End La BH24 ... 140 A2
St Ives Fst Sch BH24 ... 140 A3
St Ives Gdns BH2 ... 204 C3
St Ives Park BH24 ... 140 A3
St Ives Wood BH24 ... 140 A3
St James CE Fst Sch SP6 ... 93 A3
St James CE Prim Sch
Bournemouth BH7 ... 206 A3
Emsworth PO10 ... 136 C1
West End SO30 ... 80 C1
St James Cl Clanfield PO8 ... 88 B2
7 Poole BH15 ... 202 A1
St James Ho 23 SO14 ... 103 A2
St James Hospl PO4 ... 183 B3
St James Pk (Cvn Pk) SO53 ... 55 A4
St James Rd
Ferndown BH22 ... 165 A3
Sway SO41 ... 172 B1
West End SO30 ... 80 B1
St James Way PO16 ... 156 B4
St James' La SO22,SO23 ... 10 C4
St James' Rd PO10 ... 136 C1
St James' Terr SO23 ... 10 C4
St James' Villas SO23 ... 10 C4
St James's 20 BH5 ... 205 C2
St James's Cl SO15 ... 78 B1
St James's Park Rd SO16 ... 78 B1
St James's Rd
Portsmouth PO5 ... 215 B2
Southampton SO15 ... 102 B4
St James's Sq BH5 ... 206 A3
St James's St PO1 ... 182 A3
St John the Baptist CE Prim Sch
Titchfield PO14 ... 129 B1
Waltham Chase SO32 ... 83 C1
St John's Ave PO7 ... 134 C2
St John's Cl
Gosport PO12 ... 181 A3
Wimborne Minst BH21 ... 163 B2
St John's Coll PO5 ... 215 C1
St John's Ct
4 Bournemouth BH1, ... 205 C3
North Baddesley SO52 ... 54 A2
16 Portsmouth PO2 ... 157 B1
St John's Ctr SO30 ... 105 A3
St John's Gdns 3 BH9 ... 189 C1
St John's Hill BH21 ... 163 B3
St John's Hospital (Almshouses)(N) 27 SO23 ... 11 A4
St John's Hospital (Almshouses)(S) 38 SO23 ... 11 A4
St John's Rd
Bournemouth BH5 ... 205 C2
Christchurch BH23 ... 207 A3
Cosham PO6 ... 158 A4
Eastleigh SO50 ... 56 A2
Havant PO9 ... 135 B2
Hedge End SO30 ... 105 A3
Locks Heath SO31 ... 129 A1
Poole BH15 ... 202 B2
Southbourne PO10 ... 137 B1
Winchester SO23 ... 11 A4
St John's St Hythe SO45 ... 126 A2
Winchester SO23 ... 11 A4
St Johns CE Fst Sch BH21 ... 163 B2
St Johns CE Prim Sch PO12 ... 181 A4
St Johns Cl
Rownhams SO16 ... 77 C4
South Hayling PO11 ... 184 C1
St Johns Ct SO40 ... 101 C1
St Johns Dr SO40 ... 101 C1
St Johns Gdns SO51 ... 52 C4
St Johns Glebe SO16 ... 77 C3
St Johns Inf Sch SO14 ... 102 C2
St Johns La SO32 ... 107 C4
St Johns Mews SO31 ... 129 B2
St Johns RC Prim Sch PO1 ... 215 C3
St Johns Rd BH25 ... 195 A4
St Johns Sq 18 PO12 ... 181 A3
St Joseph Cl SO31 ... 129 A2
St Joseph's Mews PO5 ... 215 C1
St Joseph's RC Comb Sch BH12 ... 203 C4
St Joseph's RC Prim Sch BH23 ... 208 A4
St Jude's CE Prim Sch PO1 ... 182 A2
St Jude's RC Prim Sch PO14 ... 130 C1
St Judes Cl PO5 ... 215 B1
St Julien's Hospl (Almhouses) SO14 ... 103 A2
St Just Cl BH22 ... 165 B2
St Katharine's CE Prim Sch BH6 ... 207 A2
St Katherine's CE Prim Sch BH6 ... 206 A2
St Kitts Ho 4 PO6 ... 132 C1
St Lawrence Cl SO30 ... 81 B1
St Lawrence Rd
Eastleigh SO50 ... 56 A2
31 Southampton SO14 ... 103 A2
St Ledger's Pl BH1 ... 205 B3
St Ledger's Rd BH8 ... 205 B3
St Leonard's Ave PO11 ... 185 A2
St Leonard's Rd
Bournemouth BH8 ... 205 A3
Winchester SO23 ... 11 B3
St Leonards Cl PO15 ... 129 C2
St Leonards Hospl BH24 ... 139 B1
St Leonards Rd SO41 ... 199 A4
St Leonards Way BH24 ... 139 B2
St Lucia Ho 2 PO6 ... 132 C1
St Luke's CE Prim Sch
Bournemouth BH9 ... 204 C4
Sway SO41 ... 172 A1
St Luke's CE Sec Sch PO1 ... 215 B3
St Luke's Rd
Bournemouth BH3 ... 204 C4
Gosport PO12 ... 181 A3
St Lukes Cl SO30 ... 81 B1
St Margaret's Almshouses BH21 ... 163 A3
St Margaret's Ave BH23 ... 207 A3
St Margaret's Cl SO18 ... 104 A4
St Margaret's Cotts SO32 ... 59 B1
St Margaret's Rd
Bishopstoke SO50 ... 56 B2
Bournemouth BH10 ... 189 B1
Poole BH15 ... 202 B2
St Margarets BH2 ... 204 C3
St Margarets Cl BH21 ... 163 A3
St Margarets Hill BH21 ... 163 A3
St Margarets Ho 6 SO16 ... 102 C4
St Margarets La PO14 ... 129 C1
St Margarets Rd PO11 ... 185 A2
St Mark's CE Jun Sch SO15 ... 102 B4
St Mark's CE Prim Sch BH10 ... 189 B1
St Mark's Cl PO12 ... 181 A1
St Mark's Pl PO12 ... 181 A1
St Mark's Rd
Bournemouth BH11 ... 189 A2
Gosport PO12 ... 181 A1
Portsmouth PO2 ... 157 B1
St Marks Cl SO53 ... 30 C1
St Marks Ct 6 PO12 ... 181 A3
St Marks Rd
Lymington SO41 ... 197 A2
Southampton SO14 ... 103 A3
St Martin Cl SO23 ... 11 A4
St Martin's Cl
Bishopstoke SO50 ... 56 B2
Southampton SO16 ... 77 C2
St Martin's Ho 15 PO5 ... 182 B1
St Martins Rd BH16 ... 201 A4
St Martins Trad Pk SO23 ... 11 A4
St Mary Gr SO41 ... 196 A1
St Mary Magdalen Almshouses 50 SO23 ... 11 A4
St Mary St
Southampton SO14 ... 103 A2
Winchester SO22 ... 10 B3
St Mary's SO51 ... 52 C3
St Mary's Ave PO12 ... 181 A1
St Mary's Church Cl SO18 ... 79 B2
St Mary's Cl
Droxford SO32 ... 61 A1
Kings Worthy SO21 ... 2 B3
Redlynch SP5 ... 47 C2
St Mary's Coll
Southampton SO18 ... 103 C4
Winchester SO23 ... 11 A3
St Mary's Ct BH6 ... 206 C2
St Mary's Ho PO1 ... 182 C3
St Mary's Hospl East Wing PO3 ... 183 A3
St Mary's Hospl West Wing PO1 ... 182 C3
St Mary's Maternity Hospl BH15 ... 202 B2
St Mary's Mews BH22 ... 165 B2
St Mary's Pl SO14 ... 103 A2
St Mary's Prim Sch SO14 ... 103 A2
St Mary's RC Prim Sch PO12 ... 181 A3
St Mary's Rd
Bishopstoke SO50 ... 56 B2
Bournemouth BH1 ... 205 B3
Ferndown BH22 ... 165 B3
Liss GU33 ... 20 C2
Netley SO31 ... 127 B3
Poole BH15 ... 202 C2
St Mary's Rd *continued*
Portsmouth PO1 ... 182 C3
South Hayling PO11 ... 184 C2
Southampton SO14 ... 103 A3
Stubbington PO14 ... 154 B2
St Mary's Stad SO14 ... 103 A3
St Mary's Terr SO21 ... 32 A3
St Marys Cl BH23 ... 193 B4
St Matthew's Rd PO6 ... 157 C4
St Matthews Cl 22 SO14 ... 103 A3
St Matthews Ct PO12 ... 181 B3
St Matthews Rd SO22 ... 1 B1
St Merrin's Cl BH10 ... 189 B2
St Michael's 2 BH2 ... 204 B2
St Michael's CE Mid Sch BH21 ... 163 C4
St Michael's CE Prim Sch BH2 ... 204 B2
St Michael's Ct 28 PO6 ... 133 A1
St Michael's Gdns 26 SO22 ... 10 C4
St Michael's Gr PO14 ... 154 C4
St Michael's Ho 8 PO14 ... 154 C4
St Michael's Mews 16 BH2 ... 204 C2
St Michael's Pas SO23 ... 11 A3
St Michael's Pl 18 BH2 ... 204 C2
St Michael's Rd
Bournemouth BH2 ... 204 C1
Havant PO9 ... 135 B2
Portsmouth PO1 ... 215 A2
Winchester SO22 ... 10 C3
St Michael's Rdbt BH4 ... 204 B2
St Michael's Sq 16 SO14 ... 102 C2
St Michael's St 18 SO14 ... 102 C2
St Michaels Cl
Blackfield SO45 ... 150 C1
Hamworthy BH15 ... 201 C1
Verwood BH31 ... 114 C3
St Michaels Ct 1 BH6 ... 206 B2
St Michaels Rd
Locks Heath SO31 ... 129 A1
Totton SO40 ... 100 C4
Verwood BH31 ... 114 C2
St Michaels Way PO8 ... 88 B1
St Monica Inf Sch SO19 ... 104 A2
St Monica Jun Sch SO19 ... 104 A2
St Monica Rd SO19 ... 104 A2
St Nicholas Ave PO13 ... 180 B4
St Nicholas Flats 18 PO2 ... 157 B1
St Nicholas Rise SO23 ... 2 A3
St Nicholas Row PO17 ... 108 A2
St Nicholas St PO1 ... 182 A2
St Nicholas' Rd PO9 ... 135 B2
St Osmund's Rd BH14 ... 203 B2
St Patrick's Ct SO52 ... 54 A2
St Patrick's La GU33 ... 21 B3
St Patrick's RC Prim Sch SO19 ... 103 C2
St Paul's Hill SO22 ... 10 C4
St Paul's La BH1 ... 205 A2
St Paul's Pl BH1 ... 205 A2
St Paul's Rd
Bournemouth BH1 ... 205 A2
Locks Heath SO31 ... 128 C3
Portsmouth PO5 ... 215 A2
St Paul's Sq PO5 ... 215 A2
St Pauls Pl 19 SO22 ... 10 C4
St Pauls RC Prim Sch PO6 ... 157 A4
St Peter St SO23 ... 11 A4
St Peter's Ave PO11 ... 160 B1
St Peter's Cres 36 BH1 ... 204 C2
St Peter's Ct
17 Petersfield GU32 ... 40 C2
7 Poole BH14 ... 203 A2
St Peter's Gr PO5 ... 215 C1
St Peter's RC Comp Sch BH6 ... 206 C2
St Peter's RC Prim Sch SO22 ... 10 A3
St Peter's RC Sch BH7 ... 206 A4
St Peter's Rd
Bournemouth BH1 ... 205 A2
Petersfield GU32 ... 40 C2
Poole BH14 ... 203 A2
St Peter's Rdbt BH1 ... 205 A2
St Peter's Sq 6 PO10 ... 160 C4
St Peter's St SO32 ... 83 B4
St Peter's Wlk 38 BH1 ... 204 C2
St Peters Cl SO32 ... 106 B4
St Peters Ct
Bournemouth BH1 ... 205 A2
4 Emsworth PO10 ... 161 A4
St Peters RC Prim Sch PO7 ... 134 C3
St Peters Rd PO11 ... 160 B2
St Philip's Way SO18 ... 104 A4
St Pirans Ave PO3 ... 183 A4
St Quentin Ho 12 PO14 ... 154 C4
St Richards Gdns PO7 ... 134 B3
St Ronan's Ave PO4 ... 182 C1
St Ronan's Rd PO4 ... 182 C1
St Saviors Cl BH7 ... 206 B4
St Sebastian Cres PO16 ... 131 A2
St Simon Cl SO31 ... 129 A2
St Simon's Rd PO5 ... 182 B1
St Stephen's Ct 6 BH2 ... 204 C2
St Stephen's Rd
Bournemouth BH2 ... 204 C2
Portsmouth PO2 ... 182 C4
Winchester SO22 ... 1 B1
St Stephen's Way 27 BH2 ... 204 C2
St Stephens La BH31 ... 115 A4
St Swithun Cl SO32 ... 83
St Swithun St SO23 ... 11
St Swithun Wells (RC) Prim Sch SO53 ... 55
St Swithun's Cl SO51 ... 28
St Swithun's RC Prim Sch PO5 ... 182
St Swithun's Rd BH1 ... 205
St Swithun's Rd S BH1 ... 205
St Swithun's Sch SO21 ... 11
St Swithuns Ct 7 SO14 ... 103
St Swithuns Rd PO2 ... 157
St Theresas Cl PO9 ... 135
St Thomas Ave PO11 ... 184
St Thomas Cl PO16 ... 131
St Thomas Ct 7 SO50 ... 57
St Thomas Garnet's RC Sch BH5 ... 206
St Thomas Mews 22 SO23 ... 10
St Thomas More's RC Prim Sch PO9 ... 135
St Thomas Pk SO41 ... 197
St Thomas St SO22 ... 10
St Thomas's Cl BH10 ... 189
St Thomas's Ct 5 PO1 ... 182
St Thomas's Rd PO12 ... 181
St Thomas's St
Lymington SO41 ... 197
Portsmouth PO1 ... 182
St Tristan Cl SO31 ... 129
St Ursula Gr PO5 ... 215
St Valerie Rd
Bournemouth BH2 ... 204
Gosport PO12 ... 181
St Vigor Way
Colden Common SO21 ... 31
Colden Common SO21 ... 57
St Vincent Coll PO12 ... 181
St Vincent Cres PO8 ... 112
St Vincent L Ctr PO12 ... 181
St Vincent Rd
Gosport PO12 ... 181
Portsmouth PO5 ... 182
St Vincent St PO5 ... 215
St Walburga's RC Prim Sch BH9 ... 190
St Winifred's Rd
Bournemouth BH2 ... 204
Southampton SO16 ... 78
St Winifred's Sch SO17 ... 79
Salcombe Ave PO3 ... 158
Salcombe Cl SO53 ... 55
Salcombe Cres SO40 ... 100
Salcombe Rd
Southampton SO15 ... 102
Totton SO40 ... 100
Salcot Rd SO23 ... 2
Salem St SO15 ... 78
Salerno Dr PO12 ... 180
Salerno Ho
Fareham PO14 ... 154
Romsey SO51 ... 53
Salerno Pl BH15 ... 201
Salerno Rd
Portsmouth PO2 ... 157
Southampton SO16 ... 78
Salet Way PO7 ... 112
Salisbury Cl SO50 ... 56
Salisbury Ct 1 SO50 ... 56
Salisbury Rd
Awbridge SO51 ... 52
Bournemouth BH1 ... 205
Breamore SP6 ... 70
Burton BH23 ... 192
Cosham PO6 ... 158
Fordingbridge SP6 ... 70
Fordingbridge, Ibsley BH24 ... 94
Ower SO51 ... 76
Poole BH14 ... 203
Portsmouth PO4 ... 182
Ringwood BH24 ... 116
Sopley, Winkton BH23 ... 192
Southampton SO17 ... 79
Totton SO40 ... 76
West Wellow SO51 ... 50
West Wellow SO51 ... 51
Salisbury Road Arc SO40 ... 100
Salisbury St
Fordingbridge SP6 ... 69
6 Southampton SO15 ... 102
Salisbury Terr PO13 ... 179
Salmon Dr SO50 ... 56
Salt La SO32,SO24 ... 34
Salt Meat La PO12 ... 181
Salter Rd BH13 ... 214
Salterns Ave PO4 ... 183
Salterns Cl PO11 ... 185
Salterns Ct BH14 ... 214
Salterns Est PO16 ... 155
Salterns La
Bursledon SO31 ... 128
Fareham PO16 ... 155
South Hayling PO11 ... 185
Salterns Point BH14 ... 214
Salterns Quay BH14 ... 214
Salterns Rd Poole BH14 ... 203
Stubbington PO13,PO14 ... 179
Salterns Specl Sch SO40 ... 101
Salterns Way BH14 ... 214
Salters Acres SO22 ... 1
Salters La SO22 ... 1
Saltgrass La SO41 ... 212
Saltings Rd BH16 ... 201
Saltings The
Cosham PO6 ... 158

altings The *continued*
Havant PO9 159 C3
altmarsh La PO11 184 C3
altmarsh Rd SO14 103 A2
altmead SO17 79 B1
alvia Cl PO7 135 A3
alwey Rd SO30 105 B3
amber Cl SO41 197 B2
ammy Miller Motorcycle
Mus* BH25 194 C3
ampan Cl SO31 128 C1
amphire Cl SO41 197 C3
amples Way BH17 202 C4
ampson Rd
Gosport PO14 154 C3
Portsmouth PO1 181 C3
amson Cl PO13 180 B4
amson Rd BH15 201 B1
amuel Rd PO1 182 C3
an Diego Rd PO12 181 A3
an Remo Twrs 23 BH5 205 C2
ancreed Rd BH12 203 C4
ancroft BH21 164 A1
and Cl SO51 50 C2
andbanks Bsns Ctr
BH13 214 A2
andbanks Rd BH14 203 A1
andbourne Rd
Bournemouth BH4 204 B1
Poole BH15 202 B2
andcroft Cl PO12 180 C2
andecotes Rd BH14 203 B2
andell Ct SO16 79 A3
anderling Rd PO4 183 B3
anderlings BH24 141 B3
anderlings The PO11 185 A1
andford Ave PO12 180 B2
andford Cl BH9 190 B2
andford Way BH18 186 C1
andhill La PO13 180 A3
andhills Cl BH17 187 B1
andhurst Ct PO5 215 C1
andhurst Dr BH21 139 A4
andhurst Rd SO15 102 C3
andilands Way 11
SO45 126 A1
andisplatt PO14 154 B4
andle Copse SP6 69 A1
andleford Rd PO9 135 B4
andleheath Ind Est SP6 69 A1
andleheath Rd SP6 92 C4
andlewood Cl
Clanfield PO8 88 B3
Totton SO40 100 B4
andmartin Cl BH25 209 C4
andown Cl PO12 180 B2
andown Rd
Christchurch BH23 207 C3
Cosham PO6 157 C4
Southampton SO15 78 A1
andpiper Cl
Broadstone BH17 186 C1
Horndean PO8 112 A4
Marchwood SO40 101 C1
andpiper Rd SO16 78 A3
andpipers PO6 158 C4
andpit La
Beaulieu SO41 199 B3
Poole BH15 202 B2
andport Gr PO16 156 A4
andringham Cl
Bournemouth BH9 190 A2
Chandler's Ford SO53 54 C2
andringham Ct
Bournemouth BH8 205 B3
Southampton, Millbrook
SO15 102 A3
21 Southampton, Westwood Pk
SO17 79 A1
andringham Gdns BH9 190 A2
andringham La PO1 215 D3
andringham Rd
Fareham PO14 154 B4
Petersfield GU32 40 C2
Poole BH14 203 B2
Portsmouth PO1 215 D3
Southampton SO18 79 C1
andsbury La GU32 40 B3
andy Beach Est PO11 185 C1
andy Brow PO7 134 B2
andy Cl Petersfield GU31 41 B2
Wimborne Minst BH21 164 A4
andy Down SO41 173 B2
andy La
Abbotswood SO51 28 A2
Bournemouth BH6 206 A3
Christchurch BH23 191 C1
Fair Oak SO50 57 B1
Lyndhurst SO43 121 C2
North Baddesley SO52 54 A3
Pamphill BH21 162 A3
Rake GU33 21 C2
Redlynch SP5 47 C4
St Leonards BH24 140 A3
Three Legged Cross BH21 114 C1
Titchfield PO14 153 C4
Upton BH16 201 A3
Verwood BH31 115 A3
Waltham Chase SO32 83 B1
Wimborne Minst BH21 164 A4
andy Mead Rd BH8 190 C1
andy Plot BH23 207 B4
andy Point Rd PO11 185 C1
andy Way BH10 189 C2
andycroft SO31 152 B4
andyfield Cres PO8 111 C2
andyhurst Cl BH17 187 B1
anross Cl PO14 179 A3

Santoy BH13 214 B3
Sapphire Ridge PO7 135 A4
Saracen Cl SO41 197 B1
Saracens Rd SO53 55 C4
Sarah Cl BH7 206 A4
Sarah Robinson Ho 39
PO1 182 A3
Sarah Sands Cl BH23 207 B4
Sarisbury CE Jun Sch
SO31 128 C3
Sarisbury Gate SO31 129 A3
Sarisbury Inf Sch SO31 128 C2
Sark Rd BH12 203 B4
Sarnia Ct SO16 77 C2
Sarum Ave BH22 138 C2
Sarum Cl SO22 10 B4
Sarum Ct BH14 203 B2
Sarum Rd
Chandler's Ford SO53 55 C3
Winchester SO22 10 A4
Sarum Road Hospl SO22 10 B4
Sarum St 14 BH15 202 A1
Sarum View SO22 10 A4
Sarum Wlk SO41 197 B3
Satchell La SO31 128 A2
Saturn Cl SO16 77 C2
Saulfland Dr BH23 208 B4
Saulfland Ho BH23 208 B4
Saulfland Pl BH23 208 B4
Saunders Ho PO6 132 C1
Saunders La SO51 26 C3
Saunders Mews PO4 183 A1
Savernake Cl
Gosport PO13 155 B1
9 Romsey SO51 28 A1
Saville Cl
Bishopstoke SO50 56 B3
Gosport PO12 180 C2
Saville Ct 9 BH21 163 B2
Saville Gdns PO16 131 A2
Savoy Bldgs 22 PO16 131 A1
Savoy Ho SO40 101 A4
Sawmills The SO32 82 A3
Sawyer Cl SO22 1 A1
Saxholm Cl SO16 78 C3
Saxholm Dale SO16 78 C3
Saxholm Way SO16 78 C3
Saxley Ct PO9 135 B3
Saxon Cl Horndean PO8 88 B2
Locks Heath SO31 128 C1
Portchester PO16 132 A1
Saxon Gdns SO30 105 A3
Saxon Ho 17 SO14 103 B3
Saxon Hts BH6 206 C3
Saxon King Gdns BH6 207 A2
Saxon Mdw SP5 46 C4
Saxon Pl SO41 197 B3
Saxon Rd Blackfield SO45 150 C1
Southampton SO15 102 B3
Winchester SO23 2 A1
Saxon Shore Inf Sch
PO6 156 C4
Saxon Sq Sh Ctr 4
BH23 207 A3
Saxon Way Alderholt SP6 93 A3
Romsey SO51 53 A4
Saxon Wlk SO53 55 C3
Saxonbury Rd BH6 206 C3
Saxonford Rd BH23 208 B4
Saxonhurst SP5 47 A4
Saxonhurst Cl BH10 189 C3
Saxonhurst Gdns BH10 189 C2
Saxonhurst Rd BH10 189 C2
Saxton Ct 15 SO23 11 A4
Sayers Rd SO50 56 C2
Scafell Ave PO14 154 B4
Scallows La SO51 50 C3
Scantabout Ave SO53 55 C4
Scantabout Prim Sch
SO53 55 C4
Scarf Rd BH17 202 C4
Scarff Ct PO11 185 A1
Scholars' Wlk PO6 158 B4
School Cl
Chandler's Ford SO53 55 A3
Verwood BH31 115 A4
School Hill SO32 85 B3
School La Boldre SO41 197 C4
Bournemouth BH11 189 A3
Bransgore BH23 169 C2
Chandler's Ford SO53 55 A3
Compton (Sussex) PO18 90 C1
Denmead PO7 110 B3
Emsworth PO10 160 C4
Hamble-le-Rice SO31 128 A1
Kings Worthy SO23 2 A3
3 Liss GU33 20 C2
Lymington SO41 197 C2
Michelmersh SO51 6 B1
Milford on Sea SO41 211 C3
Petersfield GU32 41 A3
Poole BH15 202 B3
Ringwood BH24 141 A4
Southbourne PO18 161 C4
St Leonards BH24 140 A2
Three Legged Cross BH21 138 C4
Westbourne PO10 137 A3
Wimborne Minst BH21 163 A3
School Pl SO19 103 C2
School Rd
Bransgore BH23 169 C2
Bursledon SO31 128 A4
Fawley SO45 151 A2
Gosport PO12 155 C1
Havant PO9 135 C1
Hythe SO45 126 A2
Nomansland SP5 73 B4
Redlynch SP5 48 A3

School Rd *continued*
Romsey SO51 28 B1
Totton SO40 101 A3
Twyford SO21 31 C3
West Wellow SO51 50 C1
Wickham PO17 108 A2
Schooner Way
Locks Heath SO31 128 C1
Portsmouth PO4 183 B3
Schooners Cl PO13 179 C2
Scimitars The PO14 154 A2
Scivier's La SO32 58 B1
Scotland Cl SO50 57 C1
Scotney Ct 21 PO9 136 A3
Scott Cl
Colden Common SO21 57 A4
Poole BH12 188 C1
Stubbington PO14 154 B2
Scott Ho 2 PO2 157 B1
Scott Rd Eastleigh SO50 55 C1
Poole BH12 188 C1
Portsmouth PO1 181 C3
Portsmouth, Hilsea PO3 157 C3
Southampton SO19 103 C1
Scott's Gn BH23 207 C4
Scott-Paine Dr SO45 126 A2
Scotter Rd
Bishopstoke SO50 56 B2
Bournemouth BH7 206 A3
Scotter Sq SO50 56 B2
Scotts Hill La BH23 207 B4
Scratchface La
Havant PO9 135 A1
Waterlooville PO7 134 C2
Scullards La 1 SO14 102 C2
Sea Breeze Gdns PO4 183 B2
Sea Crest Rd PO13 179 C1
Sea Front PO11 184 C2
Sea Front Est PO11 185 A1
Sea Grove Ave PO11 185 A1
Sea Kings PO14 179 A3
Sea La PO14 179 B2
Sea Mill Gdns 24 PO1 182 A3
Sea Pines 9 SO41 211 B2
Sea Point 8 BH13 214 C4
Sea Rd
Barton on Sea BH25 209 C4
Bournemouth, Boscombe
BH5, BH6 205 C2
Bournemouth, Southbourne
BH6 206 C2
Milford on Sea SO41 211 C2
Southampton SO19 103 B2
Sea View Cotts PO10 160 C4
Sea View Est SO31 127 A3
Sea View Rd
Cosham PO6 134 B1
Poole BH12 203 A3
South Hayling PO11 185 B2
Upton BH16 201 A4
Sea Vixen Ind Est BH23 208 A4
Seabank Cl BH16 201 A4
Seabird Way PO16 155 A4
Seabourne Pl 12 BH5 206 A3
Seabourne Rd BH5 206 A3
Seacombe Gn SO16 77 B1
Seacombe Rd BH13 214 A2
Seacroft Ave BH25 209 C4
Seafarers Wlk PO11 185 C1
Seafield Cl BH25 209 C4
Seafield Dr BH6 206 C3
Seafield Park Rd PO14 179 A3
Seafield Rd
Barton on Sea BH25 209 C4
Bournemouth BH6 206 B2
Christchurch BH23 208 B4
Portchester PO16 156 A4
Portsmouth PO3 158 A1
Southampton SO16 77 C2
Seafield Terr PO12 181 B2
Seafields PO10 160 C4
Seaford Cl SO31 104 C1
Seagarth Cl SO16 78 B2
Seagarth La SO16 78 B2
Seager's Ct PO1 181 C2
Seagrove Rd PO2 157 B1
Seagull Cl PO4 183 B3
Seagull Ct PO10 136 C1
Seagull La PO10 136 C1
Seagull Rd BH8 190 B1
Seagulls The PO13 180 A2
Seahorse Wlk PO12 181 B3
Sealark Rd PO12 181 B4
Seamans La SO43 98 B2
Seamead PO14 179 B2
Seamoor La BH4 204 A2
Seamoor Rd BH4 204 A2
Searles Hill SO21 32 A3
Seathrift Cl PO13 179 C1
Seathwaite Ho 26 PO6 133 A1
Seaton Ave PO3 183 A4
Seaton Cl
Christchurch BH23 209 A4
Lymington SO41 197 C3
Stubbington PO14 179 B3
West End SO18 80 B1
Seaton Rd BH23 209 A4
Seatown Cl BH17 188 A1
Seaview Ave PO16 132 C1
Seaview Ct Gosport PO12 180 B2
14 Lee-on-the-Solent
PO13 179 C1
Seaview Rd
Barton on Sea BH25 209 B4
Christchurch BH23 194 B1
Seaward Ave BH25 209 C4
Seaward Gdns SO19 103 C2
Seaward Rd Hythe SO45 126 A2

Seaward Rd *continued*
Southampton SO19 103 C2
Seaward Twr PO12 181 C2
Seaway BH25 210 A4
Seaway Ave BH23 208 B4
Seaway Cres PO4 183 B2
Seaway Gr PO16 156 B3
Seawinds SO41 211 A3
Sebastian Gr PO7 135 A4
Second Ave Cosham PO6 157 C4
Cosham, Farlington PO6 158 C4
Emsworth PO9 136 A1
Southampton SO15 101 B4
Southbourne PO10 161 B4
Second Marine Ave
BH25 210 A3
Second St SO45 150 C4
Sedberg Ho SO16 77 B1
Sedbergh Rd SO16 77 B1
Seddul-Bahr SO30 80 C3
Sedgefield Cl
Portchester PO6 156 C4
Totton SO40 100 B4
Sedgeley Gr PO12 181 A4
Sedgemead SO31 127 A3
Sedgemead Ct SO31 127 A3
Sedgewick Cl PO13 180 B4
Sedgewick Ct SO50 56 B2
Sedgewick Rd
Bishopstoke SO50 56 B2
Southampton SO19 104 B3
Sedgley Cl PO5 215 C2
Sedgley Rd BH9 204 C4
Seed Warehouse The 15
BH15 202 B1
Segars La SO21 31 C3
Segensworth E Ind Est
PO15 129 B3
Segensworth N Ind Est
PO15 129 C3
Segensworth Rd PO15 129 C2
Segensworth W Ind Est
PO15 129 B3
Selangor Ave PO10 136 B1
Selborne Ave
Havant PO9 135 B3
Southampton SO18 104 B4
Selborne Ct 3 SO51 28 A1
Selborne Pl SO22 10 B3
Selborne Rd SO40 100 B4
Selborne Wlk SO18 104 B4
Selbourne Dr SO50 56 A2
Selbourne Gdns PO12 180 C2
Selbourne Rd PO9 135 C1
Selbourne Terr PO1 215 D3
Selby Cl BH18 187 A2
Seldon Cl SO22 10 A2
Seldown BH15 202 B2
Seldown Bridge BH15 202 B1
Seldown La BH15 202 B2
Seldown Rd BH15 202 B2
Self Rd BH15 202 A1
Selfridge Ave BH6 207 A2
Selfridge Cl BH6 207 A2
Selhurst Ho PO1 215 C4
Selhurst Way SO50 57 B1
Seliot Cl BH15 202 B3
Selkirk Cl BH21 163 C1
Sellwood Rd SO31 127 B3
Sellwood Way BH25 209 B4
Selsdon Ave SO51 53 A4
Selsey Ave Gosport PO12 181 A4
Portsmouth PO4 183 A1
Selsey Cl
South Hayling PO11 185 C1
Southampton SO16 77 C1
Selsmore Ave PO11 185 B1
Selsmore Rd PO11 185 A2
Selwood Pk BH10 189 B4
Selworth La SO32 85 A2
Selworthy Cl BH14 203 A1
Selwyn Ct 21 PO6 157 C4
Selwyn Gdns SO50 56 A3
Sengana Cl SO30 105 B3
Senlac Rd SO51 53 A4
Sennen Pl PO6 157 A4
Sentinal Ct BH15 202 C2
Sentinel Cl PO7 112 A1
Seps 4 Rd SO45 151 B2
September Cl SO30 80 B1
Serle Cl SO40 100 A4
Serle Gdns SO40 100 B3
Sermon Rd SO22 1 A1
Serpentine Rd
Fareham PO16 131 A1
Poole BH15 202 B2
26 Portsmouth PO5 182 B1
Waterlooville PO7 134 B2
Service Rd PO6 157 B4
Set Thorns Rd SO41 172 B1
Setley Gdns BH8 190 C2
Setters Cl SO21 56 C4
Settle Cl SO16 102 A4
Settlers Cl PO1 215 C4
Sevenoaks Dr BH7 206 A4
Sevenoaks Rd PO6 157 C4
Severn Cl Cosham PO6 133 A1
Portchester PO16 156 A4
Severn Rd
Ferndown BH22 166 A3
Southampton SO16 101 C4
Severn Way SO30 80 B1
Seward Ave BH6 206 B2
Seward Rise SO51 53 B4
Seymour Cl
Chandler's Ford SO53 55 C3
Portsmouth PO2 182 B4
Southampton SO16 78 B2

Seymour Cl *continued*
Totton SO40 76 B1
Seymour Ho SO16 78 B2
Seymour La SO52 53 C2
Seymour Rd
Lee-on-the-Solent PO13 180 A2
Ringwood BH24 117 A1
Southampton SO16 78 B2
Shackleton Ho 2 PO2 157 C1
Shackleton Rd PO13 180 B4
Shackleton Sq BH23 169 A1
Shadwell Ct 9 PO2 157 B1
Shadwell Rd PO2 157 B1
Shaftesbury Ave
Chandler's Ford SO53 55 B2
Southampton SO17 79 A1
Waterlooville PO7 134 C2
Shaftesbury Cl BH22 138 C1
Shaftesbury Rd
Gosport PO12 181 B2
Poole BH15 202 B2
West Moors BH22 138 C1
Shaftesbury St SP6 69 C1
Shaftsbury Rd
Bournemouth BH8 205 B3
Portsmouth PO5 182 B1
Shaggs Mdw SO43 122 A3
Shakespeare Ave SO17 103 A4
Shakespeare Bsns Ctr
SO50 56 A2
Shakespeare Dr SO40 76 B1
Shakespeare Gdns PO8 111 C2
Shakespeare Jun Sch
SO50 56 A3
Shakespeare Mews
PO14 154 A4
Shakespeare Rd
Bournemouth BH6 206 B4
Eastleigh SO50 56 A2
Portsmouth PO1 182 C4
Wimborne Minst BH21 163 B3
Shakespeare Road Inf Sch
SO50 56 A3
Shalbourne Rd PO12 181 A4
Shalcombe SO31 127 B4
Shalden Cl SO16 78 B2
Shaldon Rd 8 PO9 136 A3
Shales Rd SO18 104 A4
Shallow La SO41 197 C4
Shallows The SP6 70 B4
Shamblehurst La N SO32 81 B2
Shamblehurst La S SO30 81 B1
Shamblehurst Prim Sch
SO30 105 B4
Shamrock Cl PO12 181 B2
Shamrock Ct 2 BH21 163 B2
Shamrock Quay SO14 103 B3
Shamrock Rd SO19 103 B2
Shamrock Villas 9 SO17 79 B1
Shamrock Way SO45 126 A3
Shanklin Cres SO15 78 B1
Shanklin Rd
Portsmouth PO4 182 C2
Southampton SO15 78 B1
Shannon Cl PO15 130 B1
Shannon Ho 26 SO14 103 B3
Shannon Rd
Gosport PO14 155 A3
Stubbington PO14 154 A2
Shannon Way SO53 55 A3
Shapland Ave BH11 188 C3
Shappen Hill La BH24 142 C1
Shapton Cl SO45 150 A2
Shapwick Rd BH15 202 A1
Shard Cl BH31 115 A3
Sharlands Cl BH18 187 A2
Sharlands Rd PO14 155 A3
Sharon Ct PO12 181 B3
Sharon Rd SO30 80 B1
Sharp Rd BH12 204 A4
Sharp's Copse Inf Sch
PO9 136 A3
Sharp's Copse Jun Sch
PO9 136 A3
Sharp's Rd PO9 136 A3
Sharpley Cl SP6 69 C2
Sharpness Cl PO14 154 B4
Sharps Cl PO3 158 A2
Sharvells Rd SO41 211 B3
Shavard La SO32 61 B3
Shaves La BH25 195 A3
Shaw Cl Totton SO40 100 B4
West End SO18 80 A1
Shaw Rd BH24 117 B1
Shawcross Ind Pk PO3 158 A3
Shawfield Rd PO9 160 A4
Shawford Cl
Ashurst SO40 100 A4
8 Southampton SO16 78 C2
Shawford Gdns BH8 190 B1
Shawford Gr PO9 135 B3
Shawford Rd
Bournemouth BH8 190 B2
Twyford SO21 31 C3
Shawford Sta SO21 31 C3
Shayer Rd SO15 78 B1
Shear Hill GU31 41 A3
Sheardley La SO32 62 A1
Shearer Rd PO1 182 C4
Shears Brook Cl BH23 169 A1
Shears Rd SO50 56 C2
Shearwater Ave PO16 155 C4
Shearwater Cl PO13 155 A1
Shearwater Ct PO11 185 B1
Shearwater Dr PO6 158 C4

Sheep Pond La SO32 .... 61 A2
Sheep St GU32 .... 40 C2
Sheepwash La PO7 .... 133 C4
Sheet Prim Sch GU32 .... 41 A3
Sheffield Cl SO50 .... 56 B3
Sheffield Ct PO13 .... 180 B3
Sheffield Rd PO1 .... 215 D3
Sheiling Sch The BH24 .140 B3
Shelbourne Cl BH8 .... 205 B3
Shelbourne Rd BH8 .... 205 A3
Sheldrake Gdns
Hordle SO41 .... 196 A2
Southampton SO16 .... 78 A3
Sheldrake Rd BH23 .... 208 A3
Shelford Rd PO4 .... 183 A3
Shell Bay Sailing Ctr★
BH19 .... 214 A1
Shell Ct SO40 .... 101 C1
Shellcroft SO31 .... 152 B4
Shelley Ave PO6 .... 132 C1
Shelley Cl
Bournemouth BH1, ... 205 C3
Christchurch BH23 .... 208 B4
St Leonards BH24 .... 139 C3
Winchester SO22 .... 10 B4
Shelley Ct
Ferndown BH22 .... 165 B3
Southampton SO15 .... 102 C3
Shelley Gdns
Bournemouth BH1, ... 205 C3
Waterlooville PO8 .... 111 C2
Shelley Hamlets BH23 .. 208 B4
Shelley Hill BH23 .... 208 B4
Shelley Ho 15 BH25 .... 195 A1
Shelley La SO51 .... 75 C4
Shelley Park (Bournemouth & Poole Coll) BH5 .... 205 C2
Shelley Rd
Bournemouth BH1, BH7 .. 205 C3
Eastleigh SO50 .... 55 C1
Poole BH12 .... 203 B3
Southampton SO19 .... 104 C3
Totton SO40 .... 76 B1
Shelley Rd E BH7 .... 205 C3
Shelley Way SO41 .... 211 B3
Shelton Rd BH6 .... 206 B3
Shenley Cl PO15 .... 130 B1
Shenstone Ct 18 BH25 .. 195 A1
Shepards Cl PO14 .... 154 B4
Shepheard's Way PO12 .181 B1
Shepherd Cl BH23 .... 193 C1
Shepherds Cl
Cadnam SO40 .... 99 A3
Winchester SO22 .... 10 A2
Shepherds Down Specl Sch
SO21 .... 31 B3
Shepherds Hey Rd SO40 .76 A1
Shepherds Hill BH24 ... 116 B3
Shepherds La
Compton (Hants) SO21 .... 31 B3
Ibsley BH24 .... 116 A3
Shepherds Purse Cl
SO31 .... 128 C1
Shepherds Rd
Cadnam SO40 .... 99 B3
Winchester SO23 .... 11 B4
Shepherds Way
Bournemouth BH7 .... 206 A4
Nursling SO16 .... 77 B3
Sheppard Cl PO8 .... 112 A3
Sheppards Field 4
BH21 .... 163 A3
Sherborn Cres BH17 .... 188 A1
Sherborne Ct SO50 .... 56 A3
Sherborne Dr BH22 .... 165 B2
Sherborne House Sch
SO53 .... 55 B4
Sherborne Rd SO17 .... 79 A2
Sherborne Way SO30 .. 105 B3
Sherbrooke Cl SO23 .... 2 B4
Sherecroft Gdns SO30 .. 106 A4
Sherfield Ave PO9 .... 136 A3
Sherfield Cl BH8 .... 190 B1
Sherfield English La
SO51 .... 50 B3
Sherfield English Rd SP5 50 A2
Sherfield Ho 26 SO15 ... 102 C4
Sheridan Cl
Southampton SO19 .... 104 B3
Winchester SO22 .... 10 B3
Sheridan Gdns
Swanwick PO15 .... 129 B4
Totton SO40 .... 100 B4
Sheringham Rd
Cosham PO6 .... 133 B1
Poole BH12 .... 203 C3
Sherley Gn SO31 .... 105 A1
Sherrin Cl BH15 .... 202 B3
Sherringham Cl SO45 .. 151 A2
Sherwin Wlk PO12 .... 181 A2
Sherwood Ave
Ferndown BH22 .... 165 B2
Hedge End SO30 .... 105 B2
Poole BH14 .... 203 A2
Sherwood Cl Liss GU33 .. 21 A4
13 Southampton SO16 .... 78 C2
Sherwood Dr BH31 .... 115 A3
Sherwood Gdns SO31 .. 128 C2
Sherwood Rd
Chandler's Ford SO53 .... 30 C1
Gosport PO12 .... 181 A2
Sherwood Way SO45 ... 177 C4
Shetland Cl Cosham PO6 133 C1
Totton SO40 .... 100 A4
Shetland Rise PO15 .... 129 A4
Shetland View BH31 .... 115 A3
Shillinglee PO7 .... 134 C2
Shillingstone Dr BH9 ... 190 A2
Shillingstone Gdns
BH12 .... 203 C4
Shillito Rd BH12 .... 203 C3
Shingle Bank Dr SO41 .. 211 B2
Shinwell Ct 17 SO15 .... 78 A1
Ship Leopard St 12 PO1 182 A3
Shipbuilding Rd PO1 ... 181 C4
Shipcote La SO32 .... 59 B1
Shipley Rd SO21 .... 32 A4
Shipstal Cl BH16 .... 201 B2
Shipton Gn PO9 .... 135 B3
Shipwrights Wlk SO41 .. 212 A2
Shire Cl Swanwick PO15 .129 A4
Waterlooville PO7 .... 112 B1
Shires Cl BH24 .... 141 A2
Shires Copse BH6 .... 206 C2
Shires Mead BH31 .... 115 A3
Shires The SO30 .... 105 A3
Shires Wlk SO40 .... 100 A4
Shirley Ave
Portsmouth PO4 .... 183 B2
Southampton SO15 .... 102 B4
Shirley Cl
Bransgore BH23 .... 169 A1
West Moors BH22 .... 138 C1
Shirley High St SO15,
SO16 .... 102 A4
Shirley Holms SO41 .... 173 A1
Shirley Inf Sch SO15 .... 78 B1
Shirley Park Rd SO16 .. 102 A4
Shirley Rd
Bournemouth BH9 .... 190 A1
Poole BH12 .... 203 A3
Portsmouth PO5 .... 182 C1
Southampton SO15 .... 102 B4
Upton BH16 .... 201 B4
Shirley Twrs SO15 .... 102 B4
Shirley Warren Prim Sch
SO16 .... 78 A1
Shirrel Ct PO12 .... 180 B2
Shoblands Way 10
SO45 .... 126 A1
Shoe La Meonstoke SO32 .. 61 B3
Upham SO32 .... 58 C3
Sholing Ct PO9 .... 135 B3
Sholing Girls Sch SO19 .104 A2
Sholing Inf Sch SO19 .. 104 A3
Sholing Jun Sch SO19 .. 104 A3
Sholing Rd SO19 .... 103 C2
Sholing Sta SO19 .... 103 C1
Shoot Hill PO7&PO17 .... 109 B2
Shoot La PO13 .... 180 A4
Shooters Hill Cl SO19 .. 104 A2
Shop La SO19,SO31 .... 104 C1
Shore Ave
Portsmouth PO4 .... 183 A3
Upton BH16 .... 201 B3
Shore Cl
Milford on Sea SO41 .... 211 B2
Upton BH16 .... 201 B3
Shore Cres SO32 .... 83 B4
Shore Gdns BH16 .... 201 A3
Shore La
Bishop's Waltham SO32 .... 83 B4
Upton BH16 .... 201 B3
Shore Rd Hythe SO45 .... 126 A2
Locks Heath SO31 .... 128 B1
Poole BH13 .... 214 B3
Shoreacres BH13 .... 214 B2
Shorefield Cres SO41 .. 211 B3
Shorefield Cvn Pk SO41 211 A3
Shorefield Rd
Marchwood SO40 .... 101 C1
Milford on Sea SO41 .... 211 A3
Shorefield Way SO41 ... 211 B3
Shorehaven PO6 .... 156 C4
Shorewell SO31 .... 127 B4
Shorewood Cl SO31 .... 128 C1
Short Cl BH12 .... 204 A4
Short Hill Nomansland SP5 73 A4
Romsey SO51 .... 28 B1
Short Rd PO14 .... 179 A3
Short Row PO1 .... 182 A3
Shorts Cl BH23 .... 192 B1
Shorts Rd SO50 .... 57 B1
Shotterfield Terr GU33 ... 20 C2
Shotters Hill Cl SO30 .... 80 B1
Shotts La SO41 .... 198 C2
Shottsford Rd BH15 .... 202 B3
Shraveshill Cl SO40 .... 76 B1
Shrubb's Ave SO41 .... 197 C2
Shrubbery Cl PO16 .... 156 B4
Shrubbery The PO12 ... 180 C4
Shrubbs Hill Gdns SO43 121 C2
Shrubbs Hill Rd SO43 ... 121 C2
Shrubland Cl SO18 .... 104 A4
Sibland Cl PO14 .... 154 B4
Siblings The SO19 .... 104 C3
Sicily Ho 15 PO14 .... 154 C4
Siddal Cl SO19 .... 104 B2
Sidings The Downton SP5 .47 A4
Netley SO31 .... 127 B3
Sidlesham Cl PO11 .... 185 C1
Sidmouth Ave PO3 .... 183 A4
Sidney Gdns 11 BH9 .... 190 A2
Sidney Smith Ct BH17 .. 187 C1
Silchester Cl BH2 .... 204 C3
Silchester Rd PO3 .... 183 A4
Silhouette Ct PO11 .... 185 B1
Silkin Gdns SO40 .... 100 B3
Silkstead Ave PO9 .... 135 C3
Silkstead La SO21 .... 30 C4
Sillen La SP6 .... 43 A2
Silver Birch Ave PO14 .. 154 C4
Silver Birch Cl Liss GU33 .21 A2
Silver Birch Cl *continued*
Poole BH12 .... 204 A2
Southampton SO19 .... 104 B2
Silver Birches SO31 .... 127 C4
Silver Bsns Pk BH23 ... 207 C4
Silver Hill SO23 .... 11 A4
Silver St
Christchurch BH23 .... 207 A3
Hordle SO41 .... 196 B3
Lyndhurst SO43 .... 121 B3
1 Portsmouth PO5 .... 215 A1
Silver Way BH23 .... 208 C4
Silverdale BH25 .... 210 A4
Silverdale Cl BH18 .... 186 C2
Silverdale Cres SP6 .... 93 A3
Silverdale Ct 22 SO15 .. 102 C4
Silverdale Rd SO15 .... 102 C4
Silverlock Cl 1 PO2 .... 182 B4
Silverlock Pl PO10 .... 137 A3
Silvers End 6 SO45 .... 126 A1
Silvers Wood SO40 .... 76 B1
Silversands Gdns PO11 .185 A1
Silverthorne Way PO7 .. 134 B4
Silvertrees PO10 .... 136 C1
Silverweed Cl SO53 .... 54 C4
Silverweed Ct SO31 .... 128 C1
Silverwood Cl
Wimborne Minst BH21 ... 163 B1
Winchester SO22 .... 10 B3
Silvester Rd PO8 .... 111 C1
Silwood Cl SO22 .... 1 B1
Simmonds Cl BH15 .... 202 B3
Simmonds Gn PO11 .... 185 B2
Simmons Cl SO30 .... 105 B4
Simnel St 13 SO14 .... 102 C2
Simon Ct SO18 .... 104 C4
Simon Way SO19 .... 104 C3
Simonds Ct 5 SO23 .... 2 A1
Simpson Cl PO16 .... 156 B4
Simpson Rd PO2 .... 157 B1
Sinah La PO11 .... 184 B2
Sinclair Ct 8 BH14 .... 203 A2
Sinclair Inf Sch SO16 ... 78 A3
Sinclair Jun Sch SO16 ... 78 A3
Sinclair Rd SO16 .... 78 A3
Singleton Dr BH10 .... 189 B1
Singleton Gdns PO8 .... 88 B2
Singleton Way SO40 .... 100 A4
Sir Christopher Cl SO45 126 A2
Sir Christopher Ct 5
SO45 .... 126 A2
Sir Galahad Rd SO53 .... 54 C3
Sir George's Rd SO15 .. 102 B3
Sir Harold Hillier Gardens & Arboretum★ SO51 .... 28 B2
Sir Lancelot Cl SO53 .... 54 C3
Sirdar Ho SO17 .... 79 B2
Sirdar Rd SO17 .... 79 B2
Sirius Ct PO5 .... 215 B2
Siskin Cl
Bishop's Waltham SO32 .... 83 A4
Ferndown BH22 .... 165 A4
Southampton SO16 .... 78 A3
Siskin Gr PO7 .... 135 A3
Siskin Inf Sch PO13 .... 180 B3
Siskin Jun Sch PO13 .... 180 B3
Siskin Rd PO4 .... 183 B3
Sissinghurst Cl SO19 ... 104 A1
Sissinghurst Rd PO16 .. 156 A4
Siverdale Dr PO7 .... 111 B2
Siward Ho 20 GU32 .... 40 C2
Six Dials SO14 .... 103 A3
Six Oaks Rd SO52 .... 54 A2
Sixpenny Cl
Locks Heath PO14 .... 129 A1
Poole BH12 .... 203 C4
Sixth Ave PO6 .... 157 C4
Sizer Way SO45 .... 125 A2
Skew Rd PO17 .... 132 B1
Skinner St BH15 .... 202 B1
Skintle Gn 5 SO21 .... 56 C4
Skipper Cl SO40 .... 102 A2
Skipper Way PO13 .... 180 A3
Skipton Cl BH18 .... 187 A1
Skipton Rd SO53 .... 55 B2
Sky End La SO41 .... 196 A1
Skylark Ct PO4 .... 183 B3
Skylark Mdws PO15 .... 129 C3
Skys Wood Rd SO53 .... 54 C3
Slab La Redlynch SP5 .... 47 B3
West Wellow SO51 .... 50 C2
Slade Cl SO41 .... 196 A2
Slade's La BH10 .... 204 B4
Slades Farm Hostel
BH11 .... 189 B1
Slades Farm Rd BH10 .. 189 B1
Slades Farm Specl Sch
BH10 .... 189 B1
Slades Hill SO45 .... 150 C1
Slater App PO2 .... 157 A1
Slater Cl SO40 .... 100 A4
Sleepbrook Cl BH31 .... 114 C3
Sleeper's Hill Ho SO22 .. 10 B3
Sleeper's Hill Rd SO22 .. 10 B3
Sleepers Delle Gdns
SO22 .... 10 C3
Sleepers Hill Gdns SO22 .10 B3
Sleight La BH21 .... 186 B4
Slepe Cres BH12 .... 203 C4
Slindon Cl PO8 .... 88 B3
Slindon Gdns 15 PO9 ... 135 C1
Slindon St PO1 .... 215 B3
Slingsby Cl PO1 .... 215 A1
Slinn Rd BH23 .... 207 C4
Slip Way BH15 .... 202 A1
Slipper Rd PO10 .... 161 A4
Slipway The PO6 .... 157 A4
Sloane Ave SO45 .... 150 B2
Sloane Ct SO45 .... 150 B2
Sloane Pk SO32 .... 107 B4
Sloane Stanley Ct PO12 181 A3
Slocum Ho 17 PO12 .... 181 B2
Sloe Tree Cl PO14 .... 129 B1
Slough La BH16 .... 201 A3
Smallcutts Ave PO10 ... 137 B1
Smeaton St 7 PO2 .... 157 B1
Smeeton Rd PO13 .... 179 C1
Smith Cl SO45 .... 150 C1
Smith Gr SO30 .... 105 B3
Smith La PO10 .... 161 B1
Smith St PO12 .... 181 A3
Smith's Field SO51 .... 28 A1
Smithe Cl SO50 .... 56 A2
Smithfield Pl BH9 .... 189 C1
Smiths La SO32 .... 107 C4
Smithson Cl BH12 .... 204 B4
Smithy La BH25 .... 194 C3
Smithy The PO7 .... 110 C2
Smugglers La BH21 .... 163 C4
Smugglers La N BH23 ... 193 C1
Smugglers La S BH23 .. 208 C4
Smugglers Reach BH23 208 A3
Smugglers Wood Rd
BH23 .... 193 B1
Smythe Rd SO19 .... 104 B2
Snailing La GU33 .... 20 B4
Snails La BH24 .... 117 A2
Snakemoor La SO32 .... 81 C3
Snapdragon Cl SO31 .... 128 C1
Snape Cl PO13 .... 180 B4
Snellgrove Cl SO40 .... 76 B1
Snellgrove Pl SO40 .... 76 B1
Snooks La SO41 .... 198 A3
Snowberry Cres PO9 ... 136 B2
Snowdon Dr PO14 .... 154 C4
Snowdon Rd BH4 .... 204 B2
Snowdrop Cl SO31 .... 128 C1
Snowdrop Gdns BH23 .. 193 A1
Soake Rd PO7 .... 111 A2
Soalwood La GU32 .... 39 C4
Soberton Ho
Portsmouth PO1 .... 215 C4
34 Southampton SO17 .... 79 A1
Soberton Rd
Bournemouth BH8 .... 205 B3
Havant PO9 .... 135 C2
Soberton Twrs SO32 .... 85 B3
Solar Ct BH13 .... 204 A1
Soldridge Cl 5 PO9 .... 136 A3
Solent Ave
Lymington SO41 .... 198 A2
Southampton SO19 .... 104 C3
Solent Bsns Ctr SO15 .. 102 A3
Solent Bsns Pk PO15 ... 129 C4
Solent Cl
Chandler's Ford SO53 .... 55 C3
Lymington SO41 .... 197 C2
Solent Ct
6 Milford on Sea SO41 .. 211 B2
Southampton SO19 .... 103 C1
Stubbington PO14 .... 179 B3
Solent Ctr PO15 .... 129 C4
Solent Dr
Barton on Sea BH25 .... 210 A4
Hythe SO45 .... 125 C2
Locks Heath SO31 .... 152 B3
South Hayling PO11 .... 184 C1
Solent Gate
Gosport PO14 .... 155 A3
9 Portsmouth PO5 .... 182 B1
Solent Ho
5 Fareham PO16 .... 155 A4
Havant PO9 .... 136 A2
Solent Homes SO19 .... 104 C3
Solent Hts
12 Lee-on-the-Solent
PO13 .... 179 C1
Portsmouth PO4 .... 183 B2
Solent Ind Ctr SO15 .... 102 B3
Solent Ind Est SO30 .... 81 A1
Solent Inf Sch PO6 .... 158 B4
Solent Jun Sch PO6 .... 158 B4
Solent Lo 21 BH25 .... 195 A1
Solent Mdws SO31 .... 128 A1
Solent Pines 2 SO41 ... 211 A2
Solent Rd
Barton on Sea BH25 .... 209 B4
Bournemouth BH6 .... 207 A2
Christchurch BH23 .... 194 A1
Cosham PO6 .... 158 B4
Havant PO9 .... 135 C1
Hythe SO45 .... 149 C4
Southampton SO15 .... 102 C2
Stubbington PO14 .... 179 A3
Solent View Boldre SO41 198 A2
Bournemouth BH6 .... 207 A2
Fawley SO45 .... 178 C4
Lee-on-the-Solent PO13 .. 179 B2
Solent Village PO15 .... 129 C3
Solent Way
Gosport PO12 .... 180 C2
Milford on Sea SO41 .... 211 C2
Solihull Ho PO5 .... 215 A2
Solly Cl BH12 .... 203 C4
Solomon Way BH15 .... 201 B1
Solomons La SO32 .... 83 C1
Solona Cl SO53 .... 55 C4
Solway Ho 10 SO14 .... 103 B3
Somborne Ct 32 SO17 ... 79 A1
Somborne Dr PO9 .... 135 C3
Somborne Ho SO19 .... 103 C1
Somerby Rd BH15 .... 202 B3
Somerford Ave BH23 ... 208 A4
Somerford Bsns Pk
BH23 .... 208 A4
Somerford Cl SO19 .... 104 A3
Somerford Ct BH23 208
Somerford Cty Inf Sch
BH23 207
Somerford Cty Jun Sch
BH23 207
Somerford Rd BH23 207
Somerford Way BH23 .. 207
Somerley Rd BH9 205
Somerley View 1 BH24 .141
Somers Cl SO22 10
Somers Park Prim Sch
PO1 215
Somers Rd
Portsmouth PO1 215
Portsmouth PO1 215
Somers Rd N PO1 215
Somerset Cres SO53 55
Somerset Ct 4 SO15 102
Somerset La SO18 104
Somerset Rd
Bournemouth BH7 206
Christchurch BH23 206
Portsmouth PO5 182
Southampton SO17 79
Somerset Terr SO15 102
Somerstown Flats PO9 .136
Somerton Ave SO18 104
Somerton Cl BH25 195
Somervell Cl PO12 181
Somervell Dr PO16 131
Somerville Ct BH25 194
Somerville Pl 1 PO2 ... 157
Somerville Rd
Bournemouth BH2 204
Kings Worthy SO23 2
Ringwood BH24 141
Sommers Ct SO19 103
Sonata Ho PO6 157
Sonnet Way 1 PO7 135
Sonning Way BH8 190
Soper's La BH23 207
Sopers La BH17 187
Sopley Cl BH25 209
Sopley Ct 19 PO9 136
Sopley Farm Bldgs
BH23 192
Sopley Prim Sch BH23 .168
Sopwith Cl BH23 208
Sopwith Cres BH21 163
Sopwith Way SO31 128
Sorrel Cl Romsey SO51 28
Waterlooville PO7 135
Sorrel Dr PO15 129
Sorrel Gdns BH18 186
Sorrell Cl SO31 128
Sorrell Ct BH23 208
Sorrell Way BH23 208
South Ave Fawley SO45 .. 150
Holbury SO45 150
New Milton BH25 195
Portsmouth PO2 157
South Baddesley CE Prim Sch
SO41 198
South Baddesley Rd
SO41 198
South Bay PO10 161
South Cl Gosport PO12 .. 180
Havant PO9 160
Romsey SO51 28
South Cliff Rd BH2 204
South Cross St PO12 ... 181
South Ct SO31 127
South Downs Coll PO7 .135
South Dr Awbridge SO51 .. 27
Littleton SO22 1
South East Cres SO19 .. 104
South East Rd SO19 104
South End Cl SO21 30
South Front
18 Romsey SO51 52
Southampton SO14 103
South Gr SO41 197
South Hampshire Ind Pk
SO40 76
South Haven Cl BH16 .. 201
South Hill Alderholt SP6 .. 93
Droxford SO32 85
Southampton SO16 79
South Kinson Dr BH11 .189
South La Buriton GU31 65
Clanfield PO8 88
Downton SP5 46
Horndean PO8 89
Nomansland SP5 73
Southbourne PO10 137
Westbourne PO10 137
South Lo BH13 214
South Lodge PO15 130
South Mill Rd SO15 102
South Millers Dale SO53 .55 A
South Normandy 4
PO1 182
South Par
Portsmouth PO5 182
Totton SO40 100
South Parade Pier★
PO4 182
South Park Rd BH12 204
South Pl PO13 180
South Rd
Bournemouth BH1 205
Corfe Mullen BH21 186
Cosham PO6 158
Horndean PO8 88
Poole BH15 202
Portsmouth PO1 182
South Hayling PO11 184
Southampton SO17 103

South Rd *continued*
Southwick PO17 133 A3
South Road Comb Sch BH15 202 B1
South St Eastleigh SO50 80 A4
Emsworth PO10 160 C4
Gosport PO12 181 B2
Havant PO9 135 C1
Hythe SO45 126 A2
Lymington SO41 197 B1
Portsmouth PO5 215 B1
Titchfield PO14 153 C4
South Stoneham Ho SO18 79 B2
South Sway La SO41 196 B4
South Terr PO1 182 A3
South Trestle Rd SO45 151 B3
South View
Bournemouth BH2 204 C3
Winchester SO22 10 C4
South View Cl PO8 112 A2
South View Park Homes SO22 10 B2
South View Pl 17 BH2 204 C2
South View Rd
Christchurch BH23 207 A3
Southampton SO15 102 B4
Winchester SO22 10 A2
South Way PO15 129 C2
South Weirs SO42 172 B4
South Western Cres BH14 203 A1
Southampton Airport Parkway Sta SO18 79 C3
Southampton Central Sta SO15 102 C3
Southampton City Coll SO14 103 A2
Southampton Gen Hospl SO16 78 A1
Southampton Hill PO14 153 C4
Southampton Ho 58 PO9 136 A3
Southampton Inst ofH Ed Marine Operations Ctr SO40 102 A1
Southampton Inst(City Campus) SO14 103 A3
Southampton International Airport SO18 79 C3
Southampton Oceanography Ctr SO14 103 A1
Southampton Rd
Brockenhurst SO41,SO42 173 A2
Cadnam SO40 98 C4
Cadnam, Bartley SO40 99 A4
Cosham PO6 157 B4
Eastleigh SO50 56 A1
Fareham PO14 154 A4
Fareham PO16 131 A1
Fordingbridge SP6 70 A1
Hythe SO45 125 C2
Locks Heath SO31,PO14 129 B2
Lymington SO41 197 B3
Lyndhurst SO43 122 A3
North Baddesley SO51 53 A3
Ringwood BH24 140 C4
Romsey SO51 53 A3
Southampton St 3 SO15 102 C3
Southbourne Ave
Cosham PO6 158 A4
Hermitage PO10 161 A4
Holbury SO45 150 B2
Southbourne Coast Rd BH6 206 C2
Southbourne Cross Roads 6 BH6 206 C2
Southbourne Gr BH6 206 B2
Southbourne Jun & Inf Schs PO10 161 C4
Southbourne Overcliff Dr BH6 206 B2
Southbourne Rd
Bournemouth BH5,BH6 206 B2
Lymington SO41 197 B2
Southbourne Sands BH6 206 B2
Southbourne Sta PO10 161 C4
Southbrook Cl
Havant PO9 159 C4
Poole BH17 188 A1
Southbrook Mews 5 SO32 83 B4
Southbrook Rd
Havant PO9 159 C4
15 Southampton SO15 102 C3
Southcliff PO13 179 C2
Southcliff Rd SO14 103 A4
Southcliffe Ho 1 SO14 103 A3
Southcliffe Rd
Barton on Sea BH25 209 B4
Christchurch BH23 208 B3
Southcote Rd BH1 205 B2
Southcroft Rd PO12 180 C3
Southdale Ct SO53 55 B3
Southdene Rd SO53 55 B3
Southdown Ct 1 BH23 207 C4
Southdown Rd
Compton (Hants) SO21 31 B3
Cosham PO6 158 A4
Horndean PO8 88 B2
Southdown View PO7 111 B1
Southdown Way BH22 138 C1
Southend La SO32 109 B4
Southern Ave BH22 139 A1
Southern Gdns SO40 100 C4
Southern La BH25 209 C4
Southern Oaks BH25 194 C1
Southern Rd
Bournemouth BH6 206 B2
Fawley SO45 151 C1
Lymington SO41 197 B2
Southampton SO15 102 C2
West End SO30 80 C1
Southernhay PO7 110 C2
Southernhay Rd BH31 115 A3
Southey Rd BH23 207 C4
Southfield BH24 141 A3
Southfield La BH24 143 B1
Southfield Mews 6 BH24 141 A3
Southfield Wlk PO9 135 B4
Southfields Cl SO32 83 B4
Southgate St SO23 10 C4
Southgate Villas SO23 10 C4
Southill Ave BH12 203 B3
Southill Gdns BH9 190 A1
Southill Rd
Bournemouth BH9 190 A1
Poole BH12 203 B4
Southlands Cosham PO6 158 A4
Lymington SO41 197 B1
Southlands Ave
Bournemouth BH6 206 C2
Corfe Mullen BH21 186 C3
Southlands Cl BH21 186 B3
Southlands Ct BH18 187 A2
Southlands Sch SO41 197 C4
Southlawns Wlk BH25 194 C1
Southlea Ave BH6 206 C2
Southleigh Gr PO11 184 C2
Southleigh Rd PO9 136 B2
Southmead Rd PO15 130 C1
Southmoor La PO9 159 B4
Southsea Castle★ PO5 182 B1
Southsea Inf Sch PO4 182 C1
Southsea Terr PO5 215 A1
Southview SO32 61 A1
Southville Rd BH5 206 A3
Southwater 1 PO13 179 C1
Southway PO13 155 B2
Southways PO14 179 B3
Southwick Ave PO16 132 C1
Southwick Cl SO22 1 B2
Southwick Ct PO14 155 A3
Southwick Hill Rd PO6 133 C1
Southwick Ho 5 PO1 215 C4
Southwick Pl BH6 206 B4
Southwick Rd
Bournemouth BH6 206 B3
Cosham PO7,PO17 133 B1
Denmead PO7 110 C2
Wickham PO17 108 B2
Southwood Ave
Bournemouth BH6 206 B2
Christchurch BH23 194 A1
Southwood Cl
Christchurch BH23 194 A1
Ferndown BH22 165 B3
Southwood Ct BH23 194 A1
Southwood Gdns SO31 128 C2
Southwood Rd
Portsmouth PO2 157 C2
South Hayling PO11 185 B1
Sovereign Ave PO12 181 B4
Sovereign Bsns Ctr BH15 202 A3
Sovereign Cl
Ashurst SO40 100 B4
Bournemouth BH7 205 C4
Portsmouth PO4 183 B3
Sovereign Cres PO14 129 A1
Sovereign Ct 20 SO17 79 A1
Sovereign Ctr BH1 205 C3
Sovereign Dr
Hedge End SO30 105 B3
Portsmouth PO4 183 B3
Sovereign La PO7 134 C2
Sovereign Sq 8 BH7 205 C2
Sovereign Way SO50 55 C3
Soverign Dr SO30 105 C3
Sowden Cl SO30 105 A4
Sowley La SO41 199 B3
Spa Rd SO14 102 C2
Spain Bldgs 18 GU32 40 C2
Spain The GU32 40 C2
Spalding Rd SO19 104 C3
Spaniard's La SO51 53 A2
Sparkford Cl
Bournemouth BH7 206 A4
Winchester SO22 10 C3
Sparkford Rd SO22 10 C4
Sparrow Cl PO8 111 C2
Sparrow Ct PO13 179 C2
Sparrow Sq SO50 55 B1
Sparrowgrove SO21 31 B2
Sparrowhawk Cl PO3 158 A2
Sparsholt Cl PO9 135 A3
Sparsholt Rd
Southampton SO19 126 C4
Winchester SO21,SO22 9 B2
Spartan Cl
Stubbington PO14 154 B3
Thorney Island PO10 161 A2
Spartina Dr SO41 197 C3
Spear Rd SO14 103 A4
Specks La PO4 183 A3
Speedfields Pk PO14 155 A3
Speedwell Cl
Chandler's Ford SO53 55 A3
Locks Heath SO31 128 C1
Speedwell Dr BH23 208 A4
Speggs Wlk 2 SO30 105 B3
Speltham Hill PO7 86 B1
Spencer Cl PO11 185 A2
Spencer Ct
5 New Milton BH25 195 A1
Stubbington PO14 179 C3
Spencer Dr PO13 179 C1
Spencer Gdns PO8 111 C2
Spencer Rd
Bournemouth BH1 205 B2
Eastleigh SO50 55 C1
Emsworth PO10 136 C2
New Milton BH25 195 A1
Poole BH13 214 C4
Portsmouth PO4 182 C1
Southampton SO19 104 B3
Spenlow Cl PO2 182 B4
Spenser Cl SO31 152 B4
Spetisbury Cl BH9 190 A2
Spice Quay 16 PO1 182 A2
Spicer La BH11 188 C3
Spicer St PO1 215 B4
Spicer's Hill SO40 100 C3
Spicer's Way SO40 100 C3
Spicers Ct 5 SO22 10 C4
Spicewood PO15 130 C1
Spinacre BH25 210 A4
Spindle Cl
Broadstone BH18 186 C1
Havant PO9 136 B2
Spindle Warren PO9 136 B2
Spindlewood Cl
26 Barton on Sea BH25 195 A1
Southampton SO16 79 A3
Spindlewood Way SO40 124 C4
Spinnaker Cl
Gosport PO13 180 B4
South Hayling PO11 184 C2
Spinnaker Dr PO2 157 B2
Spinnaker Grange PO11 160 B2
Spinnaker Ho PO6 157 A4
Spinnaker View PO9 135 A1
Spinners Cl BH22 138 C1
Spinners Gdn★ SO41 173 C1
Spinney Cl
St Leonards BH24 139 B2
Waterlooville PO8 111 C2
Spinney Dale SO45 126 A1
Spinney Gdns SO45 126 A1
Spinney The
Compton (Hants) SO21 31 B4
Denmead PO7 110 C2
Fair Oak SO50 57 A1
Gosport PO13 155 B1
Portchester PO16 131 C1
Southampton SO16 79 A3
St Leonards BH24 139 C3
Totton SO40 76 B1
Waterlooville PO8 112 A3
Spinney Way BH25 195 A3
Spinney Wlk SO18 79 C2
Spinneys La BH22 165 B3
Spinningfield Ho 4 GU32 40 C2
Spitfire Ct SO19 103 B2
Spitfire End 7 SO23 11 B4
Spitfire Link SO23 11 B4
Spitfire Loop SO18 80 A4
Spitfire Quay SO19 103 B2
Spitfire Rdbt SO23 11 B4
Spitfire Way SO31 127 C1
Spithead Ave PO12 181 B1
Spithead Ho 9 PO16 155 A4
Spithead Hts PO4 183 B2
Spittlefields BH24 141 A4
Spouts La SO51 50 B3
Spring Cl Fair Oak SO50 57 B1
Southampton SO19 103 C2
Verwood BH31 114 C3
Spring Cres SO17 103 A4
Spring Ct Poole BH12 203 B3
17 Southampton SO15 102 C3
Spring Firs SO19 103 C2
Spring Garden La PO12 181 B3
Spring Gdns
1 Emsworth PO10 161 A4
North Baddesley SO52 54 A2
Poole BH12 203 B3
Portsmouth PO1 215 A3
Spring Gr SO31 105 A1
Spring House Cl SO21 32 A1
Spring La
Bishopstoke SO50 56 B2
Colden Common SO21 31 C1
New Milton BH25 195 B1
Swanmore SO32 84 A3
Spring Pl 5 SO51 52 C4
Spring Rd
Bournemouth BH1 205 B3
Hythe SO45 126 A2
Locks Heath SO31 128 C3
Lymington SO41 198 A2
Southampton SO19 103 C2
Spring St PO1 215 B4
Spring The PO7 110 C2
Spring Vale
Swanmore SO32 84 A2
Waterlooville PO8 112 A2
Spring Wlk PO1 215 B4
Springbank Rd BH7 205 C4
Springbourne Ct BH1 205 B3
Springbourne Mews BH1 205 B3
Springcroft PO13 155 A3
Springdale Ave BH18 186 C3
Springdale Ct SO40 100 C4
Springdale Fst Sch BH18 186 C2
Springdale Gr BH21 186 C2
Springdale Rd BH18, BH21 186 C2
Springfield 2 GU33 20 C2
Springfield Ave
Bournemouth BH6 207 A2
Christchurch BH23 191 B1
Holbury SO45 150 B2
Springfield Cl
Havant PO9 135 A1
Lymington SO41 198 A2
Verwood BH31 114 C3
Wickham PO17 108 A2
Springfield Cres
Poole BH14 203 A2
Redlynch SP5 47 B3
Springfield Ct SO19 103 C1
Springfield Dr SO40 100 C3
Springfield Gdns BH25 195 B1
Springfield Gr SO45 150 B2
Springfield Rd
Poole BH14 203 A2
Verwood BH31 114 C3
Springfield Sch PO6 158 B4
Springfield Way PO14 179 B3
Springfields Cl 3 SO21 31 C1
Springford Cl SO16 78 A2
Springford Cres SO16 78 A2
Springford Gdns SO16 78 A2
Springford Rd SO16 78 A2
Springhill RC Prim Sch SO15 102 C3
Springhill Rd SO53 55 B3
Springles La PO15 130 A3
Springvale Ave
Bournemouth BH7 206 A4
Kings Worthy SO23 2 A3
Springvale Rd SO23 2 A4
Springwater Cl BH11 189 A2
Springwater Ct BH23 207 B3
Springwater Dr BH23 207 B3
Springwater Rd BH11 189 A2
Springwood Ave PO7 134 C3
Spruce Ave PO7 135 A3
Spruce Cl
Broadstone BH17 186 C1
Locks Heath SO31 152 B4
Spruce Dr
Southampton SO19 104 C3
Totton SO40 100 A4
Spruce Wlk 22 PO13 179 C1
Spur Cl BH21 164 B3
Spur Hill Ave BH14 203 B2
Spur Rd Cosham PO6 157 C4
Poole BH14 203 B2
Waterlooville PO7 134 C4
Spur The Gosport PO12 180 C1
Wickham PO17 108 A2
Spurgeon Rd BH7 206 A3
Spurlings Rd PO17 131 B2
Spurlings Yd PO17 131 B2
Square The
Bournemouth BH2 204 C2
Compton (Sussex) PO18 90 C1
Fawley SO45 151 A2
Gosport PO12 181 B4
Hamble-le-Rice SO31 128 A1
Lymington SO41 197 B2
Petersfield GU32 40 C2
Sherfield English SO51 26 A2
Southbourne PO10 161 B4
Titchfield PO14 153 C4
Westbourne PO10 137 A2
Wickham PO17 108 A2
Wimborne Minst BH21 163 A3
Winchester SO23 11 A4
Squarey Cl SP5 46 C3
Squires Wlk SO19 103 C1
Squirrel Cl 7 SO50 56 C1
Squirrel Dr SO19 104 A2
Squirrel Wlk BH31 114 C3
Squirrel's Cl BH23 191 B1
Squirrels Wlk SO45 125 C1
Stable Cl PO14 129 B1
Stable La 23 GU31 40 C2
Stables The
Christchurch BH23 206 C4
Locks Heath SO31 129 A1
Stacey Cl BH12 203 B4
Stacey Ct PO9 135 B4
Stacey Gdns BH8 190 C1
Staff Rd SO51 6 A1
Stafford Rd
Bournemouth BH1 205 A2
Petersfield GU32 40 C3
Portsmouth PO5 215 C1
Southampton SO15 102 B3
Stag Bsns Pk BH24 141 A3
Stag Cl Bishopstoke SO50 56 C1
New Milton BH25 194 C2
Stag Gates SO45 150 C1
Stag Way PO15 130 B3
Stagbrake Cl SO45 150 A2
Stags La SO21 33 A3
Stagshorn Rd PO8 112 B4
Stagswood BH31 114 B3
Stainer Cl SO19 104 B2
Staith Cl SO19 104 B3
Stake's La SO32 59 C4
Stakes Hill Inf Sch PO7 134 C3
Stakes Hill Rd PO7 134 C3
Stakes La SO32 58 C2
Stakes Rd PO7 134 B2
Stalbridge Dr BH22 165 B2
Stalbridge Rd BH17 202 A4
Stalham Rd BH12 203 C3
Stallard Cl PO10 136 C1
Stallards La BH24 140 C4
Stalybridge Cl SO31 129 A3
Stamford Ave PO11 184 C2
Stamford Lodge PO11 184 C2
Stamford Rd BH6 206 B3
Stamford St PO1 215 D4
Stamford Way SO50 57 B1
Stampsey Ct 5 PO2 157 B1
Stamshaw Ct 14 PO2 157 B1
Stamshaw Inf Sch PO2 157 B1
Stamshaw Jun Sch PO2 157 B1
Stamshaw Rd PO2 157 B1
Stanbridge Earls Sch SO51 27 A2
Stanbridge La SO51 27 A2
Stanbridge Rd PO9 136 A2
Standard Way PO16 131 B2
Standen Rd SO16 77 B3
Standford St SO14 103 A2
Standing Hill SP5 3 C4
Stanfield Cl BH12 203 B4
Stanfield Rd
Bournemouth BH9 204 C4
Ferndown BH22 165 B3
Poole BH12 203 B4
Stanford Cl PO6 157 B4
Stanford Ct
42 Havant PO9 136 A3
Southampton SO19 104 B2
Stanford Hill SO41 197 B2
Stanford Rd SO41 197 B2
Stanford Rise SO41 172 A1
Stanhope Rd PO1 215 B3
Stanier Way SO30 81 B1
Staniforth Ct BH23 207 B3
Stanley Ave PO3 183 A4
Stanley Cl
Croucheston SP5 22 A4
Fareham PO15 130 C1
Gosport PO12 156 A1
Verwood BH31 115 A3
Stanley Ct
Bournemouth BH1 205 B3
Poole BH15 202 B3
Stanley Green Cres BH15 202 B3
Stanley Green Fst Sch BH15 202 B3
Stanley Green Ind Est BH15 202 B3
Stanley Green Rd BH15 202 B3
Stanley La PO5 182 B1
Stanley Pearce Ho BH17 187 B1
Stanley Rd
Bournemouth BH1 205 B3
Christchurch BH23 209 A4
Emsworth PO10 161 A4
Holbury SO45 150 B2
Lymington SO41 198 A1
Poole BH15 202 B1
Portsmouth PO2 157 B1
Southampton SO17 79 B1
Totton SO40 76 B1
Stanley St PO5 182 B1
Stanmore La SO22 10 B3
Stanmore Prim Sch SO22 10 C3
Stannington Cl BH25 195 A1
Stannington Cres SO40 100 C4
Stannington Way SO40 100 C4
Stanpit BH23 207 C3
Stanstead Rd SO50 55 C2
Stansted Cl PO9 113 B1
Stansted Cres PO9 136 A3
Stansted Ct PO9 113 B1
Stansted Rd PO5 215 D2
Stanswood Rd
Blackfield SO45 178 B3
Havant PO9 135 B3
Stanton Bldgs 20 SO15 102 A4
Stanton Lacy 17 BH13 214 C4
Stanton Rd
Bournemouth BH10 189 B1
Petersfield GU32 40 C2
Southampton SO15 102 A4
Stanton Rd Ind Est SO15 102 A4
Stanton Road Ind Est 21 SO15 102 A4
Stapehill Cres BH21 164 B3
Stapehill Mus & Gdns★ BH21 164 C3
Stapehill Rd BH21 164 C2
Staple Ash La GU32 39 B4
Staple Cl PO7 111 B1
Staple Close La BH15 202 B3
Staple Cross
Burton BH23 207 C4
Southwick PO17 132 A4
Staple Gdns SO23 10 C4
Staplecross La BH23 207 B4
Stapleford Ave BH22 165 C3
Stapleford Cl SO51 28 A1
Stapleford La SO32 81 C3
Staplehurst Cl SO19 104 A1
Staplers Reach PO13 155 A1
Stapleton Rd PO3 183 A4
Staplewood La SO40 124 B4
Star Cottage Gdn★ BH21 162 B3
Star Cotts PO17 108 A2
Star La BH24 140 C4
Stares Cl PO13 180 B4
Starina Gdns PO7 135 A4
Starlight Farm Cl BH31 115 A4
Starling Sq SO50 55 B1
Station App
Broadstone BH18 187 A2

Station App *continued*
Brockenhurst SO42 146 A1
1 Portsmouth PO1 182 A3
Station Cl PO17 108 A2
Station Cotts SO42 123 B1
Station Hill
Bursledon SO31 128 A4
Curdridge SO30 106 B4
Eastleigh SO50 56 A2
Winchester SO23 10 C4
Station La SO53 55 B3
Station Rd Alderholt SP6 92 C3
Bishop's Waltham SO32 83 B4
Burley BH24 170 B4
Bursledon SO31 128 A4
Christchurch BH23 207 A4
Christchurch, Highcliffe BH23 193 C1
Cosham PO6 158 B4
Fordingbridge SP6 69 B1
Gosport PO12 180 C4
Hamworthy BH15 202 A1
Liss GU33 20 C2
Locks Heath SO31 129 A3
Netley SO31 127 B3
New Milton BH25 195 A1
Nursling SO16 77 A3
Petersfield GU31, GU32 40 C2
Poole BH14 203 A2
Portchester PO16 156 B4
Portsmouth PO3 183 A4
Romsey SO51 52 C4
Soberton SO32 85 B4
South Hayling PO11 184 C2
Southampton, Redbridge SO15 101 B4
Southampton, Sholing SO19 103 C2
Sway SO41 172 A1
Verwood BH31 114 C4
West Meon GU32 37 B2
West Moors BH22 138 B1
Wickham PO17 108 A2
Wimborne Minst BH21 163 B2
Station Rd N SO40 101 A4
Station Rd S SO40 101 A4
Station St
Lymington SO41 197 C2
Portsmouth PO1 215 B3
Station Terr Twyford SO21 31 C3
Wimborne Minst BH21 163 B2
Station Yd SP6 92 C3
Staunton BH2 204 C1
Staunton Ave PO11 184 B2
Staunton Ctry Pk★ PO9 136 A4
Staunton Park Com Sch PO9 136 A4
Staunton Rd PO9 135 C1
Staunton St PO1 215 B4
Stead Cl PO11 185 A2
Stedman Rd BH5 206 A3
Steel St PO5 215 A1
Steele Cl SO53 55 B2
Steels Dro SP6 70 C4
Steels La SP6 68 B2
Steep CE Prim Sch GU32 40 C4
Steep Cl
Portchester PO16 132 B1
Southampton SO18 104 B4
Steepdene BH14 203 A2
Steeple Cl BH17 187 B2
Steeple Way PO14 129 B2
Steepleton Rd BH18 187 B2
Steerforth Cl PO2 182 B4
Stein Rd PO10 137 B1
Steinbeck Cl PO15 129 B4
Stella Ct
19 Christchurch BH23 209 A4
Southampton SO16 78 B2
Stem La BH25 194 C2
Stenbury Way SO31 127 B4
Stenhurst Rd BH15 202 C3
Step Terr SO22 10 C4
Stephen Cl PO8 112 A1
Stephen Langton Dr BH11 188 B3
Stephen Lodge PO5 215 B1
Stephen Martin Gdns SP6 69 C1
Stephen Rd PO15 130 C1
Stephens Ct SO51 52 C3
Stephens Wlk BH24 140 C4
Stephenson Cl PO12 181 A1
Stephenson Rd
Totton SO40 76 B1
Locks Heath PO14,PO15 129 C1
Stephenson Way SO30 81 A2
Steplake La SO51 25 B1
Steplake Rd SO51 50 B4
Stepnell Reach BH16 201 B3
Sterte Ave BH15 202 A2
Sterte Ave W BH15 202 A2
Sterte Cl BH15 202 B2
Sterte Ct BH15 202 A2
Sterte Espl BH15 202 B2
Sterte Ind Est BH15 202 A2
Sterte Rd BH15 202 B2
Steuart Rd SO18 103 B4
Stevenson Cres BH14 203 C2
Stevenson Rd BH6 207 A2
Stevensons Cl 3 BH21 163 B2
Steventon Rd SO18 104 B4
Stewart Cl 5 BH8 205 B3
Stewart Ho SO53 30 B1
Stewart Pl PO1 182 C4
Stewart Rd BH8 205 A3
Stewarts Gn PO7 86 B2
Stewarts Way BH22 165 C4
Stibbs Way BH23 169 B1
Stillmore Rd BH11 188 B2
Stinchar Dr SO53 55 A3
Stinsford Cl BH9 190 A2
Stinsford La BH17 202 B4
Stinsford Rd BH17 187 B1
Stirling Ave PO7 134 C4
Stirling Cl
New Milton BH25 195 A2
Totton SO40 77 A1
Stirling Cres
Hedge End SO30 81 B1
Totton SO40 101 A4
Stirling Ct
Bournemouth BH4 204 B1
Fareham PO15 130 C2
21 New Milton BH25 195 A2
Stirling Rd BH3 204 C4
Stirling St PO2 182 B4
Stirling Way BH23 208 A3
Stirling Wlk SO51 52 C4
Stirrup Cl Upton BH16 201 B4
Wimborne Minst BH21 164 B3
Stoborough Dr BH18 187 A1
Stock La SP5 49 B3
Stock's Cross SO43 73 C2
Stock's La SO32 61 C3
Stockbridge Cl
Havant PO9 136 A3
Poole BH17 188 A1
Stockbridge Rd SO21, SO22, SO23 1 B1
Stocker Pl PO13 155 B1
Stockers Ave SO22 1 B1
Stockheath La PO9 135 C2
Stockheath Rd PO9 135 C2
Stockheath Way PO9 135 C2
Stockholm Dr SO30 105 B3
Stockley Cl SO45 150 B2
Stockton Cl SO30 105 B4
Stoddart Ave SO19 103 C3
Stodham La GU33 20 C1
Stoke Common Rd SO50 56 C3
Stoke Gdns PO12 181 B2
Stoke Hts SO50 57 A2
Stoke Park Dr SO50 56 B2
Stoke Park Inf Sch SO50 56 C1
Stoke Park Jun Sch SO50 56 C1
Stoke Park Rd SO50 56 B2
Stoke Rd Gosport PO12 181 B2
Southampton SO16 78 A1
Winchester SO23 2 A2
Stoke Wood Cl SO50 57 A1
Stoke Wood Rd BH3 204 C3
Stokes Ave BH15 202 B2
Stokes Bay Rd PO12 180 C1
Stokesay Cl SO45 150 A4
Stokeway 4 PO12 181 B2
Stone Crop Cl SO31 128 C1
Stone Gdns BH8 191 A1
Stone La
5 Gosport PO12 181 A2
Wimborne Minst BH21 163 A3
Stone Lane Ind Est BH21 163 A3
Stone Sq PO9 135 C2
Stone St PO5 215 A1
Stone Terr SO21 31 A1
Stonechat Cl
Ferndown BH22 165 A4
Petersfield GU31 41 B1
Stonechat Ct BH23 207 C4
Stonechat Dr SO40 100 B4
Stonechat Rd PO8 112 A4
Stonecrop Cl BH18 186 C1
Stoneham Cemetery Rd SO18 79 C2
Stoneham Cl
Petersfield GU32 40 B2
Southampton SO16 79 B3
Stoneham Ct SO16 79 A3
Stoneham Gdns SO31 104 C1
Stoneham La
Chilworth SO50 79 C4
Southampton SO16 79 B3
Stoneham Pk GU32 40 B2
Stoneham Way SO16, SO18 79 C3
Stonehills SO45 151 B2
Stoneleigh 13 BH13 214 C4
Stoneleigh Ave SO41 195 C2
Stoneleigh Cl PO16 156 A4
Stoner Hill Rd GU32 19 A1
Stoners Cl PO13 155 A2
Stoney La SO22 1 B1
Stony La Burton BH23 192 B1
Froxfield Green GU32 18 C1
Portsmouth PO1 182 A3
Stony La S BH23 207 B3
Stonymoor Cl SO45 150 B2
Stopples La SO41 195 C2
Storrington Rd PO8 88 B3
Story La BH18 187 A2
Stour Cl Ferndown BH21 164 B2
Petersfield GU31 40 C1
West End SO18 80 A2
West Wellow SO51 50 B2
Stour Pk BH10 189 C3
Stour Rd
Bournemouth BH8 205 B3
Christchurch BH23 207 A3
Stour View Gdns BH21 162 C1
Stour Way BH23 191 B1
Stour Wlk
Bournemouth BH8 190 B2
11 Wimborne Minst BH21 163 B2
Stourbank Rd BH23 207 A3
Stourcliffe Ave BH6 206 B2
Stourcroft Dr BH23 191 C1
Stourfield Fst & Jun Schs BH6 206 B3
Stourfield Rd BH5 206 A2
Stourpaine Rd BH17 187 B1
Stourton Ct 17 BH4 204 B2
Stourvale Ave BH23 206 B4
Stourvale Gdns SO53 55 B3
Stourvale Pl 10 BH5 206 A3
Stourvale Rd BH5,BH6 206 B3
Stourwood Ave BH6 206 B2
Stourwood Mans 4 BH6 206 B2
Stourwood Rd BH6 206 B2
Stouts La BH23 169 A1
Stow Cres PO15 130 B1
Stowe Cl SO30 81 B1
Stowe Rd PO4 183 A2
Stradbrook PO13 155 A1
Stragwyne Cl SO52 53 C3
Straight Mile The SO51 28 C1
Strand SO14 103 A2
Strand St BH15 202 B1
Strand The PO11 185 B1
Stratfield Dr SO53 30 A1
Stratfield Gdns PO9 135 B4
Stratfield Pk PO7 134 B4
Stratfield Pl BH25 194 C2
Stratford Ct 9 SO23 2 A1
Stratford Ho PO5 215 B2
Stratford Pl
Eastleigh SO50 56 A2
Lymington SO41 197 B3
Stratford Rd PO7 135 A4
Strathmore Dr BH31 115 A3
Strathmore Rd
Bournemouth BH9 190 A2
Gosport PO12 181 B2
Stratton Cl PO6 157 B4
Stratton Rd
Bournemouth BH9 190 B2
Southampton SO15 78 B1
Winchester SO23 11 B4
Strawberry Fields
East Boldre SO42 175 B3
Hedge End SO30 105 A3
Strawberry Hill SO31 128 C2
Strawberry Mead SO50 57 A1
Streamleaze PO14 129 B1
Street End SO52 54 A3
Street The SP5 24 A2
Streets La BH24 141 B2
Strete Mount 10 BH23 207 C4
Stretton Ct BH14 203 A2
Stride Ave PO3 183 A3
Strides La BH24 140 C4
Strides Way SO40 100 A4
Strode Gdns BH24 140 A3
Strode Rd PO2 157 B1
Strongs Cl SO51 53 A4
Stroud Cl BH21 164 A3
Stroud End GU32 40 A2
Stroud Gdns BH23 207 C3
Stroud Green La PO14 154 B3
Stroud La BH23 207 C3
Stroud Park Ave BH23 207 C3
Stroud Sch SO51 53 C4
Strouden Ave BH8 205 B4
Strouden Court Prec PO9 135 B4
Strouden Ct PO9 135 B4
Strouden Rd BH9 190 A1
Stroudley Ave PO6 158 B3
Stroudley Way SO30 81 B1
Stroudwood Rd
Fair Oak SO32 58 A2
Havant PO9 136 A2
Struan Cl BH24 139 C3
Struan Ct BH24 140 A3
Struan Dr BH24 140 A3
Struan Gdns BH24 139 C3
Stuart Bridgewater Ho SO18 104 A4
Stuart Cl
Stubbington PO14 179 B3
Upton BH16 201 A4
Stuart Cres SO22 10 C3
Stuart Ct 7 PO6 157 C4
Stuart Rd BH23 209 A4
Stubbermere PO10 136 C4
Stubbington Ave PO2 157 C1
Stubbington Gn PO14 154 B2
Stubbington La PO14 179 B3
Stubbington Study Ctr PO14 179 B2
Stubbington Way SO50 57 B1
Stubbs Dro SO30 105 B4
Stubbs Rd SO19 104 B1
Stuckton Rd SP6 94 A4
Student Village BH12 204 B4
Studland Cl SO16 77 B1
Studland Dr SO41 211 B3
Studland Rd
Bournemouth BH4 204 B1
Lee-on-the-Solent PO13 179 C1
Southampton SO16 77 B1
Studley Ave SO45 150 B2
Studley Cl BH23 209 B4
Studley Ct BH25 209 B4
Sturminster Ho 4 SO16 78 A1
Sturminster Rd 10 BH9 190 A2
Styles The SP5 22 B4
Sudbury Rd PO6 157 B4
Suetts La SO32 83 C4
Suffolk Ave
Christchurch BH23 191 C1
Southampton SO15 102 B4
Suffolk Cl
Chandler's Ford SO53 55 B1
Wimborne Minst BH21 164 B3
Suffolk Dr
Chandler's Ford SO53 55 B1
Swanwick PO15 129 A4
Suffolk Gn SO53 55 B1
Suffolk Rd
Bournemouth BH2 204 B2
Bournemouth BH2 204 C2
Portsmouth PO4 183 A2
Suffolk Rd S BH2 204 B2
Sullivan Cl PO6 156 C4
Sullivan Rd SO19 104 B2
Sullivan Way PO7 134 C3
Sultan Rd
Emsworth PO10 136 C1
Portsmouth PO1, PO2 182 B4
Sumar Cl PO14 154 B3
Summer Field Cl BH21 164 A2
Summer Flds BH31 114 C2
Summerbee Comp Sch BH8 190 B1
Summerbee First Sch BH8 190 B1
Summerbee Jun Sch BH8 190 B1
Summercroft Way BH22 138 C2
Summerfield Cl BH23 192 B1
Summerfield Ct PO3 158 A2
Summerfield Gdns SO16 79 B3
Summerfields
Bournemouth BH7 205 C4
Locks Heath SO31 129 A1
Summerhill Rd PO8 112 A2
Summerlands BH22 165 B3
Summerlands Rd SO50 57 B1
Summerlands Wlk 36 PO9 136 A3
Summerleigh Wlk PO14 154 B3
Summers Ave BH11 189 A3
Summers La BH23 192 B1
Summers St SO14 103 B3
Summersfield GU33 20 C2
Summertrees Ct BH25 195 B2
Summit Way SO18 79 C1
Sumner Rd GU31 65 B3
Sun Ct PO5 215 C2
Sun St PO1 182 A3
Sunbeam Way PO12 181 A2
Sunbury Cl BH11 189 A3
Sunbury Ct
8 Bournemouth BH2 204 C2
Fareham PO15 130 C2
Suncourt Villas PO12 180 C4
Sunderland Dr BH23 208 A4
Sunderton La PO8 88 B3
Sundew Cl
Christchurch BH23 193 B1
New Milton BH25 195 B2
Sundew Rd BH18 186 C1
Sundridge Cl PO6 157 C4
Sunningdale
Christchurch BH23 206 C3
Hythe SO45 125 C2
8 Poole BH15 202 C2
Sunningdale Cl
6 Bishopstoke SO50 56 C1
Gosport PO13 155 B1
Sunningdale Cres BH10 189 B2
Sunningdale Cvn Pk SO21 31 C1
Sunningdale Gdns
Broadstone BH18 187 A3
Southampton SO18 104 A4
Sunningdale Rd
Portchester PO16 156 B4
Portsmouth PO3 183 A4
Sunny Hill Ct BH12 203 B3
Sunny Hill Rd BH12 203 B3
Sunny Way SO40 100 C4
Sunny Wlk PO1 182 A3
Sunnybank Dr BH21 164 A3
Sunnybank Rd BH21 164 A3
Sunnybank Way BH21 164 A3
Sunnydown Rd SO22 10 A2
Sunnyfield Rd BH25 210 A4
Sunnyfield Rise SO31 105 A1
Sunnyfields PO6 158 B4
Sunnyheath PO9 135 C2
Sunnyhill Rd BH6 206 B3
Sunnylands Ave BH6 206 C2
Sunnymead Dr PO7 111 B1
Sunnymoor Rd BH11 189 A1
Sunnyside Rd BH12 203 B3
Sunnyside Wlk PO9 135 B4
Sunridge Cl BH12 204 A3
Sunrise Ct BH22 165 B3
Sunset Ave SO40 100 C4
Sunset Lo BH13 204 A1
Sunset Rd SO40 100 C4
Sunshine Ave PO11 185 A1
Suntrap Gdns PO11 185 A1
Sunvale Cl SO19 104 A2
Sunwood Rd PO9 135 B3
Surbiton Rd SO50 56 A3
Surrey Cl
Christchurch BH23 191 C1
Totton SO40 100 B3
Surrey Ct SO15 102 B3
Surrey Gdns BH4 204 B2
Surrey Ho SO53 55 B2
Surrey House Inf Sch SO19 104 B2
Surrey Rd
Bournemouth BH2,BH4 204 A2
Chandler's Ford SO53 55 B2
Poole BH12 204 A2
Southampton SO19 103 B1
Surrey Rd S BH4 204 B2
Surrey St PO1 215 B3
Sussex Cl BH9 190 A2
Sussex Ct PO5 215 B1
Sussex Gdns GU31 40 C1
Sussex Pl
Portsmouth PO1 215 B4
Portsmouth PO5 215 B1
Sussex Rd
Chandler's Ford SO53 55 B2
Petersfield GU31 41 A1
Portsmouth PO5 215 B1
Southampton SO14 103 A2
Sussex St SO23 10 C4
Sussex Terr PO5 215 B1
Sutherland Ave BH18 186 C3
Sutherland Cl 6 SO51 28 A1
Sutherland Ct SO53 55 B3
Sutherland Rd
Portsmouth PO4 182 C2
Southampton SO16 77 C3
Sutherlands Way SO53 55 A4
Sutton Cl Poole BH17 188 A1
Portsmouth PO3 158 A2
Waterlooville PO8 111 B2
Sutton Gdns SO23 11 A4
Sutton Pl SO42 146 A1
Sutton Rd
Bournemouth BH9 190 A1
Totton SO40 76 C1
Waterlooville PO8 111 B2
Swale Dr SO53 55 A4
Swallow Cl
Broadstone BH17 201 C4
Havant PO9 136 A1
Totton SO40 100 A3
Swallow Ct Clanfield PO8 88 A3
Lee-on-the-Solent PO13 179 C2
Swallow Dr SO41 211 C2
Swallow Sq SO50 55 B1
Swallow Way BH21 164 A4
Swallow Wood PO16 131 A2
Swan Cl Emsworth PO10 161 A4
Swanwick SO31 128 B4
Swan Ct Bursledon SO31 128 B4
Gosport PO13 155 A2
Swan Ctr The SO50 56 A1
Swan Gn 8 BH23 207 A3
Swan La SO23 10 C4
Swan Mead BH24 141 B3
Swan Quay
Portchester PO16 155 B4
Southampton SO18 103 B4
Swan St GU32 40 C2
Swanage Cl SO19 103 C2
Swanage Rd PO13 179 C1
Swancote PO16 155 C4
Swanley Cl SO50 56 A3
Swanmore Ave SO19 104 B2
Swanmore Bsns Pk SO32 83 C3
Swanmore CE Prim Sch SO32 84 A3
Swanmore Cl
Bournemouth BH7 206 A4
Winchester SO22 1 B2
Swanmore Park Ho SO32 84 B4
Swanmore Rd
Bournemouth BH7 206 A4
Droxford SO32 84 C4
Havant PO9 135 B4
Swanmore SO32 84 A3
Swanmore Sec Sch SO32 84 A2
Swans Wlk PO11 185 A2
Swansbury Dr BH8 191 A1
Swanton Cl PO14 154 B2
Swanton Gdns SO53 55 A4
Swanwick Bsns Ctr SO31 128 B4
Swanwick La SO31 128 C4
Swanwick Nature Reserve★ SO31 128 C4
Swanwick Shore Rd SO31 128 B4
Swanwick Sta SO31 129 A3
Swarraton Rd PO9 136 A2
Sway Ct 39 Havant PO9 136 A3
Sway SO41 196 B4
Sway Gdns BH8 190 B1
Sway Park Ind Est SO41 172 A1
Sway Rd
Brockenhurst SO42 172 C4
Hordle SO41 197 A3
Lymington SO41 197 A3
New Milton BH25 195 B3
Sway Sta SO41 172 A1
Swaythling Prim Sch SO17 79 A2
Swaythling Rd
Havant PO9 135 B3
West End SO18,SO30 80 A1
Swaythling Sta SO18 79 B2
Swedish Hos SO41 198 C4
Sweep The BH24 140 C4
Sweetbriar Gdns PO7 134 C3
Sweethills Cres PO15 129 B4
Sweyns Lease SO42 175 B3
Swift Cl Broadstone BH17 201 C4
Eastleigh SO50 55 B1
Horndean PO8 112 A4
Lee-on-the-Solent PO13 179 C2
Winchester SO22 10 B3

Swift Gdns SO19 ....103 B1
Swift Hollow SO19 ....103 B1
Swift Rd
Southampton SO19 ....103 B1
Thorney Island PO10 ....161 A2
Swinburn Gdns PO8 ....111 C2
Swincombe Rise SO18 ....80 A1
Swiss Rd PO7 ....134 C4
Switch House Rd SO45 ....151 C1
Swivelton La PO17 ....132 A2
Sword Cl Clanfield PO8 ....88 A3
Gosport PO12 ....180 C1
Sword Sands Rd PO3 ....183 B4
Swordfish Dr BH23 ....208 A4
Sycamore Ave SO53 ....30 B1
Sycamore Cl
Broadstone BH17 ....186 C1
Bursledon SO31 ....127 C4
Christchurch BH23 ....206 B4
Clanfield PO8 ....88 B3
Gosport PO13 ....155 C1
Milford on Sea SO41 ....211 B3
North Baddesley SO52 ....53 C3
Romsey SO51 ....53 B3
Titchfield PO14 ....129 B1
Waterlooville PO8 ....111 C2
Sycamore Ct
Fordingbridge SP6 ....69 C1
Ringwood BH24 ....117 B1
Sycamore Dr
Holbury SO45 ....150 A3
Kings Worthy SO23 ....2 A4
South Hayling PO11 ....184 C2
Sycamore Pl BH21 ....164 B3
Sycamore Rd
Bishop's Waltham SO32 ....83 C4
Hordle SO41 ....195 C2
Hythe SO45 ....125 C2
Southampton SO16 ....78 A1
Sycamore Wlk SO30 ....105 C4
Sycamores The 9 SO45 ....126 A2
Sydenham Ct PO1 ....215 D3
Sydenham Terr
Portsmouth PO1 ....215 D3
Westbourne PO10 ....137 A3
Sydling Cl BH17 ....188 A1
Sydmanton Cl SO51 ....53 A3
Sydmonton Ct 2 PO9 ....136 A3
Sydney Ave SO31 ....127 C2
Sydney Ho PO1 ....215 B4
Sydney Rd
Bishopstoke SO50 ....56 B2
Broadstone BH18 ....187 A2
Christchurch BH23 ....191 C1
Gosport PO12 ....181 A2
Southampton SO15 ....78 A1
Syers Cl GU33 ....20 C2
Syers Rd GU33 ....20 C2
Sylmor Gdns BH9 ....190 A1
Sylvan Ave SO19 ....104 B3
Sylvan Cl Hordle SO41 ....196 A1
St Leonards BH24 ....139 B2
Sylvan Dr SO52 ....53 C2
Sylvan Fst Sch BH12 ....203 A3
Sylvan La SO31 ....128 A1
Sylvan Rd BH12 ....203 A3
Sylvan View PO7 ....134 C3
Sylvans The SO45 ....125 B2
Sylvia Cres SO40 ....76 C1
Symes Rd
Hamworthy BH15 ....201 C2
Romsey SO51 ....53 A4
Symonds Cl SO53 ....55 B2
Symonds St SO23 ....11 A4
Sywell Cres PO3 ....158 B2

T

Tadburn Cl
Chandler's Ford SO53 ....55 B3
Romsey SO51 ....53 A4
Tadburn Gn SO51 ....52 C3
Tadburn Rd SO51 ....53 A3
Tadden Cotts BH21 ....162 B4
Tadden Wlk BH18 ....186 C1
Tadfield Cres SO51 ....53 A4
Tadfield Rd SO51 ....53 A4
Tadhurst Ho 4 PO1 ....215 C3
Tait Cl BH17 ....202 C4
Tait Pl PO13 ....155 B1
Talbot Ave BH3 ....204 C4
Talbot Cl Havant PO9 ....135 B2
Southampton SO16 ....78 C2
Talbot Comb Sch BH12 ....204 A4
Talbot Ct
Bournemouth BH9 ....189 C1
11 Southampton SO14 ....103 A2
Talbot Dr
Christchurch BH23 ....193 C1
Poole BH12 ....204 A4
Talbot Heath Sch BH4 ....204 B3
Talbot Hill Rd BH9 ....204 B4
Talbot House Prep Sch
BH9 ....204 C4
Talbot Manor BH3 ....204 B4
Talbot Mdws BH12 ....204 A4
Talbot Mews BH10 ....189 A1
Talbot Rd
Bournemouth BH9 ....204 C4
Havant PO9 ....135 B2
Hythe SO45 ....125 C1
Locks Heath PO14 ....129 C1
Portsmouth PO4 ....182 C2
Talbot Rdbt BH3 ....204 B4
Talbot Rise BH10 ....189 B1
Talisman Bsns Ctr SO31 129 A3
Tall Trees BH14 ....203 A3
Talland Rd PO14 ....129 A1
Tamar Cl Ferndown BH22 166 A3
Portchester PO16 ....132 A1
Tamar Down PO7 ....135 A4
Tamar Gdns SO18 ....80 A1
Tamar Gr SO45 ....125 C2
Tamarisk Cl
Portsmouth PO4 ....183 B2
Stubbington PO14 ....179 B3
Waterlooville PO7 ....135 A3
Tamarisk Gdns SO18 ....103 C4
Tamarisk Rd SO30 ....105 A4
Tamella Rd SO30 ....105 C3
Tammys Turn PO14 ....154 A4
Tamorisk Dr SO40 ....100 B3
Tamworth Ct 9 PO12 ....181 A2
Tamworth Rd
Bournemouth BH7 ....205 C3
Portsmouth PO3 ....183 A3
Tan Howse Cl BH7 ....206 A4
Tanfield La PO17 ....108 A2
Tanfield Pk PO17 ....108 A2
Tangier La SO32 ....83 A4
Tangier Rd PO3 ....183 A4
Tanglewood
Fareham PO16 ....131 A2
Marchwood SO40 ....102 A1
Tanglewood Cl PO7 ....134 B2
Tanglewood Ct 11 BH25 195 A2
Tanglewood Lo BH17 ....201 C4
Tangley Wlk PO9 ....136 A3
Tangmere Cl BH23 ....208 A3
Tangmere Dr SO16 ....78 A2
Tangmere Pl BH17 ....202 C4
Tangyes Cl PO14 ....154 B2
Tanhouse Cl SO30 ....105 B3
Tanhouse La
Botley SO30 ....105 B2
Hedge End SO30 ....105 B3
Tankerdale La GU33 ....41 B4
Tankerton Cl 2 PO6 ....157 C4
Tankerville Rd SO19 ....103 B2
Tankerville Specl Sch
SO50 ....56 A2
Tanner St 28 SO23 ....11 A4
Tanner's Brook Way
SO15 ....101 C3
Tanner's La PO7 ....111 A3
Tanner's Ridge PO7 ....134 C2
Tanneries Ind Est The
PO9 ....135 C1
Tanners Brook Inf Sch
SO15 ....101 C4
Tanners Brook Jun Sch
SO15 ....101 C4
Tanners La Boldre SO41 ....199 A2
Gosport PO14 ....154 C3
Sandleheath SP6 ....68 C2
West Wellow SO51 ....51 B4
Tanners Rd SO52 ....54 A2
Tanners The PO14 ....129 B1
Tansy Cl PO7 ....135 A3
Tansy Mdw SO53 ....54 C2
Tanyards The SO53 ....30 A1
Taplin Dr SO30 ....105 B4
Taplings Cl SO22 ....1 B2
Taplings Rd SO22 ....1 B2
Tapper Ct BH21 ....163 C2
Taranto Rd SO16 ....78 B2
Tarbery Cres PO8 ....112 B4
Tardif Ho SO16 ....78 A1
Target Rd PO2 ....157 B1
Tarius Cl PO13 ....155 B2
Tarleton Rd PO6 ....133 A1
Tarn Dr BH17 ....201 C4
Tarn Rise PO8 ....88 B1
Tarrant Cl BH17 ....187 C1
Tarrant Gdns PO9 ....135 B2
Tarrant Rd BH9 ....190 A2
Tasman Cl
Christchurch BH23 ....206 C4
Southampton SO14 ....103 A1
Tasman Ct SO14 ....103 A1
Taswell Rd PO5 ....182 B1
Tatchbury La SO40 ....99 C4
Tatchbury Mount Hopsl
SO40 ....76 A1
Tate Ct SO15 ....101 B4
Tate Mews SO15 ....101 B4
Tate Rd SO15 ....101 B4
Tates Rd Hythe SO45 ....126 A1
Hythe SO45 ....126 A2
Tatnam Rd BH15 ....202 B2
Tattenham Rd SO42 ....172 C4
Tattershall Cres PO16 ....156 A4
Tatum Cres BH15 ....202 B2
Tatwin Cl SO19 ....104 B3
Tatwin Cres SO19 ....104 B3
Taunton Coll SO15 ....78 C1
Taunton Dr SO18 ....104 A4
Taunton Row SO53 ....55 B2
Tavell's La SO40 ....101 C1
Tavells Cl SO40 ....101 C1
Taverner Cl BH15 ....202 B1
Taverners Cl SO19 ....104 B2
Tavistock Cl 4 SO51 ....28 A1
Tavistock Gdns 10 PO9 ....136 A1
Tavy Cl SO53 ....55 A3
Taw Dr SO53 ....55 A3
Tawny Owl Cl PO14 ....154 A2
Taylor Cl SO19 ....103 B1
Taylor Dr BH8 ....190 B2
Taylor Rd PO12 ....181 B1
Taylor Way BH31 ....115 A3
Taylor's Bldgs 21 BH15 ....202 B1
Taylors Cnr SO23 ....2 A3
Teachers Terr 6 GU33 ....20 C2
Teachers Way SO45 ....150 A2
Teak Cl BH13 ....214 D4
Teal Cl Horndean PO8 ....112 A4
Portchester PO16 ....155 C4
South Hayling PO11 ....185 A2
Totton SO40 ....100 B4
Teal Wlk PO13 ....155 A2
Teapot Row PO4 ....183 A1
Teasel Way BH22 ....138 C1
Teazle Cl GU31 ....41 B1
Tebourba Cotts SO41 ....172 A1
Tebourba Dr PO12 ....181 A2
Tebourba Ho 6 PO14 ....154 C4
Tebourba Way
Curdridge SO30 ....106 B4
Southampton SO16 ....101 C4
Technology Rd BH17 ....202 A4
Ted Kelly Ct 29 PO1 ....182 A3
Tedder Cl BH11 ....189 A2
Tedder Gdns BH11 ....189 A2
Tedder Rd
Bournemouth BH11 ....189 A2
Gosport PO13 ....155 B2
Southampton SO18 ....104 A4
Tedder Way SO40 ....100 B4
Teddington Rd PO4 ....183 A2
Tees Cl SO53 ....55 A4
Tees Farm Rd SO21 ....56 C4
Tees Gn 2 SO21 ....56 C4
Teg Down GU31 ....41 A2
Teg Down Meads SO22 ....1 B1
Teglease Gn PO9 ....135 B4
Teignmouth Rd
Gosport PO12 ....180 C4
Portsmouth PO3 ....183 A4
Telegraph Rd SO30 ....80 C1
Telegraph Way SO21 ....12 A4
Telephone Rd PO4 ....182 C2
Telford Gdns SO30 ....81 C1
Telford Rd
Ferndown BH21 ....165 A4
Portsmouth PO2 ....157 C2
Telford Way PO15 ....129 B3
Teme Cres SO16 ....101 C4
Teme Rd SO16 ....101 C4
Tempest Ave PO7 ....135 A4
Templar Ct 29 SO14 ....103 A4
Templars Mede SO53 ....55 A2
Templars Way SO53 ....55 A2
Temple Gdns SO19 ....103 C1
Temple La GU32 ....63 C4
Temple Mews BH1 ....205 B3
Temple Rd Liss GU33 ....21 A3
Southampton SO19 ....103 C1
Temple St PO1 ....215 B4
Templecombe Rd SO50 ....56 C1
Templemere PO14 ....154 A4
Templer Cl BH11 ....188 C1
Templeton Cl PO2 ....157 C2
Tenby Cl SO18 ....104 A4
Tenby Dr SO53 ....55 A2
Tench Way SO51 ....52 C4
Tennyson Cl
Bishop's Waltham SO32 ....83 C4
Holbury SO45 ....150 A3
Tennyson Cres PO7 ....111 B1
Tennyson Ct
27 Southampton SO17 ....79 A1
37 Southampton SO17 ....79 A1
Tennyson Gdns PO16 ....131 A1
Tennyson Rd
Bournemouth BH9 ....189 C1
Eastleigh SO50 ....55 C1
1 Poole BH14 ....203 A2
Portsmouth PO2 ....182 C4
Southampton SO17 ....79 A1
Totton SO40 ....76 B1
Wimborne Minst BH21 ....163 B3
Tensing Cl PO16 ....131 A2
Tensing Rd BH23 ....207 C4
Tenterton Ave SO19 ....104 A1
Terence Ave BH17 ....187 B1
Terence Rd BH21 ....186 B3
Terminus Terr SO14 ....103 A2
Tern Cl SO45 ....126 A1
Tern Ct BH6 ....206 B3
Tern Wlk PO13 ....155 A2
Terrace Rd BH2 ....204 C2
Terrace The
Damerham SP6 ....68 B3
Rockbourne SP6 ....68 C4
Terrier Cl SO30 ....81 B2
Terrington Ave BH23 ....193 C1
Terriote Cl SO53 ....55 B4
Test Cl GU31 ....40 C1
Test Ho SO51 ....52 B4
Test La SO16 ....77 A1
Test Mills SO51 ....52 B4
Test Rd SO14 ....126 A4
Test Valley Bsns Ctr
SO16 ....77 B1
Test Valley Bsns Pk
SO52 ....54 A3
Testbourne Ave SO40 ....100 B4
Testbourne Cl SO40 ....100 B4
Testbourne Rd SO40 ....100 B3
Testcombe Rd PO12 ....181 A2
Testlands Ave SO16 ....77 B3
Testwood Ave SO40 ....76 C1
Testwood Cres SO40 ....76 B1
Testwood La SO40 ....101 A4
Testwood Pl SO40 ....101 A4
Testwood Rd
Havant PO9 ....135 B3
Southampton SO15 ....102 A3
Testwood Sch SO40 ....76 C1
Tethering Dro SP6 ....47 B2
Tetney Cl SO16 ....77 C2
Tetsome Cotts PO17 ....130 C4
Teviot Ho 9 SO14 ....103 B3
Teviot Rd SO53 ....55 A3
Tewkesbury Ave
Fareham PO15 ....130 B2
Gosport PO12 ....181 A4
Tewkesbury Cl PO6 ....157 B4
Texas Dr SO22 ....10 A2
Thackeray Mall 26
PO16 ....131 A1
Thackeray Rd SO17 ....103 A4
Thackeray Sq 4 PO16 ....131 B1
Thacking Gn 3 SO21 ....56 C4
Thames Alley 13 BH15 ....202 A1
Thames Cl
Ferndown BH22 ....166 A3
West End SO18 ....80 A2
Thames Ct 1 PO8 ....111 C2
Thames Dr PO15 ....130 B2
Thames Mews 12 BH15 ....202 A1
Thames St BH15 ....202 A1
Thamesmead Cl PO12 ....180 C4
Thatchers La
Boldre SO41 ....198 C4
Sopley BH23 ....168 C2
Theatre Mews 2 PO5 ....182 B1
Theobold Rd BH23 ....191 A4
Theseus Rd PO13 ....179 B2
Thessaly Ct 17 BH5 ....205 C2
Thetchers Cl BH25 ....195 A3
Thetford Gdns SO53 ....55 A4
Thetford Rd
Gosport PO12 ....180 C4
Poole BH12 ....203 C3
Thicket The
Gosport PO13 ....155 C1
Portchester PO16 ....131 C1
Portsmouth PO5 ....215 C1
Romsey SO51 ....53 B3
Waterlooville PO7 ....134 B2
Third Ave Cosham PO6 ....157 C4
Havant PO9 ....136 A1
Southampton SO15 ....101 C3
Thirlmere SO50 ....55 C1
Thirlmere Cl PO14 ....154 B2
Thirlmere Ho 23 PO6 ....133 A1
Thirlmere Rd SO16 ....77 C1
Thirlstane Firs SO53 ....55 A2
Thistle Rd
Chandler's Ford SO53 ....54 C3
Hedge End SO30 ....105 A3
Thistlebarrow Rd BH7 ....205 C3
Thistledown PO8 ....112 A3
Thistledowne Gdns
PO10 ....161 A4
Thomas Cl SO40 ....100 B3
Thomas Lewis Way SO16,
SO17 ....79 B1
Thomas Lockyer Cl
BH31 ....115 A3
Thomas Rd SO52 ....54 A2
Thompson's La SO21 ....57 B4
Thoresby Ct BH25 ....194 C2
Thorn Cl Eastleigh SO50 ....56 A3
Petersfield GU31 ....41 B1
Thorn Rd BH17 ....187 B2
Thornbrake Rd PO12 ....181 B2
Thornbury 15 BH4 ....204 B2
Thornbury Ave
Blackfield SO45 ....177 C4
Southampton SO15 ....102 C4
Thornbury Cl PO14 ....154 B4
Thornbury Ho 10 PO6 ....132 C1
Thornbury Hts SO53 ....30 C1
Thornbury Rd BH6 ....207 A2
Thornbury Wood SO53 ....30 C1
Thornby Ct PO3 ....158 A2
Thorncliffe Cl PO2 ....157 C2
Thorncombe Cl
Bournemouth BH9 ....190 A2
Poole BH17 ....187 C1
Thorncroft Rd PO1 ....182 C3
Thornden Sch SO53 ....55 C4
Thorndike Cl SO16 ....78 A1
Thorndike Rd SO16 ....77 C1
Thorne Cl BH31 ....114 C3
Thorne Way BH21 ....139 A3
Thorner's Homes,Centre Ct
10 SO15 ....102 A4
Thorner's Homes,North Ct 9
SO15 ....102 A4
Thorner's Homes,South Ct 11
SO15 ....102 A4
Thorner's Homes,West Ct 12
SO15 ....102 A4
Thorners Ct 8 SO15 ....102 C3
Thorness Cl SO16 ....77 B1
Thorney Cl PO14 ....154 B4
Thorney Island Com Prim Sch
PO10 ....161 A2
Thorney Old Pk PO10 ....161 B1
Thorney Rd
Hermitage PO10 ....161 A3
Thorney Island PO10 ....161 A3
Thorney View PO11 ....160 B1
Thornfield Cl PO8 ....88 B1
Thornfield Dr BH23 ....193 C1
Thorngate Ct 5 PO12 ....181 A3
Thorngate Way 22 PO12 181 B2
Thornham La PO10 ....161 B3
Thornham Rd BH25 ....195 B2
Thornhill Ave SO19 ....104 B3
Thornhill Cl SO45 ....150 C1
Thornhill Park Rd SO18 104 C4
Thornhill Prim Sch
SO19 ....104 B3
Thornhill Rd
Blackfield SO45 ....150 C1
Southampton SO16 ....78 B2
Thorni Ave PO15 ....130 B2
Thornleigh Rd SO19 ....103 C1
Thornley Rd BH10 ....189 B2
Thorns La SO41 ....199 C3
Thornton Ave SO31 ....128 B1
Thornton Cl
Corfe Mullen BH21 ....186 B3
Waterlooville PO7 ....134 A1
Thornton Rd PO12 ....181 A4
Thornworthy 4 SO45 ....125 C1
Thornycroft Ave SO19 ....103 B1
Thorogood Ct 4 BH15 ....202 C2
Thorold Ct SO18 ....79 C1
Thorold Rd
Chandler's Ford SO53 ....30 C1
Southampton SO18 ....79 C1
Three Acre Dr BH25 ....209 C4
Three Acres PO7 ....111 A2
Three Cross Rd BH21,
BH22 ....138 C3
Three Horse Shoes La
SO24 ....16 C1
Three Legged Cross First Sch
BH21 ....114 C1
Three Lions Cl 12 BH21 ....163 A3
Three Oaks SO19 ....104 C3
Three Tun Cl 21 PO1 ....182 A3
Threefield La SO14 ....103 A2
Thresher Cl PO7 ....112 B1
Throop Cl BH8 ....191 A1
Throop Rd
Bournemouth BH8 ....190 C2
Bournemouth BH8 ....191 A1
Throopside Ave BH9 ....190 B2
Thrush Rd BH12 ....188 B1
Thrush Wlk PO8 ....111 C2
Thruxton Ct SO19 ....103 C3
Thruxton Rd PO9 ....135 B3
Thurbern Rd PO2 ....157 C1
Thurmell Cl SO30 ....105 B2
Thurmell Wlk SO30 ....105 B2
Thurmond Cres SO22 ....10 B3
Thurmond Rd SO22 ....10 B3
Thursby Rd BH23 ....193 C1
Thurston Cl SO53 ....55 B4
Thwaite Rd BH12 ....204 A3
Thyme Ave PO15 ....129 B4
Tichborne Rd
Eastleigh SO50 ....80 A4
Southampton SO18 ....104 B4
Tichborne Way PO13 ....155 B1
Tichbourne Ho SO30 ....105 B4
Tickleford Dr SO19 ....104 A1
Tickner Cl SO30 ....105 C3
Ticonderoga Gdns
SO19 ....103 C1
Tidcombe Gn PO9 ....135 B4
Tidemill Cl BH23 ....207 A4
Tides Reach SO18 ....103 B4
Tides Way SO40 ....101 C1
Tideway Gdns PO4 ....183 B2
Tidworth Rd PO9 ....135 C2
Tiffany Cl SO41 ....195 C2
Tiffield Cl PO3 ....158 B2
Tiger Rd PO1 ....181 C4
Tilbrook Rd SO15 ....102 A4
Tilburg Rd BH23 ....207 B4
Tilden Rd SO21 ....31 B3
Tilebarn La SO42 ....173 A3
Tilford Rd PO8 ....111 C3
Tillingbourn PO14 ....129 B2
Tillinton Gdns PO8 ....88 B2
Tilmore Gdns GU32 ....40 C3
Tilmore Rd GU32 ....40 C3
Timberlane PO7 ....134 B2
Timberley Ho 2 PO1 ....215 C3
Timberley La SP5 ....48 A3
Timberly Cl SO45 ....150 B2
Timbermill Ct SP6 ....93 C4
Timbers The PO15 ....130 B1
Timor Cl PO15 ....129 B4
Timothy Cl BH10 ....189 B3
Timpson Rd PO1 ....215 D4
Timsbury Cres PO9 ....135 C1
Timsbury Ct SO19 ....103 C2
Timsbury Dr SO16 ....77 C1
Timson Cl SO40 ....100 B3
Tincleton Gdns BH9 ....190 A2
Tindale Rd SO16 ....77 C1
Tinker Alley SO18 ....80 A4
Tinkers Cross SP6 ....69 C2
Tinneys Cl SP5 ....47 B2
Tintagel Cl SO16 ....78 B3
Tintagel Way PO6 ....157 A4
Tintern Cl PO6 ....133 A1
Tintern Gr 18 SO15 ....102 C3
Tintern Rd PO12 ....181 A2
Tipner Gn PO2 ....157 B2
Tipner La PO2 ....157 B2
Tipner Rd PO2 ....157 B1
Tiptoe Gn 20 PO9 ....136 A3
Tiptoe Prim Sch SO41 ....195 B4
Tiptoe Rd BH25 ....171 A1
Tipton Ho PO5 ....215 B2
Tiptree Cl SO50 ....56 A3
Tisted Ct 28 PO9 ....136 A3
Titchborne Gr PO9 ....135 B3
Titchfield Abbey PO15 ....130 A1
Titchfield Hill PO14 ....154 A4
Titchfield Industries
PO14 ....154 A4
Titchfield La PO15, PO17 107 B2
Titchfield Park Rd PO15 129 B2
Titchfield Prim Sch
PO14 ....129 C1

Titchfield Rd PO14 154 A3
Tithe Barn SO41 197 C3
Tithe Mead SO51 27 C1
Tithe The PO7 110 C2
Tithelands La SO24 15 C2
Tithewood Cl SO53 30 A1
Titus Gdns PO7 135 A4
Tiverton Ct
 24 Bournemouth BH4 204 B2
 1 Fareham PO16 131 B1
Tivoli Cl SO53 55 C4
Toby St PO1 215 B4
Todber Cl BH11 188 C2
Tokar St PO4 183 A1
Tokio Rd PO3 158 A1
Tolefrey Gdns SO53 54 C3
Tollard Cl BH12 203 C4
Tollbar Way SO30 81 A1
Tollerford Rd BH17 187 B1
Tollgate SO53 55 B1
Tollgate Ests SO51 27 A2
Tollgate Rd SO31 128 B4
Tollgate The 20 SO23 2 A1
Tolpuddle Gdns BH9 190 A2
Tolstoi Rd BH14 203 A3
Tomkyns Cl SO53 54 C3
Toms La BH24 118 A4
Tonbridge St PO5 182 B1
Tonge Rd BH11 189 A3
Tonnant Cl PO14 179 B3
Toogoods Way SO16 77 B3
Toomer Cl SO45 150 C1
Toothill Rd SO51 53 B1
Top La BH24 141 A4
Topaz Gr PO7 135 A4
Topiary Gdns SO31 129 A2
Tor Cl Portchester PO16 131 C1
 Waterlooville PO7 134 C2
Tor Way GU31 41 A2
Torbay Rd BH14 203 B2
Torberry Dr GU31 41 A1
Torch Cl SO50 57 A1
Torcross Cl SO19 103 C1
Torfrida Ct PO4 183 B2
Tormead SO45 125 C2
Tornay Gr SO52 53 C2
Toronto Pl PO12 181 A3
Toronto Rd PO2 182 C4
Torquay Ave
 Gosport PO12 181 A4
 Southampton SO15 102 B4
Torque Cl SO19 104 C2
Torre Cl SO50 56 A3
Torridge Gdns SO18 80 A2
Torrington Cl SO19 104 A2
Torrington Rd PO2 157 C2
Tortworth Cl PO14 154 B4
Torwood Gdns SO50 56 C1
Tosson Cl SO16 101 C4
Totland Cl SO16 101 C4
Totland Ct 8 SO41 211 B2
Totland Rd Cosham PO6 157 C4
 Gosport PO13 155 B1
Totmel Rd BH17 188 A1
Totnes Cl SO50 55 C3
Tottehale Cl SO52 53 C2
Tottenham Rd PO1 215 D4
Totton & Eling Heritage Ctr★
 SO40 101 A3
Totton By Pass SO40 101 A4
Totton Coll SO40 100 B4
Totton Recn Ctr SO40 100 B4
Totton Sta SO40 101 A4
Totton Western By-Pass
 SO40 100 B3
Totton Wlk 15 PO9 135 B3
Tournerbury La PO11 185 A2
Tourney Rd BH11 188 C3
Tovey Pl SO23 2 B4
Towans The BH13 214 B2
Tower Cl PO12 180 B2
Tower Ct
 Bournemouth BH2 204 C1
 Locks Heath SO31 128 B1
 14 Winchester SO22 10 C4
Tower Gdns 4 SO16 78 C2
Tower Ho SO19 103 C1
Tower Ind Est The SO50 56 B1
Tower La Eastleigh SO50 56 B1
 Wimborne Minst BH21 163 B3
Tower Park Rdbt BH15 202 C4
Tower Pl SO30 80 B1
Tower Rd
 Bournemouth BH1 205 C3
 Poole BH13 204 A1
 Portsmouth PO4 182 C2
 Winchester SO22 10 C4
Tower Rd W BH13 204 A1
Tower St Emsworth PO10 161 A4
 Portsmouth PO1 181 C2
 Winchester SO23 10 C4
Tower The 10 PO12 181 A3
Towers Farm BH21 186 B4
Towers Gdn PO9 159 C3
Towers Way BH21 186 B4
Town Hall Rd PO9 135 C1
Town La GU32 41 A3
Town Quay
 Portsmouth PO1 181 C2
 Southampton SO14 102 C1
Towngate Bridge BH15 202 B2
Towngate Sh Ctr 1
 BH15 202 B1
Townhill Inf Sch SO18 80 A1
Townhill Jun Sch SO18 80 A1
Townhill Park House (The
 Gregg Sch) SO18 80 A2
Townhill Way SO18 80 A1
Townsend Cl BH11 189 A3
Townsend La SP6 42 C2
Townsend Prim & Com Sch
 BH8 191 A1
Townsville Rd BH9 190 A1
Towpath Mead PO4 183 B2
Toynbee Cl SO50 56 A2
Toynbee Rd SO50 56 A2
Toynbee Sch The SO53 55 C3
Tozer Cl BH11 188 C1
Tracey Ct BH23 209 A4
Trafalgar Cl SO53 55 A3
Trafalgar Ct
 Christchurch BH23 207 C3
 Fareham PO14 154 C4
 33 Portsmouth PO5 182 B1
Trafalgar Pl
 Lymington SO41 197 C2
 Portsmouth PO1 215 D4
Trafalgar Rd
 Bournemouth BH9 204 C4
 Southampton SO15 102 B3
Trafalgar Sq PO12 181 A3
Trafalgar St SO23 10 C4
Trafalgar Way 14 SO45 126 A1
Trafford Way SO50 57 B1
Trampers La PO17 109 A2
Tranby Rd SO19 103 C2
Tranmere Cl SO41 197 C1
Tranmere Rd PO4 183 A2
Treadwheel Rd PO8 113 A3
Treagore Rd SO40 76 B1
Trearnan Cl SO16 101 C4
Treble Cl SO22 10 A2
Tredegar Rd PO4 183 A2
Tree Hamlets BH16 201 B3
Tree Side Way PO7 111 C1
Treebys Cl BH23 192 B1
Treeside BH23 193 B1
Treeside Ave SO40 101 A4
Treeside Rd SO15 102 B4
Treetops 9 BH13 214 C4
Trefoil Cl 10 PO7 135 A4
Trefoil Way BH23 208 B4
Tregantle Mews PO12 181 A2
Tregaron Ave PO6 158 A4
Tregonwell Rd BH2 204 C1
Treloar Rd PO11 185 C1
Treloen Ct 3 BH8 205 A3
Treloyhan Cl SO53 55 B2
Tremona Ct SO16 78 A1
Tremona Rd SO16 78 A1
Trenley Cl SO45 150 B2
Trent Cl SO18 79 C1
Trent Ho 25 SO14 103 B3
Trent Rd SO18 79 C1
Trent Way
 Ferndown BH22 166 A3
 Lee-on-the-Solent PO13 179 C1
 West End SO30 80 B1
Trent Wlk PO16 156 A4
Trentham Ave BH7 206 A4
Trentham Cl BH7 206 A4
Tresillian Cl BH23 194 A1
Tresillian Gdns SO18 80 A1
Tresillian Way BH23 194 A1
Trevis Rd PO4 183 B2
Trevone 15 BH25 195 A2
Trevone Cl SO40 100 C3
Trevor Rd PO4 182 C2
Trevose Cl
 Chandler's Ford SO53 55 B2
 Gosport PO13 155 B1
Trevose Cres SO53 55 B3
Trevose Way PO14 129 A1
Triangle Gdns SO16 77 B2
Triangle La PO14 153 C3
Triangle The
 Bournemouth BH2 204 C2
 Upton BH16 201 A4
 Whiteparish SP5 24 A2
Tribe Rd PO12 181 A3
Tricketts La BH22 165 C3
Tricorn The PO1 215 B4
Trigon Rd BH15 202 B4
Trimaran Rd SO31 128 C1
Trimm's Dro SP6 70 C4
Trimmer's Ct PO1 181 C2
Trinadad Ho 1 PO6 132 C1
Trinidad Cres BH12 203 B4
Trinidad Fst Sch BH12 203 B4
Trinidad Ho BH12 203 B4
Trinity 2 BH1 205 A2
Trinity Cl PO12 181 C2
Trinity Ct
 Chandler's Ford SO53 55 B3
 2 Southampton SO15 102 B3
 Totton SO40 76 C1
Trinity Gdns PO16 131 A1
Trinity Gr PO12 181 C2
Trinity Ind Est
 Southampton SO15 101 C4
 Wimborne Minst BH21 163 C2
Trinity Rd
 Bournemouth BH1 205 A2
 Southampton SO14 103 A3
Trinity St PO16 131 A1
Tripps End Cvn Site
 SO30 105 B4
Tristan Cl SO45 178 C4
Tristram Cl SO53 54 C2
Triton Ctr The SO51 53 B3
Triumph Cl PO15 130 B1
Triumph Rd PO14 154 C3
Troak Cl BH23 207 C4
Trojan Way PO7 134 C2
Troon Cres PO6 134 B1
Troon Rd BH18 187 A3
Trooper Bottom GU32 19 A2
Trosnant Inf Sch PO9 135 C2
Trosnant Jun Sch PO9 135 C2
Trosnant Rd PO9 135 C1
Trotters La BH21 164 A3
Trotts La
 Marchwood SO40 101 B1
 Totton SO40 101 B2
Trowbridge Cl SO16 77 C3
Trowbridge Ct 16 SO23 11 A4
Truman Rd BH10 189 A3
Truro Ct PO13 180 B3
Truro Rd PO6 132 C1
Truro Rise SO50 56 C2
Truscott Ave BH9 205 A4
Trussell Cl SO22 1 B2
Trussell Cres SO22 1 B2
Trystworthy 10 BH2 204 C2
Tuckers La BH15 201 C1
Tucks Cl BH23 193 A4
Tuckton Cl BH6 206 B2
Tuckton Rd BH6 206 C2
Tudor Ave PO10 136 C2
Tudor Cl Alderholt SP6 93 A3
 Gosport PO13 180 B4
 Portchester PO16 132 A1
 South Hayling PO11 184 C1
 Totton SO40 100 B4
Tudor Cres PO6 157 C3
Tudor Ct
 Bournemouth BH1 205 A3
 8 Cosham PO6 157 C4
 18 Fareham PO14 154 C4
 Poole BH15 202 C3
 8 Portsmouth PO5 182 B1
Tudor Gdns SO30 105 A3
Tudor Ho (Mus)★ SO14 102 C2
Tudor Rd BH18 187 A2
Tudor Way SO23 2 A4
Tudor Wood Cl SO16 78 C4
Tuffin Cl SO16 77 B3
Tukes Ave PO13 155 A2
Tulip Gdns Havant PO9 135 B1
 Locks Heath SO31 128 C2
Tulip Rd SO16 79 B2
Tumulus Cl SO19 104 C2
Tunstall Rd SO19 104 C2
Tunworth Ct PO9 136 A3
Tupman Ho 18 PO1 182 B4
Tuppenny La PO10 161 B4
Turbary Ct
 Bournemouth BH12 189 A1
 Ferndown BH22 165 C3
 Upton BH16 201 B4
Turbary Hts BH11 188 C1
Turbary Park Ave BH11 189 A1
Turbary Rd BH22 165 C3
Turbary Ret Pk BH11 188 C2
Turbury Cl BH12 203 B4
Turbury Rd BH12 203 B4
Turf Croft Ct BH23 194 A1
Turk's La BH14 203 A1
Turlin Moor Fst Sch
 BH16 201 B2
Turlin Moor Mid Sch
 BH16 201 B2
Turlin Rd BH16 201 B2
Turnberry Cl BH23 206 C3
Turner Ave PO13 180 C4
Turner Rd PO1 182 B4
Turners Farm Cres
 SO41 196 A1
Turners Oak Ct SO15 78 B1
Turnpike Down SO23 11 B4
Turnpike Way SO30 105 A4
Turnstone Gdns SO16 78 A3
Turnworth Cl BH18 187 B2
Turtle Cl PO14 154 A2
Turvy King Ct PO7 110 C2
Tuscan Wlk SO53 55 C3
Tuscany Way PO7 135 A4
Tussocks The SO40 101 C1
Tutland Rd SO52 53 C2
Tutt's La SO51 50 C2
Tweed Cl SO53 55 A4
Tweed La SO41 197 B4
Tweedale Rd BH9 190 B2
Twemlow Ave BH14 202 C2
Twiggs End Cl SO31 128 C2
Twiggs La SO40 124 C4
Twiggs Lane End SO40 124 B3
Twin Oaks SO19 103 C2
Twin Oaks Cl BH18 187 A2
Twittens Way PO9 135 C1
Twyford Ave
 Portsmouth PO2 157 B1
 Southampton SO15 78 B1
Twyford Cl BH8 190 B1
Twyford Ct 15 SO23 2 A1
Twyford Dr PO13 179 C1
Twyford Ho SO15 102 C4
Twyford Rd SO50 56 A3
Twyford Sch SO21 32 A3
Twyford St Mary CE Prim Sch
 SO21 31 C3
Twyford Way BH17 188 A1
Twynham Ave BH23 207 A4
Twynham Cl SP5 46 C3
Twynham Rd BH6 206 C2
Twynham Sch BH23 207 A3
Twynhams Hill SO32 108 A4
Tyler Ct PO9 135 C3
Tylers Cl SO41 197 B3
Tyleshades The SO51 53 A3
Tyne Cl SO53 55 A3
Tynedale Cl
 Bournemouth BH9 190 A2
 Gosport PO12 180 C4
Tyneham Ave BH12 203 B4
Tyrells La BH24 142 C2
Tyrrel Lawn PO9 135 B4
Tyrrel Rd SO53 55 B4
Tyrrell Gdns BH8 191 A1
Tyrrells Ct BH23 169 A1
Tyseley Rd PO1 215 B2
Tytherley Gn
 Bournemouth BH8 190 B1
 24 Havant PO9 136 A3
Tytherley Rd SO18 104 B4

U

Ubsdell Cl BH25 195 A2
Uddens Dr BH21 164 B4
Uddens Trad Est BH21 164 C3
Ullswater SO50 56 A1
Ullswater Ave SO18 80 A1
Ullswater Ho 15 PO6 133 A1
Ullswater Rd
 Southampton SO16 77 C1
 Wimborne Minst BH21 163 B1
Undercliff Dr BH1, BH5 205 B1
Undercliff Gdns SO16 78 C2
Undercliff Rd BH5 205 C2
Underdown Ave PO7 134 B1
Undershore SO41 197 C3
Undershore Rd SO41 198 A2
Underwood Cl
 Poole BH17 187 A1
 Southampton SO16 78 C2
Underwood Rd
 Bishopstoke SO50 56 C2
 Southampton SO16 78 C2
Unicorn Rd
 Lee-on-the-Solent PO13 179 B2
 Portsmouth PO1 215 A4
Unicorn Trad Ctr The
 PO1 215 A4
Union La SO32 61 A1
Union Pl PO1 215 C4
Union Rd Havant PO9 135 C1
 Southampton SO14 103 B3
Union St Fareham PO16 131 B1
 8 Portsmouth PO1 182 A3
 Winchester SO23 11 A4
Univ of Portsmouth
 Portsmouth PO1 182 A3
 Portsmouth PO1 215 B2
Univ of Portsmouth
 (Langstone Campus)
 PO4 183 B3
Univ of Portsmouth (Milton
 Campus) PO4 183 A2
Universal Marina SO31 128 B3
University Cres SO17 79 A2
University Parkway SO16 54 B1
University Rd SO17 79 A2
University Rdbt BH10 204 B4
Unwin Cl SO19 103 B1
Upham CE Prim Sch
 SO32 58 C3
Upham St SO32 58 B3
Uphill Rd SO22 1 B3
Upland La GU33 20 A4
Uplands Ave BH25 210 A4
Uplands Cl BH22 166 A4
Uplands Cres PO16 131 A1
Uplands Prim Sch PO16 131 A2
Uplands Rd
 Bournemouth BH8 190 B1
 Cosham PO6 158 B4
 Denmead PO7 110 B3
 Rowland's Castle PO9 113 B1
 West Moors BH22 139 A1
 Winchester SO22 1 C2
Uplands Sch BH14 203 B2
Uplands Way SO17 79 A1
Uplyme Cl BH17 188 A1
Upmill Cl SO18 80 A2
Uppark (NT)★ GU31 90 C4
Upper Arundel St PO1 215 B3
Upper Banister St 1
 SO15 102 C3
Upper Barn Copse SO50 57 A2
Upper Bere Wood PO7 134 C4
Upper Brook Dr SO31 128 C1
Upper Brook St SO23 11 A4
Upper Brownhill Rd
 SO16 77 C2
Upper Bugle St SO14 102 C2
Upper Church Rd SO32 107 C4
Upper Common Rd
 SO41 196 C2
Upper Crabbick La PO7 110 B3
Upper Crescent Rd SO52 53 C3
Upper Deacon Rd SO19 104 B3
Upper Gn GU33 19 C4
Upper Golf Links Rd
 BH18 187 A3
Upper Gordon Rd BH23 194 A1
Upper Heyshott GU31 41 A2
Upper High St SO23 10 C4
Upper Hinton Rd BH1 204 C2
Upper House Ct PO17 108 A2
Upper Market St SO50 56 A2
Upper Mead Cl 9 SO50 57 B1
Upper Moors Rd SO21 56 C4
Upper Mount GU33 20 C2
Upper Mullins La SO45 125 C2
Upper New Rd SO30 80 B1
Upper Northam Cl
 SO30 105 A3
Upper Northam Dr
 SO30 104 C3
Upper Northam Rd
 SO30 105 A3
Upper Norwich Rd 13
 BH2 204 C2
Upper Old St PO14 154 A2
Upper Piece PO7 111 A2
Upper Rd BH12 203 B3
Upper Shaftesbury Ave
 SO17 79 A1
Upper Shirley Ave SO15 78 B1
Upper Spinney SO31 152 B4
Upper St Helens Rd
 SO30 105 A3
Upper St Michael's Gr
 PO14 154 C4
Upper Terrace Rd BH2 204 C2
Upper Toothill Rd SO16 77 C4
Upper Wardown GU31 41 A2
Upper Weston La SO19 104 A1
Upper Wharf PO16 155 B4
Uppleby Rd BH12 203 B3
Upton Cl Havant PO9 135 B4
 Upton BH16 201 A4
Upton Cres SO16 77 B4
Upton Cross Mobile Home Pk
 BH16 201 B4
Upton Ct BH16 201 B4
Upton Ctry Pk★ BH17 201 C3
Upton Grey Cl SO22 1 B2
Upton Heath Est BH16 201 B4
Upton Ho 3 SO16 78 A1
Upton Inf Sch BH16 201 A4
Upton Jun Sch BH16 201 A4
Upton La SO16 77 B3
Upton Rd
 Broadstone BH17 202 A4
 Poole BH17 201 C4
Upton Way BH18 186 C2
Upwey Ave BH15 201 C2
Utrecht Ct BH23 207 B4

V

Vadne Gdns PO12 181 A3
Vaggs La Hordle SO41 195 C3
 New Milton SO41 195 B4
Vale Cl BH14 203 C2
Vale Dr SO18 79 C1
Vale Gr PO12 181 A4
Vale Lo BH1 205 B3
Vale Mans 4 BH1 205 B2
Vale Rd
 Bournemouth BH1 205 B2
 Poole BH14 203 C2
 Redlynch SP5 47 B3
 Winchester SO23 11 B3
Vale The Horndean PO8 88 B1
 Hythe SO45 125 C2
 Locks Heath SO31 129 A1
 Petersfield GU32 41 A3
 Portsmouth PO5 182 B1
Vale View Pk SO41 195 C4
Valencia Cl BH23 191 B2
Valentine Ave SO19 104 B2
Valentine Cl PO15 130 B1
Valentine Ct
 Southampton SO19 104 B2
 Waterlooville PO7 135 A4
Valentines Inf Sch SO19 104 B2
Valerian Ave PO15 129 C2
Valerian Cl SO50 81 B3
Valerian Rd SO30 105 B3
Valetta Pk PO10 160 C4
Valetta Rd PO10 161 B1
Valette Rd BH9 190 A2
Valiant Gdns PO2 157 B2
Valiant Rd PO10 161 B1
Valiant Way BH23 208 A4
Valley Cl Blackfield SO45 150 C1
 Christchurch BH23 191 C2
 Colden Common SO21 56 C4
 Redlynch SP5 47 B3
 Waterlooville PO7 134 B2
Valley Ct The 4 SO22 10 B3
Valley La BH23 169 C2
Valley Park Dr PO8 88 B2
Valley Rd
 Bournemouth BH8 190 C2
 Chandler's Ford SO53 55 B4
 Littleton SO22 1 A3
 Totton SO40 100 C3
Valley Rise SO31 128 C2
Valley The SO22 10 B3
Valley View Poole BH12 204 A4
 Southampton SO19 104 A2
Valleydene SO45 125 C1
Vallis Cl BH15 202 B1
Valsheba Dr PO14 179 A3
Vanburgh Way SO53 30 A1
Vanguard Rd
 Bournemouth BH8 190 C1
 Gosport PO12 181 B4
 Poole BH15 202 B1
 Southampton SO18 104 A4
Vanstone Rd PO13 180 B4
Vardy Cl SO19 104 B2
Varna Rd SO15 102 B3
Varsity Rd PO10 161 B1
Vaudrey Cl SO15 78 B1
Vaughan Cl SO19 104 C3
Vaughan Rd SO45 125 B2
Vauxhall Way GU32 40 C2
Veal's La SO40 125 A4
Vear's La SO21 57 A4
Vecta Cl BH23 208 B3

ectis Ct 1 SO16 ... 78 C2
ectis Rd
Barton on Sea BH25 ... 209 B4
Gosport PO12 ... 180 C2
ectis Way PO6 ... 157 C4
elder Ave PO4 ... 183 A3
ellan Ct SO16 ... 77 B1
elmore Rd SO53 ... 55 A2
elsheda Ct 2 SO45 ... 126 A3
elvet Lawn Rd BH25 ... 194 C2
enator Pl BH21 ... 163 B3
enerable Rd PO14 ... 155 A3
engeance Rd PO13 ... 179 C2
enice Cl PO7 ... 135 A4
enning Ave BH11 ... 188 C3
entnor Ct SO16 ... 79 B3
entnor Rd
Gosport PO13 ... 155 A2
Portsmouth PO4 ... 182 C2
entnor Way PO16 ... 131 C1
entry Cl BH13 ... 203 C2
entura Ctr The BH16 ... 201 B3
entura Pl BH16 ... 201 B3
enture Ct PO3 ... 158 A3
enture Ind Pk PO3 ... 158 A3
enture Rd SO16 ... 54 B1
erbena Cres PO8 ... 112 A2
erbena Way SO30 ... 105 B3
erdon Ave SO31 ... 127 C2
erger Cl PO14 ... 129 B2
erity Cres BH17 ... 188 A1
ermont Cl SO16 ... 78 C2
ermont Sch SO16 ... 78 C2
ernalls Cl BH10 ... 189 B3
ernalls Ct BH25 ... 195 B3
ernalls Gdns BH10 ... 189 B3
erne Rd BH31 ... 115 A3
erney Cl BH11 ... 189 A2
erney Rd BH11 ... 189 A2
ernham Rd SO22 ... 1 C1
erno La BH23 ... 193 B1
ernon Ave PO4 ... 183 A3
ernon Cl
Bishop's Waltham SO32 ... 59 B1
Gosport PO12 ... 181 A3
ernon Ct 3 PO2 ... 157 C1
ernon Hill SO32 ... 59 B1
ernon Mews 2 PO4 ... 183 A3
ernon Rd Gosport PO12 181 A3
Portsmouth PO3 ... 158 A1
ernon Wlk 5 SO15 ... 102 C3
erona Ave BH6 ... 206 B3
erona Rd SO53 ... 55 C3
erulam Pl 31 BH1 ... 204 C2
erulam Rd Poole BH14 202 C2
Southampton SO14 ... 103 A4
erwood CE First Sch
BH31 ... 114 C3
erwood Cres BH6 ... 207 A2
erwood Ind Est BH31 115 A3
erwood Rd Havant PO9 136 A3
Ibsley BH24 ... 116 A1
St Leonards BH24 ... 140 B4
Three Legged Cross BH21 114 C1
Verwood BH21 ... 114 A4
Woodlands BH21 ... 114 A4
eryan PO15 ... 130 C1
esca Ho SO31 ... 129 A3
espasian Ct SO18 ... 103 B4
espasian Rd SO18 ... 103 B4
espasian Way SO53 ... 55 C4
esta Way SO53 ... 55 C4
etch Cl BH23 ... 208 B4
ian Cl PO13 ... 155 B2
ian Ct BH25 ... 194 C2
ian Pl SO23 ... 2 B4
ian Rd PO7 ... 134 C3
icarage Cotts BH8 ... 190 C2
icarage Dr SO30 ... 105 A3
icarage Farm SO50 ... 57 B3
icarage Gdns SO41 ... 196 A1
icarage La Cadnam SO40 75 A1
Curdridge SO32 ... 106 B4
Hambledon PO7 ... 86 B2
Hordle SO41 ... 196 A1
Stubbington PO14 ... 154 B2
Swanmore SO32 ... 84 B3
icarage Pk SP5 ... 47 B3
icarage Rd
Bournemouth BH9 ... 189 C1
Marchwood SO40 ... 101 C1
Poole BH15 ... 202 B3
Redlynch SP5 ... 48 A3
Verwood BH31 ... 114 C3
icarage Way BH23 ... 192 B1
ice La SO43 ... 74 A2
iceroy Rd SO19 ... 104 A2
ickers Cl BH8 ... 191 A1
ickery Way BH23 ... 207 B4
ictena Rd SO50 ... 57 B1
ictor Ct SO19 ... 104 B3
ictor Rd
Portsmouth PO1 ... 182 C4
Thorney Island PO10 ... 161 B1
ictor St SO15 ... 78 A1
ctoria Ave
Bournemouth BH9 ... 189 C1
South Hayling PO11 ... 184 C2
Waterlooville PO7 ... 134 A2
ctoria Bldgs SO32 ... 83 A4
ctoria Cl
Corfe Mullen BH21 ... 186 B3
Locks Heath SO31 ... 129 A1
ctoria Cottage Hospl
PO10 ... 160 C4
ctoria Cres BH12 ... 203 B3
ctoria Ct Durley SO32 ... 82 B4
3 Netley SO31 ... 127 A3
Victoria Ct *continued*
South Hayling PO11 ... 184 C2
Victoria Gdns
Ferndown BH22 ... 165 B3
Fordingbridge SP6 ... 69 B1
Ringwood BH24 ... 141 A3
Victoria Glade SO31 ... 127 B3
Victoria Gr PO5 ... 215 C1
Victoria Ho 11 PO16 ... 131 A1
Victoria Hospl BH21 ... 163 A3
Victoria Park Rd BH9 ... 189 C1
Victoria Pl
Bournemouth BH1 ... 205 B3
6 Gosport PO12 ... 181 A2
2 Lymington SO41 ... 197 C1
Romsey SO51 ... 52 C4
Wimborne Minst BH21 ... 163 A3
Victoria Rd
Bishop's Waltham SO32 ... 83 A4
Bournemouth BH1 ... 205 B3
Christchurch BH23 ... 207 C3
Eastleigh SO50 ... 56 A3
Emsworth PO10 ... 136 C1
Ferndown BH22 ... 165 B3
Fordingbridge SP6 ... 69 B1
Milford on Sea SO41 ... 211 B2
Netley SO31 ... 127 A3
North Hayling PO11 ... 159 C1
Poole BH12 ... 203 B3
Portsmouth PO1 ... 182 A3
Southampton SO19 ... 103 B1
Waterlooville PO7 ... 134 C4
Wimborne Minst BH21 ... 163 A3
Winchester SO23 ... 1 C1
Victoria Rd N PO5 ... 215 C2
Victoria Rd S PO5 ... 182 B1
Victoria Sq PO13 ... 179 C1
Victoria St Gosport PO12 181 B3
Portsmouth PO1 ... 182 B4
Southampton SO14 ... 103 B3
Victoria Terr
16 Cosham PO6 ... 157 C4
Hermitage PO10 ... 137 A1
Southbourne PO10 ... 161 B4
Westbourne PO10 ... 137 A2
Victoria Wlk SO30 ... 80 C1
Victory Ave PO8 ... 112 A3
Victory Cl
Chandler's Ford SO53 ... 55 A3
Three Legged Cross BH21 139 A3
Victory Cotts SO31 ... 128 B4
Victory Cres SO15 ... 102 A3
Victory Ct PO13 ... 155 B1
Victory Gn PO2 ... 157 B1
Victory Ho PO6 ... 157 A4
Victory Rd
17 Portsmouth PO1 ... 182 A3
Southampton SO15 ... 102 A3
Stubbington PO14 ... 179 B3
Victory Ret Pk PO2 ... 182 B4
Victory Sq SO15 ... 102 A3
Victory Trad Est PO3 ... 158 A1
Victory Way SO16 ... 77 C4
Viewside Cl BH21 ... 186 B3
Viking Cl Blackfield SO45 177 C4
Bournemouth BH6 ... 207 A2
Southampton SO16 ... 77 C2
Stubbington PO14 ... 154 A2
Viking Way
Bournemouth BH6 ... 207 A2
Christchurch BH23 ... 208 A3
Horndean PO8 ... 88 B2
Vikings The SO51 ... 53 A4
Villa Gdns PO7 ... 134 C4
Village Cl PO14 ... 179 B3
Village Ctr SO40 ... 101 C1
Village Gate PO14 ... 153 C4
Village Rd PO12 ... 180 C1
Village St GU32 ... 41 A3
Ville de Paris Rd PO14 155 A3
Villette Cl BH23 ... 192 A1
Villiers Rd Hythe SO45 ... 149 C4
Portsmouth PO5 ... 182 B1
Southampton SO15 ... 102 B4
Vimoutiers Ct SP6 ... 69 C1
Vimy Ho 3 PO14 ... 154 C4
Vince Cl BH11 ... 189 A3
Vincent Ave SO16 ... 78 B1
Vincent Cl 2 BH25 ... 195 A1
Vincent Gr PO16 ... 156 B4
Vincent Rd
1 New Milton BH25 ... 195 A1
Southampton SO15 ... 102 B4
Vincent St SO15 ... 102 B4
Vincent's Gr SO15 ... 102 A4
Vincent's Wlk SO14 ... 103 A2
Vine Bank SO18 ... 104 A4
Vine Cl Bournemouth BH7 206 A4
Locks Heath SO31 ... 128 B2
Vine Coppice PO7 ... 134 C2
Vine Ct 22 PO6 ... 157 C4
Vine Farm Cl BH12 ... 204 B4
Vine Farm Rd BH12 ... 204 A4
Vine Hill BH21 ... 162 C3
Vine Ho SO31 ... 129 A3
Vine Rd SO16 ... 78 A2
Vinegar Hill SO41 ... 211 B3
Vineries Cl BH21 ... 163 C3
Vineries The BH21 ... 163 C3
Vinery Gdns SO16 ... 78 B1
Vinery Rd SO16 ... 78 B1
Vinery The BH25 ... 195 A1
Vineside PO13 ... 155 C1
Viney Ave SO51 ... 53 A4
Viney Rd SO41 ... 197 C1
Vineyard Cl SO19 ... 103 B2
Vineyards The SO52 ... 54 A2
Vinnells La GU32 ... 37 B3
Vinneys Cl BH23 ... 192 B1
Vinson Rd GU33 ... 21 A2
Violet Ave PO14 ... 179 A3
Violet Cl SO53 ... 55 A3
Violet Farm Cl BH21 ... 186 B4
Violet La BH25 ... 195 A2
Violet Rd SO16 ... 79 A2
Virginia Cl BH12 ... 203 B4
Virginia Park Rd PO12 180 C3
Viscount Ct BH11 ... 188 B3
Viscount Dr BH23 ... 208 A3
Viscount Wlk BH11 ... 188 B3
Vista Marina BH13 ... 214 B3
Vita Rd PO2 ... 157 C2
Vitre Gdns SO41 ... 197 C1
Vivash Rd PO1 ... 215 D3
Vixen Cl PO14 ... 179 A3
Vixen Wlk BH25 ... 195 A3
Vokes Cl SO19 ... 104 A3
Vulcan Cl SO15 ... 101 C3
Vulcan Rd
Southampton SO15 ... 101 C3
Thorney Island PO10 ... 161 B1
Vulcan Way BH23 ... 208 A4
Vyse La 20 SO14 ... 102 C2

W

Wade Court Rd PO9 ... 160 A4
Wade La PO9 ... 160 A4
Wadham Rd PO2 ... 157 B1
Wadhurst Gdns SO19 ... 127 A4
Wadhurst Rd SO30 ... 105 B3
Wagtail Dr BH25 ... 194 C1
Wagtail Rd PO8 ... 112 A3
Wagtail Way PO16 ... 155 C4
Wainscot Rd PO4 ... 183 A1
Wainsford Cl SO41 ... 197 A1
Wainsford Rd
Hordle SO41 ... 196 C1
Lymington SO41 ... 196 C1
Wainwright Cl PO6 ... 158 A3
Wainwright Gdns SO30 ... 81 B2
Wait End Rd PO7 ... 134 C3
Waite End Prim Sch
PO7 ... 134 C3
Wake Lawn PO4 ... 183 B2
Wakefield Ave
Bournemouth BH10 ... 189 C3
Fareham PO16 ... 130 C2
Wakefield Ct 6 SO18 ... 80 A1
Wakefield Pl PO12 ... 181 A1
Wakefield Rd SO18 ... 80 A1
Wakeford Ct 17 SO51 ... 52 C4
Wakeford Pl SO31 ... 129 A1
Wakefords Way PO9 ... 136 A3
Wakely Gdns BH11 ... 189 A3
Wakely Rd BH11 ... 189 A3
Walberant Bldgs 9
PO3 ... 157 C2
Walberton Ave PO6 ... 158 A4
Walberton Ct 1 PO6 ... 158 A4
Walcheren Pl BH15 ... 201 B2
Walcott Ave BH23 ... 191 C1
Waldegrave Cl SO19 ... 103 B1
Walden Gdns PO8 ... 112 A4
Walden Rd PO2 ... 157 B1
Walditch Gdns BH17 ... 187 C1
Waldon Gdns SO18 ... 80 A1
Waldren Cl BH15 ... 202 C1
Wales St SO23 ... 11 A4
Walford Bldgs PO3 ... 183 A4
Walford Cl BH21 ... 163 B3
Walford Gdns BH21 ... 163 A3
Walford Mill Craft Ctr★
BH21 ... 163 A3
Walford Rd PO6 ... 133 B1
Walhampton Hill SO41 ... 198 A3
Walker Gdns SO30 ... 81 B1
Walker Pl PO13 ... 155 B1
Walker Rd PO2 ... 157 B1
Walker's La S SO45 ... 177 C4
Walkers Cl SO50 ... 57 B1
Walkers La N SO45 ... 150 C1
Walkford La BH25 ... 194 B2
Walkford Rd BH23 ... 194 B1
Walkford Way BH23 ... 194 A1
Walkingfield La BH15 ... 202 B1
Walkwood Ave BH7 ... 206 A4
Wallace La SO42 ... 175 B3
Wallace Rd
Broadstone BH18 ... 187 A2
Portsmouth PO2 ... 182 C4
Southampton SO19 ... 103 C1
Wallington Ct PO14 ... 154 C3
Wallington Dr SO53 ... 55 A4
Wallington Hill 3 PO16 131 B1
Wallington Rd PO2 ... 157 C1
Wallington Shore Rd
Fareham PO16 ... 131 B1
14 Portchester PO16 ... 131 B1
Wallington Way PO16 ... 131 B1
Wallis Bglws PO12 ... 180 C2
Wallis Gdns PO7 ... 111 C1
Wallis Rd
Bournemouth BH10 ... 189 A1
Waterlooville PO7 ... 111 C1
Walliscott Rd BH11 ... 189 A1
Wallisdean Ave PO14 ... 154 C4
Wallisdean Jun & Inf Schs
PO14 ... 154 C4
Wallisdean Rd PO3 ... 183 A4
Wallisdown Rd BH10,
BH11 ... 204 B4
Wallisdown Rdbt BH12 ... 189 A1
Wallrock Wlk PO10 ... 136 C2
Walmer Cl SO50 ... 56 A4
Walmer Rd PO1 ... 182 C3
Walnut Ave SO18 ... 79 C3
Walnut Cl
Chandler's Ford SO53 ... 30 B1
New Milton BH25 ... 194 C2
Southampton SO16 ... 77 C1
Walnut Dr PO14 ... 179 A3
Walnut Gr SO16 ... 77 C1
Walnut Tree Cl PO11 ... 184 C2
Walnut Tree Dr PO10 ... 137 C2
Walpole La SO31 ... 128 C4
Walpole Rd
Bournemouth BH1 ... 205 C3
Gosport PO12 ... 181 B2
Winchester SO22 ... 10 B3
Walpole Terr 8 PO12 ... 181 A2
Walsall Rd PO3 ... 183 A3
Walsford Rd BH4 ... 204 B3
Walsingham Cl PO6 ... 133 B1
Walsingham Dene BH7 205 C4
Walsingham Gdns SO18 79 C2
Waltham Bsns Pk SO32 ... 84 A2
Waltham Cl Droxford SO32 61 A1
Portchester PO16 ... 132 B1
Waltham Cres SO16 ... 78 B2
Waltham Rd BH7 ... 206 A3
Waltham St PO5 ... 215 A2
Walton Cl Gosport PO12 181 A2
Waterlooville PO7 ... 134 C3
Walton Ct Fareham PO15 130 B2
10 Portsmouth PO1 ... 182 A2
Walton Pl SO22 ... 10 B3
Walton Rd
Bournemouth BH10 ... 189 B1
Cosham PO6 ... 158 B3
Gosport PO12 ... 181 A2
Poole BH15 ... 203 A3
Southampton SO19 ... 104 B2
Waltons Ave SO45 ... 150 B2
Wandesford Pl PO12 ... 156 A1
Wandmore Cl SO45 ... 126 A2
Wangfield La SO32 ... 82 B1
Wansbeck Cl SO53 ... 55 A3
Wanstead Cl BH24 ... 117 A1
War Meml Hospl
Gosport PO12 ... 181 A2
Milford on Sea SO41 ... 211 C2
Warbler Cl
Hamworthy BH16 ... 201 A4
Horndean PO8 ... 112 A4
Southampton SO16 ... 78 A3
Warblington Ave PO9 ... 136 A1
Warblington Cl SO53 ... 55 A2
Warblington Ct 2 PO1 ... 182 A2
Warblington Halt Sta
PO9 ... 136 A1
Warblington Rd PO10 ... 160 C4
Warblington Sch PO9 ... 136 A1
Warblington St PO1 ... 182 A2
Warborne La SO41 ... 198 A4
Warbrook Ct 13 PO9 ... 136 A3
Warburton Cl SO19 ... 104 C2
Warburton Rd
Poole BH17 ... 202 C4
Southampton SO19 ... 104 C2
Warburton Way PO8 ... 88 B2
Ward Block PO12 ... 181 B3
Ward Cres PO10 ... 137 A2
Ward Ct PO11 ... 184 C1
Ward Ho 33 PO1 ... 182 A3
Ward Rd PO4 ... 183 A1
Warden Cl SO30 ... 80 B1
Wardens Cl PO11 ... 184 C3
Warders Ct 9 PO12 ... 181 A3
Wardle Rd SO50 ... 56 B4
Wardroom Rd PO2 ... 157 A1
Wareham Ct BH7 ... 206 A3
Wareham Rd BH21 ... 186 B2
Warfield Ave PO7 ... 134 C4
Warfield Cres PO7 ... 134 C4
Warland Way BH21 ... 186 C4
Warlock Cl SO19 ... 104 B2
Warmwell Cl
9 Bournemouth BH9 ... 190 A2
Poole BH17 ... 187 C1
Warnborough Ct 6
PO9 ... 136 A3
Warner Ct 11 SO23 ... 2 A1
Warnes La BH24 ... 142 C1
Warnford Cl PO12 ... 180 C2
Warnford Cres PO9 ... 135 B3
Warnford Ct SO15 ... 102 C4
Warnford Rd
Bournemouth BH6, BH7 206 B4
Meonstoke SO32 ... 61 B4
Warren Ave
Chandler's Ford SO53 ... 55 C3
Christchurch BH23 ... 207 C3
Portsmouth PO4 ... 183 A3
Southampton SO16 ... 78 A1
Warren Cl
Chandler's Ford SO53 ... 55 C3
South Hayling PO11 ... 184 B2
Southampton SO16 ... 78 A1
St Leonards BH24 ... 140 B3
Warren Cres SO16 ... 78 A1
Warren Dr BH24 ... 140 B3
Warren Edge Cl BH6 ... 206 C2
Warren Edge Ct BH6 ... 206 C2
Warren Edge Rd BH6 ... 206 C2
Warren Gdns SO51 ... 28 A1
Warren La Beaulieu SO42 200 C4
Froxfield Green GU32 ... 19 A3
Owslebury SO21 ... 33 C4
St Leonards BH24 ... 140 B3
Warren Park Prim Sch
PO9 ... 135 B4
Warren Pk SO41 ... 211 A3
Warren Pl SO40 ... 76 B1
Warren Rd
Bournemouth BH4 ... 204 A1
Liss GU33 ... 21 A4
Poole BH14 ... 203 B2
Winchester SO23 ... 11 B4
Warren The SO45 ... 150 A3
Warren Wlk BH22 ... 165 A4
Warrior Bsns Ctr The
PO6 ... 158 C4
Warrior Cl SO53 ... 55 A2
Warrior Pk SO53 ... 55 A2
Warrys Cl SO45 ... 150 C3
Warsash Cl PO9 ... 135 C3
Warsash Ct SO31 ... 128 B1
Warsash Gr PO13 ... 155 A1
Warsash Maritime Ctr (Soton
Inst) SO31 ... 152 B4
Warsash Rd PO14,SO31 ... 129 A1
Warspite Cl PO2 ... 157 B2
Warton Cl SO42 ... 175 B3
Warwick Ave BH25 ... 195 A2
Warwick Cl
Chandler's Ford SO53 ... 55 A2
Lee-on-the-Solent PO13 ... 180 A2
13 Winchester SO23 ... 2 A1
Warwick Cres PO5 ... 215 B2
Warwick Ct
14 Bournemouth BH5 ... 205 C2
4 Emsworth PO10 ... 160 C4
14 Winchester SO23 ... 2 A1
Warwick Ho 21 SO14 ... 103 B3
Warwick Pl
3 Bournemouth BH7 ... 206 A3
West Wellow SO51 ... 50 C2
Warwick Rd
Bournemouth BH7 ... 206 A3
Poole BH14 ... 203 B2
Southampton SO15 ... 78 B1
Totton SO40 ... 100 C4
Warwick Way PO17 ... 108 A2
Wasdale Cl PO8 ... 88 B1
Washbrook Rd PO6 ... 133 B1
Washington Ave BH8 ... 205 B3
Washington Ct 4 PO4 ... 183 A3
Washington Rd
Emsworth PO10 ... 136 C1
Portsmouth PO2 ... 182 B4
Wastwater Ho 25 PO6 ... 133 A1
Watcombe Rd BH6 ... 206 B3
Water Cl SO23 ... 11 A4
Water La
Bournemouth BH6 ... 206 B4
Hythe SO45 ... 125 C1
Totton SO40 ... 100 C4
Winchester SO23 ... 11 A4
Water Lane Farm BH10 ... 189 C3
Water's Edge SO30 ... 105 A3
Waterbeech Dr SO30 ... 105 B4
Waterberry Dr PO7 ... 111 B1
Waterditch Rd
Bransgore BH23 ... 193 A2
Burton BH23 ... 193 A2
Waterford Cl
Lymington SO41 ... 197 C2
Poole BH14 ... 203 A1
Waterford Ct SO41 ... 197 B1
Waterford Gdns BH23 ... 209 A4
Waterford La SO41 ... 197 C1
Waterford Lo BH23 ... 208 A3
Waterford Pl BH23 ... 209 A4
Waterford Rd
Christchurch BH23 ... 209 A4
New Milton BH25 ... 195 B2
Waterfront Mus★ BH15 202 A1
Watergate PO12 ... 181 C2
Waterhouse La SO15 ... 102 A4
Waterhouse Way SO15 ... 102 A4
Waterlock Gdns PO4 ... 183 B2
Waterloo Cl PO8 ... 111 B2
Waterloo Ho BH17 ... 187 A1
Waterloo Ind Est SO30 ... 81 A1
Waterloo Rd
Bournemouth BH9 ... 204 C4
Broadstone BH17 ... 202 B4
Corfe Mullen BH21 ... 186 A3
Gosport PO12 ... 181 B1
Havant PO9 ... 135 C1
Lymington SO41 ... 197 C2
Southampton SO15 ... 102 B3
Waterloo Sch The PO7 ... 134 C4
Waterloo St PO5 ... 215 B2
Waterloo Terr SO15 ... 102 C3
Waterloo Way BH24 ... 141 A3
Watermans La SO45 ... 125 C1
Watermead
Christchurch GU21 ... 207 A3
Winchester SO23 ... 10 C3
Watermead Rd PO6 ... 158 C4
Watermill Rd BH23 ... 207 A4
Waters Edge
Lee-on-the-Solent PO13 ... 179 C1
Poole BH13 ... 214 B3
Waters Edge Gdns
PO10 ... 160 C4
Waters Gn SO42 ... 146 A1
Waters Green Ct SO42 ... 146 A1
Waters The PO17 ... 130 C3
Watersedge PO17 ... 108 A2
Watersedge Rd PO6 ... 157 A4
Watershed Ct 2 PO6 ... 133 A1
Watership Dr BH24 ... 141 B3
Waterside
Christchurch BH23 ... 207 C2
4 Hythe SO45 ... 126 A3

Waterside Cl BH24 .....117 A1
Waterside Gdns PO16 ...131 B1
Waterside La PO16 .....156 C3
Waterside Rd SO51 .....28 A1
Waterside Sch PO2 ....157 A2
Waterside Sch (Unit)
PO4 ....183 B2
Waterside Sq SO45 ....125 C3
Watersmeet
Fareham PO16 ....155 A4
49 Winchester SO23 ......11 A4
Waterston Cl BH17 .....187 B1
Waterworks Rd
Cosham PO6 ....158 B4
Otterbourne SO21 ....31 B2
Petersfield GU32 ....41 A3
Watery La
Christchurch BH23 ......208 A4
Upton BH16 ....201 A4
Watkin Rd
19 Bournemouth BH5 ....205 C2
Hedge End SO30 ....81 B1
Watley Cl SO16 ....77 B3
Watley La SO21 ....32 A3
Watson Wlk SO40 ......100 B4
Watton Cl BH8 ....191 A1
Watton La SO32 ....61 C1
Watton Rd SO45 ....150 B2
Watts Cl SO16 ....77 C2
Watts Rd
Hedge End SO30 ....105 B4
Portsmouth PO1 ....182 B4
Wavecrest Cl SO40 .....102 A2
Wavell Ave BH17 ....187 A1
Wavell Rd
Bournemouth BH11 .....189 A2
Gosport PO13 ....155 B2
Southampton SO18 ......104 A4
Wavell Way SO22 ....10 B3
Wavendon Ave BH25 ...209 C4
Waveney Cl PO13 ......179 C1
Waveney Gn SO16 ....77 C1
Waverley Ave SO31 .....127 B3
Waverley Cl
Fordingbridge SP6 ....69 C2
Romsey SO51 ....28 A1
Waverley Cres BH15 ....202 B3
Waverley Ct SO31 ....127 B3
Waverley Gr PO4 ....182 C1
Waverley Ho 12 BH25 ...195 A1
Waverley Path PO12 ....180 C2
Waverley Rd
Cosham PO6 ....158 B4
Fordingbridge SP6 ....69 C2
New Milton BH25 ....195 A1
Portsmouth PO4 ....182 C1
Southampton SO15 ......102 B3
Wayfarer Cl
Locks Heath SO31 ......128 C1
Portsmouth PO4 ....183 B3
Wayfarers PO13 ....180 B4
Wayground Rd BH21 ....162 C1
Waylands Pl SO30 ......105 A2
Wayman Rd BH21 ....186 C3
Wayne Rd BH12 ....203 A3
Waynflete Cl 1 SO32 ....83 B4
Waynflete Pl SO22 ....10 B3
Wayside SO31 ....128 B4
Wayside Cl SO41 ....211 B3
Wayside Rd
Bournemouth BH6 ......206 C2
St Leonards BH24 ......166 C4
Wayte St PO6 ....157 C4
Waytown Cl BH17 ......187 B1
Weald Cl SO31 ....129 A2
Weardale Rd SO53 ......55 B2
Weavers Cl BH22 ....138 C1
Weavers Gn PO9 ....136 B2
Weavers Pl SO53 ....55 A4
Weavills Rd SO50 ....57 A1
Webb Cl PO11 ....185 A1
Webb La PO11 ....185 A1
Webb Rd PO16 ....156 B3
Webb's Way BH11 ......188 C1
Webbers Way PO12 .....181 B1
Webbs Cl BH24 ....139 B3
Webbs Gn SO32 ....85 B2
Webbs Way BH24 ....139 C3
Webburn Gdns SO18 ....80 A2
Webster Rd
Bournemouth BH9 ......190 A2
Winchester SO22 ....1 A1
Wedgewood Cl
Holbury SO45 ....150 B2
Stubbington PO14 ....179 A3
Wedgewood Way PO8 ...111 C1
Wedgwood Dr BH14 ....203 A1
Wedgwood Gdns BH23 ..169 B1
Wedmore Cl SO22 ....10 A2
Weeke Manor Cl SO22 ....1 B1
Weeke Prim Sch SO22 ....1 B1
Weevil La PO12 ....181 B3
Weirs The 4 SO23 ....11 A3
Welbeck Ave SO17 ....79 A1
Welburn Ct SO18 ....80 A1
Welch Rd Gosport PO12 .181 A4
Portsmouth PO4 ....182 C1
Welch Way SO16 ....77 C3
Welchwood Cl PO8 .....111 C3
Weldon Ave BH11 ......188 C3
Well Cl BH25 ....194 C1
Well Copse Cl PO8 ......88 B1
Well Hill PO7 ....110 B4
Well House Cl SP6 ......45 A2
Well House La SO22 ......1 C3
Well La
Hamble-le-Rice SO31 ....128 A1
Poole BH15 ....202 B2
Swanmore SO32 ....84 A4
Well Mdw PO9 ....135 C3
Welland Gdns SO18 ......80 A1
Welland Gn SO16 ....101 C4
Welland Rd BH21 ....163 B2
Wellands Rd SO43 ......122 A3
Wellbrooke Gdns SO53 ..55 A4
Weller Ho 16 PO1 ....182 B4
Wellers Cl SO40 ....100 A4
Welles Rd SO53 ....55 B3
Wellesley Ave BH23 ....208 B4
Wellesley Cl PO7 ....134 C4
Wellington Ave
Christchurch BH23 ......208 B4
Southampton SO18 ......104 A4
Wellington Cl
Horndean PO8 ....112 B3
Hythe SO45 ....125 B1
Wellington Ct
7 Bournemouth, Deane Pk
BH8 ....205 A3
Bournemouth, Westbourne
BH2 ....204 B2
8 Havant PO9 ....135 C1
New Milton BH25 ....195 A2
Southampton SO15 ......102 B3
West End SO30 ....80 B1
Wellington Gr PO16 ....156 B4
Wellington Pk SO30 ......81 A1
Wellington Pl SO40 ......98 C4
Wellington Rd
Bournemouth BH1, BH8 ..205 A3
Poole BH14 ....203 B2
Southampton SO18 ....79 C1
Wellington St PO5 .....215 B2
Wellington Way 9 PO7 .134 C4
Wellman Ct 10 SO16 .....78 C2
Wellow Cl Havant PO9 ...135 B2
Southampton SO18 ......104 B4
Wellow Ct 11 SO18 .....103 C4
Wellow Dro SO51 ....50 C4
Wellow Gdns PO14 ......129 B1
Wellow Sch SO51 ....50 C2
Wellow Vineyard★ SO51 .51 B4
Wellow Wood Rd SO51 ..50 B4
Wellowbrook Cl SO53 ....55 A3
Wells Cl PO15 ....129 B4
Wells Pl SO50 ....56 A1
Wells Rd SO50 ....56 A1
Wellsmoor PO14 ....129 B1
Wellswood Gdns PO9 ...113 B2
Wellsworth La PO9 .....113 B2
Wembley Gr PO6 ....158 A3
Wembley Way SO50 ......57 B1
Wendover Cl BH25 .....194 C1
Wendover Rd PO9 ......135 C1
Wendy Cres BH22 ......165 C2
Wenlock Ct 9 BH23 ....207 C4
Wensley Gdns PO10 ....136 C2
Wentwood Gdns BH25 ..195 B1
Wentworth BH14 ....214 B4
Wentworth Ave BH5 ....206 A2
Wentworth Cl BH5 .....206 A2
Wentworth Coll BH5 ....206 A2
Wentworth Dr
Broadstone BH18 ....187 A3
Christchurch BH23 ......206 C3
Horndean PO8 ....112 A4
Wentworth Gdns
Holbury SO45 ....150 B2
Southampton SO19 ......104 A1
Wentworth Gr SO45 ....150 B2
Wentworth Grange SO22 10 C3
Wescott Way BH11 .....188 C2
Wesermarsch Rd PO8 ..112 A2
Wesley Cl
8 Bournemouth BH8 ....205 B3
Southampton SO19 ......104 B2
Wesley Ct PO1 ....215 D3
Wesley Gr PO3 ....158 A2
Wesley Grange 33 BH4 .204 B2
Wesley Ho 13 SO23 ......11 A4
Wesley Rd
Kings Worthy SO23 ....2 B4
Poole BH12 ....203 B3
Wimborne Minst BH21 ..163 C3
Wessex Ave BH25 ......195 A1
Wessex Cl
Blackfield SO45 ....177 C4
Christchurch BH23 ......208 B4
Wessex Ct
Southampton, Sholing
SO19 ....104 A2
8 Southampton, Westwood Pk
SO17 ....103 A4
Wessex Dr SO22 ....1 C1
Wessex Est BH24 ....141 A4
Wessex Gate Ind Est
PO8 ....112 B3
Wessex Gate Ret Pk
BH17 ....202 A3
Wessex Gdns
Portchester PO16 ....156 A4
Romsey SO51 ....53 A4
Wessex La SO18 ....79 B2
Wessex Maternity Ctr
(private) SO18 ....80 A2
Wessex Nuffield Hospl
SO53 ....31 A1
Wessex Rd Horndean PO8 .88 B2
Poole BH14 ....203 A2
Ringwood BH24 ....141 A4
Wessex Trad Ctr BH12 ..203 A4
Wessex Way
Bournemouth BH8 ....205 B3
Wessex Way *continued*
Colden Common SO21 .....57 A4
West Ave BH21 ....138 C4
West Bargate 2 SO14 ..102 C2
West Battery Rd PO2 ...157 A1
West Bay Rd SO15 ......102 B3
West Block SO15 ....102 B3
West Borough BH21 ....163 A3
West Butts St 1 BH15 ..202 A1
West Cl Lymington SO41 .197 A1
Verwood BH31 ....114 B3
West Cliff Cotts BH2 ...204 C1
West Cliff Gdns BH2 ...204 C1
West Cliff Mews BH2 ..204 C1
West Cliff Rd BH2, BH4 .204 B1
West Close Ct BH6 .....207 A2
West Close Ho BH6 .....207 A2
West Comm SO45 ....177 C3
West Ct Portsmouth PO1 .182 C4
Portsmouth, Southsea
PO4 ....183 A2
Southampton SO19 ......103 C1
West Downs Cl PO16 ...131 A2
West Dr SO50 ....56 B2
West End Cl SO22 ....10 C4
West End Cotts 13
PO16 ....131 A1
West End Rd
Hedge End SO31 ....104 C2
Southampton SO18 ......104 A4
West End Terr SO22 .....10 C4
West Haye Rd PO11 .....185 B1
West Hayes
Lymington SO41 ....197 C2
Winchester SO22 ....10 B4
West Hill Ct SO15 ......102 C3
West Hill Dr Hythe SO45 .125 C3
Winchester SO22 ....10 C4
West Hill Park Sch
PO14 ....153 C4
West Hill Pk SO22 ....10 B4
West Hill Pl 15 BH2 ....204 C2
West Hill Rd BH2 ....204 C1
West Hoe La SO32 ....83 C4
West Horton Cl SO50 ....56 C1
West Horton La SO50 ....56 C1
West Howe Cl BH11 ....189 A2
West Howe Ind Est
BH11 ....188 C2
West La Hordle SO41 ....196 C1
North Baddesley SO52 ....53 C3
North Hayling PO11 .....184 C3
West Links SO53 ....55 B1
West Lodge PO13 ....179 B2
West Mans 8 BH4 ......204 B2
West Marlands Rd
SO14 ....102 C3
West Meon CE Prim Sch
GU32 ....37 B3
West Mills Rd SP6 ....69 C1
West Moors Mid Sch
BH22 ....138 C1
West Moors Rd
Ferndown BH22 ....165 B4
Three Legged Cross BH21 138 C4
West Moors BH22 ......138 B3
West Moors St Mary's CE Fst
Sch BH22 ....138 B2
West Overcliff Dr BH4 ..204 B1
West Park Dr SP6 ....68 B3
West Park La SP6 ....68 B3
West Park Rd SO15 .....102 C3
West Point PO13 ....179 C1
West Quay (Sh Ctr)
SO15 ....102 C2
West Quay Rd
Poole BH15 ....202 A1
Southampton SO15 ......102 C2
West Rd
Bournemouth BH5 ......206 A2
Bransgore BH23 ....193 A4
Emsworth PO10 ....160 C4
Fawley SO45 ....150 B4
Hedge End SO30 ....104 C3
Hythe SO45 ....125 B1
Milford on Sea SO41 ....211 A3
Southampton, Woolston
SO19 ....103 C1
Southwick PO17 ....133 A3
West Row BH21 ....163 A2
West Row Mews BH21 ..163 A2
West St Emsworth PO10 ..160 C4
Fareham PO16 ....131 A1
Fordingbridge SP6 ....69 C1
Hambledon PO7 ....86 B1
Havant PO9 ....135 C1
Hythe SO45 ....125 C3
Poole BH15 ....202 A1
Portchester PO16 ....156 B4
Portsmouth PO1 ....181 C2
Ringwood BH24 ....140 C4
Soberton SO32 ....85 B3
Southampton SO14 ......102 C2
Southwick PO17 ....132 C3
Titchfield PO14 ....153 C4
Wimborne Minst BH21 ..163 A3
West Station Terr BH4 ..204 B2
West Street Ct 11 BH21 .163 A3
West Tytherley CE Prim Sch
SP5 ....4 A4
West View Cotts PO10 ..137 C1
West View Rd
Christchurch BH23 ......207 C3
Poole BH15 ....202 B2
West Walk (North) Forest
Wlk★ PO17 ....108 C4
West Walk (South) Forest
Wlk★ PO17 ....108 C3
West Way
Bournemouth BH9 ......190 A1
Broadstone BH18 ....187 A2
Locks Heath PO15 ......129 C2
Lymington SO41 ....197 B1
West Way Cl BH9 ......190 A1
Westbeams Rd SO41 ....172 A1
Westborn Rd PO16 .....131 A1
Westbourne Ave
Emsworth PO10 ....137 A1
Holbury SO45 ....150 B2
Westbourne Cl
Bournemouth BH4 ......204 B2
Emsworth PO10 ....137 A1
Westbourne Cres SO17 ..79 A1
Westbourne Ct 5 PO9 ..135 C1
Westbourne Cty Prim Sch
PO10 ....137 A2
Westbourne Mans 9
SO17 ....79 A1
Westbourne Park Rd
BH4 ....204 A1
Westbourne Rd
Emsworth PO10 ....137 A2
Portsmouth PO2 ....182 C4
Westbourne PO10 ....137 A2
Westbroke Gdns SO51 ...27 C1
Westbrook Cl
Bournemouth BH10 .....189 B1
Locks Heath SO31 ......129 A3
Westbrook Ctr The 12
PO7 ....112 A1
Westbrook Gr PO7 .....134 B2
Westbrook Rd PO16 ....156 B3
Westbrook Way SO18 ....79 B2
Westbrooke Cl PO8 .....112 A3
Westbury Cl
Barton on Sea BH25 .....210 A4
Bransgore BH23 ....193 A4
Christchurch BH23 ......193 B1
31 Cosham PO6 ....133 A1
Westbury Ct
Hedge End SO30 ....105 B3
10 Poole BH14 ....203 A2
Westbury Mall 24 PO16 .131 A1
Westbury Manor Mus★
PO16 ....131 A1
Westbury Rd
Fareham PO16 ....131 A1
Ringwood BH24 ....141 A4
Southampton SO15 ......101 C4
Westbury Sq 25 PO16 ...131 A1
Westby Rd BH5 ....205 C2
Westcliff Cl PO13 ....179 C2
Westcliff Mews SO19 ...103 B2
Westcliff Wlk SO45 .....125 C3
Westcot Rd SO45 ....150 A2
Westcroft Par 10 BH25 .195 A1
Westcroft Pk BH18 .....187 B2
Westcroft Rd PO12 .....180 C3
Westdown Rd BH11 .....189 A3
Westerham Cl PO6 .....157 C4
Westerham Rd BH4 .....204 A2
Westering SO51 ....53 B4
Westerleigh BH4 ....204 B1
Westerley Cl SO31 ......128 C1
Western Ave
Barton on Sea BH25 .....209 B4
Bournemouth BH10 .....189 B2
Emsworth PO10 ....160 B4
Poole BH13 ....203 C1
Southampton SO15 ......102 A3
Western CE Prim Sch
SO22 ....10 B4
Western Cl BH10 ....189 B3
Western Com Hospl
SO16 ....77 C1
Western Ct 14 PO16 ....131 A1
Western District Cut
SO15 ....102 B4
Western Downland CE Prim
Sch
Damerham SP6 ....68 B2
Rockbourne SP6 ....44 C1
Western Espl SO14 .....102 C2
Western Par
Emsworth PO10 ....160 C4
Portsmouth PO5 ....182 A1
Western Rd
Chandler's Ford SO53 .....30 C1
Cosham PO6 ....157 B4
Fareham PO16 ....131 A1
Fawley SO45 ....151 C1
Havant PO9 ....135 C1
Liss GU33 ....20 C2
Lymington SO41 ....197 B2
Poole, Branksome Pk
BH13 ....204 A1
Poole, Canford Cliffs BH13 214 C4
West End SO30 ....80 B1
Winchester SO22 ....10 C4
Western Terr PO2 ......157 B1
Western Way
Fareham PO16 ....131 A1
Gosport PO12 ....180 C1
Portsmouth PO1 ....181 C4
Westerngate BH13 ......204 A2
Westfield 13 BH21 .....163 A3
Westfield Ave
Fareham PO14 ....154 C4
South Hayling PO11 .....184 C2
Westfield Cl
Fair Oak SO50 ....81 B4
Hamble-le-Rice SO31 ....127 C1
Wimborne Minst BH21 ..163 A3
Westfield Cnr SO18 ......79 C3
Westfield Comm SO31 ..127
Westfield Cres SO53 55
Westfield Dr SO32 84
Westfield Dro SO24 34
Westfield Gdns BH23 ...193
Westfield Ho SO18 79
Westfield Ind Est
Gosport PO12 181
Horndean PO8 112
Westfield Jun Sch PO6 .156
Westfield Oaks PO11 ...184
Westfield Rd
Bournemouth BH6 206
Chandler's Ford SO53 55
Gosport PO12 181
Littleton SO22 1
Lymington SO41 198
Portsmouth PO4 183
Southampton SO15 102
Totton SO40 100
Westgate PO14 179
Westgate Mews SO30 80
Westgate Mus★ SO23 ...10
Westgate Pk BH4 204
Westgate Sec Sch SO22 ...1
Westgate St 19 SO14 ...102
Westgrove SP6 69
Westgrove Gdns PO10 ..160
Westham Cl BH17 187
Westheath Rd BH18 187
Westland Dr PO7 134
Westland Gdns PO12 181
Westlands Ct BH23 193
Westlands Dr BH13 214
Westlands Gr PO16 156
Westley Cl SO22 1
Westley Gr PO14 154
Westmarch Ct 1 SO17 ...79
Westmead Cl PO11 184
Westminster Ct BH25 ...209
Westminster Gate SO22 .10
Westminster Gdns
PO14 129
Westminster Pl PO1 182
Westminster Rd
Milford on Sea SO41 211
Poole BH13 204
Westminster Rd E BH13 204
Westmoreland Ct SO41 .195
Westmorland Way SO53 .55
Weston Ave PO4 183
Weston Cl SO19 103
Weston Cres SO18 104
Weston Dr BH1 205
Weston Grove Rd SO19 .103
Weston Ho 19 GU32 40
Weston Homes 7 SO19 126
Weston La Buriton GU32 ..65
Nursling SO16 77
Southampton SO19 103
Weston Par SO19 126
Weston Park Boys Sch
SO19 104
Weston Park Inf Sch
SO19 104
Weston Park Jun Sch
SO19 104
Weston Rd Eastleigh SO50 56
Petersfield GU31 41
Wimborne Minst BH21 ..163
Weston Shore Inf Sch
SO19 126
Westons La 8 BH15 202
Westover La BH24 140
Westover Prim Sch
PO3 183
Westover Rd
Bournemouth BH1 204
Milford on Sea SO41 211
Portsmouth PO3 183
Southampton SO16 101
Westquay Ho 8 PO16 ...131
Westray Hall BH4 204
Westridge Ct 39 SO17 ...79
Westridge Rd SO17 103
Westrow Gdns SO15 102
Westrow Rd SO15 102
Westside View PO7 111
Westview Rd SO22 1
Westward Rd SO30 105
Westways Cosham PO9 ..158
Stubbington PO14 179
Westways Cl SO16 77
Westwood Ave BH22 165
Westwood Cl PO10 137
Westwood Ct
12 Southampton SO17 ...103
Totton SO40 76
West End SO30 80
Westwood Gdns SO53 55
Westwood Mans 28 SO17 79
Westwood Rd
Lyndhurst SO43 121
Netley SO31 127
Portsmouth PO2 157
Southampton SO17 103
Westwood View SO24 14
Westwoods & Glendene Pk
BH25 194
Wetherby Cl BH18 187
Wetherby Ct SO40 100
Wetherby Gdns SO40 ...100
Wetherdown GU31 41
Weybridge Cl SO31 128
Weyhill Cl Havant PO9 ..135
Portchester PO16 132
Weyman's Ave BH10 189
Weymans Dr BH10 189

eymouth Ave PO12 180 C4
eymouth Rd
oole BH14 203 B3
3 Portsmouth PO2 157 B1
haddon Chase PO14 179 A3
haddon Ct PO9 135 B3
haddon La
olden Common SO21 58 A4
wslebury SO21 33 A2
hale Island Way PO2 157 B1
halesmead Cl SO50 56 C1
halesmead Rd SO50 56 C1
haley Rd PO2 157 A1
harf Cl BH12 203 C3
harf Hill SO23 11 A3
harf Mill 2 SO23 11 A3
harf Rd
ortsmouth PO2 182 B4
outhampton SO19 103 B2
harfdale Rd
ournemouth BH4 204 B2
oole BH12 203 C3
harncliffe Ct BH23 208 C4
harncliffe Gdns BH23 209 A4
harncliffe Ho SO19 103 B2
harncliffe Rd
ournemouth BH5 205 B2
hristchurch BH23 209 A4
outhampton SO19 103 B2
hartons Cl SO40 100 B2
hartons La SO40 100 B2
hatleigh Cl BH15 202 B1
heat Cl SO53 54 C3
heatcroft Dr SO18 80 A1
heatcroft Rd PO13 179 C1
heatear Dr GU31 41 B1
heatears Dr SO51 50 C2
heatland Cl SO22 10 B3
heatlands PO14 129 B2
heatlands Ave PO11 185 C1
heatlands Cres PO11 185 C1
heatley Gn 2 PO9 135 B3
heaton Grange BH4 204 B2
heaton Rd BH7 206 A3
heatplot Park Homes 2
BH10 189 C2
heatsheaf Ct SO30 105 A3
heatsheaf Dr PO8 111 B2
heatstone Rd PO4 182 C2
heeler Cl PO12 181 A3
heelers La BH11 188 B3
heelers Wlk SO45 177 C4
heelwright Mews SP5 46 C4
hernside Cl SO16 101 C4
herwell Ct 33 PO9 136 A3
hichers Cl PO9 136 A4
hichers Gate Rd PO9 136 A4
himbrel Cl PO4 183 B3
himbrel Ct BH23 208 A3
hinchat Cl
areham PO15 130 B2
outhampton SO16 78 A3
hincroft Cl BH22 165 C4
hincroft Dr BH22 165 C3
hinfield Rd SO45 149 C4
hinwhistle Rd SO51 51 A1
hippingham Cl PO6 157 B4
histler Cl SO19 104 B2
histler Rd SO19 104 B2
hitaker Cres SO41 197 B2
hitby Ave BH18 187 A1
hitby Cl BH23 191 B2
hitby Cres BH18 187 A1
hitby Ct 4 SO41 211 A2
hitby Rd SO41 211 A2
hitchurch Ave BH18 187 B2
hitchurch Ct SO19 103 C2
hitcombe Cl SO40 100 C4
hitcombe Gdns PO1 182 C3
hite Barn Cres SO41 196 A2
hite Beam Rise PO8 88 B3
hite Cl BH15 203 A4
hite Cloud Pk 7 PO4 182 C2
hite Cloud Pl 8 PO4 182 C2
hite Dirt La PO8 88 B2
hite Farm Cl BH10 204 B4
hite Gates SO32 82 A3
hite Harmony Acres Ind Est
SO30 80 C3
hite Hart La
Cadnam SO40 98 C4
Portchester PO16 156 B4
hite Hart Rd
Fair Oak SO50 57 B1
4 Gosport PO12 181 A2
Portsmouth PO1 182 A2
hite Heather Ct 1
SO45 126 A3
hite Ho The SO41 211 B2
hite Horse Dr BH15 202 B3
hite Horse La PO7 111 A3
hite Horses BH25 209 C4
hite House Gdns GU32 40 C3
hite Knights BH25 209 C4
hite La SO21 32 A4
hite Ladies SO51 28 A4
hite Ladies Cl PO9 136 A1
hite Lion Ctyd BH24 140 C4
hite Lion Wlk PO12 181 B3
hite Lodge BH15 202 C2
hite Lodge Gdns
PO16 130 C2
hite Oak Wlk 31 PO9 136 A3
hite Rd SO50 56 B2
hite Row SP5 46 B4
hite Swan Rd PO1 215 A3
hite Way SO32 61 A4
hite Wings Ho PO7 110 C2
White's Rd SO19 104 A3
Whiteacres Cl 11 PO12 181 A3
Whitebeam Cl
Colden Common SO21 57 A4
2 Fareham PO14 154 C4
Waterlooville PO8 112 B3
Whitebeam Rd SO30 105 B3
Whitebeam Way
North Baddesley SO52 54 A3
Verwood BH31 115 A3
Whitechimney Row
PO10 137 A2
Whitecliff Cres BH14 203 A1
Whitecliff Rd BH14 202 C1
Whitecliffe Ave PO3 183 A4
Whitecliffe Ct PO12 180 B2
Whitecroft SO45 126 A1
Whitecross Cl BH17 187 C2
Whitecross Gdns 14
PO2 157 C2
Whitefield Lo 1 BH25 195 A2
Whitefield Rd
Holbury SO45 150 B2
New Milton BH25 195 A1
Poole BH14 203 A1
Whitehall BH23 207 A3
Whitehart Fields 2
BH24 141 B4
Whitehaugh Ct SO50 56 B2
Whitehaven
Horndean PO8 112 B3
Portchester PO16 156 A4
Whitehaven Home Pk
SO45 177 C4
Whitehayes Cl BH23 192 B1
Whitehayes Rd BH23 192 B1
Whitehill Cl SO18 104 B4
Whitehorn Dr SP5 73 B4
Whitehouse Gdns SO15 102 A3
Whitehouse Rd BH21 163 B1
Whitelands
Bransgore BH23 169 B2
Droxford SO32 85 A4
Whitelaw Rd SO15 102 A4
Whiteleaf La PO7 86 B4
Whitelegg Way BH10 189 C3
Whiteley La
Locks Heath PO15 129 C3
Swanwick PO15,SO31 106 B1
Whiteley Prim Sch
PO15 129 B4
Whiteley Way PO15 129 B3
Whitemoor La SO40,SO51 75 C2
Whitemoor Rd SO42 145 B1
Whitenap Cl SO51 53 A3
Whitenap La SO51 53 B3
Whiteparish All Saints CE
Prim Sch SP5 24 A2
Whites Ct 19 PO2 157 B1
Whites Hill SO21 33 A2
Whites La SO45 151 A2
Whiteshoot SP5 47 C2
Whiteshoot Hill SP5 47 C2
Whiteshute La SO23 10 C3
Whitestone Cl SO16 101 C4
Whitethorn Rd PO11 185 A2
Whitewater Rise SO45 125 C1
Whiteways BH21 163 C3
Whitfield Park BH24 140 A3
Whitingham Ct 8 BH5 206 A3
Whitley Cl PO10 137 A3
Whitley Row PO4 183 B3
Whitley Way BH25 195 A3
Whitmore La BH21 114 A4
Whitsbury Cl BH8 190 B1
Whitsbury Cross SP6 69 B4
Whitsbury Rd
Fordingbridge SP6 69 C2
Havant PO9 136 A3
Whitstable Rd PO6 157 C4
Whittington Cl SO45 125 C2
Whittington Ct PO10 160 C4
Whittle Ave PO15 129 B3
Whittle Rd BH21 164 C4
Whittles Way BH15 202 A1
Whitwell SO31 127 B4
Whitwell Rd PO4 182 C1
Whitworth Cl PO12 181 A2
Whitworth Cres SO18 103 B4
Whitworth Ct SO18 103 B4
Whitworth Rd
Gosport PO12 181 A3
Portsmouth PO2 182 C4
Southampton SO18 103 B4
Whyke Ct 3 PO9 135 C1
Whyte Cl SO45 150 A2
Whyteways SO50 56 A2
Wick 1 Ind Est BH25 194 C1
Wick 2 Ind Est BH25 194 C1
Wick Cl BH25 194 C1
Wick Dr BH25 194 C1
Wick Farm BH6 207 A3
Wick La
Bournemouth BH6 207 A3
Christchurch BH23 207 A3
Downton SP5 46 A4
Wicket Rd BH10 189 B3
Wicket The SO45 125 C1
Wickfield Ave BH23 207 A3
Wickfield Cl BH23 207 A3
Wickford Ho BH23 207 A3
Wickham CE Prim Sch
PO17 108 A2
Wickham Croft PO17 108 A2
Wickham Ct
Ferndown BH22 165 C3
Gosport PO12 180 B2
Wickham Dr BH21 186 B2
Wickham Ho
17 Southampton SO17 79 A1
38 Southampton SO17 79 A1
Wickham Rd
Bournemouth BH7 206 A3
Droxford SO32 85 A3
Fareham PO16,PO17 131 A3
Wickham St PO1 182 A3
Wickham Vineyard*
SO32 107 A4
Wicklea Rd BH6 207 A2
Wicklow Dr SO53 55 A3
Wickmeads Rd BH6 207 A3
Wickor Cl PO10 137 A1
Wickor Way PO10 137 A1
Wicor Mill La PO16 156 A4
Wicor Path PO16 156 B3
Wicor Prim Sch PO16 156 A4
Widbury Rd SO41 197 B1
Widden Cl SO41 172 A1
Widdicombe Ave BH14 203 C1
Wide La SO18 79 C3
Wide Lane Cl SO42 145 C1
Widecombe Dr SO45 125 C2
Widgeon Cl
Gosport PO12 181 A4
Southampton SO16 78 A3
Widgeon Ct PO16 155 C4
Widget Cl BH11 189 A1
Widlers La SO32 58 C3
Widley Court Dr PO6 158 A4
Widley Ct
4 Cosham PO6 158 A4
Fareham PO14 155 A3
Widley Gdns PO7 134 B2
Widley Rd Cosham PO6 158 A4
Portsmouth PO2 157 B1
Widley Wlk PO6,PO7 133 C2
Widworthy Dr BH18 186 C3
Wield Cl PO9 135 B2
Wigan Cres PO9 135 A1
Wight View
Lee-on-the-Solent PO13 179 B2
South Hayling PO11 185 B1
Wight Wlk BH22 165 C1
Wightway Mews SO31 128 B1
Wigmore Ho PO1 215 C4
Wilberforce Cl 2 SO22 10 B3
Wilberforce Rd
Gosport PO12 181 B1
Portsmouth PO5 215 B1
Wilby La PO3 158 B2
Wild Arum Way SO53 54 C3
Wild Cherry Way SO53 55 A3
Wild Grounds Nature Reserve
PO13 180 B3
Wild Ridings PO14 154 B4
Wild Rose Cres SO31 128 C1
Wildburn Cl SO40 76 B1
Wilde Cl SO40 100 B4
Wildern Cl SO31 128 C2
Wildern Ct SO30 105 A4
Wildern La SO30 105 B4
Wildern Sec Sch SO30 105 B4
Wilderness Hts SO18 80 B1
Wilderton Rd BH13 203 C2
Wilderton Rd W BH13 204 A2
Wildfell Cl BH23 192 A1
Wildground Inf Sch
SO45 125 C1
Wildground Jun Sch
SO45 125 C1
Wildground La 8 SO45 126 A1
Wildmoor Wlk PO9 136 A3
Wildown Gdns BH6 207 A2
Wildown Rd BH6 207 A2
Wilfred Rd BH5 205 C2
Wilkins Cl PO8 88 A3
Wilkins Way BH15 202 A1
Wilkinson Dr BH8 191 A1
Wilkinson Ho PO4 183 A1
Wilks Cl SO16 77 B3
Willersley Cl PO6 133 B1
Willett Rd BH21 163 A1
William Booth Ho 37
PO1 182 A3
William Cl
Christchurch BH23 194 A1
Stubbington PO14 179 B3
William Ct 17 BH23 209 A4
William George Ct 9
PO13 179 C1
William Gilpin CE Prim Sch
SO41 173 C1
William Macleod Way
SO16 78 A1
William Price Gdns
PO16 131 A1
William Rd
Bournemouth BH7 205 C4
Lymington SO41 197 C3
William St SO14 103 B3
William's Ind Pk BH25 194 C1
Williams Cl
Gosport PO13 180 B4
Holbury SO45 150 B2
Williams Rd PO3 158 A2
Willis Ave SO52 54 A2
Willis Rd Gosport PO12 181 B2
Portsmouth PO1 215 B3
Southampton SO16 79 B3
Willis Way BH15 202 A3
Willis Waye SO23 2 B3
Willment Marine & Bsns Pk
SO19 103 B3
Willow Ave SP6 69 C1
Willow Cl
Bournemouth BH4 204 A3
Willow Cl *continued*
Havant PO9 136 A1
Hedge End SO30 105 B3
St Leonards BH24 139 B2
Upton BH16 201 B3
West End SO30 80 C2
Willow Ct
Bournemouth BH7 206 B3
Fareham PO14 130 B1
Southampton SO16 78 A2
Willow Dr
Christchurch BH23 207 A3
Marchwood SO40 124 C4
Ringwood BH24 141 A3
Wimborne Minst BH21 164 B3
Willow Gdns
North Baddesley SO52 53 C3
Westbourne PO10 137 A2
Willow Gn SO21 57 A4
Willow Gr 11 SO50 57 B1
Willow Herb Cl SO31 128 C1
Willow La BH23 169 B2
Willow Lo 1 BH1 205 B2
Willow Mead
Bournemouth BH8 190 B2
Hedge End SO30 105 A4
Willow Pk BH14 203 A2
Willow Pl
Christchurch BH23 207 B3
Gosport PO12 181 A3
Willow Rd
Bishop's Waltham SO32 83 C4
Liss GU33 21 A2
Willow Tree Ave PO8 112 A1
Willow Tree Gdns PO14 154 C4
Willow Tree Ho SO41 197 B1
Willow Tree Rise BH11 189 A2
Willow Tree Wlk SO19 104 A2
Willow View BH16 201 B2
Willow Way
Christchurch BH23 207 A3
Ferndown BH22 165 B4
Willow Wlk BH25 210 A4
Willow Wood Rd PO11 185 A2
Willowdale Cl GU32 40 A2
Willowdene Cl
Havant PO9 135 A2
New Milton BH25 195 B2
Willows The
Barton on Sea BH25 210 A4
Chandler's Ford SO53 55 B2
Denmead PO7 110 C2
Wills Cl BH21 186 B2
Wills Rd BH12 203 C2
Wills Way SO51 53 A3
Willwood Cl BH17 187 C2
Wilmcote Gdns 5 PO1 215 C3
Wilmcote Ho PO1 215 C3
Wilmer Rd SO50 56 A1
Wilmington Cl SO18 79 C2
Wilmot Cl SO50 56 C3
Wilmott Cl PO12 180 C3
Wilmott La PO12 180 C3
Wilmur Cres BH15 202 C3
Wilson Ct Fair Oak SO50 81 B4
Fordingbridge SP6 69 C1
Wilson Gr PO5 215 D1
Wilson Rd
Bournemouth BH1 205 C3
Poole BH14 203 B2
Portsmouth PO2 157 B1
Wilson St SO14 103 B3
Wilton Ave SO15 102 C3
Wilton Cl
Christchurch BH23 191 B1
Gosport PO12 180 C2
Wilton Cres SO15 78 B1
Wilton Ct SO15 102 B4
Wilton Dr PO8 112 A3
Wilton Gdns
New Milton BH25 194 C2
Southampton SO15 78 B1
Wilton Pl PO5 182 B1
Wilton Rd
Bournemouth BH7 205 C3
Southampton SO15 78 B1
Wilton Terr PO5 182 B1
Wiltshire Gdns BH23 192 C4
Wiltshire Rd
Bransgore BH23 192 C4
Chandler's Ford SO53 55 B2
Wiltshire St PO5 215 A2
Wilverley Ave
Bournemouth BH8 190 C1
Havant PO9 136 A2
Wilverley Cl SO41 197 A1
Wilverley Pl SO45 150 C1
Wilverley Rd
Brockenhurst SO42 145 C1
Brockenhurst, Wootton
BH25 170 C2
Christchurch BH23 208 A4
Wimbledon Park Rd
PO5 182 B1
Wimborne Fst Sch
BH21 163 A3
Wimborne Ho SO16 77 C1
Wimborne Inf & Jun Schs
PO4 183 A2
Wimborne Minster Model
Town & Gdns* BH21 163 A2
Wimborne Rd
Bournemouth BH10, BH11,
BH2, BH3, BH9 204 C3
Bournemouth, Kinson
BH10, BH11, BH2, BH3,
BH9 189 B3
Broadstone BH21 162 C1
Wimborne Rd *continued*
Poole BH15 202 B3
Portsmouth PO4 183 A2
Wimborne Minst BH21 163 A3
Wimborne Minster, Colehill
BH21 163 C3
Wimborne Rd E BH22 165 B3
Wimborne Rd W
Ferndown BH21 164 B3
Wimborne Minst BH21 164 B3
Wimpole Ct PO1 215 C4
Wimpole St PO1 215 C4
Wimpson Gdns SO16 77 C1
Wimpson La SO16 101 C4
Wincanton Way PO7 112 A1
Winchcombe Rd PO6 133 A1
Winchelsea Sch BH12 188 B1
Winchester Cath* SO23 11 A4
Winchester Cl 7 SO31 127 A3
Winchester Coll
Winchester SO22 10 C3
Winchester SO23 11 A3
Winchester Ct
Gosport PO13 180 B3
5 Romsey SO51 28 A1
Southampton SO15 78 B1
Winchester Cty Mill*
SO23 11 A4
Winchester Cty Mus*
SO23 11 A4
Winchester Hill SO51 53 A4
Winchester Ho 10 PO9 136 A3
Winchester Pl 3 BH15 202 B1
Winchester Rd
Bishop's Waltham SO32 83 A4
Chandler's Ford SO53 55 C4
Durley SO32 81 C2
Langrish GU32 39 C2
Langrish GU32 39 C2
New Milton BH25 195 B2
Owslebury SO21, SO32 58 B2
Petersfield GU32 40 B2
Portsmouth PO2 182 C4
Romsey SO51 52 C4
Romsey, Woodley SO51 28 B1
Southampton SO16 78 B1
Upham SO32 58 B2
Waltham Chase SO32 83 C1
Winchester Sch of Art
SO23 11 A4
Winchester St
Botley SO30 106 A4
4 Southampton SO15 102 C3
Winchester Sta SO22 10 C4
Winchester Way SO40 100 B4
Winchfield Cl SO19 104 A1
Winchfield Cres PO9 135 B2
Winchfield Ho PO12 181 C2
Wincombe Cl BH22 165 B2
Wincombe Dr BH22 165 B2
Windbury Rd SO16 77 C1
Windermere Ave
Southampton SO16 77 C1
Stubbington PO14 154 B2
Windermere Gdns SO40 100 C4
Windermere Ho PO6 157 A4
Windermere Rd
Bournemouth BH3 205 A4
Portsmouth PO2 157 C2
West End SO18 80 A1
Windfield Dr SO51 53 A4
Windgreen Est BH21 186 C4
Windham Mews BH1 205 B3
Windham Rd BH1 205 B3
Windhill Field PO7 111 A2
Windmill Cl Clanfield PO8 88 B3
5 Milford on Sea SO41 211 B3
St Leonards BH24 140 B2
Windmill Copse SO45 125 C1
Windmill Gr PO16 156 B3
Windmill La
Bursledon SO31 105 A1
St Leonards BH24 140 B2
Windover Cl SO19 104 B3
Windrush Gdns PO7 134 B4
Windrush Rd SO16 101 C4
Windrush Way SO45 126 A2
Windsor Cl Hordle SO41 195 C2
St Leonards BH24 139 C2
Windsor Ct
5 Christchurch BH23 209 A4
9 Cosham PO6 157 C4
Poole BH14 203 A2
14 Southampton SO17 103 A4
13 Southampton, Bitterne
SO18 103 C4
Southampton, Millbrook
SO15 102 A3
6 Southampton, Westwood Pk
SO17 103 A4
Windsor Gate SO50 56 A3
Windsor Ho
3 Portsmouth PO1 215 C3
25 Winchester SO23 11 A4
Windsor Rd
Bournemouth BH5 205 C2
Christchurch BH23 206 C4
Cosham PO6 157 C4
Gosport PO12 181 A2
Petersfield GU32 40 C2
Poole BH14 203 A2
Portchester PO16 156 B3
Windsor Way SP6 93 A3
Windward Ct 11 PO12 181 B2
Wine Cross PO17 109 A1

Winecross PO17 .109 A1
Winfield Way PO10 .136 C2
Winfrid Ho SO40 .100 B4
Winfrith Cres BH12 .203 C4
Winfrith Way SO16 .77 B3
Wingate Dr SO19 .104 A3
Wingate Rd
Gosport PO12 .155 C1
Totton SO40 .100 B4
Wingfield Ave
Christchurch BH23 .193 B1
Poole BH15 .202 B3
Wingfield Ct BH1 .205 B2
Wingfield St PO1 .182 B4
Wingrove Rd SO40 .100 B2
Winifred Cl SO50 .57 B2
Winifred Rd Poole BH15 .202 C3
Waterlooville PO7 .134 C4
Winkfield Row PO8 .112 A3
Winkle St SO14 .103 A1
Winkton Cl Burton BH23 .192 B2
Havant PO9 .135 B2
Winkton Ho BH23 .192 B2
Winn Ct SO17 .102 C4
Winn Mans 25 SO17 .79 A1
Winn Rd SO17 .79 A1
Winnall Cl SO23 .2 B1
Winnall Manor Rd SO23 .11 B4
Winnall Prim Sch SO23 .11 B4
Winnall Trad Est SO23 .11 B4
Winnall Valley Rd SO23 .11 B4
Winnards Cl BH22 .165 C1
Winnards Pk SO31 .128 B2
Winnham Dr PO16 .132 A1
Winnington PO15 .130 B2
Winnington Cl PO15 .130 B2
Winscombe Ave PO8 .112 A1
Winsford Ave SO50 .57 A1
Winsford Cl
Bishopstoke SO50 .57 A1
Christchurch BH23 .193 B1
Winsford Gdns SO50 .57 A1
Winslade Rd Havant PO9 135 B3
Winchester SO22 .1 B2
Winsley Ave BH6 .206 B2
Winslow Ct PO6 .158 B4
Winsor Cl PO11 .185 B1
Winsor Ct SO50 .56 B2
Winsor La SO40 .99 C4
Winsor Rd Cadnam SO40 .75 B1
Totton SO40 .101 A3
Waterlooville PO7 .111 B1
Winspit Cl BH15 .201 C2
Winstanley Rd
Nursling SO16 .77 B3
Portsmouth PO2 .157 B1
Winston Ave BH12 .204 A3
Winston Churchill Ave
PO5 .215 B2
Winston Cl Eastleigh SO50 56 A2
South Hayling PO11 .184 C2
Southampton SO16 .77 C1
Winston Ct
1 Christchurch BH23 .207 A4
20 New Milton BH25 .195 A1
Winston Gdns BH12 .204 A3
Winston Par 22 BH25 .195 A1
Winston Pk BH12 .204 A3
Winston Rd BH9 .190 A2
Winston Way BH24 .141 A4
Winstone Bldgs SO16 .78 C2
Winstone Cres SO52 .54 A2
Winter Rd PO4 .183 A2
Winterbarrow Cotts
SO32 .36 C2
Winterbourne Cl BH15 .202 B2
Winterbourne Rd
Cosham PO6 .132 C1
Poole BH15 .202 B3
Romsey SO51 .28 A1
Winterhayes Cl BH17 .187 C2
Winterhill Rd PO6 .157 B4
Winters Cl SO45 .150 B2
Winters Hill
Bishop's Waltham SO32 .82 C4
Durley SO32 .82 C4
Winters Rd SO32 .84 A1
Winterslow Dr PO9 .135 C3
Winton (Boys) Sch
BH10 .189 B1
Winton Cl
Lymington SO41 .197 C2
Winchester SO22 .1 C1
Winton Ct
11 Petersfield GU32 .40 C2
West End SO30 .80 B1
Winton Prim Sch BH9 .189 C1
Winton Rd
Petersfield GU32 .40 C2
Portsmouth PO2 .157 C1
Winton St 14 SO14 .103 A3
Winton Way
Bournemouth BH10 .189 B1
New Milton BH25 .195 A3
Wisbech Way SO41 .195 C2
Wisborough Rd PO5 .182 C1
Wises Ct PO12 .181 C2
Wish Pl PO5 .215 D1
Wishart Gdns BH9 .190 A3
Wistaria Ho 7 BH10 .189 C2
Wisteria Dr BH31 .115 B2
Wisteria Gdns PO9 .136 A2
Witchampton Cl PO9 .136 A3
Witchampton Rd BH18 .186 C1
Witham Cl SO53 .55 A3
Withedwood Ave SO15 .102 B4
Witherbed La
Locks Heath PO15 .129 B2
Locks Heath PO15 .129 C3
Withermoor Rd BH9 .204 C4
Withers La SO42 .175 B4
Withewood Mans 2
SO15 .102 B4
Withies Rd PO13 .180 B4
Withingham Rd BH13 .203 C2
Withington Cl 8 PO6 .133 A1
Withy Cl SO51 .52 C4
Witley BH14 .214 B4
Witley Rd PO8 .111 C3
Witney Rd BH17 .187 B1
Witt Rd SO50 .57 B1
Wittensford La SO43 .98 B4
Wittering Rd
South Hayling PO11 .185 C1
Southampton SO16 .78 A2
Witts Hill SO18 .79 C1
Woburn Cl SO50 .56 A3
Woburn Ct PO13 .179 C1
Woburn Rd SO16 .78 B3
Wode Cl PO8 .88 B2
Wodehouse Rd SO19 .103 C2
Woking Rd BH14 .203 B2
Wolfe Cl
Christchurch BH23 .207 B4
Winchester SO22 .10 B3
Wollaston Rd BH6 .206 C2
Wollaton Cres BH22 .165 B2
Wollaton Rd BH22 .165 B2
Wollstonecraft Rd 25
BH5 .205 C2
Wolseley Rd Poole BH12 .203 B3
Southampton SO15 .102 B4
Wolsey Way SO41 .211 B3
Wolterton Rd BH12 .204 A3
Wolverley Ct
16 Bournemouth BH4 .204 B2
Southampton SO16 .78 B2
Wolverton Rd
Bournemouth BH7 .205 C3
Havant PO9 .135 C3
Southampton SO14 .103 A3
Wolvesey Castle (Old Bishop's Palace)*
SO23 .11 A3
Wolvesey Pl SO53 .55 A2
Wolvesey Terr 3 SO23 .11 A3
Wonderholm Par BH11 .189 A1
Wonston Ct PO9 .136 B3
Wonston Rd SO16 .78 A2
Wood Cl SO19 .104 B2
Wood End Rd BH24 .141 C3
Wood End Way SO53 .55 A3
Wood Glade Cl SO40 .101 C1
Wood House La SO41 .174 A1
Wood La
Bournemouth BH11 .188 C3
Bramdean SO24 .15 C3
Milford on Sea SO41 .211 B2
Southwick PO17 .133 A3
Wood Lark Gdns GU31 .41 B2
Wood Lawn Cl BH25 .209 C4
Wood Lodge SO40 .76 A1
Wood Rd SO40 .100 A1
Wood Row BH9 .190 C2
Wood View BH21 .164 A4
Wood's Cnr BH24 .143 B3
Woodacre Gdns BH22 .165 C2
Woodberry La PO9,PO10 136 C4
Woodbind Wlk SO31 .128 C1
Woodbourne Cl
Fareham PO15 .130 B1
Liss GU33 .21 A2
Woodbury
Bournemouth BH1 .205 A1
Brockenhurst SO42 .145 B1
Woodbury Ave
Bournemouth BH8 .190 C1
Havant PO9 .159 C4
Petersfield GU32 .40 C3
Woodbury Cl BH23 .191 C2
Woodbury Gr PO8 .111 C3
Woodcock La SO41 .196 A2
Woodcocks Cres BH7 .206 A4
Woodcot Cres PO9 .136 A3
Woodcot Prim Sch
PO13 .155 A2
Woodcote Cotts SO24 .15 B2
Woodcote Dr BH16 .201 A3
Woodcote La PO14 .155 A2
Woodcote Rd SO17 .79 B2
Woodcroft Gdns PO8 .111 C3
Woodcroft La PO8 .111 C3
Woodend Rd BH9 .204 C4
Wooderson Cl SO50 .57 A2
Woodfern SP6 .70 B1
Woodfield Ave PO6 .134 C1
Woodfield Cotts GU32 .19 A2
Woodfield Dr SO22 .10 A3
Woodfield Gdns BH23 .193 B1
Woodfield Ho 22 PO2 .157 C2
Woodfield Park Rd
PO10 .161 A4
Woodfield Rd BH11 .189 A3
Woodford Cl BH24 .141 B4
Woodford Ho PO15 .130 B1
Woodford Rd BH1 .205 B2
Woodgaston La PO11 .160 B1
Woodgreen Ave PO9 .135 B2
Woodgreen Dr BH11 .188 B2
Woodgreen Rd SO22 .1 B2
Woodgreen Wlk SO40 .76 A1
Woodhall Way PO15 .130 C2
Woodhay SO43 .121 C3
Woodhay Wlk 22 PO9 .136 A3
Woodhayes Ave BH23 .193 C1
Woodhill Sch
Botley SO30 .105 C4
Chandler's Ford SO53 .55 B4
Woodhouse La
Finchdean PO8 .113 A3
Hedge End SO30 .105 C4
Rowland's Castle PO8,
PO9 .113 B2
Woodhouse Rd PO8 .112 C4
Woodington Cl 55 PO9 .136 A3
Woodington Rd SO51 .51 B3
Woodlake Cl BH17 .187 B1
Woodland Ave BH5 .206 A2
Woodland Cl
Southampton SO18 .104 B4
Verwood BH31 .114 C4
West Wellow SO51 .51 A1
Woodland Ct BH7 .205 C3
Woodland Dro SO21 .32 A2
Woodland Mans BH14 .203 A3
Woodland Mews SO30 .80 B1
Woodland Pl 18 SO15 .102 C4
Woodland St PO1 .215 D4
Woodland Vale SO19 .104 A2
Woodland View
Bursledon SO31 .127 C4
Horndean PO8 .111 C3
Woodland Way
Christchurch BH23 .208 B4
Milford on Sea SO41 .211 B2
Woodland Wlk
Bournemouth BH5 .206 A2
Ferndown BH22 .165 C4
* Mottisfont SO51 .5 B2
Woodlands PO16 .131 B1
Woodlands Ave
Emsworth PO10 .136 C2
Hamworthy BH15 .201 C2
Woodlands Cl
Bransgore BH23 .193 A4
Chandler's Ford SO53 .30 B1
Gosport PO13 .180 B3
Hythe SO45 .125 C1
Locks Heath SO31 .128 C3
Woodlands Com Sch
SO18 .104 B4
Woodlands Cres BH15 .201 C2
Woodlands Ct
5 Hythe SO45 .125 C1
18 Winchester SO23 .2 A1
Woodlands Dr SO31 .127 B3
Woodlands Dro SO40 .99 C2
Woodlands Gdns 8
SO51 .28 A1
Woodlands Gr PO7 .134 B3
Woodlands La Liss GU33 .21 A2
South Hayling PO11 .184 C3
Woodlands Prim Sch
PO8 .111 B2
Woodlands Rd
Ashurst SO40 .99 C2
Barton on Sea BH25 .209 C4
Brockenhurst SO42 .172 C4
Netley Marsh SO40 .99 C2
Woodlands The
Chandler's Ford SO53 .30 A1
Kings Worthy SO23 .2 B3
Woodlands Way
Bursledon SO31 .127 C4
Havant PO9 .135 C2
New Milton BH25 .195 A3
North Baddesley SO52 .53 C2
Southampton SO15 .102 C4
St Leonards BH24 .139 C2
Woodlane Cl SO24 .15 B3
Woodlea Cl SO22 .1 C1
Woodlea Gdns SO30 .80 C1
Woodlea Ho SO53 .55 B2
Woodlea Way SO51 .29 C1
Woodleaze Cl BH18 .187 A3
Woodleigh Cl PO9 .136 B2
Woodley Cl SO51 .28 B1
Woodley Close Flats
SO51 .28 B1
Woodley Gdns SO41 .197 B3
Woodley La SO51 .28 A1
Woodley Rd
Gosport PO12 .181 B2
Southampton SO19 .103 B2
Woodley Way SO51 .28 B1
Woodling Cres SP6 .70 B1
Woodlinken Cl BH31 .115 A2
Woodlinken Dr BH31 .115 A3
Woodlinken Way BH31 .115 B2
Woodmancote La PO10 .137 C2
Woodmancote Rd PO4 .183 A2
Woodmill La SO18 .79 C1
Woodmoor Cl SO40 .102 A1
Woodpath PO5 .215 B1
Woodpath Ho PO5 .215 B1
Woodpecker Cl
Havant PO9 .136 A1
Verwood BH31 .114 C3
Woodpecker Copse
SO31 .129 A2
Woodpecker Dr
Broadstone BH17 .201 C4
Marchwood SO40 .101 C1
Woodpecker Way
Eastleigh SO50 .55 B1
Portsmouth PO3 .158 A2
Woodpeckers Dr SO22 .1 B1
Woodrising BH13 .214 A2
Woodrisings The BH2 .204 B2
Woodroffe Wlk PO10 .136 C2
Woodrow PO7 .110 C2
Woodruff Cl BH23 .208 B4
Woodrush Cres SO31 .128 C1
Woods Ho 5 GU32 .40 C2
Woods View Rd BH9 .204 B4
Woodsedge PO7 .135 A3
Woodside
Brockenhurst SO42 .173 A4
Chilworth SO16 .54 C1
Gosport PO13 .155 A3
Portsmouth PO5 .215 B1
Woodside Ave
Eastleigh SO50 .56 A3
Lymington SO41 .197 C1
Woodside Cl
Ferndown BH22 .165 C3
13 Lymington SO41 .197 C1
Marchwood SO40 .101 C1
Woodside Cres SO16 .54 C1
Woodside Ct 23 SO17 .103 A4
Woodside Gdns SO40 .100 B2
Woodside La SO41 .197 C1
Woodside Rd
Bournemouth BH5 .206 A2
Eastleigh SO50 .55 C2
Ferndown BH22 .165 C3
North Baddesley SO52 .53 C2
Poole BH14 .203 B2
Southampton SO17 .103 A4
West Moors BH22 .138 B2
Woodside Way SO30 .105 A3
Woodstock Ave PO8 .112 A3
Woodstock Cl
Fareham PO15 .130 C1
Hedge End SO30 .105 B3
Poole BH14 .203 A1
Woodstock Ct BH22 .165 C2
Woodstock Dr SO17 .79 A1
Woodstock La BH24 .141 A3
Woodstock Rd
Burton BH23 .192 B1
Gosport PO12 .181 B2
Havant PO9 .135 B1
Poole BH14 .203 A1
Woodthorpe Gdns SO31 128 C3
Woodvale PO15 .130 B1
Woodvale Gdns BH25 .195 B2
Woodview Cl SO16 .79 A3
Woodville Dr PO1 .182 A2
Woodville Rd
Fawley SO45 .151 A2
Havant PO9 .135 A1
Woodward Cl PO12 .180 C2
Woofferton Rd PO6 .133 A1
Wool Rd BH12 .203 A4
Woolfield La GU32,GU34 .18 A2
Woolford Cl 1 SO22 .10 B3
Woolley Ho 17 SO14 .103 A3
Woolmer Ct 30 PO9 .136 A3
Woolmer La BH24 .117 A1
Woolmer St PO10 .136 C2
Woolner Ave
Cosham PO6 .158 A4
Petersfield GU32 .40 C2
Woolsbridge Ind Est
BH21 .139 A3
Woolsbridge Rd BH24 .139 C3
Woolslope Cl BH22 .138 C1
Woolslope Gdns BH22 .138 C1
Woolslope Rd BH22 .138 C1
Woolston Ct PO12 .180 B2
Woolston Inf Sch SO19 .103 C1
Woolston Rd Havant PO9 135 B3
Netley SO31 .127 B4
Woolston Sch (Annexe)
SO19 .103 C2
Woolston Sec Sch SO19 103 C1
Woolston Sta SO19 .103 B2
Woolven Cl BH14 .203 A3
Woolwich Cl SO31 .104 C1
Wootton SO31 .127 B4
Wootton Farm Rd BH25 170 C1
Wootton Gdns BH1 .205 A2
Wootton Mount BH1 .205 A2
Wootton Rd
Lee-on-the-Solent PO13 .180 A2
New Milton BH25 .195 B4
Wootton Rough BH25 .195 A4
Wootton St PO6 .157 C4
Worbarrow Gdns BH12 .203 B4
Worcester Cl 5 PO1 .215 C2
Worcester Ct PO13 .180 B3
Worcester Pl
7 Lymington SO41 .197 C1
Southampton SO19 .104 A1
Wordsworth Ave
Bournemouth BH8 .190 C1
Portchester PO6 .132 C1
Wordsworth Cl
Bishop's Waltham SO32 .83 C4
Winchester SO22 .10 B4
Wordsworth Inf Sch
SO15 .78 A1
Wordsworth Pl PO15 .106 B1
Wordsworth Rd SO15 .78 B1
Worgret Rd BH15 .202 B4
Workhouse La GU32 .38 B1
Worldham Rd PO9 .136 A3
Worrell Dr BH12 .203 B4
Worsley Rd PO5 .215 B1
Worsley St PO4 .183 A1
Worth The PO5 .182 B1
Worthing Ave PO12 .180 C4
Worthing Rd PO5 .182 B1
Worthington Cres BH14 203 A2
Worthy Ct 46 PO9 .136 A3
Worthy Ho SO16 .78 A1
Worthy La SO23 .1 C1
Worthy Rd
New Milton BH25 .195
Winchester SO23 .2
Wortley Rd BH23 .209
Wr Twr Rd BH18 .187
Wraxall Cl BH17 .187
Wraysbury Park Dr
PO10 .136
Wren Cl
Christchurch BH23 .208
New Milton BH25 .194
Ringwood BH24 .141
Winchester SO22 .10
Wren Cres BH12 .204
Wren Ctr The PO10 .137
Wren Gdns SP6 .93
Wren Rd SO50 .55
Wrenway PO16 .155
Wrexham Gr PO8 .88
Wright Way SO45 .151
Wright's Hill SO19 .104
Wrights Wlk SO31 .104
Wriothesley Ct PO14 .153
Wroxham Rd BH12 .203
Wryneck Cl SO16 .78
Wuthering Hts SO22 .10
Wyatts Cl BH21 .186
Wyatts La BH21 .186
Wyborn Cl PO11 .185
Wych La PO13 .155
Wychwood Cl BH2 .204
Wychwood Dr
Blackfield SO45 .177
Bournemouth BH2 .204
Wychwood Gr SO53 .55
Wychwood Grange 1
BH2 .204
Wycliffe Rd
Bournemouth BH9 .204
Southampton SO18 .80
Wycote Rd PO13 .155
Wyeford Cl 4 PO9 .136
Wyelands Ave BH21 .164
Wykeham Ave PO2 .157
Wykeham Cl
6 Netley SO31 .127
Poole BH17 .202
Southampton SO16 .78
Wykeham Field PO17 .108
Wykeham House Sch
PO16 .131
Wykeham Ind Est The
SO23 .2
Wykeham Lo BH13 .214
Wykeham Pk SO21 .12
Wykeham Pl
Lymington SO41 .197
Winchester SO22 .10
Wykeham Rd
Netley SO31 .127
Portsmouth PO2 .157
Wyld Green La GU33 .21
Wylds La GU32 .65
Wyllie Rd PO2 .157
Wylye Cl SO18 .80
Wymering La PO6 .133
Wymering Manor (Youth
Hostel) PO6 .157
Wymering Manor Cl 9
PO6 .157
Wymering Rd PO2 .182
Wyn Sutcliffe Ct 9 PO4 183
Wyncombe Rd BH5 .206
Wyndcliffe Rd PO4 .182
Wyndham Cl
Christchurch BH23 .194
Waterlooville PO8 .112
Wyndham Ct SO15 .102
Wyndham Mews PO1 .182
Wyndham Pl 14 SO15 .102
Wyndham Rd
Christchurch BH23 .194
Poole BH14 .203
Wynford Ind Pk SO51 .27
Wynford Rd
Bournemouth BH9 .190
Poole BH14 .203
Wynne Cl BH18 .186
Wynter Cl BH7 .205
Wynter Rd SO18 .104
Wynton Way PO15 .130
Wynyards Gap SO52 .53
Wyre Cl SO53 .55
Wyvern Cl
Chandler's Ford SO53 .55
Poole BH12 .203
Wyvern Tech Coll SO50 .57

Y

Yachtsman Cl SO31 .128
Yaldhurst Ct 23 PO9 .136
Yaldhurst La SO41 .197
Yapton St PO1 .215
Yarborough Rd PO5 .215
Yardlea Cl PO9 .113
Yardley Cl PO3 .158
Yardley Rd SO30 .105
Yarmouth Cl BH12 .204
Yarmouth Gdns 14 SO15 .78
Yarmouth Rd BH12 .203
Yarrell Mead SO41 .197
Yarrells Cl BH16 .201
Yarrells Dr BH16 .201
Yarrells La BH16 .201
Yarrells Sch BH16 .201
Yarrow Cl BH23 .208

'arrow Rd BH12 ....203 A4
'arrow Way SO31 ......128 C1
'ateley Cl PO9 ....135 B3
'averland SO31 ....127 B3
'eatminster Rd BH17 ..187 C1
'eatton Ho SO41 ......196 A1
'elverton Ave SO45 ....150 A4
'elverton Rd 33 BH1 ...204 C2
'eo Ct PO4 ....183 B2
'eoman Pk SO16 ....77 B1
'eomans Ind Pk BH8 ...190 C1
'eomans Rd BH8 ......190 C2
'eomans Way
Bournemouth BH8 ......190 C1
Totton SO40 ....100 C4
'eovil Chase SO18 .....104 A4
'eovilton Cl SO41 ......196 C1
'erville Gdns SO41 .....195 C2
'ew La BH25 ....195 B2
Yew Rd SO18 ....104 A4
Yew Tree Ave PO8 ......112 A1
Yew Tree Cl
Fair Oak SO50 ....57 B2
Hedge End SO30 ....105 A3
Wimborne Minst BH21 ...163 B3
Yew Tree Ct
Fordingbridge SP6 ....93 C4
Locks Heath PO15 ......129 A4
30 New Milton BH25 .....195 A1
Yew Tree Dr PO15 ......129 A4
Yew Tree Gdns
Denmead PO7 ....110 C2
3 Ringwood BH24 ....141 A3
Yew Tree Pl GU33 ....21 A2
Yew Tree Rd PO11 .....185 A4
Yewberry Way SO53 .....54 C3
Yews The PO8 ....112 B4
Yewside PO13 ....155 B1
Yewtree Cl SO45 ....150 A4
Yewtree La SO16 ....77 B2
Yoells Cres PO8 ....111 C3
Yoells La PO8 ....111 C3
Yokesford Hill SO51 .....27 C2
Yokesford Hill Est SO51 .27 C3
Yonge Cl SO50 ....56 A2
York Ave BH25 ....195 A2
York Bldgs SO14 ....103 A2
York Cl Broadstone BH18 .187 A1
Chandler's Ford SO53 .....54 C2
Christchurch BH23 ......206 C4
Fair Oak SO50 ....81 B4
Petersfield GU32 ....40 B2
Southampton SO14 ......103 B3
Totton SO40 ....101 A4
York Cres PO13 ....180 A2
York Dro Nomansland SP5 .73 B4
Southampton SO18 ......104 A4
York Gdns PO16 ....156 C3
York Ho 26 Gosport PO12 181 B2
7 Southampton SO14 ...103 B3
32 Winchester SO23 ....2 A1
York Pl Bournemouth BH7 206 A3
17 New Milton BH25 .....195 A2
Portsmouth PO1 ....182 A3
York Rd
Bournemouth BH1 ......205 A2
Broadstone BH18 ....187 A1
Eastleigh SO50 ....80 A4
Netley SO31 ....127 A3
Southampton SO15 ......102 B4
York Terr PO2 ....157 C3
Yorkdale SO31 ....128 B2
Yorke St PO5 ....215 A2
Yorke Way SO31 ....127 C2
Yorkwood GU33 ....20 C2
Youngbridge Ct 12
PO16 ....155 A4
Youngs Rd BH11 ....189 A3
Yves Mews PO5 ....182 B1

Z

Zamek Cl BH11 ....189 A3
Zetland Ct BH4 ....204 A1
Zetland Rd Cosham PO6 .158 B4
Gosport PO12 ....181 A3
Zeus La PO7 ....134 C2
Zinnia Cl BH10 ....189 C1

Notes

Using the Ordnance Survey National Grid

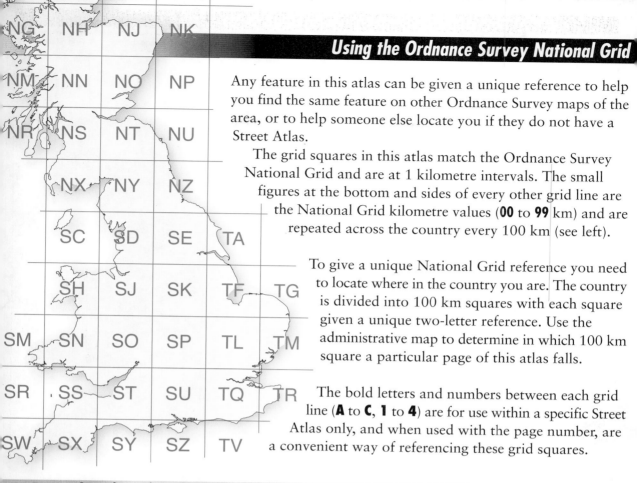

Any feature in this atlas can be given a unique reference to help you find the same feature on other Ordnance Survey maps of the area, or to help someone else locate you if they do not have a Street Atlas.

The grid squares in this atlas match the Ordnance Survey National Grid and are at 1 kilometre intervals. The small figures at the bottom and sides of every other grid line are the National Grid kilometre values (**00** to **99** km) and are repeated across the country every 100 km (see left).

To give a unique National Grid reference you need to locate where in the country you are. The country is divided into 100 km squares with each square given a unique two-letter reference. Use the administrative map to determine in which 100 km square a particular page of this atlas falls.

The bold letters and numbers between each grid line (**A** to **C**, **1** to **4**) are for use within a specific Street Atlas only, and when used with the page number, are a convenient way of referencing these grid squares.

Example The railway bridge over DARLEY GREEN RD in grid square A1

Step 1: Identify the two-letter reference, in this example the page is in **SP**

Step 2: Identify the 1 km square in which the railway bridge falls. Use the figures in the southwest corner of this square: Eastings **17**, Northings **74**. This gives a unique reference: **SP 17 74**, accurate to 1 km.

Step 3: To give a more precise reference accurate to 100 m you need to estimate how many tenths along and how many tenths up this 1 km square the feature is. This makes the bridge about **8** tenths along and about **1** tenth up from the southwest corner.

This gives a unique reference: **SP 178 741**, accurate to 100 m.

Eastings (read from left to right along the bottom) come before Northings (read from bottom to top). If you have trouble remembering say to yourself "Along the hall, THEN up the stairs"!

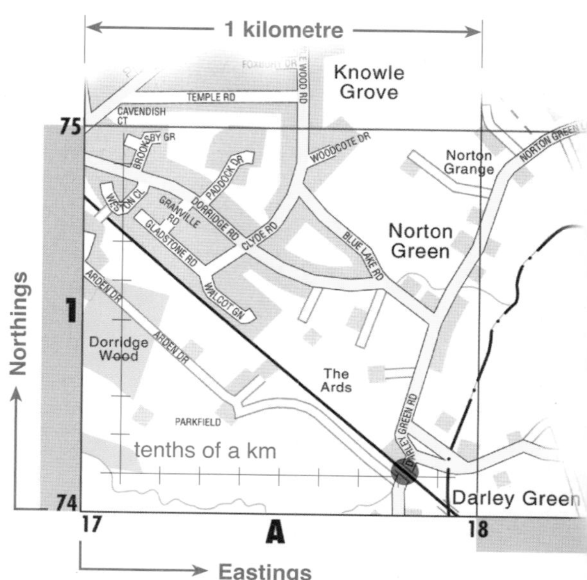

Addresses

Name and Address	Telephone	Page	Grid reference

Name and Address	Telephone	Page	Grid reference

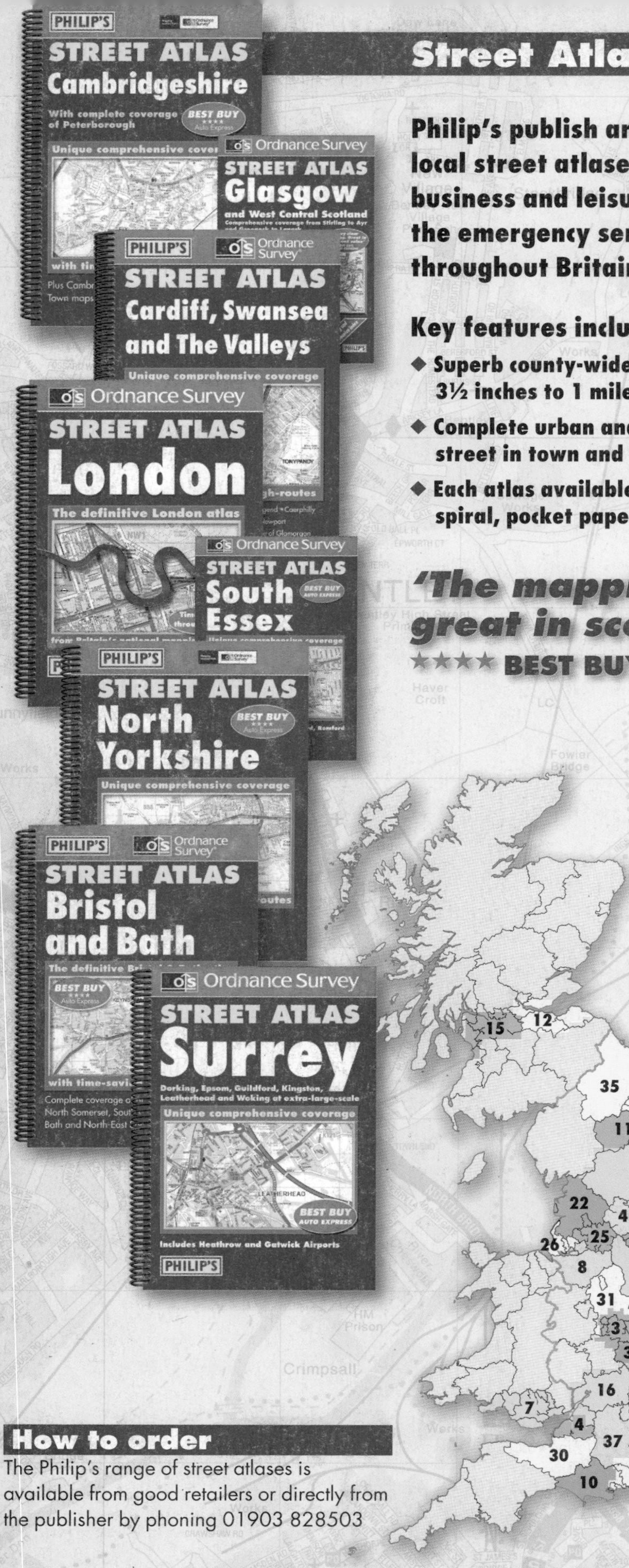

Street Atlases from Philip's

Philip's publish an extensive range of regional and local street atlases which are ideal for motoring, business and leisure use. They are widely used by the emergency services and local authorities throughout Britain.

Key features include:

- **Superb county-wide mapping at an extra-large scale of 3½ inches to 1 mile, or 2½ inches to 1 mile in pocket editio**
- **Complete urban and rural coverage, detailing every named street in town and country**
- **Each atlas available in three handy formats – hardback, spiral, pocket paperback**

'The mapping is very clear... great in scope and value'

★★★★ BEST BUY AUTO EXPRESS

1 Bedfordshire
2 Berkshire
3 Birmingham and West Midlands
4 Bristol and Bath
5 Buckinghamshire
6 Cambridgeshire
7 Cardiff, Swansea and The Valleys
8 Cheshire
9 Derbyshire
10 Dorset
11 County Durham and Teesside
12 Edinburgh and Eas Central Scotland
13 North Essex
14 South Essex
15 Glasgow and Wes Central Scotland
16 Gloucestershire
17 North Hampshire
18 South Hampshire
19 Hertfordshire
20 East Kent
21 West Kent
22 Lancashire
23 Leicestershire and Rutland
24 London
25 Greater Mancheste
26 Merseyside
27 Northamptonshire
28 Nottinghamshire
29 Oxfordshire
30 Somerset
31 Staffordshire
32 Surrey
33 East Sussex
34 West Sussex
35 Tyne and Wear an Northumberland
36 Warwickshire
37 Wiltshire and Swindon
38 East Yorkshire and Northern Lincolnsh
39 North Yorkshire
40 South Yorkshire
41 West Yorkshire

How to order

The Philip's range of street atlases is available from good retailers or directly from the publisher by phoning 01903 828503